THE DIARY OF
JOHN EVELYN

THE DIARY OF
JOHN
EVELYN

Now first printed in full from the
manuscripts belonging to Mr. John Evelyn
and edited by

E. S. de Beer

In six volumes

Volume VI

ADDITIONS & CORRECTIONS
INDEX

OXFORD
AT THE CLARENDON PRESS
1955

Oxford University Press, Amen House, London E.C.4
GLASGOW NEW YORK TORONTO MELBOURNE WELLINGTON
BOMBAY CALCUTTA MADRAS KARACHI CAPE TOWN IBADAN
Geoffrey Cumberlege, Publisher to the University

PRINTED IN GREAT BRITAIN

PREFACE

THE present volume contains an appendix; additions and corrections to the preceding five volumes; and the index to the whole work. The introduction to the index sets out its aims and its treatment of some matters, more especially those in which alternative courses are possible; if it states aspirations rather than achievement, I must plead the magnitude of the task and the absence of an adequate pilot-index for the Diary. The work of indexing has brought to light a number of errors in the text and notes; corrections to them are given in the additions and corrections.

In the preface to vol. i I should have thanked the Warden and Fellows of All Souls College for permission to make use of Narcissus Luttrell's manuscripts. Although it came too late to affect the notes, I am indebted to Dr. Folke Dahl for his advice about the use of newspapers.

The compilation of the index has occupied most of my time during the last three years. During this period I have troubled most of my friends and acquaintances with my difficulties; I owe them apologies for what I have inflicted on them and thanks for their patience and their suggestions. My more especial thanks are due to the staff of the Clarendon Press, who have settled many technical problems, and to my constant adviser in this part of my task, Dr. L. F. Powell.

RAASAY; LONDON

1953–4

CONTENTS

APPENDIX: GOTHIC AND SOME OTHER ARCHITECTURAL TERMS 1

ADDITIONS AND CORRECTIONS 8

INDEX: INTRODUCTION 26

INDEX 39

ADDENDA: ADDITIONAL CORRECTIONS TO THE TEXT 627

ADDITIONS TO THE INDEX 627

APPENDIX

GOTHIC AND SOME OTHER ARCHITECTURAL TERMS

EVELYN'S Diary is one of the books most frequently cited for the early use of the word 'Gothic' as an architectural term. This is largely due to the accessibility of the Diary; occurrences in other contemporary writings have scarcely been noticed, except by the *Oxford English Dictionary*; but also it is used frequently in the Diary, and occurrences elsewhere in English writings are rare until near the end of the seventeenth century.

I have investigated the early use of the term in an article in the *Journal* of the Warburg and Courtauld Institutes.[1] The term originated through the historical study of architecture. 'Architecture differs from painting and sculpture in that, owing to its nature, there is in it a far greater element of that common form which the individual artist shares with his contemporaries. This common form shows itself very clearly in ornamentation; and the latter lends itself to codification. Hence the architectural styles of the textbooks, compiled and named for the convenience of archæologists and designers, the creation of a sophisticated age, detached and reflective; in themselves only lists of the elements most frequently found in architectural practice within more or less reasonably selected limits of time and place.' In the Middle Ages there was no idea of architectural styles in our sense. Building had gone on continuously from time immemorial, and at best men could distinguish between customary and strange, whether old-fashioned or outlandish.[2] The way was prepared

[1] 'Gothic: origin and diffusion of the term; the idea of style in architecture': xi (1948), 143–62. Since the article was written I have seen, by the kindness of Mr. Ellic Howe, C. Wehmer, *Die Namen der gotischen Buchschriften*, 1930–2 (also published in *Zentralblatt für Bibliothekswesen*, vol. xlix). Wehmer gives examples of the application of the term Gothic to handwriting in the Middle Ages; and shows how readily the humanists turned it into a term of abuse.

[2] Villard de Honnecourt gives a drawing of 'li sepouture d'un sarrazin', a Roman monument; his interest was confined to its general arrangement and he alters the style freely.

for the idea when Brunelleschi, dissatisfied with the forms current in Florence in his time, by studying the ruins of Rome created for himself a complete and homogeneous architectural system.[1]

Contemporary or slightly later architects and writers equated this with the ancient Roman style, and noted the sharp contrast between the Roman style, whether old or new, and the style or styles of the intervening period. According to the life of Brunelleschi attributed to Antonio Manetti, the antique style disappeared when the Empire was invaded by the barbarians. The invaders, Vandals, Goths, Lombards, Huns, and others, being inexperienced, employed German craftsmen for their buildings. When Charlemagne expelled the Lombards from Italy, he employed Roman workmen who built some buildings in Florence in the Roman style. Then the Germans overran Charlemagne's empire and reintroduced their own manner of building, which lasted until the time of Brunelleschi. It is to be noted here that the Goths are only one horde among the barbarian invaders, and are not directly responsible for any architectural style.

Raphael, or some member of his circle, writing about 1518–19, holds similar views, but has to fit them to Rome instead of Florence. There are three kinds of building in Rome. The oldest style lasted until Rome was laid waste by the Goths and other barbarians. The next lasted so long as Rome was ruled by the Goths and for a century thereafter. Their architecture reflects the misery of their time; as an example of it the Torre della Milizia is cited. But then the Germans (Tedeschi) began to revive architecture a little; they established the third style, from the description the medieval pointed style, which lasted until the writer's own time. The writer clearly distinguishes between the style of the Goths

[1] Brunelleschi appears to have turned to ancient buildings for their formal qualities; he was seeking an adequate means of expression, not trying to revive the architecture of antiquity for the sake of the glories of the Greek and Roman past. Medieval artists, notably a sculptor at Rheims and Nicolo Pisano, had used antique motives; the buildings of the Florentine proto-renaissance and some of those erected for Frederick II also show a close dependence on the ancient Roman.

building, which we have since call'd *Modern* (or *Gothic* rather)'.[1] Ultimately, when Evelyn was composing the 'De Vita Propria', where he had first described the gates of Amsterdam as 'some of them modern', they were now in the 'antien, & best manner'.[2]

In the notice of S. Maria Maggiore the statement that 'the designe is mixt' probably refers not to the style of the building as a whole, but to the irregular nature of the building, its parts in different styles. In the notice of the Château at Richelieu mixed is a stylistic term: it is built 'upon an old designe, not altogether gotique, but mix'd'.[3] The term is used with greater clarity in the description of Audley End quoted above, but in a later notice of the house Evelyn finds a more suitable term: 'It is indeede a cherefull piece of Gotic-building, or rather *antico-moderno*'.[4]

Evelyn's other stylistic terms do not call for special discussion.

[1] *Parallel of Architecture*, 1707, p. 9 (Misc. writings, p. 365). Not in the earlier version.

[2] ii. 48; i. 34.

[3] ii. 151. Cf. the account of St.-Germain: 'the style of the magnificence then in fashion, which was with to greate a mixture of the Gotic': ii. 111.

[4] iii. 556. I take it that the terms are not alternative, but that the second corrects the first; cf. the earlier notice of the house. Evelyn might have found 'antico-moderno' in Baglione's *Le nove chiese* (above, ii. 575), where it is frequently applied to sculpture, twice with the word 'Gotico' attached.

ADDITIONS AND CORRECTIONS

AMONG books which appeared too late for me to use in the notes to the text there are four of great importance for Evelyn and the Diary:

W. G. Hiscock, *John Evelyn and Mrs. Godolphin*, 1951.
B. H. Johnson, *Berkeley Square to Bond Street*, 1952.
Sir Tresham Lever, *Godolphin*, 1952.
John Ehrman, *The Navy in the War of William III, 1689–1697*, 1953

I have incorporated very little information from these in the following pages; readers concerned with the special subjects must consult the books for themselves. Mr. Johnson identifies Evelyn's house in Dover Street—the house in which he died—as one on the site of the present no. 11.

i, introduction: p. *5*, l. 3. Southborough is an error for Southover.

i. *5*, n. 2. Mr. Hiscock informs me that, at least largely as a result of his son's conduct, Evelyn was in financial difficulties about 1694; his removal from Sayes Court to Wotton was connected with his troubles. This appears in a letter to George Evelyn, 2 November 1694. How hard pressed Evelyn was in fact is not very clear, but the letter is strongly worded.

i. *73*, n. 2. The entry for 9 July 1689 presents a problem which I cannot solve. Evelyn apparently wrote the whole notice at one time. He sat to Kneller again on 24 July, presumably for the same portrait. In a letter to Pepys written late in August (Bohn, iii. 294–5; there dated 12 August; the reference to Lady Sunderland provides a date after 21 August, and Pepys's reply of 30 August a still later date) he states that he is surprised to find that his portrait has been placed in Pepys's library. There are breaks, or apparent breaks, in the manuscript at the beginnings of the entries for 8 July; 21, 24, 29 July, 18, 21 August, 1 September.

The succeeding entry, for 11 July, is also problematical: see iv. 644, nn. 2, 3.

i. *74*. That V was begun by 1704 is clear from the notice of Dr. Ralph Bathurst on p. 13: see the notice of his death, v. 571.

i. *87*, l. 15. Add note: the library catalogue is that dated 1687: for it see Keynes, *John Evelyn*, pp. 14–17.

i. *129*, l. 14. Add note: the principal files of newspapers that I have used are those in the Bodleian Library and the British Museum (a large number of papers of the period 1679–1706 in the two libraries once belonged to Narcissus Luttrell); further I have used the papers available in the London Library (prior to 1945) and a broken run of the *London Gazette* in the Institute of Historical Research. For the *Votes* of the House of Commons I have used the files in the British Museum and the Institute of Historical Research. There were frequently, if not generally, two editions of the issues of the *London Gazette* and of the *Votes*, and possibly further editions; for the other papers it is possible that there was more than one edition at least for some issues.

i, De Vita Propria: p. 60, l. 6 from foot. The 'List' is presumably Millet, *Le Tresor sacré*: see ii. 86, n. 1.

i. 86–7. The stories of the tulip-bulb and the anemone-seed. A version of the former story, in which a sailor finds the bulb on a merchant's counter, is told by J. B. Schupp as a reminiscence of his visit to Holland in 1634–5: cited by Graf H. zu Solms-Laubach, *Weizen und Tulpe*, 1899, p. 76, from Schupp, *Salomo- oder Regentenspiel*, 1659. A version of the second story is told in N. A. Pluche, *Le spectacle de la nature*, vol. ii, 1735, pp. 52, 53; the victim is M. Bachelier, the thief a *conseiller au parlement*; the latter drops his robe on the plants in seed; his servant picks it up, folding it so as to conceal the seed.

ii. 9 and n. 7. For Southover Grange and the Newtons see also *Sussex Notes and Queries*, xiii (1950–3), 1–4; A. Millward Flack, *Southover Grange*, 1948.

ii. 30 and n. 4. The word frigate was already in use apparently for merchant or passenger vessels; for the first naval frigates see v. 9–11 and n.; i. 22, n. 6.

ii. 41, l. 16. Artificial music. Artificial is used in the obsolete sense, skilfully made or contrived. In his use of the word Evelyn generally appears to imply some degree of skill, even where it is directly opposed to natural: e.g. 'Curiosities naturall or artificial' (ii. 100); 'hills, meadows, growne Wood, & Upland, both artificial and naturall' (ii. 102); 'these artificial Miracles . . . the so famous natural Precipice' (ii. 397). It is sometimes commendatory: 'an artificial fountain' (ii. 406; iv. 347). See also v. 75 and n. 4.

ii. 53, l. 15 (i. 37). The head of the rhinoceros. This may be, not the mammal but the rhinoceros-bird, i.e. the horn-bill: see Hegenitius, p. 109.

ii. 73, n. 7. Marchantius: i.e. J. Marchantius, *Flandria*, 1596.

ii. 86, n. 1. The Bonfons figures of monuments at St.-Denis are by J. Rabel, and appeared first in N. Bonfons, *Les antiquitez et singularitez de Paris, Livre second*, 1588.

ii. 90, n. 3. Browne became Sir Richard not later than December 1646: *Cal. Clarendon S.P.*, i. 348. There is an interesting short account of his early life in J. W. Stoye, *English Travellers Abroad, 1604–1667*, 1952, p. 431.

ii. 91, n. 1. Louisa Maria Theresa is an error for Louisa Maria.

ii. 95 and n. 1 (i. 63). The choir-screen was reconstructed about 1630: *Revue de l'art ancien et moderne*, xliii (1923), 110–14.

ii. 95, n. 2. Gothic is used at least once by Varennes as a stylistic term: see above, p. 4, n. 3.

ii. 96, n. 2. St. Isidore's College is Franciscan, not Dominican.

ii. 96, n. 3. The church is now called St.-Paul-St.-Louis.

ii. 120, n. 10. There is a view by I. Silvestre.

ii. 178 and n. 9 (i. 113). Pliny gives 'Delphini Portus', not 'Promontorium': Pflaumern's error.

ii. 181 and n. 3 (i. 114). Full account of the vase in G. A. Dosio, *Das Skizzenbuch*, &c., ed. C. Huelsen, 1933, p. 12 (and plate).

ii. 212, n. 2. For the population of Rome, 1600–1739, see F. Cerasoli, in Accademia di Conferenze storico-giuridiche, *Studi e documenti di storia e diritto*, xii (1891), 169–99. This gives figures based on annual censuses, including the numbers of clergy, Jews, &c.

ii. 223 and n. 4. Alex: is Alexander Severus; Mammea (Julia Avita Mamaea) was his mother.

ii. 226 and nn. 4, 5. The flight of steps ascended by the devotees was apparently that from the Arch of Septimius Severus to the

Capitol; it was wrongly identified as the Centum Gradus of Tacitus: O. Panciroli, *Tesori nascosti . . . di Roma,* 2nd ed., 1625, p. 73 (followed by Totti). The flight of steps from the Piazza d'Ara cœli to the west front of the church consists of 121 steps: ibid.

ii. 236, n. 7. For Angeloni see also *La Bibliofilia,* xxxv (1933), 221.

ii. 242, n. 5. Totti here copies Panciroli (see above), p. 251. The antecedent there of 'Doppo' is Nero's burning the Christians after the fire of Rome.

ii. 248 and n. 5. The remains of the Meta Sudante were demolished in 1936: G. Lugli, *Roma antica,* 1946, p. 313.

ii. 251, l. 15: '. . . divers excellent marble statues': the statues are an addition of Evelyn's; Totti has simply 'nobilissimi marmi'.

ii. 259 and n. 1. For Bernini's tower see especially Dagobert Frey, in *Jahrbuch der kunsthistorischen Sammlungen in Wien,* new ser., xii (1938), 203–26.

ii. 260, l. 10: 'marble)': the closing bracket has been substituted for a comma in MS.

ii. 263 and n. 2. For Bernini's hostility to Duquesnoy see also G. B. Passeri, *Die Künstlerbiographien,* ed. J. Hess, 1934, p. 111, n. 2.

ii. 265, n. 3. The mosaic is now in the portico. In Evelyn's time it was inside the church above the main door; it was moved to the entrance of the Vatican by Innocent X and to its present position in 1674: F. Martinelli, *Roma ricercata,* 2nd ed., [1650], p. 11; [M. A. Rossi], *Ritratto di Roma moderna,* 1689, p. 21.

ii. 270, n. 2. Innocent XI is an error for Innocent X.

ii. 317 and n. 1. The association of the Aqua Marcia with Ancus Martius goes back to Pliny: T. Ashby, *The Aqueducts of Ancient Rome,* ed. I. A. Richmond, 1935, p. 90.

ii. 330, n. 4. Evelyn has already used the word *cavallerizzo* incorrectly: ii. 195.

ii. 342, n. 6. Pflaumern presumably quoted St. Peter Damianus from Capaccio.

ii. 355. The omitted lines resemble a passage in Carew's 'The Rapture'. See further addition to ii. 512, n. 1.

ii. 359, n. 2. The church is generally called S. Stefano alle Carrozze: Huelsen, *Chiese*, p. 484.

ii. 373, n. 1. For the church, &c., see further F. Bonnard, *Histoire du couvent royal de la Trinité du Mont Pincio à Rome*, 1933.

ii. 391, n. 1. For the palace occupied by the Ministry of Justice see L. Càllari, *I palazzi di Roma*, 3rd ed., 1944, pp. 275–9.

ii. 391, n. 4. Parinoli is an error for Primoli.

ii. 393–4. For Mammea see above, addition to ii. 223. Alexander Severus.

ii. 408, l. 4: 'deale wood': followed in MS. by: 'Also in the *Domo* lies buried *Hen*: the 7th who was poyson'd by a Monk in the Eucharist:', all deleted.

ii. 410, n. 5. I think that Evelyn went from Lucca to Florence in one day, and visited Poggio Imperiale early next morning.

ii. 429, n. 6. It seems certain that, for his account of Venice, Evelyn also made some use of *Coryats crudities*: see ii. 442, n. 6, 444, n. 1, 445, n. 7, and below, additions to notes on ii. 443, 446, 460, 461; for further possible influence see ii. 483, n. 9.

ii. 432, n. 2. St. Didier says that half the people at the ceremony were 'en masque': p. 387.

ii. 443, n. 9. Coryat uses the word 'tribunal' in this sense in his account of the Sala dello Scrutinio: p. 202. This was presumably Evelyn's source for it; compare ii. 444, n. 1, and addition to ii. 446, n. 9.

ii. 446, n. 9. Coryat describes the Loggetta as 'a place where some of the Procurators of Saint Markes doe use to sit in judgement, and discusse matters of controversies . . . of that singular and incomparable beauty . . .', and also uses the word 'tribunal': 'over the tribunal where the Procurators sit, the image . . .': pp. 185–6. The use, here and on ii. 443, is Italian rather than English.

ii. 453, n. 1. On Evelyn at Padua there is an article by A. Favaro: Reale Accademia di Scienze, Lettere, ed Arti in Padova, *Atti e memorie*, new ser., xxx (1914), 79–90.

ii. 460, n. 1. The statements about the statues and paintings are very close to Coryat, p. 228, and presumably derive from him.

ii. 461, n. 7. The statements about the garden and orchard are fairly close to Coryat, p. 245; but the olives are original, and the notice may be independent of him.

ii. 466, n. 5. Evelyn's *hortus siccus* is now at Christ Church, Oxford.

ii. 467, l. 8. The ancient theatre was an amphitheatre.

ii. 469–70. Favaro (see above, addition to ii. 453, n. 1) states that Evelyn was not elected *syndicus artistarum*; presumably he was invited to stand for the office and refused to do so.

ii. 508, n. 5. There is now an admirable history of the pass, P. Arnold, *Der Simplon*, N.D. (*c.* 1948). That the seventeenth-century route ran at the bottom of the ravine of Gondo is clear from C. Bascapè, *Novaria*, 1612, pp. 214–17 (extract, with notes, in *Notes and Queries*, cxciii (1948), 356–7).

ii. 512, n. 1. Carew has 'the grim Swisse' in 'The Rapture', l. 10; he is writing about a door-keeper.

ii. 521, n. 1. Jean Diodati apparently visited England a second time in 1627: D. C. Dorian, *The English Diodatis*, 1950, pp. 119–20.

ii. 522, n. 1. For the younger Buckingham's travels see also Hist. MSS. Comm., *Denbigh MSS.* (pt. v), pp. 79–80.

ii. 523, n. 1. For the rocks see also F. Stähelin, *Die Schweiz in römischer Zeit*, 3rd ed., 1948, p. 544 (as Pierres-à-Niton). He thinks that the derivation of the name from Neptune is possible.

ii. 529, n. 1. There are two editions of Minutoli ('V.M.G.'), neither with a date; my citation is from the first.

ii. 537, n. 2. Sir John Cotton died, not in 1656, but in 1646 (possibly 1646/7).

ii. 537, n. 6 *ad fin.* For plans of Sayes Court see also addition to iii. 80, n. 1.

ii. 539, l. 6. 1648 is a marginal date.

ii. 564, n. 4. Coventry was knighted, not on 3 March, but on 26 June 1665: iii. 414, n. 5.

iii. 17, n. 2. Evelyn probably means Charles de Créqui, d. 1638, prince de Poix, duke of Lesdiguières; marshal of France 1621: *Nouvelle biog. gén.* Marines was his grandson.

iii. 23, n. 3. Squire was not knighted.

iii. 28, n. 3. Senneterre appears as St.-Nectaire in de la Chenaye-Desbois and Badier, xviii. 128.

iii. 35, n. 5. William Stafford is an error for William Howard.

iii. 46, n. 3. On the *Orarium* see the introduction to the reprint published by the Parker Society, 1851 (*Private Prayers*, &c., ed. W. K. Clay).

iii. 69, n. 1 Locksbottom is in Farnborough, about three miles from the centre of Bromley, and just outside the parish boundary.

iii. 71, l. 13. The drought lasted for some years: J. Childrey, *Britannia Baconica*, 1661, pp. 55*–48, 66.

iii. 80, n. 1. Mr. Hiscock has published, in *The Illustrated London News*, 30 August 1952, pp. 348–9, a plan of Sayes Court dated 1653, made by or for Evelyn, and with a full key to it in his writing (it was made to be sent to Sir Richard Browne). This shows the principal rooms on the ground-floor (it also gives some statements about the rooms above them); the gardens and yards; and part of the adjoining fields.

The oval garden is marked, to the south-west of the house; it had disappeared by 1692.

iii. 104, l. 3. For the heat see Childrey (see above), pp. 55*–48.

iii. 140 and n. 3. These were the books later returned to Lambeth: for their history see *D.N.B.*, art. Bancroft.

iii. 151, n. 5. Gillingham had been sequestered from Chalton in 1646: A. G. Matthews, *Walker revised*, 1948, p. 183.

iii. 172, n. 1. The Parliamentary Committee is an error for the Commissioners for the Approbation of Public Preachers (the

'Triers'), instituted by Cromwell in 1654: G. B. Tatham, *The Puritans in Power*, 1913, pp. 241–5.

iii. 188, n. 3, &c. This is the fight celebrated by Waller in 'Of a war with Spain, and a fight at sea'.

iii. 201, nn. 1, 2. James Darell was also a son of Sir Robert Darell.

iii. 202, n. 2. Reynolds gives the date of the delivery of the sermon as 4 December; but the service for the Company was ordered to be held on 2 December, and there are other grounds for believing that it was held on that day: *Cal. Court Minutes*, as cited, pp. 191–2.

iii. 209, n. 1, 210, n. 3. The passages relating to Richard Evelyn in the dedication of the *Golden Book*, and his epitaph, are reprinted in C. Barksdale, *Memorials of worthy persons. Two decads*, 1661, pp. 76–85. The epitaph is there stated to be by Wase.

iii. 214 and n. 1. Massam is perhaps Masterson (iii. 212 and n. 7), rather than Mossom.

iii. 235, n. 4, 237–8 and n., 240 and nn. 4, 5, 245 and n. 3. On this negotiation see also A. H. Nethercot, 'John Evelyn and Colonel Herbert Morley in 1659–60', in *Huntington Library Quarterly*, i (1937–8), 439–46. This includes a note made by Evelyn about 1700; in it he writes that Morley, not believing that Monck intended to march on London, had procrastinated, and continues: 'Had he [Morley] taken my Advise in time, he had ben Duke, & I God knows what:'. He then gives some biographical details: 'I was Morleys Schole fellow & Bedfellow at *Lewes* in Sussex', &c.

iii. 259, l. 3. By 'in the Presence of the King' Evelyn means either in sight of his palace or in time of his presence in England. Charles did not attend any of the executions.

iii. 262, n. 6. For the Dutch gift to Charles II see *Burlington Magazine*, xci (1949), 303–5, 349–50; xcii (1950), 12–18. The second painting by 'Douce' is probably a work by, or attributed to, Elsheimer.

iii. 265, n. 2. The cross-reference should be to 1672 (iii. 627, n. 1).

iii. 266, n. 6 *ad fin.* The article in Institute of Historical Research, *Bulletin*, vol. xv, is superseded by a revised version, in *Notes and Records of the Royal Society of London*, vii (1950), 172–92.

iii. 274, n. 4. For Tuke in Paris see also Christian Huygens, diary, in Brugmans, *Le séjour*, &c. (see iii. 286, n. 2), pp. 170–1.

iii. 275 and n. 1. As yet the Society had no curator: compare iii. 292, n. 2.

iii. 285–6. Huygens (Zuylichem) mentions meeting Evelyn at Sir Robert Moray's about this time: diary, in Brugmans (iii. 286, n. 2), p. 170.

iii. 297–8 and n. The ambassadors' encounter. For the events leading up to it, Louis XIV's views on it, and a French translation of one of the English pamphlets, see *Mémoriaux du Conseil de 1661*, ed. J. de Boislisle (Soc. de l'hist. de France, 1905–7), iii. 140–76, &c.; for Vatteville, *Dictionnaire hist. et biog. de la Suisse*, vii. 238 b.

iii. 306, n. 3. Thomas Howard, the duke of Norfolk attainted in 1572, should be reckoned as fourth, rather than as third duke.

iii. 314, n. 4. Alsop is presumably Josias Alsop, M.A., rector of St. Clement, Eastcheap, 1660–6: Matthews, *Walker revised*, p. 308.

iii. 322, n. 5. D. Stoup is an error for D. Stoop.

iii. 335, n. 3. Lloyd was deprived in 1690, not 1692.

iii. 352, n. 2. The Surveyor-General is perhaps not Denham, but the Surveyor-general of the Crown Lands, Sir Charles Harbord; for him see iii. 175, n. 6.

iii. 363, n. 1. Huygens met Evelyn this day at Lady Needham's: diary, in Brugmans (iii. 286, n. 2), p. 175.

iii. 390 and n. 7. Evelyn presumably followed the notice in *The Intelligencer* cited in the note.

iii. 396, n. 4. The Sir Peter Wyche mentioned in this note was a son of the elder Sir Peter (see v. 359 and n. 4) and a brother of Sir Cyril.

iii. 400, n. 3. Rich was knighted in 1670.

iii. 412 and n. 6. The Royal Society's vacation this year was on account of the plague; regular summer vacations began in 1667.

iii. 443, n. 1. Legge was Lieutenant of the Ordnance, not a commissioner. On Compton's death in 1663 the existing commissioners were empowered to perform the Master's duties: *Cal. S.P., Dom., 1663–4*, p. 350.

iii. 447, n. 5. For Fox see further Lord Ilchester (G. S. H. Fox-Strangways, sixth earl of Ilchester), *Henry Fox, Lord Holland*, 1920, i. 5–16.

iii. 462, n. 1. Moorgate is an error for Moorfields.

iii. 471, n. 3. Sylvius, like Kievit, was concerned in Buat's plot: K. Feiling, *British Foreign Policy, 1660–1672*, 1930, pp. 197–201.

iii. 480, l. 12. The guns at the Tower were on Tower Wharf: *A New and Compleat Survey of London*, 1742, i. 172; see also the younger Clarendon, as cited at v. 28, n. 2.

iii. 483 and n. 6. For the Commissioners of the Treasury see iii. 487, n. 7.

iii. 492, l. 4. I take it that 'published' means denounced: compare *The Winter's Tale*, II. i. 98. The passage makes good sense if one reads it as, 'the cruel contrivers, [who were doing it] to get money ...'

iii. 523, n. 1. On the dates of Evelyn's letters to Clifford see further *Notes and Queries*, clxxiv (1937), 130–1. The letter dated 14 November 1671 (14 September?) was probably addressed to Arlington.

iii. 529, n. 1. Berkshire was created Viscount Andover as well as Baron Howard in 1622.

iii. 551, n. 6 *ad fin.* For Stanhope see also G. van der Haute, *Les relations anglo-hollandaises ... d'après la correspondance d'Alexandre Stanhope, 1700–1706*, 1932.

iii. 575, n. 5. Ragni's father was François de Bonne de Créqui, duke of Lesdiguières, a son of the Marshal de Créqui, for whom see above (add. to iii. 17, n. 2).

iii. 578, n. 2. Carteret was appointed a member of this council at this time: Harris, *Life of Sandwich*, ii. 307.

iii. 611 and n. 4. What appears to be a weather-cock of this description, at Stoke, near Rochester, is described in *Hogarth's Peregrination* (1732), ed. C. Mitchell, 1952, p. 8.

iii. 613 and n. 3. The ambassador is Don Pedro de Jouar y Velasco, marqués de Fresno, here from 2 March of this year until 1674.

iii. 618, n. 6. Mountagu (Sandwich) did not serve in Sweden, but acted as a mediator between Sweden and Denmark.

iii. 630 and n. 3. The preacher is perhaps the other Dr. William Lloyd, the nonjuror.

iv. 4, n. 5. Rector of Deptford is an error for vicar.

iv. 6, l. 1. For 'imcomparable' read 'incomparable'.

iv. 6, ll. 8–10. This probably refers to the Chapel Royal, Whitehall.

iv. 50 and n. 3. Evelyn's new lodgings were in Bell Yard, King Street, to the south of the palace: W. G. Hiscock, *John Evelyn and Mrs. Godolphin*, 1951, p. 114.

iv. 58, n. 1. The cross-reference should read, 'iii. 369, 392'.

iv. 60, n. 3. The best statement of the case against Petty's authorship of the *Observations* is probably that by M. Greenwood, in Royal Statistical Society, *Journal*, xci (1928), 79–85; xcvi (1933), 76–81.

iv. 72, n. 1. The Rev. Thomas Hutchinson is perhaps identifiable with a Dr. or Mr. Hutchins, who preaches occasionally at Deptford between 1684 and 1688. The latter is identifiable with a Dr. Hutchinson at Lee in 1680 (iv. 386, n. 2) and with Dr. Thomas Hutchinson, who was buried there on '9 Jan. 1706': Drake's Hasted, p. 235.

iv. 78 and n. 4, 493 and n. 4. Tutor at Oxford of John Evelyn, jnr. The Turner who was at Trinity was William; his brother Thomas was principally at Corpus Christi, and never at Trinity. The younger Evelyn's tutor was therefore presumably William; and the notice on p. 78 ought to refer to him. He died on 20 April 1685 (Wood, *Life*, iii. 139), so the preacher on p. 493 must be Thomas,

and Evelyn's identification of him there as his son's tutor must be erroneous.

It is possible that the identification on p. 78 is also wrong, and that the preacher here is Dr. Francis Turner, a third brother.

iv. 84, ll. 8–9. For 'gravely a wittily' read 'gravely & wittily'.

iv. 90 and n. 6. William Charleton the collector was at present living at Montpellier in France: J. Locke, *Locke's Travels in France*, ed. J. Lough, 1953, p. 4 and n. 6, &c. Evelyn presumably means Dr. Walter Charleton.

iv. 98 and n. 1. There are notices relating to the house in R. Hooke, *Diary*, 15, 18, 20, 22, 25, 27 July; 16 October.

iv. 115, n. 8, 116, nn. 1, 2. Evelyn may himself have used Blome's *Britannia*.

iv. 118, ll. 12, 11 from foot. Brederode is an error for Beverweerd; and Henry Frederick for Maurice of Orange.

iv. 124, n. 9. Grew was secretary of the Royal Society from 1677 to 1679.

iv. 144, l. 5: 'surprizing'. See above, iii. 120, n. 1.

iv. 155, n. 2. The text is Deuteronomy xxix. 29.

iv. 196, n. 1. George Evelyn, George Evelyn of Wotton's son by his first wife, had died in 1676: v. 358, n. 7.

iv. 207, n. 4. Ibach is probably identifiable with Josiah Ibeck, who worked as a coppersmith for or at Chatsworth about 1692: Francis Thompson, *A History of Chatsworth*, 1949, pp. 36, 87, 124, 204.

iv. 218 and n. 1. Lord Ilchester questions Duppa's share in Fox's advancement: *Henry Fox* (see above, addition to iii. 447, n. 5), i. 5. Fox had left school before Duppa became bishop of Salisbury; he may have attracted Duppa's attention when he came to court.

iv. 226, n. 5. There is a good view of the trial in *Historical Collections: or, a brief account . . . of the two last Parliaments*, 2nd ed., 1685.

iv. 257, n. 5. For Foubert see further advertisement in *London Gazette*, 27 Oct. 1679.

iv. 269, n. 5. On Chelsea Hospital see further C. G. T. Dean, *The Royal Hospital, Chelsea*, 1950.

iv. 271, n. 5. A letter written by Isaac is printed in M. Arnold-Forster, *Basset Down*, [1950], pp. 112–13; see also pp. 114, 115, 125.

iv. 320, n. 1. Heneage Finch: the cross-reference should be to 12 February 1686, i.e. iv. 500.

iv. 324, notice for 11 July: 'A Club of our *Society*'. Pepys mentions 'a club supper' of fellows, and later 'the club', on both occasions at the Crown (Threadneedle Street): 15 February 1665, 4 June 1666; Hooke says that there was 'noe meeting of the Society nor noe Lecture nor noe club' on one meeting-day: *Diary*, 11 June 1674. The meetings were apparently informal and open to all fellows. Other notices by both diarists probably refer to gatherings of the kind.

iv. 328, n. 4. Evelyn visited Shaftesbury twice in 1676: iv. 82, 88.

iv. 354, n. 6. Peregrine Osborne was at this time Danby's second surviving son. In 1674 Danby had surrendered his Scottish peerage, which was then conferred on Peregrine; the title was altered from Viscount Osborne of Dunblane to Viscount Dunblane: A. Browning, *Thomas Osborne, earl of Danby*, &c., 1944–51, i. 137.

iv. 366, n. 4. Tyrone was imprisoned in the Gatehouse, not the Tower.

iv. 386, n. 2. See above, addition to iv. 72, n. 1.

iv. 397, n. 4. St. James's, Piccadilly. The services here in 1697 were:

Daily: Prayers at 10 and 3.

Sundays: Prayers and Sermons at 10 and 3; Prayers at 7 and 5.

Additional Prayers and Sermons: New Year, 30 January, Ash Wednesday, all Thursdays in Lent, Good Friday, 5 November, and all public fasts or thanksgivings.

Additional Prayers: 29 May; all festivals in the year.

Prayers and Catechising: all Thursdays from Michaelmas to Midsummer Day, except between Christmas and Epiphany, and during Lent.

Sacraments: every second Sunday of the month; every Sunday from Palm Sunday to Trinity Sunday; New Year; two each on Palm Sunday, Easter Day, Whitsunday, Christmas.

The services in the Tabernacle belonging to it (v. 132 and n. 2) were:

Daily: Prayers at 11 and 3.

Sundays: Prayers and Sermons before 10 and before 3.

Additional Sermons: Christmas and 'any solemn casual fast'.

Sacraments: last Sunday of every month, Christmas, Easter Day, Whitsunday.

(*Select Psalms and Hymns for the use of the Parish-Church and Tabernacle of St. James's Westminster*, 1697, pp. 58–60.)

iv. 406, n. 1. Charles had had a sore on his heel.

iv. 407, l. 13: 'both the Court Chapells'. Evelyn presumably means the Chapel Royal and the Private Oratory. The 'Closet' in the passage from Horne quoted in n. 5 may refer to the latter, or perhaps only to private prayer.

iv. 434, n. 3. George Evelyn's intention to stand seems to have attracted some notice: *Epistolary curiosities*, ed. Rebecca Warner, 1818, i. 129.

iv. 474 and n. 4. Evelyn had visited Portsmouth in both years; the Isle of Wight only in 1638.

iv. 477, n. 1. From Evelyn's note on Pepys's letter of 2 October it seems certain that what he saw was attested copies of the two papers: Bohn, iii. 279, n. 1.

iv. 479, n. 2. The painting formerly at Wotton (now at Christ Church, Oxford) is more probably the 1689 portrait (iv. 644). Sir John Evelyn bought the latter on 24 April 1724 for £12 12*s*. from Mrs. Ann Jackson (presumably wife or widow of Pepys's nephew John Jackson): information from Mr. Hiscock. What became of the 1685 portrait is unknown.

iv. 480, notice for 15 October. James's birthday fell on 14 October; according to Luttrell the celebration took place on that day and not on the 15th.

iv. 481, n. 1. Thomas Pitt was Chatham's grandfather, not his father.

iv. 493 and n. 4. Dr. Thomas Turner. See above, addition to iv. 78 and n. 4.

iv. 502 and n. 4. The bishop is John Lake, 1624–89; D.D. 1661; bishop of Sodor and Man 1682; of Bristol 1684; of Chichester 1685: *D.N.B.*

iv. 541, n. 2. Salisbury died in 1694, not 1693: iv. 261, n. 5.

iv. 544, n. 5. For services here see above, addition to iv. 397, n. 4.

iv. 565, first notice for 20 December (Wake's sermon). Presumably the date should be Sunday, 18 December.

iv. 604 and n. 3, 606 and n. 2. The Prince's Declaration is that dated 10 October N.S.

iv. 606 and n. 3. An account of this ceremony, or another about this time, is given by H. Misson de Valmont, *Memoires*, 1698, pp. 117–18.

iv. 608, n. 8. Sir Tresham Lever has found a copy of the instructions, and summarizes them in his *Godolphin*, 1952, pp. 70–1.

iv. 632, n. 5. 1660 is an error for 1661.

iv. 641, notice for 7 June. Louis XIV was to some extent involved in 1687 in the censures of the bull *In Cœna Domini* (ii. 385 and n. 5); there was never any question of an express excommunication: Pastor, *Geschichte der Päpste*, xiv. 927, n. 4; J. Orcibal, *Louis XIV contre Innocent XI*, 1949, pp. 11–13, 26, &c.

iv. 642, n. 6. The duke of Holstein is Christian Albrecht, duke of Gottorp: iv. 525, n. 1.

iv. 643, ll. 1, 2. In April, May, and June, there were several petitions to the house of commons against the East India Company, but there appears to have been no ground for a general attack: *C.J.*, x. 92, 120, 135, 167.

iv. 644 and nn. 1–3. See above, additions to i. *73*, n. 2; iv. 479, n. 2.

v. 7, critical note. Coleton is Sir Peter Colleton, 1635–94; second

baronet 1666; M.P. for Bossiney 1681, 1689–94: G. E. C., *Baronetage*, iii. 161–2.

v. 9 and n. 1. Lumley was a convert from Roman Catholicism; but receiving the Sacrament according to the rites of the Church of England was a qualification required of all office-holders by the Test Act. By being a witness Evelyn perhaps means that he signed a certificate that Lumley had received it.

v. 27, n. 2, 29, n. 3. On Torrington's conduct see further J. C. M. Warnsinck, *De vloot van den Koning-Stadhouder, 1689–90*, 1934, pp. 142–4, &c.

v. 44, n. 6. On the Arundel statues at Oxford see further Dr. J. Hess, in *English Miscellany*, i (1950), 197–220.

v. 90, n. 3. The warrant for Fermor was for a barony, not an earldom.

v. 91 and n. 1. 'Metaschematism' occurs again, v. 295.

v. 111, n. 4, 112, n. 1. For Leinster see v. 139, n. 2.

v. 128, notice for 15 January. By the Reader of St. Martin's Evelyn may mean Dr. W. Lancaster (v. 121, n. 1); see v. 147, notice of Lancaster's sermon on 16 July.

v. 147 and n. 1. The earlier sermon may be that preached by the Reader of St. Martin's on 15 January 1693: see preceding addition.

v. 150, n. 3. 'Luttrell, 31 July' is an error for 'Luttrell, 1 July'. See further Luttrell, 27 June (iii. 124, 127).

v. 159, 164. The house in Dover Street was occupied by the dowager countess of Clancarty (Elizabeth Maccarty) in 1696: E. to Wotton, 30 March 1696 (Bohn, iii. 347). It was perhaps occupied by the younger William Glanville in 1694: see v. 169.

v. 166 and n. 3. St. James's chapel is perhaps that of the Palace; if so, one of its set of six or eight chaplains may be meant: for them see Chamberlayne, *Angliae Notitia*, 1692, i. 175; 1694, p. 216.

v. 170, n. 3. Quin was father of James Quin, the actor.

v. 182, n. 3. The first earl of Dartmouth is an error for the first Baron Dartmouth.

v. 184, notice for 13 June. The fast, for the preservation of the king and queen, and for prosperity in the war, was ordered by a proclamation dated 14 May; it was to be kept on 23 May in London and on 13 June in the country: *London Gazette*, 17 May.

v. 192 and n. 1. A variant of this story is found in London about 1630; it is there told of a monk of Westminster Abbey, who, seeing first a 'maske' at the court of Henry VII, and then its aftermath the next morning, became so convinced of 'the mutability of the glories of this world' that he became an anchorite: *Archaeologia*, xciii (1949), 159–60, quoting *Autobiography of Thomas Raymond*.

v. 205, n. 5. Lloyd is at least as likely as Tenison to have been Evelyn's informant regarding Mary's papers.

v. 209, n. 7. Charles II had complained about the increase in the number of private acts in a speech to Parliament on 19 May 1662: *L.J.*, xi. 474.

v. 228, n. 2. Fleetwood is an error; he was lecturer at St. Dunstan in the West: v. 220, n. 2. The lecturer at St. Clement Danes was John Adams: v. 240 and n. 5.

v. 228, n. 3. On the condition or the currency at this time, and its reform, see Macaulay, v. 2562–80; vi. 2632–6, 2651–4.

v. 257, n. 1. The note is badly worded. It was through Dr. Gabriel Offley, and not through his wife, that Mrs. Graham was related to Lady Cotton.

v. 258 and n. 6. The two generals are Count Donat Heissler and — Pollant. For them and the battle (best called the battle on the Bega river) see O. Redlich, *Geschichte Österreichs*, vol. vi (in 'Allgemeine Staatengeschichte', ed. H. Oncken), 1921, pp. 585–6.

v. 264, n. 2. Precautions were being taken at court against possible assassins: *Post-Boy*, 16 January.

v. 275, n. 1. For the controversy see *Journal of Modern History*, xviii (1946), 306–13.

v. 284, notice for 30 January. Presumably there was no service at Wotton on 31 January, as there should have been according to the statute. The fast was held on 31 January this year in London. Compare a similar irregularity at Deptford in 1670: iii. 542.

v. 292, n. 3. Master of the Savoy is an error for minister at the Savoy.

v. 299 and n. 1. Evelyn perhaps refers to his dangers by weather on the Ligurian coast in October 1644: ii. 170 (i. 107–8), 178 (i. 112–13).

v. 330, n. 1. St. Saviour's Dock was (and is) in Bermondsey, a little to the west of the boundary between it and Rotherhithe.

v. 514, n. 2. The report about Portugal was false; the Methuen Treaty was not signed until May 1703, and Portugal did not participate actively in the war until 1704.

v. 545, n. 3. For the Archduke Charles as king of Spain see M. Landau, *Geschichte Kaiser Karls VI als König von Spanien*, 1889.

v. 553 and n. 2. Ragotski is Francis II Rákóczy, prince of Transylvania, 1676–1735: *Encyclopaedia Britannica*, 11th ed.; for his rebellion see Klopp, vols. x, xi.

v. 595 and n. 4. Come is Coombe House in Kingston: *V.C.H. Surrey*, iii. 502.

INDEX

INTRODUCTION

This index is intended both for scholars consulting Evelyn's Diary from time to time for more or less detached statements of fact or opinion, and for readers of the Diary who want to recapture passages in what they have read. Although the interest of the Diary extends far beyond England, the majority of consultants are likely to be English or English-speaking, and it is for them, rather than for a hypothetical universal public, that the index is designed. There are some qualitative differences in treatment, corresponding to the relative importance of the various subjects. The large number of very short notices in the Diary has made the utmost compression necessary; I have tried, however (apart from some omissions stated below), to include all proper names and the principal subjects emerging in the Diary.

While I have tried to keep the occasional consultant in view, and to make the index as generally intelligible as possible, the repetition of some passages in the Diary, and more especially the later recension of its opening part ('De Vita Propria'), presents a major problem. This I have tried to solve by the use of brackets where the recension (in vol. i) repeats more or less exactly passages in the principal text (in vol. ii), and elsewhere by using the word 'repeated', or sometimes by simple normal references. For practical reasons it was impossible to grade the repetitions into the more or less faithful; if fresh matter appears in the repetitions, it is indexed in the normal way.

References are to the text, to the text and notes, or to the notes alone.

Many of Evelyn's statements are so fragmentary as to require completion rather than explanation in the notes; the index is obliged to deal with the completed statements and must ignore the fragments; as a result, where a reference is to text and note, consultants will often find it most quickly by turning first to the note. This is especially the case with works

of art: for example, Cellini's Perseus, which bears a false name in the text (ii. 193 and n. 4; repeated i. 120); it may also occur with battles and even sometimes with persons; in a few cases names occur only in the index (e.g. the Seven Bishops). I have omitted references to the notes when they are simple cross-references and generally when they consist only of citations of authorities.

The following paragraphs deal with particular matters:

Abbreviations and Symbols

add. Additions and Corrections, in the present volume.

And. This is used as a convenient abbreviation for 'in connexion with' or 'in relation to'; sometimes it has to cover a relationship which cannot be precisely stated except at some length.

E. This is used exclusively to indicate John Evelyn the diarist.

Geneal. See *Genealogical* below.

Select. Used in subject and similar entries, to indicate that significant notices alone are indexed.

(?) This is used to imply that a statement in the text or notes is doubtful. Where statements in the text are certainly wrong, I have occasionally used '(error)' instead of '(?)'. See also below, p. 30.

All other abbreviations are in current use.

Arrangement in entries

The general principle is to follow the alphabet for the order of the subheadings, and of the individual items within them. But this principle cannot be applied in indexing chronological sequences of notices, or where items are defined by phrases or sentences; nor is it altogether suitable for entries containing important and miscellaneous sections. I have therefore modified or abandoned it on occasion.

For towns described by Evelyn the most important passages are generally his descriptions. The references to these are given first, and, if a description is indexed in detail, the various items follow, first the general statements, then the topographical details. After this the other sub-headings follow in alphabetical order.

For persons (apart from those mentioned only once) the first reference, without further specification, is to the principal biographical and bibliographical note (further similar references may follow). The first subheadings are generally Character, containing references to Evelyn's principal descriptive notices for the person,

and Chronological series, the main series of events in the person's life (it is liable to contain miscellaneous unspecialized activities). Then follow, in alphabetical order, subheadings giving the person's principal specialized activities and interests, then subheadings for social life and genealogy, and references for notices of associates and dependants.

Artists and Musicians

The more celebrated are generally indexed under the names by which they are most commonly known (Raphael, and not Sanzio), with cross-references from the surname where they seem necessary.

Books

All books mentioned in the Diary, apart from those written by Evelyn, all books used by Evelyn as sources for the Diary, and some other books mentioned in the notes, are entered under BOOKS; the contents and arrangement of the section are set out in an explanatory note. Books and other writings by Evelyn are indexed under EVELYN.

Cathedral Clergy

All clerics, apart from the popes, are indexed under their surnames, with cross-references from their benefices. The cross-references for bishops, deans, and diocesan and cathedral clergy, are given in special entries, separate from any other entries, under the place-name concerned.

Cross-references

The dates following the names in lists of dignitaries and office-holders are those of their tenure of the dignity or office concerned.

In some cases where there are cross-references from dignities to their holders, the particular dignity is not mentioned in the entry for the holder; it will be found in the principal biographical note relating to him.

'De Vita Propria'

For its treatment see above, p. 26.

Diplomatists

The diplomatic representatives sent from and to the various states are all listed in the entry DIPLOMATISTS; they do not appear in the entries for the various states, except in such cases as Bantam.

Double entries and Double references

If a man is known more or less equally by two names, provided that there are very few references, full entries may be found under both names: thus Scipione Pulzone, commonly called Gaetano, has two full entries.

Some entries for dignitaries consist of a heading followed by a cross-reference to the proper name and, in brackets, unspecified references to the text and notes. This occurs only where there are very few references. Details are given in the entry under the proper name.

In lists of dignitaries references are occasionally inserted after the names. These references are to where the dignitary is mentioned in text or notes as holder of the dignity; there may be further notices of him, and if the individual rather than the office is required, the consultant should turn to the proper name.

Evelyn family

In the entries for the various members, apart from the more recent, I have inserted the relationship to Evelyn. The principal members, when they are mentioned in entries other than their own, are distinguished thus:

E .. John Evelyn the Diarist.
Mrs. Evelyn .. Mrs. Mary Evelyn, Evelyn's wife.
George Evelyn .. Evelyn's brother.
George Evelyn, sen. .. Evelyn's grandfather.
John Evelyn, jnr. .. Evelyn's son.
(Sir) John Evelyn .. Evelyn's grandson.
Mary Evelyn .. Evelyn's daughter.
Richard Evelyn .. Evelyn's brother.
Richard Evelyn, sen. .. Evelyn's father.
Little Richard Evelyn .. Evelyn's eldest son.

Other members of the family are more fully particularized.

Genealogical

Statements of family relationships in text or notes are indexed as 'Geneal.' (for genealogical or genealogy). All passages in the notes referred to under this term are exclusively genealogical; those in the text may contain other matter.

Names

False names and false spellings. Where proper names in the text are completely false (e.g. Baker for Halley, iv. 314), they are in-

dexed with cross-references to the correct names. Where spellings are false, if an error occurs in the first three letters, I have generally indexed them, with a cross-reference to the conventional form; if, however, the true form is sufficiently obvious the false spelling is not indexed (e.g. Licester for Leicester). If an error occurs only after the first three letters, the name is indexed only under the conventional form. In the entries under the conventional forms I have inserted (in brackets) the form or forms used by Evelyn if they are at all likely to be difficult to recognize. In a few cases names have gone wrong in the notes. I have used Montagu and Montague for the same man, Neile and Neale, and so on. In the index all notices relating to an individual or a place are either dealt with in a single entry, with cross-references as required, or, if divided into separate entries, are provided with cross-references.

Foreign names of persons. I have tried to follow the rules for the British Museum catalogue. All foreign names possessing prefixes are indexed under their principal component (Pozzo and not dal Pozzo, Ruyter, not de Ruyter), except French names and names in common use in England. For French names, if there is a preceding definite article, it is regarded as part of the principal component; a preceding preposition, unless it is combined in a single word with the article, is disregarded. Names in common use in England are indexed under the English forms (Vandyck, Vanbrugh). Cross-references are given where they seem desirable.

Names with queries. When Evelyn names a man and no identification is possible, he is indexed under his surname, with a dash for his Christian name: Smith, Rev. —: sermon by, iv. 136. If there is a possible identification, it is inserted, in brackets, with a query: Smith, Rev. — (John Smith ?): sermon by, iv. 136 and n. 1, with a cross-reference from the full name: Smith, Rev. John: *see* Smith, Rev. —; or sometimes there is a cross-reference to the full name: Smith, Rev. —: *see* Smith, Rev. John. If there is a probable identification, but short of full proof, there is only an entry under the full name; a query is inserted at some point: Smith, Rev. John: sermon by (?), iv. 136 and n. 1; or: Smith, Rev. John, iv. 136, n. 1; sermons by (?), iv. 136, 141. The consultant searching for minor personalities should examine the entries for all bearers of the surnames of the persons whom he is pursuing.

Omissions

The contents of certain lists are not indexed: the dignitaries appearing in some processions (ii. 279–81; iii. 41–3, 278–81), ex-

cept where their proper names are given; and the dancers in the ballet, *Les festes de Bacchus* (iii. 31–2).

The appendixes in vol. i are not indexed, and the indexing of the introduction is summary.

I have not indexed, or not in detail, the ordinary comings and goings of Evelyn, Mrs. Evelyn, and his brothers and sisters-in-law; and ordinary services at churches which he habitually attended. Under Evelyn I have omitted, so far as possible, those of his activities in which other persons were directly concerned, and generally whatever the consultant should search for in other entries.

I have not indexed notes of sermons for ordinary theological or moral topics, or the three persons of the Trinity; and I have not indexed texts of sermons, except where they are the subject of historical comment, &c. I have tried to index these notes for all persons, other than the Trinity (but the Trinity as such is indexed); I have included some parables, but not all; and I have indexed them for politics, religious controversies (against Roman Catholics, Nonconformists, atheists, &c.), and for some special topics, notably death-bed repentance and the duration of the world. The indexing is necessarily defective, partly because I did not recognize the importance of some topics at the outset, partly because Evelyn's notes are sometimes too loose or too allusive to be reached through the index.

When place-names occur in the notes as the homes of persons, they are not indexed (I have generally indexed them when they occur in the text, unless they are little more than parts of the persons' names). Constituencies of members of parliament are not indexed. Benefices held by clergy are indexed. Inclusions and exclusions of this kind are determined by the available books of reference.

Books, manuscripts, maps, paintings, and engravings, cited in the notes as authorities for statements, in general are not indexed; there are some exceptions: Evelyn's own writings; letters to and from him; and a few books and so on, selected as being likely to be of special interest to scholars. Newspapers are treated more fully, on account of their peculiar interest in the period of the Diary.

Peers and Foreign Nobility

English, Scottish, and Irish peers and peeresses and holders of courtesy titles, other than members of the royal family, and Jacobite peers and peeresses, are indexed under their family names, with cross-references from their titles: e.g. Bennet, Sir Henry, earl of Arlington, with cross-reference from Arlington.

Peeresses who remarry into a lower rank are indexed under the surname of the higher rank, with cross-references from their titles and lower-ranking surnames: e.g. Fitzroy, Isabella, duchess of Grafton, later wife of Sir Thomas Hanmer, with cross-references from Grafton and Hanmer. In a very few cases, where peers are mentioned only by their titles, they are indexed only under their titles. The titles are given in the shortest form compatible with clearness.

Foreign noblemen and noblewomen, other than members of royal and reigning families, are indexed under either their titles or their family names, whichever appear to be the more commonly used; there are cross-references from their less frequently used names or titles, when the latter are given in text or notes.

Royalty

Rulers, their wives, sons, daughters, and daughters-in-law, are indexed under their christian or regnal names. Cross-references from kingdoms or principalities are given for a few minor rulers: e.g. Honorato II, prince of Monaco. The principal contemporary rulers are listed in vol. i, app. iii. (p. 145).

Sermons. See *Omissions* above.

Social

Simple notices, such as 'I visited Lord Arlington', 'Lord Arlington visited me', 'I dined with Lord Arlington', &c., are all indexed as 'Arlington: Social'. If, however, other persons besides Evelyn and Arlington are mentioned, the formula is 'Arlington: Social: parties', the visits, &c., in which Arlington alone is mentioned being distinguished as 'Arlington: Social: alone, &c.' In smaller entries I have not divided Social into the two classes. The term also includes some other social activities; these are precisely stated in the index.

Evelyn writes almost indifferently 'I dined with Lord Arlington', 'I dine with Lady Arlington', and 'I dined at Arlington House'; in the second and third forms, unless Arlington's absence is stated or clearly implied, it cannot be assumed (it may, of course, be known from other sources). I have not attempted to give cross-references in such cases; the consultant must search all the relevant entries.

The term is used residually; notices of social intercourse in which some more specific statement is made about the other per-

son concerned are indexed only for the latter, and are not usually inserted again under Social.

States and Rulers

Evelyn, in notices concerning French political activities after about 1660, practically equates France as a state, the king of France as its ruler, and Louis XIV, the individual king: France denotes Louis XIV. I have brought the notices together so far as possible, and, in view of Louis XIV's personality, have indexed them under Louis XIV. In the case of other states, apart from England, Spain, and the United Provinces, I have generally used the ruler's name in the same way.

The governmental activities of the States General of the United Provinces, and the political activities of the Princes of Orange, are so distinct that no problem arises. England presents serious difficulties, arising partly from the large number of notices to be indexed (necessitating a detailed classification of the entries), partly from the nature of the English polity: although the king was the chief governor of the state, there is a sharp difference between the actions which express the personalities of the kings and those in which the nation was an active or at least acquiescent participant; the Secret Treaty of Dover, the religious policy of James II, the Partition Treaty of 1699, are the work of the various kings. In general I have indexed all political activities (including religious policy) under England, with additional references or cross-references where the kings' personal concern is clear.

Subject-entries

See Synopsis of Subject-headings below.

Women

Women are generally indexed under their married names, and, if married more than once, under their latest married names, with cross-references from their earlier names: if, however, a woman previously married to a man possessing a title marries later a man of lower rank, I have followed seventeenth-century usage, and indexed her under the higher rank: thus George Evelyn's second wife is indexed as Lady Cotton.

Single women, in their own entries or in those relating to other persons, are generally distinguished by surname and Christian name, without further prefix; I have generally omitted 'Lady' as a courtesy title for the unmarried daughters of dukes and earls.

Married women, in their own entries or in those relating to

other persons, are generally distinguished by the word 'Mrs.' or, if titled, by their titles; for the wives of knights I have used 'Lady', where 'Dame' would be more correct; I have also occasionally used 'Lady' for peeresses. In the headings to the entries for married women, I have generally given their husbands' names and, if they appear in the text under both their maiden and their married names, their maiden names are also given.

Words and Phrases

These are all indexed in a single alphabetical sequence headed WORDS AND PHRASES. Its contents are explained in a preliminary note.

Synopsis of Subject-headings

All subjects are entered in the general alphabetical sequence of the index. Those defined by proper names are entered under them. Those not defined by proper names are grouped, as far as is practicable, under general headings. The following classified list gives these headings; it is confined to them except in a few cases, where there is a choice of proper names:

Special Headings

Books. Diplomatists. Words and Phrases.

Amusements

Amusements. Entertainers and Entertainments. Lotteries. Puzzles. Waterworks.

Billiards. Cards and Card-playing. Gaming.

Dancing. Masquerades.

Bear-baiting. Bull-baiting. Cock-fighting. Dog-fighting. Horse-baiting. Tiger-baiting.

Boat-racing. Bowls. Coach-racing. Field-sports. Horse-racing. Jousting. Pall-mall. Skating. Swimming. Tennis. Wrestling.

Applied Science

General

Mensuration.

Engineering

Automata. Bridges. Canals and Water-ways. Inventions and Mechanical Curiosities. Land-drainage. Paving. Roads. Street-lighting. Water-mills. Water-supply.

Land-utilization

Agriculture. Fruit-trees and Fruits. Gardening. Trees and Timber. Vineyards and Viticulture.

Medicine and Hygiene

Anatomy and Physiology. Baths and Bathing. Corpses. Embryology, Human. Epidemics. Illnesses. Medicine and Surgery. Monstrosities (human). Plague. Poisons. Soap.

Metal-working

Gold and Silver. Metals.

Bibliographical

Book-bindings. Libraries. Manuscripts. Newspapers, Newsletters, and other Periodicals. Printing. Publishing and Bookselling. Shorthand.

Culture and Learning

Academies and Learned Societies. Antiquities. Inscriptions. Learning. Museums and Miscellaneous Collections. Philology.

Genealogy and Heraldry

Baronets. Heraldry and Heralds. Knights and Orders of Knighthood.

Geography

Civilized World. Exploration. Geography. Maps and Engraved Views.

Literary

Ballads. Diaries. Dictionaries. Hymns. Libels and Lampoons. Proverbs and Mottoes. Psalms. Romances.

Military and Naval

Arms and Armour. Arsenals. Explosions. Fortifications. Gunpowder and Salt-petre. Light-houses. Military. Navigation. Pirates and Privateers. Ships and Shipping.

Music and Theatre

Music

Music. Opera.

Theatre

Plays, Operas, Masques, and Ballets. Theatre.

Religion (apart from churches, sects, &c., with distinctive names)

Angels. Anti-Trinitarianism. Atheism and Atheists. Church. Enthusiasts. Libertines. Miracles. Naturalists. Nonconformists, Puritans, and Sectaries. Pilgrims. Preaching and Sermons. Prophecies. Sermons, Printed. Theists or Deists.

Science

General

Natural History Collections. Science. Scientific Instruments.

Astronomy and Chronology

Astronomy. Chronology. Clocks and Watches. Sundials.

Biology and Zoology

Animals (mammals). Aviaries. Biology and Zoology. Birds. Coral. Deer. Dog. Fish, Crustaceans, &c. Horses and Horsemanship. Insects. Monsters. Reptiles. Shells. Toads. Worms. Zoological Gardens.

Botany

Botany. Flowers. Plants. Vegetation.

Chemistry

Alchemy. Chemistry.

Geology and Mineralogy

Amber. Caves. Crystal or Rock-crystal. Earthquakes. Fossils. Gems and Semi-precious Stones. Geology. Medicinal and Hot Springs. Minerals. Petrifactions. Volcanoes.

Mathematics

Mathematics.

Physics

Perpetual Motion. Physics. Vacuum.
Compass. Magnetism.
Acoustics. Echoes.
Camera obscura. Optics.

Weather, &c.

Exhalation, Fiery. Floods. Weather and Climate.

Sociology

Education

Education. Schools and Colleges. Universities.

Finance

Banks and Bankers. Currency. Mints.

Folklore

Animals, Fabulous. Astrology. Folklore. Giants. Legends. Signs and Portents. Witches.

Food and Drink

Decoys. Drinking and Drunkenness. Fish-ponds. Food and Drink. Meals. Wines.

Law, &c.

Crime. Duels. Justice: Administration of. Law. Oaths.

Politics

Politics. Slaves.

Public Celebrations, &c.

Ceremonies. Fireworks and Illuminations. Popular Celebrations. Processions.

Trade and Industry

Auction-sales. Fairs and Markets. Fuel. Glass. Leather. Paper. Pottery and Porcelain. Textiles. Trade and Industry.

Transport and Travel

Bills of Health. Coaches. Inns and Travellers' Lodgings. Passes and Passports. Transport. Travel.

Miscellaneous

Charity and Charitable Collections. Hospitals and Charitable Institutions.
Curiosity Shops, &c.
Dress. Cosmetics.
Fires and Fire-fighting.
Holidays, Secular.
Housing. Lighting.
Mountebanks.
Promenade. Pleasure-gardens.
Tobacco. Snuff.

Visual Arts

General

Art-collections. Art-dealers. Effigies. Funeral Portraits.

Architecture

Architecture (features; styles and stylistic terms). Building Materials. Fountains. Gardens. Grottoes. Town-planning.

Decorative and Minor

Embroidery. Enamel. Furniture. Straw-work. Tapestry. Turning. Waxworks.

Graphic Arts

Engraving and Etching. Mosaic. Painting and Drawing. Stained Glass.

Sculpture

Brasses, Sepulchral. Coins and Medals. Ivory. Sculpture: Ancient. Sculpture: Materials. Sculpture: Medieval and Modern. Wood-Carving.

Miscellaneous

Memory. Transmigration of Souls. Views.

~ is used to avoid ambiguity, and indicates that the entry belongs with the preceding reference.

INDEX

Aaron (Aron): rod of (relic), ii. 275 & n. 3; in sermons, v. 63, 309.
Abano, Pietro d' (Petrus de Apono): bust of, ii. 463 & n. 4.
Abbate, Niccolo dell': painting by, ii. 113 & n. 11 (i. 73).
Abbeville (Abb-Ville, Albe-Vill): notice, 1643, ii. 85 & nn. 1, 3 (i. 57–8); E at, 1650, 1652, iii. 12 & n. 3, 17, 54 & n. 3; house at, ii. 141, n. 3.
Abbigenses: *see* Albigenses.
Abbot, Rev. —: sermon by, iii. 75.
Abbot, George, archbishop of Canterbury: tomb, &c., of, at Guildford, iii. 88 & n. 5.
Abbot, Robert, uncle of Sir R. Clayton: account of, iv. 185–6 & n.
Abburie: *see* Albury.
Abdy, —: *see* Abdy, Sir J.
Abdy, Anthony: geneal., ii. 480, n. 4.
Abdy, Sir John; baronet 1662, ii. 480, n. 4; at Padua, 1646 (?), ii. 480 & n. 4; poem by, ii. 479, n. 2; social (?), iii. 83 & n. 3.
Abel: in sermons, iv. 26, 499.
Abell, John, singer: performs, iv. 270 & n. 2.
Abercrombie, Duncombe: geneal., iii. 358, n. 5.
Abergavenny (Bergavenny): twelfth Lord, 1666–95: *see* Nevill, George.
Abiathar: in sermon, v. 298 & n. 3.
Abigail: in comparison, iii. 615.
Abimelech: in sermon, v. 347.
Abingdon (Abington), Berks., ii. 23 (i. 17).
Abingdon: second Earl of, 1699–1743: *see* Bertie, Montague.
Abinger, Surrey: Evelyn property in, i. 2, 3; mill in, v. 606, n. 1; *manors in*: Abinger: as part of Wotton estate, v. 337; Abinger, Paddington Bray, Paddington Pembroke: courts held, v. 478 & n. 1; mentioned, ii. 5 (i. 2); i. 4.
church: advowson of, ii. 5 & n. 1 (i. 2); services at: for fast-day, iii. 423; ~ ordinary, iii. 220, 561 *bis*; iv. 111 *bis*, 377, 558 *bis*; v. 202–3, 206–7, 207–8, 216, 445; *rectors of*: *see* Geree, Stephen (1646–65); Offley, Gabriel (1665–83); Crawley, T.
Abinger (*cont.*)
(1683–5); Offley, Robert (1690–1743); *curates at*: *see* Andrews, — (*c.* 1665); Evans, Rev. John (1677); Wye, R. (*c.* 1678–80); Wells, W. (*c.* 1692–5); Nasson, — (*c.* 1700–5).
Abraham: in sermons, iii. 11; iv. 31, 32, 170 & n. 8, 237, 243, 495, 532; v. 63, 251, 268, 271, 274, 296, 306, 308, 334, 347, 387, 397, 405, 414, 463, 499, 509, 554.
Absalom: in sermon, v. 603.
Abs-Court: *see* Walton-on-Thames.
Abyssinia: books from, ii. 301.
Academies and Learned Societies: Italian, ii. 364 & n. 5; individual societies: della Crusca, ii. 415–16 & n.; Filomati (Siena), ii. 202, n. 3; Olimpica (Vicenza), ii. 482 & n. 2; Umoristi, ii. 364–5 & nn.; the Sarottis' society at Venice, iv. 278, 279, n. 1; mathematical college proposed by E, iii. 232 & n. 2; *see also* London: topography: Gresham College; London: environs: Chelsea College; Royal Society.
Achaia: relic from, ii. 263.
Achan: in sermon, iii. 312.
Acheron: lake of, ii. 347 & n. 5.
Acherusia: lake of, ii. 347 & n. 5.
Achitophel (Ahitophel): in sermons, iii. 203; v. 48, 345.
Acoustics [*see also* Echoes]: walls of room constructed for resonance, ii. 467; experiment, iii. 563; discourse on, iv. 370.
Acquapendente: notice, ii. 209 & nn. 2–4; mentioned, ii. 407, n. 5.
Acquapendente, Fabritius de, ii. 209 & n. 5.
Acre: pillars from, in Venice, ii. 443, n. 1.
Acteon (Heleon): at Lake Nemi, ii. 317 & n. 4.
Actors: *see* Theatre.
Adam: in sermons, iii. 159, 168; iv. 26, 135, 239; v. 165, 181, 274–5, 387, 503, 613; and Eve ('our first parents', &c.): in sermons, iii. 27; iv. 166, 433; v. 28, 62, 73, 274, 397.
Adams, —, servant of E: dies, &c., iii. 631; iv. 1.

Adams, John; D.D. 1705; provost of King's College, Cambridge, 1712–20, v. 240, n. 5; as Boyle Lecturer: sermon, v. 528; as lecturer at St. Clement Danes: sermons, v. 228 & n. 2; *add.*; v. 240–55 *passim*, 275, 276–7, 292.
Adams, Sir Thomas, bt.: as president of St. Thomas's Hospital, iii. 391 & nn. 4, 5.
Adda, Ferdinando, conte d'; cardinal 1690, iv. 494, n. 1; as apostolic minister in England, iv. 493–4; attends lord mayor's feast, iv. 562–3 & n.
Addey, John: *see* Adye, J.
Addiscombe, in Croydon, Surrey: Sir Purbeck Temple's house, v. 214 & n. 2, 219 & n. 1; Lady Temple dies at, v. 385; inherited by William Draper, v. 385–6, 425; E visits, v. 425–8, 470; rebuilding, v. 509; the new house: notice, v. 541 & n. 1; ~ E visits, v. 605; *see also* v. 139, n. 6, 287, n. 6.
Addresses: *see* England: addresses.
Adige (Adice, Athesis), river, ii. 428 & n. 7; at Verona, ii. 485 & n. 4; French and Imperialists campaign on, 1701, v. 465, n. 2, 467 & n. 1, 471.
Adria: ruins of, ii. 428 & n. 6.
Adrian: *see* Hadrian.
Adrian IV, pope: tomb of, ii. 289 & n. 7.
Adrianople: Sir W. Hussey dies at, v. 71, n. 6.
Adriatic Sea, ii. 428–9 & n., 446; Venetian supremacy over, &c., ii. 431–2.
Adrumetum: Bishop of (*in partibus*): *see* Leyburn, J.
Adye *or* Addey, John: charitable bequest of, at Deptford, iii. 223, n. 4.
Aelius Aristides: statue of, ii. 301 & n. 1.
Æmiliana, Margareta, supposed courtesan, ii. 468 & n. 4.
Æmilius Macer: statue of (modern), ii. 486–7 & n.
Aemilius Paulus, Lucius: medallion of, iv. 397 & n. 2.
Aeneas: at Lake Avernus, ii. 346; trumpeter of (Misenus), ii. 350 & n. 1.
Aeneas Silvius: *see* Pius II.
Aerskin, —: *see* Erskine, W.
Aesculapius: object sacred to, ii. 500, n. 4.
Affonso VI, king of Portugal: and Castelmelhor, iv. 130 & n. 1, 454; mourning for, in England, iv. 351 & n. 1.
Africa: hostilities between English and Dutch in, 1664, iii. 387, n. 5; imports from, at Marseilles, ii. 166 (i. 105); desert of: monster in, iv. 630; locusts in, iv. 54; scorpion from, iv. 632.
Africa Company: *see* Guinea Company.
African Church: preaching in, &c.: in sermon, iv. 288.
Agen: J. J. Scaliger born at, ii. 487, n. 1.
Agesandrus, sculptor, ii. 304.
Agincourt, battle of: prisoner taken at, iv. 40 & n. 2.
Agnano, Lago d', ii. 339–40 & nn.; Grotta del Cane at, *ib.*
Agrate, Marco d': statue by, ii. 493 & n. 3.
Agriculture:
 enclosure: progress of, in Leicestershire, iii. 122 & n. 3.
 equipment, &c.: farm-buildings, &c., iv. 256; ploughs: Col. Blount's, iii. 170; ~ sembrador, iii. 519 & n. 2.
 method: cultivation of newly-drained fenland, iii. 555; use of salts in: discourse on, iii. 318.
 particular crops: cole-seed (rape), iii. 555 & n. 5; hemp, iii. 555; liquorice, iii. 131 & n. 3; saffron, iii. 556; wheat: in Huntingdonshire, iii. 135.
 special areas: England: Lincolnshire, iii. 131; Thanet, iii. 611, 615–16; Yorkshire, iii. 128; Italy: Lombardy, ii. 491 & n. 1; Padua-Vicenza, ii. 481 & n. 1; Terra di Lavoro, ii. 324–5 & n.; Verona, environs, ii. 488 & n. 1; Switzerland: Valais, ii. 515 & n. 4.
 See also Fruit; Gardens; Vegetation; Vineyards.
Agrippa (Herod Agrippa II): in sermons, iii. 249; iv. 531; v. 75, 266.
Agrippa, Marcus: builds Pantheon, ii. 371 & n. 2; forms Portus Julius, ii. 345, n. 2.
Agrippina: Lavacrum of, ii. 247.
Agrippina, the elder: funerary cyst of, ii. 223 & n. 6.
Agrippina, the younger: murder and tomb of, ii. 349 & nn. 5, 6.

Ahab: in sermons, iv. 33; v. 165 & n. 3, 347, 487, 556–7.
Ahimelech, v. 298, n. 3.
Ahitophel: *see* Achitophel.
Ahlefeldt, Frederik, Count, Danish ambassador to England 1660–1, iii. 270, n. 2; presents condolences (?), iii. 257; attends meeting of Philosophical Society (Royal Society), iii. 270, 271; social (?), iii. 255 & n. 2.
Ahmad III, sultan of Turkey: accession of, v. 545–6 & n.
Ahmed Hadu (Mohammed Ohadu), Moroccan ambassador to England 1682, iv. 265, n. 5, 266; audience for, iv. 265–6 & nn.; entertained by: duchess of Portsmouth, iv. 267–8 & n.; ~ earl of Berkeley, iv. 285; displays of horsemanship by, iv. 268–9 & n.; goes to theatres, iv. 269 & n. 2; admitted F.R.S., iv. 283 & n. 3; visits New Hall, Essex, iv. 287.
Aiguillon, Duchess of, ii. 133, n. 4 *ad fin.*
Ailesbury: Earls of: *see* Bruce, Robert, earl of Elgin, &c., first earl, 1664–85; Bruce, Thomas, second earl, 1685–1741.
Aisne, river: in campaign, 1650, iii. 17, n. 3.
Aix-en-Provence: notice, ii. 162–3 & nn. (i. 103).
Aix-en-Provence: Archbishop of, 1687–1708: *see* Cosnac, D. de.
Alassio (Araisso), Liguria: coral-fishery at, ii. 169 & n. 11 (i. 107).
Alba: Duke of: *see* Alva.
Alba Julia, Transylvania: occupied by Count E. Tökölyi, v. 35 & n. 7.
Albani, Francesco, ii. 420, n. 5; paintings by, ii. 369 & n. 2.
Albani, Giovanni Francesco: *see* Clement XI.
Albano: notice, ii. 356 & nn. 1–3; the Curiatii of, ii. 361.
Albemarle: Dukes, &c., of: *see* Monck, George, first duke, 1660–70; Monck, Anne, his duchess; Monck, Christopher, second duke, 1670–88; Montagu, Elizabeth, formerly Monck, his duchess, later duchess of Montagu.
Albemarle: Earl of: *see* Keppel, A. J. van, first earl, 1696–1718.
Albenga, Liguria, ii. 169 (i. 107 & n. 1).
Albert: *see* Dürer.
Albert, Archduke: geneal., &c., ii. 70, n. 4.
Alberti, Cherubino, ii. 273, n. 4; tomb of, ii. 374, n. 7; paintings by, ii. 273 & n. 4, 296 & n. 5, 298.
Alberti, Durante: painting by, ii. 366 & n. 1.
Alberti, Giovanni, ii. 273, n. 4; tomb of, ii. 374, n. 7; paintings by, ii. 267 & n. 3, 273 & n. 4.
Alberto Eremitano (Alberto di Padova): bust of, ii. 463 & n. 4.
Albe-Vill: *see* Abbeville.
Albigenses (Abbigenses): supposed progenitors of Waldenses, iii. 152 & n. 1; as one of the Two Witnesses, iv. 637, n. 1.
Albury, Surrey: George Evelyn married at, ii. 24 (i. 18); Weston in, iii. 14, n. 8; *see also* ii. 24, n. 2.
Albury Park: (i) as property of Arundel and later of Henry Howard, sixth duke of Norfolk, &c., ii. 27, n. 4 *ad fin.*, 77 & n. 2; E hopes to buy, 1652, iii. 59, n. 1; art-collection at, iii. 155 & nn. 1–3; great room in, ii. 551 & n. 5; garden: altering, iii. 154–5; ~ E designs, iii. 496 & n. 2, 561–2 & n.; iv. 111; *see also* iv. 558; park, iii. 326; E visits, ii. 77 (i. 51), 543; iii. 88, 154–5, 325–6, 496, 561–2; iv. 111.
— (ii) as property of Heneage Finch, later baron of Gernsey and earl of Aylesford: purchase of, iv. 558 & n. 1; garden, *ib.*; visits to, iv. 558; v. 219, 581 & n. 1(?); Rev. William Wotton at, v. 184, n. 2.
church: services in, iii. 326 *bis*, 496; *rectors of*: *see* Oughtred, W. (1610–60); Hansley, J. (1660–7); Duncombe, Rev. George (1691–1714).
Alchemy [called chymistry by E when he names it]: alkahest: examined, iii. 302 & n. 1; elixir or philosopher's stone: MS. relating to, iv. 215; ~ attainability of: views on, iii. 158 & n. 1; v. 599; mercury of metals, iii. 28, n. 2; transmutation of metals: powder of projection, iii. 483 & n. 4; ~ attempts at, &c., i. 118; iii. 24; v. 599; ~ supposed specimen of, ii. 192 & n. 1

Alchemy (*cont.*)
(i. 119); ~ stories concerning, iii. 52–3.
practitioners, adepts, &c.: Dr. E. Dickinson, v. 599 & n. 1; du Menie, iii. 34; N. Flamel, ii. 131–2 & n. (i. 85); Grand-duke of Tuscany, i. 118; T. Mundanus, v. 599 & n. 1; L. Thurneisser, ii. 192 & n. 1 (i. 119); *see also* v. 176.
Alcini, Mount: *see* Montalcino.
Alcock, —: buys impropriation of South Malling, ii. 541.
Aldermaston, Berks.: house of Sir H. Forster at, iii. 100 & n. 4; *see also* iii. 99, n. 4.
Alderson, Rev. Samuel: notice of, &c. (?), iv. 217 & n. 1.
Aldobrandini, Ippolito, cardinal: bequest of, ii. 284, n. 2; ~ alluded to, ii. 392, n. 2.
Aldobrandini, Pietro, cardinal: villa of, at Frascati, ii. 392–3 & nn.
Aldrich, Henry; D.D. 1682; dean of Christ Church, Oxford, 1689, iv. 519, n. 4; v. 210, n. 10; candidate for promotion, 1686, iv. 519; sermons by, v. 210, 388–90.
Aldus (Aldo Manuzio): books printed by, iv. 330 & n. 5.
Alençon, Duke of, 1649, ii. 563 & n. 1.
Aleppo: English consul (Levant Company) at: *see* Wandesford, J. (iii. 24–5 & n.); English factory at: chaplain of: *see* Frampton, R.
Alesbury: Earl of: *see* Ailesbury.
Alessandro family, of Naples: chapel belonging to, ii. 328, n. 7.
Alessandro, musician at Paris, 1650, iii. 1.
Alessandro, musician at Rome, 1644, ii. 287.
Alessandro, Alessandro d': tomb of, ii. 328 & n. 7.
Alessi, G.: building designed by, ii. 495, n. 3.
Alestree, Dr. —: *see* Allestree, R.
Alex *or* Alexer, —: *see* Allix, P.
Alexander the Great: conquests of, iv. 486; destruction of Persepolis by, iv. 213; effect of music on, iii. 168 & n. 3; in sermon, v. 156.
Alexander III, pope: birth-place of, ii. 203 & n. 6; submission of Frederick Barbarossa to, ii. 439 & n. 3; ~ picture and inscription commemorating, ii. 297 & nn. 4, 5.
Alexander VI, pope (Roderigo Borgia): letter from Bajazet II to, ii. 499 & n. 2.
Alexander VII, pope (Fabio Chigi), ii. 203, n. 6; buildings erected by, ii. 299, n. 6, 370, nn. 1, 6 *ad fin.*, 371, n. 4; conduct of, towards Queen Christina, iv. 221 & n. 2; mission to (Sir R. Bellings, jnr.), iii. 381, n. 2.
Alexander VIII, pope (P. Ottoboni): elected, iv. 650 & n. 1, 651.
Alexander, Richard Zinzano *alias*, i. 54, n. 2.
Alexander Severus, Roman emperor: supposed sarcophagus of, ii. 223 & n. 4; as Severus: geneal., ii. 393–4.
Alexandria: body of St. Mark brought to Venice from, ii. 441 & n. 5; obelisk from, ii. 269 & n. 7, 270.
Alexandria: patriarch of: Nathaniel Conopius as, i. 14.
Alexis Romanov, tsar of Russia: relations of, with Charles II during his exile, iii. 344 & n. 5; sends envoys to England, 1662, 1667, iii. 344, 494 & n. 6.
Alfonso IV (d'Este), duke of Modena: geneal., iv. 27, nn. 5, 6, 28, n. 4.
Alford, Lord, *rectè* Orford: *see* Russell, Edward, earl of Orford.
Algardi, Alessandro, ii. 399 & n. 6; sculptures by, ii. 234 & n. 2.
Algiers: preparations for expedition against, v. 287, n. 3.
Alibon, —, judge: *see* Allibone, Sir R.
Alington, William; Baron Alington (Allington) 1660, iii. 553, n. 3; house of, at Horseheath, iii. 553 & n. 3; as member of Council for Foreign Plantations, iii. 578; as Constable of the Tower: social, iv. 383 & n. 6.
Alington of Killard: third Baron, 1660–85: *see* Alington, William.
Alington of Wymondley: Baron, 1682–5: *see* Alington, William.
Alippius, St.: baptism of, ii. 500.
Allen, William: *Killing no Murder* attributed to, iii. 526, n. 5.
Allestree (Alestree), Richard, D.D., iii. 266, n. 3; examines scholars from Westminster School, iii. 288 & n. 5; as Regius professor of Divinity at Oxford, iii. 533, n. 8; ~ speech of, at Act, iii. 533; ~ visits E, iii. 535; ~ visit to, iv. 69; as

Allestree, R. (*cont.*)
provost of Eton, iii. 560, n. 1; ~ visits to, at Eton, iii. 559–60; iv. 176 & n. 2(?), 208; *Whole Duty of Man* attributed to, v. 112, n. 5 *ad fin.*; as preacher, iv. 61; sermons by: printed, iii. 266 & n. 3, 321 & n. 4, 353 & n. 2, 403 & n. 2; iv. 132–3 & n.(?), 157 & n. 5(?), 158 & n. 1(?), 185 & n. 4(?); ~ unprinted, iii. 301; iv. 49, 61, 124, 187; accident to, iv. 211 & n. 5; dies, iv. 211, n. 5.
Allestry, James: appointed printer to Royal Society, iii. 340, n. 1.
Allexton, Leics.: rector of: *see* Cradocke, M.
Alleyn (Allen), Edward, the actor: as founder of Dulwich College, iv. 74 & n. 1.
Allibone (Alibon), Sir Richard, judge: in trial of Seven Bishops, iv. 587 & n. 2, 589.
Allier (Alice), river: at Moulins, ii. 154 (i. 99).
Allin (Allen), Sir Thomas; knighted 1665, iii. 404, n. 4; captures Dutch sailors, &c., iii. 404 & n. 4, 407; elected master of Trinity House, iii. 581 & n. 3.
Allington, Rev. John: sermon by, iii. 134 & n. 1.
Allington: Baron: *see* Alington.
Allix (Alex, Alexer), Pierre (Peter); D.D. 1690: seeks refuge in England, iv. 485–6 & n., 518.
Alost (Ouse), ii. 73 & n. 2 (i. 48).
Alphonso, king of Portugal: *see* Affonso.
Alps, the: characteristics of, ii. 509–10, 513; covered with snow since the Creation, ii. 513 & n. 1; 'foot of the Alps', ii. 505, 507, 515; 'the rubbish of the earth', ii. 507; sudden rise of, ii. 507 & n. 5; views of: from Lake of Geneva, ii. 520; from Lago Maggiore, ii. 506 *bis*; from Lyons, ii. 157 (i. 101).
animals of, ii. 509, 510, 515, 516 & n. 1, 517; crystal found in, ii. 501 & n. 8; goitre in, ii. 510 & nn. 3, 4; ~ alluded to, ii. 530; petrified man found in, ii. 235 & n. 10, 391.
in comparison, iii. 103.
Alresford, Hants: house at, designed by W. Samwell, iii. 554, n. 3.
Alsop, Rev. Josias: sermon by (?), iii. 314 & n. 4; *add.*
Alsted (Alstedius), J. H., encyclopaedist: teacher of Sir W. Curtius, iii. 36 & n. 2, 379; *see also* Books mentioned in text.
Alston, Sir Edward, M.D.: social, iii. 379 & n. 2.
Alston, Sir Joseph: geneal., v. 337, n. 1.
Alston, Penelope, Lady Alston, born Evelyn, wife of Sir Joseph: as heiress, v. 337, n. 1.
Altemps, Cardinal (Marcus Sittich von Hohenems): builds villa at Frascati, ii. 393, n. 5.
Althorp, Northants.: Sunderland's house at: visits to, 1675, 1688, iv. 69–70, 592–6 & nn.; notices, iv. 69–70 & n., 594; storm at, 1689 (?), iv. 644; earthquake at, v. 36 & n. 3; William III visits, v. 223 & n. 3; Sunderland dies at, v. 516, n. 9; view of (painting), iv. 128 & n. 4; paintings at (since E's time), iv. 162, nn. 2, 3, 403, n. 8, 404, nn. 2–4.
minister of: *see* Jessop, C.
Alto, Giovanni (Hans Gross): guide in Rome, ii. 214, n. 2.
Alva (Alba), Duke of: builds citadel at Antwerp, i. 45; *see also* ii. 66, n. 4; persecution by, in Netherlands: fugitive from, iv. 475 & n. 2.
Amalech: in sermons, iv. 85, 239.
Amalia von Solms, princess of Orange: meets Marie de Médicis, ii. 57 & n. 4 (i. 39).
Amazon river: electric eel of, iv. 196–7 & n.
Amazons: supposed to exist near the Caucasus, iv. 214 & n. 4.
Amber: carved, ii. 87 (i. 59), 190 (i. 119) (repeated, ii. 414), 191, critical note (repeated, ii. 413), 298; iv. 531; cabinet, &c., of, v. 147; containing insects, &c., ii. 471, 502; iv. 138, 275; spirit of: in medicine, iv. 77.
Amboise: notice, 1644, ii. 143–4 & nn. (i. 93); staircase in chateau at: in comparison, ii. 303.
Amboise, Cardinal d' (error), ii. 161 & n. 10.
Ambrose, St.: recites Te Deum, &c., ii. 500 & nn. 2, 3.
America: penguin of, iii. 399; English colonies in: proposed intro-

America (*cont.*)
duction of useful plants into, iii. 602–3; ~ ships of: ordered to sail in convoy, 1672, iii. 603 & n. 2; the Evelyns (Robert and his son George) in, i. 2; ii. 551, n. 3; v. 574, n. 2; *see also* New England; Spanish Indies; West Indies; *and the various colonies and territories, &c.*
Amiata, Monte (Monte Mantumiato), ii. 207 & n. 5.
Amiclas: *see* Amyclae.
Amiens: French court at, 1649, ii. 561, n. 1.
Amiens: Bishop of: *see* la Grange, J. de (ii. 161, n. 10).
Ammanati, Bartolomeo, architect and sculptor, ii. 186, n. 5; buildings by: Florence, Palazzo Pitti, courtyard or garden front, i. 81, n. 2; ii. 186 & n. 5; Rome, Palazzo Ruspoli, ii. 372–3 & n.; sculpture by: Florence: Apostles in Baptistery, ii. 197 & n. 12; ~ Neptune fountain, ii. 193 & nn. 6, 7 (i. 120); Padua, Hercules, ii. 466–7 & n.
Ammanati, Vincenzo: error for Bartolomeo Ammanati, ii. 372–3 & n.
Amsterdam: notice, 1641, ii. 42–9 & nn. (i. 31–5).
civic: gives yachts to Charles II, iii. 296, n. 5, 297, n. 2; accused of corrupt relations with Louis XIV, 1684, iv. 367 & n. 3; opposes new levies of troops, iv. 369 & n. 2, 378, n. 1.
miscellaneous: goldsmith at: story of, iii. 52–3; Petty's map of Ireland engraved at, iv. 58 & n. 2; shells bought at, iii. 10; wind-gun made at, iv. 520–1.
personal: E in danger of robbery at, iii. 71 & n. 1; Shaftesbury dies at, iv. 329, n. 1.
topography, &c.: (i) general: canals, &c., ii. 46 (i. 33); charitable institutions, ii. 45–6 (i. 32–3); church-bells, ii. 48 & n. 4 (i. 34 & nn. 1–2); extension, *c.* 1657, i. 35 & n. 3; foundations of buildings, ii. 48 (i. 34); gates: architecture of, ii. 48 & n. 2 (i. 34); Jews at, ii. 42–3 & nn. (i. 31); port, ii. 48 (i. 34); *see also* ii. 46 (i. 33); sectaries at, ii. 44 & nn. 1–3 (i. 32).
— (ii) particular buildings, &c.: Begijnhof: English Reformed

Amsterdam (*cont.*)
church in, ii. 44, n. 1; Bourse, ii. 46 & n. 2 (i. 33); Bruyloft, ii. 46–7 & n. (i. 33); churches (Oude Kerk, &c.), ii. 48–9 & nn. (i. 34); dog-market, ii. 46 & n. 1 (i. 33); Dolhuis, ii. 45 & n. 5 (i. 32); English Presbyterian congregation, ii. 44 & n. 1 (i. 32); hospitals: Gasthuis, ii. 43 & n. 2 (i. 31); ~ section of, for soldiers, ii. 45 & n. 6 (i. 32); St. Elizabethsgasthuis, ii. 43, n. 2; Keizers-Gracht, ii. 47–8 & nn. (i. 33–4); Kloeveniersdoelen: picture in, ii. 43 & nn. 4, 5 (i. 32); Oost-Indisch Huis, i. 35 & n. 2; Outer Singel, i. 35, n. 3; Rasphuis, ii. 45 & n. 4 (i. 32); Rijksmuseum: painting in, iii. 263, n. 3; ~ trophies of *Royal Charles* in, iii. 149, n. 6; Spinhuis, ii. 43 & n. 1 (i. 31); Stadhuis: new, ii. 43 & n. 3 (i. 31–2); ~ old, ii. 43, nn. 2, 3; i. 32; synagogue, ii. 42 (i. 31); Weeshuis, ii. 45 & n. 3 (i. 32).
Amunclae, ii. 322, n. 5.
Amusements: unsuitable in times of public trouble, iii. 229, 466; ~ in sermon, iii. 153.
Amwell, Herts.: springs at, iv. 515, n. 4.
Amyas, Christopher, carver in ordinary, iii. 343, n. 5.
Amyclae (Amiclas): legend concerning, ii. 322 & n. 5.
Anabaptists [E uses the word to designate the Baptists or, more loosely, as a term of abuse for the sectaries; all occurrences are indexed here]: obstruct proceedings at East India Company's meeting, iii. 201 & n. 5; in Monmouth's rebellion, iv. 452; participate in address to James II, iv. 553; an Anabaptist elected lord mayor of London, iv. 562 & n. 4; individuals, ii. 46 & n. 4 (i. 33); iii. 223, n. 1.
equated with Donatists by E, iv. 346, n. 2; anabaptistical sermon, iii. 91.
in sermons: views of, on baptism, attacked, iii. 202 & n. 4; v. 285, 374, 461; other sermons against, iii. 512, 513 & n. 3; iv. 550–1.
Anacletus, St., pope: builds tomb of St. Peter, ii. 258 & n. 3.

Ananias and Sapphira: in sermons, v. 219, 347, 596.
Anastasius IV, pope: tomb of, ii. 274, n. 5.
Anastasius, St.: tomb of, ii. 380 & n. 6.
Anathema Maranatha: explained in sermons, iii. 337 & n. 1; iv. 164, 436.
Anatomy and Physiology: anatomical drawings, iii. 385 & n. 4; anatomical tables: *see* Evelyn: collections; anatomy theatres: Leyden, ii. 53 (i. 37); ~ London, Royal College of Physicians, iii. 338, 379; iv. 308; ~ Padua, ii. 464; dissections, ii. 475, 553–4; lectures, ii. 475–6; vivisection of dog, iii. 497–8.
blood: transfusion of, iii. 478, 503; bones: composition of, iv. 278; embryology: discourse on, iv. 297; ~ abortions, iii. 255–6; iv. 145–6; eye: optic nerve demonstrated, iv. 275; ~ described in sermon, v. 11; Fallopian tubes, iv. 146; heart: lecture on, iv. 308 & n. 3; liver, iii. 210; lymph ducts: discoverer of, ii. 551 & n. 2; iii. 186; morbid growth, iv. 202; ovarium, iv. 146; pineal gland, iv. 530 & n. 2; pulse: discourse on, iii. 525–6; suffocation in Grotta del Cane, ii. 339–40 & nn.; worms found in human bodies, iv. 289–90.
Ancus Martius: aqueduct of (error), ii. 317 & n. 1; *add.*
Anderson, Mrs. Elizabeth, wife of Richard Anderson: *see* Harcourt, Elizabeth, Viscountess Harcourt.
Anderson, Elizabeth, Lady Anderson, wife of Sir Richard, iv. 224, n. 3; social, iv. 224, 313; godmother of Elizabeth Evelyn (later Mrs. Harcourt), iv. 396.
Anderson, Richard, d. 1695: social, iv. 224 & n. 3.
Anderson, Sir Richard, bt., iv. 224, n. 3; social, iv. 224, 313.
Andover, Hants: Arlington wounded at, iv. 119, n. 4.
Andoyne: Abbot of, ii. 74 (i. 48).
Andrea, Giovanni d': tomb of, ii. 421 & n. 7.
Andrelini, P. F.: inscription by, ii. 141 & n. 2.
Andrew, St.: patron of Royal Society, iii. 366; relic of, ii. 263; in sermon, v. 80.
Andrewes, Lancelot, D.D., bishop of Winchester, iii. 139, n. 4; as master of St. Catharine's Hall, Cambridge (error), iii. 139 & n. 4; style of, as preacher, iv. 84, n. 2, 166 & n. 6, 330; employs Rev. H. Wotton (?), iv. 172 & n. 4.
Andrews, Rev. —, curate of Abinger, *c.* 1665: sermon by, iii. 425.
Angelico, Fra (Giovanni da Fiesole, called il Beato Angelico): painting by (?) and tomb of, ii. 377 & nn. 6, 7.
Angelico, Angelo, of Vicenza (Michelangelo Angelico ?): art-collection of, ii. 484 & n. 2.
Angeloni, Francesco, ii. 236 & n. 7; *add.*; art-collection, &c., of, ii. 236–7 & nn., 356–7 & n.
Angels [select; all notices are in sermons]: dialogue between two: Psalm xxiv as, v. 99; guardian, v. 362; joy of, at Christ's birth, iii. 367; knowledge possessed by, iii. 169; orders of: number of, iii. 246–7 & n.; Sadducees' views on, &c., v. 96; *see also* v. 228; status of, v. 395–6; Trisagion: use of, by, iii. 236; visions of, v. 170; worship of, iv. 88, 153, 649 *bis*.
Angera, on Lake Maggiore, ii. 506.
Anglesey: first Earl of, 1661–86: *see* Annesley, Arthur.
Angoulême, Jean d'Orléans, count of: kept prisoner at Groombridge, iii. 72, n. 2; iv. 40, n. 2.
Angus: sixth Earl of: *see* Douglas, Archibald.
Aniene (Anio) *or* Teverone, river: bridges over, ii. 393–4 & nn.; falls of, ii. 397 & n. 1.
Animals [mammals; select notices; for other animals *see* Birds; Fish; Insects; Reptiles; Toads; Worms; Monsters; Animals, fabulous]:
general: animals in relation to man: in sermons, iii. 234; iv. 106, 311.
antelopes, iii. 400; horns of, iii. 323.
asses: in races, ii. 382; riding on, ii. 508 *bis*; hide of, inscribed (?), iii. 107 & n. 4.
bats, large, iii. 20.

Animals (*cont.*)
bears: in Alps, ii. 509, 510, 515, 517; in zoos, ii. 107 (i. 69), 195 (i. 120); performing, ii. 183 (i. 115); iv. 217; bear-baiting, iii. 549 & n. 4; bear-gardens, ii. 14, n. 4; iii. 549 & n. 4; skins of: worn, ii. 125 (i. 80).
buffaloes, ii. 182–3 (i. 115); in races, ii. 382.
camels or dromedaries, iii. 27 & n. 4, 292.
capricorn, ii. 516 & n. 1.
cats: as generic term, iii. 194–5; in comparisons, iii. 93, 194–5; wild (?), ii. 195 (i. 121).
cattle: murrain, ii. 546; effects of severe winter on, iv. 362, 364; cattle-fair, iv. 311 & n. 2; ox: huge, ii. 554 & n. 2; oxen for draught, ii. 382; *see also* Bull-baiting.
chamois, ii. 516, n. 1.
deer: *see* Deer.
dogs: *see* Dog.
elephants, ii. 39–40 & n. (i. 29); tusks of, iv. 54–5 & n.; skeleton, &c., of, ii. 53 (i. 37); iii. 334 & n. 9 *ad fin.*
elks, iii. 400; stuffed, ii. 414; horns of, iii. 323.
ermines: fur, iii. 349; iv. 262.
foxes, ii. 66 (i. 44); heads of, nailed to doors, ii. 515; black: fur, iii. 349.
goats: wild, in Alps, ii. 509; Guinea, iii. 400.
hares: hare-park, iii. 324 & n. 5; warren and coursing, iii. 114, 115, n. 1.
horses: *see* Horse.
jackal: skin, iii. 108.
lemur, iii. 194–5 & n.
leo marinus, preserved, ii. 53 (i. 37).
leopard, ii. 107 (i. 69).
lions, i. 69; ii. 195 (i. 120–1); iii. 93; iv. 266 & n. 3.
lynx, ii. 116 (i. 75).
moles: not found in Ireland, iii. 303 & n. 6.
monkeys or apes, ii. 66 (i. 44); performing, iii. 256, 549 & n. 4; iv. 253; kill children, iv. 349–50.
mules: in procession, ii. 280–1; *see also* Transport.
otter: hunted, iii. 306.
pigs: hogs used to find truffles, ii.

Animals (*cont.*)
158–9 (i. 101 & n. 1); wild boar: in France, &c., ii. 107, 112 (i. 72), 116 (i. 75), 141 & n. 3 (i. 92), 206; ~ rib of (Guy of Warwick), iii. 121.
porcupine, iii. 222 & n. 5.
rabbits or conies: yellow, ii. 72 (i. 47); warren, iii. 161; shooting, v. 199.
rats: rare in Ireland, iii. 303 & n. 6; and plague, iii. 412, n. 6 *ad fin.*
ratton, Egyptian (ichneumon): in comparison, iii. 194, 195, n. 1.
rhinoceros (unicorn), iv. 389–90 & n.; head of (?), ii. 53 (i. 37); *add.*; horns of, ii. 441, n. 3; iii. 373; ~ error for unicorn's, ii. 457 & n. 4; skin of: piece of, iii. 334, n. 9 *ad fin.*
sables: fur, iii. 349; iv. 262.
sea-morse: teeth of, iii. 349.
sheep: on Salisbury Plain, iii. 115; Arabian, iii. 400; Mauretanian, ii. 467.
squirrels: fur, ii. 448.
steinbock, ii. 516, n. 1.
tigers, ii. 195 (i. 120); baited by dogs, v. 317 & n. 1; skeleton of, ii. 53 (i. 37).
whales: stranded at Greenwich, &c., 1658, 1699, iii. 214–15 & nn.; v. 318–19 & n.; Greenland and Bermuda: taking of, iv. 146–7 & n.; skeleton, &c., of, ii. 53 (i. 37); iii. 121.
wolves: in Alps, ii. 509, 510, 515, 517; in France, ii. 112 (i. 72), 116 (i. 75), 122 (i. 78), 141, 142 (i. 92 *bis*); iii. 54; in zoos, ii. 107 (i. 69), 195 (i. 120).
Animals, fabulous: dragon: painting of, &c., at Rouen, ii. 123 & n. 5 (i. 79); griffon: claw of, ii. 89 & n. 3 (i. 60); hydra: spurious specimen, ii. 391–2 & n.; phoenix: wing-feather of, iii. 199 & n. 1; sphinxes: in Jewish symbolism (in sermon), iv. 45; unicorns: horns of, ii. 89 (i. 60), 441 & n. 3; iii. 263 & n. 4; ~ power of horns of (called rhinoceros), ii. 457 & n. 4.
monsters: African, iv. 630; in Lake of Geneva, ii. 520.
Anjou: Dukes of: *see* Philip, duke of Orleans (duke 1640–60); Philip V, king of Spain (duke 1683–1700).

Anna Maria, duchess of Savoy, later queen of Sicily and Sardinia: position of, in succession to English crown, v. 421 & n. 3.
Anne, queen of England [b. 1665; styled the Lady Anne; married, 1683, Prince George of Denmark, and thenceforward called princess; succeeded to the crown 1702; d. 1714]:
— as princess: chronological series: tutor of: *see* Lake, E.; performs in *Calisto*, iv. 49–50 & n.; marries Prince George of Denmark, iv. 332 & n. 3, 333; at opening of parliament, 1685, iv. 442; conduct of, at Revolution, v. 205, n. 6; position of, in succession to crown: in Declaration of Rights, iv. 616 & n. 1, 621, 622, n. 1; ~ in succession bill, 1689, iv. 645 & n. 8; subservience of, to Lord and Lady Marlborough (later duke and duchess), v. 86, n. 1; refuses to dismiss Lady Marlborough and retires from court, v. 90 & n. 2; quarrel of, with Queen Mary, v. 98 & n. 1, 201 & n. 4; reconciled with William III, v. 201 & n. 4; insignificant in politics, v. 213 & n. 6.
— — children, &c.: general, v. 421 & n. 1; pregnancy, 1683–4, iv. 358 & n. 2; ~ sermon alluding to, iv. 357–8 & n.; pregnancy, 1689 (for William, duke of Gloucester), iv. 645–6 & n.; son, born 1692, v. 98, n. 1; miscarriages, 1696, v. 213, n. 6, 259 & n. 2; unlikely to have a child living (1701), v. 445.
— — household of, iv. 333 & n. 3; v. 201; member of, iv. 222, n. 2.
— — religious: attends service at St. James's Palace, iv. 357; seat occupied by, in Chapel Royal, Whitehall, 1685, iv. 433, 491; attends services in: Chapel Royal, Whitehall, iv. 499, 502, 528, 529, 532, 539, 541, 544, 545, 570, 577, 590, 630; ~ Chapel Royal, St. James's, v. 388, 394.
— — residences: Syon House, v. 90 & n. 2, 98, n. 1; Berkeley House, v. 201; invited to live in Whitehall, *ib.*
Anne, Queen (*cont.*)
— — views of: on pregnancy of Queen Mary of Modena, iv. 587, n. 1; on Lord and Lady Sunderland, iv. 595, n. 1; on James II's relations with Anglican bishops, Oct. 1688, iv. 600, n. 4 *ad fin.*
— as queen: accession of: proclaimed, &c., v. 492, 493 & n. 3.
— — coronation of: proclamation relating to, v. 495 & n. 6; ceremony, v. 498 & n. 5
— — speeches of, to parliament: 1702, v. 517 & n. 4, 520, n. 1; 1703, v. 553, n. 1; 1704, v. 581 & n. 3; 1705, v. 615.
— — ministers of: good relations of, with parliament, 1702, v. 518, 521.
— — proposed grant by, to Marlborough: parliament opposes, v. 524–5 & nn.
— — entertains Archduke Charles at Windsor, v. 555 & n. 3.
— — complimented by Leopold I on capture of the Schellenberg, v. 573 & n. 2.
— — receives news of Blenheim, v. 574–5 & n.
— — Godolphin as adviser of, 1705, v. 612, n. 1, 619, n. 1.
— — attends thanksgiving services, v. 521, 578 & n. 1.
— — visits: Bath, &c., v. 514 *bis* & n. 7, 516 & n. 2, 517 & n. 3; Cambridge, &c., v. 591 & n. 3, 592 & n. 2 (as Oxford, in error).
— — at Windsor, 1705, v. 602, n. 2.
— — birthday of, v. 528 & n. 6.
— miscellaneous: E kisses hand of, iv. 358; builds orangery at Kensington Palace, v. 8, n. 2; friendship of, with Frances Apsley (Lady Bathurst), iv. 264, n. 3.
Anne Boleyn, queen of England: geneal., iii. 388, n. 3.
Anne of Cleves, queen of England: grant to, iii. 156, n. 2.
Anne of Austria, queen of France, ii. 91, n. 3.
as regent: receives ambassadors, ii. 91 (i. 61), 566; attends review, ii. 135 (i. 88); awarded Golden Rose, ii. 384, n. 6; orders C. Le Prévost to apologize to Sir R. Browne, iii. 7; termination of regency of, iii. 41.

Anne of Austria (*cont.*)
in procession for Louis XIV's majority, iii. 43; gives audience with Louis XIV to diplomatists, iii. 43–4 & nn.; English court in mourning for, iii. 429 & n. 2.
thank-offering of, for birth of Louis XIV, ii. 105–6 (i. 68); founds Val-de-Grâce, Paris, i. 84; bridge named after, ii. 93, n. 5 *ad fin.*; changes name of Palais-Cardinal, ii. 133, n. 4; E presented to, &c., ii. 562 & n. 2, 566; doctor of: *see* Yvelin, P.; guards, &c., of: in procession, iii. 41, 43; secretary of, ii. 31.
Anne of Brittany, queen of France: mantle of, ii. 88 (i. 60).
Anne, duchess of York, daughter of Sir Edward Hyde, earl of Clarendon, first wife of James, duke of York, later James II, iii. 258, n. 4; birth-place of, iv. 527 & n. 4; in Paris, 1656: acquainted with Sir R. Browne, iii. 264 & n. 2; marriage of, to James: officiating divine, ii. 564, n. 5; ~ Henrietta Maria's opposition to, iii. 258 & n. 4; ~ made public, &c., iii. 264 & n. 1; Clarendon's alleged ambition for, iv. 338, n. 4; supposed to have involved Clarendon in debt, iv. 339; sees comedy at Whitehall, iii. 315; dines at Durdans, iii. 334; children of, iii. 380 & nn. 2, 3; in childbirth, iii. 569, n. 2; spiritual adviser of (Dr. G. Morley), iv. 283, n. 1; conversion of, to Roman Catholicism: grounds for, iv. 282–3 & nn.; ~ paper by, relating to, iv. 477, n. 1.
geneal., iv. 12 & n. 5, 122.
maids of honour of, iii. 495, n. 2; individuals: *see* Godolphin, Mrs. Margaret (Blagge) (iii. 530, n. 1, 621, n. 5); Graham, Mrs. Dorothy (Howard) (iii. 529, n. 6, 621, n. 5); Howard, Mrs. Anne (Ogle) (iv. 70, 71, n. 1); Lyttelton, Anne, Lady Lyttelton (Temple) (iv. 576, n. 3); Talbot, Frances, duchess of Tyrconnel (Jennings) (iv. 79 & n. 3).
physician of: *see* Wedderburn, Sir J.
Anne of Gonzaga, wife of Prince Edward of the Palatinate, ii. 567, n. 1.
Anne, St.: relic of, ii. 307.
Annesley, Arthur; second Viscount Valentia 1660; first earl of Anglesey 1661, iii. 515, n. 2; created earl, iii. 277; in ceremony, iii. 515.
Annius of Viterbo: forgery by (?), ii. 210–11 & n.
Annoni, J. A., ii. 498, n. 8.
'Annus mirabilis', 1660, iii. 239 & n. 1; 'Annus mirabilis tertius', 1688, iv. 566.
Anslowe, Sir Richard: *see* Onslow.
Antenor: founder of Padua, ii. 453 & n. 2; tomb of, ii. 454 & n. 3.
Anthonides, Johannes: water-works of, ii. 46–7 & n. (i. 33).
Anthony, St., of Padua: miracle performed by, ii. 319, n. 2; tomb of, ii. 454.
Anthony, Francis: on use of gold in medicine, iii. 86, n. 6.
Antibes (Antibo), ii. 168 & n. 2 (i. 106).
Antichi, Prospero, called Bresciano: statues by, ii. 260, n. 5.
Antichrist: destruction of, in prophecies, iv. 636–7 & n.; v. 322; kingdom of: duration of, v. 26; alluded to, in sermon, iii. 238.
Antigua: *see* Leeward Islands.
Antinomians: views of, on impeccability: attacked in sermons, v. 131 & n. 3, 364 & n. 2, 386.
Antinous: portraits of: engraved gem, ii. 314; ~ statue (error), ii. 305 & n. 1.
Antiquities [generally exclusive of sculptures, buildings, coins and medals, and inscriptions. Collections of unspecified antiquities, forming part of museums or art-collections, are not indexed]:
collections: Aix: duke of Guise, ii. 163 & n. 4 (i. 103); Bolsena: S. Cristina, ii. 210 & n. 1; Lyons: Hôtel de Ville, ii. 158 (i. 101); Padua: S. Giustina, ii. 456 & n. 7; Rome: F. Gualdi, ii. 314–15 & nn.; Sion, Valais: castle, ii. 516 & n. 3.
archeological sites in England: Banstead: foundations, &c., at, iii. 221 & nn. 6, 7; Camberwell: urns from, iv. 483; Leicester: ruins of temple at, iii. 123 & n. 2.

Antiquities (*cont.*)
sites elsewhere: Nineveh, iv. 214; Palmyra: drawings of, v. 224 & n. 3; Persepolis, iv. 213; *see also* Rome; Pozzuoli; &c.
individual objects [select and incomplete]: aries: relief showing, ii. 220; armour, Roman, iii. 199; balls, bronze, ii. 222 & n. 2, 256, n. 2; bath, stone, ii. 287 & n. 1; chairs, perforated, of red marble, ii. 268, n. 2; fasces: relief showing, ii. 247 & n. 3; lamps, &c., ii. 356; milestones, ii. 220, n. 3, 222 & n. 2, 321; rostrum, ii. 433; sacrificial instruments, ii. 314 & n. 2, 314–15; ~ relief showing, ii. 218; sistrum, ii. 314 & n. 1; stater, ii. 314; stylus, *ib.*; talus, ii. 237 & n. 1; tombs, wayside (nameless), ii. 317, 319–20, 351 & n. 2, 394; tripod of Apollo, ii. 314 & n. 1; urns: at Geneva, ii. 526 & n. 1; ~ at Pisa, ii. 181 (i. 114); vase: marble, ii. 286 & n. 11; ~ porphyry, ii. 370, n. 6, 371.
Anti-Trinitarianism [the principal form in the Diary is Socinianism; E very nearly identifies Arianism with the latter. Only the more general notices are indexed under the present heading; *see further* Arianism; Socinianism; Theism; Unitarianism]: in England, iii. 227, n. 1; anti-Trinitarian pamphlet (by W. Penn), iii. 521 & n. 1; sermons against, iii. 521; iv. 160–1; mentioned in sermon, v. 390 [all other anti-Trinitarian sermons are indexed under Socinianism, except three, which occur only under Arianism (v. 292, 511, 512)].
Antoninus Pius, Roman emperor: baths of (Baths of Caracalla), ii. 361 & n. 3; builds Ponte Sisto (error), ii. 384 & n. 2; column of (Column of Marcus Aurelius), ii. 370 & n. 3; palace of (Temple of Hadrian), ii. 370 & n. 5.
Antonio: *see* Marc' Antonio (iii. 52–3).
Antonio da Viterbo: painting by (?), ii. 224 & n. 3.
Antony: wager of, with Cleopatra, ii. 372, n. 5.
Antwerp: notice, 1641, ii. 63–7 & nn. (i. 43–5).
Antwerp (*cont.*)
general statement, ii. 67 & n. 4 (i. 45); dog-wagons at, ii. 73 (i. 48).
cathedral, ii. 64–5 & nn. (i. 43–4); ~ organist of: *see* Liberti, H.; churches: Jerusalem (error), ii. 65 & n. 3 (i. 44); ~ Jesuits' (St. Charles Borromée), ii. 63–4 & n. (i. 43); ~ St. Mary (error?), ii. 65 & nn. 3, 4 (i. 44; not named); citadel, ii. 66–7 & n. (i. 44–5); convent at (error?), ii. 65 & nn. 3, 4 (i. 44); Jesuits' school (Gymnasium), ii. 65–6 & nn. (i. 44); Oostershuis, ii. 66 & n. 3 (i. 44); Place de Meir, ii. 66 & n. 2 (i. 44); Senate-house, ii. 65 (i. 44).
entry into, of Cardinal-Infante Ferdinand of Austria: paintings relating to, ii. 71, n. 3; East India Company of (error), ii. 66 & n. 3 (i. 44); Jesuits at: convert W. Hollar to Roman Catholicism, i. 21.
Lady Arundel at, ii. 479, n. 4; Sir E. Hyde (Clarendon) travels to, 1651, iii. 32, n. 5 *ad fin.*; Lady Hyde (Clarendon) at, iii. 383, n. 5; Rev. H. Nash at, *ib.*; mentioned, ii. 62 (i. 42), 72 (i. 47).
Anxur: ancient name of Terracina, ii. 320.
Apelles: in comparison, ii. 412.
Apennine mountains: at Florence, ii. 184 (i. 117); in Liguria, ii. 170 (i. 107); pass over, ii. 419 & n. 4; in view from Rome, ii. 313; statue representing, ii. 419 & n. 2.
Apollodorus, architect, ii. 379 & n. 2.
Apollodorus, father of Cleomenes, ii. 286, n. 5.
Apollonius: sculptor of Toro Farnese, ii. 216.
Apono, Petrus de (P. d'Abano): bust of, ii. 463 & n. 4.
Appenzell, canton, ii. 518, n. 1.
Appian way: *see* Via Appia.
Appii Forum, ii. 318 & nn. 2, 8.
Appius Claudius Caecus: builds Via Appia, ii. 319 & n. 4.
Apsley, Sir Allen, sen.: geneal., ii. 36, n. 4.
Apsley, Frances: *see* Bathurst, Frances, Lady Bathurst.
Apsley, Jane: *see* Newton, Mrs. J.
Apsley, John: geneal., ii. 9, n. 7.

Apsley, Peter, captain in Dutch service, ii. 36, n. 4; company of, &c., ii. 36 (i. 27).
Apulia: revenue of, ii. 352 & n. 6.
Aquapendente: *see* Acquapendente.
Aquinas, Thomas: *see* Thomas, St., Aquinas.
Aquitaine: Duke of: representative of, in Charles II's coronation procession, iii. 280 & n. 1.
Aquitaine: Primate of, ii. 154 & n. 4 (i. 99).
Arabic language: scholars, &c., iv. 172, 213; examination in, iii. 287; study of: Archbishop Ussher's views on, iii. 156; translation into, from Grotius, v. 82 & n. 2; writing, iii. 108; chessmen inscribed in, ii. 89 (i. 60).
Arabs: account of, iii. 25.
Aragon, Don P. A. d', viceroy of Naples, ii. 327, n. 2.
Archimedes: burning-glass of: discourse on, iv. 54 & n. 4; water-screw of, ii. 58, n. 1.
Archangel, Russia, iii. 344, n. 5.
Araisso: *see* Alassio.
ARCHITECTURE:
— features [some terms, in both architecture and building, are indexed under Words and Phrases; they are not necessarily repeated in the present entry]:
— — arcaded houses, ii. 422, 453, 490; *see also* ii. 524 & n. 4.
— — baths or bathing-rooms, ii. 121 (i. 78), 134 (i. 87); iv. 118.
— — ceilings: plaster, in England, ii. 308–9; wooden, in Italy, *ib.*
— — chimney-pieces or mantles, iii. 114; iv. 98, 199 *bis*; notable, ii. 118 & n. 1 (i. 76); iii. 156 & n. 2.
— — decorations: ceiling or wall paintings: in England, ii. 300; iii. 338 & n. 6, 385–6 & n., 386 & n. 4, 625–6 & n.; iv. 180(?), 288(?); *see also* Verrio, A.; ~ in France, ii. 103 & n. 3 (i. 67), 117–18 (i. 76), 123 (i. 79), 151 (i. 98); ~ at Geneva, ii. 529 & n. 6; ~ in Italy: not indexed collectively; ~ in Netherlands, ii. 56 (i. 38–9); trophies of arms, iii. 560; iv. 473; v. 103 & n. 4.
— — domes and cupolas: cupolas (E's usual term), ii. 60 & n. 4 (i.

ARCHITECTURE (*cont.*)
41); &c.; variants ('cupoled', &c.), ii. 112, 191, 337 & n. 2; not used in church-building in England, 1666, iii. 449; arches to support: drawings for, iii. 598 & n. 4; cupola on house at Kew, iv. 347; domes (domo), ii. 56 & n. 2 (i. 38); ~ term used, ii. 197 *bis*, 199 (passages from V); 'domo or cupola', ii. 493–4.
— — *dômes*: at Geneva, ii. 524 & n. 4.
— — doors: bronze (brass, &c.), ii. 180 (i. 114), 197, 219 *bis*, 258, 306 & n. 7, 372, 439; or gates: wolves' heads, &c., nailed to, ii. 141 & n. 3 (i. 92), 515.
— — façades: encrusted with antique reliefs, ii. 231 (& 286), 252 & n. 2 (& 390); painted, ii. 184 (i. 116), 196, 434, 454, 485.
— — fire-places: corner, iii. 554 & n. 4.
— — floors: inlaid marble, &c., ii. 48–9 (i. 34), 96 (i. 63), 103 (i. 67), 105 (i. 68), 150, 197, 204 & n. 7 (& p. 407), 242, 265, 272, 296, 307, 311, 329 & n. 4, 372, 396, 411, 416, 437 & n. 4, 455, 461; parquet, iii. 21 & n. 1; iv. 141, 177, 199; paved: notable, iii. 382; plaster, ii. 174 & n. 1 (i. 110 & n. 1).
— — foundations: at Amsterdam and Venice, ii. 48 (i. 34), 446 & n. 4, 459.
— — fret, ii. 366 & n. 6; other occurrences, ii. 98; iv. 288; fretted, ii. 103 (i. 67).
— — moats: dry, round houses in France, i. 70; ii. 151 (i. 98), 563; iii. 18.
— — mosaic: *see* Mosaic.
— — panelling or wainscot, iii. 398, 625; iv. 116–17, 140.
— — stairs or staircases: notable, ii. 56 (i. 38), 129 (i. 82 *bis*), 295–6 & n., 461 & n. 7; iii. 18, 109, 180; paintings for, iv. 316; winding or spiral, ii. 104 (i. 67–8), 139–40 & n. (i. 91), 186 & n. 6 (i. 117); iii. 114 & n. 3(?); ~ oval, ii. 229; ~ for carriages, ii. 143 (i. 93), 303.
— — tympanum, iv. 199–200.
— — volto, ii. 229, 258, 259, 296; iv. 316.

ARCHITECTURE (*cont.*)
— styles and stylistic terms:
— — general and historical: the almost lost art restored by Michelangelo, ii. 214 & n. 4, 238; of age of Henry VIII and Elizabeth, v. 427; after the ancient building of gentlemen's houses, iv. 481; eastern manner of building houses, ii. 156 (i. 100); exact architecture, &c., ii. 150 (i. 97); iii. 140 & n. 1; French manner or French pavilion way, iii. 591; iv. 90 & n. 7, 184, 345; chimney-pieces after the French best manner, iii. 114; open manner of architecture, iii. 2.
— — particular terms [for E's terminology see appendix on Gothic, &c., above, pp. 1–7. Terms used casually in notes are not indexed]:
— — — ancient, i. 34 (*see* ii. 48, n. 2), 93 (*see* ii. 144); ii. 214; iii. 99 (doubtful use); *see also* Words.
— — — antico-moderno, iii. 556.
— — — antique or a l'antique, i. 76; ii. 259; iii. 96; applied to royal barge, iii. 333; *see also* Words.
— — — baroque, ii. 212, n. 2, 214, n. 4.
— — — classical renaissance, ii. 214, n. 4.
— — — Gothic (Gotick, Gotique, Gotish, à la Gotic, &c.), i. 27; ii. 48 (i. 34), 50 (i. 35), 64 (i. 43); i. 55; ii. 85 (i. 57), 95 (i. 63), 99 (i. 65), 126 (i. 80), 141, 144 (*see* i. 93), 153 (i. 99), 157 (i. 101), 246, 266 & n. 5, 271, 307, 319, 380, 381 & n. 7, 408, 436 *bis*, 494 & n. 2, 528, 567; iii. 99, 108, 113, 121, 129, 192, 323, 427, 556; iv. 113; the Gothic barbarity, ii. 214.
— — — Greek or a la Greca, ii. 440 & n. 4, 454; of Greek building (not stylistic), ii. 460 & n. 3.
— — — Italian, ii. 34, n. 7 *ad fin.*, 35, 66 (i. 44); i. 54 & n. 3.
— — — mixed, ii. 103 & n. 2 (i. 67) (possibly not stylistic); mixed, partly antique, partly modern (doubtful use), ii. 242 & n. 4; mixed, 'twixt antique and modern, iii. 140–1; mixed with Gothic, ii. 111 (i. 71), 151.

ARCHITECTURE (*cont.*)
— — — modern or a la moderna, ii. 48 & n. 2 (*see* i. 34), 97 (i. 64), 111 (i. 71); i. 76; ii. 118 (i. 76), 150 (i. 97), 202 & n. 1, 482 & n. 1, 495; iii. 100, 117, 124, 134; iv. 70, 594; modern built part of a house (doubtful use), iii. 113; not altogether modern, iv. 593; in quotations from E's writings, iii. 459, n. 1, 637; applied to garden, iii. 315–16.
— — — modern Gothic, i. 76.
— — — Roman, i. 67 (*see* ii. 104); ii. 129 (i. 82) (probably not stylistic), 436; used by Wren, iii. 449, n. 2 *ad fin.*
— — — rustic, ii. 129 (i. 82), 186 *bis* (i. 117 *bis*).
— — orders: five or all, ii. 249 & n. 8, 417 & n. 2; three, ii. 214 & n. 4; Doric, Ionic, Corinthian, ii. 186 (i. 117); Composita, ii. 248; Corinthian, i. 55; ii. 188 (i. 118), 370, 482, 483; iii. 333; Doric, i. 55; ii. 481; first, *ib.*; Tuscan, ii. 489.
Arco Felice, Phlegraean Fields, ii. 347 & n. 3.
Arconati, Galeazzo, Cavaliere: gives Leonardo's drawings, &c., to Ambrosiana, ii. 497–8 & nn.
Arcueil: aqueduct at, ii. 129 & n. 3 (i. 82).
Arents, Maritjen, ii. 56, n. 7.
Aresfeild, —: *see* Eversfield, J.
Aretino, Pietro: tomb of, ii. 460 & n. 5.
Argenti, Bonaventura, singer, ii. 400 & n. 1.
Argos: battle near, 1695, v. 215 & n. 6.
Argyll: Earls, Marquises, and Dukes of: *see* Campbell, Archibald, eighth earl, 1638–41, and marquis, 1641–61; Campbell, Archibald, ninth earl, 1663–85 (wrongly called 'the young Marquis'); Campbell, Archibald, tenth earl, 1689–1701, and first duke, 1701–3.
Arianism: growth of, in England, 1691, 1700, v. 65, 408; new sect of Arians, 1702, v. 512; sermons against, iv. 35, 435–6 & n.; v. 278 & n. 6, 292, 342, 414, 465, 511, 512; *see also* Anti-Trinitarianism; Socinianism.
Ariccia, ii. 356, n. 3.
Arignie, Marquis: *see* Ragni.

Ariosto: tomb of, ii. 427 & n. 10.
Aristides: *see* Aelius Aristides.
Aristobulus: in Britain, iii. 333 & n. 4.
Aristotle: views of: in sermons, iv. 561; v. 613; on influence of climate: in sermon, v. 156.
Arius, the heresiarch: date of, v. 278, n. 6; tenets of: boy's knowledge of, iv. 617; in sermon, v. 414.
Ark, the: in sermons, iv. 314–15, 379.
Arlington, village: *see* Harlington.
Arlington: Baron, Earl of, &c.: *see* Bennet, Sir Henry, first baron, 1665–72, and first earl, 1672–85; Bennet, Isabella, his countess; FitzRoy, Isabella, duchess of Grafton, countess *suo jure* 1685–1723.
Armagh: Archbishops of: *see* Ussher, James (1625–56); Bramhall, John (1661–3); dean of: *see* Wentworth, Peter (1637–41).
Armagnac, Louis de Lorraine, count of, 'Monsieur le Grand': visits England, iii. 575, n. 6.
Armenia, ancient: statues from, ii. 237; war against: reliefs representing, ii. 370.
Armenians: at Venice, ii. 449.
Arminians: attacked at Synod of Dort, ii. 32 (i. 25).
Armorer, Sir James: error for Sir William Armourer (?), iii. 487 & n. 8.
Armorer, Sir Nicholas: social, iii. 488 & n. 4; geneal., iii. 487, n. 8 *ad fin.*
Armourer, Sir William: house of (?; as Sir James Armorer), iii. 487 & n. 8.
Arms and Armour [select: notices of ordinary weapons, such as cannon or swords, are not indexed collectively unless they contain matter of special interest. *See further* Arsenals; Gunpowder and Salt-petre]:
— antique and exotic arms, &c.: collections, ii. 192 & nn. 5–8 (i. 119), 414 & n. 7; iii. 199; Guy of Warwick's arms, &c., iii. 120; Hannibal's helmet, ii. 192 & n. 6 (i. 119); Indian, iii. 107; Turkish, iv. 399; bows and arrows from Russia, iii. 344, 349; poisoned daggers, from

Arms and Armour (*cont.*)
Bantam, iv. 285; knives: Chinese, &c., iii. 373–4; scimetars, iv. 266.
— armour: suit of: ordered by E, ii. 55 (i. 38); ~ worn by E (?), ii. 79 (i. 53); in procession, ii. 281; casque, iii. 57.
— manufacture of: general, ii. 502; gunsmiths, ii. 85 (i. 57–8), 489 & nn. 3–6, 524 & n. 8; ordnance, ii. 457 & n. 6; sword-blades, ii. 159 (i. 102).
— ordnance:
— — *balistae*, ii. 528 & n. 4.
— — guns or cannon [for firing of guns for salutes, &c., *see* Military: salutes]: at Geneva: on cathedral, ii. 527–8 & n.; Genoa: first used at, ii. 175–6 (i. 111); granadoes fired from, iii. 483; Havre: inscribed, at, ii. 125 & n. 4 (i. 80); inventions relating to, iii. 307 & n. 1; in Italy: outside noblemen's houses, ii. 252–3 & n.; monster, ii. 73–4 & n. (i. 48), 417; at Venice, in Arsenal: captured, &c., ii. 458 & n. 10; ~ cast while Henri III dined, ii. 457 & n. 7; ~ firing six times at once, ii. 458 & n. 7.
— — — great guns, ii. 528; iii. 44, 437; iv. 42, 46; ~ name given to drinking measure, ii. 469 & n. 2; whole cannon, iii. 413.
— — — brass cannon, i. 22; ii. 125; iii. 60, 413, 439, 506; leather great guns (1544), ii. 84 & n. 3 (i. 57).
— — — gunfire: sound of, at distance, iii. 84 & n. 5, 409, n. 3, 437 & nn. 4, 7, 438 *bis*, 445, n. 7; v. 518; in comparison, iv. 395.
— — mortars: bombs shot from, iv. 543; large, ii. 458.
— — bombs [for bombardments of towns *see* Military: operations], iv. 381; v. 234; tested, iv. 543 & n. 4; mentioned in error, iii. 485 & n. 4.
— — granadoes [*see also* hand-grenades *below*], iii. 368, n. 5; iv. 42; glass, iii. 368; tested, iii. 483; at Venice in Arsenal, ii. 458; in comparison, iii. 454; iv. 395.
— — mines, i. 27; ii. 37 (i. 28); iv. 42.

Arms and Armour (*cont.*)
— small arms: general: as decoration of rooms, iii. 560; iv. 473 & n. 5; v. 103 & n. 4; the traveller's: given up on entering towns, ii. 160 (i.103), 427.
— — bows, long, ii. 526, 528.
— — carbines, ii. 116 (i. 75), 160 (i. 103), 475, 512, 513; made by L. Cominazzo, ii. 489, 528.
— — cross-bows, ii. 526 & n. 2, 528, n. 4.
— — guns, ii. 427; iii. 5; accident with (shot-gun ?), v. 199; manufacture of, ii. 85 (i. 57–8), 489 & nn. 3–6; practice with, ii. 526 & n. 2; shooting for wager, iii. 21; screwed: manufacture of, ii. 524 & n. 8; wind-gun, iv. 520–1.
— — halberds, iii. 42.
— — hand-grenades (granadoes), iii. 368, n. 5; soldiers armed with, iv. 137, 354.
— — hooks: in 'Bataille de Vambre', iii. 5.
— — javelins: carried by sheriff's train, i. 9; in riding exercises, iv. 400.
— — knives: pointed: forbidden at Genoa, ii. 173 (i. 109).
— — lances, ii. 279, 281; iv. 269.
— — muskets, iii. 204; practice with, ii. 528; story concerning musket-shot, iii. 49–50; in comparison, iv. 395.
— — pikes, iii. 357 & n. 2.
— — pistols, ii. 160 (i. 103), 472, 504; iii. 5; iv. 400, 452; manufacture of, ii. 85 (i. 57–8).
— — spears, iv. 269.
— — swords, iii. 5, 57; iv. 71; manufacture of, ii. 159 (i. 102), 489; not worn by Bantam ambassadors, iv. 285; broadsword, v. 592; two-handed (Guy of Warwick), iii. 120.
Armstrong (Arme-Strong), Sir Thomas, iv. 323, n. 4; proclamation against, for complicity in Rye-House plot, iv. 322, n. 1, 323 & n. 1; flies abroad, iv. 323, n. 4; proceedings against, and execution of, iv. 382 & n. 4, 466, n. 5; quarter of, set up on Temple Bar, v. 235 & n. 3; geneal., iv. 452, n. 8.
Arnhem: review of forces near, v. 352 & n. 4.
Arno, river: at Florence, ii. 185 (i. 117); at Pisa, ii. 182 (i. 114).
Arnold of Egmont, duke of Gelderland, &c.: heart of, ii. 58, n. 3.
Arona, on Lake Maggiore, ii. 506.
Arpino: Giuseppe Cesari, called the Cavaliere d'Arpino, ii. 224, n. 4; mosaic designed by, ii. 259; paintings by, ii. 224 & n. 4, 233 & n. 7, 244 & n. 1, 267 & n. 4, 272 & n. 7, 393 & n. 2; mosaic copy of painting by, ii. 260 & n. 4.
Arran: Earls of (Ireland): *see* Butler, Lord Richard, earl 1662–86; new creation: *see* Butler, Charles, earl 1693–1758.
Arran: Earl and Countess of (Scotland): *see* Douglas, James, styled earl *c.* 1658–98, later fourth duke of Hamilton; Douglas, Lady Anne, his countess (1688–90).
Arronches, Henrique de Sousa Tavares, marquez d', Portuguese ambassador to England 1679–81, iv. 169, n. 3; entry of, iv. 169 & n. 3; residence of, iv. 190; social, iv. 190, 191; secretary of, *ib.*
Arsenals: Antwerp, ii. 66–7 & n. (i. 44–5); Chatham (the dockyard), i. 23 & n. 2; Florence, ii. 417 & n. 4; Geneva, ii. 529 & n. 7; Genoa, ii. 175–6 (i. 111); Milan: in castle, ii. 501–2; Rome: Vatican, ii. 302–3 & n.; Venice: Arsenal, ii. 456–9 & nn.; ~ in Doges' Palace, ii. 444 & n. 8; Windsor: small arms at, iii. 560; v. 103 & n. 4.
Art-collections [collections containing European paintings or statues, &c.; they may also contain miscellaneous antiquities and natural objects prized for their beauty, such as shells and agates. More miscellaneous collections, comprising both works of art and natural history specimens, are indexed under Museums (the more important notices are indexed here also), as also are collections of non-European works of art, &c.; specialized collections are indexed under Coins and Medals; Engraving and Etching; Gems and Semi-precious Stones; Portraits; Pottery and Porcelain; &c. Houses containing a single picture, and churches, are not indexed collectively. Only collections mentioned by E, or

Art-collections (*cont.*)
existing in his time, &c., are indexed here; later private owners of works of art are not indexed. The arrangement is by places]:
Antwerp: Duarte, ii. 67, n. 6.
Blois: chateau (Gaston, duke of Orleans), ii. 141 (i. 92).
Brussels: Cour, ii. 70–1 & nn. (i. 46).
Chenonceaux: chateau, ii. 152 (i. 98).
Ditchley Park, Oxon.: Sir F. H. Lee, iii. 383 & n. 4.
Easton Neston: Sir W. Fermor, later Lord Leominster, v. 44–5 & n.
England: Arundel: *see* Howard, Thomas, earl of Arundel; Howard, Henry, sixth duke of Norfolk; royal collections: *see* Charles I: art-collections; Charles II: culture, &c.; ~ paintings belonging to, at Kensington Palace, v. 237.
Essonne: L. Hesselin, ii. 120–1 (i. 77).
Florence: J. Gaddi, ii. 415 & nn. 5–8; P. Giovio (Uffizi), ii. 189 & n. 6 (i. 119); Grand dukes: Pitti palace, ii. 186 (i. 117); ~ Uffizi, ii. 188–93 & nn. (i. 118–19), 413–14 & nn.; Prince Leopold de' Medici, ii. 415 & nn. 2–4.
Fontainebleau: French kings, ii. 117–20 & nn., *passim* (i. 76–7).
Genoa: Palazzo Doria a Fássolo, ii. 174 (i. 110).
Greenwich: J. Lanière, iii. 74–5 & nn., 79–80 & n.
Hackney: Tombs, iii. 96 & nn. 2–4.
Isleworth: G. Barrell, ii. 540 & n. 3; Sir C. Crewe, ii. 540 & n. 1; P. Oliver, ii. 540 & n. 2.
Leyton: Forest House (Lord Goring), iii. 538 & n. 1.
London [*see also* England *above*]: Arlington, iv. 102 & nn. 1–6; J. van Belkamp, ii. 549 & nn. 5, 6; Lord Bradford (as Viscount Newport), iv. 402–3 & nn.; Lady Bristol, at Chelsea, iv. 162 & nn. 2, 3; T. Chiffinch, iii. 305; Clarendon: collection of portraits, i. *21*; iii. 379, n. 8 *ad fin.*, 520 & n. 3; Clifford, iv. 18 & n. 3; Delabarr, ii. 555 & n.

Art-collections (*cont.*)
4; Viscount Downe (as Mr. or Sir W. Ducie), ii. 549–50 & nn.; iii. 96 & n. 5; Du Bois, ii. 549 & nn. 3, 4; Friar (?), ii. 548 & n. 3; G. Geldorp, ii. 554 & n. 3; Grinling Gibbons, iv. 179; La Neve, ii. 548 & nn. 4, 5; R. van Leemput (Remée), iv. 3; Sir P. Lely, iv. 312 & n. 3, 404, n. 3; John Drummond, earl of Melfort: sale of, 1693, v. 144–5 & nn.; Dom F. de Mello, iv. 2; R. Montagu, later duke of Montagu, iv. 344; earl of Northumberland, iii. 216 & nn. 2–6; Painters' Hall, iii. 390 & n. 4; Lord Pembroke, v. 245 & nn. 2, 3; Sir F. Prujean, iii. 294; Sunderland, iv. 128 & n. 4, 403–4 & nn.; F. Trion, ii. 548, n. 3; Van Dyck, iv. 312, n. 3; Col. W. Webb, ii. 549 & nn. 1, 2; J. M. Wright, iii. 339 & nn. 3–6; *see also* iii. 372; unnamed hatmaker in Blackfriars (agates, &c.), iii. 143; unnamed collector (?), iv. 23.
Mantua: ducal, iii. 323 & n. 2.
Milan: Ambrosiana, ii. 497–8 & nn.
Monaco: princes, ii. 169 (i. 106).
Naples: dukes of Maddaloni, ii. 330 & n. 1.
Paris: S. della Bella, iii. 3; du Houssay, ii. 114–15 & nn. (i. 74); Fresne, ii. 114 & n. 7, &c. (i. 74); Liancourt, ii. 113–14 & nn. (i. 73–4); Lincler (at the Samaritaine), iii. 10–11 & nn., 20; Louvre: Salle des Antiques, ii. 104–5 & nn. (i. 68); Luxembourg, ii. 131 (i. 84); Mazarin: agent for, to buy paintings in England, iii. 82 & n. 2; Perruchot, ii. 114 & n. 6 (i. 74); Poignant, iii. 35; de Richaumont, ii. 132 & n. 2 (i. 85).
Richelieu: chateau, ii. 151 (i. 98).
Rome: F. Angeloni, ii. 236–7 & nn., 356–7 & n.; Barberini, ii. 229 & nn. 4, 5; Conservatori, ii. 222–6 & nn.; Farnese, ii. 214, n. 3, 215–16 & nn., 308–11 & nn.; Gottifredi, ii. 391 & n. 4; *add.*; Pichini, ii. 217 & n. 1; C. dal Pozzo, ii. 277–8 & nn.; Vatican, ii. 303–5 & nn.; H. Vitelleschi, ii. 283 & n. 4, 365.

Art-collections (*cont.*)
— villas: Aldobrandini, ii. 284–5 & nn.; Borghese, ii. 252–4 & nn., 390; Giustiniani, ii. 382–3 & nn.; Ludovisi, ii. 234–6 & nn., 391–2 & nn.; Medici, ii. 230–2 & nn., 286–7 & nn.; Montalto, ii. 240.
Sheen: earl of Leicester (as Lord Lisle), iv. 143 & nn. 3, 4; Sir C. Lyttelton, iv. 576 & n. 5; Sir W. Temple, iv. 576.
Venice: F. Contarini, ii. 470, n. 5; Grimani, ii. 459, n. 4.
Verona: Curtoni (Cortoni), ii. 487 & n. 3; Muselli, ii. 487 & n. 4.
Vicenza: Angelico, ii. 484 & n. 2.
Windsor Castle: Prince Rupert, iii. 560.
Art-dealers, &c. [*see also* Auction-sales]: — Daun (M. Dahl?), v. 148 & n. 1; J. M. Wright (?), iii. 339, n. 6; paintings on sale, ii. 39 & n. 4 (i. 29), 100 (i. 65), 368.
Artemidorus, sculptor: error for Athenodorus, ii. 304 & n. 1.
Arthur, King: round table, &c., of, ii. 79 (i. 52).
Arundel, Sussex: document at Arundel Castle, ii. 479, n. 5.
Arundel: Earls and Countesses of: *see* FitzAlan, Henry, twelfth earl, 1544–80; *new creation*: *see* Howard, Thomas, second earl, 1604–46; Howard, Alathea, his countess; Howard, Henry Frederick, third earl, 1646–52; Howard, Elizabeth, his countess; Howard, Thomas, fourth earl, 1652–60, later fifth duke of Norfolk; Howard, Henry, courtesy title, 1677–84, later seventh duke of Norfolk.
Arundel: Duke of (Henry Howard?), iii. 515, n. 1.
Arundell, Henry, third Baron Arundell of Wardour, iii. 62, n. 1; as prisoner in Tower 1678–84: *see* London: Tower: prisoners: the Roman Catholic peers; appointed Lord Privy Seal, iv. 540 & n. 2; gives music-party, iv. 404, 422; as godfather, iii. 585; social, iii. 62, 239, 577; geneal., iii. 373 & n. 1.
Arundell, Mary: *see* Somerset, Mary.
Arundell, Thomas, first Baron Arundell of Wardour: geneal., ii. 367, n. 2.
Arundell of Wardour: Barons: *see* Arundell, Thomas, first baron; Arundell, Henry, third baron, 1643–94.
Ascension, island: Captain W. Dampier at, v. 295, n. 3.
Ashburnham, John, iii. 360, n. 7; commissioner for London streets, iii. 319, n. 1; social (?), iii. 360, 494 & n. 4.
Ashburnham, William, iii. 360, n. 7; social (?), iii. 360, 494 & n. 4.
Ashley: error for Ashtead, Surrey (?), iii. 425 & n. 5.
Ashley, Dr. —: *see* Astley, H.
Ashley: first Baron, 1661–72: *see* Cooper, Sir A. A., later earl of Shaftesbury.
Ashmole, Elias, antiquary, &c., iii. 159, n. 3; character of, iv. 138; chamber of, in Middle Temple, ii. 24, n. 4; museum, &c., of, iii. 198, n. 4 *ad fin.*, 199 & n. 2; iv. 138–9 & nn.; social, iii. 159, 217; iv. 454 & n. 2.
Ashtead (Ashsted, Ashted), Surrey: Sir Robert Howard's seat at, iv. 376–7 & n.; Lady Mordaunt at, iii. 425 & n. 5 (?; in text as Ashley); iv. 557 & n. 1; church: service in, interrupted by Quaker, iii. 220; the living, v. 181 & n. 2; *see also* v. 207, n. 2; rectors of: *see* King William (1643–62); Duncombe, Rev. William (1683–99).
Ashton, John, conspirator: executed, v. 42 & n. 2.
Ashurst, Henry, sen., v. 88, n. 1.
Ashurst, Sir Henry, bt., v. 88, nn. 1, 2; trustee for Boyle Lectures, v. 88 (as Sir Robert Ashwood, in error), 238.
Ashwell, George, ii. 18, n. 4.
Ashwood, Sir Robert: error for Sir Henry Ashurst, v. 88 & n. 1.
Asia *or* Asia Minor: Dr. I. Basire's missionary work in, iii. 303 & n. 3; churches of: subscribe to Anglican tenets, iii. 342 & n. 5; columns from, ii. 272–3 & n.; risings in: 1689, iv. 645 & n. 7; ~ 1692, v. 101 & n. 4; Asiatic troops in Turkish service: disturbances among, 1693, v. 150 & n. 3.
Asiatics: effeminacy of: in sermon, v. 156.
Asinelli family, ii. 420, n. 10.
Aspetti, Titiano: sculpture by, ii. 445 & n. 5.

Assassination Plot, 1696: discovered, &c., v. 231–3 & nn.; Association for maintenance of government, &c., v. 232 & n. 2, 233, n. 3, 242–3 & n.; invasion from France prevented, v. 233–4 & nn.; conspirators in: arrested, tried, &c., v. 234 & n. 8, 235 & nn. 1–4, 238 & n. 2, 243 & n. 2, 245 & n. 4, 264 *bis* & nn. 3, 6; ~ two absolved on scaffold, v. 236 & n. 1; i. 8; ~ attainted, v. 264, n. 2.
Asseph: *see* Azov.
Association for maintenance of government, 1696, v. 232 & n. 2, 233, n. 3; office-holders, &c., required to join, v. 242–3 & n.
Astley (Ashley), Herbert, LL.D., dean of Norwich: sermon by, iv. 86 & n. 6.
Aston (Austine), Francis: elected secretary of Royal Society, iv. 263 & nn. 3, 6.
Aston, Walter, third Lord Aston of Forfar: Lord Stafford and Stephen Dugdale meet at house of, iv. 228 & n. 6, 232.
Aston: third Lord: *see* Aston, Walter.
Astrakhan: pelican from, iii. 399.
Astrea: in paintings, iii. 338; iv. 377.
Astrology: books and MSS. relating to, iv. 126, 138 & n. 4; almanack-maker (Sir G. Wharton), iii. 443 & n. 3; students of, iv. 138, 200; predictions concerning eclipses, iii. 63; v. 354 & n. 2; horoscope (Clifford), iv. 22 & n. 2; time of laying foundation-stone taken, v. 249; time of planting orchard: phase of moon at, iii. 81 & n. 3.
Astronomy:
  Greenwich Observatory: foundation of, iv. 98 & n. 3; ~ visits to, iv. 205, 383; demonstration at Royal Society, iii. 444; observations from Bologna, iii. 563.
  instruments: clock showing equation of times, iii. 450 & n. 1; quadrant, the great, at Greenwich, iv. 205 & n. 4; selenoscope, iii. 85 & n. 10; telescopes (optical glasses, perspectives), ii. 64 (i. 44); iii. 110, 293, 384; Sir Paul Neile's, iii. 172 & n. 6, 286, nn. 2, 4; Newton's, iii. 601 & n. 2; Whitehall, 35-foot, iii. 286 & nn. 2, 4; maker of, iii. 64.
  sun: Oughtred on, iii. 158; ~ meridian laid down, for checking clocks, iv. 333; moon: nature of, ii. 64 & n. 2 (i. 43–4); ~ Oughtred on, iii. 158; ~ discourse on, iv. 54 & n. 4; ~ Mons Porphyrites in, iii. 286 & n. 3.
  Jupiter: observed, &c., iii. 286.
  Mercury, transit of: attempt to observe, iii. 384–5 & n.
  Saturn: its ring demonstrated, &c., iii. 276 & n. 1, 285–6 & nn.; mentioned, iii. 288.
  comets: as portents, ii. 7 & n. 1 (i. 7); iv. 235; by date: 1618, ii. 7 & n. 1 (i. 7); 1664–5, iii. 392 & n. 1, 393 *bis* & n. 4, 396, 397; ~ alluded to, iii. 477 & n. 3; 1680, iv. 235 & n. 1, 237 & n. 1; 1682 (Halley's), iv. 291.
  eclipses: solar: 1652 (Black Monday), iii. 63 & n. 3; v. 354 & n. 2; 1684, iv. 383 & n. 7; 1688 (error), iv. 601 & n. 4; 1699, v. 354 & n. 1; lunar, iii. 62 & n. 7; v. 540.
  shining cloud or meteor: 1643, ii. 80 (i. 54); iv. 235; ~ 1680 (comet), iv. 235 & n. 1; pillar of light, iii. 403.
Atalanta: in sermon, v. 217.
Atestinus: *see* Leonius, J.
Athaliah, v. 165, n. 3.
Athanasius, St.: creed of: in sermon, v. 57.
Atheism and Atheists [*see also* Infidels; Libertines]:
  cause of: in sermon, v. 73; prevalence or growth of, in England: general remarks, iii. 558; iv. 331; v. 331, 408, 415; ~ in reports of sermons (E's or the preacher's remarks), iii. 605; iv. 402, 416, 512; v. 23, 65, 75–7, 121, 143, 283, 290, 292, 293, 319, 327–9, 335, 340, 342, 378, 390–1, 414, 548; sermons against: endowment for (Boyle Lectures), v. 82, 88 & n. 3; societies formed to oppose, v. 366 & n. 5, 391 & n. 1.
  sermons against (*see also above*), iv. 43, 236–7, 294, 295, 334, 383, 405, 433, 551, 649; v. 50, 60, 107, 146, 157, 178–9, 345,

Atheism (*cont.*)
360, 386, 423–4, 432–4, 454, 511, 512, 596–7; minor reports, iii. 19, 238, 239, 304, 467, 534, 544; iv. 44, 62, 179, 333, 368; v. 43, 67, 71, 164 *bis*, 184, 185, 257, 295, 584; *see also* iv. 379–80.
Athenodorus (Artimadorus), sculptor, ii. 304 & n. 1.
Athens: Venetian occupation of, 1394–1402, ii. 439, n. 5; captured by Venice, 1687, iv. 560, n. 3; columns from, in Venice, ii. 439 & n. 5; St. Paul at: in sermons, iii. 22–3; v. 384–5, 395, 523.
Athesis, river: *see* Adige.
Athlone (Athlane): taken by English, v. 59 & n. 4.
Athlone: Earl of, 1692–1703: *see* Ginkel, Godard van Reede, heer van.
Atholl (Athole): second Earl, 1642–70, and first Marquis, 1676–1703, of: *see* Murray, John.
Atkins, Sir Edward, judge, iv. 417, n. 6 *ad fin.*
Atkins, Sir Jonas *or* Jonathan, iii. 619, n. 4; at military funeral, iii. 619–20 & n.; appointed governor of Barbados, iv. 25 & n. 6.
Atria: *see* Adria.
Atterbury, Francis, D.D.; bishop of Rochester 1713: in Convocation controversy, 1701, v. 460 & n. 1.
Atterbury, Rev. Lewis, jnr.: sermon by (?), v. 612 & n. 2.
Attica: Sir G. Wheler's account of his travels in, iv. 358 & n. 1.
Aubette river, at Rouen, ii. 122 & n. 4 (i. 78).
Aubigné, Françoise d', Madame de Maintenon: *see* Maintenon.
Aubigny, Lord: *see* Stuart, Ludovic, seigneur d'Aubigny.
Aubrey, John: character-drawing by, i. *109* & n. 1; obtains information from E, ii. 1, n. 1; iii. 158, n. 1, 496, n. 2 *ad fin.*; *see also* i. 21, n. 1; ii. 4, n. 1; iii. 104, n. 2; accepts legend of Greek philosophers at Cricklade, iii. 117, n. 3.
Aubusson, Jacques d': *see* Villac, seigneur de.
Aucher, Sir Anthony, sen.: geneal., iii. 196, n. 4.
Aucher (Auger), Sir Anthony, bt.: social, iii. 488 & n. 6.
Aucher, Hester: *see* Bowyer, Hester, Lady Bowyer.
Auction-sales: art-collections, iv. 566, n. 2; v. 144–5 & n.; books, iv. 126, n. 3, 330 & n. 3; v. 206 & n. 1; rhinoceros, iv. 390, n. 1.
Audley: Baron, 1633–84: *see* Touchet, James, third earl of Castlehaven.
Audley End, Essex: notices, iii. 140–2 & nn., 556 & n. 2; mentioned, iv. 120.
Auger, Sir Anthony: *see* Aucher.
Aughrim: battle of, v. 66 & n. 2.
Augsburg: taken by Bavarians, 1703, v. 553, n. 2; the Hairy Maid born at (error), iii. 198 & n. 1.
Augustine, St.: baptized and recites Te Deum, ii. 500 & n. 3; in sermons, iii. 24, 39; iv. 225, 361; v. 56; mentioned, iv. 256.
Augustus, Roman emperor: buildings of: aqueduct, ii. 312, 313; ~ obelisks, ii. 256 & n. 2, 374–5; ~ temple of Jupiter Tonans, ii. 218 & n. 3; ~ Theatre of Marcellus, ii. 228; portraits of: gem, ii. 89 (i. 60); ~ statues (false), ii. 222 & n. 4; temple of, at Pozzuoli, ii. 343–4 & nn.; tomb of, ii. 245, 375–6 & n.; mentioned, ii. 253, n. 2.
Augustus the Strong (Friedrich August), 1670–1733; elector of Saxony 1694; king of Poland (as Augustus II), 1697, v. 267, n. 2; elected king of Poland, v. 267 & n. 2, 269 & n. 5; becomes a Roman Catholic, v. 270–1 & n.; treaty of, with Cardinal Primate of Poland, v. 288 & n. 5; seizes Warsaw, 1704, v. 580 & n. 2.
Aungier, Elizabeth: *see* Caryl, Mrs. E.
Aungier, Sir Francis, first Baron Aungier of Longford (here called Lord Longford in error): geneal., ii. 29, n. 4.
Aungier, Francis; third Baron Aungier 1655; viscount, 1675, and earl, 1677, of Longford, iv. 137, n. 3; social, iv. 137; defeated in parliamentary election, 1679, iv. 164–5 & n.
Aungier, Gerald, second Baron Aungier of Longford, iii. 142, n. 5; social, iii. 142; geneal., &c., iv. 137.

Aungier: Barons: *see* Aungier, Sir Francis, first baron, 1621–32; Aungier, Gerald, second baron, 1632–55; Aungier, Francis, third baron, 1655–75, later earl of Longford, &c.
Aurach, near Kufstein (?): taken by Bavarians, 1703, v. 529 & n. 2.
Aurelian, Roman emperor: builder of walls of Rome, ii. 375, n. 3.
Aurunca: *see* Sessa Aurunca.
Ausburg: *see* Augsburg.
Austine, —: *see* Aston, Francis.
Authie, river: and frontier of France, ii. 84, n. 1.
Automata: chariot, ii. 408; on clock, Venice, Piazza, ii. 435.
Auxerre, Peter of Courtenay, count of: crowned emperor of Byzantium, ii. 381 & n. 3.
Auzout (Azoule), Adrien: at Royal Society's meeting, iv. 287 & nn. 1, 3.
Avaux (Aveaux), Jean-Antoine de Mesmes, comte d', iv. 635, n. 1; accompanies James II to Ireland, iv. 634–5; as French ambassador to United Provinces: recalled, 1701, v. 472 & n. 5.
Avebury, Wilts.: standing stones at, iii. 116 & n. 1.
Avelyn *or* Evelyn, William, i. *1*.
Avernus, lake, ii. 346–7 & nn.; Grotta di Pietro la Pace near, ii. 338, n. 4, 346, n. 9 *ad fin.*; mentioned, ii. 338, n. 3, 345, n. 2, 349, n. 7.
Aversa, ii. 325.
Avery *or* Every, John, pirate: associates of, executed, v. 261 & n. 5.
Aviaries [also called Volaries by E; for mixed collections of birds and mammals *see* Zoological Gardens]: E's, at Sayes Court, iii. 175; Fontainebleau, ii. 118 & n. 4 (i. 76); Genoa, Palazzo Doria, ii. 175 & nn. 2, 3 (i. 110–11); Rueil, ii. 110 (i. 71); others, ii. 105 (i. 68), 106 (i. 69), 108 (i. 70), 112 (i. 73), 238, 362, 383, 419; iii. 96, 376; iv. 144; artificial (waterworks), ii. 392, 396 & n. 5.
Avignon: notice, ii. 160–2 & nn. (i. 102–3); the pope's return from, to Rome: monument commemorating, ii. 248 & n. 4; mentioned, ii. 158.
Avila, Monsieur Zanches d', iii. 17; as Don Sanchez (?), ii. 560 & n. 7.
Avon, river, Bristol, iii. 102, n. 7; at St. Vincent's Rocks, iii. 103 & n. 2; mouth of, iii. 119, n. 3.
Avon, river, Warwickshire: at Warwick, iii. 119, n. 6, 120.
Axtel, Col. Daniel: executed, iii. 259 & n. 2.
Aylard, Alice, wife of Roger Evelyn, i. *1*.
Aylesbury, Frances: *see* Hyde, Frances, countess of Clarendon.
Aylesbury, Sir Thomas: geneal., &c., iii. 263, n. 7; iv. 527, n. 4.
Aylesford: first Earl of, 1714–19: *see* Finch, Heneage, baron of Gernsey.
Ayre, Anthony: commissioner for London streets, iii. 319, n. 1.
Ayscue (Ayscogh), Sir George, iii. 414 & n. 3; taken prisoner in Four Days' Battle, iii. 439 & n. 4.
Ayton, Sir John, Black Rod: in Grand Feast of Order of the Garter, iii. 479 & n. 7
Aytoun, Sir Robert, the poet: geneal., iii. 479, n. 7.
Azoule, —: *see* Auzout, A.
Azov (Asseph): taken by Russians, 1696, v. 258 & n. 5.

Babel, Tower of, iv. 29 & n. 1.
Baber, Sir John: geneal., iii. 218, n. 4.
Babylon: monarchy of: duration of, ii. 431, n. 3; ~ mentioned, iv. 617.
Babylonian Captivity: in sermons, iv. 577–8; v. 227; return of Jews from: in comparison, iii. 246.
Baccano, near Rome, ii. 211, n. 4.
Bacharach on the Rhine: Dr. A. Horneck born at, v. 317, n. 4.
Bachelier, —: theft of anemone-seed from, *add.* (i. 86–7).
Backhouse, Flower: *see* Hyde, Flower, countess of Clarendon.
Backhouse, Sir John, K.B.: geneal., iv. 2, n. 1.
Backhouse, Sir William, bt.: geneal., iv. 2, n. 1.
Bacoli, Phlegraean Fields, ii. 349, nn. 4, 5, 8.
Bacon, Sir Edmund, bt. (either of Redgrave or of Gillingham): visits Ipswich, iv. 114–15 & n.
Bacon, Francis, Baron Verulam, Viscount St. Albans; Lord Chancellor, &c.: experiments propounded by, to be examined by

Bacon, Francis (*cont.*)
Royal Society, iv. 205 & n. 5, 206; said to have introduced plane-trees into England, iii. 386, n. 6; as occupant of York House, iii. 162, n. 1; tomb of, ii. 78 & n. 4 (i. 51); geneal., iv. 115 & n. 1; secretary of: *see* Bushell, T. (iii. 382 & n. 6).
Bacon, Matthew, M.D.: at Rome, ii. 213 & n. 4.
Badajoz: action at, 1705, v. 614 & n. 5.
Baden: Margrave of, 1677–1707: *see* Ludwig Wilhelm I.
Baden: Prince of, 1675: lodging of, at Naples, ii. 325, n. 5.
Badminton, Gloucs.: duke of Beaufort dies at, v. 379, n. 4.
Badoaro, G. A. (Balduarius): tomb of, ii. 461 & n. 3.
Bagdad (Bagdat): traveller to, iv. 213.
Baglione, Giovanni, Cavaliere, ii. 219, n. 2; paintings by, ii. 219 & n. 2, 244 & n. 1, 365 & n. 5; *see also* Books: sources.
Bagnacavallo, B. Ramenghi, called: paintings by, ii. 423, n. 7 *ad fin.*
Bagshaw, Henry, D.D.: sermon by (?), iv. 71 & n. 2.
Bagshot, Surrey, iv. 467 & n. 2, 468; Bagshot Park at: visits to, iv. 467–8 & n., 480–1, 558 *ter*, 559.
Bahama Islands: Hispaniola, wreck near, iv. 552.
Baia (Baiæ): notice, ii. 348–9 & nn.; former splendour of, ii. 352; in view, ii. 334; mentioned, ii. 336, 344, 351.
Baides, Marquis of: *see* Lopez de Zuñiga, Don Francisco.
Baily, Dr. Richard: *see* Baylie.
Baines *or* Blackiston, Charles: *alias* of J. Cosin, jnr., iii. 26, n. 6.
Baios, ii. 348 & n. 4.
Bajazet II, sultan of Turkey: sends Holy Lance to Innocent VIII, ii. 262; letters from, to popes, ii. 499–500 & n.
Baker, —: in Paris, 1651, iii. 37.
Baker, —: error for Edmond Halley, iv. 314 & n. 2.
Baker, Captain —: on expedition to seek North-West Passage, iv. 96 & n. 5.
Baker, Thomas, of Fressingfield, iii. 538, n. 1; owner of Forest House, Leyton, iii. 538 & n. 1; iv. 306; geneal., *ib.*
Baldassare: *see* Peruzzi, B.
Baldero, Dr. —: *see* Boldero, E.
Balduarius, Andreas (G. A. Badoaro): tomb of, ii. 461 & n. 3.
Bales, Thomas: commissioner for London streets, iii. 319, n. 1.
Ball, M.: letters of news written by, i. *128*, n. 1.
Ball, Peter, M.D.: gift of, to Royal Society, &c. (error), iii. 366 & n. 3; geneal., iii. 310, n. 2.
Ball, Sir Peter: drafts parliamentary bill for E, iii. 310 & n. 2.
Ball, Richard, D.D., iii. 627, n. 1; sermons by, iii. 265 & n. 2(?), 627, 631; iv. 125, 155, 258–9.
Ball *or* Balle, William, astronomer, iii. 286, n. 1; at examination of Saturn's rings, iii. 286; as treasurer of Royal Society: gift of, to Society (in text as P. Ball), iii. 366 & n. 3; geneal., iii. 310, n. 2.
Ballads: sale of, &c., during frost fair, 1683–4, iv. 362 & n. 2.
Ballet: *see* Plays, &c.
Ballion: Duke of: *see* Bouillon.
Balls Park, Herts., ii. 81 & n. 1 (i. 54).
Balsham, Cambs.: sermon preached at, v. 207, n. 5.
Baltazar di Sienna: *see* Peruzzi, B.
Baltic Sea: fear of Russian activities in, v. 439.
Baltimore: third Lord: *see* Calvert, Charles.
Baltzar, Thomas, violinist: as Lubicer: performs, iii. 167–8 & nn.
Bambino, the Santo: procession to, ii. 291 & n. 7.
Banastre, Margaret: *see* Lewis, Mrs. M.
Banbury: Earls of: *see* Knollys, William, earl, 1626–32; Knollys, Edward, styled second earl, 1632–45.
Bancroft, John, D.D., bishop of Oxford, ii. 8, n. 2, 23, n. 3; confirms E, ii. 23 (i. 17).
Bancroft, Richard, archbishop of Canterbury: books bequeathed by, to Cambridge University, iii. 140 & n. 3; *add.*; founds library at Lambeth Palace, iii. 527, n. 1.
Bandinelli, Baccio, sculptor, ii. 188, n. 3; works by: Clement VII, ii. 188 & n. 6 (i. 118); God supporting the dead Christ, ii. 195 & n. 2 (i. 120); Hercules and Cacus, ii. 188 & n. 3 (i. 118), 193 (i. 120);

Bandinelli (*cont.*)
Laocoon (copy of antique group), ii. 413 & n. 6; Leo X, ii. 188 & n. 6 (i. 118); altar figures, Florence Cathedral, ii. 197 & n. 2.
Bandini, Giovanni, sculptor: statue of Ferdinand I, Leghorn, by, ii. 183 & n. 7 (i. 116).
Bangor: cathedral clergy:
bishops: *see* Roberts, William (1637–65); Humphreys, Humphrey (1689–1701); Evans, John (1701–16).
dean: *see* Lloyd, William, the apocalyptic (1672–80).
Bankes (Banks), Sir John, bt.: house of, &c., iv. 96 & n. 4.
Bank of England: foundation of, and subscription for, v. 185 & n. 3, 185–6; makes loan to king, 1696, v. 255 & n. 1; first governor of: *see* Houblon, Sir John (iv. 162, n. 6); director of: *see* Houblon, Sir James (*ib.*); mentioned, v. 246, n. 3.
Banks and Bankers:
banks: *see* Bank of England; new: establishment of, 1696, v. 246 & n. 3.
bankers: as purchasers of Albemarle House, iv. 339 & n. 4; misdemeanours of (Sir C. Duncomb, &c.), v. 246, 256; London bankers: Sir S. Fox and, iv. 218, 267; Sir R. Viner as banker, iv. 170.
Banstead, Surrey: Sir C. Buckle's seat in: antiquities found near, iii. 221 & nn. 6, 7.
Banstead Down, Surrey: mishap to coach on, v. 467.
Bantam: ambassadors from, &c., iv. 284–6 & nn.; river near, iv. 313.
Banting: *see* Bentinck, H. W., earl of Portland.
Bantry: Countess of: title proposed for Frances Hamilton, Lady Hamilton, later Frances Talbot, duchess of Tyrconnel, iv. 79, n. 3, 108, n. 3.
Bantry Bay: battle of, iv. 639 & n. 1.
Baptists [called Anabaptists by E]: increase of, iii. 202 & n. 4, 513 & n. 3; sermons against: *see* Anabaptists; church of, at Deptford (?), iv. 546, n. 6 *ad fin.*
Barattiero, Niccolò, architect, ii. 445 & n. 1.
Barbados: account of: mentioned, iii. 327; pine-apples from, iii. 293 & n. 2, 513; fish found near, iii. 372, n. 6.
discontent in: report of, iii. 583 & n. 2; governorship, &c., of: discussed by Council of Trade and Plantations, iii. 605 & n. 1; iv. 6; negro conspiracy in, v. 130 & n. 2; prisoners of war to go to, iii. 412; merchant ships for, v. 68, 79.
governors of: *see* Willoughby, Francis, Baron Willoughby of Parham (1650–2, 1660–6); Willoughby, William, Baron Willoughby of Parham (1667–73); Atkins, Sir J. (1674–80).
Barbarians: at Rome, ii. 256, 257, 265 & n. 3.
Barbaro *or* Gauro, Monte, ii. 345 & n. 1.
Barberini family: arms of, ii. 261, 305; chapel of, at S. Andrea della Valle, Rome, ii. 376.
Barberini, Antonio, cardinal (Cardinal Onufrio), ii. 369 & n. 6; mentioned in inscription, ii. 245.
Barberini, Francesco, cardinal, Protector of the English nation, ii. 266 & n. 3; occupies Cancelleria, ii. 367 & n. 4; admits E to papal audience, ii. 391; building restored by, ii. 275 & n. 5.
Barberini, Maffeo: *see* Urban VIII.
Barberino (Barbarino), in Tuscany, ii. 200 & n. 11.
Barcelona: siege of, 1694: attempted relief, v. 186; taken by French, 1697, v. 270 & n. 1; Allied attack on, 1705: *see* Catalonia.
Museum: paintings in, ii. 369, n. 2.
Barckley: *see* Berkeley.
Barckman, John: *see* Leijonberg, Baron.
Bargrave, John, D.D., canon of Canterbury, iii. 614 & n. 6; helps J. Raymond to write his *Itinerary*, i. 99 & n. 1; mentioned, ii. 23, n. 1.
Barillon *or* Barrillon, Paul, seigneur d'Amoncourt, marquis de Branges; French ambassador to England 1677–88, iv. 128, n. 5; character, iv. 493; social, iv. 128; obstructs collection for French protestant refugees, iv. 508 & n. 3; ascendancy of, in England, iv. 510–11 & n., 515; chapel of: cele-

Barillon (*cont.*)
brations in, for Louis XIV's recovery from illness, iv. 533, n. 6.
Baritiere, —, at Florence, ii. 184 (i. 116).
Barker, Henry, Clerk of the Crown 1685, iv. 494 & n. 2.
Barker, Rev. Samuel, v. 469, n. 4; sermons by (?), v. 469, 552.
Barkley: — *see* Berkeley.
Barkstead, Col. John: regiment of: soldiers from, ii. 541 & n. 2.
Barlow, Francis, the painter, iii. 166–7 & n.; paintings by, belonging to D. Onslow, iv. 255 & n. 5.
Barlow, Mrs. Lucy, formerly Walter, mother of James Scott, duke of Monmouth, ii. 561, n. 12; appearance of, ii. 561–2; career of, iv. 457; attempt to remove her son from, ii. 560, n. 2; Charles II denies marrying, iv. 457 & n. 7; supposed certificate of marriage to him, iv. 502, n. 5; alluded to, iv. 189.
Barlow, Thomas; D.D. 1660; bishop of Lincoln 1675, iii. 106, n. 4, 384, n. 5; addresses book to E, iii. 106, n. 4; as Bodley's Librarian: shows the library, iii. 106; as Provost of Queen's College: visits Lord Cornbury, iii. 384; and Arundelian inscriptions: arranges removal of, to Oxford, iii. 498; ~ bears University's thanks for, iii. 498–500; social, iii. 534; consecrated bishop of Lincoln, iv. 66–7 & n.
Barnard, Mrs. S. L.: sometime owner of E MSS., i. *48*, n. 2.
Barnard: first Baron, 1698–1723: *see* Vane, Christopher.
Barne *or* Barnes, Miles; D.D. 1682: sermon by (?), iv. 76 & n. 4.
Barnes, Surrey: Abraham Cowley at, iii. 355 & n. 4; Barn Elms in: Cowley at, iii. 355, n. 4, 367.
Barnet, Herts.: highway-robbery near, v. 122 & n. 2.
Barnevelt (Johan van Oldenbarnevelt): imprisonment of, i. 29 & n. 1.
Barnstaple, Devon: earthquake at, 1690, v. 36 & n. 3.
Baroccio, Federico: paintings by, ii. 233 & n. 4.
Baron, Mrs. —, iv. 13.
Baron, the Black, iv. 393 & n. 2.
Baronets: fees of: inquiry concerning payment of, 1686, iv. 513–14 & n.
Baroni, Adriana, singer, ii. 400, n. 1.
Baroni, Leonora, singer, ii. 400, n. 1.
Baronio (Baronius), Cesare, cardinal, the historian, ii. 233, n. 8; tomb of, ii. 233; views of, on origin of Candlemas, iii. 241, n. 1; *see also* Books mentioned in text.
Barrell (Barill), Gilbert: garden and art-collection, &c., of, ii. 540 & n. 3.
Barrow, Isaac, D.D., iv. 62 & n. 2; sermon by, iv. 62; printed sermon by: read, iv. 517 & n. 2.
Bartholomew, St.: relics of, ii. 88 (i. 59), 358.
Bartleme *or* Bartholomew, harpsichord player: *see* Bartolomeo.
Bartolomeo, Signor, harpsichord player: here identified as Bartleme or Bartholomew, iv. 186, n. 6; as Batholomeo: performs, iv. 186; teaches Mary Evelyn, iv. 271, 421; alluded to, iv. 428.
Bartolommeo, painter: legend concerning, ii. 412 & n. 4.
Barton, Adrian: geneal., iii. 84, n. 4.
Barton, Francis: geneal., iii. 490, n. 5.
Barton, John, barrister: last illness and funeral of, iii. 84 & n. 4, 85 & n. 2.
Barton, John, serjeant-at-law: reader at Middle Temple, iii. 490 & n. 5.
Barton-upon-Humber, Lincs., iii. 131.
Baruch: in sermon, iv. 197.
Baruth (Beirut ?): Evelinus, lord of, iii. 548, n. 3.
Barzillai: in sermon, v. 365.
Basel (Basil): Council of: copy of Synodal Epistles of, iii. 106 & n. 6; editions of Early Christian Fathers published at, iv. 145 & n. 1; projected French winter-quarters near, 1690, v. 35, n. 8; O. Walker at, iii. 193, n. 3.
Basingstoke, Hants: vicar of: *see* Wheler, Sir George.
Basire (Basiere), Isaac, D.D., iii. 303 & n. 3; shows subscriptions of Orthodox bishops to Anglican tenets, iii. 342 & n. 5; sermon by, iii. 303.
Bassano: painters [E recognized at least two members of the family (ii. 356): Old Bassano, presumably Giacomo da Ponte, called Bassano (ii. 114, n. 2), and an-

Bassano (*cont.*)
other, presumably Francesco da Ponte, jnr., called Bassano (ii. 113, n. 8)]: paintings by: Giacomo, ii. 114 (i. 73), 356; Francesco, ii. 113 (i. 73), 356, 444 & n. 2; 'Bassano', ii. 235 & n. 3, 284; iv. 162, 404 & n. 4; v. 145, 237.
Bassano, Dominico, music-teacher at Padua, ii. 473.
Basso, Girolamo, cardinal: tomb of, ii. 374 & n. 5.
Bassompierre, François, maréchal de, ii. 90 & n. 5; mentioned (error ?), i. 61 & n. 2; house of, at Chaillot, ii. 90–1 & n. (i. 61); doctor of, iii. 547, n. 3.
'Bataille de Vambre' (Vanves, near Paris), iii. 4–8 & nn.
Batavia: name for Netherlands, ii. 51.
Batavia (New Batavia): earthquake and volcanic eruption at, 1699, v. 357 & n. 2.
Bate, George, M.D.: E consults, iii. 191 & n. 4.
Bath, Somerset: notice, 1654, iii. 101–2 & nn.; baths at: in comparison, ii. 155 (i. 100); water: drunk at Wotton, &c., v. 283 & n. 2.
visitors to: Queen Anne, 1702, v. 514–17 & nn., *passim*; Lord and Lady Arlington, 1674, iv. 44 & n. 5; Charles II and Queen Catherine, 1663, iii. 361 & n. 3; E, 1639, 1640, ii. 23 (i. 17), 25 (i. 18); ~ 1654, iii. 101–2, 103; Mrs. Evelyn and Susanna Evelyn (Mrs. Draper), 1691, v. 58, 61; George Evelyn, 1640, ii. 25 (i. 18); Richard Evelyn, sen., 1640, ii. 25 (i. 18); James II, 1687, iv. 560, n. 1; Queen Mary of Modena, 1687, iv. 560 & n. 2.
Bath: Earls of: *see* Grenville, John, first earl, 1661–1701; Granville, Charles, second earl, 1701.
Bath and Wells: diocese of: see declined by Dr. W. Beveridge, 1691, v. 43, n. 3, 52 & n. 1.
bishops: *see* Montagu, James (1608–16); Laud, W. (1626–8); Piers, W. (1632–70); Creighton, Robert, sen. (1670–2); Mews, P. (1673–84); Ken, T. (1684–91); Kidder, R. (1691–1703); Hooper, G. (1704–27).
Batholomeo, harpsichord player: *see* Bartolomeo.
Baths and Bathing [ancient thermae and basins are not indexed collectively; for medicinal baths *see* Medicinal and Hot Springs]:
bathrooms, &c.: Essonne, ii. 121 (i. 78); Euston, iv. 118; Paris: Palais-Royal, ii. 134 (i. 87); ~ Pont-Neuf: Lincler's under, iii. 20.
Turkish bath at Venice, ii. 430–1 & n.; bathing: at Bath, iii. 101–2 *bis* & n.; ~ in Seine at Conflans, iii. 38 & n. 7; ~ in Wotton pond, iii. 15.
Bathsheba: in sermon, v. 414.
Bathurst, —, Spanish merchant, iv. 64.
Bathurst, Allen, Earl Bathurst: geneal., iv. 264, n. 3.
Bathurst, Sir Benjamin; knighted 1682: social, iv. 264 & n. 3.
Bathurst, Elizabeth: *see* Bohun, Mrs. E.
Bathurst, Frances, Lady Bathurst, wife of Sir Benjamin, iv. 264, n. 3.
Bathurst, George (?), ii. 16 & n. 4.
Bathurst, Ralph; M.D. 1654; president of Trinity College, Oxford, 1664, iii. 401, n. 5; notice, i. 13; as E's prospective tutor at Oxford (error), ii. 16–17 & n. (i. 13); sermons by, iii. 401, 433; iv. 3; recommends Dr. Ralph Bohun to E, iii. 416; superintends John Evelyn, jnr., at Oxford, iii. 474; iv. 68; concern of, in gift of Arundelian inscriptions to Oxford, iii. 496, n. 1, 497; social, iii. 510; as vice-chancellor of Oxford: entertains E, iv. 68, 69; proposed for bishop of Bristol, v. 49, critical note & n. 1; dies, v. 571 & n. 1; benefactions of, i. 13 & n. 1; v. 571 & n. 2; library of, v. 571; geneal., ii. 16, n. 4; iii. 416, n. 1; iv. 264, n. 3; *see also add.* (i. 74).
Bathurst: first Earl Bathurst: *see* Bathurst, Allen.
Battle (Battel), Sussex: anniversary of William I's victory at, iv. 601.
Baugency: *see* Beaugency.
Bauli, Phlegraean Fields, ii. 349 & nn. 4–6.
Baux, Samuel, sieur de l'Angle, D.D.: at Windsor, iv. 318–19 & n.

Bavaria: forces of, in War of Spanish Succession, v. 529, 535, 574; Elector of: driven out of, v. 577 & n. 2, 580; *see also* Maximilian II Emanuel.
Bavaria: Elector of, 1679–1726: *see* Maximilian II Emanuel; Electress of: *see* Maria Antonia.
Baveno: granite from, ii. 493, n. 1.
Bavent, Madeleine, iii. 547, n. 3.
Baxter, Rev. Richard: chapel built by, iv. 242 & n. 4; friends of: *see* Ashurst, Sir Henry, &c. (v. 88, nn. 1, 2); Bridges, Col. J. (ii. 545, n. 3).
Bayard: birth-place of, ii. 156, n. 7.
Baylie (Baily), Richard, D.D.: as vice-chancellor of Oxford, ii. 16 & n. 3 (i. 13).
Bayly, Mary, of Deptford: miraculous cure of: alluded to (?), iv. 469 & n. 3.
Baynards, Ewhurst, Surrey: estate of Richard Evelyn, ii. 539 & n. 4; described, iii. 193 & nn. 1, 2; G. Tuke considers taking, iii. 192–3; entail relating to: broken, iv. 582–3 & n.; v. 86; ~ alluded to, iv. 569.
Bayntun (Baynton), Sir Edward, sen.: character, house of, &c., iii. 112–13 & nn.
Bayntun, Sir Edward, K.B.: geneal., iii. 112, n. 2.
Bayntun, Sir Henry: geneal., iii. 112, n. 2.
Beach, Sir Richard: at Portsmouth, iv. 474 & n. 2.
Beachy Head, Sussex: battle of, 1690, v. 27 & n. 2, 29; ~ Torrington's conduct in, v. 29 & n. 3; *add.*; ~ C. Evertsen the youngest in, iii. 406, n. 2.
Beaconsfield, Bucks., iii. 386.
Beade: *see* Bede.
Bear-baiting, &c., iii. 549 & n. 4.
Beardmore, Rev. Thomas: sermon by (?), v. 350–1 & n.
Beauce (Beaulse), province, ii. 138 & n. 4 (i. 90).
Beauchamp: Lord and Lady: *see* Seymour, Henry, styled Lord Beauchamp 1646–54; Somerset, Mary, duchess of Beaufort, &c., formerly Lady Beauchamp.
Beauclerk, Charles; earl of Burford 1676; duke of St. Albans 1684, iv. 374, n. 6; receives Sacrament at Whitehall, iv. 374; character of, &c., iv. 392; mentioned, iv. 408, n. 3; chaplain of: sermon by, v. 110–11.
Beaufort: Duke and Duchess of: *see* Somerset, Henry, first duke, 1682–1700; Somerset, Mary, his duchess.
Beaufort, Henry, cardinal, bishop of Winchester: tomb of, iv. 472 & n. 4.
Beaufort, Margaret, countess of Richmond, &c., mother of Henry VII: gifts made by, iii. 137 & n. 3.
Beaugency (Baugency), on the Loire, ii. 139 (i. 91).
Beaumaris Castle, Anglesey: governor of: *see* Wray, Sir William (ii. 480, n. 3).
Beaumont-sur-Oise, ii. 85 (i. 58); iii. 12, 17, 54.
Beaumont, Francis, and John Fletcher: *The Scornful Lady* by: acted, iii. 268 & n. 5.
Beaumont, Joseph, D.D., iii. 351, n. 1; sermons by, iii. 351, 474; iv. 30, 51.
Beauvais (Beavais), ii. 85 & n. 5 (i. 58); iii. 12, 17, 54; Sir G. Radcliffe at, iii. 2, n. 1.
Beauvoir, Richard, jeweller: crown made by, iv. 441 & n. 3.
Beaw, William, D.D.; bishop of Llandaff 1679: appointed to preach, iv. 306, n. 3.
Bec (Bec-Hellouin): abbey of: manor belonging to, ii. 544, n. 2.
Beccadelli, Antonio, called Panormita, ii. 328–9 & n.
Beccafumi, Domenico, sometimes called Macarino: pavement designed by, ii. 407 & n. 8.
Bechworth Castle, *see* Betchworth.
Beck, Michael Van: geneal., iii. 198, n. 1.
Becket, Thomas à: *see* Thomas à Becket, St.
Beckford, Mary, Lady Beckford, wife of Sir Thomas, and previously of J. Eversfield, iv. 196, n. 1; negotiates her daughter's marriage, iv. 195–6 & n.; house of: wedding-party at, iv. 238.
Beckford, Sir Thomas, iv. 196, n. 1; social, iv. 282.
Beddingham, Sussex: manor of Preston Beckhelvyn in, ii. 544, n. 2; ~ E visits, ii. 544; ~ lease relating to, ii. 552; ~ sale of, &c., iii. 151 *bis*.

Beddington (Bedington), Surrey: the Carews' estate in: notices: 1632 and *c.* 1700, i. 9 & n. 2; 1632, ii. 11; 1658, iii. 221; 1700, v. 427 & n. 1.
Bede (Beade), the Venerable: MS. of work by, iii. 106–7 & n.
Bedel, Gabriel, and T. Collins: sometime E's publishers, iii. 284, n. 4.
Bedford: Earls and Dukes of: *see* Russell, Francis, fourth earl, 1627–41; Russell, William, fifth earl, 1641–94, and first duke, 1694–1700; *see also* Russell family.
Bedloe (Bedlow), William: evidence of, in Stafford's trial, iv. 174 & n. 1.
Beecher, —: sells land in Deptford to E, iii. 508 & n. 4; iv. 37 & n. 6.
Beecher, Henry, of Deptford, iii. 508, n. 4 *ad fin.*
Bega river: battle on (near Temesvar), 1696, *add.* (v. 258 & n. 6).
Beirut, Syria: Evelinus, lord of (?), iii. 548, n. 3.
Belasyse, John, Baron Belasyse, iii. 351, n. 7; as prisoner in Tower, 1678–84; *see* London: Tower: prisoners: the Roman Catholic peers; appointed a commissioner of the Treasury, iv. 533; social: at parties, iii. 351, 386, 512.
Belasyse, Mary, countess of Fauconberg: geneal., iv. 125, n. 1.
Belasyse, Thomas, second viscount and earl of Fauconberg, iv. 125, n. 1; social, iv. 125, 318.
Belasyse: first Baron, 1645–89: *see* Belasyse, John.
Belchamp, John (J. van Belkamp ?), ii. 549, n. 5.
Belgrade: taken by Imperialists from Turks, 1688, iv. 598 & n. 3; recaptured by Turks, 1690, v. 37 & n. 2; besieged by Imperialists, 1693, v. 155 & n. 6; W. Harbord dies at, v. 117 & n. 4.
Belin, —: *see* Bellings, Sir R.
Belisarius: water-mills invented by, ii. 357.
Belkamp, Jan van (Bellcan): painting owned by, ii. 549 & n. 5.
Bell, William, D.D., iv. 182, n. 5; sermons by, iv. 182, 222.
Bella, Stefano della: E buys prints from, iii. 3 & n. 3.
Bellarmino, Roberto, cardinal, ii. 230, n. 3; tomb of, ii. 230 & n. 3; views of: attacked in sermon, iv. 533; ~ on tyrannicide: attacked in sermon, v. 166 & n. 1.
Bellegarde: Perte du Rhône at, ii. 523 & n. 3.
Belli, Valerio (Valerio Vincentino), gem engraver: gem attributed to, iii. 79 & n. 2.
Bellings (Belin), Sir Richard, jnr.; knighted 1666: visits Cornbury (?), iii. 381 & n. 2.
Bellini, Giovanni (Jo: Belino): portrait by (?), iii. 262 & n. 7.
Bellomont: Earl of, 1680–3: *see* Kirkhoven, C. H.
Bellot, Sir Thomas, bt.: negotiates proposed marriage of R. Wilbraham to Mary Evelyn, iv. 324 & n. 3.
Belluccio, Dr. Tommaso, ii. 408 & n. 6; *see also* ii. 181, n. 8.
Belvoir Castle, Leics.: notice, iii. 124–5 & n.
Bembo, Pietro, cardinal: tomb of, ii. 378 & n. 3.
Benavidii family, called Mantoa: palace of, at Padua, ii. 466–7 & n.
Benbow, John, admiral, v. 160, n. 1, 244, n. 1; bombards St. Malo, 1693, v. 160 & n. 1; and Sayes Court: takes it on lease, i. *34*, n. 1; v. 244 & n. 1, 245; ~ furniture of, at: compensated for damage done to, by Peter the Great, v. 284, n. 5, 290, n. 6; action of, in West Indies, 1702, v. 526–7 & n.
Bendish, Susanna: *see* Hooker, Susanna, Lady Hooker.
Bendish, Sir Thomas, bt.: geneal., iv. 349, n. 1.
Benedict VII, pope: tomb of, ii. 380 & n. 7.
Benedict XIII, pope, ii. 275, n. 5.
Benedict XIV, pope, ii. 380, n. 1.
Bengeo, Herts.: Sir Richard and Lady Fanshawe resident at, iii. 184, n. 4.
Benlowes (Benlous), Edward, poet: gifts of, to St. John's College, Cambridge, iii. 136 & nn. 3, 4.
Benn, Amabella: *see* Grey, Amabella, countess of Kent.
Benn, Sir Anthony: geneal., i. 3, n. 3.
Benn, Joan *or* Jane, Lady Benn, born Evelyn, wife of Sir Anthony Benn: *see* Hart, Joan, Lady Hart.
Bennet, Elizabeth: *see* Carr, Elizabeth, Lady Carr.

Bennet, Sir Henry; Baron Arlington 1665; earl of Arlington 1672, iii. 299, n. 2 [from 1674 he is frequently designated Lord Chamberlain].
— character, &c.: general account, iv. 118–20 & nn.; hospitality at Euston, iii. 590–1; indebtedness, iv. 118–19, 120; indolence, iv. 19, 38; as political patron, iv. 39 & n. 1, 119 & n. 7.
— chronological series: parentage, &c., iv. 119 & nn. 2, 3; wounded in Civil War, iv. 119 & n. 4; appointed secretary of state, 1662, iii. 343 & n. 4; at Lord Mayor's feast, 1664, iii. 388–9; created baron, iii. 406 & n. 6; accident to, iii. 498; at consecration of Dr. J. Wilkins, iii. 518; as participant in Secret Treaty of Dover, 1670, iii. 608, n. 1; at Windsor, 1670, iii. 558; as member of Council for Foreign Plantations (later of Trade and Plantations), 1671–2: promoter of the council (?), iv. 14 & n. 3; ~ reports Charles II's proposal for building council-chamber, iii. 582–3; ~ commission for governor of Barbados submitted to, iii. 612, n. 2; ~ attends meetings, iii. 578, 584, 604–5, 629; ~ attends Council dinner, iii. 599; concurs in Declaration of Indulgence, 1672, iii. 607–8 & n.; created earl and K.G., iv. 119 & n. 5; at Buoy of the Nore, iii. 620; appointed Lord Chamberlain, 1674, iii. 591, n. 1; iv. 47, n. 2; at Bath, 1674, iv. 44 & n. 5; at Windsor: 1678, iv. 136–7; ~ 1679, iv. 171 & n. 10; high steward of manor of Sayes Court, 1683, iv. 346; reappointed Lord Chamberlain, 1685, iv. 416; received into Roman Catholic church and dies, iii. 608 & n. 1; iv. 476 & n. 1; grave of, iv. 118 & n. 1.
— political relations: opposes Clarendon, iii. 494, n. 2; advances Clifford, &c., iii. 470; iv. 18 & n. 4, 19–20 & n.; ~ alluded to, iv. 39 & n. 1, 119 & n. 7; hated by Danby (Sir T. Osborne, later duke of Leeds), iv. 14; ~ *see also* iv. 39, n. 1; hostility to, of James, duke of York, iv. 119; employs, and is succeeded by, Sir J. Williamson, iii. 471 & n. 4, 526 & n. 6; iv. 38–9 & n.; ~ alluded to, iv. 119 & n. 7.

Bennet, Sir H. (Arlington) (*cont.*)
— social: visits Enfield (Henry Coventry), &c., iv. 91–2; visits Wimbledon (earl of Bristol), iii. 316; at parties: as guest, iii. 446, 576–7, 586, 600; iv. 179; ~ as host, iii. 524, 528–9, 539, 549–50, 558, 564; iv. 6, 77, 78, 91–8 *passim*, 103, 130, 326, 337, 344, 358, 393; *see also* iii. 562, 623 (Goring House).
— relations with E: general, i. *22*; iii. 571, 591.
— — official and business: attends reading of E's account of the ambassadors' encounter, &c., 1661, iii. 299, 300; receives petition from E, iii. 343; discusses provision of fuel with E, iii. 487; gives E order to visit H. Oldenburg in Tower, iii. 491; other business interviews, iii. 344, 406, 521 & n. 3, 537, 562–3, 568(?); iv. 16.
— — literary: E dedicates *History of Three Impostors* to, iii. 523; desires E to write history of second Dutch War, iii. 523 & n. 1, 550, 558; John Evelyn, jnr., dedicates translation of Rapin to, iv. 1.
— — patronage: gives employment at E's request to: E. Phillips, iv. 120–1 & n.; ~ Lady Tuke, iv. 8; ~ C. Wase, iii. 525 & n. 1; *see also* iii. 526.
— — social: announces to E Charles II's intended visit to Sayes Court, iii. 302; greets E after plague, iii. 429; visits E at Sayes Court, iii. 302, 526; iv. 102, 271; E visits at Euston: 1671, iii. 589–92, 595–6 & nn.; ~ 1677, iv. 113–20 & nn.; ~ *see also* iii. 554; E visits, &c., in London, iii. 355, 371, 372, 397, 571, 574; iv. 9, 30, 47, 82, 91–108 *passim*, 122–35 *passim*, 156, 160, 163, 167, 168, 169, 182–3, 197, 202, 239, 240, 254, 260, 266, 273, 352, 361; *see also* iii. 541 (Goring House).

Bennet, Sir H. (Arlington) (*cont.*)
— culture, &c.: art-collection of, iv. 102 & nn. 1–6; looks at paintings, iv. 23; library of, iv. 121; employs Edward Phillips as reader, &c., iv. 120–1 & n.; visits Grinling Gibbons, iv. 179; examines Montagu House, iv. 344; at demonstration of phosphorus, iv. 263.
— property: Goring House: acquired by, iii. 404 & n. 2; ~ loss by fire at, iv. 44; *see also* London: topography: Goring House.
— — Euston: notices, iii. 589–92, 595–6 & nn.; iv. 113–20 & nn.; ~ travels to, iii, 553–4; rebuilds church at, iv. 114 & n. 5, 118 & n. 1; *see also* Euston.
— — Whitehall: official lodgings in, iii. 568, n. 2; iv. 77, 184 & n. 4; reversion granted to, v. 161, n. 4.
— geneal., iii. 358 & n. 4 (repeated, iii. 372; iv. 13 & n. 3), 622 & nn. 4, 5; iv. 119 & n. 2, 498, n. 3.
Bennet, Isabella: *see* FitzRoy, Isabella, duchess of Grafton.
Bennet, Isabella, countess of Arlington, wife of Henry Bennet, earl of Arlington, iii. 622, n. 5; character, &c., of, iv. 118; as Groom of the Stole to Queen Catherine: attendance required, iv. 318 & n. 8; ~ resides in Somerset House, iv. 498, 531, 565; and her daughter's marriage, iii. 622; iv. 184; assists Lady Tuke, iv. 8; dressing-room of, at Goring House, *ib.*; apartment of, at Euston, iv. 117; visits Bath, iv. 44 & n. 5; at Windsor, iv. 383; visits Grinling Gibbons, iv. 179; letter of, to E, iv. 341; affection of, for Mary Evelyn, iv. 428; social: parties, iv. 102, 105, 179; geneal., iv. 97, n. 7, 102 & nn. 9, 10, 222, n. 2.
Bennet, Sir John, B.A.: geneal., iv. 119 & n. 2.
Bennet, Sir John, D.C.L.: geneal., iv. 119, n. 2.
Bennett, Frances: *see* Cecil, Frances, countess of Salisbury.
Benotti, Domenico, Florentine mosaicist, ii. 191 & n. 12 (i. 119), 417; work by: E buys, ii. 191 & n. 13 (i. 119).
Benson, George, D.D.; dean of Hereford 1672: sermon by, iii. 629 & n. 3; geneal., iv. 27 & n. 2.
Benson, Rev. Samuel: administers Sacrament (?), iv. 27 & n. 2.
Bentinck, Hans Willem; first earl of Portland 1689, v. 230, n. 1; as Banting or Benting: grants to, to be withdrawn, v. 229–30 & n.; ~ comes to London for money for army, 1696, v. 253 & n. 2, 256, n. 3; impeachment of, 1701, v. 456, n. 1; ~ alluded to, v. 466 & n. 1, 481; ~ dismissed, v. 468 & n. 1.
Bentivoglio, castle, near Bologna, ii. 427 & n. 1.
Bentivoglio, Guido, cardinal: garden of, at Rome, ii. 379 & n. 4.
Bentley, Richard; D.D. 1696; master of Trinity College, Cambridge, 1700, v. 88, n. 4; relations of, with E, i. 35; as Boyle lecturer: appointed for 1692, v. 88–9; lecture by, v. 94 & n. 1; ~ consults E about printing, v. 94; trustees' satisfaction with, v. 123; re-appointed for 1694, v. 159, 160–1 & n., 196–7, 199; lecture by, v. 164; as library-keeper at St. James's Palace: appointed, v. 196 & n. 7; proposals of: for increasing accommodation of library, v. 224, n. 2; ~ for converting library into a public institution, v. 280, n. 5.
sermon by, v. 160; social, v. 171, 280.
Bentley Hall, Staffs.: Charles II at, iii. 51, n. 2.
Bereans: in sermons, iv. 223; v. 152.
Berettini (Berettieri), Pietro: *see* Cortona, P. da.
Bergamo, Fra Damiano (Zambelli) da: intarsio by, ii. 421 & n. 5.
Bergavenny (Abergavenny): twelfth Lord, 1666–95: *see* Nevill, George.
Bergen, Norway: English attack on Dutch East India ships at, 1665, iii. 562 & n. 5, 617 & nn. 2, 4; ~ Clifford's responsibility for, iii. 618 & n. 3; iv. 21 & n. 4; fire at, 1702, v. 504.
Bergen-op-Zoom: E visits, 1641, ii. 61 & n. 5 (i. 42).
Beringhen, Henri de, 'Monsieur le Premier': visits English court (?), iii. 575 & n. 7.

Berkeley (Barkley), — (George Berkeley, later first earl of Berkeley ?): social, iii. 169 & n. 6.
Berkeley, Lady (Christian Berkeley, Lady Berkeley of Stratton ?): social, iv. 363 & n. 3.
Berkeley, Charles; second Baron Berkeley of Stratton 1678, iv. 330 & n. 2; tutor of, iv. 330; proposed marriage of, iv. 86, n. 3.
Berkeley, Charles; second earl of Berkeley 1698: sells Durdans, iii. 15, n. 1.
Berkeley, Sir Charles, 1630–65; first Viscount Fitzhardinge 1663; earl of Falmouth 1664: at the ambassadors' encounter, 1661, iii. 298 & n. 2, 299.
Berkeley, Sir Charles, 1599–1668; second Viscount Fitzhardinge 1665, iii. 251, n. 1; as Comptroller of the Household, iii. 251; ~ successor of, iii. 344, n. 2; as Treasurer of the Household, iii. 351, n. 5; ~ successor of, iv. 19 & n. 4; commissioner for London streets, iii. 319, n. 1; social: party, iii. 351; ~ alone, &c., iii. 308, 355 & n. 6(?), 444 & n. 6; geneal., iii. 445, n. 2.
Berkeley, Christian, Lady Berkeley, wife of John Berkeley, Baron Berkeley of Stratton, and friend of Mrs. Godolphin, iv. 3, n. 2; visits art-collection, iv. 3; visits Royal Society's museum, iv. 34; at Southborough (Tunbridge Wells), iv. 40–1; and Lord Berkeley's embassy to France: accompanies Berkeley, iv. 79; ~ asks E to act as Berkeley's agent during, iv. 77; ~ thanks him for doing so, iv. 110; lets Berkeley House garden for building, iv. 381–2 & n.; friend of Lady Hamilton, later duchess of Tyrconnel, iv. 79 & n. 3; social: parties, &c., iv. 11, 15, 34, 64; ~ visit of condolence to, iv. 152; ~ other visits to, iv. 363 & n. 3(?), 398; *see further* Berkeley, John, Baron Berkeley of Stratton; London: topography: Berkeley House.
Berkeley, Mrs. Elizabeth, wife of Robert Berkeley of Spetchley: *see* Burnet, Mrs. E.
Berkeley, Elizabeth, Lady Berkeley, widow of Sir William: *see* Howard, Elizabeth, countess of Carlisle.
Berkeley, Elizabeth, d. 1708, countess of Berkeley, wife of George Berkeley, ninth Lord and first earl of Berkeley, iii. 230, n. 1; social, iii. 230; iv. 18, n. 1; connexion of, with East India Company, iv. 285, n. 1.
Berkeley, George, eighth Lord Berkeley (of Berkeley Castle); geneal., iii. 166 & n. 2; dies, iii. 220, n. 6.
Berkeley, George; ninth Lord Berkeley (of Berkeley Castle) 1658; first earl of Berkeley 1679, iii. 166, n. 2; invites E to accompany commissioners to Charles II, May 1660, iii. 244–5 & n.; elected Master of Trinity House, iv. 248; attends Trinity House feast, iv. 380; entertains Bantam ambassadors, iv. 285 & n. 1.
property: Durdans: as owner, iii. 15, n. 1, 219, n. 6, 220, n. 6, 291; ~ entertains Charles II, &c., at, iii. 334 & nn. 5–7; house of, at St. John's, Clerkenwell: bought for Roman Catholic nunnery (?), iv. 607 & n. 4.
social: wedding anniversary, iv. 18 & n. 1; parties, visits, &c., iii. 166, 169 & n. 6(?), 220 & n. 6, 230, 231, 291, 369, 507, 514.
chaplain of: *see* Rogers, J.
Berkeley, Isabel: *see* Packer, Mrs. I.
Berkeley, Lord John: appellation given by E to Sir John Berkeley, Baron Berkeley of Stratton, iii. 470 & n. 3; iv. 11.
Berkeley, Sir John, 1607–78; created Baron Berkeley of Stratton 1658, iii. 445, n. 2; as commissioner: of the Ordnance, iii. 443, n. 1, 445, n. 2; ~ for Saltpetre, iii. 443, n. 1, 445; as Lord Lieutenant of Ireland, 1670–2: returns to London, iii. 624 & n. 5; ~ London agent of, iv. 77 & n. 5; as ambassador to France, &c., 1675–7: instructions, &c., for, iv. 76 & n. 3; accompanied by: John Evelyn, jun., iv. 76; ~ Mrs. Godolphin, iv. 73, n. 7, &c.; departure of: delayed by illness, iv. 77; journey of, to Dover, iv. 78–80 & nn.; journey of, to Nimeguen, iv. 90 & n. 3; returns to London, iv. 110 & n. 1; allowance to, for expenses, iv. 110, n. 1; appoints

Berkeley, Sir John (*cont.*)
E as his agent during embassy, iv. 77–8, 79–80; E acts on behalf of, iv. 86, 96, 99, 107; E renders accounts to, &c., iv. 110 *ter* & n. 1.
property: *see* London: topography: Berkeley House; Twickenham Park, iv. 23, n. 1; ~ bailiff, &c., at, iv. 86, 99.
ill, iv. 75; social: parties, iii. 445–6; iv. 11; ~ alone, &c., iii. 470 & n. 3(?); iv. 124, 134 [*see further* London: topography: Berkeley House. In some notices 'at my Lord Berkeley's' may be merely an equivalent for 'at Berkeley House'; similarly Berkeley or Lady Berkeley may have been present when the house alone is mentioned]; dies, iv. 152 & n. 2; geneal., iv. 86 & n. 3, 330 & n. 2.
Berkeley, Sir John, first Baron Berkeley of Stratton, and Lady Berkeley: E dines with 'L. Berkeley', iv. 1, 30.
Berkeley, John, 1663–97; third Baron Berkeley of Stratton 1682: as admiral: bombards Dieppe, &c., 1694, v. 186 & n. 2; mentioned, iv. 86, n. 3.
Berkeley, Robert, of Spetchley, iv. 345 & n. 4; house of, &c., iv. 363 & nn. 4, 5.
Berkeley, Sir Robert, judge, iv. 345 & n. 4; geneal., ii. 548, n. 1; iv. 345.
Berkeley, Theophila: *see* Coke, Theophila, Lady Coke.
Berkeley, Sir William: geneal., iii. 475, n. 1; iv. 561, n. 2.
Berkeley: Earls, &c., of: *see* Berkeley, George, first earl, 1679–98, formerly ninth Lord Berkeley; Berkeley, Elizabeth, his countess; Berkeley, Charles, second earl.
Berkeley (of Berkeley Castle): Lords and Ladies [for the designation *see* iii. 166, n. 2]: *see* Berkeley, George, eighth Lord, 1613–58; Berkeley, George, ninth Lord, 1658–79, later first earl of Berkeley; Berkeley, Elizabeth, his lady.
Berkeley of Stratton: Barons, &c.: *see* Berkeley, Sir John, first baron, 1658–78; Berkeley, Christian, his baroness; Berkeley, Charles, second baron, 1678–82; Berkeley, John, third baron, 1682–97.
Berkeley Castle, Gloucs.: as distinctive appellation of Lords Berkeley, iii. 166, n. 2.
Berkenshaw, —: *see* Birchensha, J.
Berkshire: stinking fog in, v. 298 & n. 1.
Berkshire: Earls of: *see* Howard, Thomas, first earl, 1626–69, formerly Baron Howard of Charleton; Howard, Charles, second earl, 1669–79; Howard, Thomas, third earl, 1679–1706.
Berlin: Kaiser Friedrich Museum: painting in, ii. 487, n. 3.
Bermuda: Bermuda whale: method of catching, &c., iv. 146–7 & n.; estate of Sir R. Clayton in, iv. 147 & n. 1.
Bern (Bearn), canton: geographical, ii. 520 & n. 2; alliance of, with Geneva, ii. 526.
Bernard, St.: picture of, ii. 310, 311, n. 1.
Bernay (Bernée), in Picardy: E's night at, iii. 54 & n. 3.
Bernina pass, ii. 489, n. 6.
Bernini, Giovanni Lorenzo, architect and sculptor, ii. 229, n. 1, 261 & n. 4; opera by, ii. 261 & n. 5.
— as architect: general, ii. 212, n. 2, 399; buildings by (all in Rome): Fountain, Piazza Navona, ii. 362 & n. 6, 368, n. 1; Palazzo Barberini, ii. 228–9 & n.; Pantheon: bell-towers, ii. 371; n. 1; S. Maria del Popolo, ii. 373, n. 9 *ad fin.*; St. Peter's: canopy of high altar, ii. 261 & nn. 1–4; ~ tower, ii. 258–9 & n.; *add.*; Vatican: Sala Ducale, ii. 294, n. 3 *ad fin.*; ~ Scala Regia, *ib.*
— as sculptor: rivalry of, with F. Duquesnoy, ii. 263 & n. 2; *add.*
— — works by: in Rome: Apollo and Daphne, ii. 253 & n. 7, 404; Cathedra Petri: first and present settings, ii. 264, n. 4; David, ii. 253 & n. 8; Longinus, ii. 262, 308; Rape of Proserpine, ii. 235–6 & n.; St. Theresa, ii. 239, n. 10; tombs: A. Emmanuele (Nigrita) (school-piece), ii. 244 & n. 5; ~ Countess Matilda, ii. 265 & n. 2; ~ Paul III: rearranged by, ii. 265 & n. 2; ~ Urban VIII, ii. 265, n. 2.

Bernini, Giovanni Lorenzo (*cont.*)
— — works by: outside Rome: Florence: bust (Costanza Buonarelli ?), ii. 413 & n. 7; Paris, Palais-Royal, chapel: St. John and Virgin Mary, ii. 566 & n. 7; Velletri: Urban VIII, ii. 317 & n. 6.
Bernini, Pietro: sculpture by, ii. 253, n. 5.
Berny, Louis-Hugues de Lionne, marquis of: social (?; as M. Brizasiere), iii. 411 & n. 3.
Berry: *see* Bury St. Edmunds.
Berry, French province, ii. 152 (i. 98); *drap de*, i. 99 & n. 2.
Berry: Duke of (Jean de France): chapel built by, ii. 153 & nn. 10–12 (i. 99); 'La Couronne du Duc de', ii. 153 & n. 13 (i. 99).
Bertie, — (Charles Bertie ?): letter from, iii. 438 & n. 4.
Bertie, Bridget: *see* Osborne, Bridget, duchess of Leeds.
Bertie, Charles: letter from (?), iii. 438 & n. 4.
Bertie, Elizabeth, countess of Lindsey, wife of Robert Bertie, third earl, and previously of Sir F. H. Lee: social (as Lady Lee), iii. 383 & n. 1.
Bertie, Montagu, second earl of Abingdon: removed from offices, 1705, v. 611 & n. 4.
Bertie, Montague, second earl of Lindsey, iii. 251, n. 1; as lord great chamberlain: in ceremonies, iii. 251 & n. 1(?), 283 & n. 5; geneal., iii. 438, n. 4; iv. 354, n. 5.
Bertie, Robert, first earl of Lindsey: request of, to Richard Evelyn, sen., ii. 12 & n. 1 (i. 10); killed, i. 53.
Bertie, Robert, third earl of Lindsey: geneal., iii. 383, n. 1.
Berwick: Duke of: *see* Fitzjames, James.
Bess of Hardwick: *see* Talbot, Elizabeth, countess of Shrewsbury.
Betchworth, Surrey: Betchworth Castle at: visits to, iii. 143 & n. 1, 219–20 & nn., 326 & n. 4(?); house of S. Harvey at, v. 547, n. 4.
Bethel: in sermon, v. 63.
Bethlehem: relic from, ii. 244; in sermons, v. 84 *bis*, 524.
Beuningen (Beverning), Koenraad van, Dutch ambassador to England 1674–9, iv. 77, n. 1; social: parties, &c., iv. 77, 91, 94, 105 & n. 3, 164.
Beveretta: *see* Le Bouveret.
Beveridge (Beverwich), William; D.D.; bishop of St. Asaph, 1704, v. 43, n. 3; and bishopric of Bath and Wells: nominated for, 1691, v. 49 & n. 1; ~ consults Sancroft and refuses, v. 52 & n. 1; sermon by, v. 43.
Beverland, Adrianus: library of (?), v. 322, n. 1.
Beverley, Yorks.: notice, iii. 130 & n. 4.
Beverning, —: *see* Beuningen, K. van.
Beverweerd, Mlle de: social, iv. 102 & n. 10.
Beverweerd, Amelia (Emilia) van: *see* Butler, Amelia, countess of Ossory.
Beverweerd, Charlotta Philibert van: as godmother (?), iv. 222 & n. 2.
Beverweerd, Isabella van: *see* Bennet, Isabella, countess of Arlington.
Beverweerd, Louis of Nassau, Baron or Lord of: geneal., iii. 622, n. 5; iv. 102, n. 10, 222, n. 2; called Bredrode in error, iv. 118; *add.*
Bexhill, Sussex: vicar of: *see* Bradford, J.
Beza, Theodore: church discipline of, ii. 527; views of: attacked in sermon, iv. 86; translation of Bible by: *see* Bible.
Bianchi, Francesco, singer, ii. 400 & n. 1.
Biard, P., jnr.: statue of Louis XIII by, ii. 101 & n. 1 (i. 66).
Bible:
— versions:
— — Polyglot: *Biblia sacra polyglotta*, ed. B. Walton, 1655–7: proposals for publishing, iii. 78 & nn. 3, 4.
— — English: authorized version: translation defended in sermon, iv. 537; ~ disparaged by a Jesuit, iv. 599 & n. 1.
— — Greek: Septuagint: Ussher's views and book on, iii. 156 & n. 4.
— — Hebrew: Ussher on value of, iii. 156.
— — Italian: translation by J. Diodati, ii. 521 & n. 1.

Bible (*cont.*)
— — Latin: Vulgate (St. Jerome): Ussher on, iii. 156; ~ quoted, iv. 385, n. 3; Old Testament, trans. Tremellius and Junius: quoted, v. 105 & n. 2; Psalm civ: paraphrase of, by Sir W. Petty, iv. 61 & n. 2; New Testament, trans. Beza, v. 105, n. 2; ~ quoted, iii. 454 & n. 2; iv. 385, n. 3, 402 & n. 2.
— — various languages: translations published at charge of R. Boyle, v. 82 & n. 2.
— particular copies:
— — MSS.: Bibles: Old English (Wycliffe), Bodleian Library, iii. 106 & n. 5; ~ French, Geneva, University, ii. 529–30 & n.; New Testament (part) from Scotland (Book of Deer?), v. 206 & n. 3; separate books: Esdras, Bologna, S. Domenico, ii. 421 & n. 6; St. Mark, Venice, St. Mark's, ii. 441 & n. 4; St. John, Florence, Palazzo Vecchio, ii. 188 & n. 8 (i. 118); Acts, Vatican, ii. 301 & n. 6.
— — printed: Bible given to York Minster by Charles I, iii. 129 & n. 3.
— criticism, &c. [all references, except that to ii. 247 & n. 3, are to notes of sermons]:
— — general: canon settled, v. 331; east and west in: significance of, iii. 25.
— — particular books and passages, &c.: Old Testament: chronology of, v. 268–9 & n.; Psalms: double significance of, iv. 567–8; ~ xxiv: as a dialogue, v. 99; ~ xxvii: origin of, v. 298; ~ xlviii: origin of, iv. 348 & n. 1; Jonah: period of, iv. 244 & n. 3; St. Mark xi. 13: translation of, iv. 46 & n. 7; 1 Corinthians xiii. 3: translation of, v. 450 & n. 1; Galatians: Luther on, iii. 31 & n. 2; Philippians iii. 20: meaning of, v. 498 & n. 6; Hebrews vi. 4: meaning of, v. 389; 1 Peter: date of, v. 128–9 & n.; 1 John: purpose of, v. 131.
— — commentaries on, by St. Jerome: passage in, ii. 247 & n. 3.
— use, &c., of [all references are to notes of sermons]:

Bible (*cont.*)
— — interpretation of, iii. 24, 60; nations deprived of, iii. 229; only rule of Faith, iv. 545–6, 599; v. 143, 221; superior to conscience, iii. 563; word of God, iii. 191; reading: duty of, &c., iii. 104, 232, 391; iv. 223, 229, 448, 513, 516, 570; v. 105–6, 127, 152, 183, 482; ~ not to be forbidden to laity, iv. 277; sufficiency, authority, &c., of, iii. 226–7, 510; iv. 138, 155, 170, 344, 538–9, 623, 643, 646–7; v. 57–8, 143, 540–1; veracity, &c., of, iv. 18.
— E's citations and quotations:
— — Leviticus (error), ii. 247 & n. 3; Acts xxviii, ii. 318, 343 & n. 3; Hebrews, xiii. 14, iii. 454 & n. 2.
— miscellaneous [for prophecies based on Revelations *see* Antichrist; Witnesses, the Two; all references here are to notes of sermons]: Apostles and, iii. 509; Beasts in Revelations, iv. 348; Christ and, iv. 104, 298; Covenant of Grace in, iii. 512; St. John the Baptist and, iv. 356; word 'new' in, v. 2–3; perversion of, iv. 541; the 'terrible text' (Hebrews x. 26–8), iv. 81; and Transubstantiation, iv. 539.
Bichi, Alessandro, cardinal: eunuch of, ii. 400 & n. 1.
Bicker van Swieten, C., captain: in painting, ii. 43, n. 5 *ad fin.*
Bickerstaffe, Sir Charles: payment by, to E, iv. 378 & n. 2.
Bickerton, Jane: *see* Howard, Jane, duchess of Norfolk.
Bickerton, Robert: geneal., iii. 592, n. 5.
Biddulph, Sir Theophilus, bt.: social, iii. 348 & n. 6.
Bièvre, river, at Arcueil, ii. 129, n. 3.
Bifrons, near Canterbury: owned by Sir Arthur Slingsby, ii. 560, n. 2.
Billiards: table, iv. 116 & n. 6; ~ for 'French billiards', iv. 190 & n. 4.
Billingshurst, Sussex, ii. 544 & n. 4.
Bills of health: in Italy, ii. 167–8 & n. (i. 106), 426 & n. 9, 429; pratique granted, ii. 171 & n. 4 (i. 108).
Bindley, James: helps Bray to edit the Diary, i. *55* & n. 5, *115*.

Bingham, Rev. Joseph: sermon by, v. 231, n. 1.
Biology and Zoology [for experiments on, and dissections of, particular kinds of animals, *see* Dogs; Reptiles]: equivocal generation, iii. 341 & n. 4; iv. 290; microscopic examinations, iii. 356–7 & n.; iv. 126 & n. 4, 128, 171; experiments on respiration of fish, iii. 353–4.
Birch, Andrew, major: encamps on Blackheath, v. 29–30 & n.
Birch, Peter; D.D. 1688; rector of St. James's, Piccadilly, 1692–5, iv. 488, n. 1; v. 136, n. 5; sermons by, iv. 488(?), 529(?); v. 23 & n. 1, 24, 39–47 *passim*, 136–40 *passim*, 170, 193.
Birchensha (Berkenshaw), John, musician: system of composition of, &c., iii. 377 & n. 4.
Bird (Byrd), William, stone-cutter at Oxford: discovers method of staining marble, iii. 111, n. 1; makes model of Sheldonian Theatre, iii. 385, n. 5.
Birdlip, Gloucs.: view from towards Gloucester, iii. 118, n. 5.
Birds [select notices; *see also* Aviaries; Zoological Gardens]: general: discourse on names of, iii. 341.
barnacles (Orcades anates): preserved, ii. 331 & n. 3.
birds of paradise (manucodiata): preserved, ii. 331 & n. 4; iii. 325 & n. 4.
bustards: captive, ii. 72 (i. 47).
cranes: captive, ii. 72 (i. 47), 251, 467; in Norfolk, iii. 594; Balearian, iii. 399 & n. 5.
crows: in severe winter, iii. 211.
eagles: captive, ii. 66 (i. 44), 72 (i. 47), 467; in Norfolk, iii. 594.
hawks: from Russia, iii. 344, 349.
herons, iv. 70, 255; heronry, ii. 71 (i. 47).
hornbills (as rhinoceros or rhinoceros bird): heads, ii. 53 (i. 37); *add.*; iii. 33 & n. 4.
humming-birds: preserved, iii. 108.
jackatroo (parrot): preserved, iii. 108 & n. 5.
nightingales, ii. 147 (i. 95), 383 & n. 5; captive, ii. 434.
ostriches (estriges), ii. 251, 390; iv. 266 & n. 3; thigh-bone of, iii. 338.
Birds (*cont.*)
parrot, iv. 618; preserved, iii. 108.
peacocks, ii. 251.
pelicans (onocrotalus), ii. 40 & nn. 1, 2 (i. 30); iii. 398–9; preserved, ii. 331 & n. 2; in wood-carving, iv. 397.
penguin: bird resembling, iii. 399.
pheasants: captive, ii. 72 (i. 47).
ravens: white, iii. 222, 399 & n. 4.
rhinoceros-birds: *see* hornbills *above*.
solan geese: captive, iii. 399.
sparrow: tame, iv. 336.
storks, ii. 32 & n. 7 (i. 25); iii. 399; in Norfolk, iii. 594 & n. 1; captive, ii. 72.
swans, ii. 251.
turkeys: egg of, as measure of size, iii. 3.
turtle-doves: in E's aviary, iii. 175.
vultures: captive, i. 44.
woodcocks: nets to catch, ii. 390.
Birkhead, Henry: geneal., iii. 230, n. 3.
Biron: Barons: *see* Byron.
Birstall *or* Burstall, Robert, agent for Sick and Wounded at Gravesend: misconduct of, iv. 132 & n. 7.
Bisaccioni, M.: libretto by, ii. 450 & n. 2.
Bisagno, river, near Genoa (?), ii. 178 & n. 1 (i. 112).
Biscay, Spain: man from (Garro), ii. 149 (i. 96).
Biscay, Bay of: ship lost in, iv. 58.
Bisentina, island in lake of Bolsena, ii. 209 & n. 7.
Bishop, William: geneal., iv. 2, n. 1.
Bishop's Stortford (Bishop Stratford), Herts.: notice, iii. 142 & n. 2; E at, iii. 556, 588, 597; iv. 120.
Bishopston, Wilts.: hare-warren at, iii. 114, 115, n. 1.
Bishopthorpe, Yorks., W.R.: palace of archbishops of York at, iii. 128 & n. 4; Archbishop Dolben and: first goes to, iv. 335, n. 1; ~ dies at, iv. 507, n. 1.
Black Monday: day of solar eclipse, 1652, v. 354 & n. 2.
Black *or* Euxine Sea: Chardin's travels about, iv. 213; Peter the Great builds navy on, v. 316.
Blackall (Blackwall), Offspring; D.D. 1700; bishop of Exeter 1708, v. 366, n. 2; appointed Boyle lecturer for 1700, v. 362, n. 1, 366; lecture by, v. 398 & n. 3.

Blackheath: alternative name for Wotton, Surrey (error?), ii. 3 & n. 2 (i. 5).
Blackheath, Kent (now county of London): fair on, iv. 311 & n. 2; military: bombs, &c., tested on, iv. 543 & n. 4; encampments on: 1673, iv. 13 & n. 1, 15; ~ 1685, iv. 458 & n. 1; ~ 1690, v. 30 & n. 1, 31, 32 & n. 6; review on, 1657, iii. 192, n. 6; places about: Sir John Morden's Hospital (in Charlton), v. 212 & n. 5; Wricklemarsh near (in Charlton), iii. 70, n. 2, 161, n. 1.
Blackheath, hundred, Surrey, ii. 3, n. 2.
Blackiston *or* Baines, Charles: *alias* of J. Cosin, jnr., iii. 26, n. 6.
Blacklow: *alias* of Father T. White, iii. 33, n. 5.
Blaeu (Bleaw), Joan: atlases by, ii. 49 & n. 4 (i. 35); *see also* Books mentioned in text.
Blaeu, W. J., ii. 49, n. 4.
Blagge, Henrietta Maria: *see* Yarborough, Henrietta Maria, Lady Yarborough.
Blagge, Margaret: *see* Godolphin, Mrs. M.
Blagrave, Jonathan; D.D. 1693, iv. 180, n. 4; v. 40 & n. 3; sermons by, iv. 180(?); v. 40.
Blake, Elizabeth: *see* Burnet, Mrs. E.
Blake, Sir Richard: geneal., iv. 345, n. 4.
Blake, Robert, the admiral: engagement of, with Tromp, 1652, iii. 67 & n. 4.
Blanc, Mont, ii. 506, n. 3.
Blanchot, Friar Nicholas, physician, &c.: notice (?), iii. 27–8 & nn.
Blandford: Marquis of, 1702–3 (courtesy title): *see* Churchill, John, 1686–1703.
Blandford, Walter; D.D.; bishop of Oxford 1665; of Worcester 1671, iii. 626 & n. 4; officiates at Whitehall, iii. 626; appointed to preach, iv. 52, n. 5.
Blaney, —: makes shorthand report of trial of Seven Bishops, iv. 615, n. 2.
Blathwayt, Mrs. Mary, wife of William Blathwayt: alluded to, iv. 554 & n. 3.
Blathwayt, William: notice, iv. 554–5 & n.; as secretary at war: orders quartering of soldiers in private houses, iv. 458 & n. 2.
Bleaw, —: *see* Blaeu, Joan.
Blechingley, Surrey: manor of: descent of, iii. 156, n. 2; ~ sale of, by Lord Peterborough: E trustee for, iv. 108–9 & n.; ~ bought by Sir R. Clayton, iv. 110–11 & n.; manor-house: chimney-piece from, iii. 156 & n. 2; ~ demolished, iv. 111, n. 1; Sir Ralph Whitfield resident at, ii. 82 & n. 3 (i. 55).
Bleike, on Simplon road, ii. 508, n. 5 *ad fin.*
Blenheim, battle of, 1704, v. 574–9 *passim*; news of, brought to Queen Anne, v. 574–5 & nn.; pursuit after, v. 576 & n. 1; effects of, French losses, &c., v. 577 & nn. 2–5; thanksgiving for, v. 578–9 & nn.; alluded to, v. 581.
Blenheim Palace, Woodstock, Oxon.: Sunderland library at, v. 322, n. 1.
Blith: *see* Blyth.
Blocklandt, Anthonie van (A. van Montfort): painting by, ii. 32 & n. 6 (i. 25).
Blois: notice, 1644, ii. 140–2 & nn. (i. 92–3); château: proposed for residence of James II, 1697, v. 271, n. 2; Forest of, ii. 142 (i. 92); E's journey to, ii. 139 *bis* (i. 91 *bis*).
Blois: Earls of: tombs of, ii. 142 (i. 92).
Blood (Bloud), Thomas: notice, iii. 576 & n. 2.
Bloody Assize, 1685, iv. 466 & n. 5, 484.
Blount, Lady (Hester Blount?), and family: social, iv. 15 & n. 2.
Blount, Edward: supposed author of *Microcosmographie*, iii. 346 & n. 2.
Blount, Sir Henry, the traveller, iii. 233 & n. 2; social, iii. 233, 252; geneal., iv. 15, n. 2.
Blount, Hester, Lady Blount, wife of Sir Henry, iii. 233, n. 3; iv. 15, n. 2; social, iii. 252; iv. 15(?).
Blount, Montjoy, first earl of Newport: in ceremony, iii. 277; commissioner for London streets, iii. 319, n. 1.
Blount *or* Blunt, Col. Thomas, iii. 70 & n. 2; as magistrate, iii. 70; warren and vineyard of, iii. 161 & n. 1; ploughs invented by, iii. 170; shows waywiser, iii. 196; social, iii. 233.

Bludworth, Sir Thomas, lord mayor of London 1665–6, iii. 429, n. 3; speech of, to Charles II, iii. 429 & n. 3; at launching of *Loyal London*, iii. 440; conduct of, during Great Fire, iii. 452, n. 3, 455, n. 3; social, iii. 443.
Blunt, Col. Thomas: *see* Blount.
Blyth (Blith), Notts., iii. 127.
Boat-racing: at Venice, &c., ii. 433 & n. 3.
Bobart, Jacob, sen.: plants cultivated by, iii. 386 & n. 7.
Bobart, Jacob, jnr.: information given by, iv. 362, n. 4.
Bobbing (Bobing), Kent: Lady Smith at, iii. 417 & n. 5.
Boby, Lucerne valley, Piedmont, iv. 515, n. 1.
Boccaccio, Giovanni: tomb of, ii. 199–200 & n.
Bochton: *see* Boughton Malherbe.
Bocking, Essex: dean of: *see* Gauden, John.
Bodly, Jane, Lady Bodly, wife of Sir John: geneal., i. 10, n. 1.
Bodly, Sir John, of Streatham, i. 10 & n. 1.
Bodmin: Lord, 1679–82 (courtesy title): *see* Robartes, Robert.
Bodvile, John: will of: disputed, iii. 473 & n. 3.
Bodvile, Sarah: *see* Robartes, Mrs. Sarah, styled countess of Radnor.
Boet, Dr. —: *see* Boot, A.
Boggi, —: *see* Bolgi, A.
Bohemia: revolt of, 1618, ii. 7 & n. 1 (i. 7).
Bohun, —, of Lee: *see* Boone, Christopher.
Bohun, Abraham: geneal., iii. 416, n. 1.
Bohun, Mrs. Elizabeth, wife of Abraham Bohun: geneal., iii. 416, n. 1.
Bohun, Rev. Ralph; D.C.L. 1685; rector of Wotton 1701–16, iii. 416, n. 1; relations of, with E, i. *24*, *36*; 'Character' of Mrs. Evelyn by, ii. 535, n. 4; as tutor to John Evelyn, jnr.: accompanies him to Wotton, iii. 416; ~ accompanies him to Oxford, iii. 474, 482, 506; ~ leaves E's service, iii. 566 & n. 3; recommended to Archbishop Tenison, v. 256; as canon of Salisbury, v. 473 & n. 1; legacy to, v. 571; kinsman of: *see* Boone, Christopher.
Bohun, Rev. Ralph (*cont.*)
as rector of Wotton: presented, &c., v. 447 & n. 3; introduced, v. 456; qualifies, v. 477 & n. 3.; curate of: *see* Tomson (Thompson), Rev. —; sermons by, at Wotton, v. 456, 470–82, 509–21, 537–49, 569–71, 605 *passim & separatim*; *see also* v. 597, n. 1; catechises at evening prayer, v. 478, 510–14 *passim*, 542–8 *passim*; officiates at Wotton House, v. 550.
sermons, &c., by, elsewhere than at Wotton: Abinger, iv. 111; Deptford, iv. 25, 108, 133, 165, 167–8, 191–2, 204, 248, 264–5, 293, 295, 296–7, 312, 334, 386, 389, 402, 520, 522, 586–7; v. 57–8, 60; Lee, iv. 179; London: St. James's, Piccadilly, iv. 590; St. James's Palace, iv. 76; Trinity Chapel, v. 522, 556, 561, 566–7; officiates: at Deptford, iv. 524; at Sayes Court, iv. 517.
sermons by: general: on dress; and quarrels with E, v. 542; repeats sermons, iv. 586–7 & 590; v. 512 & 515–16, 543 & 547, 544 & 548(?).
Boile: *see* Boyle.
Boine: *see* Boyne.
Bois-le-Duc: *see* 's Hertogenbosch.
Boldero (Baldero), Edmund, D.D.: sermon by, iii. 270–1 & n.
Bolgi (Boggi), Andrea: statue by, ii. 262 & n. 4.
Bolles (Bowles), Sir John, bt.: geneal., iv. 352 & n. 3.
Bollogne: *see* Boulogne.
Bolney Court (Boyne), near Henley-on-Thames, ii. 540 & n. 5.
Bologna: notice, 1645, ii. 420–6 & nn.
general remarks, ii. 420 & nn. 5–9, 426 & nn. 1–8; arcades at, ii. 422 & n. 1, 453; use of brick at, ii. 421 & nn. 10, 11.
buildings, &c.: Archiginnasio, ii. 421 & n. 2; Biblioteca Universitaria, ii. 422, n. 7; churches: S. Domenico and convent, ii. 421 & nn. 3–8; S. Francesco, ii. 422 & n. 8; S. Giovanni in Monte, ii. 424 & n. 1; S. Gregorio, ii. 424 & n. 2; S. Maria della Pietà (Mendicanti), ii. 424 & nn. 4, 5; S. Petronio, ii. 421 & n. 1, 423, n. 6; S. Salvatore, ii.

Bologna (*cont.*)
423–4 & n.; ~ library of, ii. 422 & n. 7; Museo Civico: sculptures in, ii. 421, n. 7, 422, n. 3; ~ Liceo Musicale: theorbo in, ii. 426, n. 6; Palace of the Legate (Palazzo Comunale), ii. 421 & n. 9, 422 & nn. 2–4; Palazzo Magnani-Salem: frescoes in, ii. 424 & n. 6; Piazza Maggiore, ii. 422 & n. 5; Pinacoteca: paintings in, ii. 423, n. 7 *ad fin.*, 424, nn. 1, 2, 4, 5; Torre Asinelli, ii. 420 & nn. 10, 11; ~ height of, ii. 425 & n. 3; Torre Garisenda, ii. 420–1 & n.; University, ii. 420 & n. 5; ~ building, ii. 421 & n. 2.
environs: cattle in, ii. 426; fertility of, ii. 420 & n. 6, 426; road to, from Pratolino, ii. 419, n. 3; S. Michele in Bosco, ii. 423 & nn. 2–6; ~ convent of, ii. 425.
art: school of painting at, ii. 420, n. 5; statue found at, ii. 415 & n. 4; woman artists at, ii. 307, 424 & n. 3.
history: Charles V crowned at, ii. 422, n. 4; Sir N. Carew at, 1529–30, i. 9, n. 2.
products of: lap-dogs, ii. 425 & n. 1; lutes, ii. 426 & nn. 4–7; provisions, &c., ii. 426 & nn. 1–3.
science: astronomical observations from, iii. 563; *lapis illuminabilis* (Bologna stone), ii. 398, n. 3, 422–3 & n.; iv. 251; treatise from, iii. 599.
E sets out for, ii. 418; E sees Persian at, ii. 422; iii. 465, n. 3.
Bologna, Baldassare di (B. Croce): paintings by, ii. 239 & n. 7.
Bologna, Giovanni (John di Bolognia, &c.), sculptor, ii. 93, n. 1.
works by: Bologna: Neptune fountain, ii. 422 & n. 6; Florence: Cosimo I, ii. 194 & nn. 4, 5 (i. 120); Ferdinand I, ii. 194 & n. 6 (i. 120); Hercules killing Nessus (Centaur), ii. 194 & n. 2 (i. 120); Labours of Hercules (silver), ii. 190 & n. 3 (i. 119); Mercury (seen by E at Rome), ii. 231 & n. 4; Rape of the Sabines, ii. 193 & n. 5 (i. 120); reliefs in SS. Annunziata, ii. 195 & n. 1 (i. 120);
Bologna, Giovanni (*cont.*)
Genoa: S. Francesco di Castelletto: tombs in, ii. 176, n. 8; Paris: Henri IV, ii. 92–3 & n. (i. 62), 101 (i. 66).
works designed by: Pisa: cathedral: west doors of, ii. 180 & n. 6 (i. 114); Cosimo I, ii. 180 & n. 1 (i. 113); Ferdinand I, ii. 182 & n. 4 (i. 114).
works falsely attributed to: Leghorn: Ferdinand I and Slaves, i. 116 (*see* ii. 183, n. 7); Rotterdam: Erasmus, i. 25 (*see* ii. 33, n. 4).
chapel at S. Marco, Florence, designed by, ii. 200 & n. 4.
Bologna stone: name for *lapis illuminabilis* or heavy-spar, ii. 398, n. 3, 422–3 & n.; iv. 251.
Bolsano (Botzen), ii. 489, n. 6.
Bolsena: lake of, and town, ii. 209–10 & nn.; mentioned, ii. 407, n. 5.
Bolsover Castle, Derbyshire: fireplace at, iii. 554, n. 4.
Bolteele, — (John Bulteel?), iii. 392 & n. 5.
Bolton, Lancs.: James Stanley, seventh earl of Derby, executed at, iii. 48 & n. 7.
Bolton, Samuel, D.D., iii. 312, n. 3, 345, n. 6; sermons by, iii. 312, 345–6.
Bolton, Sir William; knighted 1663; lord mayor of London 1666–7, iii. 266, n. 2; as sheriff: social, iii. 266; as lord mayor: consults about fuel for London, iii. 487.
Bolton: first Duke of, 1689–99: *see* Paulet, Charles, sixth marquis of Winchester, &c.
Bombay (Bombain): governor and deputy-governor of: *see* Child, Sir John; Wyborne, Sir J. (iv. 438 & n. 2).
Bommel, on the Waal: English in garrison at, 1641, ii. 38 & n. 6 (i. 29); marauders near, ii. 59 (i. 40).
Bond, Sir Thomas, bt., iv. 93, n. 2; house of, at Peckham, iv. 93 & n. 2, 258; joint-purchaser of Clarendon (Albemarle) House, iv. 339, n. 4.
Boniface VIII, pope: statue of, ii. 422, n. 3.
Bonifacio, confessor of Marques de la Fuente, ii. 477.
Bonn: siege of, 1689, iv. 645 & n. 5, 649 & n. 7.

Bonython, Charles: commits suicide, v. 593 & n. 2.
Book-bindings: jewelled, ii. 88 (i. 60); iv. 216; morocco, ii. 128 (i. 82); iii. 11; velvet, iii. 129; in Essex's library, iv. 200; MSS. bound in red and chained, ii. 417.
Bookham, Surrey: road to Wotton from, v. 228, n. 4.
Books [divided into three sections: books used, or possibly used, by E when writing the Diary (apart from those supplying occasional quotations, such as Ovid); books mentioned, or alluded to, by E in the Diary (including the sources of the occasional quotations); and other books described, or the subjects of statements, in the introduction and notes, with a few miscellaneous books. Titles are abbreviated as far as possible. References to i. *1–131* are to the introduction; to ii. 569–79 to bibliographical notes.
E's own works are indexed under Evelyn: books and miscellaneous writings; the Bible under Bible; books in manuscript, under Manuscripts; newspapers and periodicals, under Newspapers, Newsletters, and other Periodicals; and proclamations, under Proclamations. Printed sermons are traceable under Sermons, printed.
Books cited only in the notes as authorities for statements are not as a rule entered under the present heading; a list of those most frequently cited is given at i. 153–71.
General notices, &c., are indexed under Printing; Publishing and Bookselling].
— sources [books and other materials, apart from newspapers, used, or possibly used, by E when writing the Diary]:
— — *Account how the Earl of Essex Killed Himself*, 1683, iv. 326, n. 4 *ad fin.*
— — Aubrey, J., *Natural history of Wiltshire*, iii. 104, n. 2, 113, n. 6; cited, iii. 114–15, nn.
— — Bacon, F., Viscount St. Albans, *Sylva Sylvarum*, 1627, ii. 467, n. 5; *see also* books mentioned in text *below*.
— — Baglione, G., *Le nove chiese di Roma*, 1639, ii. 575 (note); cited as source, &c., ii. 255, n. 1, 256, n. 5, 261, n. 3, 266, nn. 4, 5, 267, n. 1, 381, nn. 2, 7.
— — — *Le vite*, 1642, ii. 310, n. 2.
— — Blaeu, J., *Theatrum urbium Belgicæ liberæ*: *see* books mentioned in text *below*.
— — Blome, R., *Britannia*, 1673, iv. 113, nn. 5, 6, 115, n. 8, 116, nn. 1, 2; *add.*
— — Blount, Sir Henry, *Voyage into the Levant*, 1638, ii. 467, n. 5; *see also* books mentioned in text *below*.
— — Burnet, Gilbert, *History of my own time*: passages in, related to Diary, iv. 353, n. 1, 409, n. 2.
— — — *Sermon at funeral of Mr. James Houblon*, 1682, iv. 475, n. 2.
— — Camden, W., *Britannia*, ed. 1607: notice related to, iii. 98, n. 5; as possible source for, or alluded to by, E, i. 57, n. 1; iii. 100, n. 3, 119, n. 6, 120, nn. 4, 6, 129, n. 1, 131, n. 5, 133, n. 1, 135, n. 5, 138, n. 1, 140, n. 6, 180, n. 2, 221, n. 7; iv. 116, nn. 1, 2, 474, n. 1. For Gibson's edition, 1695, *see* books mentioned in text *below*.
— — Carew, Thomas, 'The Rapture': influences poem by E, *add.* (ii. 355, n. 1); phrase in, *add.* (ii. 512, n. 1).
— — Childrey, J., *Britannia Baconica*, 1661, iii. 116, n. 1.
— — Claudian, 'De sene Veronensi': influences poems by E, ii. 355, n. 1, 402, n. 1; *see also* i. *41* & n. 1.
— — Coryat, T., *Coryats crudities*, 1611: probably used by E, *add.* (ii. 429, n. 6), and references there; cited as source or for parallels, &c., ii. 433–49, nn., *passim*, 459, n. 5, 467, n. 7, 468, n. 5, 474, nn. 1, 5.
— — Donatus, A., *Roma vetus ac recens*, 1639, ii. 357, n. 4.
— — Dryden, J., *Annus mirabilis*, 1667, iii. 439, n. 4; its title, iii. 239, n. 1.

BOOKS: sources (*cont.*)
— — — *Conquest of Granada*, 1672, iii. 304, n. 6 *ad fin.*
— — Fuller, T., *Worthies of England*, 1662, iv. 304, n. 5.
— — Gölnitz, A., *Ulysses Belgico-Gallicus*, 1631: as source, ii. 569–70 (note); character of, i. *81*, 97 & n. 1; quoted or cited as source, ii. 64, n. 2, 66, n. 3, 67, n. 4, 70, nn. 2, 3, 73, nn. 6, 7, 74, n. 5.
— — Heath, James, *Chronicle*, 1676, iii. 228, n. 9 *ad fin.*
— — Hegenitius, G., *Itinerarium Frisio-Hollandicum*, 1630: as source, ii. 569 (note); quoted or cited as source, ii. 50, n. 3, 51, n. 5, 52, n. 2, 54, n. 2; *see also* ii. 32, n. 3, &c.
— — Heylyn, P., *Cosmographie*, ed. 1657: as source, ii. 569 (note); quoted or cited as source, i. 23, n. 4, 24, n. 1; ii. 32, nn. 1, 4, 34, nn. 5, 6, 35, n. 4, 44, n. 2, 73, nn. 3, 5, 7, 74, n. 2; *see also* ii. 331, n. 4; iii. 189, n. 1, 325, n. 4.
— — Howard, Thomas, earl of Arundel, instructions for E's journey from Padua to Milan (MS.): as source, i. *87*; ii. 479 & n. 5, 573 (note); cited as source, ii. 481–7, nn., *passim*, 491–9, nn., *passim*.
— — *Itinerarium Italiae totius*, 1602, ii. 489, n. 6.
— — Jacob, L., *Traicté des plus belles bibliothèques*, 1644, ii. 128, nn. 1, 3.
— — James, T., *Treatise of the Corruption of Scripture*, &c., 1611, &c., iv. 145, n. 1.
— — Kircher, A., *Latium*, 1671, ii. 396, n. 3, 397, nn. 1, 3.
— — — *Musurgia universalis*, iii. 168, n. 3.
— — Lassels, R., *Voyage of Italy*, 1670: as source, i. *87*, *89*, *117*; ii. 573 (note); character of, i. *100*; cited as source, i. 112, n. 1; ii. 198, n. 12, 371–2, nn., 378, n. 7, 379, n. 3, 387, n. 6, 388, n. 2, 397, n. 1, 415, n. 1, 420–3, nn., *passim*, 429, n. 6, 436, n. 6, 453, n. 1, 455–6, nn., 459, nn. 1, 2, 461, n. 7, 520, n. 6; &c.
— — *Letter from a Person of Quality*, 1675, iii. 609, n. 4.

BOOKS: sources (*cont.*)
— — Mayerne Turquet, Sir T. de, *Sommaire description de la France*, ed. 1604, ii. 151, n. 3 *ad fin.*; cited, ii. 152, nn. 5–7, 154, nn. 7–10, 156, n. 5.
— — Monconys, B. de, *Journal des Voyages*, 1665–6: as source, i. *80–1* & n., *87*, *88–9* & nn.; ii. 573 (note); ~ bearing of, on dates of composition of Diary, i. *72* & nn. 4, 5; character of, i. *99–100*; quoted or cited as source, ii. 186–99, nn., 227, n. 7, 284, n. 2, 286, n. 6, 294, n. 3, 299, n. 1, 301, n. 2, 406–44, nn., 456–61, nn., 480, n. 2, 491, n. 3, 493, nn. 1, 4, 502, nn. 3, 5, 503, n. 2 *passim & separatim*; further citations, iii. 322, n. 5, 324, n. 7. *See also* books mentioned in text *below*.
— — Neri, A., *L'arte vetraria* (*Art of Glass*, 1662), ii. 467, n. 5.
— — Palladio, A., *Architettura*, 1570, ii. 140, n. 1. *See also* books mentioned in text *below*.
— — Petit, P., *De l'antiquité . . . de Paris*, 1662, ii. 91, n. 5, 98, n. 1, 103, n. 1, 104, n. 6, 105, nn. 1, 5.
— — Pflaumern, J. H. von, *Mercurius Italicus*, 1628: as source, i. *80–1* & n., *87*; ii. 573 (note); E's copy of, i. *87* & n. 2; ii. 171, n. 3, 214, n. 1; character of, &c., i. *97–8* & nn.; uses: Boissard, ii. 224, n. 1; Capaccio, *add.* (ii. 342, n. 6); Schott, *Itinerario*, ii. 224, n. 1; *see also* i. *88*, n. 1; used by J. Raymond, i. *99*; quoted (specimen), i. *91–2*; quoted or cited as source, ii. 171–502, nn., *passim*; the author at Siena, ii. 203, n. 5.
— — Phipps, Sir William, letter concerning Salem witches, v. 130, n. 1.
— — Pliny, *Naturalis historia*, ii. 372, n. 5. *See also* books mentioned in text *below*.
— — Raymond, J., *An Itinerary* (*Il Mercurio Italico*), 1648: as source, i. *80–1* & n., *87–8* & nn., *118–19*; ii. 573 (note); character of, i. *99* & nn. 1, 2, *100*; uses: Pflaumern, i. *99*; Schott, *Itinerario*, i. *87–8*, *99*; Totti, i. *99*; quoted (specimen), i. *95–6*; quoted or cited as source, ii.

BOOKS: sources (*cont.*)
168–526, nn., *passim*; figures in: cited, ii. 229, n. 4, 318, n. 2, 322, n. 9, 334, n. 1, 496, n. 2.
— — Sanderson, Sir W., *King Charles*, 1658: as source: alluded to, i. *85*, n. 1; quoted or cited as source, i. 53, n. 1, 54, n. 1; ii. 26, n. 1; further citations, iii. 50, n. 3, 118, n. 4. *See also* books mentioned in text *below*.
— — Sandys, George, *Relation of a Journey*, ed. 1637: as source, ii. 42, n. 3, 578 (note); E's copy of, i. *87*; ii. 578; character of, i. *101*; ii. 578–9; uses Schott, *Itinerario*, i. *87–8*; other derivative matter in: *see* ii. 578–9; quoted or cited as source, ii. 47, n. 4, 315, n. 1 *ad fin.*, 321, n. 5, 332–54, nn., *passim*, 467, n. 5; further citation, iii. 85, n. 7; figure in: cited, ii. 353, n. 6.
— — Scamozzi, V., *L'idea dell' architettura universale*, 1615, ii. 484, n. 1.
— — Speed, J., *Theatre of the empire of Great Britaine*, 1610, iii. 98, n. 5, 122, n. 6, 177, n. 1.
— — Sprat, T., life of Cowley, iii. 490, n. 2.
— — Tempesta, A., etching of papal procession to Lateran (*Possesso*), ii. 279, n. 3.
— — Totti, P., *Ritratto di Roma antica*, 1633: as source, i. *100*; ii. 575 (note); used by J. Raymond, i. *99*; quoted (specimen), i. *92–5*; quoted or cited as source, ii. 245, n. 6, 247–50, nn., *passim*, 256, nn., 269–70, nn., 278, n. 2, 279, n. 1, 371, n. 1, 374, n. 9, 375, n. 5, 378, n. 7.
— — — *Ritratto di Roma moderna*, 1638: as source, ii. 575 (note); E's copy of, i. *87*; character of, i. *100–1* & nn.; used by J. Raymond, i. *99*; quoted (specimen), i. *95*; quoted or cited as source, ii. 214–313, nn., *passim*, 357–96, nn., *passim*.
— — *True and Perfect Account of the Taking of James late Duke of Monmouth*, 1685, iv. 452, n. 3.
— — *Tryal of William Viscount Stafford*, 1681, iv. 225, n. 3; cited, as source, &c., iv. 226–8, nn., *passim*, 230–4, nn., *passim*.
BOOKS: sources (*cont.*)
— — Varennes, C. de, *Voyage de France*, ed. 1643: as source, i. *65*; character of, &c., i. *96–7*; ii. 571–2 (note); E's copy of, i. *87*; ii. 572; quoted or cited as source, ii. 84–167, nn., *passim*, 520–33, nn., *passim*.
— — Virgil, *Georgics*: influences poem by E, ii. 402, n. 1.
— — Watson, Richard, letter to Sir R. Browne, in I. Basire, *Ancient liberty of the Britannick Church*, iii. 248, n. 1.
— — William III, *Directions to our Archbishops . . . concerning the Holy Trinity*, 1696, v. 231, n. 1.
— — Wood, Anthony, *Athenæ Oxonienses*, 1691–2, ii. 18, n. 4; alluded to, i. *85*, n. 1.
— — — *Historia Universitatis Oxoniensis*, 1674, i. 15, n. 2.
— — Wotton, Sir Henry, *Elements of Architecture*, ed. 1624, ii. 418, n. 4, 419, n. 1.
— books mentioned in text [books named, or alluded to, by E in the text of the Diary. A book both used by him as a source and named by him appears in both this and the preceding sections]:
— — general: libels against government: dispersal of, 1640, ii. 25 & n. 3 (i. 18); pamphlets, &c.: active publication of: 1679, iv. 172 & n. 3; ~ *c.* 1682, iv. 319; ~ 1688, iv. 609 & n. 5; Roman antiquities: books on, iv. 330; Roman Catholic pamphlets, &c.: on public sale, 1685, iv. 489 & n. 4; ~ licences for, iv. 503–4 & n., 512 & n. 1; controversy relating to alteration of Anglican liturgy, 1690, v. 6; Socinian publications: diffusion of, 1696, v. 230–1 & n.
— — *Account of the Proposals of the Arch-bishop of Canterbury*, &c., 1688: published, iv. 601 & n. 1.
— — Aesop, iii. 207.
— — Allen, W.: see *Killing no Murder* below.
— — Allestree, R.: see *Whole Duty of Man* below.
— — Allington, J., *The grand conspiracy*, &c., 1653, iii. 134 & n. 1.
— — almanacks: by Sir George Wharton, iii. 443 & n. 3.

Books: in text (*cont.*)
— — Alsted, J. H., *Encyclopædia*, 1630, and *Triumphus Bibliorum sacrorum*, 1625: prophecy in, v. 178 & n. 2; alluded to, iii. 36, 379.
— — Ammianus Marcellinus: cited, ii. 269 & n. 8.
— — Antoninus, *Itinerarium*: cited, iii. 221 & n. 7.
— — Arnauld, A., and P. Nicole, *La nouvelle hérésie des Jésuites*, 1662: translation of, by E, iii. 393 & n. 6.
— — Ashmole, E., *Order of the Garter*, 1672, iv. 138 & n. 4; illustrated by Hollar, i. 22 & n. 3.
— — Athanasius, &c., epistles: error for St. Ignatius, iii. 246–7 & n.
— — Athenaeus, *Deipnosophistae*: alluded to, iv. 300 & n. 7.
— — atlases and maps: publications of J. Blaeu and H. Hondius, ii. 49 & nn. 3, 4 (i. 34–5).
— — Atterbury, F., *Rights of Convocation*, 1701: alluded to, v. 460 & n. 1.
— — Augustine, St., *De baptismo contra Donatistas*: alluded to, in sermon, iv. 346 & n. 2.
— — Bacon, Francis, Viscount St. Albans, *Essays* (*Sermones fideles*): cited, ii. 175 & n. 2 (i. 110).
— — — *New Atlantis*: cited, iii. 374 & n. 2.
— — — *Sylva Sylvarum*: experiments based on, to be made by Royal Society, iv. 205 & n. 5. *See also* sources *above*.
— — Barclay, John, *Icon Animarum*, 1614: description of view in, iii. 76 & n. 3.
— — Baronius, C., *Annales*, 1588–1607: cited, ii. 370 & n. 4; alluded to, ii. 233 & n. 8.
— — Bentley, Richard, *Folly of Atheism*, &c., 1693: printing of part of, v. 94 & n. 1.
— — Blaeu, J., *Theatrum urbium Belgicæ liberæ*, 1649: cited, ii. 37 & n. 4 (i. 28); as possible source for Diary, ii. 35, n. 7 *ad fin.*; *see also* ii. 569 (note).
— — — *see also* atlases *above*.
— — Blount, Sir Henry, *Voyage into the Levant*, 1636: alluded to, iii. 233 & n. 3. *See also* sources *above*.

Books: in text (*cont.*)
— — Bonnefons, N. de, *Le jardinier françois*, 1651: translation of, by E, iii. 225 & n. 3.
— — Bosio, A., *Roma sotterranea*, 1632: cited, ii. 388 & n. 1.
— — Bosse, A., *Maniere universelle, pour pratiquer la perspective*, 1648: questions concerning, ii. 568 & n. 3.
— — Bossuet, J. B., *Exposition de la doctrine de l'Eglise catholique*, 1671: answered by Wake, iv. 532 & n. 3.
— — Boyle, Robert, *Memoirs for the natural history of Humane Blood*, 1684: Boyle gives copy to E, iv. 370 & n. 3, 371.
— — Braccius, I., *Remoræ effigies*, 1634, ii. 314 & n. 4.
— — Browne, Sir Thomas, *Pseudodoxia epidemica* and *Religio Medici*, iii. 592 & n. 2.
— — Burnet, Gilbert, *History of the Reformation*, 1679, &c., iv. 47–8 & n., 205 & n. 3; materials for, iv. 216 & n. 3; ~ lent by E, iv. 241 & n. 3.
— — — *Pastoral letter*, 1689: burnt by house of commons, v. 131 & n. 2.
— — Busbecq, O.-G. de, *Legationis Turcicæ epistolæ iv*: cited, iv. 398–9 & n.
— — Camden, W., *Britannia*, ed. Gibson, 1695: publication of, and E's contribution to, v. 206 & n. 2.
— — Cappel, L., *Commentarii in Vetus Testamentum*, 1689: copy given to Bishop Lloyd, iv. 641 & n. 4.
— — Catullus: his Lesbia, iv. 336 & n. 2.
— — Cave, W., *Apostolici*, 1677, and *Ecclesiastici*, 1682, iv. 299 & n. 5.
— — — *Primitive Christianity*, 1673, iv. 192 & n. 4, 299.
— — Cavendish, Margaret, duchess of Newcastle, poetical and philosophical works, iii. 482–3 & n.
— — Chardin, Sir John, travels in Persia, pt. i (English and French versions), 1686: in preparation, iv. 358; plates for, &c., iv. 369 & n. 1.
— — Ciccarelli, life of Sixtus V: cited, ii. 257 & n. 1.

Books: in text (*cont.*)
— — Cicero, *De Officiis*: early edition of, v. 322 & n. 2; cited in sermon, v. 249.
— — — *Pro Rege Deiotaro*: cited in sermon, v. 165.
— — — praise of Tusculum by, ii. 393 & n. 1.
— — Claude, Jean, *Les Plaintes des Protestans*, 1686, and English translation: burnt by public hangman, iv. 510–11 & n., 515.
— — Claudian, 'De hystrice': cited, iii. 222 & n. 5.
— — *Collection of Cases to recover Dissenters to the Church of England*, 1685: publication of, iv. 418 & n. 2.
— — *Collection of Private Devotions* (by J. Cosin), 1627: origin of, iii. 45–6 & nn., 635–6.
— — Collins, Greenville, *Great Britain's Coasting Pilot*, 1693: charts for, iv. 301 & n. 3.
— — Colonna, Maria Mancini, princess of Paliano, *Apologie*, v. 330 & n. 3.
— — Comber, T., *Companion to the altar*: alluded to, v. 405 & n. 1.
— — Comenius, J. A., *Janua linguarum reserata*: little Richard Evelyn's progress in, iii. 207 & n. 3.
— — Cosin, J.: see *Collection of Private Devotions* above.
— — Cowley, A., poems by: set to music, iv. 220 & n. 5; *see also* Cowley, A.
— — Creech, T., translation of Lucretius, &c., v. 417 & n. 2.
— — Creighton *or* Crichton, R., edition of S. Sgouropoulos, *Vera historia*, 1660, ii. 563 & n. 5.
— — Cresollius, L., *Anthologia sacra*, 1632: given by E to Balliol College, ii. 19 & n. 3 (i. 15).
— — Cressy, S. (H. P.), *Roman-Catholick doctrines no novelties*, 1663: in controversy, iii. 360 & n. 5.
— — Croft, Herbert, *The Naked Truth*, 1675: attacked in sermon, iv. 83 & n. 5.
— — Culmann, L., *Sententiae pueriles*: little Richard Evelyn's progress in, iii. 207 & n. 1.
— — Dampier, W., *New voyage*, 1697, v. 295 & n. 2.

Books: in text (*cont.*)
— — Davenant, Charles, *Essays*, 1701: attacked by Convocation, v. 452 & n. 3.
— — Defoe, D., *The Storm*, 1704, v. 550 & n. 2.
— — Descartes, R., *Principia Philosophiæ*, 1644: dedication of, i. 25–6 & n.
— — Dickinson, E., *Epistola ad Theodorum Mundanum*, 1686, v. 599 & n. 1.
— — Digby, Sir Kenelm, *Discourse concerning the Vegetation of Plants*, 1661: given to members of Philosophical Society, iii. 294 & n. 2.
— — — *Two treatises*, 1644: alluded to, iii. 550 & n. 5.
— — Dionysius the Areopagite, on the Celestial Hierarchy (spurious work): in sermon, iii. 246, 247, n. 1.
— — Dryden, J., translation of Virgil: in preparation, v. 164.
— — Dudley, Sir Robert, titular duke of Northumberland, *Dell' arcano del mare*, 1646–7, i. 115–16 & n.
— — Dugdale, Sir W., *Monasticon Anglicanum*, 1655–73, iv. 441 & n. 2.
— — — various works: illustrated by Hollar, i. 22 & n. 2.
— — Earles, J., *Microcosmographie*: authorship of, iii. 346 & n. 2.
— — *Eikon Basilike*: alluded to, i. 20 & n. 2; Latin translation of, by Earles, iii. 346 & n. 3.
— — *Enquiry into the miscarriage of the Scots colony at Darien*, 1700: burnt by order of house of commons, v. 376 & n. 4.
— — Euclid, iii. 207.
— — Eustachius of Matera: cited, ii. 346 & n. 4.
— — Evelyn, John, jnr., *Of Gardens* (translation from R. Rapin), 1673: published, &c., iv. 1 & n. 4.
— — *Extract of the States General their Resolution, 28 Oct. 1688*: circulated, iv. 604 & n. 2.
— — Fathers, Early Christian: editions of, published at Basel and Rome, iv. 145 & n. 1.
— — Filmer, Sir Robert, *Patriarcha*: Algernon Sidney's reply to, iv. 353 & nn. 2, 3; sermon influenced by, iv. 336 & n. 4.

Books: in text (*cont.*)
— — Flamel, Nicolas, alchemical works: hieroglyphics relating to, ii. 131–2 & n. (i. 85).
— — Fréart, R., sieur de Chambray, *Idée de la perfection de la peinture*: translation of, by E, iii. 514 & n. 2.
— — — *Parallele de l'Architecture*: translation of, by E, iii. 380 & n. 4, 387; i. *17–18*.
— — Gassendi, P., life of Peiresc: English translation of, by W. Rand, dedicated to E, iii. 189, n. 6; *see also* ii. 14, n. 3.
— — Goodman, J., *Old Religion*, 1684, and *Penitent Pardoned*, 1683, iv. 392 & n. 3.
— — Granadus, L., *Commentarii*, 1624: given by E to Balliol College, ii. 19 & n. 3 (i. 15).
— — Graunt, John: *see* Petty, Sir William *below*.
— — Grotius, M., *De veritate Religionis Christianæ*: Arabic translation of, 1660, v. 82 & n. 2.
— — Hammond, Henry, *Paraphrase of the New Testament*: read by Mary Evelyn, iv. 421 & n. 1.
— — Harvey, W., *Exercitationes de generatione animalium*: advises bleeding, iv. 425 & n. 1.
— — Henry VIII, *Assertio septem sacramentorum*, 1521: copy of, in Vatican Library, ii. 302 & n. 2.
— — Herbert, Edward, Lord Herbert of Cherbury, *De Veritate*: copy of, given to E, iii. 58 & n. 3.
— — — *King Henry VIII*: cited, ii. 84 & n. 3 (i. 57).
— — Hevelius, J., *Selenographia*, 1647, i. 44: *see* ii. 64, n. 2, *ad fin.*
— — Heylyn, P., *Microcosmus*, 1621, &c., iii. 275 & n. 2.
— — *His Majesties Declaration* (Rye-House Plot): read in church, iv. 335 & n. 2, 336.
— — Hobbes, T., *Leviathan*: answer to, by A. Rosse, iii. 81 & n. 2.
— — *Hollandia illustrata*: *see* Blaeu, J., *above*.
— — Homer, iv. 423; early edition of, v. 322 & n. 2.
— — Hooke, R., *Lampas*, 1677: experiment based on, iv. 162 & n. 4.

Books: in text (*cont.*)
— — — *Micrographia*, 1665: plates for, iii. 356–7 & n.
— — Horace, iv. 423; quoted or cited, ii. 348 & n. 5; iv. 318 & n. 9.
— — Horneck, A., *Great Law of Consideration*, iv. 307 & n. 1.
— — — devotional works, v. 329 & n. 1.
— — Huygens, Constantijn, sen., Latin poems, iii. 377 & n. 1.
— — Hyde, Edward, earl of Clarendon, *History of the Rebellion*, 1702–4: given to E, v. 583 & n. 4.
— — Iamblichus, *De vita Pythagorica*: projected edition of, by T. Gale, v. 221 & n. 1.
— — Ignatius, St., Epistle to the Trallians: interpolation in: in sermon, iii. 246–7 & n.
— — 'Index expurgatorius', iv. 145 & n. 1.
— — James I, *Opera*, 1619: copy given to Cambridge University Library, iii. 140 & n. 4.
— — James II: coronation of: published accounts of, iv. 437 & n. 2.
— — Jerome, St., Biblical commentaries: passage in, ii. 247 & n. 3; *see also* Bible.
— — *The Jesuits Morals*, translated by E. Tonge from N. Perrault, 1670, iv. 154 & n. 1.
— — John Chrysostom, St., *Homilies*: in sermon, v. 168 & n. 2.
— — Johnson, Rev. Samuel, *Julian the Apostate*, 1682: author tried for, iv. 367 & n. 2.
— — Juvenal: quoted, ii. 510 & n. 4; translation by Sir R. Stapleton, iii. 98 & n. 2.
— — *Killing no Murder*: authorship of, iii. 526 & n. 5.
— — Kircher, A., *Obeliscus Pamphilius*, 1650, and *Oedipus Aegyptiacus*, 1652–4: in preparation, ii. 270 & n. 2; E sends drawing for, ii. 469 & n. 4; E sees copy of one or both, iii. 171–2 & n.
— — la Mothe le Vayer, F. de, *De la Liberté et de la Servitude*: translation of, by E, ii. 547 & n. 3.
— — Ligon, R., *History of Barbados*, 1657: cited, iii. 513–14 & n.

Books: in text (*cont.*)
— — Lilly, W., *Annus tenebrosus*, 1652: prophecies in, v. 354 & n. 2.
— — Lloyd, W., *Historical account of Church-Government*, 1684, v. 12 & n. 2.
— — Lucretius: edited and translated by T. Creech, v. 417 & n. 2; *see also* iii. 173, n. 4 *ad fin.*; quoted in sermon, iv. 129 & n. 2; E's *Essay* on: published, iii. 173 & n. 2.
— — Luther, Martin, commentary on Galatians and *De servo arbitrio*: in sermon, iii. 31 & n. 2.
— — Mackenzie, Sir George, *Antiquity of the Royal Line of Scotland*, 1685: controversy relating to, v. 12 & n. 2.
— — — *Moral Essay*, 1665: E's reply to: published, iii. 475 & n. 8; ~ alluded to, v. 12.
— — Maillard, Mary: account of miraculous cure of, v. 164 & n. 1.
— — Maimbourg, L., *Histoire du Calvinisme*, 1682: account in, of conversion of Anne, duchess of York, iv. 282–3 & nn.
— — Maiolus, S., *Dies caniculares*, 1597: cited, ii. 340 & n. 3.
— — Malpighi, M., 'Anatomes plantarum idea': sent to Royal Society, iii. 599 & n. 4.
— — — *Dissertatio de Bombyce*, 1669: sent to Royal Society, iii. 524 & n. 3.
— — Martial: quoted, &c., ii. 250 & n. 1, 349 & n. 1; iv. 619 & n. 1.
— — Mazarin, Hortense Mancini, Duchesse, *Memoires*, 1675, v. 330 & n. 2; alluded to, iv. 97 & n. 5.
— — Millet, S.-G., *Le Tresor sacre de S. Denis*, 1636, &c.: alluded to, i. 60; *add.*; *see also* ii. 86, n. 1.
— — Milton, John, *Pro populo Anglicano defensio*, 1651: alluded to, iii. 364–5 & n.; iv. 514.
— — *Missale ad usum ecclesiæ Sarum*: copy of, in Bodleian Library, iii. 107 & n. 2.
— — Monconys, B. de, *Journal des voyages*: cited, iii. 557–8 & n. *See also* sources *above*.
— — Moyle, W.: *see* Trenchard, J., *below*.

Books: in text (*cont.*)
— — Naudé, G., *Advis pour dresser une bibliotheque*: translation of, by E, iii. 303–4 & n.
— — Needham, M., *Newes from Brussels*, 1660: E replies to, iii. 243 & n. 3.
— — Nicole, P., *L'Hérésie imaginaire*: translation of, by E, iii. 393 & n. 6.
— — — *Les Pernicienses Consequences de la nouvelle Heresie des Jesuites*: translation of, by E, iii. 431 & n. 7.
— — — *see also* Arnauld, A. *above*.
— — Nostradamus, *Prophéties*: alarm based on, v. 273 & n. 2.
— — Novarinus, A., *Electa sacra*, 1629: given by E to Balliol College, ii. 19 & n. 3 (i. 15).
— — Oates, T., *Eikon basilike*, 1696: dedicated to William III, v. 238 & n. 3.
— — Ovid, iv. 423; *Metamorphoses*: sculptures representing, ii. 396 & n. 3; quoted, ii. 5 & n. 4 (i. 6), 32 & n. 2 (i. 24).
— — Palladio, A., *Architettura*: design in, iii. 625 & n. 3. *See also* sources *above*.
— — Panciroli, G., *Rerum memorabilium* . . . : cited, ii. 320 & n. 1.
— — Papin, D., *New Digester*, 1681: cited, iv. 278, 279, n. 1.
— — Parker, Samuel, *Reasons for abrogating the Test*, 1688, iv. 574 & n. 2.
— — Parr, R., *Life of Usher*, 1686: publication of, delayed, iv. 507–8 & n. *See also* books mentioned in notes *below*.
— — Penn, W., *The Sandy Foundation shaken*, 1668: publication of, iii. 521 & n. 1.
— — Pepys, S., *Memoires relating to the Royal Navy*, 1690: read to E, v. 24 & n. 2; copy of, for Godolphin, v. 39; mentioned, v. 538.
— — — projected history of the navy, v. 538 & n. 4.
— — Perrault, N.: see *The Jesuits Morals* above.
— — Petty, Sir William, *or* John Graunt, *Observations upon the Bills of Mortality*: authorship of, iv. 60 & n. 3; *add.*
— — Petty, Sir William, further works, iv. 58 & n. 3, 60–1 & nn.

Books: in text (*cont.*)
— — Platina, B., *Historia pontificum Romanorum*: cited, ii. 257 & n. 1.
— — Plato, *Republic*: alluded to, iv. 328 & n. 5.
— — Plautus, iii. 207; iv. 423.
— — Pliny, *Naturalis historia*: cited, ii. 40 & n. 1 (i. 30), 178 & n. 9 (i. 113); *add.*; ii. 209 & n. 8, 216 & n. 3, 232 & n. 3, 235 & n. 6, 277 & n. 4, 304 & n. 1; iv. 391 & n. 1; v. 179 & n. 1. *See also* sources *above*.
— — Pliny the younger, *Epistolae*: cited, ii. 388 & n. 3.
— — Plot, R., *Natural history of Oxford-shire*, 1677, iv. 68 & n. 4, 263.
— — — *Natural history of Staffordshire*, 1686: in preparation, iv. 68 & n. 4.
— — Plutarch, *Vitae*: cited, ii. 5 & n. 2 (i. 6).
— — *The Poor-Whores Petition*, 1668: circulated, iii. 507 & n. 6.
— — Porta, G. B. della, *Magiae naturalis* . . .: cited, ii. 398 & n. 4; iv. 253.
— — Prideaux, H., *Marmora Oxoniensia*, 1676: copies presented to E, &c., iv. 89 & n. 2.
— — *The proceedings and tryal* [of the Seven Bishops], 1689: publication of, iv. 615 & n. 2.
— — *Puerilis*: *see* Culmann, L., *above*.
— — Rapin, R., *Hortorum libri IV*: translation of, by John Evelyn, jnr., iv. 1 & n. 4.
— — Ray, J.: *see* Willoughby, F., *below*.
— — *The report . . . Irish forfeitures*, 1700: published, v. 404 & n. 2.
— — Rogers, George, *Oratio anniversaria*, 1682: copy given to E, iv. 291 & n. 1.
— — Rosse, Alexander, *Leviathan drawn out with a hook*, 1653: copy given to E, iii. 81 & n. 2.
— — — *Virgilius evangelisans*, iii. 81 & n. 1.
— — Rubens, Sir P. P., *Palazzi di Genova*, ii. 173 & n. 1 (i. 109), 176.
— — Russell, William, Lord Russell, *Speech to the Sheriffs*, 1683: influence of, iv. 332 & n. 5.
— — Salmasius, C., *Defensio regia pro Carolo I*: Milton's reply to, iii. 364, n. 6 *ad fin.*, 365.
— — Sanderson, Sir W., *Mary Queen of Scotland* and *King Charles*, iv. 94 & n. 4. *See also* sources *above*.
— — Santa Clara, Franciscus a (C. Davenport), *Religio Philosophi Peripati discutienda*: miracle described in, &c., iv. 469 & n. 1.
— — Sarayna, Torellus, *Verona*: copy of, iv. 330 & n. 4.
— — Scaliger, J. C., poems on Verona, ii. 487 & n. 5.
— — Scaliger, J. J., poem on Verona, *ib.*; quoted, ii. 488 & n. 2.
— — Selden, J., *Titles of honor*: Ussher's opinion of, iii. 156–7 & n.
— — Sexby, E.: see *Killing no Murder* above.
— — Sgouropoulos, S., *Vera historia*, edited by R. Creighton, ii. 563 & n. 5.
— — Sidney, Algernon, reply to Filmer: use made of, at Sidney's trial, iv. 353 & n. 2.
— — Sloane, Sir Hans, writings on Jamaica: E encourages, v. 48 & n. 1.
— — Spanheim, E., *Dissertatio de praestantia et usu numismatum antiquorum*, iv. 78 & n. 1.
— — Spinoza, B., *Tractatus theologico-politicus*: alluded to, iv. 381 & n. 2.
— — Sprat, T., *The Lord Bishop of Rochester's Letter*, 1688: publication of, iv. 596 & n. 2.
— — Stillingfleet, E., *Vindication of their Majesties authority*, 1691: alluded to, v. 59 & n. 3; printed sermon, iv. 368.
— — Stokes, W., *The Vaulting Master*, 1641, ii. 21 & n. 1 (i. 16).
— — Suarez, F., unidentified work: cited in sermon, iv. 562 & n. 3.
— — Suidas: early edition of, v. 322 & n. 2.
— — Sylvius, F. de la Boe: gives book by himself to Royal Society, iii. 583 & n. 8.
— — Taylor, Jeremy, *Answer to a letter written by the bishop of Rochester*, 1656: discussed, iii. 171 & n. 4.

BOOKS: in text (*cont.*)
— — — *Ductor Dubitantium*, 1660: MS. of, iii. 190 & n. 6.
— — — *Unum necessarium*, 1655: discussed, iii. 158 & n. 5.
— — Te Deum: recited by SS. Ambrose and Augustine, ii. 500 & n. 3.
— — Terence, iv. 423.
— — Tertullian: quoted in sermon, v. 231 & n. 2.
— — Titus, S.: see *Killing no Murder* above.
— — Tonge, E.: see *The Jesuits Morals* above.
— — Tradescant, J., jnr., &c., *Musæum Tradescantianum*, 1656: cited, iii. 198–9 & nn.
— — Trenchard, J., and W. Moyle, *An argument, shewing, that a standing army*, &c., 1697, and succeeding controversy, v. 275 & n. 1; *add.*
— — trials, published *c.* 1679: reliability of, iv. 175 & n. 3.
— — *True and Compleat List of the Present Parliament*, 1685, iv. 444 & n. 4.
— — *Tryal* [of the Seven Bishops], 1689: publication of, iv. 615 & n. 2.
— — Turner, Francis, *Animadversions upon The Naked Truth*, iv. 83 & n. 5.
— — Ussher, J., *De Græca septuaginta interpretum versione syntagma*, 1655: in preparation, iii. 156 & n. 4.
— — — edition of epistles of St. Ignatius: cited in sermon, iii. 246–7 & n.
— — Vane, Sir Henry, jnr., *A healing question*, 1656: author imprisoned for, iii. 183 & n. 2.
— — Varo, F., *Arte de la lengua mandarina*: MS. copy of (?), iii. 374 & n. 7.
— — Vasari, G., *Vite*: cited, ii. 415 & n. 7.
— — Vincent of Lérins, *Commonitoria*: cited in sermon, iii. 30 & n. 5.
— — Virgil, iv. 423; works: Dryden engaged in translating, v. 164; *Aeneid*: quoted, ii. 26 & n. 2 (i. 19); ~ cited, ii. 318 & n. 6, 346; ~ imitated, iii. 454 & n. 3; fourth *Eclogue*: in sermon, iv. 357–8 & n.; phrase falsely attributed to, ii. 125 & n. 4; *Virgilius evangelisans* (A. Rosse), iii. 81 & n. 1.
— — Vorstius, A., catalogue of botanic garden, Leyden, ii. 53 & n. 1.
— — Vossius, I., edition of epistles of St. Ignatius: cited in sermon, iii. 246–7 & n.
— — Wake, W., *Exposition of the Doctrine of the Church of England*, 1686, iv. 532 & n. 3.
— — — in Convocation controversy, 1701, v. 460 & n. 1.
— — Wallis, J., *Treatise of Algebra*, 1685: presented to Royal Society, iv. 439 & n. 2.
— — Walsh, Peter, works: alluded to, iv. 496 & n. 4.
— — Walton, Brian: *see* Bible.
— — Wecker, J. J., *De secretis*: cited, iv. 253 & n. 4.
— — Wheler, Sir George, *Journey into Greece*, 1682, iv. 358 & n. 1, 528.
— — White, Father Thomas, *De mundo*, iii. 33 & n. 5.
— — *Whole Duty of Man*, 1658: authorship of, v. 112 & n. 5.
— — Wilkins, John, paper on the Ark: cited in sermon, iv. 315 & n. 1.
— — William III, declarations, 1688, as Prince of Orange: *see* William III.
— — Willis, T., 'De sanguinis accensione': cited, iv. 252 & n. 1.
— — Willoughby, F., *De historia piscium*, ed. J. Ray, 1686: published by Royal Society, iv. 503 & n. 5.
— — Zanchius, H., *Omnia opera theologica*, 1619: given by E to Balliol College, ii. 19 & n. 3 (i. 15).
— books mentioned in notes and introduction [books mentioned in the introduction, other than E's sources; books appearing in the notes, but not in the text, which are the subjects of statements (other than criticism of secondary works cited as authorities); and a few other books, cited as authorities, &c., to which references may be useful (in some cases supplementing the finding list, i. 153–71)]:

Books: in notes, &c. (*cont.*)
— — *Account of the times . . . Morning and Evening Prayers . . . within the Bills of Mortality*, 1703, iv. 305, n. 1.
— — Aitzema, L. van, *Saken van Staet en Oorlogh*, vol. i: influence of, on E's projected history of the Second Dutch War, iii. 523, n. 1.
— — Albertini, F., *Opusculum de mirabilibus Romae*, 1510, &c., i. *100*, n. 4.
— — ambassadors' dispute, 1661: accounts of, other than E's, iii. 297, n. 4 *ad fin.*; *add.*
— — Ambrose, Isaac, *Media*, 1650: on diary-keeping, i. *82*.
— — Aubrey, J., *Brief lives*: information from E in, ii. 1, n. 1; iii. 158, n. 1; *see also* i. 21, n. 2.
— — — *Natural history of Surrey*: information from E in, ii. 4, n. 1; iii. 496, n. 2 *ad fin.*
— — — *Natural history of Wiltshire*: E adds notes to, iii. 104, n. 2; *see also* sources *above*.
— — Baker, Sir Richard, *Chronicle*, ed. E. Phillips, 1665, &c.: contains E's account of ambassadors' encounter, &c., iii. 297, n. 4 *ad fin.*, 364, n. 6; i. *24* & n. 2.
— — Barlow, T., *Letter concerning invocation of saints*, 1679: written to E, iii. 534, n. 1.
— — Beadle, J., *Journal or Diary of a Thankful Christian*, 1656: on diary-keeping, i. *82*, *83* & n. 3.
— — Benthem, H. L., *Engelandischer Kirch- und Schulen-Staat*, 1694: cited, iv. 538, n. 1, 539, n. 2; v. 399, n. 1.
— — *Biographia Britannica*: account of E in, i. *39* & n. 3, *57*, *116*.
— — Blount, Charles, *King William and Queen Mary conquerors*, 1693: burnt by house of commons, v. 131, n. 2.
— — Bonfons, N., *Les antiquitez de Paris, Livre second*, 1588: figures in, *add.* (ii. 86, n. 1).
— — Boyle, R., *Origine of formes and qualities*, 1666: theory of atomism in, iii. 173, n. 4 *ad fin.*

Books: in notes, &c. (*cont.*)
— — Browne, Sir Thomas, *Christian Morals*: on diary-keeping, i. *82*.
— — *Bulstrode papers*: newsletters, i. *105*, n. 2, *127*, n. 1.
— — Bunyan, John, *Grace Abounding*, i. *82*, n. 3.
— — Burnet, Gilbert, *History of my own time*: genesis of, iv. 178, n. 5.
— — Camden, W., *Britannia*: on foundation of St. Paul's, iii. 459, n. 6. *See also* sources *above*.
— — Cary, Lucius, second Viscount Falkland, *Discourse of infallibility*: edition of, by T. Triplet, iii. 168, n. 5.
— — Chalmers, A., *Biographical Dictionary*: account of E in, i. *116*.
— — Charles II, *Copies of Two Papers*, 1686, iv. 477, n. 1.
— — Charleton, W., works on Epicurus, iii. 173, n. 4.
— — Clutterbuck, R., *History of the county of Hertford*, vol. i, 1815: use of Diary in, i. *56*, n. 1.
— — Cook, Moses, *Manner of raising Forrest-Trees*, 1676, &c., iv. 200, n. 4.
— — Cowley, Abraham, 'The Garden': account of E in, i. *37*; *see also* Cowley, A.
— — Crashaw, R., 'Music's Duel': local setting of, ii. 383, n. 5.
— — Culpeper, N.: joint-translator of J. Riolan's *Sure guide to Physick*, iii. 189, n. 5.
— — Dallington, Sir R., *Method for Travell*, i. *80*, n. 1.
— — *Declaration of the nobility at Nottingham, Nov. 22, 1688*, iv. 608, n. 3.
— — Derham, Rev. W., weather-diaries, 1697–9 (in *Philosophical Transactions*), v. 263, n. 2; cited occasionally, v. 263–367, nn.
— — 'De tribus impostoribus': title, iii. 522, n. 2.
— — Donatus, A., *Roma vetus ac recens*, 1638, &c., i. *100*; ii. 575 (note). *See also* sources *above*.
— — Dryden, J., *Conquest of Granada*: preface to, quoted, iii. 309, n. 1.

BOOKS: in notes, &c. (*cont.*)
— — — *Poem upon the death of his late Highness*: quoted, iii. 215, n. 3.
— — Felini, P. M., *Trattato nuovo*, &c., 1610, &c.: used by P. Totti, i. *100*, n. 3.
— — Flatman, T., elegy on Ossory, iv. 211, n. 1.
— — Ford, John, *Broken Heart*: chair in, ii. 254, n. 3.
— — Franco, J., *Thesaurus Hieroglyphicorum*, 1600: given by E to Bodleian Library, iii. 385, n. 2.
— — frost-fair, 1684: descriptive poems, plans, &c., iv. 360, n. 4, 362, nn. 1, 2, 365.
— — Glanvill, Joseph, *Plus Ultra*, 1668: remarks on E in: quoted, i. *36*.
— — Glisson, F., *Anatomia hepatis*, 1654, ii. 551, n. 2.
— — Hartlib, S., *Reformed commonwealth of bees*, 1655: cited, iii. 110, n. 1.
— — — *Samuel Hartlib, His Legacie*, 1651, &c.: quoted, &c., iii. 85, n. 10, 110, n. 4.
— — *Historical Manuscripts Commission, Le Fleming Manuscripts*: newsletters, i. *105*, n. 2, *127*, n. 1.
— — Hobbes, T., *Leviathan*: date of publication of, iii. 41, n. 1.
— — Howell, James, *Instructions for Forreine Travell*, i. *80*, n. 1.
— — Jarrige, P., *Further discovery of the Mystery of Jesuitisme*, 1658 (translations from Jarrige, &c.): title, iii. 393, n. 6 *ad fin.*
— — Jones, Thomas, *Elymas the Sorcerer*, 1682: Dr. G. Morley attacked in, iv. 283, n. 1.
— — la Quintinye, J. de: translation from, by E (*The Compleat Gard'ner*), i. *35*.
— — *Lent Preachers appointed by the Lord-Bishop of London for 1684/5*, iv. 436, n. 1.
— — *Lent-preachers at court*, 1661, iii. 272, n. 1.
— — Letsome, S., *Preacher's Assistant*, 1753: bibliography of printed sermons, i. *130*, n. 6.
— — *Lex Talionis*, 1676: attributed to P. Gunning, iv. 83, n. 5.
— — Lilly, W., *Monarchy or no monarchy in England*, 1651: on Grebner, iii. 137, n. 2.

BOOKS: in notes, &c. (*cont.*)
— — Lovelace, Richard, poem by, iii. 216, n. 5.
— — Luttrell, Narcissus, *Brief Relation*: use of newsletters in, &c., i. *128* & nn. 2, 4.
— — Malingre, C., *Histoire de l'Italie*, 1627, i. *98*, n. 4.
— — Mancini, G., *Viaggio per Roma*, i. *100*, n. 4.
— — Manning, O., and W. Bray, *History of Surrey*: use of Diary in, i. *52*.
— — Marchantius, J., *Flandria*, 1596, *add.* (ii. 73, n. 7).
— — Mary II, queen of England, *Memoirs, 1689–93*, i. *82*, n. 3.
— — Marvell, A., 'An historicall poem' (spurious): quoted, iv. 21, n. 1.
— — — *Mr. Smirke*: in controversy, iv. 83, n. 5.
— — Minutoli, V., *L'embrasement du Pont du Rhône à Genève*, *add.* (ii. 529, n. 1).
— — *Mirabilis annus*, 1661, 1662: title, iii. 239, n. 1.
— — More, Henry: on sectarian preachers, iii. 551, n. 2.
— — Morin, J. B., *Vincentii Panurgi epistola*: title, iii. 522, n. 2.
— —Moryson, Fynes, *Itinerary*, 1617, i. *80*, n. 1.
— — Neale, T., *A Treatise*, 1643, i. *80*, n. 1.
— — Nicolson, W., *English historical library*, pt. iii, 1699: E complimented in, v. 508, n. 2.
— — Oxford, Physick Garden, *Catalogus*, 1648, and *Catalogus*, 1658: cited, iii. 109, n. 7, 386, nn. 5, 6.
— — Panciroli, O., *Tesori nascosti di Roma*: used by P. Totti, i. *100* & n. 3.
— — Parr, R., *Life of Usher*: forged letters in, v. 13, n. 1. *See also* books mentioned in text *above*.
— — Pascal, B., *Les Provinciales*, English translation, 1657: title, iii. 393, n. 6 *ad fin.*
— — Pepys, S., *Diary*: publication of, i. *54*.
— — Perrier, F., *Icones et segmenta*, &c.: given by E to Bodleian Library, iii. 385, n. 2.
— — Perry, W., *Bibliotheca Norfolciana*, 1681, iii. 472, n. 3.

Books: in notes, &c. (*cont.*)
— — Phillips, E., *New World of Words*, 1671, &c.: E supplies information for, i. *24* & n. 1; fourth edition, 1678: dedication of, iv. 120, n. 7.
— — Pierce, T., writings in controversy with S. (H. P.) Cressy, iii. 360, n. 5.
— — Plat, Sir H., *A new Fire of Cole-balles*: copied in *Sylva*, iii. 487, n. 6.
— — Pope, Walter, 'The Old Man's Wish': translated into Latin by Sir W. Petty, iv. 58, n. 3.
— — Racan, H. de Bueil, marquis de, *Les Bergeries*: local setting of, ii. 564, n. 3.
— — Riolan, J., *Sure guide to physick*: English translation of, iii. 189, n. 5.
— — Rome, *Regionary Catalogue*, ii. 249, n. 3.
— — Schott, François, *Itinerarii Italiae libri tres*, 1600, &c., i. *97* & n. 2; ii. 573–4 (note); used by: C. Malingre, i. *98*, n. 4; J. H. von Pflaumern, i. *88*, n. 1; J. Raymond, i. *87–8*, *99*; ii. 573, 574; G. Sandys, i. *87–8*; ii. 574, 579; derivation of passages in, ii. 332, n. 2, 336, n. 6, 394, n. 4.
— — Scott, Sir Walter, *Kenilworth*: notice of E in, i. *58*.
— — Selden, J., *Marmora Arundelliana*, iii. 496, n. 1.
— — Sidney, Sir Philip, *Arcadia*: paintings of scenes from, iii. 114, n. 1; associated with Wilton, iii. 72, n. 5, 115, n. 5; *see also* iii. 103, n. 6.
— — Sincerus, Jodocus (J. Zinzerling), *Itinerarium Galliae*, 1616, &c., i. *97*; ii. 571 (note).
— — Smith, Dr. Thomas, *Vitae*, 1707: E supplies extracts from Diary for, iii. 632 & nn. 1, 2.
— — Sophocles, *Electra*: translation of, by C. Wase, iii. 55, n. 1.
— — Sprat, T., *History of the Royal Society*: frontispiece of: designed by Mrs. Evelyn (?), ii. 535, n. 4; ~ cited, iii. 286, n. 4.
— — Stanley, T., *History of philosophy*: Epicurus's system described in, iii. 173, n. 4.
— — Stillingfleet, E., *Origines Britannicæ*, 1685, v. 12, n. 2.
Books: in notes, &c. (*cont.*)
— — Talmud: passage based on: in sermon, iv. 496, n. 1.
— — Taylor, Jeremy, *Deus justificatus*, 1656, iii. 171, n. 4.
— — Tenison, T., various works, iv. 537, n. 4, 540, n. 1, 546, n. 1, 550, n. 3.
— — Ussher, James, *Prophecy of Bishop Usher*, 1688: forged letters in, v. 13, n. 1.
— — Vickars, J., works illustrated by Hollar, i. 22, n. 1.
— — Waller, E., 'Of a war with Spain, and a fight at sea': cited, *add.* (iii. 188, n. 3).
— — Wase, C., translation of Sophocles, *Electra*, iii. 55, n. 1.
— — Wotton, William, *Reflections upon ancient and modern learning*, 1694: given by Wotton to E, v. 184, n. 2.
Boom, Brabant, ii. 68, n. 1.
Boone (Bohune), Christopher, iv. 180 & n. 3; house and garden of, at Lee, iv. 180 & n. 3, 288, 337 & n. 4; almshouses of, at Lee, iv. 288–9 & n.; social, iv. 386.
Boone, Mrs. Mary, wife of Christopher Boone, iv. 180, n. 3; cabinet of, iv. 180, 288.
boord, Madame de: *see* Bordes d'Assigny, H. de.
Booreman, —: *see* Boreman, Sir W.
Boot (Boet), Arnold *or* Aarnt: social, iii. 24 & n. 2.
Booth, Sir George, first Baron Delamer: created a baron, iii. 277 & n. 4.
Booth, Henry, Charles II's agent at Calais, iii. 12 & n. 7, 55.
Booth, Henry; second Baron Delamer 1684; earl of Warrington 1690, iv. 608, n. 2; declares for William of Orange, iv. 608; dies, v. 165 & n. 1.
Borcht, Hendrik van der: portrait of E by, ii. 29 & n. 1 (i. 21).
Bordeaux: opposes Louis XIV, iii. 23 & n. 1; Parlement of: *présidents* of: *see* Pontac, A. de; Pontac, F.-A. de (iv. 329 & n. 3).
Bordes d'Assigny, Henriette de (Madame de boord), iii. 572 & n. 3.
Bordley, Rev. Stephen: sermon by (?), v. 35 & n. 2.
Boreel, Johan, Dutch ambassador in England, *c.* 1667, iii. 502, n. 6.

Boreman, Robert, D.D.: geneal., iii. 270, n. 3.
Boreman (Booreman), Sir William; knighted 1661, iii. 270 & n. 3; social, iii. 270, 463, 503; information from, iv. 492.
Borgh, —, Dutch traveller, ii. 316.
Borghese family: arms of, ii. 312 & n. 7.
Borghese, —, cardinal, 1644 (error for Prince Paolo Borghese?), ii. 284 & n. 2, 285.
Borghese, Camillo: *see* Paul V.
Borghese, Camillo, Prince, *c.* 1806, ii. 252, n. 5.
Borghese, Paolo, Prince: in succession to Aldobrandini property, ii. 284, n. 2; as Cardinal Borghese (?), ii. 284, 285.
Borghese, Scipione, cardinal, ii. 251, n. 4; builds Villa Borghese, Rome, *ib.*; collection of paintings of, at Villa Borghese, ii. 252, n. 5 *ad fin.*; restores S. Sebastiano, Rome, ii. 363, n. 3; completes Villa Mondragone, Frascati, ii. 393 & n. 5; gift made by, ii. 236, n. 1.
Borgia, Roderigo: *see* Alexander VI.
Borgianni, O.: painting by, ii. 365 & n. 1.
Borgoforte *or* Santa Vittoria, near Mantua: engagement at, 1702, v. 512 & n. 4.
Borgo San Sepolcro, Guerrino dal, architect, ii. 202, n. 8 *ad fin.*
Borough Green, Cambs.: *see* Burrough Green.
Borri (Borrhi), G. F.: communication from, to Royal Society, iii. 293–4 & n.
Borromean Islands: notice, ii. 506–7 & nn.
Borromeo family, ii. 507, n. 2.
Borromeo, Count Carlo, ii. 506, n. 8.
Borromeo, St. Charles: *see* Charles, St., Borromeo.
Borromeo, Federigo, cardinal, ii. 491, n. 2; colleges founded by, ii. 496 & n. 1; as founder of the Ambrosiana, ii. 497 & n. 4.
Borromeo, Countess Isabella, ii. 506, n. 8.
Borromini, Francesco, architect: general, ii. 212, n. 2; buildings by (all in Rome): Palazzo Barberini, ii. 229, n. 1; S. Carlo alle Quattro Fontane, ii. 242, n. 1; S. Giovanni in Laterano, nave, ii. 266, n. 4, 273, n. 5.
Boscawen, — (Edward Boscawen?): social, iv. 189, 289.
Boscawen, Anne: *see* Evelyn, Anne, Lady Evelyn.
Boscawen, Dorothy: *see* Meadows, Mrs. D., later Lady Meadows.
Boscawen, Edward, iv. 189, n. 2; social, iv. 189(?), 212, 289(?); geneal., iv. 147, n. 6; v. 258, n. 1.
Boscawen, Edward, jnr.: dies, 1705, v. 618.
Boscawen, Hugh; Viscount Falmouth 1720, v. 618 & n. 3.
Boscawen, Mrs. Jael, born Godolphin, wife of Edward Boscawen, iv. 147 & n. 6; godmother of Francis Godolphin, second earl of Godolphin, iv. 147; lives with Dr. Henry Godolphin, iv. 606; at Cranbourn Lodge, iv. 642; daughters of: weddings of, v. 258 & n. 1, 609, 609–10; son of: dies, &c., v. 618, 619; social, iv. 156, 212, 337, 339, 450, 463, 475, 520; v. 127, 171, 600; mentioned, iv. 133, n. 4.
Boscobel, Salop: royal oak at, represented in Lord Mayor's show, iii. 259 & n. 4; view of, by R. Streater, iii. 375, n. 3.
Bosleduke: *see* 's Hertogenbosch.
Bosse, Abraham, engraver: consulted by E, ii. 568 & n. 3.
Boston, Lincs.: in view, iii. 133 & n. 2.
Boston, Mass.: project for controlling, iii. 582; shipping at: order to, 1672, iii. 603, n. 2.
Boswell, James: house occupied by, in London, iii. 578, n. 1.
Boswell, Sir William: letter from, about Roman Catholic emissaries in England, iv. 508, n. 1; v. 13, n. 1.
Bosworth, Leics., battle of, iii. 122, n. 6.
Botany: lectures, ii. 565 & n. 3; iv. 68; microscopic observations, iii. 629; vegetation without earth discussed, iii. 316; R. Waller's tables of plants, iv. 632 & n. 3.
  herbals, MS., with miniatures, iv. 215–16, 330; *hortus siccus*: E's, ii. 466 & n. 5; *add.*; ~ Sir H. Sloane's, v. 48; paintings of flowers, &c., ii. 133 & iii. 33; iii. 236; iv. 289, 531–2 & n.

Boteler, Joan, Lady Boteler, wife of Sir William: *see* Warwick, Joan, Lady Warwick.
Boteler, Sir William: geneal., iii. 368, n. 3.
Bothwell Bridge, Lanarkshire, battle of, iv. 171, n. 1.
Bothwell Castle, Lanarkshire: part of Clarendon Collection of portraits at, iii. 520, n. 3.
Botzen (Bolsano), ii. 489, n. 6.
Bouchavannes, M. E. de (abbess of Boucharvant): befriended by E, iii. 34 & n. 5.
Bouche, P. P., engraver, iv. 369, n. 1.
Boughton Malherbe (Bochton), Kent: Chilston *or* Chilson in: visits to, iii. 436 & n. 3, 468.
Bouillon, Frédéric-Maurice de la Tour-d'Auvergne, duke of: at Rome, ii. 382 & n. 3; geneal., iv. 77 & n. 2.
Bouillon, Godefroy-Maurice de la Tour-d'Auvergne, duke of: visits English court, iii. 575 & n. 4.
Bouillon, Isabella de la Tour-d'Auvergne (born de 's Heerenberg), duchess of: at Rome, ii. 382 & n. 3.
Boulogne (Bollogne): notice, 1643, ii. 84 & n. 2 (i. 57); journey to, from Calais, ii. 83–4 & nn. (i. 56–7); Henry VIII besieges, ii. 84 & n. 3 (i. 57); English troops embark for, 1657, iii. 192, n. 6; E at, 1650, 1652, iii. 12, 17, 54.
Bourbon: Duchy of, ii. 155 (i. 100); dukes of: seat of, ii. 154 & n. 12 (i. 99).
Bourbon: House of: name of: origin of, ii. 155 (i. 100).
Bourbon: Armand de: *see* Conti, prince of; Armand de: *see* Miremont, marquis de; François-Louis de: *see* Conti, prince of; Henri de: *see* Verneuil, duke of; Louis II de: *see* Condé, prince of.
Bourbon-l'Archambault: notice, ii. 155–6 & nn. (i. 100).
Bourbonnais, the, ii. 154 (i. 99).
Bourchier, Anne: *see* Rich, Mrs. A.
Bourchier, Christian: *see* Stephens, Mrs. C.
Bourchier, Mary: *see* Prettyman, Mary, Lady Prettyman.
Bourchier, Mary (Mrs. Fanshawe): geneal., iii. 19, n. 5.
Bourchier, Thomas, of Barnsley: geneal., iii. 400, n. 3.
Bourchier, William, of Barnsley: geneal., ii. 535, n. 3; iii. 19, n. 5, 78, n. 2, 111, n. 6.
Bourchier, Winifred: *see* Glanville, Winifred, Lady Glanville.
Bourdon, Sebastian: portrait of Mrs. Evelyn by, ii. 551 & n. 7; iii. 56, 62.
Bourges: notice, ii. 152–4 & nn. (i. 98–9).
Bovey, James: social (?), iii. 186 & n. 3.
Bow, Middlesex: scarlet dye named from, iii. 446, n. 6.
Bowles, Sir John: *see* Bolles.
Bowls: games of, iii. 68, 219; bowling-greens, &c., ii. 527; iii. 112, 192, 383, 595 & n. 4; iv. 311, 482, 594.
Bowyer, Anthony, iv. 387, n. 3; social, iv. 387(?); member of Greenwich Hospital site committee, v. 211, n. 1.
Bowyer, Sir Edmund, iii. 196, n. 4; seat of, at Camberwell, iii. 197 & n. 2; social, iii. 196, 197, 211, 218, 488, 490; geneal., iv. 387, n. 3.
Bowyer, Hester, Lady Bowyer, wife of Sir Edmund, iii. 196, n. 4, 488, n. 6; social, iii. 196, 211.
Box Hill, near Dorking, Surrey: box-trees on, iii. 157 & n. 3; Mole river at, ii. 523, n. 3; iii. 157; road by, v. 168 & n. 1; in *Sylva*, iii. 143, n. 1.
Boxley Hill, near Maidstone, Kent: accident on, iii. 468 & n. 3.
Boyle family: Sir Richard Browne's connexion with, iii. 169, n. 7; iv. 304, n. 2.
Boyle, Lady Catherine: *see* Brett.
Boyle, Catherine, countess of Cork, wife of Richard Boyle, first earl; geneal., iii. 169, nn. 2, 7.
Boyle, Charles; second earl of Burlington 1698, v. 353, n. 4; chaplain of: *see* Roe, J.
Boyle, Charles; styled Viscount Dungarvan 1643–91; succeeded as Baron Clifford 1691: tutor for, iii. 182 & n. 3.
Boyle, Elizabeth: *see* Tufton, Elizabeth, countess of Thanet.
Boyle, Elizabeth, countess of Cork and Burlington, wife of Richard Boyle, second earl of Cork, &c.; Baroness Clifford *suo jure* 1643, iv. 428, n. 2; affection of, for Mary Evelyn, iv. 428; mentioned, iii. 182, n. 3, 242, n. 1.

Boyle, Elizabeth, Viscountess Boyle of Kinalmeaky ('Lady Kinalmeaky'); created countess of Guildford 1660: social, iii. 263 & n. 8.
Boyle, Henry, of Castlemartyr: social (?), iv. 570 & n. 3.
Boyle, Henry; Baron Carleton 1714: social (?), v. 597 & n. 5.
Boyle, Joan: *see* Fitzgerald, Joan, countess of Kildare.
Boyle, Katherine: *see* Jones, Katherine, Viscountess Ranelagh.
Boyle, Lewis, Viscount Boyle of Kinalmeaky: geneal., iii. 263, n. 8.
Boyle, Lionel, third earl of Orrery: house of, at Charleville, destroyed by James II's adherents, v. 37 & n. 1.
Boyle, Richard, first earl of Cork: geneal. (connexion with Mrs. Evelyn, &c.), iii. 169, nn. 2, 7, 232.
Boyle, Richard, 1612–98; second earl of Cork 1643; created earl of Burlington 1664, iii. 242, n. 1, 379, n. 7; requires tutor for his sons, iii. 182 & n. 3; buys site of Burlington House, London, iii. 379, n. 7; house of, at Chiswick, iv. 294 & n. 5; social: parties, &c., iii. 242, 379; iv. 88, 603; geneal., iii. 446, n. 2; iv. 222, n. 8, 244 & n. 5.
Boyle, Richard, d. 1665, younger son of Richard Boyle, earl of Cork and Burlington: tutor for, iii. 182 & n. 3.
Boyle, Hon. Robert, the scientist, iii. 169, n. 7.
as scientist: presides at meeting of Philosophical Society (Royal Society), iii. 327; elected president of Royal Society, iv. 225 & n. 1; views of, on relations of religion and science, i. *110*, n. 1; introduces atomism into England, iii. 173, n. 4 *ad fin.*; air-pump of (vacuum Boylianum): experiments with, &c., iii. 255 & n. 3, 271 & n. 3, 284–5, 318; iv. 271, 381; chemical demonstration by, iii. 337; method of, of making phosphorus, iv. 252 & n. 2; on use of gold in medicine, iii. 86, n. 6; demonstrates adhesive power of polished surfaces, iii. 291–2; observes transit of Mercury, iii. 384–5 & n.; and machine for purifying sea-water, iv. 388–9 & n.
Boyle, Hon. Robert (*cont.*)
relations of with E: friendship of, with E, i. *12* & n. 1; influence of, on E, i. *43* & n. 1; E proposes scientific college to, iii. 232 & n. 2; E dedicates *Sculptura* to, iii. 325; gives E *History of Humane Blood*, iv. 370 & n. 3, 371; appoints E a trustee for Boyle Lectures, i. *35*; v. 88. *See also* social *below*.
residences of: at Chelsea, iii. 255 & n. 3, 272; at Oxford, iii. 384; in Pall Mall, with Lady Ranelagh, iv. 124, n. 6; v. 83, n. 2; ~ laboratory of, in, iv. 124 & n. 6.
social: parties, &c., iii. 169–70; iv. 84, 603, 630; v. 26; alone, &c., iii. 232, 241, 255, 272; iv. 258, 371, 392, 570 & n. 3(?), 585.
dies, v. 81 & n. 2; funeral, benefactions, &c., of, v. 81–3 & nn.; *see also* Boyle Lectures.
See also Books mentioned in text; Books mentioned in notes.
Boyle, Roger; Baron Broghill 1628; first earl of Orrery 1660, iii. 405, n. 2; *Mustapha* by: performed, iii. 405 & n. 2, 465 & n. 4, 466; geneal., iv. 261, n. 2.
Boyle of Kinalmeaky: Viscount, &c.: *see* Boyle, Lewis; Boyle, Elizabeth, his viscountess, later countess of Guildford.
Boyle Lectures: foundation of, v. 82, 88 & n. 3.
— trustees for: appointed, v. 88 & nn. 1, 2; E as one, i. *35*; meet, &c., v. 88–9 & nn., 123, 159, 160–1 & n., 196–7, 198–9 & n., 224, 238, 273, 362, 366, 536, 583; propose altering settlement for lectures, v. 197; make investment to provide for lectures, v. 238; sermons (lectures) dedicated to, v. 94, n. 1, 199, n. 1, 273, n. 4, 442, n. 2.
— lecturers: appointments of, sermons by, &c. [the lecturers are also indexed under their names]:
— — 1692: (Dr.) Richard Bentley, v. 88–9 & n., 94 & n. 1, 123.
— — 1693: Dr. Richard Kidder, bishop of Bath and Wells, v. 123 & n. 3, 126, 161 & n. 1.

Boyle Lectures (*cont.*)
— — 1694: Bentley again, v. 159, 160–1 & n., 164, 196–7, 199.
— — 1695: Dr. John Williams, later bishop of Chichester, v. 198–9 & n., 222 & n. 5.
— — 1696: Williams again, v. 224 & n. 4, 239 & n. 1.
— — 1698: (Dr.) John Harris, v. 273 & n. 4.
— — 1700: Dr. Offspring Blackall, later bishop of Exeter, v. 362 & n. 1, 366 & n. 2, 398 & n. 3.
— — 1701: Dr. George Stanhope, v. 442–3 & n.
— — 1703: (Dr.) John Adams, v. 528.
— — 1704: (Dr.) Samuel Clarke, v. 536 & n. 1.
— — 1705: Clarke again, v. 583.
Boyne, near Henley-on-Thames: *see* Bolney Court.
Boyne, river: Battle of the Boyne, v. 28 & nn. 2, 4; William III wounded on eve of, v. 27–8 & n., 28 & n. 4; de la Caillemotte wounded at, v. 30 & n. 2; Sir Charles Tuke wounded at, v. 32–3.
Boynton, Katherine: *see* Talbot, Mrs. K.
Boynton, Col. Matthew: geneal., iv. 15, n. 8.
Brabant: Duke of: *see* John IV (ii. 32, n. 3).
Brabourne, Kent: yew-tree at, iii. 359 & n. 3.
Bracciano: district, ii. 313.
Bracciano: Duke of: palace of, at Rome, ii. 288 & n. 4.
Braddon, Lawrence: views of, on Essex's death, iv. 326, n. 4 *ad fin.*; tried, iv. 367, n. 1.
Bradford, John; D.D. 1671, iii. 562, n. 3; sermon by, iii. 562; social, iv. 334 & n. 3.
Bradford: Earls and Countesses of: *see* Newport, Francis, formerly Lord Newport, first earl, 1694–1708; Newport, Diana, his countess; Newport, Richard, second earl, 1708–23.
Bradshaw, George: E's tutor at Oxford, ii. 17 & n. 2 (i. 13); alluded to, ii. 21 (i. 16).
Bradshaw, John, the regicide, ii. 547 & n. 2; passes signed by, ii. 557 & n. 1; iii. 16 & n. 1; Somerhill granted to, iii. 71–2 & n.; sermon dedicated to, iii. 212, n. 7; corpse of, exhumed and exposed, iii. 269 & n. 2; alluded to, &c., ii. 17 & n. 2 (i. 13).
Bradshaw, Rev. Nicholas, rector of Ockham, ii. 17 & n. 2 (i. 13).
Brady, Nicholas, D.D.: sermon by (?), v. 556–7 & n.
Braganza: Duke of: *see* John IV, king of Portugal.
Brahal, Lord, *rectè* Broghill: *see* Boyle, Roger, later earl of Orrery.
Braham (Breames), Sir Richard, bt.: in proceedings against Mordaunt, iii. 469 & n. 1.
Brahe, Count N. N., Swedish ambassador to England, 1661: state entry of, into London, iii. 297 & n. 4.
Brainford: *see* Brentford.
Bramante, Donato, architect, i. 81, n. 2; buildings by: Rome: Tempietto, ii. 313 & nn. 3, 4; ~ Vatican, staircase, ii. 303 & n. 1; buildings attributed to: Milan: S. Maria presso S. Celso, ii. 495 & nn. 1, 2; Paris: Palais du Luxembourg, i. 81 & n. 2; Rome: Palazzo della Cancelleria, ii. 367 & n. 5; ~ Palazzo di Venezia, ii. 378 & n. 6.
Bramantino: building attributed to, ii. 495, n. 2.
Bramber, Sussex, ii. 544 & n. 4.
Bramhall (Bramall), John, D.D.; bishop of Derry 1634; archbishop of Armagh 1661, iii. 253, n. 1; presents Irish divines to Charles II, ii. 252–3 & n.; letter from, about Roman Catholic emissaries in England, iii. 157, n. 2; iv. 507, 508, n. 1; v. 13, n. 1.
Brampton, Rev. — (error for Rev. William Bramston ?): sermon by, v. 92–3 & n.
Bramston, Sir Francis, judge; knighted 1678, ii. 470, n. 3; at Padua, ii. 470 & n. 3, 473; as Reader at Middle Temple: feast of, iii. 512; social, iii. 514; geneal., iv. 529, n. 2.
Bramston, Sir John, sen.: geneal., ii. 473 & n. 2; iii. 512; iv. 529 & n. 2.
Bramston, Sir John, jnr.: geneal., ii. 470, n. 3.
Bramston (Branston), William; D.D. 1705, iv. 529, n. 2; v. 224,

Bramston, William, D.D. (*cont.*) n. 1; sermons by, iv. 529; v. 92–3 & n.(?), 224.
Brandenburg: Electors (called Dukes in error) and Electresses of: *see* Frederick William, elector 1640–88; Louise Henriette, his electress; Frederick III, elector 1688–1701, later king in Prussia.
Brandon, Charles, duke of Suffolk: in painting (error), iv. 141 & n. 1.
Brandon: Duke of, 1711–12: *see* Douglas, James, fourth duke of Hamilton.
Brandon: Viscount, 1679–94 (courtesy title): *see* Gerard, Charles, second earl of Macclesfield.
Brasses, sepulchral: destruction of, at Lincoln, iii. 132.
Brattle, Sir John, assay-master of the Mint, iv. 138 & n. 1.
Bray, Edward, of Shere, i. *52*.
Bray, William, first editor of the Diary: notice, i. *52*.
as editor of Diary: first edition, i. *54–6*; second edition, i. *58*; third edition, i. *62–3*; views of, i. *56–8*; text of, i. *58–63*; annotation of, i. *115–16*, *120*; treatment by, of E's correspondence, i. *129*–30.
markings made by, on MS Diary, i. *45*, n. 2; mentioned, i. *53*, *54*; identification by, of work by E, iii. 284, n. 4; conjecture by, iii. 425, n. 5.
Braybroke, Robert de, bishop of London: corpse of, iii. 459 & n. 5.
Brazen serpent: relic of, ii. 500 & n. 4; in sermons, iii. 506, 526.
Brazil (Brazeele): siren from, iii. 517 & n. 4; treasure from, 1703, v. 530 & n. 2.
Brazil: Princess of: *see* Theresa Josepha.
Breage, Cornwall: burial-place of Godolphin family, iv. 150 & n. 1; Mrs. Margaret Godolphin buried at, iv. 150, 152.
Breakspear, Nicholas: *see* Hadrian IV.
Breames, Sir Richard: *see* Braham.
Brechin: Bishop of: *see* Sydserff, T. (1634–5).
Brecknock: Earl of, 1660–82: *see* Butler, James, first duke of Ormond.
Brecknockshire: in view, iii. 119.
Breda: belongs to Princes of Orange, i. 41 & n. 1; Charles II at: 1650, iii. 2, n. 2; ~ 1660, iii. 245 & n. 1; Declaration of, iii. 244 & n. 2; Treaties of, 1667: *see* Wars: second Dutch War; Dr. G. Morley goes to, iii. 2, n. 2; knighthood conferred at, iii. 473, n. 5.
Brederode (Bredrode) — (error), iv. 118; *add.*
Brederode, J. W. van: accompanies Marie de Médicis to Cologne, ii. 57 & n. 3 (i. 39).
Bredox *or* Bredoy, Dr. —: *see* Brideoake, R.
Bremhill, Wilts.: Cadenham manor in: *see* Cadenham.
Brent, —, an official, iv. 297.
Brent, Mrs. —: godmother of William Draper, 1698, v. 288.
Brenta, river: journey on, ii. 452 & nn. 2–5.
Brentford (Brainford), Middlesex: battle of, &c., ii. 79 (i. 52–3 & n.); review at (?), iv. 463 & n. 2; encampment at (at Hounslow), 1686, iv. 514; *see also* Hounslow; house of T. Povey at, iii. 447 & n. 3; mentioned, iv. 119.
Brentwood, Essex, iii. 91, 225.
'Brereton', near 'Carthope', Lincs: storm at, 1701, v. 473 & n. 3.
Brereton, Edward, controller of Inner Temple, Christmas 1697, v. 280 & nn. 1, 2.
Brereton, Frances, Baroness Brereton, wife of William Brereton, third baron, iii. 218, n. 7; as Frances Willoughby: social, iii. 218; as Mrs. Brereton: social, iii. 232 & n. 3.
Brereton, William, second Baron Brereton: geneal., iii. 232.
Brereton, William, third Baron Brereton, iii. 232 & n. 3; as Mr. Brereton: social, iii. 232; as Lord Brereton: social, iii. 488; geneal., iii. 218, n. 7.
Brereton: Barons and Baronesses: *see* Brereton, William, second baron, d. 1664; Brereton, William, third baron, 1664–80; Brereton, Frances, his baroness.
Brescia: notice, ii. 489–90 & nn.; feud of, with Vicenza, ii. 483 & nn. 4–6; fire-arms manufactured at, ii. 489 & nn. 3–6; E's carbine from, ii. 528.

Bresciano, Prospero Antichi, called: statues by, ii. 260, n. 5.
Bressanone (Brixen), ii. 489, n. 6.
Brest: Sir Richard Browne and the Comte de Kéroualle at, iv. 66 & nn. 1, 2; in War of League of Augsburg: English fleet before, 1689, iv. 645; Allied attack on, 1694, v. 184 *bis* & n. 3; ~ revenge for failure of, v. 186; French fleets at: 1690, v. 31 & n. 7; ~ 1693, v. 142, n. 1; ~ 1696, v. 242; Pointis at, 1697, v. 266 & n. 4.
Bret, Col. —: *see* Brett, Richard.
Bretel de Gremonville, Nicolas, French ambassador to Venice, ii. 440 & n. 5.
Breton, John, D.D., master of Emmanuel College, Cambridge: sermon by, iii. 542–3 & nn.
Breton, John, son of Dr. Robert: godson of E, iii. 369 & n. 6.
Breton, Robert; D.D. 1663; vicar of Deptford 1662–72, iii. 302, n. 4; probation sermon by, at Deptford, &c., iii. 302; instituted vicar, iii. 317, n. 2; remains at Deptford during plague, iii. 424; sermons by, at Deptford (as 'our vicar', 'our doctor', or 'our minister'), iii. 317–601 *passim*; sermons by: commended, iii. 317 *bis*; funeral sermon by, iii. 363; baptizes Richard Evelyn (1664) and Elizabeth Evelyn, iii. 368, 495.
appointed a chaplain in ordinary, iii. 347 & n. 3; sermon by, at court, iii. 517; as rector of St. Martin, Ludgate: sermon by, iii. 367; as prebendary of St. Paul's: sermon by, *ib*.
ill, 1664, iii. 389; dies, funeral sermon, &c., iii. 603–4 & nn.; geneal., iii. 369, 542; mentioned, iii. 296, n. 1; iv. 5.
Breton language: similarity of, to Welsh, iv. 66.
Brett, Lady Catherine, wife of Richard Brett: geneal., iv. 261, n. 2.
Brett, Sir Edward: military, iii. 422 & n. 4.
Brett, Richard (Col. Bret): complicity of, in marriage of Lady Ogle to Thomas Thynne, iv. 261 & n. 2.
Breugill *or* Breugle: *see* Bruegel.
Bréval, François Durant de; D.D. 1675, iii. 602 & n. 3; sermons by, iii. 556 & n. 5(?), 602; iv. 244.
Brevint (Brevent), Daniel, D.D., dean of Lincoln, iii. 8, n. 5; ordained, iii. 8–9 & nn., 632–3.
Brewer, Mary: *see* Boone, Mrs. M.
Briat (Briot), giant: bones of, ii. 153 & n. 11 (i. 99).
Brickhill, Beds., iv. 71.
Bridekirk, Cumberland: living of Rev. Joseph Williamson, iv. 38 & n. 4.
Brideoake (Bredox, Bredoy), Ralph, D.D.; dean of Salisbury 1667; bishop of Chichester 1675, iv. 2, n. 2; elected bishop, iv. 61 & n. 3; sermons by: as dean, iv. 2, 4, 29–30; ~ as bishop, iv. 61, 85 & n. 5; appointed to preach, iv. 107, n. 3, 132 & n. 4 (error).
Brides, Rev. —, preacher at Cadenham, iii. 117.
Bridgeman, — (William Bridgeman ?): social, iv. 96 & n. 3.
Bridgeman, Mrs. —: plays guitar, iv. 360.
Bridgeman, Sir Orlando; lord keeper 1667–72, iii. 518, n. 3; and Council for Foreign Plantations: *ex officio* member, iii. 571, n. 1; ~ attends meetings, iii. 578, 584; swears in members of Council of Trade and Foreign Plantations, iii. 627 & n. 5; London house of, iii. 627 & n. 4; social, iii. 518, 574; request of, to E(?), iii. 394 & n. 3.
Bridgeman, William, clerk of the council, iv. 197 & n. 2; character, v. 325; admitted F.R.S., iv. 197; master of Clothworkers' Company, iv. 518 & n. 3; trustee for grant of reversion to Arlington, &c., v. 161, n. 4; social, iv. 96(?); dies, v. 325 & n. 7.
Bridges [select: bridges notable for their construction or other features; those merely mentioned, or with ordinary commendations, are not indexed collectively]:
special features, &c.: bridge of boats, ii. 122 & n. 5 (i. 79); ~ military, ii. 38 & n. 3 (i. 28–9); drawbridges: at Brussels, ii. 69 (i. 46); ~ military, ii. 151 (i. 98); with echo, ii. 115 & n. 6 (i. 75); houses, &c., built on, ii. 93 (i. 62), 127 (i. 81), 152 (i.

Bridges (*cont.*)
98), 185 (i. 117), 433, 528–9 & n.; iii. 128, 451; with monument, &c., ii. 136–7 & nn. (i. 89–90); in mountains (Simplon pass), ii. 509; ruinous, ii. 122 & n. 5 (ii. 78–9), 161 & n. 3 (i. 102); with water-houses, ii. 93–4 & nn. (i. 62); wheel-bridge, military, ii. 37 & n. 2 (i. 28); wooden, ii. 93–4 & n. (i. 62), 528–9 & n.
notable bridges [*see also* London: topography; Rome: topography; environs]: Caen, ii. 126 & n. 3, 127 (i. 80, 81); Florence, ii. 185 & nn. 2–4 (i. 117); Lyons, ii. 157 & n. 2 (i. 101); Paris: Pont-Neuf, ii. 92–3 & nn. (i. 61–2), 99 & n. 7 (i. 65); iii. 10–11 & nn., 20 & n. 6; Pisa, ii. 182 & n. 3 (i. 114); Pont St. Esprit, ii. 160 (i. 102); Pozzuoli: Caligula's at, ii. 344 & n. 3; Rochester, i. 23; Venice: Rialto, ii. 433 & n. 2; York, iii. 128 & n. 7.
Bridges, George Rodney: geneal., iii. 596, n. 4.
Bridges, Col. John: buys Hurcott, ii. 545 & n. 3.
Bridget, St., of Sweden: relics, &c., of, ii. 246 & n. 8, 306 & n. 10.
Bridgewater: Earl, &c., of: *see* Egerton, Scroop, fourth earl, 1701–20, and first duke, 1720–45; Egerton, Elizabeth, his countess.
Brieg (Briga): notice, ii. 514–15 & nn.; roads to, ii. 508, n. 5 *ad fin.*, 515, n. 3; Hospital of St. Antony at, ii. 511, n. 5.
Brigg, Lincs.: liquorice cultivated at, iii. 131 & n. 3.
Brigges, Martha: *see* Stonhouse, Martha, Lady Stonhouse.
Brigges, Robert: geneal., iv. 189, n. 3.
Bright, George, D.D., dean of St. Asaph, v. 13, n. 2; sermons by, v. 13, 14.
Brightman, Rev. Thomas: prophecies by, v. 26 & n. 3.
Brighton: error for Brington, Northants, iii. 183.
Brill: as cautionary town, i. 23, n. 4; William of Orange and Princess Mary part at, iv. 604 & n. 4.
Brill, Paul, ii. 113, n. 10; paintings by, ii. 113 (i. 73), 299 & n. 1.
Brindisi (Brundusium): end of Via Appia, ii. 319.
Brington (Brighton), Northants.: rectory (house) at, iv. 593 & n. 2; rectors: *see* Jessop, C.; Pierce, T. (presentation, iii. 234, n. 2).
Briosco, Andrea Riccio called: sculptures by, ii. 454–5 & n.
Brisacier family, iii. 411, n. 3.
Brisbane, John, secretary to the Admiralty, iv. 178, n. 5; social, iv. 178, 241, 258, 347.
Brisbane, Mrs. Margaret, wife of John Brisbane, later Baroness Napier of Merchiston, iv. 178, n. 5.
Bristol: notice, 1654, iii. 102–3 & nn.; E at, 1639, ii. 23 (i. 17); size of, iii. 102, n. 5, 594, n. 2; environs of: Avon gorge, &c., iii. 103 & nn. 2–6; ~ King Road (channel), iii. 119 & n. 3.
declares for William of Orange, 1688, iv. 609; grand jury of: asks for enforcement of laws against profanity, &c., v. 366, n. 5 *ad fin.*; governor of, *c.* 1654: *see* Scrope, Col. Adrian.
Bristol: Earl and Countess of: *see* Digby, George, second earl, 1653–77; Digby, Anne, his countess.
Bristol: cathedral clergy:
bishops: *see* Ironside, Gilbert, sen. (1660–71); Carleton, G. (1671–9); Trelawney, Sir Jonathan (1685–9); Ironside, Gilbert, jnr. (1689–91); Hall, Dr. John (1691–1710); Smalridge, G. (1714–19).
— Dr. R. Bathurst proposed for bishop, 1691, v. 49, n. 1; Dr. Thomas Watson called bishop in error, 1696, v. 256 & n. 7.
prebendary: *see* Crespion, Rev. S.
British Museum:
original constituent collections, v. 48, n. 1; Cottonian MSS., iii. 507, n. 1; Harleian MSS.: include Dr. N. Marsh's collection, v. 323, n. 3.
other collections: Arundel MSS., iii. 472, n. 3; Royal Society's museum, iii. 433, n. 3; J. M. Wright's collections, iii. 339, n. 6; *see also* iv. 214, n. 8 (Old Royal and King's MSS.).
particular objects: anatomical tables prepared for E, ii. 475, n. 5; drawings: by E, ii. 334, n. 3; ~ by Leonardo (Arundel Codex), ii. 498, n. 8 *ad fin.*; ~ by A. Marshall, iv. 289, n. 2;

British Museum (*cont.*)
etching by R. Gaywood or F. Barlow, iii. 166, n. 5; manuscripts: Edward VI's journal, &c., iv. 216, nn. 1, 3; ~ Queen Mary's Psalter, iv. 215, n. 1; ~ Vitruvius (Arundel), iv. 145, n. 2; maps: book of (I. Klencke), iii. 260, n. 5.
site of: *see* London: topography: British Museum.
Brittany: Sir Richard Browne in, as Charles II's agent, iii. 248, n. 1; iv. 66 & n. 2.
Brittany, Anne of: *see* Anne.
Brixen (Bressanone), ii. 489, n. 6.
Brixham, Devon: William of Orange lands at, iv. 605 & n. 2.
Brizasiere (Brisacier?), Monsieur: social (error?), iii. 411 & n. 3.
Broad Chalk, Wilts., iii. 115, n. 1.
Broad Hinton, Wilts.: house of Sir J. Glanville at, iii. 111 & n. 7.
Brocchi, Vincenzo, modeller: E buys statuettes from, ii. 198, 417.
Broderick, Sir Alan: challenges Sir William Petty, iv. 59 & n. 1.
Broghill: Baron: *see* Boyle, Roger, earl of Orrery.
Bromfeild, manor (Denbighshire): granted to Portland, &c., v. 230, n. 1.
Bromham, Wilts.: house of Sir E. Bayntun at, iii. 112, n. 2.
Bromley, Kent: James II's accession proclaimed at, iv. 414–15 & nn.; bishops' palace at: repaired by Dr. J. Dolben, iii. 537–8 & n.; ~ E visits Dolben at, iii. 537; iv. 73, 153, 211, 288, 334; Procession Oak near: E robbed at, iii. 69–70 & nn.; *add.*; mentioned, iii. 375.
Bronzino, Agnolo, ii. 191, n. 7; paintings by, ii. 191 & n. 7, 416 & n. 3.
Brooke, Rutland: house of Lady Campden at, iii. 124 & n. 1.
Brooke: Barons, &c.: *see* Greville, Sir Fulke, first baron; Greville, Robert, second baron; Greville, Catherine, his baroness; Greville, Francis, third baron; Greville, Fulke, fifth baron.
Brosse, Salomon de, architect: buildings by: Palais du Luxembourg, Paris, i. 81, n. 2; the Temple, Charenton, ii. 115, n. 2.
Brossin family, lords of Méré, ii. 145, n. 6.
Brough (Burgh), William, D.D., dean of Gloucester, iii. 239, n. 4; sermons by, iii. 239(?), 295.
Brouncker (Broncher, &c.), Henry; third Viscount Brouncker 1684, iii. 578, n. 8; character, &c., iv. 575 & nn. 2, 3; misconduct of, after battle of Lowestoft, iii. 410 & n. 3; as member of Council for Foreign Plantations, iii. 578, 599; as Cofferer of the Household, iv. 219 & n. 3; house of, at Sheen, iv. 142–3 & n.; ~ bequeathed to Sir C. Lyttelton, iv. 575.
Brouncker (Brounchar), William; second Viscount Brouncker 1645; scientist, iii. 285, n. 6; at observation of Saturn, iii. 285–6 & nn.; paper by, iii. 307, n. 1; designs *Jemmy* yacht, iii. 327, n. 5.
as first president of Royal Society: nominated, iii. 332; makes speeches to Charles II and Clarendon, iii. 334 & n. 2; receives duchess of Newcastle, iii. 483; signs *imprimatur* for *Sylva*, iii. 340, n. 1; experiments by, iii. 353; E reports new plough to, iii. 519, n. 2; tenure of office of, iv. 125 & n. 3.
as commissioner of the Navy: in charge of Dutch prizes, iii. 420 & n. 3.
takes Dulwich waters, iv. 112 & n. 3; social: parties, iii. 332, 369–70, 418, n. 1, 463; iv. 25 & n. 2, 105, 136; alone, &c., iii. 419 & n. 1; iv. 75, 104, 138.
Brouncker: Viscounts: *see* Brouncker, William, second viscount, 1645–84; Brouncker, Henry, third viscount, 1684–8.
Brown, John, clerk of the parliament *c.* 1671, iii. 588, n. 1.
Browne family of Betchworth, ii. 36, n. 5.
Browne family of Sayes Court: Gonson descent of, iii. 55, n. 3; iv. 304, n. 1, 313, n. 3; burial-place of, iii. 76; iv. 304; epitaph of, iii. 93, n. 1; iv. 303, n. 3.
Browne, Sir Adam, bt., of Betchworth, iii. 326, n. 4; elected M.P. for Surrey, 1685, iv. 433–4 & n.; social, iii. 326.

Browne, Alexander: publishes account of mezzotint engraving, iii. 274, n. 2.
Browne, Sir Ambrose, bt., of Betchworth, iii. 143, n. 2; owner of Box Hill, iii. 157, n. 3; social, iii. 143, 219–20 & nn.; geneal., iii. 326, n. 4.
Browne, Sir Anthony: owner, 1547, of West Horsley manor, ii. 545, n. 5.
Browne, Christopher, father of Sir Richard: tenant of Sayes Court, &c., ii. 537, n. 6; iii. 508, n. 4 *ad fin.*; interest of, in Sayes Court garden, ii. 537, n. 6 *ad fin.*; iii. 80, n. 1; acquires Great Warley manor, ii. 554, n. 1; letters of: cited, ii. 535, n. 4, 537, n. 6 *ad fin.*; will of: witness to, ii. 558, n. 7 *ad fin.*; ~ executor of: *see* Prettyman, W.
Browne, Elizabeth, Lady Browne, born Prettyman, wife of Sir Richard, ii. 535 & n. 3; house of, in Paris: receives English exiles at, iii. 77; concerned in marriage of marquis (later duke) of Newcastle, iii. 480 & n. 8; visits St. Cloud, ii. 536; takes charge of Mrs. Evelyn, 1647, *ib.*; in Paris during siege, 1649, ii. 550; in 'Bataille de Vambre', iii. 4, 5; accompanies Mrs. Evelyn to England, 1652, iii. 68; visits Tunbridge Wells, iii. 68–9, &c.; comes to Deptford, iii. 73; proposed visit of, to Wotton and Wiltshire, iii. 76; death, funeral, &c., of, iii. 76–7 & n.; burial-place of, iii. 93, n. 1; iv. 430; Mrs. Evelyn's grief for, iii. 77, 87; joint-owner of Great Warley manor, ii. 554, n. 1; portrait of, iii. 9, n. 3; geneal., ii. 558, n. 7; iii. 19, n. 5, 55, n. 1, 78, n. 2, 81, n. 7, 89, n. 5; mentioned, i. *8*, *10*, *11*.
Browne, Elizabeth, Viscountess Montagu, wife of Francis Browne, third viscount, ii. 551, n. 8; social, ii. 551; iii. 76, 354.
Browne, Francis; third Viscount Montagu 1629, ii. 545, n. 4; mortgages West Horsley manor to E, ii. 545 & n. 5; iii. 418; social, ii. 546, 554; iii. 15, 61–2, 239.
Browne, Mary, daughter of Sir Richard: *see* Evelyn, Mrs. M.
Browne, Richard, son of Sir Richard, ii. 537, n. 6 *ad fin*.
Browne, Sir Richard, sen., 1539–1604: notice, iv. 303–4 & n.; tomb of, iii. 93 & n. 1.
Browne, Sir Richard, bt., 1605–83; diplomatist; father of Mrs. Evelyn, ii. 90, n. 3; *add.*
  baptism of: date of, iv. 302, n. 4.
  residence of, in Paris, 1641–52, as English agent, later English Resident, in France: instructions to, 1641, iii. 67, n. 2; in Paris during siege, 1649, ii. 550 & n. 5; accredited by Charles II: first audience, ii. 566; in 'Bataille de Vambre', iii. 4–8; Lord Hatton quarrels with, iii. 38 & n. 4; audience to, on Louis XIV's attaining his majority, 1651, iii. 43 & n. 4; hears of Charles II's escape after Worcester, iii. 47 & n. 4; in Paris during siege, 1652, iii. 77 & n. 1; houses of, in Paris, iii. 21 & n. 3, 22 & n. 7; Cosin dines with, iii. 45, 635; Lord Hatton resides with, ii. 558; Sir Arthur Hopton resides with, ii. 555–6 & n.; Sir Thomas Osborne (later earl of Danby, &c.) entertained by, iii. 22; iv. 14, 20; *see also* iii. 77; chapel of: maintains Anglican worship in, iii. 247–8 & n.; ~ regarded as evidence of visibility of Church of England, *ib.*; iv. 303; services in, ii. 562–7 *passim*; iii. 1–12 *passim*, 17–54 *passim*, 632–5; ~ Charles II attends, iii. 48, 49, 51 *bis*, 53; ~ James, duke of York, attends, iii. 51, 53; special services, &c., in: baptism, ii. 567; marriages: marquis (later duke) of Newcastle, iii. 480 & n. 8; ~ E, ii. 536; burial service, ii. 565; ordination, iii. 8–9 & nn., 632–3; Christmas, ii. 567; iii. 51; Epiphany, iii. 53 & n. 2; fasts, iii. 38, 39.
  residence of, in Brittany, 1652–4: activities of, iv. 66 & n. 2; mentioned, iii. 248, n. 1.
  life in England after the Restoration: arrives at Dover, 1660, iii. 247; candidate for wardenship of Merton College, Oxford, iii. 273 & n. 3; interests of, at court, *ib.*; influence of, iii. 313,

Browne, Sir Richard (*cont.*)
n. 2; ill, 1667, iii. 482; lodgings of, in Whitehall, iii. 571–2 & n.; resigns office of Clerk of the Council, 1672, iii. 601; gives land at Deptford for Trinity House almshouses, 1671, iii. 577 & n. 6; iv. 303; Master of Trinity House, 1672–3, iv. 6, 11–12, 302; death, funeral, &c., of, iv. 302–4 & nn.; will of: clause in, relating to his burial, iv. 304; ~ probate of, iv. 305 *bis*; ~ E as executor of, iv. 340, 551.
miscellaneous: interest of, in gardening, ii. 127, n. 5; portrait of, iii. 9, n. 3; servants of: *see* Hoare, R. (ii. 559, n. 2, &c.); ~ former secretary of: dies, iii. 241.
relations of, with E: E visits, 1643, ii. 90 (i. 61); helps E to recover stolen property, 1647, ii. 535; E marries his daughter Mary, ii. 536; E resides with, iii. 634 (and, presumably, ii. 536, 561–8; iii. 1–12, 17–54); Mrs. Evelyn at his house, iii. 17 (and, presumably, ii. 536–iii. 66); E's son Richard (1652) named after, iii. 75; godfather: of E's children, iii. 368, 421, 495, 528; ~ of E's grandson Richard, iv. 236; correspondence of, with E, ii. 552 & n. 4; iii. 200, n. 1; letters of, to E: mentioned, iii. 65; ~ cited, ii. 555, n. 7, 558, n. 7 *ad fin.*; iii. 12, n. 7, 19, n. 2, 142, n. 4, 222, n. 3, 248, n. 1; for E's letters to, *see* Evelyn, John: correspondence; mentioned, iii. 371; iv. 23.
relations of, with other persons: friendships of: with Anne Hyde, later duchess of York, iii. 264 & n. 2; ~ with the Comte de Kéroualle, &c., iv. 66 & n. 2; correspondence of, with Clarendon: publication of, i. *56*; letters to, from Sir T. Hanmer, iii. 191, n. 2.
property, claims, &c., of: *Sayes Court*: the Brownes' tenancy, ii. 537, n. 6; Browne as owner, ii. 546; iii. 58; agent of, for (W. Prettyman), ii. 538 & n. 1; interest of, in: E negotiates for, iii. 74 & n. 4; grants to, of adjoining land, iii. 59, n. 1, 600 & n. 2; desire of, to extend estate, iii. 509; claim of, to fee-farm of, iii. 600; iv. 129, n. 3; *Great Warley*: sells it to E, ii. 554 & n. 1.
— claims on crown for expenditure as Resident in France, ii. 538, n. 1; iii. 600, n. 2; iv. 14, n. 1, 20; ~ petition relating to, iv. 394 & n. 3; ~ part settlement of, iv. 551 & n. 1; ~ alluded to, iii. 273; iv. 535 & n. 2; financial dealings of, with W. Prettyman, iii. 171, n. 1; iv. 339; *see also* Prettyman, W.; debt of, to J. Stephens: paid, iii. 75; business of, with Lord Chancellor, 1667, iii. 482; case in chancery of, iv. 67.
geneal., ii. 558, n. 7 *ad fin.*; iii. 55 & n. 1, 91, n. 5, 169, n. 7; iv. 303–4 & nn.; genealogical table, i. 142–3 (table no. 7).
See also i. *8*, *10*, *14–15*.
Browne, Sir Richard, lord mayor of London 1660–1, iii. 259 & n. 4; his show, *ib.*; as Major-General Browne: use by, of word Rump, iii. 242, n. 2.
Browne, Robert, founder of the Brownists, ii. 44, n. 3.
Browne, Sir Thomas, author of *Religio Medici*, iii. 592 & n. 2; house and collections of, iii. 594 & n. 1; shows E the sights of Norwich, iii. 594–5.
Browne, Mrs. Thomasine; born Gonson; wife (1) of Captain E. Fenton; (2) of Christopher Browne: geneal., ii. 554, n. 1; iii. 169, n. 7, 209, n. 2; iv. 304 & nn. 1, 2.
Brownists: at Amsterdam, ii. 44 & n. 3 (i. 32); mentioned, i. 18, n. 1.
Bruce, Christian: *see* Cavendish Christian, countess of Devonshire.
Bruce, Edward, Baron Bruce of Kinloss: geneal., iii. 329, n. 3.
Bruce, Robert, second earl of Elgin and Baron Bruce of Whorlton 1663; first earl of Ailesbury 1664, ii. 449, n. 7; as Lord Bruce: in Venice, ii. 449 & n. 7; ~ social, iii. 166; as Ailesbury: social, iv. 296.

Bruce, Thomas; styled Lord Bruce 1664–85; second earl of Ailesbury 1685, iv. 360, n. 2; as Lord Bruce: social, iv. 360; as Ailesbury: at meeting to discuss settlement of the crown, 1689, iv. 613–15.
Bruce: Lord, 1664–85 (courtesy title): *see* Bruce, Thomas, second earl of Ailesbury.
Bruce of Kinloss: Baron: *see* Bruce, Edward.
Bruce of Whorlton: second Baron: *see* Bruce, Robert, earl of Ailesbury.
Brudenell, Anna Maria: *see* Talbot, Anna Maria, countess of Shrewsbury.
Brudenell, Robert, second earl of Cardigan: geneal., iii. 596, n. 4.
Brudenell, Sir Thomas, Baron Brudenell: created earl of Cardigan, iii. 277.
Brudenell: Baron: *see* Brudenell, Sir Thomas, later earl of Cardigan.
Bruegel (Breugle, &c.): painters [E recognized at least two members of the family (ii. 70): Old Bruegel, presumably Pieter the elder (ii. 70, n. 5), and Young Bruegel, presumably Jan the eldest (*ib.*; called Hans, ii. 497)]: paintings by: Pieter, ii. 70 (i. 46); iii. 538; Jan, ii. 70 (i. 46), 497 & n. 5; 'Bruegel', ii. 540 & n. 4, 549.
Bruges: notice, 1641, ii. 74–5 & nn. (i. 49); Jerusalem Church at, ii. 65 & n. 3 (i. 44); Col. Gage's regiment at, &c.(?), ii. 65 & n. 4 (i. 44); journey to, from Ghent, ii. 74 & nn. 4, 5 (i. 48–9); Arundel at, ii. 74–5 (i. 49).
Bruggen, Louis van der, called Hans (Haunce): portrait of E by, ii. 133 & n. 2 (i. 87).
Brundusium (Brindisi): end of Via Appia, ii. 319.
Brunelleschi, Filippo, architect: tomb of, ii. 197 & n. 5; designs Pitti Palace, Florence, i. 81, n. 2.
Bruno, Giordano: execution of: place of, ii. 367, n. 1.
Brunswick: Prince of, 1675: lodging of, at Naples, ii. 325, n. 5.
Brunswick-Lüneburg: Dukes of: *see* Georg Wilhelm, duke of Celle; Johann Friedrich.
Brunswick-Lüneburg-Bevern: Duke of: *see* Ferdinand Albrecht I (iii. 396 & n. 5).
Brussels (Bruxelles, &c.): notice 1641, ii. 69–72 & nn. (i. 46–7).
buildings, &c.: Abbey of the Glorious Assumption, ii. 69–70 & n. (i. 46); Boucherie, ii. 69 & n. 5 (i. 46); Cour, ii. 70–2 & nn. (i. 46–7); Hôtel de Ville, ii. 69 & n. 4 (i. 46); Parc, ii. 71–2 & nn. (i. 46–7); iv. 115 & n. 5; Ste.-Gudule, ii. 69 & n. 7 (i. 46); walls, ii. 69, 71 (i. 46 *bis*).
environs: journey to, from Antwerp, ii. 68–9 & nn. (i. 45–6).
social: court at: in mourning, &c., ii. 72 *bis* (i. 47); dogs used for transport at, ii. 72 (i. 48); English nuns at, ii. 69–70 & n. (i. 46).
historical: false report about Charles II from, 1660, iii. 243 & n. 3; French bombardment of, 1695: damage caused by, ii. 69, nn. 4, 5.
persons at: James, duke of York, and his duchess, 1679, iv. 167, n. 6; Maximilian II of Bavaria, 1704, v. 580 & n. 5; Ossory, 1677, iv. 112, n. 2; Sir Arthur Slingsby, 1656–7, ii. 560, n. 2.
Brussels (Bruxells): the Jesuit of: *see* Seghers, D.
Brutus, Marcus: busts of, ii. 283; iv. 404.
Buat, Henri de Fleury de Culan, heer van: plot, &c., of, iii. 471 & n. 1; *add.*
Buccleugh: Dukedom of, iv. 6 & n. 1, 456 & n. 5.
Buccleugh: Duke, &c., of: *see* Scott, James, duke of Monmouth, first duke 1663–85; Scott, Anne, duchess of Monmouth, countess of Buccleugh 1661–3, duchess 1663–1732.
Buck, James, D.D.: sermon by, iii. 271 & n. 2.
Buckhurst: Lord, 1652–75 (courtesy title): *see* Sackville, Charles, later earl of Dorset, &c.
Buckingham: Dukes, &c., of: *see* Villiers, George, first duke, 1623–8; Villiers, George, second duke, 1628–87; Villiers, Mary, his duchess.
Buckingham: Duke of the county of: *see* Sheffield, John, earl of Mulgrave, &c., first duke, 1703–21.
Buckinghamshire: Millenarians in, 1694, v. 177–8 & n.; jurymen from, v. 248.

Buckle, Sir Christopher: house of, iii. 221 & n. 6.
Buckle, Sir Cuthbert: geneal., iii. 221, n. 6.
Buda, Hungary: besieged by Imperialists, 1684, iv. 394 & n. 1; capture of, by Imperialists, 1686: thanksgiving services for, in London, &c., iv. 524 & n. 2.
Building materials [select notices. In some cases, such as tombs, it is impracticable to distinguish between architecture and sculpture; for further references to some of the materials indexed below see Sculpture: materials]:
alabaster, oriental, ii. 438 & n. 5.
brass, copper, or Corinthian brass (i.e. bronze), ii. 261, 272, 372 *bis*, 416 & n. 8.
brick: use of, at: Addiscombe, v. 541; Bologna, ii. 420, 421–2; Genoa, i. 109; Nice, ii. 168 (i. 106); Siena, ii. 201, 202; in United Provinces, i. 24; *see also* clinker-brick *below*.
Caen stone, ii. 127 (i. 81).
clinker-brick (clincard, white Flanders brick): building of, iii. 555; paving of, in United Provinces, i. 24; ii. 47–8 & n. (i. 34); project for making, &c., iii. 471, 476, 477–8, 495.
enamelled terracotta (as earth painted like porcelain), iii. 3 & n. 1.
flint, worked: at Norwich, iii. 594 & n. 3.
free-stone: at Paris, ii. 92 & n. 6 (i. 61), 131 (i. 84); iii. 637; cave-dwellings cut in, ii. 144 (i. 93); *see also* stone *below*.
granite, Egyptian, ii. 493 & n. 1.
jasper, ii. 118 *bis* (i. 76).
lead: church-roofs, &c., of, ii. 260 *bis*; iii. 459 & n. 2.
marble: inlay or incrustation, ii. 63 (i. 43), 96 (i. 63), 103 (i. 67), 105 (i. 68), 118 (i. 76), 177 (i. 111), 199, 260, 265–6 & n., 296, 367 & n. 6, 376, 437 & n. 5, 460, 468; mountains or quarries of, ii. 170 (i. 107), 179 (i. 113); white: stained red, iii. 111 & n. 1.
— kinds of: Irish, iv. 199; Parian, ii. 176 & n. 8 (i. 111); Sussex, iii. 113, n. 2; Theban, ii. 371 & n. 4; Verona, ii. 462 & n. 4, 463 & n. 3.
Building materials: marble (*cont.*)
— use of: in England, iv. 122; ~ warehouse for, iv. 98; at Genoa, i. 109; ii. 174 (i. 110), 176 & n. 7 (i. 111).
mud: in Leicestershire, iii. 122.
ophite (serpentine), ii. 181 & n. 4 (i. 114), 185 (i. 117), 438 & n. 4 (error), 444.
paragon, ii. 416 (*see* ii. 199, n. 2).
piles: as foundations, ii. 48 (i. 34), 446, n. 4, 459.
plaster, ii. 350; ceilings of, ii. 308–9; floors of, ii. 174 & n. 1 (i. 110 & n. 1); pargeting, ii. 235.
porphyry, ii. 460 & n. 7.
Portland stone, i. 81 & n. 1, 84; iii. 459; v. 541; quarries of: sinkage at, v. 230 & n. 6.
pozzolana, ii. 344 & n. 2.
slate: quarries of, ii. 122 (i. 78); blue: use of: at Euston, iv. 116; ~ in Loire towns, ii. 143 & n. 3 (i. 93).
Spartan stone, ii. 460 & n. 7.
stone: in Leicestershire, iii. 122 & n. 2; *see also* free-stone *above*.
Tiburtine stone (i.e. travertine), ii. 249 & n. 6.
timber: houses of, ii. 124 (i. 79); iv. 144, 255; use of, at Geneva (the *dômes*), ii. 524 & n. 4.
touch, ii. 199 & n. 2.
Bulkeley, Sir Richard, bt.: chariot invented by, iv. 483–4 & n.
Bull, Dr. — (Richard Ball?): sermon by, iii. 265 & n. 2.
Bull, George, D.D.; bishop of St. Davids 1705: ordination of, iii. 172, n. 1.
Bullack, John, of Dover, iv. 80 & n. 2.
Bull-baiting: in London, iii. 549; iv. 362; in Paris, ii. 567; at Venice, ii. 474 & n. 2.
Bullion: Duke of: *see* Bouillon.
Bulteel, John: social (?; as Bolteele), iii. 392 & n. 5.
Bunyan, John: called Sir John Shorter's chaplain, iv. 562, n. 4.
Buonarotti, Michelangelo: *see* Michelangelo.
Buonconvento, ii. 206 & n. 6.
Buontalenti, Bernardo: ciborium designed by, ii. 191 & n. 9 (i. 119), 199.
Buoy of the Nore, the, iii. 413, n. 2; fleet at: 1665, iii. 413–14 & n.; ~ 1666, iii. 436 & n. 2, 441 & n. 4;

Buoy of the Nore (*cont.*)
~ 1672, iii. 620, 623; Sandwich at, 1665, iii. 418, n. 5; Dutch fleet near, 1667, iii. 486 & n. 2, 489 & n. 1; captured Spanish ship at, 1702, v. 522 & n. 1.
Burch, Hendrik van der, painter, ii. 29, n. 1.
Burckhorst, Jacob, iii. 420 & n. 4.
Burford: Earl of, 1676–84; *see* Beauclerk, Charles, duke of St. Albans.
Burgh, Dr. —: error for W. Brough (?), iii. 239 & n. 4.
Burghesi: *see* Borghese.
Burghley: Baron: *see* Cecil, William.
Burgundy: French protestants seek refuge in, iv. 448; Burgundian Jew at Leyden, ii. 54–5 & n. (i. 37–8).
Burgundy: Duke of, 1682–1711: *see* Louis de France.
Burleigh House, Stamford: garden of: plan for, iv. 350–1.
Burley-on-the-Hill (Burleigh House), Rutland: notice, iii. 124 & n. 2; marriage at, v. 208 & n. 2; stable of: burnt, v. 586 & n. 2.
Burlington: Earls, &c., of: *see* Boyle, Richard, second earl of Cork, &c., first earl, 1664–98; Boyle, Elizabeth, Baroness Clifford, his countess; Boyle, Charles, second earl, 1698–1704.
Burnet, Col. Alexander: death of, &c., ii. 503–5 & nn.
Burnet, Mrs. Elizabeth, wife of (1) Robert Berkeley; (2) Dr. Gilbert Burnet (his third wife), iv. 345, n. 4; estate of, in Clerkenwell, iv. 363, n. 4; sister of, iv. 363 & n. 5.
Burnet, Gilbert; D.D. 1680; bishop of Salisbury 1689–1715; author of *History of my own time*, &c., iv. 47–8 & n.
personal: doctorate of, iv. 205, n. 3; *see also* iv. 47, n. 5; lodgings of, 1682–3, iv. 301, n. 1; house of, in Clerkenwell, iv. 363, n. 4; portrait of, iv. 642 & n. 3; geneal., ii. 503, n. 3; third wife of: *see* Burnet, Mrs. Elizabeth.
appointments: minister of Rolls Chapel, iv. 282, n. 2; Thursday lecturer at St. Clement Danes, iv. 309, n. 2; nominated bishop of Salisbury, &c., iv. 632, n. 6.
miscellaneous activities, &c.: recognizes character of Titus Oates, iv. 153, n. 4 *ad fin.*; on William Wotton's precocity, iv. 172–3; attends Col. Vratz at his execution, iv. 274, n. 1; warns Dr. G. Morley of impending attack on him, iv. 283, n. 1; investigates Essex's death, iv. 326, n. 4 *ad fin.*; comes to London, Dec. 1688, iv. 612, n. 1; on case of conscience, v. 338–9; on frequent communion, i. *30*, n. 1; social, iv. 124, 205, 300–1; mentioned, iv. 633, n. 3.
relations with E: E lends MSS. to, &c., iv. 241 & n. 3; as possible informant of E, iv. 274, n. 1, 624, n. 1; has informant in common with E, iv. 409, nn. 2, 3; on E's character, i. *39*; iv. 241, n. 3.
as preacher: manner, iv. 47–8 & n.; v. 619; sermons by: printed: coronation of William and Mary, iv. 632 & n. 6; funeral of R. Boyle, v. 81–3 & nn.; thanksgiving for Peace of Ryswick, v. 277 & n. 3; Reformation of Manners, v. 391–2 & n.; unprinted, iv. 47–8, 121, 282, 309, 623, 641 & n. 1; v. 11–12, 559 & n. 3, 618–19.
See also Books mentioned in text; Books mentioned in notes.
Burnett family, of Leys, ii. 503, n. 3.
Burnham, Bucks.: manor of: *see* Huntercombe.
Burnham, Somerset: church at: sculpture from Whitehall in, iv. 534, n. 1.
Burning Bush, the: in sermon, iv. 87–8.
Burrough Green (Borough Green, &c.), Cambs.: house of Henry Slingsby at, iii. 335, n. 2, 552–3 & nn., 556.
Burstall, Robert: *see* Birstall.
Burton *or* Buxton, —, of Thorpe, Derbyshire (?), iv. 415.
Burton, Rev. —: sermon by, iv. 192.
Burton, Anne, Lady Burton, wife of Sir Thomas, third bt.: mentioned (?), iv. 461 & n. 1.
Burton, Elizabeth, Lady Burton, wife of Sir Thomas, second bt., and secondly of Sir William Halford: mentioned (?), iv. 461 & n. 1.
Burton, James, sheriff of Surrey 1673: his daughter's wedding, iv. 352 & n. 1; mentioned, iv. 484, n. 2.

Burton, Sir Thomas, of Stockerston, second bt.: geneal., iv. 461, n. 1.
Burton, Sir Thomas, of Stockerston, third bt.: geneal., iv. 461, n. 1.
Bury St. Edmunds (St. Edmondsbury, Berry), Suffolk: notice, 1677, iv. 113 & nn. 5, 6; mentioned, iv. 113, 120; preacher at: *see* Clagett, W. (iv. 113, n. 2); house of Lord Crofts near, iv. 113 & n. 4.
Busby, Richard, master of Westminster School: dies, v. 208 & n. 3.
Buschetus (Busqueto Delichio), architect, ii. 408 & n. 5.
Buscot, Berks.: rector of: *see* Hungerford, W.
Bushell, Thomas: waterworks of, at Enstone, iii. 382 & n. 6.
Bushey Park, Hampton Court, iii. 324, nn. 5, 6.
Bushnell, John, sculptor: monument by, to Lord Mordaunt, iv. 86 & n. 5; statue given to, iii. 460, n. 8.
Businello, G. F.: opera libretti by, ii. 474, n. 6.
Busse, the: *see* 's Hertogenbosch.
Butler, —, daughter of Thomas Butler, earl of Ossory: visits E, 1684, iv. 361 & n. 1.
Butler, Amelia (Emilia), countess of Ossory, d. 1688; born de Beverweerd; wife of Thomas Butler, styled earl of Ossory, iv. 102, n. 9; letter to, iv. 211 & n. 3; social: parties, iv. 102, 105, 368 & n. 4; alone, &c., iv. 112 *bis*, 131, 545(?); geneal., iii. 622, n. 5; iv. 102, n. 10, 222, n. 2.
Butler, Anne, countess of Ossory 1682–5; born Hyde; first wife of James Butler, styled earl of Ossory, later second duke of Ormond, iv. 297 & n. 6, 483, n. 1; marriage of, iv. 297; social, iv. 368 & n. 4.
Butler, Charles, earl of Arran: appointment for, v. 321, n. 1.
Butler, Lady Elizabeth: *see* Stanhope, Elizabeth, countess of Chesterfield.
Butler, Elizabeth: *see* Stanley, Elizabeth, countess of Derby.
Butler, Elizabeth, duchess of Ormond, d. 1684; wife of James Butler, first duke, &c., iii. 76, n. 1; in England: 1652, iii. 76 & n. 1; ~ 1660, iii. 263; goes to Ireland, 1662, iii. 326; visits Roehampton House, iv. 105; mentioned, iii. 2, n. 4.
Butler, James, 1610–88; twelfth earl, 1633, marquis, 1642, and first duke, 1661, of Ormond, iii. 2, n. 6.
life to 1662: in Paris, 1651, iii. 26 & n. 1; at Caen, iii. 26, n 2, 47, n. 1; as intermediary between Charles II and Dr. J. Hewit, 1658, iii. 216 & n. 9; act of parliament restoring Irish estates of, 1660, iii. 252; created duke, 1661, iii. 284 & n. 5; takes part in Twelfth Night gaming at court, iii. 308; dines with James, duke of York, at Deptford, iii. 312–13.
appointments, &c.: as Lord Steward of the Household: orders survey of ground at Sayes Court, iii. 262 & n. 3; ~ attends the king in parliament, 1665, iii. 402 & n. 3; as Lord Lieutenant of Ireland, first term, 1662–9 [he was in England in 1664–5 and 1668–9]: appointed, iii. 326, n. 7; ~ goes to Ireland, iii. 326 & n. 7; ~ mock-criticism of, by Sir W. Petty, iv. 59–60; as Chancellor of University of Oxford: created D.C.L., iii. 535–6 & n.; ~ E asks for patronage of, iv. 111–12 & n.; as member of Council for Foreign Plantations, &c., iii. 571, n. 1; ~ attends meetings, iii. 598, 629; as Lord Lieutenant of Ireland, second term, 1677–85: goes to Ireland, iv. 111.
life from 1662: views of, on Lord Russell's trial, &c., iv. 327, nn. 2, 3, 328, nn. 2, 3; services of, to the crown, &c., iv. 209, 210; social: parties, &c., iii. 379, 389, 512; iv. 2, 65, 67, 103; residences of: lodgings in Whitehall, iii. 284, n. 5; ~ occupied by Ossory, iv. 208, n. 7; in Chelsea, 1664, iii. 376 & n. 5; at Clarendon House, 1672, iii. 629 & n. 2.
relations of, with E: describes Ireland for E, iii. 303; presents E to Queen Catherine, iii. 321; social, iii. 376, 537, 624; iv. 108.

Butler, James (*cont.*)
relations of, with other persons: friendship of, with Col. E. Cooke, iv. 360, n. 3; sends letter by (Sir) A. Slingsby, ii. 560, n. 2; Lady Isabella Thynne as mistress of (?), ii. 549, n. 9 *ad fin.*; secretary of: *see* Lane, Sir George, Viscount Lanesborough.
geneal., iii. 2 & nn. 4, 5, 535, n. 5; iv. 105, 498, n. 2.
Butler, James, 1665–1745; styled earl of Ossory 1680–8; second duke of Ormond 1688, iv. 287, n. 5.
as Lord Ossory: marriages of: first, iv. 297 & n. 6; ~ second, iv. 483, n. 1; social, iv. 287, 483.
as duke: wounded at Landen, &c., v. 149 & nn. 5, 6; protests against promotion of Albemarle (Keppel), v. 320–1 & n., 323 & n. 2, 325 & n. 5; in command of English troops in expedition to Cadiz, 1702: declaration of, concerning Spanish Succession, v. 515 & n. 3; ~ success of, at Vigo, v. 519 & n. 2; returns to London, v. 520 & n. 4.
Butler, John, D.D.: sermon by, iv. 157 & n. 2.
Butler, Mary, duchess of Ormond, second wife of James Butler, second duke, iv. 483 & n. 1; as Lady Ossory: social, iv. 483, 545 (?).
Butler, Lady Mary: *see* Cavendish, Lady Mary, duchess of Devonshire, &c.
Butler, Lord Richard; created earl of Arran (Ireland) 1662, iii. 2, n. 5; in Paris, 1650–1: at del Campo's academy, iii. 2 & n. 4; ~ in 'Bataille de Vambre', iii. 4; ~ visits E, iii. 37; goes to Caen, iii. 47; in Ireland, 1682, iv. 296, n. 3; social (?), iv. 466 & n. 1; attends James II at Winchester (?), iv. 468, 470 & n. 1.
Butler, Thomas; styled earl of Ossory 1642–80, iii. 2, n. 4; character, iv. 209, 210–11.
in Paris 1650–1: at del Campo's academy, iii. 2 & n. 4; iv. 210; ~ in 'Bataille de Vambre', iii. 4, 8; ~ visits E, iii. 37; goes to Caen, iii. 47; in London 1653–6, iii. 251, n. 7; ~ visits E, iii. 87, 91; returns to London, 1660, iii. 251 & n. 7.
and attack on Dutch Smyrna fleet, 1672: takes part in, iii. 605–6 & n.; ~ disapproves of, iv. 211; created K.G., iii. 629 & n. 2; and Trinity House: sworn a younger brother, iv. 6; ~ as Master of, 1675–6, iv. 64, 91; journeys of, to Netherlands: July 1677, iv. 112 & n. 2; ~ Jan. 1678, first and second sailings, iv. 127 *bis* & nn. 1, 3; ~ July 1678, iv. 137 & n. 5; at French church in London, iv. 168; quarrel of, with Sunderland, iv. 209 & n. 1; last illness, death, &c., iv. 208–11 & nn.
letters of, to Ormond and Sunderland, July 1680, iv. 208–9 & n.; social: parties, iii. 600; iv. 94, 95, 105, 136, 187, 190, 191; ~ alone, &c., iv. 2, 103, 107, 122; lodgings of, in Whitehall, iv. 64, 208 & n. 7, 210.
chaplain(s) of: sermons by, iv. 8, 91; ~ *see also* Young, Rev. Edward; secretary of, 1680 (R. Mulys), iv. 208, n. 8; servant of: wedding of, iv. 194; geneal., iii. 4, n. 2; iv. 97–8, 287 & n. 5, 361 & n. 1.
Butler of Moore Park: Baron: *see* Butler, Thomas, earl of Ossory.
Buxton *or* Burton, —, of Thorpe, Derbyshire (?), iv. 415.
Buyster, P., sculptor: statues by (?), iii. 18 & n. 3.
Buzzi, Carlo, architect: design by, for façade of Milan cathedral, ii. 492, n. 2.
Byfleet, Surrey: Manor House, iv. 141 & n. 3; paper-mill at, iv. 141–2 & n.
Byrd, William, of Oxford: *see* Bird.
Byron, Elizabeth, Baroness Byron; born Stonhouse: wife of (1) Sir Richard Stiddolph (*d.* 1677); (2) William Byron, Baron Byron: as Lady Stiddolph: social, iv. 137 & n. 4.
Byron, Sir John, first Baron Byron (Biron): attends Charles II in Paris, 1651, iii. 51 & n. 5.

Byron, Richard, second Baron Byron (Biron): owner of Newstead Abbey, iii. 126 & n. 7.
Byron, William, third Baron Byron: geneal., iv. 137, n. 4.
Byron: Barons, &c.: *see* Byron, Sir John, first baron, 1643–52; Byron, Richard, second baron, 1652–79; Byron, William, third baron, 1679–95; Byron, Elizabeth, his baroness.
Bysshe, Sir Edward, Clarenceux king of arms: in Garter feast, 1667, iii. 479 & n. 7.
Byzantium: *see* Constantinople.

Cabo Verde: *see* Santiago de Cabo Verde.
Caccini, G. B., sculptor, &c., ii. 187, n. 8; statue by, ii. 185 & n. 3 (i. 117); altar designed by, ii. 187–8 & n. (i. 118).
Cacus, ii. 228 & n. 1.
Cade, Salusbury, M.D., v. 190, n. 5; attends Mrs. Susanna Draper, v. 190; and Greenwich Hospital, v. 399, n. 2.
Cadenham, Bremhill, Wilts.: house of Edward Hungerford, iii. 100–1 & n.; E and Mrs. Evelyn at, iii. 100–1, 103, 111–13, 116–17; mentioned, iii. 99, n. 4, 118, n. 5.
Cadet-la-Perle: see Harcourt, Henri de Lorraine, comte d'.
Cadiz (Cales): capture of Spanish plate ships near, 1656, iii. 188, n. 3; attack on Dutch Smyrna convoy near, 1664, iii. 407 & n. 6; *see also* iii. 404 & n. 4; English Smyrna fleet at, 1691, v. 60 & n. 3; French fleet near, 1693, v. 145, n. 4; ships from Allies' Smyrna fleet at, 1693, v. 150 & n. 2; Allied expedition against, 1702, v. 515–19 & nn., *passim*.
Cadogan, William, first Earl Cadogan: owner of Caversham Park, iii. 99, n. 3.
Cadogan, first Earl: *see* Cadogan, William.
Caecubus, Mount, ii. 322 & n. 7.
Caen (Cane), Normandy: notice, 1644, ii. 126–7 & nn. (i. 80–1); Ormond at, 1651, iii. 26, n. 2; ~ and his sons, iii. 47 & n. 1; Lord Inchiquin at, iii. 26, n. 2; students at, iii. 633; ~ Sir William Petty, iv. 56, n. 6 *ad fin*.
Caesar: generic, &c.: tribute to: from Pisa, ii. 181 (i. 114); ~ in sermon, v. 288; portraits of: in sermon, iv. 561; ~ gold coin or medal of, iii. 339; ~ *see also* Claudius. For Caesar meaning Julius Caesar *see* Julius Caesar.
Caesar, Charles: accuses Godolphin, v. 619 & n. 1.
Caesar, Rev. John, vicar of Croydon: sermon by, v. 427 & n. 2.
Caesars, the Twelve: sets of busts of: *see* Sculpture, Ancient; Sculpture, Medieval and Modern.
Caetani (Cajetan, Gaetani), Enrico, cardinal: tomb of, ii. 246 & n. 5.
Cage, Ann: *see* Slingsby, Mrs. A.
Cage, Sir Anthony: geneal., &c., iii. 335, n. 2, 553, n. 1.
Cain, &c.: in sermons, iv. 26; v. 62.
Cairasca, river, ii. 508, n. 5.
Cairo: inscribed stone from, ii. 469 & nn. 3, 4; iii. 171–2; trade in mummies at, ii. 469, n. 5.
Cajeta: *see* Gaeta.
Cajetan, Cardinal: *see* Caetani, E.
Calabria: revenue of, ii. 352 & n. 6.
Calais (Calis, Calice): notices: 1643, ii. 82–3 & nn. (i. 56); ~ 1649, ii. 560 & nn.; castle at, ii. 559; environs: marshes, ii. 83; ~ capable of being flooded for defence of Calais, ii. 560 & n. 6; ~ in comparison, iii. 130; road from, towards Paris: dangers of, 1650, iii. 16; straits of: *see* Dover Straits.
  E at, &c.: 1641, ii. 76 (i. 50); 1643, ii. 82–3 & nn. (i. 56); 1647, ii. 537; 1649, ii. 559–60; June 1650, iii. 12–13 (journey from Paris to, iii. 12); Aug. 1650, iii. 16; 1652, iii. 54–6 (packages sent to, iii. 53).
  Henrietta Anne (Madame) at, 1670, iii. 549 & n. 1; accident at pier, 1685, iv. 432; Queen Mary of Modena and James Edward at, 1688, iv. 612, n. 4; bombarded, 1695, v. 216 & n. 3, 218; James II and French army at, 1696, v. 231–2 & n.; French fleet at, 1696, v. 234.
  Lieutenant-governor of, 1649, ii. 560; Charles II's agent at, 1649–50: *see* Booth, Henry (iii. 12 & n. 7, 55); various English persons (named) at, 1649, 1650, ii. 560; iii. 55.

Calamy, Benjamin, D.D., iv. 229 & n. 2; sermons by: printed (?), iv. 397 & n. 3, 398 & n. 1; unprinted, iv. 229, 297.
Calamy, Rev. Edmund, sen.: geneal., iv. 229 & n. 2.
Caldara, Polidoro, da Caravaggio, iii. 75, n. 2; as Polydor: paintings by, iii. 75, 339.
Calderon de la Barca, Pedro: *see* Plays.
Caldwell (Colwall) family, v. 358 & n. 3.
Caldwell, Daniel: geneal., ii. 24, n. 2.
Caldwell, Mary: *see* Evelyn, Mrs. Mary, wife of George Evelyn.
Caldwell, Mrs. Mary: geneal., ii. 24, n. 2.
Cales: *see* Cadiz.
Calf, the Golden: in sermon, v. 347.
Calf *or* Colfe, Rev. Abraham, vicar of Lewisham, iii. 60, n. 1.
Caligula: obelisk erected by, ii. 256, n. 1; bridge of, at Pozzuoli, ii. 344 & n. 3.
Calixtus I, pope, ii. 289, n. 3.
Callao, Peru: flooded, 1687, iv. 586, n. 1.
Calloo, fort on the Scheldt, ii. 62 & n. 7 (i. 43).
Callot (Calot), Jacques: prints by, ii. 133 & n. 1.
Callwell, Daniel: *see* Colwall.
Calpurnius, L., ii. 343 & n. 7.
Calvert, Charles, third Lord Baltimore: inherits Woodcote Park, ii. 542, n. 3.
Calverton, Notts.: incumbent of: *see* Lee, William.
Calvin, Jean, the Reformer: church discipline of, ii. 527; heterodox opinion of, v. 137 & n. 2; allows regicide: in sermon, iv. 405; views of: attacked in sermon, iv. 86.
Calvinists ('those of Geneva'): censured in sermon, iii. 34.
Cam, river: at Audley End, iii. 141 & n. 1.
Camaret Bay: attempted English landing at, 1694, v. 184 *bis* & n. 3.
Cambert, R.: composes music for *Ariane*, iv. 30, n. 1.
Cambio, Arnolfo di (Arnulpho Lupo): builds Florence cathedral, ii. 196 & n. 8.
Cambrai: military operations near, 1649, ii. 561, n. 1.
Cambridge: notice, 1654, iii. 136–40 & nn.
Cambridge (*cont.*)
— the town: streets, &c., iii. 140 & nn. 5, 6; St. Mary's church, iii. 140; Sturbridge fair, iii. 138 & n. 4; John Churchill, marquis of Blandford, dies at, v. 530; Queen Anne visits, 1705, v. 591 & n. 3, 592, n. 2.
— University: puritanism at, iii. 139, n. 5; Dr. J. Wilkins as preserver of, during Protectorate, iii. 165 & n. 8; Schools building, iii. 140 & n. 2; University Library, iii. 140 & nn. 3, 4; ~ books from Lambeth Palace library (Archbishop Bancroft's bequest) at, iii. 140 & n. 3; *add.*; iii. 527, n. 1; ~ gift to, from George I, v. 206, n. 3, 325, n. 8.
— — dignitaries, &c.: chancellor, 1674–82: *see* Scott, James, duke of Monmouth; Regius professors: of Divinity: *see* Gunning, P. (1661–72); James, Henry (1699–1717); ~ of Greek: *see* Duport, J. (1639–54); Creighton, Robert, jnr. (1666–72); the *Praevaricator*, iii. 104, n. 6.
— — colleges: general: in comparison, i. 62 (*see also* ii. 94, n. 1); Caius, iii. 138; Christ's, iii. 139–40 & n.; ~ master, 1688–1722: *see* Covel, J.; Clare, iii. 138 & n. 6; Corpus Christi: master, 1693–8: *see* Stanley, William; Emmanuel, iii. 139 & nn. 5–8; ~ master, 1665–76: *see* Breton, John; Jesus, iii. 139 & n. 9; ~ masters: *see* Beaumont, Joseph (1662–3); Boldero, E. (1663–79); King's, iii. 138 & nn. 1–3; ~ scholars at: election of, at Eton, iv. 208 & n. 2; ~ provost, 1712–20: *see* Adams, John; ~ fellows: *see* Wase, C.; Wells, Rev. William; ~ member of: *see* Churchill, John, marquis of Blandford (v. 531 & n. 3); Magdalene: Pepysian Library: MSS. in, iv. 241, n. 3, 303, n. 3; ~ master, 1668–79: *see* Duport, J.; Pembroke: masters: *see* Andrewes, L. (1589–1605); Frank, Mark (1662–4); Peterhouse, iii. 138–9 & nn.; ~ masters: *see* Cosin, John, sen.

Cambridge: Colleges (*cont.*) (1634–44, 1660); Beaumont, Joseph (1663–99); ~ fellows: R. Crashaw and three others converted to Roman Catholicism, iii. 46, n. 4; ~ member of: *see* Keightley, T.; Queens': president, 1675–1717: *see* James, Henry; St. Catharine's Hall (Kathrine Hall), iii. 139 & nn. 3, 4; St. John's, iii. 136 & nn. 2–6; ~ books given to, iii. 137 & nn. 3, 4; ~ president, 1661–70: *see* Gunning, P.; Sidney Sussex, iii. 139 & n. 2; Trinity, iii. 136–8 & nn.; ~ scholars at: election of, at Westminster, iii. 287–8 & n.; ~ masters: *ex officio* electors of scholars from Westminster, iii. 287, n. 5; ~ individual masters: *see* Comber, Thomas (1631–45); North, John (1677–83); Montagu, John (1683–1700); Bentley, R. (1700–42); ~ fellows: *see* Pearson, John (master, 1662–72); a fellow, unnamed: preaches at Deptford, iv. 172.

Cambridge: Duke of, 1664–7: *see* Stuart, James.

Camera obscura, iii. 549 & n. 2.

Camilla (*Aeneid*): birth-place of, ii. 318.

Camisards, v. 545, n. 4, 563, n. 1.

Campagna, Girolamo (H. Compagno): sculptures by, ii. 445 & n. 5, 454 & n. 7.

Campania: plains of (Terra di Lavoro): fertility of, ii. 324–5 & nn.

Campbell, Archibald; eighth earl, 1638, and marquis, 1641, of Argyll, iii. 175, n. 2; visits E, iii. 175, 186; execution of, iii. 318 & n. 2.

Campbell, Archibald; ninth earl of Argyll 1663, iii. 318, n. 2; visits Sayes Court, iii. 318; rebellion of, 1685, iv. 443 & n. 1, 446 & n. 3; ~ suppression of: thanksgiving for, iv. 460 & n. 1; captured, &c., iv. 450 & n. 4.

Campbell, Archibald; tenth earl and first duke of Argyll: geneal., v. 41 & n. 1.

Campbell, Captain James: abducts Mary Wharton, v. 41 & n. 1.

Campbell, Dr. John : on E (1750), i. *39*.

Campden: Viscounts, &c.: *see* Hicks, Baptist, first viscount; Noel, Edward, second viscount; Noel, Juliana, his viscountess.

Campion (Champion), Edmund, S.J.: in painting, ii. 366 & n. 2.

Campo, — del: riding-academy of, in Paris: display at, iii. 2 & n. 3.

Campo, G. B. del: children of, baptized, iv. 222 & n. 3.

Camulodunum (Camelodunum, &c.): identified as Maldon, Essex, iii. 180 & n. 2.

Can *or* Cann, Dr. —: *see* Ken, T.

Cana in Galilee: water-pot from, ii. 89 (i. 60); miracle at: in sermon, iii. 29.

Canaan *or* the Promised Land: in sermons, v. 14, 114, 268–9, 273–5, 306, 309, 564.

Canaanites: in sermons, iv. 556; v. 63.

Canals and Waterways [described or traversed by E, excluding his journey from Dort to Antwerp (ii. 59–63 & i. 41–3) and the Thames. Canals as means of communication in towns (as at Amsterdam) and as features of gardens or parks are not indexed collectively]: Amsterdam-Haarlem, ii. 49 (i. 35); Antwerp-Brussels, ii. 67–9 & n. (i. 45–6); Avernus-Ostia (Nero's project), ii. 347 & n. 1; Bologna-Ferrara, ii. 426–7 & nn.; Brenta, ii. 452 & nn. 2–5; Bruges-Ostend, ii. 75 (i. 49); Ferrara-[Brondolo ?], ii. 428 & nn. 5, 6; Ghent-Bruges, ii. 74 & n. 5 (i. 48–9); The Hague-Leyden-Utrecht: alluded to, ii. 34 (i. 27); Pisa-Leghorn, ii. 183 & n. 4 (i. 115); ~ alluded to, ii. 182 (i. 114); Richelieu, ii. 150 (i. 97); Rotterdam-The Hague, ii. 33 & n. 6 (i. 25); 's Hertogenbosch, ii. 58 (i. 39–40); 's Hertogenbosch-Dort, ii. 59 (i. 40); Waal, ii. 38–9 (i. 28–9).

— sluices (locks), ii. 426–7 & n., 452 & n. 4.

Canary Company: charter, iii. 388 & n. 5; governor of: *see* Ingram, Sir A. (iii. 448 & n. 1).

Canary Islands: English traders to, petition for charter, &c., iii. 388 & n. 5; *see also* Tenerife.

Candia (Candy), Crete: Venetian conquest of, ii. 431; attacked by Turks: 1645, ii. 452 & n. 1; ~ 1668, iii. 515 & n. 4; English ship pressed to go to, ii. 451–2, 468; Venetian galleys for, ii. 470, 475; officer going to, ii. 476–7; a Candiot, ii. 460.
Canea, Crete: attacked by Turks, ii. 452, n. 1.
Cannes (Canes), Provence, ii. 167 & n. 6 (i. 105–6); journey to, ii. 166 (i. 105).
Cante, Matthew: miraculous cure of, iv. 469 & n. 2.
Canterbury: E visits: 1641, ii. 76 (i. 50); 1650, iii. 13, 15–16; 1652, iii. 56; 1665, iii. 395, 409 *bis*, 410; 1672, iii. 610, 614, 616; 1675, iv. 79, 80.
— cathedral: windows of, and their destruction, ii. 76 & n. 3 (i. 50); repairs to, after 1660, iii. 395 & n. 2; history of the archbishops (MS.) displayed in, ii. 559, n. 2; services, &c., in, iii. 610, 616 (?); iv. 79, 80.
— cathedral clergy:
— — archbishops: *ex officio* visitors of Merton College, Oxford, iii. 273; palace of, at Croydon, iv. 73, n. 6; v. 426; history (MS.) of, displayed in Canterbury cathedral, ii. 559, n. 2; tombs of, at Croydon, v. 426 & n. 5; Prerogative Court of: judge of: *see* Meyrick, Sir W.; ~ registrar of: *see* Cottle, M.; ~ R. Hoare employed in, ii. 559, n. 2; Vicar-general of: *see* Chaworth, Sir R.
— — individual archbishops: *see* Bancroft, R. (1604–10); Abbot, George (1611–33); Laud, W. (1633–45); Juxon, W. (1660–3); Sheldon, Gilbert (1663–77); Sancroft, W. (1678–90); Tillotson, J. (1691–4); Tenison, T. (1694–1715); Wake, William (1716–37); *see also* v. 426, n. 5.
— — deans: *see* Turner, Thomas (1644–72); Tillotson, J. (1672–89); Sharp, John (1689–91); Hooper, George (1691–1703); Stanhope, George (1704–28).
— — canons, &c.: *see* Bargrave, J.; Castillion, J.; Gostling, J.; Hérault, L.
Canterbury (*cont.*)
— — archdeacon: error for dean (Dr. G. Hooper), v. 380 & n. 4.
— dean of the Arches, 1660–72: *see* Sweet, Sir G.
— province of: Convocation of: *see* Church of England: organization.
Canterbury: Thomas of: *see* Thomas, St., à Becket.
Canton: book published at, by Franciscans, iii. 374, n. 7.
Cap fino (Portofino), ii. 178 & n. 9 (i. 113); *add.*
Cape of Good Hope: Sir J. Chardin at, iv. 212, n. 2.
Capel, Surrey: minister of: *see* Higham, John.
Capel, Algernon; second earl of Essex 1683, iv. 201 & n. 4; education of, *ib.*; appointed constable of the Tower 1705, v. 611, n. 4 *ad fin.*; social, iv. 383; mentioned, iv. 328, n. 2.
Capel, Anne: *see* Howard, Anne, countess of Carlisle.
Capel, Arthur, 1610–49; first Baron Capel of Hadham 1641, ii. 548, n. 2; trial and execution of, ii. 548 & n. 2, 552 & n. 1; ~ account of, by Col. S. Tuke (?), iii. 249–50 & n.; ~ mentioned, &c., iv. 201, 328, n. 2; acquires Cassiobury Park, iv. 199, n. 2; geneal., iii. 159 & n. 7, 482, n. 2; iv. 559, n. 2.
Capel, Arthur, 1632–83; second Baron Capel of Hadham 1649; earl of Essex 1661, iii. 371, n. 1; character and political career of, iv. 200–2 & nn.; created earl, iii. 277; as lord lieutenant of Ireland, iv. 199 & n. 6, 201; account by, of Lady Ogle's marriage to T. Thynne, iv. 260–1 & nn.; social: parties, iii. 371; iv. 181; ~ alone, iv. 238; imprisoned for Rye-House Plot, iv. 322 & n. 3; complicity of, in general plot, iv. 323 & n. 7, 329; commits suicide, iv. 326–9 & nn.; Charles II's attitude towards, iv. 328 & n. 2; generally regretted, iv. 329; *see also* i. 29 *bis*; attempt to prove that he was murdered, iv. 326, n. 4 *ad fin.*, 367 & n. 1; houses of: Cassiobury Park, iv. 199–200 & nn., ~ in London, iv. 199 & n. 3, 238; geneal., iii. 482, n. 2; iv. 327–8 & n.

Capel, Dorothy, Lady Capell, wife of Sir Henry Capel, Baron Capell, mentioned (name not stated), iv. 144, n. 1.
Capel, Elizabeth, Baroness Capel, wife of Arthur Capel, first baron: petition of, to house of lords, iii. 250, n. 1.
Capel, Elizabeth, countess of Essex, wife of Arthur Capel, first earl, iv. 201 & n. 2; asks Burnet to investigate Essex's suicide, iv. 326, n. 4 *ad fin.*; geneal., iv. 260 & n. 4, 261, n. 1, 327, n. 3.
Capel, Sir Henry; created Baron Capell of Tewkesbury 1692, iii. 482, n. 2; appointed a commissioner of the Admiralty, 1679, iv. 171 & n. 2; at Cassiobury, iv. 347; created baron, v. 90 & n. 3; appointed a lord justice of Ireland, 1693, v. 150 & n. 5; house and garden of, at Kew, iv. 144 & n. 1, 347, 576; social, iii. 482; iv. 465.
Capel, Theodosia: *see* Hyde, Theodosia, Lady Cornbury.
Capel of Hadham: Barons: *see* Capel, Arthur, first baron, 1641–9; Capel, Arthur, second baron, 1649–61, later earl of Essex.
Capell of Tewkesbury: Baron: *see* Capel, Sir Henry.
Cappel (Capellus), Jacques-Louis: gift from, to Bishop Lloyd, iv. 641 & n. 4.
Cappel, Louis: *see* Books mentioned in text.
Capponi, Luigi, cardinal, ii. 213 & n. 6.
Capponi (Caponi), Pietro, Count, envoy from Tuscany, 1686, iv. 499 & nn. 1, 2.
Capra, Count Mario: villa of, at Vicenza, ii. 484 & n. 3.
Capranica: road through, ii. 211 & n. 2.
Caprarola: palace and town of, ii. 406–7 & nn.
Capri (Capra): in views, ii. 326 & n. 2, 329, 334.
Capriani, Francesco, called Francesco da Volterra: building designed by, ii. 373 & n. 8.
Capua, ii. 324 & n. 6; ancient: ruins of, ii. 324 & nn. 3–5; mentioned, ii. 315, n. 1, 319.
Caracalla, Roman emperor: buildings of, at Rome: baths, ii. 361 & n. 3; ~ bridge (Ponte Sisto), ii. 384 & n. 2; ~ circus (error), ii. 362 & nn. 3–6; bust of, ii. 310, n. 1.
Caraccio: *see* Carracci.
Carafa, dukes of Maddaloni: palace of, at Naples, ii. 330 & n. 1.
Caravaggio, Michelangelo Merisi, called, ii. 113, n. 4; paintings: by, ii. 113 & n. 4 (i. 73), 233 & n. 5, 374 & n. 6; in manner of, ii. 424 & n. 4.
Caravaggio, Polidoro Caldara da: *see* Caldara.
Carbery: third Earl of, 1686–1713: *see* Vaughan, John.
Cardano (Cardan), Girolamo: on Edward VI, iv. 216 & n. 2.
Cardigan: Earls of: *see* Brudenell, Sir Thomas, first earl; Brudenell, Robert, second earl.
Cardinal Infante: *see* Ferdinand of Austria.
Cardinals [select references]: a titular church, ii. 359; lodgings of, during papal elections, ii. 302 & n. 7; red hats of, i. 103; *see also* ii. 400 & n. 2; present: at ceremonies, ii. 281, 377–8, 384; ~ at an opera, ii. 388–9; ~ at a play (Jesuit), ii. 291.
Cards and card-playing, iii. 308, 590; iv. 338, 422; basset: in Venice, ii. 451 & n. 1, 474; ~ at court, iv. 413, 519, 625. *See also* Gaming.
Carew (Carie) family: seat of, at Beddington, i. 9 & n. 2; iii. 221; v. 427; owners of Sutton, ii. 11, n. 3.
Carew, —, cousin of E, v. 183 & n. 2.
Carew, —, performer on Welsh harp, ii. 556.
Carew, —: social, iii. 378.
Carew, Anne: *see* Throckmorton, Anne, Lady Throckmorton.
Carew, Elizabeth, *rectè* Carey: *see* Mordaunt, Elizabeth, Viscountess Mordaunt.
Carew, John, regicide: executed, iii. 259 & n. 2.
Carew, Sir Nicholas, d. 1539: geneal., &c., i. 9, n. 2.
Carew, Sir Nicholas, formerly Throckmorton, d. 1644: owner of Beddington, i. 9 & n. 2.
Carew, Sir Nicholas, bt., 1687–1727: owner of Beddington, v. 427 & n. 1.

Carey, Abigail, countess of Dover, wife of John Carey, second earl: social (?), iv. 498 & n. 3.
Carey (Cary), Anthony; fifth viscount of Falkland 1663, iv. 318, n. 4; character and career of, v. 182–3 & n.; as Treasurer of the Navy, iv. 384 & n. 4; ~ occupies Treasurer's house at Deptford, iv. 386 & n. 3, 427 *bis*; stands for parliament 1685, iv. 427 & n. 2; love of music of, iv. 384-5, 427; attends Mary Evelyn's funeral, iv. 430; congratulates E on appointment, iv. 465; social, iv. 318, 385–8 *passim*; dies, &c., v. 182–3 & n.
Carey, Catherine: *see* Howard, Catherine, countess of Nottingham.
Carey (Carew), Elizabeth: *see* Mordaunt, Elizabeth, Viscountess Mordaunt.
Carey, Henry, first earl of Dover: daughters of: visit E, iii. 189 & n. 4.
Carey (Cary), Henry, third Viscount Falkland: tutor of: *see* Triplet, T.
Carey, John, second earl of Dover: geneal., iv. 498, n. 3.
Carey (Cary), Lucius, second Viscount Falkland, ii. 213 & n. 3; geneal., ii. 213; v. 182, 183; chaplain of: *see* Gataker, C.; *see also* Books mentioned in notes.
Carey, Mrs. Margaret: *see* Herbert, Margaret, Lady Herbert.
Carey (Cary), Patrick: in Rome, ii. 213 & n. 3.
Carey (Cary), Rebecca, Viscountess of Falkland, wife of Anthony Carey, fifth viscount, iv. 386, n. 1; fortune of, v. 182; Mary Evelyn stays with, &c., iv. 425, 427–8; v. 183; social, iv. 386, 387.
Carey, Robert, first earl of Monmouth: geneal., iii. 1, n. 2, 155, n. 7, 156, n. 1.
Carey, Thomas: geneal., iii. 1, n. 2, 155, n. 7.
Caribbee Islands: governor of, 1667–71: *see* Willoughby, William, sixth Baron Willoughby of Parham (iii. 612 & n. 2).
Carie family: *see* Carew.
Carie, John, iii. 280, n. 1.
Carisbrooke, I.O.W.: Charles I's flight to, iii. 360, n. 7; *see also* iii. 445, n. 2, 494, n. 5; Sir Henry
Carisbrooke, I.O.W. (*cont.*)
Vane, jnr., imprisoned at, iii. 183 & n. 2.
Carleton, Guy, D.D.; bishop of Bristol 1671; of Chichester 1679: sermon by, iii. 321 & n. 6.
Carleton: Baron, 1714–25: *see* Boyle, Henry.
Carlingford: Earl of, 1661–77: *see* Taafe, Theobald.
Carlisle: captain in garrison at, 1661, iii. 619, n. 4.
— cathedral clergy:
— — bishops: *see* White, Francis (1626–9); Sterne, R. (1660–4); Rainbowe, E. (1664–84); Smith, Thomas (1684–1702) (proposed successor to Smith, 1696, v. 257); Nicolson, W. (1702–18).
— — dean: *see* Graham, William (1686–1704).
— Earls and Countesses of: *see* Howard, Charles, first earl, 1661–85; Howard, Anne, his countess; Howard, Edward, second earl, 1685–92; Howard, Elizabeth, his countess; Howard, Charles, third earl, 1692–1738; Howard, Anne, his countess.
Carlisle, John, clerk of the passage at Dover: complaint against, iii. 434 & n. 2.
Carlone, Taddeo, sculptor: fountain by, ii. 175 & n. 1 (i. 110).
Carlowitz, Peace of, 1699: negotiations for, v. 307 & n. 2; settled, v. 316 & n. 2; alluded to (?), v. 345 & n. 3.
Carmagnola (Carmaliona): taken by duke of Savoy, 1691, v. 71 & n. 4.
Carmarthen: Marquises of: *see* Osborne, Sir Thomas, marquis 1689–94, later first duke of Leeds; Osborne, Peregrine, styled marquis (courtesy title) 1694–1712, later second duke of Leeds.
Carnarvon: second Earl of, 1643–1709: *see* Dormer, Charles.
Caro, Annibal, ii. 407, n. 1.
Caroline of Ansbach, queen of England: lays out Kensington Gardens, v. 8, n. 2.
Carondelet, Ferry, cardinal: portrait of (as Guicciardini), iv. 102 & n. 2.
Carpi: battle at, 1701, v. 471 & n. 2.
Carpi, Girolamo da, ii. 113, n. 13; paintings by, ii. 113 (i. 73), 423, n. 7 *ad fin.*

Carr, Elizabeth, Lady Carr, wife of Sir Robert, third bt., iii. 358, n. 4; as Elizabeth Bennet: courted by Carr, iii. 372; ~ social, iii. 358; as Lady Carr: social, iv. 13 & nn. 3, 4.
Carr, Mary: *see* Scrope, Mary, Lady Scrope.
Carr, Sir Robert, second bt.: geneal., iii. 275, n. 6.
Carr, Sir Robert, third bt., iii. 372, n. 3; courts Elizabeth Bennet, iii. 372; social, iii. 491; geneal., iii. 358, n. 4; iv. 13 & n. 3.
Carr, William: punished for libel, iii. 503 & n. 4.
Carracci, painters: Agostino, ii. 423, n. 7; painting by, ii. 423 & n. 7; engraving by, iii. 567, n. 4; Annibale, ii. 215, n. 1; paintings by: Rome, Palazzo Farnese, frescoes, ii. 215 & nn. 1, 2, 310 & n. 2; ~ payment for, ii. 310 & n. 2; Charles I's collection, Agony in the Garden, iii. 262–3 & n.; other paintings, ii. 285 & n. 1, 356 & n. 5, 369 & n. 2 (school-pieces); false attributions, &c., ii. 229 & n. 5, 407 & n. 1, 424 & n. 5; engraving by, ii. 407 & n. 2; Lodovico, ii. 423, n. 5; paintings by, ii. 423 & n. 5, 424 & n. 5; false attribution, iv. 403 & n. 8; the three Carracci: together: paintings by, ii. 424 & n. 6; one or other: paintings by, ii. 309 & n. 10; iii. 294.
Carragio: painting by, ii. 284.
Carrara: marble quarries at, ii. 179 (i. 113).
Carrell: *see* Caryl.
Carrickfergus (Karric firgus), Antrim: surrendered to English, 1689, iv. 648 & n. 1; William III lands at, 1690, v. 24, n. 4.
Carshalton (Cassalton), Surrey: Carshalton Park: notice, iii. 221 & n. 5.
Cartagena, port in Caribbean Sea: sacked by Pointis, 1697, v. 266 *bis* & n. 2.
Carter, Rev. Edward (as Dr. Cartwrite, in error): library of: sale of, iv. 589 & n. 4.
Carteret, Anne: *see* Slanning, Anne, Lady Slanning.
Carteret, Caroline: *see* Scott, Caroline, Lady Scott.
Carteret, Elizabeth, Lady Carteret, wife of Sir George, iii. 252, n. 4; social, iii. 252, 325, 327, 364, 506.
Carteret, Sir George, bt., ii. 561, n. 7 [he is frequently called 'Mr. Vice-Chamberlain' and occasionally 'Mr. Treasurer of the Navy']:
as governor of Jersey: in Paris, 1649, ii. 561 & n. 7; as Vice-Chamberlain of the Household: appointed, iii. 251 & n. 5; ~ apartment of, at Hampton Court: E and Mrs. Evelyn stay in, iii. 320; as Treasurer of the Navy: appointed, iii. 252 & n. 5; ~ occupies Treasurer's House at Deptford, iii. 312, n. 4, &c.; ~ entertains James, duke of York, iii. 312–13; ~ payment to, iii. 412; ~ visits fleet at Buoy of the Nore, iii. 414; ~ accusation against, 1669, iii. 540 & n. 6; as keeper of Cranbourn Lodge, Windsor Great Park: rebuilds the lodge, iv. 527 & nn. 3, 5; as member of Council for Foreign Plantations: sworn in, iii. 578 & n. 2; *add.*
promotes recommendation made by E, iii. 251 & nn. 5, 6; takes E to Scot's Hall, iii. 358–9 & n.; social: parties, iii. 252, 327, 363, 506; ~ for his daughter's wedding, iii. 343 & n. 1; alone, &c., iii. 292, 331, 355 & n. 6 (?), 356 & n. 5 (?), 358, 364, 379, 392 *bis*, 403, 408, 478, 482, 492 & n. 1 (?), 498, 503, 556, 563, 584, 597, 602; iv. 4, 27, 28–9, 49.
geneal., iii. 327 & n. 2, 343, n. 1, 358 & n. 5, 401; iv. 561, n. 3.
Carteret, George; Baron Carteret 1681: social, iv. 561 & n. 3.
Carteret, Lady Jemima, born Mountagu, wife of Sir Philip, iii. 401, n. 6; as Lady Jemima Mountagu: treated for deformity, iii. 317, n. 4; as Lady Jemima Carteret: social, iii. 506.
Carteret (Cartrite), Sir Philip; knighted 1667, iii. 401, n. 6; as Mr. Carteret: admitted F.R.S., iii. 401 & n. 6; as Sir Philip: social, iii. 506.
Carteret, Sir Philip de: geneal., iii. 252, n. 4.
Carteret: Baron, 1681–95: *see* Carteret, George.
Cartesians: views of, on pineal gland, iv. 530 & n. 2; in sermon, v. 412 & n. 1.

Carthage: wars of, with Pisa, ii. 179 (i. 113); Capua as rival of, ii. 324.
Cartwright (Cartrite), Col. George: report of, on New England, 1671, iii. 581–2 & n.
Cartwright, Thomas, of Ossington, Notts: geneal., iii. 581, n. 5.
Cartwright (Cartwrite), Thomas, D.D.; bishop of Chester 1686–9, iii. 438, n. 2; iv. 518, n. 5; *congé d'élire* for, iv. 525; sermons by, iii. 438; iv. 518.
Cartwrite, Dr. —: *see* Carter, Rev. Edward.
Cary: for members of the Falkland family *see* Carey.
Cary, —, iv. 111–12 & n.
Caryl, Mrs. Elizabeth: geneal., ii. 29, n. 4.
Caryl *or* Caryll (Carill, &c.), John, ii. 29, n. 4; home of, ii. 28, n. 5 *ad fin.*; travels with E in Netherlands, 1641, ii. 29 (i. 22); i. 47; matriculates at Leyden, ii. 52, n. 4.
Caryl *or* Carrell, Judith: *see* Duncombe, Mrs. J.
Caryl, Simon: geneal., ii. 29, n. 4.
Casa Bianca, near Sezze, ii. 318, n. 2.
Casale (Cassal): besieged by duke of Savoy, 1695, v. 209 & n. 2; surrender of, v. 215 & n. 3; ~ thanksgiving for, in England, v. 218 & n. 3.
Casa Nuova, near Sezze, ii. 318, n. 2.
Caserta: palace of: statue in, ii. 215, n. 4.
Cashel and Emly: Archbishop of, 1727: *see* Nicolson, W.
Caspian Sea: traveller to, iv. 213.
Cassalton: *see* Carshalton.
Cassano: battle at, 1705 (?), v. 607 & n. 4.
Cassillis: Earl of: *see* Kennedy, John.
Cassiobury Park, Watford, Herts.: notice, iv. 199–200 & nn., 201; Sir Henry Capel at, iv. 347.
Castelfranco, Giorgio: *see* Giorgione.
Castellanza, ii. 505 & n. 3.
Castelli, O.: libretto by, ii. 389, n. 1.
Castellion, Sébastien: on sinlessness, iii. 363, n. 2.
Castelmelhor, Luis de Vasconcellos e Sousa, conde de: account of, iv. 130 & n. 1; visits repository of Royal Society, &c., iv. 133; attends meeting of Royal Society, iv. 191; at demonstration of phosphorus, iv. 263; returning to Portugal, iv. 454 & n. 4.
Casterton Magna: *see* Great Casterton.
Castile: Admiral of: *see* Medina de Riosecco, duke of; Constable of: *see* Frias, duke of.
Castillion, John; D.D. 1660; dean of Rochester 1676, iii. 8, n. 1; iv. 3, n. 6, 94, n. 2; sermons by, iii. 8; iv. 3, 94.
Castle, Mrs. —: wedding of, 1683, iv. 352.
Castle Ashby, Northants.: notice, iv. 593–4 & n.
Castlehaven: Earls of: *see* Tuchet, Mervyn, second earl 1617–31; Touchet, James, third earl 1631–84.
Castlemaine: Earl and Countess of: *see* Palmer, Roger; Palmer, Barbara, later duchess of Cleveland.
Castleton: Earl of (Scottish), v. 150 & n. 6.
Castleton: Viscount and Viscountess (Ireland): *see* Saunderson, George; Saunderson, Sarah.
Castro: War of: *see* Wars.
Catalonia: Allied naval expedition to, 1705, v. 605 & n. 2; ~ lands near Barcelona, v. 607 & n. 2; ~ takes Barcelona, v. 610 & n. 2 (report), 614 & n. 4; ~ conquers Catalonia, v. 617.
Catania, Sicily: lava-flow at, 1669, iii. 539 & n. 2; destroyed by earthquake, 1693, v. 133 & n. 3.
Cathari, iii. 363, n. 2.
Catherine of Aragon, queen of England: tomb of, iii. 134–5 & n.
Catherine of Braganza, queen of England, consort of Charles II, formerly Portuguese infanta, iii. 286, n. 6.
— appearance of, iii. 321 & nn. 2, 3.
— biography: marriage, 1662: negotiations for, iii. 275, n. 5, 305; Charles II announces his intention of marrying, iii. 286 & n. 6; marriage-treaty signed, iii. 290, n. 8, 305, n. 4; dowry of, iii. 290, n. 8; ~ includes Tangier, iii. 305 & n. 4, 311; fleet sent to bring her to England, iii. 306, 311 & n. 5, 618, n. 6; Portuguese attendants of, iii. 320–1 & nn., 321 & n. 8,

Catherine of Braganza (*cont.*)
481, n. 5; ~ musicians, iii. 322 & n. 4; music prepared for arrival of: performance, iii. 310; arrives at Portsmouth and is married, iii. 320 & n. 2; arrives at Hampton Court, iii. 320 & n. 3; compliments and wedding-presents for, iii. 321 & nn. 5, 7, 323–4; water-procession of, to Whitehall, iii. 333 & n. 2; *see also* iii. 322, n. 2; sterility of, iv. 158, 338 & n. 4; Charles II's only wife, iv. 457, n. 7.
— — later life and movements: visits Bath, 1663, iii. 361 & n. 3; Charles II shows her Crucifixion carved by G. Gibbons, iii. 572; visits Norwich, 1671, iii. 593 & n. 3; gift to, from Charles II, iv. 9; accused by Titus Oates of trying to poison Charles II, 1678, iv. 158 & nn. 5, 6; Roman Catholic servants of, to be dismissed, iv. 159 & n. 2; goes to Windsor, 1679, iv. 171, n. 10; visits Newmarket, 1679, iv. 183, n. 1; at Windsor, 1682, iv. 280 & n. 2; in mourning for Dom Affonso VI, 1683, iv. 351 & n. 1; and Charles II's death, 1685: his and her mutual requests for pardon, &c., iv. 408–9 & nn.; ~ visit of condolence to, iv. 419 & n. 3; retires from Whitehall to Somerset House, iv. 433 & n. 4; abandons intention of returning to Portugal, 1688, iv. 585 & n. 5; attends meeting authenticating birth of James Edward, iv. 602 & n. 3; returns to Portugal, 1692, v. 93 & n. 5; *see also* iii. 511, n. 2.
— ceremonies, social, amusements, &c.: attends audiences of ambassadors, iii. 356, 412, 494; iv. 262, 265; attends review, iii. 357; spectator at Garter feast, 1667, iii. 480 & n. 5; does not watch Lord Mayor's show, 1662, iii. 341–2 & nn.; at balls, &c., at court, iii. 350, n. 2, 351–2, 476, 569 & n. 2 [some birthday celebrations also include balls]; birthdays of: song for one, iii. 230, n. 3; ~ celebrated, iii. 518, 630; iv. 48, 101, 123–4,

Catherine of Braganza (*cont.*)
157, 395; plays acted before, iii. 341, 465, 505; entertained: at Durdans, iii. 334; ~ by Sir R. Holmes, iv. 38; receives French visitors, iii. 575; watches skating, iii. 347; wins prize in Sir A. Slingsby's lottery, iii. 376; at meals, iii. 321, 322, 491, n. 1; walks in Windsor Great Park, iv. 318.
— dress: Portuguese, iii. 320–1 & n.; riding-habit, 1666, iii. 463 & n. 3.
— relations of, with E: E presented to, iii. 321; conversations of, with E, iii. 379, 463; visits Mrs. Evelyn at Sayes Court, iv. 89.
— geneal., iii. 481–2; iv. 130, n. 1.
— residences, apartments, &c.: Hampton Court: bed-chamber at, iii. 322; ~ bed, iii. 323 & n. 5; oriental furniture of, at, iii. 324 & n. 2; St. James's Palace: chapel of, at, iii. 373, n. 2; ~ music for, iii. 310; ~ marriages in, iii. 373, 511, n. 2; ~ mentioned, iv. 159, n. 2; Somerset House: granted to, iv. 90, n. 4; ~ goes into residence at, iv. 433 & n. 4; *see also* London: topography: Somerset House [entries relating to members of her household living there, &c.]; Whitehall: *see* Whitehall: structure: Queen's Bed-chamber, &c.; ~ apartment of, at: compared with Duchess of Portsmouth's, iv. 74, 343.
— household [for her Portuguese attendants in 1662 *see* biography *above*]: clergy, &c.: Grand Almoner (Lord Almoner): *see* Stuart, Ludovic, seigneur d'Aubigny (1662–5); Howard, Philip Thomas (1665–94); first chaplain, 1662–5: *see* Howard, Philip Thomas; organist: *see* Draghi, G. B.
— — Council: grants lease to Mrs. Godolphin, iv. 90 & n. 4, 93 *bis*, 101; members: Lord Chamberlain: *see* Stanhope, Philip, second earl of Chesterfield (1662–5); Hyde, Henry, second earl of Clarendon (1665–76?); Duras, Louis de, earl of Feversham (1680–1705); Chancellor:

Catherine of Braganza (*cont.*)
see Brouncker, William, Viscount Brouncker (iv. 25, n. 2; not identified as chancellor in notes); Savile, George, marquis of Halifax (1684–5); secretary and master of requests: *see* Bellings, Sir R.; treasurer: *see* Hervey, John (1662?–79?); Hyde, Henry, earl of Clarendon (1680–5); attorney-general, 1662–76: *see* Montagu, William, sen.
— — other members of the household: private secretary: *see* Hyde, Henry, earl of Clarendon; gentleman usher of the privy chamber: *see* Stanhope, Alexander; physician: *see* Wakeman, Sir G.; page of the back-stairs: *see* Del Campo, G. B.
— — women: Groom of the Stole: *see* Howard, Barbara, countess of Suffolk (1662–81); Bennet, Isabella, countess of Arlington (1682–92); maids of honour: collective notices: watch Lord Mayor's show, 1662, iii. 342; ~ taken by E to comedy, iii. 622; ~ visit Mrs. Evelyn, iii. 623; ~ social, iii. 495, 621; iv. 2, 28, 34, 52; individuals: list, 1672, iii. 621, n. 5; *see also* Sheldon, Frances; Sylvius, Ann, Lady Sylvius (formerly Howard); Talbot, Mrs. Katherine (formerly Boynton); appointments, &c.: Mrs. Godolphin (formerly Blagge) granted leave to retire, iv. 1; ~ proposed or expected: *see* Kéroualle, Louise de, duchess of Portsmouth (iii. 564 & n. 1); Evelyn, Mary (iv. 428); ~ woman wrongly described as former maid, iv. 576 & n. 3; mother of the maids: *see* Sanderson, Bridget, Lady Sanderson (1669?–82); Madam Nurse: *see* Scrope, Mary, Lady Scrope; dressers: *see* Bordes d'Assigny, H. de; Scrope, Mary, Lady Scrope; Thornhill, Mrs. J.; Tuke, Mary, Lady Tuke, born Sheldon; Lady of the Jewels: Charles II promises to appoint Mrs. Evelyn, iii. 275 & n. 5.

Catherine de Médicis, queen of France: lays out Tuileries garden, ii. 106, n. 1; builds Chenonceaux, ii. 152 (i. 98).
Catherine, St., of Siena: relics of, ii. 204 & n. 3, 377 & n. 4; cell of, ii. 408 & n. 2.
Cati, Pasquale: painting by, ii. 246 & n. 9.
Catinat, Nicolas, marshal of France, v. 31, n. 5; in Savoy (Piedmont), 1690, v. 31; in battle of Staffarda, v. 33 *bis* & n. 6.
Cato (the Censor), iv. 256, n. 1; in comparison, iv. 256; in sermon, iv. 274.
Cato (Uticensis): in sermon, v. 179 & n. 2.
Catta Malata: *see* Gattamelata.
Caumont: Antoine-Nompar de: *see* Lauzun, duke of; Jacques-Nompar de: *see* la Force, duc de.
Caus: *see* de Caus.
Causam: *see* Caversham.
Cavalcaselle (Cavalli Caschieri), near Peschiera: inn at, ii. 488 & n. 4, 489.
Cavalli, F., composer: opera by, ii. 474, n. 6.
Cavan, co. Cavan: fight at, 1690, v. 8 & n. 4.
Cave, William, D.D., iv. 192, n. 4; books by, iv. 192 & n. 4, 299 & n. 5; sermons by: printed, iv. 402 & n. 4; ~ unprinted, iv. 192, 299.
Cavedoni, Giacomo: paintings by, ii. 424 & n. 4.
Cavendish, Arabella: *see* Spencer, Arabella, Lady Spencer.
Cavendish, Catherine: *see* Tufton, Catherine, countess of Thanet.
Cavendish, Christian, countess of Devonshire, wife of William Cavendish, second earl: social, iii. 329 & n. 3.
Cavendish, Elizabeth: *see* Montagu, Elizabeth, duchess of Montagu, &c.
Cavendish, Elizabeth, countess of Devonshire, wife of William Cavendish, third earl: social (?), iv. 498 & n. 2.
Cavendish, Henry, second duke of Newcastle: regiment of, 1688, iv. 599, n. 6; geneal., iv. 15, n. 7, 260, n. 4 *ad fin.*, 505, nn. 3, 4 *ad fin.*; v. 202 & n. 4.
Cavendish, Henry; styled Lord Ogle 1676–80: geneal., iv. 260 & n. 4.

Cavendish, Margaret, duchess of Newcastle, wife of William Cavendish, first duke, iii. 478, n. 3; marriage of, iii. 480 & n. 8; visits Royal Society, iii. 482–3 & n.; literary activities of, *ib.*; dress of, iii. 478 & n. 5, 481; social, iii. 478, 481 *bis*, 482; mentioned, iii. 126, n. 8.

Cavendish, Lady Mary, later countess and duchess of Devonshire, wife of William Cavendish, Lord Cavendish, later fourth earl and first duke of Devonshire, iv. 105 & n. 4; as Lady Mary Cavendish: social, iv. 105; as countess of Devonshire: social (?), iv. 498 & n. 2.

Cavendish, William, second earl of Devonshire: geneal., iii. 329, n. 3.

Cavendish, William; third earl of Devonshire 1628–84, iii. 65, n. 1; employs C. Wase as tutor to his son, iii. 65 & n. 3; visits E, iii. 329; as owner of Roehampton House, iv. 105, n. 5.

Cavendish, William, 1641–1707; styled Lord Cavendish 1641–84; fourth earl, 1684, and first duke, 1694, of Devonshire, iii. 65, n. 2; education of, iii. 65; quarrel of, with Col. T. Colepeper, 1685, iv. 453–4 & n.; appointed lord steward of the household, 1689, iv. 627; created duke, v. 180 & n. 2; tenant of Montague House, iv. 497, n. 2; buys Berkeley House, iii. 436, n. 6; loss of, on horse race, v. 320 & n. 1; social: as Lord Cavendish, iv. 191; as earl, v. 147.

Cavendish, William, d. 1729; second duke of Devonshire 1707: as marquis of Hartington: conduct of, in parliament, v. 311, n. 1.

Cavendish, William, 1593–1676; earl, 1628, marquis, 1643, and first duke, 1665, of Newcastle, iii. 126, n. 8; property of: Nottingham Castle, iii. 126, n. 2; ~ Welbeck Abbey, iii. 126 & n. 8; house of, in Clerkenwell, iii. 478 & n. 4; social, iii. 478, 480–1, 482; *see also* Plays.

Cavendish: Lord, 1641–84: *see* Cavendish, William, fourth earl and first duke of Devonshire.

Caversham (Causam), Oxon.: Lord Craven's house at, iii. 99 & n. 3.

Caves [for cave-dwellings *see* Housing]: at Deepdene, iii. 154; in Phlegraean Fields, ii. 339–40 & n., 346–7 & nn.; Ste.-Baume, ii. 167 (i. 105); Caves-Gouttières, near Tours, ii. 148 & n. 1 (i. 95–6).

Caves-Gouttières, near Tours, ii. 148 & n. 1 (i. 95–6).

Cecchino del Frate: paintings by, ii. 414 & n. 6.

Cecil, Sir Edward, Viscount Wimbledon: owner of Wimbledon Park, iii. 315, n. 5.

Cecil, Elizabeth: *see* Cavendish, Elizabeth, countess of Devonshire.

Cecil, Frances, countess of Salisbury, wife of James Cecil, fourth earl, v. 445, n. 1; chaplain of: sermon by, v. 445.

Cecil, James; fourth earl of Salisbury 1683, iv. 261, n. 5; as Lord Cranborne: marriage project for, iv. 261; converted to Roman Catholicism, iv. 541, n. 2.

Cecil, John; fifth earl of Exeter 1678, iv. 350, n. 4; garden of, at Burleigh House: plan for, iv. 350–1.

Cecil, Sir Robert, first earl of Salisbury: portrait of, ii. 80 & n. 5 (i. 54; there as William Cecil).

Cecil, Sir Thomas, first earl of Exeter: builds Wimbledon Park, iii. 315, n. 5; mentioned (as son of Burleigh), iii. 203, n. 3.

Cecil, William, Baron Burghley: builds Exeter House, London, iii. 203, n. 3.

Cecil, William, second earl of Salisbury: as owner of Hatfield (not identified in notes), ii. 80 (i. 54); geneal., iv. 498, n. 2.

Cecilia, St.: relics and bath of, ii. 357–8 & nn.; commemoration of, iii. 23 & n. 4.

Celle (Tell): Duke of: *see* Georg Wilhelm (v. 352 & n. 5).

Cellini, Benvenuto: Perseus by (also called Medusa in text), ii. 193 *bis* & n. 4 (i. 120 *bis*).

Celsus, author of *The True Word*: in sermon, v. 143.

Cencovius, S., ii. 337 & n. 1.

Centeno, Tuscany, ii. 208, n. 4.

Centurion, the (St. Matthew, ch. viii; &c.): in sermons, iii. 25; v. 65–6, 116, 499.

Cerasi family: chapel of, Rome, ii. 374 & n. 6.
Ceremonies [notices of strictly religious ceremonies are indexed under the various religious bodies, and not under this heading; notices of secular ceremonies accompanying religious festivals are indexed in the miscellaneous section below. Household ceremonies, revels, &c., are indexed under England: social: calendar festivals, family, &c. *See further* Popular celebrations; Processions]:
academic: Act, Oxford, 1654, iii. 104–5 & nn.; Act, Encænia, &c., Oxford, 1669, iii. 530–6 & nn.
coronations, &c.: coronations of: Charles II, iii. 281–4 & nn.; ~ James II, iv. 437 & nn. 2–4; ~ William and Mary, iv. 632–3 & nn.; enthronement of pope (*possesso*): thrones used for, ii. 268 & n. 2; translation of bishop to archbishopric, iii. 361–3 & nn.
diplomatic: Louis XIV gives audiences: general, on attaining his majority, iii. 43–4; ~ to Sir R. Browne, 1649, ii. 566; Charles II: gives audiences, iii. 256, 349 & n. 1, 412, 494 & n. 6, 506, 537; iv. 262 & n. 3, 265–6.
political, &c.: creations of: Knights of the Bath, iii. 276 & n. 5; ~ peers, iii. 277–8 & nn.; Rome: *conservatori* sworn in, ii. 291 & n. 5; ~ town standard blessed, ii. 387 & n. 1.
miscellaneous: *Cathedra Petri*: papal almsgiving on, ii. 300 & n. 2; *chapelle ardente*, ii. 368–9; funeral of bishop in Westminster Abbey, iii. 307; Golden Rose: consecration of, ii. 384 & n. 6; King's Evil: touching for, iii. 250–1 & n.; iv. 606 & n. 3; *add.*; Lady Day: papal charity on, ii. 377–8 & n., 384 & nn. 4, 5; Maundy Thursday: popes and English kings wash poor folk's feet, ii. 385 & n. 5.
Cerquozzi, Michelangelo (Michelangelo delle Battaglie): painting by, v. 245 & n. 3.
Certaldo di Val d'Elsa: Boccaccio buried at, ii. 200, n. 1.
Cesari, Giuseppe: *see* Arpino.
Cestius, C.: tomb of, ii. 360–1 & n.
Ceuta: captured by English, 1704 (error), v. 575 & n. 3.
Cevennes (Scevenies, Sevenes), mountains: protestants in: destruction of, as one of the Two Witnesses, iv. 636–7 & n.; risings of (the Camisards), 1703, 1704, v. 545 & n. 4, 563 & n. 1.
Cew: *see* Kew.
Chabot, Henri de: *see* Rohan, duke of.
Chadwell, Herts.: springs at, iv. 515, n. 4.
Chadwick, James: greenhouse of, v. 80 & n. 3.
Chadwick, Mrs. Mary: geneal., v. 80, n. 3.
Chafford, Penshurst, Kent: *see* Penshurst.
Chagres: base for Col. H. Morgan's attack on Panama, iii. 585, n. 2.
Chailey (Chaylie), Sussex: road near, ii. 544.
Chaldean astronomers: in sermon, v. 526.
Chalton, Hants: rector of: *see* Gillingham, G.
Chamberlaine, Rev. — (1659–60): sermons by, iii. 230, 235–40 *passim*, 245 *bis*, 248; ill, iii. 233; social, iii. 237.
Chambord: chateau and environs of, ii. 139–40 & nn. (i. 91–2).
Champneyes, William, carver in ordinary, iii. 343, n. 5.
Channel, English [*see also* Dover Straits]: fleet in, 1696, v. 233 & n. 2.
Channel Islands: translation of Book of Common Prayer used in, iii. 545, n. 4; projected French attack on, 1692, v. 97, n. 2.
Channoveau, John, iii. 306, n. 5.
Chantemesle: *see* Essonnes.
Chanterell, —: paints E's portrait, ii. 7 (i. 7).
Chantilly: stone from, iii. 18 & n. 2; Musée Condé at: painting in, ii. 309, n. 10 *ad fin*.
Chaplin, Dr. —: error in Bray's text for Dr. (Arthur) Charlett, v. 112, n. 5.
Charcas, Los, district in South America, iii. 188–9 & n.
Chardin (Jardine, Chartin), Sir John; knighted 1681; the traveller, iv. 212, n. 1; notice of, and of

Chardin, Sir John (*cont.*)
his travels, 1680, iv. 212–14 & nn.; welcomed by Royal Society, *ib.*; account by, of his travels: in preparation, iv. 358; ~ plates for, iv. 369 & n. 1; drawings made for, iv. 213 & n. 2, 369 & n. 1, 372; information from, iv. 337 & n. 4(?), 358 & n. 4; visits Montague House, iv. 345; introduced to Lord Keeper Guilford, iv. 372; resides at Greenwich, 1686, &c., iv. 520 & n. 2, 561; house of, at Turnham Green, *c.* 1705, v. 594 & n. 4; son of, baptised, iv. 561 & nn. 1–4; social, iv. 521, 548, 586, 587; v. 204.

Chardin, Sir John, bt.: baptised, iv. 561 & nn. 1, 2; mentioned, v. 204.

Charenton, near Paris: the Temple at: notice, 1644, ii. 115 & nn. 2–5 (i. 74–5); burial and cemetery at, ii. 565 & n. 5; ministers from, iv. 318–19 & n., 485, nn. 4, 5; bridge over Marne at, ii. 115 & n. 6 (i. 75).

Charity and Charitable collections [for institutions *see* Hospitals and Charitable Institutions]:
— charity: recommended in sermons, iii. 195, 201, 315, 358, 422, 473, 541; iv. 195; v. 160, 554, 599; offerings for, at Communion, v. 477 & n. 4.
— collections: for: ministers from Palatinate, 1636, ii. 15 & n. 5 (i. 12); Waldensians, 1655, iii. 152 & n. 1; Anglican clergy, 1658, iii. 213–14; sick and wounded, 1666, iii. 444; sufferers from plague in Deptford, &c., 1666, iii. 445, n. 6; Great Fire of London, iii. 464; London poor, &c., winter, 1683–4, iv. 361 & n. 3, 363; Waldensians, 1690, v. 3 & n. 1; redemption of slaves in Morocco, 1702, v. 485 & n. 1.
— — for French protestant refugees: on briefs of 1686 and 1688, iv. 447, n. 3 *ad fin*; ~ mentioned, v. 36; brief of 1686, sermons, &c., iv. 485, n. 3, 504 & n. 3, 506 & n. 1, 508–9 & nn., 510–11, 515 & n. 2; brief of 1688, &c., iv. 572 & n. 2, 574, 581; Boyle's gifts to, v. 82; proclamation and sermons for, 1699, v. 319–20 & n., 321 & n. 2; brief, &c., for refugees from Orange, 1704, v. 559 & n. 3.
— — on Church briefs (*see also above*): for: St. Albans abbey church, 1681, iv. 589 & n. 5; fire at Newmarket, 1683, iv. 340, 341, n. 1; fugitive Irish clergy, 1689, iv. 647, n. 5; Yalding (?), 1694, v. 188 & n. 1; *see also* v. 3 & n. 1, 485, n. 1.
— gifts and bequests: for imprisoned debtors, poor, &c., iv. 29 & n. 2, 81 *ter*, 139 & n. 5, 140, 150; v. 386; miscellaneous benefactions: *see* Boyle, Robert (v. 82 & n. 2; &c.); Rustat, T. (iv. 207); Tenison, T. (v. 65–6; &c.).
— papal donations, &c., in Rome, ii. 291 & n. 3, 300 & n. 2, 385 & n. 5; dowries for *zitelle*, ii. 378 & n. 1, 384 & n. 4.
— visit to almshouse, iv. 28.

Charlbury, Oxon: sermon at, iii. 383 & n. 5.

Charlemagne: ancestors of, ii. 86 (i. 58); relics of, ii. 87, 88, 89 (i. 58, 59, 60); sword of, ii. 192 (i. 119); residence of, at Nijmegen (called Charles V, in error), ii. 35 & n. 4 (i. 27).

Charleroi: besieged and taken by French, 1693, v. 155 *bis* & nn. 1, 2.

CHARLES I, king of England:
— chronological series:
— — *c.* 1614–23: Spanish Marriage project, ii. 6–7 & n. (i. 6–7).
— — 1623: return of, from Spain: chapel at Groombridge built to commemorate, iii. 72 & n. 3; iv. 40.
— — 1625: proclamation of, as king: the ceremonial, iv. 412, n. 5; coronation oath of, iii. 282, n. 4.
— — 1629: eldest child of, i. 8 & n. 3.
— — 1633: visits Scotland, ii. 12 & n. 2 (i. 10); reception of, at Godmanchester, iii. 135, n. 5.
— — *c.* 1637–41: disaffection towards, due to building *Sovereign of the Seas*, ii. 30 & n. 3 (i. 22–3); v. 230 & n. 5.
— — 1637–9: Scottish opposition to, ii. 22 & n. 3 (i. 17); Puritan opposition to: stories concerning, v. 13, n. 1.

CHARLES I: chronological (*cont.*)
— — 1640: opens Short Parliament, ii. 23–4 & n. (i. 17); and Scottish invasion of England: strength of royal army, iii. 50 & n. 2; ~ betrayed by marquis of Hamilton, iii. 50 & n. 3; ~ returns from expedition against, ii. 25 (i. 19); opens Long Parliament, ii. 25–6 (i. 19).
— — 1641: attends Strafford's trial, ii. 27 (i. 20); signs Strafford's death-warrant, i. 20 & n. 2; returns from Scotland, ii. 77 (i. 51).
— — 1642: Hull held against, iii. 130–1 & n.; raises his standard at Nottingham, iii. 126; forces of, in Civil War: munitions for, iii. 24, n. 6; ~ officer in, iii. 144, n. 1; at Edgehill, i. 53–4 & n.; at Brentford, ii. 79 (i. 52–3).
— — 1643: Oxford colleges surrender their plate to, i. 15 & n. 1; Commission of Array issued by: men concerned in, ii. 478; iv. 186 & n. 1; marches to Gloucester, ii. 79 & n. 6 (i. 53); siege of Gloucester fatal to, iii. 118 & n. 4.
— — 1643–6: holds Donnington Castle, iii. 100, n. 3.
— — 1646: orders Newark to surrender, iii. 125, n. 1.
— — 1647: prisoner at: Holmby House, iv. 70, n. 3; ~ Caversham Park, iii. 99, n. 3; ~ Hampton Court, ii. 537 & n. 4; flight of, to Carisbrooke: companions of, on, iii. 360, n. 7, 445, n. 2, 494, n. 5.
— — 1648: projected escape of, from Newport, iv. 360, n. 3; removal of, to Hurst Castle: debated, ii. 545, n. 6.
— — 1649: trial, execution, &c.
— — — trial: story relating to, v. 13, n. 1; participants in: *see* Bradshaw, John; Dorislaus, I.; Peters, Hugh; St. John, Oliver.
— — — execution: notice, ii. 547; service before: questions Juxon on lesson for the day, iv. 193, n. 2; passage of, to: route through Whitehall, iii. 474, n. 4; ~ insulted by Lady Norton during, iii. 90 & n. 1; influence of, on Tsar Alexis of Russia, iii. 344, n. 5; commemoration of: annual fast (30 January) established, iii. 269 & n. 1; ~ observance of: *see* Church of England: worship: feasts and fasts; vindicators of: in sermon, v. 165–6; *see also* Milton, John; mentioned or alluded to, ii. 79, 537, 566; iv. 411; v. 290.
— — — burial-place of, iii. 98–9 & n.; statues of, at Royal Exchange, &c., removed, ii. 555 & n. 6; Dr. R. Parr's grief for, iii. 604; cures effected by blood of, iv. 469 & n. 3.
— — — regicides: sermons, &c., against, iii. 134 & n. 1; trial and executions of, iii. 258 & n. 6, 259 & nn. 1, 2; reprieves of: censured in sermon, 1662, iii. 312; further executions of: bill for, iii. 312, n. 1; survivors excepted from pardon, 1690, v. 23, n. 4; show no remorse: in sermon, iv. 405.
— art-collections.
— — formation of: Arundel's attempt to buy drawings by Leonardo, ii. 498 & n. 8; Endymion Porter helps in, ii. 555, n. 1; gifts to, iii. 147–8 & n., 260.
— — paintings in, by: Annibale Carracci, iii. 262–3 & n.; Correggio, ii. 549 & n. 6; Giulio Romano, iii. 75 & n. 1; Holbein, iii. 263 & n. 2; Leonardo, ii. 120, n. 3; Mantegna, iii. 323 & n. 2; Rottenhammer, ii. 550, n. 1; Titian, iii. 166, n. 5; Van Dyck, ii. 548, n. 3; artist not named, ii. 550 & n. 4.
— — various objects in: agate cup (?), iii. 148 & n. 4; cameo of Claudius, iii. 260 & n. 4; clock, iii. 147–8 & n.; embroidery, iii. 260.
— — dispersal of: gifts of paintings, ii. 114 *bis* (i. 73); sale, 1649, ii. 549 & nn. 1, 5, 7.
— — recovery of: order for return of king's goods, 1660, iii. 249 & n. 2; discovery, &c., ii. 554, n. 3.
— household, &c.
— — clergy: dean of the chapel,

CHARLES I: household (*cont.*)
1643: *see* Steward, R.; chaplains: *see* Gillingham, G.; Laurence, T.; Stokes, D.; Turner, Thomas; Wolley, E.; Wood, Thomas.
— — various: Lord Chamberlain, 1626–41: *see* Herbert, Philip, earl of Pembroke; Comptroller, 1643–6: *see* Hatton, Christopher, Baron Hatton; gentleman of the privy chamber: *see* Hawarde, Sir W.; cup-bearer: *see* Erskine, W.; page (?): *see* Rustat, T.; grooms of the bedchamber: *see* Legge, William; Porter, Endymion; clerks of the kitchen: *see* Boreman, Sir W.; Crane, John; Master of the Revels: *see* Herbert, Sir Henry; musician: *see* Mercure, J.; jewellers in ordinary: *see* Simpson, F. and J.; equerry: *see* Armourer, Sir W.; horse-trainer: *see* Zinzano *alias* Alexander, R.
— palaces: Newmarket, iii. 138, n. 5; Royston, *ib*; Theobalds: notice, 1643, ii. 81 & n. 2 (i. 54–5); Windsor Castle: neglected by Charles, iii. 98, n. 6; for other palaces *see* chronological series *above*.
— personal relations.
— — E: Charles helped by E and his brother(s), 1642–3, i. 53; ii. 81 (i. 54); grants E licence to travel, ii. 82 & n. 2 (i. 53 & n. 2); E visits, 1647, ii. 537; i. *9*.
— — Arthur Capel, Lord Capel, loses his life for, iv. 201; Sir Kenelm Digby fixes mercury in presence of, iii. 48; Sir John Evelyn of West Dean: excluded by, from pardon, 1642, ii. 553, n. 7; J. Hobson: employed by, ii. 476, n. 3; William Howard, Viscount Stafford: ennobled by, iv. 233; Marie de Médicis: influence of, on Charles, i. 39 & n. 1; Sir Edward Nicholas: correspondence of, with Charles: publication of, i. *56*; Sir James Palmer: friend of, ii. 549, n. 2; William Prettyman: carries letters between Charles and Henrietta Maria, ii. 538, n. 1; Algernon Sidney: hostility of, to Charles, iv. 353; Sir John Winter: grant from, to, iii. 343, n. 3.
— religion: concern of, in Cosin's *Collection of Private Devotions*, iii. 45–6, 635; builds portico of St. Paul's, &c., iii. 458, 459, n. 1; gifts from, to York Minster, iii. 129 & n. 3; as martyr for protestant religion or Church of England (in contrast to his sons), iv. 7, 478. [Remarks about Charles's sufferings, &c., occur frequently in sermons for 30 Jan.]
— miscellaneous notices: geneal., v. 421; portrait of, with James, duke of York, by Lely, iii. 216 & n. 5; prophecy by P. Grebner applied to, iii. 137 & n. 2; reign of, represented in etchings by Hollar, i. 22 & n. 1; visits Bushell's Wells, iii. 382, n. 6; error for Charles II, iv. 612 & n. 5.
CHARLES II, king of England:
[Born 1630; succeeded as king in 1649, while in exile; returned to England in 1660 (the Restoration); married Catherine of Braganza in 1662; died in 1685.
The notices indexed under this heading are those in which Charles is more or less explicitly concerned ('the court' in a few cases, in text or notes, is treated as a synonym). When the entries refer to his connexion with persons or places, or to his intervention in independent activities, these are all fully indexed under their own appropriate headings.]:
— character: general, iv. 409–11 & nn., 478; defended by E in *The Late News*, 1660, iii. 243 & n. 3; extravagance, i. 14–15; v. 401, 402; immorality: attacked in sermons, iv. 85, 398; *see also* court and social life *below*; love of dogs, iv. 410 & n. 1; interest in shipping, iii. 303 & n. 5; iv. 409.
— early life and reign (to 1660):
— — as Prince of Wales (1630–49):
— — — 1630: birth of: rejoicing for, ii. 10 (i. 8).
— — — 1641: attends Strafford's trial, ii. 27 (i. 20).

CHARLES II: early life, &c. (*cont.*)
— — — 1642: leaves London, iii. 246, n. 1.
— — — 1646: sails from Falmouth and from Scilly Islands, *ib.*
— — — 1646–8: resides in Paris, &c., ii. 536 & n. 1.
— — — called prince after his succession, ii. 559; for his household as prince *see below*, at end of this section.
— — as king in exile (1649–60):
— — — 1649: at St.-Germain, ii. 561 & n. 10; ~ visited by French nobility, ii. 562–3 & nn.
— — — 1650: at Breda, iii. 2, n. 2; in Scotland, iii. 14, n. 6, 20, n. 4.
— — — 1651: prayer for, iii. 40; occupies Worcester, iii. 119, n. 5; defeat of, at Worcester: false mention, iii. 178 & n. 1; escape after: assisted by: Father J. Huddlestone, iv. 408, n. 1; ~ Jane Lane, iii. 51 & n. 2; ~ Col. Robert Phelips, iv. 513, n. 1; news of: reaches Paris, iii. 47 & n. 4; commemorated in sermons, iii. 47, 49; represented in Lord Mayor's show, iii. 259 & n. 4.
— — — — arrives in Fécamp and in Paris, iii. 47, n. 4.
— — — 1651–2: attends divine service in Paris, iii. 48, 49, 51, 53.
— — — 1654–6: resides at Cologne, iii. 251 & n. 2.
— — — foreign relations during exile: France: renewal of friendship with Louis XIV on Louis's attaining his majority, iii. 43; credentials to Sir Richard Browne as representative in, ii. 566; *see also* iii. 58; employs Sir R. Browne at Brest, 1652–4, iv. 66 & n. 2; agent of, at Calais: *see* Booth, Henry (iii. 12 & n. 7, 55); Russia: obtains loan from Tsar Alexis, iii. 344 & n. 5; Spain: treaty with, iii. 257, n. 2; United Provinces: refuse to assist him, iii. 236.
— — — naval affairs during exile: privateer of, ii. 559; royalists' prizes at Brest, &c., iv. 66 & n. 2.

CHARLES II: early life, &c. (*cont.*)
— — — general statements, &c., relating to exile: E sends political information to, iii. 59, 200 & n. 1; help given to, by C. Evertsen, sen., iii. 407 & n. 2; Dr. J. Hewit communicates with, iii. 216 & n. 9; praying for Charles Stuart, London, 1657, iii. 204; penury of, during exile, iv. 338; influence of period of exile on public taste, iii. 304.
— — household of, as Prince of Wales and as king during exile [for his household after the Restoration *see* Royal Household]: clergy: dean of the chapel, 1646–51: *see* Steward, Dr. R.; clerk of the closet, *c.* 1651: *see* Earles, J.; chaplains of, iii. 633; ~ individuals: *see* Earles, J.; Wolley, E.; other members of: chamberlain, 1653, &c.: *see* Percy, Henry, Baron Percy (iv. 218, n. 3); comptroller: *see* Hatton, Christopher, first Baron Hatton (iii. 6 & n. 1, 22); gentleman (later groom) of the bedchamber: *see* Eliot, Thomas (iii. 588, n. 8); (Sir) Stephen Fox, iv. 218 & n. 3.
— political and public life:
— — chronological series:
— — — 1660: the Restoration: E's negotiation with Col. H. Morley for (begins in 1659), iii. 235, n. 4, 237–40 & nn., *passim*, 245 & n. 3; i. *13–14*; Monck's intentions, Jan. 1660, iii. 240 & n. 5; action to assist, by Edward Mountagu (later earl of Sandwich), iii. 619 & n. 2; Declaration of Breda, &c., iii. 244 & n. 2; Charles proclaimed king in London, iii. 244 & n. 3; iv. 412, n. 5; receives commissioners bearing invitation to return to England, iii. 245, n. 1; enters London, iii. 246 & n. 2; ~ the procession, v. 273; audiences given by, at Whitehall, iii. 247 & n. 3; receives addresses and congratulations from: foreign protestant churches in London, iii. 248 & n. 3; ~ English counties, iii. 249 & nn. 4, 5; ~ city of Cologne, iii. 251 & n. 2; ~

CHARLES II: political, &c. (*cont.*)
Philip, duke of Anjou (later of Orleans), iii. 254 & n. 7; ~ Tsar Alexis (1662), iii. 344 & n. 5; general statements, &c.: annual thanksgiving for (29 May): established, iii. 289 & n. 5; ~ for services *see* Church of England: worship: feasts and fasts; as divine dispensation, iii. 464; saved England from anarchy, &c., v. 102; treatment of bishops and impoverished royalists at time of, iii. 609; execution of the regicides in the king's presence, iii. 259; *add.*
— — — 1660–85: the reign: general accounts of, i. *25–30*; iv. 411; troubles during, iv. 478; frequent changes of favourites (ministers, &c.) during, iv. 410 & n. 3.
— — — 1661: coronation: creations prior to, of: Knights of the Bath, iii. 276 & n. 5; ~ peers, iii. 277–8 & nn.; procession from Tower to Whitehall preceding, iii. 276–7, 278–81 & nn.; ~ triumphal arches, &c., for, iii. 278 & n. 2, 281; ceremony: notice, iii. 281–4 & nn.; ~ E attends, iii. 278; iv. 438; ~ procession for, from Westminster Hall to Abbey, and return, iii. 281, n. 3, 284 & nn. 2, 3; ~ coronation oath, iii. 282 & n. 4; iv. 632, n. 5; ~ regalia, iii. 281 & n. 3, 283 & nn. 7, 9, 284 & n. 1; coronation feast, iii. 284 & n. 3; Charles, &c., give suits worn for, to actors, iii. 303, n. 4; day of, commemorated, iii. 407.
— — — 1661: procession to open parliament, iii. 286 & n. 5. [For Charles's further relations with Parliament *see* analytical series *below*.]
— — — 1662: marriage: *see* personal relations *below*.
— — — 1667: advice to, not to set out a fleet: men giving, iii. 486, 489 & n. 2; dismisses Clarendon, iii. 493–4 & nn.
— — — 1669: proposes union of English and Scottish parliaments, iii. 570, n. 7.
— — — 1670: meets Madame (Henrietta Anne) at Dover, iii. 548–9 & nn.
— — — 1672: responsibility of, for Third Dutch War, iv. 16, n. 1; concern of, in: Stop of the Exchequer, iii. 606–7 & n.; ~ Declaration of Indulgence, iii. 607–8 & n.
— — — 1678: Popish Plot: *see* analytical series *below*.
— — — 1679: illness of, iv. 180 & n. 1, 181 *bis* & n. 1.
— — — 1680: unwilling to let parliament sit, iv. 192–3 & n.; attends Stafford's trial, iv. 226 & nn. 2, 6.
— — — 1681: Surrey address presented to, iv. 248 & nn. 4, 5.
— — — 1683: Rye House plot: *see* analytical series *below*; at Tower at time of Essex's suicide, iv. 326; additional guards for, &c., iv. 331 & n. 1.
— — — 1685: dies: last illness, death, character, &c., iv. 405–11 & nn.; last illness: prayers for, during, iv. 407 & nn. 4, 5, 414; ~ incident during, iv. 470–1 & n.; grief for, iv. 407 & n. 4; mourning for, iv. 414 & n. 3, 492 & n. 3(?); buried, iv. 415 & n. 3; death: attributed to poison, v. 197–8 & nn.; ~ diplomatic condolences for, iv. 419 & n. 3, 492, n. 1; ~ commemorated in sermon, iv. 440; ~ day of: observed as festival for James II's accession, iv. 499 & n. 8.
— — analytical series:
— — — ceremonies: (i) diplomatic: intervenes to prevent contest between French and Spanish ambassadors, iii. 297, n. 4; regulates entries of foreign ambassadors, iii. 352 & n. 3; gives audiences, &c., to ambassadors from: Morocco, iv. 265–6; ~ Russia, iii. 349 & n. 1, 356 & n. 7, 494; iv. 262–3; ~ Spain, iii. 256, 412.
— — — (ii) domestic: for Coronation, &c., *see* chronological series *above*; touches for King's Evil, iii. 250–1 & n.; in Garter celebrations, iii. 479–80 & nn., 559; *see also* iii. 580 & n. 6.

CHARLES II: political, &c. (*cont.*)
— — — charities and benefactions: gives money for London poor, 1684, iv. 361 & n. 3; *see also* iv. 365; as founder of Chelsea Hospital: negotiates for site, &c., iv. 257 & n. 3, 269–70 & n.; founds Mathematical School, Christ's Hospital, iv. 542 & n. 2; for his gifts to Royal Society *see* culture, &c.: scientific interests *below*.
— — — charters, &c., granted by, to: Canary Company, iii. 388 & n. 5; Clothworkers' Company, iv. 518, n. 3; Royal College of Physicians, iii. 337, n. 3; Royal Society: *see* culture, &c.: scientific interests *below*.
— — — colonial: recommends Council for Foreign Plantations to investigate condition of New England, iii. 579 & n. 2; abolishes Council of Trade and Plantations, iv. 50, n. 4.
— — — ecclesiastical: divines suitable for Irish bishoprics presented to, 1660, iii. 253 & n. 1; founds French Conformist church in the Savoy, iii. 545 & nn. 3, 4; issues Declaration of Indulgence, 1672, iii. 607–8 & n.; i. 26.
— — — foreign relations [including treaties, negotiations, &c.]: bound by treaty to assist Portugal against Spain, 1661, iii. 290, n. 8; sells Dunkirk to Louis XIV, 1662, i. 50; letter from, to Tsar Alexis, 1663, iii. 356, n. 7; confers with Dutch ambassador, 1664, iii. 390 & n. 7; Louis XIV's attitude towards, 1664–5, iii. 405, n. 1; negotiates for alliance with Spain, &c., 1665, iii. 434, n. 1; and Secret Treaty of Dover: negotiation for, 1669–70, iii. 548, n. 1; ~ provision of, iii. 559, n. 4; sends commissioners to Surinam, 1674, iv. 36, n. 1; offers to mediate between France and United Provinces, 1675, iv. 76, n. 3; averse to war with France, 1678, iv. 136, n. 4; money-treaties with France, 1681, iv. 331, n. 5; relations of, with Tsar Theodore II, *c.* 1681, iv. 262, n. 3; concern of, in trial of Count K. J. von Königsmarck, 1682, iv. 274, n. 1; relations with France, *c.* 1683, as cause of Rye-House plot, iv. 323; selfish desire of, for peace, iv. 331 & n. 5; financial dependence of, on Louis XIV, iv. 331, n. 5; ~ alluded to (?), iv. 340.
— — — London: Charles in connexion with: attends civic feast, 1660, iii. 250 & n. 2; does not watch Lord Mayor's show, 1662, iii. 341, 342 & nn. 1, 2; and Great Fire: gives orders for fighting, iii. 454–5 & n.; activity in fighting, iii. 457 & n. 5; views of, on causes of, iii. 457, n. 4; visits Tower after, iii. 458 & n. 4; fugitives from: care of, for, iii. 461 & n. 5; ~ speech of, to, iii. 462, n. 1; fails to control rebuilding of London after, iv. 307 & n. 6.
— — — — congratulated by Lord Mayor, &c., on recovery from illness, 1679, iv. 181; sups with sheriffs, 1680, iv. 208, n. 3, 210 & n. 1; receives submission of the City on *Quo Warranto* proceedings, 1683, iv. 319 & n. 1; disaffection of the City towards, iv. 322; obtains forfeiture of City charter, iv. 341–3 & nn.
— — — military: at reviews, iii. 357; iv. 13, n. 1, 136 & n. 4; interest of, in grenades, iii. 368, 483; visits new fortifications at Sheerness, iii. 610, n. 1; increases his forces, iv. 354 & n. 3; founds Chelsea Hospital, &c.: *see* charities *above*.
— — — naval and maritime: (i) as commander-in-chief, &c.: visits fleet at Buoy of the Nore, &c.: 1665–6, iii. 413–14 & nn., 436, n. 2, 441 & n. 5; ~ 1672, iii. 620, 623; at launching of ships, iii. 392, 440, 506; iv. 58; acts as Lord High Admiral in conjunction with James, duke of York, 1684, iv. 377.
— — — — (ii) private interest: general, iii. 303 & n. 5; iv. 409; takes part in yacht-race, iii. 296–7; sails to Ports-

CHARLES II: political, &c. (*cont.*) mouth, 1679, iv. 178 & n. 3; discusses new varnish for ships, iii. 512; gives name to Sir W. Petty's double-bottom, iii. 392; iv. 58.
— — — — (iii) persons: assists Captain G. Collins, the hydrographer, iv. 301, n. 3; intervenes on behalf of Captain C. Gunman, iv. 432, n. 1; shipwright (Withers) introduced to, iv. 12.
— — — parliamentary: speeches, &c., of, in parliament: notices, iii. 252 & n. 9, 401–2 & nn. [for Charles's other speeches, &c. *see* Parliament]; refuses to accept Sir E. Seymour as Speaker, 1679, v. 476, n. 2; unwilling to let parliament sit, 1680, iv. 192–3 & n.; attends debates in house of lords, iii. 545, 546, n. 1; submits to tacking (error), v. 401 & n. 1, 402.
— — — plots against: escapes from: in sermons, iv. 336, 337, 446; Popish Plot (alleged assassination plot): general notice, i. *27–8*; revealed, iv. 153–4 & nn.; attempts to assassinate Charles: Queen Catherine accused, iv. 158 & nn. 5, 6; ~ Sir G. Wakeman accused, iv. 174; ~ Stafford accused, iv. 228, 234; Rye House Plot: general notice, i. *29*; discovered, &c., iv. 321–4 & nn.; Charles's policy as cause of, iv. 329; effects on, of, iv. 331; Declaration of, concerning, iv. 335 & n. 2, 336; escape of: thanksgiving for, iv. 336–7; ~ due to Providence, iv. 340–1; ~ in sermon, iv. 333.
— — — Privy Council [for Charles's activities in Council *see* Privy Council].
— — — revenue: amount of, iii. 361 & n. 1; inadequacy of, iv. 410, n. 2; squandered on favourites, i. 14–15; v. 401 & n. 1, 402; collection of, continued by James II after his accession, iv. 417 & n. 6; accounts of, shown to E by Sir P. Warwick, iii. 361.
— court and social life:
— — court [for the members of the royal household from 1660 onwards *see* Royal Household]: character of, i. *24, 111*; immorality or dissoluteness of: general remarks on, iii. 316, 464, 596; iv. 403, 413–14, 416, 428, 437, 478; Charles dines in public, iii. 251, 490–1 & n., 513; dances in balls at court, iii. 350 *bis*, 351–2, 476; opens Twelfth Night gaming at court, iii. 308.
— — dress: new fashion adopted by, 1666, iii. 464–5 & n., 467.
— — gifts to: book of maps, iii. 260 & n. 5; queen-pine from Barbados, iii. 293; from: Amsterdam: yachts, iii. 296 & n. 5, 297, n. 2; emperor of Morocco: animals, iv. 266 & n. 3; Russian tsars: furs, animals, &c., iii. 349, 398–9 & n.; iv. 262; United Provinces: paintings, iii. 262, n. 6; *add.*; ~ bed, iii. 323 & n. 5; Venice: gondolas, iii. 322 & n. 2.
— — movements [migrations of Charles and his court from London, and some journeys of Charles by himself; for his visits to the fleet at the Nore *see* political, &c: naval *above*; for his day-visits to friends *see* social *below*. In some notices in text or notes the court alone is mentioned; if Charles is clearly involved they are entered here]:
— — — 1660: goes to meet Henrietta Maria, iii. 259 & n. 3.
— — — 1661: goes to Portsmouth, to take leave of Henrietta Maria, iii. 267 & n. 2.
— — — 1662: goes to Portsmouth to marry Queen Catherine, iii. 320, n. 2; at Hampton Court, iii. 320, n. 3, 322; goes to Downs to meet Henrietta Maria, iii. 328 & n. 1; comes from Hampton Court to London, iii. 333.
— — — 1663: goes to Bath, iii. 361, n. 3.
— — — 1665–6: movements to avoid Plague: to Hampton Court, iii. 415, n. 1; at Salisbury, &c., and Oxford, iii. 423 & n. 7; at Hampton Court and

CHARLES II: court (*cont.*)
returns to London, iii. 428–9 & nn.
— — — 1670: at Dover, to meet Henrietta Anne, iii. 548 *bis* & n. 1; at Windsor, iii. 558–60; returns from Newmarket, iii. 562.
— — — 1671: at Windsor, iii. 580, n. 6; at Newmarket, Euston, and Norwich, iii. 588–9 & n., 590, 592, n. 1, 593 & n. 3, 596.
— — — 1674: at Windsor, iv. 38, 41; *see also* p. 42.
— — — 1675: at Newmarket, iv. 55 & n. 5; at Windsor, iv. 73 & n. 2.
— — — 1676: at Newmarket, iv. 99, n. 2.
— — — 1677: at Newmarket, iv. 122, n. 3.
— — — 1678: at Windsor, iv. 142 & n. 6, 147.
— — — 1679: at Windsor, iv. 171 & n. 10, 176–7; goes to Hampton Court, iv. 177–8; sails to Portsmouth, iv. 178, n. 3; at Windsor, iv. 180 & n. 1, 180–1 & n.; at Newmarket, iv. 183 & n. 1.
— — — 1680: at Windsor, iv. 207, n. 6, 214 & n. 7.
— — — 1681: at Oxford (for parliament), iv. 239 & n. 3, 240, n. 3; at Windsor and Hampton Court, iv. 248 & n. 4.
— — — 1682: at Newmarket, iv. 282, n. 1; at Windsor, iv. 280 & n. 2.
— — — 1683: at Newmarket, iv. 321, 340–1 & n.; at Windsor, iv. 317–19 (*see* p. 317, n. 7).
— — — 1684: at Newmarket, iv. 372 & n. 1, 373, n. 2; at Windsor and Winchester, iv. 383 & n. 2, 387 & n. 4.
— — social life: meals on his yachts, iii. 297; French visitors to, iii. 575; in Hyde Park, iii. 249, 285; in St. James's Park, iii. 437, 614; ~ watches skating, iii. 346–7; attends Christmas revels at Lincoln's Inn, iii. 307–8; dines at Durdans, iii. 334; attends marriage-ceremonies of duke of Grafton, iii. 622; iv. 184–5; at ball given by earl of St. Albans, iv. 30; entertained by Sir R. Holmes, iv. 38; at entertainment for Moroccan ambassador, iv. 268.

CHARLES II: social life (*cont.*)
— culture and amusements:
— — amusements: music: at concert, iv. 82; hears Mrs. Packer sing, iv. 404; plays, &c.: attends performances, iii. 313, 341, 344, 347, 351 & n. 14(?), 465, 505; T. Fiorilli acts before, iv. 75; absent from performance at court, iii. 315; gives his coronation suit to actors, iii. 303, n. 4.
— — artistic interests: loved building, iv. 409; *see also* iii. 297; introduces corner fireplaces (?), iii. 554 & n. 4; Grinling Gibbons introduced to, &c., iii. 567–8, 571–2; buys clock made by S. Watson, iii. 112, n. 1; art-collections, &c., of: notices, iii. 260–1 & nn., 262–3 & nn., 323 & n. 2; iv. 216–17 & n.; mentioned, iii. 262, 300; Charles I's property returned to, iii. 249 & n. 2; Dutch gift to, iii. 262, n. 6; *add.*; gem owned by, iii. 79, n. 2; miniatures owned by, iii. 287; paintings belonging to: in duchess of Portsmouth's apartments, iv. 343.
— — library of: notice, iv. 214–16 & nn.; mentioned, iv. 257.
— — scientific interests, &c.: interest of, in Saturn, iii. 286 & n. 2 (error), 288; great telescope of (?), iii. 286 & n. 4; founds Greenwich Observatory, &c., iv. 98 & n. 3; laboratory of, iv. 409; watches preparation of cordial, iii. 336.
— — — — and Royal Society: approves of Philosophical Society, &c., iii. 266, n. 6 *ad fin.*, 288; offers himself as member of Philosophical Society, iii. 306, n. 1; as founder of Royal Society: petition to, for incorporation, iii. 296 & n. 3, 306, n. 1; ~ grants first charter to, iii. 332 & n. 1, 334 & n. 2; grants arms to (by second charter), iii. 332 & n. 2, 336; gives mace to, iii. 332 & n. 3; grants Chelsea College to, iii. 496–7 & n., 527 & n. 2; grants third

CHARLES II: culture, &c. (*cont.*).
charter to, iii. 527, n. 2; buys Chelsea College back from, iv. 257 & n. 3, 269 & n. 5; visit of, to: preparation for, iii. 357, 364; gives objects to, iii. 268 & n. 4, 272 & n. 2, 372 & n. 6; gives venison to, for anniversary dinners, iii. 366, 501, 519, 565; iv. 190, 351.

— — sport: for Charles's visits to Newmarket *see* court and social life: movements *above*; intends to substitute Winchester for Newmarket, iv. 341 & n. 2; race-horse of, iii. 588; captured Turkish horses shown to, iv. 398–9; goes otter-hunting, iii. 306; goes stag-hunting, iii. 560; watches wrestling-match, iii. 476.

— palaces and property [the notices indexed here are only those concerning Charles II's dealings with the various buildings. For his art-collection, &c., *see* culture and amusements *above*]:

— — Audley End: buys, iii. 140, n. 7 *ad fin.*, 556, n. 2; Berkshire House, London: buys for Lady Castlemaine, iii. 470, n. 5; Eltham: owner of, iii. 170 & n. 3; Euston House (property of Arlington): apartment for, at, iv. 116; Greenwich: project of, for rebuilding palace, iii. 300–1 & n., 313; ~ plants park, iii. 370 & n. 5; Hampton Court: constructs canal, lays out garden, &c., iii. 322, n. 5, 324 & n. 4; Holmby or Holdenby House: owner of, iv. 70 & n. 3; ~ grants to Louis de Duras, earl of Feversham, iv. 77; Newmarket: rebuilds, &c., iii. 138, n. 5, 554–5 & nn.; ~ mentioned, iv. 341, n. 1; Nonsuch: grants to duchess of Cleveland, iii. 426, n. 4; *see also* p. 428; Royston: owner of, iii. 138, n. 5; St. James's Park: lays out, &c., iii. 346, n. 4, 399, n. 6, 404; Whitehall: projects alterations, iii. 387 & n. 4; ~ employs Hugh May at, iii. 381, n. 3; ~ proposes building room at, for Council of Foreign Plantations, iii. 582–3 & n.; ~ project of, for rebuilding King Street (adjoining Whitehall), v. 204 & n. 4; Winchester: builds palace, &c., at, iv. 341 & n. 2, 471–2 & n. Windsor Castle: project of, for repairing, iii. 560 & n. 2, 573 & n. 1; ~ employs Hugh May at, iii. 381, n. 3, 573; ~ employs Grinling Gibbons at, iii. 573 & n. 1; ~ new buildings of, &c., at: notices, iv. 136 & n. 3, 207 & nn. 3–5, 316–17 & nn.; *see also* Windsor; ~ plants park, iii. 560; iv. 317.

— personal or private:

— — birthday, iii. 246; for commemoration *see* Church of England: worship: feasts and fasts.

— — geneal., iii. 271, n. 4, 316, 412, n. 4; v. 421, n. 3.

— — health: endangered by smoke of London, iii. 310; illness of, 1679, iv. 180 & n. 1, 181 *bis* & n. 1; ~ Jesuits' bark (quinine) administered to, during, v. 197 & n. 3; last illness of, iv. 405–9 & nn.

— — portraits, &c., of: by S. Cooper, drawing of head for coinage, iii. 309–10; by Van Dyck, as child: cited, iii. 468, n. 4; by Verrio: at Chelsea Hospital, v. 53; ~ at Windsor, iv. 465, n. 7 *ad fin.*; statues: by G. Gibbons: bronze, at Chelsea Hospital, iv. 317, n. 2; v. 53 & n. 2 (called James II in text, in error); ~ marble, at Royal Exchange, iv. 317, n. 2; at Windsor Castle, iv. 207 & n. 4; silver statuette, iv. 138 & n. 2.

— personal relations [notices indexed in this section are those in which the various persons named are mentioned in connexion with Charles (where the relations are political only select references are given)]:

— — Queen Catherine: (i) marriage: announced, iii. 286 & n. 6; Charles entertains Portuguese ambassador, iii. 290–1 & n.; negotiator for marriage, iii. 305; Tangier as part of dowry, iii. 305 & n. 4, 311 & n. 5; ceremonies, iii. 320 & n. 2;

CHARLES II: personal (*cont.*)
Clarendon accused of knowing that Catherine would be sterile, iv. 338 & n. 4; project for Charles's separation from Catherine and re-marriage, iv. 158 & n. 6.
— — — (ii) Charles's conduct towards, &c.: on her features, iii. 321, n. 3; displeased with her dress, iii. 320, n. 4; likes her musicians, iii. 322, n. 4; present of, to her, iv. 9; she is accused of intending to poison him, iv. 158 & nn. 5, 6; mutual requests for pardon, iv. 408–9 & n.; concerned in appointment of member of her household, iv. 8; promises to appoint Mrs. Evelyn as lady of her jewels, iii. 275.
— — mistresses and children:
— — — mistresses: (i) collective: Charles's addiction to women, iv. 410 & n. 2; general remarks on, i. *24, 30*; called concubines, &c., iv. 268, 374, 403, 409, 413; hostility of, to Clarendon, iii. 493; iv. 338–9; actresses as, iii. 466 & n. 5; lodgings of, in Whitehall, v. 47 & n. 2; Charles's expenditure on, i. 14–15; iv. 410 & n. 2; v. 401 & n. 1, 402.
— — — — (ii) individuals: Lucy Barlow, formerly Walter, ii. 561–2 & n.; alleged marriage of, to Charles: he contradicts, iv. 457 & n. 7; ~ supposed certificate of, iv. 502, n. 5; Barbara Palmer, countess of Castlemaine, later duchess of Cleveland, iii. 505, n. 4; Charles visits, iii. 573; Charles with, at court, 1685, iv. 403, 413; gifts of property to, iii. 426, n. 4, 470, n. 5; his death-bed concern for, iv. 409 & n. 2; Mary Davis, iii. 466, n. 5; Nell Gwynn, *ib.*; introduction of, to Charles, iii. 230, n. 3; Charles converses with, iii. 573, & n. 4; his death-bed concern for, iv. 409 & n. 2; Moll Knight, iii. 230, n. 3; Hortense Mancini, Duchesse Mazarin, iv. 97, n. 5; Charles with, at court, iv. 403, 413; Louise de Kéroualle, duchess of Portsmouth, iii. 564, n. 1; becomes Charles's mistress, iii. 589–90 & n.; he visits, iv. 343; with her at court, iv. 403, 413; his death-bed concern for, iv. 409 & n. 2.
— — — children: (i) collective: Charles's death-bed concern for, iv. 408 & n. 3; daughters: mentioned, iv. 268; sons: at Communion with Charles, iv. 374; comparisons among, iv. 185, 391–2.
— — — — (ii) individuals: Charles Beauclerk, duke of St. Albans, iv. 374, n. 6; Charles FitzCharles, earl of Plymouth, iv. 181, n. 6; Charles Fitzroy, duke of Southampton, iv. 392, n. 1; George Fitzroy, duke of Northumberland, iv. 374, n. 4; Henry Fitzroy, duke of Grafton, iii. 622, n. 4; ~ Charles attends marriage-ceremonies of, iii. 622; iv. 184–5 ~ grant of, to, v. 161 & n. 4; Anne Lennard, formerly Fitzroy, countess of Sussex, iii. 592, n. 4; Charlotte Lee, formerly Fitzroy, countess of Lichfield, iv. 268, n. 2; Charles Lennox, duke of Richmond, iv. 268, n. 6; James Scott, duke of Monmouth, ii. 562, n. 1; ~ told by Charles that he was illegitimate, iv. 456; *see also* iv. 457, n. 7; ~ Charles's paternity of, doubtful, iv. 457 & n. 6; ~ in disfavour, iv. 181 & n. 1, 189, n. 6, 353–4 & n., 408 & n. 3.
— — kinsfolk: Elizabeth, queen of Bohemia: his conduct towards, 1661, iii. 316 & n. 2; Henrietta Anne, later duchess of Orleans: visits Charles, 1660–1, 1670, iii. 262, 267, n. 2, &c., 548 *bis* & n. 1; Henrietta Maria, queen of England: letter from, to Charles, iii. 247; ~ he goes to meet, &c., 1661, 1662, iii. 259 & n. 3, 262, 267, n. 2, 328 & n. 1; James, duke of York, later James II: Charles exempts from attending Chapel Royal services, iv. 87, n. 4; ~ treats him as his chief adviser, iv. 294, n. 1, 323 & n. 6; ~ death-bed commendations to,

CHARLES II: personal (*cont.*)
iv. 408 & n. 3, 409 & n. 2; ~ death-bed gift to, iv. 408 & n. 2, 470–1 & nn.; Mary, Princess Royal, princess of Orange: visits Charles, iii. 264, &c.; William III, prince of Orange, later William III: visits Charles, 1670, iii. 563–4 & n.
— — various persons: Henry Bennet, earl of Arlington: Charles's conduct to, 1672, iv. 19 & n. 6; ~ grant of, to, v. 161 & n. 4; Thomas Blood: serves Charles as a spy, iii. 576 & n. 2; Sir Thomas Clifford, Baron Clifford: Charles advances, iv. 19 & n. 6; &c.; George Legge, Baron Dartmouth: grant to, iv. 311, n. 2; Arthur Capel, earl of Essex: Charles's attitude towards, 1683, iv. 328 & n. 2; Cornelis Evertsen, jnr.: Charles receives, &c., iii. 407; Sir Charles Berkeley, earl of Falmouth: as favourite, iii. 298; Mrs. Margaret Godolphin: Charles allows her to leave court, iv. 1; ~ grief of, for, iv. 149; William O'Brien, earl of Inchiquin: Charles displeased with, iv. 208, n. 6; Jan Kievit: Charles creates baronet, iii. 470, n. 6, 471; John Maitland, duke of Lauderdale: as favourite, iii. 370; Sir Robert Moray: Charles buries, iv. 15; Henry Howard, sixth duke of Norfolk: advice of Charles to, iii. 592; Titus Oates: Charles's views on, iv. 158, n. 6; Thomas Butler, earl of Ossory: Charles's lack of consideration for, iv. 209–10; Sir W. Petty: Charles on, iv. 58, n. 4; William Russell, Lord Russell: Charles's attitude towards, 1683, iv. 328 & n. 3; Tobias Rustat: gratitude of, to Charles, iv. 207; Mary Scrope, Lady Scrope: bribes Charles, iii. 275; Sir A. Slingsby: Charles and lottery run by, iii. 376; William Howard, Viscount Stafford: Charles's favours to, iv. 233; Robert Spencer, earl of Sunderland: Charles displeased with, iv. 245 & nn. 5, 6; Sir Charles Tuke: Charles godfather of, iii. 585; Col. C. Vratz:

CHARLES II: personal (*cont.*)
Charles and burial of, iv. 276; Sir Joseph Williamson: Charles attends promotion of, iii. 601.
— — Charles II and E:
— — — general series: Charles's friendliness, iv. 411; E's increasing dissatisfaction with, i. *29–30*.
— — — E compliments, &c.: 1641, ii. 28; ~ 1647, 1649, ii. 536, 561; ~ 1674, iv. 38; ~ 1679, iv. 180–1; E corresponds with, during exile, iii. 59, 200 & n. 1; E works for recall of, i. *13–14*; Charles sends E message from Breda, iii. 245; E presented to, iii. 247; compliments E, iii. 249; takes E yachting, iii. 296–8; takes E otter-hunting, iii. 306; visits Sayes Court: project, iii. 302; ~ the visit, iii. 110 & n. 2, 354; receives E after the Plague, iii. 428–9; wishes to knight E, iii. 428, n. 6; hears foreign news from E, iii. 434; orders E to search for fuel for London, 1667, iii. 486, 487; gives E piece of king-pine, iii. 513; E presents John Evelyn, jnr., to, iii. 440; Charles and Mrs. Evelyn, iii. 261–2, 275 & n. 5, 287.
— — — appointments: Charles nominates E a member of council of Royal Society, iii. 266 & n. 6; wants E to qualify as J. P., iii. 433–4; *for* Commission for Sick and Wounded *see below*; nominates E a commissioner for Saltpetre, iii. 442–3 & n.; appoints E a member of Council for Foreign Plantations, iii. 570–1; prepared to grant E office arising from forfeiture of London City Charter, iv. 341–2; promised appointments: Latin secretary (reversion), iii. 546–7 & n.; ~ Clerk of the Council, iii. 601.
— — — E as Commissioner for Sick and Wounded: Charles's dealings with: 1664: nominates E a commissioner, iii. 387–8 & n.; disposal of prisoners of war, iii. 391–2; 1665: disposal of prisoners of war, &c., iii. 406–

CHARLES II: personal (*cont.*)
12 *passim*; 1666: examines E's project for infirmary, iii. 430 & n. 2; E reports news to, iii. 437; orders of, to E, iii. 439; E reports to, on French prisoners, iii. 457 & n. 4; 1672: E reports progress to, &c., iii. 612, 616, 620 *bis*, 623 *bis*; orders of, to E, iii. 614; 1673: E reports progress to, &c., iv. 2(?), 16, 18(?); sends E to City to raise money, iv. 9.

— — — grants, &c., to E: Sayes Court: promises to grant in fee-farm to E and Sir R. Browne, iii. 59 & n. 1, 600; authorizes E to occupy, iii. 59; receives petition from E concerning (?), iii. 336; grants E ground adjoining, iii. 512 & n. 8, 530; renews lease of pastures adjoining, iii. 600 & n. 2.

— — — E's project, with Sir J. Kievit, for brick wharf along Thames: audience relating to, iii. 477; Charles's indebtedness to Sir Richard Browne: E's claim to recompense, iv. 20; ~ E petitions, concerning, iv. 394.

— — — patronage [E as intermediary with Charles II]: presents petition on behalf of Deptford poor, 1684, iv. 365; solicits for supplies for John Berkeley, Baron Berkeley of Stratton, during his embassy, iv. 110; solicits, to exempt Sir John Evelyn of Godstone from shrievalty of Surrey, iii. 365; assists Sir D. Gauden, iv. 176; introduces Grinling Gibbons, &c., iii. 568, 571–2, 573; introduces — Withers, iv. 12.

— — — conversations [apart from those concerning E's writings]: subjects stated: bees, iii. 304, 322; caleche, iii. 475; Cliveden and Windsor compared, iv. 177; E's proposals for replanning London after Fire, iii. 462–3 & n.; experiments, iii. 477; gardens, &c., iii. 297; Greenwich Palace: Charles's project for rebuilding, iii. 313; glass grenades, iii. 368; painting, &c., iii. 310; Philosophical

CHARLES II: personal (*cont.*)
Society (Royal Society), &c., iii. 288; shipping, &c., iii. 303, 512–13; swimming, iii. 490; subjects not stated, iii. 352, 369, 481, 521, 537; iv. 131.

— — — E's writings: Charles's reception of, &c.: Account of ambassadors' encounter: Charles orders E to prepare, &c., iii. 297–300 & nn.; ~ E gives copy to, iii. 352; *Fumifugium*: dedicated to Charles and published by command, iii. 295–6 & n., 456 & n. 8; ~ Charles orders E to prepare bill for parliament in accordance with, iii. 297 & n. 3, 310; History of Second Dutch War (project): Charles's interest in, i. *22–3*; ~ desires E to compose, iii. 523, n. 1, 550; ~ gives instructions to E, &c., for, iii. 559 & n. 4; ~ inquires about progress of, iii. 568; ~ specimen of, shown to, iii. 573; see also *Navigation and Commerce* below; *History of the Three Impostors*: E gives copy to Charles, iii. 522; *Late News*: E defends Charles in, iii. 243 & n. 3; *London revived* E presents to Charles, iii. 462–3 & n.; *Mystery of Jesuitism*: Charles commends, &c., iii. 397; *Navigation and Commerce*: Charles orders E to write, iv. 30; ~ remarks of, concerning, iv. 41 & n. 1; *Panegyric*: E presents to Charles, iii. 284 & n. 4; *Parallel of Architecture* (Fréart): dedicated to Charles, i. *18*; iv. 409, n. 5; ~ E gives copy to Charles, iii. 380; ~ Charles praises, &c., iii. 386–7; *Pernicious Consequences*: E gives copy to Charles, iii. 431; *Sylva*: dedicated to Charles, iii. 369; iv. 409, n. 5; *see also* i. *16–17*; iii. 541, n. 4; ~ Charles thanks E for, iii. 369, 386–7; *Tyrannus*: E gives copy to Charles, iii. 465.

— religion [Charles's conduct and views; for his ecclesiastical policy, &c., *see* political and public life: analytical series *above*]:

— — worship: attends divine ser-

CHARLES II: religion (*cont.*)
vice in Paris, 1651–2, iii. 20 & n. 4 (error), 48, 49, 51, 53 & n. 2; attends services, 1660–85, iii. 262–iv. 403 *passim*; makes offerings at Epiphany, &c., iii. 53 & n. 2, 501 & n. 3; iv. 171 & n. 8; receives Sacrament, iii. 51; iv. 7, 374–5 & n.
— — conversion to Roman Catholicism: exhorted to be a steadfast protestant (in sermon), iv. 157; Anglican devotions at his death-bed, iv. 407; reception into Roman Catholic Church rumoured, iv. 407–8 & n., 476; his two papers on doctrine, iv. 476–9 & n.; *add.*; influence of conversion on E, i. *31–2*.
— — miscellaneous: Charles's innovation in Chapel Royal music, iii. 347–8 & n.; hears A. Morus preach, iii. 310–11; gold cross, &c., belonging to, iv. 470–1 & n.
— miscellaneous: prophecy by P. Grebner applied to Charles, iii. 137, n. 2; remarks on a good omen, iii. 321–2.
Charles V, Emperor: birth-place of, ii. 73 & n. 7 (i. 48); armour of, ii. 414 & n. 7; monuments commemorating, ii. 73 & n. 8 (i. 48), 422 & n. 4; error for Charlemagne, ii. 35 & n. 4 (i. 27).
Charles VI, Emperor, v. 545, n. 3; *add.*; as Archduke Charles: in second Partition Treaty, v. 434, n. 4; as pretender to Spanish crown (styled Charles III, king of Spain): sets out from Vienna, v. 545 & n. 3; journey of, to Portsmouth, v. 548 & n. 2, 550, 551 & n. 2, 554 & n. 1; visits Windsor, v. 554, 555 & n. 3; journey of, to Lisbon, v. 555–8 & nn., *passim*; arrives at Lisbon, v. 560 & n. 1, 561; marriage project for, v. 560 & n. 1; embarks for Catalonia, v. 605 & n. 2; parliamentary grant to, v. 616–17 & n.
Charles V, king of France: chapel of, at St. Denis, ii. 86 (i. 58); buildings of: part of Louvre, ii. 103, n. 1; old chateau at St.-Germain-en-Laye, ii. 110–11 (i. 71).
Charles VI, king of France: geneal., iii. 72, n. 2.
Charles VII, king of France: victories of: in painting, ii. 117–18 (i. 76); statue of, ii. 137 (i. 90).
Charles VIII, king of France: imprisons Louis, duke of Orleans (later Louis XII), ii. 154 & n. 1 (i. 99); church built by, at Rome, ii. 373.
Charles IX, king of France: tomb of, ii. 86 (i. 58); statue of, ii. 108 (i. 70); buildings of: parts of Louvre and Tuileries, ii. 103, n. 1, 104, n. 2; at Fontainebleau, ii. 117, n. 4.
Charles of Anjou, king of Naples, ii. 160, n. 5.
Charles II, king of Spain, v. 287, n. 3.
1696–7: ill, v. 263–4 & n.
1698: ill, v. 287 & n. 3; in good health, v. 307 & n. 1.
1699: dominions of: French claims to succession to, iii. 316 & n. 3; ~ in Partition treaties, v. 434 & n. 4; reported ill, v. 324 & n. 6; consultations for defence of Empire in case of death of, v. 345 & n. 1; recovers, v. 352 & n. 2, 355 & n. 1; reported relapse of, v. 368 & n. 2.
1700: death of, reported, v. 429 & n. 3, 431 & n. 1; dies, v. 431, n. 1, 434; mourning for, in England, v. 437 & n. 1; will of, v. 434 & n. 2, 436 & n. 2, 445; ~ contrived by Louis XIV, &c., v. 445 & n. 5; Emperor claims escheatage of Milan, v. 440–1.
Charles III, king of Spain: *see* Charles VI, Emperor.
Charles X Gustavus, king of Sweden, ii. 521, n. 4; at Geneva, *ib.*; project for marriage of, to Queen Christina, iv. 221 & n. 1; invades Poland, 1655, iii. 161 & n. 3; march of, across the ice, winter 1657–8, iii. 211, n. 2; second Danish war of: Dutch intervene in, iii. 236 & n. 5.
Charles XI, king of Sweden, iv. 295, n. 2; birthday of: celebrated, iv. 295–6; at battle of Landskrona, iv. 333 & n. 1.
Charles XII, king of Sweden, v. 384, n. 2; hostilities of, with Denmark, 1700, v. 384 & n. 2, 386 & n. 1; ~ attempted mediation in, v. 417 & n. 1; defeats Russians at Narva, v. 438–9 & n., 440; takes Mittau, 1701, v. 472 & n. 4;

Charles XII (*cont.*)
threatens and takes Warsaw, 1702, v. 486 & n. 2, 504 & n. 5; threatens Cracow, v. 510 & n. 5; alluded to (the Northern princes), v. 446.
Charles IV, duke of Lorraine: assists Condé, 1652, iii. 67, n. 1.
Charles V Leopold, duke of Lorraine, iv. 394, n. 1; at siege of Buda, 1684, iv. 394; dies, v. 22 & n. 2.
Charles, Archduke: *see* Charles VI, Emperor.
Charles, duke of Kendal: born, iii. 444 & n. 2.
Charles, duke of Orleans: kept prisoner at Groombridge (error), iv. 40 & n. 2.
Charles, St.: chapel dedicated to (error), iv. 40 & n. 3.
Charles, St., Borromeo, ii. 496, n. 1; favours Inquisition at Milan, ii. 491, n. 2; colleges founded by, ii. 496 & n. 1; miracles of: represented, ii. 493 & n. 6; relics of, ii. 493 & n. 7; *ex voto* to, ii. 414 & n. 9; mentioned, iv. 40 & n. 3.
Charles Louis, Elector Palatine: agent of, in Paris, ii. 567 & n. 2.
Charles Martel: tomb of, ii. 86 (i. 58).
Charleton, Walter, M.D., iii. 289, n. 3; lectures, &c., by, iii. 289, 341; iv. 308 & n. 3; social(?), iv. 90 & n. 6; *add.*
Charleton *or* Courten, William, iv. 531, n. 3; museum of, iv. 531–2 & nn.; v. 13–14 & n., 81, 224; false mention of, iv. 90, n. 6; *add.*
Charlett, Arthur, D.D.: *The Whole Duty of Man* attributed to, v. 112 & n. 5.
Charleville, co. Cork: Lord Orrery's house at: destroyed, v. 37 & n. 1.
Charlotte Felicitas, duchess of Modena, iv. 28, n. 4.
Charlton, Kent: E visits or dines at (presumably at Charlton House), iii. 159, 162, 169, 525; Charlton House, iii. 66 & n. 3, 377; ~ view from, &c., iii. 85; ~ sold by Sir H. Puckering (formerly Newton), iii. 182, n. 6; ~ bought by Sir William Ducie (later Viscount Downe), ii. 539, n. 7; iii. 233, n. 2; ~ E dines at, iii. 414.
— church: monument in, iii. 66 & n. 3; marriage in, iii. 77 & n. 3; funeral at, iii. 185 & n. 4; other services in, iii. 66, 85, 86, 154, 174; v. 350–1; rector, 1687–1702: *see* Beardmore, T.
— Sir John Morden's Hospital, v. 212 & n. 5; Wricklemarsh, iii. 70, n. 2, 161, n. 1.
Charmont: *see* Chaumont.
Charnock, Robert: trial of, &c., v. 234 *bis* & nn. 4, 8.
Charon's Cave *or* Grotta del Cane, ii. 339–40 & nn.
Chartres: consecration of Henri IV at, ii. 147, n. 1; as error for Chastres, ii. 135 & n. 4 (i. 89).
Chastres (called Chartres, in error), ii. 135 & n. 4 (i. 89).
Châteillon, Sébastien: on sinlessness, iii. 363, n. 2.
Chatham, Kent: E visits: 1641, ii. 30 (i. 22); 1663, iii. 359; as Commissioner for Sick and Wounded: 1665, iii. 395, 411, 413–14, 417, 422, 432; 1666, iii. 436, 441–2, 468; 1667, iii. 486; 1672, iii. 614.
James II at, May 1688, iv. 582 & n. 1.
as naval station: Commissioners of the Navy at: *see* Cox, Sir J.; Middleton, Col. T.; Pett, Peter (1610–70; also master-builder of the Navy at Chatham); Dockyard, i. 23; ~ chaplain of: *see* Loton, J.; infirmary at: project for, iii. 430 & n. 2; ~ site for, iii. 432; money sent to, for Sick and Wounded, iii. 433; fleet at: Dutch attack, 1667, iii. 484–7 & nn.; ~ fortifications to protect, iii. 609–10; *Loyal London* burnt at, iii. 440, n. 6; *Sovereign of the Seas* at, ii. 30 (i. 22–3); ~ burnt at, v. 230 & n. 5.
church: service in, iii. 414; perpetual curates of: *see* Loton, J., Roswell, W.
house of Commissioner Peter Pett at, iii. 359; river of: *see* Medway.
Pett of: error for Peter Pett of Deptford, v. 10 & n. 1.
Chatsworth, Derbyshire: works by J. Ibach at, *add.* (iv. 207, n. 4).
Chaucer, Geoffrey: tomb of, iii. 490; and Dennington Castle, iii. 100 & n. 3.

Chaucer, Thomas, iii. 100, n. 3.
Chaumont (Charmont), on the Loire: chateau, ii. 143 & n. 2 (i. 93).
Chaworth, Patricius, third Viscount Chaworth: owner of Wiverton, iii. 125 & n. 2.
Chaworth, Sir Richard, D.C.L.: as vicar-general of the archbishop of Canterbury, iii. 362 *bis* & nn. 6, 8.
Chaworth, third Viscount: *see* Chaworth, Patricius.
Cheam (Cheme), Surrey: church: tombs in, iii. 221 & n. 2; ~ service in, iii. 221; ~ rectors of: *see* Doughty, J.; Hacket, J.
Cheke (Cheeke) family, iii. 553 & n. 1.
Cheke, Sir John: owner of Burrough Green (error), iii. 553 & n. 1.
Cheke, Thomas, lieutenant of the Tower, &c., iv. 226, n. 7; at Stafford's trial, iv. 226, 232.
Chelmsford, Essex: E visits, iii. 179, 180.
Chemistry [*see also* Alchemy; Medicine and Surgery; E uses the term in all three fields; here they are separated as far as possible]: E studies, ii. 534–5, 547; iii. 49; Sir K. Digby on, iii. 48 & nn. 2–6; iatro-chemical phase of, iii. 48, n. 2.
chymists: pharmacists, ii. 276 & n. 3; iii. 27–8 & n.; lady interested in distilling, iv. 121; other persons called, iii. 13, 88; *see also* Alchemy; le Fèvre, N.
chemicals: aqua fortis, iii. 293: aqua regalis, iv. 276; corrosive powder, iii. 317; phosphorus: demonstrations of, &c., iv. 251–4 & nn., 263, 271, 491; ~ segregation of, ii. 398, n. 3; ~ Bologna stone called, ii. 422–3 & n.; sal ammoniac, iv. 325 & n. 1; spirit of sulphur, iii. 293; iv. 325; spirit of vinegar, iv. 324.
laboratories or elaboratories, ii. 187 & n. 4 (i. 118); iii. 154 & n. 6, 294; iv. 118, 124.
Chenies, Bucks.: Col. J. Russell buried at, iv. 562, n. 1.
Chenonceaux: chateau, ii. 152 & nn. 3, 4 (i. 98).
Cher river, at Tours, ii. 144, n. 4.
Cherbury, Lord: *see* Herbert, Edward, Baron Herbert of Cherbury.
Cheriton, Hants.: battle of: Edward Stowell at, iii. 37, n. 3.
Chesewick: *see* Chiswick.
Cheshire: rising in, on behalf of William of Orange, iv. 608; Stansfield family of (error), iii. 89 & n. 3.
Chester: Schomberg at, iv. 647, n. 1.
Chester: County Palatine of: chief justices of: *see* Herbert, Sir Edward, earl of Portland (Jacobite creation); Jeffreys, George, Baron Jeffreys.
Chester: diocese: Bishops: *see* Walton, Brian (1660–1); Ferne, H. (1662); Hall, George (1662–8); Wilkins, John (1668–72); Pearson, John (1672–86); Cartwright, T. (1686–9); Stratford, N. (1689–1707).
Chesterfield: Earls and Countesses of: *see* Stanhope, Philip, first earl, 1628–56; Stanhope, Catherine, Lady Stanhope, countess *suo jure* 1660–7; Stanhope, Philip, second earl, 1656–1713; Stanhope, Elizabeth, his countess.
Chesterford, Essex, iii. 588.
Chetwin, Rev. —: error for K. Chetwood, iv. 502 & n. 1(?), 539 & n. 2.
Chetwood, Knightly; D.D. 1691, iv. 502, n. 3; sermons by, iv. 502; ~ as 'Mr. Chetwin', iv. 502 & n. 1(?), 539 & n. 2.
Chetwynd, Rev. John: sermon by (?), iv. 502 & n. 1.
Chevareux, near Tours: chateau, ii. 148 (i. 96).
Chewney (Chunie), Rev. Nicholas: sermon by, iii. 615 & n. 4.
Cheyne, Charles, first Viscount Newhaven and Lord Cheyne 1681, v. 100, n. 4; geneal., v. 100, 585, n. 2; social, v. 247.
Cheyne, Mrs. Gertrude, later Lady Cheyne, &c., born Pierrepont, wife of William Cheyne, second Viscount Newhaven and Lord Cheyne, v. 7, n. 5; geneal., v. 7, 100; dies (error), v. 518 & n. 4.
Cheyne, William; second Viscount Newhaven and Lord Cheyne 1698, v. 7 & n. 5; appointed a commissioner of the Privy Seal, *ib.*; social, v. 100, 469.

Cheyne (Cheny): Lords and Lady: *see* Cheyne, Charles, first Viscount Newhaven and Lord Cheyne, 1681–98; Cheyne, William, second Viscount Newhaven and Lord Cheyne, 1698–1728; Cheyne, Gertrude, his lady.
Chicheley, —: social, iv. 257.
Chicheley, Mrs. —, iii. 437 & n. 2.
Chicheley, Sir John, admiral: social (?), iii. 390 & n. 6.
Chicheley, Sir Thomas; knighted 1670; Master of the Ordnance 1670–4, iii. 390, n. 6; as privy councillor, iii. 442 & n. 9; as commissioner for Saltpetre, iii. 442–3 & n.; and proposed repair of St. Paul's, iii. 448–9 & n.; drains Fens about Soham Mere, &c., iii. 555 & nn. 2, 4; social (?), iii. 390; geneal., iii. 437, n. 2.
Chichester, Sussex: notice, ii. 22 (i. 16 & n. 2); E at, ii. 79; recorder of: *see* Peckham, Sir H.
Chichester: cathedral clergy:
bishops: *see* Andrewes, L. (1605–9); Duppa, B. (1638–41); King, Henry (1642–69); Gunning, P. (1670–5); Brideoake, R. (1675–8); Carleton, G. (1679–85); Lake, John (1685–9); Patrick, S. (1689–91); Grove, R. (1691–6); Williams, John (1696–1709); Hare, F. (1731–40).
— R. Kidder called bishop in error, v. 161 & n. 1.
deans: *see* Ryves, Bruno (1646, 1660); Gulson, J. (1663–9); Stradling, G. (1672–88); Hayley, W. (1699–1715).
Chichester, Sir John, iv. 378, n. 2.
Chiffinch (Chiffing), Thomas, iii. 305 & n. 1; social, iii. 305; garden of, iii. 293, n. 1, 305, n. 1.
Chiffinch, William, iii. 305, n. 1.
Chigi (Ghisi) family: chapel belonging to, ii. 374 & n. 4.
Chigi (Ghisi), Agostino: palace of, in Rome, ii. 287–8 & n.
Chigi, Fabio: *see* Alexander VII.
Child, Sir John, iv. 438, n. 2.
Child, Sir Josiah, bt., iv. 305–6 & n.; estate of, at Wanstead, *ib.*
Child, Rebecca: *see* Somerset, Rebecca, marchioness of Worcester.
Childebert, king of France: statue of, ii. 95 (i. 63).
Chile: governor of: *see* Lopez de Zuñiga, Don F. (iii. 188, n. 5).
Chilston, Boughton Malherbe, Kent: *see* Boughton Malherbe.
China: account of: mentioned, iv. 214; geography of: in sermon, v. 49; objects from: books, ii. 301; furnishings, v. 147; lacquer, iii. 324, n. 2; screens, iv. 288; porable barber's shop, v. 303 & n. 1; royal dress, ii. 192 (i. 119); works of art, &c., iii. 373–4 & nn.; other curiosities, ii. 53 (i. 37); i. 65; v. 427.
China oranges, iv. 182; tea, i. 14.
Chinese language: grammar (book) of (?), iii. 374 & n. 7; writing, iii. 374.
Chioggia (Chioza), ii. 429 & n. 1.
Chios: relic from, ii. 438–9 & n.
Chippenham, Wilts.: vicar of: *see* Barker, S.
Chislehurst, Kent: Frogpoole or Frognal in, iii. 253, n. 2; E visits, iii. 253; iv. 73.
Chiswell, Richard, publisher, iv. 241, n. 3.
Chiswick (Chesewick), Middlesex: Mary Evelyn (later Lady Wyche) at, ii. 558; Chiswick House (Lord Burlington), iv. 294 & n. 5; Sir Stephen Fox's house at, iv. 185, n. 2, 294 & n. 4, 316; mentioned, iv. 467.
Choiseul, César de, duke of Choiseul, &c.: *see* du Plessis, Maréchal.
Choiseul, Gilbert de, bishop of Tournai, &c.: visits England, iii. 548 & n. 2.
Cholmley, Sir Hugh: work of, on mole at Tangier, iv. 54, n. 5.
Christ [passages in sermons relating to Him are not indexed]:
— legends associated with: Nativity: Temple of Peace at Rome burnt on night of, ii. 218 & n. 1; ~: fountain of oil at time of, ii. 289 & n. 1; Passion: rock at Gaeta cleft during, ii. 323 & n. 3; ascended from hell at Avernus, ii. 346; appearance of, at Domine Quo Vadis, ii. 363.
— miscellaneous notices: portraits of, ii. 269 & n. 4, 311 & n. 1; monogram of, ii. 383 & n. 4, 388 & n. 2; symbol of crucifixion, ii. 500, n. 4; in Bajazet II's letter, ii. 499–500; opinions of a Jew on, ii. 54 (i. 38).
— Second Coming: views of Lactan-

Christ (*cont.*)
tius on: in sermons, v. 448 & n. 1, 613 & n. 1; Oughtred's views on, iii. 158 & n. 3; John Mason announces, v. 177–8 & n.
— relics of: collections: Rome: S. Croce in Gerusalemme, ii. 380 & nn. 8–10; ~ S. Giovanni in Laterano, ii. 273–5 & nn.; St.-Denis, ii. 87–9 (i. 58–60); Venice, St. Mark's, ii. 441 & nn. 6–10.
— — single:
— — — Nativity: crib, ii. 244; ~ exhibited, ii. 291 & n. 2; swaddling-clothes, ii. 87 (i. 59); gold offered by Magi: piece of, ii. 496 & n. 2.
— — — water-pot from Cana, ii. 89 (i. 60).
— — — towel used for disciples' feet, ii. 87 (i. 59), 275.
— — — Last Supper: table, ii. 272, n. 6, 275; ~ exhibited, ii. 385; vessel used at, ii. 177, n. 1.
— — — Thirty Pieces of Silver, ii. 380 & n. 10.
— — — Crown of Thorns, ii. 87, 88 (i. 59 *bis*), 99 (i. 65), 155 (i. 100), 380, 441 & n. 9; iv. 470.
— — — pillar to which Christ was tied, ii. 246 & n. 2, 441.
— — — sudarium (St. Veronica), ii. 262; ~ exhibited, ii. 385 & n. 3, 386.
— — — cross: nails, ii. 87 (i. 58), 205, 380, 441; title, ii. 87 (i. 59), 380; wood, ii. 87 (i. 58), 155 (i. 100), 256, 262, 274, 298, 380, 441 & n. 7; iv. 470, n. 3 *ad fin.*, 471; ~ exhibited (Rome, St. Peter's), ii. 385, n. 4, 386 & n. 2.
— — — lance, ii. 262; exhibited, ii. 385 & n. 4, 386; letter relating to, ii. 499–500 & n.
— — — reed, ii. 275.
— — — sponge, ii. 87 (i. 59), 275.
— — — blood, ii. 87 (i. 59), 268, 275, 380, 441 & n. 6.
— — — other relics of Passion, ii. 273 & nn. 7, 8.
— miscellaneous: clothes, hair, &c., ii. 87 (i. 59); column from the Temple associated with, ii. 264; foot-prints, ii. 363 & n. 7; stone from Tyre associated with, ii. 438 & n. 8; table showing height of, ii. 273 & n. 6; Volto Santo (Lucca), ii. 409–10 & n.
Christian V, king of Denmark, iii. 342, n. 3; as prince: attends Lord Mayor's show, London, iii. 342 & n. 3; at battle of Landskrona, iv. 333 & n. 1; besieges Hamburg, &c., iv. 524–5 & nn.; offers to support Emperor, &c., iv. 642 & n. 6; dies, v. 353 & n. 2, 354; geneal., v. 582 & n. 1.
Christian, Prince, of Brunswick, brother of George I: drowned, v. 543 & n. 2.
Christian Albrecht, duke of Gottorp, iv. 525, n. 1; and Christian V of Denmark: driven from his duchy by, &c., iv. 525 & n. 1; ~ treaty with, iv. 642, n. 6; *add.*; geneal., v. 582, n. 1.
Christian Ernest, margrave of Kulmbach: crosses Simplon pass, ii. 505, n. 2.
Christina, queen of Sweden, iv. 220, n. 6; character of, &c., iv. 221 & nn. 1–3; entry of, into Rome, ii. 375, n. 1; palace of, at Rome, ii. 379, n. 4; musician at court of (Pietro Reggio), iv. 220.
Christmas, — (W. Christmas ?), ii. 545 & n. 7.
Christmas, Mrs. Susannah, born Evelyn, wife of W. Christmas: geneal., ii. 545, n. 7.
Christmas, William: payment by (?), ii. 545 & n. 7.
Christopher, St.: relic of, ii. 290; statue of, ii. 95–6 & n. (i. 63).
Chronology [*see also* Prophecies]: boy's knowledge of, iv. 617; coincidences of dates of death, &c., v. 195–6 & n.; diluvian period, iii. 158 & n. 3; equinoxes: dates of, iii. 477, n. 2; v. 515, n. 1; four ancient monarchies, ii. 431 & n. 3; new style calendar used by English in Paris for Church festivals, iii. 2, n. 7; Pie: rules called the, iv. 300 & n. 4; year: reckonings of the, v. 26.
Chrysostom, John, St.: *see* John, St., Chrysostom.
Chudleigh, Sir George: geneal., iii. 470, n. 2.
Chudleigh, Mary: *see* Cole, Mrs. M.
Chunie, Rev. —: *see* Chewney, N.
Chur, Switzerland, ii. 489, n. 6.
CHURCH, the [the Church in general, including the Early Christians and the Fathers; a few notices indexed under Church of Eng-

CHURCH (*cont.*)
land also refer to the Church in general; notices relating to the various churches, sects, &c., are indexed under their own names]:
— Councils: Basle: copy of synodal epistles of, iii. 106 & n. 6; Ferrara, later Florence: history of, by S. Sgouropoulos, ii. 563 & n. 5; ~ man attending, ii. 200, n. 2; Lateran, ii. 274 & n. 4; Milan, S. Ambrogio, ii. 500; Orleans, ii. 138 (i. 90–1); Trent: *see* Trent, Council of.
— early Christians [the Primitive Saints, &c.]: antiquities from time of, at Sion, ii. 516; build Baths of Diocletian, &c., ii. 238, 240 & n. 3; catacombs of, at Rome, ii. 363–4 & n., 387–8 & nn.; churches of: first consecration of, with existing ceremonies, ii. 271–2; ~ first use of stone altars in, ii. 272; faith of; survives among Pyrennean Christians, iv. 636; martyrs: places of general martyrdoms, ii. 307 & n. 7, 456; Millenarians imitate, v. 178; miracle of: represented on Column of Marcus Aurelius, ii. 370 & n. 4; ten persecutions of, ii. 238 & n. 4, 240 & n. 3; ~ in comparison, iv. 575; ~ instruments of torture for, ii. 307; alluded to ('maiden of primitive life'), iv. 482–3.
— — in sermons: All Saints' day celebrated by, iii. 342; articles of belief, iv. 570; assemblies for worship, iv. 283; Bible not forbidden to laity, iv. 277; choice of Christian names, v. 125; church buildings, v. 64; confession, iv. 256; discipline or penance, &c., iv. 204, 290–1, 538, 573; v. 131–2; dispersal of, iii. 377; excommunication: use of, by, iv. 346; faith of: Church of England adheres to, iv. 73; fasting, v. 325, 379; hymns: use of, by, iv. 527; martyrs in first persecution, iii. 238; mutual love of, v. 231 & n. 2, 471, 488; obedience of, to princes, iv. 336, 522; period of: Nonconformists appeal to, v. 64; purity and piety of, iv. 501;

CHURCH (*cont.*)
v. 328; renunciation by, of worldly things, v. 120–1; Sacrament: frequency of receiving, v. 590 & n. 4; ~ views on, iv. 580; Trinity: views on, v. 414.
— Fathers: editions of works of, iv. 145 & n. 1; Greek: do not mention original sin, iii. 158; patristic learning of R. Boyle, v. 82.
— — in sermons: on ascension of the just, v. 536; on Bible-reading, v. 106; on eternal punishment, v. 107; on irremissible sin (Hebrews vi. 4), v. 389; on submission to kings, v. 165; zeal of, v. 57; minor reports, iii. 11, 21–2 *bis*, 35; iv. 539.
— miscellaneous: history of: boy's knowledge of, iv. 617; toleration: at Amsterdam, ii. 44 & n. 2; in England: *see* Nonconformists, &c.; Roman Catholic Church; in Switzerland, ii. 518.
— — in sermons [select]: compared to ship, iv. 459; deliverances of: *see* Church of England: chronological series; garden of the Spouse, &c., iii. 133, 167, 169; interpreter of Scripture, iii. 60; and persecution: submission to, iv. 493; ~ unlawfulness of, v. 223; schisms and heresies in: causes of, iii. 233; iv. 229; Sunday substituted by, for Sabbath, v. 591; unity, former, of, iv. 24–5.
Church, Percy, royalist: in Paris, iii. 6 & n. 5.
Churchill, Lady Anne: *see* Spencer, Anne, countess of Sunderland.
Churchill, Arabella: *see* Godfrey, Mrs. A.
Churchill, Charles, General: as Lieutenant of the Tower, v. 611 & n. 4.
Churchill, Lady Elizabeth: *see* Egerton, Elizabeth, countess of Bridgewater.
Churchill, Lady Henrietta: *see* Godolphin, Henrietta, duchess of Marlborough.
Churchill, John, 1686–1703; styled Lord Churchill 1689; marquis of Blandford 1702: dies, v. 530 & n. 5, 531 & n. 3.
Churchill, John, 1650–1722; Baron Churchill 1682; earl of Marlborough 1689; duke 1702, v.

Churchill, John, 1650–1722 (*cont.*) 35, n. 4; colonel, King's Own Dragoons, iv. 354, n. 3.
1685: at Sedgemoor, iv. 452, n. 1.
1690: captures Kinsale, v. 35 & n. 4.
1692: dismissed by William III, v. 86 & n. 1, 90 & n. 2, 98, n. 1.
1700: appointed Master of the Ordnance (error), v. 438 & n. 3.
1701: joins in lords' protest, v. 466 & n. 2.
1702: elected K.G. and appointed captain-general, &c., v. 495 & n. 2; captured by French and released, v. 519 & n. 1; returns to England, v. 521 & n. 3; created duke, and proposed grant to, v. 524–5 & n.
1703: death of his son, v. 530 & n. 5, 531; goes to United Provinces, v. 531 & n. 3; takes Limburg, &c., v. 546 & n. 4; prepares for England, v. 548, n. 2.
1704: goes to The Hague, v. 555 & n. 2; goes to United Provinces as general, v. 563 & n. 2; march of, to the Danube, v. 572 & n. 1; capture of the Schellenberg, v. 572 & n. 3, 573 & n. 1; created a prince of the Empire, v. 573 & n. 2; victory of, at Blenheim, v. 574–5 & nn.; movements of, after Blenheim, v. 577 & n. 3; prisoners allotted to, v. 577, n. 4; returns to England, v. 583 & n. 5; complimented by parliament, v. 583 & n. 7.
1705: goes to United Provinces to take command, v. 590 *bis* & nn. 1, 3; forces French lines at Elixem, v. 602 & n. 3, 604–5 & n.; besieges Leuwe, v. 607 & n. 3.
appearance, manner, &c., of, v. 525–6 & n.; courtesy of, to E, v. 584 & n. 1; alleged corruption of, v. 86 & n. 1; income of, 1702, 1704, v. 525 & n. 3; relations of, with James II, v. 86, 90; grants to: Woodstock manor, iii. 381, n. 5; principality of Mindelheim, v. 573, n. 2; geneal., iv. 497, n. 4 *ad fin.*; v. 86 & n. 2, 290 & n. 5, 525 & nn. 4–8, 530 & n. 5, 611 & n. 4; aide-

Churchill, John, 1650–1722 (*cont.*) de-camp of, 1704: *see* Parke, D.; chaplain of (F. Hare?): sermon by, v. 620 & n. 4.
Churchill, Sarah; born Jennings; wife of John Churchill, duke of Marlborough; Baroness Churchill 1682; countess, 1689, and duchess, 1702, of Marlborough, v. 90 & n. 2; origin of, v. 525 & n. 4; influence of, over Princess Anne, v. 86, n. 1; forbidden the court, 1692, v. 90 & n. 2; income of, 1704, v. 525, n. 3; the Blenheim letter to, v. 574, n. 1; at thanksgiving for Blenheim, v. 578 & n. 1; letters from, to E, i. *53*; geneal., iv. 79, n. 3.
Churchill, Sir Winston: conduct of, &c., v. 86 & n. 2, 525.
Churchill, Baron, 1682–9: *see* Churchill, John, later duke of Marlborough.
Churchill, Lord, 1689–1702: *see* Churchill, John, later marquis of Blandford.
Churchill, Lord, 1705 (error): *see* Churchill, Charles.
CHURCH OF ENGLAND [the name, 'the Church of England', has different implications before and after the outbreak of the Civil War in 1642; the Act of Uniformity of 1662 was, in one aspect, an expression of the change in the relationship between the Church and the national community. The chronological section below is divided in accordance with the different implications or meanings of the name.
For the Diary as a source for the history of the Church *see* i. *111–12* & nn.]:
— chronological series: (i) from the Reformation to 1642:
— — — Puritan opposition to: stories of origin of, iii. 157, n. 2; iv. 507, 508, n. 1; v. 13 & n. 1; the Church in its splendour, ii. 6 & n. 1 (i. 6 & n. 1), 19–20 (i. 15); Laud and Lambeth Palace attacked, 1640, ii. 25 & nn. 1, 3 (i. 18).
— — (ii) the general community of English protestants, 1642–62:
— — — the solemn Vow and Covenant to be taken, ii. 81–2 & n.

CHURCH OF ENGLAND (*cont.*)
(i. 55); general state of the Church, 1647–60, i. *8–9* & n., *11*; parish churches occupied by the sectaries, 1649, &c., ii. 552 & n. 3; iii. 60, 181, 185; 'honest' sermons, 1652, iii. 60, 79; various sectaries, enthusiasts, &c., as preachers, iii. 14, 15, 67, 91, 147, 150; *see also* iii. 80–1, 185; ~ sermons on theological problems, iii. 160, 184; festivals, &c.: abolished, iii. 79, n. 1, 145 & n. 1, 204 & n. 5; ~ non-observance of, iii. 78–9, 92, 97, 144 & n. 3, 164, 225; ~ sermons against abolition of, &c., iii. 145, 225; neglect of Communion, ii. 552; iii. 94, 95; v. 180, n. 1; neglect of piety and ignorance of the laity, 1655, &c., iii. 153, 160 & n. 5, 184 & n. 2, 254 & n. 1; Gauden tries to reconcile Anglicans and sectaries, iii. 187, n. 6; rise of heresies and schisms, 1657, &c., iii. 197, 227 & n. 1; ~ in sermons, iii. 233, 236.

— — (iii) the orthodox Anglicans, 1642–62:

— — — general: time of affliction, &c., *c.* 1650–1, iii. 9, 37, 46, 633; ~ fast on account of, iii. 39; ~ prayer for Church, iii. 40; ~ in sermons, iii. 32, 44, 47; ~ alluded to, in sermons, iii. 1–54 *passim*; Anglicans preach infrequently in parish churches, iii. 60 [notices of particular Anglican divines preaching 1649–60 are not indexed collectively]; incumbent dispossessed for using Prayer Book, iii. 134, n. 1; views of clergy on communicating with sectaries, &c., iii. 184, n. 2; ejected clergy: forbidden to conduct services, &c., 1655, iii. 163 & n. 1, 164; ~ poverty of, iii. 172 ~ collection for, iii. 213–14 & n.; the Church first reduced to a conventicle, 1656, iii. 181; devoutness of members in time of persecution, *ib.*; raid on London congregations, Christmas, 1657, iii. 203–4 & nn.; sufferings of the Church, 1658, 1659, iii. 214, 231; ~ fast for, iii. 234, 235; ~ end,

CHURCH OF ENGLAND (*cont.*)
iii. 246; restoration of the Church, iii. 464; v. 102; ~ in sermons (other than on 29 May), iii. 253–4, 262, 304; its powers restored, iii. 312 & n. 2.

— — — the Church in France: the Anglican exiles in Paris, i. *8*, *10*; services in Paris, 1649–52, ii. 562–7; iii. 1–12, 17–54, all *passim*; iii. 632–5; service at Calais, iii. 55; the Anglicans at the Louvre, iii. 36 & n. 5; services in Sir Richard Browne's chapel as proof of visibility of the Church, iii. 247–8 & n.; iv. 303.

— — — the Church in London, 1649–60: places of worship [for full references for the various churches, &c., *see* London: topography; references here are to decisive notices]: Exeter House chapel (earl of Rutland), iii. 95, n. 5, 203, n. 3; ~ congregation at, called 'the Church of England', iii. 204, n. 6 *ad fin.*; ~ ministry of Peter Gunning at, iii. 190, n. 3; ~ monthly communion at (?), iii. 233; ~ fasts at (?), iii. 226 & n. 6, 234–41 *passim* [many of the Anglican services, iii. 190–248, if no other place is named, were probably held here]; church by Garlick Hill, iii. 204, n. 6 *ad fin.*; private houses, iii. 181 & n. 3, 185, 190, 204, n. 6 *ad fin.*, 211, 212, 222; St. Gregory by St. Paul's, iii. 61, n. 4, 150 & n. 2; St. Peter, Paul's Wharf, ii. 552 & n. 5; Westminster, congregation of T. Thurscross, iii. 204, n. 6 *ad fin.*; [the following are uncertain; E records Easter celebrations (Communion or sermon) at them:] St. Clement, Eastcheap, iii. 64 & n. 5, 82, 150; St. Mary Woolchurch Haw, iii. 212 (identification, iii. 197, n. 3); St. Mary Magdalen, Old Fish Street, iii. 82 & n. 4 [places, in London or in the country, at which Anglicans preached, either as incumbents or occasionally, but which presumably conformed to the government's orders, are not indexed collectively].

CHURCH OF ENGLAND (*cont.*)
— — — — services attended by E in London [Anglican services or services at which Anglicans preach, but excluding baptisms, &c., and services in French and Italian], ii. 552–6; iii. 13–15, 61 *bis*, 64, 82 *bis*, 94–5, 148–52, 158–70, 181–204, 211–14, 222–45 *passim & singulatim*; Communion, ii. 556; iii. 61, 64, 82, 150–243, as above, *passim*; monthly Communion and fasts: *see* Exeter House chapel *in preceding section*.
— — (iv) 1662–1706: time of heresies, &c., 1670, iii. 558; effect of Declaration of Indulgence 1672, iii. 608; attitude of Rye-House conspirators to the Church, iv. 323; Charles II's death-bed silence concerning, iv. 409 & n. 3; James II promises to maintain, iv. 411, 442–3; ~ confidence in his promise, iv. 479; ~ his promise broken, iv. 509–10, 582; supported by L'Estrange in *The Observator*, iv. 439 & n. 3; defended in parliament, iv. 495 & n. 2; weakened by deaths of Dolben and Fell, iv. 507, 519; *see also* Commission for Ecclesiastical Affairs.
— — — 1687: the Declaration of Indulgence as an attempt to ruin, iv. 546.
— — — 1688: the Declaration: ordered to be read in all churches, iv. 583–4 & n.; ~ clergy not reading: impending attack on, iv. 590 & n. 3, 596; Nonconformists ally themselves with the Church, iv. 590; royal declaration promising to maintain the Church, iv. 597 & n. 4; protestant officers removed, iv. 599 & n. 6; deliverance of the Church from James II (general), v. 475.
— — — sermons during reign of James II: on perseverance in true faith, &c., iv. 414, 419–20, 503, 504, 512, 544, 564, 567, 569, 571–2, 576–7, 577–8, 581, 589, 590, 591, 601; on submission to persecutors, iv. 493; on deliverances of the Church, iv. 607.

CHURCH OF ENGLAND (*cont.*)
— — — 1689: votes of parliament to maintain the Church as established by law, iv. 631 & n. 4; promise to maintain, in coronation oath, iv. 632 & n. 5; prosperity of: threatened by republicans in office, iv. 635; 1691: fear of schism arising from deprivation of nonjuring bishops, v. 52, 59; for the Nonjurors *see* Nonjurors; 1698–9: time of schisms, &c.: in sermons, v. 292, 307, 319; Church weakened by death of Stillingfleet, v. 319.
— — (v) sermons on God's deliverances of the Church, &c.:
— — — God's care of the Church, against wickedness, iv. 84; deliverances: general (1689), iv. 621, 623; from James II, v. 559; in 5 November sermons, iii. 47–8 & n., 235, 423, 501, 597; iv. 101, 348, 563; v. 72, 118, 156, 271–2, 582; ~ including William III, iv. 650; v. 362; in other sermons, v. 89, 240.
— buildings [structure, &c.]:
— — reverence due to churches: in sermons, iv. 160, 526; v. 265, 317, 610; benefits to be obtained in: in sermon, iii. 482; consecration of a church, ii. 8 (i. 7); inauguration of Trinity Chapel, v. 61–6; orientation of a chapel, iii. 139 & n. 7; altars: arrangement of, iii. 109, 317 & n. 7; iv. 132 & n. 8; ~ decoration of, iv. 397 & n. 4; altar-plate, &c., iii. 129 & n. 4; iv. 397; pews: effect of, ii. 115 & n. 4 (i. 75); burying in churches: opposed, iv. 304 & n. 4, 634; v. 119; tabernacles: used during rebuilding of a church, iv. 180 & n. 6; ~ chapels of ease called, iv. 242 & n. 4; v. 132 & n. 2, 170 & n. 2.
— — iconoclasm: damage to churches by Puritans and in Civil War: alluded to, ii. 49 & n. 1 (i. 34), 528; at Cambridge, Peterhouse chapel, iii. 139, n. 1; Canterbury cathedral: windows destroyed, &c., ii. 76 & n. 3 (i. 50); ~ repairs to, iii. 395 & n. 2; at Lambeth Palace chapel, iii. 361, n. 5; at Lincoln cathe-

CHURCH OF ENGLAND (*cont.*)
dral, &c., iii. 131, n. 6, 132 *bis* & nn. 3, 4; London, Cheapside Cross: destroyed, ii. 81 & n. 3 (i. 55); Oxford: windows in cathedral destroyed, iii. 109 & n. 3; ~ chapels of New College and Magdalen unharmed, iii. 108 & n. 7, 109 & n. 5; at Peterborough cathedral, &c., iii. 134 & nn. 2, 3; at Worcester cathedral, iii. 119 & n. 5; York Minster: preserved unharmed, iii. 128–9 & n.

— the Church overseas [for the Church in exile in France *see* chronological series *above*]:

— — missions, &c.: travels of I. Basire in Levant, &c., iii. 303 & n. 3, 342 & n. 5; Plantation negroes: James II desires baptism of, iv. 471 & n. 3; translations of Bible, &c., into Turkish, &c., made for R. Boyle, v. 82 & n. 2; Society for Propagation of the Gospel: activities of, v. 507 & n. 1.

— — chaplains [excluding those of ambassadors at Paris, regiments, and ships]: at Bombay, iv. 438; at Constantinople, iv. 545 & n. 3; v. 224, n. 7; in India, v. 568, n. 1; at Leghorn (?), iv. 156, n. 2.

— doctrines, &c. [all notices of controversies, including writings and sermons relating to them, and sermons relating to other churches, sects, &c., are indexed under the opponents alone: *see* Nonconformists; Roman Catholic Church]:

— — general: subscriptions to, by Orthodox bishops (?), iii. 342 & n. 5; the Church as Protestant or Reformed, iv. 600, n. 4, 632, n. 5; Anglicans influenced by Socinus, iii. 227, n. 1; doctrines asserted in sermon, iv. 182; the Church or its doctrines praised in sermons, iii. 152, 303; iv. 73, 394, 541–2, 555; v. 546–7; particular subjects: Christian liberty: in sermons, iii. 31 & n. 2, 101; v. 19–20; faith and works: in sermon, v. 70–1; free will, iii. 235, 236, 237; immutable decrees: in sermon, v. 612; persecution: unlawfulness of: in sermon, v. 223; Sacrament: in sermon, v. 17–18; ~ corporal presence of Christ in: discussed, iv. 129–30.

— — political teaching: loyalty of the Church praised by James II, iv. 442; views of clergy on passive obedience prior to 1689, iv. 620 & n. 1; v. 59.

— — — in sermons: ministers of state not to be criticized in sermons, v. 467; monarchy: best form of government, iv. 135, 336; v. 165–6; obedience to kings or magistrates (select), iii. 365; iv. 35, 63, 192, 242, 277, 381, 455; ~ necessity of, in all lawful things, iv. 522; v. 237; ~ to tyrannous princes, iv. 578; patriarchal dominion, &c., iv. 336 & n. 4; primogeniture, iv. 135; v. 165–6; princes: good prince the life of his people, iv. 237; duty of: to God, to govern justly, &c., iv. 621; v. 22; ~ to take care of Church, iii. 49; v. 22; ~ to their subjects, v. 378 & n. 2; God's care of, iv. 361; God's vicegerents, iv. 621; powers of, in church-government, iv. 264–5.

— — — — rebellion, &c.: condemned, iii. 421; iv. 105, 128–9, 163, 250, 458, 643; ~ not authorized by Christian liberty, iv. 182; regal office, iv. 499; regicide condemned, iii. 569; iv. 364, 404–5; v. 165–6, 364–5; sovereignty necessary in every government (anti-papal), v. 271–2; subjects: duty of, to pray for rulers, iii. 528; subordination, iii. 542–3; minor notices, iii. 521, 580; iv. 47, 52, 91, 168, 247, 550, 568, 621.

— organization:

— — clergy: (i) chronological series: depletion of, *c.* 1650, iii. 9, 633; during Civil War, &c.: persecution of, iv. 634; ~ not inclined towards Roman Catholicism (in sermon), iv. 394; required to use Book of Common Prayer, &c., 1662, iii. 331 & n. 3; preach and write against Roman Catholicism, 1687, iv.

CHURCH OF ENGLAND (*cont.*)
541 & n. 3; attitude of, towards Revolution, iv. 620 & n. 1; required to take Oath of Allegiance to William and Mary, iv. 637; *see also* iv. 634; for the Nonjurors *see* Nonjurors; entitled by Toleration Act to dues from Nonconformists, iv. 640; the two parties, Feb. 1690, v. 6; *see also* i. *29*, *30* & n. 1, *112* & n. 1.
— — — (ii) the ministerial function: in sermons: dignity, &c., of, iii. 248, 317, 354; iv. 68, 75, 136, 168, 647; v. 224; usurped by sectaries, iii. 330; duties of, v. 124, 553; Apostolic ministry, iv. 440; *see also* v. 546–7.
— — — (iii) miscellaneous: ordination: services, iii. 8–9 & nn. (repeated, iii. 632–3), 254; iv. 54; ~ episcopal, during Protectorate, i. *9*, n. 1; iii. 172 & n. 1; ~ fasting before (in sermon), iv. 572; ~ Ordination Sunday, iv. 75 & n. 1, 81; benefice: qualifying to hold, after induction, v. 477 & n. 3; impropriation: E's, at South Malling, ii. 8 & n. 4 (i. 7–8), 541; ~ 'a poor preacher to the impropriation', iii. 133; pluralities: remarks concerning Rev. W. Duncombe at Wotton, &c., v. 181, 216, 266–7; ~ Rev. R. Holden at Deptford, &c., iv. 4, n. 5, 179 & n. 4, 522 & n. 2, 563 *bis* [other cases are not indexed collectively]; tithes: tithe-ale, iii. 133; chaplains and tutors in London: need of library for, iv. 367; clergy: benefaction for (R. Boyle), v. 82 & n. 4; censure of, by the wicked: in sermon, v. 487–8; corruption of: attack on, iv. 83; excess of, in dress, v. 542 & n. 3; inadequate training of, for preaching, v. 68; country: *see* Duncombe, William (iv. 558; v. 207); Offley, Robert (v. 182, 216); ~ sermons by, iii. 111 (*see also* iii. 101); v. 152 *bis*.
— — episcopate: (i) chronological series:
— — — — 1650, &c.: small number of bishops left in England, iii. 9, 633; rise of heresies in absence of (in sermons), iii. 233, 236; episcopal ordination during Protectorate, i. *9*, n. 1; iii. 172 & n. 1.
— — — — 1660, &c.: almost extinct in the three kingdoms, iii. 253 & n. 1; restored to its rights, iii. 312, n. 2; selfish conduct of bishops at Restoration, iii. 609 & n. 1.
— — — — 1672: weakened by Declaration of Indulgence, iii. 608.
— — — — 1686: opposed to Roman Catholicism, iv. 504; ~ resultant popularity of (1689; alludes to Seven Bishops ?), iv. 631.
— — — — 1688, Oct., Nov.: James II appeals to, to appease disaffection, &c., iv. 600 & n. 4, 601 & n. 1; at meeting to authenticate birth of James Edward, iv. 602 & n. 3; James II questions bishops in London about invitation to William of Orange, iv. 604 & n. 3, 605–6 & n.
— — — — 1689: views of, on settlement of crown, iv. 614, 625, 626–7; votes and protests of, iv. 619 & n. 4, 622 & n. 2, 626, n. 3; bishops not attending parliament: proposed exclusion of, from house of lords (?), iv. 619–20 & n., 631 & n. 5; and oath of allegiance to William and Mary, iv. 628 & n. 4, 637; bishops participating in coronation of William and Mary, iv. 633 & n. 3; suspension of nonjuring bishops, iv. 648, n. 6; for the nonjurors *see* Nonjurors.
— — — — 1691: vacation of Nonjurors' sees: Sancroft's views on, &c., v. 51–2 & nn.; necessity of accepting new bishops, v. 59 & n. 3.
— — — — 1696: in controversy with Jeremy Collier, v. 236, n. 1.
— — — — 1700: politics of, v. 402.
— — — — 1702: bishops congratulate Queen Anne on her accession, v. 493, n. 3.
— — — (ii) episcopacy as an institution: sermon on, iv. 67; apostolic succession: in sermons, iii. 8, 632–3; v. 546–7; *see also* iv. 440; Jean Diodati on episcopal government, ii.

CHURCH OF ENGLAND (*cont.*)
521; J. Owen attacks, iii. 105; Shaftesbury's views on, iv. 328; hierarchy: in *Naked Truth* controversy, iv. 83 & n. 5.
— — — (iii) creation, &c., of bishops: *congé d'élire*: procedure, iv. 525; consecrations, iii. 266, 345–6, 517–18; iv. 66–7; translation of bishop to archbishopric, iii. 361–3 & nn.
— — discipline: ecclesiastical jurisdiction: restored, iii. 312, n. 2; ~ the duke of Norfolk's divorce and, v. 90, n. 7 *ad fin.*, 127, n. 1; canons: proposed reform of, 1689, iv. 634, 652; canon law: Tenison on, v. 256; case of simony, v. 256, 346; necessity of church government: in sermon, iv. 566; Church's powers: in sermons, iv. 9, 403; use of excommunication: in sermons, iii. 234–5 *bis*; iv. 346; exhortations to unity, &c.: in sermons, iii. 336, 352, 569; iv. 140.
— — convocation: Seven Bishops refer themselves to decision of, on toleration, iv. 583–4 & n.; province of Canterbury: 1689: meets, iv. 652 & n. 1; ~ adjourned, &c., v. 6 & n. 3; 1701: disapproves of work by C. Davenant, v. 452 & n. 3; ~ dispute in, v. 460 & n. 1.
— — societies: the Religious Societies, v. 366, n. 5; Societies for Reformation of Manners, v. 366 & n. 5; ~ sermons for, v. 391–2 & nn.; Society for Propagation of the Gospel, v. 507 & n. 1; Society of Sons of the Clergy, v. 79, n. 2.
— worship:
— — services: (i) general: duty of attending public worship, public worship preferred to private prayers, &c.: in sermons, iii. 214, 538; iv. 28, 194; v. 155, 290, 429, 589, 603–4; requirements of divine service: in sermon, v. 576–7; Sunday observance: travel prohibited, iii. 13 & n. 2; ~ in sermons, iii. 245, 519, 574–5 *bis*, 576; iv. 102, 387, 458; v. 589; ~ taking purges on Sunday reproved in sermon,

CHURCH OF ENGLAND (*cont.*)
iv. 108 & n. 2; stated hours of prayer commended: in sermons, iv. 156, 160; evening prayer: time of, indicated, iv. 466; week-day services: daily advocated by S. Patrick, iv. 136, n. 2; ~ Wednesday, iv. 136; ~ Thursday, iv. 309 & n. 2; ~ Friday, iv. 305 & n. 1; *see also* London: topography: St. Martin in the Fields *and* Trinity Chapel; adoration towards the East: in sermon, iii. 630; men's wearing hats during services, ii. 527, n. 5; *see also* i. 75; kneeling at prayer: in sermon, iii. 568; *see also* iv. 254; music with services: revived at Chapel Royal, iii. 262 & n. 2; ~ revived at Westminster Abbey, iii. 265 & n. 4; ~ innovations at Chapel Royal, iii. 347–8 & n.; use of surplices during services: in Sir R. Browne's and royal chapels in Paris, iii. 9 & n. 2; ~ revived at Chapel Royal, iii. 262 & n. 2; ~ in sermon, iv. 264–5; perfume burnt before service in Chapel Royal, iv. 375.
— — — (ii) particular services [baptism, communion, &c.; select notices; for consecrations of churches and bishops, and ordinations of clerics, *see* buildings *and* organization *above*; for annual and specially appointed services *see* feasts and fasts *and* special services *below*]:
— — — — baptism: general significance, &c., of: in sermons, iii. 202, 238, 514, 630; iv. 61, 126, 139, 292, 569; v. 124–6, 373–4, 554; necessity of: in sermon, v. 67–8; use of Cross in: in sermon, iv. 264–5; private, ii. 5–6 (i. 6); iv. 634; ~ in sermon, v. 374; ~ occurrences of, iii. 421; iv. 147, 395–6; *see also* Sayes Court.
— — — — burial [the more general features of burials are indexed under England: social: funerals]: burials at night, ii. 15 (i. 12), 26 (i. 19), 28 (i. 20); iii. 210, 541; iv. 15, 415 & n. 3; *see also* ii. 556; Anglican service

CHURCH OF ENGLAND (*cont.*)
for: in Paris, ii. 565; iii. 39, 49; ~ at Deptford, 1652, iii. 76–7; French officer in Rochester cathedral, iii. 619–20 & n.; nonjuring bishop, v. 289 & n. 3; pall at, iv. 203–4; v. 55, 538; *see also* iii. 57, 224; services with sermons, ii. 26 (i. 19); iii. 185, 378, 603–4, 622; iv. 43, 111, 131, 183, 203–4, 292, 302–3, 430, 432, 507; v. 81–3, 158–9; commemorative sermon, v. 365–6.

— — — — churching of women: disused at Deptford, 1653, iii. 90; ~ Mrs. Evelyn, at Sayes Court, 1652–7, iii. 76, 90, 147, 195.

— — — — communion: administration of [to individuals, &c.]: at court, iii. 51 & n. 5; iv. 374–5 & n.; to king, in coronation ceremony, iii. 284; ~ omitted for James II, iv. 437; to sick or dying persons in private houses, iii. 244; iv. 210, 420, 463, 509, 605, 651; v. 190, 532; ~ receiving with sick, &c., strangers, iv. 27, 32 & n. 4, 52, 56, 84; private celebration(?), iv. 90; *see also* Sayes Court (services 1653–7); to sinners: in sermon, iv. 346 & n. 2; ~ as mixed communion: lawfulness of, in sermons, iii. 514 & n. 4, 524; ~ refused to man dying impenitent, iv. 455–6 & n.; celebrations [ordinary celebrations, including those on the usual feasts, are indexed or indicated under Evelyn: religion]: disused or rare in parish churches, 1649, &c., ii. 552 & n. 3; iii. 94; at Deptford, 1654, 1659, iii. 95, 228; at Greenwich, 1659, iii. 228; frequency of, v. 180, n. 1; monthly celebration: by name, iii. 233; iv. 136, 422; ~ omitted on Sunday before Palm Sunday, iv. 277; ~ neglect of, at Wotton, v. 180; offering for poor at, v. 477 & n. 4; on Ascension Day: *see* London: topography: St. Martin in the Fields; on New Year's Day (not being Sunday), iv. 359, 532–3; v. 81; names: generally Communion; Sacrament fairly frequently; Agape, v. 290; Eucharist, ii. 206; iii. 243, 364, 425, 476, 511, 538; iv. 50, 280, 522, 580; v. 249, 322, 397 (eucharistical in general sense, iii. 431 & n. 6, 517; iv. 460); Heavenly Viaticum, iv. 150; Synaxis, i. 16 & n. 1, &c.; iv. 32 & n. 4, 106, 107 *bis*, 134, &c.; preparation for: notices, iii. 79; iv. 7, 26, 46, 183, 223, 376, 462, 475, 545; v. 536–7; with fasting, iii. 623 & n. 6; iv. 27 & n. 1, 29, 35, 422, 528–9; preparatory sermons, iii. 24, 89 (continued, pp. 89, 90 *bis*), 202, 228, 244, 254, 317, 417; iv. 387, 388, 560, 646; v. 123, 124, 170, 305, 397, 413, 435, 439, 443, 477, 483 *bis*, 545, 546, 553, 563, 580, 617–18, 620; the worthy communicant: in sermons, iii. 197; v. 16–18; the unworthy communicant: danger to, in sermon, iv. 25; reception: obligatory, ii. 19, n. 4; *see also* v. 180, n. 1; neglect of: 1654, iii. 95; ~ at Wotton, 1700, &c., v. 422 & n. 2, 580; ~ in sermons, iii. 291; iv. 402; v. 163; frequent: Latitudinarians on, i. 30 & n. 1; ~ urged in sermons, iii. 258, 329, 522, 569; iv. 61, 239; v. 154, 459, 476, 493, 585–6, 590; miscellaneous: words of consecration: meaning of, in sermon, iii. 525; married couple first receive together, ii. 562; betrothed couple receive together, v. 608; sacramental test in politics (Test Act), iv. 7, n. 4, 10 & n. 3; mental communion, iv. 30 *bis* & n. 5.

— — — — confirmation: receiving sacrament before, ii. 19 & n. 4 (i. 15); E confirmed, ii. 23 (i. 17); John Evelyn, jnr.: confirmed, iii. 472; ~ instructed before first Communion, iv. 6–7; services, with sermons, iii. 471–2; iv. 167, 292; v. 70–1; in sermons, v. 310, 405, 562.

— — feasts and fasts [all holy days, whether observed or not, the State Services, and special seasons such as Lent; and some secular days closely associated

CHURCH OF ENGLAND (*cont.*)
with the Church calendar. If the festivals, apart from Easter Day, &c., fall on Sundays, the celebrations are not indexed under this heading, unless they present unusual features. For specially appointed services *see* special services *below*; for the abolition of festivals during the Commonwealth *see* chronological series above]:
— — — Advent: Advent Sunday, by name, iii. 144, 565; iv. 80, 103; v. 77, 122, 160, 198, 552, 582, 618 (error); later Sundays in, iv. 236; v. 305; mentioned more generally, iii. 24, 78, 225, 392, 519, 520; iv. 565 *bis*, 612; v. 228, 276, 482 [sermons alluding to Advent are not indexed].
— — — All Saints: celebration in Chapel Royal, iii. 501 & n. 3; fast postponed for, iii. 423, n. 4; in sermons, iii. 235 & n. 2, 342 [services at Deptford on 1 November are for a local charity: *see* iii. 223, n. 4, 318, n. 3; and are not connected with the festival.]
— — — Annunciation of our Lady (Lady Day): celebrated, iii. 190, 275; iv. 630; services for (?), iii. 353, 610; *see also* iv. 33 & n. 1; named, iii. 574; iv. 277.
— — — Ascension: celebrated, iii. 246, 547; iv. 168, 204; v. 99; ~ with Communion (all at St. Martin in the Fields), iv. 10, 35, 63, 90, 109, 134, 244, 313, 512, 549, 584–5; v. 23, 53–4; named, iii. 509, 528, 614; iv. 281; v. 141, 461.
— — — Ash Wednesday: Cromwell feasts on, iii. 93; celebrated, iii. 272, 431, 505–6; iv. 52–3, 83, 106, 130, 195, 272, 366, 418, 538; v. 9, 43 & n. 2, 489, 585; named, iii. 397.
— — — Charles the Martyr (30 January): fast instituted, iii. 269 & n. 1; E gives notices for 1661–81, 1683–92, 1694, 1698–9, 1704; Form of Prayer for, 1686, iv. 499, n. 7; service altered (?), 1689, iv. 620 & n. 5; sermon to house of commons, 1700, v. 378 & n. 2; fast postponed for Sundays, iv. 82, 237, 537; v. 557; ~ irregular observances, iii. 542 & n. 3; v. 284; *add.*
— — — Christmas: celebrations, 1649–59: in Paris, ii. 567; iii. 24, 51; in London, iii. 185, 238; ~ congregation raided, iii. 203–4 & nn. [later celebrations are not indexed].
— — — Circumcision: celebrations, iii. 1, 52; iv. 1, 402, 495; v. 620; ~ held in private, 1655–8, iii. 146, 164, 186, 205; ~ with sermons, iii. 350, 367, 472, 504, 521, 542, 600; ~ with sermons, falling on Sundays, iii. 239; v. 124–6, 309; Communion services (with sermons) for, iv. 359, 532–3; v. 81; ~ falling on Sundays, iii. 24, 393, 566; iv. 265, 566; ignored at Wotton, v. 229 [private prayers for, are not indexed].
— — — Conversion of St. Paul: celebration, iv. 128; sermons relating to, iii. 240 & n. 6; iv. 128; v. 42, 487.
— — — Easter Day: celebrations to 1660: 1639, ii. 22; 1649, London (not identified as Easter), ii. 552–3; 1650–1, Paris, iii. 2, 30; 1652–3, 1655–8, London, iii. 64 & n. 4, 82 & n. 3, 150, 169, 190, 211–12; 1659, Greenwich, iii. 228 & n. 2; 1660, Wotton, iii. 244 [later celebrations are not indexed]; preparation for: *see* Holy Week *below*.
— — — Ember Week: named, iv. 44 & n. 4, 64, 75 & n. 1, 81.
— — — Epiphany: E's observance of, v. 621; *see also* iii. 165; celebrations, iii. 53, 308, 395(?); sermons relating to, iii. 24, 472; named as date, v. 164.
— — — Good Friday: celebrated every year (frequently with Communion), 1660–94, 1696, 1700, 1704, 1705; indifference to, at Wotton, v. 207.
— — — Gunpower Plot (5 November): celebrations (including some Sunday occurrences), 1651, 1654, 1659, 1663–74, 1676, 1678, 1680–93, 1695, 1697–1700, 1704 (no sermons,

CHURCH OF ENGLAND (*cont.*)
1664, 1672; E absent, 1685, 1698, 1700); lesson in service for, iii. 48, n. 1; preachers commemorate William III's landing, iv. 650–1; v. 362; neglect of, at Wotton, v. 520; secular rejoicings, iii. 77; iv. 487 & n. 3.
— — — Holy Week: named, iv. 107, 198, 435, 629; v. 170; ~ as Passion Week, iii. 30; iv. 6, 277; preparation for (or for Easter, &c.), iv. 240, 308; ~ in sermons, iii. 354, 612; iv. 277; v. 206–7.
— — — Innocents' Day: sermon, iii. 238 & n. 3.
— — — James II's accession day (6 February): celebration instituted and held, iv. 499 & nn. 7, 8; ordered not to be observed, iv. 621 & n. 2.
— — — Lent [for Lenten sermons at court *see* Whitehall: religion]: as time of fasting: in sermons, iii. 27, 352–3; iv. 132, 197; v. 314, 379 & n. 5, 381, 388–9, 494; general observance of: in sermons, v. 380, 448; ~ neglect of, at Wotton, v. 207; Lenten sermons in London, iv. 305, n. 1, 436, n. 1.
— — — Palm Sunday: named, iii. 94, 317, 611; iv. 33, 107, 167, 277, 308–9, 629; v. 92, 563 [celebrations not indexed].
— — — Pentecost: *see* Whitsunday *below*.
— — — Purification of the Virgin Mary (Candlemas): service on, iv. 538; origin of: in sermon, iii. 240–1 & n.; named, iii. 314, 397; iv. 2, 164.
— — — Quadragesima Sunday: named, ii. 78 (i. 51).
— — — Restoration of Charles II (29 May): commemoration instituted, iii. 289 & n. 5; service for, *ib.*; ~ altered, 1686, iv. 446 & n. 4; celebrations, 1661–3, 1669, 1671–6, 1678–81, 1684–7, 1698; ~ E absent from, iv. 109, 283 & n. 2; ~ no sermons at Deptford, iv. 204, 513 & n. 2; not observed at Trinity Chapel, 1692, v. 102 & n. 2.
— — — Rogation Sunday: named,

CHURCH OF ENGLAND (*cont.*)
iv. 35, 63, 89, 134; sermon for, iii. 32.
— — — St. Andrew's Day: named, iii. 345; iv. 27, 396; and for Royal Society's anniversary meetings; for them *see* Royal Society.
— — — St. Bartholomew's Day: named, ii. 49 (i. 34); iv. 386; v. 39 & n. 3 (error).
— — — St. George's Day: Charles II crowned on, iii. 281 (James II and Anne were also crowned on this day; E does not name it as St. George's); Garter celebration on, iii. 479 & n. 1; named, iv. 89, 202.
— — — St. James's Day: named, iv. 72, 384; v. 543.
— — — St. John Baptist's Day, iv. 171, n. 8.
— — — St. John the Evangelist's Day: celebrated, iii. 238 & n. 3.
— — — St. Luke's Day: service, iii. 234; named, iv. 527; v. 260.
— — — St. Mark's Day: named, iv. 508; v. 22 & n. 1 (error).
— — — St. Matthew's Day: service on, iv. 598; sermon relating to, iv. 388 & n. 3; named, iv. 648.
— — — St. Matthias's Day: named, iv. 627.
— — — St. Michael's Day (Michaelmas): named: Sunday celebrations, iv. 649; v. 428; ~ as date, ii. 13 (i. 11); v. 478.
— — — St. Peter's Day: celebration of, in Chapel Royal, iv. 171 & n. 8; named, iii. 249; v. 27.
— — — SS. Simon and Jude: named, iv. 393 & n. 4.
— — — St. Thomas's Day: named, iv. 401; v. 483.
— — — Septuagesima (period): sermon on, iii. 26 & n. 5.
— — — Shrovetide: named, iii. 148.
— — — Shrove Tuesday: marriage on, iv. 194; named, iii. 81, 369; v. 560.
— — — Trinity Monday: for services for Trinity House held on this day *see* Trinity House.
— — — Trinity Sunday: named 1674–9, 1687–92, and in some other years; celebrations to

CHURCH OF ENGLAND (*cont.*)
1659: 1650, Paris, iii. 8–9 and pp. 632–3; ~ 1651, Paris, iii. 34; 1658, Deptford, iii. 216; sermons for, relating to the Trinity as against the Unitarians, &c., iv. 135, 169; v. 56–7, 143, 414, 465, 502–3, 537; *see also* v. 210; minor sermons, iii. 290, 372.

— — — Whit Monday: celebrated, iv. 378–9 & n.

— — — Whit Sunday: named in most years from 1650 to 1705; celebrations to 1659: 1650, 1651, in Paris, iii. 8, 34; 1652, at Rye, iii. 67; 1654, 1655, at Sayes Court, iii. 97–8, 151; 1657–9, in London, iii. 193, 214, 230; as Pentecost: in sermon, iii. 34; ~ preparation for, v. 410; ~ Millenarian expectations for, v. 177.

— — special services and fasts [mainly services, &c., ordered by government for particular occasions; for the annual State Services *see* feasts and fasts *above*. The services for which special *Forms of Prayer* are cited are indicated]:

— — — thanksgivings with *Forms of Prayer*: Rye-House plot, 1683: king's *Declaration* read in church, iv. 335 & n. 2, 336; ~ service, iv. 336 & n. 3; defeat of Argyll's and Monmouth's rebellions, 1685, iv. 460 & n. 1; capture of Buda, 1686, iv. 524 & n. 2; queen's pregnancy, 1688, iv. 567 & n. 4; birth of James Edward, iv. 588 & n. 7; deliverance effected by William of Orange, 1689, iv. 621 & n. 1; Blenheim, 1704, v. 578–9 & n.

— — — thanksgivings without *Forms of Prayer*: William III's success in Ireland, 1690, v. 36 & n. 5; La Hogue, 1692: unofficial, v. 102 & n. 3; ~ official, v. 119 & n. 2; William III's preservation, 1694, v. 199 & n. 3; capture of Namur, 1695, v. 218 & n. 3; peace of Ryswick, 1697, v. 277 & n. 2; Vigo, v. 519, n. 2.

— — — intercessions: for Charles

CHURCH OF ENGLAND (*cont.*)
II in his last illness (with *Prayers*), iv. 407 & nn. 4, 5, 414; time of public danger, Oct. 1688: orders for drafting *Prayers*, &c., iv. 600, n. 4, 601 *bis* & n. 6; i. 33; for armies, 1702 (with *Prayers*), v. 504 & n. 1.

— — — services for special bodies: regiment's thanksgiving for success, ii. 36 (i. 27); prayer for Church, Paris, 1651, iii. 40; trading-company's prayers, &c., for enterprise, iii. 201, 202 [for services held regularly by or for other bodies, *see* Deptford: parochial, &c., Societies for Reformation of Manners; Trinity House].

— — — fasts: Church, Paris, 1651, iii. 39; ordered by Protectoral government, for: Waldenses, 1655, iii. 152, n. 1; ~ sickness, 1657, iii. 196–7 & nn.; ~ plague, 1658, iii. 213 & n. 3; Anglicans in London, 1659–60, iii. 226 & n. 6, 234–41 *passim*; ordered by government for: weather, 1662, iii. 311–12 & nn.; (second) Dutch war, 1665, iii. 404–5 & n.; plague, &c., 1665 (monthly; *Form of Prayer* issued), iii. 415–16 & n., 421, 423 & n. 4, 424; plague, 1666 (monthly), iii. 430, 432 & n. 3, 435 & n. 11, 439, 443, 446; Fire of London, 1666, iii. 464 & n. 3; calamities of war, &c., 1674, iv. 31 & nn. 3, 4; Popish Plot: 1678, iv. 157 & n. 3; ~ 1679, iv. 166 & n. 8; king and parliament, 1680, iv. 236 & n. 1; success of fleet, 1689, iv. 640–1 & n.; war in Ireland, 1690 (monthly), v. 14 & n. 1, 21, 23 & n. 1, 24, 29, 34; war against France: 1691 (monthly), v. 51 & n. 2, 53, 58, 60–1; ~ 1692 (monthly), v. 94 & n. 2, 100 & n. 3, 109, 113, 115 & n. 3; ~ 1693 (monthly), v. 151 & n. 2, 153; ~ 1694, v. 184; *add.*; ~ 1695, v. 213 & n. 1; parliament, 1695, v. 227 & n. 1; king's safety, &c., 1696, v. 248 & n. 1; distressed foreign protestants, 1699, v. 319 & n. 4; parliament, protestant religion, &c., 1701, v. 452 & n. 4, 453; war against

CHURCH OF ENGLAND (*cont.*)
France: 1702, v. 504 & n. 2, 505; ~ 1703, v. 539 & n. 2; great storm, 1704, v. 556 & n. 2; war against France, 1705, v. 590 & n. 2.
— — liturgical [notices relating to *Book of Common Prayer*, and some miscellaneous notices]:
— — — *Book of Common Prayer*: (i) chronological series: attempt to introduce, into Scotland, ii. 22 & n. 3 (i. 17); disuse of: at Deptford, iii. 76; ~ in 1654, iii. 144 & n. 3; use of: at particular churches during Commonwealth, ii. 552 & n. 5; iii. 150 & n. 2; ~ by orthodox clergy, iii. 144; ~ restored, 1660, iii. 251–2 & n.; revised edition: use of, made compulsory, 1662, iii. 331 & n. 3; proposed revision of, 1689–90, iv. 634, 652 & n. 1; v. 6.
— — — — (ii) text and contents: abused by sectaries, iii. 204; French translation of, used by French Conformist churches, iii. 545 & nn. 3, 4; ~ used at Greenwich, iv. 548, 565, 598; Nonjurors' modifications of, v. 142–3 & n.; lesson for 30 January in, iv. 193 & n. 2; prayer for Prince James Edward disused, iv. 613 & n. 1; prayers for James II and his queen curtailed, iv. 620 & n. 5; burial service, v. 289; 'Rules called the Pie' in preface, iv. 300 & n. 4; State Services and service for James II's accession-day: *see* feasts and fasts *above*.
— — — — (iii) in sermons [mainly allusions to it]: liturgy to be adhered to, iii. 315; opponents of, iii. 551; set forms preferable to extemporary prayers, iv. 298, 414; v. 573, 603–4.
— — — miscellaneous: copy of *Book of Common Prayer* given by Charles I to York Minster, iii. 129 & n. 3; service when king touches for King's Evil, iii. 250–1 & n.; *see also* iv. 606, n. 3; Church censured by Henrietta Maria for lacking books of hours, iii. 45, 635; *Collection of private devotions* (J. Cosin): origin and sources

CHURCH OF ENGLAND (*cont.*)
of, iii. 45–6 & n.; *add.*; iii. 635–6.
— — preaching and catechizing, &c. [notices relating to the art of preaching are indexed under Preaching and Sermons; the notices indexed here relate to specifically Anglican preaching]:
— — — preaching: during Lent at Whitehall (?), iv. 6; lenten sermons: in London, iv. 305, n. 1, 436, n. 1; ~ at court: *see* Whitehall: religion; collect for the day included in sermon, iv. 414; 'opus diei', iii. 507 & n. 3, 509 & n. 2; iv. 11 & n. 1; blessings before and after sermons: in sermon, iii. 22; ~ omitted by sectary, iii. 67; prayers before sermon, v. 155, 237, 266–7; preacher's voice tested, v. 27; homily read owing to preacher's illness, iii. 233; Thirty-nine Articles read before sermon, 1660, iii. 254; clergy required to preach against immorality, v. 8 & n. 1; clergy required to read acts, &c., against immorality, &c., 1690, 1698, v. 24 & n. 3, 327–8 & n.
— — — catechizing: need for: in country parishes, v. 415; ~ sermon on, iv. 289; in place of Sunday afternoon sermons: at Greenwich, iii. 361, 378; ~ at Wotton, iv. 111; v. 415–24 *passim*; on Fridays in London, iv. 259–60, 269.
— — fasting [for national fasts *see* special services and fasts *above*; for fasting as preparation for Communion *see* services *above*]:
— — — attendance at church on fast-day, v. 556; effects of fasts: in 1662, iii. 312; ~ sermon on, v. 21; Friday as fast-day, iii. 604; iv. 187 & n. 4; duty, &c., of fasting: in sermons, iii. 2, 273; iv. 26, 293, 504, 572; v. 136, 325–6, 429–30, 449, 489, 557; *see also* iii. 613.
— — private devotions:
— — — general: little Richard Evelyn's training and piety, iii. 207–8; *see also* Evelyn: religion; Godolphin, Mrs. Margaret.

CHURCH OF ENGLAND (*cont.*)
— — — confession: Earles on desirability of: in sermon, iii. 39; general or private: recommended in sermons, iii. 211 *bis*, 233, 303, 402; iv. 36, 139; v. 4, 92, 131–6 *passim*, 169; death-bed repentance: sermons against, iii. 213; iv. 283, 293, 370–1, 573–4, 577, 578; v. 50, 70, 116, 137, 146–7, 162, 169, 186, 407, 437, 520–1, 539–40, 568–9, 570–1; devotional papers, &c.: of Mary Evelyn, iv. 421, 431; of Mrs. Godolphin, iv. 152; books of devotions composed by E, ii. 559, n. 2; iv. 126 & n. 5; *see also* liturgical: miscellaneous *above*; family prayers: in sermons, iii. 356(?), 358(?); iv. 292–3; private prayer: E on, iv. 414; in sermons, iii. 497, 538; iv. 53, 158, 572, 575; v. 429, 461; *see also* worship: services (i) general *above*; spiritual guides, iii. 149 & n. 2; iv. 283, n. 1, 431; in sermon, v. 92.
— miscellaneous:
— — Church: converts to and from: for Roman Catholics *see* Roman Catholics; others are not indexed collectively; hostility to: of Jesuits, iv. 174; ~ of Scots Presbyterians, v. 12; Ussher prophesies destruction of, iii. 157 & n. 2; will endure to end of the world, iv. 479.
— — alms-giving: in sermon, iv. 293; case of conscience, v. 338–9 & n.; charitable collections: *see* Charity, &c.; charitable foundations: in sermon, iv. 436–7; England: favoured with means of salvation, iv. 254; ~ Gospel declared to, iv. 153; French conformists: churches: *see* Greenwich; London: topography: Savoy; ~ translation of liturgy used by, iii. 545 & n. 4; High and Low Churchmen in politics, v. 612 & n. 1, 614; perjury, i. *27* & n. 1; profanity: proclamation against, to be read in church, v. 327–8 & n.; spiritual entertainment, iii. 511 & n. 1.
Ciampelli, Agostino: paintings by, ii. 272, n. 3.
Cicero: death and tomb of, ii. 322–3 & n.; praise of Tusculum by, ii. 393; statue of, ii. 225 & n. 10; his daughter Tulliola: supposed corpse of, ii. 320 & nn. 1, 2; academy and baths of, at Pozzuoli: ruins of, ii. 344–5 & n., 348, n. 2; grotto of, at Formia, ii. 323 & n. 5; palace of, at Rome: ruins of, ii. 219 & n. 7; villas of: Cumanum, ii. 344, n. 4; Formiana, ii. 322 & n. 9; Puteolanum, ii. 344–5 & n.; Tusculanum, ii. 392 & n. 1; *see also* Books mentioned in text.
Cifeccio *or* Cifacca: *see* Siface (G. F. Grossi).
Cigala, J. M. (Mahomed Bei), impostor, iii. 522, n. 2.
Cigoli, Lodovico, ii. 113, n. 3; paintings by, ii. 113 (i. 73), 244, n. 1.
Cimbrians: defeat of, by Marius, ii. 485 & n. 3; ~ trophies of, at Rome (sculpture), ii. 222, 379.
Ciminus: lake and mountain, ii. 211 & n. 3.
Cimmerians, Cimmeria, ii. 338 & nn. 1, 3, 349 & n. 7.
Cioli, Valerio: statue by, ii. 418–19 & n.
Circean promontory, &c. (Monte Circeo), ii. 320 & n. 4, 321 & nn. 5, 6.
Circei: ruins of, ii. 321, n. 6.
Cirencester, Glos., ii. 23 (i. 17); Lord Lovelace arrested at, 1688, iv. 607, n. 1; Queen Anne at, v. 516, n. 2; road from, to Gloucester, iii. 118, n. 5.
Cisij, Pietro: describes Turkey, &c., iii. 516 & n. 2, 522, n. 2.
Cisner, Rev. Christophe: social, iii. 171 & n. 2.
Citinburne: *see* Sittingbourne.
Citolin, Martyr, schoolmaster at Lewes, ii. 8 & n. 5 (i. 8).
Civil Wars, 1642–6, 1648 [for origins, &c., *see* Great Rebellion. The military operations are not indexed collectively]:
opening of, iii. 126; progress of, ii. 79 (i. 52); i. 55; portent during, ii. 80 (i. 54); iv. 235 & n. 1; hand-grenades: use of, in, iii. 368, n. 5; Henrietta Maria's escapes in, iii. 341 & n. 2; rebel officers in, ii. 480 & n. 3; iv. 474 & n. 5; royalists,

Civil Wars (*cont.*)
impoverished, at Restoration, iii. 609; taxation for, iii. 159 & n. 2.
cathedrals damaged in: Canterbury, ii. 76 & n. 3 (i. 50); iii. 395, n. 2; Lincoln, iii. 131, n. 6, 132 & n. 3; Peterborough, iii. 134, n. 3; St. Paul's, iii. 448, n. 3; Winchester, iv. 472 & n. 2; Worcester, iii. 119 & n. 5.
particular places and areas: Belvoir Castle: royalist garrison at, &c., iii. 124–5 & n.; Bramber: held by parliament, ii. 544, n. 4; Broad Hinton: Sir J. Glanville's house at, burnt, iii. 111 & n. 7; Bromley: bishop's palace at, damaged, iii. 537–8; Burley-on-the-Hill: burnt, iii. 124, n. 2; Essex: effects of Second Civil War on, iii. 159, n. 2; Faringdon: burnt, iii. 111 & n. 2; Forest of Dean: effects of war on, iii. 343 & n. 3; Holmby House: demolished, iv. 70 & n. 3; Lincoln: ruined, iii. 132 & n. 4; London: defences of, during war, ii. 80 & n. 1; iii. 461, n. 2; Newark: royalist garrison at, iii. 125 & n. 1; Nonsuch: trees felled at, iii. 428 & n. 2; Nottingham Castle: demolition of, iii. 126, n. 2; Pontefract Castle: demolition of, &c., iii. 127 & n. 6; Woodstock: destruction at, iii. 381 & n. 5; York: cathedral preserved from damage in, iii. 128–9 & n.
Civilized world: limits of, ii. 354 & n. 4.
Clagett, Rev. Nicholas: sermon by (?), iv. 113 & n. 2.
Clagett, William, D.D.: sermon by (?), iv. 113 & n. 2.
Clancarne: Earl of: *see* Cunningham, Alexander, earl of Glencairn.
Clancarty: Earls and Countesses of: *see* Maccarty, Callaghan, third earl, 1666–76; Maccarty, Elizabeth, his countess; Maccarty, Donogh, fourth earl, 1676–91 (1734); Maccarty, Elizabeth, his countess.
Clandon: *see* West Clandon.
Clanricarde (Clainricharde): fifth Earl and first Marquis of: *see* de Burgh, Ulick.
Clare, Andrew, D.D., iii. 39, n. 1; sermons by, iii. 39, 47, 48, 51.
Clare, Gilbert de, earl of Gloucester: boundary of lands of, iii. 119, n. 2.
Clare: Earls of: *see* Holles, John, first earl; Holles, John, second earl, 1637–66; Holles, John, fourth earl, later duke of Newcastle.
Clarence: Duke of: *see* Thomas of Lancaster.
Clarendon: Earls and Countesses of: *see* Hyde, Sir Edward, first earl, 1661–74; Hyde, Frances, his countess; Hyde, Henry, second earl, 1674–1709; Hyde, Flower, his countess; Hyde, Edward, third earl, 1709–23; Hyde, Henry, fourth earl, 1723–53, formerly earl of Rochester.
Clarges, Anne: *see* Monck, Anne, duchess of Albemarle.
Clarges, John: geneal., iii. 425, n. 2.
Clarges, Sir Walter, bt.: in Albemarle inheritance dispute, v. 410–11 & n.
Clark (Cleark, Clarke), —, performer on the Irish harp, iii. 92 & n. 2, 518.
Clarke, Dr. —: *see* Clarke, Timothy, M.D.
Clarke (Cleark), Rev. —: sermons by, iii. 236, 240.
Clarke, Col. Charles, of Ockley: geneal., v. 582, n. 3.
Clarke, Elizabeth: *see* Neile, Elizabeth, Lady Neile.
Clarke, Mrs. Evelyn, born Draper, wife of Col. Charles Clarke: born, &c., v. 582 *bis* & n. 3.
Clarke, Rev. Gabriel: geneal., iii. 172, n. 6 *ad fin*.
Clarke, Samuel; D.D. 1710, v. 536, n. 1; appointed Boyle lecturer for 1704 and 1705, v. 536 & n. 1, 583.
Clarke, Timothy, M.D., iii. 183, n. 4; ill (?), iii. 183, 185; proposes Sir P. Carteret for Royal Society, iii. 401, n. 6; inspects Sick and Wounded in E's district, iii. 403 & n. 5; social(?), iii. 442 & n. 6.
Clarke, William, D.D.; dean of Winchester 1665, iii. 605, n. 2; sermon by, iii. 605; appointed to preach, iv. 56, n. 2, 84, n. 1.
Claud, Dr. —: attends E, 1660, iii. 243.

Claude, Jean, French protestant divine: seeks refuge in Holland, iv. 485 & n. 4; *see also* Books mentioned in text.
Claudius, Roman emperor: aqueduct of, at Rome, ii. 317 & n. 2, 383 & n. 6; grant by, of privileges to Lyons: inscription containing, ii. 158 & n. 6 (i. 101); portrait of (cameo), iii. 260 & n. 4.
Clayhidon, Devon: rector of: *see* Pemberton, Matthew.
Clayton family: property of, in Blechingley and Godstone, iv. 111, n. 1, 121, n. 2.
Clayton, — (of Norfolk?): social, iii. 186 & n. 2.
Clayton, Bridget, Lady Clayton, wife of Sir Thomas: geneal., iii. 273, n. 2.
Clayton, Sir John: social, iv. 96 & n. 2.
Clayton, Martha, Lady Clayton, wife of Sir Robert, iv. 121, n. 5; character, iv. 121, 186; social, iv. 121, 122; v. 426.
Clayton, Rebecca: *see* Paston, Mrs. Rebecca, later countess of Yarmouth.
Clayton, Sir Robert, lord mayor of London 1679–80, iii. 625, n. 5; career and character, iv. 185–6 & nn.; as friend of E, i. *29*.
— official career, &c.: as sheriff of London: social, iii. 625; as lord mayor elect: social, iv. 182 & nn. 1, 3; as lord mayor: social: parties, on solemn and private days, &c., iv. 185 & n. 6, 187 & n. 4, 191, 195; ~ alone, &c., iv. 183, 190, 193, 198, 219.
— — deprived of aldermanship, iv. 342, n. 6 *ad fin.*; promotes foundation of Mathematical School, Christ's Hospital, iv. 542, n. 2; as commissioner of Greenwich Hospital: attends meeting, &c., v. 209–10, 211.
— other activities: trustee for duke of Buckingham's estate, iv. 186 & n. 4; at Royal Society meeting, iv. 170, n. 5; social (apart from terms as lord mayor, &c.): parties, iv. 170, 173; ~ alone, &c., iv. 81, 125, 173, 180, 248, 292; ~ at Marden, iv. 121–2; v. 425–6.
— property: London house: notice, &c., iii. 625–6 & nn.; iv. 185; Blechingley: buys manor, iv.
Clayton, Sir Robert (*cont.*)
110–11 & n.; Marden (in Godstone): buys, iv. 121 & n. 3; ~ notice, iv. 121–2 & n.; ~ improvements of, at, v. 425–6 & n.; Bermuda: plantations of, in, iv. 147 & n. 1.
— son of, iv. 186, n. 2; servant of: account by, of Clifford's death, iv. 21.
Clayton, Sir Thomas, M.D.: elected warden of Merton College, Oxford, iii. 273 & nn. 2, 3.
Cleark: *see* Clark *and* Clarke.
Clegett, Rev. — (Dr. William Clagett?): sermon by, iv. 113 & n. 2.
Clement III, pope: crucifix carved by, ii. 87 (i. 58–9).
Clement VI, pope: acquires Avignon, ii. 160 & n. 5 (i. 102).
Clement VII, anti-pope: tomb of (as Clement VIII, in error), ii. 161 & n. 12 (i. 103).
Clement VII, pope: crowns Charles V at Bologna, ii. 422, n. 4; statue of, at Florence, ii. 188 & n. 6 (i. 118).
Clement VIII, pope: consecrates high altar, St. Peter's, Rome, ii. 261; decorates transept, St. John Lateran, ii. 272, n. 2, 273, n. 1; arms of, ii. 296, n. 7; error for Clement VII, anti-pope, ii. 161 & n. 12 (i. 103).
Clement X, pope: constructs fountain before St. Peter's, Rome, ii. 255, n. 3.
Clement XI, pope (Francesco Albani), v. 440, n. 4; crowned, v. 440; policy of, in Spanish Succession, v. 462 & n. 5; intervenes in Polish dispute, v. 577 & n. 6.
Clement XII, pope: sarcophagus of, ii. 370, n. 6.
Clement XIV, pope: expands Vatican museums, ii. 294, n. 3 *ad fin.*
Clement, Gregory, regicide: executed, iii. 259 & nn. 1, 2.
Clément, Jacques, murderer of Henri III, ii. 108, n. 1.
Clement, William, M.D.: attends Mrs. Eleanor Evelyn, ii. 14 & n. 2 (i. 11).
Clench, Andrew, M.D., iv. 616, n. 3; murdered, v. 83 & n. 4; precocious son of, iv. 616–19 & nn.; v. 83.
Clench, Edmund, iv. 616, n. 3 *ad fin.*
Clench, John, iv. 616, n. 3 *ad fin.*

Cleomenes, sculptor, ii. 286, n. 5.
Cleopatra: wager of, with Antony, ii. 372 & n. 5; portrait-gem of, ii. 89 (i. 60); figure of, on cup (modern), iii. 148 & n. 4; statue of: *see* Sculpture, Ancient: Ariadne.
Clerke, Henry, M.D., iii. 183, n. 4.
Cleve: Duke of: heart of, ii. 58 & n. 3 (i. 40).
Cleveland: Duchess of: *see* Palmer, Barbara.
Cleveland: Earl of, 1626–67: *see* Wentworth, Thomas.
Cleves: Duke of: *see* William V, duke of Juliers and Cleves.
Cleworth: Baron of, 1689–1715 (Jacobite creation): *see* Drummond, John, duke of Melfort, &c.
Cliffe, The, near Lewes, Sussex: *see* Lewes.
Clifford family, iv. 18, n. 4.
Clifford, Anne, Baroness Clifford: *see* Herbert, Anne, countess of Pembroke and Montgomery.
Clifford, Elizabeth, Baroness Clifford: *see* Boyle, Elizabeth, countess of Cork and of Burlington.
Clifford, Henry, fifth earl of Cumberland: geneal., iv. 428, n. 2.
Clifford, Hugh: geneal., iii. 470, n. 2.
Clifford, Mrs. Mary: *see* Cole, Mrs. M.
Clifford, Sir Thomas, 1630–73; first Baron Clifford of Chudleigh 1672; Lord High Treasurer 1672–3, iii. 388, n. 2 [from 1668 to 1672 he is generally called 'Mr. Treasurer'].
— character, &c.: general accounts, iii. 470; iv. 18–23 & nn.; horoscope of, iv. 22 & n. 2; paintings owned by, iv. 18 & n. 3.
— chronological series:
— — origin, &c., iii. 470 & n. 2; iv. 18 & n. 4.
— — 1664: commissioner for Sick and Wounded: appointed, iii. 387–8; ~ district of, iii. 394–5 & n.
— — 1665: concerned in attack on Dutch East India ships at Bergen, iii. 562 & n. 5, 618 & n. 3; iv. 21.
— — 1666: brings news of St. James's fight to Whitehall, iii. 446, n. 3; appointed Comptroller of the Household, iii. 469–70 & n.; iv. 19 & n. 3; appointed Privy Councillor, iii. 526 & n. 8; iv. 19 & n. 3.

Clifford, Lord (*cont.*)
— — 1667: appointed commissioner of the Treasury, iii. 487, n. 7; iv. 19 & n. 5; opposes Clarendon, iii. 494, n. 2.
— — 1668: appointed Treasurer of the Household, iii. 470, n. 1, 526, nn. 2, 8; iv. 19 & n. 4.
— — 1671: attends Council for Foreign Plantations, iii. 578, 584.
— — 1671–2: inclining towards Roman Catholicism, iii. 577 & n. 5, 608.
— — 1672: responsible for Third Dutch War, iv. 16 & n. 1, 21; advises Stop of the Exchequer, 606–7 & n.; iv. 16; advises Declaration of Indulgence, iii. 608 & n. 1; alleged remark of, about bridling London, iii. 609, n. 4; created baron, iii. 613 & n. 5; appointed Lord High Treasurer, iii. 621, n. 2; iv. 1, n. 5, 19 & n. 6.
— — 1673: received into Roman Catholic church, iv. 14 & n. 1; E applies to, for money, iv. 12; resigns Treasurership, iv. 14 & n. 1, 16 & n. 1; ill health of, &c., iv. 16 & n. 1; visits Tunbridge Wells, iv. 16–17; returns to London and removes to Devon, iv. 18, 20; alleged suicide of, &c., 20–1 & n.
— political relations, &c.: with Arlington, iii. 470; iv. 19–20 & n.; ~ Clifford's supposed ingratitude to: alluded to, iv. 39 & n. 1, 119 & n. 7; with James, duke of York, iv. 14 & n. 1, 20 & n. 1; questions Sandwich's courage(?), iii. 617 & n. 4.
— relations with E: general, i. *22*, *109*; iv. 9, 20; family connexion, iii. 470 & n. 2; correspondence: general note on, iii. 523, n. 1; *add.*; announces E's appointment to Council for Foreign Plantations, iii. 570–1; and E's projected History of Second Dutch War: interest in, iii. 523, n. 1, 558, 559; ~ provides materials for, iii. 562, 563, 587–8; iv. 18; ~ E submits passages to, iii. 586, 624; iv. 41, n. 1 *ad fin.*; ~ business interviews, mainly relating to,

Clifford, Lord (*cont.*)
iii. 556, 562 *bis*, 565, 568, 586; takes E to visit Newmarket and Euston, iii. 588, 589, 597; takes leave of E, iv. 20.
— social: parties, iii. 526 *bis*, 529, 547, 565, 576 *bis*, 586, 587, 600, 626; iv. 1, 2; alone, &c., iii. 563, 568, 569, 574, 597, 600, 621 & n. 2; iv. 3, 9.
— miscellaneous: eldest son of, dies, iii. 574 & n. 5; trustee of, iv. 21 & n. 3; chaplain of: *see* Lloyd, William, D.D., the Nonjuror; servant of: account by, of Clifford's death, iv. 21.
Clifford, Thomas, 1652–71, son of Clifford: dies, iii. 574 & n. 5.
Clifford: Baronesses, &c.: *see* Herbert, Anne, countess of Pembroke (1605–76); another creation: *see* Boyle, Elizabeth, countess of Cork and Burlington (1643–91); Boyle, Charles, sometimes styled Viscount Dungarvan (1691–4).
Clifford of Chudleigh: first Baron, 1672–3: *see* Clifford, Sir Thomas.
Clifford of Lanesborough: Baron, 1644–64: *see* Boyle, Richard, second earl of Cork and first earl of Burlington (iii. 242, n. 1).
Clifton, Baroness, 1672–1702: *see* O'Brien, Katherine, styled Lady O'Brien, &c.
Climate: *see* Weather and Climate.
Cliveden Park (Clifden), Taplow, Bucks.: notice, iv. 176–7 & nn.
Clocks and Watches:
— mechanism: pendulum clocks: C. Huygens as inventor of, iii. 276 & n. 1; made by A. Fromanteel on Huygens's system, iii. 261, n. 1, 285 & n. 4; devised by R. Hooke, iii. 441 & n. 2, 450, 539; improvement of: discussed by Royal Society, iii. 473 & n. 1; owned by: Charles II, iv. 217; ~ E, iv. 333; ~ other owners, iii. 293; iv. 288, 343.
— — rolling ball and spring, iii. 147–8 & n.
— makers, &c.: England: A. Fromanteel, iii. 260–1 & n., 285 & n. 4; S. Watson, T. Tompion, &c., iii. 111–12 & n.
— — German clocks, ii. 235, 254, 310.
Clocks and Watches (*cont.*)
— — watch-makers at: Blois, ii. 142 (i. 93); Geneva, ii. 524 & n. 6, 529, n. 1; Paris, ii. 99 (i. 65); i. 68.
— astronomical, ii. 192 & n. 3; iii. 112, n. 1, 260–1 & n., 450 & n. 1.
— public: Lyons, St. Jean, ii. 157 & n. 4 (i. 101); Paris, La Samaritaine, ii. 93 (i. 62); Strassburg, cathedral, ii. 434 & n. 5; Tours, St. Gatien, ii. 145 (i. 94); Venice, Piazza, ii. 434–5 & nn.
— collections, &c.: Charles II, iii. 112, n. 1, 260–1 & n.; iv. 217; Gaston, duke of Orleans, iii. 21; D. Palmer, iii. 293.
— miscellaneous: clockwork, ii. 47; musical clock, iii. 293; chimes, iv. 326; clocks, &c.: not used in Persia, iv. 358.
— — mensuration of time: discussed at Royal Society, iii. 313.
Clonfert and Kilmacduagh: bishop of, 1665–84: *see* Wolley, E.
Cloyne: bishop of, 1683–92: *see* Jones, Edward.
Clutterbuck, Anne: *see* Burton, Anne, Lady Burton.
Clutterbuck, Sir Thomas, iv. 156, n. 2; chaplain of: sermon by, iv. 156; geneal., iv. 461, n. 1.
Coaches [select. Coaches appear in town use at ii. 92 (i. 61), 93 (i. 62), and then frequently; for travel at ii. 72 (i. 47), 182 (i. 115), 184 (i. 116), 392, 393, 406, and then frequently]:
— the vehicle: design for, iii. 65; improvements in, iii. 405; way-wiser applied to, iii. 196; parts, &c.: carriage and perch, iii. 475 & n. 5; cushions, &c., iv. 72; glasses, iv. 72, 301; leather: in comparisons, iii. 215; iv. 390; silver fittings, &c., ii. 257–8 & nn.; velvet, iv. 259.
— team: two: stone-horses, iii. 169; ~ two only, on country road, v. 547; four, iii. 98; iv. 592–3; six, ii. 72 (i. 47), 90; iii. 256, 358, 381, 545, 552, 588; iv. 113, 151, 207, 430, 467, 528, 592–3; v. 175, 578; eight, v. 578; mishaps, &c., with, iii. 116(?), 193, 226, 295.

Coaches (*cont.*)
— use: (i) special occasions: processions, ii. 281; iii. 43; iv. 412–13; v. 578; arrival of dignitary, &c., ii. 389, n. 4 *ad fin.*; iv. 491; ambassadorial: in entries, &c., iii. 256, 344, 513; iv. 492; v. 238; ~ lent by king, iii. 515; ~ not allowed to enter Whitehall, iv. 262; funerals, iii. 76, 185, 490, 545; iv. 151, 430; v. 56.
— — (ii) at particular places: Genoa: not used in, ii. 178 (i. 112).
— — — London: hackney: commission for regulating, iii. 319 & n. 1, 358 & n. 2, 379; in Hyde Park, iii. 285, 357; ~ pay for admission to, iii. 82–3 & n.; on frozen Thames, 1684, iv. 360–5 *passim*.
— — — Milan, ii. 503; Naples, ii. 353; ~ in carnival, ii. 331, 332; Paris, iii. 637 (extract from *State of France*); ~ at Cours la Reine, ii. 106–7 (i. 69); Rome, ii. 257–8 & n.; ~ in Piazza Farnese, ii. 217.
— — (iii) miscellaneous: coach-races, iii. 213; iv. 362; at embarkation, iv. 80; hired for sightseeing, ii. 325; service for travel, ii. 182, n. 7.
— accidents, mishaps, &c. [*see also* team *above*], ii. 543; iii. 192, 206, 411, 468 (chariot); iv. 301, 568–9; v. 467, 618.
— miscellaneous notices: coach-house, &c., iv. 72, 117, 259; coachman: accident to, iii. 295; ~ made drunk while his master pays visit, iii. 112–13 & n., 525; coaches: discomfort of, i. 18; E's, iii. 65, 75, 94, 98, 433, 468 (chariot); iv. 170; v. 470; miscarriage in, iv. 282; murder in, v. 83 & n. 4; staircase, &c., fit for, ii. 143 (i. 93), 303, 445–6.
Coach-racing, iii. 213; iv. 362.
Coale, Dr. —: *see* Cole.
Cocceius Auctus, L., engineer, &c., ii. 338 & n. 4, 343.
Cock, —: *see* le Coq, F.
Cock, Mrs. —, and her son, iv. 511.
Cock, — (Capt. George Cocke?): E brings action against, iii. 565 *bis* & n. 3, 580 *bis*.
Cockayne, Jane: *see* Needham, Jane, Lady Needham.
Cockayne, Sir William: geneal., iii. 363, n. 1.
Cocke, George, Captain, iii. 390, n. 2; as treasurer to Commissioners for Sick and Wounded: appointed, iii. 390 & n. 2; ~ payments to, iii. 409, 412 & n. 2; ~ accounts of, iii. 477, 481 & n. 4, 565, n. 3, 597, n. 5; ~ E brings action against (?), iii. 565 *bis* & n. 3, 580 *bis*; social: parties, iii. 392, 418, n. 1; ~ alone, &c., iii. 477; iv. 121.
Cockes, Elizabeth: *see* Evelyn, Elizabeth, Lady Evelyn.
Cockes, Robert: geneal., ii. 553, n. 7 *ad fin.*
Cock-fighting, iii. 549.
Codd, John, D.D.: as Dr. Cod: sermon by, iii. 619, n. 3.
Coel, duke of Colchester and king of England: legend of, iii. 176, n. 5.
Cœur, Jacques: house of, at Bourges, ii. 153, n. 5, 154 (i. 99).
Coilus, King: legends relating to, &c., iii. 176–7 & n.
Coins and Medals [as antiquities; for coins in use in the various countries *see* Currency]:
— collecting: 'the curiosi of antiquities and medals', iv. 340; coins, &c.: on sale at Pozzuoli and Rome, ii. 343, 368; treatises on: by E. Spanheim, iv. 78 & n. 1; ~ by O. Walker, iv. 531, n. 3; *see also* Evelyn: books.
— collections:
— — Florence: Uffizi, ii. 190, 191 (i. 119).
— — Isleworth: G. Barrell, ii. 540.
— — London: W. Charleton or Courten, iv. 531 & n. 3; v. 13; royal collections, iv. 216; v. 44 & n. 3; R. Sheldon (deceased), iv. 396–7 & n.; J. M. Wright, iii. 339 & n. 6.
— — Norwich: Sir T. Browne, iii. 594.
— — Oxford: Bodleian Library, iii. 106, 108, 385 & n. 3.
— — Paris: Gaston, duke of Orleans, ii. 128 (i. 82); Perruchot, ii. 114 (i. 74); Poignant, iii. 35.
— — Rome: Angeloni, ii. 236, 356; Barberini, ii. 229; dal Pozzo, ii. 277; Gottifredi, ii. 391 & n. 4.
— — Sion, Valais: private, ii. 516.
— — Venice: Ruzini, ii. 471.

Coins and Medals (*cont.*)
— miscellaneous: Roman coins: values of, ii. 398–9 & nn.; ancient medals: found near Banstead, iii. 221; ~ shown, &c., to Royal Society, iii. 445, 566; relics: gold coin offered by Magi to Christ, ii. 496 & n. 2; ~ one of Thirty Pieces of Silver, ii. 380 & n. 10; angel gold (touch-piece), iii. 250, 251, n. 1; angel gold (coin), iv. 340 & n. 2; Maundy Thursday medals, Rome, ii. 385; commemorative medals: coronation of William and Mary, iv. 633 & n. 2; ~ martyrdom of J. Hus, iv. 396 & n. 5.
Cokayne, Abigail: *see* Carey, Abigail, countess of Dover.
Cokayne, Sir William: geneal., iv. 498, n. 3.
Coke, Sir Edward, Lord Chief Justice: geneal., iii. 14, n. 4; *see also* iii. 15, n. 2.
Coke, Henry: as patron of Dr. John Pearson, iii. 15, n. 2.
Coke (Cook), Sir Robert, of Durdans, iii. 14, n. 4; social, iii. 14, 15; geneal., iii. 15, nn. 1, 2.
Coke, Theophila, Lady Coke, wife of Sir Robert: inherits Durdans, iii. 15, n. 1.
Colbert, Charles, marquis de Croissy (Colbert de Croissy), French ambassador in England 1668–74, iii. 513, n. 2; arrives in England, iii. 468, n. 1; visits Charles II, iii. 513; public audience for, iii. 513 & n. 4; at Euston, iii. 589, 590; exhibits Easter sepulchre at York House, iii. 612; Arlington complains to, about Clifford, iv. 19, n. 6; *see also* iii. 467–8 & n.
Colbert, Jean-Baptiste, marquis de Seignelay: sends gift to French prisoners of war in England (?), iii. 467–8 & n.
Colchester, Essex: notice, iii. 176–8 & nn.; mentioned, iii. 179.
castle, iii. 176 & n. 5; Dutch settlers at, iii. 177, n. 4; King Coel's Pump, iii. 176, n. 5; oysters, ii. 468; iii. 178; population of, iii. 176, n. 4; Quaker fasting at: *see* Parnell, J. (iii. 179 & n. 2, 207); sectaries at, iii. 177 & n. 3; town-walls, iii. 177 & n. 1.
Colchester, Essex (*cont.*)
siege of, ii. 541 & n. 4; iii. 176 & n. 4, 177 & n. 2, 178 & n. 1; Ireton's conduct at, iii. 58 & n. 1; executions following: Sir S. Tuke's account of, iii. 249–50 & n.; men present at, iv. 575; mentioned, v. 112, 336.
Colchester: Duke of: *see* Coel.
Colchis, iv. 213, n. 1.
Cold brook (name of stream ?), iv. 200 & n. 2.
Cold Norton, Essex: rector of: *see* Middleton, W.
Cole (Coale), Dr. — (Rev. N. Cole ?): sermon by, iv. 295 & n. 1.
Cole, Frances: *see* Thornhill, Mrs. F.
Cole (Coale), Gregory, E's 'nearest kinsman': geneal., iii. 470 & n. 2; iv. 9, n. 4.
Cole, Mrs. Mary, previously Mrs. Clifford: geneal., iii. 470 & n. 2.
Cole, Rev. Nathaniel, iv. 295, n. 1.
Cole, Robert, iii. 470, n. 2.
Colebrande, Richard, D.D., iv. 1, n. 2; sermons by, iv. 1, 2 & n. 3.
Coleman, Edward, iv. 155, n. 4; correspondence of, i. 27; iv. 153, nn. 3, 4 *ad fin.*, 174, 231, n. 3; intimacy of, with Sir E. B. Godfrey, iv. 155, 175; tried and executed, iv. 158 & n. 3; evidence against, of Titus Oates, iv. 174, 231 & n. 3, 232.
Colepeper (Culpeper), Col. Thomas: assaults earl of Devonshire, iv. 453–4 & n.
Colepeper, Thomas, second Baron Colepeper (Culpeper), iii. 422, n. 1; lets Leeds Castle to Commissioners for Sick and Wounded, iii. 422 & n. 1, 436; as member of Council for Foreign Plantations, iii. 571, n. 1, 578, 629.
Colepeper: second Baron, 1660–89: *see* Colepeper, Thomas.
Coleraine, second Baron, 1667–1708: *see* Hare, Henry.
Colfe *or* Calf, Rev. Abraham, vicar of Lewisham, iii. 60, n. 1.
Coligni, Admiral: assassination of: painting representing, ii. 297 & nn. 2, 3.
Colin: *see* Cologne.
Colladon (Colidon), Sir John, M.D.: social, iii. 623 & n. 3.
Colleoni, Bartolommeo: statue of, ii. 459 & n. 6.

Colleton, Sir Peter, bt., v. 7, critical note; *add.*
Collier, Rev. Jeremy: absolves Sir W. Perkins and Sir J. Friend, i. 8, n. 2; v. 235, n. 4, 236 & n. 1.
Collin: see Cologne.
Collins, Frances: *see* Heath, Mrs. F.
Collins, Captain Greenville: charts by, &c., iv. 301 & n. 3.
Collins, Increased: geneal., iii. 502, n. 5.
Collins, Samuel, D.D., Latinist: tomb of, iii. 138 & n. 3.
Collins, Thomas, and G. Bedel: sometime E's publishers, iii. 284, n. 4.
Cologne (Colin, Collin): Charles II resident at, iii. 251 & n. 2; congratulates Charles II on Restoration, *ib.*; peace negotiations at, 1673–4, iv. 8, n. 2, 310, n. 3; garrison for, 1688, iv. 598 & n. 2; relics at, ii. 496 & n. 2; perpetual motion sent to E from, iii. 513 & n. 1; visitors, &c., to: Arundel, ii. 57 (i. 39), 72, n. 4; Sir K. Digby, ii. 59 (i. 40); Dr. Lloyd, iii. 53, n. 4; Marie de Médicis, ii. 57 (i. 39).
— Electorate: disputed election, 1688, iv. 596 & n. 3, 598; archbishop-elector, 1688–1723: *see* Joseph Clemens.
Colombiers (Colombieres), near Tours: caves near, ii. 148 & n. 1 (i. 95–6).
Colonna, Alban hills (Ager Columnae), ii. 238 & n. 7.
Colonna family: tombs of, ii. 273, n. 3.
Colonna, Filippo, Constable Colonna, duke of Paliano: tomb of (error), ii. 273 & n. 3.
Colonna, Lorenzo Onofrio, prince of Paliano, &c.: geneal., v. 330, n. 3.
Colonna, Lucrezia, born Tomacelli, wife of Constable (Filippo) Colonna: tomb of, ii. 273 & n. 3.
Colonna, Maria, born Mancini, wife of L. O. Colonna, prince of Paliano; writes her memoirs, v. 330 & n. 3.
Colonna, Pompeo, prince of Gallicano: opera by, &c., ii. 388–9 & n.
Columbus: portrait of, iv. 403.
Colusius, lake of, ii. 347, n. 5.
Colwall: *see also* Caldwell.
Colwall (Callwell), Daniel, F.R.S.: letter to, iv. 273 & n. 5.
Colyear, Sir David, earl of Portmore: geneal., iv. 13, n. 6.
Combefis, F., editor of St. John Chrysostom, iii. 220, n. 4.
Comber, Eleanor (Hellena): *see* Stansfield, Mrs. E.
Comber, Mrs. Elizabeth, wife of Richard Comber: marriage of, ii. 5, n. 7.
Comber, Richard: marriage of, ii. 5, n. 7.
Comber, Thomas, of West Allington: geneal., ii. 3, n. 1.
Comber, Thomas, 1576–1654; D.D. 1616: epitaph composed by, i. 4 & n. 2.
Comber, Thomas, 1645–99; D.D. 1678, iv. 286, n. 2; sermon by, iv. 286; appointed dean of Durham, v. 49, n. 1.
Comber, William, of Wotton: godfather of E, ii. 5 & n. 5 (i. 6); geneal., ii. 5, n. 7.
Comberland, —: *see* Cumberland, R.
Come (Coombe House): *see* Kingston, Surrey.
Comer, Henry, violinist, iii. 348, n. 3.
Cominazzo, Lazzaro, gunsmith at Brescia, ii. 489 & n. 3.
Cominges, G.-J.-B. de, comte de Cominges, French ambassador in England 1662–5, iii. 357, n. 2; at review, iii. 357; at Lord Mayor's banquet, iii. 389; social, iii. 412.
Commin, Faithful: legend of, v. 13, n. 1.
Comminges: Bishop of: *see* Choiseul, G. de.
[Commissions and Commissioners: commissioners replacing an officer of state or other official are indexed with the officer or office: *e.g.* commissioners for the Privy Seal with the Lord Privy Seal; of the Treasury with the Treasury. The commissioners of the Navy are indexed with the Navy.]
Commission for Ecclesiastical Affairs, 1686–8: appointed, iv. 519–20 & n.; suspends Bishop Compton, iv. 524 & n. 1; inquires into reading of Declaration of Indulgence, iv. 590, n. 3; Bishop Sprat resigns from, iv. 596 & n. 2; dissolved, iv. 599 & n. 3.
Commission for government of City of London, 1683, iv. 342 & n. 6.

Commission for Saltpetre, 1666: members of, iii. 443 & n. 1; secretary of: *see* Wharton, Sir G. (iii. 443 & n. 3); meets, iii. 443–6 *passim*, 447(?).

Commission of Accounts, 1667–9 (Brooke House commission), iii. 536, n. 2; E before, iii. 536; charges of, against Sir G. Carteret, iii. 540 & n. 6.

Commission or committee for the Mint, 1663, &c.: *see* Royal Mint.

Commissioners for the Approbation of Public Preachers (called Parliamentary Committee in error): Anglicans and, iii. 172, n. 1; *add.*

Commissioners for Charities: inquiry of, concerning Gresham College, iii. 328 & n. 2, 330 & n. 4, 334–5 & n.

Commissioners for licensing hackney-coaches in London: E appointed, iii. 318–19 & n.; meet, iii. 358 & n. 2, 379.

Commissioners for new buildings near London, 1657: E before, iii. 223 & n. 2, 224–5; alluded to, iii. 227.

Commissioners for reforming London streets, 1662–4: *see* London: improvements.

Commissioners for repair of St. Paul's: *see* London: topography: St. Paul's.

Commissioners for Sick and Wounded Mariners and Prisoners of War, 1664–7 [including E's activities as a commissioner]:

— general notice, i. *18–21*.

— organization: appointment, instructions, &c., iii. 387–8 & nn.; commission, iii. 391 & n. 2; offices: Painters' Hall, iii. 390; ~ Star Chamber, iii. 444; power of appointing subordinate officers, iii. 388; ~ subordinates appointed, iii. 389, 390 & n. 2; salaries, iii. 387, n. 5, 388; seal, iii. 390 & n. 3; treasurer: *see* Cocke, G.

— individual commissioners: appointment, 1664 (Sir T. Clifford, later Baron Clifford (*see also* iv. 19); Sir W. Doyley; E (for his decision to stay in Deptford during plague *see* iii. 417, 429); B. Reymes), iii. 388; Sir G. Downing appointed (May 1666), iii. 444–5 & n.; special commission to E for prisoners (?), iii. 409 & n. 4; the commissioners' districts, iii. 388, 394–5 & n., 620 & n. 1; importance of Ipswich, iv. 115, n. 7.

— proceedings: commissioners: meet (meetings are indicated frequently only by the names of the meeting-places, Painters' Hall and Star Chamber), iii. 389–405, 430, 435 *bis*, 441–50, 462–82, 487–95, 504 *passim & singulatim*; disperse to districts, iii. 392, 405; and casualties, &c., due to explosion of *London* frigate, iii. 403 & n. 1, 408; charitable gift to, for casualties, iii. 444.

— — E: sits alone as commissioner, iii. 405 *bis*; has business with: Albemarle, iii. 411 & n. 4, 416–24 *passim*, 431, 434; ~ Charles II, iii. 391–2, 406, 407, 411 *bis*, 430, 437, 439, 441; ~ Commissioners of the Navy, iii. 405, 418, 431; guards for, for conveyance of money, iii. 421.

— — E: activities in his district (Kent, &c.): establishes subordinates, physicians, &c., at ports, iii. 394; visits ports, &c.: 1665, iii. 394–6, 409, 410–11, 413–14, 417, 422–3; ~ 1666, iii. 432, 436, 437, 441–2, 467–8; ~ 1667, iii. 486–7, 489; sends Dr. T. Clarke to inspect sick and wounded, in, iii. 403; sends dispatches to, iii. 405; sends surgeons and surgical supplies to, iii. 439, 440; money sent to, iii. 417, 433; daily expenses in, iii. 419, n. 3; allocation of money for, iii. 420; accounts for, iii. 409; ~ at Deal, *ib.*; proceedings relating to quarters at Deal, iii. 541 & n. 3; difficulties at Dover, iii. 434 & n. 2.

— finance [some notices may refer to E and his district rather than to the commissioners in general; those relating specifically to E are distinguished below; see also preceding section]: requests for money for commissioners and payments to them, iii. 405–15 *passim*, 420, 421, 431–3 *passim*, 487,

Commissioners for Sick, &c. (*cont.*) 490 & n. 4, 492(?), 494(?); weekly cost, iii. 409; urgent need of money, iii. 419 & n. 3; fund to be assigned to commissioners, iii. 483 & n. 6.
— — accounts: to be shown to Treasury Board, iii. 597 & n. 5; cited, iii. 422, n. 1; E's accounts: made up with G. Cocke, iii. 477, 481 & n. 4; completed, &c., iii. 491, 508 & n. 1, 514, 516(?); dispute with Cocke concerning, iii. 565 & n. 3, 580 *bis*; E reports on expenditure to Commission of Accounts(?), iii. 536 & n. 2.
— hospitals: commissioners' powers regarding, iii. 388; use of, iii. 405; inspector of, iii. 445; accounts relating to(?), iii. 516; sick, &c.: at St. Bartholomew's, iii. 455 & n. 4; at St. Thomas's: accommodation for, iii. 391 & n. 4; at Savoy, iii. 409–10, 448, 458; *see also* iii. 456; pest-ship for: E applies for, iii. 418; quarters for (or for prisoners), iii. 420, 432; infirmary for: E projects, &c., iii. 430 & n. 2, 431 & n. 3, 432.
— prisoners of war: in general, iii. 405; committed to E by special commission(?), iii. 409 & n. 4; number of, in E's charge, iii. 419, n. 3; exchange or discharge of, &c., iii. 403, 406–8 *passim*, 412; ~ Sir G. Downing and, iii. 445; French, iii. 457 & n. 4, 467–8 & n., 492; ~ allowances to, iii. 521, n. 3; guards for, iii. 406, 409, 411, 419, 422, 457 & n. 4; marshals or provost-marshals for, iii. 388, 392, 394, 397, 406; reception of, &c., iii. 392, 404, 406, 418–19, 420, 448; subsistence of, iii. 419; general release of, ordered, iii. 492 & n. 4, 494–5.
— — accommodation for: shortage of, 1665, iii. 418–19; ships used as, iii. 419 & n. 4; Chelsea College, iii. 397–8 & n., 406, 496–7 & n.; Dover Castle, iii. 409; Leeds Castle: hired, &c., iii. 422 & n. 1; adapted for, iii. 436; prisoners at: muster of, &c., iii. 467–8 & n.; ~ release of, iii. 492 & n. 4.

Commissioners for Sick and Wounded Mariners and Prisoners of War, 1672–4 [including E's activities as a commissioner]:
— general notice, i. *22–3*.
— organization: appointment, &c., iii. 602 & n. 1; commissioners' districts, iii. 620 & n. 1; treasurers, iii. 602, n. 1; messenger: *see* Strickland, J. (v. 98, n. 3).
— proceedings: commissioners meet, iii. 612–13 & n.; iv. 27; E as commissioner: business with: Charles II, iii. 612; iv. 9, 16; ~ Commissioners of the Admiralty, iv. 23, 24 *bis*; ~ James, duke of York, iv. 93; visits his district, iii. 609–12, 614–16, 616–20, 623, 624; ~ attended by king's surgeon, &c., iii. 611 & nn. 2, 3; agents, &c., of, at: Dover, iv. 80 & n. 2; ~ Gravesend, iv. 132 & n. 7; ~ Margate, iii. 611 & n. 1; ~ Rochester, iv. 79 & n. 2, 80.
— finance: requests for money, iii. 620–4 *passim*, 631; iv. 12, 31; payment to E, iv. 24; E borrows money, iv. 9 & n. 5; E's dependence on Lord Treasurer for supply, iv. 14, n. 1.
— — accounts: general, iv. 93, n. 5, 243, n. 1, 264, n. 1; E's accounts [some notices may refer to the 1664–7 Commission, and some may not refer to the Sick and Wounded at all], iv. 85, 95, 242, 243 & n. 1, 244, 248, 249 *ter*, 570, 571; *see also* iv. 568; E petitions for allowances, iv. 581–2, 589(?).
— hospitals, iv. 24.
— prisoners of war: accommodation, &c., for: Chelsea College (?), iii. 497, n. 1; iv. 257, n. 3; Dover Castle, iii. 615; Hartlip: Dane House at, iii. 611 & n. 5.

Commissioners of Prizes: and *Golden Phoenix* and *Slothany*, 1665, iii. 419 & n. 3, 420, n. 3, 424, n. 1; two to attend opening of prize-ship, 1702, v. 522, n. 1; (Sir) John Evelyn appointed a commissioner, v. 601–2 & n.

Commissions of Sewers: statute relating to, 1660, iii. 252; *see also* Surrey and Kent Commission of Sewers.

Committee for Trade and Navigation, 1655–7: inefficiency of, iii. 187 & n. 4.
Commodus, Roman emperor: statues of: colossus, ii. 248 & n. 7; ~ falsely named, ii. 223 & nn. 1, 2, 304, n. 8.
Commonwealth and Protectorate, 1649–60 [*see also* Great Rebellion; Cromwell, Oliver; Charles II]: kingship abolished, ii. 555 & n. 6.
Commonwealth: established, iii. 14, n. 6; called the State, iii. 14 & n. 6, 57, 83; arms of, iii. 57; affairs of, 1651: discussed, iii. 37; stability of, 1652, iii. 58; occupies Sayes Court, iii. 58–9 & n.
Protectorate: Englishman represented on figurehead of *Naseby*, iii. 149–50 & n.; as time of calamity or danger, iii. 153, 196, 214; ~ Dutch ambassador on, iii. 174.
period after fall of Richard Cromwell: as time of anarchy or danger, iii. 228, 229, 231 & n. 4, 234 & n. 3, 235, 241; ~ Dutch ambassador on, iii. 229.
Council of State: *see* Council of State.
High Courts of Justice: trials by: 1649, ii. 548 & n. 2, 556 & n. 2; 1651, iii. 384, n. 2; 1658, iii. 214 & nn. 3, 4.
Major-generals, iii. 163, n. 1, 204, nn. 2, 3; Committee of Safety, Oct. 1659, iii. 234, n. 3.
Como: Pliny born at, ii. 486, n. 6 *ad fin*.
Compagno, Hieron: *see* Campagna, G.
Company for the Propagation of the Gospel in New England, v. 88, n. 1.
Company of Scotland trading to Africa and the Indies (Darien Company), v. 245, n. 5; subscriptions to (as Scottish East India Company), v. 245 & n. 5; expedition sent by, to Darien, v. 345 & n. 2; votes of English parliament relating to, v. 376 & n. 4, 379 & n. 1.
Compass: variation of the pole: paper on, v. 97 & n. 1.
Compiègne: Marie de Médicis resides at, ii. 146, n. 2; French court at, 1649, ii. 561, n. 1.
Compton, Surrey: rector of: *see* Fulham, G.
Compton, George; fourth earl of Northampton 1681, iv. 593, n. 3; Lady Sunderland visits, at Castle Ashby, iv. 593–4; geneal., iv. 245, n. 2.
Compton, Henry, D.D.; bishop of Oxford 1674; of London 1675, iii. 533, n. 5.
character, iv. 9, 97.
early life, iv. 97 & n. 3; commences D.D., iii. 533; appointed dean of Chapel Royal, iv. 83, n. 1; as bishop of London: translated to London, *ib.*; attends Charles II on his death-bed, iv. 407; dismissed from deanery of Chapel Royal, iv. 495 & n. 2; ordered to suspend Dr. J. Sharp, iv. 516, n. 1; suspended from episcopal functions, iv. 524 & n. 1; denies inviting William of Orange to England, iv. 604, n. 3; orders prayers for Prince James Edward to be omitted from services, iv. 613, n. 1; officiates at coronation of William and Mary, iv. 633 & n. 6; opposes reform of administration of Sacrament in Chapel Royal, iv. 375, n. 1; claims right of presentation to St. Martin in the Fields, &c., against William and Mary, v. 112, n. 4, 136, n. 5, 169 *bis* & n. 1, 376 & n. 1; *see also* v. 121, n. 1; attends service at Chapel Royal, v. 271; at reopening of St. Paul's, v. 278–9; at meeting of Society for Propagation of Gospel, v. 507; charitable activities, &c., of: authorized to make collections for London poor, 1683–4, iv. 361 & n. 3; ~ letters of, for collections, v. 3 & n. 1, 485 & n. 1; ~ letter to, from William III for moral reform, v. 8 & n. 1, 24, n. 3; presentations made by, iv. 127 & n. 2; v. 112, n. 4, 136, n. 5, 204, n. 5; at Fulham: plants grounds, &c., iv. 258 & n. 3
Chapel Royal services: officiates at communion, iv. 103, 106, 125, 129, 167, 182, 193, 260, 271, 308, 374 *bis*; confirms, iv. 167.

Compton, Henry, D.D. (*cont.*)
as preacher: lacks gifts, iv. 9; sermons by: in Chapel Royal, iv. 9, 10, 33, 83 & n. 1, 106 & n. 1, 130 & n. 2, 195 & n. 1; ~ at St. Martin in the Fields, iv. 63 & n. 3.
possible informant of E, iv. 624, n. 1; social: parties, &c., iv. 97, 152, 291, 318, 488, 489; v. 25; ~ visits to, at Fulham, iv. 182, 258, 289, 379.
chaplains of: sermons by, v. 111–12 & n., 621.
Compton, James; third earl of Northampton 1643, iii. 228, n. 3; presents Warwickshire address to Charles II, 1660, iii. 249; appointed Constable of the Tower, iv. 78 & n. 2· social, iii. 228; iv. 78; geneal., iii. 533; iv. 9.
Compton, Jane, countess of Northampton, born Fox, first wife of George Compton, fourth earl, iv. 245, n. 2; as Jane Fox: proposed marriage to Lord Spencer, iv. 245–7, 248; ~ dowry of, iv. 248; ~ visits E(?), iv. 288; as countess: behaviour of, to Lady Sunderland, iv. 594.
Compton, Sir William, Master of the Ordnance: witness of the Ambassadors' encounter, 1661, iii. 298 & n. 1, 299.
Condé, Louis II de Bourbon, prince of, ii. 550, n. 5; besieges Paris, 1649, ii. 550 & n. 5; visits Charles II, &c., ii. 563 *bis*; imprisoned at Vincennes, iii. 1 & n. 3; manœuvres about and occupies Paris, 1652, iii. 66–7 & n., 77, n. 1; Sir R. Walsh joins, iii. 6, n. 4; geneal., iii. 1 & n. 3.
Congregationalists: church of, at Deptford, iv. 546, n. 6; divine (Rev. T. Malory), iii. 80, n. 5.
Coni, in Piedmont: siege of, 1691, v. 60, n. 1.
Coningsby, Thomas: appointed a lord justice of Ireland, v. 34, n. 2.
Coningsmark, Count: *see* Königsmarck.
Connecticut: governor of: *see* Winthrop, John, jnr.
Connor: Bishops of: *see* Down and Connor.
Conny (Cony), John, of Rochester, iv. 79 & n. 2, 80.
Conopios, Nathaniel: at Oxford, ii. 18 & n. 2 (i. 14).
Constance: martyrdom of John Hus at: medal showing, iv. 396 & n. 5.
Constans I, Roman emperor: statues of, ii. 223 & n. 2, 226 & n. 6.
Constantia, daughter of Constantine the Great: mausoleum of, ii. 241 & n. 2.
Constantine the Great, Roman emperor: expedition of, against Maxentius: in comparison, iv. 618; victory of, over Maxentius, ii. 250, 380, 383 & n. 4; baptism of, ii. 267 & n. 1; ~ in inscription, ii. 271; vision of the Cross to, ii. 380, 383 & n. 4; ~ relic of, ii. 490 & n. 3; *labarum* of, ii. 236 & n. 8, 383 & n. 4, 441–2 & n.; in Colchester legend, iii. 176–7 & n.
buildings, &c., of: as founder of churches: in sermon, v. 64; churches founded by, ii. 258, 306, 380, 381; monuments in churches, &c., transported by, ii. 264, n. 3, 272–3 & n.; secular buildings, &c. (all at Rome): Arch, ii. 250 & n. 3; ~ painted copy of, ii. 109 (i. 70); Basilica, ii. 217, n. 2, 218 & n. 1; ~ column from, ii. 245 & n. 4; Baths, ii. 379 & n. 5; ~ statues from, ii. 226; palace and bedchamber of, ii. 266–7 & nn.; *monuments associated with*: obelisk, ii. 269, n. 7, 270 *bis* (inscriptions); Horses of St. Mark, Venice, ii. 437 & n. 3.
statues of, ii. 221 & nn. 1, 5, 6, 222 & n. 8, 223 & nn. 1, 5, 226 & nn. 4, 6; modern paintings of life of, ii. 272.
geneal., ii. 241, n. 2, 262, 270.
Constantinople (Byzantium):
disturbances at, 1688, &c., iv. 581 & n. 2; v. 60, 101 & n. 4.
appearance of, ii. 47, n. 4; ~ in comparison, iii. 85; monuments associated with: bronze doors made at, ii. 306 & n. 7; ~ obelisk intended to be sent to, ii. 269 & n. 7, 270 (inscription); relic from, ii. 456, n. 4; sculptures from: Horses of St. Mark, Venice, ii. 437 & n. 3; ~ relief at Venice, ii. 440 & n. 2.
emperor of: *see* Peter of Auxerre.

Constantinople (*cont.*)
patriarchs of: *see* Joseph II; Lukaris, K.
persons at: English ambassadors: *see* Diplomatists; Dr. Isaac Barrow, iv. 62, n. 2; N. Conopios, i. 14; *see also* ii. 18; Dr. J. Covel, v. 224, n. 7; Dr. W. Hayley, iv. 545, n. 3; Sir Henry Hyde, iii. 384, n. 2.
Constantius II, Roman emperor: obelisk of, at Rome, ii. 269–70 & nn.
Contarini, Alessandro: tomb of, ii. 455 & n. 3.
Contarini, Federico: collection of antiques of, ii. 470, n. 5.
Contelori, F., ii. 297, n. 5.
Conti, Armand de Bourbon, prince of: imprisoned, iii. 1 & n. 3.
Conti (Conty), François-Louis de Bourbon, prince of, v. 259, n. 5 *ad fin.*; as candidate for throne of Poland, 1696, v. 259, 267 & n. 2, 269 & n. 5; holds principality of Orange, 1702–3, v. 545, n. 1.
Conti, Nicolò de: sculpture by, ii. 444 & n. 11.
Conti Guidi di Bagno, N. de', cardinal: as papal nuncio in Paris, ii. 566 & n. 2.
Contucci, Andrea: *see* Sansovino, A.
Conturbia, ii. 289, n. 8 *ad fin.*
Conway, Edward, third Viscount and first earl of Conway: visits Wimbledon House, iv. 130–1 & n.
Conway, Popham Seymour, also called Conway Seymour: killed in duel, v. 331 & n. 1.
Conway: third Viscount and first earl of: *see* Conway, Edward.
Conway of Ragley: Baron, 1703–32: *see* Seymour, later Seymour-Conway, Francis.
Conyers (Coniers), —, a friar, *alias* Mr. Paynter: attends conference on T. Keightley's conversion, iii. 36, 634.
Conyers (Conniers), Sir John, bt.: social, v. 288 & n. 1.
Cook, —, of Greenwich: buried, iv. 507.
Cook, John, regicide: executed, iii. 259 & n. 1.
Cook (Cooke), Moses, gardener, &c., iv. 200 & n. 4.
Cook, Sir Robert: *see* Coke, Sir R.
Cook, Rev. Shadrach: absolves Sir W. Perkins and Sir J. Friend, i. 8, n. 2; v. 235, n. 4, 236 & n. 1.
Cooke, Col. —: at St. Germain, 1649, ii. 563.
Cooke (Coock), Col. Edward, of Highnam: social, iv. 360 & n. 3.
Cooke, Capt. Henry, singer, iii. 144, n. 1; performs, iii. 144; social, iii. 183.
Cooke, Sir Thomas: examined by house of commons, v. 209 & n. 5.
Cooper: *see also* Cowper.
Cooper, Mrs. —, wet-nurse of Prince James Edward, iv. 597 & n. 2.
Cooper, Sir Anthony Ashley, bt.; first Baron Ashley 1661; first earl of Shaftesbury 1672, iii. 411, n. 8.
created baron, iii. 277 & n. 4; commissioner for London streets, iii. 319, n. 1; as Chancellor of the Exchequer: to provide funds for Sick and Wounded, iii. 411–12, 412; appointed a commissioner of the Treasury, 1667, iii. 487, n. 7; said to have advised Stop of the Exchequer, iii. 607; share of, in Declaration of Indulgence, 1672, iii. 608, n. 1; created earl, iii. 599, n. 5; appointed Lord Chancellor, *ib.*; iv. 1, n. 6; opposes the court, iv. 50, n. 4; share of, in Rye-House Plot, &c., flight, and death, iv. 322, n. 1, 328–9 & nn.
colonizing interests: Council for Foreign Plantations: attends meeting, &c., iii. 578, 599; ~ Council meets at his house, iii. 624 & n. 1; Council of Trade and Plantations: president of, i. *23*; iii. 627, n. 5; ~ attends meetings, iii. 628, 629; iv. 10; ~ chief promoter of, iv. 14, n. 3; *see also* iv. 50, n. 4.
views of, on government and religion, iv. 328 & nn. 4–6; *add.*; anecdote told by, of Clifford's belief in astrology, iv. 21–2.
proposes marriage between his son and E's niece, iii. 519 & n. 3.
social: parties, iii. 526, 600; iv. 1, 2, 88; alone, &c., iv. 18, 82.
Cooper, Anthony Ashley, second earl of Shaftesbury 1683: projected marriage for, iii. 519 & n. 3.

Cooper, Benjamin, registrar of Oxford University: certifies document, iii. 499.
Cooper, Dorothy, countess of Shaftesbury, wife of Anthony Ashley Cooper, second earl, iii. 519, n. 3.
Cooper, John, carver in ordinary, iii. 343, n. 5.
Cooper, Samuel, miniaturist: takes Charles II's portrait, iii. 309–10 & n.
Coote, Charles, third earl of Mountrath: at Swallowfield, iv. 559 & n. 2.
Coote, Isabella, countess of Mountrath; wife of Charles Coote, third earl: at Swallowfield, iv. 559 & n. 2.
Copenhagen: relief of, 1658, iii. 236, n. 5; book, &c., sent from, iii. 563.
Copts: bread used by, for Sacrament, ii. 469.
Corah: in sermon, v. 347.
Coral: fishery, ii. 169 (i. 107); in collections, ii. 133 (i. 86) & iii. 33; iii. 10; v. 48; carved, ii. 133 (i. 86); special pieces, ii. 191 & n. 8 (i. 119), 408; as decoration of grottoes, i. 47; ii. 396.
Corans, —, iii. 94, critical note & n. 3.
Corbeil: notice, ii. 121 & n. 1 (i. 78).
Corbetta, Francesco, guitar player, iv. 49, n. 5.
Corbola (Corbua, Corbula), ii. 428 & n. 6.
Cordier, Nicholas, called il Franciosino, sculptor, ii. 241, n. 1; works by, *ib.*; ii. 275 *bis* & nn. 2, 7.
Corinth: Church of, &c.: in sermons, iv. 346, 638–9; v. 74, 131, 290.
Cork: French troops land at, 1690, v. 19, n. 2; surrendered to English forces, v. 35 *bis* & n. 1; explosion in harbour of, v. 37, n. 1; duke of Grafton dies at, v. 37, n. 3; Lord Clancarty captured at, v. 38, n. 1.
Cork: Earls and Countesses of: *see* Boyle, Richard, first earl; Boyle, Catherine, his countess; Boyle, Richard, second earl, 1643–98, and earl of Burlington; Boyle, Elizabeth, his countess.
Cork and Ross: Bishop of, 1679–99: *see* Wetenhall, E.
Corker, James (Maurus), O.S.B.: trial of, iv. 173–6 & nn.
Cornaro, —, iv. 492.
Cornaro, Luigi (Alvise): represented in ballet, iii. 32 & n. 1; house of, at Padua, ii. 467, n. 1.
Cornbury House, Charlbury, Oxon.: visit to, 1664; notice of, and proposed alterations to, iii. 381–3 & nn.; as suitable refuge for Clarendon, iii. 502; Henry Hyde, second earl of Clarendon and: allowed to reside at, 1691, v. 60 & n. 5; ~ sells, iv. 339, n. 2.
Cornbury, Lords and Ladies (courtesy title): *see* Hyde, Henry, second earl of Clarendon, styled Lord Cornbury 1661–74; Hyde, Theodosia, Lady Cornbury, his first wife; Hyde, Flower, countess of Clarendon, his second wife; Hyde, Edward, third earl of Clarendon, styled Lord Cornbury 1674–1709.
Corneille, Pierre: *see* Plays.
Cornelius, the centurion: in sermons, iii. 227; iv. 364; v. 141, 511.
Cornelius Nepos: statue of (modern), ii. 486–7 & n.
Cornia, Antonio della, painter, ii. 399 & n. 8.
Cornwall: control of Sick and Wounded in, 1664, iii. 395, n. 1; elections to parliament for, 1685, iv. 444 & nn. 2, 3; sheriff of, 1660–1: *see* Edgcumbe, Piers.
Cornwallis, Charles, third Baron Cornwallis, iv. 219, n. 4; estate of, iv. 246 & n. 1; visits Foubert's academy, iv. 400; at proclamation of James II's accession, iv. 413; marriages of: first, iv. 219 & n. 4, 246; ~ second, iv. 6, n. 1.
Cornwallis, Elizabeth, Baroness Cornwallis, born Fox, wife of Charles Cornwallis, third baron: marriage of, &c., iv. 219 & n. 4, 245, n. 3, 246.
Cornwallis, Sir Frederick, first Baron Cornwallis: created baron, iii. 277.
Cornwallis: Barons, &c.: *see* Cornwallis, Sir Frederick, first baron; Cornwallis, Charles, third baron, 1673–98; Cornwallis, Elizabeth, his baroness.
Corpses: consumption of, by soil, in various cemeteries, ii. 131 & n. 4 (i. 85), 181 & n. 1 (i. 114), 290; em-

Corpses (*cont.*)
balmment of: instance of, iv. 151; ~ process of, of W. Russell, iv. 276 & n. 3; frozen: in Iceland, &c., iv. 146; girl's, found in ancient tomb, ii. 320 & n. 1; man's, petrified, ii. 235 & n. 10, 391; hair of a, iv. 202.

Correggio, Antonio Allegri, called, ii. 113, n. 5; drawings by, ii. 356, n. 5; paintings by (or attributed to): Jupiter and Antiope: copy of, ii. 549 & n. 6; Madonna (Uffizi), ii. 190 & n. 14; Marriage of St. Catherine, ii. 229 & n. 5; ~ E obtains copy of, *ib.*; self-portrait, ii. 356 & n. 5; Venus (false attribution), v. 147–8 & n.; unidentifiable, &c., ii. 113 (i. 73), 115 (i. 74), 190 & nn. 13, 14, 356 & n. 5; iii. 339; v. 237.

Corsica: in views, ii. 169 & n. 7 (i. 106), 178 (i. 112); Corsicans: in garrison at Genoa, ii. 176 & n. 2 (i. 111).

Cortnèe, Father: *see* Courtney, Thomas.

Cortona, Pietro Berettini da, ii. 229, n. 3; notices, ii. 399 & n. 9, 417 & n. 8; paintings by, ii. 229 & n. 3, 234 & n. 1.

Cortone, Dr. —: *see* Curtoni, G. P.

Corunna: English fleet near, 1702, v. 513, n. 1, 514, n. 5.

Cosen (Cosin), Rev. Samuel: sermon by, iii. 219 & n. 7.

Cosimo I, grand duke of Tuscany: creator of Leghorn, ii. 183, n. 3; buildings of: at Florence: column with statue of Justice, ii. 185–6 & n. (i. 117), 415; ~ Palazzo Vecchio: interior decorated for, ii. 188, n. 2; ~ Pitti Palace: extended by, ii. 186 & n. 5 (i. 117); at Siena: fort, ii. 203, n. 8.
gift to, ii. 304, n. 6; paintings relating to, ii. 188 & n. 7 (i. 118); statues of: at Florence, ii. 194 & n. 4 (i. 120); at Pisa, ii. 180 & n. 1 (i. 113).

Cosimo II, grand duke of Tuscany: gift from, to Marie de Médicis, ii. 92–3 (i. 62); votive statuette of, ii. 414 & n. 9; geneal., ii. 410, n. 5.

Cosimo III, grand duke of Tuscany: as prince of Tuscany: proposed visit of, to Royal Society, iii. 527 & n. 3; ~ visits Althorp, iv. 69, n. 3.

Cosin (Cousin), John, D.D.; bishop of Durham 1660, ii. 562, n. 7.
Collection of Private Devotions by: origin, &c., of, iii. 45–6 & nn., 635–6.
as master of Peterhouse, Cambridge, iii. 138 & n. 7; introduces ritual into college services, iii. 139, n. 1; fellows in time of: converts to Roman Catholicism among, iii. 46, n. 4; student under(?), iii. 634.
as dean of Peterborough, iii. 138, n. 7; [he was living in Paris in the period to which the following references belong; he is frequently called 'the Dean'] visits St.-Germain, ii. 562; aversion of, to Roman Catholicism, &c., iii. 46 & n. 4, 636; takes part in conferences relating to T. Keightley's conversion to Roman Catholicism, iii. 36, 36–7 & nn., 634; and conversion of his son to Roman Catholicism, iii. 51, 636; reconciles Lord Hatton and Sir R. Browne, iii. 38; libraries of: at the Louvre, iii. 36, 634; ~ in England, iii. 62 & n. 8, 636; social, iii. 24; officiates, &c.: baptism, ii. 567; ordination: preaches at, &c., iii. 8–9, 632–3; sermons by, ii. 566, 567; iii. 2 *bis*, 7–10, 17–39, 44, 47, 50, 51 *passim & singulatim*; ~ printed, iii. 19, n. 1, 26, n. 5, 27, n. 7, 30, nn. 2, 4, 33, n. 1, 51, n. 4.
as bishop of Durham: at coronation of Charles II, iii. 282, n. 2; attends consecration of Bishop Wilkins, iii. 517.
relations of, with E: informs E about accusation against him, iii. 52 & n. 2; library of: E proposes buying, iii. 62 & n. 8, 636; ingratitude of, to E, iii. 355; social, iii. 26, 39, 49, 54.
geneal., iii. 636 & n. 3; iv. 502, n. 5.

Cosin, John, jnr., iii. 26, n. 6; visits E, iii. 26; as convert to Roman Catholicism, iii. 46, n. 4 *ad fin.*; ~ letter from, requesting E to mediate with his father, &c., iii. 51 & n. 3, 52 & n. 2, 62, 636.

Cosin, Mary: *see* Gerard, Mary, Lady Gerard.

Cosin-Gerard, Sir Gilbert, bt.: projected marriage of, to Susanna Evelyn (Mrs. Draper), iv. 502–3 & n.
Cosmas and Damian, SS.: relics of, ii. 219.
Cosmetics: depilatory (rusma), ii. 430–1 & n.; hair, dyed, of Venetian ladies, ii. 447 & nn. 1–3; paint: English ladies use, 1654, iii. 97 & n. 2; ~ ladies using, iv. 336.
Cosnac, Daniel de, bishop of Valence: speech of, to Louis XIV, 1685, iv. 486–7 & n.
Coster, Laurence, supposed inventor of printing: statue of, ii. 54 & n. 2 (i. 37).
Cotentin, A.-H. de, comte de Tourville: *see* Tourville.
Cotta, John: on use of gold in medicine, iii. 86, n. 6.
Cotterel, Bridget: *see* Clayton, Bridget, Lady Clayton.
Cotterell, Sir Charles, master of ceremonies, iii. 515, n. 3; at ceremonies, iii. 515; iv. 262; geneal., iii. 273, n. 2, 616.
Cotterell, Clement: killed, iii. 616–17 & n.
Cottesmore, Rutland, iii. 124 & n. 3.
Cottington, Francis, Baron Cottington, ii. 561, n. 4; visits E, ii. 561; going ambassador to Spain, 1651 (error), iii. 32–3 & n., 33.
Cottington, Baron: *see* Cottington, Francis.
Cottle (Cottyles), Mark, iii. 421, n. 2; office of, ii. 559, n. 2; social, iii. 421; *see also* iii. 148 & n. 6, 169.
Cotton, Captain —, ii. 36, n. 4.
Cotton, Gertrude, Lady Cotton, born Morice, wife of Sir Robert, iii. 442, nn. 2, 3.
Cotton, Sir John, d. 1646: geneal., ii. 537, n. 2; *add.*; v. 359.
Cotton, Sir John, third bt., iii. 443, n. 2; as scholar, iii. 443 & n. 2; library of, iii. 507 & n. 1.
Cotton, Sir John, of Landwade, first bt.: travels with E, ii. 121 & n. 2 (i. 78).
Cotton, Mary, Lady Cotton; born Offley; wife of (1) Sir John Cotton; (2) George Evelyn (his second wife), ii. 537, n. 2; i. *4*; as mistress of Wotton House, ii. 5; children of: births of, ii. 544; iii. 62, 63, 89, 154; godmother of George Evelyn (E's son), iii. 194; ill, iii. 216; dies, iii. 377 & n. 5; buried, iii. 378 & nn. 1, 2.
social (some notices may relate to Mrs. Elizabeth Evelyn), ii. 537, 548; iii. 14, 56, 74, 78, 94, 98, 151, 161, 171, 230, 355, 358.
geneal., ii. 542, n. 2, 544, n. 5, 553, n. 3; iii. 58, n. 2, 154, n. 7, 213, n. 1, 218, n. 6; v. 56, n. 2, 182 & n. 1, 257, n. 1, 359 & n. 2; *see also* ii. 537, n. 2.
Cotton, Sir Robert, bt., iii. 442, n. 2.
Cotton, Sir Robert, of Hatley St. George, iii. 442, n. 2; social (?), iii. 442; geneal., iii. 443, n. 2.
Cotton, Sir Robert Bruce, iii. 443, n. 2; library of, iii. 507 & n. 1; geneal., iii. 442, n. 2, 443 & n. 2.
Cottyles *or* Cotyles, — (Mark Cottle ?), iii. 148 & n. 6, 169; *see also* Cottle, M.
Coubert: Count of: *see* Schomberg, F. H., first duke of Schomberg.
Couleuvre, ii. 154 & n. 8 (i. 99).
Coulsdon, Surrey: rectory of: man recommended for, iv. 641, n. 5.
Council for Foreign Plantations, 1670–2, i. *23*; iii. 571, n. 1; membership of, iii. 571, n. 1, 574, 578–9 & nn.; E appointed a member, &c., iii. 570–1, 577; president of: *see* Mountagu, Edward, earl of Sandwich (iii. 578); secretary and treasurer of: *see* Slingsby, Henry (iii. 578–9 & n.); clerks of, iii. 579; commission to and instructions for, iii. 578, n. 13, 579 & n. 1; council-chamber, &c., of, iii. 577–8 & n.; ~ proposed new, iii. 582–3 & n., 584 & n. 1; ~ moved to Whitehall, iii. 603 & n. 4; meetings of, iii. 573, n. 6, 577–87, 597–605, 612, 613, 621–4 *passim & singulatim*; members dine together, iii. 599; Council of Trade amalgamated with, iii. 624 & n. 2, 627 & n. 5; for further proceedings *see* Council of Trade and Plantations.
Council of the Marches: justice in court of: *see* Eyton, Sir K.
Council of State: closes Spring Garden, iii. 83, n. 1; appoints consul at Venice, iii. 86, n. 1; Sir Henry Vane, jnr., before, iii. 183, n. 2; enforces ordinance against observance of Christmas,

Council of State (*cont.*) iii. 204, n. 5; tries J. Mordaunt and Dr. Hewit (error), iii. 214 & nn. 3, 4; deprived of its power, 1659, iii. 234, n. 3; members of, iii. 64, n. 2, 65 & n. 9, 164–5 & nn.; presidents of: *see* Bradshaw, J. (1649–53); Lawrence, H. (1653–9).
Council of Trade: member of the various councils, 1660–74, iii. 335, n. 2 (H. Slingsby); council, 1668–72: under-secretary of: *see* Worsley, B. (iii. 603, n. 1); amalgamated with Council for Foreign Plantations, 1672, iii. 624 & n. 2, 627 & n. 5.
Council of Trade and Plantations, 1672–4, i. *23*; successor to Council for Foreign Plantations, iii. 571, n. 1; members sworn in, &c., iii. 627 & n. 5; E as member: complies with Test Act, iv. 10; president of: *see* Cooper, Anthony Ashley, earl of Shaftesbury (iii. 627, n. 5, &c.; iv. 328, n. 4); secretary of: J. Locke sworn in (error), iii. 628 & n. 3; ~ Locke succeeds B. Worsley, iv. 24, 25 & n. 1; clerks of, iii. 628; meetings of, iii. 628–31; iv. 1–17, 24–37, 44–50, all *passim*; accounts of, iv. 28; committee of, for an inquiry, iii. 629 & n. 6; conversation at meeting of, iv. 21–2; congratulates new Lord Treasurer on his appointment, iv. 14; abolition of, iv. 50, n. 4; ~ alluded to, iv. 14 & n. 3.
Councils, Church: *see* Church: Councils; Trent, Council of.
Coupe de Chosroès II, ii. 89 & n. 2 (i. 60).
Coupe des Ptolomées, ii. 88–9 & n. (i. 60).
Courten, William: *see* Charleton *or* Courten, William.
Courtenay, Peter of, count of Auxerre: *see* Peter of Auxerre.
Courtney (Cortnèe), Father Thomas, S.J.: at Rome, ii. 213 & n. 7.
Cousin, Dean: *see* Cosin, John, D.D.
Couwenberch, Christiaen van: paintings by, ii. 56 & nn. 3, 4 (i. 38–9).
Covel (Cowell), John, D.D.: social, v. 224 & n. 7.
Coventry, Warwickshire: notice, 1654, iii. 121 & nn. 2–7; address of thanks from, to James II, 1687, iv. 553–4 & n.; Watson, the blacksmith of, iii. 112, n. 1.
Coventry, Henry, iv. 91, n. 5; house of, in Enfield Chase, iv. 91–2 & n.; social, iv. 142; secretary of: *see* Thynne, H. F.
Coventry, Thomas, Baron Coventry, Lord Keeper: geneal., iii. 233–4 & n.
Coventry, Sir William; knighted 1665, ii. 564 & n. 4; *add.*; character, &c., iii. 233–4 & n.; in Paris, 1649–50, ii. 564; iii. 19, 22; business interviews with (Sick and Wounded, &c.), iii. 414 *bis* & n. 5, 415, 444, 448; appointed a commissioner of the Treasury, 1667, iii. 487, n. 7; advises against setting out a fleet, 1667(?), iii. 489 & n. 2; opposes Clarendon, iii. 494, n. 2; social, iii. 233–4, 351 & n. 10, 429; geneal., iii. 336, n. 5; iv. 91, n. 5.
Cow Bay, Jamaica: French force in, 1694, v. 188 & n. 4.
Cowell, Dr. —: *see* Covel, J.
Cowes, I.O.W.: storm at, 1702, v. 486, n. 4.
Cowley, Abraham, the poet, iii. 355 & n. 4; E visits, *ib.*; ill, iii. 367; death of, funeral, and monument, iii. 489–90 & nn.; *poems, &c., by*: compared with Milton's, iii. 364, n. 6; some set to music, iv. 220 & n. 5; commendatory poem for Sir S. Tuke, iii. 348, n. 4; essay, 'The Garden', addressed to E, iii. 355, n. 4; ~ quoted, i. *37*.
Cowper (Cooper), Rev. Edward: sermon by, ii. 19 & n. 5 (i. 15).
Cowper (Cooper), William, first Earl Cowper: appointed Lord Keeper, v. 611 & nn. 1, 2.
Cowper (Cooper), William, surgeon, v. 487 & n. 1; account by, of E's anatomical tables, *ib.*; *see also* ii. 475, n. 5 *ad fin.*
Cowper: Baron and first Earl Cowper: *see* Cowper, William.
Cows, James and Mrs. Jane: geneal., iv. 139, n. 3.
Cowse, Anne: *see* Fowler, Mrs. A.
Cox, John, Captain, later Sir John, commissioner of the Navy, iii. 509 & n. 3; provides yacht for E, iii. 609; social, iii. 509, 610.
Coxall, Rev. Esdras: sermon by, ii. 8 & n. 3 (i. 7).
Coxcyen, Michiel van: painting by, ii. 65 & n. 2 (i. 44).

Cracow (Cracovia, Kracovia): Swedes take, 1655, iii. 161, n. 3; Swedes threaten, 1702, v. 510 & n. 5; Swedes take, 1704, v. 561 & n. 2.
Cradock, Zachary, D.D.; provost of Eton 1681, iv. 4, n. 1; as preacher: merits of, iv. 196; sermons by, iv. 4, 32, 105, 129, 132, 164, 165, 193, 196, 277–8, 302, 309, 373, 435–6, 505, 578–9; appointed to preach, iv. 56, n. 3; visits to, at Eton, iv. 176 & n. 2(?), 181.
Cradocke, Rev. Mountjoy: sermon by, iii. 133 & n. 6.
Craford *or* Crayford (Crafford), John, traveller in Italy, ii. 22–3 & n. (i. 17).
Cranach, Lucas, sen.: paintings by, ii. 414 & n. 4.
Cranborne, Lord: *see* Cecil, James, fourth earl of Salisbury.
Cranbourn Lodge, Windsor Forest: notice, 1686, iv. 527–8 & nn.; Charles II, &c., entertained at, iv. 38 & n. 2; E visits, iv. 558 *bis*, 642; v. 110.
Crane, John, Clerk of the Green Cloth: social, iii. 265 & n. 7.
Cranes, —, iii. 94 & n. 3.
Cranfield, Frances: *see* Sackville, Frances, countess of Dorset.
Cranfield, Lionel, earl of Middlesex: geneal., iii. 203, n. 5.
Crashaw, Richard, iii. 46, n. 4.
Craven, William; Baron Craven 1627; earl of Craven 1665, iii. 99, n. 3; house of, at Caversham, iii. 99 & n. 3; welcomes Elizabeth, queen of Bohemia, iii. 316, n. 2; master of Trinity House, iii. 581; at Trinity House feast, iv. 380; social, iii. 548.
Craven: Baron, 1627–65, and Earl of, 1665–97: *see* Craven, William.
Crawley, Mrs. Elizabeth, wife of Rev. Thomas, iv. 377, n. 1.
Crawley, Rev. Thomas: sermon by (?), iv. 377 & n. 1.
Crécy: Forest of, iii. 54, n. 3.
Creech, Thomas, B.D.: commits suicide, v. 417 & n. 2; translation of Lucretius by, iii. 173, n. 4 *ad fin.*
Creighton *or* Crichton, Robert, sen., 1593–1672; D.D.; bishop of Bath and Wells 1670, ii. 563 & n. 5; as preacher: merit of, iii. 623–4; iv. 23; sermons by: to house of commons, iii. 356; ~ others, ii. 563; iii. 304.
Creighton (Crighton), Robert, jnr., 1636–1734; D.D. 1678, iii. 623–4 & n.; sermons by, iii. 623; iv. 23, 97, 181, 465; appointed to preach, iv. 502, n. 1.
Crema, ii. 490 & nn. 7, 8.
Cremona: taken and evacuated by Imperialists, 1702, v. 488 & n. 2.
Créqui: Charles de, marshal of France: *see* Lesdiguières, duke of; Charles-Nicolas de: *see* Ragni, marquis de; François de: *see* Marines, marquis de; François de Bonne de: *see* Lesdiguières, duke of.
Crespion (Crispin), Rev. Stephen: sermon by, iv. 207 & n. 1.
Cresset, James: occupies Sayes Court, v. 600 & n. 7.
Cressing Temple, Essex: George Tuke's estate at, iii. 182, n. 7; E and Mrs. Evelyn keep Christmas at, iii. 225–6; sale of: negotiations for, iii. 435, 542 *bis*.
Cressy, Hugh Paulinus, *otherwise* Serenus Cressy, O.S.B., iii. 360, n. 5; controversy of, with T. Pierce, iii. 360 & n. 5; as friend of Clifford, iii. 577, n. 5.
Crete: *see* Candia.
Crèvecœur, N.-A. Gouffier, marquis of, &c.: ball given by, iii. 30 & n. 1.
Crew, Jemima: *see* Mountagu, Jemima, countess of Sandwich.
Crew, John, first Baron Crew of Stene: created baron, iii. 277; geneal., iii. 621, n. 1.
Crew, Nathaniel, D.C.L.; bishop of Oxford 1671; of Durham 1674; third Baron Crew of Stene 1697, iv. 4, n. 4; as bishop of Durham: leases granted by, iv. 502–3; attends Charles II on death-bed, iv. 407; as Clerk of the Closet: orders King's Private Oratory to be closed, 1685, iv. 418 & n. 1; appointed Dean of the Chapel, iv. 495 & n. 2; as a Commissioner for Ecclesiastical Affairs, 1686: appointed, iv. 519; ~ joins in proceedings against Bishop Compton, iv. 524; sermons by, iv. 4, 538 & n. 1; attends services at Whitehall, iv. 374, 433 & n. 3; chaplain of: *see* Offley, Rev. Robert.
Crew of Stene: Barons: *see* Crew, John, first baron, 1661–79; Crew, Nathaniel, third baron, 1697–1721.

Crewe, Sir Clipsby: social, ii. 539–40 & n.
Crewe, Randolph, artist, ii. 540, n. 1.
Cricklade (Greekelade), Wilts.: university at, iii. 117 & n. 3.
Crighton: *see* Creighton.
Crime [general statements; *see further* England: justice, administration of; England: social; Justice: administration of; Travel]: murders, &c.: at Genoa, ii. 173 & n. 2 (i. 109); ~ at Padua, ii. 472 & n. 2; ~ in Paris, iii. 638 (extract from *State of France*); parricide: in sermons, v. 146, 149 & n. 1.
Crisp, Sir Nicholas, inventor, iii. 75, n. 3; project of, for dock at Sayes Court, iii. 161 & n. 2, 162, 313 & n. 2; business meetings with, iii. 75, 318.
Crispin, Rev. —: *see* Crespion, S.
Croatia, ii. 446, n. 6.
Croce, Baldassare (B. di Bologna): paintings by, ii. 239 & n. 7.
Croft, Herbert, D.D., bishop of Hereford, iii. 524, n. 6; social, iii. 524; preaches to house of lords, iv. 31, n. 4; *see also* Books mentioned in text.
Croft (Crofts), John, D.D., dean of Norwich: sermon by, iii. 381 & n. 1.
Crofts, William; created Baron Crofts 1658, ii. 562, n. 6; in Paris, 1649, ii. 562; last illness of, iv. 113 & n. 4.
Crofts, Baron, 1658–77: *see* Crofts, William.
Croke, Sir George: introduces plane-trees into England, &c., iii. 386, n. 6.
Crombe, Col. Christoffel, ii. 59 & n. 3 (i. 40).
Crombe, Courtenay, ii. 59, n. 3.
Cromer, —, musician (H. Comer?), iii. 348 & n. 3.
Cromwell, Mary: *see* Belasyse, Mary, countess of Fauconberg.
Cromwell, Oliver, the Protector [called 'Oliver'; 'the pretended Protector'; 'the Tyrant'; 'the Usurper']:
— political: (i) chronological series:
— — — 1652: at Ireton's funeral, iii. 57; act of oblivion promoted by, iii. 61 & n. 3.
— — — 1654: feasts with Lord Mayor on Ash Wednesday, iii. 93; projected rising against: participants in, iii. 463, n. 6; closes Spring Garden, iii. 97 & n. 1; enforces suppression of Book of Common Prayer, iii. 144, n. 3.
— — — 1655: proclamation of, against Anglican clergy, iii. 163 & n. 1, 164.
— — — 1656: summons parliament, iii. 182 & n. 5; imprisons royalists, iii. 183 & n. 3.
— — — 1657: releases Spanish captives, iii. 189; petitioned to adopt title of king, iii. 190–1 & n.
— — — 1658: death of, iii. 220; ~ portent of (whale), iii. 215, n. 3; v. 319; ~ storm at time of, iii. 220 & n. 2; v. 2 & n. 3; funeral of, iii. 224 & nn. 1–4; ~ alluded to, iii. 269 & n. 2; corpse of, exhumed and exposed (1661), *ib.*
— — (ii) miscellaneous: addresses to, v. 279 & n. 2; court lords of, iii. 193; relations of, with Russia, iii. 344, n. 5 *ad fin.*; dignities conferred by: peerages, iii. 239, n. 3, 252, n. 7; iv. 28, n. 2; ~ knighthoods, iii. 165, n. 7, 540, n. 4; iv. 28, n. 2; appointments by, and adherents of: consul at Venice: J. Hobson, ii. 476, n. 3; president of the council: Henry Lawrence, iii. 193 & n. 5; served by Edward Mountagu, later earl of Sandwich, iii. 619 & n. 2; friend: Col. R. Norton, iv. 474, n. 5; spy: Sir R. Stone, ii. 38, n. 1.
— military: troops of: damage Peterborough cathedral, iii. 134, n. 3; guards of: murder Surrey petitioners, 1648, ii. 541 & n. 2; *see also* iii. 58, n. 1.
— naval: at launching of *Diamond* and *Ruby*, iii. 60; builds *Naseby* (later *Royal Charles*), iii. 149–50 & n.
— Oxford University: as chancellor of: influence of, iii. 165 & n. 8; ~ vice-chancellor of: Dr. J. Owen, iii. 105 & n. 1.
— residences of: Hampton Court, iii. 179, n. 3, 323, n. 2; New Hall, near Chelmsford, iii. 179–80 & n.; Whitehall, iii. 166, n. 1.
— miscellaneous: clock owned by, iii. 147–8; queen-pines sent to, iii. 293; imitates Julian the Apostate, iii. 163 & n. 1;

Cromwell, Oliver (*cont.*)
represented on figurehead of *Naseby*, iii. 149–50 & n.
— geneal., iii. 52, n. 1, 104, n. 8; iv. 125, n. 1.
Cromwell, Richard: marriage of, iv. 474, n. 5; as Protector: addresses to, v. 279; ~ fall of, iii. 228 & n. 9, 231, n. 4; ~ presents T. Plume to vicarage of Greenwich, iii. 228, n. 2.
Cromwell, Robina: *see* Wilkins, Mrs. R.
Croom, G., printer, iv. 362, n. 2.
Croone *or* Croune, William, M.D., iii. 475, n. 4; caleche invented by, iii. 475 & n. 5; views of, on freezing, iv. 146.
Cropley, Dame Martha: geneal., iii. 196, n. 4.
Cropredy Bridge, Oxon.: battle of: man killed at, iii. 368, n. 3.
Crosse, Mary: patron of rectory of Wotton, iv. 220, n. 1.
Crowe, Sir Sackville, bt.: social, iii. 406 & n. 7.
Crowne, John: *Calisto* by: performed, iv. 49–50 & nn., 50–1 & n.; ~ performers in, iii. 230, n. 3; iv. 186, n. 6, 271, n. 5, 455, n. 5.
Crowther (Crowder), Joseph, D.D., chaplain to James, duke of York, ii. 564, n. 5; powers of, as preacher, iii. 19, 38; sermons by, ii. 564; iii. 19, 37, 38, 39, 44, 47, 49, 53.
Croyden, George, D.C.L., iii. 34 & n. 3; in Paris, *ib.*; social, iii. 442.
Croydon, Surrey: church: monuments in, v. 426 & n. 5; ~ services in, v. 426 *bis*, 427 *bis*; palace of archbishops of Canterbury at, iv. 73, n. 6; v. 426; road through, v. 168 & n. 1; Sir Purbeck Temple's house near: *see* Addiscombe; Archbishop Sheldon at, iv. 73; vicar of: *see* Caesar, J.
Crystal *or* Rock-crystal:
natural history specimens: containing uncongealed water, ii. 331 & n. 7, 408, 471, 502; from Iceland, iii. 563; other specimens, iii. 10; iv. 68, 531.
carved: worked at: Geneva, ii. 524 & n. 7; ~ Milan, ii. 501 & n. 8; altar-set, ii. 310 & n. 5; other pieces, ii. 87–9 *passim* (i. 59–60), 417, 493 & n. 7, 566 (?); iii. 35(?), 262.
Cuddington, Surrey: Nonsuch Palace in: *see* Nonsuch Palace.
Cudworth, Ralph, D.D.: sermon by, iv. 163 & n. 2.
Cue: *see* Kew.
Cuke-Land: *see* Cuyk: Land van.
Cullen, co. Tipperary: raid on English cannon at, v. 33 & n. 2.
Culmer, Richard, iconoclast: at Canterbury, ii. 76, n. 3.
Culpeper: *see* Colepeper.
Cuma, ii. 347 & nn. 2–4; tunnel leading to, ii. 346–7 & n.; in view, ii. 334.
Cumberland: white raven from, iii. 222.
Cumberland: Duke of, 1644–82: *see* Rupert, Prince.
Cumberland: fifth Earl of: *see* Clifford, Henry.
Cumberland (Comberland), Richard, D.D.; bishop of Peterborough 1691, v. 49, n. 1; character, v. 59; nominated bishop, v. 49 & n. 1, 59 & n. 1; consulted on case of conscience, v. 338–9.
Cunningham, Alexander, tenth earl of Glencairn: social, iii. 463 & n. 6.
Curiatii, ii. 356, 361.
Curiosity shops and sale of curios in streets, &c., ii. 49 & n. 5 (i. 35), 100 (i. 65–6), 124 (i. 79), 343, 368.
Curradi, Raffaello: statue by (?), ii. 186–7 & n. (i. 117).
Currency [coins as antiquities are indexed under Coins and Medals]:
— coins, &c.:
— — ancient Roman: various coins, iii. 398–9 & nn.
— — England: (i) general: new coinage, 1662–3, iii. 309 & n. 6, 370 & n. 6; ~ motto for, iii. 335, n. 2; transport of and payment in specie, iii. 417; iv. 196; v. 122 & n. 2; condition, 1694, and clipping, v. 186 & n. 4; reform, 1695–6: parliament's concern for, v. 228 & n. 3, 230 & n. 3; *add.*; ~ proclamation for, v. 228 & n. 3; distress due to shortage of currency, clipping, &c., v. 229, 233, 242 & n. 3, 245–6, 253, 256 & n. 3; new money coined, v. 231 & n. 3, 242 & n. 3, 246; clipping, 1696, v. 256 & n. 6; continued scarcity of currency, 1697, v. 263.
— — — (ii) particular coins [select

Currency (*cont.*)
notices]: angel, iv. 340 & n. 2; broad-piece, &c., iii. 49 & n. 5, 407 & n. 5; Carolus, iii. 49, n. 5; guinea: introduced, *ib.*; iii. 370 & n. 6; ~ price of, June 1696, v. 245; Jacobus, iii. 49, n. 5; pound: rate of exchange with livre, iii. 24.
— — France: crown, ii. 149 (i. 96); iii. 10; livre (liver french), iii. 24 & n. 3, 34; louis d'or (loise), iii. 21 & n. 6; pistole, ii. 130 & n. 4 (i. 83), 534; iii. 12 & n. 2.
— — Italy [each state had its own currency; here the various states are disregarded]: baiocco, ii. 300, n. 2, 398 & n. 7; ducat, ii. 399, 477; *ducato di banco*, ii. 401 & n. 6, 480; gazzetta, ii. 445, n. 7; giulio, ii. 300, n. 2, 398 & n. 7, 429 & n. 6; lira, ii. 429, n. 5, 450, n. 1, 452, n. 2; mezzo grosso, ii. 300 & n. 2; paolo, ii. 398, n. 7; pistole, ii. 429 & n. 6, 489 *bis*, 530, n. 5; quattrino, ii. 398 & n. 7; scudo or crown, ii. 213 & n. 1, 398 & n. 7, 425, n. 1, 475, n. 5 *ad fin.*, 508.
— — Spanish Netherlands: guilder, ii. 63 & n. 1.
— — Switzerland: pistole, ii. 512, 530 & n. 5.
— — United Provinces: dollar, i. 42 & n. 1; guilder, ii. 63 & n. 1; rix-dollar, ii. 52, 62 & n. 1 (i. 42, n. 1); shilling, ii. 62 & n. 1 (i. 42); stiver, ii. 62 & n. 1 (i. 42 & n. 1), 63, n. 1.
— bills of exchange, &c.: bills of exchange, ii. 60 & n. 5 (i. 41), 182 (i. 115), 401, 408, n. 8, 477, 480, 558; iii. 14, 47, 49; iv. 78, 339; Exchequer bills, v. 255 & n. 2; Exchequer tallies, v. 253 & n. 3, 255, 256; letters of credit, ii. 408 & n. 8.
Curtius, Adolphus, iii. 36, n. 1.
Curtius, Sir Charles, bt., iii. 36, n. 1.
Curtius, Marcus *or* Mettus: exploit of: site of, ii. 218 & n. 2; reliefs representing, ii. 222, n. 6, 252 & n. 3.
Curtius, Sir William, bt.: notices of, iii. 36 & n. 1, 379 & n. 5.
Curtoni *or* Cortoni, G. P.: art-collection of, ii. 487 & n. 3.
Cutler (Cuttler), Sir John, iii. 227, n. 4; as patron of vicarage of Deptford, iii. 227–8, 302, 604, 613; geneal., iii. 540, n. 5.
Cuttance, Sir Roger: knighted, iii. 413 & n. 4.
Cuyk: Land van (Cuke-Land, Kukeland), ii. 35 & n. 6 (i. 27).
Cyprian, St.: controversy of, with Pope Stephen I, iv. 617 & n. 1; in sermons, iv. 361; v. 56.
Cyprus, iii. 52; a queen of: gift from, ii. 301, n. 6.
Cyril, patriarch of Constantinople: *see* Lukaris, K.

Dacia: Trajan's war in: reliefs representing, ii. 378; mentioned in error, ii. 431 & n. 3.
Dacre: Lords, &c.: *see* Lennard, Francis, fourteenth Lord; Lennard, Elizabeth, his lady; Lennard, Thomas, fifteenth Lord, later earl of Sussex.
d'Adda (Dadi): *see* Adda, Ferdinando, conte d'.
Dagobert, king of France: founder of St.-Denis; tomb of, ii. 86 *bis* (i. 58 *bis*).
Dahl, Michael: sells painting (?; as Mr. Daun), v. 148 & n. 1.
Dalkeith, Lord: *see* Douglas, Robert, earl of Morton.
Dalkeith: Earl of, 1685–1705: *see* Scott, James.
Dalmahoy, Thomas: social (?), iv. 35 & n. 7.
Dalmatia: in view, ii. 446; Venetian conquests in (in text as Dacia, in error), ii. 431 & n. 3.
Damascus: and the Arabs, iii. 25.
Damian, SS. Cosmas and: relics of, ii. 219.
Damiano da Bergamo, Fra: *see* Bergamo.
Damietta: siege of: commemorated, &c., ii. 50 & n. 3 (i. 35), 51 & n. 1 (i. 36).
Dampier, William, Captain: voyages of, &c., v. 295 & nn. 2, 3; ship of, v. 369, n. 2.
Danby: Earls, &c., of: *see* Danvers, Henry, earl 1626–44; *new creation*: *see* Osborne, Sir Thomas, earl 1674–89, later first duke of Leeds; Osborne, Bridget, his countess, later duchess; Osborne, Peregrine, styled earl 1689–94, later second duke of Leeds.

Dancing [ball-room, &c.; *see also* England: social; Whitehall: social]: ball: in Paris, iii. 30; lessons, &c., ii. 134 (i. 87), 534; iv. 271, 423; wanton: in sermon, v. 508.
Dandridge, Martha, later wife of George Washington: geneal., v. 574, n. 2 *ad fin*.
Dangerfield, Thomas: punished, &c., iv. 451 & n. 3.
Daniel: visions of: interpretation of, &c., v. 26, 322; in sermons, iv. 447, 638; v. 156.
Daniele da Volterra: *see* Volterra.
Dante: tomb of (error), ii. 197 & n. 3; statue of, ii. 411 & n. 2.
Danvers, Henry, earl of Danby: builds Cornbury House, iii. 381 & nn. 6, 7.
Danzig: as home of Hevelius, iii. 583.
da Ponte, Count: *see* Mello, Dom Francisco de, marquis of Sande.
Darcy, Sir Christopher: geneal., ii. 544, n. 5.
Darcy, Edward, ii. 10, n. 7; character, ii. 12 (i. 10); marries Elizabeth Evelyn, ii. 10–11 & n. (i. 8); i. *3*; second marriage of, i. 10–11; geneal., i. 9 & n. 2.
Darcy, Elizabeth, 1634–5, ii. 12 & n. 3 (i. 10 & n. 2); i. *3*.
Darcy, Mrs. Elizabeth, 1614–34; daughter of Richard Evelyn, sen.; first wife of Edward Darcy: born, ii. 1; marries Darcy, ii. 10–11 & n. (i. 8); dies, &c., ii. 12–13 & nn. (i. 10); jointure of, i. 11; grave of, ii. 15 (i. 12); portrait of, v. 359, n. 9; *see also* i. *3*; i. 1.
Darcy, Mrs. Elizabeth, born Stanhope, second wife of Edward Darcy, ii. 10, n. 7; i. 10; geneal., iii. 551, n. 6 *ad fin*.
Darcy, Grace, Lady Darcy, wife of Sir Robert: house of, ii. 11 & n. 3 (i. 9).
Darcy, Mary, Lady Darcy, wife of Sir Christopher and secondly of T. Offley, ii. 544, n. 5.
Darcy, Sir Robert: geneal., ii. 11, n. 3.
Darcy, Thomas, Lord Darcy: geneal., ii. 10, n. 7.
Darcy, Lord: *see* Darcy, Thomas, Lord Darcy.
Darell family: property of, iii. 620, n. 5.
Darell, Mrs. Anne, wife of James Darell: *see* Henshaw, Mrs. A.
Darell, Mrs. Dorothy, wife of Edward Darell, iii. 201, n. 2.
Darell (Dorrell, &c.), Edward, iii. 201, n. 2; social, iii. 85 & n. 9(?), 201, 217 *bis*; geneal., iii. 620, n. 5.
Darell, James: geneal., iii. 201, n. 1; *add*.
Darell (Dorel), Nathaniel, Major, governor of Sheerness: social, iii. 620 & n. 5.
Darell, Sir Robert: geneal., iii. 201, n. 2; *add*.
Darien: Scottish expedition to, 1699, v. 345 & n. 2; ~ English opposition to, v. 376 & n. 4, 379 & n. 1; ~ *see also* v. 245, n. 5.
Darking: *see* Dorking.
Darneford Magna: *see* Great Durnford.
Darnel, Rev. —: sermon by, iii. 158–9.
Dartford, Kent: Kentish insurgents at, 1648, ii. 541, n. 4; Lord Berkeley, &c., at, iv. 79; Dartford Place in, ii. 10, n. 7; property at, i. 11.
Dartmouth: first Baron, 1682–91: *see* Legge, George.
Daun, — (Michael Dahl?), v. 148 & n. 1.
Dauphin: source of title, ii. 158 (i. 101).
Dauphiné, ii. 158 (i. 101); duke of Savoy retires from, 1692, v. 117 & n. 2; beech-leaves used in mattresses in, ii. 507, n. 6.
Dauphins: *see* Louis (1661–1711); Louis, duke of Burgundy (1711–12).
Davenant, Charles, LL.D., v. 147, n. 6; offends the clergy, v. 452 & n. 3; social, v. 147.
Davenant, Sir William: opera of: performance, iii. 229 & n. 2; theatres used for, iii. 95, n. 5, 268, n. 6; women perform in, iii. 465, n. 5; cessation of: alluded to, iii. 309, n. 1.
plays, &c., by: performances of: version of *Hamlet* attributed to, iii. 304 & n. 6; *Law against Lovers*, iii. 347 & n. 4; *Love and Honour*, iii. 303 & n. 4; *Siege of Rhodes*, pt. ii, iii. 309 & n. 1; *see also* iii. 229, n. 2.
theatrical company of (Duke's Company): *see* London: topography: theatres.
geneal., v. 147, n. 6.

Davenport, Christopher: *see* Santa Clara, Franciscus a.
Davenport, Elizabeth, known as Roxalana: becomes Lord Oxford's mistress, iii. 309 & n. 2; alluded to, iii. 466 & n. 1.
Daventry, Northants.: sermon preached at, v. 207, n. 5.
Davia, Maria Vittoria, iv. 93, n. 1.
David: harp of: effect of, on evil spirits, &c., iii. 168 & n. 3.
in sermons: biographical: Saul's hatred of, v. 298–9; sin of, iv. 349; v. 414; ~ alluded to, iv. 579; Nathan reproves, iv. 205, 638; v. 557; preservation of, iv. 333, 336; numbers the people, iv. 165–6; v. 151; prepares materials for Temple, v. 63.
— as author of Psalms, &c., iii. 19; iv. 53, 567–8, 654; v. 74–5, 85, 113, 119–20, 123, 229, 243, 319, 380, 397, 432, 467, 484, 487, 603; minor mentions, iii. 20, 598; iv. 81, 100, 156, 206, 324, 447; v. 110, 128, 172, 179, 281, 323, 333, 345, 387, 457, 473, 499, 509.
David II, king of Scotland: imprisoned at Nottingham, iii. 126 & n. 3.
Davies, Sir John: geneal., iii. 543, n. 3.
Davies, Lucy: *see* Hastings, Lucy, countess of Huntingdon.
Davies, Mary: *see* Grosvenor, Mary, Lady Grosvenor.
Davinson (D'avison) Charles, Polish envoy in England, 1660, iii. 255, n. 1; social, iii. 255, 257.
Davis, Mrs. — (Mary Grosvenor, Lady Grosvenor?), iv. 86 & n. 3.
Davis, —, servant of Anne Howard (later Lady Sylvius), iv. 100–1.
Davis, Mary *or* Moll, actress, mistress of Charles II: alluded to (?), iii. 466 & n. 5.
Davis, Sir William, Irish judge, iv. 244, n. 5; remarks of, on condition of Ireland, iv. 527 & n. 2; social, iv. 385 & n. 1(?), 531.
Davison *or* Davidson (D'Avinson), William, M.D.; botanical professor in Paris, &c., ii. 565 & n. 3; i. 67 & n. 2; lectures by, ii. 565 & n. 3; iii. 41, n. 1; ill, iii. 20; geneal., iii. 255, n. 1.
Davydge, Richard: gift from, to Bodleian Library, iii. 108, n. 1.
Day, — (Rev. Matthew Day?): sermon by, iii. 217 & n. 5.
Day, Rev. Matthew, master of Colfe's School: sermon by(?), iii. 217 & n. 5.
Deal, Kent: E visits, as commissioner for Sick and Wounded: 1665, iii. 395, 409, 410–11; ~ 1672, iii. 610; business relating to Sick and Wounded at, iii. 541 & n. 3, 542 & n. 4; Four Days' Battle not heard at, iii. 437 & n. 7; fleet at, 1691, v. 57, n. 4; the 'small forts' at or near, iii. 395 & n. 5, 409; rector of: *see* Ibbot, E.; ~ sermons by(?), iii. 410–11 & n.; J. Diodati at, ii. 521; Queen Maria Anna of Spain at, v. 2, n. 2.
'Dean', 'the', 1649–52: *see* Cosin, John, D.D.
Dean, Forest of: *see* Forest of Dean.
Deane, Anthony: purchases by: part of Hyde Park, iii. 82, n. 6; ~ the Mulberry Garden iii. 96, n. 7 *ad fin*.
Deane, Sir Anthony, iv. 270, n. 5; MS. treatise by, on shipbuilding, &c., iv. 270–1; views of, on naval administration, frigates, &c., v. 9–11 & nn.; alleged maladministration by, v. 24; social, iv. 273.
Deborah, iii. 615; in sermon, iv. 249.
de Burgh, Ulick, marquis of Clanricarde: owner of Somerhill, iii. 71 & n. 3.
de Carteret: *see* Carteret.
de Caus, Isaac, architect, &c.: at Wilton House, iii. 114, n. 4.
de Caus, Salomon, architect, &c.: at Wilton House, iii. 114, n. 4.
Decio, Filippo: tomb of, ii. 181 & n. 2 (i. 114).
Decius, Roman emperor, ii. 439, n. 1.
Decoys (for wild fowl), ii. 59 & n. 6 (i. 40); iii. 399–400 & n.; iv. 114, 118, 255.
De Critz, —: purchase by, iii. 148, n. 1.
de Critz (De Creete), Emanuel: paintings by, at Wilton House, iii. 114 & n. 1.
Dedham, Essex, iii. 178 & n. 3, 179.
Deepdene (Dipden), near Dorking, Surrey: Charles Howard's garden at, iii. 154 & n. 5, 377, 561.

Deeping Fen, Lincs., iii. 135, n. 3.
Deer, Aberdeenshire: Book of Deer (?), v. 206 & n. 3.
Deer [select notices]: effect on, of severe winter, iv. 363, 364; about Siena (as venison), ii. 206; various kinds of: collection, iii. 400; fallow, ii. 71 (i. 47); iv. 117; bucks in Hyde Park, iv. 388; buck-hunting, ii. 542; iii. 326; iv. 113; red deer, ii. 71 (i. 47), iv. 117, 468; stag-hunting, iii. 560; sorrel: hunting, iii. 117 & n. 1; antlers: as decoration, iii. 323; ~ representation of, &c., ii. 141 & n. 9 (i. 92), 143–4 & n. (i. 93).
Deering, Sir Edward: *see* Dering.
Dehague, Jeanne, wife of J. Le Franc, iii. 160, n. 4.
Deianira: in painting, iv. 344.
Deists: *see* Theists.
del, della: *for foreign surnames beginning with these prefixes (as separate words) see the part following the prefix.*
Delabar, John: art-collection of (?), ii. 555 & n. 4.
Delamer: Barons: *see* Booth, Sir George, first baron, 1661–84; Booth, Henry, second baron, 1684–90, later earl of Warrington.
Delaval, John, of Dover, iii. 13, n. 3; *see also* De la Vall, —.
Delaval, Sir Ralph, admiral: commission to, 1693, v. 131 & n. 1, 161 & n. 2.
Delaval, Sir Ralph, bt.: geneal., iii. 13, n. 3.
De la Vall, —, of Dover, *c.* 1650–2, iii. 13 & n. 3, 56; alluded to (?), iii. 56 & n. 1.
Del Boeuf: *see* Elbeuf, duke of.
Del Campo, G. B.: children of, baptized, iv. 222 & n. 3.
Delfshaven, ii. 56 (i. 39).
Delft: E visits, 1641, (1), ii. 33 (i. 25); (2), with notice, ii. 40–1 & nn. (i. 30); (3), ii. 41; (4), ii. 55 (i. 38).
Delphi: temple of Apollo: statue from, ii. 189 & n. 4 (i. 118).
Delphini Promontorium (error for Portus) (Portofino), ii. 178 & n. 9 (i. 113); *add.*
Demelhoy, — (T. Dalmahoy ?): social, iv. 35 & n. 7.
Denbigh, manor: granted to Portland, &c., v. 230, n. 1.
Denbigh: Earls of: *see* Feilding, William, first earl; Feilding, William, third earl.
Denby, *rectè* Danby: Earl of: *see* Danvers, Henry.
Denham, — (Sir John ?): social, iii. 94 & n. 6.
Denham, Sir John; K.B. 1661; the poet and architect, iii. 94, n. 6; as Surveyor-General of the Works: consults E about rebuilding Greenwich Palace, iii. 300–1 & nn.; ~ office (rooms) of, iii. 319 & n. 2; gives E possession of ground at Deptford (?), iii. 352 & n. 2; *add.*; commissioner for London streets, iii. 319, n. 1; employed on repair of St. Paul's, iii. 449, n. 2; translates part of Corneille's *Horace*, iii. 505, n. 2; book dedicated to, i. *18*; social, iii. 94 & n. 6(?), 164–5.
Denis, St.: *see* Dionysius.
Denmark:
foreign policy [*see also* the various kings]: treaty of peace with England, 1667, iii. 491, n. 1, 492, n. 5; assisted by France against Sweden, 1683, iv. 332; activities of, in French interest, 1693–4, v. 150, 163.
general: controls the Sound, i. 50, n. 1; condition of, 1687, iv. 559 & n. 1; despotic power in, v. 402; French protestants seek refuge in, iv. 448, 485; Danish troops in English service, v. 6 & n. 4.
kings of: *see* Erik Eiegod; Frederick III (1648–70); Christian V (1670–99); Frederick IV (1699–1730); governor of, in Norway: *see* Gyldenløve, U. F.
princes of: *see* Christian V, king of Denmark; George, Prince.
Dennington Castle, now Donnington, Berks., iii. 100 & n. 3.
Denton, near Lewes, Sussex: manor of, ii. 27, n. 2; rector of: *see* Edwards, W.
Deodatus: baptism of, ii. 500.
Deptford, Kent:
[Where Deptford is used as a synonym for Sayes Court, notices are indexed under Sayes Court.]
— general: (i) chronological series:
— — — 1648: Kentish insurgents at, ii. 541 & n. 4.

Deptford, Kent (*cont.*)
— — — 1665–6: plague at, iii. 415–19, 424–30, 435, 445–8, 462, 467, & nn., *passim & singulatim*; ~ numbers of deaths from, iii. 426 (1665), 467, n.1 (1666).
— — — 1666: disorders feared at, iii. 433–4.
— — — 1667: soldiers quartered at: removal of, desired, &c., iii. 475; alarm at, of Dutch landing, iii. 485 & n. 6.
— — — 1679: Charles II at, iv. 178, n. 3.
— — — 1684: sickness, &c., at, iv. 389.
— — — 1695: poll-tax list for: preparation of, v. 214 & n. 1.
— — (ii) miscellaneous: Nonconformists: churches of, at, iv. 546 & n. 6; storms at, iii. 71; iv. 644 & n. 3; camel shown at, iii. 292; funeral-procession starts from, iii. 621, n. 4.
— parochial and charitable: vestries for parish business, iii. 317–18, 482; parish officers, iii. 475; poor of: condition of, 1671, iii. 577; Dr. Breton's bequest to, 1672, iii. 604; feoffees for, iii. 223, n. 4; ~ John Evelyn, jnr., appointed a feoffee, iv. 202; ~ meetings of [generally a sermon and a dinner; held on 1 May and 1 Nov. in each year], iii. 223, 318, 342, 371–2, 481, 517, 540, 563, 575; iv. 47, 63, 90, 101, n. 2, 108, 123, 156, 183, 202, 243, 260, 295, 311, 347, 376, 393, 509, 581, 638; v. 118; money for (?), iv. 50; relief of, winter 1683–4, iv. 361 & n. 3, 365 *bis*.
— places, &c.:
— — Brick Close: E petitions for ground in, iii. 482, n. 4, 504 & n. 3, 511, 512 & n. 8, 530.
— — Brook Mill, iii. 508, n. 4 *ad fin.*
— — Broomfield: occupied by Kentish insurgents, 1648, ii. 541 & n. 4; West: lease of, granted to E, &c., iii. 600 & n. 2.
— — Congregationalist church, iv. 546 & n. 6.
— — Creek Street, iii. 352, n. 2.
— — Deptford Bridge: held by Kentish insurgents, 1648, ii. 541, n. 4.

Deptford, Kent (*cont.*)
— — Dockyard or King's Yard: fire in, 1667, iii. 485 & n. 6; Peter the Great visits, v. 284, n. 5; ships built or launched at, iii. 60 & n. 2, 322, n. 1, 506 & n. 4; iv. 310 & n. 2; Brick Close in: *see* Brick Close *above*; Treasurer of the Navy's house in, iii. 312, n. 4; ~ occupied by Sir George Carteret, *ib.*; iii. 325, n. 8, 364, n. 2; ~ occupied by Lord Falkland, iv. 386, 427 *bis*; ~ James, duke of York, dines at, iii. 312; ~ Venetian ambassador at, iii. 515, n. 1; ~ housekeeper of, 1669, iii. 345, n. 4; water-dock in, iii. 292; officials: clerks of the survey: J. Uthwat, iv. 43, n. 2; J. Sheere, iv. 292, n. 1; master-attendants: Captain J. Tinker, iv. 131, n. 4; Admiral J. Benbow, v. 244, n. 1; master-shipwrights, &c.: Jonas Shish and members of Shish family, iii. 506–7 & n.; iv. 203, 310; storekeeper: T. Turner, iii. 622, n. 2; unspecified: brother of A. Cowley, iii. 355, n. 4.
— — King's Yard: *see* Dockyard *above.*
— — New Cross: occupied by Kentish insurgents, 1648, ii. 541, n. 4; roads at, iv. 78 & n. 5.
— — Oldcourt manor, Greenwich: lands of, in Deptford, iii. 355, n. 4.
— — Ravensbourne mills, &c.: bought by E, iii. 508–9 & n.; iv. 37 & n. 6.
— — St. Nicholas's church: connexion of, with Trinity House, iv. 247–8 & n.; *see also* iii. 313, n. 6 *ad fin.*
— — — fabric, &c.: repairs to, 1678, iv. 132 & n. 8; rebuilding of: proposed, v. 119; ~ completed, 1697, v. 348 & n. 2; *see also* iii. 93, n. 1; communion-table: to be set altarwise, iii. 317 & n. 7; iv. 132 & n. 8; graves and epitaphs of Brownes and Evelyns in, iii. 76 & n. 4, 93 & n. 1; iv. 303, n. 3, 304, 430 & n. 1; churchyard: Sir R. Browne buried in, iv. 304.
— — — vestry: meets for church repairs, &c., iii. 317; v. 119;

Deptford, Kent (*cont.*)
see also parochial and charitable *above*.
— — — congregation: character of, iii. 604; iv. 5, 126, 291, 375; complains about reading of sermons, iv. 581 & n. 3; small, on Restoration day, 1680, iv. 204; effect on, of Declaration of Indulgence, 1687, iv. 546 & n. 6.
— — — services, iii. 75–v. 179; v. 191–200, 211–14, all *passim*; v. 239–40, 348; Anglican burial-service, 1652, iii. 76–7; orthodox preachers at, 1653, iii. 80; fanatical preachers at, 1653–5, iii. 91, 147, 150; no afternoon sermon, 1681, iv. 254; no sermon, Restoration day, 1686, iv. 513 & n. 2; brief read, iv. 508; *see also* iv. 340, 341, n. 1, 572; prayer for Prince James Edward omitted, iv. 613 & n. 1; diocesan preaches, iii. 471–2, 537; Communion: celebrations, 1653–9, iii. 89(?), 94 & 95, 228(?); ~ [from the Restoration the Communion was celebrated apparently on the three major festivals, and on the first Sunday of every month except those in which the three festivals fell; later there were rather more frequent celebrations; E's participation and record depend on his presence in Deptford]; three celebrations in Holy Week, iv. 277; confirmation services, iii. 471–2; iv. 292; burials, iii. 76–7, 92–3, 210 & n. 3, 211 & n. 1, 603–4 & n., 622 & n. 2; iv. 43 & n. 2, 131 & n. 4, 203–4, 292 & n. 1, 302–4, 335, 430 & n. 1, 464; v. 158–9.
— — — clergy: presentations: patron (Sir J. Cutler) requested to make suitable, &c., iii. 227–8, 302, 604, 613; vicars: *see* Malory, T. (1644–59); Littler, R. (1659–61); Breton, R. (1662–72); Holden, R. (1673–1702); Stanhope, G. (1702–28); curates: first mention (1658), iii. 212 & n. 3; new, iii. 356; iv. 557; S. Alderson, iv. 217 & n. 1; — Dolby, iv. 244 & n. 1; — Holland, iv. 5, n. 2, 11; Dr. William Lloyd, the nonjuror, iii. 335 & n. 3, &c.; J. Loton,

Deptford, Kent (*cont.*)
iii. 432, n. 2, 468, &c.; — Saunders, iv. 35, n. 6; — Smith, iv. 243; — Woodward, iii. 365, n. 5; lecturer: sermons by, iv. 563–623 *passim*; reader: sermon by, iv. 649 & n. 4.
— — Sayes Court: *see* Sayes Court.
— — Slaughter-house: granted to E, iii. 352 & n. 2.
— — Trinity Hospital: gift of land for, iii. 577 & n. 6; iv. 303.
— — Trinity House: for its general activities, &c., *see* Trinity House; buildings of, in Deptford, iii. 313, n. 6 *ad fin.*, 441 & n. 1, 581; almshouses and hospital of, at Deptford, iii. 577 & n. 6; iv. 303; connexion of, with St. Nicholas's church, iv. 248, n. 1 [anniversary meetings all begin with sermon here]; feasts of, at Deptford, iii. 441, 483, 510 (?), 581; iv. 12(?), 36(?).
— — Upper Brockley Farm, iii. 227, n. 4 *ad fin.*
— — Upper Deptford, iii. 508.
— residents and personal [the references give the connexion with Deptford; for the dockyard officials, clergy, &c., *see* Dockyard; St. Nicholas's church *above*]: Sir J. Cutler, iii. 227, n. 4; Grinling Gibbons, iii. 567–8, 572; Sir George Jeffreys, Baron Jeffreys, iv. 484 & n. 2; Count K. J. von Königsmark, iv. 274, n. 1; Peter the Great, v. 284 & n. 5; Captain A. Young, iii. 188 & n. 4; girl with cross-shaped marks, iii. 556–8.
Derby: Earls and Countesses of: *see* Stanley, William, sixth earl; Stanley, James, seventh earl, 1642–51; Stanley, William G. R., ninth earl, 1672–1702; Stanley, Elizabeth, his countess.
Derbyshire: in view (?), iii. 119 & n. 2.
Derham, Rev. William: weather diaries kept by, v. 263, n. 2.
Dering (Deering), Sir Edward, bt.: social, iv. 203 & n. 1.
Dering, Elizabeth: *see* Southwell, Elizabeth, Lady Southwell.
Derry: Bishops of: *see* Bramhall, J. (1634–61); Wild, G. (1661–5); Mossom, R. (1666–79); King,

Derry (*cont.*)
William (1691–1703); Hickman, C. (1703–13); Nicolson, W. (1718–27).
de Ruyter, M. A.: Albemarle's contempt for, iii. 425, n. 1; attacks English fleet in Medway, iii. 484, n. 1.
Der-Veere: *see* Veere.
Dery, —, singer, iv. 413, n. 5; performs (?), iv. 404, 413.
Descartes, René: praises Princess Elizabeth of the Palatinate, i. 25–6 & n.; on the pineal gland, iv. 530, n. 2.
des Essarts, Antoine, ii. 95, n. 7.
Desjean, J. B. L., baron de Pointis: *see* Pointis.
Desmond: Earls of: *see* Preston, Richard; Feilding, Sir George.
d'Espagne, Jean, French divine, iii. 181, n. 5; catechizes, iii. 181, 202–3.
Des Rabesnières-Treillebois (Rabiniere tres le bois): death and burial of, iii. 619–20 & nn.
Dethick, Sir John, lord mayor of London: at St. Paul's, iii. 165 & n. 7.
De Vere, earls of Oxford: original home of (?), i. 24 & n. 1.
de Vere, Aubrey, twentieth earl of Oxford, iii. 309, n. 3; mistress of, iii. 309 & n. 2, 466; in Garter celebration, iii. 559; gift from, to Duke's Company, iii. 303, n. 4; social, iii. 351, 360; regiment of: *see* England: army: regiments.
Devereux, Leicester, sixth Viscount Hereford: house of, at Ipswich, iii. 178 & n. 7.
Devereux, Leicester, seventh Viscount Hereford: house of, at Ipswich, iv. 115 & nn. 4–6.
Devereux, Robert, second earl of Essex: Essex House, Strand, named after, iii. 627, n. 4.
Devereux, Robert, third earl of Essex, the general, i. 53, n. 1; relieves Brentford, i. 53; occupies Worcester, iii. 119, n. 5; Cassiobury Park granted to, iv. 199, n. 2; death of, iii. 627, n. 4.
Devereux, Lord: *see* Devereux, Leicester, sixth Viscount Hereford.
de Vic, Sir Henry, bt., ii. 72, n. 3; as English resident at Brussels, ii. 72 (i. 47); as secretary for French tongue, iii. 294 & nn. 3, 4; as chancellor of the Order of the Garter, iii. 479.
Devizes, Wilts., iii. 116 & n. 2.
Devois de Martignargues, Gard: engagement with Camisards at, v. 563 & n. 1.
Devon: Sick and Wounded in: control of, 1664, iii. 395, n. 1; Monmouth's progress in, 1680, iv. 189, n. 6; elections to parliament in, 1685, iv. 444 & n. 2; Treasury business in, 1687, iv. 565; militia, &c., called out, 1690, v. 31, n. 7.
persons, &c., connected with: — Clarke, iii. 92 & n. 2, 518, n. 7; Clifford, iii. 470; Glanville family, v. 497; Sir W. Morice, iii. 476, n. 1.
Devonshire: Earls and Dukes of, &c.: *see* Cavendish, William, second earl; Cavendish, Christian, his countess; Cavendish, William, third earl, 1628–84; Cavendish, Elizabeth, his countess; Cavendish, William, fourth earl, 1684–94, and first duke, 1694–1707; Cavendish, Lady Mary, his countess, later duchess; Cavendish, William, second duke, 1707–29.
de Witt, Cornelis: portrait of, iii. 559, n. 4.
Diana: wood and lake associated with, ii. 317 & n. 4.
Diano (Drano), Liguria, ii. 169 & n. 10 (i. 107).
Diaries: Edward VI's, iv. 216 & n. 3; Mrs. Godolphin's, iv. 152; diary-keeping, i. *79* & n. 1, *82* & n. 3; memoranda of Richard Evelyn, sen., ii. 10 (i. 8).
Dickinson (Dikinson), Edmund, M.D.: account by, of the philosophers' elixir, v. 599 & n. 1.
Dickson, — (Matthew Dixon ?): paints portrait of Mrs. Godolphin, iv. 13 & n. 7, 14.
Dickvelt, Heer van: *see* Dijkveld.
Dictionaries: defect in: means of rectifying, iii. 341.
Dido: in paintings, iv. 344.
Dieppe: notice, 1644, ii. 124 & n. 6 (i. 79); women's dress at, ii. 125–6 & n. (i. 80); E at, 1647, ii. 536; bombarded, 1694, v. 186 & n. 2.
Digby, Anne: *see* Spencer, Anne, countess of Sunderland.

Digby, Anne, countess of Bristol, wife of George Digby, second earl, iv. 95, n. 1; at Wimbledon House, iv. 95; sells Wimbledon House, iii. 315, n. 5; iv. 130, n. 4; house of, in Chelsea, iv. 161–2 & nn.; ~ visits to her at, iv. 168, 180, 182; ~ projected sale or lease of, iv. 170, 185 & n. 2, 257–8; ~ sold, iv. 335; at Windsor, iv. 383, 466; attachment of, to Lady Sunderland, &c., iv. 595; social: visit of condolence to E, iv. 432; ~ parties, iv. 254, 266, 283, 333, 450, 549, 586, 643; ~ alone, &c., iv. 271, 571, 636; v. 38; geneal., iv. 170, n. 2, 333, n. 6.

Digby, Sir Everard: letters of, iv. 156–7 & n.

Digby, George; second earl of Bristol 1653, iii. 295, n. 7; conversion of, to Roman Catholicism, iii. 311, n. 3; hears A. Morus preach, iii. 311; social, iii. 295, 300.
houses of: Chelsea, iv. 161–2 & n.; Queen street, London: occupied by Council for Foreign Plantations, iii. 577–8 & n.; Wimbledon: consults E about gardens of, iii. 315–16 & n.; ~ E visits, at, iii. 322; iv. 72; ~ library of, at, iv. 126 & n. 3; ~ sold, iv. 130 & n. 4, 162 & n. 1.
portrait of, iv. 162 & n. 3, 403–4; geneal., iii. 40 & n. 1, 589, n. 4; iv. 95, n. 1; secretary of (Sir A. Slingsby ?), ii. 560, n. 2.

Digby, John: at Padua, ii. 479 & n. 7.

Digby, John, first earl of Bristol: buys house in London, iii. 578, n. 1.

Digby, Sir Kenelm, ii. 59, n. 5; character, iii. 48 & n. 6, 550; in Netherlands, ii. 59 (i. 40); in Paris, iii. 20; in London, 1654, iii. 94; books collected by, iv. 126, n. 3; MSS. given by, to Bodleian Library, iii. 107 & n. 6; interest of, in chemistry, iii. 48 & nn. 2–6, 49; presents his *Discourse concerning Plants* to Philosophical Society, iii. 294 & n. 2; thanks E for *Sylva*, iii. 344 & n. 4; on case of antipathy to roses, iii. 550 & n. 5; portrait of, iv. 404 & n. 2; geneal., ii. 479–80; iv. 157, n. 1; *see also* Books mentioned in text.

Digby: Earl of: error for George Digby, earl of Bristol, iv. 403.

Dijkveld (Dickvelt), Everard van Weede, heer van, Dutch ambassador in England, 1687: views of, on English foreign policy, iv. 548–9 & nn.

Dikinson, Dr. —: *see* Dickinson, Edmund.

Dillon, Elizabeth, countess of Roscommon, wife of James Dillon, third earl: social, iii. 91 & n. 2.

Dillon, James, third earl of Roscommon: geneal., iii. 91, n. 2.

Dillon: Viscounts: owners of Ditchley Park, iii. 382, n. 8.

Dinegro family: villa of, at Genoa, ii. 173–4 & n. (i. 109–10).

Diocletian, Roman emperor: Baths of, ii. 238 & nn. 2–5, 240; *see also* ii. 212, n. 2; persecutes Christians, ii. 238 & n. 4, 240 & n. 3, 307; ~ in sermon, v. 64.

Diodati, Carlo: geneal., ii. 521, n. 1.

Diodati, Charles: geneal., ii. 521, n. 1.

Diodati, Jean, the divine, ii. 521 & n. 1; *add.*; views of, on church-government, &c., ii. 521; sermons by, ii. 523, 527.

Diogenes Laertius, iii. 173, n. 4 *ad fin.*

Dionysius (Denis), St., bishop of Paris: relics of, ii. 86 (i. 58), 88 (i. 59); miraculous journey of, ii. 90 & n. 1 (i. 60–1).

Dionysius, St., pope, ii. 359, n. 4.

Dipden: *see* Deepdene.

Diplomatists [this section comprises diplomatists and diplomatic agents of all ranks, including consuls. The list is arranged under the states which the diplomatists represent; within these groups, by the states to which they are accredited; in each case chronologically. The English representatives at peace-conferences and English consuls are placed at the end of England (no foreign members of these two classes appear in the Diary). The identifications of some less important persons, &c., are not repeated here. The references are to the first or to the principal (sometimes the only) statement or statements about the persons in the parti-

DIPLOMATISTS (*cont.*)
cular capacities; further references are to be sought under their own names. The designations are generally shortened. Some dates of terms of office have been added from Bittner and Gross, &c.]:
— general notices:
— — collective notices: ambassadors at Rome, 1644–5, ii. 282, 389; 'the Ambassadors', Paris, 1651 (Hyde and Cottington?: *see* iii. 32 & n. 5, 33), iii. 31; diplomatists attending Cromwell's funeral, iii. 224, n. 4; diplomatists at The Hague: declaration circulated among, 1688, iv. 604 & n. 2.
— — English consulage: at Leghorn(?), iii. 629 & n. 5; at Venice: examined, &c., iii. 630 *bis* & n. 1, 631 & n. 4.
— — foreign ambassadors in London: state entry of: practice, iii. 297, n. 4; ~ regulated, iii. 352 & n. 3; audiences to: admission of coaches to Whitehall for, iv. 262–3; houses occupied by: Wild House, iv. 242 & n. 6; ~ York House, iii. 162, n. 1, 612.
— list:
— — Bantam:
— — — England: ambassadors, 1682, iv. 284–6 & nn.
— — Bohemia, Elizabeth, queen of:
— — — England: agent, *c.* 1633: Sir William Curtius, iii. 36, n. 1.
— — Brandenburg:
— — — England: envoy, 1660: G. B. von Pöllnitz, iii. 249, n. 3.
— — Congo:
— — — Papacy: ambassador, 1608, ii. 244 & n. 5.
— — Denmark:
— — — England: resident, 1651–60: H. V. Rosenvinge, iii. 255 & n. 2; ambassador, 1660–1: Frederik, Count Ahlefeldt, *ib.*; iii. 270, n. 2; ambassador, 1669–70: U. F. Gyldenløve, iii. 537 & n. 5; mission of condolence, 1685, iv. 419, n. 3.
— — Empire:
— — — England: *ablegatus*, 1680–5: F. S., Graf von Thun, iv. 365, n. 5; resident, 1704, v. 573, n. 2.

DIPLOMATISTS (*cont.*)
— — England: Brandenburg (Prussia): envoy, 1680: Sir R. Southwell, iv. 203 & n. 2; envoy, 1700: J. Cresset, v. 600, n. 7.
— — — Brunswick-Lüneburg: envoy, 1694–1703: J. Cresset, v. 600, n. 7.
— — — Denmark: envoy, 1664–6: Sir Gilbert Talbot, iii. 332, n. 3; ambassador, 1670: Arthur Capel, earl of Essex, iv. 201 & n. 6; ambassador, 1671–2: Charles Stuart, duke of Richmond, iv. 76 & n. 1; envoy, 1672–4: T. Henshaw, *ib.*; envoy, 1685–9: Sir G. Sylvius, iv. 447 & n. 2; envoy, 1699–1700: J. Cresset, v. 600, n. 7.
— — — Empire: ambassador, 1529–30: Sir Nicholas Carew, i. 9, n. 2; ambassador, 1636: Thomas Howard, earl of Arundel, i. 21 & n. 1.
— — — France: agent, later resident, 1641–57: Sir Richard Browne, ii. 90 & n. 3, 566; iii. 43 & n. 4, 67, n. 2; ambassador, 1643–4: George Goring, Baron Goring, later earl of Norwich, ii. 90–1 & n.; envoy from Protector, 1655: G. Downing, later Sir George, iii. 445, n. 1; ambassador, 1660–2: Henry Jermyn, earl of St. Albans, iii. 299 & n. 5 (for his later missions see *ib.*; iv. 338, n. 1); envoy, 1661 (Mazarin's death): S. Tuke, later Sir Samuel, iii. 274 & n. 4; secret negotiator, *c.* 1670: Sir R. Bellings, jnr., iii. 381, n. 2; ambassador, 1672–3: Robert Spencer, earl of Sunderland, iii. 626 & n. 8; ambassador, 1673–5: Sir William Lockhart, iv. 28 & n. 2; ambassador, 1675–6: Sir John Berkeley, Baron Berkeley of Stratton, iv. 76 & n. 3; ambassador, 1678–9: Sunderland (as above), iv. 593, n. 2; ambassador, 1688: Henry Waldegrave, Baron Waldegrave, iv. 497, n. 4; ambassador, 1699–1701: Charles Montague, fourth earl (later duke) of Manchester, v. 476 & n. 4.
— — — Genoa; envoy, 1675–6: Bernard Granville, iv. 11, n. 2.

DIPLOMATISTS: England (*cont.*)
——— Germany (princes, &c.): resident, *c.* 1639–61: Sir W. Curtius, iii. 36 & n. 1, 379 & n. 5.
——— Morocco: ambassador, 1669–70: Henry Howard, Baron Howard, later sixth duke of Norfolk, iii. 528 & n. 4.
——— Papacy: agent, 1662–3: R. Bellings, jnr., later Sir Richard, iii. 381, n. 2; ambassador, 1686–7: Roger Palmer, earl of Castlemaine, iv. 558 & n. 6; agent, 1687–8: Sir John Litcott, iv. 498, n. 1; ambassador from James II (in exile), 1689–91: John Drummond, earl (later duke) of Melfort, v. 144 & n. 3.
——— Portugal: ambassador, 1661–2: Edward Mountagu, earl of Sandwich, iii. 618, n. 6; ambassador, 1662–3: Sir R. Fanshawe, iii. 329 & n. 6; envoy, 1666–9: Sir R. Southwell, iv. 203, n. 2; envoy designate, 1684: J. Brisbane, iv. 178, n. 5.
——— Prussia: *see* Brandenburg.
——— Russia: ambassadors from Charles II, 1650, and Protector, 1655, 1657, iii. 344, n. 5; ambassador, 1664: Charles Howard, earl of Carlisle, *ib.*
——— Savoy: envoy, 1675–6: Bernard Granville, iv. 11, n. 2; envoy, 1678–81: Sir W. Soame, iv. 466, n. 3.
——— Saxony: agent, 1680: Sir R. Southwell, iv. 203, n. 2.
——— Spain: ambassador, 1638–42: Sir A. Hopton, ii. 555 & n. 7; ambassadors from Charles II, 1649–51: Francis Cottington, Baron Cottington, and Sir Edward Hyde, later earl of Clarendon, iii. 32, n. 5; resident for Charles II, 1657–61: Sir Henry Bennet, later earl of Arlington, iii. 299, n. 2; agent, 1666: Sir R. Southwell, iv. 203, n. 2; ambassador, 1666–8: Edward Mountagu, earl of Sandwich, iii. 519 & n. 1; envoy, &c., 1669–80: Sir W. Godolphin, v. 506 & n. 1; ambassador, 1672: Robert Spencer, earl of Sunderland, iii. 587 & n. 6; envoy, 1689–99: Alexander Stanhope, iii. 551, n. 6 *ad fin.*
——— Spanish Netherlands: resident, 1641–61: Sir Henry de Vic, ii. 72 & n. 3; agent, 1671–2: Sir R. Southwell, iv. 203, n. 2.
——— Sweden: agent, from R. Cromwell as Protector, 1659: Edward Mountagu, later earl of Sandwich, iii. 618, n. 6; envoy, 1689–92: W. Duncombe, v. 150, n. 5.
——— Turkey: ambassador, 1627–39: Sir Peter Wyche, v. 359 & n. 4; ambassador, 1638–47: Sir S. Crowe, iii. 406 & n. 7; ambassador for Commonwealth, 1650, iii. 384, n. 2; proposed appointment, 1660: T. Henshaw, iii. 248–9; ambassador, 1660–7: Heneage Finch, earl of Winchilsea, iii. 249, n. 1; ambassador, 1668–72: Sir Daniel Harvey, iii. 439, n. 2; ambassador designate, 1684–6: Sir W. Soame, iv. 466 & n. 3; ambassador, 1687–91: Sir W. Trumbull, iv. 545 & n. 4; ambassador, 1690–1: Sir W. Hussey, v. 71 & n. 6; ambassador, 1691–2: William Harbord, v. 117 & n. 4; ambassador, 1692–1702: William Paget, Baron Paget, *ib.*
——— Tuscany: resident, 1665–71: Sir John Finch, iii. 578, n. 10.
——— United Provinces: ambassador, 1657–65, from Protector, &c., and later from Charles II: G. Downing, later Sir George, iii. 445, n. 1; ambassador, 1668–70, 1674–6, 1678–9: Sir W. Temple, iv. 143 & n. 2; envoy, 1679–81: Henry Sidney, later earl of Romney, iv. 254 & n. 1; ambassador designate, 1694: Anthony Cary, Viscount Falkland, v. 182, 183, n. 1; envoy, 1700–6: Alexander Stanhope, iii. 551, n. 6; ambassador extraordinary, 1702, &c.: John Churchill, earl (later duke) of Marlborough, v. 495 & n. 2.
——— Venice: resident, 1638–45: G. Talbot, later Sir Gilbert, iii. 332, n. 3; envoy, 1674–9: Sir Thomas Higgons, iv. 528 & n. 3.

DIPLOMATISTS: England (*cont.*)
— — — plenipotentiaries, &c., at peace conferences: Cologne, 1673: Sir J. Williamson, Sir L. Jenkins, and Robert Spencer, earl of Sunderland, iv. 8 & n. 2; Nimeguen, 1676: Sir John Berkeley, Baron Berkeley of Stratton, Sir W. Temple, and Sir L. Jenkins, iv. 76 & n. 3; *see also* iv. 310, n. 3; Nimeguen, 1677: Laurence Hyde, later earl of Rochester, iv. 188 & n. 6.
— — — consuls: Aleppo, 1630–8: J. Wandesford, iii. 24–5 & n.; Greece, 1649–50: Sir Henry Hyde, iii. 384, n. 2; Leghorn: Sir T. Clutterbuck, iv. 156, n. 2; Smyrna, 1667–77: P. Rycaut, later Sir Paul, iv. 489, n. 2; Venice, *c.* 1643–54: J. Hobson, ii. 476, n. 3; ~1653(?): M. Phillips, iii. 86 & n. 1.
— — France:
— — — England: envoy, from duke of Anjou, 1660, iii. 254 & n. 7; ambassador, 1661: Godefroi, comte d'Estrades, iii. 297 & n. 4; ambassador, 1662–5: G.-J.-B. de Cominges, comte de Cominges, iii. 357 & n. 2; 'la célèbre ambassade', 1665 (duke of Verneuil, &c.), iii. 405, n. 1, 412, n. 4; envoy, 1667–8: Henri de Massué, first marquis de Ruvigny, ii. 504–5 & n. (for his earlier missions see iv. 523, n. 1); ambassador, 1668–74: Charles Colbert, marquis de Croissy, iii. 513 & n. 2; *see also* iii. 467–8 & n.; envoy, 1671, iii. 575, n. 5; ambassador, 1674–6: Ruvigny (as above), iv. 523 & n. 1; ambassador, 1677–88: Paul Barillon, seigneur d'Amoncourt, &c., iv. 128 & n. 5; mission of condolence, 1685, iv. 419, n. 3; ambassador to James II in Ireland, 1689–90: J.-A. de Mesmes, comte d'Avaux, iv. 634–5 & n.; ambassador to England, 1698–1701: C. d'Hostun, comte de Tallard, v. 285 & n. 3.
— — — Papacy: ambassador, *c.* 1644, ii. 282 & n. 2.
— — — United Provinces: ambassador, 1701: Avaux (as above), v. 472 & n. 5.

DIPLOMATISTS: France (*cont.*)
— — — Venice: ambassador, 1638–40: C. de Mallier, seigneur du Houssay, ii. 114–15 & n.; ambassador, 1645–7: N. Bretel de Gremonville, ii. 440 & n. 5.
— — Genoa:
— — — England: ambassador, 1661–2: Count G. L. Durazzo, iii. 314 & n. 2; *proconsole*, 1670–95: C. Ottone, iv. 365, n. 7.
— — Germany (princes):
— — — France: agents, 1651, iii. 43.
— — Hamburg:
— — — England: ambassador, 1661: V. Garmers, iii. 288 & n. 9; envoys, 1671–3: V. Garmers and F. Matfeld, iii. 585 & n. 3.
— — Lucca:
— — — Papacy: ambassadors, 1645, ii. 391 & n. 2.
— — Morocco:
— — — England: ambassador, 1682: Ahmed Hadu, iv. 265 & n. 5.
— — Palatinate (Elector Palatine):
— — — England: envoy, 1675: E. Spanheim, iv. 78 & n. 1; house of, in London, 1688 (i.e. used by agent), iv. 599, n. 1.
— — — France: agent, 1649, ii. 567 & n. 2.
— — Papacy:
— — — England: apostolic minister, later nunzio, 1685–8: Ferdinando, conte d'Adda, later cardinal, iv. 493–4 & n.
— — — France: nunzio, 1644–56, ii. 566 & n. 2.
— — Poland:
— — — England: envoy, 1660: C. Davinson, iii. 255 & n. 1.
— — Portugal:
— — — England: ambassador, 1652–4, iii. 83 & n. 2; ambassador, 1661, &c.: Dom Francisco de Mello, marquis of Sande, &c., iii. 290 & n. 8; agent, 1661: Richard Russell, later bishop of Vizeu, &c., iii. 305 & n. 2; *chargé d'affaires*, 1663–7, and ambassador, 1671–8: Dom Francisco de Mello (Manuel da Camara), iii. 481–2 & n.; iv. 2 & n. 7; ambassador, 1678: Don M. F. de Lira y Castillo (error), iv. 133 & n. 6; ambassador, 1679–81:

DIPLOMATISTS: Portugal (*cont.*)
Henrique de Sousa Tavares, marquez d'Arronches, iv. 169 & n. 3.
— — — United Provinces: ambassador, 1667–70: Dom Francisco de Mello (Manuel da Camara), iii. 481, n. 5 *ad fin.*
— — Russia:
— — — England: ambassadors: 1662–3: Prince P. Prozorovsky, &c., iii. 344 & n. 5; envoys, 1667, iii. 494 & n. 6; ambassador, 1681–2: Prince P. Potemkin, iv. 262-3 & n.
— — Savoy:
— — — France: agent, 1651, iii. 43–4.
— — Saxony:
— — — England: envoy, 1683: G. L., Graf von Zinzendorf, iv. 316 & n. 1.
— — Siam:
— — — England and France: ambassadors, 1684, iv. 388 & n. 2.
— — Spain:
— — — Empire: envoy, 1673–4: Don P. Ronquillo, iv. 242, n. 5.
— — — England: ambassador, 1613–22: Count of Gondomar, ii. 6 & n. 5; ambassador, 1660: C. L., prince de Ligne, iii. 256 & n. 1; ambassador, 1660–2: Charles, baron de Vatteville, iii. 297 & n. 4; *add.*; ambassador, 1665–9, 1670–1: Conde de Molina, iii. 412 & n. 5; envoy, later ambassador, 1670–2: Don M. A. de Oñate, iii. 553–4 & n.; ambassador 1672–4: Marqués de Fresno, *add.* (iii. 613 & n. 3); agent, 1674(?), iv. 133, n. 6; envoy, 1675–6, and ambassador, 1680–91: Don P. Ronquillo, iv. 242 & n. 5.
— — — France: ambassador, 1671–3: Conde de Molina, iii. 412, n. 5.
— — — Papacy: ambassador, *c.* 1644, ii. 281–2 & n.
— — — United Provinces: envoy, 1673–9: Don M. F. de Lira y Castillo, iv. 133, n. 6.
— — — Venice: ambassador, 1646: marques de la Fuente, ii. 477.
— — Spanish Netherlands:
— — — England: mission of condolence, 1685, iv. 419, n. 3.
— — Sweden:
— — — England: ambassador,

DIPLOMATISTS: Sweden (*cont.*)
1661: Count N. N. Brahe, iii. 297 & n. 4; resident, 1661–91: J. Barckman, Baron Leijonberg, iii. 497–8 & n.; ambassador, 1667, iii. 479, n. 1; ambassador, 1668: Count von Dohna, iii. 506 & n. 1.
— — Tuscany:
— — — England: envoy, 1686: P. Capponi, iv. 499 & n. 2.
— — — Papacy: ambassador, 1645, ii. 389 & n. 4.
— — United Provinces:
— — — England: ambassador, 1653–60: W. Nieupoort, iii. 174 & n. 3; ambassador, 1660–2, 1664–5: M. van Goch, iii. 390 & n. 7; ambassadors, 1667, &c.: J. Meerman and J. Boreel, iii. 502 & n. 6; ambassador, 1674–9: K. van Beuningen, iv. 77, n. 1; *see also* iv. 41; mission of condolence, 1685, iv. 419, n. 3; ambassador, 1687: E. van Weede, heer van Dijkveld, iv. 548 & n. 2; ambassadors, 1689, iv. 640 & n. 3; ambassador, 1701–11: M. van Vrijberghe, v. 495 & n. 3.
— — Venice:
— — — England: ambassador, 1661, iii. 297, n. 4; ambassador, 1668–70: P. Mocenigo, iii. 515 & n. 1; resident, 1675–81: P. Sarotti, iv. 278, 279, n. 1; secretary, 1681–6: G. Vignola, iv. 365, n. 6; ambassadors, 1685–6: G. Zen and A. Giustinian, iv. 492–3 & n.; ambassadors, 1696: L. Soranzo and G. Venier, v. 238 & n. 1.
— — — France: ambassador, 1651: M. Morosini, iii. 43 & n. 5.
— — — Papacy: ambassador, 1672–5: P. Mocenigo, iii. 515 & n. 1.
Disraeli, Benjamin, earl of Beaconsfield: on E, i. *39*, n. 5.
Ditchley (Dichley) Park, Spelsbury, Oxon.: notice, iii. 382–3 & nn.
Ditton: *see* Long Ditton.
Dive, —, iv. 350.
Diveria, river, ii. 508, n. 5.
Dives: in sermons, iii. 11, 503; iv. 176, 299; v. 60, 215, 405; as the rich Epulo: in sermon, iv. 138; alluded to, in sermon, iii. 35.
Dives, Sir Lowes: *see* Dyve.

Dixmude: taken by French, 1693, v. 126 & n. 2; surrendered to French, 1695, v. 215 & n. 5.
Dixon, Matthew: portrait of Mrs. Godolphin by (?), iv. 13 & n. 7, 14.
Djem, Turkish prince, ii. 499, n. 2.
Dobson, Austin: on E, i. *39–40*; as editor of the Diary, i. *63, 69, 115, 116–17*.
Dobson, William: painting by, iv. 402–3 & n.
Doeg: in sermon, v. 299.
Does, Johan van der (Janus Dousa): geneal., &c., iv. 312 & n. 4.
Does, Johan van der, jnr.: tries to buy drawings, iv. 312 & n. 4.
Dog (dogs): used for transport (Brussels, &c.), ii. 72–3 (i. 48); used to catch salmon, iii. 303; at Grotta del Cane, ii. 339 & n. 4, 340; in Royal Society's experiments, iii. 288, 289, 290, 403, 478; vivisection of a, iii. 497–8; embryo puppies, iii. 325 & n. 6; dog-fighting, iii. 549; performing dog, iv. 359.
  dogs owned by: Charles II, iv. 410 & n. 1; E, ii. 533, 560–1; Henrietta Maria, iii. 331; James, duke of York, iii. 412; pension and epitaph for a dog, ii. 175 (i. 111).
  kinds of dog: various, iii. 549; Bolognese lap-dogs, ii. 425 & n. 1; Island, iii. 198 & n. 2; mastiffs, ii. 72 (i. 48); spaniels, ii. 425, 533, 560; iv. 410; tumbler, iv. 114 & n. 3; water-spaniel, ii. 511.
Dog-fighting: in Bear-garden, iii. 549.
Dohna, Christopher Delphicus von, count von Dohna, Swedish ambassador in England: audience for, iii. 506 & n. 1.
D'oily, Sir William: *see* Doyley.
Dolben, Anne, Lady Dolben, wife of Sir Gilbert, iv. 282, n. 5.
Dolben, Mrs. Catherine, wife of the bishop, iv. 257 & n. 2.
Dolben, Sir Gilbert; bt. 1704: marriage of, iv. 282 & n. 5.
Dolben, John, D.D.; dean of Westminster 1662–83; bishop of Rochester 1666; archbishop of York 1683, iii. 444, n. 1.
  as dean: delivers charitable gift to E, iii. 443–4.
Dolben, John, D.D. (*cont.*)
  as bishop: consecrated, iii. 471, n. 6; repairs his palace at Bromley, iii. 537–8 & n.; consulted about new vicar for Deptford, iii. 604; becomes Lord Almoner, iv. 61, n. 6; opposes Parliamentary Test Act, iv. 159, n. 4; and controversy, iv. 282; attends: consecration of Bishop Wilkins, iii. 517; ~ funeral of Sir Richard Browne, iv. 302; relations of, with: Danby, iv. 267 & nn. 3–5; ~ Sir W. Temple, iv. 266–7 & n.
  as archbishop: elected, &c., iv. 334 & n. 2; goes to York, iv. 335 & n. 1; at Chapel Royal service, iv. 436; at opening of parliament, 1685, iv. 442; dies, iv. 507 & n. 1.
  officiates: confirms, iii. 471–2; iv. 292; at marriages, iv. 123, 238; at remarriage of duke and duchess of Grafton, iv. 184 & n. 3; sermons by: at Deptford, iii. 471–2, 537; iv. 292; ~ for Trinity House, iv. 11, 36; to House of Lords, iv. 31 & n. 4; elsewhere, iv. 6, 34, 61, 62, 91, 132, 168, 193, 300; appointed to preach, iv. 133 & n. 2, 167, n. 3, 309 & n. 3.
  social: wedding anniversary of, iv. 266; visits to, &c.: at Bromley, iv. 73, 153, 211, 288; ~ at Greenwich (Captain Cocke), iv. 73; ~ at Ham Court (D. Sheldon), iv. 142 & n. 2; elsewhere: parties, iv. 44, 89, 152, 291, 488, 496; alone, &c., iii. 472, 602, 614; iv. 32, 87, 95, 165, 188, 240, 257, 277, 299, 309, 439.
  geneal., iv. 257 & n. 2, 282 & n. 5.
  chaplain of: sermon by, iii. 516.
Dolben, Sir William, judge: dismissal of: alluded to (?), iv. 320 & n. 1.
Dolby, Rev. — (Thomas Dolby ?), curate at Deptford, iv. 244 & n. 1; style of preaching of (?), iv. 247, 250 [his sermons are not indexed].
Dolcebuono, G. G.: building designed by, ii. 495, n. 2.
Domenichino: paintings by, ii. 276, n. 1, 289 & n. 2, 376, n. 6; ~ as by Domenico, ii. 424 & n. 3.

Domenico, painter: *see* Domenichino.
Dominic, St.: cell of, ii. 421 & n. 8; relics of, ii. 359 & n. 10, 421 & n. 4; portrait of, ii. 439 & n. 2.
Domitian, Roman emperor: additions by, to Coliseum, ii. 248, n. 8; triumphal arch of, ii. 370 & n. 2.
Domodossola (Duomo), ii. 508 & nn. 2, 3.
Donatello, ii. 193, n. 3; sculptures by: Judith, ii. 193 & n. 3 (i. 120), 193–4; ~ Gattamelata, ii. 454 & n. 5; ~ in choir, S. Antonio, Padua, ii. 455, n. 1; named in error, ii. 267, n. 3.
Donatists: views of: revived by Nonconformists (in sermon), iv. 346 & n. 2.
Doncaster, Yorks., W.R.: notice, iii. 127 & n. 5.
Doncaster: Earl of, 1674–85: *see* Scott, James, later earl of Dalkeith.
Donghi, Gianstefano, cardinal, ii. 207 & n. 3.
Donna, Count: *see* Dohna.
Donneau de Vizé, family, iii. 23, n. 3.
Donnington (Dennington) Castle, Berks.: notice, iii. 100 & n. 3.
Dorchester, Oxon.: former episcopal see at, iii. 131, n. 7.
Dorchester: Countess of, 1686–1717: *see* Sedley, Catherine.
Dorchester: Marquises of: *see* Pierrepont, Henry, marquis 1645–80; *new creation*: *see* Pierrepont, Evelyn, marquis 1706–15, later duke of Kingston.
Dordrecht (Dort): E visits, 1641, ii. 32 & nn. 3–6 (i. 24–5), 59 *bis* & n. 6 (i. 40, 41), 60 *bis* (i. 41).
notice, ii. 32 & nn. 3–6 (i. 24–5); decoys at, ii. 59 & n. 6 (i. 40); Stadhuis: portrait in, *c.* 1670, iii. 559, n. 4; Marie de Médicis at, ii. 57 & n. 1 (i. 39); Synod of Dort, ii. 32 & n. 5 (i. 25), 521, n. 1.
Dordsche-Kil (the Keele), ii. 60 *ter* & n. 1 (i. 41 *bis*).
Dorel, Major —: *see* Darell, N.
Dorislaus, Isaac: buried, ii. 556 & n. 5.
Dorking (Darking), Surrey: distance of Wotton from, ii. 4 & n. 2 (i. 5–6); manors in: Milton, v. 478 & n. 1, 547; ~ Westcote, v. 478 & n. 1; places in: Comb Hill, &c., v. 547, n. 4, 548, critical note; ~ Westcote, v. 547 & n. 4; ~ *see also* Deepdene; river of: *see* Mole; road through, v. 168 & n. 1; vicar of: *see* Cosen, S.
Dormer, Charles, second earl of Carnarvon, ii. 521 & n. 3; at Geneva, *ib.*; geneal., iv. 559, n. 2.
Dormer, Isabella: *see* Coote, Isabella, countess of Mountrath.
Dormer, Mrs. Mary, wife of Robert Dormer: as amateur artist (?), iv. 363 & n. 5.
Dormer, Robert, of Lee Grange: geneal., iv. 363, n. 5.
Dorrell, —: *see* Darell, E.
Dorset: in comparison, ii. 488.
Dorset: Earls, &c., of: *see* Sackville, Richard, third earl, 1609–24; Herbert, Anne, countess of Pembroke, his countess; Sackville, Richard, fifth earl, 1652–77; Sackville, Frances, his countess; Sackville, Charles, sixth earl, 1677–1706.
Dort: *see* Dordrecht.
Dou (Douce), Gerrit: paintings by, presented to Charles II, iii. 262 & n. 6; *add.*; iii. 323, n. 5.
Douai (Doway): English college at: member of, ii. 213 & n. 2.
Douce, painter: *see* Dou, G.
Doughty, John, D.D.: sermon by, iii. 524 & n. 7.
Doughty, Thomas, D.D., iv. 87, n. 2; sermons by, iv. 87, 103.
Douglas: regiment of, in French army, iii. 12, n. 5.
Douglas, Lady Anne, countess of Arran; born Spencer; wife of James Douglas, styled earl of Arran, later fourth duke of Hamilton, &c., iv. 567, n. 2; married, iv. 567; social, iv. 567, 594; character, iv. 595.
Douglas, Anne, duchess of Hamilton *suo jure*; born Hamilton; wife of William Douglas, third duke of Hamilton: geneal., iii. 254, n. 2; iv. 296, n. 3.
Douglas, Anne, countess of Morton; born Villiers; wife of Robert Douglas, earl of Morton, ii. 564, n. 7; in Paris, 1649–52, ii. 564–5; iii. 22, 54; mentioned, iii. 44, n. 5.
Douglas, Archibald, sixth earl of Angus: geneal., iv. 215, n. 2.

Douglas, Lord George, first earl of Dumbarton: in camp on Hounslow Heath, iv. 514 & n. 3.
Douglas, Lt.-Gen. James: describes condition of English troops in Ireland, v. 7 & n. 3.
Douglas, James; styled earl of Arran (Scotland) 1658–98; fourth duke of Hamilton 1698; &c., iv. 296, n. 3; as Lord Arran: character, iv. 595; attends James II at Winchester(?), iv. 468, 470, n. 1; marriage of, iv. 567 & n. 2; prisoner in the Tower, iv. 640 & n. 4; social, iv. 296, 466 & n. 1(?), 567.
Douglas, Robert, earl of Morton: geneal., ii. 564, n. 7.
Douglas, William; third duke of Hamilton 1660, iii. 254, n. 2; iv. 603, n. 3; account by, of Mary, queen of Scots, iv. 603; social, iii. 254; iv. 296, 567; dies, v. 177 & n. 2; geneal., iv. 296, n. 3.
Douglas, William, first duke of Queensberry: opens Scottish parliament, 1685, iv. 440 & n. 2.
Douleroy: *see* Dun-le-Roy.
Dousa, Janus (Johan van der Does), and his grandson, iv. 312 & n. 4.
Douse, — van der: *see* Does, Johan van der, jnr.
Dove, Henry; D.D. 1677, iv. 100, n. 1; sermons by: funeral, iv. 183; printed, iv. 403 & n. 3; others, iv. 100, 363.
Dovedro (Vedra), ii. 508 & n. 5.
Dover, Kent: E visits: 1641, ii. 76 (i. 50); 1643, ii. 82 (i. 56); 1647, ii. 537; 1649, ii. 559; 1650, iii. 13, 16; 1652, iii. 56; 1675, iv. 79–80; as commissioner for Sick and Wounded: 1665, iii. 394, 395, 408 & n. 3, 409, 411; ~ 1672, iii. 610, 614–15.
  Four Days' Battle: not heard at, &c., iii. 437, n. 7, 438, n. 1; Charles II and Henrietta Anne (Madame) meet at, iii. 548 *bis* & n. 1.
  officials at: clerks of the passage, iii. 56, 434 & n. 2; customs officials, &c., iii. 13, 16 & n. 1, 395; mayors, iii. 13 & n. 2, 395; iv. 80 & n. 2.
  Dover Castle: cliff beneath, ii. 335; prisoners of war in, iii. 409 & n. 2, 615; salute from, iv. 80; E at, iii. 395, 411;
Dover, Kent (*cont.*)
  governors of: *see* Manwood, Sir J. (1637–40); Strode, Col. John (1660–86); Hales, Sir Edward, third bt. (1686–).
  other places in: harbour, i. 50; St. Mary's church: sermons at, iii. 395; iv. 80; ~ incumbent of: *see* Hinde, S.; environs of: Dover Cliff, v. 231; the downs, i. 57.
  personal: Lord Berkeley and his train at, iv. 79–80; Sir Richard Browne at, iii. 247; J. Delaval of, iii. 13 & n. 3, 56 *bis* & nn. 1, 2; John Evelyn, jnr., at, iii. 548; iv. 80; Mrs. Godolphin at, iv. 79–80, 88; Henry Howard, sixth duke of Norfolk, going to, iv. 236; Dr. P. Yvelin at, iii. 547–8 & n.; French merchant of, iii. 56.
Dover: Baron, 1685–1703, &c.: *see* Jermyn, Henry, third Baron Jermyn, &c.; Jermyn, Judith, his baroness.
Dover: Earls, &c., of: *see* Carey, Henry, first earl, 1628–66; Carey, John, second earl, 1666–77; Carey, Abigail, his countess; *Jacobite creation*: *see* Jermyn, Henry, Baron Jermyn, &c., earl 1689–1708.
Dover: Secret Treaty of, 1670, iii. 523, n. 1, 548, n. 1; iv. 7, n. 3; provisions, &c., of, iii. 559, n. 4, 608, n. 1; unknown to Buckingham, iii. 596, n. 3; Clifford's share in, iii. 577, n. 5, 608, n. 1; signatory of, iii. 381, n. 2.
Dover Straits [also called English Channel, &c]: origin of, i. 57 & n. 1; control of, i. 50; English and French fleet in, 1672, iii. 615 & n. 1; French warships allowed to pass through, 1683, iv. 331–2 & n.; fleet movement in, 1702, v. 510.
Doway: *see* Douai.
Down and Connor: Bishops of: *see* Leslie, H. (1635–61); Taylor, Jeremy (1661–7).
Downe: second Earl of: *see* Pope, Thomas.
Downe: Viscount, 1675–9: *see* Ducie, Sir W.
Downes, —: buried, ii. 565.
Downham (Santon Downham), Suffolk: travelling sands (sand-flood) at, iv. 120 & n. 2.

Downing, Sir George, bt., iii. 445, n. 1; character, &c., iii. 445 & n. 1; appointed a commissioner for Sick and Wounded, iii. 444–5 & n.; to provide materials for E's History of Second Dutch War, iii. 568; social, iii. 514.
Downs: the English (the hills): in comparisons, i. 57; ii. 121 (i. 78), 485.
Downs, The (the sea, within the Goodwin Sands): shipping movements, &c., in, iii. 68, n. 3, 328, n. 1, 438, 609, n. 3; iv. 552; v. 97, n. 3, 112, n. 1; E visits, for Sick and Wounded, iii. 410, 437.
Doyley (D'oily), Sir William, bt., iii. 388, n. 1.
as a commissioner for Sick and Wounded, 1664–7, 1672–4: appointed, iii. 387–8, 602, n. 1; district controlled by, iii. 394–5 & n., 620, n. 1; iv. 115, n. 7; activities of, iii. 391, 490, n. 4.
agent for tax-collectors, 1664–7, iii. 464, n. 1; ill, iii. 433, 448; social, iii. 402, 448, 463, 491, 514, 548, 614.
Draghi, Giovanni Battista, organist, &c., iv. 384, n. 6; performs(?), iv. 384–5, 404, 422.
Drake, —: garden of, at Hackney, iii. 96, n. 2.
Drake, Sir Francis, ii. 355; iii. 585; fight of, 1588: painting representing, iii. 180.
Drano: *see* Diano.
Draper, Mrs. —, mother of William Draper (E's son-in-law), v. 146, n. 1; visits E, v. 146; godmother of Mary Draper, v. 218; buried, v. 451 & n. 2.
Draper, Evelyn: *see* Clarke, Mrs. E.
Draper, George, b. 1697: born and baptized, v. 263 & n. 1; dies(?), v. 423 & n. 1.
Draper, Jasper, v. 451, n. 2.
Draper, Mary, b. 1695: born and baptized, v. 217 & n. 1, 218–19.
Draper, Richard, b. 1699: born and baptized, v. 351 & n. 3; dies(?), v. 423 & n. 1.
Draper, Roger, v. 218 & n. 4.
Draper, Sarah: *see* Temple, Sarah, Lady Temple.
Draper, Susannah, 1701–72, v. 459, n. 1; born, v. 459; baptized, v. 461.
Draper, Mrs. Susanna, 1669–1754; daughter of E; wife of William Draper, iii. 528, n. 1; character, iv. 462; v. 138.
as Susanna Evelyn: born and baptized, iii. 528; i. *23*; confirmed, iv. 292; ill, iv. 359, 564 *bis*; alluded to, iv. 424, 426 *bis*; receives Sacrament, iv. 437, 479; v. 24, 119; portrait of: drawn, iv. 475; marriage-proposal for, 1686, iv. 502–3 & n.; i. *32*; visits: Wotton, iv. 557; Tunbridge Wells, iv. 646; Bath, v. 58, 61 & n. 1.
marriage with William Draper: proposed, v. 133; celebrated, v. 138; dowry of, *ib.*; ~ paid, iv. 153–4, 154.
as Mrs. Draper [*see also* Draper, William *and* Mrs. Susanna, where joint-notices are indexed. Notices in which Draper alone is named, although his wife's participation is to be assumed, are indexed under Draper, William]: visits to, as bride, v. 138–9; pregnancies, &c., of, v. 158, 190–4 *passim*, 215, 217, 262–3 & n., 286, 287 & n. 6, 351 & n. 3, 459 & n. 1, 582 *bis*; receives Sacrament, v. 171, 190, 243; visits: Wotton, v. 259; ~ Greenwich, v. 600; dress of, v. 542; death of, i. *36*.
Draper, Thomas, 1694–5: born, v. 190; baptized, v. 191, 193–4; dies, v. 215.
Draper, Sir Thomas, bt., v. 191, n. 1; as godfather of T. Draper, v. 191, 194; geneal., v. 133, n. 2, 194.
Draper, William, d. 1718, husband of Susanna Evelyn, v. 133, n. 2; i. *34* [*see also* Draper, William *and* Mrs. Susanna, where joint-notices, except those relating to houses, are indexed].
marriage: proposed, v. 133; celebrated, v. 138; dowry paid, v. 154.
houses of: in 1693, v. 139 & n. 6; occupies Sayes Court, 1694, v. 179; in London, 1694, 1696, v. 199, 219, n. 6, 235; ~ fire in, 1697, v. 268; at Addiscombe: inherits, v. 383, 385–6; ~ resides at, v. 425, 470; ~ rebuilds, v. 509, 541 & n. 1.
personal, &c.: and estate of Sir Purbeck and Lady Temple:

Draper, William (*cont.*)
prospective heir to, v. 219, 247–8; ~ inherits, v. 383, 385–6; and Greenwich Hospital: member of Grand Committee, v. 236, n. 2; ~ appointed treasurer of, v. 544 & n. 1; ~ clerk of, as treasurer of, v. 98, n. 3; visits Wotton, v. 187, 259; travels to Land's End, v. 515, n. 4; on jury(?), v. 528, n. 8; receives Sacrament, v. 171.
geneal., v. 146, n. 1, 194, n. 1, 218, n. 4, 288, 351; for his children *see* Draper, Mrs. Susanna.
Draper, William and Mrs. Susanna [notices in which the two are expressly mentioned together, except those relating to houses]: visit E at Sayes Court, v. 146, 158, 163, 164; visit Draper's relations, v. 148, 158; anniversary of marriage, v. 178; visit Wotton, v. 214, 259, 421, 478, 508–9; escape from fire, v. 268; visited by E and Mrs. Evelyn, v. 425–8; wish their children to be christened Evelyn, v. 287, 582.
Draper, William, 1698–1759(?), v. 287, n. 6; born, v. 287; baptized, v. 287–8.
Drawing: *see* Painting and Drawing.
Drebbel, Catherina: *see* Kuffeler, Mrs. C.
Drebbel (Drebbell), Cornelius, iii. 446 & nn. 5, 6, 447, n. 1.
Dress [select notices. For materials *see* Textiles]:
— national dress, classes, &c.: (i) England: academic dress: lambskin as part of, iv. 217; ~ at Oxford during Commonwealth, iii. 105 & n. 4; ~ at Oxford: in comparison, ii. 448; Charles II's new fashion, 1666 (so-called Persian vest), iii. 464–5 & n., 467, 476; children at Christ's Hospital, ii. 311; coronation robes (Charles II), iii. 283 & nn. 3, 4, 6; coronation suits (Charles II, &c.), iii. 303, n. 4; duchess of Newcastle, iii. 478 & n. 5; fantastic old costumes in coronation procession, iii. 280; lawyers: gowns of, iv. 227; London aldermen: gowns and gold chains of, iv. 342; members

Dress (*cont.*)
of parliament: cloaks and swords of, iv. 227; peers: mantles, coronets, &c., of, in creation ceremony, iii. 277–8 & n.; public mourning: orders for, &c., iv. 414 & n. 3; v. 201, 202, n. 1, 493 & n. 1, 494.
— — (ii) other nationalities, &c.: various, ii. 449; iii. 150; Arab shash, iv. 285; Bantam ambassadors and slaves, iv. 285, 286; eastern, ii. 432; iii. 344, 349, 464; iv. 212; French, iii. 465 *bis*, 575; iv. 263; ~ dislike of, at Naples, ii. 354 & n. 1; ~ protestant preachers', i. 75; ii. 527 & n. 5; ~ women's, on coast of Normandy, &c., ii. 125–6 & n. (i. 80); ~ petticoats, &c.: woman bringing, to London, iii. 572; Genoese: imitates Spanish, ii. 178 (i. 112); Irish, i. 80; Jewish: at synagogue service, ii. 42 (i. 31); ~ bride's, at Venice, ii. 477; ~ hats worn by Jews at Rome, &c.: colours of, ii. 162 & n. 5 (i. 103), 294, 400 & n. 2; Moroccan, iv. 266; Neapolitan: imitates Spanish, ii. 353 & n. 5; Persian: described, ii. 422; ~ imitated, &c., iii. 465 *bis* & n. 1; Polish, iv. 354; Roman: classical, iv. 266; ~ children's, in orphanage, ii. 311; Spanish: in use at Genoa and Naples, ii. 178 (i. 112), 353 & n. 5; ~ dislike of, in Paris, ii. 97 (i. 64); Swiss, iii. 41; ~ in Valais, &c., ii. 510–11 & n., 517; Turkish, iv. 266; ~ shash, iv. 285; ~ vestments, iii. 108 & n. 1; Venetian: ladies', &c., ii. 446–8 & nn.; ~ noblemens', ii. 442, 448–9 & nn.; iv. 493; ~ doge's, ii. 432, 449 & n. 5; ~ *see also* ii. 429, n. 6 *ad fin.*
— — (iii) miscellaneous costumes: antique or al' antique, ii. 473; iii. 32; cardinals: red hats of, i. 103; ii. 400 & n. 2; courtesans: travel in mens' clothing, ii. 316; fools, iv. 137 & n. 1; galley-slaves, ii. 165 (i. 104), 184 (i. 116); masquerade: *see* Masquerades; strange fashions or excess in dress: sermons against, v. 15, 121, 542.

Dress (*cont.*)
— garments and accessories [notices giving definitions, indicating use, &c. Ordinary garments, such as coats, are generally not indexed]:
— — alhaga (i.e. haik), iv. 266 & n. 1.
— — beards: cut of, *c.* 1620–40, ii. 1–2 (i. 1); worn by Russians, iv. 263.
— — bonnets or caps of galley-slaves, ii. 165 (i. 104); i. 116.
— — buff, i. 64.
— — buskins, iii. 349.
— — caps: dragoons', iv. 354; graduates', i. 75; grenadiers', iv. 137 & n. 1; noblemens', &c., iii. 41, 42; Russian, iii. 344, 349; Venetian, ii. 448–9; iv. 493.
— — casaques, iii. 41 & n. 4.
— — cassocks: Moroccan, iv. 266; of clergy, v. 542.
— — choppines (*zoccoli*, &c.), ii. 446–7 & n., 448.
— — cloaks: mourning, v. 204; of priests, i. 86, 87; of sheriff's retinue, i. 9; red: fashionable in France, ii. 354; and swords: dress of members of parliament, iv. 227.
— — coat of Tartar lamb, iii. 107, n. 9.
— — coats: long, for little boys, iii. 468 & n. 4.
— — cravat, iv. 21.
— — doublets, ii. 11 (i. 9), 31 (i. 24).
— — drawers: of galley-slaves, ii. 165 (i. 104); of Bantam ambassadors, &c., iv. 285, 286.
— — fans, iii. 374, 572.
— — farthingales, iii. 320 & n. 4.
— — furs (various kinds), ii. 125 (i. 80), 448, 511; iii. 344, 349; iv. 262, 399.
— — garlands: at Ironmongers' Company feast, iii. 587 & n. 2.
— — girdle, jewelled, oriental, iii. 373.
— — gowns, iv. 227, 342; Venetian, iv. 493; worn by poor men at state-funeral, iii. 57.
— — guarda-infantes, iii. 320 & n. 4.
— — haik (alhaga), iv. 266 & n. 1.
— — hats: wearing of, iii. 313 & n. 1; ~ in church, i. 75; ii. 527 & n. 5; ~ in house of lords, iii. 545; red or yellow: worn by Jews in Rome, &c., ii. 162 & n. 5 (i. 103), 294, 400 & n. 2.
— — hose: narrow, i. 64.
— — lambskin: as academic costume, iv. 217.
— — mantle: Moroccan and Roman, Roman, iv. 266.
— — masks: wearing of, at Venice, ii. 451, n. 2, 473, n. 7.
— — morning loose garment: lady's, iv. 343.
— — perukes: powdered, of clergy, clergy, v. 542 & n. 3.
— — petticoats: from France, iii. 572.
— — plod (plaid), iii. 339.
— — points, ii. 448 & n. 1.
— — riding-habit: women's, 1666, iii. 463 & n. 3.
— — sashes (shashes): as turbans, iv. 266 & n. 2, 285; in Charles II's fashion, iii. 465.
— — scarfs, iii. 42, 57, 349, 494.
— — shirts: at Venice, ii. 449 & n. 2; sleeved, iv. 266.
— — shoes: Jewish: in sermon, iii. 542–3.
— — slop (sloope), i. 116 & n. 2.
— — socks, leather: worn by Moors, &c., iv. 266.
— — stockings: knitted at Doncaster, iii. 127 & n. 5; machine for knitting, iii. 285 & n. 3; throwing the stocking, iii. 589.
— — stomachers: men's, ii. 410.
— — suit, iii. 42.
— — surcoat, iii. 467.
— — toques, ii. 280 & n. 3; iii. 41.
— — tunics, iii. 349, 467.
— — turban *or* turbant, iv. 266.
— — umbrellas, ii. 166 & n. 6 (i. 105).
— — undress: woman's, iii. 589, 590, n. 1; iv. 625; man's, iv. 413.
— — veils: at Venice, ii. 448 & n. 4; Jewish bride's, ii. 477.
— — vests: Charles II's fashion, iii. 464–5 & n., 467, 476; oriental, iii. 373; of Oxford bachelors of arts, ii. 448; Persian, ii. 422; iii. 465 & n. 1; Russian, iii. 344, 349, 494; Vene-

Dress (*cont.*)
tian noblemens', &c., ii. 448, 449 & n. 5.
— — waist-coats, iii. 282 & n. 6, 283; iv. 285.
Driffield (Dryfield), Glos.: Sir J. Prettyman's house at, iii. 117 & n. 4; *see also* iii. 73, n. 3.
Drinking and drunkenness: at parties, ii. 38 (i. 28), 473, 503–4; iii. 21, 54; ~ 'great guns', ii. 469 & n. 2; ~ to be expected at 'a Dutch feast', iv. 296; among Leicestershire gentry, iii. 122; at Orleans, ii. 138 (i. 90); death from excessive, v. 54; making visitors' servants drunk, iii. 112–13 & n., 525; sermons against, iii. 254, 258; iv. 196; v. 15, 234, 543, 547.
Drogheda: capture of, 1649, ii. 565 & n. 2; surrender of, 1690, v. 28 & n. 7.
Drummond, John, earl of Melfort, &c.: art-collection of: sold, v. 144–5 & nn.
Drury, Bridget: *see* Needham, Bridget, Viscountess Kilmorey.
Drury, Sir William: geneal., iii. 218, n. 4.
Dryden, John, iv. 37, n. 1; visits E, iv. 37; at dinner-party, iv. 318; converted, with his sons, to Roman Catholicism, iv. 497 & n. 1, 541, n. 2; engaged on translation of Virgil, &c., v. 164 & n. 5; plays by, acted: *Conquest of Granada*, iii. 569–70 & n.; *Evening's Love*, iii. 510–11 & n.; *Indian Queen* (with Sir R. Howard), iii. 368–9 & n.; *Secret Love*, iii. 477 & n. 4; *Wild Gallant*, iii. 351 & n. 14. *See also* Books: sources.
Dryfield: *see* Driffield.
Duarte (Duert) family at Antwerp, ii. 67 & n. 6 (i. 45).
Dublin: Tyrconnel arrives at, 1686, iv. 514, n. 4; surrendered, 1690, v. 28 & n. 7; William III at, v. 31, n. 1; earthquake at, v. 36; mentioned, iii. 369, n. 4; iv. 300.
places in: Castle: seizure of, 1660, ii. 545, n. 3; ~ declaration dated from, 1689, iv. 642, n. 5; Christ Church: suicide in, v. 170 & n. 3; French conformist church: minister of: *see* Severin, J.; Marsh's Library, v. 323, n. 3.
persons: de la Caillemotte dies at, v. 30, n. 2; John Evelyn, jnr., arrives at, v. 116.
Dublin: diocese: archbishops: *see* Marsh, Francis (1682–93); King, William, D.D. (1703–29).
Du Bois, —, of London: art-collection of, ii. 549 & nn. 3, 4; social (?), iii. 13.
Dubois, Jean, painter, at Fontainebleau (?), ii. 119–20 & n. (i. 77).
Dubois, John: candidate for office of sheriff, London, 1682, iv. 319 & n. 1.
Du Bosse, engraver: *see* Bosse, A.
du Bouchet, Jean: *see* Sourches, Marquis of.
Ducie, Sir William; third bt. 1657; created Viscount Downe 1675, ii. 539, n. 7; as traveller, &c., iii. 181 & n. 2; art-collection of, ii. 549–50 & nn.; iii. 96 & n. 5; buys Charlton House, iii. 233, n. 2, 377; visits art-collections, ii. 539–40; social, iii. 83, 233, 414, 525.
Dudley, Duchess, i. 115, n. 2.
Dudley, Robert, earl of Leicester, iii. 143, n. 4; employs Sir Richard Browne, sen., iv. 303 & n. 3; letters to, iv. 241, n. 3; hospital at Amsterdam founded by, ii. 45, n. 6; house of, at Wanstead, iv. 305, n. 4 *ad fin.*; agate vase belonging to, iii. 143; illegitimate son of, i. 115 & n. 2.
Dudley, Sir Robert, titular duke of Northumberland: designs mole at Leghorn, &c., i. 115–16 & n.
Duels: in sermon, v. 121; frequent, 1684, 1686, iv. 401, 501 & n. 2; Sir A. Broderick and Sir W. Petty: challenge, iv. 59 & n. 1; Buckingham and Shrewsbury, 1668, iii. 596, n. 4; ~ participant in, iv. 453, n. 2; Captain Love and S. Talbot, 1685, iv. 453 & n. 2; Grafton and J. Talbot, 1686, iv. 501 & n. 2; J. Law and E. Wilson, 1694, v. 175, 176, n. 1; Conway Seymour (P. S. Conway) and Captain G. Kirke, 1699, v. 331 & n. 1; Carmarthen and Halifax, 1702: prevented, v. 523 & n. 1; Sir R. Onslow and L. Oglethorpe, 1703, v. 527 & n. 2.
Duert: *see* Duarte.

Dugdale, Stephen, iv. 228, n. 3; as witness at Stafford's trial, iv. 228 & nn. 6, 8, 230; alluded to, iv. 232.
Dugdale, Sir William; knighted 1677; the herald, iii. 171 & n. 5; obtains MSS. from Arundel Library for College of Arms, iv. 144 & n. 3; social, iii. 171, 237 & n. 4; iv. 441 & n. 2.
Duglas: *see* Douglas.
du Guesclin, Bertrand: tomb of, ii. 86 & n. 4 (i. 58).
du Houssay (de Hausse), Claude de Mallier, Seigneur: art-collection of, ii. 114–15 & n. (i. 74).
Duilius: Columna rostrata of, ii. 222 & n. 6.
Duke, Edward, M.D.: social(?), iii. 426 & n. 2.
Duke's Company: *see* London: topography: theatres.
Dukeson, Richard, D.D.: sermon, by, iii. 159 & n. 1.
Duleek, co. Meath: William III at, v. 28, n. 4.
Dumah: the burden of: in sermon, iv. 75.
Dumbarton: first Earl of, 1675–92: *see* Douglas, Lord George.
du Menie, —, alchemist, iii. 34.
du Moulin, Dr. Lewis, physician, ii. 553, n. 4.
Duna river: crossed by Swedes, v. 472 & n. 1.
Dunbar: battle of, iii. 14, n. 6, 19 & n. 7.
Dunblane: Viscount, 1674–89: *see* Osborne, Peregrine, second duke of Leeds, &c.
Duncan, Dr. —: *see* Duncon, E.
Duncannon, co. Wexford: James II embarks at, 1690, v. 28, n. 6; William III takes, v. 31 & n. 1.
Duncomb family: owns Weston in Albury, iii. 14, n. 8.
Duncombe, —, 1640, ii. 25.
Duncomb, —, 1650, iii. 14 & n. 8.
Duncombe, Sir Charles: knighted 1699, v. 246 & n. 2; rise of, to wealth, *ib.*; imprisoned, &c., v. 284 & n. 4, 285 *bis* & nn. 2, 5.
Duncombe, George, of Shalford: geneal., ii. 14, n. 4, 24, n. 2.
Duncombe (Duncumb), George, of Weston, ii. 77, n. 2.
Duncomb, Rev. George, rector of Albury, v. 185, n. 1; sermons by, v. 185, 214, 217, 473.
Duncombe, Sir John, iii. 442, n. 8; as commissioner: for Ordnance, iii. 442–3 & n.; ~ for Saltpetre, iii. 443, n. 1, 445; ~: of the Treasury, iii. 487, n. 7; attends Council for Foreign Plantations, iii. 578 & n. 5; as chancellor of the Exchequer, iv. 24, n. 2, 32 & n. 3; ~: dismissal of, iv. 267 & n. 3; social, iii. 446; geneal., v. 150, n. 5.
Duncombe, Mrs. Judith, wife of George Duncombe of Shalford: geneal., ii. 24, n. 2, 29, n. 4.
Duncombe, Mary: *see* Caldwell, Mrs. M.
Duncombe, Sir Sanders, ii. 14, n. 4; attends Mrs. Eleanor Evelyn, ii. 14 (i. 11); introduces sedan-chairs into England, i. 11–12; ii. 353.
Duncombe, Thomas, D.D., rector of Shere, iv. 111, n. 5; house of, iv. 111 & n. 5; geneal., v. 185, n. 1.
Duncombe, William: appointed a Lord Justice of Ireland, 1693, v. 150 & n. 5.
Duncombe, Rev. William, rector of Wotton, iv. 558 & n. 3; officiates at Wotton (sermons, &c.), *ib.*; v. 207, 266–7; negligence, &c., of, v. 180, 181, 188, 207, 266–7; dies, v. 377; alluded to, v. 216.
Duncon (Duncan), Eleazar, D.D., iii. 11, n. 6; sermons by, iii. 11–12, 19–26 *passim*; goes to Italy, iii. 30 & n. 3.
'Dundas', 'Lowthiel', iii. 345, n. 4.
Dundee: Viscount of, 1688–9: *see* Graham, John.
Dunes: Battle of the, iii. 395, n. 3.
Dungarvan: Viscounts (courtesy title): *see* Boyle, Richard, second earl of Cork, &c.; Boyle, Charles, Baron Clifford.
Dungeness, Kent: French fleet off, 1690, v. 29, n. 1.
Dunkirk (Dynkirk): notice, 1641, ii. 75–6 & nn. (i. 49–50).
  possessed by France, 1646–52, iii. 55, n. 8; English blockade, 1657, iii. 199 & n. 3; taken by French and English, 1658, iii. 217 & n. 3; sold by Charles II, i. 50 & n. 1; Louis XIV at, 1671, iii. 575 & n. 1; French fleet at, 1696, v. 234, 242; English prepare to besiege, 1696, v. 251 & n. 2, 252 & n. 2.

Dunkirk (*cont.*)
Louis XIV's harbour-works at, i. 49–50 & n.; privateers of, ii. 30, n. 5, 75 & n. 11 (i. 49); v. 10, 67 & n. 3, 528, n. 2; ~ seize Mrs. Evelyn's portrait, &c., ii. 551; iii. 56, 62.
regiment from, 1662, iii. 357, n. 2; Conti embarks at, v. 267, n. 2.
governor of, 1649–52: *see* Estrades, G., comte d'; deputy-governor of, 1662: *see* Norwood, Col. H.
Dun-le-Roy (Douleroy), ii. 154 & n. 6 (i. 99).
Duns Scotus: picture of (?), iii. 339 & n. 3.
Dunstable, Beds., iv. 593 *bis* & n. 1.
Dunstaffnage, Lorne: Argyll at, 1685, iv. 443, n. 1.
Dunster, Samuel, D.D., v. 587, n. 3; sermons by (?), v. 587, 603.
Duomo: *see* Domodossola.
du Plessis *or* de Plessis, —: riding academy of, ii. 134 (i. 87–8); iii. 2, n. 4.
du Plessis, Alphonse Louis, cardinal: and the Jews at Rome, ii. 400 & n. 2.
du Plessis, Armand-Jean: *see* Richelieu, Cardinal.
du Plessis, Armand-Jean: *see* Richelieu, Duc de.
du Plessis, C. de Choiseul, sieur du Plessis-Praslin, duke of Choiseul, Maréchal: in London, iii. 548 & n. 2.
Duport, James, D.D.; Regius professor of Greek at Cambridge 1639–54, iii. 137, n. 5, 524, n. 1, 624, n. 3; entertains E, iii. 137–8; examines at Westminster School, iii. 288; sermons by, iii. 524, 624; iv. 52, 83.
Duppa, Brian, bishop of Winchester, &c.: as patron of (Sir) Stephen Fox, iv. 218 & n. 1; *add.*
Du Prue (Du Pre ?), —, lutanist, iv. 186 & n. 5.
Duquesnoy, François (Francesco Fiammingo), sculptor, ii. 253, n. 6; death of, ii. 263 & n. 2; *add.*; ii. 399; works by: St. Andrew, in St. Peter's, Rome, ii. 263 & n. 2, 399; other works by (?), ii. 253 & n. 6; iii. 10 & n. 4, 11 & n. 2.
Durance, river, ii. 162 & n. 9 (i. 103).
Durant de Bréval, François: *see* Bréval.
Durante: *see* Alberti, D.
Duras, Guy-Aldonce de Durfort, marquis de, and his wife Elizabeth: geneal., iv. 77, n. 2.
Duras, Louis de; created Baron Duras of Holdenby 1673; second earl of Feversham 1677, iv. 77 & n. 2, 222 & n. 1; acquires Holmby House, iv. 70, n. 3, 77; present at Charles II's reception into Roman Catholic church, iv. 408; commands royal forces at Sedgemoor, iv. 451, 452, n. 1; attends James II at Winchester, iv. 468; tent of, in camp on Hounslow Heath(?), iv. 517 & n. 4; sent by James II to William of Orange and arrested, iv. 610, 611, n. 1; social, iv. 77; as godfather, iv. 222; nephew of, iv. 400 & n. 4.
Duras: Baron, 1673–7: *see* Duras, Louis de, later earl of Feversham.
Durazzo, Count G. L.: attends meeting of Philosophical Society, iii. 314 & n. 2.
Durdans (Durdens), Epsom, Surrey, iii. 15, n. 1; as property of Sir R. Coke: E visits, iii. 14 & n. 4(?), 15; as property of George Berkeley, first earl of Berkeley, &c.: Charles II, &c., dine at, iii. 334 & nn. 5–7; ~: Dr. J. Wilkins, &c., at, iii. 416 & n. 3; ~: E visits, iii. 219, 291, 377; iv. 18; *see also* iii. 220 & n. 6.
Durel (Durell), John, D.D., dean of Windsor, iii. 8, n. 4; iv. 15, n. 4, 164; ordained, iii. 8–9 & nn., 632–3; translation by, of *Book of Common Prayer*, iii. 545 & n. 4; sermons by, iv. 15, 106, 164 & nn. 1, 2, 194; dies, iv. 318 & n. 7.
Dürer, Albrecht (Albert, &c.), ii. 114, n. 3; works by or attributed to: paintings, ii. 190–1 & n., 285 & n. 3, 411 & n. 3, 414 & n. 4; iii. 155 & n. 4; drawings, ii. 114 (i. 73); engravings, ii. 133 (i. 86); carvings, ii. 411 & n. 4; iii. 155 & n. 3; *see also* ii. 190–1 & n.
Durfort, Guy-Aldonce de *and* Elizabeth de: *see* Duras.
Durham (Duresme), iii. 129.
Durham, county: Lord Lieutenant of, *c.* 1690: *see* Lumley, Richard, earl of Scarborough (v. 9, n. 1).
Durham: cathedral clergy:
bishops: *see* Montaigne *or* Mountain, G. (1628); Morton, T. (1632–59); Cosin, John (1660–72); Crew, Nathaniel, Baron

Durham (*cont.*)
Crew (1674–1721); Talbot, William (1721–30).
deans: *see* Sudbury, J. (1661–84); Comber, Thomas (1691–9); Montagu, John (1700–28); *see also* Brevint, D., wrongly called dean (iii. 8–9 & n.).
prebendaries: *see* Brevint, D.; Jessop, C.; Offley, Rev. Robert; Wheler, Sir George.
archdeacon: *see* Clarke, Rev. Gabriel.
Durier, —: inn kept by, at St.-Cloud, ii. 108 & n. 3.
Dutch East India Company: headquarters of, in Amsterdam, i. 35 & n. 2; men-of-war of, in Indies, &c., iii. 187 & n. 2; yacht built for, &c., iii. 296 & n. 5.
Dutch Republic, Dutchmen, &c.: *see* United Provinces.
Dynkirk: *see* Dunkirk.
Dyott, Mrs. Elizabeth, born Evelyn, wife of Richard Dyott, v. 54, n. 2, 358, n. 7.
Dyott, Jane, v. 358, n. 7; legacy to, v. 359 & n. 8.
Dyott, Richard: geneal., v. 54, n. 2, 358, n. 7.
Dysart: Earls and Countess of: *see* Murray, William; Maitland, Elizabeth, duchess of Lauderdale; Tollemache, Sir Lionel, earl 1698–1727.
Dyve (Dives), Sir Lewis, iii. 40 & n. 1; adventures of, *ib.*; iii. 49–50 & nn.

Eachard (Etcher), John, D.D.: sermon by (?), iv. 397–8 & n.
Earles, Mrs. Bridget, wife of Dr. John Earles, iii. 153 & n. 3.
Earles *or* Earle, John, D.D.; dean of Westminster 1660; bishop of Worcester 1662; of Salisbury 1663, ii. 536 & n. 2; character, &c., iii. 346; marries E, ii. 536; and T. Keightley's conversion to Roman Catholicism, iii. 36, 634; in Flanders, iii. 153; as dean of Westminster: at coronation of Charles II, iii. 281 & n. 3, 282, n. 2, 283; ~ examines at Westminster School, iii. 288; consecrated bishop, iii. 345–6 & nn.; sermons by, ii. 562; iii. 37–8, 39 *bis*, 47, 49, 51, 54, 265; social, ii. 561; iii. 44, 54, 265, 320, 348, 363;
Earles *or* Earle, John, D.D. (*cont.*)
geneal., iii. 153; *see also* Books mentioned in text.
Early Christians: *see* Church.
Earnley, Sir John: *see* Ernle.
Earthquakes: as portents, iv. 598; frequent at: Leghorn, ii. 184 (i. 116); ~ Pozzuoli, &c., ii. 344, 345–6, 350; at Rome: effects of, ii. 257.
— earthquake separating England and France, i. 57 & n. 1.
— particular earthquakes: England: 1687 (?), iv. 550 & n. 2; 1690, v. 36 & n. 3; 1692, v. 115 & n. 4; 1696: sinkage of ground at Portland, v. 230 & n. 6.
— — Italy, &c.: Naples, 1688, iv. 598 & n. 4; Sicily and Malta, 1693, v. 133 & n. 3, 134 & n. 2, 135; Genoa (?) and Turin, 1699, v. 353 & n. 1; Rome, &c., 1703, v. 531 & n. 1.
— — Lima, &c.: 1687, iv. 585–6 & n.; ~ 1688 (?), iv. 598 & n. 4; Smyrna, 1688, *ib.*; Jamaica (Port Royal), 1692, v. 113 & n. 1, 115–16 & n., 133; Batavia, 1699, v. 357 & n. 2; Portugal, 1699, v. 368 & n. 3.
East Clandon, Surrey: manor of: owned by Lord Aungier, iii. 142, n. 5.
East Horsley, Surrey: Bishop's Manor in, now Horsley Towers, sometime seat of Henry Hildyard (called by E Horsley or East Horsley), ii. 551, n. 9; iii. 87 & n. 6; v. 56, n. 1; ~ E visits, ii. 551; 87, 157, 423; Rowbarnes in, iii. 85, n. 4.
East India Company: new charter for, 1657, iii. 201, n. 5; New General Stock, 1657, *ib.*; ~ courts for, iii. 201 & n. 5, 203 & n. 1; ~ prayers for success of, &c., iii. 201, 202 & n. 2; *add.*; ~ pays dividend, iii. 365 & n. 1; and embassy from Bantam, 1682, iv. 284, n. 3, 285, n. 1; attacked in parliament, 1689, iv. 643; *add.*; dissolution of: proposed, 1692, v. 90 & n. 6; shares in: price of, falls, 1694, v. 174 & n. 6; bribes members of parliament, 1695, v. 207, n. 7 *ad fin.*, 209 & n. 5; New East India Company established, &c., 1698, v. 288 & n. 7, 291–2 & n.; old Company: bills and

East India Company (*cont.*)
act for continuance of, 1699, 1700, v. 317 & n. 1, 378 & n. 3, 404 & n. 3.
factory at Bantam, iv. 284, n. 3; gifts from: animals to Charles II, iii. 398, n. 4; ~ to Royal Society, v. 303 & n. 1; ships belonging to: taken by French, v. 218 & n. 1; takes Addiscombe as training-college, 1809, v. 541, n. 1.
governors of: *see* Bathurst, Sir B.; Child, Sir Josiah; Riccard, Sir A.; Smith, Sir Thomas; treasurer of: *see* Massingberd, J.; members of committee: C. Boone, iv. 180, n. 3; ~ Sir P. Paravicini, iii. 508, n. 2; connexion with, of George Berkeley, earl of Berkeley, iv. 285, n. 1.
investments in: E's in New General Stock, iii. 201–2, 203 & n. 1; ~ sold, iv. 297, 298; ~ letter relating to (?), iv. 273, n. 5; transfer of a holding, iii. 508 & n. 2.
East India Company, Antwerp (error), ii. 66 & n. 3 (i. 44).
East India Company, Dutch: *see* Dutch East India Company.
East India Company of Scotland: *see* Company of Scotland trading to Africa and the Indies.
East Indies [notices relating expressly or clearly to the East Indies; *see further* Dutch East India Company; East India Company; India; Indies]:
commerce, &c.: commercial disputes in, between English and Dutch, a cause of Third Dutch War, iii. 606, n. 1; English trade with: regulated, v. 288, n. 7; ~ interlopers in, v. 404.
products, &c.: shop for, at Amsterdam, i. 35 & n. 2; furniture, &c., iii. 324 & n. 2; iv. 288; v. 147; textiles: hangings, ii. 540; ~ of pintado, iii. 425–6 & n.; various: wearing of, in England, to be prohibited, 1700, v. 377–8 & n.
shipping, &c.: ships, iii. 313, 373; captured Dutch ships, 1665: *see* Ships and Shipping: *Golden Phoenix* and *Slothany*; Dutch ships from: attacked at Bergen, 1665: *see* Bergen; losses to, by
East Indies (*cont.*)
French action, 1694, 1695, v. 174 & n. 4, 218 & n. 1, 220 & n. 4; ships from: come home safe, 1696, &c., v. 251, 516 & n. 5, 520 & n. 3, 616 & n. 1; sea-captain's voyages to, iii. 63; Dutch merchant from, iii. 420 & n. 4; Sir J. Chardin in, iv. 212 & n. 2; Canary wine sent to, and brought back from, iii. 313.
miscellaneous: animals from, iii. 194–5 & n.; iv. 389–90 & n.; curiosities from, ii. 124 (i. 79); v. 303 & n. 1; stone with curative properties from, iii. 288.
Eastern Churches: Dr. I. Basire's relations with, iii. 342 & n. 5; in sermons: preaching in, iv. 288; condition of, under Turkish rule, v. 378.
Eastern Empire: ruin of: in sermon, v. 378.
Easton Neston, Northants.: house at, built by Wren, iv. 170, n. 1; Arundel sculptures at, v. 44–5 & n.
Eaton, —: *see* Eyton, Sir K.
Ebsham: *see* Epsom.
Ecbatana: in sermon, v. 84.
Echoes: discourse on, iii. 335; in square room, ii. 406 & n. 6; individual echoes, ii. 106 (i. 69), 115 & n. 6 (i. 75), 181 (i. 114); iii. 118 & n. 1.
Eckington, near Lewes, Sussex: property in, ii. 27, n. 2.
Edelinck, G.: engraving by, v. 92, n. 2.
Eden, Garden of: in sermon, v. 114.
Edgar, Thomas, recorder of Ipswich, iv. 114, n. 6.
Edgcumbe, Mrs. Mary, born Glanville, wife of Piers Edgcumbe, iii. 78, n. 2; social, iii. 83; geneal., iii. 81, n. 7, 182, n. 4.
Edgcumbe (Edgecomb), Piers, iii. 78, n. 2; social, iii. 78, 83; geneal., iii. 182, n. 4.
Edgcumbe (Edgecomb), Sir Richard; K.B. 1661, iii. 182, n. 4; social, iii. 182(?), 509.
Edgehill, Warw.: battle of, ii. 79 & n. 3 (i. 52); ~ account of, i. 53–4 & n.; ~ Sir R. Walsh at, iii. 6, n. 4.
Edinburgh: James, duke of York, arrives at, 1679, iv. 189, n. 6; Sir R. Sibbald's recantation at, iv.

Edinburgh (*cont.*)
515 & n. 3; William Douglas, duke of Hamilton, dies at, v. 177 & n. 2.
Edmonton, Middlesex: William Draper's mother buried at, v. 146, n. 1, 451 & n. 2; W. Draper, jnr., buried at, v. 287, n. 6.
Edomites: in sermon, iv. 578.
Education [*see also* Schools and Colleges; Universities]:
exercise-book (Edward VI), iv. 216 & n. 1.
exercises: by candidates at Westminster for university scholarships, iii. 287–8 & n.; formal, on anniversary, &c., iii. 408 & n. 1; v. 79.
Inns of Court: gentlemen reside at, for general instruction in law, i. 12; v. 358; readers at, iii. 400 & n. 3, 490, 512, 536.
Jesuits: methods of, ii. 65–6 & n. (i. 44).
public speaking: training in, ii. 233.
studies and accomplishments: Dr. Clench's son, iv. 617–18; E's children, iii. 206–7 & nn.; iv. 421, 423; v. 138; *see also* iv. 350; W. Wotton, iv. 172–3.
tutors and governors [individual tutors are not indexed collectively]: salary for, iii. 364, n. 6; travelling tutors, ii. 550; iii. 354 & n. 2, 401, n. 4; iv. 38; tutor accompanies pupil to Oxford, iii. 474; *see also* iii. 482, 506 & n. 3.
miscellaneous: Anglican boy attends Jesuit school in Paris, iii. 636; ejected clergy not to be employed as school-masters, 1655, iii. 163 & n. 1, 164; literacy and Bible-reading: in sermon, v. 106; maternal care, iv. 595; sermons on education, iv. 121, 364, 479, 570.
Edward, St., the Confessor: laws of: kings swear to keep, iii. 282, n. 4; crown of, iii. 283, n. 7; gold cross from coffin of, iv. 470–1 & nn.
Edward I, king of England: lays out Winchelsea, iii. 67, n. 6; wound of: Queen Eleanor sucks poison from, iii. 131 & n. 6.
Edward III, king of England: receives Black Prince: in painting, iv. 316 & n. 4, 465 & n. 7.
Edward VI, king of England: exercise-book, journal, &c., of, iv. 216 & nn. 1–3; founds Christ's Hospital, London, iv. 543; ~ in painting, iii. 192 & n. 3; grants church in London to French protestants, iii. 160, n. 3; portraits of, ii. 549; iv. 543 & n. 1; statue of, iv. 543 & n. 2; tutor of: *see* Cheke, Sir J.
Edward, prince of Wales, the Black Prince: triumph of: in painting, iv. 316 & n. 4, 465 & n. 7.
Edward, Prince, of the Palatinate, ii. 567 & n. 1; in Paris, 1649 (?), *ib.*; at Durdans, 1662, iii. 334 & n. 7.
Edwards, Sir James, lord mayor of London 1678–9, iv. 181, n. 9; visits Charles II, iv. 181; social (?), iv. 182 & n. 3.
Edwards, Rev. William, rector of Denton, Sussex: sermon by, &c., v. 183 & n. 3.
Edwin, Sir Humphrey, lord mayor of London 1697–8: in St. Paul's, v. 278 & n. 4.
Effigies, funeral: Cromwell, iii. 224; duke of Richmond, ii. 28 (i. 20); French and English kings, ii. 90 (i. 60).
Effingham, Surrey: road from, to Wotton, v. 228, n. 4; rector of: *see* Miller, J.
Egerton family: buys Cleveland House, London, iii. 470, n. 5.
Egerton, Lady Elizabeth, countess of Bridgewater, wife of Scroop Egerton, fourth earl, &c., v. 525 & n. 8.
Egerton, Scroop, fourth earl and first duke of Bridgewater: marriage of, v. 525 & n. 8.
Egypt:
modern: E wishes to visit, ii. 451; traveller to, iii. 52; form of capital punishment in, iv. 206 & n. 5; exports from, to Marseilles, ii. 166 (i. 105); crocodile of: in comparison, iv. 391; ratton of: in comparison, iii. 194, 195, n. 1.
antiquities from: inscribed stones, ii. 315; ~ stone given to E, ii. 469 & nn. 3, 4; iii. 171–2 & n. [inscriptions (hieroglyphics) on obelisks are not indexed]; mummies, ii. 53 (i. 37), 408, 469 & n. 5; iii. 382; obelisks: *see* Rome: topography: obelisks;

Egypt (*cont.*)
sistrum, ii. 314 & n. 1; statues, &c.: Canopus, ii. 314; Horus, ii. 229, n. 4; Isis, ii. 53 (i. 37), 309 & n. 4, 314, 356; Osiris, ii. 229 & n. 4; unspecified, ii. 469 & n. 4; iii. 75; votive offering to Isis, ii. 226, n. 8.
in sermons, iv. 348, 556, 592; v. 271, 309, 347, 526.
Eland: Lords, &c. (courtesy title): *see* Savile, Henry, Lord Eland 1679–87; Savile, Esther, his lady; Savile, William, Lord Eland 1687–95.
Elbeuf, Charles II, duke of (Delboeuf): visits Charles II, ii. 562–3 & n.
Elbing, East Prussia: S. Hartlib born at, iii. 162, n. 2.
Eleanor of Castile, queen of England: tomb and legend of, iii. 131 & n. 6.
Elector Palatine: chapel of, in London, 1688, iv. 599, n. 1.
Eleutherius, St.: relics of, ii. 86 (i. 58).
Elgin: second Earl of: *see* Bruce, Robert, earl of Ailesbury.
Eli: in sermons, v. 299, 375.
Elijah (Elias): in sermons, iii. 569; iv. 447; v. 114, 228, 306, 556, 572.
Eliot, John: translation of Bible by, v. 82, n. 2.
Eliot, Thomas, courtier: race-horse belonging to, iii. 588–9 & n.
Elixem: Marlborough forces French lines at, 1705, v. 602 & n. 3, 604–5 & n.
Elizabeth I, queen of England:
association to defend, v. 233, n. 3; at Tilbury, ii. 30 & n. 1 (i. 22); holds cautionary towns in United Provinces, i. 23 & n. 4; plots against: in sermon, iv. 336; prizes taken during reign of, v. 516; book of prayers published by authority of, iii. 46 & n. 3, 635–6; in comparison, v. 205.
buildings, &c.: acquires Nonsuch Palace, iii. 426, n. 4; builds Upnor Castle, iii. 485, n. 3; repairs Windsor Castle, &c., iii. 98, n. 6; iv. 317, n. 4.
grants, &c., by: founds scholarships at Westminster School, iii. 287, n. 5; to George Evelyn, sen., &c., for manufacture of

Elizabeth I (*cont.*)
gunpowder, i. 52 & n. 2; grants New Hall to Lord Sussex, iii. 180; founds hospital at Amsterdam, ii. 43 & n. 2 (i. 31), 45, n. 6.
letter of, iv. 241, n. 3.
portraits of: painting, ii. 549; gem, iii. 79–80 & n.; statue, iii. 460–1 & n.
favourite of: *see* Dudley, Robert, earl of Leicester (iv. 303); servant of: *see* Laniere, J.
Elizabeth of York, queen of England: portrait of, iii. 166, n. 1.
Elizabeth, queen of Bohemia, ii. 33, n. 8; court and family of, at The Hague, ii. 33–4 & nn. (i. 25–6 & nn.); palace of, at Rhenen, ii. 34–5 & n. (i. 27); burial of, iii. 316 & n. 2; ~ storm at time of, v. 2 & n. 4; geneal., ii. 567, n. 1; v. 421 & n. 2; agent of: *see* Curtius, Sir W.; attendant on, ii. 38, n. 1.
Elizabeth, St., queen of Hungary, ii. 43, n. 2.
Elizabeth of Bourbon, queen of Spain: mourning for, ii. 331, n. 9 *ad fin.*; *chapelle ardente* for, ii. 368–9 & n.
Elizabeth, Princess, daughter of Charles I: book dedicated to, iii. 55, n. 1.
Elizabeth, Princess Palatine, abbess of Herford, i. 25–6 & nn.; ii. 34, n. 1.
Elmes, —, of Bolney Court, Henley, ii. 540 & n. 5.
Elmley, Kent: rector of: *see* Creech, T.
Elois, &c.: *see* Elwes.
Eltham, Kent: subsidy business at, 1671, iii. 576 & n. 3; visit to, iii. 165; Eltham House (palace), iii. 170 & n. 3; Sir John Cotton buried at, ii. 537, n. 2; *add.*; Lady Gerrard (Garrard) at, ii. 542 & n. 2, 554; Sir John Shaw at: house of, iii. 375–6 & n.; ~ visit to, iii. 437; vicar of: *see* Owen, Richard; ~ visit to, at, iii. 217; recommendation for vicar, iii. 195 & n. 3.
Elwes (Elouis), Frances, Lady Elwes, wife of Sir Gervase, sen.: social, iii. 58 & n. 4.
Elwes, Sir Gervase, sen.: geneal., iii. 58, n. 4.

Elwes (Elois, &c.), Sir Gervase; bt. 1660, iii. 31 & nn. 3, 4; in Paris, iii. 31, 38; social, iii. 58; geneal., iv. 247, n. 2.
Elwes, Sir John: social, iv. 247 & n. 2.
Ely (Elie): in view, iii. 138.
Ely: cathedral clergy:
bishops: London house of, iii. 231, n. 6, 270, n. 5; individual bishops: *see* Andrewes, L. (1609–19); White, Francis (1631–8); Wren, Matthew, D.D. (1638–67); Laney, B. (1667–75); Gunning, P. (1675–84); Turner, Francis (1684–90); Patrick, S. (1691–1707); Moore, John, D.D. (1707–14); Fleetwood, W. (1714–23).
deans: *see* Love, R. (1660–1); Lambe, J. (1693–1708).
Ely: Isle of: Family of Love in, iv. 554.
Elysian Fields, near Miseno, ii. 334, 351 & nn. 1, 2.
Elzevier family: printing-press of, at Leyden, ii. 52 & n. 6 (i. 36).
Embroidery: on clothes or robes, ii. 298; iii. 41, 42, 280, 373, 476; on furnishings, saddle, &c., ii. 224, 281; iii. 57, 224, 323; iv. 399; ecclesiastical, ii. 298 & n. 3; iv. 397; needlework landscape, iii. 260; silkwork flowers, ii. 473.
Embrun (Morbrun): burnt by duke of Savoy, 1692, v. 117 & n. 2.
Embryology, human: discourse on, iv. 297; abortions, iii. 255–6; iv. 145–6.
Emden, Germany: men from, iii. 412.
Emerton, Mrs. Bridget: *see* Osborne, Bridget, duchess of Leeds, wife of Peregrine Osborne, second duke.
Emerton, John: marriage of, iv. 354 & n. 6.
Emiliani *or* Miani, Giovanni, ii. 468, n. 4.
Emilius Marcus: *see* Æmilius Macer.
Emmanuele, Antonio, called Nigrita: tomb of, ii. 244 & n. 5.
Empire (Holy Roman Empire) [for the Empire as a territory *see* Germany]: general: place of coronation of Emperors, ii. 500–1 & n.; Diet of the: political activities of, iv. 608, n. 6, 622, n. 5; Milan as fief of the, v. 440–1; count of: Lord Lansdowne created a, iv. 400–1 & n.; v. 476; prince of: Marlborough created a, v. 573 & n. 2.
state of the Hapsburgs [including Leopold I's political activities; for the Empire in the various wars *see* Wars: Turkish-Imperial war; War of the League of Augsburg; War of the Spanish Succession]: intervenes in dispute between Denmark and Hamburg, iv. 525 & n. 1; and election of Archbishop-Elector of Cologne, 1688, iv. 596, n. 3; relations of, with Savoy, v. 247; court of: does not mourn death of William III, v. 594; effect on, of Hungarian rebellion, &c., v. 553; Bavarians appeal to, after Blenheim, v. 577.
emperors, unnamed: gifts from, ii. 193, 235.
Empoli, ii. 184 (i. 116).
Enamel: artist in, iii. 52; crucifix with, iv. 471; portrait, &c., in, iii. 21, 260; painting compared to, iii. 262.
Enfield, Middlesex: garden at, iv. 91 & n. 4.
Enfield Chase, Middlesex: notice, iv. 91–2 & n.
Engelen (Ingle), near 's Hertogenbosch, ii. 57 & n. 7 (i. 39).
Engham, Sir Edward: geneal., ii. 36, n. 5.
ENGLAND:
— addresses [*see also* petitions *below*]: congratulatory, &c.: origin and progress of, v. 279 & n. 2; from counties, &c., to Charles II at Restoration, iii. 249 & nn. 4, 5; Surrey gentlemen to Charles II, 1681, iv. 248; Nonconformists, &c., to James II for Declaration of Indulgence, iv. 553–4 & nn., 560 & n. 1; fleet at Portsmouth to James II, 1 Dec. 1688, iv. 609 & n. 8; general to William III on Assassination Plot, v. 232 & n. 2; Surrey gentlemen to William III, 1697, v. 279 & n. 1; general, promising to support William III against Pretender, v. 480–1 & n.
— Admiralty:
— — department: occupies Derby

ENGLAND: Admiralty (*cont.*)
House, iii. 222, n. 4; administration of: misdemeanours in, *c.* 1673–9, iv. 169 & n. 1; commissioners for [some notices relating to similar business are indexed under James II: naval *and* relations with E]: Sick and Wounded business with, iv. 17(?), 18(?), 23, 24 *bis*; ~ visit E, 1679, iv. 171; ~ examine project for hospital at Greenwich, 1693, v. 203, n. 1; ~ attend meeting of commissioners for Greenwich Hospital, v. 209–10; ~ parliamentary inquiry to, 1699, v. 369, n. 2.
— — personal: lord high admiral or committees or commissioners of the Admiralty:
— — — 1660–73: James, duke of York: appointed, iii. 389, n. 2; resigns, iv. 14, n. 1.
— — — 1673–9: successive committees of Privy Council: *see* iv. 17, n. 6, 377, n. 3.
— — — 1679–84: successive commissions: first commission (Sir H. Capel, &c.), iv. 171 & n. 2; commissioners abolished, iv. 377 & n. 3.
— — — 1684–5: Charles II, assisted by James, duke of York, *ib.*
— — — 1689–1702: successive commissions: first appointed, iv. 629 & n. 2; commissioners dismissed, Nov. 1693 (error), v. 157; Orford resigns from commission, 1699, v. 325 & n. 4.
— — — 1702: Thomas Herbert, earl of Pembroke: *see* v. 496 & n. 1.
— — — secretaries to the lords high admiral, committees, and commissioners: *see* Coventry, Sir W. (1660–7); Wren, Matthew (1667–72); Pepys, S. (1673–9, 1684–9); Brisbane, J. (1680–4); Bridgeman, W. (1694–8).
— — — judges of the admiralty court: *see* Exton, J.; Jenkins, Sir L.
— antiquities: student of, iii. 598.
— arms of: right to use, granted to Royal Society, iii. 332 & n. 2, 336 & n. 1.
— army [select: notices relating to the organization, general conduct, and political activities of the army (including the militia forces). Notices relating to campaigns, battles, sieges, &c., are indexed in general under the various wars (*see* Wars) and in detail under their names]:
— — chronological series:
— — — Charles I: levy, 1628 (?), ii. 8, 9, n. 1 (i. 8); commissary-general of victuals to, 1639, iii. 330, n. 1; commission of array, 1643: E. Waller, &c., and, ii. 478; ~ R. Abbot and, iv. 185–6 & n.
— — — parliamentary, later Cromwell's army: (i) general notices: alarms London, Apr. 1648, ii. 540 & n. 6; Pride's Purge, ii. 545 & n. 6; council of officers at Whitehall, Dec. 1648, ii. 546 & n. 1; distribution to, of lands in Ireland, iv. 57 & n. 3; hostile to universities and learning, iii. 165 & n. 8; Sir G. Downing's services to, iii. 445, n. 1; fanatics in, oppose Cromwell's adopting title of king, iii. 190–1 & n.; regiments going to Flanders, 1657, iii. 192 & n. 6; and capture of Mardyke, iii. 200 & n. 5; and capture of Dunkirk, iii. 217 & n. 3; officers and soldiers at Cromwell's funeral, iii. 224 & n. 4; and fall of Richard Cromwell, iii. 228, n. 9; political activity of, May 1659, iii. 231 & n. 4; expels Long Parliament, 1659, iii. 234 & n. 1; as 'the old army of the fanatics': dispersed, Feb. 1660, iii. 241 & n. 4; commissioners for control of, Feb. 1660, iii. 242, n. 2; soldiers of, in Charles II's entry into London, 29 May 1660, iii. 246 & n. 2; disbandment of: tax for, iii. 258 & n. 1.
— — — — (ii) detachments: kill Surrey petitioners, 1648, ii. 541 & n. 2; in scuffle in Fleet Street, 1649, ii. 556 & n. 1; taking horses for Commonwealth, 1650, iii. 14 & n. 6; examine E at Canterbury, iii. 15; raid Exeter House chapel, Christmas 1657, iii. 203–4 & nn.
— — — — (iii) former soldiers in: projected rising of, 1662, iii. 341, 342, n. 1; in Rye House plot, iv. 322, n. 1.

ENGLAND: army (*cont.*)
— — — Charles II: at entry of Russian ambassadors, 1662, iii. 344; supervises refugees from Fire of London, iii. 462; forces sent to Medway, 1667, iii. 484–5 & nn., 486–7 & nn.; encamped on Blackheath, 1673, iv. 13 & n. 1, 15; newly raised forces, 1678: camp, &c., on Hounslow Heath, iv. 136–7 & n.; grenadiers introduced, *ib.*; English forces in Netherlands, 1678: Ossory commands, iv. 137; extra guards for Charles II, 1683, iv. 331 & n. 1; dragoons introduced, iv. 354 & n. 3.
— — — James II: (i) general: forces engaged at Sedgemoor, iv. 451–2 & n.; forces about London, 1686: review of, iv. 504; as instrument of James II's religious policy, iv. 582 & n. 3; Scots and Irish reinforcements, &c., for, 1688, iv. 599 & nn. 5, 6; disaffection in, iv. 600; pressing for, iv. 601; prepares to repel William of Orange, &c., iv. 605, 607, 608; desertions from, iv. 607 & n. 3; disbanded by Feversham, iv. 611, n. 1; control of, assumed by William of Orange, iv. 612, n. 2; forces dispersed, iv. 612 & n. 2; discontented with William, &c., *ib.*; iv. 620 & n. 4, 629 & n. 4.
— — — — (ii): encampments of, on Hounslow Heath: general, iv. 629; in 1686, iv. 513 & n. 5, 514, 516, 517, 519; in 1687, iv. 553 & n. 1; ~ Roman Catholic chapel for, v. 61–2 & n.; in 1688, iv. 590 & n. 1.
— — — — (iii): Roman Catholics in: commissioned by James II, &c., iv. 488 *bis*, 489, 599, n. 6(?); Irish: crimes committed by, iv. 596–7 & n.; ~ stationed at Portsmouth, &c., iv. 599 & n. 6.
— — — William III: difficulty in recruiting for, 1689, iv. 629, 637; discontent in, iv. 631; forces in Ireland: sent, Feb. 1689, iv. 622 & n. 4; ~ condition of, 1690, v. 7; encampment on Blackheath, 1690, v. 30 & n. 1, 31, 32 & n. 6; prepares to repel projected French invasion, 1692, v. 97, 99 & n. 1; commander

ENGLAND: army (*cont.*)
of, under William III: to be British born, 1693, v. 135 & n. 1; votes of supply for, 1693, 1694, v. 161 & n. 3, 202, n. 6; regiments brought from Netherlands to repel French invasion, 1696, v. 233; pay for forces in Netherlands, 1696, v. 245–6, 253 & n. 2, 255 & n. 1, 256 & n. 3; need for, &c., 1697, v. 275 & n. 1; *add.*; v. 278 & n. 2; arrears due to, v. 280; to be reduced: votes for, 1698–9, v. 309 & n. 2, 311 & n. 1, 315–16 & n.; all troops to be British born, v. 311 & n. 1; forces voted, 1702, v. 485 & n. 2.
— — — Queen Anne: prayers for success of, 1702, v. 504 & n. 1; force on Cadiz expedition, 1702, v. 515, n. 3.
— — command (general officers, &c.): commanders-in-chief or captains-general: *see* Monck, George, duke of Albemarle (Scotland 1654–9; Scotland and England 1659–60; England 1660–70); Scott, James, duke of Monmouth (1678–9); Duras, Louis de, earl of Feversham (lieutenant-general 1685; general 1688); Churchill, John, duke of Marlborough (commander in England 1690–2; captain-general 1702–11).
— — — generals: *see* Hamilton, Richard (1686–8); Kirke, Percy (1685–91); chaplain-general, Flanders, 1704: *see* Hare, Francis; paymasters-general: *see* Fox, Sir Stephen (1660–76; *see especially* iv. 218–19 & nn.); Fox, Charles (1682–5); comptroller of accounts, 1703–4: *see* Duncombe, William.
— — militia: disaffection in, 1685, iv. 449; concerned in capture, &c., of Monmouth, iv. 451, 453 *bis*; James II wishes to replace, by standing army, iv. 488; Devon, &c.: called out, 1690, v. 31 *bis* & n. 7; Kent: regiment of horse in, 1660, iii. 254 & n. 4; ~ horsemen for, 1685, iv. 450, 458–9; ~ and Sussex: called out, 1696, v. 233 & n. 1; London: *see* London: military.

ENGLAND: army (*cont.*)
— — regiments and regimental officers:
— — — Guards: at ambassadors' entry, iii. 344.
— — — — horse: in procession, iii. 280; reviews of, iii. 357 & n. 2; iv. 526 & n. 4; commands in: dispute between A. J. van Keppel, earl of Albemarle, and James Butler, second duke of Ormond, concerning, 1699, v. 320–1 & n., 323 & n. 2, 325 & n. 5; duke of York's troop: in procession, iii. 278–9; ~ at ambassador's entry, iii. 298; ~ officer in: *see* Berkeley, Charles, earl of Falmouth.
— — — — foot: in procession, iii. 280; at ambassador's entry(?), iii. 298; review of, iii. 357 & n. 2; First (later Grenadier): officers in: *see* Atkins, Sir J.; Cheke, Thomas; Fairfax, General Thomas; Russell, Col. John; Strode, Col. John; Coldstream: officer in: *see* Graham, James.
— — — other regiments:
— — — — horse: Oxford's Blues: troop in Kent, 1665(?), iii. 422 & n. 4; officers in: *see* Brett, Sir E.; Compton, Henry, bishop of London; Hawley, Francis, Baron Hawley; Jones, Sir Henry; Slingsby, Col. Henry.
— — — — — Royal Dragoons: formation of, iv. 354 & n. 3; Col. Henry Slingsby's regiment, iv. 473, n. 4; Scottish dragoon regiments serving in England, 1694, v. 175 & n. 1.
— — — — foot: Lord High Admiral's regiment: officer in: *see* Darell, N.; Barbados regiment: officer in: *see* Stapleton, Sir W.; Brigadier Charles Churchill's regiment: on Blackheath, 1690, v. 29–30 & n.; ~ officer in: *see* Birch, A.; Fifth and Sixth Foot: origin of, iv. 458, n. 1; Fifth Foot: officer in: *see* Fairfax, General Thomas; Sir H. Goodrick's regiment: officer in: *see* Fairfax, General Thomas; Holland regiment: officers in: *see* Birch, A.; Fitzpatrick, E.; Woodcock, Sir T.; Queen's: officer in: *see* Kirke, P.; Royal Fusiliers: officer in: *see* Fitz-

ENGLAND: army (*cont.*)
patrick, E.; commissions to raise regiments, 1688 (Col. H. Gage; Henry Cavendish, duke of Newcastle), iv. 599, n. 6; troop of volunteers: in coronation procession, 1661, iii. 280 & n. 4; officer (regiment not specified): *see* Evelyn, Major Edward.
— — standing army, &c.: encampments, 1673, 1678: feared by parliament, &c., iv. 13 & n. 1, 136 & n. 4; James II desires, in place of militia, iv. 488; encampment, 1686: fear of, iv. 514; James II uses to advance Roman Catholicism, iv. 582 & n. 3; formation of feared, 1693, v. 140 & n. 1; controversy relating to, 1697–8, v. 275 & n. 1; *add.*; v. 278 & n. 2.
— — miscellaneous: garrisons: at Portsmouth, 1685, &c., iv. 472–3, 599 & n. 6; ~ at Tangier, iii. 311 & n. 5; iv. 208 & n. 5, 209 & n. 2; hospitals: *see* London: Environs: Chelsea; quartering of soldiers in private houses, iii. 192 & n. 6; iv. 458 & n. 2, 490 & n. 5, 613; recruiting: levy (muster), 1628, ii. 8, 9, n. 1 (i. 8); ~ pressing, iv. 601; v. 449 & n. 1; reviews or musters, iii. 357 & n. 2; iv. 136, 458 & n. 1, 463 & n. 2, 504, 526; uniforms: grenadiers, iv. 137 & n. 1; ~ Royal Dragoons, iv. 354.
— Civil War: *see* Civil War.
— climate: *see* weather and climate *below*.
— commissions and commissioners: for commissions for special purposes and standing commissions *see* Commission *and* Commissioners; for commissioners replacing an officer of state *see* officers *below*, &c.
— Commonwealth and Protectorate: *see* Commonwealth and Protectorate.
— Council of State: *see* Council of State.
— Council of the North, iii. 128, n. 6.
— Councils for Foreign Plantations, of Trade, and of Trade and Plantations: *see* Council for Foreign Plantations; Council of Trade; Council of Trade and Plantations.

ENGLAND (*cont.*)
— court [the sovereigns and the officers of state and of the household immediately about them, treated collectively and principally in their social aspect; in most of the notices indexed here the term 'the court' is used. It moved about with the sovereigns unless they were on progress or campaign; it was usually kept at Whitehall until 1688 or later, and after 1698 at St. James's Palace (so v. 518 & n. 2); for its movements 1660–84 *see* Charles II: court & social life; for movements 1685–7 *see* iv. 465–7, 467, n. 1, 526, n. 2, 558, n. 5. Notices relating to its religious life, to theatrical performances, and to parties, are indexed under Whitehall and the other palaces; notices relating to the individual members and their duties, under England: officers; Royal Household; &c.; and under the various queens]:
— — as an institution, &c.: jurisdiction over, iv. 454, n. 1; gaming at, on Twelfth Night, iii. 308 & n. 4, 504 & n. 1; courtiers: servitude of, iv. 318.
— — character of, under Charles II, &c.: dissolute, &c., iii. 316, 464, 596; iv. 416, 428, 437, 478; ~ on 25 Jan. 1685, iv. 403, 413–14; splendour of: at balls, &c., iii. 476, 518, 630; iv. 48, 157, 395; ~ at Windsor, iv. 142; reformed by James II, iv. 415; little affected by Revolution, iv. 625.
— — particular notices: alarm at, during Fire of London, iii. 454 & n. 8; and alarm due to reports of invasion, 1666, iii. 462 & n. 1; ceremonial at, revived after Treaty of Breda, iii. 491 & n. 1; and dismissal of Clarendon: hostility of the buffoons and mistresses to him, iii. 493–4 & nn.; iv. 338–9; French visitors to, 1671, iii. 575; Clifford leaves for good, iv. 20; grief of, for death of Mrs. Godolphin, iv. 149; Roman Catholics at, 1685, iv. 418, 419; alarm at, due to William of Orange's expedition, iv. 597–9 & nn., *passim*, 605

ENGLAND: court (*cont.*)
bis; flight of, Dec. 1688, iv. 609; the old courtiers, Mar. 1689, iv. 627; crowds at, soliciting office, *ib.*
— — in mourning: for Henry, duke of Gloucester, iii. 257; for Mary, princess of Orange, iii. 264–5; for Charles II, iv. 492 & n. 3; for foreign rulers, &c., iii. 429; iv. 351 & n. 1; v. 126 & n. 1, 437 & n. 1, 582 & n. 1; no mourning for Leopold I, v. 594 & n. 2.
— crown: exclusion bills and succession to, iv. 236 & n. 1, 239 & n. 3.
— — settlement of, at Revolution: proposals for Regency, iv. 613–14, 619 & n. 4, 624, n. 3, 625; transferred to William and Mary, &c., iv. 616 & n. 1, 621, 623 & n. 4; too hasty, &c., iv. 635; v. 148 & n. 3, 152 & n. 1.
— — succession to: proposed regulation of, iv. 616 & n. 1; threatened by republicans, iv. 635; bill to regulate, iv. 645 & n. 8; uncertainty of, 1700, v. 421 & n. 2; referred to parliament, v. 445, 448 & n. 5; Act of Settlement, v. 464–5 & n.; Regency Act, 1706, v. 620 & n. 2.
— — king's absence abroad: Queen Mary II appointed to govern during, v. 24 & n. 1, 25; Lords Justices appointed, 1695, &c., v. 238 & n. 4, 294 & n. 2, 327 & n. 2, 469 & nn. 2, 6.
— — crown lands: resumption of, 1660, &c., i. 14; grant of, by William III: withdrawn, v. 229–30 & n.; *see also* Sayes Court.
— currency: *see* Currency.
— customs: collection of, at James II's accession, iv. 417 & n. 6; as error for excise, iv. 419; commissioners of: and prize-ships, v. 522, n. 1; receiver of, 1691–7: *see* Knight, J.
— — at ports: Dover: examination at, iii. 13; officers of, at: and passes, iii. 16 & n. 1; ~ conduct of, to E, iii. 395; clerk of the passage at, iii. 56; Gravesend: searcher at (R. Birstall), iv. 132 & n. 7; London: Customs-house: pass obtained at, ii. 29 & n. 3;

ENGLAND: customs (*cont.*)
Margate: officer at (J. Glover), iii. 611 & n. 1; Rye: searchers at, iii. 66.
— European possessions, &c.: Calais: traces of English occupation of, ii. 83 & n. 3 (i. 56); cautionary towns in Zeeland, i. 23 & n. 4; Dunkirk: delivered to English, 1658, iii. 217, n. 3; ~ sold by Charles II, i. 50 & n. 1; Orleans: siege of, by English: monument commemorating relief from, ii. 137 & nn. 1–4 (i. 90); Paris: threatened by English (error), ii. 100 & n. 6 (i. 66); Rochecorbon: castle at, built by English, ii. 148 (i. 96); Rouen: cathedral at, built by English, ii. 122–3 & n. (i. 79); ~ Joan of Arc burnt at, by English, i. 90; *see also* ii. 137; Tours: church at, built by English, ii. 145 & n. 3 (i. 94).
— Exchequer: *see* Treasury, *below*.
— excise: farm of, at James II's accession, iv. 417 & n. 6, 419 (called customs in error).
— foreign policy [indexed under the various states having relations with England, wars, treaties, &c.]: E's comments on selfishness, &c., of: 1683–4, iv. 331–2 & nn., 369, 380, 549; ~ in Peace of Ryswick, v. 270–1 & n.
— French protestants in: *see* French protestants.
— geographical: coasts: charts of, iv. 301 & n. 3; ~ open to invasion, &c., v. 160; earthquake dividing, from France, i. 57 & n. 1; stone buildings in: rare in Leicestershire, &c., iii. 122; trench dividing, from Wales, iii. 119 & n. 2; Trent separates north and south of, iii. 125; York second city of, iii. 128 & n. 6.
— Great Rebellion: *see* Great Rebellion.
— harvests [the years run from Sept. to Sept.]:
— — 1630: dearth, ii. 10 & n. 2 (i. 8).
— — 1666–7: sowing-time bad, iii. 466.
— — 1692–1700: general note, v. 301, n. 1.
— — 1692–3: plentiful, v. 157.

ENGLAND: harvests (*cont.*)
— — 1693–4: promise of plenty and failure, v. 186, 188 & n. 6; *see also* v. 157, n. 3.
— — 1694–5: backward, v. 216.
— — 1695–6: good after wet summer, v. 253, 257, 259.
— — 1696–7: sowing-time bad, v. 259, 260, 261, 263; corn dear, May 1698, v. 287.
— — 1697–8: cold summer and corn dear, v. 287, 288, 301 & n. 1; satisfactory supply, Jan. 1699, v. 312 & n. 2.
— — 1699–1700: plentiful, v. 408, 415, 422.
— — 1700–1: famine feared, v. 459.
— — 1701–2: excellent after wet weather, v. 513, 514; fall in price of corn, Jan. 1703(?), v. 528 & n. 3; ~ alluded to, v. 540.
— — 1702–3: good harvest weather after wet, v. 539, 540, 542 & n. 4, 543, 544.
— — 1703–4: plentiful, v. 580.
— heralds: *see* Heraldry and Heralds.
— justice: administration of:
— — courts:
— — — Chancery: place of sitting, iv. 226, n. 5; importance of, *c.* 1700, v. 438; E qualifies in, for office under Test Act, iv. 10; officers of state sworn in in, iv. 417 & n. 5; signing Association in, v. 242–3 & n.; depositions relating to birth of Prince James Edward enrolled in, iv. 602 & n. 3; proceedings in: abuse in, iv. 67; Master in Chancery consulted, iv. 273; cases in: Sir R. Browne, iv. 67; W. Prettyman *v.* E and Mrs. Evelyn, iv. 339–40, 344, 361(?), 389(?), 393, 546(?), 551; Lady Tuke, iv. 489, 530(?), 535.
— — — Common Pleas: cases, &c., in, iv. 105–6; v. 247–8.
— — — Delegates, iv. 267, n. 1; cases before, &c., iv. 266–7, 354 & n. 6; v. 528, n. 8 *ad fin.*
— — — Exchequer [for Treasury business, &c., in, *see* Treasury *below*]: officers of state sworn in in, iv. 417 & n. 5; Lord Mayor of London sworn in in, iii. 259, n. 4; trial in, iv. 368.
— — — High Commission: in comparison, iv. 519, 520, n. 1.

ENGLAND: justice (*cont.*)
— — — High Court of Justice: court, 1649: tries Hamilton, &c., ii. 548 & n. 2; ~ alluded to, ii. 556; court, 1658: tries Mordaunt, &c., iii. 214 & nn. 3, 4.
— — — King's Bench: place of sitting, iv. 226, n. 5, 587–8 & n.; jurisdiction of, v. 41, n. 4; E qualifies in, for office under Test Act, v. 212 & n. 2; *see also* iv. 500 & n. 3; signing Association in, v. 243 & n. 1; chief clerkship of: reversion of, disputed, v. 161 & n. 4; trials in [many of the political trials, &c. (*see below*) took place here]: E. Fenwick *v.* Lady Grosvenor, v. 528 & n. 8; J. Lewknor *v.* W. Montague, v. 3 & n. 2; duke of Norfolk *v.* Sir J. Germaine, v. 127, n. 1.
— — — Star Chamber: meeting-place of, iii. 444, n. 3.
— — — Wards: meeting-place of, iii. 435 & n. 5.
— — trials, proceedings, &c.:
— — — trials in general: right of accused in, to counsel, iv. 234, n. 2; jury: a corrupt, iv. 273, 274, n. 1; ~ given supper by successful litigant, v. 248; reports of: reliability of, for Popish Plot trials, iv. 175 & n. 3; ~ publication of, iv. 438, 439, n. 1, 615 & n. 2; for high treason: two witnesses required for conviction in, &c., iv. 232, 352–3 & n., 354; v. 264 & n. 6.
— — — procedure and miscellaneous: Habeas Corpus: release of prisoners in accordance with, iv. 354, 366; ~ proceedings under, iv. 587 & n. 2; hue and cry, iii. 70; libel: punishment for, iii. 503 & n. 4; office, ii. 27 & n. 1 (i. 20); robbery: circulating description of stolen property, iii. 70, 71; ~ proceedings in court relating to, iii. 73, 74; *scandalum magnatum*: action for, iv. 636, n. 1; writ of error, iv. 636; v. 161 & n. 4.
— — — punishments [beheading and hanging not indexed collectively]: burning to death (woman), iii. 64 & n. 3; guillotine at Halifax, ii. 401 & n. 2;

ENGLAND : justice (*cont.*)
hanging, drawing, and quartering, iv. 233; *see also* iii. 259; pillory, iii. 503; ~ with whipping, iv. 440 & n. 4, 445, 451 & n. 3; *præmunire*: as penalty, &c., iv. 602–3, 631; v. 242, 243, n. 1; pressing to death, iii. 74 & n. 2; traitors' heads, &c., exposed on Temple Bar, &c., v. 235 & n. 3.
— — — — places of execution, &c.: Charing Cross, iii. 259, 503; Lincoln's Inn Fields, iv. 332; Palace Yard, Westminster, iv. 440, n. 4; Pall Mall, iv. 274, n. 1; Smithfield, iii. 64; Tower Hill, ii. 28 (i. 20); iv. 236, 353, 456; v. 264; Tyburn, iv. 332, 382; v. 186, n. 4, 236.
— — — particular cases [*see also* courts *above*. Select: generally only those trials are indexed for which there is a substantial notice of proceedings or comment, or which are cited for special reasons]: (i) for High Treason [including impeachments, &c.]: Sir T. Armstrong, iv. 382 & n. 4; Charles Gerard, Viscount Brandon (later earl of Macclesfield), iv. 490; Sir R. Graham (Viscount Preston), v. 41 & n. 4, 42 & n. 1; Forde Grey, Baron Grey of Wark (later earl of Tankerville), iv. 490; James Hamilton, duke of Hamilton, &c., ii. 548 & n. 2; Dr. J. Hewit, iii. 214 & n. 4; John Mordaunt (later Viscount Mordaunt), iii. 214 & n. 3; the Regicides, iii. 258 & n. 6; William Russell, Lord Russell, iv. 326, 327 & nn. 1, 2, 329, n. 1; Algernon Sidney, iv. 352–3 & nn.; William Howard, Viscount Stafford, iv. 225–34 & nn.; Thomas Wentworth, earl of Strafford, ii. 27 & nn. 3, 4, 28 & n. 5 (i. 20 *bis*); ~ mentioned, iv. 226; Sir G. Wakeman, &c., iv. 173–6 & nn.; ~ mentioned, iv. 435.
— — — — (ii) cases connected with politics: *Quo Warranto* proceedings against City of London, 1681–3, iv. 319–20 & nn.; F. Dangerfield, for scandalous libel, 1685, iv. 451, n. 3; Titus

ENGLAND: justice (*cont.*)
Oates, for perjury, &c., 1684, 1685, iv. 435, n. 2, 438–9 & n., 636 & n. 1, 643 & n. 1; Seven Bishops, for seditious libel, 1688, iv. 585, nn. 3, 4, 587–8 & n., 589 & n. 1, 590.
— — — — (iii) ordinary crimes: abduction: Sir J. Johnston, v. 41 & n. 1; robbery, &c.: J. Thompson, iii. 73, 74 & n. 2; murder: Count K. J. von Königsmarck, &c., iv. 273–4 & n.; Charles Mohun, Baron Mohun: tried by Lord Steward's court, v. 129 & n. 2; Henry St. John (later Viscount St. John) and Col. E. Webb, iv. 401 & n. 1.
— — — — (iv) civil cases: Albemarle inheritance disputes, 1694–1700, v. 167 & n. 1, 246 & n. 5, 288 & n. 6, 410–11 & n., 475; Crispe *v.* Lady Cranborne, iv. 65, n. 2; Godden *v.* Hales, iv. 517, n. 1; Craven Howard *v.* Mrs. W. Howard, &c., iv. 67, 70–1; Shirley *v.* Fagg, iv. 65, n. 1; Stoughton *v.* Onslow, *ib.*; Lady Tuke, &c., iv. 276 & n. 4, 280, 281.
— — personal and professional:
— — — lawyers: anecdote relating to conduct of, iv. 530; practising: obliged to swear allegiance to William III, 1696, v. 242–3 & n.; attorneys: bill for reducing number of, v. 379 & n. 2; decline of legal learning, *c.* 1700, v. 438.
— — — judges: in general: dismissals and appointments of, in reign of James II, iv. 508 & n. 2, 514 & n. 6, 536, 589 & n. 1, 590; appointment of: delay in, 1689, iv. 627; opinions of: on ship-money, i. 23 & n. 1; on liability of corporations to forfeiture, iv. 320 & n. 1; on continued validity of farm of excise after king's death, iv. 417 & n. 6, 419.
— — — — in ceremonies [judges and other law officers in Charles II's coronation procession (iii. 279) are not indexed separately]: presented to Queen Catherine, iii. 321 & n. 5; attend meeting to authenticate birth of James Edward, iv. 602 & n. 3; at coronation of William and Mary, iv. 633 & n. 4; at Queen Mary's funeral, v. 204; at divine service(?), iv. 284 & n. 1.
— — — — miscellaneous notices: assize at Worcester, 1654, iii. 119 & n. 4; Fire Judges: portraits of, iii. 338 & n. 5; iv. 17 & n. 5; at Reader's feast, iii. 400; E dines with: at Old Bailey, iv. 175; ~ at assize in Southwark, iv. 276–7.
— — — judges and law officers: individuals:
— — — — lord chancellor, lord keeper, &c.: *see* officers and departments of state *below*.
— — — — attorney-general (king's attorney): *see* Palmer, Sir G. (1660–70); Finch, Sir Heneage, later earl of Nottingham (1670–3); Jones, Sir William (1675–9); Sawyer, Sir R. (1681–7); Powys, Sir T. (1687–8); Somers, Sir John, later Baron Somers (1692–3).
— — — — solicitor-general (king's solicitor): *see* Finch, Sir Heneage, later earl of Nottingham (1660–70); North, Sir Francis, later Baron Guilford (1671–3); Winnington, Sir F. (1674–9); Finch, Heneage, later earl of Aylesford, &c. (1679–86); Powys, Sir T. (1686–7); Somers, Sir John, later Baron Somers (1689–92); Harcourt, Sir Simon, later Viscount Harcourt (1702–7).
— — — — Common Pleas: Lord Chief Justice: *see* Richardson, Sir T. (1626–31); Finch, Sir John, later Baron Finch (1634–40); St. John, O. (1648–60); Bridgeman, Sir O. (1660–7); Vaughan, Sir John (1668–74); North, Sir Francis, later Baron Guilford (1675–82); Pemberton, Sir F. (1683); Herbert, Sir Edward, later titular earl of Portland (1687–8); Treby, Sir G. (1692–1700).
— — — — — other judges: *see* Jenner, Sir T.; Milton, Sir C.
— — — — Exchequer: Lord Chief

ENGLAND: justice (*cont.*)
Baron: *see* Hale, Sir M. (1660–71); Turnor, Sir E. (1671–6); Montagu, William, sen. (1676–86).
— — — — — other barons: *see* Jenner, Sir T.; Milton, Sir C.; Thurland, Sir E.
— — — — King's Bench (and Queen's Bench): Lord Chief Justice: *see* Richardson, Sir T. (1631–5); Foster, Sir R. (1660–3); Hyde, Sir R. (1663–5); Hale, Sir M. (1671–6); Pemberton, Sir F. (1681–3); Jeffreys, Sir George, later Baron Jeffreys (1683–5); Herbert, Sir Edward, later titular earl of Portland (1685–7); Wright, Sir Robert (1687–8).
— — — — — other judges: *see* Allibone, Sir R.; Holloway, Sir R.; Powell, Sir J.; Powys, Sir T.; Walcot, Sir T.; Wilde, Sir W.; Wythens, Sir F.
— — — — judges casually mentioned: *see* Berkeley, Sir R.; Bramston, Sir J.; Heath, Sir R.; Littleton, Sir Thomas.
— — — — judges, &c., in other courts: Admiralty: *see* Jenkins, Sir L.; Exton, J.; Chester: chief justice of: *see* Jeffreys, Sir George, later Baron Jeffreys (1680–3); Herbert, Sir Edward, later titular earl of Portland (1683–5); Council of the Marches: *see* Eyton, Sir K.
— — — — masters in chancery: *see* Hoskins, Sir J.; Strode, Sir N.; Master of the Rolls: *see* Trevor, Sir J. (1685–8).
— — — subordinate officials:
— — — — axe-bearer: at Stafford's trial, iv. 226; alluded to, iv. 233 & n. 2.
— — — — common or public hangman: burns books, iv. 510, 515; v. 131, 376 & n. 4; burns libel, iii. 503 & n. 4; burns Monmouth's Declaration, 1685, iv. 449 & n. 3; burns Solemn League and Covenant, iii. 288–9 & n.; as executioner of Monmouth, iv. 456 & n. 2.
— justices of the peace: commission for: E on, &c., iii. 433–4 & n.; Roman Catholics appointed, iv. 536 & n. 3.

ENGLAND (*cont.*)
— kings [collective notices, &c.]:
— — accession of: order of proclaiming, iv. 412–13 & nn.; ~ commemoration of, iv. 499 & n. 8; birthdays of: salute for, iv. 601; burials of: place of, ii. 85 (i. 58); ~ wax effigies for, ii. 90 (i. 60); ~ coffins of, at Winchester (Saxon kings), ii. 79 (i. 52); iv. 472 & n. 2; health of: rules for bleeding, iv. 406 & n. 1; meeting at Godmanchester with hundred ploughs: custom of, iii. 135 & n. 5; religious practices of: receive Communion with royalty, &c., alone, iii. 51 & n. 5; iv. 374–5 & n.; ~ in Maundy Thursday ceremony, ii. 385 & n. 5; ~ offerings of, at Epiphany, &c., iii. 53 & n. 2; iv. 171 & n. 8; statues of: in Royal Exchange, iii. 460 & n. 8; ~ in York Minster, iii. 129 & n. 2; touch for King's Evil, iii. 250–1 & n.; iv. 606 & n. 3; ~ applicants for touching: accident to, iv. 374 & n. 2.
— — regalia, iii. 283, 402 & n. 3; Imperial crown: in coronation, iii. 283 & n. 7, 284 & n. 1; ~ worn by king in parliament, iii. 286, 402; *see also* iv. 442; ~ T. Blood tries to steal, iii. 576 & n. 2; St. Edward's crown, iii. 283, n. 7; crowns worn by Queen Mary of Modena, iv. 441 & n. 3.
— landed property: tenures: entail, v. 336–7, 339, n. 2; ~ clandestine breaking of, iv. 569, 582–3 & n.; v. 86; fee-farm, iii. 59 & n. 1; tail male, v. 314, n. 1; right belonging to Lord Harington at Oakham, iii. 123 & n. 5.
— — Roman Catholics rendered incapable of inheriting, v. 403 & n. 1.
— laws [notices relating to the operation, &c., of particular statutes or groups of statutes or laws, and general notices concerning the laws of England, &c. For the passing of acts of parliament *see* Parliament; for the administration of justice *see* justice: administration of *above*]:

ENGLAND: laws (*cont.*)
— — general and miscellaneous: all acts and ordinances passed since 3 March 1642 held void after Restoration, iii. 252, n. 1; crown's right of dispensing with the laws, &c.: claimed by or for James II, iv. 517, n. 1, 583–4 & n., 599 & n. 4; James II attempts to subvert the laws, iv. 616; declarations for maintenance of the laws, 1688, iv. 609; legal learning: decline of, *c.* 1700, v. 438; property secured by law, iv. 286; corporations: liability of to forfeiture, iv. 320 & n. 1; suicides: goods of, liable to forfeiture, iv. 327, n. 3.
— — groups of laws: Licensing Acts, 1662, 1685, iv. 172, n. 3, 508, n. 1; ~ general operation of press laws, i. *101–5*; laws against profanity, &c.: enforcement of, 1699, v. 366 & n. 5.
— — — penal laws against Roman Catholics: speech against, 1661, iii. 249–50 & n.; with laws against protestant Nonconformists: suspended by Declaration of Indulgence, 1672, iii. 608, n. 1; speech against, 1673(?), iv. 5 & n. 5; including Test Acts: project for repeal of, 1687, iv. 540–1 & n., 544; ~ abrogated by Declaration of Indulgence, 1687, iv. 546 & n. 5, 585 & n. 2; ~ abrogation of: advocated by Bishop S. Parker, iv. 574 & n. 2.
— — — — acts forbidding printing of Roman Catholic prayer-books, &c., iv. 504; acts requiring oaths of Allegiance, &c., from fellows of colleges, &c., iv. 509.
— — — — Test Act, 1673 (*see also above*): provisions of, iv. 7, n. 4; alluded to, iv. 159 & n. 3; qualifying for office in compliance with, iv. 10 & n. 3, 496, 500 *bis*; v. 212 & n. 2, 568 & n. 2; refusals to comply with, iv. 14 & n. 1, 16, 25, n. 1; disqualification due to, iii. 596, n. 1; evasion of, iv. 377 & n. 3; James II's dispensations from, iv. 488 *bis*, 489, 509–10, 514; abrogated by Herbert's judgement in Godden *v.* Hales, iv. 517 & n. 1.

ENGLAND: laws (*cont.*)
— — — — Parliamentary Test Act: provisions of, iv. 158–9 & n.; compliance with, iv. 442 & n. 4, 476 & n. 1.
— — — — act disqualifying Roman Catholics from inheriting land, &c., 1700, v. 403 & n. 1.
— — particular statutes [select: omits some statutes cited in notes. The ordinances of the Long Parliament are included with the statutes]: statute of Merchants, 1285, and Ordinance of the Staple, 1353: loan under, ii. 545 & n. 2; against perjury, 1563: read in church, v. 24 & n. 3; Petition of Right, 1628: infringed, iv. 458 & n. 2; abolishing Court of High Commission, 1641, and explanatory act, 1661, iv. 519, 520, n. 1; imposing Solemn Vow and Covenant, 1643, ii. 81–2 & n.; exiling Edmund Waller, 1644, ii. 478 & n. 3; ~ revoked, 1651, iii. 53, n. 3; abolishing Church festivals, 1647: enforced, iii. 79 & n. 1, 145 & n. 1, 204 & n. 5; confiscating impropriations held by bishops, 1648, ii. 8, n. 4; establishing High Court of Justice, 1649, ii. 548, n. 2; for sale of Charles I's goods, 1649, ii. 549, nn. 5, 7; establishing the Commonwealth, 1649, iii. 14, n. 6; for sale of crown lands, 1649, iii. 59, n. 1; granting property to J. Bradshaw, 1649, iii. 71, n. 3; against scandalous ministers, 1654: enforced, iii. 144, n. 3; regulating new buildings near London, 1657: E and, iii. 223 & n. 2, 224–5, 227; Act of Oblivion, 1660: and trial of Algernon Sidney, iv. 353 & n. 2; for commemorating Restoration, 1660, iii. 289 & n. 5; establishing annual fast on 30 January, 1660, iii. 269, n. 1; restoring dukedom of Norfolk, 1660, and confirmatory act, 1661, iii. 306, n. 3; empowering bishops to resume their seats in parliament, 1661, iii. 312, n. 2; restoring ecclesiastical jurisdiction, 1661, *ib.*; Corporation Act, *ib.*; for London street-improvements, &c., 1662, iii.

ENGLAND: laws (*cont.*) 319, n. 1; Act of Uniformity, 1662: comes into operation, iii. 331 & n. 3; ~ effect of, iii. 252, n. 1; for rebuilding London, 1667 and 1670: provisions in, iii. 476, n. 3; iv. 17, n. 5, 243, n. 7; for Forest of Dean, 1668, iii. 343, n. 3; for building thirty ships for Navy, 1677: ships built under, iv. 310 & n. 2; v. 24; creating parish of St. Anne, Soho, 1678, 1685, iv. 544, n. 1; forbidding quartering soldiers in private houses, 1679: breach of, iv. 458 & n. 2; Declaration of Rights, 1689: settlement of crown in, iv. 616 & n. 1, 621–2 & n.; v. 421 & n. 2; for Coronation Oath of William and Mary, 1689: the oath, iv. 632 & n. 5; for Oath of Allegiance to William and Mary, 1689: enforced, iv. 648, n. 6; v. 51, n. 5; Toleration Act, 1689: alluded to, v. 616; appointing Queen Mary regent in king's absence, 1690, v. 24, n. 1; establishing Bank of England, 1694, v. 185 & n. 3; for preventing expense in elections, 1696, v. 446 & n. 3; enabling parliament to continue sitting after sovereign's death, 1696, v. 232, n. 2, 492, n. 1; regulating county elections, 1696, v. 442, n. 1; for Land Bank, 1696, v. 246, n. 3; ~ authorizes issue of Exchequer bills, v. 255, n. 2; Act of Settlement, 1701: proposed repeal of clause in, v. 621 & n. 3.

— legendary history: *see* Arthur; Coel; Guy of Warwick; Helena, St.; Hengist.

— — Britain received the Gospel earlier than Rome, iii. 333 & n. 4; siege of Paris by English raised by St. Geneviève, ii. 100 & n. 6 (i. 66).

— merchant shipping [for notices relating to ships in general and for individual ships *see* Ships and Shipping]:

— — Bristol trade with America, &c., iii. 102; at Venice, ii. 429; ~ ship at, pressed for Cretan war, ii. 451–2, 468–9.

— — 1652: embargo on, iii. 67 & n. 4.

ENGLAND: merchant shipping (*cont.*)

— — 1672: captures of, by French, near Leeward Islands, iii. 605; from Plantations: ordered to sail in convoys, iii. 603 & n. 2.

— — 1689: captures of, by French, lack of convoys for, &c., iv. 642, 651–2 & n.

— — 1690: movements of, v. 2, 31 & n. 2, 33 & n. 5; losses of, by capture, &c., v. 37.

— — 1691: Barbados and Jamaica fleets: losses from, v. 68, 79; Russia fleet: losses from, v. 67 & n. 3; Smyrna fleet: movements of, v. 60 & n. 3, 67 & n. 1; West Indies fleet: movements of, v. 67, 77 & n. 3.

— — 1693: Smyrna fleet (called Turkey merchants, &c.): in danger of French attack, v. 142 & n. 1, 145 & n. 4; attacked, &c., v. 148 & n. 2; losses and survivors, v. 150 & n. 2; disaster: mentioned, v. 151–2, 155 & n. 7; ~ parliamentary inquiry into, v. 158 & n. 1.

— — 1694: East India ship: sunk by French, v. 174 & n. 4; Smyrna fleet (Turkey merchants): loss by storm, iv. 169 & n. 3; privateering against, v. 174–5.

— — 1695: East India ships: captured by French, v. 218 & n. 1, 220 & n. 4.

— — 1696: wrecks, v. 230 & n. 4; East India ships: come home, v. 251.

— — 1701: care of, recommended to parliament, v. 445; excluded from French and Spanish ports, v. 477 & n. 1.

— — 1702: East India and Virginia fleets: come home, v. 516 & n. 5, 520 & n. 3.

— — 1705: ships from Lisbon: come home, v. 601 & n. 1; losses of, by storms and capture, v. 614 & n. 6.

— military: regiments and soldiers in foreign service [there are similar sections under Ireland and Scotland]:

— — France: Monmouth's regiment or Royal Anglais, iii. 587 & n. 3; Sir H. Jones, *ib.*

— — Spain (Spanish Netherlands:) Sir H. Gage's regiment, ii. 65 & n. 4. (i. 44).

ENGLAND: military: foreign service (*cont.*)
— — United Provinces: sixteenth century, &c.: at Bergen-op-Zoom, ii. 61 & n. 5; hospital for, ii. 43, n. 2, 45, n. 6; the Veres, i. 24 & n. 1.
— — — at siege of Gennep, 1641, ii. 36–8 & nn. (i. 27–8); garrisons, &c., 1641, ii. 38 (i. 29), 56 (i. 39), 60 (i. 41); Ossory and his soldiers, 1677–8, iv. 127, n. 1; the three regiments, 1674–88: come to England, 1685, iv. 458 & n. 1; ~ captain in: *see* Lanham, H. (iv. 604, n. 1).
— — Venice and Parma (military?): *see* Kingston, — (iii. 13).
— militia: *see* army *above*.
— navy [select: notices relating to the organization and general conduct of the navy. Notices relating to fleet movements are indexed under the various wars (*see* Wars); those relating to sea-fights, &c., under their names; those relating to individual ships under Ships and Shipping]:
— — administration [the Navy Office, and Commissioners and other officers of the Navy]:
— — — general notices: Navy Office moves to Greenwich during plague, 1665, iii. 418, n. 2; change of officers at Revolution, v. 9, 24, 111.
— — — commissioners: in general: attend Trinity House annual meeting, iv. 459; attend meeting of commissioners for Greenwich Hospital, v. 209–10; Sick and Wounded business with(?), iii. 405, 418; iv. 95; examine E's project for infirmary, iii. 430, n. 2, 431 & n. 3; in charge of prize ships, iii. 420 & n. 3; E's private, &c., business with, iii. 482 & n. 4; iv. 171, 264 & n. 1.
— — — — individuals: the Gonsons as naval officials, iv. 304 & n. 1; Clerk of the Acts: *see* Pepys, S. (1660–73); commissioners (at Navy Office): *see* Brouncker, William, Viscount Brouncker (iii. 419, n. 1, 420, n. 3); Deane, Sir A.; Haddock, Sir R.; Hewer, W.; Smith, Sir Jeremiah.

ENGLAND: navy (*cont.*)
— — — commissioners (at ports): *see* Beach, Sir R.; Cox, Sir John; Middleton, Col. T.; Pett, Peter (iii. 359 & n. 4; &c.); Tippetts, Sir J.
— — — comptroller: *see* Mennes, Sir J. (1661–71); Haddock, Sir R. (1682–1715); judge-advocate: *see* Brisbane, J.; deputy judge-advocate: *see* Hewer, W.; surveyor: *see* Tippetts, Sir J.; treasurer: house of, in Deptford Dockyard, iii. 312 & n. 4; iv. 386 & n. 3; individual treasurers: *see* Carteret, Sir G. (1660–7); Seymour, Sir Edward (1673–81); Carey, Anthony, Viscount Falkland, (1681–9); Russell, Edward, earl of Orford (1689–99); Caesar, C. (1711–14).
— — — victualler: *see* Gauden, B.; minor officials: *see* Crane, J.; Turner, Thomas.
— — historical notices [excluding notices of war-time manœuvres, &c.]:
— — — the navy in general: ship-money, for, i. 23, 26; ~ alluded to, ii. 30 & n. 3; v. 230 & n. 5; strength of, 1683, iv. 332; decay of, *c.* 1684, iv. 377 & n. 3; unprepared, May 1688, iv. 582 *bis*; disaffection in, Oct. 1688, iv. 600 & n. 3; lack of convoys, 1689, iv. 651–2 & n.; mock sea-fight, 1698, v. 285 & n. 4; losses by storms, 1703, 1704, v. 551 & n. 3, 552, 556 & n. 3.
— — — — parliamentary proceedings relating to: thirty new ships voted, 1677, iv. 310 & n. 2; ~ building of: Pepys, &c., accused of embezzlement in, v. 24; votes of supply for, 1693–5, v. 161 & n. 3, 202, n. 6; need for, in king's speech, 1697, v. 278; arrears due to: discussed, v. 280; strength of: voted, 1699, 1702, v. 316 & n. 1, 485 & n. 2.
— — — particular fleets, &c.: to bring Queen Catherine to England, 1662, iii. 306, 311 & n. 5; for Tangier, 1662, iii. 311 & n. 5, 312; at Chatham, 1663, iii. 359; decision not to set out fleet, 1667: responsibility for, &c., iii. 484, n. 1, 486, 489 & n. 2;

ENGLAND: navy (*cont.*)
at Portsmouth: 1685, iv. 474; ~ address from, to James II, 1688, iv. 609 & n. 8; delay in setting out, 1689, iv. 631, 639, 642; inferior to French fleet, 1690, v. 27 & n. 2; escorting Queen Maria Anna to Spain, 1690, v. 2 & n. 2; command of, 1693, v. 131 & n. 1; failure of, 1693: complaints in parliament about, v. 161 & n. 2; at sea, 1701, v. 462 & n. 2.
— — — officers and seamen: gentlemen or tarpaulins, v. 10 & n. 3, 11; *see also* v. 27; difficulty of raising seamen, 1689, iv. 637; pressing, iv. 601; v. 449 & n. 1, 587; losses by sickness in West Indies, 1697, v. 268 & n. 1.
— — — admirals of the fleet: *see*: Percy, Algernon, earl of Northumberland (v. 586–7); James, duke of York (1664–5; appointed, iii. 389, n. 2; superseded, iii. 413, n. 1, 414 & n. 2); Mountagu, Edward, earl of Sandwich (1665; iii. 413 & n. 1); Monck, George, duke of Albemarle, and Rupert, Prince (joint command, 1665–6; iii. 424–5 & n.); James, duke of York (1672; iii. 614 *bis*); Russell, Edward, earl of Orford (appointed, 1693, v. 157 & n. 2; resigns, 1699, v. 325 & n. 4).
— — miscellaneous notices: books or MSS. relating to navy, iv. 215; projected history of navy (by Pepys), v. 538 & n. 4; council of war: trial by, v. 526–7; at Deptford: uses Slaughter-house, iii. 352 & n. 2; dockyards: *see* Chatham; Deptford; &c.; prizes: rules relating to opening, v. 522 & n. 1; *see also* Ships and Shipping: *Golden Phoenix* and *Slothany*; timber: felling of, for navy, 1649–60, iii. 170 & n. 3, 343 & n. 3, 428, n. 2; supply of: inquiries concerning, by Commissioners of the Navy, i. *16*; iii. 340 & n. 1.
— oaths [for general notices on use of, *see* Oaths]:
— — Oaths of Supremacy and Allegiance: office-holders required to take, iv. 7, n. 4; taken by: E, iv. 10, 491, 494; ~ Sir J. Williamson, iii. 601; ~ peers, iv. 442 & n. 4; dispensed with, 1686, iv. 509–10 & n.
— — Oath of Allegiance: J.P.s' right of imposing, iv. 159, n. 3; to Charles I: E takes, ii. 16, 29; to Commonwealth, &c.: E refuses, iii. 15–16, 223; to James II: bishops desire to salve theirs to, iv. 614, 626; to William and Mary: imposition of, on office-holders, iv. 634 & n. 3; ~ bishops, &c., and, iv. 628 & n. 4, 637 & n. 3; v. 59; ~ abstention from: penalty for, iv. 648, n. 6; v. 48–9 & n.; to William III: required of lawyers, 1696, v. 242–3 & n.
— — Oath of Supremacy: obligatory on members of house of commons, iv. 159, n. 1.
— — other national or political oaths: Association, 1696, v. 242–3 & n.; coronation: Charles II takes, iii. 282 & n. 4; ~ new, for William and Mary, iv. 631 & n. 3, 632 & n. 5; Solemn League and Covenant: attacked in sermons, iii. 47, 274; ~ C. Wase refuses, iii. 55; ~ burnt by hangman, iii. 288–9 & n.; ~ to be abjured by all incumbents, iii. 331 & n. 3; Solemn Vow and Covenant (1643): E evades, ii. 81–2 & n. (i. 55).
— — officers' oaths: Clerk of the Council, iii. 601; Lord Privy Seal, iv. 494 & n. 3; members of Council for Foreign Plantations, &c., iii. 578, 627; Privy Councillor, iii. 578.
— — miscellaneous: administrator of estate of deceased person, v. 340; admission at Oxford, ii. 16; president of Royal Society, iv. 125; v. 305.
— officers and departments of state [the section comprises the officers and departments of state, &c., engaged in the general political and administrative activities of the government, apart from readily definable entities, such as the Customs, the Privy Council, and the Treasury. Notices relating to specialized departments and their officers, such as the Ad-

ENGLAND: officers of state, &c. (*cont.*) miralty and the Lord High Admirals, are indexed under the departments. The officers, &c., taking part in Charles II's coronation procession (iii. 278–81) are not indexed separately]:
— — general notices, relating to officers of state and members of the royal household:
— — — white staffs: officers bearing: list of, iv. 536, n. 2; Lord High Steward breaks his on completion of duty, iv. 233; broken by bearers on king's burial, iv. 415 & n. 3; mentioned as insignia of office, iv. 416, 417, 627.
— — — officers in general (including white-staff officers): imprisoned, &c., 1641, i. 26; changes among, Aug. 1684, iv. 387–8; retain their offices on James II's accession, iv. 412; appointments, Feb. 1685, iv. 416–17 & nn.; attend Lord Lieutenant of Ireland on his departure from London, iv. 491; dismissals of, closeting, &c., 1687, iv. 536 & n. 2, 540–1 & n., 544; appointments, 1689: delay in, &c., iv. 627 & n. 2; ~ given to members of parliament, iv. 629, 631 & n. 6; ~ generally unsatisfactory, iv. 629, 639, 646; conduct of former: inquiry into, v. 4 & n. 1; salaries of: proposed reduction of, during French war, v. 78 & n. 2; appointments, 1694, v. 177 & n. 1; all office-holders required to sign Association, 1696, v. 242–3 & n.; expected changes of, 1699, v. 325; new appointments, 1700, v. 406 & nn. 1–3, 431 & n. 3, 432 & nn. 2, 3, 438 & nn. 2–4; resignations of, 1701, v. 452 & n. 1; expected dismissals of, 1704, v. 567 & n. 1; changes in, 1705, v. 612 & n. 1.
— — — — exclusion of, from house of commons: bill for, rejected, 1693, v. 126 & n. 3; clause enacting, in Act of Succession, repealed, v. 621 & n. 3.
— — particular officers of state and their departments, &c.:
— — — Earl Marshal: dignity of, iii. 596, n. 1; office of: books, &c., relating to, iv. 144; individual Earls Marshal: *see* Howard, Thomas, earl of Arundel (1621–46; ii. 27, n. 4, &c.); Howard, James, earl of Suffolk (acting, 18–24 April 1661; iii. 277, n. 3, 280); Howard, Henry, sixth duke of Norfolk (1672–84; acquires dignity, iii. 595–6 & n.); Howard, Henry, seventh duke of Norfolk (1684–1701; iv. 412 & n. 7); Howard, Charles, third earl of Carlisle (acting, 1702; v. 493, n. 1).
— — — Lord Chancellor [in connexion with the Great Seal, and holders of the office; for the High Court of Chancery and its officers *see* justice: administration of *above*]:
— — — Great Seal (the object): brought to Windsor on Lord Keeper's death, 1685, iv. 466; carried away by James II, iv. 616 & n. 1; new: delay in preparing, 1689, iv. 627; procedure: grant under, iv. 533, n. 2; dockets for, iv. 503 & n. 6, 509; immediate warrants for, iv. 510 & n. 1.
— — — Lord Chancellor or Lord Keeper: *ex officio* member of Council for Foreign Plantations, iii. 571, n. 1; office of: emoluments of, v. 611 & n. 2; occupies York House, iii. 162, n. 1; individual keepers of the Great Seal, &c. (distinguished as Chancellor, (Lord) Keeper, &c.):
— — — — 1587–91: Sir C. Hatton, Chancellor.
— — — — 1621–5: John Williams, archbishop of York, Keeper.
— — — — 1625–40: Thomas Coventry, Baron Coventry, Keeper.
— — — — 1640–1: Sir John Finch, Baron Finch, Keeper.
— — — — 1645–50: Sir Richard Lane, Keeper.
— — — — 1649–53: B. Whitelocke, Commissioner (parliamentary).
— — — — 1653–4: Sir Edward Herbert, Keeper.
— — — — 1658–67: Sir Edward

ENGLAND: officers of state, &c. (*cont.*)
Hyde, earl of Clarendon, Chancellor; dismissal of, &c., iii. 493–4 & nn., 498 & n. 1, 502 & nn. 1–4.
— — — — 1667–72: Sir O. Bridgeman, Keeper.
— — — — 1672–3: Sir A. A. Cooper, earl of Shaftesbury, Chancellor.
— — — — 1673–82: Sir Heneage Finch, earl of Nottingham, Keeper to 1675, then Chancellor.
— — — — 1682–5: Sir Francis North, Baron Guilford, Keeper.
— — — — 1685–8: Sir George Jeffreys, Baron Jeffreys, Chancellor; appointed, iv. 466 & n. 5.
— — — — 1689–93: commissioners, including Sir J. Maynard; appointed, iv. 629 & n. 2.
— — — — 1693–1700: Sir John Somers, Baron Somers, Keeper to 1697, then Chancellor; appointed, v. 135; dismissed, v. 406 & n. 1, 407 & n. 1.
— — — — 1700, April-May: office vacant, v. 407–8 & n., 413.
— — — — 1700–5: Sir Nathan Wright, Keeper: appointed, v. 413 & n. 3.
— — — — 1705–10, 1714–18: William Cowper, Earl Cowper, Keeper to 1707, then Chancellor; appointed, v. 611 & nn. 1, 2.
— — — Lord Great Chamberlain: *see* Bertie, Robert, earl of Lindsey (1625–42); Bertie, Montague, earl of Lindsey (1642–66).
— — — Lord High Steward: trials by, ii. 10, n. 4; v. 129 & n. 2; presides at impeachments, ii. 27 (i. 20); iv. 226, 232–3; individual stewards: *see* Howard, Thomas, earl of Arundel (1641); Finch, Heneage, earl of Nottingham (1680).
— — — Lord President of the Council: *see* Hyde, Lawrence, earl of Rochester (1684–5; appointed, iv. 387); Savile, George, marquis of Halifax (1685; appointed, iv. 417); Spencer, Robert, earl of Sunderland (1685–8; appointed, iv. 490; dismissed, iv. 602, n. 2); Osborne, Thomas, duke of Leeds (1689–99; appointed, iv. 627); Herbert, Thomas, earl of Pembroke (1699–1702, 1702–8; appointed, v. 325 & n. 2).
— — — Lord Privy Seal:
— — — Privy Seal: the object, iv. 493, 513; procedure, &c.: commissioners for, 1685–7 (for appointment, &c., *see below*): activities of, iv. 494–535 *passim*; to be applied to dockets for Great Seal, iv. 503–4 & n., 509–10; use of, evaded, iv. 510 & n. 1; warrants for money and grants under, iii. 409 *bis*; iv. 498, 533 & n. 2; grant under, to E, iv. 550–5 *passim*.
— — — Lord Privy Seal: oath of, iv. 494 & n. 3; lodgings of, in Whitehall, iv. 500 *bis*; individual Lords Privy Seal, &c.:
— — — — 1661–73: John Robartes, Baron Robartes, later earl of Radnor.
— — — — 1682–5: George Savile, marquis of Halifax.
— — — — 1685: Henry Hyde, earl of Clarendon; appointed, iv. 417 & n. 3; not reappointed, 1687, iv. 540.
— — — — 1685–7: commissioners (E; Robert Spencer, Viscount of Teviot; Col. R. Phelips); to be appointed, iv. 464; sworn in, &c., iv. 493–4 & nn.; qualify under Test Act, iv. 500 *bis*; activities of: *see above*; superseded, iv. 540.
— — — — 1687–8: Henry Arundell, Baron Arundell of Wardour; appointed, iv. 540 & n. 2.
— — — — 1689–90: Halifax, *as above*.
— — — — 1690–2: commissioners (William Cheyne, Lord Cheyne; Sir J. Knatchbull; Sir W. Poultney); appointed, v. 7 & n. 5.
— — — — 1692–9: Thomas Herbert, earl of Pembroke.
— — — — 1700–1: Forde Grey, earl of Tankerville.
— — — Clerks of the Privy Seal, iv. 494, n. 4; *see also* Bickerstaffe, Sir C. (iv. 378, n. 2).
— — — Lords Justices: *see* crown *above*.

ENGLAND: officers of state, &c. (*cont.*)
— — — Secretaries of State:
— — — — general: status of, iii. 526, n. 7; payments made by, to predecessors, on entering office, iv. 39, n. 1, 245, n. 5; *ex officio* members of Council for Foreign Plantations, iii. 571, n. 1; lodgings of, iv. 191, n. 3, 403, n. 5; in ceremonies, iii. 277 & n. 7, 349; as political agents, iii. 300, 431, 434; order issued by, 1688, iv. 585 & n. 3; ordered to help E with History of Dutch War, iii. 550, 559; *see also* iii. 568; clerks in office of: *see* Bridgeman, W.; Williamson, Sir J.
— — — — principal secretary: as keeper of the Signet, iv. 494, n. 4; clerks of the Signet, iv. 494 & n. 4; *see also* iv. 378, n. 2.
— — — — individual secretaries: see Carey, Lucius, Viscount Falkland (1633–43); Nicholas, Sir Edward (1641–9, 1652–62); Morice, Sir W. (1660–8); Bennet, Henry, earl of Arlington (1662–74); Trevor, Sir John (1668–72); Coventry, H. (1672–80); Williamson, Sir J. (1674–9; appointed, &c., iv. 38–9 & n.); Spencer, Robert, earl of Sunderland (1679–81, 1683–8; dismissals of, 1681, 1688, iv. 245 & n. 5, 602 & n. 2; rumoured reappointment of, v. 49, n. 2); Jenkins, Sir L. (1680–4); Conway, Edward, earl of Conway (1681–3); Godolphin, Sidney, earl of Godolphin (1684); Middleton, Charles, earl of Middleton (1684–8; appointed, iv. 387–8 & n.); Graham, Richard, Viscount Preston (1688); Talbot, Charles, duke of Shrewsbury (1689–90, 1694–8; appointed, v. 177 & n. 2); Finch, Daniel, earl of Nottingham (1689–93); Sidney, Henry, Viscount Sydney, later earl of Romney (1690–2); Trenchard, Sir J. (1693–5); Trumbull, Sir W. (1695–7); Vernon, J. (1697–1702); Villiers, Edward, earl of Jersey (1699–1700); Hedges, Sir C. (1700–1, 1702–6).
— — minor officers:
— — — alienation office: commissioner of the, 1689–1702: *see* Glanville, William, sen.
— — — clerk of the crown, 1685: *see* Barker, H. (iv. 494 & n. 2).
— — — keeper (master) of the state paper office: *see* Williamson, Sir J. (iii. 526 & n. 6, 563).
— — — master of requests, 1661: *see* Fanshawe, Sir R.
— — — master of the rolls: chapel of: *see* London: topography; individual master: *see* Trevor, Sir J. (iv. 590, n. 4).
— — — postmaster-general (joint): *see* Cotton, Sir Robert (1691–1708); Evelyn, (Sir) John (1708–).
— — — receiver and remembrancer of the First Fruits, &c.: *see* Treasury *below*.
— — — secretary at war, 1683–9, 1689–1704: *see* Blathwayt, W.
— — — secretary for Ireland, 1690–1702: *see* Southwell, Sir R.
— — — secretary to Lords of Trade, 1679–96: *see* Blathwayt, W.
— — — stamp duties: receiver for, 1704–8: *see* Evelyn, (Sir) John (appointed, &c., v. 556 & n. 1).
— — — surveyor-general, 1649–60: *see* Webb, Col. W.
— — — surveyor-general of crown lands: *see* Harbord, Sir C. (1633–79); Travers, S. (1693–1710).
— — — vicar-general: powers of, iv. 519.
— Ordnance: officers of the:
— — master: *see* Compton, Sir W. (1660–3); Chicheley, Sir Thomas (1670–4); Legge, George, Baron Dartmouth (1682–8); Sidney, Henry, earl of Romney (1693–1702); Churchill, John, duke of Marlborough (1702–11; appointed, 1700 (error), v. 438 & n. 3).
— — lieutenant: *see* Legge, Col. W. (1660–70; iii. 443, n. 1; *add.*; iv. 314 & n. 3); Walter, D. (1670–9).
— — commissioners and other officers, 1666 (John Berkeley, Baron Berkeley of Stratton, &c.), iii. 442–3 & n.; *add.*

ENGLAND (*cont.*)
— pardons, general: act of amnesty desirable, 1689, iv. 628; act for, 1690, v. 23 & n. 4; James II offers: 1689, iv. 642; ~ 1693, v. 140.
— peerage: *see* Parliament.
— petitions:
— — political [*see also* addresses *above*]: to Monck (Albemarle) for re-establishment of parliament, 1660, iii. 241 & n. 2; to Charles II, for meeting of parliament, Dec. 1679, &c., iv. 193, n. 1; City of London to Charles II, on *Quo Warranto* proceedings, 1683, iv. 319 & n. 1; peers in London to James II for parliament, Nov. 1688, iv. 608 & n. 4; Kentish Petition, 1701, v. 457 & n. 2, 461.
— — miscellaneous: merchants to Charles II about Jamaica, 1660, iii. 257 & n. 2; to Charles II for relief of poor of Deptford, 1684, iv. 365.
— plots [*see also* Gunpowder Plot; Popish Plot; Rye-House Plot; Lancashire Plot; Assassination Plot; *and* Jacobites]: 1658: Mordaunt and Hewit tried for, iii. 214 & nn. 3, 4; 1689: arrests for, iv. 643 & n. 3; 1691: sham (W. Fuller), v. 78 & n. 1; 1697: reported, v. 264 & n. 2; *add.*
— political: constitutional [general subjects and terms; particular constitutions]:
— — constitution in general: future of, on extinction of house of Stuart, iv. 646; ~ reflections on, 1700, v. 402–3, 408; the monarchy: Shaftesbury's views on, iv. 328; ~ James II's attempt to make himself absolute, v. 475; ~ the king can do no wrong: in lords' debate on settlement of crown, iv. 619; fear of military rule, &c.: *see* army: standing army *above*.
— — — Agreement of the People: discussed, ii. 546, n. 1; Humble Petition and Advice: alluded to, iii. 190–1 & n.
— — — terms: civil list, v. 282 & n. 1; premier minister, iv. 501 & n. 4; prime favourite, iv. 549; prime minister, iv. 118 & n. 4; *see also* iv. 130.

ENGLAND: political (*cont.*)
— — miscellanea: right of the flag: claim to, iii. 606 & n. 1; ~ in E's *Navigation and Commerce*, iv. 30, 41; Charles II's death-bed silence about the country's future, &c., iv. 409 & n. 3; economic exhaustion, 1696, v. 255.
— — public opinion and the condition of the country [*see also* Commonwealth and Protectorate, *and* army: standing army *above*]: the halcyon days, 1625–40, ii. 21 & n. 7 (i. 16); unrest, 1640–96: cause of, v. 230 & n. 5; burning of the Rumps, 1660, iii. 242 & n. 2; hope of re-establishment of constitution, iii. 243; Charles II's return to London, iii. 246; time of judgements, &c., 1666, iii. 464, 466; Stop of the Exchequer: destroys public confidence, iii. 607 & n. 1; general unrest, 1681, iv. 239–40; instability, 1683, iv. 320 & n. 2, 338; fear of arbitrary government, iv. 329; effects of Rye-House plot, iv. 330–1 & n.; apathy in foreign policy, iv. 331 & n. 5; disaffection: fear of, 1685, iv. 449, 460 & n. 3; suspension of Bishop Compton resented, 1686, iv. 524; discontent, 1688, iv. 590, 597 *bis*, 600; settlement of the crown, 1689: views on, iv. 614 & n. 4, 628; Queen Mary censured, iv. 625; bishops' conduct in Revolution questioned, iv. 626–7; discontent, &c., with new government: 1689, iv. 629–32 *passim*, 637, 639, 642, 646, 651, 654; ~ 1690, v. 4, 6, 21, 22, 39 *bis*; instability of the government, 1691, v. 60; rumours of rebellion, 1692, v. 97; unsettled state, 1694, v. 178; grief for Queen Mary, v. 201 & n. 3, 203, 207; nation in decline, 1696, v. 246; risings, 1697(?), v. 263 & n. 5; death of William III: effects of, on, v. 491–2 & n.; popularity of Queen Anne's government, &c., 1702, v. 516, 521; political instability, 1705, v. 611–12.
— — sermons [sermons dealing with or mentioning historical events

ENGLAND: political (*cont.*)
or current politics, apart from Gunpowder Plot, the execution of Charles I, the Restoration, and the Revolution, when they occur in sermons in the commemorative services]: Reformation, v. 227; Spanish Armada, *ib.*; Gunpowder Plot, *ib.*; Civil War, *ib.*; state of England, 1650–1, iii. 18, 37, 44; changes of government, 1657, iii. 197; miseries following sin, 1659, iii. 232; Restoration, iii. 262, 304; time of calamity, &c., 1679–80, iv. 168 *bis*, 193, 197, 223; sedition, &c., 1681, iv. 250; dangerous times, &c., 1682, iv. 275, 281; recent rebellions, 1685, iv. 458; Revolution, v. 227, 319, 559; growth of faction, &c., 1689–90, iv. 652; v. 23.
— Post Office [*see also* London: topography]: pension on, iv. 533; ~ proposed, v. 525 & n. 2; as security for Exchequer tallies, v. 253.
— Privy Council: *see* Privy Council.
— proclamations: *see* Proclamations.
— regents: *see* crown *above*.
— regicides: *see* Charles I.
— religion [notices are indexed as far as possible under the various churches and sects to which they apply more particularly; those relating to the Nonconformists in general, and to toleration, under Nonconformists, Puritans, and Sectaries; and general comments on the growth of atheism, &c., under Atheism and Atheists]: speech of bishop of Valence relating to, 1685, iv. 486 & n. 3.
— republicans: obtain recall of Long Parliament, 1659, iii. 228, n. 9; army officers displaced, 1660, iii. 241, n. 4 *ad fin.*; republican aims of Rye-House plotters, iv. 329; A. Sidney as, iv. 353; views, &c., of, 1689: *see* Parliament: parties.
— revenue [*see also* customs *and* excise *above*; taxation and taxes *below*]: crown lands: former income from, i. 14–15; grants to Charles II for life, iv.

ENGLAND: revenue (*cont.*)
417 & n. 6; inadequacy of, in Charles II's reign, iii. 607, n. 1; iv. 410 & n. 2; v. 401 & n. 1; James II demands, for life, iv. 443; granted to James II for life, iv. 443–4; further demands of James II, iv. 488 & n. 3; deficiency of, 1697, v. 278, 280; civil list voted, 1697, v. 282 & n. 1; public accounts: bill for taking, 1704, v. 560, 561, n. 1.
— royal household: *see* Royal Household.
— royal mint: *see* Royal Mint.
— royalists: *see* Royalists.
— seals: *see* officers, &c.: Lord Chancellor; Lord Privy Seal; Secretaries of State *above*.
— shipping: *see* merchant shipping *and* navy *above*.
— social:
— — calendar festivals: Christmastide: revels at Inns of Court, ii. 77 (i. 51); iii. 307–8 & n., 504; v. 280; at Wotton, ii. 11, n. 4; v. 283; at Sayes Court [E entertains his neighbours in most years from 1655–6 to 1684–5; *see also* iv. 495, 613. He mentions his tenants in 1656–7 and 1664–5; he specifies his parish neighbours in 1662–3 and his poor neighbours in 1664–5; the vicar attends in 1685–6]; proper enjoyment of: in sermons, v. 373, 483.
— — — New Year: rewards and gifts to servants, v. 554, 620; Twelfth Night: gaming at court, iii. 308 & n. 4, 504 & n. 1; ~ party, ii. 473; Plow Monday, iii. 396, n. 3; Shrove Tuesday: party (casual), iii. 369; May Day: in Hyde Park, iii. 285; St. Thomas à Becket's day: at English College, Rome, ii. 291 & n. 4.
— — coffee, tea, &c.: introduced, &c., i. 14–15 & n.; coffee-houses: news circulated by, i. *128*.
— — cosmetics: paint: women first use, iii. 97 & n. 2; ~ ladies using, iv. 336.
— — country gentry, iii. 552; iv. 255.
— — crime: prevalent: 1684, iv. 401; ~ 1699, v. 366 & n. 4;

ENGLAND: social (*cont.*)
abduction of heiress, v. 41 & n. 1; clipping money: *see* Currency; forgery, v. 246, 248, 288, 475; murders, iv. 274, n. 1, 401 & n. 1, 596–7 & n.; v. 83 & n. 4, 129 & n. 2, 175; perjury, v. 196; ~ trial for, &c.: *see* Oates, T.
— — dancing: balls: at court, iii. 350 *bis*, 351–2, 569 & n. 2, 630; iv. 101, 123–4; v. 362, 528; ~ given by duchess of York, iv. 103; ~ private, iv. 30 *bis*; masques at court, iii. 357 & n. 1, 397; lessons, ii. 20 (i. 16); iv. 271, 423.
— — debt: arrest for, in private house, iv. 333–4; imprisonment for: in sermon, v. 346; prisoners for: relief of: *see* Charity.
— — duelling: *see* Duels.
— — family:
— — — children: the mother's upsitting after child-birth, iv. 591; wet-nurses employed, ii. 6 (i. 6); iii. 211(?), 371(?); nurse and nursemaid (?), iii. 145, 208, 209; nursery: conditions in, iii. 206, 209; child's coats, iii. 468 & n. 4.
— — — marriages: courtship and negotiations for, ii. 535, 536; iii. 475, 519; iv. 69, 123, 189, 192, 193, 194, 195–6, 245–7, 248, 425–6, 454–5, 502–3; v. 133, 138, 588, 602, 605, 606, 607; suitable age and parties' consent required, iv. 246, 247, 248, 425; contract, iv. 194; settlements, iii. 172; iv. 192, 193, 194; v. 605, 606, 607; dowry (portion), i. 8; iv. 426; v. 138; ~ father-in-law and, iv. 196, 415; jointure, i. 11; iv. 194; v. 138; weddings, ii. 536; iii. 343, 551; iv. 194–5, 238, 352; v. 138, 609; ~ favours for guests, &c., iii. 622; iv. 567; ~ wedding-night, iii. 373, 511; ~ wedding-night customs, iii. 589, 590, n. 1; ~ complimentary visits, &c., following, iv. 567; v. 138–9, 609–10; ~ anniversaries of: feasts for, iii. 237; iv. 18, 34, 266, 644 & n. 2(?); irregularities: marriage between children and remarriage, iii. 622; iv. 184–5; ~ clandestine marriage, iv.

ENGLAND: social (*cont.*)
70; ~ elopement, iv. 460–1; ~ misalliances, iii. 592 & n. 5 and iv. 128 & n. 2; iv. 39, 461–2, 505 & n. 4; ~ abductions, &c., iv. 260–1 & nn., 354 & n. 6; v. 41 & n. 1, 528 & n. 8.
— — — divorce, &c.: cases: John Manners, Lord Ros, later duke of Rutland, iii. 545–6 & n.; Henry Howard, seventh duke of Norfolk, v. 90 & n. 7, 127 & n. 1, 380 & n. 3, 393–4 & n.; marriage annulled, v. 41, n. 1; marriage declared void, v. 528, n. 8 *ad fin.*
— — — in sermons: family prayers, iii. 356(?), 358(?); iv. 292–3; husbands and wives: relations of, &c., iii. 123, 518; iv. 359; parents and children: relations of, &c., iii. 226, 514, 558; iv. 257.
— — funerals [select; notices relating to the burial-service and funeral sermons are indexed under Church of England: worship, and appear under the present heading only for special features]: state, iii. 57, 224; v. 204 & n. 6; ~ 'private' (Charles II), iv. 415 & n. 3; public or quasi-public, iii. 307, 490, 619–20, 621; iv. 302; v. 289; nobleman's, ii. 28 & n. 3 (i. 20); ~ in comparison, v. 359–60; deceased desires simple, ii. 13 (i. 11); *see also* v. 205; burial in sea, v. 497 & n. 3.
— — — corpse: embalmed, &c., iv. 151, 276; encased in lead, iii. 378; v. 319, 497; transported to distant burial-place, iv. 151–2; *see also* iv. 161; ~ shorter journeys, iii. 76, 545; v. 319, 385; custom of family staying at home from death until burial, iv. 302, 464.
— — — burial: attendance at service, iii. 378; v. 360 & n. 1; ~ coaches, iii. 76, 185, 490, 545; iv. 430; funeral effigies, ii. 28 (i. 20); iii. 224; herald attends, v. 55; *see also* iii. 57, 224; mourning: gift of, v. 538 & n. 6; ~ rings, iii. 210; iv. 430; v. 538, n. 6; night or evening as time of, ii. 15 (i. 12), 26 (i. 19), 28 (i. 20), 556; iii. 210, 541; iv.

ENGLAND: social (*cont.*)
15, 415 & n. 3; pall at, iii. 57, 224; iv. 203–4; v. 55, 538.
— — — panegyric after burial, v. 365–6; visits of condolence, iv. 152, 432; intended transfer of remains, iii. 210; iv. 430.
— — hospitality [select; ordinary visits to houses, dinner-parties, &c., are not indexed collectively; for select dinner-parties, &c., *see* Meals]: the ancient: houses suitable for, ii. 4 (i. 5); iii. 553; iv. 481; v. 427; ~ practised, v. 357, n. 3, 358; house-parties: large or noble, iii. 589–92; iv. 113–20, 480–2, 592–6; ~ visits to relations, iii. 101–3, 111–17, 121–3, 133–4; *see also* iii. 76; house-warmings, iv. 50, 504, 606; welcoming visitors by intoxicating their servants, iii. 112–13 & n., 525.
— — household (family): management of, &c., iv. 594; *see also* ii. 3 (i. 5); numbers in: Euston, iv. 118; ~ Wotton, 1702–3, v. 509, 550; servants: master dines at house of, v. 600; ~ New Year's gifts, &c., for, v. 554, 620; ~ wedding of: masters attend, iv. 194; ~ duties to, of masters (in sermons), iii. 226, 558; iv. 372; *see also* hospitality *above*.
— — housing, &c.: of gentry in country: in comparison, ii. 139 (i. 91); lodgings in Inns of Court: improvement of, 1640–1700, i. 18; fine bedsteads: former delight in, ii. 236.
— — jewellery: at court, iii. 505; iv. 51; *see also* iv. 268.
— — literacy: and Bible-reading: in sermon, v. 106.
— — lodging-house, v. 175.
— — manners: 'this refined age' (1661), iii. 304 & n. 6; influence on, of Charles II, iv. 409–10; reformation of: *see* morals *below*; old English, iv. 339; ~ George Evelyn as example of, v. 357–8 & n.; French: imitation of, iv. 339; ~ in sermon, iv. 308.
— — — 'journey of adventure and knight-errantry', iv. 71; bedroom: visitors received in, &c., iii. 397, 558; iv. 588; dressing-room: visitors in, iv. 8.
— — morals: immorality: prevalence of, iv. 585; v. 160, 331; ~ judgements on, iii. 316, 464, 569; v. 550; ~ on the stage: *see* Theatre; nation's failure to respond to good preaching, iv. 330; influence of Charles II on, iv. 478; youth contaminated, iv. 595.
— — — reform: James II and profanity, &c., iv. 437; sermons against sexual immorality ordered, v. 7–8 & n.; proclamations against immorality, v. 327–8 & n., 495 & n. 4; Societies for Reformation of Manners, v. 366 & n. 5; ~ sermons for, v. 391–2 & nn.
— — — in sermons: sins in general, iii. 222; iv. 84, 163, 271, 592; v. 4, 87, 335, 366, 378, 379, 390–1, 467; dishonesty, v. 249; ingratitude to God, iv. 488, 512; profanity or swearing, &c., iv. 182, 220, 229, 385, 387, 416, 459, 501, 512, 527, 556, 560; need for reform, &c., iii. 244, 537; v. 89–90, 121, 293, 319–20, 327–9, 484.
— — mourning: for kings, &c., iv. 414; v. 201, 204, 493, 494; room hung with black (royal), iv. 419; rings, &c.: *see* funerals *above*.
— — pressing: for army and navy, iv. 601; v. 449 & n. 1, 587.
— — promenade: in Hyde Park, iii. 82–3, 175, 213, 249, 285, 447, 481; iv. 171; pleasure-parties on Thames, iii. 372, 529–30.
— — sedan-chairs: early reputation of, i. 11–12.
— — servants: *see* household *above*; Evelyn: servants.
— — sheriff's following, ii. 11–12 & n. (i. 9–10).
— — suicides: frequent: 1694, v. 165 & n. 2; ~ 1702, v. 506; ~ 1705, v. 593; individual cases, iv. 20–1 & n.(?), 71, 326–7 & nn.; v. 170 & n. 3, 182 & nn. 2, 3(?), 417 & n. 2, 475–6 & n., 505–6 & n., 528 & n. 7, 593 & n. 2.
— — wealth and poverty: growth of luxury, iv. 8; private acts

ENGLAND: social (*cont.*)
relating to property: increasing number of, v. 209 & n. 7; *add.*; desire for wealth, v. 408; poor: condition of, in Leicestershire, iii. 122; ~ in winter, 1683–4, iv. 363, 364; ~ proposed tax for, v. 445; vagabonds, i. 32.
— — miscellaneous: May 1661 as time of universal joy, &c., iii. 285; reception of Arlington at Ipswich, iv. 115.
— state papers: borrowed by E from Clifford, iv. 18; collection formed by Sir Richard Browne, sen., iv. 303, n. 3; ~ papers from, lent to Burnet, iv. 241 & n. 3; State Paper Office: E borrows documents from, iii. 563 & n. 1; keeper of: *see* Williamson, Sir J.
— taxation and taxes:
— — general notices: heaviness of, 1692–6, v. 119, 169 & n. 4, 233, 246; in Essex after Civil War, iii. 159 & n. 2; collectors of taxes in Second Dutch War: London agents for, iii. 464, n. 1; for war in Ireland, 1689–90, v. 22; parliamentary inquiry concerning proceeds of, 1703, v. 529 & n. 1.
— — named taxes: customs (tunnage and poundage) and excise: granted, 1660, iii. 252; ~ king's powers under acts for, iv. 417 & n. 6; the Decimation, 1655, iii. 163 & n. 1; Hearth (or Chimney) Money: abolished, iv. 628 & n. 5; ~ suggested revival of, v. 202 & n. 6; Land Tax: bill for, 1689, iv. 628 & n. 5; ~ act for, 1693, v. 135 & n. 1; ~ bill for, 1699, v. 324, nn. 4, 5; poll-tax, 1660, 1689, 1690, iii. 258 & n. 1; iv. 639 & n. 3; v. 19 & n. 1; Ship Money, ii. 30 & n. 3 (i. 23); i. 26; ~ alluded to, v. 230 & n. 5.
— — taxes sometimes called subsidies or aids: grant, 1671: E commissioner for, iii. 576 & n. 3; grant, 1673: E commissioner for, *ib.*; ~ E raises money on, iv. 9 & n. 5; grants or votes, 1689, 1690, iv. 628, n. 5, 651 & n. 2; v. 4 & n. 1, 36 & n. 4; grant, 1701, v. 466 & n. 1, 468; grant, 1704, v. 559 & n. 2.

ENGLAND: taxation, &c. (*cont.*)
— — miscellaneous: coal: farm of export duty on, iv. 259 & n. 2; Million pound lottery loan, 1694: duties granted to finance, v. 177, n. 4; tax on births, marriages, &c., 1695, v. 202 & n. 6, 209 & n. 6; ~ preparation for collecting, v. 214 & n. 1; taxes on tea, coffee, &c., i. 14–15.
— trade and industry [*see also* merchant shipping *above*; Council of Trade and Plantations; &c.; East India Company; Guinea Company; Levant Company; Muscovy Company; *and* Trade and Industry]: mismanaged during Protectorate, iii. 187 & n. 4; injured by French attacks on shipping, 1689–95 [select notices], iv. 651–2; v. 145, 148, 174–5, 218; fall in value of East India Company shares, &c., 1694, v. 174 & n. 6; proposal for encouraging, 1700, v. 377–8 & n.
— — fishery: in E's *Navigation and Commerce*, iv. 30, 41; ironwork, iii. 112; leather: reported imposition on, 1640, i. 39 & n. 1; wool: former staple for, i. 56; *see also* ii. 83, n. 3; ~ transport of, discussed, iv. 17.
— — Canary Islands: merchants trading to, petition for charter, iii. 388 & n. 5; France: prohibits English imports, &c., 1701, v. 477 & n. 1; Jamaica: merchants' petition concerning, iii. 257 & n. 2; plantation trade: Darien adventure prejudicial to, v. 379 & n. 1; Russia: Tsar stops English trade with, 1649, &c., iii. 344 & n. 5; consulage: at Leghorn, iii. 629 & n. 5; ~ at Venice, iii. 630 *bis* & n. 1, 631 & n. 4.
— — retail trade: effect on, of William III's death, v. 493; shops: at Bristol, &c., iii. 102, 121, 130; in London, iii. 638 (extract from *State of France*).
— Treasury.
— — Lord High Treasurer: *ex officio* member of Council for Foreign Plantations, iii. 571, n. 1.
— — the Commissioners of the

ENGLAND: Treasury (*cont.*)
Treasury (or the Treasury): *ex officio* members of Council for Foreign Plantations, iii. 571, n. 1; as error for Lord High Treasurer, iv. 24 & n. 2, 28 *bis* & n. 3; administrative activities, &c. [similar notices, if particular Lord High Treasurers are concerned in them, are indexed under the Treasurers' names]: arrange three years' farm of Excise, 5 Feb. 1685, iv. 417 & n. 6; employ John Evelyn, jnr., iv. 565; and H. Slingsby's debts, iv. 567 & n. 1; payment by, for Greenwich Hospital, v. 244; report to, on damage at Sayes Court, v. 290 & n. 6; E's relations with: Sick and Wounded business (requests for money, accounts, &c.): 1667, iii. 483 & n. 6, 487, 490 & n. 4, 492, 494; ~ 1669–71, iii. 541 & n. 3, 565, n. 3, 597 & n. 5; ~ 1681, iv. 243 & n. 1, 244 & n. 2, 249; ~ 1688, iv. 570, 571, 581–2, 589(?); ~ alluded to, iv. 568; private claims, 1684, 1687, iv. 394 & n. 3, 398 *bis*, 537, 547; E opposes petition of duke of Leeds relating to Sayes Court, v. 195 & n. 2; unknown business, 1680, iv. 203.

— — the Exchequer: receipt of: removed to Nonsuch Palace, 1665–6, iii. 426–7 & n.; ~ removal of, to Nonsuch, ordered, 1666, iii. 454, n. 8; Stop of the Exchequer, 1672, iii. 606–7 & n.; ~ advised by Clifford, iv. 16; loan to, iv. 559 & n. 3; tallies and bills: discount on, 1696, v. 253 & n. 3, 255 & n. 2, 256; E and Auditor of, iv. 244; Chancellor of: *ex officio* member of Council for Foreign Plantations, iii. 571, n. 1.

— — personal: (i) Treasury:

— — — Lord High Treasurer or Commissioners of the Treasury (distinguished as Commissioners): *see*:

— — — — 1614–19: Thomas Howard, earl of Suffolk (iii. 140 & n. 7).

— — — — 1636–41: Dr. W. Juxon, bishop of London, &c. (iii. 274 & n. 1).

ENGLAND: Treasury (*cont.*)

— — — — 1643–6: Francis Cottington, Baron Cottington (ii. 561 & n. 4).

— — — — 1660: commissioners: secretary to (Sir P. Warwick), iii. 253, n. 2.

— — — — 1660–7: Thomas Wriothesley, earl of Southampton (iii. 253, n. 2).

— — — — 1667–72: commissioners: George Monck, duke of Albemarle (d. 1670), A. A. Cooper, Baron Ashley (later earl of Shaftesbury), Sir Thomas Clifford (later Baron Clifford), Sir W. Coventry, Sir J. Duncombe, iii. 487, n. 7; iv. 19.

— — — — 1672–3: Sir Thomas Clifford, Baron Clifford (iv. 19–20).

— — — — 1673–9: Sir Thomas Osborne, earl of Danby, &c., later duke of Leeds (iv. 13–14 & n.).

— — — — 1679–85: commissioners (appointed, iv. 166, n. 2; new commissions, Nov. 1679; four in 1684): Arthur Capel, earl of Essex (resigned Nov. 1679: iv. 201, n. 7), Sir E. Dering (iv. 203 & n. 1), Sir J. Ernle (iv. 533, n. 5), Sidney Godolphin, later earl of Godolphin (iv. 166, 387), Laurence Hyde, later earl of Rochester (until 1684: iv. 188, n. 6, 387), Sir S. Fox (Nov. 1679: iv. 193, n. 3); H. F. Thynne (1684: iv. 178, n. 4).

— — — — 1685–7: Laurence Hyde, earl of Rochester (iv. 417 & n. 3).

— — — — 1687–9: commissioners: John Belasyse, Baron Belasyse, Henry Jermyn, Baron Dover, Sir J. Ernle, Sir S. Fox, Godolphin, iv. 533 & nn. 2–5.

— — — — 1689–1702: commissioners (frequent new commissions): appointed, 1689, iv. 629 & n. 2, 631, n. 6; new commission, including Godolphin, 1690, v. 39 & n. 1; new commission, 1692, v. 90 & n. 4; Godolphin resigns, 1696, v. 261 & n. 1; Godolphin reappointed, 1700, v. 432 & n. 2, 438 & n. 2; other commissioners: Sir

ENGLAND: Treasury (*cont.*)
Thomas Pelham, later Baron Pelham (1697–9, &c.), v. 309 & n. 2; John Smith (1694–1701), v. 452 & n. 1.
— — — — 1702–10: Godolphin (v. 500 & n. 1).
— — — secretary to the Lord High Treasurer or to the Treasury: *see* Warwick, Sir P. (1660–); Lowndes, W. (1695–1724).
— — — solicitor to the Treasury: *see* Horneck, P. (1716–28).
— — personal: (ii) Exchequer:
— — — auditor: *see* Howard, Sir Robert (1673–98).
— — — chamberlain: *see* Hildyard, H., sen. (1660–74); Hildyard, P. (1674–93).
— — — chancellor: *see* Hyde, Sir Edward, later earl of Clarendon (1643–60); Cooper, Sir A. A., Baron Ashley, later earl of Shaftesbury (1661–72); Duncombe, Sir J. (1672–6; supersession of, iv. 267 & n. 3); Ernle, Sir J. (1679–89); Hampden, R. (1690–4); Montagu, Charles, later earl of Halifax (1694–9); Smith, John (1699–1701; resignation of, v. 452 & n. 1); Boyle, Henry, later Baron Carleton (1701–8).
— — — receiver of the first fruits and tenths: *see* Prettyman, Sir John (1660–3); Prettyman, W. (deputy or acting, 1663–78).
— — — remembrancer of the first fruits and tenths: office of: situation of, iii. 567 & n. 1; ~ mentioned, iii. 565, n. 2; individual remembrancers: *see* Prettyman, W. (deputy, 1669–76; sole, 1676–82); Farrington, G. (deputy, 1671–6); Porter, Sir Charles (1682–).
— — — tellers: *see* Downing, Sir G. (1657–84); Pinckney, L. (1660–1); Howard, Thomas (1689–1701).
— — — usher of the receipt of: reversion of (P. Packer, &c.), iii. 427, n. 2.
— weather and climate:
— — general: E's notices: reliability of, i. *106–7* & nn.; rain-gauge at Gresham College, 1695–6, v. 216, n. 5 (readings cited in later notes); weather diaries kept by W. Derham, 1697–9, v. 263, n. 2 (cited in later notes); England requires cold winters, v. 133; atmosphere, iv. 29; Bloomsbury: good air of, iii. 398 & n. 3; fogs, &c., iii. 565; iv. 101, 161 & n. 1; v. 363; ~ stinking, v. 298 & n. 1; hurricanes: by name, iv. 549; v. 2, 550; luminous cloud, 1643, ii. 80 (i. 54); ~ or meteor, 1680 (comet ?), iv. 235 & n. 1; pillar of light, 1665, iii. 403; storms: notable, *see below*, 1658, 1661–2, 1689, 1703; ~ notices from newspapers, v. 69 & n. 2, 261, 263, 473 & n. 3, 486 & n. 4 [some other notices are in part dependent on newspapers]; two suns, 1696, v. 229.
— — chronological series [E's notices are at first infrequent; they become increasingly more frequent from about 1684, and there is a constant stream from 1691 to the end. References to all notices are given until 1691; thereafter references only to general statements or to notices of extraordinary events. Footnotes are cited only in special cases. The characterization of the seasons is E's, so far as he provides it; general statements after 1691, if not followed by page references, are summarized from E's notices. All general statements, apart from E's, are necessarily rough]:
— — — 1647–8: wet winter(?), v. 336.
— — — 1648: wet summer and autumn, ii. 546; v. 112.
— — — 1649: cold January, Thames frozen, ii. 547 & n. 5, 548.
— — — 1652: drought, heavy hail-storm, iii. 71; *add.*
— — — 1654: hot summer, iii. 104; *add.*
— — — 1655: storm, iii. 162.
— — — 1655–6: cold and long winter, iii. 165 & n. 4; storms, iii. 169 *bis*.
— — — 1656: hot July, iii. 176; snow, iii. 185.

ENGLAND: weather, &c. (*cont.*)
— — — 1657: wet and sickly summer, &c., iii. 196 & n. 5, 197.
— — — 1657–8: extremely cold winter, Thames frozen, iii. 206 & n. 1, 211 & n. 2; ~ false statement, v. 2.
— — — 1658: cold spring, iii. 214; storm, 30 Aug., iii. 220 & n. 2; ~ and Cromwell's death, v. 2 & n. 3.
— — — 1660: seasonable spring, iv. 636; *see also* iv. 635; rain, iii. 250.
— — — 1661: wet summer and autumn, iii. 296.
— — — 1661–2: wet and warm winter, iii. 311 & n. 4; storm, 17–18 Feb., and Queen of Bohemia's death, iii. 316 & n. 3; v. 2 & n. 4.
— — — 1662: wet but healthy, iii. 350; storm, iii. 328 & n. 1; Thames frozen, Dec., iii. 347 & n. 2.
— — — 1663: wet and cold July, iii. 358.
— — — 1664–5: cold winter, iii. 393, 394 & n. 4.
— — — 1665: storm, iii. 417.
— — — 1666: dry summer, iii. 451 & n. 6, 452, 466; east wind, 1–4 Sept., and Fire of London, iii. 451 & n. 6, 454 & nn. 1, 7, 456; wet October, iii. 466.
— — — 1667: cold winter, backward spring, iii. 472, 477 & n. 2, 478.
— — — 1669: cold December, iii. 541.
— — — 1670: wet and stormy, iii. 569; gale, Jan., iii. 542; fog, Dec., iii. 565.
— — — 1671: storm, iii. 586 & n. 3.
— — — 1672: snow, Feb., iii. 601.
— — — 1675: dry summer and autumn, iv. 76.
— — — 1676: mist, iv. 101; cold December, Thames frozen, iv. 103 *ter* & n. 3, 104.
— — — 1678: hot and sickly autumn, iv. 148, 152; casual notices, iv. 136, 144.
— — — 1679: 'black Sunday', 12 Jan., iv. 161 & n. 1; wet and sickly October, iv. 182.
— — — 1680: casual notices, iv. 204 *bis*, 207.

ENGLAND: weather, &c. (*cont.*)
— — — 1680–1: cold winter and spring, iv. 235, 237, 239.
— — — 1681: dry early summer, &c., iv. 243, 247, 249 *ter*.
— — — 1682: wet April, iv. 280.
— — — 1683: cold February, iv. 305; hot March, wet April, iv. 311–12.
— — — 1683–4: extremely cold winter, frost fair on Thames, &c., iv. 357–66 & nn., *passim*, 394, 450; ~ effects of: E's account of, iv. 362, n. 4, 365, n. 1, 376 & n. 1; ~ in comparison, v. 263.
— — — 1684: late spring, &c., iv. 374, 375, 379; dry summer, iv. 383–6 *passim*, 450; rain, iv. 388.
— — — 1684–5: cold winter, Thames frozen, iv. 394, 401, 402 & n. 1, 450.
— — — 1685: dry May and June, iv. 446, 449, 450 *bis* & n. 3; casual notices, iv. 433, 472.
— — — 1685–6: wet and mild winter, iv. 487, 490 & n. 1, 495, 497; frost, iv. 498.
— — — 1686: wet summer, iv. 509–23 *passim*.
— — — 1687: mild January, iv. 535; wind, iv. 549, 550, 556.
— — — 1687–8: stormy winter, backward spring, iv. 564, 567, 581 *bis*.
— — — 1688: bad June, iv. 590, n. 1; wind, Oct.: direction of, iv. 600 & n. 2, 601; storm at sea, 20 Oct., iv. 603 & n. 7; wind, early Nov., iv. 605 & n. 2.
— — — 1688–9: cold winter, Thames frozen, iv. 607, 613 & n. 3.
— — — 1689: seasonable spring and summer, iv. 635 & n. 4, 636, 648; casual notices, iv. 643, 644, 647, 649; storm, 11 July (?), iv. 644 & n. 3.
— — — 1689–90: wet winter, iv. 651 *bis*, 654; v. 2, 4; gale, v. 2 & n. 1.
— — — 1690: stormy autumn, v. 31–6 *passim*.
— — — 1690–1: mild winter, later cold, v. 38–41 *passim*.
— — — 1691: very hot summer, &c., v. 58, 67–70 *passim*.

ENGLAND: weather, &c. (*cont.*)
— — — [From this passage to the end notices appear frequently, except on pp. 118–27 and 392–400; page-references are given henceforward only for general statements or extraordinary events.]
— — — 1691–2: warm winter, later snowy.
— — — 1692: backward spring, &c.; wet summer, v. 112 & n. 2.
— — — 1692–3: mild or warm winter, v. 130, 133.
— — — 1693: very wet summer and autumn, v. 157.
— — — 1693–4: cold winter; hard frost, v. 164.
— — — 1694: hot dry April; fine July; wet August.
— — — 1694–5: extremely cold winter, Thames frozen, v. 199–202 & nn., *passim*, 207–9 & nn., *passim*.
— — — 1695: dry summer, then wet and cold, v. 213, 215.
— — — 1695–6: mild winter, backward spring.
— — — 1696: wet and cold summer, v. 257.
— — — 1696–7: cold winter.
— — — [The text between February and August is missing.]
— — — 1697–8: cold winter, backward spring.
— — — 1698: dark and wet summer and autumn, v. 301.
— — — 1698–9: very wet winter, v. 336.
— — — 1699: fine dry year, v. 367; very hot June, v. 336; pleasant autumn, v. 361; fog, 8 Nov., v. 363 & n. 2.
— — — 1699–1700: mild winter.
— — — 1700: promising spring, v. 408; fine summer, v. 422, 429.
— — — 1700–1: mild winter; cold March, v. 452.
— — — 1701: dry spring; hot summer, v. 473.
— — — 1701–2: wet and warm winter, v. 487, 489.
— — — 1702: good harvest weather, &c., v. 514.
— — — 1702–3: mild winter; pleasant spring, v. 533.
— — — 1703: good harvest

ENGLAND: weather, &c. (*cont.*)
weather, v. 543, 544; the great storm, 26 Nov., v. 550 & n. 2; effects of: at sea, v. 551 & n. 2, 552 & n. 4; ~ on land, v. 552, 558; fast for, v. 556 & n. 2.
— — — 1703–4: mild winter.
— — — 1704: dry spring, v. 570; hot summer, v. 573; good harvest year, v. 580.
— — — [The text between December and February is missing.]
— — — 1705: hot and dry summer and autumn, v. 602, 604, 613.
— — — 1705–6: mild and stormy winter.
English Channel: *see* Dover Straits.
English language: the language of Queen Mary's days, iii. 130; improvement of: committee of Royal Society for, &c., iii. 396 & n. 4.
English residents abroad [men and women residing or travelling abroad for private business, &c. Diplomatists and consuls are indexed under Diplomatists; soldiers in foreign service under England: military. Ordinary travellers and royalist and Jacobite exiles are not indexed collectively]: Antwerp: ~ Lewkner, ii. 63 (i. 43); Florence: Sir Robert Dudley, titular duke of Northumberland, i. 115–16 & nn.; Genoa: Zacharias, — Tomson, ii. 171–2 (i. 108–9); Leghorn: general, ii. 183, n. 2; Leyden: wife of a Jew, ii. 54 (i. 37); Lisbon: Lady Tuke, iii. 511, n. 2; Naples: merchants, ii. 330 & n. 3; Orleans: English avoid residing at, ii. 138; Padua: unnamed, ii. 470, 473; ~ Thomas Howard, fifth duke of Norfolk, iii. 329; iv. 128 & n. 1; Paris: English at, use new style calendar for church festivals, iii. 2, n. 7; ~ noblemen at del Campo's academy, iii. 2; Rome: named residents, ii. 213 & nn. 2–8, 251, 311, 367 & n. 2, 400 & n. 3; iii. 33 & n. 6, 595; Venice: ships, ii. 429 & n. 3; ~ J. Hobson, ii. 476 & n. 3; *see also* ii. 469 & n. 6, 475; ~ Captain Powell, ii. 451–2, 468–9.
English spa, the (Harrogate), iii. 129, n. 6.

Engraving and Etching:
collections of prints: James, duke of York, iii. 44; Lincler, iii. 11; P. Morin, ii. 133 (i. 86); iii. 33; Poignant, iii. 35; E: buys prints, ii. 198; iii. 3.
engravers [personal notices]: F. Barlow, iii. 166 & n. 5; A. Bosse, ii. 568 & n. 3; S. della Bella, iii. 3 & n. 3; W. Hollar, i. 21–2 & nn.; R. Nanteuil, iii. 9–10 & n., 22 & n. 9; Perelle, iii. 3 & n. 4; Richett (P. Richer?), iii. 82; R. Waller, v. 176.
processes, &c.: mezzotint: Prince Rupert shows E the process, &c., i. *15–16*; iii. 271 & n. 4, 274 & n. 2; rolling-press, i. 35 & n. 1; taille douce, iii. 387 & n. 2; method of copying prints, iii. 163.
miscellaneous notices: Charles II discusses, iii. 310; drawings approved for engraving, iii. 356–7 & n.; v. 487 & n. 1; E takes drawings to France for engraving, ii. 557 & n. 3; Petty's map of Ireland engraved in Amsterdam, iv. 58 & n. 2; plates for: Chardin's *Travels*, iv. 369; ~ E's *Parallel of Architecture*, iii. 387; engraved views, &c.: frost fair, 1684, iv. 365; Greenwich Hospital, v. 399 & n. 2; Japanese and Chinese landscapes, &c., iii. 374 & n. 3.
— A. Tempesta, etching of a *Possesso*: as source for Diary, ii. 279, n. 3.
Enoch: in sermons, v. 114, 572.
Enos: in sermon, v. 62.
Enriquez de Cabrera, Don J. A.: *see* Medina de Riosecco, duke of.
Enstone (Ensham), Oxon.: Bushell's Wells at, iii. 382 & n. 6.
Entertainers and entertainments: animals, performing, iii. 256, 549 & n. 4; iv. 359; fire-eater(s), iii. 626–7 & n.; iv. 359; knife-eater, iv. 87; pantomimes, iv. 253; 'Paradise', Hatton Garden, iv. 24 & n. 6; puppet plays, &c.: *see* Theatre: miscellaneous; rope-dancers, iii. 27, 197–8 & n., 256; water-spouter, iii. 27 & n. 5; weight-lifter, iii. 256.
Enthusiasts: censured in sermons, iv. 521, 550, 646; v. 42, 253–4, 332, 348.
Ephesus: temple of Diana at: statue from, ii. 105 (i. 68); column from (?), ii. 202 & n. 4.
Ephraim: in sermon, iii. 188.
Epicurus: philosophy of: little known in England *c.* 1656, iii. 173 & n. 4; views of: in sermons, v. 94, 613.
Epidemics [*see also* Plague; Illnesses: smallpox]: rare in Paris, iii. 639 (extract from *State of France*); in England: sickly seasons, &c.: 1657, iii. 196 & n. 5; ~ 1658, iii. 213 & n. 3; ~ 1661, iii. 295, 296 & n. 4; cold, 1675, iv. 76; 'the new fever', 1678, iv. 148; ~ alluded to (?), iv. 152; fevers, 1684, iv. 386; ague, 1705, v. 585.
Epping Forest, Essex: houses, &c., in, iii. 538 & n. 1; iv. 305–6 & n.
Epsom (Ebsham, &c.), Surrey: as watering-place, iii. 544, n. 1; the waters, iii. 544 & n. 1; v. 250 & n. 1, 255; church: burials in: Richard Evelyn, iii. 545 & n. 6; ~ Mrs. Elizabeth Evelyn, v. 86, n. 3; vicar of: *see* Morehouse, Rev. John; road through, v. 168, n. 1; Richard Evelyn at, ii. 542; iii. 291; E at, iii. 14; ~ with Sir S. Tuke, iii. 371; *see also* Durdans; Woodcote Park.
Epte, river, ii. 121, n. 5.
Epulo, the rich: *see* Dives.
Erasmus: statue and birth-place of, at Rotterdam, ii. 33 & nn. 4, 5 (i. 25); portraits of, iii. 155 & n. 1, 263 & n. 2.
Eremitano, Alberto: bust of, ii. 463 & n. 4.
Ericis (Erycis) castellum, ii. 178, n. 10, 179, n. 2.
Eridanus, river (the Po), ii. 428 & n. 5.
Erik Eiegod, king of Denmark: influence of music on, iii. 168 & n. 3.
Erith, Kent, iii. 420, n. 2; Charles II at, iii. 414, n. 7; captured Dutch ships at, iii. 420 & n. 3; plague at, iii. 435, n. 1; Captain J. Cox at, iii. 509.
Ernle (Earnley), Sir John: appointed a commissioner of the Treasury, iv. 533 & n. 5.
Ernst August, elector of Hanover: geneal., v. 352, n. 5.
Ersfield, —: *see* Eversfield. J.
Erskin, —: *see* Eversfield, J.
Erskine, John, second earl of Mar: geneal., iv. 262, n. 1.

Erskine, John, sixth earl and titular duke of Mar: appointed secretary of state of Scotland, v. 611 & n. 3.
Erskine (Aerskin), William, Master of the Charterhouse: character, &c., iv. 262 & n. 1.
Esau: in sermons, v. 306 & n. 1, 564.
Escorial, the: P. Tibaldi employed at, ii. 494 & n. 6.
Esdras: autograph MS. by, ii. 421 & n. 6.
Esher, Surrey: rectory: held by E. Sclater, iv. 510, n. 1.
Espagne, Jean d', divine, iii. 181, n. 5; catechizes, iii, 181, 202–3.
Esseck (Eszek) on the Drave: the Turks at, 1690, v. 37 & n. 2.
Essex: the Essex petitioners, 1648, ii. 540–1 & n.; taxation in, during Civil War, iii. 159 & n. 2; control of Sick and Wounded in, 1664, &c., iii. 395, n. 1, 620, n. 1; clothing trade in, iii. 178; puritanism, &c., in, iii. 177, n. 3.
ruled by Coel, iii. 176, n. 5; 'the unwholesome Hundreds', iii. 178 & n. 5; ague contracted in, i. 14; former home of Browne family, iv. 304; Mrs. Evelyn and G. Tuke visit, iii. 182 & n. 7.
Essex: Earls of: own Cassiobury Park, iv. 199, n. 2.
Essex: Earls, &c., of: *see* Devereux, Robert, second earl; Devereux, Robert, third earl 1604–46; *new creation*: *see* Capel, Arthur, first earl, 1661–83; Capel, Elizabeth, his countess; Capel, Algernon, second earl, 1683–1710.
Essling, —: *see* Hesselin, L.
Essones: house of L. Hesselin at, ii. 120–1 & n. (i. 77–8).
Estampes: *see* Étampes.
Estcourt, Sir William: murdered, iv. 401 & n. 1.
Este family: owns Villa d'Este, Tivoli, ii. 394, n. 4.
Este, Ippolito d', cardinal: builds Villa d'Este, Tivoli, ii. 394, n. 4.
Este, Rinaldo d', cardinal: gives jousting, ii. 389, n. 3.
Estensis: *see* Leonius, J., called Estensis.
Estrades, Godefroi d'Estrades, comte d' (Count de la Strade or de Strade), iii. 55, n. 8; as governor of Dunkirk: sends E stolen portrait of Mrs. Evelyn, iii. 55–6, 62; ~ letter to, iii. 56; as French ambassador in England: encounter of, with Spanish ambassador, &c., iii. 297–300 & nn.; *add.*; ~ hears A. Morus preach, iii. 311 & n. 2.
Estrées, Gabrielle d': geneal., ii. 152, n. 4.
Eszek: *see* Esseck.
Étampes (Estampes), ii. 135 & n. 5 (i. 89).
Etcher, Dr. — (J. Eachard?): sermon by, iv. 397–8 & n.
Ethelbert, king of Kent: founds St. Paul's Cathedral, iii. 459, n. 6.
Etherege, Sir George: *see* Plays.
Etna (Ætna), Mount: eruption of, 1669: map, &c., of, iii. 539 & n. 2; crater of, ii. 335, n. 4.
Eton, Bucks.: in view, iii. 99.
Eton (Eaton) College, iv. 519; school: discipline in, ii. 11 & n. 1; election of scholars from, iv. 208 & n. 2; proposal to send E to, ii. 11 (i. 8–9); (Sir) John Evelyn at, v. 103, 110, 162, 201, 236; Sir W. Wyndham at, v. 237.
provosts: *see* Murray, T.; Monck, N. (1660–1); Allestree, R. (1665–81); Cradock, Z. (1681–95); Godolphin, Henry (1695–1733); vice-provost, 1686: *see* Godolphin, Henry; fellow: *see* Horne, T.; schoolmaster, v. 236.
E at, iii. 559–60; iv. 176 & n. 2, 181, 519; v. 110, 236–7.
Etruria: border of, ii. 208 & n. 4.
Eu: E at (?; as Ville-Dieu), ii. 536 & n. 6.
Euganean Hills: vegetation of, &c., ii. 480–1 & n.
Eugene (Eugenius), pope: picture of, ii. 310.
Eugene II and III, popes, ii. 242 & n. 6.
Eugene, Prince, v. 472, n. 3; campaigns of, in Italy: 1701, v. 472; ~ 1702, v. 488 & n. 2, 504 & n. 4, 510, 512 & n. 4; in battle of Luzzara, v. 514 *ter* & nn. 1, 4, 8; in battle of Blenheim, v. 574; prisoners taken at Blenheim allotted to, v. 577, n. 4; advances on Landau, v. 577, n. 3; in battle at Cassano (?), v. 607 & n. 4.

Eunuch, the (Acts, ch. viii): in sermon, iii. 227.
Eure: *see* Newry.
Eure, river: *see* Yèvre.
Eustace, St.: relics of, ii. 86 (i. 58).
Euston, Suffolk: Arlington's house and park at: E visits: 1671, iii. 589–92, 595–6; ~ 1677, iv. 113–20; notices, iii. 591–2 & nn.; iv. 116–18 & nn.; *see also* iii. 589, n. 1; chapel in: service in, iii. 590; library, iv. 121; mentioned, iii. 553, 554; iv. 112.
church: rebuilt by Arlington, iv. 114 & n. 5, 118; ~ service in, iv. 114; rector: *see* Mathew(s), R.
Euston: Earls of: *see* Fitzroy, Henry, earl 1672–5, later first duke of Grafton; Fitzroy, Charles, earl (courtesy title) 1683–90, later second duke of Grafton.
Euxine Sea: *see* Black Sea.
Evans, Rev. John, iv. 111, n. 3; presented to St. Ethelburga's, London, iv. 127 & n. 2; sermons by, iv. 111, 173.
Evans, John, D.D.; bishop of Bangor 1701–16; of Meath 1716–24: social, v. 568 & n. 1.
Eve: in sermons, iii. 26; iv. 75, 155; v. 316; *see also* Adam.
Evelin, Monsieur: *see* Yvelin, P.
Eveliniere, fief, iii. 548 & n. 3.
Evelinus (Ibelinus), lord of Baruth, iii. 548, n. 3.
Evelyn family: genealogical tables, i. 135–44; origin of, i. *1*; relationship of, with Yvelins of Normandy, iii. 548 & n. 3; views of, in Civil War, i. *6–7*; and Sir Edward Nicholas, i. 53 & n. 2; extinction of: prospect of, v. 337.
Wotton branch: continued ownership of Wotton desired by E, v. 337, 339, n. 2; (Sir) John Evelyn as only hope of continuance of, v. 318; burial-place of, in Wotton church, ii. 12–13 (i. 10); iii. 210, 378; iv. 430; v. 56, 319.
Evelyn, —, niece: marriage proposal for, 1668, iii. 519 & n. 3.
Evelyn, Anne, E's first cousin, daughter of John Evelyn of Godstone: *see* Hartop, Mrs. A.
Evelyn, Anne, E's niece, daughter of Richard Evelyn: *see* Montague, Mrs. A.
Evelyn, Anne, Lady Evelyn, wife of Sir John of Wotton, first bt., E's grandson, v. 600, n. 4.
as Anne Boscawen: geneal., iv. 147, n. 6; v. 258, n. 1; marriage of: proposal for, v. 588, 600, 602; settlement, v. 605, 607; receives Sacrament with her fiancé, v. 608; celebrated, &c., v. 609, 609–10; i. *36*.
as Mrs. Evelyn: visits Wotton, v. 613.
Evelyn, Arthur, brother of Sir Edward Evelyn, bt., E's first cousin once removed, v. 100 & n. 2.
Evelyn, Arthur, brother of Sir John Evelyn of Wilts, E's first cousin once removed: inherits land in Godstone, ii. 557, n. 4.
Evelyn, Catherine, E's aunt: *see* Stoughton, Mrs. C.
Evelyn, Catherine, E's great-niece, daughter of George Evelyn, jnr., of Wotton: *see* Fulham, Mrs. C.
Evelyn, Mrs. Catherine, born Gore, wife of George Evelyn, jnr., of Wotton, E's nephew, iv. 14, n. 2; v. 358 & n. 6; visits E, iv. 14; geneal., iv. 132, n. 6.
Evelyn, Catherine: *see also* Evelyn, Katherine.
Evelyn, Sir Edward, bt., of Long Ditton, E's first cousin once removed, iv. 434, n. 1; elected M.P. for Surrey, 1685, iv. 433–4 & n.; death, will, &c., of, v. 100 & n. 2, 337 & n. 1.
Evelyn, Edward, major, son of George Evelyn of Nutfield, E's first cousin once removed, v. 520 & n. 5.
Evelyn, Mrs. Eleanor (Hellen), E's mother, born Stansfield, wife of Richard Evelyn, sen.: appearance, character, &c., of, ii. 2–3 & n. (i. 4–5); birth of, ii. 1 & n. 2, 3; marriage of, ii. 1 & n. 3, 5, n. 7 *ad fin.*; children of, ii. 1; puts E out to nurse, ii. 6 (i. 6); dies, &c., ii. 12, 13–15 (i. 10, 11–12); grave of, ii. 26 (i. 19); portrait of, v. 359 & n. 9; property of, ii. 27, n. 2; v. 441, n. 5; geneal., i. 4 & n. 2; ii. 5 & n. 5 (i. 6).
Evelyn, Elizabeth, E's sister: *see* Darcy, Mrs. Elizabeth (1614–34).
Evelyn, Elizabeth, daughter of George Evelyn of the Six Clerks

Evelyn, Elizabeth, dau. of Geo. (*cont.*) (of West Dean), E's first cousin: *see* Tyrell, Elizabeth, Lady Tyrell.
Evelyn, Elizabeth, E's grand-daughter, daughter of John Evelyn, jnr.: *see* Harcourt, Mrs. E.
Evelyn, Elizabeth, E's great-niece, daughter of John Evelyn of Wotton: *see* Dyott, Mrs. E.
Evelyn, Elizabeth, daughter of Sir John Evelyn of Godstone, E's first cousin: *see* Hales, Mrs. E.
Evelyn, Elizabeth, daughter of Sir John Evelyn of Wilts, E's first cousin once removed: *see* Pierrepont, Mrs. E.
Evelyn, Elizabeth, 1667–85, E's daughter [her married name is unknown]: born and baptized, iii. 495 *bis* & n. 3; entrusted to Margaret Blagge (Mrs. Godolphin), iv. 35 & n. 4; confirmed, iv. 292; alluded to, iv. 424, 426 *bis*; elopes, iv. 460–2 & nn.; i. *31*; ill, iv. 463 *bis*; death and burial of, iv. 463–4; i. *31*; ~ alluded to, iv. 495; v. 432.
Evelyn, Elizabeth, E's niece, daughter of George Evelyn of Wotton, v. 359 & n. 2.
Evelyn, Mrs. Elizabeth, E's sister-in-law, born Mynne, wife of Richard Evelyn, ii. 542 & n. 3; wedding of, ii. 542–3 & n.; children of: births, &c., of, iii. 334, 376; ~ *see also* iii. 77, 155, 218; as godmother of children of E, iii. 75, 495; visits Whitehall(?), iii. 262; summons E to Richard Evelyn's sick-bed, iii. 517; and entail of Baynards, iv. 569, 582–3 & n.; v. 86; lodgings of, in London, iii. 510, 551; social, ii. 543; iii. 61, 63, 74, 78, 94(?), 98, 151, 171, 190, 194, 229–30(?), 358, 378, 428, 437, 495, 510 *bis*; ~ at time of Richard Evelyn's death, iii. 544, 545; ~ later, iii. 547, 581, 621 *bis*, 623; iv. 13, 14, 18; dies, &c., v. 86 & n. 3; geneal., iii. 183, n. 1, 218, n. 2.
Evelyn, Mrs. Elizabeth, formerly Mrs. Walsham, wife of George Evelyn of Huntercombe, E's first cousin once removed, iv. 177 & n. 2.
Evelyn, Elizabeth, Lady Evelyn, born Cockes, wife of Sir John Evelyn of Wilts, E's first cousin once removed, ii. 553, n. 7, 557.
Evelyn, Frances, E's aunt, i. 2, n. 2.
Evelyn, Frances, daughter of William Evelyn, E's first cousin twice removed, v. 340, n. 2.
Evelyn, Mrs. Frances, born Harvey, second wife of Thomas Evelyn of Long Ditton, E's uncle, iii. 63, n. 2.
Evelyn, Mrs. Frances, E's great-niece; daughter of William Glanville, jnr., and wife (1718) of William Evelyn, E's first cousin twice removed, v. 340, n. 2; as Frances Glanville, v. 340, 497.
Evelyn, Sir Frederick, third bt., i. *52*; v. 339, n. 2.
Evelyn, George, sen., 1526–1603, E's grandfather [he is distinguished elsewhere as 'George Evelyn, sen.'], i. *1–2*, 2–4 & nn.; as manufacturer of gunpowder, i. 2–3 & n., 52, n. 2; bequeathes Wotton to Richard Evelyn, sen., ii. 3–4; property of, ii. 557, n. 4; v. 478, n. 1; E names a son after, iii. 194; geneal., iii. 136, n. 6.
Evelyn, George, b. 1593, E's first cousin, son of Robert Evelyn: for possible identification *see* Evelyn, Captain George, traveller, &c. (ii. 551, n. 3; &c.); geneal., v. 574, n. 2.
Evelyn, George, 1657–8, E's son: born, &c., iii. 194 & n. 6; dies, iii. 210–11 & n.; mentioned, iii. 368, n. 1.
Evelyn, George, 1658, E's nephew, son of Richard Evelyn: baptized, iii. 218 & n. 1; dies, iii. 219.
Evelyn, Captain George, traveller and architect, E's kinsman, ii. 551 & n. 3; designs portico in garden at Wotton, *ib.*; i. 55; iii. 61, n. 1; social, ii. 551; iii. 85.
Evelyn, George, 1581–1637, of Everley and West Dean, one of the Six Clerks, E's first cousin: geneal., i. 3, n. 2; ii. 553, n. 7; iii. 91, n. 5; patronage of, i. 53, n. 2.
Evelyn, George, 1593–1657, of Huntercombe, E's first cousin, son of Thomas Evelyn: for possible identification *see* Evelyn, Captain George, traveller, &c. (ii. 551, n. 3, &c.).

Evelyn, George, 1630–99, of Huntercombe, E's first cousin once removed: house of, at Huntercombe, iv. 177 & n. 2.
Evelyn, George, 1641–99, of Nutfield, E's first cousin once removed, v. 56, n. 3; quarrels with his brother, i. 51–2 & n.; at funeral of John Evelyn of Wotton, v. 56; his ten children, &c., v. 187 & n. 1; appointed a deputy-lieutenant for Surrey, v. 169–70; dies, v. 333 & n. 1; geneal., iii. 84, n. 1; v. 202 & n. 5, 339, n. 2, 340, n. 2, 520, n. 5.
Evelyn, George, 1678–1724, of Nutfield, E's first cousin twice removed, v. 520, n. 5.
Evelyn, George, of Surrey: geneal., v. 574, n. 2.
Evelyn, George, 1617–99, of Wotton, E's brother [he is distinguished elsewhere as 'George Evelyn' or 'George Evelyn of Wotton'. Notices relating to 'my brother' between 1638 and 1669 may refer to George or to Richard Evelyn; when the abbreviated form 'my bro:' is used, both may be concerned. Such notices, when they record simple social intercourse, are not indexed; the remainder, unless they clearly refer to one or the other, are entered, with queries, under both brothers. Notices specifically relating to the two are entered under both]:
— character and career, v. 357–9 & nn.; i. *3–4*.
— chronological series:
— — born, ii. 1 & n. 5; education: at Guildford free school, v. 358; at Trinity College, Oxford, ii. 15 & n. 1, 17, 20 (i. 12, 13, 15–16); ~ advises sending E to Balliol, i. 13; at Middle Temple: admitted, ii. 15 & n. 4 (i. 12); ~ lodgings at, i. 12; ii. 24 & nn. 1, 4 (i. 18).
— — visits Lewes, &c.: 1638(?), ii. 21 (i. 16); ~ 1641, 1642, ii. 77 (i. 51), 79; marries Mary Caldwell, ii. 24 (i. 18); at Bath, 1640, ii. 25 (i. 18); visits: London, 1641, ii. 28(?); ~ Northampton Fair, 1642, ii. 78 (i. 51); views of, on Civil War, i. *6–7*; sends money to Charles I(?), i. 53;

Evelyn, George, 1617–99 (*cont.*)
visits Godstone, 1643(?), ii. 81; his wife dies, ii. 146 & n. 3 (i. 94); marries Lady Cotton, ii. 537, n. 2; describes Charles I's execution, ii. 547; ill, 1654, iii. 142; Lady Cotton dies, iii. 377.
— — as M.P.: service, 1645, &c., v. 358, n. 1; ~ elected for Surrey, Feb. 1679, iv. 164–5 & n.; ~ elected for Surrey, Aug. 1679, iv. 165, n. 1, 224 & n. 2; ~ candidate for Surrey, 1685, iv. 433–4 & nn.; *add.*; i. *31*, *32*, n. 1; as deputy-lieutenant for Surrey, v. 169–70; ill health of, v. 180; dies, v. 357 & n. 3; funeral, &c., of, v. 359–60 & nn.
— children, &c.: George: born, ii. 97 & n. 5 (i. 64); by Lady Cotton, ii. 537, n. 2; v. 359; ~ births of, ii. 544; iii. 62, 89 & n. 3; John Evelyn: negotiates marriage for, iv. 195–6 & n., 238; ~ announces death of, to E, v. 54, 55; surviving descendants of: 1691, v. 54 & n. 2; ~ 1699, v. 358 & n. 7, 359 & n. 2; *see further* property *below*.
— property:
— — business relating to his father's estate, ii. 26–7 & n. (i. 20); pays debt to E, 1649, ii. 557; E transfers mortgage to, 1668, iii. 509; payments to, from E, 1684, iv. 378, 380.
— — estates, &c.: Baynards: residuary interest in, iv. 582–3 & n.; v. 86; ~ alluded to, iv. 569; Denton: inherits, ii. 27, n. 2; Hurcott: sells manor of, to E, ii. 541 & n. 5; North Stoke: orders sale of, v. 441 & n. 5; Wotton: as owner of, ii. 4, 5; v. 478, n. 1; improves gardens, ii. 81 & n. 4 (i. 55), 551 & n. 4; iii. 24, 60–1 & n.; E becomes heir to, 1691, v. 54–5; business relating to(?), v. 67; makes agreement with E about timber at, 1692, v. 89, 93; settles on E, 1692, v. 103, 105, 359; invites E to live at, 1694, v. 179; proposed new settlement of: quarrels about, with E, 1698–9, v. 288 & n. 3, 292, 314 & n. 1, 336–9; ~ alluded to (?), v. 497.

Evelyn, George, 1617–99 (*cont.*)
— as patron of livings: Abinger, v. 181–2, 207, 216; Denton, v. 183; Wotton, iv. 558; v. 180, 181, 207, 216, 266–7.
— will, v. 359 & nn. 8, 9; cited, ii. 539, n. 2; executors of, v. 359, 377; provision in, for his granddaughters, &c., v. 337–9, 441; goods of: sold, v. 377.
— relations with E [exclusive of those concerning property, for which *see above*]: E's regard for, v. 55; books dedicated to, by E, ii. 547, n. 3; iii. 209, n. 1, 220; godfather to: E's son Richard, iii. 75; ~ grandsons of E, iv. 236; v. 263; E godfather to his daughter Mary (Lady Wyche), ii. 544; letters from, to E, 1685, iv. 434, n. 3; bequest made by, to E, v. 359 & n. 9; social [ordinary social intercourse is not indexed; notices of meetings in London and Deptford are frequent between ii. 546 and iv. 321; George's latest visit occurs at iv. 525, 526. E's visits to Wotton are indexed under Wotton]: takes leave of E, 1643, ii. 82 (i. 56); entertains E at Spring Garden(?), iii. 213.
— miscellaneous: letters from, ii. 15, n. 1; library of, v. 359; painting owned by, ii. 56 & n. 4; godfather to: — Smith, ii. 78; ~ son of Richard Evelyn, iii. 218; meets P. Yvelin, iii. 548; influence on, of William Glanville, sen., v. 497; stonehorse belonging to, ii. 557; residences: Wotton [notices relating to him as resident at are not indexed; for his improvements to the gardens *see* property *above*]; winters in London, 1653–4, iii. 92; lodgings of, in Covent Garden, 1655–8(?), iii. 148 & n. 2, 192, 212 & n. 5, 216, n. 1.
Evelyn, George, jnr., 1644–76, of Wotton, E's nephew, ii. 97, n. 5; v. 358–9 & n.; born, ii. 97 (i. 64); E visits, ii. 539 & n. 3; to live with E, iii. 64; to be educated with Lord Cavendish, iii. 65; travels abroad, iii. 354 & nn. 1, 2; visits E, iv. 14; wife of: *see* Evelyn, Mrs. Catherine; geneal., v. 54, n. 2, 282, n. 2, 358, n. 7; mentioned, ii. 146, n. 3; iii. 77; iv. 196, n. 1; *add.*
Evelyn, Mrs. Hellen: *see* Evelyn, Mrs. Eleanor.
Evelyn, Jane, E's sister: *see* Glanville, Mrs. J.
Evelyn, Jane, b. 1691, E's granddaughter: born and baptized, v. 80 & n. 1, 84.
Evelyn, Jane, d. 1662, niece, daughter of George Evelyn of Wotton, v. 359 & n. 2.
Evelyn, Jane, d. 1723, niece, daughter of George Evelyn (error ?), ii. 537, n. 2; v. 359, n. 2.
Evelyn, Jane, E's first cousin once removed, daughter of Sir John Evelyn of Godstone: *see* Leech, Jane, Lady Leech.
Evelyn, Jane, E's first cousin, daughter of Thomas Evelyn of Long Ditton: *see* Bodly, Jane, Lady Bodly.
Evelyn, Joan *or* Jane, E's first cousin, daughter of John Evelyn of Godstone: *see* Hart, Joan, Lady Hart.
Evelyn, Mrs. Joan (Joanna), E's grandmother, second wife of George Evelyn, sen., i. 2 & n. 2.
Evelyn, John:
— accidents and dangers [falls, &c., affecting E's health are indexed under Evelyn: health *below*; *see also* robberies and thefts *below*]:
— — thanksgiving for escape, v. 299 & n. 1; *add.*; escapes falling into fire, 1703, v. 549.
— — by road: coaches: accidents to, iii. 192, 411, 468; iv. 301; v. 547, 548, critical note; ~ way lost, v. 228; horse: in flood, ii. 83 (i. 56); ~ E escapes falling from, ii. 543–4; ~ E struck by, ii. 557.
— — by water: boats on rivers: accidents to, ii. 58 (i. 40), 547; iii. 522; bad landings at Calais, ii. 82 (i. 56); iii. 16; storms: danger by, ii. 82 (i. 56), 170 (i. 107–8), 178 (i. 112–13).
— — dangers, &c., due to persons: in Forest of Orleans, ii. 136 (i. 89); disturbances in Padua, 1645, ii. 472; shot at in Venice,

EVELYN, JOHN: accidents, &c. (*cont.*) ii. 475; arrested at Simplon hospice, ii. 512–13 & nn., 516, 518; threatened on account of preface to *Of Liberty and Servitude*, ii. 547 & n. 3; Bataille de Vambre, iii. 4–8; examined by soldiers at Canterbury, iii. 15; taken in Christmas raid on Anglican churches, 1657, iii. 203–4.

— — unspecified, iii. 185.

— and architecture:

— — taste in general, i. *17*, n. 1.

— — criticism of particular buildings [select: remarks expressing rather more than simple commendation or the reverse. *See further* Architecture: styles, &c.]:

— — — Byzantine and Romanesque: Pisa: Leaning Tower, &c., ii. 180 (i. 113–14); Venice: St. Mark's, ii. 436–7, 440.

— — — Gothic: Cambridge: King's College Chapel, iii. 138; Salisbury Cathedral, iii. 113; York Minster, iii. 129.

— — — sixteenth century, &c., to 1621: Frascati: Villa Aldobrandini, ii. 392, 393; Rome: Quirinal palace, ii. 237; ∼ S. Maria Maggiore, Cappella Paolina, ii. 243; ∼ St. Peter's, façade, ii. 258; ∼ Villa Medici, ii. 231; Chambord, ii. 139–40 (i. 91); Louvre, Grande Galerie, ii. 104 (i. 67); Audley End, iii. 140–1, 556; Hatfield House, ii. 80.

— — — contemporary, 1621–1706: Florence: Chapel of the Princes, ii. 198–9, 416–17; Rome: Palazzo Barberini, ii. 229; ∼ S. Carlo alle Quattro Fontane, ii. 242; ∼ S. Maria della Vittoria, façade, ii. 239; ∼ St. Peter's, baldacchino, ii. 261; Maisons, ii. 563; iii. 18; Paris: Luxembourg, ii. 128, 129 (i. 81, 82); ∼ St.-Louis, ii. 96 (i. 63–4); ∼ Sorbonne, ii. 97 (i. 64); Richelieu: the town, ii. 150 (i. 97); Amsterdam: new Stadhuis, ii. 43 (i. 31–2); Addiscombe: Draper's new house, v. 541; Althorp, iv. 70, 594; Eltham: Sir J. Shaw's house, iii. 375–6; Euston, iii. 591; iv. 116–17;

EVELYN, JOHN: architecture (*cont.*) London: Berkeley House, iii. 625; ∼ Clarendon House, iii. 470; ∼ Montague House, iv. 344–5; ∼ Northumberland House, garden front, iii. 216; ∼ St. Paul's, apse, v. 192; Newmarket: new palace (1670), iii. 554; Wotton House, portico in garden, i. 55; ii. 551.

— — Evelyn consulted about buildings, &c. [*see also* gardens and gardening *below*]: Fulham: monument to Lord Mordaunt in church, iv. 86; Greenwich Palace: Sir J. Denham's plan for rebuilding, iii. 300–1; ∼ Charles II's proposals for, iii. 313; London: E's suggestions for replanning, 1666, i. *20*; iii. 463 & n. 2; ∼ Berkeley House gardens: development of, iv. 381–2 & n.; ∼ Godolphin's house: construction of, iv. 98 *bis*, 99, 100; ∼ St. Paul's: E as a surveyor for repair of, 1666, iii. 448–9 & nn.; Norwich: Duke's Palace, iii. 593, 595; Oxford: Sheldonian Theatre, iii. 385.

— artistic interest [*see also* architecture *above*; collections; drawings and etchings; *and* gardens and gardening *below*]:

— — general: value of notices of works of art, &c., in Diary, i. *107–8*; origin of, i. *5*; E indebted to Arundel, iii. 326; influence of C. Maratti on E's taste, ii. 287, n. 7 *ad fin.*, 299, n. 4.

— — criticism of particular works of art [select]: paintings: C. Alberti, Sala Clementina ceiling, ii. 296; Carracci, Farnese gallery, ii. 215; Holbein, *Noli me tangere*, iv. 216–17; Kneller, portrait of E, 1689, iv. 644; Raphael, Galatea, ii. 357; Verrio, Windsor, St. George's Hall, &c., iv. 176, 316–17, 465.

— — — sculpture: ancient: Laocoon, ii. 304; ∼ Niobe and children, ii. 232; Florence, Baptistery doors, ii. 197; Michelangelo, tomb of Julius II, ii. 278.

— — miscellaneous: advises concerning Clarendon collection of

EVELYN, JOHN: artistic (*cont.*) portraits, i. *21*; iii. 520 & n. 3; interest in mezzotint engraving, iii. 271 & n. 4, 274 & n. 2; discovers Grinling Gibbons, &c., iii. 567–8, 571–2; admires rock-crystal, ii. 310.

— biographical miscellanea: birth, ii. 1 & n. 1 (i. 1); baptism and godparents of, ii. 5 & n. 5 (i. 6); marriage, ii. 536; climacterical year of, iv. 294, 298, 347; desires to be buried at Wotton, iii. 210; iv. 430; death and epitaph, v. 622, n. 1, 623.

— books and miscellaneous writings [notices of E's books and other formal compositions, printed or manuscript, and quotations from, and citations of, them in notes. Very short quotations, and especially those illustrating vocabulary, are generally entered among the citations]:

— — list of E's published writings, i. 122–34 [no further references are given to this list]; literary characteristics, i. *41–2*; punctuation, i. *51*; E's earlier publishers, iii. 284, n. 4.

— — 'Account of Architects': see *Parallel of Architecture* below.

— — *Acetaria*: presented to Lord Somers, &c., v. 361 & n. 3; added to *Sylva*, 1706, i. *16*; v. 361, n. 3; Milton in, iii. 364, n. 6 *ad fin.*; cited, i. 101, n. 1; ii. 158, n. 9, 425, n. 2; iii. 365, n. 3, 538, n. 2; iv. 269, n. 4; v. 13, n. 4 *ad fin.*, 552, n. 3.

— — 'Animadversions upon Spinoza' (MS.), iv. 381, n. 2.

— — *Apology for the Royal Party*, i. *13*; published, iii. 235 & n. 4, 243, n. 3; quoted, ii. 28, n. 5; cited, iii. 242, n. 2 *ad fin.*

— — Aubrey, J., *Natural history of Surrey*: notes, &c., by E in: cited, ii. 4, n. 1, 551, n. 5; iii. 193, n. 1, 221, n. 7 *ad fin.*, 496, n. 2 *ad fin.*; E gives information to Aubrey, ii. 1, n. 1.

— — Bosse, A., *Traicté des manieres de graver*, &c.: E translates part of, ii. 568, n. 3.

— — Camden, *Britannia*, 1695: E's notes in, &c., v. 206 & n. 2; ~ alluded to (?), i. 5 & n. 1;

EVELYN, JOHN: books (*cont.*) cited, i. 9, n. 2; ii. 4, n. 1; iii. 496, n. 2 *ad fin.*

— — *Case of George Evelyn of Wotton . . . with some remarks thereon, by John Evelyn of Deptford*: delivered to house of commons, v. 314 & n. 1; alluded to, v. 337.

— — *Character of England*, i. *14*, *17*; quoted, ii. 50, n. 5, 115, n. 4, 552, n. 3; iii. 82, n. 6, 160, n. 5; v. 577, n. 1; cited, ii. 48, n. 2, 106, n. 4, 556, n. 4; iii. 213, n. 4, 459, n. 1, 568, n. 3; iv. 164, n. 2.

— — *Compleat Gard'ner* (translation from J. de la Quintinye), i. *35*; poem translated by Creech in, v. 417, n. 2; advertisement to: cited, iii. 538, n. 2; v. 176, n. 3.

— — *Devotionarie Book*: cited, iii. 511, n. 1, 522, n. 1; iv. 30, n. 5.

— — Devotionary books for Mrs. Godolphin (MS.), iv. 126, n. 5.

— — *Directions for the Gardiner at Says-Court*, iv. 521, n. 3.

— — *Elysium Britannicum* (synopsis), i. *12*; quoted, iii. 103, n. 6.

— — Encounter between the French and Spanish ambassadors: composed, circulated, &c., iii. 297–300 & nn.; copy for Charles II, iii. 352; mentioned, i. *24*, n. 2.

— — *English Vineyard Vindicated*: cited, iv. 84, n. 3.

— — *French Gardiner* (translation from N. de Bonnefons): published, iii. 225 & n. 3; dedication of, ii. 179, n. 6; cited, ii. 223, n. 8; iv. 84, n. 3.

— — *Fumifugium*, i. *17*; presented to Charles II, &c., iii. 295–6 & n., 297 & n. 3; alluded to, iii. 456–7 & n.; quoted, ii. 171, n. 2; cited, ii. 339, n. 4, 341, nn. 3, 5; iii. 24, n. 2, 291, n. 2.

— — *Golden Book of St. John Chrysostom*, i. *13*; published, iii. 220 & n. 4; dedication, iv. 619; ~ quoted, iii. 206, n. 3; ~ cited, iii. 209, n. 1, 210, n. 3; *add.*

— — 'History of Chalcography': see *Sculptura* below.

— — *History of Religion*, i. *42*; completed (?), iv. 568 & n. 1;

EVELYN, JOHN: books (*cont.*)
quoted, i. 18, n. 1; iv. 346, n. 2, 435, n. 5; v. 137, n. 2, 542, n. 2; cited, ii. 44, n. 3, 238, n. 4, 460, n. 2; iii. 22, n. 6, 30, n. 5, 152, n. 1, 179, n. 2, 202, n. 4, 227, n. 1, 247, n. 1, 363, n. 2, 365, n. 3; iv. 35, n. 5, 259, n. 8, 334, n. 6, 363, n. 7, 381, n. 2, 554, n. 2, 634, n. 2; v. 107, n. 2, 130, n. 3, 131, n. 3, 278, n. 6 *ad fin*, 364, n. 2, 412, n. 1.
— — History of Second Dutch War (project), i. *22–3*; iii. 523, n. 1; E invited to write, iii. 523, 550; E reports progress, &c., iii. 558, 559 *bis*, 568, 573, 586, 624; materials for, &c., iii. 559, 562, 563, 568, 588; iv. 18; referred to, for account of battle, iii. 411; preface of: published as *Navigation and Commerce* (see below), iv. 41 & n. 1.
— — *History of the Three Impostors*, iii. 522, n. 2; presented to Charles II, &c., iii. 522–3; materials for, iii. 516, n. 2; iv. 489, n. 2; cited, iii. 515, n. 4.
— — History of Trades (project): presented to Royal Society, iii. 268 & n. 2.
— — *Idea of the Perfection of Painting* (translation from R. Fréart): published, iii. 514 & n. 2; cited, iv. 329, n. 4; preface, &c.: cited, i. *42* & n. 4; ii. 214, n. 4, 261, n. 5, 264, n. 5, 298, n. 1, 382, n. 4 *ad fin.*; iii. 496, n. 1.
— — *Instructions concerning Erecting of a Library* (translation from G. Naudé), iii. 303, n. 7; presented to Clarendon, iii. 303–4; dedication: passage in, on Royal Society, iii. 306 & n. 1; ~ quoted, i. *42–3*.
— — *Kalendarium Hortense*: published with *Sylva*, i. *16*; iii. 340, n. 1; second edition dedicated to Cowley, iii. 355, n. 4, 490, n. 1; in comparison, ii. 132, n. 3; cited, ii. 109, n. 2; eighth edition, 1691, cited, iv. 462, n. 5; v. 80, n. 3.
— — *Late News from Bruxels Unmasked*: composed and published, iii. 243 & n. 3.
— — letter to John Cosin, jnr.: suggested publication of, iii. 62.
— — *Life of Mrs. Godolphin*, i. *25*;

EVELYN, JOHN: books (*cont.*)
E plans to write, iv. 149 & n. 1; dedicated to Lady Sylvius, iii. 471, n. 3; iv. 429 & n. 1; not intended to be printed, i. *85*, n. 2; E's handwriting in (Rosenbach MS.), i. *49*, *74*, n. 1; on Mrs. Godolphin's diary, i. *82*; read to Mary Evelyn, iv. 429; cited, ii. 246, n. 1; iii. 149, n. 2, 155, n. 7, 263, n. 8; iv. 13, n. 7, 30, n. 5, and then frequently to p. 152, n. 3.
— — *London revived*: presented to Charles II, iii. 462–3 & n.; cited, iv. 304, n. 4, 423, n. 2; v. 419, n. 1.
— — Lucretius: translation of *De rerum natura*, book I, i. *12*; published, &c., iii. 173 & n. 2; notes to: use of Diary in, i. *84*, n. 4; commendatory letter in, iii. 123, n. 3; frontispiece: design of, ii. 535, n. 4; presentation copy of, v. 187, n. 2; quoted, ii. 288, n. 3; cited, ii. 148, n. 1, 269, n. 1, 335, n. 4.
— — *Memoires for my Grand-son*: quoted, iii. 149, n. 2; iv. 126, n. 5; v. 339, n. 2.
— — *Mundus Muliebris*: *see* Evelyn, Mary.
— — *Mysterion tes Anomias*: published, iii. 393 & n. 6; Charles II thanks E for, iii. 397; alluded to, iv. 539 & n. 3; supposed notice of, iii. 431, n. 7 *ad fin.*
— — *Navigation and Commerce*, i. *22–3*; E ordered to write against the Dutch, iv. 30; suppressed, &c., iv. 41 & n. 1; cited, ii. 48, n. 1, 50, n. 3, 166, n. 4, 222, n. 6; v. 120, n. 2.
— — *Numismata*, i. *35*; published, &c., v. 283 & n. 3; E complimented on, v. 508, n. 2; dedication, iv. 595, n. 2; quoted, ii. 54, n. 2, 57, n. 1; iii. 85, n. 5, 112, n. 1; iv. 328, n. 5, 409, n. 4; cited, i. 25, n. 1 *ad fin.*; ii. 21, n. 7, 23, n. 5, 39, n. 2, 157, n. 4, 185, n. 5, 188, n. 13 *ad fin.*, 247, n. 4, 391, n. 4, 398, n. 5, 399, n. 2, 535, n. 1, 559, n. 2; iii. 79, n. 2, 96, n. 5, 191, n. 2, 196, n. 1, 197, n. 4, 285, n. 3, 335, n. 2, 359, n. 5, 364, n. 6 *ad fin.*, 446, n. 6; iv. 68, n. 4, 138, n. 2, 186, n. 5, 287, n. 2,

EVELYN, JOHN: books (*cont.*) 325, n. 1, 358, n. 1, 396, n. 4, 397, n. 1, 531, n. 3; v. 44, n. 3, 186, n. 4 *ad fin.*, 295, n. 2.
— — Office for John Evelyn, jnr., &c. (MS.), iv. 126 & n. 5.
— — 'Officium Sanctæ Trinitatis' (MS.), ii. 559, n. 2.
— — *Of Liberty and Servitude*, i. *11*, *81*; published, &c., ii. 547 & n. 3; quoted, ii. 21, n. 7; iv. 328, n. 5.
— — 'Paneficium' (MS.): read to Royal Society, iii. 401, n. 8.
— — *Panegyric to Charles II*: presented to Charles, iii. 284 & n. 4; passage in, relating to Royal Society, iii. 306, n. 1; mentioned, i. *42*, n. 2.
— — *Parallel of Architecture* (translation from R. Fréart), i. *17–18*, *35*; iii. 380, n. 4; dedicated to Charles II, iv. 409, n. 5; gifts of copies, &c., iii. 380 & n. 4, 385, n. 2; Charles II commends, iii. 386–7; Henrietta Maria thanks E for, iii. 389; cited, ii. 366, n. 6.
— — — 'Account of Architects' published with, i. *18*, *35*; edition of 1664: quoted, ii. 221, n. 3; ~ cited, ii. 260, n. 4, 261, n. 2, 354, n. 2; edition of 1707: cited, ii. 10, n. 5, 182, n. 3, 222, n. 6, 265, n. 3; iii. 448, n. 3.
— — *Pernicious Consequences of the New Heresie of the Jesuits*: presented to Charles II, iii. 431 & n. 7; preface of: Milton named in, iii. 364, n. 6 *ad fin.*
— — Phillips, E., *New World of Words*: E supplies information for, i. *24* & n. 1.
— — *Philosophical Discourse of Earth* (*Terra*): read to Royal Society, &c., iv. 62 & n. 4; cited, iii. 271, n. 6; iv. 253, n. 1, 313, n. 2; v. 202, n. 2; attached to *Sylva*, i. *16*.
— — *Philosophical Transactions*: contributions to, by E, ii. 475, n. 5 *ad fin.*; iii. 519, n. 2; iv. 376 & n. 1; v. 487, n. 1; ~ cited, ii. 105, n. 2; iv. 362, n. 4, 365, n. 1.
— — poems: commendatory: for T. Creech, v. 417, n. 2; ~ for Sir S. Tuke, iii. 348, n. 4; Latin, to Dr. G. Rogers, ii. 464, n. 1,

EVELYN, JOHN: books (*cont.*) 479, n. 2; iv. 291, n. 1; on duchess of Newcastle's visit to Royal Society (attributed), iii. 483, n. 2; on Charles II's coronation (?; attributed by Bray), iii. 284, n. 4.
— — Pomona: see *Sylva* below.
— — *Preamble to the Subscriptions to Greenwich Hospital*, v. 211 & n. 5.
— — *Publick Employment*: published, iii. 475 & n. 8; alluded to, v. 12; passage on Sir R. Browne in, iii. 248, n. 1; cited, i. *43*, n. 1; ii. 111, n. 1; iii. 455, n. 1.
— — religious treatise, 1688 (*History of Religion*?): completed, iv. 568 & n. 1.
— — *Sculptura*, i. *15–16*; iii. 325, n. 2; publication of, recommended by Royal Society, iii. 268 & n. 3; presented to Royal Society, iii. 325 & n. 2; mezzotint process announced in, iii. 274 & n. 2; Prince Rupert makes mezzotint for, iii. 271, n. 4; dedication of, to R. Boyle: quoted, i. *43*; book II, ii. 568, n. 3; iii. 325, n. 2; quoted, ii. 54, n. 2, 299, n. 4, 407, n. 2; iii. 10, n. 3, 11, n. 1; cited, i. 21, n. 2; ii. 9, n. 2, 49, n. 4, 64, n. 2 *ad fin.*, 91, n. 5, 92, n. 3, 111, n. 1, 324, n. 8, 549, n. 4; iii. 3, nn. 3, 4, 9, n. 3, 22, n. 9, 79, n. 2, 82, n. 2, 86, n. 3, 166, n. 5, 276, n. 1, 387, nn. 2, 3; book ii: cited, i. 35, n. 1.
— — *State of France*, i. *11*, *41*, n. 1, *81*; description of Paris in: reprinted, iii. 637–9; poem in, i. *66*; ii. 355, n. 1; quoted, ii. 125, n. 4, 354, n. 4; cited, i. *41*, n. 3, *80*, n. 2; ii. 26, nn. 4, 5, 44, n. 4, 48, n. 2, 94, n. 3, 131, n. 3, 354, nn. 2, 3, 512, n. 1, 534, n. 2; iii. 142, n. 3, 154, n. 6, 365, n. 3.
— — *Sylva*, i. *16–17*, *35*, *41–2* & n.; origin, &c., of, iii. 340 & n. 1; printing of: ordered by Royal Society, iii. 353; in press, iii. 369; dedicated to Charles II, iv. 409, n. 5; gifts of copies, iii. 369 *bis* & nn. 2, 8; E thanked for, iii. 344 & n. 4, 369; Charles II commends, iii. 386–7; in portrait of E, iv. 644; second

EVELYN, JOHN: books (*cont.*)
edition (1670), i. *22*; ~ published, &c., iii. 541 & n. 4; third edition (1679): source of passage in, ii. 408, n. 7; Latin poem by R. Bohun in (second and later editions), iii. 416, n. 1; essay by Cowley in (third and later editions), iii. 355, n. 4; use of Diary in, i. *84*, n. 4; Hunter's editions of, &c., i. *57* & nn. 2, 3; mentioned in quotations, i. *38*, *58*.
— — — two or more editions quoted or cited, iii. 324, n. 7 (hedge at Hampton Court), 386, n. 6 (plane-trees), 487 & n. 6 (houllies); iv. 117, n. 1 (Norway oak, &c.), 304, n. 4 (burials in churches), 312, n. 1 (E's holly-hedge); first edition (1664): quoted, ii. 47, n. 4, 60, n. 3, 127, n. 5, 130, n. 1, 507, n. 6; ~ cited, ii. 6, n. 3, 73, n. 4, 81, n. 2, 182, n. 8, 208, n. 1, 324, n. 8, 428, n. 5, 514, n. 3; iii. 81, n. 3, 100, n. 3, 127, n. 2, 143, n. 1, 157, nn. 3, 5, 180, n. 1, 193, n. 1, 359, nn. 2, 3, 386, n. 5; second edition (1670): quoted, ii. 349, n. 6; ~ cited, ii. 446, n. 11; iii. 133, n. 7, 396, n. 2, 625, n. 1; iv. 253, n. 1; v. 552, n. 3; third edition (1679): cited, ii. 295, n. 3, 459, n. 5; iii. 382, n. 4, 591, n. 3; iv. 121, n. 4, 142, n. 3, 200, n. 4; fourth edition (1706): quoted, v. 550, n. 2; ~ cited, ii. 12, n. 5; iv. 337, n. 4; v. 176, n. 3, 290, n. 6 *ad fin.*
— — — 'Pomona' published with, i. *16*; materials for, iii. 351, n. 4; *see also* iii. 340, n. 1; third edition (1679): note by Sir T. Hanmer in, iii. 191, n. 2; cited, iii. 118, n. 6; first edition (1664): cited, ii. 105, n. 2; v. 416, n. 1.
— — — see also *Acetaria*, *Kalendarium Hortense*, and *Philosophical Discourse* above.
— — *Terra*: see *Philosophical Discourse* above.
— — *Tyrannus*, i. *42*, n. 2; published, iii. 306 & n. 4; and new fashion, 1666, iii. 465 & n. 3; cited, ii. 10, n. 5, 331, n. 4, 449, n. 1; iii. 374, n. 4.
— character [passages in introduction; passages in text in which E calls attention to his feelings or conduct. *See also* religion *below*]:
— — general: contemporary accounts of, i. *36–9*; later estimates of, i. *39–43*; in early manhood, ii. 26 & n. 4 (i. 19); epitaph, v. 623.
— — court-life: distaste for, &c., iii. 313; iv. 344, 403, 413–14; drinking: dislike of heavy, iv. 296; *see also* ii. 38 (i. 28); gaming: regrets excessive, at court, iii. 308; iv. 403, 413; grief: for Church of England, 1655, iii. 164; ~ for little Richard Evelyn, iii. 210; hospitality to neighbours, &c., at Christmastide, iii. 185; *see also* iii. 348, 393, &c.
— — humanity: bombardment of towns: censured, iv. 381 & n. 3(?); v. 186, 216, 218; cruelty to animals: dislike of, iii. 492, 498, 549; suffering: distressed at watching surgical operations and torture, ii. 476; iii. 29 & n. 2, 610; trials involving death-penalty: unwilling to promote or attend, &c., ii. 535; iii. 73; iv. 175–6.
— — idleness: period of, ii. 534; immorality: dislike of, on stage, iii. 465; London: pride in, i. *112–13*; natural scenery: appreciation of landscape, i. *107*; ~ love of woodlands, ii. 6 & n. 3 (i. 6); political: general attitude, i. *113–14*; ~ subservience, i. *32* & n. 1, *113*; ~ on effects of ambition of princes, iii. 610; scurrility: disapproval of (speech of *Terræ filius*), iii. 532–3; sightseeing: eager for, ii. 20 (i. 15), 213, 431, 489; sincerity: praises James II's, iv. 479; theatre-going in bad times: disapproves of, iii. 229, 466.
— and charity: gifts of money to, for charitable distribution, iv. 29 & n. 2, 81 *ter*, 139 & n. 5, 140; Chelsea Hospital: advises on establishment of, &c., iv. 269–70, 281; Deptford: seeks help for poor of, winter, 1683–4, iv. 361, 365 *bis*; Greenwich Hospital: treasurer of: *see* Green-

EVELYN, JOHN: charity (*cont.*) wich Hospital; St. Thomas's Hospital: invited to be a governor of, iv. 560; Society for Propagation of the Gospel: elected member of, v. 507 & n. 1.
— children [collective notices, &c. Notices relating to the family's receiving the Sacrament are not indexed]: E's religious duties as a father, iv. 7; the younger children: burial-place of, iv. 430; daughters: education of, iv. 350; E's 'six sons', iii. 421 & n. 3; the children's health, iv. 152, 153, 156, 381 *bis*, 386; v. 519.
— collections [*see also* library *below*]:
— — general: expenditure on, at Rome, ii. 401; Italian: sent to England, ii. 402, 553; P. Lombard comes to see, iii. 86; paintings moved to Wotton, 1694, v. 179.
— — particular objects, &c.: anatomical tables: preparation of, ii. 475 & n. 5; ~ shown to surgeon, ii. 553; ~ lent to Royal College of Physicians, iii. 77–8; ~ given to Royal Society, iii. 501 & n. 2; *see also* v. 487 & n. 1; antiquities: bought at Rome, &c., ii. 343, 368; ~ Egyptian, ii. 469 & nn. 3–5; ~ drawing of Egyptian inscription sent to Kircher, iii. 171–2 & n.; drawings: bought at Florence, ii. 198; ~ by Charles II of new plan for Whitehall, iii. 387 & n. 4; ~ by C. Maratti of Roman reliefs, ii. 223, 247; Florentine mosaic: pieces of, for cabinet, ii. 191 & n. 3 (i. 119), 198; glass: Venetian, &c., ii. 467, 478; horns of steinbock (refused), ii. 516; *hortus siccus*, ii. 466 & n. 5; *add.*; Indian curiosities, ii. 49 (i. 35); medals, ii. 343; *see also* ii. 368.
— — — paintings: bought in Italy, ii. 401, 478; *see also* ii. 368; bought in United Provinces, ii. 39 (i. 29); by C. van Couwenberch, ii. 56 & n. 4; copies after: Correggio, ii. 229 & n. 5; ~ Tintoretto, iii. 567 & n. 4; bought by E for Sir C. Crewe, ii. 540.

EVELYN, JOHN: collections (*cont.*)
— — — pendules, iv. 333; prints: bought at Florence, ii. 198; ~ bought from S. della Bella, iii. 3; ~ by Hollar, i. 22; ~ F. Perrier, *Icones*, iii. 11, n. 1; ~ A. Tempesta, *Possesso* of a pope, ii. 279, n. 3; ~ portraits, i. *21*; ~ sieges and battles, iii. 37; shells, ii. 49; statuettes: by V. Brocchi, ii. 198, 417; ~ ivory copy of Borghese Hermaphrodite, ii. 253; Turkish bridle, &c. (gift), ii. 504, 508; Venice treacle, ii. 478 & n. 2; Vesuvius: pumices from, ii. 334.
— as commissioner and office-holder in government service:
— — commissions:
— — — Greenwich Hospital: E as treasurer of, 1695–1703, i. *34, 36*; for activities *see* Greenwich Hospital.
— — — Gresham College: inquiry into finances of, 1662, iii. 328 & n. 2, 330, 335.
— — — London street improvements, 1662: E appointed to, i. *17*; iii. 318–19 & n.; activities of: *see* London: improvements.
— — — Privy Seal, 1685–7: E appointed to, i. *31–2*; iv. 464–5; seal delivered to commissioners, &c., iv. 493–4 & n.; E takes Test for, iv. 500 *bis*; occupies Lord Privy Seal's lodgings, Whitehall, iv. 500 *bis*; at seals, iv. 494–9, 508–35 *passim*; refuses to apply seal to grants, iv. 504, 512; evades sealing grant, iv. 504; effect of E's unwillingness to seal dispensations, iv. 510, n. 1; commissioners discharged, iv. 540.
— — — Privy Seal, 1690: possibility of E's appointment to, v. 7.
— — — Royal Mint, 1663–4, 1666: E appointed to, i. *19*; activities of: *see* Royal Mint.
— — — St. Paul's Cathedral, repair of: E as a surveyor of, 1666, i. *19–20*; iii. 448–9 & nn.
— — — Saltpetre, 1666: E appointed to, i. *19*; iii. 442–3 & n.; activities of, iii. 443–6 *passim*, 447(?).

EVELYN, JOHN: commissioner, &c. (*cont.*)
— — — sewers: *see* Surrey and Kent Commissioners of Sewers.
— — — Sick and Wounded Mariners, &c., 1664–7, 1672–4: *see* Commissioners for Sick and Wounded.
— — — subsidies, 1671, 1673, iii. 576 & n. 3.
— — other appointments, &c.:
— — — Council for Foreign Plantations, &c., 1671–4: E appointed member of, i. *23*; iii. 570–1 & n.; takes Test for, iv. 10 & n. 3; for activities *see* Council for Foreign Plantations; Council of Trade and Plantations.
— — — Clerk of the Council: sells reversion of, 1672, iii. 601.
— — — Latin secretary: reversion of, 1670, iii. 546–7 & n.
— — — J.P.: Charles II asks E to qualify as, 1666, iii. 433–4.
— — — office arising from forfeiture of City Charter, 1683: offered to E, iv. 341–2.
— correspondence:
— — general: publication of, i. *129–30* & nn.; E's letter-book, iii. 239; iv. 273; E receives letters from: France, ii. 553; iii. 62, 434; ~ England, ii. 566; E writes letters to: England, iii. 18, 20; ~ Paris, &c., iii. 55, 58.
— — general notices or citations of correspondence with various persons: F. Barlow, iii. 166, n. 5; R. Bentley, v. 88, n. 4; ~ cited, v. 283, n. 3; R. Berkeley, iv. 345, n. 4; R. Boyle, iii. 169, n. 7 *ad fin.*; Sir Richard Browne, 1647–9, 1657, ii. 552 & n. 4; iii. 200 & n. 1; Sir Thomas Browne, iii. 592, n. 2, 594; Charles II and his ministers in exile, iii. 59; Henry Hyde, earl of Clarendon, as Lord Cornbury, 1669–73, iii. 523, n. 1; Clifford, 1669–73, *ib.*; *add.*; Sir K. Eyton, *c.* 1649–50, ii. 558 & n. 4; Mrs. Godolphin, iv. 151; Sir T. Hanmer, iii. 191, n. 2; Sir G. Mackenzie, 1668, iii. 475, n. 8 *ad fin.*; Dr. W. Nicolson, v. 508 & n. 2; Sir E. Thurland, iii. 219, n. 2; William Wotton, iv. 172, n. 4.
— — letters from E to various

EVELYN, JOHN: correspondence (*cont.*) persons, mentioned, cited, &c.: Albemarle, 1665: cited, iii. 409, n. 2; E. Ashmole, 1664: cited, ii. 389, n. 3; J. Aubrey: *see* books, &c. *above*; Dr. R. Bathurst: 1667, iii. 496, n. 1, 497, n. 3 (cited); ~ 1669, iii. 500, n. 4; Dr. J. Beale, 1668: cited, iii. 87, n. 5; R. Bentley: 7 Jan. 1695, v. 200, n. 4 (cited); ~ 20 Jan. 1697, i. *42* & n. 3 (cited); ~ Dec. 1697, v. 282, n. 2 (quoted), 283, n. 1 (cited); Dr. R. Bohun, 1697, i. *89* & n. 4 (quoted); v. 264, n. 6; R. Boyle: 9 Aug. 1659, iii. 162, n. 2 (quoted), 268, n. 2 (cited); ~ 3 Sept. 1659, iii. 232, n. 2 (cited); ~ 29 Sept. 1659, ii. 39, n. 2 (cited); ~ 23 Nov. 1664, iii. 393, n. 6 *ad fin.* (cited); Viscount Brouncker, 1670, iii. 519, n. 2; Sir Richard Browne: various letters, 1648–9: mentioned, ii. 553 & n. 2, 554 & n. 1; quoted, ii. 540, n. 5, 546, n. 3; cited, ii. 541, nn. 1, 2, 543, n. 5, 556, n. 1, 559, n. 2, 564, n. 1; iii. 38, n. 3; ~ 14 Feb. 1658, iii. 209, n. 1; Sir Thomas Browne, 28 Jan. 1660: quoted, iii. 103, n. 6; cited, ii. 41, n. 4, 80, n. 4, 81, n. 4, 173, n. 3; Dr. M. Casaubon, 1674: cited, iii. 173, n. 2; Henry Hyde, earl of Clarendon, as Lord Cornbury, various letters, 1665–6: cited, ii. 451, n. 4; iii. 140, n. 7 *ad fin.*, 416, n. 3, 417, n. 4, 418, n. 3, 431, n. 7, 437, n. 1, 470, n. 4; v. 491, n. 1; Clifford: 20 Apr. 1665, iii. 406, n. 1 (cited); ~ 16 June 1665, iii. 410, nn. 1, 4, 411, n. 4; iv. 77, n. 3 (all citations); ~ 23 Nov. 1670, ii. 78, n. 1, 82, n. 2 (citations); D. Colwall, 1682, iv. 273 & n. 5; John Cosin, jnr., 1652, iii. 52, n. 2, 636; publication of, suggested, iii. 62; Sir W. Coventry, 1665: cited, iii. 422, n. 1; A. Cowley, 1667: cited, iii. 475, n. 8 *ad fin.*, 490, n. 1; W. Cowper, F.R.S., *c.* 1702, v. 487, n. 1; cited, ii. 475, n. 5 *ad fin.*; Comte d'Estrades, 1652, iii. 56; George Evelyn, 1685, iv. 434 & n. 3; John Evelyn, jnr., 1688, iv.

EVELYN, JOHN: correspondence (*cont.*) 610, n. 4, 611, n. 1; Mrs. Evelyn: 1649, ii. 550; ~ 1652, iii. 62 *bis*; ~ 1666, iii. 428, n. 6 (cited); Dr. J. Fell, 1667, iii. 496 & n. 1; Lady Garret, 1651: cited, ii. 542, n. 2; Joseph Glanvill, 1668, iv. 53, n. 4 *ad fin.*; Dr. H. Godolphin, 1698: cited, v. 283, n. 3; Mrs. Godolphin, 1676, iv. 84; Godolphin, 1705, v. 602; T. Henshaw, 1698: cited, v. 298, n. 2; J. Jackson, 1703, v. 537, n. 1; Sir J. Langham, 1667: cited, iii. 364, n. 6, 401, n. 4; — Maddox, 1657: cited, i. *41*, n. 3; iii. 222, n. 3; Dr. G. Morley, 1682, iv. 283 & n. 1; Col. H. Morley, 1660, iii. 239 & n. 5; Dr. W. Nicolson, 1699: quoted, iv. 241, n. 3; Henry Howard, sixth duke of Norfolk, as Howard, 1667, iii. 496, n. 1; Lady Ossory, 1680, iv. 211; Father Patrick (Maginn), 1671: cited, v. 240, n. 6; *see also* iii. 365, n. 3; Pepys: on Sick and Wounded business, 1665–6, 1672: cited, iii. 419, n. 4, 420, n. 2, 423, nn. 1, 5, 430, n. 2, 431, n. 3, 433, n. 2, 623, n. 5; ~ 12 Aug. 1689: quoted, iii. 493, n. 6; cited, i. *32*, n. 1; iii. 14, n. 4, 62, n. 8, 79, n. 2, 379, n. 8 *ad fin.*, 472, n. 3, 520, n. 3; iv. 287, n. 2, 396, n. 4, 531, n. 3, 644, n. 1; v. 44, n. 3, 419, n. 1; ~ 4 Oct. 1689, iii. 396, n. 4; cited, iv. 531, n. 3; ~ other letters, various dates: cited, i. *88*, n. 3, *89–90*; iv. 6, n. 2, 41, n. 1 *ad fin.*, 267, n. 5; v. 24, n. 2, 215, n. 3, 420, n. 1, 422, n. 3, 484, n. 1, 515, n. 4, 521, n. 1, 583, n. 4; T. Pierce, 1663, iii. 360 & n. 5; cited, iii. 363, n. 6; Sancroft: 10 Oct. 1688, i. *33*; iv. 600 & n. 4, 601, n. 1, 614 (Sancroft's thanks for), 632, n. 5; ~ 10 May 1689, iv. 641, n. 5; Sandwich, 1667, iii. 519, n. 2; Lady Sunderland: Dec. 1688, iv. 610; ~ 4 Aug. 1690, ii. 6, n. 3 (cited); Charles Spencer, earl of Sunderland, as Lord Spencer, 1688, 1693: cited, iv. 595, n. 2; Jeremy Taylor, various letters, 1655–6: cited,

EVELYN, JOHN: correspondence (*cont.* iii. 158, n. 4, 163, n. 1, 164, n. 1, 171, nn. 1, 3, 4, 173, n. 2; Tenison, 1692: cited, ii. 332, n. 2; Sir E. Thurland, 1652, 1658: cited, iii. 59, n. 1, 65, n. 4, 84, n. 4, 142, n. 3; Sir S. Tuke, 1666: cited, iii. 459, n. 3; Sir P. Warwick, 1665: cited, iii. 419, n. 3, 420, n. 3; Dr. J. Wilkins, 1666: cited, iii. 431, n. 7 *ad fin.*; Sir J. Williamson, various letters, 1661–72, iii. 297, n. 4 *ad fin.*, 523, n. 1, 546, n. 4; cited, iii. 574, n. 5, 619, n. 3; W. Wotton: 30 March 1696, i. *41*, n. 4; v. 83, n. 3; **add.** (v. 159) (citations); ~ 12 Sept. 1703, iii. 106, n. 1, 162, n. 2, 169, n. 7 *ad fin.*, 268, n. 2; iv. 56, n. 4; v. 532, nn. 1, 2 (all citations); Sir C. Wren, 1665: quoted, iii. 364, n. 6; Sir P. Wyche, 1665, iii. 396, n. 4; without address or date, *ib.*

— — letters to E from various persons, mentioned, cited, &c.: Albemarle, 1665, iii. 416; Lady Arlington, 1683, iv. 341–2; Dr. T. Barlow: 1655, iii. 385, n. 2 (cited); ~ 1664, iii. 393, n. 6 *ad fin.* (cited); ~ 28 Sept. 1669, iii. 106, n. 4, 534, n. 1; Dr. I. Basire, 1647: cited, iii. 303, n. 3; Dr. R. Bathurst, 1669, iii. 500, n. 4; R. Bentley, 22 Feb. 1696, v. 224, n. 2; Sir R. Browne: *see* Browne, Sir Richard; Henry Hyde, earl of Clarendon, 1685, iv. 464; John Cosin, jnr., 1651, iii. 51 & n. 3, 52 & n. 2, 636; *see also* iii. 62; A. Cowley, 1663, 1667: cited, iii. 355, n. 4, 490, n. 1; Mrs. Susanna Draper, as S. Evelyn, Bath, 1691: cited, v. 61, n. 1; George Evelyn, 20 Feb., 30 Mar. 1685, iv. 434, n. 3; (Sir) John Evelyn: various letters, 1699–1701, v. 322 & n. 4, 417, n. 2 (cited), 434, 484, n. 1 (cited); Mrs. Evelyn: 1649, ii. 552; ~ 1652, iii. 61, 65; Dr. J. Fell, 24 Sept., 21 Oct. 1667, iii. 498–9 & n., 500 & n. 3; ~ 1676, iv. 89; Godolphin, 1678, iv. 148; S. Hartlib, 1660, iii. 162, n. 2; Queen Henrietta Maria, 1660, iii. 247; J. Jackson, 1703;

EVELYN, JOHN: correspondence (*cont.*) cited, v. 537, n. 1, 538, nn. 6, 7; James II, as duke of York, 1665, iii. 406; Dr. R. Mander, &c., 1700, v. 432; John Mordaunt, Viscount Mordaunt, 1661: cited, iii. 284, n. 4; Henry Howard, sixth duke of Norfolk, as Howard, 1668: cited, iii. 515, n. 1, 522, n. 2; Pepys: 2 Oct. 1685, iv. 475 & n. 1 (quoted); *add.* (iv. 477, n. 1); ~ 7 Nov. 1694, v. 203, n. 1 *bis* (cited); J. Quinn, 1694–5: cited, v. 170, n. 3; A. Rosse, 1650: cited, iii. 81, n. 1; Sandwich, 1665, iii. 418; Somers, 1699, v. 361 & n. 4; Lady Sunderland, Oct. 1688: cited, iv. 602, n. 2; Charles Spencer, earl of Sunderland, as Lord Spencer, 1690, v. 36; Robert Spencer, earl of Sunderland, secretary of, 1686, iv. 525; Jeremy Taylor 1655–6, 1659: cited, &c., iii. 171, n. 4, 173, n. 2, 363, n. 2; Tenison: 1694, v. 174, n. 3 (cited); ~ 1704, v. 583 & n. 3; Sir P. Warwick, 16 Sept. 1665: quoted, iii. 253, n. 2; cited, iii. 419, n. 3; servant at Sayes Court, spring 1698: quoted, v. 284, n. 5.

— dangers: *see* accidents and dangers *above*.

— Diary:

— — almanacs containing notes by E, i. *44, 48* & n. 2; the notes, i. *75–7*.

— — chronology: notes on E's: Netherlands tour, ii. 571; Easter, 1644, ii. 124 & n. 4; journeys in: France, &c., ii. 151, n. 3, 162, n. 7, 167, n. 4, 169, n. 6; ~ Italy, &c., ii. 206, n. 1, 315, n. 1, 405, n, 2, 488, n. 1, 511, n. 6; for 1646, ii. 479, n. 2, 534, n. 1.

— — composition:

— — — E's original notes, i. *74–9*; E begins making, i. *75, 79*; ii. 10 (i. 8); text of surviving (1636–7), i. *75–7*; alluded to, ii. 20.

— — — Kalendarium (K): dates of writing, i. *69–74, 116, 117, 118*; forward references in, i. *70, 71–2*; *select specimens*: notices based on repeated experiences, ii. 128, n. 1, 134; iv. 106, n. 4; events entered prematurely, iii. 199, n. 2, 217, n. 7, 239, n. 1, 338 & nn. 5, 7, 340 & n. 1, 500 & n. 4, 591 & nn. 1, 5; iv. 149, n. 1; E's changes of opinion, iii. 607, n. 1, 608, n. 2; conflated and problematical notices, iv. 587, n. 2, 644, nn. 1–3; *add.* (i. *73*, n. 2).

— — — — methods of composing, i. *83–4, 91*; expanded extracts from, iii. 632–6 & nn.; notice omitted from (?), iv. 124, n. 9.

— — — De Vita Propria (V): date of writing, i. *74*; *add.*; as expansion of K, i. *84, 85*, n. 1.

— — contents: general: credibility of, i. *105–7*; historical value of, i. *107–14* & nn.

— — — value of, for special topics, &c.,: art-history, i. *107–8*; character-drawing, i. *108–9*; landscape, i. *107*; London history, i. *112–13*; religion, i. *109–12*; Royal Society, i. *108*; science, *ib.*

— — — notices of Italian towns, ii. 398, n. 5, 426, n. 4; sermons: reports of, i. *82–3* & n.

— — dates: omission of, for first of the month, iii. 149, n. 3.

— — editions:

— — — text: first and second editions, i. *56–62*; ~ Bray's concern in, i. *54–6*; ~ Upcott and, i. *52–6, 58*, n. 3; third edition, i. *62–3*; fourth edition, i. *63*; ~ Upcott's transcripts in, *ib.*; i. *69*, n. 1; later editions and extracts, i. *63*; present edition, i. *64–8*; ~ corrections to: *add.* (ii. 260, 408, 539; iv. 6, 84).

— — — notes and commentaries: in former editions and extracts, ii. *115–20*; in present edition, i. *120–31*.

— — errors and doubtful statements in [select specimens; errors due to E; *see also* sources *below*]: facts, ii. 72, n. 2, 204, n. 3, 247, n. 3, 400, n. 3; doubtful or false chronology [*see also* composition: Kalendarium *above*], ii. 28, n. 3; iii. 31, nn. 1, 5; iv. 49, n. 7; confusions: persons, ii. 229, n. 5, 244, n. 7, 356, n. 5, 407, n. 1; ~ topo-

EVELYN, JOHN: Diary (*cont.*)
graphical, ii. 65, nn. 3, 4, 167, n. 3, 246, n. 2, 284, n. 2, 489, n. 6; false routes, ii. 121, n. 3, 151, n. 3, 158, n. 7, 159, n. 2, 162, n. 9, 169, n. 6, 316, n. 3, 419, n. 3; spurious legend about St. Paul, ii. 306, n. 2; alleged exhibitions of relics, &c., ii. 262, n. 3, 328, n. 3, 412, n. 4.
— — manuscripts of: described, i. *44–8* & nn.; hand-writing of, i. *48–51*; history and ownership of, i. *44*, *51–5*.
— — names: E's, for, i. *44*, *84*; ii. 1; iv. 23.
— — notes: E's original: *see* composition *above*.
— — publication: Diary not written for, i. *84–5*; for editions *see* editions *above*.
— — punctuation: E's, i. *51*.
— — purpose and use of, i. *79–85*; as record of extraordinary events, &c., iv. 23; use of: in E's books, i. *84* & n. 4, *121*; ~ for spiritual purposes, i. *83*; E reads over year's notes on birthday, v. 518; extracts from, sent to biographer of Cosin, iii. 632.
— — sources for [notes on sources used by E for various passages (mainly descriptions of places) are prefixed to the passages; for particular books, newspapers, &c., used by him *see* Books: sources; Newspapers]: general, i. *83–105*, *120–1*; books, miscellaneous, i. *85* & n. 1; MS. instructions for sight-seeing (Arundel's), i. *87*; ii. 479, n. 5; newspapers, i. *84*, *89–90* & nn., *101–5* & nn.; oral information, iv. 274, n. 1, 409, n. 2, 456, 588, n. 1, 603, n. 1, 624, n. 1; v. 205, n. 5; *add.*; published sources of information: mentioned or alluded to, iv. 175, 635; v. 101, 514, 518; travel-books, &c., i. *80*, *86–9* & nn., *90–101* & nn., *107*, *108*, *117*, *118–19*; mistranslations, &c., from books [select], ii. 92, n. 1, 187, n. 1, 193, n. 6, 225, n. 6, 241, n. 2, 244, n. 3, 265, n. 3, 267, n. 1, 311, n. 7, 319, n. 3; iii. 41, nn. 3, 4, 6.
— dignities: knighthood: reported to be knighted, 1649, ii. 563; declines being made K.B., 1661, iii. 276; avoids being knighted, 1666, i. *19*; iii. 428, n. 6.
— — created D.C.L., Oxford, 1669, i. *21*; iii. 535–6; *see also* iii. 500.
— — sworn a younger Brother of Trinity House, 1673, iv. 6.
— domestic life [for the family's changes of residence *see* London residences *below*; Sayes Court; Wotton]: starts housekeeping on his own account, iii. 149.
— drawings and etchings by:
— — general: early interest in drawing, ii. 9; i. 12; consults A. Bosse about perspective, ii. 568.
— — drawings by: views: Putney, &c., ii. 557 & n. 3; Radicofani, ii. 208 & n. 3; Tarare, ii. 156; Tournon, ii. 159–60 (i. 102); Wotton House, i. *3*; *see also* ii. 334, n. 3.
— — — map of Medway, &c., showing Dutch raid, 1667, iii. 484, n. 1; plan of Deptford: cited, iii. 504, n. 3; E's Egyptian inscription, ii. 469, n. 4; iii. 172.
— — etchings by: Tres Tabernæ, ii. 318, n. 2; Vesuvius: crater, ii. 335, nn. 3, 4; ~ view from summit, ii. 334, n. 3; etching dedicated to Lady Isabella Thynne, ii. 549, n. 9 *ad fin.*; other etchings by, ii. 208, n. 3, 557, n. 3.
— — frontispieces designed by: for: *Sculptura*, iii. 325, n. 2; T. Sprat, *History of Royal Society* (?), iii. 266, n. 6 *ad fin.*, 533, n. 7.
— education:
— — intended by his father to study law (?), ii. 24 (i. 12).
— — rudiments, ii. 6 (i. 6).
— — at Lewes, 1628–37: starts Latin, &c., ii. 8 (i. 8); under Mr. Potts, ii. 9; at Southover free school, ii. 9, 11, 15–16 (i. 8, 9, 12); ~ school-fellows at, iii. 65, 238, 502 & n. 5; evades going to Eton, ii. 11 (i. 8–9); studies hand-writing, ii. 8 (i. 8), 13, critical note; i. *48–9*.
— — at Balliol College, Oxford,

EVELYN, JOHN: education (*cont.*) 1637–40, ii. 16–23, 24 (i. 12–18); *see also* i. 76–7; mentioned, iii. 105; fellow-student at(?), iii. 72–3 & n.
— — Middle Temple: admitted to, ii. 15 & n. 4 (i. 12); surety for, iii. 470, n. 2; goes into residence, ii. 24 *bis* & nn. 1, 4 (i. 18 *bis*); elected comptroller of Christmas revels, ii. 77 (i. 51); for E's further residence at, *see* London: topography: Middle Temple.
— — at Padua university, 1645–6: matriculates, ii. 464–6 & nn.; *add.* (ii. 453); studies anatomy, &c., ii. 464, 475–6; elected a syndic, ii. 469–70 & n.; *add.*
— — other studies, &c.: matriculates at Leyden, ii. 52 & n. 4 (i. 36); studies French, ii. 97, 146; studies German and Spanish, ii. 534; attends botanical lecture, ii. 565 & n. 3; chemistry: studies, ii. 534–5; ~ E's teacher of, iii. 336; ~ goes through course of, ii. 547.
— — miscellaneous courses: dancing, ii. 20 (i. 16), 534; music, ii. 22, 287, 473, 535; vaulting, ii. 20 (i. 16).
— as executor: *see* (Evelyn) as trustee, executor, or agent *below*.
— as farmer: harvests, &c., at Wotton, v. 422, 470–1, 514, 574.
— and field sports: takes part in, ii. 542; iii. 117, 133, 306, 326; iv. 113 *bis*.
— gardens and gardening [*see also* tree-planting *below*; Sayes Court *and* Wotton]:
— — acquires taste for woods and solitudes, ii. 6 & n. 3 (i. 6); greenhouse furnace of, v. 80 & n. 3; orange-trees given to, iv. 162.
— — gardens, &c., designed by, or for which E was consulted: Albury, iii. 496 & n. 2, 561–2 & n.; iv. 111, 558; Clarendon House, Piccadilly, iii. 379–80; Oatlands (Sir E. Herbert), iv. 566; Wimbledon House, iii. 315–16; iv. 130–1; Wotton: 1643, ii. 81 (i. 55); iii. 61; ~ 1651–2, iii. 24, 60–1.

EVELYN, JOHN: gardens (*cont.*)
— gifts and benefactions made by [ordinary presents to persons are not indexed collectively]: books: to Balliol College library, ii. 19 & n. 3 (i. 15); ~ to Bodleian Library, iii. 385 & n. 2; *see also* ii. 469, n. 4; iii. 11, n. 1.
— — church repairs, &c.: subscribes to, v. 348, n. 2, 603; society for Propagation of the Gospel: annual subscription to, v. 507; pays ordination fees for J. Le Franc, iii. 172; invited to subscribe to Walton's *Polyglot*, iii. 78 & n. 3.
— — Royal Society: gives anatomical tables to, iii. 501 & n. 2; ~ proposed gift to, for building, iii. 507; gives burning-glass to Dr. J. Wilkins, iii. 170.
— godchildren of: John Breton, iii. 369; Sir John Chardin, bt., iv. 561 & n. 1; — Del Campo, iv. 222; Thomas Draper, v. 194; William Draper, v. 287–8; George Evelyn, son of Richard Evelyn, iii. 218, 219; (Sir) John Evelyn, iv. 272; Mary Evelyn, later Lady Wyche, ii. 544; Mary Prettyman, iii. 166 & n. 4; Andrew Rilie, ii. 567; — Wase, iii. 369; Baptist Watson, iv. 49; William Wren, iv. 169 & n. 4.
— — invited to stand godfather to Mrs. Jane Glanville's expected child, iii. 51 & n. 1; godfather of: — Smith, as proxy for George Evelyn(?), ii. 78 (i. 51); ~ converted Turk or Jew, ii. 376–7.
— habits: bathing: in pond, &c., iii. 15, 38, 101–2; ~ Turkish bath, ii. 430–1 & nn.; ~ for health, iii. 63; ~ head washed annually, iii. 87 & n. 5; drinking, heavy, ii. 38 (i. 28); iii. 21, 54; ~ E avoids, iv. 296; food: first eats oysters, ii. 468; smoking, ii. 522; wagers, &c.: shooting, iii. 21; ~ bowling-match, iii. 219; walking: between Deptford and London, ii. 548; iii. 90, 147, 170, 212; iv. 73, 613; ~ and return, iii. 149; other journeys, iii. 165; iv. 76.

EVELYN, JOHN (*cont.*)
— health:
— — general: Le Duchat's regimen, ii. 530–2; consults Dr. G. Bate, iii. 191; statements for year (31 Oct.), v. 118, 430–1, 518–19; ~ without detail, ii. 568 (31 Dec.); v. 38, 71, 480, 548.
— — major illnesses: small-pox (1646), ii. 519 & n. 4, 521–2 & nn.; haemorrhoids (1658), iii. 212; malignant fever (1660), iii. 243–4; notices of ill-health in old age become increasingly frequent from about v. 520.
— — illnesses and ailments [ordinary illnesses, &c., named or described by E]:
— — — ague [*see also* fever *below*], iii. 26, 81–2; v. 431, 436, 545, 549, 609; ague-like attacks, v. 543, 609, 611; tertian, iii. 94; ~ treatment for, &c., iv. 271–2; double tertian, iii. 243; quartan, ii. 22 (i. 16–17); v. 541.
— — — angina (quinsy), ii. 472 & n. 3.
— — — cold, &c.: ordinary cold, ii. 42 (i. 31); iii. 163, 212; iv. 76, 192, 223, 271, 632; v. 155, 195, 478; cold, later colic, v. 196; cold and rheum, ii. 431; iv. 401; defluxion, v. 38; ~ salt, ii. 478–9 & n.; hoarseness and rheum, v. 235; rheum, iii. 165 & n. 4; iv. 487; v. 483; sore throat, iii. 30, 223; ~ with fever, iii. 220.
— — — colic, iii. 218; v. 196.
— — — constipation (described, not named), v. 499, 560, 606.
— — — dizziness or vertigo, iv. 388; v. 496.
— — — eyes, sore, ii. 535; iii. 186.
— — — face swollen, iv. 10.
— — — fainting fits or faintness, iii. 418; iv. 296; v. 213.
— — — fever [*see also* ague *above*], ii. 7 (i. 7); iii. 81–2, 220; v. 420, 621; ~ malignant, iii. 243.
— — — gripes or gripings, iv. 161, 249; v. 69, 298.
— — — haemorrhoids or piles, iii. 38, 63, 212; v. 543, 552.
— — — head (no details), ii. 554.
— — — kidneys: pains in, iv. 275; v. 118, 518, 616, 621; gravel, v. 91, 230 *bis*, 527, 528, 591;

EVELYN, JOHN: health (*cont.*)
stone, v. 597, 602, 603, 605, 606, 611, 616.
— — — melancholy, v. 213.
— — — muscular pains, &c., iii. 538; iv. 341; v. 254.
— — — palpitations of the heart, v. 286.
— — — pleurisy: prevention of, iii. 77.
— — — scorbut (scurvy): prevention of, iii. 464 & n. 2.
— — — sea-sickness, ii. 559; iii. 16.
— — — smallpox, ii. 519 & n. 4, 521–2 & nn.
— — — spleen, iii. 243.
— — — stitch, ii. 31 (i. 24).
— — — stomach trouble, iii. 62.
— — — strangury, &c., v. 420; *see also* v. 421, 422.
— — — teeth: trouble with, ii. 149 (i. 96); iii. 538.
— — — vapours, v. 213.
— — — accidental injuries, &c.: due to falls, ii. 20 (i. 16); iii. 468; iv. 99, 101; v. 181, 299, n. 1, 532, 601; face peels, ii. 513; iii. 12; hurt on shoulder, iii. 5; sore hand, ii. 318; sore foot, iii. 1; struck by horse, ii. 557.
— — sleepiness at Sunday afternoon services [notices begin at iv. 207 and gradually, and with some notable intervals, become frequent; the most interesting notices are at iv. 249, 279–80, 313; v. 351, 470, 584; there is only one notice for a morning service, v. 273].
— — minor and undescribed ailments, &c., iii. 262, 356, 429, 476, 516, 584; iv. 104, 105, 160, 191, 375, 381, 639; v. 134, 135, 155, 156, 168, 213, 219, 262, 297, 452, 456, 516, 522–8 *passim*, 538 & n. 7, 567, 582, 583, 592, 609, 614, 619–22 *passim*.
— — treatment:
— — — more important notices: angina, ii. 472; smallpox, ii. 521–2; head trouble, ii. 554; sore teeth, iii. 538; ague, iv. 271–2.
— — — bleeding, ii. 479, 522, 535, 554; iii. 30, 38, 63, 77, 94, 143, 186, 212, 220, 232, 252, 356, 476, 538; iv. 99, 388; v. 496, 543; ~ from foot, iii. 212.
— — — blistering, ii. 554; iii. 538.

EVELYN, JOHN: health (*cont.*)
— — — cupping, &c., ii. 472.
— — — drinks medicinal waters: Epsom, v. 250, 255; Shooter's Hill, v. 351 & n. 2; Tunbridge, iii. 69, 71.
— — — lancing a gum, ii. 149 (i. 96).
— — — leeches, ii. 522 & n. 2; iii. 538.
— — — physick, iii. 30, 62, 77, 81, 212, 232; iv. 160, 192, 280, 361, 375; v. 297; course of, iii. 62, 94; preventing, &c., ii. 553; iii. 47, 191, 192; iv. 96, 388, 562, 632; v. 286.
— — — purging, ii. 522; iii. 212.
— — — sweating, &c., iii. 63.
— — — vomit, iv. 375, 562; v. 496; of mercury of life, iii. 220 & n. 3.
— legal:
— — Garro's claim against E, Tours, 1644, ii. 149 (i. 96); arrested on Simplon, ii. 512–13 & nn., 516, 518; law-suits: *v.* Captain G. Cocke, iii. 565 *bis* & n. 3, 580 *bis*; *v.* Lady Micklethwaite, iv. 368; *v.* W. Prettyman: *see* Prettyman William.
— — in case(?) at Guildhall, iv. 65.
— letters of recommendation for, ii. 422, 492; *see also* ii. 213.
— library:
— — general: moves books to Wotton, 1694, v. 179; George Evelyn bequeaths his library to E, v. 359.
— — catalogues: written by Richard Hoare, 1653, ii. 559, n. 2; dated 1687, *add.* (i. *87*); ~ books listed in, i. *87*; ii. 86, n. 1, 569 *bis*, 572, 578; *see also* ii. 257, n. 1 (book owned by E).
— — gifts of books to E, iii. 81 & n. 1, 294 & n. 2; v. 184, n. 2, 206 & n. 2, 583 & n. 4.
— — MSS. in: Elizabethan state papers: loan of, to G. Burnet, &c., iv. 241 & n. 3; ~ gift of, to Pepys, iv. 303, n. 3; pedigree of Yvelin family, iii. 548 & n. 3.
— — purchases for: books, ii. 67, 104 (i. 68), 401, 470, 478; Pflaumern, *Mercurius Italicus*, i. *87*, *98*; ii. 214, n. 1; maps, ii. 49; E desires copies of Bajazet II's letters to popes, ii. 499; E proposes to buy books from Dr. J. Cosin, iii. 62 & n. 8, 636.

EVELYN, JOHN (*cont.*)
— London residences:
— — E's personal lodgings: *see* London: topography: Middle Temple; Whitehall: personal.
— — family lodgings during winters:
— — — 1659–60: E seeks, iii. 233; Three Feathers, Russell Street, iii. 233 & n. 4; return to Sayes Court, iii. 244.
— — — 1661–2: near Westminster Abbey, iii. 301, n. 3, 317.
— — — 1683–4: family to winter in London, iv. 347 *bis*; takes Mr. Dive's house, Villiers Street, iv. 350 & n. 1; return to Sayes Court, iv. 375.
— — — 1686–7: at house of John Evelyn, jnr., Arundel Street, iv. 530; return to Sayes Court, iv. 546.
— — — 1689–90: in Soho Square, iv. 652 & n. 2; return to Sayes Court, v. 23.
— — — 1690–1: family to winter in London, v. 36; at house of John Evelyn, jnr., Dover Street, v. 37; return to Sayes Court, v. 53.
— — — 1691–2 (until August): in London, v. 72 (house not stated; probably that of John Evelyn, jnr., in Dover Street); return to Sayes Court, v. 114.
— — — 1692–3 (until June): 'our house in Dover Street' (that of John Evelyn, jnr.), v. 119; return to Sayes Court, v. 143; house to be let, v. 159, 164.
— — later residences:
— — — 1695–8 (with intervals): apparently in William Draper's house, Surrey Street, Strand: *see* v. 219, n. 6, 235; the churches attended by E indicate this or a neighbouring house.
— — — 1698–9: house in Berkeley Street, v. 292 & n. 5, 340.
— — — 1699–1706: takes lease of house of John Evelyn, jnr., Dover Street, v. 339–40.
— military: at siege of Gennep, i. *6*; ii. 33, 35–8 & nn. (i. 27–8); at Heusden: given complimentary command, ii. 59 (i. 40); orders horseman's armour, ii. 55 (i. 38); conduct in Civil War, i. *7*;

Evelyn, John: military (*cont.*)
joins Charles I at Brentford, ii. 79–80 (i. 53); sends horse to Charles I, ii. 81 & n. 5 (i. 54 & n. 2); advised to leave England, i. 53 & n. 2; offered captaincy in militia, 1660, iii. 254; required to provide horseman during Monmouth's rebellion, iv. 450, 458–9.
— motto of, i. *41* & n. 2; source of, iv. 168, n. 1.
— and music [for E's general interest, &c., *see* Music]: takes lessons: general, ii. 22; ~ on theorbo, &c., ii. 287, 473, 535.
— offices held by, in government service: *see* (Evelyn) as commissioner, &c., *above*.
— patronage [recommendations, &c.; E made only one presentation to a living (R. Bohun to Wotton)]:
— — ecclesiastical preferment: R. Bohun: recommended to Tenison, v. 256; E presents to Wotton, &c., v. 447, 456; E obtains prebend for, v. 473.
— — — recommendations for: J. Evans to Compton, iv. 127; Dr. W. Graham to Tenison for bishopric of Carlisle, v. 257; L. Moody for Eltham, iii. 195 & n 3; W. Strengfellow: to Sancroft, iv. 641 & n. 5; ~ to Tenison, v. 27, 61–2, 376; W. Wells to Tenison, v. 199.
— — — recommends chaplain to Godolphin, v. 534; pays J. Le Franc's ordination fees, iii. 172.
— — recommendations for secular employment: T. Henshaw: for embassy to Turkey, iii. 248–9; ~ for French secretary, iii. 294; Dr. T. Hoy to Sunderland, &c., v. 298 & n. 2; — Messervy for office in Jersey, iii. 251 & n. 4; — Spelman to Lord Mordaunt, iii. 263; W. Vanbrugh for secretary to Greenwich Hospital commissioners, v. 211–12.
— — miscellaneous: befriends C. Wase, iii. 55; books dedicated to: by T. Barlow, iii. 106, n. 4, 534, n. 1; ~ by W. Rand, iii. 189 & n. 6; etching dedicated to, iii. 166, n. 5; introduces Grinling Gibbons to Charles II, &c., iii. 568, 571–3; invited to

Evelyn, John: patronage (*cont.*)
subscribe to Walton's *Polyglot*, iii. 78 & nn. 3, 4; persuades Henry Howard, duke of Norfolk, to give: Arundel inscriptions to Oxford, iii. 495–6 & n., 497, 498–500; ~ Arundel library to Royal Society, iii. 472–3; iv. 144–5.
— petitions: *see* Prettyman, W.: litigation with E; Sayes Court: estate.
— political [select; E's activities and general views; casual comments on particular occurrences, &c., are not indexed collectively. For offices, &c., held by E *see* (Evelyn) as commissioner, &c. *above*]:
— — general attitude, i. *113–14*; constitutional views, i. *28*; moderation, i. *29*, *31*; dislike of party names, 1685, &c., iv. 439, 614; v. 612; on violent conduct of parliaments, iv. 628.
— — conduct in Civil War, i. *7*; ii. 79–80 (i. 53), 81 & n. 5 (i. 54 & n. 2); evades taking Solemn Vow and Covenant, 1643, ii. 81–2 & n. (i. 55); visits Charles I, 1647, ii. 537; fasts on day of Charles I's execution, ii. 547; reception of, by exiled royalists, i. *10*; sends political information to king, &c., abroad, ii. 552 & n. 4; iii. 59, 200 & n. 1; correspondent of, in England, 1649–50, ii. 558 & n. 4; never took oaths to Commonwealth, &c., iii. 15–16, 223; negotiation with Col. H. Morley, 1659–60, i. *13–14*; iii. 235, n. 4, 237–40 & nn., *passim*, 245; ~ account of, i. *24*, n. 2; invited to go with commissioners to Charles II, 1660, iii. 244–5 & n.; reception of, by Charles II, iii. 247; signs Sussex address to Charles II, 1660, iii. 249 & n. 5; subservience of, to James II, i. *31*, *32* & n. 1; writes to warn Sancroft against Roman Catholic ruses, Oct. 1688, i. *33*; iv. 600 & n. 4; *see also* iv. 601, n. 1, 614; views on crisis, 1688–9, i. *33*; iv. 606; Jacobites attempt to win, i. *33*; v. 92 & n. 2; attends services in Jacobite's chapel, v. 142–3 & nn.; attends presentation of

EVELYN, JOHN: political (*cont.*)
Surrey address to William III, 1697, v. 279; hatred of Louis XIV, i. 67, n. 1, 68, n. 2; conduct of, in Surrey elections: 1701, v. 482 *bis*; ~ 1705, v. 595.
— portraits: engraved: account of, mentioned, i. *120*; by: Chanterell, ii. 7 (i. 7); Mrs. Evelyn, on frontispiece of E's *Lucretius*, iii. 173, n. 2; Sir G. Kneller: 1685, iv. 479 & n. 2; *add.*; ~ for Pepys, iv. 644 & n. 1, 646; *add.* (iv. 479); R. Nanteuil, iii. 9–10 & n., 22 & n. 9; H. van der Borcht, ii. 29 & n. 1 (i. 21); L. van der Bruggen (Hans), ii. 133 & n. 2 (i. 87); R. Walker, ii. 541 & n. 6; anon., with helmet, at Wotton, ii. 55, n. 2.
— property, income, &c.:
— — general: heritage, i. 5, 12; ii. 27, n. 2; ~ business relating to, ii. 26–7 & n. (i. 20); income, i. 5, n. 2; *add.*; settles his estate on John Evelyn, jnr., 1680, iv. 193; ~ alluded to, iv. 194; settles his estate on (Sir) John Evelyn, 1705, v. 606, 607; settlement on daughter-in-law (Mrs. Martha Evelyn), iv. 194; marriage-settlement on daughter (Mrs. Susanna Draper), v. 138; ~ land sold, to pay, v. 153–4 *bis*.
— — accounts [E apparently made up his accounts annually on or about 31 Dec.: notices, 1650–3, 1655, 1669, 1684–5, 1690–9, &c.; more vaguely, as his domestic affairs, 1656–7, 1659, 1661–4; in other years there is only an annual thanksgiving. He states the amount only once, in 1650: iii. 24. Accounts made up on other dates, iii. 44, 77. Private accounts, 1698 (for Sayes Court?), v. 284.]
— — claims on Crown [as Sir Richard Browne's executor (iv. 305 *bis*, 340, 551) E inherited Browne's claims for repayment of money lent to the king; for them *see* Browne, Sir Richard: property; for the dispute arising from them *see* Prettyman, William.]
— — investments and speculations:

EVELYN, JOHN: property, &c. (*cont.*)
in project for reduction of Ireland, 1642: proposed, ii. 78 (i. 52); in East India Company's New General Stock, 1657, iii. 201–2 & n., 203 & n. 1; ~ dividend on, iii. 365 & n. 1; ~ alluded to(?), iv. 273 & n. 5; ~ sold to Royal Society, iv. 297, 298; project with Sir. J. Kievit for making clinker-brick, &c., iii. 471, 476 & n. 3, 477–8 *bis*, 495; ~ E's loss on, i. 5, n. 2; project for making houllies: offer of share in, iii. 487; loans by E on mortgage, &c., ii. 545 *bis* (& iii. 418); iii. 151, 152, 153; payments to E, ii. 545, 557; iii. 93.
— — land, estates, houses, &c.:
— — — general: inherited property, ii. 27, n. 2; property in Sussex: influence of, on E's conduct in Civil War, i. 53; *see also* ii. 79; ~ tenants near Lewes, ii. 27 & n. 2 (i. 20); rent-charge terminates, iii. 25.
— — — particular properties:
— — — — The Cliffe, Lewes, house at, ii. 27, n. 2; visit to, ii. 544; sold, iii. 65.
— — — — Great Warley: *see* Great Warley.
— — — — Hanson or Honson Grange: sold, &c., iv. 415 & n. 2.
— — — — Hurcott, manor of: bought and sold, ii. 541 & n. 5, 545 & n. 3.
— — — — North Stoke: sold, &c., v. 441 & n. 5.
— — — — Pilton, fee-farm of: sold, iv. 378 & n. 2.
— — — — Preston Beckhelvyn in Beddingham, manor of: visit to, ii. 544 & n. 2; farm in, leased(?), ii. 552; sold, iii. 151 *bis*.
— — — — Ripe, farm in, ii. 27, n. 2; lease of, ii. 555 & n. 5; visit to, iv. 40.
— — — — Sayes Court: *see* Sayes Court: manor of *and* estate.
— — — — South Malling, land in, ii. 27, n. 2; *see also below*.
— — — — Wotton: *see* Wotton: Wotton estate.
— — — — London: leasehold property [long leases; for other London houses occupied by E

EVELYN, JOHN: property, &c. (*cont.*) *see* London residences *above*]: part of chamber in Middle Temple: *see* London: topography: Middle Temple (ii. 24, n. 4, &c.); lodgings in Bell Yard, near Whitehall, iv. 50 & n. 3; *add.*; ~ mentioned or implied (?), iv. 72, 194, 271, 592; house in Dover Street, v. 339–40.
— — — miscellaneous: impropriation of St. Michael's, South Malling, ii. 8 & n. 4 (i. 7–8), 27, n. 2; ~ sold, ii. 541; interest in entail of Baynards, iv. 582–3 & n.
— — — proposed purchases: Albury, iii. 59, n. 1; Bolney Court, ii. 540 & n. 5.
— — offices and salaries [for other offices held by E, &c., *see* (Evelyn) as Commissioner, &c. *above*]: Clerk of the Council: E sells reversion of, iii. 601; Commissioner for Sick and Wounded, 1664, &c.: salary as, iii. 387, n. 5, 388; member of Council for Foreign Plantations (later of Trade and Plantations), 1671–4: salary as, iii. 571, 574 & n. 2.
— — personal property [*see also* collections *and* library *above*]:
— — — general: goods dispersed during Civil War, &c., ii. 553; inventory of, 1649, *ib.*; receives books, &c., from England, 1651, iii. 39; goods from France, 1652, iii. 53, 62, 63, 68; inventory, Sayes Court, 1682, iv. 272; bequest from George Evelyn, v. 359 & n. 9.
— — — particular [*see also* robberies and thefts *below*]: furniture: removals, &c., v. 164, 179, 340; cabinet, ii. 191 & n. 13 (i. 119), 198; coaches, new: 1652, iii. 65, 75; ~ 1654, iii. 94, 98; ~ 1666, iii. 433; ~ 1679, iv. 170; ~ 1701, v. 470; chariot: 1666, iii. 468 & n. 2; ~ new, 1701, v. 470; carbine, ii. 489, 528.
— — — miscellaneous: starts managing his own expenses, 1638, ii. 21 (i. 16); repays minor debts, iii. 13, 200; clear of debt, 1653, iii. 85; mortgage: E transfers to George Evelyn, iii. 509; ~ payments on, iv. 378, 380; pays poll-tax as esquire, 1660, iii. 258 & n. 1; relations with Clifford and Danby, iv. 14 & n. 1, 20.

EVELYN, JOHN: property, &c. (*cont.*)

— relations [most of E's relations are traceable through the genealogical tables at i. 136–44. The persons entered below do not appear in the tables, but are described by E or in the notes as his relations. References are given only to the passages or notes in which the relationship is claimed or defined]: — Carew, v. 183 & n. 2; Gertrude Cheyne, Lady Cheyne and Viscountess Newhaven, v. 7 & n. 5, 100, 518; Elizabeth Maccarty, countess of Clancarty, iv. 244, n. 5; Gregory Cole, iii. 470 & n. 2; Dr. T. Comber, iv. 286, n. 2; Sir Humphrey Forster, second bt., iv. 313 & n. 3; — Hall, iii. 370 & n. 7; Robert Heath, iii. 502, n. 5; T. and W. Keightley, ii. 149 & n. 2 (i. 97); Anthony Grey, earl of Kent, iii. 372 & n. 1; v. 518; George FitzGerald, earl of Kildare, iv. 244; Lady Langham (error ?), iii. 143 & n. 5; Sir R. Langley, iii. 394 & n. 1; Sir R. Lechford, iii. 561 & n. 4; Mrs. Jane Myddelton, iv. 334 & n. 5; Sir R. Needham, iii. 198 & n. 3; iv. 334; Thomas Offley, iii. 458; *see* ii. 537, n. 2, 544, n. 5; Col. Daniel Parke, v. 574 & n. 2; Lady Shaen, iv. 244, n. 5; Mrs. Joanna Thornhill, iv. 9 & n. 4; — Verney, iv. 382 & n. 3; Sir F. Vincent, v. 55, n. 3; John Williams, archbishop of York, iii. 136 & n. 6.
— religion [notices relating to E's own religious life and activities; similar notices of a less personal nature are indexed under Church of England and the religious bodies named in section on E's views *below*.
— — general: Church of England: E attached to, i. 5, 7; ~ adherence to, during Commonwealth, iii. 90; ~ durability of, &c.: E's belief in, iv. 479; belief in Providence, iv. 575, 581.

EVELYN, JOHN: religion (*cont.*)
— — religious history: first Communion, ii. 19 (i. 15); confirmed, ii. 23 (i. 17); ~ alluded to, iv. 6; avoids taking Covenant, ii. 81–2 & n. (i. 55); church-going during Commonwealth, &c.: remarks on, iii. 60, 144, 185; first hears sectary, &c., preach, iii. 67, 91; adopts spiritual father, iii. 149 & n. 2; usually spends Holy Week in London, iv. 6, 435, 629; resolves to lead more holy life, &c., iv. 47, 75; composes devotional works, &c., iv. 126 & n. 5, 272, 568 & n. 1; self-examination, &c., on sixtieth birthday, iv. 223–4 *bis*; repents his errors, &c., v. 153, 192; his 'funeral sermon', v. 550.
— — habits:
— — — Communion [notices of Communion services. In the earlier notices as a rule E only mentions the services; from about 1684 he generally states explicitly that he received the Sacrament; this appears to be only a change of formula. In 1650 and 1651 and from 1660 to 1706 only the number of celebrations in each year is given below. For E's preparation for the Sacrament *see* Church of England: worship]:
— — — — early period: 1637–9, ii. 19–23 *passim* (i. 15–17) (9 occasions); 1640–July 1641, ii. 23, 28, 29 (i. 17, 21); Nov. 1641–1643, ii. 77–81 *passim* (i. 51–5) (6 occasions).
— — — — London, 1649, ii. 552, 556.
— — — — Paris, 1649–52: 1649, ii. 562, 564, 566, 567 *bis*; 1650, 8 celebrations; 1651, 12 celebrations (notice, iii. 45, repeated, iii. 635).
— — — — England, 1652–May 1660: 1652, iii. 61, 64; 1653, iii. 79, 82, 89; 1654, iii. 94, 95, 145; 1655, iii. 150, 152, 160, 164; 1656, iii. 167, 169, 181, 185; 1657, iii. 189, 190, 195, 197, 201, 203–4; 1658, iii. 211, 214, 222, 225; 1659, iii. 228, 230, 232, 233, 236, 238; 1660, iii. 239, 243 *bis*, 244.

EVELYN, JOHN: religion (*cont.*)
— — — — England, June 1660–Feb. 1706: numbers of celebrations: 1660 (part), 3; 1661–4, 5, 6, 10, 5; 1665–8, 8 (or 9), 6, 12, 12; 1669–72, 11, 10, 12, 12; 1673–6, 17, 22, 33, 27 (or 28); 1677–80, 21, 25, 21, 18; 1681–4, 15, 16, 17, 18; 1685–8, 14, 19, 21, 17; 1689–92, 17, 17, 20, 16; 1693–6, 13, 12, 8, 9; 1697 (incomplete), 6; 1698 (incomplete), 11; 1699–1700, 10, 10; 1701–3, 6, 9, 6; 1704 (incomplete), 8; 1705 (incomplete), 10; 1706 (part), 1.
— — — notes of sermons [for the reports in the Diary *see* i. *82–3* & nn., *111*. E also made separate reports of more important sermons, 1650–87; for them *see* i. *83* & n. 1. They are mentioned by E, as 'your notes', &c., at iii. 8, 12, 38, 39, 61, and onwards to iv. 546, but the citations are unevenly distributed, none occurring between iii. 245 and iii. 505. For E's remarks about sermons *see* Preaching and Sermons.]
— — — annual thanksgivings and prayers, ejaculations, reflections, &c. [in most years, beginning in 1649–50, E closes the old year with thanks and opens the new with a prayer; he generally gives thanks on his birthday (31 Oct.) from 1652 onwards. Pious ejaculations occur frequently for reception of the Sacrament and the ordinary incidents of life, such as recoveries from illnesses; and on political or public occasions (*e.g.* iii. 164, 244, 259; v. 2, 27, 29); they become more frequent as E grows older. Reflections are comparatively rare; specimens: on surgical operations or torture, iii. 4, 29, 610; on moral and political topics, iii. 189, 246, 269, 464; iv. 344, 530. There is a special prayer in time of danger on E's birthday in 1688: iv. 603.]
— — parochial activities, &c.: E's influence on clergy, i. *111*; concern in presentation of vicars to Deptford, iii. 227–8, 302, 604,

EVELYN, JOHN: religion (*cont.*) 613; for concern in other presentations, &c., *see* Evelyn: patronage *above*; complains about services at Wotton, i. *36*; v. 180, 181; concern in conduct of Wotton parishioners at divine service, v. 577; feoffee for poor of Deptford, iii. 223 & n. 4(?), 318 & n. 3, &c.; vestryman, St. Nicholas, Deptford, iii. 317; subscribes to rebuilding St. Nicholas, Deptford, v. 348, n. 2; contributes to repairing Oakwood chapel, v. 603; urges Sir R. Clayton to rebuild Woldingham church, iv. 121–2 & n.

— — views on religious bodies other than the Church of England:

— — — French protestants: persecution of: E's views on, i. *29*, *32*; for E's further remarks, attendance at services, &c., *see* French protestants; persuades J. Le Franc to join Church of England, iii. 172.

— — — Greek rite: interest in, ii. 399, 460 & n. 2.

— — — Jews: attends ceremonies, &c., ii. 42–3 & nn. (i. 31), 292–4, 477; hears sermons to, at Rome, &c., ii. 291–2, 376–7; projects visit to Holy Land, ii. 451–2, 468; interest in spoils of the Temple, ii. 247 & n. 4.

— — — Protestant Nonconformists: tolerance towards, i. *29–30*; iii. 608–9 & n.

— — — Quakers: visits, in Ipswich gaol, iii. 179 & n. 2.

— — — Roman Catholic church: attitude towards, i. *26*; believes in Popish Plot, i. *28*; attends services and sermons, ii. 290, 384, 385–6; iii. 23; iv. 534–5; anti-Romanist remarks, iii. 585, 612; iv. 408, 599; on priestly fraud, &c., ii. 290; iii. 118; iv. 251–2; sceptical about relics, &c. (the stronger expressions), ii. 87–90 (i. 58–60); i. 65; ii. 273–4 & n., 275, 319, 365, 380, 500; discussions: with H. Holden, ii. 567; ~ with Don P. Ronquillo, iv. 242–3; ~ on corporal presence in Sacrament, iv. 129–30; concern in controversy,

EVELYN, JOHN: religion (*cont.*) iv. 282–3 & n.; *see also* Evelyn: books *above*.

— — miscellaneous: Biblical knowledge: error in, ii. 268–9 & nn.; ~ quotes Beza's translation, iii. 454 & n. 2; catechizes his family, &c., iii. 160; views: on burial in churches, iv. 304, 634; ~ on private baptism, iv. 634; *see also* ii. 5 (i. 6).

— robberies and thefts from:

— — general: precaution against theft or seizure of goods, ii. 553.

— — personal: clothing, &c., stolen by valet, Paris, 1647, ii. 535; rings, &c., taken by foot-pads, Bromley, 1652, iii. 69–71, 73, 74 & nn.; dogs stolen or lost, ii. 533, 560–1; E in danger of robbery at Amsterdam, iii. 71 & n. 1.

— — piracy: Mrs. Evelyn's portrait: taken, ii. 551; ~ recovered, iii. 56 & n. 1, 62; ~ alluded to(?), iii. 71 & n. 1.

— — Sayes Court: thefts of plate, &c., from, iii. 226, 352; attempted theft at, iii. 265; coach-house at: thefts from, iv. 72, 259.

— — E's footman robbed on road, iii. 378.

— and Royal Society:

— — general notice, i. *15* & n. 1; projects mathematical college, 1659, iii. 232 & n. 2; elected to, iii. 266 & n. 6; thanked for calling it Royal Society, iii. 306 & n. 1; sketches arms for, &c., iii. 332, n. 2.

— — service on council, &c.: nominated member of council in first and second charters, iii. 266 & n. 6, 332 & n. 1, 355, n. 2; elected member of council, &c., iii. 519, 565; iv. 103, 190, 263, 396, 652; v. 198, 304; elected member, but excused, iii. 434 & n. 3; iv. 225; elected secretary, iii. 630 & n. 5; proposed, &c., for president, iv. 296 & n. 6; v. 39, 160; as vice-president, iv. 450; as member of committees, iii. 351 & n. 4, 374 & n. 8, 396 & n. 4, 400–1 & n., 433 & n. 3; takes chair at society's meetings, iv. 128, 259, 275, 299, n. 1, 395 & n. 4, 450

EVELYN, JOHN: Royal Society (*cont.*) & n. 1; deputed to administer oath to new president, iv. 125 & n. 7; v. 304; deputed to compliment strangers, iv. 212 & n. 3, 283; on deputation concerning Stillingfleet's library, v. 324.

— — miscellaneous services to society: persuades Henry Howard (later sixth duke of Norfolk) to give Norfolcian library to, iii. 472–3; iv. 144; gives anatomical tables to, iii. 501 & n. 2; *see also* ii. 475 & n. 5; projected building for society: helps to lay out, iii. 505; ~ subscribes bricks for, iii. 507; negotiates sale of Chelsea College, iv. 257 & n. 3; sells East India Company stock to society, iv. 297, 298; ~ letter relating to(?), iv. 273 & n. 5; proposes candidate for fellowship, iii. 401, n. 7.

— — scientific activities, &c.: presents books: *Parallel of Architecture*, iii. 380, n. 4; *Sculptura*, iii. 325 & nn. 2, 3; *Sylva*: as MS. discourse, iii. 340 & n. 1; ~ first edition, iii. 369 & n. 2; ~ second edition, iii. 541 & n. 4.

— — — reads papers, ii. 568, n. 3; iii. 359, n. 3; iv. 62 & n. 4; writes papers for, iii. 271, n. 4, 401, n. 8; iv. 376 & n. 1; ordered to make experiments, iii. 293 & n. 1, 316; forwards account of Tenerife, iii. 274 & n. 3; proposes planting Forest of Dean to society, iii. 343 & n. 3.

— and science [for his studies *see* education *above*; for his general interest see the various subjects; for his activities as F.R.S. *see* (Evelyn) and Royal Society *above*]: E's scientific attainments, i. *12*; anatomy: interest in monsters, ii. 40, n. 3; ~ E's anatomical tables, ii. 475 & n. 5, 553; iii. 77–8, 501 & n. 2; v. 487 & n. 1; ~ attends dissection, ii. 553–4; ~ attends vivisection of dog, iii. 497–8; astronomy: views on comets as portents, iv. 235; botany: E's *hortus siccus*, ii. 466 & n. 5;

EVELYN, JOHN: science (*cont.*) chemistry: interest in phosphorus, ii. 397–8 & n., 422–3 & n.; iv. 251–3 & nn., 263, 491; surgery: sees operations for stone, iii. 3–4.

— servants:

— — on E's travels: unnamed: in United Provinces, ii. 57 (i. 39); in France, iii. 12, 17; passes for E and, ii. 477–8; iii. 16, n. 1.

— — — named valets: Garro, at Tours: action of, against E, ii. 149 (i. 96); Hebert, at Paris: steals from E, ii. 535; La Roch: in Bataille de Vamber, iii. 5; ~ discharged, iii. 44.

— — — *see also* Hoare, R.

— — at Sayes Court and Wotton, &c.: collective: left at Sayes Court, winter 1683–4, iv. 350; divided between Wotton and Sayes Court, 1694, v. 179; household or staff at Wotton: number of, 1702, 1703, v. 509, 550; women-servants: dress of, v. 542.

— — — men, by employ: butler (H. Prideaux): dies, iv. 357 *bis* & n. 1; ~ alluded to (?), iv. 464; coachman: made drunk while E pays visit, iii. 112, 525; ~ accident to, iii. 295; ~ dies, &c., iv. 508, 509, 511; ~ wins lottery-prize, v. 158; footman: sent ahead on journey, iii. 69; ~ robbed on journey, iii. 378; gardener, v. 478; ~ (J. Mosse): apprenticed to E, iv. 521 & n. 3; lackey (T. Heath): apprenticed to carpenter, iii. 95; ~ in Royal Society experiment, iii. 292; ~ (Adams) dies, iii. 631; ~ ill, iv. 153; steward at Wotton, 1702, v. 499.

— — — men, duties not stated: at Sayes Court, 1698: letter from, quoted, v. 284, n. 5; at Wotton, 1699, v. 360; married, &c., iii. 167; ill, iv. 638; (J. Smith) dies, iii. 566; (Jo:) accident to, iv. 654; *see also* Hoare, R.; Strickland, J.

— — — women: maid of Mrs. Evelyn ill, &c., iv. 432–3; marriages of, &c., iii. 167; iv. 194; children's nurses or maids, iii. 145, 208, 209 *bis*, 371; iv. 350.

EVELYN, JOHN (*cont.*)
— travelling expenses: in Italy: drawings of money, ii. 401 & n. 6, 408, 480 & n. 1; fails to obtain credit in Rome, ii. 401, 408; bills of exchange for, ii. 401, 408, n. 8, 477; letter of credit of, ii. 408 & n. 8.
— — costs: illness, &c., at Geneva, ii. 530 & n. 5; journeys: Rome–Venice, ii. 429 & n. 6; Paris–Calais, iii. 12; lodgings, &c., ii. 212–13, 325, n. 5, 429, n. 5, 534.
— and tree-planting [*see also* gardens and gardening *above*]: at Sayes Court, iii. 370 & n. 4, 393 & n. 3(?); *see also* i. *38*; iii. 80; at Wotton, 1701, v. 480; plane-tree given to E, iii. 386, n. 6; advises on, at: Cassiobury, iv. 201; Cornbury, iii. 381, 382 & n. 4; Cranbourn Lodge, iv. 527; Euston, iii. 591; iv. 117.
— as trustee, executor, or agent:
— — as executor or trustee appointed by will, &c.: for: R. Boyle: *see* Boyle Lectures; Sir Richard Browne, iv. 340, 551 (for litigation arising from executorship *see* Prettyman, W.); ~ former servant of, iii. 241; John Evelyn, jnr., v. 340 & n. 3; Richard Evelyn, iii. 545; William Howard: E trustee for Mrs. Howard and daughters, iv. 67, 70–1 & n., 105–6, 106; Elizabeth Mordaunt, Lady Mordaunt: care of children of, iv. 173, 188–9, 202, 258, 259, 289, 335; George Tuke: *see* Tuke, G.
— — as agent for living persons: for: Lord Berkeley: during embassy, 1675–7: *see* Berkeley, John, Lord Berkeley of Stratton; Anne Digby, countess of Bristol: for sale of house, iv. 170, 185 & n. 2, 335; Francis Godolphin, later second earl of Godolphin: for his education, &c., iv. 155, 182, 337, 463; ~ investment for, iv. 559; Mrs. Godolphin: miscellaneous: *see* Godolphin, Mrs. Margaret: property; Henry Mordaunt, earl of Peterborough: for sale of Blechingley, &c., iv. 108–9 & n., 110–11; Mr. & Mrs. Thayre: trust, iv. 446 & n. 6, 489; George Tuke: trust, iii. 190; Sir Samuel Tuke: for sale of Cressing Temple, iii. 542.

EVELYN, JOHN: trustee, &c. (*cont.*)
— — uncertain: *see* Tuke, Mary, (second) Lady Tuke.
— wills: new or revised, 1647–55, ii. 536, 557; iii. 12, 77, 160; new, 1682, iv. 272; ~ altered, iv. 462; new, 1700–1, v. 422, 461; ~ revised, 1704, v. 560; E transfers real estate to (Sir) John Evelyn, &c., 1705, v. 606; last will, 1706: witness to, v. 98, n. 3; ~ alluded to, iii. 69, n. 2.
— and Wotton: *see* Wotton.
Evelyn, John, jnr., 1655–99, E's son [he is distinguished elsewhere in the index as 'John Evelyn, jnr.']:
— early life: born, iii. 146–7 & n.; baptized, iii. 147; little Richard Evelyn's advice to, iii. 208; visits Wotton, iii. 218; presented to Henrietta Maria, 1660, iii. 263 & n. 6.
— education: brought up with sons of Henry Howard, later sixth duke of Norfolk, 1662–3, iii. 326, 329, 355; iv. 142; tutors of, i. *23–4*; tutor required, 1663, iii. 364; Edward Phillips as, iii. 364–5 & n., 401; Dr. Ralph Bohun as, iii. 416.
— — goes to Trinity College, Oxford, accompanied by R. Bohun, 1667, iii. 474 *ter* & nn. 3, 5; Dr. R. Bathurst in charge of, iv. 68; tutor of, at Oxford, iv. 78 & n. 4, 493 & n. 4; *add.*; vacations, iii. 482, 506; leaves Oxford, 1669, iii. 525; admitted to Middle Temple, 1672, iii. 613–14 & n.; called to the bar, 1683, and proposes to study further, iv. 375 & n. 3.
— boyhood and early manhood: accompanies E to Kentish ports, iii. 409, 468; taken to Wotton to avoid plague, iii. 416; presented to Charles II, iii. 440; watches Fire of London, iii. 451; in coach-accident, iii. 468 & n. 4; confirmed, iii. 472; presented to Clarendon, iii. 474; visits Calais, &c., 1670, iii. 548–9; translates Rapin, iv. 1 & n. 4; religious instruction

Evelyn, John, jnr., 1655–99 (*cont.*) for, iv. 6; first Communion, iv. 7; later Communions, iv. 28, 31, 32; sworn younger brother of Trinity House, iv. 12; visits Windsor, iv. 38; dines at Arlington's, iv. 78, 102; visits France, 1675–6, iv. 76, 78, 79, 80, 91; i. *25*.

— marriage and later life: proposed marriage for, 1677, iv. 112; given book of devotions by E, iv. 126 & n. 5; marriage of, with Martha Spencer: negotiation for, 1679–80, iv. 189–94 *passim*; ~ celebrated, iv. 194–5; appointed feoffee for poor at Deptford, iv. 202; sends horseman to Kentish militia, 1685, iv. 458–9; visits Wotton, iv. 557; employed by Treasury, 1687, iv. 565; visits Althorp, iv. 592; joins William of Orange, iv. 609 & n. 10; visits Tunbridge Wells, iv. 646; attends funeral of John Evelyn of Wotton, 1691, v. 55; appointed a commissioner of Irish Treasury, &c., 1692, v. 92 & n. 1, 240, n. 1; visits Cranbourn, v. 110–11; goes to Ireland, v. 113, 116; returns from Ireland, 1696, v. 240; visits Wotton, 1697–8, v. 266, 282, 286; concern of, in Wotton estate, 1699, v. 337, n. 5; death and burial of, v. 318 & n. 1, 319 & n. 3; estate of: administration of, v. 340 & n. 3.

— health: early illnesses, iii. 232, 233, 265, 290, 367; crooked leg to be rectified, iii. 317; smallpox, iv. 72 *bis*; further illnesses: 1679, iv. 180; ~ 1693, v. 93 & n. 3, 103; in perfect health, 1695, v. 219; illness in last years, v. 240, 265, 266, 269, 282, 283, 318, 340; E's prayers for, v. 269, 299.

— residences, 1680–99: at Sayes Court, 1680, iv. 196; sets up house in London, 1684, iv. 375; house in Arundel Street, iv. 392, 395 & n. 5, 530; *see also* iv. 523, 546, 603, 606; new house (in Dover Street?), 1689, iv. 642 & n. 2; house in Dover Street (same?), 1690, v. 37 & n. 4; ~ Trinity Chapel erected near, &c., v. 61, 62; ~ occupied by E during Evelyn's absence in Ireland, v. 119; ~ to be let, 1693, v. 159, 164; ~ lease of: taken over by E, 1699, v. 339–40; *see also* v. 27, 292, n. 5 *ad fin.*; house in Berkeley Street, 1698 (error?), v. 292 & n. 5.

Evelyn, John, 1554–1627, of Godstone, E's uncle, i. 2 & nn. 4, 5; as manufacturer of gunpowder, i. 3, n. 1, 52, n. 2; builds Lee Place, Godstone, ii. 557, n. 4; iii. 219; geneal., ii. 553, n. 7; iii. 198, n. 3, 372, n. 1.

Evelyn, Sir John, 1591–1664, of Godstone, E's first cousin, ii. 553, n. 7; as manufacturer of gunpowder, i. 52 & n. 2; views of, on Civil War, i. *6* & n. 2; acquires Godstone, ii. 557, n. 4; buys Squerryes, iii. 90 & nn. 3, 4; godfather of John Evelyn, jnr. (?), iii. 147 & n. 1; wedding anniversary of, iii. 237 & n. 1; excused serving as sheriff for Surrey, iii. 365 & n. 4; tomb, &c., of, iv. 122 & n. 2; social, ii. 78 (i. 51), 81, 553, 557; iii. 174, 213(?), 219, 236 & n. 3; geneal., iii. 174, n. 2, 219 & n. 3; iv. 121, n. 3; v. 56, n. 3, 218, n. 6, 340.

Evelyn, Sir John, bt., 1633–71, of Godstone, E's first cousin once removed, iv. 121, n. 3; ii. 553, n. 7 *ad fin.*; and Godstone estate: inherits, ii. 557 & n. 4; ~ demolishes house (Lee Place), i. 51–2 & n.; sells Marden, iv. 121 & n. 3; v. 426; estate of: passes from the Evelyns, v. 337 & n. 1.

Evelyn, John, of Kingston, E's great-grandfather, i. *1*; as manufacturer of gunpowder, i. 2–3; geneal., iii. 470, n. 2.

Evelyn, John, 1677–1702, of Nutfield, E's first cousin twice removed: dies, v. 520 & n. 5.

Evelyn, Sir John, 1601–85, of West Dean and Everley, E's first cousin once removed [he is distinguished elsewhere as 'Sir John Evelyn of Wilts'], ii. 553, n. 7; conduct of, in Civil War, i. *6*; estate of: passes from the Evelyns, v. 337 & n. 1; social, ii. 553, 557; iii. 213(?); geneal., i. 3, n. 2; iv. 551; v. 7, n. 5, 150, n. 6 *ad fin.*, 310; *see also* iii. 147 & n. 1.

Evelyn, John, 1653–91, of Wotton, E's nephew, son of George Evelyn: born, iii. 89 & n. 2; marriage negotiation for, iv. 195–6 & n.; marriage of, iv. 238; v. 359; godfather of (Sir) John Evelyn, iv. 272; death, character, &c., of, v. 54 & n. 1, 55; buried, v. 55–6 & nn.

Evelyn, Sir John, first bt., 1682–1763, of Wotton, E's grandson; created baronet 1713 [he is distinguished elsewhere as '(Sir) John Evelyn'], iv. 272, n. 2.
early life: born, &c., iv. 272, 277; ill, iv. 337, 653, 654; at Sayes Court, iv. 350, 360.
education: attends French school at Greenwich, 1689, iv. 653; formal exercises at school of, v. 79 & n. 3; goes to Eton, 1692, v. 103, 110; proficiency of, at Eton, v. 162, 236; school holidays, v. 162, 201; at Oxford: enters Balliol College, 1699, v. 314 & n. 8, 318; prepares for first Communion, v. 322; vacations, v. 367, 373 (receives Sacrament), 422, 439; has smallpox (at Oxford), v. 431–2, 434, 435, 480; leaves, 1701, v. 484 & n. 1.
appointments: receiver for Stamp Duties, 1704, v. 556 & n. 1; commissioner of Prizes, 1705, v. 601–2 & n.; joint Postmaster-general, 1708, iii. 442, n. 2.
marriage with Anne Boscawen, 1705: negotiation for, v. 588, 600, 602; settlement on, v. 605, 606, 607; receives Sacrament with her, v. 608; ceremony, v. 609; entertainment for, v. 609–10.
miscellaneous: concern of, in Wotton estate, v. 337, n. 5; obtains grant in fee-farm of Sayes Court, iii. 59, n. 1; E bequeaths ring to, iii. 69, n. 2; buys portrait of E, *add.* (iv. 479, n. 2); visits: Land's End, 1702, v. 515 & n. 4; ~ Wotton, v. 521, 591, 613; ~ Greenwich, v. 600; attends parliamentary election, 1705, v. 595; godfather of Evelyn Draper, v. 582; receives mourning-ring for Pepys, v. 538, n. 6; letters of, v. 322 & n. 4, 417, n. 2, 434, 484, n. 1; transcribes part of Diary, i. *47*, *47–8*, *52*.

Evelyn, Sir John, 2nd bt., of Wotton, i. *52*.

Evelyn, John, 1743–1827: inherits Wotton estate, 1817, v. 339, n. 2.

Evelyn, John Stansfield, 1653–4, E's son: born and baptized, iii. 89 & n. 3; ill, iii. 91 *bis*; dies, &c., iii. 92–3 & n.

Evelyn, Katherine, E's great-niece, daughter of George Evelyn, jnr., of Wotton: *see* Fulham, Mrs. Catherine.

Evelyn, Katherine, first cousin, daughter of Thomas Evelyn: *see* Kendrick, Mrs. K.

Evelyn, Mrs. Katherine, born Eversfield, wife of John Evelyn of Wotton, E's nephew, iv. 196, n. 1; v. 359 & n. 6; marriage negotiation for, iv. 195–6; wedding, &c., iv. 238; miscarries, iv. 282; character, v. 54.

Evelyn, Katherine: *see also* Evelyn, Catherine.

Evelyn, Margaret, daughter of George Evelyn of Nutfield, E's first cousin once removed: *see* Hussey, Mrs. M.

Evelyn, Mrs. Martha, E's daughter-in-law, born Spencer, wife of John Evelyn, jnr., iv. 189, n. 4; character, iv. 569; marriage negotiation for, iv. 189, 192, 193, 194; dowry of, iv. 194, 196, 415 & n. 2; wedding, iv. 194–5; comes to live at Sayes Court, iv. 196; sets up house in London, iv. 375; visits Wotton, iv. 557; coach accident to, iv. 568–9; visits Tunbridge Wells, iv. 646; journey to Ireland, 1692: farewell visits, v. 103, 110–11; ~ sets out, v. 113; ~ returns, 1696, v. 240; ill, 1697–8, v. 269, 282, 283, 285, 286; visits Wotton, v. 282, 286; children of: births, &c., of, iv. 235, 237, 272, 277, 392, 395–6; v. 80; *see also* iv. 324; geneal., iv. 224 & n. 3; v. 448, n. 4.

Evelyn, Martha Maria, E's granddaughter: born and baptized, iv. 324 *bis*; dies, iv. 335; buried, *ib*.

Evelyn, Mrs. Mary, *c*. 1635–1709, E's wife, daughter of Sir Richard Browne [she is dis-

Evelyn, Mrs. Mary (*cont.*)
tinguished elsewhere as 'Mrs. Evelyn'], ii. 535, n. 4.
— chronological series: absent from England for twelve years, 1641–52, iii. 67 & n. 2; E's affection for, ii. 535; marries E, 1647, ii. 536 & n. 3; i. *8*; continues to reside with her parents, ii. 536, 561; iii. 12, 17; in Paris during Condé's siege, ii. 550; makes excursions, &c.: St. Cloud, ii. 536; ~ Cours-la-Reine, iii. 1; ~ 'Bataille de Vambre', iii. 4; ~ Maisons, iii. 18; ~ Conflans, iii. 38, attends ball, iii. 30; return of, to England, 1652: preparations for, &c., iii. 59, 62, 65, 66; ~ pass for, iii. 65–6; ~ arrives at Rye, &c., iii. 68; visits Tunbridge Wells, iii. 68–9, 71–2; comes to Sayes Court, iii. 73; tour of, in England, summer 1654, iii. 98–142; *see also* iii. 103–4 & n., 117, 134; presented by Charles II to Henrietta Maria and Henrietta Anne, &c., 1660, iii. 261–2; gives Henrietta Anne a 'Character', iii. 264; Charles II promises place to, in household of future queen, iii. 275 & n. 5; gives Charles II painting by herself, iii. 287; visits Hampton Court, 1662, iii. 320; watches Fire of London, iii. 451; shown Queen Catherine's dressing-room, iv. 9; entertains Queen Catherine at Sayes Court, 1676, iv. 89.
— artistic and literary pursuits: general, ii. 535, n. 4; drawings, &c., by, i. *39*; designs frontispieces for: E's *Lucretius*, iii. 173, n. 2; ~ Sprat's *History of Royal Society*(?), iii. 266, n. 6 *ad fin.*, 533, n. 7; miniature painting by, iii. 287; commendatory poem attributed to, iii. 348, n. 4; unidentified publication by, iii. 264 & n. 7.
— children: pregnancies, confinements, &c.: Richard, 1652, iii. 65 *bis*, 75, 76; John Stansfield, 1653, iii. 84, 89, 90; John, 1655, iii. 145, 146, 147; George, 1657, iii. 194, 195; the second Richard, 1664, iii. 368; Mary, 1665, iii. 421 & n. 3; [she is not named in connexion with the birth of Elizabeth, 1667 (iii. 495)]; Susanna, 1669, iii. 528; miscarriages, iii. 31, 259, 435.
— — further relations with: Elizabeth: tends, in last illness, iv. 463–4; John: attachment of, to, iv. 194; ~ visits, in last illness, v. 265, 266, 286; Mary: care of, in her upbringing, iv. 427, 428; ~ grief of, for, iv. 421, 424, 438, 461; Richard (the first): distress of, for, iii. 146; ~ *see also* iii. 145, 209; Susanna (Mrs. Draper): attends, at confinements, v. 190, 217, 286, 582; ~ other visits of, to, v. 425, 541.
— friends, relations, &c.: Dr. R. Bohun: friendship, i. *24*; ~ account (character) of, by him, ii. 535, n. 4; ~ obtains prebend for, v. 473; Dr. R. Breton: regard of, for, iii. 302, n. 4; Lady and Sir Richard Browne: grief of, for deaths of, iii. 77, 87; iv. 302; Lady Cotton: nurses, iii. 216; William Glanville, sen.: entertained by, iii. 96; ~ he quarrels with, v. 497; Margaret Blagge, *later* Mrs. Godolphin: meets first, iii. 529–30; ~ visits to, &c., iv. 8, 63–4, 73–4, 100, 140, 140, n. 3, 147–8; ~ on cause of last illness of, iv. 148 & n. 1; ~ affection of, for, iv. 150; duchess of Newcastle: promise made to, by the duchess, iii. 480–1; ~ visits, iii. 481 *bis*; Sir G. Sylvius: attends wedding of, iv. 123.
— — other social intercourse with: Alessandro, iii. 1; Arlington, iv. 94 *bis*; Sir R. Clayton, iv. 173; Sir John Evelyn of Godstone, iii. 219; Sir D. Gauden, iii. 510; S. Harvey, v. 547, 548, critical note; Mrs. Howard and her daughters, iii. 529–30; iv. 109; Jane Lane, iii. 51; Lady Mordaunt, iv. 75, 103, 109; the Mordaunt children, iv. 335; Archbishop Sheldon, iv. 73; H. Slingsby, iv. 186; G. Tuke, iii. 182, 225–6; Lady Tuke, iii. 568.
— — relations of: visit E, iii. 14; ~ in Wiltshire, iii. 76, 98.

Evelyn, Mrs. Mary (*cont.*)
— genealogical: table, i. 142–3; various relationships (select references): Boyle, iii. 169, n. 7; Clancarty, iv. 244, n. 5; Edgcumbe, iii. 78, n. 2; Fanshawe, iii. 19, n. 5; Farrington, iii. 491, n. 6; Glanville, iii. 111, n. 6; Hungerford, ii. 22, n. 1; iii. 89, n. 5; Kildare, iii. 169, n. 2; Rich, iii. 400, n. 3; Shaen, iv. 244, n. 5; Tuke, ii. 564, n. 1; Warwick, iii. 253, n. 2; Wase, iii. 55, n. 1; Wells, iii. 209, n. 2; Willoughby de Broke, iii. 184, n. 6.
— godchildren: daughter of Edmund Waller, iii. 19 & n. 2(?), 20, n. 3, 39, 40; other children, iii. 154, 376; iv. 324; v. 461.
— health: drinks waters at Tunbridge Wells, 1661, iii. 292, 294; ~ 1681, iv. 250, 256; visits Bath, 1691, v. 58, 61 & n. 1; usual winter rheumatism of, v. 155; visits Greenwich and consults Sloane, 1701, v. 456 *ter*, 459, 461, 463; various ailments, &c., iii. 184; iv. 564–7 *passim*, 569(?), 586, 592, 596, 605, 607; v. 18, 187, 198, 199 *bis*, 519, 585, 586, 591.
— letters: written by: mentioned or cited, ii. 552; iii. 14, 61, 481, n. 1, 511, n. 2, 524, n. 2, 566, n. 3, 570, n. 1, 603, n. 5; iv. 13, n. 3, 197, n. 4, 201, n. 1, 420, n. 2; letter to, iii. 62.
— portraits: as child(?), ii. 535, n. 4; by S. Bourdon: stolen by pirates and recovered, ii. 551 & n. 7; iii. 55–6, 62, 71, n. 1; drawing by Nanteuil, ii. 535, n. 4; iii. 9, n. 3; drawing, 1685, iv. 475.
— property: E settles Great Warley manor on, ii. 554, n. 1; consents to Sir R. Browne's gift of land to Trinity House, iii. 577; as heiress of Sir R. Browne, iv. 303; involved in Chancery suit, &c., iv. 340, 344, 394, n. 3, 551, n. 1; E bequeaths lease of Dover Street house, &c., to, v. 606; will of: quoted, i. 37; ~ cited, iv. 446, n. 6.
— religion: first receives Sacrament with E, ii. 562; first goes with E to Deptford parish church,

Evelyn, Mrs. Mary (*cont.*)
iii. 83; attends further services during Protectorate, &c., iii. 164, 203, 228; receives Sacrament at home, iv. 605, 651; [her other receptions of Sacrament are not indexed]; churched after childbirth, iii. 76, 90, 147, 195.
— travel and movements in England [*see also* chronological series; children; *and* health *above*; her visits to London are not indexed]: visits, &c., to: Cranbourn, &c., v. 110–11; Cressing Temple, iii. 225–6; Essex, iii. 182 & n. 7, 183; Greenwich, 1705, v. 600; Thames mouth (excursion by water), iii. 529–30; Windsor, iv. 38, 207–8; Woodcot, iii. 76, 218, 244, 326, 371, 428, 467; Wotton, iii. 76 (proposed visit), 87–8, 154–8, 218, 417–30 *passim* (during plague; *see also* iv. 428), 561; iv. 219, 557; v. 179, 200, 221, 250, 467, 482, 499, 500, 521, 605, 613.
— miscellaneous: as member of E's projected mathematical college, iii. 232, n. 2; at house-warming for E's new lodging, iv. 50; visits Blackwall, iv. 99; visits Ashmole's museum, iv. 139; sample of cooking in Papin's digester sent to, iv. 278; in coach accident, v. 467; dress of (general), v. 542; gives portrait of E to Royal Society, iv. 479, n. 2 *ad fin.*; gift to, i. 26 & n. 3.
Evelyn, Mary, 1665–85, E's daughter: born and baptized, iii. 421 & nn. 3, 5; at Windsor with Lady Tuke, iv. 38; birthday of, iv. 153; confirmed, iv. 167; receives Sacrament, iv. 167, 418, 420; visits Windsor, iv. 207–8; ill, iv. 224; drinks waters at Tunbridge Wells, iv. 250, 256; taught music and dancing, iv. 271 & n. 5, 421–2, 427; sings, iv. 404 *bis*, 422; proposed appointment for, as maid of honour, iv. 428; marriage proposals for, iv. 324, 425–6, 454–5; authoress of *Mundus Muliebris*, iv. 423–4 & n.; last illness, death, burial, character, &c., iv. 418, 420–31

Evelyn, Mary, 1665–85 (*cont.*)
& nn., 433; condolences for, iv. 432; grave of, iv. 464; death, &c., of: mentioned or alluded to, iv. 461, 464, 495; v. 183, 432; i. *31*.
Evelyn, Mary, E's aunt: *see* Hatton, Mrs. M.
Evelyn, Mrs. Mary, E's sister-in-law, born Caldwell, first wife of George Evelyn of Wotton, ii. 24, n. 2; v. 358 & nn. 3, 4; married, ii. 24 (i. 18); dies, ii. 146 & n. 3 (i. 94); geneal., ii. 25, 29, n. 4; iii. 14, n. 8; iv. 111, n. 5, 558, n. 3.
Evelyn, (Mrs.) Mary, E's sister-in-law, second wife of George Evelyn of Wotton: *see* Cotton, Mary, Lady Cotton.
Evelyn, Mary, E's niece, daughter of George Evelyn of Wotton: *see* Wyche, Mary, Lady Wyche.
Evelyn, Mary (later Mrs. Stonhouse?), E's greatniece, daughter of George Evelyn, jnr., of Wotton, v. 54, n. 2, 358, n. 7, 359, n. 8.
Evelyn, Mary, daughter of Sir Edward Evelyn, E's first cousin once removed: *see* Glynn, Mary, Lady Glynn.
Evelyn, Mary, Lady Evelyn, wife of Sir Frederick: bequeaths Wotton estate to John Evelyn, 1817, v. 339, n. 2; i. *51–2*; treatment by, of family MSS. (Upcott's account), i. *53–4*; permits publication of Diary, i. *54*, *55*.
Evelyn, Penelope, daughter of Sir Edward Evelyn, E's first cousin once removed: *see* Alston, Penelope, Lady Alston.
Evelyn, Rebecca: *see* Parke, Mrs. R.
Evelyn, Richard, sen., *c.* 1589–1640, E's father [he is distinguished elsewhere as 'Richard Evelyn, sen.'], ii. 1–26 & nn., *passim* (i. 1–19); i. *2–3*.
character, &c., ii. 1–2 & nn. (i. 1–2); birth of, ii. 1, n. 2; i. *2*, n. 2; marriage of, ii. 1 & n. 3, 5, n. 7 *ad fin.*; refuses knighthood, ii. 2 & n. 2; as sheriff of Surrey and Sussex, ii. 2 & n. 1 (i. 1), 11–12 & nn. (i. 9–10); as trustee for purchase of Albury, ii. 77, n. 2; concern of, in his sons' education, ii. 9, n. 7 *ad fin.*, 11 (i. 8–9), 13, critical note; i. 12; ii. 16–17 (i. 13), 21 (i. 16); last illness, journey to Bath, death, &c., ii. 23–6 *passim* (i. 17–19).
memoranda written by: imitated by E, ii. 10 (i. 8); i. *79–80*; ~ cited, ii. 6; letter of, ii. 16 (i. 13); portrait of, ii. 1, n. 6; v. 359 & n. 9.
property, ii. 2 & n. 3, 5 (i. 2 & n. 1, 4); Wotton (specifically), ii. 3 (i. 5); v. 478, n. 1; ~ views of, on descent of, v. 54, n. 3, 338; other estates, ii. 27, n. 2, 539, n. 4; v. 441, n. 5; will of, ii. 26–7 & nn. (i. 20), 78, n. 1; iv. 583, n. 1; provides for his younger sons, i. 12.
grandchildren named after, iii. 63, 75.
Evelyn, Richard, 1622–70, of Woodcote, E's brother [he is distinguished elsewhere as 'Richard Evelyn'. Notices relating to 'my brother' between 1638 and 1669 may refer to Richard or to George Evelyn; when the abbreviated form 'my bro:' is used, both may be concerned. Such notices, when they record simple social intercourse, are not indexed; the remainder, unless they clearly refer to one or the other, are entered, with queries, under both brothers. Notices specifically relating to the two are entered under both]:
— character and career, iii. 544; i. *3–4*.
— chronological series: born, ii. 1, 6; education: at school at Lewes (Southover), ii. 13, 15 (i. 11, 12); ~ *see also* ii. 9, n. 7 *ad fin.*; at Balliol College, Oxford, ii. 23 (i. 17); at Middle Temple: admitted, ii. 15 & n. 4 (i. 12); ~ lodgings at, i. 12; ii. 24 & n. 4 (i. 18).
— — movements, 1638–42 (visits to Lewes, London, &c.), ii. 21–2 (i. 16), 27 (i. 20), 28(?), 77 *bis* (i. 51 *bis*), 78 (i. 51), 79; sends money to Charles I(?), i. 53; visits Godstone, 1643(?), ii. 81; at Baynards, 1648, ii. 539; at Epsom, ii. 542; marries Elizabeth Mynne, ii. 542–3 & n.; visits Lewes, &c., ii. 543–4; godfather

Evelyn, Richard, 1622–70 (*contd.*) of son of George Evelyn, iii. 63; lodgings of, in Covent Garden, 1655–8(?), iii. 148 & n. 2, 192, 212 & n. 5; visits Whitehall, 1660(?), iii. 262; and death of Lady Cotton, iii. 377; illnesses of: 1666, iii. 464, 467; ~ 1667, iii. 472; ~ 1668, iii. 517, 518, 519; ~ 1669–70, iii. 536–43 *passim*; encouraged by Pepys to be operated on for stone, iii. 529; last days, death, &c., iii. 543–5 & nn.
— children: births, &c., iii. 77, 155 & n. 5, 218, 334, 376.
— property: inheritance from his father, i. 12; Baynards: inherited by (life-interest), ii. 539, n. 4; iv. 583, n. 1; ~ proposed lease of, iii. 192–3; ~ succession to, altered, iv. 569 (allusion), 582–3 & n.; v. 86; Woodcote Park: acquired by, ii. 542–3 & n.; payment by, to E, iii. 93; will of, iii. 545; ~ set aside, iv. 582–3 & n.; v. 86; ~ cited, ii. 539, n. 2.
— relations with E [exclusive of those concerning property, for which see above. Ordinary social intercourse is not indexed; notices occur frequently between ii. 543 and iii. 528. E's visits to Woodcote are indexed under Woodcote Park]: takes leave of E, 1643, ii. 82 (i. 56); entertains E at Spring Garden (?), iii. 213; book dedicated to, by E, iii. 209, n. 1, 220; godfather to E's son George, iii. 194; E and Mrs. Evelyn godparents to children of, iii. 218, 219, 376.
Evelyn, Richard, 1652–8, E's eldest son [he is distinguished elsewhere as 'Little Richard Evelyn']: born and baptized, iii. 75 *bis*; mentioned, iii. 104; accident to, iii. 145–6 & nn.; birthday of, iii. 182; ill, iii. 86, 183, 197; last illness, death, accomplishments, &c., of, iii. 206–10 & nn.; *add.*; precocity and death of, iv. 619; i. *12–13*.
Evelyn, Richard, 1664, E's second son of the name: born and baptized, iii. 368 *bis* & n. 1; dies, &c., iii. 371 *bis*.
Evelyn, Richard, 1680–1, E's grandson: born, iv. 235; baptized, iv. 236; dies, &c., iv. 256.
Evelyn, Richard, b. 1652, E's nephew, son of George Evelyn: born, &c., iii. 62, 63 & n. 1.
Evelyn, Richard, b. 1656, E's nephew, George Evelyn's second son of this name, iii. 63, n. 1.
Evelyn, Richard, b. 1664, E's nephew, son of Richard Evelyn: born, &c., iii. 376 & n. 6.
Evelyn, Robert, E's uncle, emigrant to Virginia, i. *2*; i. 2, n. 4; as gunpowder-manufacturer, i. 52, n. 2; geneal., ii. 551, n. 3; v. 574, n. 2.
Evelyn, Roger, of Great Stanmore, i. *1*.
Evelyn, Rose, E's first cousin, daughter of Thomas Evelyn: *see* Keightley, Mrs. R.
Evelyn, Mrs. Rose, born Williams, first wife of George Evelyn, sen., E's grandfather, i. 2 & n. 2; iii. 136, n. 6.
Evelyn, Sarah, daughter of Sir John Evelyn of Wilts., E's first cousin once removed: *see* Saunderson, Sarah, Viscountess Castleton.
Evelyn, Stansfield, E's nephew, son of George Evelyn: born, iii. 154 & n. 4; baptized, iii. 155 & n. 6; mentioned, iii. 89, n. 3.
Evelyn, Susanna, E's first cousin, daughter of Thomas Evelyn: *see* Christmas, Mrs. S.
Evelyn, Susanna, E's daughter: *see* Draper, Mrs. S.
Evelyn, Thomas, of Long Ditton, E's uncle, i. 2 & n. 4, 3; geneal., i. 10, n. 1; ii. 5, n. 5, 545, n. 7, 551, n. 3; iii. 63, n. 2; iv. 177, n. 2.
Evelyn, Sir Thomas, of Long Ditton, E's first cousin: geneal., ii. 5 & n. 5 (i. 6); iv. 238–9, 434, n. 1.
Evelyn, Thomasine, Lady Evelyn, born Heynes or Haines, wife of Sir John Evelyn of Godstone, E's first cousin, ii. 553, n. 7 *ad fin.*; iii. 174, n. 1; social, ii. 557; iii. 174; tomb of, iv. 122.
Evelyn, W. J.: concern of, in publication of part of Diary, i. *63*.
Evelyn *or* Avelyn, William, of Harrow, i. *1*.
Evelyn *or* Glanville, William, son of George Evelyn, of Nutfield, E's first cousin once removed, iii. 84, n. 1; v. 340, n. 2.

Everard, Mrs. —, a 'chymist', iii. 13.
Everard, Edmund, perjurer: statements by, iii. 6, n. 4.
Everley, Wilts.: Evelyn property at, i. *2*; i. 3 & n. 2.
Eversfield (Ersfield, Erskin, Aresfeild), John: geneal., iv. 196 & n. 1, 238; v. 359 & n. 6.
Eversfield, Katherine: *see* Evelyn, Mrs. K.
Eversfield, Mrs. Mary, born Thomas, wife of John Eversfield: *see* Beckford, Mary, Lady Beckford.
Evertsen, Cornelis, the Old, iii. 407 & n. 2.
Evertsen, Cornelis, the Youngest: taken prisoner, 1665, presented to Charles II, &c., iii. 406 & nn. 2, 3, 407 & n. 2.
Evertsen, Johan, iii. 407 & n. 2.
Every *or* Avery, John, pirate: associates of: executed, v. 261 & n. 5.
Evett, Rev. William: sermon by, ii. 21 & n. 5.
Evreux, ii. 127 (i. 81).
Ewers, —: *see* Hewer, W.
Ewhurst, Surrey: Baynards in: *see* Baynards; Somersbury in, ii. 539, n. 4.
Exeter (Excester, &c.): Henrietta Maria at, 1644, i. 96–7 & n.; attendant on Henrietta Anne at, iii. 270, n. 3; Bishop J. Gauden at, iii. 263, n. 5; William of Orange at, 1688, iv. 605 & n. 3; recorder of: *see* Ball, Sir Peter.
Exeter: Earls of: *see* Cecil, Thomas, first earl; Cecil, John, fifth earl, 1678–1700.
Exeter: diocese:
  bishops: *see* Hall, Joseph (1627–41); Gauden, J. (1660–2); Ward, Seth (1662–7); Sparrow, A. (1667–76); Lamplugh, T. (1676–88); Trelawny, Sir Jonathan (1689–1707); Blackall, O. (1708–16).
  chancellor: *see* James, J.
Exhalation, fiery, near Harlech, v. 174 & n. 3.
Exploration: expedition to seek North-West Passage, iv. 96 & n. 5; Dampier's voyages to Pacific, v. 295 & nn. 2, 3.
Explosions: near Wapping, iii. 195 & n. 2; ships, iii. 403 & n. 1; v. 37 & n. 1.
Exton, John, LL.D., Admiralty judge: at Sheldon's translation to Canterbury, iii. 362 & n. 2.
Eynsham, Oxon., iii. 382, n. 6.
Eyton, Sir Kenrick (Mr. Eaton): maintains secret correspondence with E (?), ii. 558 & n. 4.

Faber, Dr. A. O.: on use of gold in medicine, iii. 86, n. 6.
Fabius Maximus: place where Hannibal escaped from, ii. 324 & n. 1.
Fabrici, Girolamo, of Acquapendente, ii. 209 & n. 5.
Faenza, Antonio da (A. Gentili): silver cross made by, ii. 329 & n. 5.
Fagg, Sir John, bt.; created baronet 1660, iii. 238, n. 1; as Mr. Fay: E desires him to assist Charles II, iii. 238; imprisoned in Tower, 1675, iv. 65, n. 1.
Fairfax, Mary: *see* Villiers, Mary, duchess of Buckingham.
Fairfax, Thomas, 1633–1712, general: as Major Fairfax: character, &c., iv. 120 & n. 6.
Fairfax, Thomas, third Baron Fairfax, the general: takes Leicester, iii. 122, n. 4; besieges Bristol, iii. 102, n. 5; besieges Colchester, iii. 176, n. 4; influenced by Ireton, iii. 58, n. 1; occupies Lord Bristol's house in London, iii. 578, n. 1; granted York House, iii. 162, n. 1; geneal., iv. 120 & n. 6, 517, n. 5.
Fairfax, Sir William, of Steeton: geneal., iv. 120, n. 6.
Fairfax: third Baron: *see* Fairfax, Thomas.
Fairs and Markets: Bartholomew Fair, ii. 543 & n. 1; ~ Polichinelli at, iii. 492, n. 2; Blackheath Fair, iv. 311 & n. 2; frost-fair on Thames, 1684, iv. 359–65 *passim* & nn.; Northampton: fair at, ii. 78 (i. 51); Padua: St. Anthony's fair, ii. 452 & n. 2, 453; Paris: Vallée de Misere, ii. 99–100 & n. (i. 65–6); Richelieu, ii. 151 (i. 98); Rome: Piazza Navona, ii. 367–8 & nn.; iv. 253; Rotterdam: *kermis*, ii. 39–40 & nn. (i. 29–30); Southwark Fair (also called St. Margaret's Fair, &c.), iii. 255–6 & n.; ~ shortened for misconduct, v. 115–16 & n.; Sturbridge Fair, iii. 138 & n. 4; Utrecht: *kermis*, ii. 34 (i. 27); Venice: Ascensiontide

Fairs and Markets (*cont.*)
fair, ii. 446 & n. 10; ~ Merceria (shopping-street), ii. 434.
Falerium (Falerii), ii. 210, n. 3.
Falernus, Ager (Falernum), ii. 210 & n. 3, 323 & n. 6.
Falisci, ii. 210.
Falkenberg, Viscount, *rectè* Fauconberg: *see* Belasyse, Thomas, earl of Fauconberg.
Falkland: Viscounts, &c., of: *see* Carey, Lucius, second viscount, 1633–43; Carey, Henry, third viscount; Carey, Anthony, fifth viscount, 1663–94; Carey, Rebecca, his viscountess.
Falls, the, near Goodwin Sands, Kent: fleet near, 1672, iii. 615, n. 1.
Falmouth, Cornwall: Henrietta Maria sails from, ii. 149, n. 1; Charles II, as Prince of Wales, sails from, iii. 246, n. 1.
Falmouth: Earl of, 1664–5: *see* Berkeley, Sir Charles.
Falmouth: first Viscount, 1720–34: *see* Boscawen, Hugh.
Family of Love: address from, to James II, iv. 554 & n. 2.
Fane, Mrs. Amabella, wife of Anthony Fane: *see* Grey, Amabella, countess of Kent.
Fane, Anthony: geneal., i. 3, n. 3.
Fane, Charles, first Viscount Fane: geneal., v. 147, n. 7.
Fane, Charles, third earl of Westmorland: social, iv. 78 & n. 3.
Fane, Francis, first earl of Westmorland: geneal., i. 3, n. 3; v. 147, n. 7.
Fane (Vane), Sir Henry, K.B.: social, v. 147 & n. 7.
Fane, Vere, fourth earl of Westmorland: dies, v. 165 & n. 1.
Fane: first Viscount: *see* Fane, Charles.
Fanelli, Francesco, sculptor: fountain at Hampton Court by, iii. 324 & n. 6.
Fanshawe, —, of Fenchington: visits E, iii. 184 & n. 5.
Fanshawe, Ann, Lady Fanshawe, wife of Sir Richard, authoress of the *Memoirs*, iii. 19, n. 5; on passes, iii. 16, n. 1; godmother of daughter of Edmund Waller, iii. 20, n. 3; social, iii. 184 & n. 4.
Fanshawe, Joan: *see* Warwick, Joan, Lady Warwick.
Fanshawe, Sir Richard, bt., iii. 19, n. 5; commendatory letter from, to E, iii. 123, n. 3; consults E on behalf of Lord Cork, iii. 182 & n. 1; in Charles II's coronation procession, iii. 280 & n. 1; going as ambassador to Portugal, 1662, iii. 329 & n. 6; social, iii. 19, 57 & n. 2, 58, 123 & n. 3, 143 & n. 3, 184 & n. 4; geneal., iii. 253 & n. 2.
Faringdon, Berks., iii. 111 & n. 2; garrison at, ii. 16, n. 4 *ad fin.*; Faringdon House near, iii. 111, n. 3.
Farmor, Sir William: *see* Fermor.
Farnborough, Kent: Locksbottom in, iii. 69, n. 1; *add.*
Farnese family: as dukes of Parma, ii. 310, n. 4; territories of, about Ronciglione, ii. 211, n. 2; own the Farnesina, ii. 287, n. 7; tombs of, ii. 209 & n. 7.
Farnese, Alessandro, cardinal: builds Caprarola, ii. 406 & n. 4.
Farnese, Alexander, duke of Parma: *see* Parma.
Farnese, Odoardo, duke of Parma: *see* Parma.
Farnese, Ranuccio, cardinal: tomb of, ii. 274 & n. 6.
Farnham, Surrey, ii. 79 (i. 52); vicar of: *see* Cosen, S.
Farringdon —: buried, iii. 491 & n. 6.
Farrington, Mrs. Dorothy, wife of John Farrington: geneal., iii. 491, n. 6.
Farrington, George, deputy for Remembrancer of First Fruits, iii. 491, n. 6, 567, n. 1.
Farrington, John: geneal., iii. 491, n. 6.
Fathers of the Church: *see* Church.
Faubert, Monsieur: *see* Foubert, S.
Fauconberg: second Viscount, and Earl of, &c.: *see* Belasyse, Thomas; Belasyse, Mary, his countess.
Faustulus, ii. 276.
Faversham (Feversham), Kent: E at, 1672, iii. 611; James II taken at sea near, 1688, iv. 610 & n. 5; Sir E. Hales taken near, iv. 611 & n. 6.
Faversham, *rectè* Feversham: Earl of: *see* Duras, Louis de.
Fay, —: *see* Fagg, Sir John.
Fearne, Dr. —: *see* Ferne, H.
Febur(e), —: *see* le Fèvre, N.
Fécamp: Charles II arrives at, 1651, iii. 47, n. 4.

Feild, Robert, D.D.: sermon by (?), iv. 7 & n. 1.
Feilding, Elizabeth: *see* Boyle, Elizabeth, countess of Guildford.
Feilding, Sir George, earl of Desmond: sometime owner of Euston, iii. 591, n. 2.
Feilding, Mary: *see* Pierrepont, Mary, countess of Kingston.
Feilding, William, first earl of Denbigh: geneal., iii. 263, n. 8.
Feilding, William, third earl of Denbigh: geneal., iv. 551, n. 2 *ad fin.*
Felbrigg Hall, Norfolk: architect of, iii. 554, n. 3.
Felix: in sermons, iv. 123, 273, 435; v. 58, 209, 294, 477, 513, 586.
Felix, St., of Cantalice: relic of, ii. 369 & n. 7.
Fell, John, D.D.; dean of Christ Church, Oxford, 1660–86; bishop of Oxford 1676–86, iii. 288, n. 3; iv. 89, n. 3; as dean: examines scholars at Westminster School, iii. 288; ~ visits Lord Cornbury, iii. 384; ~ E visits, iv. 69; as vice-chancellor of Oxford university: receives Arundelian marbles (inscriptions) on behalf of university, iii. 496–500 & nn.; ~ promises to protect Arundelian marbles, iii. 534 & n. 4; ~ presides at Encænia and Act, 1669, &c., iii. 531–6 & nn.; as bishop: asks E to introduce H. Prideaux to Lord Norwich (Henry Howard, later duke of Norfolk), iv. 89; dies, iv. 519 & n. 1.
and author of *Whole Duty of Man*, v. 112, n. 5 *ad fin.*; as preacher: style of, iii. 401 & n. 2; iv. 106; sermons by, iii. 401; iv. 10, 106, 132; appointed to preach, iii. 609, n. 2; iv. 372, n. 4.
Felton, Sir Henry, bt. (as Sir John): social, iv. 115 & n. 2.
Felton, Lieut. John: assassinates Buckingham, ii. 9 & n. 1 (i. 8).
Felton, Sir John: error for Sir Henry (?), iv. 115 & n. 2.
Fenchington: Mr. Fanshawe of, iii. 184 & n. 5.
Fens: atmosphere of, iii. 140 & n. 6; drainage of, in Lincolnshire, iii. 135 & n. 3; drained area: visit to, iii. 553, 555–6 & n.
Fenton, Captain Edward: geneal., iii. 169, n. 7.
Fenton, Elizabeth, Lady Fenton: *see* Petty, Elizabeth, Baroness Shelburne, &c.
Fenton, Sir Maurice: geneal., iv. 57, n. 4.
Fenwick, Edward: claims of, against Lady (Mary) Grosvenor, v. 528 & n. 8.
Fenwick, Sir John, bt., iv. 561, n. 4; arrested for Assassination Plot, v. 245 & n. 4; attainted and executed, v. 264 & nn. 3, 6; social, iv. 561.
Fenwick, Lady Mary, wife of Sir John: geneal., iv. 561, n. 4.
Ferdinand I, Emperor: gift from, to Sulaiman the Magnificent, iii. 112, n. 1.
Ferdinand II, Emperor: grants English title to Sir R. Dudley, i. 115, n. 2; geneal., ii. 410, n. 5, 411.
Ferdinand I, grand duke of Tuscany: creator of Leghorn, ii. 183 & n. 3 (i. 115); chapel of, in Florence, ii. 416; inn at Radicofani built by, ii. 207; buys Villa Medici, Rome, ii. 230, n. 8 *ad fin.*; gift from, to Marie de Médicis, ii. 92–3 (i. 62); statues of, ii. 182 & n. 4 (i. 114), 183 & n. 7 (i. 116), 194 & n. 6 (i. 120).
Ferdinand II, grand duke of Tuscany: gift to, ii. 193; statue bought by, ii. 415, n. 4; mentioned, ii. 194, 412; geneal., ii. 206, n. 5, 415, n. 2; error for Ferdinand I, ii. 183 & n. 3 (i. 115).
Ferdinand III, grand duke of Tuscany: error for Ferdinand I, ii. 182 & n. 4 (i. 114).
Ferdinand Albrecht I, duke of Brunswick-Lüneburg-Bevern: admitted F.R.S., iii. 396 & n. 5.
Ferdinand of Austria, the Cardinal Infante, viceroy of the Spanish Netherlands, ii. 59, n. 7; pass from, ii. 59, 62, 63 (i. 40, 42, 43); entry of, into Antwerp, ii. 63, n. 3; ~ paintings for, ii. 71 & n. 3 (i. 46); death of, &c., ii. 72 & n. 2 (i. 47).
Ferguson, Robert, the 'Plotter', iv. 323, n. 5; complicity of, in Rye-House Plot, &c., iv. 322, n. 1, 323 & nn. 5, 6, 329 & n. 2; in Monmouth's rebellion, iv. 452 & n. 7; blamed by Monmouth, iv. 455.

Feria, Don Gomez Suarez de Figueróa y Cordóba, duke of, governor of Milan: and negotiation for drawings by Leonardo, ii. 498 & nn. 7, 8.
Fermor, Henrietta Louisa, countess of Pomfret: gives Arundel sculptures to Oxford University, v. 44, n. 6.
Fermor, Sir William, bt.; first Baron Leominster 1692, iv. 170, n. 1; godfather of William Wren, iv. 169–70; art-collection of, &c., v. 44–5 & n.; created baron, v. 90 & n. 3; *add.*; social, iv. 243.
Fernandez de Velasco y Tovar, Don Bernardino, duke of Frias: *see* Frias.
Ferne (Fearne), Henry, D.D.; bishop of Chester 1662: social, iii. 237 & n. 6.
Ferrara: notice, 1645, ii. 427–8 & nn.; E sets out for, ii. 426; Imperial army near, 1701, v. 471.
Ferrara: Council of, ii. 200, n. 2.
Ferrara: Marquis of: *see* Niccolò III d'Este.
Ferrari, F. B., prefect of the Ambrosiana, ii. 492 & n. 1, 497.
Ferrucci, F.: statue by, ii. 185 & n. 5 (i. 117), 415 & n. 1.
Festus: in sermons, v. 75, 395.
Fetherby, Sir John: *see* Fotherby.
Feversham: *see* Faversham.
Feversham (Faversham): second Earl of, 1677–1709: *see* Duras, Louis de.
Fiammingo, Francesco: *see* Duquesnoy, F.
Fiammingo, Gerardo: *see* Honthorst, G.
Fiammingo, Hans: error (?), ii. 253 & n. 6.
Fiat, —: *see* Fiott, P.
Ficino, Marsiglio: tomb of, ii. 197 & n. 4.
Field, Rev. — (Dr. R. Feild?): sermon by, iv. 7 & n. 1.
Field, Theophilus, D.D.; bishop of Hereford, &c.: consecrates church at South Malling (?), ii. 8 & n. 2 (i. 7).
Field-sports: Euston well situated for, iv. 117; buck-hunting, ii. 542; iii. 326; iv. 113; ~ as sorrel, iii. 117 & n. 1; hawking, iii. 133; iv. 113; otter-hunting, iii. 306; setting, iii. 133; stag-hunting: Charles II goes, iii. 560.
Fiennes (Finnes), Rev. Pharamus: sermon by (?), iv. 396 & n. 2.
Fiennes, William, first Viscount Saye and Sele: geneal., iv. 396, n. 2.
Fiery Furnace, the: in sermon, v. 308.
Fiesole, Fra Giovanni da (il Beato Angelico): painting by (?) and tomb of, ii. 377 & nn. 6, 7.
Fifth Monarchy Men, iii. 196 & n. 3; rising of (Venner's revolt), iii. 266 & n. 5, 266–7 & n.; sermon against, iii. 196.
Filarete, Antonio: bronze doors by, at St. Peter's, ii. 258 & n. 6.
Filigare, ii. 419, nn. 3, 5.
Finale, Liguria, ii. 169 & n. 13 (i. 107).
Finch, Daniel; second earl of Nottingham 1682; sixth earl of Winchilsea 1729, iv. 171, n. 3; as Mr. Finch: commissioner of the Admiralty, 1679, iv. 171 & n. 2; as earl of Nottingham: refuses to sit in Privy Council with Roman Catholics, iv. 602–3 & n.; commissioner for James II to William of Orange, iv. 608 & n. 8; *add.*; protests against vote, that James II has abdicated, iv. 622; as secretary of state: quarrels with Admiral E. Russell (later Lord Orford), v. 127 & n. 2; ~ dismissed, 1693, v. 157 & n. 2, 177 & n. 2; attacked in parliament, 1704, v. 560–1 & n.; leaves office, 1704, v. 567, n. 1; book dedicated to, v. 184, n. 2; owns Burley-on-the-Hill, iii. 124, n. 2; loss of, by fire at Burley, v. 586; sells Kensington Palace to William III, v. 8 & n. 2; geneal., v. 208 & n. 2.
Finch, Heneage, 1649–1719; baron of Gernsey 1703; earl of Aylesford 1714, iv. 500, n. 5; as solicitor-general: in *Quo Warranto* case, iv. 320, n. 1; ~ pleads before Lord Chancellor Jeffreys, iv. 500; ~ dismissed, iv. 546, n. 3; counsel against E, iv. 546; counsel for Seven Bishops, iv. 587 & n. 2; employs W. Wotton as tutor, v. 184, n. 2; created baron, v. 532 & n. 2; buys Albury, ii. 77, n. 2; iv. 558 & n. 1; social: as Mr. Finch, v. 219, 473 & n. 2(?); ~ as Lord Gernsey, v. 532, 564, 581.

Finch, Sir Heneage, 1621–82; first Baron Finch of Daventry 1674; first earl of Nottingham 1681; Lord Keeper 1673–5; Lord Chancellor 1675–82, iii. 388, n. 4; as pleader, iii. 388, 473 & n. 2; as Lord Keeper, &c.: proceedings before, iv. 67 & n. 4, 275, 281; as Lord High Steward at Stafford's trial, iv. 226 & n. 4, 228, n. 1, 232–3 & nn.; house of, at Kensington, iii. 447, n. 4; social, iii. 574 & n. 4; iv. 67 & n. 3; geneal., iv. 171, 500, n. 5, 546; death of, iv. 299 & n. 3.

Finch, Heneage, 1620–89; second earl of Winchilsea 1639, iii. 159, n. 6; as ambassador to Turkey: appointed, iii. 249 & n. 1; ~ returns home, iii. 537, n. 1; social, iii. 159, 537; geneal., v. 484, n. 4.

Finch, Sir John, 1584–1660; Baron Finch of Fordwich 1640; Lord Keeper 1640–1, ii. 34, n. 3; impeachment of, *ib.*; i. 23, n. 1; as refugee in Holland, ii. 34 (i. 26), 44 (i. 32); geneal., ii. 45, n. 1.

Finch, Sir John, 1626–82, physician, iii. 289, n. 2; commendatory poem by, ii. 472, n. 5; describes a poison, iii. 289; gift of, to Philosophical Society (Royal Society), iii. 295 & n. 6; attends Council for Foreign Plantations (?), iii. 578 & n. 10.

Finch, Leopold, D.D.: sermon by, v. 484–5 & n.

Finch, Mary: *see* Savile, Mary, marchioness of Halifax.

Finch of Daventry: first Baron, 1674–81: *see* Finch, Sir Heneage, later earl of Nottingham.

Finch of Fordwich: Baron, 1640–60: *see* Finch, Sir John.

Finisterre, cape: fleet near, 1702, v. 512 & n. 5.

Finland: recovering drowned men in (in text as Greenland, in error), iii. 601 & n. 2.

Finnes, Dr. — (Rev. P. Fiennes?): sermon by, iv. 396 & n. 2.

Fioravanti, —, ii. 399 & n. 10; paintings by, ii. 399, n. 10; iii. 11.

Fiorenzuolo: *see* Firenzuola.

Fiorilli, Tiberio, called Scaramouche, iv. 12, n. 3; troupe of: performs at Whitehall, iv. 12, 75 & nn. 4, 5.

Fiott (Fiat), Peter, D.Med.: social, iii. 105 & n. 8.

Firenzuola (Fiorenzuolo), ii. 419 & nn. 3, 4.

Fires and Fire-fighting [for fires as divine warnings, &c., *see* London: Great Fire: commemoration, &c.]:

— fire-extinguishers, iii. 173, 488; fire-fighting in Fire of London, iii. 455.

— particular fires: Bergen, 1702, v. 504; Burley-on-the-Hill, 1705, v. 586 & n. 2; Denton, 1694, v. 183; Deptford: Dockyard, 1667, iii. 485 & n. 6; Faringdon, *c.* 1646, iii. 111 & n. 2; Greenwich, 1662, iii. 316 & n. 4; Kensington Palace, 1691, v. 74 & n. 1; London: Fire of, 1666: *see* London: Great Fire; fires in, 1655, iii. 150 & n. 4, 153; Beaufort Buildings, 1695, v. 222–3 & n.; Goring House, 1674, iv. 44; Middle Temple, 1704, v. 563 & n. 3; Montague House, 1686, iv. 497 & n. 2; Red Lion Square (as Golden Square), &c., 1700, v. 376 & n. 5; Southwark, 1689, iv. 649.

— — Marlborough, 1653, iii. 99 & n. 4; Moscow, 1699, v. 352 & n. 3; Tsar's palace in, 1702, v. 504; Newmarket, 1683, iv. 340–1 & n.; Northampton, 1675, iv. 69–70 & n., 596 & n. 1; ~ mentioned, iii. 130, n. 3; Port Royal, Jamaica (as St. James Town), 1703, v. 532 & n. 4; Rotherhithe, 1699, v. 330 & n. 1; Upsala, 1702, v. 504; Whitehall: 1662, 1691, and 1698, iii. 316 & n. 4; v. 47 & n. 2, 283 & n. 5; Wilton House, 1704, v. 586 & n. 3.

— — tenant of E, 1705, v. 614; York in need of a fire, iii. 130, n. 3.

Fireworks and Illuminations:

firework-displays: Rome, 1644, ii. 281–2; London: 1684, iv. 395; ~ 1688, iv. 591 & n. 2; ~ 1695, v. 223 & n. 4; ~ 1697, v. 269 & n. 4, 277–8 & n.; minor notices, i. 27; ii. 390–1 & n.; iii. 518; iv. 589; v. 528, n. 6.

squibs: in London, iv. 393; ~ forbidden, &c., iv. 487, n. 3; v. 72; in Moscow, v. 352.

bonfires: in London, iii. 242, 281, 410, 440; iv. 588 & n. 2, 589, 623;

Fireworks, &c. (*cont.*)
v. 578; ~ forbidden, &c., iv. 487 & n. 3; v. 72.
illuminations: in France and Italy, v. 72; in Rome, ii. 282, 391; in London, v. 72, 277, 578.
Firmin, Thomas: social (?), iv. 647 & n. 5.
Firstenberge: Prince of: *see* Fürstenberg, W. E. von.
Fish, crustaceans, &c. [select notices]:
respiration of fish: experiments on, iii. 353–4.
bream, iv. 481; carp, ii. 119 & n. 5 (i. 77); iv. 117, 481–2; crabs from Red Sea, iii. 33; devil-fish, iii. 338 & n. 1; electric eel, iv. 196–7 & n.; flounders, iii. 399; lampreys, ii. 348–9; lobster: dissected, iii. 526; oysters, ii. 345 & n. 3, 467–8; iii. 178, 627; pike, iv. 481; ~ teeth of, iii. 341; pinna marina, &c., ii. 330–1 & n.; plaice, iii. 399; remora, ii. 314 & n. 4; salmon: caught with dogs, iii. 303; sharks: teeth of, iv. 253; ~ fossil teeth of, iii. 511; tench, iv. 481; torpedo, ii. 53 (i. 37); trout, ii. 488; iii. 104 & n. 2; iv. 200; ~ giant, &c., ii. 520 & n. 5, 523 & n. 2; ~ spearing, at night, iii. 115 & n. 4.
horn of a fish, iii. 372 & n. 6; legendary fish, ii. 51–2 (i. 36).
Fisher, Sir Clement, bt.: geneal., iii. 51, n. 2.
Fisher, Jane, Lady Fisher, born Lane, wife of Sir Clement, iii. 51, n. 2; as Jane Lane: in Paris, 1651–2, iii. 51, 54.
Fish-ponds, &c., ii. 81 (i. 55), 121 (i. 77), 238, 240, 396, 523 & n. 2; iv. 115, 117, 256, 306, 481–2, 594.
FitzAlan, Henry, twelfth earl of Arundel: buys Arundel House, London, iii. 234, n. 4; acquires Nonsuch Palace, iii. 426, n. 4.
FitzCharles, Charles; earl of Plymouth 1675–80: social, iv. 181 & n. 6.
FitzGerald, Lady Catherine: social, iv. 385 & n. 2.
FitzGerald, Elizabeth: *see* Maccarty, Elizabeth, countess of Clancarty.
FitzGerald, Frances: *see* Shaen, Frances, Lady Shaen.
FitzGerald, George, sixteenth earl of Kildare, iii. 169, n. 2; commission concerning, iii. 169; geneal., iv. 244 & n. 5.
FitzGerald, Joan, countess of Kildare, wife of George FitzGerald, sixteenth earl: geneal., iii. 169, nn. 2, 7.
FitzGerald, John, eighteenth earl of Kildare, iv. 247, n. 3; social, iv. 247, 249.
Fitzgerald, Captain R.: machine of, for purifying sea-water, iv. 388–9 & n.
Fitzhardinge: Viscounts: *see* Berkeley, Sir Charles, later earl of Falmouth, first Viscount, 1663–5 (1664); Berkeley, Sir Charles, second Viscount, 1665–8.
FitzJames, Henrietta: *see* Waldegrave, Henrietta, Baroness Waldegrave.
Fitzjames, James, duke of Berwick, v. 149, n. 6; captured at Landen and exchanged, v. 149 & nn. 5, 6; in London to lead rising, 1696, v. 232; reported to be in London, 1697, v. 273 & n. 3.
Fitzpatrick, Col. Edward: social (?), iv. 548 & n. 6.
Fitzpatrick, Richard, first Baron Gowran: geneal., iv. 548, n. 6.
Fitzroy family, dukes of Grafton: art-collection of, iv. 102, n. 1.
Fitzroy, Anne, *otherwise* Palmer: *see* Lennard, Anne, countess of Sussex.
Fitzroy, Catherine, duchess of Northumberland, first wife of George Fitzroy, duke of Northumberland: abducted, iv. 505 & n. 4.
Fitzroy, Charles; second duke of Grafton 1690, iv. 351, n. 4; born, iv. 351; grant of reversion to, v. 161 & n. 4.
Fitzroy, Charles; duke of Southampton, 1674; alluded to, iv. 391–2 & n.
Fitzroy, Charlotte: *see* Lee, Charlotte, countess of Lichfield.
Fitzroy, George; earl, 1674, and duke, 1683, of Northumberland, iv. 374, n. 4; character of, &c., iv. 391–2; receives Sacrament at Whitehall, iv. 374; as horseman, iv. 400; Charles II's concern for, iv. 408, n. 3; abducts his duchess, iv. 505 & n. 4.

FitzRoy, Henry; earl of Euston 1672; first duke of Grafton 1675, iii. 622, n. 4; character of, &c., iv. 184, 185 & n. 1; marriage of, to Isabella Bennet: first ceremony, iii. 622 & n. 4; ~ second ceremony, iv. 184–5 & nn.; ~ mentioned, iv. 119; to be given Euston, iv. 117; inherits Goring (Arlington) House, iii. 404, n. 2; grant of reversion to, v. 161 & n. 4; at demonstration of phosphorus, iv. 263; at Trinity House feasts, iv. 264, 459; Charles II's concern for, iv. 408, n. 3; fights duel with J. Talbot, iv. 501 & n. 2; helps duke of Northumberland to abduct his duchess, iv. 505; social: parties, iv. 191, 287, 326, 589; ~ alone, iv. 314; sets out for Ireland, 1690, v. 30; wounded and dies, v. 35 *bis* & n. 1, 37 & n. 3; geneal., iv. 97, n. 6; alluded to, iv. 391–2 & n.

FitzRoy, Isabella, duchess of Grafton, born Bennet, wife of Henry FitzRoy, first duke; &c., iii. 622, n. 4; character, iv. 117, 119, 184–5, 351; marriage of, to Grafton: first ceremony, iii. 622 & n. 4; ~ second ceremony, iv. 184–5 & nn.; ~ mentioned, iv. 119; education of, iv. 120, n. 7; book dedicated to, *ib.*; lays foundation-stone of Euston church, iv. 114, n. 5; to be given Euston, iv. 117; visits Grinling Gibbons, iv. 179; godmother to — Del Campo, iv. 222; at demonstration of phosphorus, iv. 263; pregnant, iv. 337, 344; son born to, iv. 351; attends service at St. James's Palace, iv. 357; affection of, for Mary Evelyn, iv. 428; grant of reversion to: appeals to house of lords about, v. 161 & n. 4; social: parties, iv. 102, 108, 271, 361; ~ alone, iv. 475; v. 143.

Fitzwilliam, Mrs. Eleanor, later Viscountess Fitzwilliam and countess of Tyrconnel, wife of Col. O. Fitzwilliam, later earl of Tyrconnel, &c.: at Calais, iii. 16 & n. 3.

Fitzwilliam, John, D.D., the nonjuror: sermon by, iv. 503 & n. 3.

Fitzwilliam, Col. Oliver; Viscount Fitzwilliam *c.* 1650; earl of Tyrconnel 1661: at Calais, iii. 16 & n. 3.

Fitzwilliam: Viscount, &c.: *see* Fitzwilliam, Oliver, later earl of Tyrconnel, second viscount *c.* 1650–61; Fitzwilliam, Eleanor, later countess of Tyrconnel, his viscountess.

Flacket family: property of, iv. 415, n. 2.

Flamarens, François de Grossolles, marquis de: social, iv. 393 & n. 3.

Flamel (Flamen), Nicolas: monument of, &c., ii. 131–2 & n. (i. 85).

Flaminius, L. V.: and amphitheatre at Verona, ii. 486 & n. 2.

Flamsteed (Flamested), John, Astronomer Royal, iv. 98 & n. 2; social, iv. 98; at Greenwich Observatory, iv. 205 & n. 4; draws meridian for E, iv. 333; observes solar eclipse, iv. 383 & n. 7; attends laying of foundation-stone of Greenwich Hospital, v. 249 & n. 2; letter of, to Royal Society, iv. 196, n. 3.

Flanders: *see* Spanish Netherlands.

Flea *or* Fly, Rev. —, curate at Cadenham: sermons by, iii. 101 *bis* & n. 3, 111(?), 116, 117.

Fleetwood, James, D.D.; bishop of Worcester 1675–83: sermon by, iv. 86 & n. 1.

Fleetwood, William; D.D. 1705; bishop of St. Asaph 1708; of Ely 1714, v. 220, n. 2; as lecturer at St. Dunstan's in the West: sermons by, v. 220, 222; ~ false identification, v. 228, n. 2; *add.*; mentioned, v. 221, n. 5.

Fleming, the, sculptor: *see* Duquesnoy, F.

Fletcher, Rev. —: sermons by, iv. 37 & nn. 5, 7, 8, 39 & n. 5(?), 47.

Fletcher, John: part-author of *The Widdow* (?), iii. 313, n. 4; and F. Beaumont: *The Scornful Lady* by: acted, iii. 268 & n. 5.

Fleury, Normandy, ii. 121 (i. 78).

Fleury de Culan, Henri de, heer van Buat: plot, &c., of, iii. 471 & n. 1; *add.*

Floods: at Callao, 1687, iv. 586 & n. 1; submerging Zealand, ii. 31–2 & n. (i. 24).

Flora, Joachim of: *see* Joachim.

Florence:

— descriptions: 1644, ii. 184–200 & nn. (i. 117–21); 1645, ii. 410–17 & nn.

— general and miscellaneous: artists

Florence (*cont.*)
at, ii. 417 & nn. 5–8; in comparisons: with Lucca, ii. 410; ~ with Paris, iii. 637; houses, ii. 200; manufactures: *pietra commessa*, ii. 411; ~ porcelain (*c.* 1580), ii. 100, n. 1; ~ silks, &c., ii. 200; merchants: privileges of, at Lyons, ii. 158 (i. 101); population, ii. 200; prostitutes: tax on, ii. 417; St. John's day festival, ii. 193 & n. 1 (i. 119), 199, n. 4; situation, ii. 184–5 (i. 117); streets: paving of, &c., ii. 200.

— buildings, &c.: Accademia della Crusca: rooms of, ii. 415–16 & n.; ~ mentioned, ii. 364, n. 5 *ad fin.*; Accademia di Belle Arti: statue in, ii. 188, n. 3; Archaeological Museum: statues in, ii. 189, nn. 2, 4; Arsenal, ii. 417 & n. 4; Bargello: statues, &c., in, ii. 231, n. 4, 403, n. 1 *ad fin.*, 413, nn. 5, 7, 414, nn. 1, 7; Biblioteca Laurenziana, ii. 198 & nn. 10, 11, 417 & nn. 1–3; ~ MSS. in, ii. 188, nn. 8, 9; Boboli gardens, ii. 186 & n. 4, 187 & nn. 3–6 (i. 117–18); ~ obelisk, &c., in, ii. 232, n. 4, 287, n. 1; bridges: Ponte S. Trinità, ii. 185 & n. 3 (i. 117); ~ Ponte Vecchio, ii. 185 & n. 4 (i. 117); Canto de' Carnesecchi, ii. 194, n. 2; Canto della Paglia, ii. 197 & n. 8.

— — churches: Baptistery, ii. 197–8 & nn.; Cathedral (S. Maria del Fiore), ii. 196–7 & nn.; ~ statues from, ii. 411 & n. 2; ~ campanile, ii. 197 & nn. 6–8; Or San Michele, ii. 196 & n. 6; SS. Annunziata and convent, ii. 194–5 & nn. (i. 120), 411–13 & nn.; S. Croce, ii. 195–6 & nn.; S. Lorenzo, ii. 198–9 & nn., 416–17 & nn.; ~ Chapel of the Princes at, ii. 184, n. 7 *ad fin.*, 198–9 & nn., 216, n. 6, 416–17 & nn.; ~ ciborium for Chapel of the Princes at, ii. 191 *bis* & n. 9 (i. 119), 199, 416–17 & n.; ~ New Sacristy, ii. 198, nn. 5, 7, 9, 416 & n. 5; S. Marco, ii. 200 & nn. 3–5; S. Maria Novella, ii. 199–200 & nn.; S. Spirito, ii. 187–8 & n. (i. 118).

Florence (*cont.*)
— — column with statue of Justice, ii. 185–6 & nn. (i. 117), 415 & n. 1; Forte di Belvedere, ii. 187 & n. 5 (i. 118); Fortezza da Basso, ii. 417, n. 4; fountains: Boar, ii. 194 & n. 7 (i. 120); ~ Neptune, ii. 193 & nn. 6, 7 (i. 120), 194 & n. 3; Grand-dukes: art-collections of: *see* Palazzo degli Uffizi *below*; ~ ateliers of, ii. 188 (i. 118); ~ riding-school and zoo of, ii. 195 & nn. 5, 6 (i. 120–1); law-courts, ii. 188 & n. 11 (i. 118); Loggia dei Lanzi, ii. 193 & nn. 2–5 (i. 120); ~ statues in, ii. 194, n. 2, 231, nn. 2, 5; Mercato Nuovo, ii. 194, n. 7.

— — palaces: dell' Antella, ii. 196, n. 5; Pitti, ii. 186–7 & nn. (i. 117 & n. 1); ~ imitated at Luxembourg, Paris, i. 81, n. 2; ~ Museo degli Argenti in, ii. 414, n. 9; ~ paintings in, ii. 190, n. 12, 191, n. 6, 411, n. 3, 413, n. 14; Strozzi, ii. 186 (i. 117); degli Uffizi and its collections, ii. 188–93 & nn. (i. 118–19), 413–14 & nn.; ~ armoury in, ii. 192 & nn. 5–8 (i. 119), 414; ~ Tribuna, ii. 190 & nn. 1, 8 (i. 119); ~ statues, &c., in, ii. 232, n. 2, 286, nn. 2, &c., 304, n. 6, 415, nn. 4, 8; Palazzo Vecchio, ii. 188 & nn. 2–10 (i. 118), 194, 414 & nn. 8–10; ~ hall in, i. 117, n. 1; ~ wardrobe, ii. 192, n. 11.

— — Piazza di S. Maria Novella, ii. 199 & n. 4; Piazza S. Spirito: E lodges in, ii. 184 (i. 117); Piazza della Signoria: statues and fountain in, ii. 193–4 & nn. (i. 120); Serraglio delle fiere, ii. 195 & n. 6 (i. 120–1); Spedale degli Innocenti, ii. 195 & n. 4 (i. 120).

— environs: beauty of, ii. 184–5 (i. 117); cultivation of, ii. 410; Poggio a Caiano, ii. 410, n. 5 *ad fin.*; Poggio Imperiale, ii. 200, 410–11 & nn.; *add.*; ~ statue at, ii. 403, n. 1.

— political: wars of, with Pisa, ii. 179 (i. 113); Pisa as subject to, ii. 182, n. 6; victory of, over Siena, ii. 186, n. 1.

— persons: T. Clifford dies at, iii.

Florence (*cont.*)
574 & n. 5; Sir Robert Dudley, titular duke of Northumberland, resides at, i. 115.
Florence: Council of, ii. 200, n. 2; ~ history of, ii. 563 & n. 5; iii. 304.
Florence: Dukes of: *see* Tuscany: Grand dukes of.
Florival, —, private tutor, v. 322 & n. 3.
Flowers [the several kinds; for general notices *see* Gardening; for some other flowering plants *see* Plants; Trees and Timber]: anemones, ii. 114 (i. 74), 133 (i. 86), 528; ~ story relating to, i. 86–7; *add.*; crocus, ii. 133 (i. 86); polyanthus, i. 86; ranunculus, ii. 133 (i. 86); roses: rose grafted on orange-tree, ii. 187 & n. 6 (i. 118); ~ antipathy to, iii. 550 & n. 5; tulips, ii. 114 (i. 74), 133 (i. 86), 528; ~ kinds of: number of, iii. 33; ~ story relating to, i. 86; *add.*
Flushing: notice, 1641, ii. 31 & nn. 1–3 (i. 23 & n. 4); journey to, ii. 30–1 (i. 23); English fleet at, 1690, v. 2, n. 2.
Fly *or* Flea, Rev. —, curate at Cadenham: sermons by, iii. 101 *bis* & n. 3, 111 (?), 116, 117.
Foate, Sir Thomas: *see* Foote.
Foley, Thomas: buys Hurcott, ii. 545, n. 3.
Folkestone, Kent: sea-fight off, 1652, iii. 67, n. 4.
Folklore [*see also* Giants; Legends; Witches]: charms: roll of, iii. 108; death-watches: fear of, iii. 325; possession: supposed case of, iii. 547, n. 3; second sight: instance of, iv. 470; siren: arm of, iii. 517 & n. 4; tritons: in Lake of Geneva, ii. 520; ~ near Brazil, iii. 517, n. 1.
customs: throwing the stocking, iii. 589, 590, n. 1; weathercocks on trees, in Thanet, &c., iii. 611; *add.*; Delft: punishment at, of woman committing bigamy, ii. 41 (i. 30); Godmanchester: kings met at, by hundred ploughs, iii. 135 & n. 5.
Fondi (Fundi), ii. 322 *bis* & nn. 1, 5; Via Appia near, ii. 319, n. 3, 322 & n. 4.
Fontaine (Vilvorde ?), ii. 68, n. 3.
Fontaine, Mrs. Mary: *see* Fountaine.
Fontainebleau, ii. 116 & n. 3 (i. 75), 119 (i. 77); palace, ii. 116 (i. 75), 116–20 & nn. (i. 76–7); ~ in comparison, iii. 126; ~ execution of G. R. Monaldesco at, iv. 221 & n. 3.
Fontainebleau: Forest of, ii. 116 & n. 1 (i. 75), 119 (i. 77).
Fontana, Annibale: sculptures by, ii. 495 & nn. 3, 4.
Fontana, Domenico, architect, ii. 243, n. 4; work of, in general, ii. 212, n. 2; buildings (all in Rome): Acqua Felice: fountain, ii. 238 & n. 6; Lateran palace, ii. 271; Palazzo della Cancelleria: doorway, ii. 367; S. Maria Maggiore: Cappella Sistina, ii. 243; obelisks erected by: Vatican, ii. 256, 257; ~machines for removal of: paintings of, ii. 302 & n. 5; others, ii. 245, 270, 375.
Fontana, Lavinia: paintings by, ii. 307 & n. 3, 359 & n. 9.
Food and Drink [select: notices relating to kinds of food and drink, cooking, &c.; notices relating to meals are indexed under Meals]:
kinds of food: ale: Margate or Northdown, iii. 615 & n. 5; beef: powdered, ii. 469 & n. 1; betel nut: chewing, iv. 285; botargo, ii. 426 & n. 2; bread: Dutch prisoners of war complain about, iii. 397–8; broth, iii. 145; butter: at Bruges, ii. 75 (i. 49); ~ at Vanves, iii. 4; caviare: at Bologna, ii. 426 & n. 2; cheese: at Bruges, ii. 75 (i. 49); ~ Lodi, ii. 490 & n. 9; ~ Parmesan, ii. 426, 490 & n. 9; ~ on Simplon, ii. 511; ~ mites in, iii. 341; chocolate (jacolatte), iv. 268 & n. 5; cider: *see* Fruit-trees and Fruits; coffee: introduction of, into England, &c., ii. 18 & n. 4 (i. 14–15); cream: at Blois, ii. 142 & n. 5 (i. 92); eryngoes, iii. 178 & n. 2; fish: sea and fresh-water available at Wotton, i. 6; fruit: *see* Fruit-trees and Fruits; hartshorn: jelly made from, iv. 278; milk: on Simplon, ii. 511; olio, iv. 190; oysters, iii. 627; ~ Colchester, iii. 178; ~ Lago Lucrino, ii. 345 & n. 3; ~ Murano, ii. 467–8; pilaw, iv.

Food and Drink (*cont.*)
286; potatoes: proposed paper on cultivation of, iii. 340, n. 1; pottage, iv. 286; punch, iii. 313 & n. 3; rice: grown in kingdom of Naples, ii. 325, 353; sausages: at Bologna, ii. 426 & n. 1; sorbet, iv. 268; sugar: grown in kingdom of Naples, ii. 325, 353; ~ refining of, iii. 102–3 & n.; sweet-meats: as dessert or banquets, iii. 480 & n. 5; iv. 268, 492; tea: introduction of, into England, &c., i. 14–15 & n.; truffles, ii. 158–9 (i. 101); venison (frequent notices): of sorrel deer (?), iii. 117 & n. 1; potted, ii. 476; gifts of: private, iii. 219; iv. 171, 220; ~ by Charles II, &c., for Royal Society's anniversary dinners, iii. 366, &c.; wine: *see* Wines.
cookery: for Bantam ambassadors, iv. 286; Portuguese, iv. 190; Spanish and English, iv. 242; test of a cook, iv. 483.
miscellaneous: brewers, iv. 363; kitchen-stuff, iv. 352 & n. 2; spoon-meat, iv. 286; provisions for sea-voyage, ii. 451; 'a very honourable table', iii. 437; food cooked in digester, iv. 171–2, 278–9.
Foote (Foate), Sir Thomas, bt.: arbitration to, &c., iii. 540 & nn. 4, 5.
Foots Cray, Kent: road to, from Deptford, iii. 253, n. 2.
Forbus, —: shows plan for garden at Burleigh House, iv. 350–1.
Ford, —, Lady Ford (Sarah Ford ?), iii. 14–15 & n.
Ford, Sir Edward: geneal., iii. 14, n. 9.
Ford, Sir Henry: commissioner for Sick and Wounded 1672–4, iii. 602, n. 1.
Ford, Sarah, Lady Ford, wife of Sir Edward, iii. 14, n. 9.
Forest of Dean: proposal for planting, iii. 343 & n. 3; effects of storm in, 1703, v. 550, n. 2 *ad fin.*
Forges, —: *see* Hubert, R. (iii. 433, n. 3).
Formello, Donato da, artist: works by, ii. 267, n. 3, 297 & n. 1.
Formia (Formiana, Formiae): Cicero's tomb, &c., at, ii. 322–3 & nn.
Forster, Captain — (William Forster ?), iii. 91 & n. 5.
Forster, Mrs. Elizabeth, born Tyrell, wife of William Forster: geneal., iii. 91, n. 5; *see also* iv. 313, n. 3.
Forster, Sir Humphrey, first bt., iii. 100, n. 4; house of, at Aldermaston, iii. 100 & n. 4; geneal., iii. 91, n. 5.
Forster, Sir Humphrey, second bt., iv. 313, n. 3; travels in Spain, iv. 313; geneal., iii. 91, n. 5.
Forster, John: as editor of: Diary, i. *69*, *115*, *116–17*; ~ E's correspondence, i. *130*.
Forster, William, iii. 91, n. 5.
Fortifications [select: fortifications mentioned in notices of sieges, &c., town gates and walls mentioned casually, and castellated houses, are not indexed collectively]:
— general: fortification: teaching of, ii. 134 (i. 87); model fort, for instruction of Louis XIV in, iii. 44.
— — fortifications: in England: rare before Civil War, ii. 21 (i. 16); in France, v. 160; siege: for display, iv. 42; special features: blockhouses, ii. 30 (i. 22); iii. 130 & nn. 5, 6; chains across rivers, &c., ii. 164 (i. 104); iii. 485; sconces, ii. 57, n. 7, 62 (i. 42), 183 & n. 6 (?).
— particular fortifications:
— — towns with general systems (walls with or without castles, &c.): Abbeville, ii. 85 (i. 57); Antwerp, ii. 67 (i. 45); Avignon, ii. 161 (i. 102); Bergen-op-Zoom, ii. 61 & n. 5 (i. 42); Bologna, ii. 420; Bruges, ii. 75 (i. 49); Brussels, ii. 69 (i. 46); Calais, ii. 82–3 (i. 56), 560 & n. 6; Colchester, iii. 176–7 & n.; Coventry, iii. 121 & n. 4; Dieppe, ii. 124 (i. 79); Dunkirk, ii. 75, 76 & n. 2 (i. 50); ~ new fortifications, i. 49–50 & n.; Ferrara, ii. 427; Geneva, ii. 524 & n. 2; Genoa, ii. 177 & nn. 6, 7 (i. 112); Ghent, ii. 73 (i. 48); Gloucester, iii. 118 & n. 3; Hull, iii. 130 & n. 6; Leghorn, ii. 183 (i. 115); London: line of communication, 1642, ii. 80 & n. 1; Lucca, ii. 409, 410; Maas-

Fortifications (*cont.*)
tricht: imitation of, iv. 42 & n. 1; Marseilles (town and harbour), ii. 164 & nn. 3–5 (i. 104); Milan, ii. 491, n. 3 *ad fin.*, 501; Monaco, ii. 168–9 (i. 106); Montreuil, ii. 85 (i. 57); Ostend, ii. 75 (i. 49); Portsmouth: in 1638, ii. 21 & n. 7 (i. 16); ~ in 1685, iv. 472 & n. 6, 473 *bis*; Richelieu, ii. 150–1 (i. 98); 's Hertogenbosch and environs, ii. 57–8 & n. (i. 39); Siena, ii. 201; Tours, ii. 145 (i. 94); Verona, ii. 486 & n. 4; York, iii. 128, 130 & n. 2.
— — towns dominated by citadels: Antwerp, ii. 66–7 & n. (i. 44–5); London: the Tower: *see* London: topography; Milan: Castle, ii. 501–2 & nn.; Naples, ii. 326 & nn. 1–6; Paris: the Bastille, ii. 102 (i. 67); Siena, ii. 203–4 & n.
— — towns with castles or forts for defence: Boulogne, ii. 84 (i. 57); Bourges, ii. 153–4 & n. (i. 99); Bristol, iii. 102 & n. 6; Caen, ii. 127 (i. 81); Dover: Castle, iii. 395; Florence, ii. 187 & n. 5 (i. 118), 417, n. 4; Havre, ii. 125 (i. 80); Lyons, ii. 157 (i. 101); Margate, iii. 615 & n. 5; Nice, ii. 168 (i. 106); Nijmegen, ii. 35 & n. 1 (i. 27); Nottingham, iii. 126 & n. 2; Pontefract, iii. 127 & n. 6; Tournon, ii. 159 (i. 102); Valence, ii. 160 (i. 102); Villeneuve-lès-Avignon, ii. 161 & n. 4 (i. 102); Woolwich, iii. 485.
— — fortresses or small garrison or frontier towns: Arona, ii. 506; Gennep, Huys te, ii. 35 & n. 5 (i. 27); Heusden, ii. 59 (i. 40); Orzinuovi, ii. 490 & n. 6; Peschiera, ii. 488; Radicofani, ii. 208; Sheerness, 1666–72, iii. 441 & n. 7, 487 & n. 1, 511 & n. 4, 609–10 & n.; Steenbergen, ii. 61 (i. 41); Willemstad, ii. 60 & n. 3 (i. 41).
— — castles and isolated forts: Baia, ii. 349; Belvoir, iii. 124–5 & nn.; Bramber, ii. 544 & n. 4; Deal: forts near, iii. 395 & n. 5; Donnington, iii. 100 & n. 3; Knodsenburg, ii. 35 (i. 27); Leeds Castle, iii. 422, n. 1, 436;

Fortifications (*cont.*)
Loevestein, ii. 39 & n. 1 (i. 29); Terracina (?), ii. 321 & n. 6; Tickhill, iii. 127 & n. 4; Upnor Castle, iii. 485, 620.
— — defences for waterways, &c.: Ghent-Bruges canal, ii. 74 (i. 48–9); Golfo della Spezia, ii. 179 (i. 113); Medway and Swale, &c., iii. 485, 610; Scheldt, on Dutch-Spanish border, ii. 61–3 & nn. (i. 42–3); Thames, at Gravesend and Tilbury, ii. 30 & n. 1 (i. 22); iii. 609 & n. 4.
Fort James, Gambia river: taken by French, 1694(?), v. 174 & n. 5.
Forum Julii (Fréjus), ii. 167 & n. 3 (i. 105).
Fossanova (Nova fossa), ii. 318–19 & nn.
Fossils, iii. 511 & n. 4; *see also* ii. 398 & n. 1; discussed by Royal Society, iv. 355.
Foster, Sir Robert, judge: attends Gresham College commission, iii. 335 & n. 1.
Fotherby (Fetherby), Sir John: at Amsterdam, ii. 45 & n. 1 (i. 32).
Fotherby, Martin, bishop of Salisbury: geneal., ii. 45, n. 1.
Foubert, Major Henri, riding-master, iv. 257, n. 5, 399.
Foubert (Faubert), Solomon, iv. 257, n. 5; *add.*; and Count K. J. von Königsmarck, iv. 274, n. 1; watches Turkish horses, iv. 399; academy of: negotiations for house for, iv. 257–8 & n.; proposed supervision of, by Royal Society, iv. 290 & n. 2; *see also* iv. 289, n. 4; exercises of, in manage, iv. 400–1 & n.; mentioned, ii. 134, n. 2; iv. 201, n. 4.
Fountaine, Mrs. Mary, widow of Peter Fountaine: *see* Tuke, Mrs. M.
Fountaine, Peter: geneal., iii. 172, n. 5.
Fountaine, Rebecca: *see* Paravicini, Mrs. R.
Fountains [for street-fountains *see* Water-supply; for those in fanciful displays *see* Waterworks]:
general: discussed at Royal Society, iv. 65.
in gardens [select: notices of gardens in which the water-schemes are principal ele-

Fountains (*cont.*)
ments, &c. Fountains forming ordinary features of gardens are not indexed]: Brussels: Cour, &c., ii. 71–2 (i. 47); Essonne, ii. 121 (i. 77–8); Euston, iii. 591; iv. 117; Florence: Pitti palace, ii. 186–7 & nn. (i. 117–18); Fontainebleau, ii. 118–19 & nn. (i. 76–7); Frascati: Villas Aldobrandini, &c., ii. 392–3 & nn.; Genoa: Palazzo Doria a Fassolo, ii. 175 (i. 110–11); Hampton Court, iii. 322, n. 5, 324 & n. 6; iv. 645; Maison Rouge, ii. 120 (i. 77); Paris: Luxembourg, ii. 129, 130 (i. 82, 83); ~ Palais-Royal, ii. 134 (i. 87), 567; iii. 44; Pisa: botanic garden, ii. 181 (i. 114); Pratolino, ii. 418–19 & nn.; Rome: Villa Borghese, ii. 251, 390 & n. 3; Rueil, ii. 109–10 (i. 70–1), 564; St.-Cloud, ii. 107–8 (i. 69), 564; Tivoli: Villa d'Este, ii. 395–6 & nn.; Wilton, iii. 114; Wotton, i. 5; ii. 81 (i. 55); iii. 24, 61.

Fowler, —: petition of, 1687, iv. 565.

Fowler, Rev. —: sermon by, iv. 286–7.

Fowler, Mrs. Anne, wife of Captain T. Fowler: marriage of, iv. 139 & n. 3.

Fowler, Edward, D.D.; bishop of Gloucester 1691: nominated bishop, v. 49, n. 1.

Fowler, Captain Thomas: marriage of, iv. 139 & n. 3.

Fowler, Sir Thomas, bt.: aviary of, iii. 96 & n. 6.

Fox, — (Stephen, later Sir Stephen, Fox ?): social, iii. 356.

Fox, Charles, iv. 219, n. 5; marriage of, iv. 219 & n. 5; health of, 1681, iv. 248; social, iv. 288.

Fox, Elizabeth: *see* Cornwallis, Elizabeth, Lady Cornwallis.

Fox, Mrs. Elizabeth, wife of Charles Fox, iv. 219 & n. 5, 288, n. 1.

Fox, Elizabeth, Lady Fox, wife of Sir Stephen, iv. 170 & n. 3, 219; and Fox's house at Chiswick, iv. 294; condoles for Mary Evelyn, iv. 432; social, iv. 170, 288.

Fox, Rev. Henry: sermon by (?), iv. 416 & n. 2.

Fox, Jane: *see* Compton, Jane, countess of Northampton.

Fox, Margaret, daughter of Sir Stephen, iv. 245, n. 3.

Fox, Sir Stephen; knighted 1665, iii. 447, n. 5; *add.*; account of, iv. 217–19 & nn.; *add.*; as paymaster to the forces, iv. 218–19 & nn.; ~ supersession of, iv. 267 & n. 4; ~ alluded to, iv. 270; as clerk comptroller of the Green Cloth, iii. 261, n. 4; as commissioner for London streets, iii. 319, n. 1; as commissioner of the Treasury: appointed, 1680, iv. 193 & n. 3; ~ appointed, 1687, iv. 533; as originator of Chelsea Hospital: consults E, i. *34*; ~ negotiates for site for, iv. 257 & n. 3; ~ proposals of, for establishment for, iv. 269–70 & n.; ~ submits plans of, to Sancroft, iv. 281; ~ inspects foundations of building, iv. 289; wealth and credit of, iv. 218–19, 248, 267, 270; house of, in Whitehall, iv. 179, n. 3; tries to buy house at Chelsea, iv. 170, 185 & n. 2; house of, at Chiswick: building, &c., iv. 294 & n. 4, 316; and marriage-negotiation for his daughter Jane, iv. 245–7 & nn., 248; condolences of, &c., for Mary Evelyn, iv. 430, 432; recommends cook to Henry Hyde, earl of Clarendon, 1685, iv. 483; social, iii. 356 & n. 3 (?), 447; iv. 44, 75, 94, 103, 106, 107, 124, 179, 266, 273, 276, 282, 288, 339, 344, 359, 391, 467, 603; geneal., iv. 219, n. 6.

Foxham Common, near Calne, Wilts., iii. 100, n. 6 *ad fin.*

Foy, Dr. —: *see* Hoy, T.

Fraiser, Carey: *see* Mordaunt, Carey, countess of Peterborough, &c.

Fraizer *or* Fraiser (Frasier), Sir Alexander, bt., M.D., iii. 351, n. 11; social, iii. 351, 440; geneal., iv. 499, n. 5.

Frampton, Robert; D.D. 1673; bishop of Gloucester 1681–90; nonjuror, iii. 604, n. 3, 629 & n. 1; iv. 85, n. 6; proposed for vicar of Deptford (?), iii. 604; as preacher: eloquence, &c., of, iii. 629; iv. 55; ~ sermons by, iii. 629; iv. 32, 55, 85, 107; ~ appointed to preach, iv. 165; superseded as bishop, v. 48–9 & n.

Francavilla, Pietro, sculptor: statues by, ii. 180 & n. 1 (i. 113), 182 & n. 4 (i. 114), 185 & n. 3 (i. 117).

France [in political and public matters from 1661 onwards E treats France and the king of France as being practically identical. All notices from 1661 onwards relating to the king of France in his public capacity as head of the French state, as well as those in which France itself is named, are indexed under the present heading, or the headings mentioned below; those in which Louis XIV's personality is concerned are also indexed under Louis XIV].

— Evelyn in France: travels and residence in: 1643–4, ii. 82–168 & nn. (i. 56–106 & nn.); ~ 1646–7, ii. 532–7 & nn.; ~ 1649–52 (mainly in Paris), ii. 559–iii. 13, 16–56 & nn.; account of France: bibliographical note on, &c., i. *96–7*; ii. 571–3; journey to, 1649: preparations for, &c., ii. 557 & n. 3, 558 *bis* & n. 4; E's goods from France, iii. 62, 63, 66, 68.

— chronological series:

— — (i) to 1661: general [*see also* Wars: War between France and Spain]: civil wars, ii. 138 (i. 91), 160 (i. 102); treaty of Rueil, 1649, ii. 553 & n. 6; court at Amiens, &c., 1649, ii. 561, n. 1; Paris exposed to invaders, 1650, iii. 17 & n. 3; *see also* iii. 638–9 (extract from *State of France*); Mazarin banished, 1651, iii. 26 & n. 4.

— — — foreign relations: England: Frenchman represented on figurehead of *Naseby*, iii. 149–50 & n.; Monaco: placed under French protection, ii. 169 & n. 1 (i. 106); Naples: French hated in, ii. 354 & n. 1; Spanish Netherlands: frontier towards, ii. 84, n. 1; ~ Dunkirk as French possession, iii. 55, n. 8; Switzerland: general, ii. 518.

— — (ii) from 1661 onwards: general: relations of, with Charles II, i. *27, 28, 30*; initiates bombardment of towns from sea, v. 186, 216, 218; use of

France (*cont.*)
corruption by, in foreign policy, iv. 367 & n. 3, 378 & n. 1; v. 546; *see also* iv. 136, n. 4, 331, n. 5; v. 104; pensions John Sobieski, king of Poland, v. 247.

— — — 1661: establishes precedence of French ambassadors over Spanish, iii. 297 & n. 4; *add.*

— — — 1662: acquires Dunkirk, &c., i. 50 & n. 1; *see also* ii. 75, n. 11 *ad fin.*

— — — 1664: king's health drunk at Lord Mayor's banquet, iii. 389; instigates Second Dutch War (?), iii. 405 & n. 1.

— — — 1666: declares war on England, iii. 457, n. 4; offers to mediate between Spain and Portugal, iii. 434 & n. 1; Fire of London attributed to French and Dutch incendiaries, iii. 457, n. 4, 462; reported French landing in England, iii. 462 & n. 1.

— — — 1667: makes peace with England, iii. 491, n. 1, 492, n. 5.

— — — 1670: Secret Treaty of Dover: *see* Dover: Secret Treaty of; seizes Lorraine, iii. 587 & n. 4.

— — — 1671: French army at Dunkirk, iii. 575 & n. 1.

— — — 1672–8: war with United Provinces, &c.: *see* Wars.

— — — 1678: bribes Country party members of English parliament, iv. 136, n. 4.

— — — 1681: secret money-treaties with Charles II, iv. 331, n. 5.

— — — 1683: Charles II's conduct towards, iv. 331 & n. 5; ~ alluded to (?), iv. 340; ~ English dislike of, iv. 323; men-of-war of, permitted by England to pass up Channel, iv. 331–2 & n.; encourages Turkey to invade Empire, iv. 331 & n. 3, 340; threatens Spanish Netherlands, United Provinces, &c., iv. 331 & n. 4, 340.

— — — 1684: induces Amsterdam to oppose William of Orange, iv. 367 & n. 3, 378 & n. 1; *see also* iv. 369 & n. 2; England

France (*cont.*)
adheres to, iv. 369, 380; takes Luxemburg, iv. 378 & n. 1, 380 & n. 3, 549; bombards Genoa, iv. 381 & n. 3; Siamese embassy to, iv. 388, n. 2.
— — — 1686: attempts to involve protestant powers in war among themselves, iv. 524–5 *bis*.
— — — 1687: Louis XIV visits Luxemburg, iv. 549, n. 1.
— — — 1688: attitude of, in disputed election of Archbishop-Elector of Cologne, iv. 596 & n. 3.
— — — 1688–97: war of the League of Augsburg: *see* Wars; for the war in Ireland, 1689–91, *see* Ireland: chronological series.
— — — 1689: concern in Turkish negotiations for peace with Empire, v. 36, n. 1, 37.
— — — 1690: relations with Savoy, v. 25 & n. 2; rejoicings for supposed death, &c., of William III, v. 32; relations with Switzerland, v. 35 & n. 8, 39 & n. 5.
— — — 1691: Jacobites' dependence on, v. 42.
— — — 1696: interest of, in Polish succession, v. 247, 270 & n. 2; *see also* Conti, F. L. de Bourbon, prince of.
— — — 1697: ambition of, checked: in sermon, v. 277; cost of war of League of Augsburg to, v. 270, n. 2.
— — — 1698–1713: for the war of the Spanish Succession and the preparations, &c., for it, *see* Wars.
— — — 1701: relations with Switzerland and Venice, v. 441.
— — — 1703: annexes Orange, v. 545, n. 1, 559; intrigues of, in Scotland, v. 546, 553 & n. 1.
— army:
— — general: condition of soldiers, 1650, iii. 17; subsistence of troops: method of providing for, iii. 587 & n. 5; review, 1644, ii. 135 & n. 1 (i. 88); sent against Waldenses in Piedmont, iv. 511, n. 2, 515 & n. 1; dragoon missioners persecute protestants, iv. 575; new levy, 1688, iv. 596, n. 3.
— — regiments, &c.: household

France (*cont.*)
troops, &c.: in procession, 1651, iii. 41–3 & nn.; Picardy: death of captain in, ii. 136 (i. 89); ~ on march, iii. 17; Royal Anglais (horse): raising of, iii. 587 & n. 3; Irish, commanded by Sir G. Hamilton, iv. 79, n. 3; Scottish, 1650–1, iii. 12, n. 5, 43; Swiss guards, &c., iii. 41, 43.
— — mercenaries: Irish, iii. 6, n. 4; Scottish, iii. 12 & n. 5; Swiss, ii. 517; ~ officers, ii. 136 (i. 89), 516.
— climate [select notices]: winters: 1655–6, iii. 165, n. 4; ~ 1657–8, iii. 211, n. 2; churches, &c., struck by lightning, 1687, iv. 560; dearth: 1693, v. 130; ~ 1699, v. 311–12 & n.
— colonies: in Leeward Islands, iii. 605 & n. 1; West Indian: negroes in, to be baptized, iv. 471, n. 3.
— commerce and manufactures:
— — commerce: at Marseilles, ii. 166 (i. 105); merchants at Lyons, ii. 158 (i. 101); booksellers, ii. 98; curio dealers, ii. 100 (i. 65–6), 124 (i. 79); fancy goods, ii. 98 *bis* (i. 64).
— — manufactures: cutlery, gunmaking, &c., ii. 85 (i. 57–8), 154–5 (i. 100), 159 (i. 102); ivory-working, ii. 124 (i. 79); textiles: silk-weaving, ii. 145–6 & n. (i. 94); ~ tapestry, iv. 343 & n. 2; watch-making, goldsmiths' work, &c., ii. 99 *bis* (i. 65), 142 (i. 93).
— geographical: centre of France, ii. 153 (i. 99); roads: paving of, ii. 135 & n. 3 (i. 89); towns and villages protected against hostile incursions, v. 160; vegetation: about Tarare, ii. 156 (i. 100); ~ in Provence, ii. 162 & n. 10, 163 (i. 103 *bis*); vineyards: northerly limits of, ii. 85 (i. 58), 121 (i. 78); 'the best that all France affords' (at Roanne), ii. 533; mentioned, ii. 168 (i. 106), 514, 524; iv. 618.
— kings: absolute power of, v. 402, 475; ~ dislike of, *c.* 1700, i. 88 & n. 2; use of term 'royal', i. 66–7 & n.; king of France as part of English royal style, iv. 621.

France (*cont.*)
— — as art-patrons, ii. 105 (i. 68); burial place of, ii. 85 (i. 58); children of: residence of, ii. 142 (i. 92); coronation of: Sainte Ampoule in, ii. 147 (i. 95); cup-bearers of: oath of, ii. 138 (i. 90); heirs-apparent of: source of title of, ii. 158 (i. 101); house of Bourbon: source of name of, ii. 155 (i. 100); portraits of: in Louvre, ii. 104 (i. 68); at Rome, ii. 373; ~ statues, ii. 95 (i. 63); ~ wax effigies, ii. 90 (i. 60); queens of: dowry of, ii. 155 (i. 100).
— — one kept prisoner at Groombridge (error), iii. 72 & n. 2; one ascends Campanile at Venice on horseback, ii. 445 & n. 8.
— — palaces of: views of: in paintings, ii. 117 & n. 3 (i. 76); ~ on tapestries, iv. 343 & n. 2; individual palaces &c.: Amboise, ii. 143–4 & nn. (i. 93); Chambord, ii. 139–40 & n. (i. 91–2); Fontainebleau, ii. 116–20 & nn. (ii. 75–7); Madrid, Château de, ii. 112 & n. 1 (i. 72); Paris: *see* Paris: topography: Louvre and Tuileries; Palais-Cardinal; Plessis-lez-Tours, ii. 147 & n. 3 (i. 95); Rouen: lodgings at, ii. 123 (i. 79); St.-Germain-en-Laye: *see* St.-Germain; Tours: lodgings at, ii. 146 & n. 1 (i. 94); Vincennes, Château de, ii. 102 (i. 67); iii. 1 & n. 3.
— officers and members of royal household: in Louis XIV's procession, 1651 (not indexed separately), iii. 41–3; grand écuyer de France: *see* Armagnac, L. de Lorraine, count of; premier écuyer de la petite-écurie du roi: *see* Beringhem, M. de; grand master of the Artillery: residence of, ii. 102 (i. 67); grand-prévot: *see* Sourches, Marquis de; secretary of state: *see* Lionne, M. de.
— religion [for the French protestants and their persecution *see* French protestants]: conversion of France to protestantism prophesied, v. 322; French share in persecuting Waldenses, iv. 511 *bis* & n. 2, 515 & n. 1; v. 3, 25; church-music, iii. 347; clergy: join in persecuting protestants, iv. 447, n. 3, 575; ~ speech of bishop of Valence on behalf of, 1685, iv. 486 & n. 3; preaching, iv. 164 & n. 2.
— social [*see also* Paris: social]: *baume de Lucatel*: use of, in, iii. 146, n. 1; caleche: introduced into, iii. 475, n. 5; celebrations: illuminations used for, v. 72; dress: men's, iii. 465 *bis*, 467; ~ farthingale, iii. 320, n. 4; ~ petticoats, &c., for English court ladies, iii. 572; duelling: banishment on account of, iv. 393 & n. 3; forests: public security in, ii. 116 (i. 75), 135–6 (i. 89); frontier areas (northern France): marauding, &c., in, ii. 83–4 & n. (i. 56), 84–5 & n. (i. 57), 561 & n. 1; iii. 12, 16, 17, 54; horsemanship, ii. 327, n. 4; ~ Neapolitan horses brought to France, iii. 50; ~ proficiency in, of nobility, i. 88; iii. 2; ~ riding academies: English youths sent to, iv. 290; housing: cave-dwellings, ii. 144 & n. 2 (i. 93); ~ in comparison (?), iii. 122; manners, i. 47; ~ influence of, i. 88 & n. 2; ~ imitated in England, iv. 308 (in sermon), 339; population, &c.: effect on, of persecution of protestants, iv. 447, n. 3, 448, 486 & n. 1; poverty in: in comparison, iii. 122; torture: use of, in, iii. 29, n. 1; wolves, &c., in, ii. 116 (i. 75), 122 (i. 78), 141 & n. 3, 142 (i. 92 *bis*).
— miscellaneous: 'as good as home' for Englishman travelling further afield, ii. 518; portrait of Prince James Edward from, 1692, v. 92; French convent in Rome, ii. 373 & n. 1.
— personal:
— — Frenchmen and women: in France: attend English ambassador's chapel on Christmas day, ii. 567; E's acquaintances, iii. 54; virtuosi: communication from, to Royal Society, iii. 473.
— — — in England (mainly not named): clergy: chaplain of Sir

France (*cont.*)
G. Sylvius, iv. 447; ~ preacher before James II, iv. 465; converts to Church of England, v. 204, 269; *see also* Bréval, F. Durant de; merchants: at Dover, iii. 56 & n. 1; ~ in London (J. Houblon), iv. 128, 162, 306; mountebank (J. Punteus), iii. 293, n. 4; musicians, iii. 310; iv. 186, 385, 404 & n. 7, 413 & n. 5; nobleman with second sight, iv. 470; servant, v. 44; tutor, iv. 618; visitors (some named), iii. 548, 575, 576, 577; iv. 442; ~ to E, iii. 76, 258.

— — — at sea, ii. 169 (i. 107); in Venice, ii. 442.

— — — named, outside France [apart from diplomatists and French protestants, for whom *see* Diplomatists *and* French protestants. The present list is probably very incomplete]: in England: *see* Auzout, A.; Bordes d'Assigny, H. de; Flamarens, marquis de; Hubin, L.; Isaac, —; Kéroualle, Louise de, duchess of Portsmouth; la Varenne, Mlle; Mazarin, Hortense Mancini, Duchesse; Pontac, F.-A. de; Pontack, —; Richett, —; Sessac, marquis de; Vendôme, P. de; Yvelin, Dr. P.; *see further* iii. 575 & nn. 2–7; at Rome: *see* Bouillon, duke and duchess of; Petit, —; Poussin, N.

— — English persons in France: unnamed: at Bourges, 1644, ii. 154 (i. 99); France full of royalists, 1650, iii. 17.

— — — named [apart from diplomatists, royalties, and persons named as then present in E's account of his travels and residence in France]: George Villiers, first duke of Buckingham, in, ii. 522, n. 1; Philip Stanhope, second earl of Chesterfield, 1655, iii. 153 & n. 5; A. Cowley, iii. 355, n. 4; C. Davinson: going to, 1660, iii. 257; George Evelyn of Wotton (E's nephew): going to, 1663, iii. 354; John Evelyn, jnr., 1675–6, iv. 76, 91; Mrs. Margaret Godolphin, 1675–6, iv. 79–80, 88; George Goring, Lord Goring, 1642, ii. 79 (i. 52); Henry Hildyard, jnr., and Charles Hildyard, iii. 61; Lord Thomas Howard, 1664–7, iii. 373, 482; Sir George Lane, Viscount Lanesborough, iii. 285; Sir B. Maddox (?), iii. 222 & n. 3; Dr. J. Needham, iii. 175 & n. 1; William and Margaret Cavendish, duke and duchess of Newcastle, iii. 480 & n. 8; Henry Howard, sixth duke of Norfolk: comes from, 1663, iii. 352; Henry Howard, seventh duke of Norfolk, 1664–7, iii. 373, 482; Charles Mordaunt, earl of Peterborough, as Viscount Mordaunt, 1676, iv. 84; W. Prettyman, 1648–9, ii. 543 & n. 3, 551; Lady Scrope, iii. 275, n. 6; Lady Isabella Thynne, ii. 549, n. 9 *ad fin.*; Sir S. Tuke, 1658, &c., iii. 223 & n. 5, 274 & n. 4, 373, 488 & n. 5; Lady Tuke, iii. 373; Dr. F. Turner, nonjuring bishop of Ely: reported to have fled to, 1691, v. 42, n. 4.

Francesco I, grand-duke of Tuscany: and Leghorn, ii. 183, n. 3; geneal., ii. 43, n. 5 *ad fin.*

Franchesse (Franchede), ii. 154 & n. 9 (i. 99).

Francini, A. and T., constructors of water-works, ii. 111, n. 2.

Francino (Franco), G.B., gunsmith, ii. 489 & n. 4.

Franciosino, Il: *see* Cordier, N.

Francis I, king of France: victory of, at Marignano, ii. 490, n. 10; captivity of, in Spain, ii. 112 & n. 2 (i. 72); iii. 2; called a virtuoso, ii. 111 & n. 1 (i. 71), 497; buildings: Chambord, ii. 139 (i. 91); Fontainebleau, ii. 117 *bis* & n. 3 (i. 76 *bis*), 118, n. 3, 119, n. 10; Madrid, Château de, ii. 112 (i. 72); iii. 2; St.-Germain-en-Laye, ii. 111 (i. 71).
opens Laura's tomb, ii. 162, n. 1; attachment of, to Leonardo, ii. 497 & n. 1; wants to take Leonardo's Last Supper to France, *ib.*; praises Orleans, ii. 139 (i. 91); gift to, ii. 119, n. 2; portrait of, ii. 550 & n. 4; tomb of, ii. 86 (i. 58).

Francis II, king of France: tomb of, ii. 86 (i. 58).
Francis, St., of Assisi: tree growing from staff of, ii. 205 & n. 8; mosaic portrait of, ii. 439 & n. 2.
Francis, St., of Paola: convent founded by, and tomb of, ii. 147 & nn. 5, 6 (i. 95); miracles of: paintings of, *ib.*; ii. 373.
Francis, St., Xavier.: relic of, ii. 230; sermon on, iii. 23.
Francis, Michael, English consul at Venice, ii. 469, n. 6.
Francisco, Signor, harpsichord player: performs, iv. 49 & n. 5, 270 & n. 3(?).
Franco, J. B.: *see* Francino, G. B.
Frank (Franck), Mark, D.D.: as chaplain to Dr. Sheldon, iii. 362 & n. 4.
Frankfort: English resident at: *see* Curtius, Sir W. (iii. 36 & n. 1).
Frascati, ii. 316, n. 3, 317; Villa Aldobrandini, ii. 392–3 & nn.; iv. 177 & n. 1; Villa Mondragone, ii. 393 & nn. 5, 6.
Frasier, —, iv. 454, n. 3.
Frasier, Dr. —: *see* Fraizer, Sir A.
Frassinodo, ii. 508, n. 5.
Frate, Cecchino del: paintings by, ii. 414 & n. 6.
Frazier, —: books bought by, &c., iv. 330 & n. 1.
Frederick I Barbarossa, Emperor: destroys Milan, &c., ii. 496, n. 2; submission of, to Alexander III: site of, ii. 439 & n. 3; ~ painting of, ii. 297 & nn. 4, 5; in legend, ii. 50, n. 3.
Frederick III, Emperor: at Venice, ii. 445, n. 8.
Frederick III, king of Denmark: United Provinces assist, 1658, iii. 236 & n. 5; natural son of, iii. 537, n. 5; *see also* iii. 270.
Frederick IV, king of Denmark, v. 384, n. 2; hostility of, towards Sweden, 1700, v. 384 & n. 2, 386 & n. 1; ~ attempt to terminate, v. 417 & n. 1; alluded to (the Northern princes), v. 446.
Frederick III, elector of Brandenburg, later king in Prussia as Frederick I, v. 147, n. 3; present from, to Queen Mary II, v. 147 & n. 3; court of: singer going to, v. 531.
Frederick V, Elector Palatine and king of Bohemia ('the Winter King'): geneal., ii. 33, n. 8, 567, n. 1.
Frederick, prince of Wales, son of George II: occupies Leicester House, iii. 626, n. 9.
Frederick, Sir John, lord mayor of London 1661–2, iii. 301, n. 4; as lord mayor, iii. 321 & n. 7, 330 & n. 4; ~ show of, iii. 301 & n. 4.
Frederick Augustus, elector of Saxony: *see* Augustus the Strong.
Frederick Henry, prince of Orange, ii. 37, n. 3; at siege of Huis te Gennep, ii. 36–8 & nn. (i. 28–9); pass from, ii. 59 (i. 40), 62 (i. 42); geneal., ii. 382, n. 3; natural son of, iii. 565, n. 6; as error for Maurice of Orange, iv. 118; *add.*; secretary of: *see* Huygens, Constantijn, sen.
Frederick Magnus, prince of Salm, Rhinegrave, ii. 61 & n. 4 (i. 42).
Frederick William, elector of Brandenburg (the Great Elector), iv. 275, n. 4; sends amber to Royal Society, iv. 275 & n. 4; geneal., ii. 57, n. 5.
Freeman, Sir Ralph, joint master of the Mint: social, iii. 345 & n. 2; mentioned, iii. 335, n. 2.
Freeman, Samuel, D.D.; dean of Peterborough 1691, v. 205, n. 2; sermons by, v. 205, 226, 383–4 & n.(?).
Freeman, William: acquires Baynards estate, ii. 539, n. 4.
Freising: Bishop of, 1684–94: *see* Joseph Clemens, archbishop-elector of Cologne.
Fréjus (called Périgueux, in error): notice, ii. 167 & nn. 3, 4 (i. 105).
French, Elizabeth: *see* Tillotson, Mrs. E.
French, Peter, D.D.: sermon by, iii. 104 & n. 8.
French, Mrs. Robina: *see* Wilkins, Mrs. R.
French language: improvement of: foundation for, ii. 150 (i. 97); influence of, on Simplon dialect, &c., ii. 511 & n. 2; purity of, as spoken at: Blois, ii. 142 (i. 92); ~ Bourges, ii. 153 (i. 99); ~ Orleans, ii. 138 (i. 90); in use at Geneva, ii. 524.
scholars, &c.: Arlington, iv. 118; — Clench, iv. 618; E's children,

French language (*cont.*)
iii. 206–7 & n.; iv. 421; v. 138; at school display, v. 79.
discourse in, before Charles II, iii. 336; spoken by Prince George of Denmark, iv. 332.
French protestants [*see also* Geneva]:
— before the persecution of 1680–1720:
— — in France: services: conduct of, &c., ii. 115 & nn. 2–4 (i. 74–5), 527 & n. 5; views of, on episcopal government, ii. 521; deputy-general of, iv. 522–3 & n.; representative of, in Parlement of Paris, v. 196 & n. 6; churches: *see* Charenton; Rouen; cemeteries, ii. 565 & n. 5; iii. 48, n. 10 *ad fin.*; iconoclasm of, in civil wars, ii. 126 (i. 80), 137, n. 1, 138 & n. 7 (i. 91), 147 (i. 95), 160 (i. 102).
— — in England: address from, to Charles II, 1660, iii. 248 & n. 3; services, iv. 168; ~ catechizing during, iii. 160, 181, 202–3; churches: *see* London: topography: Somerset House *and* Threadneedle Street; Anglican conformist church in the Savoy, iii. 545 & n. 3; ~ translation of liturgy used at, iii. 545 & n. 4; ~ services at, iii. 181 & n. 4 (error), 202–3 (error), 545, 556, 570(?); iv. 531; v. 269.
— the persecution of 1680–1720 and its effects:
— — in France: the first period, 1680–8 [for Louis XIV's share in the persecution of the Waldenses, 1686–9, *see* Louis XIV: religion]: influence of, on E, i. *29–30*; major notices, June, Nov., 1685, iv. 447–8 & nn., 484–7 & nn.; ~ March, 1688, iv. 574–5 & n.; Revocation of the Edict of Nantes, i. *32*; iv. 447, n. 3, 484 & n. 4; general notices or allusions to, iv. 490, 493, 498 & n. 4, 514–15, 518, 525, 533, 552, 560, 581; mentioned in sermons, iv. 504, 531, 548; account of, by J. Claude, burnt in London, iv. 510–11 & n., 515; *particular features*: churches: closed, iv. 447–8 & n.; ~ demolished, iv. 484; converts to Roman Catholicism: treatment of relapsed, iv. 447, n. 3,
French protestants (*cont.*)
485, 574–5; dragonnades, iv. 213, n. 3, 447, n. 3, 485, 575; estates: confiscated, iv. 485; v. 469; ministers: sent to galleys, iv. 485; St. Ruth as persecutor, v. 66.
— — — renewed persecution, 1699, &c.: notices, v. 319, 363, 431; effect of, on treatment of Roman Catholics in England, v. 403; fast for, in England, v. 319; mentioned in sermon, v. 380.
— — — the churches of the Desert: formed, iv. 447, n. 3, 575; the Cevennes protestants, &c., iv. 636–7; rising in Cevennes, 1703–4, v. 545 & n. 4, 563 & n. 1.
— — the dispersion: in 1685, &c., iv. 447, n. 3, 448, 484–6 & nn., 487 & n. 2; settlement in Germany, 1699, v. 317 & n. 2; expulsion from Orange, 1703, v. 544–5 & n., 559; collections in England for fugitives abroad: 1699, v. 319–20 & n., 321 & n. 2; ~ 1704, v. 559 & n. 3.
— — the refugees in England: general statements, 1685–8, iv. 448, 485–6 & nn., 574; arrested on English ships, iv. 490 & n. 8; James II protects, &c., iv. 515 & n. 2; R. Boyle relieves, v. 82; individual fugitives: 1680–3, iv. 213 & n. 3, 257–8 & n., 318–19 & n.; ~ 1686, iv. 517–18 & n., 522–3 & n.; noblemen as, iv. 531, 581; churches founded by, iv. 447, n. 3 *ad fin.*
— — — collections for relief of, iv. 447, n. 3 *ad fin.*; in 1686, iv. 485, n. 3, 504–11 & nn., *passim*, 515 & n. 2; in 1688, iv. 572 & n. 2, 574, 581; mentioned in sermon, v. 36.
— — — at Greenwich: number of, 1687, iv. 548; social, iv. 640; school: (Sir) John Evelyn at, iv. 653 & n. 2; ~ ceremony at (?), v. 79 & n. 3; church: general, iv. 548, n. 1; uses Anglican liturgy, iv. 548, 565, 598; minister of (J. Severin), v. 23 & n. 5; services, 1687–90 [for details *see* Greenwich], iv. 548, 552, 557, 565, 568, 573, 592, 597 *bis*, 598 *bis*, 607, 615, 650; v. 23–4, 36.

French protestants (*cont.*)
— individuals in England:
— — residents and new-comers before 1680 [some of these may never have been Calvinists]: *see* Basire, I.; Bréval, F. Durant de; Brevint, D.; Cisner, C.; Citolin, M.; Durel, J.; Espagne, J. d'; Hérault, L.; Houblon, Sir James (iv. 162, n. 6); Le Franc, J.; Stouppe, J.-B.
— — refugees from Louis XIV's persecution: *see* Allix, P.; Chardin, Sir J.; Foubert, S.; Gouvernet, Marquise de; Justel, H.; la Caillemotte, P. de Massue, sieur de; la Mothe, C.-G. de; l'Angle, S. Baux, sieur de; le Coq, F.; Maillard, M.; Ruvigny, H. de Massue, marquis de; &c.; Schomberg, F. H., duke of Schomberg; &c.; Severin, J.
Fresne, Nicolas Hennequin, baron d'Ecquevilly, sieur de: art-collection of, ii. 114 & n. 7 (i. 74).
Fresno, Don Pedro de Jouar y Velasco, marqués de, Spanish ambassador in England 1672–4: complaint of, iii. 613 & n. 3; *add.*
Fretcheville, Lady: in Blenheim procession, v. 578, n. 1.
Frey, Hans, lute-maker, ii. 426 & n. 6.
Friars *or* Friar, —: art-collection of, ii. 548 & n. 3.
Frias, Don Bernardino Fernandez de Velasco y Tovar, duke of, constable of Castile, &c., governor of Milan, ii. 494 & n. 8.
Friderica Amalia, duchess of Gottorp, wife of Duke Christian Albert: dies, v. 582 & n. 1.
Friend, Sir John, v. 235, n. 1; tried and executed, v. 235 *bis* & nn. 1, 3; absolution of, v. 235, n. 4, 236 & n. 1; i. 8 & n. 2.
Frier, —: school-teacher at Wotton, ii. 6.
Frobenius: portrait of, iii. 263, n. 2.
Fromanteel, Ahasuerus, iii. 261, n. 1; clocks made by, iii. 260–1, 285 & n. 4.
Frowde, C.: clerk of Council of Trade and Foreign Plantations, iii. 628 & n. 4.
Fruit-trees and Fruits [*see also* Vineyards and Viticulture; for walnuts *see* Trees and Timber]:
— general: collations, &c., of fruit, iii. 110, 123; fruit-trees: in Italy, supporting vines, ii. 324–5, 481 & n. 1, 491; ~ sent to Wotton, v. 119, 530; orchard at Swallowfield, iv. 481; wall-fruit, iii. 415; ~ nailing of, iv. 576; ~ *see also* citron *below*; crops and effects of weather on: 1658, iii. 220; 1692, v. 104, 117; 1693, v. 151, 157; 1694, v. 186, 188; 1698, v. 287, 288 & n. 2; 1700, v. 408, 415, 419.
— the several kinds:
— — apple: *see* cider fruit *below.*
— — apricot, ii. 176; fruit, ii. 353.
— — cherry, ii. 523; iii. 221; fruit, ii. 353.
— — cider fruit (apples and pears), ii. 122 (i. 78); iii. 118; iv. 481; Royal Society and: inquiries concerning, iii. 340, n. 1; ~ committee for, iii. 351 & n. 4.
— — citron (E equates citron and lemon: ii. 171 & i. 108; see *O.E.D.*), ii. 169 (i. 106), 175 (i. 111), 240, 322, 325, 488, 507; as wall-trees, ii. 176 (i. 111), 285; 'citroniere', &c., ii. 109 & n. 1 (i. 70); iii. 18 & n. 5; flowers: scent of, ii. 171.
— — date-palms: in Liguria, ii. 169 (i. 106).
— — fig, ii. 325, 452, 488.
— — lemon (*see also* citron *above*), ii. 338, 393; flowers: scent of, i. 108.
— — melon: fruit: at Tours, ii. 148 (i. 96); at Naples, ii. 353; at Leicester, iii. 123; in comparison, iii. 514.
— — olive, ii. 163 (i. 103), 179 (i. 113), 252, 317, 323, 325, 393, 410, 461, 488, 491 & n. 1; at Oxford, iii. 110.
— — oranges and orangeries: in England: Althorp, iv. 70; Beddington, i. 9 & n. 2; iii. 221; v. 427 & n. 1; Chelsea, Lady Bristol, iv. 162; Eltham, iii. 376; Euston, iv. 117; Ham House, iv. 144; Kew, Sir H. Capel (later Baron Capell), iv. 347, 576; Marden, iv. 121; Sayes Court, iv. 182, 365; Sheen, Sir W. Temple, iv. 576;

Fruit-trees and Fruits (*cont.*)
Swallowfield, iv. 481; China oranges, iv. 182.
— — — in France: Marseilles, ii. 163; Paris, ii. 102, 106 (i. 69); ~ trees on sale in, ii. 100 (i. 65); *see also* citron *above* (citroniere, &c.).
— — — in Italy, ii. 169 (i. 106), 175 (i. 111); i. 112; ii. 287, 322, 325, 338, 393, 452, 488, 507; 'cedrario', ii. 484 & n. 1; flowers: scent of, ii. 171 (i. 108); tree with rose grafted on it, ii. 187 & n. 6 (i. 118).
— — pear: *see* cider fruit *above*.
— — pine-apple: fruit: queen-pine, iii. 293 & n. 2; king-pine, iii. 513–14 & n.
— — pomegranate, ii. 106 (i. 69), 163 (i. 103), 175 (i. 111), 322, 325 338; at Beddington, iii. 221.
— — quince: in comparison, iii. 514.
— — strawberry, iii. 96.
Fryer, Leonard, sergeant-painter, ii. 548, n. 3.
Fuel: in London: scarcity of, 1667, 1683–4, iii. 486 & n. 1, 487 *bis*, 488; iv. 363; ~ wharfs for, in Great Fire, iii. 456 & n. 7; in Paris, i. 63; ii. 105 (i. 68 & n. 1).
charcoal: preparation of, ii. 514.
coal or sea-coal: coal-farm, iv. 259 & n. 2; coking: project for, iii. 180–1 & n.; mines (coal-pits), iv. 502; smoke of, in London, iv. 363, 380; ~ book against: *see* Evelyn: books: *Fumifugium*; ~ projected act of parliament against, iii. 297, 310; transport of, iv. 115 & n. 8.
houllies (hotshots, &c.): trial of, iii. 487 & n. 6.
Fuente, Don Gaspar de Teves y Guzman, marques de la: pass for E issued by, ii. 477–8 & nn., 508.
Fuga, F., architect: building by, ii. 242, n. 6.
Fulgosus, Raphael: tomb of, ii. 455 & n. 2.
Fulham, Mrs. Catherine, born Evelyn, wife of Dr. George Fulham: geneal., v. 54, n. 2, 282 & n. 2, 336, 358, n. 7; legacy to, v. 359 & n. 8.
Fulham (Fullham), George, D.D., v. 282, n. 2; opposes original settlement of Wotton estate on E, v. 292, 314, n. 1, 336–9; sermons by, at Wotton, v. 282–7 *passim*.
Fuller, Dr. — (Thomas Fuller?): sermon by, iii. 266 & n. 4.
Fuller, Dr. — (Samuel Fuller or Fulwar?): sermon by, iv. 383 & n. 3.
Fuller, Isaac: paintings by, iii. 386 *bis* & nn. 1, 4.
Fuller *or* Fulwar, Samuel, D.D.; dean of Lincoln 1695: sermon by (?), iv. 383 & n. 3.
Fuller, Thomas, D.D., author of the *Worthies*: sermon by (?), iii. 266 & n. 4.
Fuller, William: announces fictitious plot, v. 78 & n. 1.
Fuller, William, D.C.L.; bishop of Lincoln 1667, iv. 33, n. 3; restores tomb of Remigius, iii. 131, n. 7 *ad fin.*; appointed to preach, iii. 605, n. 2; social, iv. 33.
Funen, island, Denmark: Charles X's winter march to, iii. 211, n. 2.
Fundi: *see* Fondi.
Fuorigrotta, ii. 338–9 & n.
Furnes: taken by French, 1693, v. 126 & n. 2.
Furniture [select. *See also* Tapestry]:
beds: in Italy and England, ii. 236; cupboard-beds, ii. 511; damask, ii. 533 & n. 2; embroidered, iii. 323 & n. 5; iv. 537; inlaid with gems, &c., ii. 174 (i. 110), 236, 471; iron, ii. 471; silver, ii. 174 (i. 110); tester of a bed, iv. 21.
bedding: feather quilts, &c., ii. 511; mattress stuffed with leaves, ii. 507 & n. 6.
billiard-tables, iv. 116 & n. 6, 190 & n. 4.
braseras, iv. 343 & n. 3.
cabinets: in comparison, ii. 393; in Uffizi collection, ii. 189–91 & nn. (i. 119), 413–14; amber, v. 147; Chinese, v. 147; East Indian: on sale, ii. 100, 124 (i. 79); Indian, iii. 324 & n. 2; iv. 92; v. 147; inlaid with gems, i. 110; Japan, iv. 190, 343; *pietra commessa*, ii. 286; ~ E's, ii. 191 & n. 13 (i. 119); silver, i. 110; silver filigree, v. 147.
candlesticks: amber, ii. 413; bronze, at Padua, ii. 454–5 & n.

Furniture (*cont.*)
carpets: Persian, iii. 349; iv. 262.
chairs: adjustable, ii. 236 & n. 6, 286; arm-chairs: as armed chairs, iii. 362, 633; ~ as chairs of (or with) arms, ii. 378 & n. 1; iv. 534–5; chair that entraps sitter, ii. 254 & n. 3, 285, critical note; wheel-chairs (for invalids), iii. 310, 502.
chandeliers (branches, &c.): church, ii. 47 (i. 33); silver, iv. 343; at Haarlem, ii. 50 & n. 4 (i. 35); Couronne du Duc de Berry, ii. 153 & n. 13 (i. 99).
cradle, &c., iii. 209.
hangings, iii. 578; v. 147; of sweet flag, iv. 482; *see also* Textiles.
japanning: process, iii. 324, n. 2.
joint-stool, iv. 60 & n. 1.
lac, iii. 324, n. 2.
lacquer chests, iii. 324 & n. 2.
locks for doors: iron, iii. 111–12 & n.
looking-glasses, iii. 11, 21, 323–4 & n.; iv. 8(?); with amber frame, v. 147; manufacture of, iv. 98–9.
mattresses: as floor-covering, ii. 174.
sconces, ii. 113 (i. 73); iv. 343.
screens: Chinese or Indian, v. 147; Japan, iv. 288 & n. 7, 343(?).
stands: silver (?), iv. 74.
stoves: in Germany, iii. 162; in Simplon hospice, ii. 511; in Sweden, iv. 221.
tables: silver, ii. 174 (i. 110); iv. 74(?).
toilet-sets: gold, iii. 323–4; iv. 9.
trunks (chests), iii. 324 & n. 2.
furnishing of particular rooms, &c.: Lady Arlington: dressing-room, iv. 8; C. Boone, iv. 180, 288; Cardinal Doughi: travels with his own furniture, ii. 207; Sir James Houblon, iv. 162–3; Queen Mary II, v. 147; duchess of Portsmouth, iv. 74, 343.
Fürstenberg (Firstenberge), W. E. von, bishop of Strassburg and cardinal: candidate for archbishopric-electorate of Cologne, iv. 596, n. 3, 598.
Fusàro, Lago del (Acherutia, &c.), ii. 347 & n. 5.
Fusconi, G. B., *Argiope*: performer in, ii. 450, n. 3.
Gabbard: battle off the, iii. 84 & n. 5.
Gadarenes *or* Gadarites: in sermons, iv. 82, 525; v. 159.
Gadbury, John: horoscope by, iv. 22, n. 2.
Gaddi family, Florence: chapel of, ii. 199–200 & nn.
Gaddi, Giovanni, ii. 415, n. 7.
Gaddi, Jacopo: art-collection of, ii. 415 & nn. 5–8.
Gaeta (Cajeta), ii. 323 & nn. 2, 3; inscription at, ii. 278, n. 2.
Gaetani (Cajetan, Caetani), Enrico, cardinal: tomb of, ii. 246 & n. 5.
Gaetano, Scipione Pulzone, called, ii. 233, n. 3; paintings by, ii. 233, 274 & n. 8.
Gage, Col. Henry: commissioned to raise a regiment, 1688, iv. 599, n. 6.
Gage, Sir Henry: regiment of, in Spanish Netherlands, ii. 65 & n. 4 (i. 44).
Gaillon: Château, ii. 121 & n. 3 (i. 78).
Galatians: in sermons, iv. 516; v. 348.
Galba, Roman emperor: villa of, near Terracina, ii. 321, n. 5, 322 & n. 2.
Gale, Thomas, D.D.; high master of St. Paul's school; dean of York 1697, iv. 300 & n. 1; v. 280, n. 4; shows E MS. Bible, v. 206 & n. 3; extracts by, from Platonist MSS., v. 220–1 & n.; E gives copy of *Numismata* to, v. 283, n. 3; as secretary of Royal Society, iv. 263, n. 3; social, iv. 300; v. 124, 127, 221, 280.
Galeazzo II Visconti: builds castle at Milan, ii. 501 & n. 10.
Galileo: observations by: of the moon, ii. 64, n. 2 *ad fin.*; ~ of Saturn, iii. 286, n. 3; tomb of, ii. 196 & n. 3.
Gallicano, Pompeo Colonna, prince of: opera by, &c., ii. 388–9 & n.
Galloper sand: *Royal Prince* grounded on, iii. 439, n. 4.
Galloway (Scotland): second Earl of, 1649–71: *see* Stewart, Sir James.
Galloway (Scotland): diocese: bishops: *see* Sydserff, T. (1635–8); Hamilton, James (1661–74).
Galway (Galloway), in Ireland: French troops enter, 1690, v. 33 & n. 3; taken by English, 1691, v. 67 & n. 4, 68.

Galway: Viscount, 1692–7, and Earl of, 1697–1720: *see* Ruvigny, Henri de Massue, second marquis de.
Gambia river, v. 174, n. 5.
Gambo, in Guinea: taken by French, 1694, v. 174 & n. 5.
Gaming [dice or cards], iii. 590; at court, iv. 403, 413; ~ on Twelfth Night, &c., iii. 308 & n. 4, 504 & n. 1; loss at, iv. 96; as means of recruiting galley-slaves, ii. 184 & n. 1 (i. 116); passage (game at dice), iii. 308 & n. 4; alluded to (?), i. 51 (*see* ii. 77, n. 4).
habitual or noted gamblers: Lord Cornwallis, iv. 246 & n. 1; Sir J. Germain, v. 393–4; St. Albans, iv. 338; Sunderland, iv. 245 & n. 4.
See also Cards and Card-playing.
Ganter, river, ii. 508, n. 5 *ad fin.*, 513, n. 3.
Gaoler, the Converted (Acts, ch. xvi): in sermon, iii. 561.
Garda: Lake of, ii. 488–9 & nn.
Gardening: progress of, in England, ii. 4–5; at Norwich, iii. 595 & n. 1; Charles II discusses, iii. 297; books on: *see* Evelyn: books.
features of gardens, words, &c.: conservatory or greenhouse (E apparently equates the two words: ii. 109, n. 2; iv. 462, n. 5), iv. 117 (both words used, for separate buildings), 347; ~ heating for, iv. 462 & n. 5; v. 80 & n. 3; grottoes: *see* Grottoes; hortulan (word), i. 70 & n. 1; v. 151; ice-house, ii. 130 (i. 83); mazes (labyrinths), ii. 106 (i. 69), 484; nursery garden (Brompton Park), v. 176 & n. 3, 532; plashing, iv. 347; pole work: cupola of, *ib.*; potagere, iii. 538 & n. 2; shrubs: on sale in Paris, ii. 100 (i. 65); topiary work, ii. 127 (i. 81), 187 (i. 118); *see also* Trees: cypress; watering: fountain for, iii. 444.
gardeners, professional, ii. 53, 130–1 (i. 83), 132 (i. 85–6), 408, 466; iii. 386 & n. 7; iv. 200 & n. 4, 350, 521 & n. 3; v. 290 & n. 6, 478, 606 & n. 4; florist, i. 86 & n. 1; fontaniers, ii. 72, 109 (i. 70), 110.
Gardens:
— botanical:
— — Chelsea: Society of Apothecaries, iii. 217, n. 1; iv. 462 & nn. 3–5; Leyden, ii. 52–3 & n. (i. 36–7); Oxford: Physick Garden, iii. 109–10 & n., 386 & nn. 5–7; ~ lecture in, iv. 68; Padua, ii. 466 & nn. 4, 6, 480, n. 5; Paris: Jardin Royale, ii. 102 & n. 2 (i. 66–7); ~ lecture at, ii. 565 & n. 3; Pisa, ii. 181–2 & n. (i. 114), 408 & nn. 6, 7; Westminster: medical garden, iii. 217 & n. 1.
— pleasure: *see* Pleasure.
— royal or private:
— — (i) subjects of important notices: Albury: Henry Howard later sixth duke of Norfolk, &c.: E plans alterations, &c., iii. 154–5, 496 & n. 2, 561–2 & n.; iv. 111, 558; Althorp, iv. 70, 594; Beddington: orange-trees at, &c., i. 9 & n. 2 (*see also* ii. 11); iii. 221; v. 427 & n. 1; Blois: Château, ii. 141 & nn. 5–9 (i. 92); Brenta: villas on banks of, ii. 452; Brompton Park, nursery garden, v. 176 & n. 3, 532; Brussels: Cour (the Park), ii. 71–2 & nn. (i. 46–7); Burleigh House: plan for, iv. 350–1; Caen: unknown cleric, ii. 127 (i. 81); Cassiobury Park, iv. 200; Castle Ashby, iv. 593–4 & n.; Chatham: Commissioner Peter Pett, iii. 359; Chelsea: Lady Bristol, iv. 162; Cliveden Park, iv. 177; Deepdene: Charles Howard, iii. 154 & n. 5, 561; Essonne: L. Hesselin, ii. 120–1 & n. (i. 77–8); Euston, iii. 591; iv. 117; Florence: Pitti palace (Boboli), ii. 187 & nn. 3–6 (i. 117–18); Fontainebleau, ii. 118–19 & nn. (i. 76–7); Frascati: Villa Aldobrandini, ii. 392–3 & nn.; Villa Mondragone, ii. 393 & nn. 5, 6; Fulham Palace: Bishop H. Compton, iv. 258 & n. 3; Geneva, environs, ii. 523, 528; Genoa: Dinegro, ii. 173–4 & n. (i. 109–10); Palazzo Doria a Fássolo, ii. 174–5 & nn. (i. 110–11); Palazzo Spinola, ii. 176 (i. 111); Hackney: Lady Brooke, iii. 96 & n. 1, 169; — Tombs, iii. 96

Gardens (*cont.*)
& n. 2; The Hague: Binnenhof, ii. 41 & n. 4 (i. 30); Ham House, iv. 143–4; Hampton Court, iii. 322, n. 5, 324–5 & nn.; iv. 645 & n. 2; Isola Bella, ii. 506–7 & n.; Kensington Palace, v. 8 & n. 2, 237, 606 & nn. 3, 4; Kew: Sir Henry Capel, later Baron Capell, iv. 144 & n. 1, 347, 576; Lee, Kent: Lee Place (C. Boone), iv. 288, 337 & n. 4; London: Berkeley House, iii. 625; ~ partially built over, iv. 381–2 & n.; Clarendon House: project for, &c., iii. 380, 502; ~ mentioned, &c., iv. 339, 382; St. James's Park: royal garden in, iii. 573 & n. 3; ~ occupied by A. Verrio, iv. 522 & n. 1; Maison Rouge, ii. 120 (i. 77); Maisons: Château, ii. 563 & n. 3; iii. 18; Marden: Sir R. Clayton, iv. 121; v. 425–6; Norwich: flower-gardens, iii. 595 & n. 1; Oatlands: Sir E. Herbert, L.C.J., iv. 566; Paris: Hôtel de Liancourt, ii. 112–13 (i. 72–3); Louvre, &c., ii. 104–7 & nn., *passim* (i. 68–9); Luxembourg, ii. 128–31 & nn. (i. 81–4); P. Morin, ii. 132–3 & n. (i. 85–7; *add.*); iii. 33; Palais-Royal, ii. 134 (i. 87), 567; iii. 44 & n. 1; Perruchot, ii. 114 (i. 74); Pratolino, ii. 418–19 & nn.; Rome: Quirinal, ii. 237–8 & n., 287; Vatican, ii. 305 & nn. 5, 6; Villas: Aldobrandini, ii. 284, 285; Borghese, ii. 251–2 & nn., 390 & nn. 1–3; Giustiniani, ii. 382–3 & nn.; Ludovisi, ii. 234–5 & nn.; Mattei, ii. 362 & n. 1; Medici, ii. 230–2 & nn., 287; Montalto, ii. 240; Rueil: Richelieu, ii. 108–10 & nn. (i. 70–1); St.-Cloud, ii. 107–8 & n. (i. 69–70); St.-Germain-en-Laye, ii. 110–12 & nn. (i. 71–2); Sayes Court: *see* Sayes Court; Sheen: Sir William Temple, iv. 143 & nn. 1, 2, 576; Swallowfield, Berks.: Henry Hyde, earl of Clarendon, iv. 481–2 & nn.; Theobalds Palace, ii. 81 & n. 2 (i. 55); Tivoli: Villa d'Este, ii. 394–6 & nn.; Verona: Giusti, ii. 487 & n. 2; Vicenza: Valmarana, ii. 483–4 & nn.; Weybridge: Ham Court (D. Sheldon), iv. 142 & nn. 1, 3; Wilton House, iii. 114 & n. 4; Wimbledon Park: E consulted for, &c., iii. 315–16 & n.; iv. 130–1; Windsor: Castle, i. 72; iv. 317; A. Verrio, iv. 176 & n. 4, 207–8; Wotton: *see* Wotton.

— — (ii) subjects of minor notices: gardens at: Audley End, iii. 141; Bourges, ii. 154 (i. 99); Brington, iv. 593; Camberwell, iii. 197 & n. 2; Caprarola, ii. 407; Chaillot, ii. 91 (i. 61); iii. 27; Chevareux, near Tours, ii. 148 (i. 96); Chiswick, iv. 294 & n. 4; Clapham, v. 428; Enfield, iv. 91 & n. 4; Enfield Chase, iv. 92 & n. 1; Gaillon, ii. 121 (i. 78); Godstone, iii. 219; Greenwich, v. 348; The Hague, i. 27; Hammersmith, iv. 523; Hampstead (Belsize House), iv. 92 & n. 2; Hatfield House, ii. 80 & n. 4 (i. 54); Hondsholredijk, ii. 56 (i. 39); Huntercombe, iv. 177 & n. 2; Isleworth (G. Barrell), ii. 540; Kirby Hall, iii. 134; Lambeth Palace, v. 80, 213; Leyton, iii. 538 & nn. 1, 2; Liancourt, Oise, i. 74; London: various, iii. 162 & n. 1, 192, 200, 231 & n. 6, 398, 573 & n. 4, 578; iv. 184 & 344–5, 190; Lyons, ii. 158 (i. 101); Moulins, ii. 154–5 (i. 99); Murano, ii. 468; New Hall, Essex, iii. 180; Norwich, iii. 594, 595; Padua, ii. 466–7 & n.; Paris, ii. 101 (i. 66), 102 (i. 67); Parson's Green (Lord Mordaunt), iii. 271, n. 6; Peckham, iv. 93 & n. 2, 258; Penshurst Place, iii. 72; Plessis-lez-Tours, ii. 147 (i. 95); Richelieu, ii. 151 (i. 98); Roehampton House, iv. 105; Rome: various, ii. 373, 374, 379 & n. 4; Ryswick, ii. 41 & nn. 3, 4 (i. 30); Salisbury, iii. 113; Sheen, iv. 143 & nn. 1, 3, 575; Syon House, Isleworth, iii. 415; Tours, ii. 145 *bis* (i. 94 *bis*); Turnham Green, v. 594 & n. 4; Venice, ii. 461; Warwick Castle, iii. 119–20 & n.; York, iii. 129 & n. 7.

Gardiner, Mrs. Anne, wife of Dr. J. Gardiner, bishop of Lincoln: commits suicide, v. 528 & n. 7.
Gardiner, James, D.D.; bishop of Lincoln 1695: social, v. 224 & n. 5; geneal., v. 528 & n. 7.
Gardiner, Mary: *see* Wood, Mary, Lady Wood.
Gardiner, Sir Thomas: geneal., iii. 22, n. 5.
Gardone, Val Trómpia: gunsmiths at, ii. 489, nn. 3, 4.
Garigliano, river and village, ii. 323 & n. 6.
Garmers (Garmus), Vincent, ambassador, &c., from Hamburg to England, iii. 288 & n. 9, 585, n. 3; gives feast, iii. 288; social iii. 585(?), 621; iv. 10 & n. 1(?).
Garndsey, Lord, *rectè* Gernsey *or* Guernsey: *see* Finch, Heneage, later earl of Aylesford.
Garo, Monte, ii. 323 & n. 6.
Garrard, Jane: *see* Spencer, Jane, Lady Spencer.
Garrard (Gerrard), Jane, Lady Garrard, born Lowe, wife of Sir John, first bt., and previously of Sir M. Lambarde, ii. 542, n. 2; geneal., iii. 90, n. 4, 176, n. 2, 222, n. 3, 252, n. 3; further notices, all relating to her or all to the younger Lady Garrard: godmother of: Mary Evelyn, later Lady Wyche, ii. 544; ~ John Evelyn, jnr., iii. 147; collection of porcelain of, iii. 60 & n. 6; at Mulberry Garden, iii. 96–7; social, ii. 542, 554; iii. 74, 86, 89, 176, 214, 218, 252.
Garrard, Jane, Lady Garrard, born Lambarde, wife of Sir John, second bt., ii. 542, n. 2; geneal., iii. 176, n. 2, 252, n. 3; *for further possible notices see preceding entry*.
Garrard, Sir John, first bt.: geneal., ii. 542, n. 2.
Garrard, Sir John, second bt.: geneal., ii. 542, n. 2; iii. 252, n. 3.
Garret, —: dines with E, iii. 450.
Garro, E's valet at Tours: claims money from E, ii. 149 (i. 96).
Garse, Monsieur: incognito of Gustavus Adolphus, ii. 521 & n. 4.
Garsington, Oxon.: Dr. Ralph Bathurst and, v. 571, n. 2.
Garter: Order of the:
ceremonies: Grand Feasts: 1667, iii. 479–80 & nn.; ~ 1671, iii. 580 & n. 6; celebration, 1670, iii. 558–9 & n.
officers: chancellor, iii. 479, 559; dean (error), iii. 479 & n. 5, 559 & n. 2; deputy-chancellor, iii. 280, n. 1; prelate, iii. 479 & n. 4; register, iii. 479, n. 5, 559, n. 2.
knights: Godolphin, v. 572 *bis* & n. 4; duke of Hamilton, v. 177 & n. 2; Marlborough, v. 495 & n. 2, 525; ~ his George, v. 584; Monmouth, iv. 457 & n. 2; ~ his George, iv. 452 & n. 3; Ossory, iii. 629 & n. 2; Shrewsbury, v. 177 & n. 2; Sunderland, iv. 549 & n. 2.
Gary, Rev. —: *see* Geree, Rev. Simon.
Gascoigne, Sir Bernard (Bernardino Guasconi), iii. 554, n. 1; as associate of Arlington, iii. 553–4, 597; visits Wimbledon House, iv. 130–1; social, iv. 258.
Gassendi (Gassend), Pierre, iii. 189, n. 6 *ad fin.*; revives Epicurus's atomism, iii. 173, n. 4; *see also* Books mentioned in text.
Gassion, Jean, comte de, marshal of France, ii. 565 & n. 5; tomb of, *ib.*; victory of, at Rocroi, iii. 638–9 (extract from *State of France*).
Gaston-Jean-Baptiste, duke of Orleans, ii. 128, n. 1; in procession for Louis XIV's majority, iii. 43 & n. 2; apanage of, ii. 563, n. 1; at Blois: building of, in Château, ii. 141 & n. 4 (i. 92); ~ rights of sovereignty of: protects wolves, ii. 142 (i. 92); as owner of the Luxembourg, Paris, ii. 128 & n. 1, 130 (i. 82, 83); iii. 20, n. 7; and flowers: delights in, ii. 128 (i. 82), 130 (i. 83), 141 (i. 92); ~ artist employed by, to draw, iv. 532 & n. 1; library and other collections of, ii. 128 & n. 3 (i. 82).
Gataker, Rev. Charles, iii. 149, n. 3; sermons by (?), iii. 149, 219.
Gattamelata (Catta Malata), Erasmo da Narni, called: statue of, ii. 454 & n. 5.
Gauden, —, iv. 105 & n. 1.
Gauden, Benjamin: social (?), iv. 172 & n. 2.

Gauden, Sir Dennis, iii. 510, n. 2; business meetings, iv. 45, 264; has business with Charles II, iv. 176; house of, at Clapham, iv. 176 & n. 1; v. 111; social, iii. 510, 512; iv. 172; geneal., iv. 105, n. 1, 172 & n. 2.
Gauden, Lady, wife of Sir Dennis: social, iii. 512 & n. 1.
Gauden, John, D.D.; bishop of Exeter 1660; of Worcester 1662, iii. 187, n. 6; becomes bishop of Exeter, iii. 263 and & n. 5; sermons by, iii. 187–8, 194, 249, 261, 263; geneal., iii. 510, n. 2; iv. 105, n. 1.
Gaudy, Sir John: *see* Gawdy.
Gaunt, John of: *see* John.
Gauro *or* Barbaro, Monte, ii. 345 & n. 1.
Gawdy (Gaudy), Sir John, bt., and family, iv. 113 & n. 3.
Gayer, John: geneal., iv. 3, n. 2.
Gayer *or* Gayre (Geere), Sir Robert: gift from, to St. James's, Piccadilly, iv. 397 & n. 5.
Gaywood, Richard, etcher: collaborates with F. Barlow, iii. 166, n. 5.
Geere, Sir Robert: *see* Gayer.
Geery, Mrs. Mary Knight *alias*: *see* Knight, Mrs. M.
Gelasius I, pope: originates Candlemas (?), iii. 241, n. 1.
Gelderland, ii. 35 (i. 27); dukes of, ii. 58, n. 3.
Geldorp (Geldrop), George, artist: art-collection of, &c., ii. 554–5 & nn.
Gembloux: French forces at, 1693, v. 142, n. 2.
Gems and Semi-precious Stones [select notices]:
collections: Albury: Henry Howard, later sixth duke of Norfolk, iii. 155; Florence: Uffizi, ii. 189–93 (i. 119), 414; London: hatmaker in Blackfriars, iii. 143; ~ W. Courten or Charleton, iv. 531; ~ royal, iii. 260; iv. 216; ~ J. M. Wright, iii. 339 & n. 6; Oxford: Plot, iv. 68; Paris: Gaston, duke of Orleans, ii. 128 (i. 82); ~ Lincler, iii. 10; ~ Poignant, iii. 35; ~ de Richaumont, ii. 132 & n. 2 (i. 85); Rome: Farnese, ii. 310; ~ Gualdi, ii. 314; St.-Denis, ii. 87–9 (i. 58–

Gems, &c. (*cont.*)
60); Venice: Ruzini, ii. 471; ~ St. Mark's, ii. 441.
engraved: distinction between cameo and intaglio, iii. 79, n. 2; portraits, &c.: Antinous, ii. 314; Apollo, ii. 89 (i. 60); Augustus, *ib.*; Claudius, iii. 260 & n. 4; Cleopatra, ii. 89 (i. 60); dog, ii. 471; Queen Elizabeth, iii. 79–80 & n.; Garter jewel, v. 584; Grande camée de la France, ii. 99 & n. 2 (i. 65); Hercules, ii. 314; Julius Caesar, ii. 89 (i. 60), 192 & n. 4 (i. 119), 314; Mark Anthony, ii. 89 (i. 60); Nero, *ib.*; Scipio, iii. 339 & n. 6; queen of Sheba, ii. 89 (i. 60); Tiberius, ii. 471; woman in bath, *ib.*
particular stones or kinds of stone [select]: agate (achate), ii. 88 & n. 1; amethysts: table, iv. 471; balas rubies, iii. 373 & n. 7; Bristol diamonds, iii. 103 & n. 4; carbuncle, ii. 277 & n. 5, 278; enhydros, ii. 277 & n. 4; marcasites, iii. 10 & n. 2; onyx: seal-ring, iii. 69 & n. 2; pearls: Cleopatra's, ii. 372 & n. 5; ~ use of, at Venice, ii. 449; ~ worn by Moroccan ambassador, iv. 266; ruby: in doge's cap, ii. 441 & n. 2.
vases of semi-precious materials, &c.: Coupe de Chosroès II, ii. 89 & n. 2 (i. 60); Coupe des Ptolomées, ii. 88–9 & n. (i. 60); Sacro Catino, ii. 177 & n. 1 (i. 111); cup with Cleopatra, iii. 148 & n. 4.
miscellaneous: (Sir) J. Chardin travels to obtain jewels, iv. 212; inlay with gems, &c.: beds, ii. 174 (i. 110), 236, 471; ~ Chapel of the Princes, Florence, ii. 199, 416–17; pastes and counterfeits: makers of, at Venice, ii. 480 & n. 2.
Geneva: Church of ('those of Geneva'): attacked in sermon, iii. 34.
— city and republic:
— — E at, 1646, ii. 519, 520–30 & nn.
— — general: allied with Swiss cantons, ii. 518 & n. 1, 520, n. 6; capital punishment at, ii. 527 & nn. 3, 4; church govern-

Geneva (*cont.*)
ment, ii. 527; city arms, ii. 525 & n. 4; trade and industry at, ii. 524 & nn. 5–8, 529 & n. 1; Italian sermons at, ii. 523 & n. 4; languages spoken at, ii. 524; military exercises at, ii. 526–7 & nn., 528 & n. 4; population of, ii. 520, n. 6; sentinel at, ii. 528; situation of, ii. 524; Sunday observance at, ii. 526; territory of, ii. 525; women at: appearance of, ii. 530 & n. 4.
— — buildings, places, &c.: Académie: *see* university *below*; antiquities found at, ii. 523, n. 1, 526 & n. 1; arsenal, ii. 529 & n. 7; bishops' castle, ii. 529, n. 2; bishops' palace, ii. 530 & n. 3; bridges, ii. 528–9 & n.; cathedral (St. Pierre), ii. 527–8 & nn.; ~ inscription in, ii. 525, n. 3; la Coulouvrenière (Campus Martius), ii. 526–7 & nn., 528; *dômes*, ii. 524 & n. 4; environs, ii. 522–3; fortifications, ii. 524 & n. 2; hospital, ii. 530 & n. 2; Maison de ville, ii. 525–6 & nn., 529 & nn. 5–7; mall, &c., ii. 527; Mint, ii. 529 & n. 3; Musée archéologique, ii. 525, n. 5 *ad fin.*, 528, n. 2; Palais de Justice, ii. 530, n. 2; prison, ii. 530 & n. 3; rue de Coutance, ii. 520, n. 6; St. Germain, ii. 523, n. 4, 528, n. 6; St. Gervais (as St. Germain, in error): church and suburb of, ii. 528 & n. 6; la Serve, ii. 523 & n. 2; Tour de l'Isle, ii. 529 & n. 2; university (Académie, &c.), ii. 529–30 & nn.; ~ professor at: *see* Morus, A.; White Cross inn, ii. 520 & n. 6; ~ E's expenses at (as 'my host'), ii. 530.
— — historical, &c.: protestant refugees from Lucca at, ii. 523–4 & n.; Charles X Gustavus, king of Sweden, at, ii. 521, n. 4; French protestant refugees at, 1685, iv. 485 & n. 1; attack feared, 1690, v. 39 & n. 5; refugees from Orange at, 1703, v. 544.
— — — Florival of, v. 322 & n. 3.
— Lake of (Lacus Lemanus): E sails along, ii. 519–20 & nn.; journey from Brieg to, ii. 515 & n. 3; course of Rhone through, ii. 520 & n. 4; Pierres du Niton (Neptune's Rock), ii. 523 & n. 1; *add.*; trout in, ii. 520 & n. 5, 523 & n. 2; mentioned, ii. 528.
Geneviève, St.: protectress of Paris, ii. 100–1 & n. (i. 66).
Gennari, Benedetto: painting by, iv. 534, n. 1.
Gennep: Huys te: siege-works at, &c., ii. 31 (i. 24), 35–8 & nn. (i. 27–9); St. Aechten Clooster, ii. 37 & n. 1 (i. 28).
Genner, —: *see* Jenner, Sir T.
Genoa: city and republic:
— the city: notice, 1644, ii. 172–8 (i. 109–12); E's journey to, ii. 166, 167 (i. 105–6 *bis*); E arrives at, ii. 171 & n. 4 (i. 108).
— — general and miscellaneous: in comparison, iii. 637; dress at, ii. 178 (i. 112); iii. 320, n. 4; galley of, ii. 170 (i. 107); garrison, ii. 176 & n. 2 (i. 111); gunpower: imported into England from, i. 3; marble from, iv. 98; merchants of: expenditure of, on houses, ii. 39, n. 4, 174 & n. 2 (i. 110); murders in, ii. 173 & n. 2 (i. 109); site, &c., ii. 172–3 & nn. (i. 109); traffic in, ii. 178 (i. 112).
— — topography, &c.: Arsenal, ii. 178 & n. 3 (i. 112); churches: S. Ambrogio (Jesuits), i. 109; ii. 177 (i. 111); SS. Annunziata, ii. 177 & n. 3 (i. 111–12); *see also* ii. 176, n. 8; S. Francesco, ii. 176 & n. 8 (i. 111); S. Lorenzo, ii. 176–7 & nn. (i. 111).
— — — Darsena, ii. 178, n. 3; Forte Castellaccio, ii. 178, n. 1; harbour, ii. 171 & n. 3 (i. 108), 177 & n. 4 (i. 112); ~ boatmen in, ii. 173 (i. 109); lighthouse, ii. 171 & n. 3 (i. 108), 172 (i. 109), 177 (i. 112); Loggia dei Banchi, ii. 175 & n. 7 (i. 111); Mole, ii. 171 & n. 3 (i. 108), 172 (i. 109), 177 & n. 4 (i. 112); ~ in comparisons, ii. 183 (i. 115), 327; palaces: general, ii. 174 (i. 110); in Strada Nuova: published by Rubens, ii. 173 & n. 1 (i. 109), 176 & n. 3 (i. 111); Dinegro (Villa Rolla-Rosazza), ii. 173–4 & nn. (i. 109–10);

Genoa (*cont.*)
Doge's, ii. 175 & n. 6 (i. 111); ~ travellers registered at, ii. 171 (i. 108); Doria, Don Carlo (Doria-Tursi), ii. 176 & n. 5 (i. 111); Doria a Fássolo, ii. 174–5 & nn. (i. 110–11); Spinola, old Marquis, ii. 176 & n. 6 (i. 111).
— — — Pratique-house, ii. 171 (i. 108); public armoury, ii. 175–6 (i. 111); Sacro Catino, ii. 177 & n. 1 (i. 111); Strada Nuova, ii. 176 & n. 3 (i. 111); *see also* ii. 173 (i. 109); walls, ii. 177 & nn. 6, 7 (i. 112).
— — environs: Bisagno river, ii. 178 & n. 1 (i. 112); Sampierdarena, &c., ii. 170–1 & n. (i. 108), 178 (i. 112).
— — historical: bombarded by French, 1684, iv. 381 & n. 3; French protestants escape through, 1685, iv. 485, n. 1; earthquake at, 1699 (?), v. 353 & n. 1.
— — English residents at: M. Phillips, &c., iii. 86, n. 1; — Tomson, ii. 172 (i. 108–9); Zachary (inn-keeper), ii. 171–2 (i. 108).
— the Republic: guns first used in service of, ii. 175–6 (i. 111); territory of: limit of, ii. 169 (i. 106); ~ errors relating to, i. 106 & n. 1, 107 & n. 1.
— Genoese: Cardinal G. S. Donghi, ii. 207; Grimaldi family, ii. 169 (i. 106); jeweller possessing the great arcanum, iii. 52; singer, ii. 450, 475.
Gentileschi, Orazio: paintings, ii. 365 & n. 4.
Gentili, Antonio (A. da Faenza): silver cross made by, ii. 329 & n. 5.
Genuarius, St.: *see* Januarius.
Geoffries, Sir George: *see* Jeffreys.
Geography: measurement of degrees of the earth, iii. 539; errors in, iv. 214.
Geology [miscellaneous notices; *see also* Caves; Earthquakes; Fossils; Medicinal and Hot Springs; Volcanoes; &c.]: mountains: origin of, v. 30; ~ highest in Europe, ii. 334, 506; travelling sands at Downham, Suffolk, iv. 120 & n. 2.
George I, king of England; elector of Hanover, as George Louis, 1698, v. 421, n. 2; as elector: in succession to English crown, v. 421, 464–5 & n.; as king: establishes later Order of the Bath, iii. 276, n. 5; ~ gift of, to Cambridge University Library, v. 206, n. 3, 325, n. 8; ~ alters Kensington Palace, v. 8, n. 2; geneal., ii. 34, n. 1; iv. 28, n. 4; v. 317, n. 3, 543, n. 2.
George II, king of England: and Leicester House, iii. 626, n. 9.
George III, king of England: at Kew, iv. 144, n. 1.
George IV, king of England: reconstruction by, of Windsor Castle, iv. 316, n. 4.
George I, prince of Transylvania: geneal., ii. 34, n. 1.
George of Denmark, Prince, husband of Queen Anne, iv. 332, n. 3; comes to London, 1683, iv. 332 & n. 3; appearance and character, iv. 332–3 & n.; marries Anne, iv. 333; views horses, &c., iv. 399, 400; at Charles II's funeral, iv. 415, n. 3; visits Denmark, 1687, iv. 558, n. 7 *ad fin.*, 559; journey to Bath, 1702, v. 516, n. 2; revenue for, voted, v. 527 & n. 3; at thanksgiving for Blenheim, v. 578, n. 1; children of, v. 421 & n. 1; household of, iv. 333, n. 3; ~ master of the horse, iv. 558, n. 7 *ad fin.*; geneal., v. 582, n. 1.
George, Landgraf of Hesse-Darmstadt: killed, v. 610 & n. 2.
Georgia, in Asia, iv. 213, n. 1; women of, iv. 214 & n. 3.
Georgion: *see* Giorgione.
Georg Wilhelm, duke of Celle (Tell): visits William III, v. 352 & n. 5.
Gerard, Charles, 1618–94; first Baron Gerard of Brandon 1645; first earl of Macclesfield 1679, iii. 37, n. 6; as Lord Gerard: in Paris, 1651 (?), iii. 37 & n. 6; ~ judge at wrestling-match (?), iii. 476 & n. 1; ~ petition against, iii. 503, n. 4; ~ discusses theology, iv. 129–30; ~ social, iii. 351(?); iv. 167; as earl: social, v. 139; ~ dies, v. 165 & n. 1.
Gerard, Charles, 1659–1701; styled Viscount Brandon 1679–94; second earl of Macclesfield 1694: tried for complicity in Rye House Plot, iv. 490 & n. 6.

Gerard, Charles, 1634–67; fourth Baron Gerard of Gerard's Bromley 1640, iii. 37, n. 6; mentioned (?), iii. 37, 351, 476.
Gerard (Gerrard), Sir Gilbert, bt., iv. 502, n. 5; proposes marriage between his son and Susanna Evelyn (later Mrs. Draper), iv. 502–3; i. *32*; geneal., iii. 636, n. 3.
Gerard, Mary, Lady Gerard, born Cosin, wife of Sir Gilbert, iii. 636, n. 3; negotiates proposed sale of Cosin's library, iii. 636; geneal., iv. 502, n. 5.
Gerard of Brandon, Baron: *see* Gerard, Charles, later first earl of Macclesfield.
Gerard of Gerard's Bromley, Baron: *see* Gerard, Charles.
Gerbier, Sir Balthasar: academy of, ii. 134, n. 2.
Geree (Gerey), Rev. Simon: fatal accident to (?), v. 199 & n. 5.
Geree (Gere), Rev. Stephen, rector of Abinger: sermon by, iii 220 & n. 5.
Germain: Sieur de: *see* le Coq, F.
Germaine, Sir John, v. 394, n. 1; adultery of, with duchess of Norfolk, &c., v. 127, n. 1, 393–4 & n.
Germaine, Lady Mary, wife of Sir John: *see* Mordaunt, Lady Mary, Baroness Mordaunt.
German, Lord, *rectè* Jermyn: *see* Jermyn, Henry, earl of St. Albans, &c.
German language: in Upper Valais, ii. 511 & n. 2; at Geneva, ii. 524; E studies, ii. 534.
Germany and the Germans [Germany as the Empire (Holy Roman Empire) in its territorial aspects]:
— geographical, ii. 514, 524; travellers in, &c.: unnamed, ii. 45 (i. 32), 60; H. van der Borcht, i. 21; John Wall, ii. 96 (i. 63).
— social and miscellaneous: bleeding in, v. 352; feasts in, iii. 288; *see also* iv. 296; stoves in, iii. 162; products of, at Dort, ii. 32 & n. 4 (i. 24); Colchester cloth trade with, iii. 177, n. 4; balsams from, iii. 88; letters from, at Royal Society meetings, iv. 162 & n. 4, 202.
— historical and political [for campaigns in, &c., *see* Wars: Thirty Years' War; War of the League of Augsburg; War of the Spanish Succession]: Swiss mercenaries in, ii. 517; French hostility to, 1683, iv. 331, 340; exposed to French invasion: 1684, iv. 380; ∼ 1697, v. 270; French protestants seek refuge in, iv. 448, 485 & n. 2; v. 317 & n. 2.
— Germans: the ancient: victories of Marcus Aurelius over, commemorated, ii. 370.
— — unnamed individuals or groups [including some men described as Dutch; some others said to be Dutch may be Germans; for them *see* United Provinces]: E's acquaintances in Paris, iii. 54; visitors to E in England, iv. 220; bishop, buried at Montefiascone, ii. 210 & n. 4; gunsmiths at Brescia (error), ii. 489 & n. 6; horse-dealer, with Turkish horses, iv. 399; interpreter for Russian envoys, iii. 494; inventor of grenades, iii. 483; lute-makers at Bologna, ii. 426; musician, iv. 187; preacher at Deptford, iii. 182; prince: present from a, to Charles I, iii. 147–8; sculptor, iv. 207, n. 4; *add.*; soldiers: in Danish army, iv. 559 & n. 1; ∼ at Genoa, ii. 176 & n. 2 (i. 111); students and travellers: at Bourges, ii. 152–3 & n. (i. 98); at Orleans, ii. 138 (i. 90); at Padua University, ii. 470 & n. 1; *see also* pp. 465, 466 & n. 2; in Rome: inn for, ii. 214, n. 2; at Siena University: privileges of, ii. 203; at Venice: merchants' depot, ii. 434.
— — named individuals said to be Germans: *see* Faber, A. O.; Horneck, A.; Oenipont, J.; Vratz, C.
Gernsey: Baron of, 1703–14: *see* Finch, Heneage, later earl of Aylesford.
Gerrard: *see* Garrard *and* Gerard.
Ghent: notice, ii. 73–4 & nn. (i. 48); E's journey to, ii. 72–3 (i. 47–8).
Ghisi: *see* Chigi.
Ghrame, —: *see* Graham, Col. James.
Giants [*see also* Monstrosities]: bones of, ii. 153 & n. 11 (i. 99), 314, 344 & n. 1.

Gibbes, Dr. James Alban: at Rome, ii. 213 & n. 5, 311.
Gibbons, Christopher, organist: performs (?; as Mr. Gibbon), iii. 109 & n. 6.
Gibbons (Gibson), Grinling, the wood-carver, &c., iii. 567, n. 3; at work in Deptford, iii. 567; E introduces to Charles II, &c., iii. 568, 571–3 & nn.; house of, &c., iv. 179 & n. 2; sculpture (in stone or bronze): statues, &c., iv. 317 & n. 2; Charles II, Chelsea Hospital, v. 53 & n. 2; Charles II (?) and pedestal, Windsor Castle, iv. 207 & n. 4; *add.*; reredos, &c., Roman Catholic chapel, Whitehall, iv. 534 & n. 1; wood-carvings: copy of Tintoretto's Crucifixion, iii. 567–8 & n.; ~ shown to Wren and Pepys, iii. 570; ~ shown to Charles II, &c., iii. 571–2; ~ sold, iii. 572–3 & n.; at Cassiobury Park, iv. 199; at Lee Place, iv. 180, 288 *bis*; at St. James's, Piccadilly, iv. 397 & n. 4; at Whitehall, iv. 537 & n. 2; at Windsor, iv. 136 & n. 3, 316–17 & n.; at Woodcote Park, ii. 542, n. 3.
Gibeonites: in sermon, iii. 312.
Gibraltar: loss of ships near, 1694, v. 169 & n. 3; captured by Allies, 1704, v. 575 & n. 3; besieged by Spaniards, 1704–5, v. 583 & n. 2, 587 & n. 2, 591 & n. 2; ~ siege raised, v. 594 & n. 3; ~ *see also* v. 610, n. 2.
Gibraltar: Straits of: Sir Thomas Allin attacks Dutch Smyrna fleet near, 1664, iii. 404, n. 4; *see also* iii. 407 (as before Cadiz); Sir George Rooke in, 1696, v. 233 & n. 2; battle in, 1704 (Malaga), v. 579 & n. 2, 579–80 & n., 580 & n. 4.
Gibson, —: error for G. Gibbons, iii. 567.
Gibson, Edmund; D.D. 1702; bishop of Lincoln 1716; of London 1723, v. 533, n. 2; edition by, of Camden's *Britannia*, v. 206 & n. 2; sermon by, v. 533–4.
Gifford, Captain —: venture of, lost, &c., 1695, v. 218 & n. 1.
Giglio, C.: painting by, ii. 529 & n. 6.
Gilbert, lapidary, ii. 480 & n. 2.
Gilbert, William, M.D., iii. 338, n. 3; portrait of, iii. 338; uses Terrella, iii. 152, n. 5.
Gilford: *see* Guildford.
Gillam, Captain Zachary: leads expedition to seek North-West Passage, iv. 96, n. 5.
Gillingham, Kent: chain across the Medway near, iii. 484, n. 1, 485 & n. 4; fortifications at, 1672, iii. 610.
Gillingham, George, D.D., iii. 151, n. 5; *add.*; sermons by, iii. 151, 152, 160, 190.
Ginkel, Godard van Reede, heer van; earl of Athlone 1692: conduct of, at Landen, v. 150 & n. 1.
Giolo (Jolo, Jeoly), Prince, v. 295 & n. 2.
Giorgione (Georgion): Giorgio da Castelfranco, called, ii. 413, n. 12; paintings by: Fondaco dei Tedeschi, Venice (frescoes), ii. 434 & n. 1; ~ others, ii. 413; iii. 216.
Giotto: Navicella mosaic by, ii. 265 & n. 3; *add.*
Giovanni, Signor, and his fellow, ii. 417–18; as two Italian gentlemen, ii. 406.
Giovanni Battista (Signor Jo. Baptist), ii. 316; as the Capitano, ii. 325.
Giovanni d'Andrea: tomb of, ii. 421 & n. 7.
Giovanni da Fiesole, Fra (il Beato Angelico): painting by (?) and tomb of, ii. 377 & nn. 6, 7.
Giovanni da Salerno, Blessed: tomb of, ii. 199 & n. 7.
Giovio, Paolo (Paulus Jovius), ii. 189, n. 6; collection of, of portraits, ii. 189 & n. 6 (i. 119); tomb of, ii. 198 & n. 8, 416.
Gipping, river, iv. 115, n. 7.
Gittings, Mary: and Marden, iv. 121, n. 3; v. 337, n. 1.
Giulio (Julio) Romano: Giulio Pippi, called, ii. 114, n. 9; paintings by, ii. 114 (i. 74), 299 & n. 3; ~ at Kensington Palace, v. 237.
Giuseppe, Cavaliere: *see* Arpino.
Giusti, Count —: garden of, at Verona, ii. 487 & n. 2.
Giustiniani (Justinian) family, Venice: tombs of, ii. 468 & n. 6.
Giustiniani (Justiniani), Ascanio, Venetian ambassador to James II: audience for, &c., iv. 492–3 & nn.; at court ceremony, iv. 493.
Giustiniani, Blessed Niccolò: tomb of, ii. 468 & n. 6.
Givet: French magazine at, destroyed, 1696, v. 234 & n. 5.

Glanvill, Rev. Joseph, the author, iv. 53, n. 4; sermons by (?), iv. 53–4, 123.
Glanville, Elizabeth, daughter of William Glanville, jnr., v. 169 & n. 2, 340 & n. 2(?), 497(?).
Glanville, Frances, daughter of William Glanville, jnr.: *see* Evelyn, Mrs. Frances.
Glanville, Mrs. Frances, born Hales, wife of William Glanville, jnr., iii. 84, n. 1; v. 218, n. 6; at baptism of Mary Draper, v. 218–19; dies, v. 340 & n. 2.
Glanville, Sir Francis: geneal., ii. 539, n. 2.
Glanville, George: geneal., ii. 539, n. 2.
Glanville, Jane, sister of William Glanville, sen.: *see* Cows, Mrs. J.
Glanville, Mrs. Jane, 1616–51, sister of E, wife of William Glanville, sen.: character, iii. 57.
as Jane Evelyn: birth, ii. 1 & n. 4; visits Lewes, &c., ii. 21 (i. 16), 29 (i. 21), 79 (i. 52); E gives portraits of himself to, ii. 29, 133 (i. 87); at Wotton, 1647, ii. 537.
as Mrs. Glanville: announces her marriage to E, ii. 539; accompanies E to Gravesend, ii. 558–9; E visits, iii. 14 & n. 5, 15; child or children of, iii. 1 & n. 4, 15, 51 & n. 1, 84; dies, &c., iii. 52 & n. 3; mourning for, &c., iii. 57.
mentioned, i. 1; v. 497 *bis*; i. *3–4*.
Glanville, Sir John, the Speaker, iii. 111 & n. 6; seat of, at Broad Hinton, iii. 111 & n. 7; geneal., iii. 78, n. 2, 81.
Glanville, Mary: *see* Edgcumbe, Mrs. M.
Glanville, William: *see* Evelyn *or* Glanville, W.
Glanville, William, sen., 1618–1702, husband of Jane Evelyn, ii. 539 & n. 2; visits Sussex, ii. 544; employs R. Hoare, ii. 559, n. 2; mourns his wife, iii. 57; godfather of: Richard, son of George Evelyn, iii. 63; ~ J. S. Evelyn, iii. 89; ill, iii. 151; attends funeral of John Evelyn of Wotton, v. 55; at Greenwich, v. 71; intervention of, in settlement of Wotton estate, v. 103, 497; member of Greenwich Hospital Grand Committee, v. 236, n. 2; quarrels with E and
Glanville, William, senr. (*cont.*) Mrs. Evelyn, v. 497, 497–8; social, ii. 552; iii. 62, 81, 84, 96, 467 & n. 3; geneal., iv. 139 & n. 3; death, character, &c., v. 496–7 & n., 497–8 & nn.
Glanville, William, jnr., *c.* 1650–1718, nephew of E, iii. 84, n. 1; birth (?), iii. 1 & n. 4; as child, iii. 15(?), 84; trustee for John Evelyn, jnr., iv. 194; godfather of Elizabeth Evelyn (later Mrs. Harcourt), iv. 396; attends funeral of John Evelyn of Wotton, v. 55; daughter of: baptized, v. 169; executor of George Evelyn, v. 377; house of, v. 211; buys picture, v. 145 & n. 3; owns portrait of E, i. 87; mentioned, v. 497 *bis*.
Glanville, William, of Heavitree: geneal., ii. 539, n. 2.
Glanville, William, son of Sir John, the Speaker, iii. 81, n. 7; social, &c., iii. 81, 111–12.
Glanville, Winifred, Lady Glanville, wife of Sir John, iii. 111, n. 6; social, iii. 194; geneal., iii. 78, n. 2.
Glascocke, William: commissioner for London streets, iii. 319, n. 1.
Glasgow: University: professor of theology at, 1669–74: *see* Burnet, G.
Glasgow: diocese: archbishop of, 1687–1708: *see* Paterson, J.
Glass [*see also* Stained Glass]: 'artificial glass or porcelain', 'kind of', iii. 310; a beer glass, iii. 626; coach-windows, iii. 468; iv. 72, 301; a flint glass a yard long, iv. 415; grenades, iii. 368 & n. 5; manufacture of: at Murano, ii. 467 & n. 5; at Greenwich, iv. 13 & n. 2; at Vauxhall (Buckingham), iv. 98–9 & n.; crucibles used in, iii. 180.
Glencairn: tenth Earl of: *see* Cunningham, Alexander.
Glisson, Francis, M.D.: on the lymph ducts, ii. 551, n. 2.
Gloucester: notice, 1654, iii. 117–18 & nn.; Charles I's march to, ii. 79 & n. 6 (i. 53); siege of, iii. 118 & n. 4; defended by (Sir) E. Massey, iii. 257, n. 3; case of clipping at, v. 256 & n. 6.
Gloucester: Dukes of: *see* Humphrey; Richard III, king of England; Henry, duke 1640–60; William, duke 1689–1700.

Gloucester: Earl of: *see* Clare, Gilbert de.
Gloucester: cathedral clergy:
bishops: *see* Goodman, G. (1624–56); Nicholson, W. (1661–72); Prichett *or* Pritchett, J. (1672–81); Frampton, R. (1681–91); Fowler, E. (1691–1714).
deans: *see* Brough, W. (1643–71); Frampton, R. (1673–81); Jane, W. (1685–1707); Chetwood, K. (1707–20).
prebendary: *see* Nash, H.
Gloucestershire: in view, iii. 119; receiver of, 1662–7: *see* Scawen, R.
Glover, Captain John, customs officers at Margate, &c., iii. 611 & n. 1.
Glycon: Farnese Hercules by, ii. 216, n. 1.
Glynn, Mary, Lady Glynn, born Evelyn, wife of Sir William: as heiress, v. 337, n. 1.
Glynn, Sir William: geneal., v. 337, n. 1.
Gnesen: Archbishop of, 1687–1705: *see* Radziejowski, M. S.
Gnostics: tenets of, iv. 617; in sermons, iv. 363 & n. 7; v. 131.
Goa: Portuguese possess, iii. 324, n. 2.
Goad, Thomas, LL.D.: sermon by (?), iii. 314 & n. 1.
Goade, Dr. —: *see* Goad, T.; Good, T.; Gouge, N.
Goare *or* Gore, Catherine: *see* Evelyn, Mrs. C.
Gobelins: tapestries, iv. 343, n. 2.
Goch, Michiel van, Dutch ambassador to England, iii. 390, n. 7 *ad fin.*; Charles II's negotiation with, iii. 390 & n. 7; E negotiates exchange, &c., of prisoners of war with, iii. 406, 407 *bis*, 408.
Godalming, Surrey: Westbrook in, seat of L. Oglethorpe, v. 527 & n. 2.
Godard, —: sermon by, 1652, iii. 61.
Goddard, Jonathan, M.D.: dissects chameleon, iii. 302, n. 6; Royal Society refers inquiries to, &c., iii. 340, n. 1.
Goddard, Rev. Thomas, v. 615, n. 3; sermons by (?), v. 615–16, 617–18.
Godfrey (Godfery), — (John Godfrey?): in Paris, 1651, iii. 31 & n. 4, 38.
Godfrey, Mrs. Arabella, born Churchill, wife of Col. Charles Godfrey, iv. 497, n. 4; as Arabella Churchill: mistress of James, duke of York (later James II), v. 86, 525; ~ children of, by James, iv. 497–8 & n.; v. 149, n. 6.
Godfrey, Col. Charles: geneal., iv. 497, n. 4 *ad fin.*
Godfrey, Sir Edmund Berry, iv. 155, n. 3; death of, iv. 153, n. 3, 155 & n. 3, 175, 188, 231, n. 3; intimacy of, with E. Coleman, iv. 155, 175; *see also* i. 27.
Godfrey, John: in Paris, 1651 (?), iii. 31 & n. 4, 38.
Godman *or* Goodman, Henry, Congregationalist minister in Deptford: church of, iv. 546, n. 6.
Godmanchester, Hunts.: plough custom at, iii. 135 & n. 5.
Godolphin: parish church: *see* Breage.
Godolphin family: burial-place, iv. 150 & n. 1.
Godolphin, Mrs. Den (Penelope Godolphin?), v. 171 & n. 2.
Godolphin, Francis, *c.* 1661–1702: commits suicide, v. 505–6 & n.
Godolphin, Francis, of Coulston, Wilts.: geneal., iv. 206, n. 1.
Godolphin, Sir Francis, K.B.: geneal., iv. 147 & n. 7.
Godolphin, Francis, 1678–1766; second earl of Godolphin 1712, iv. 147, n. 2; born and baptized, iv. 147 & nn. 3–7; i. *25*; E as trustee for, iv. 155, 182; maintenance of: provision for, iv. 559; weaning of, iv. 179; education of: E supervises, iv. 463; i. *25*; illnesses, iv. 178, 507, 508; as child, &c.: visits E, iv. 212, 337, 448, 450, 463; v. 127; marriage of, v. 290 & n. 5, 525.
Godolphin, Lady Henrietta; born Churchill; countess of Godolphin, 1712, as wife of Francis Godolphin, second earl; duchess of Marlborough *sui juris* 1722, v. 290, n. 5; marriage of, v. 290 & n. 5, 525.
Godolphin, Henry; D.D. 1685; provost of Eton 1695, iv. 181, n. 8; as prebendary of St. Paul's: admitted, iv. 372, n. 3; ~ house-warming, iv. 606 & n. 4; buys library, iv. 589 & n. 4; sermon by, iv. 372; social, iv. 181, 337, 519; v. 236, 279, 290.

Godolphin, Jael: *see* Boscawen, Mrs. J.
Godolphin, Mrs. Margaret, born Blagge, wife of Sidney Godolphin, later Baron and earl of Godolphin, iii. 530, n. 1. [She is called Mrs. Blagge until iv. 63; Mrs. Blagge or Mrs. Godolphin from iv. 64 to iv. 75; and thenceforward Mrs. Godolphin. She is also represented by two symbols, the pentacle (iv. 1) and the sign for Libra (iv. 27, n. 4).]
— chronological series: Lady Guildford in charge of, iii. 263, n. 8; as maid of honour, iii. 621, n. 5.
— — 1669: on journey of pleasure, iii. 529–30.
— — 1672: friendship of, with E begins (visits, &c.), iii. 622 & n. 3, 623, 626; makes compact of friendship with E, iii. 628 & n. 1.
— — 1673: leaves court and goes to reside at Berkeley House, iv. 1.
— — 1674: performs in *Calisto*, iv. 49–50 & n., 51 & n. 1.
— — 1675: marries Godolphin, iv. 63 & n. 4; ~ anniversary, iv. 134–5; travels to France, iv. 73, n. 7, 79–80.
— — 1676: returns to London, iv. 88, 91; announces her marriage, iv. 89, 90; *see also* iv. 63, n. 4; starts house-keeping at Berkeley House, iv. 94 & n. 1; lodgings preparing for, in Whitehall, iv. 98 *bis* & n. 1, 99, 100; *add.*
— — 1677: moves to Whitehall, iv. 107.
— — 1678: pregnant, iv. 135, 139; gives birth to son, iv. 147–8 & nn.; last illness, death, character, &c., iv. 148–51 & nn.; buried at Breage, &c., iv. 150, 151–2, 161; condolences for, iv. 154; death of: alluded to or commemorated, iv. 156, 161, 219, 256–7, 292.
— amusements, &c.: at comedy, iii. 622; at musical performance, iv. 51; visits to exhibitions, &c.: Ashmole's collection, iv. 138–9; Blackwall: Indian curiosities at, iv. 99; Lambeth: marble-warehouse, &c., at, iv. 98–9; 'Paradise', iv. 24; Royal Society museum, iv. 34.

Godolphin, Mrs. Margaret (*cont.*)
— charity: general, iv. 150; visits almshouse, iv. 28; gifts: to imprisoned debtors, iv. 29 & n. 2; ~ to poor, iv. 139.
— friends [these include Lady Berkeley, with whom she resides, visits Twickenham Park (iv. 23, 72–3, 73–4), &c.; Mrs. Elizabeth Howard and her daughters, Dorothy, later Mrs. Graham, and Ann, whose marriage to Sir G. Sylvius she promotes (iv. 123); Lady Mordaunt, whose son is recommended to her care (iv. 84); and Lady Sunderland].
— miscellaneous: chaplain of (?), iv. 147; diary, i. *82*; health: ill, iv. 1; ~ faints, iv. 26; ~ drinks waters at Tunbridge Wells, iv. 40–1; landlady of: *see* Warner, Mrs. —; papers of, iv. 152; portrait of, iv. 13 & n. 7, 14.
— property: value of, 1675, iv. 79; lease at Spalding granted to, iv. 90, 93 *bis*, 101; lends money to Sunderland, iv. 94, 559; settlement on, made by Godolphin, iv. 124; E as trustee for, iv. 43, 44, 78, 124; *see also* iii. 628; gives E power of attorney, iv. 73 & n. 7; E renders accounts, iv. 88, 155; requires form of will, iv. 34; will of, 1675, iv. 79; letter of, about disposal of property, iv. 150 & n. 2; bills of exchange for, 1675, iv. 78.
— relations with E [apart from those concerned with property]: general, i. *24–5*; in period before compact of friendship: *see* chronological series *above*; social intercourse with E and Mrs. Evelyn, 1673–8, iv. 1–15, 23–80, 88–111, 121–40 *passim*; special passages, &c.: compact of friendship: anniversaries of, iv. 25, 45, 76, 100, 122, 155, 182; v. 299, n. 1; ~ alluded to, iv. 150; Tuesday as visiting-day, iv. 147; E's gifts to: locket, iv. 1; ~ engraved gem, iv. 46 & n. 5; ~ MS. devotionary books, ii. 559, n. 2; iv. 126, n. 5; attends E's house-warming at new lodgings, iv. 50; visits (other than day) to Sayes Court, iv. 67, 99 & n. 2, 100;

Godolphin, Mrs. Margaret (*cont.*) engages E to act as Berkeley's agent, 1675, &c., iv. 77, 99, 110; marriage of: E informed of, iv. 89, 90; *see also* iv. 63, n. 4; takes charge of Elizabeth Evelyn, iv. 35; supervises John Evelyn, jnr., in France, iv. 79, 91; E's account of life of: *see* Evelyn: books.
— religion: piety of, &c., iv. 429; uses mental communion, iv. 30 *bis* & n. 5; Communion at her landlady's, iv. 90; visits sick, &c., iv. 25, 28, 29; receives Sacrament with sick, iv. 27, 32 & n. 4, 52, 56, 103(?); visits widow(s), iv. 31, 33, 36, 54, 71; godmother to B. Watson, iv. 49.
— genealogical: sisters of: *see* Yarborough, H. M., Lady Yarborough; ~ unnamed: dies, iv. 387; relation of: *see* Warner, Mrs. —.
Godolphin, Penelope, iv. 432, n. 2; social, iv. 432, 643; v. 171 & n. 2(?).
Godolphin, Sidney; first Baron Godolphin 1684; first earl of Godolphin 1706, iv. 10, n. 6.
— public life, appointments, &c.:
— — 1678: Master of the Robes, iv. 139 & n. 4.
— — 1679: commissioner of the Treasury, iv. 166 & n. 2; privy councillor (error), *ib.*
— — 1684: secretary of state, iv. 383 & n. 1; created baron, iv. 387 *bis* & n. 1; commissioner of the Treasury, iv. 387 & n. 5.
— — 1685: chamberlain to Queen Mary (of Modena), iv. 416–17 & n.
— — 1687: commissioner of the Treasury, iv. 533.
— — 1688: commissioner from James II to William of Orange, iv. 608 & n. 8; *add.*
— — 1690: commissioner of the Treasury, v. 39 & n. 1; Pepys's *Memoires relating to the Navy* shown to, v. 39.
— — 1695: commissioner for Greenwich Hospital: attends meeting, v. 209–10; ~ subscribes to Hospital, v. 249 & n. 3.
— — 1696: resigns from Treasury, v. 261 & n. 1.

Godolphin, Sidney (*cont.*)
— — 1700: commissioner of the Treasury, v. 432 & n. 2, 438 & n. 2; member of Cabinet Council, v. 438 & n. 2.
— — 1701: joins in Lords' protest, v. 466 & n. 2; Lord Justice, v. 469 & n. 6.
— — 1702: Lord High Treasurer, v. 500 & n. 1.
— — 1704: elected K.G., v. 572 *bis* & n. 4.
— — 1705: advises ministerial changes, v. 612, n. 1; accused of Jacobite intrigues, v. 619 & n. 1.
— married life, relations with E, &c.: general, i. *25*; marriage, iv. 63 & n. 4; *see further* Godolphin, Mrs. M.; allows Mrs. Godolphin to dispose of her property, iv. 79; lodgings of, in Whitehall: *see* Godolphin, Mrs. M.; makes settlement on Mrs. Godolphin, iv. 124; grief of, for Mrs. Godolphin's death, &c., iv. 148–52 *passim*; attends Mrs. Godolphin's funeral, iv. 161; E accounts to, for his management of Mrs. Godolphin's affairs, iv. 155; E sends copy of his *Life of Mrs. Godolphin* to, iv. 429, n. 1; E accounts to, as trustee for Francis Godolphin, iv. 182; entrusts Francis Godolphin's early education to E, iv. 463; provides for Francis Godolphin, iv. 559; attends Mary Evelyn's funeral (?), iv. 430; congratulates E on appointment, iv. 465; business interviews with E, 1686–7, iv. 517, 535 & n. 2, 551, 558; offers E treasurership of Greenwich Hospital, v. 203; E recommends chaplain to, v. 534; gives appointments to (Sir) John Evelyn, v. 556 & n. 1, 601–2 & n.; and marriage of Anne Boscawen to (Sir) John Evelyn, v. 588, 602; *see also* v. 609–10.
— further private affairs, &c.: at Newmarket, 1676, iv. 99, n. 2; at Windsor, 1678, iv. 147; returns to London, iv. 148; and Cranbourn Lodge: as keeper, iv. 527–8 & n., 558; ~ entertains E, &c., at, v. 110; ill, 1684, iv. 383 *ter*, 384; buys painting(s),

Godolphin, Sidney (*cont.*)
v. 145 & n. 2; burial-place of, iv. 150, n. 1.
— social: parties, iv. 10, 11, 67, 133, 181, 192, 437, 589; v. 584 & n. 1; alone, or with Mrs. Godolphin, &c., iv. 99, 106, 122, 140, 173, 547; v. 500, 609.
— genealogical, iv. 133 & n. 4, 151, 372; v. 258 & n. 1, 505–6 & n.
Godolphin, Sir William, 1605–63, of Spargor: social (?), iii. 62 & n. 2.
Godolphin, Sir William, 1635–96, diplomatist: geneal., v. 506 & n. 1.
Godolphin, Sir William, bt., 1640–1710, iv. 133, n. 3; godfather of Francis Godolphin (late second earl of Godolphin), iv. 147; accompanies Mrs. Margaret Godolphin's hearse, iv. 151; questions Parliamentary Test Act, iv. 159 & n. 4; attends Mary Evelyn's funeral (?), iv. 430; learning, &c., of, iv. 171, 178, n. 2, 589; six horses (team) of, iv. 207; in Hyde Park, iv. 171; visits Cranbourn Lodge, iv. 642; goes to see rhinoceros, iv. 389; social, iv. 133, 178, 179, 192, 202, 271, 300, 337, 395, 414, 448, 520, 529, 531, 546, 564, 592, 602, 643, 646, 652; v. 2, 5, 9, 19, 38, 39, 81, 143, 204, 214, 222, 226, 273.
Godolphin: sisters of Sidney Godolphin, first earl of Godolphin, and of Sir William Godolphin, iv. 133, n. 4; accompany Mrs. Margaret Godolphin's hearse, iv. 151; social, iv. 133, 179, 448, 450.
Godolphin: Baron and Earls, &c., of: *see* Godolphin, Sidney, first baron, 1684–1706; first earl, 1706–12; Godolphin, Francis, second earl, 1712–66; Godolphin, Lady Henrietta, his countess, later duchess of Marlborough *sui juris*.
Godstone, Surrey: E visits Sir John Evelyn at, ii. 78 & n. 5 (i. 51–2), 81, 557–8; iii. 219; church: tomb of Sir John Evelyn, &c., in, iv. 122 & n. 2; ~ sermon in, iv. 122; the Evelyns in, i. *2*, 2 & nn. 4, 5; ~ powder-works of, i. *1*, 2–3 & n.; iii. 219; ~ property of, ii. 557, n. 4; Lee Place in, *ib.*; ~ notice of, iii. 219; ~ demolished, i. 51–2 & n.; ~ position of, iv. 121, n. 2.
Godstone, Surrey (*cont.*)
Marden in: succession to, v. 337, n. 1; acquired and improved by Sir R. Clayton, iv. 121–2 & nn.; v. 425–6 & n.; residence of Clayton family, iv. 111, n. 1; paintings by Streater at, iii. 626, n. 1.
Goffe, Stephen, D.D., ii. 36 & n. 3 (i. 27); sermon by, *ib.*; intervenes in controversy, iii. 360 & n. 5; geneal., iii. 204, n. 3.
Goffe, Col. William, regicide: takes part in Christmas raid on Exeter House chapel, 1657, iii. 204 & n. 3.
Gold and Silver [select. The goldsmiths' work in the various collections of relics is not indexed under the present heading, or elsewhere in detail; for the collections *see* Roman Catholic Church: relics; for the English regalia *see* England: kings; *see also* Alchemy]:
general: discourse on, to Royal Society, iv. 275–6; specimens of, in natural state, iv. 288; cups of plate, ii. 518; goldsmiths [general notices; named individuals are not indexed collectively], ii. 99 *bis* (i. 65), 105 (i. 68), 142 (i. 93); ~ as bankers: misdemeanours of, v. 246, 256.
gold: dissolvant of, iii. 48; experiment on, iii. 84; gold-beater, iv. 340; in medicine, iii. 86 & n. 6; plating on iron, ii. 192, n. 1; refining: discourse on, iii. 325; specimen of, in natural state, ii. 413; used for: church fittings, &c., ii. 298, 414, 438 & n. 3; iii. 35; cross of Edward the Confessor, iv. 470–1 & nn.; furniture, &c., iii. 323–4; iv. 9; v. 147; service, ii. 192 (i. 119); statuette, ii. 106 (i. 68).
silver: church fittings, &c., ii. 272 & n. 6, 329 & n. 5, 412; coachwork, ii. 257; furniture, ii. 174 (i. 110); iii. 21; iv. 8, 74, 343; ~ filigree cabinet, v. 147; services, ii. 192 (i. 119); statuette, iv. 138 & n. 2; vases, iii. 35.
Goldesborough, William, clerk of the house of commons: E borrows Journals of the house from (?), iii. 588 & n. 1.
Gondi family: as owners of St.-Cloud, ii. 107, n. 3.

Gondi, Jean-François de, archbishop of Paris: as owner of St.-Cloud, ii. 107 & n. 3 (i. 69).
Gondo: ravine of, ii. 508, n. 5, 510, n. 2; *add.*
Gondomar (Gundamar), Don Diego Sarmiento de Acuña, count of: as Spanish ambassador in England, ii. 6 & n. 5 (i. 6).
Gonson family: geneal., iii. 55, n. 3, 91, n. 5; iv. 304 & n. 1, 313, n. 3.
Gonson, Benjamin, sen., iv. 304, n. 1; owned Great Warley manor, ii. 554, n. 1.
Gonson, Benjamin, jnr., iv. 304, n. 1.
Gonson, Thomasine: *see* Browne, Mrs. T.
Gonson, William, iv. 304, n. 1.
Gonzaga, Anne of, wife of Prince Edward of the Palatinate, ii. 567, n. 1.
Good, Thomas, D.D.: sermon by (?), iii. 314 & n. 1.
Goodman, Godfrey, bishop of Gloucester: project of, for cathedral library, iii. 117, n. 6.
Goodman, Henry: *see* Godman *or* Goodman, H.
Goodman, John, D.D., iv. 198, n. 4; books by, iv. 392 & n. 3; sermons by, iv. 198, 222, 392, 480.
Goodwin Sands: fleets near: 1672, iii. 614, n. 4, 615, n. 1; ~ 1690, v. 31, n. 2; body of W. Glanville, sen., thrown into sea near, v. 497 & n. 3.
Gorcum *or* Gorinchem, ii. 39 & n. 3 (i. 29), 59 (i. 40).
Gore, —, iv. 132 & n. 6.
Gore (Goare), Catherine: *see* Evelyn, Mrs. C.
Gore, Lucie (Sir William Leveson Gower?): social, iv. 11 & n. 6.
Gore (Goare), Robert: geneal., iv. 14, n. 2; v. 358, n. 6.
Gore, Sir William, lord mayor of London 1701–2: signs charitable appeal, v. 485, n. 1.
Gorges, Sir Arthur, the poet: house of, at Chelsea, iii. 315, n. 2; geneal., ii. 546, n. 6.
Gorges, Sir Arthur, jnr., ii. 546, n. 6; social, ii. 546; house of, at Chelsea (?), iii. 315 & n. 2.
Gorges, Arthur, d. 1668, iii. 315, n. 2.
Gorges, Ferdinando, iii. 582, n. 2; claim of, to Maine: negotiation for, iii. 582 & n. 2, 584.
Gorges, Sir Ferdinando: geneal., iii. 582, n. 2.
Gorges, Richard, second Baron Gorges, iii. 599, n. 6; as member of Council for Foreign Plantations (later of Trade and Plantations), iii. 578, n. 13 *ad fin.*, 599, 629; social, iv. 642.
Gorges: second Baron, 1650–1712: *see* Gorges, Richard.
Gorinchem: *see* Gorcum.
Goring, Alice, countess of Norwich, wife of Charles Goring, second earl, and previously of Thomas Baker: house of, at Leyton, iii. 538, n. 2; iv. 306.
Goring, Lady Catherine: *see* Scott, Lady Catherine.
Goring, Charles; styled Lord Goring 1657–63; second earl of Norwich 1663, iii. 245, n. 2; house of, at Leyton in Epping Forest: notice, iii. 538 & n. 1; ~ mentioned, iv. 306; social, iii. 245, 270, 537, 562.
Goring, George, jnr., styled Lord Goring 1644–57, ii. 36, n. 1; regiment of, in Dutch service, ii. 36 & n. 1 (i. 27); winter-quarters of, ii. 56 (i. 39); besieged in Portsmouth, 1642, ii. 79 (i. 52); treachery of, i. 52 & n. 3.
Goring, George, sen.; first Baron Goring 1628–44; first earl of Norwich 1644, ii. 36, n. 2; as ambassador to France, 1643: audience to, &c., ii. 90–1 (i. 61); leads Kentish rising, 1648, ii. 541 & n. 4; at Colchester, iii. 176, n. 4; tried by High Court of Justice, 1649, ii. 548 & n. 2; in Paris, 1651, iii. 48; and ownership of Goring House and Mulberry Garden, iii. 96, n. 7; helps E to recover stolen property, iii. 56; E writes to, iii. 62; letter to, from Louisa Hollandina, i. 26; geneal., ii. 36, 560.
Goring: Lord (courtesy title): *see* Goring, George, jnr. (1644–57); Goring, Charles, later earl of Norwich (1657–63).
Goshen: England as land of: in sermon, iii. 303.
Gostling (Gosling), Rev. John: sings before Charles II, iv. 404 & n. 9.
Gothic: architecture: *see* Architecture: styles; lettering, ii. 123 (i. 79); printing-type, iii. 206.
Goths, the: destruction by, ii. 257, 324.

Gottenberg, John: *see* Gutenberg.
Gottifredi (Gotefredi), B. and F.: collection of, of medals, ii. 391 & n. 4; *add.*
Gottorp: Duke and Duchess of: *see* Christian Albrecht; Friderica Amalia.
Gouffier, N.-A., marquis of Crèvecœur: *see* Crèvecœur.
Gouge, Nicholas, D.D., vicar of St. Martin in the Fields 1694, v. 169, n. 5; sermon by (as Dr. Goade), v. 169; mentioned, v. 112, n. 4, 204, n. 5.
Gough *or* Goffe, Stephen: *see* Goffe.
Goujon, Jean: sculpture by, ii. 132 & n. 1 (i. 85).
Gouvernet, Charles de la Tour, marquis de: geneal., iv. 517, n. 6.
Gouvernet (Governè), Esther de la Tour, marquise de: describes persecution of French protestants, iv. 517–18 & n.; geneal., *ib.*
Gower, Sir William Leveson: *see* Leveson-Gower.
Gowran: first Baron: *see* Fitzpatrick, Richard.
Grafton: Dukes, &c., of: *see* FitzRoy, Henry, first duke, 1675–90; FitzRoy, Isabella, his duchess; FitzRoy, Charles, second duke, 1690–1757.
Grafton Flyford, Worcs.: rector of: *see* Evett, W.
Graham (Grahame), Mrs. Dorothy, born Howard, wife of Col. James Graham, iii. 529, n. 6.
as Dorothy Howard: on pleasure journey, iii. 529; E as trustee for, iv. 67, 70–1 & n., 105–6, 106; attends assize at Northampton, 1675, iv. 67–71 & nn.; courted by Graham, iv. 69; married, iv. 88, n. 6; social, iv. 11, 12–13, 34–5, 50, 67.
as Mrs. Graham: at wedding of Sir G. Sylvius, iv. 123; house and family of, at Bagshot, iv. 467–8 & n., 480–1, 558; social, iv. 88, 134–5.
Graham (Ghrame, Grahame), Col. James, iv. 69, n. 2; courts and marries Dorothy Howard, iv. 69, 88, n. 6; commission for, in army, iv. 95, n. 4; as Master of the Buckhounds, &c., iv. 558; apartment of, in St. James's Palace, iv. 123 & n. 5; as keeper of Bagshot Park: house of, iv. 467–8 & n., 480, 558; as Jacobite: search, &c., for, 1691, 1692, v. 42 & n. 5, 100, n. 1; ~ imprisoned, 1696, v. 235 & n. 2; children of, iv. 468; social, iv. 95, 97, 123; geneal., iv. 548, n. 5.
Graham, James, marquis of Montrose: betrayed by marquis of Hamilton, iii. 50 & n. 3; execution of, iii. 40 & n. 1.
Graham, John, of Claverhouse, viscount of Dundee: killed, iv. 647 & n. 3.
Graham, Mrs. Mary, wife of Dr. William Graham: geneal., v. 257, n. 1; *add.*
Graham, Reynold: commissioner for London streets, iii. 319, n. 1.
Graham, Sir Richard, bt.; created Viscount Preston (Scotland) 1681; Viscount Preston in Amoundernesse (Jacobite creation) 1689, iv. 548, n. 5; appointed secretary of state, iv. 603 & n. 2; Jacobite peerage of, v. 41, n. 4; imprisoned in Tower, 1689, iv. 640 & n. 4; captured and imprisoned, 1691, v. 41, 42, n. 2; tried, v. 41 & n. 4, 42 & n. 1; confessions of, v. 52–3 & n.; pardoned and released, v. 57 & n. 2; social, iv. 548, 603 *bis.*
Graham (Grahame), William, D.D.; dean of Carlisle 1686; of Wells 1704, v. 257, n. 1, 560, n. 5; recommended for bishopric of Carlisle, 1696, v. 257; sermons by, v. 560, 586; social, v. 221 & n. 4(?).
Gramont, Philibert, comte de: social, iii. 576 & n. 1.
Grand Cairo: *see* Cairo.
Grand Camée de la France, ii. 99 & n. 2 (i. 65).
Grande Chartreuse, ii. 141, n. 3.
Grand St. Bernard: *see* St. Bernard.
Grant, John; D.D. 1709: sermon by (?), v. 249 & n. 4.
Grantham, Lincs.: notice, iii. 132–3 & nn.
Grantham: Dean of: error for Dr. W. Graham (?), v. 221 & n. 4.
Granville: *see also* Grenville.
Granville (Greenevill), Mrs. Anne, wife of Bernard Granville: social, iv. 11 & nn. 2, 3.
Granville (Greenevill, Grinvill), Bernard, iv. 11, n. 2; at Apps Court, iv. 24 & n. 4; social, iv. 11, 32.

Granville, Charles; styled Lord Lansdown 1661–1701; second earl of Bath 1701, iv. 400–1 & n.; visits Foubert's academy, iv. 400; death of, &c., v. 475–6 & n.
Granville, Denis, D.D., dean of Durham: on frequent communion, i. *30*, n. 1.
Granville, George, Lord Lansdowne: geneal., iv. 11, n. 2.
Granville, John; Baron Granville of Potheridge 1703: geneal., iv. 306, n. 1.
Granville of Potheridge: Baron, 1703–7: *see* Granville, John.
Granville: Lord, 1689–1701: title conferred on Charles Granville, Lord Lansdowne, later second earl of Bath, iv. 400, n. 7 *ad fin*.
Gravelines: frontier near, ii. 84, n. 1.
Gravesend, Kent: notice, 1641, ii. 29–30 & n. (i. 22).
E at: in transit, 1641–63, ii. 29–30 (i. 22, 23), 76 (i. 50), 558–9; iii. 13, 15, 56, 358, 359; as commissioner for Sick and Wounded: 1665–7, iii. 395–6, 409, 422, 422–3, 489; ~ 1672, iii. 609, 623 *bis*, 624; journey towards, 1678, iv. 127.
yacht-race to, iii. 297; mayor of, 1665, iii. 396; Dutch fleet near, 1667, iii. 484, n. 1; Albemarle at, iii. 484, n. 3; naval engagement near, iii. 489 & n. 1; Sick and Wounded at: mismanagement of, iv. 132 & n. 7; troops land at, 1685, iv. 458, n. 1; James II goes to, 1688, iv. 611; William III at (transit), v. 136, 177 & n. 5.
block-house, ii. 30 & n. 1 (i. 22); ~ and its governor, iii. 396 & n. 1; fort: governor of, 1665, iii. 422–3 & n.; route through, ii. 82, n. 4.
Gravina: Dukes of (Orsini): palace of, at Naples, ii. 330 & n. 2.
Grays-in: *see* Gravesend.
Great Bookham, Surrey: Slyfield mill in: Sir J. Fenwick said to have been arrested near (error), v. 245, n. 4.
Great Casterton with Pickworth, Rutland: Rev. R. Holden and: as rector, iv. 4, n. 5; ~ visits, iv. 179 & n. 4; ~ resigns living, iv. 522 & n. 2.
Great Durnford (Darneford Magna), Wilts.: E. Hungerford's farm at, iii. 115 & n. 3.
Great Ellingham, Norfolk: rector of: *see* Clagett, N.
Great Faringdon, Berks.: *see* Faringdon.
Great Level of the Fens: draining of, iii. 135, n. 3.
Great Malvern (Maubern), Worcs.: notice, iii. 118–19 & nn.
Greatorex (Greatorix), Ralph: fire-engine of, iii. 173 & n. 1.
Great Rebellion, 1640–60 [*see also* Civil Wars; Commonwealth and Protectorate]: *Sovereign of the Seas*, &c., as cause of, ii. 30 & n. 2 (i. 22–3); v. 230 & n. 5; troubles fomented by friars disguised as puritans, iii. 157, n. 2; *see also* v. 13, n. 1; initial disturbances, ii. 24–5 & nn. (i. 18), 29 & n. 2 (i. 22); v. 263; J. Diodati deplores, ii. 521; Anglican clergy during [*see also* Church of England: chronological series], iv. 394, 634; punishment for (?), v. 152 & n. 1.
Great Tangley, near Guildford, Surrey: E at, ii. 28, n. 5 *ad fin*.
Great Warley (Warley Magna), Essex: manor: bought by E, ii. 554 *bis* & n. 1; courts, ii. 557; iii. 65 & n. 4, 84, 91, 93, 150; ~ alluded to, iv. 70; other business, iii. 146; manager, iii. 84, n. 4; woods, iii. 89; E sells, iii. 158, 159 & n. 2.
Grebner, Paulus: prophetic MS. by, iii. 137 & n. 2.
Greece: Ancient: history, &c.: study of, iv. 617, 618; monarchy of (Macedonia): duration of, ii. 431, n. 3; Seven Sages of: in sermon, v. 49.
Greece: Modern: Venetian conquests in, ii. 431; earthquake in, 1688, iv. 598; architecture of: *see* Architecture: styles; columns, &c., from, ii. 264, n. 3, 439 & n. 5, 445; inscriptions from: Arundel's collection, iii. 495–6 & n., &c.; sculptures in, iv. 213; Dr. I. Basire in, iii. 303, n. 3; Charles II's consul in, 1649–50, iii. 384, n. 2; Sir G. Wheeler in, iv. 358 & n. 1, 528.
Greek (Orthodox) Church: bishops of, and Dr. I. Basire, iii. 342 & n. 5; views of, on Procession of

Greek Church (*cont.*)
Holy Ghost: discussed, ii. 460 & n. 2; ~ in sermon, iii. 193; has its own church at Venice, &c., ii. 460; rite: use of, in church at Rome, ii. 291, n. 6; benediction in, ii. 399; *see also* Eastern Churches.
Greekelade: *see* Cricklade.
Greek language: in England: scholars, &c., i. 14; ii. 563; iii. 304, 359, 443; iv. 172, 213(?), 216, 302, 618; v. 82; ~ studies of little Richard Evelyn and John Evelyn, jnr., iii. 207, 208, 474; ~ school examinations, &c., iii. 287; v. 79; ~ used in sermons, iii. 186; iv. 375; in Italy: present state of studies, iii. 156.
Greek language: modern: knowledge of, iv. 213(?).
Greeks:
ancient: build Cuma, ii. 347 & n. 2; philosophers: at Cricklade, iii. 117, n. 3; ~ deride St. Paul, &c. (in sermon), v. 75–6; sculptors: works by, ii. 309.
modern: sailors, iii. 52; in England, iii. 161; ~ N. Conopius, ii. 18 (i. 14); ~ Signora Lucretia, ii. 556; at Venice, ii. 449.
Greenbury (Greeneborow), Richard: painting by, iii. 386 & n. 3.
Greene, Anne: revival of, after hanging, iv. 57 & n. 1.
Greenevill, Bernard: *see* Granville.
Greenland: Greenland whale, iv. 146 & n. 3; error for Finland, iii. 601 & n. 2.
Greenwich (Greenewich, &c.), Kent:
— general and miscellaneous: Kentish insurgents at, 1648, ii. 541, n. 4; yacht-race at, iii. 297; fire at, 1662, iii. 316, n. 4; Henrietta Maria at, 1662, iii. 328 & n. 1; Charles II at: 1665, 1667, iii. 414, n. 7, 483; plague at, 1665, 1666, iii. 417, n. 4, 435, n. 1; prince of Neuburg at, iv. 65, n. 4; Commission of Sewers at: E sworn a member of, 1685, iv. 490–1; French refugees at, 1689, iv. 640; storms: damage by, at, iii. 71; iv. 644 & n. 3(?); lemur at, iii. 194–5; whales at, 1658, 1699, iii. 214–15 & nn.; v. 318–19 & n.
— places, &c.:
— — Billingsgate, iii. 180, n. 4.
Greenwich, Kent (*cont.*)
— — College: *see* Trinity Hospital *below*.
— — Combe, v. 211, n. 3.
— — Croome's Hill, iv. 349, n. 1; Dr. Mason's house in: view from, iii. 76 & n. 2.
— — Ferry (Potter's Ferry), iii. 180 & n. 4, 538.
— — French protestant church, i. *32*; iv. 548 & n. 1; minister of, 1687–93: *see* Severin, J.; services: in St. Alphege's church, iv. 548; in the older Ruvigny's chapel in Queen's House, iv. 565, 568, 592, 597, 598, 607; in the younger Ruvigny's lodgings, v. 23–4; place not stated, iv. 552, 557, 573, 597, 598, 615, 650; v. 36.
— — French school, iv. 653 & n. 2; v. 79 & n. 3(?).
— — gardens: anchorsmiths', &c., v. 348.
— — Green Coat School: founder of, iii. 270, n. 3.
— — heath: air on, v. 456.
— — Italian glass-house, iv. 13 & n. 2.
— — National Maritime Museum, ii. 543, n. 2.
— — Norfolk College: *see* Trinity Hospital *below*.
— — Oldcourt Manor: granted to A. Cowley, iii. 355, n. 4.
— — Palace, ii. 543, n. 2; iii. 170, n. 3; visit to (?), ii. 543; rebuilding of: Charles II's project for, iii. 300–1 & n., 313; slaughter-house for, iii. 352 & n. 2; Commissioners of the Navy at, 1665, iii. 418 & n. 2; for its later use see Greenwich Hospital; King's House: used as hospital, 1692, v. 203, n. 1; ~ proposed adaptation of, v. 211 & n. 4; Queen's House, ii. 543, n. 2; visit to, ii. 543; occupied by B. Whitelocke, 1652 (?), iii. 64 & n. 2; in Charles II's rebuilding project, iii. 300–1 & n.; mentioned (?), iii. 483 & n. 3; Sir J. Chardin resident in, iv. 520, n. 2, 561; first Marquis de Ruvigny resident in: *see* Ruvigny; French protestant services at: *see* French protestant church *above*.
— — Park: planting of, iii. 270, n. 3,

Greenwich, Kent (*cont.*)
370 & n. 5; view of London from, iii. 76, n. 3; grenades tested in, iii. 483 & n. 3; high stewards of, iii. 64, n. 2; Castle Hill, Duke Humphrey's Tower, and the house in, iii. 483 & n. 3; observatory in: *see* Royal Observatory *below*.
— — Potter's Ferry, iii. 180 & n. 4, 538.
— — Queen's House: *see* Palace *above*.
— — Royal Hospital: *see* Greenwich Hospital.
— — Royal Naval College, ii. 543, n. 2.
— — Royal Observatory: site of, iii. 483, n. 3; founded, &c., iv. 98 & n. 3; visits to, iv. 205 & n. 4, 383; mentioned, iv. 333.
— — St. Alphege's church: used by French protestant (Conformist) church, iv. 548; French services in: *see* French protestant church *above*; little Richard Evelyn attends service at, iii. 208 & n. 2; burials at, ii. 538, n. 1; iii. 181, n. 6; services: catechism expounded, &c., iii. 361, 378; ~ christening, iv. 561; ~ communion, iii. 228 & n. 2 (1659); iv. 8, 10–11; ~ confirmation (with sermon), v. 70–1; ~ funeral sermon, iv. 507; ~ prayers (Sunday services), iii. 445, 467; ~ sermons, iii. 75 *bis*, 88, 145, 152, 153, 195, 366, 418–22 *passim*, 425, 428 *bis*, 444, 463 *bis*, 467, 474, 508, 510, 512, 546, 551, 582, 587, 597 *bis*, 604, 612, 613, 616, 621; iv. 8, 10–11, 16, 18, 56, 64, 67, 73, 81, 89, 96, 108 *bis*, 121, 345, 349, 532, 548; v. 34, 71, 101; vicars: *see* Plume T. (1658–1704); Turner, John, D.D. (1704–20); curate(s): sermons by, at Deptford [the curates' sermons explicitly delivered at Greenwich are included in the sermons listed above; some in the following references may have been delivered at Greenwich rather than Deptford], iv. 34, 37, 46, 280, 291, 293, 295, 334, 347, 376, 382, 388, 450, 489, 495, 496, 511, 520, 526, 562, 642, 651, 654; v. 32.

Greenwich, Kent (*cont.*)
— — Thames at: and site of Palace, iii. 300–1 & n.
— — Trinity Hospital (the College), ii. 76 & n. 4 (i. 50).
— — Westcombe: owners of, ii. 542, n. 2; iii. 348, n. 6.
— E at Greenwich: visits not covered by references above, iii. 87, 166, 192, 366; stays at, &c., v. 346–51, 456 *bis*.
— residents at and visitors to: Sir T. Biddulph, iii. 348, n. 6; Sir W. Boreman, iii. 270, n. 3; Lord Brouncker, 1665, iii. 419, n. 1; Dr. S. Cade, v. 190, n. 5; Sir J. Chardin, iv. 520 & n. 2, 561; — Cook, iv. 507; M. Cottle, iii. 421, n. 2; Mrs. Evelyn, 1701, v. 456, 463; *see also* v. 461; Rebecca Fountaine, later Mrs. (Lady) Paravicini, iii. 508, n. 2; William Glanville, sen., v. 71; ~ dies at, &c., v. 497 & n. 3; Sir W. Hooker, iv. 349, n. 1; James, duke of York: house of, at (?), iii. 515, n. 1; Sir M. Lambarde, ii. 542, n. 2; Jerome Laniere, iii. 74, n. 5, 79–80; Sir T. Lynch, iii. 574; Dr. R. Mason, iii. 76 & n. 2; Elizabeth Newton, Lady Newton, iii. 87 & n. 1; E. Peto, iii. 87 & n. 2; William Prettyman: married at, iii. 77 & n. 3; Captain R. Sanderson, v. 211, n. 3; Sandwich, 1665, iii. 419; J. Strickland, v. 600; Tuke, George: married at, iii. 181 & n. 6; Sir J. Vaughan, 1667, iii. 492, 497; B. Wells, physician, iii. 209, n. 2; B. Whitelocke, iii. 64 & n. 2; *see also* Flamsteed, J.; Ruvigny, Henri de Massue, first marquis de; Ruvigny, Henri de Massue, second marquis de, earl of Galway; Ruvigny, Marie de Massue, marquise de.

Greenwich Hospital:
foundation of: proposed, v. 203 & n. 1; Queen Mary's project for (?), v. 205 & n. 4.
commissions: Mar. 1695, v. 209, n. 8; ~ read, v. 210; ~ insufficient, v. 212; Sept. 1695: issued, &c., v. 219 & n. 2; 1703: read, &c., v. 543–4 & n.; 1704:

Greenwich Hospital (*cont.*)
commissioners, &c., qualify, v. 568 & n. 2.
commissioners: meet, v. 209–14 *passim*, 219, 220, 240(?); chairman of: *see* Bridgeman, W. (v. 325); secretary of: *see* Vanbrugh, W. (v. 211–12 & n.); treasurers: E, 1695–1703: appointed, i. *34*; v. 203, 209, n. 8; ~ qualifies for, v. 212 & n. 2; ~ resigns, i. *36*; v. 544; William Draper, 1703–15: appointed, v. 544 & n. 1; ~ clerk of: *see* Strickland, J. (v. 98, n. 3).
committees: Directors, v. 544, n. 1, 568; Fabric Committee: meets, v. 236, n. 2, 243(?), 244 & n. 2(?), 334, n. 1; ~ at Greenwich, v. 249 & n. 1(?), 326 & n. 2; ~ mentioned (?), v. 268 & n. 3; Grand Committee, v. 236, n. 2; ~ meets, v. 236, 240(?); ~ attends laying of foundation-stone, v. 249 & n. 1; Site Committee: appointed, v. 210 & n. 9; ~ visits Greenwich and reports, v. 211 & nn. 1, 4.
buildings [for general notices of Greenwich Palace before 1695 *see* Greenwich]: King Charles's block: built, iii. 300, n. 4 *ad fin.*; ~ used for sick and wounded after La Hogue, v. 203, n. 1; Greenwich Palace: examined for use as hospital, &c., v. 210 & n. 9, 211 & nn. 1, 4; officers for, &c.: appointed, v. 243; to be started, &c., v. 244 & n. 2; foundation-stone laid, v. 249 & n. 1; foundations of hall, &c., v. 290–1 & n.; Fabric Committee visits, v. 326 & n. 2; model, &c., shown to William III, v. 399 & n. 2; E visits, v. 334 & n. 1, 346, 450; viewed by committee of House of Commons, 1702, v. 498 & n. 4, 499 & n. 1; accounts for, submitted to: House of Commons, 1701, v. 447 & n. 1; ~ Commons' committee, 1702, v. 492 & n. 4, 499 & n. 1; ~ Lord High Admiral, v. 496; expenditure on, 1696–1703, v. 544 & n. 1; occupation of: begins, 1705, v. 600 & n. 5.
funds for: E ordered to prepare subscription-book, v. 211 & n. 5; rolls for subscribers' names, v. 212; subscriptions received, v. 213 & n. 4, 249 & n. 3; lottery for, 1699, v. 325 & n. 6.
miscellaneous: called a college, v. 447 & n. 1; mentioned, v. 541, n. 1.
Gregory I, St., pope: relics of, ii. 251.
Gregory VII, pope: Countess Matilda's gift to, ii. 208 & n. 4.
Gregory IX, pope, ii. 374, n. 3.
Gregory X, pope: crosses the Simplon, ii. 508, n. 5.
Gregory XI, pope: tomb of, ii. 248 & n. 4.
Gregory XIII, pope: establishes sermons for Jews in Rome, ii. 291, n. 8; buildings, &c., of, ii. 209 & n. 1, 237, 299, n. 5, 366, n. 10 *ad fin.*, 370, n. 6; tomb of, ii. 260 & n. 5; statues of, ii. 221 & n. 2, 422, n. 3.
Gregory XV, pope: sings Te Deum for battle of the White Hill, ii. 239 & n. 11; bust of, ii. 234, n. 2.
Gregory, Francis, D.D., iv. 92, n. 3; sermons by, iv. 92–3; v. 139(?).
Grelot, G. J.: draws Persian monuments for Chardin, iv. 213 & n. 2, 369 & n. 1.
Grenville: *see also* Granville.
Grenville, Sir Bevil: geneal., iv. 9, n. 4, 95, n. 3.
Grenville, Bridget: *see* Higgons, Bridget, Lady Higgons.
Grenville, Jane: *see* Leveson-Gower, Jane, Lady Leveson-Gower.
Grenville, Jane, countess of Bath, wife of John Grenville, first earl: geneal., v. 237, n. 1.
Grenville, Joanna: *see* Thornhill, Mrs. J.
Grenville, John; first earl of Bath 1661, iv. 95, n. 3; created earl, iii. 277; present at Charles II's reception into Roman Catholic church, iv. 408; superseded as groom of the stole, iv. 417 & n. 2; as the 'Prince Elector': influence of, on Cornish elections, 1685, iv. 444 & n. 3; declares for William of Orange at Plymouth, iv. 608–9 & n.; claims Albemarle inheritance, v. 167 & n. 1, 246 & n. 5, 288 & n. 6, 475; dies, v. 475 & n. 3; as godfather, iv. 95, 561; social: parties, iv. 125, 191, 296, 318; geneal., iv. 9 & n. 4, 11 & n. 2, 32,

Grenville, John (*cont.*)
400–1 & n., 528 & n. 3; v. 237, n. 1; chaplain of: sermon by, iv. 309.
Gresham, Sir Thomas, ii. 46, n. 2; Royal Exchange built by, ii. 46 & n. 2 (i. 33); house of (Gresham College), iii. 266, n. 6 *ad fin.*; will of: inquiry concerning, iii. 330 & n. 4, 335; statue of, iii. 460 & n. 8.
Gretton, Northants.: Kirby Hall in, iii. 133–4 & n.
Greuter: *see* Gruter, J.
Greville, Catherine, Baroness Brooke, wife of Robert Greville, second baron, iii. 96, n. 1; garden of, at Hackney, iii. 96 & n. 1, 169.
Greville, Elizabeth: *see* North, Elizabeth, Baroness Guilford.
Greville, Francis, third Baron Brooke: owner of Warwick Castle, iii. 120 & n. 2.
Greville, Sir Fulke, first Baron Brooke: as owner of Warwick Castle, iii. 119, n. 6 *ad fin.*
Greville, Fulke, fifth Baron Brooke, v. 528, n. 4; geneal., v. 366, n. 1; chaplain of: sermon by, v. 528.
Greville, Robert, second Baron Brooke: geneal., iii. 96, n. 1.
Grew, Nehemiah, M.D., iv. 124, n. 9; *add.*; paper by, on London medicinal waters, iv. 170 & n. 6; social, iv. 124.
Grey family, earls of Kent: connexion of, with Evelyn family, i. 3 & n. 3.
Grey, Amabella, countess of Kent, wife of Henry Grey, tenth earl, i. 3, n. 3; geneal., *ib.*; social (?), iii. 541 & n. 2.
Grey, Lady Anabel: dies, v. 521 & n. 7.
Grey, Anthony; eleventh earl of Kent 1651, iii. 372, n. 1; social, iii. 372; v. 469 *bis*; dies, v. 518 & n. 3, 521 & n. 7; geneal., iii. 521 & n. 7; chaplain(s) of: sermons by, iv. 91; v. 403–4, 438.
Grey, Forde; third Baron Grey of Warke 1675; earl of Tankerville 1695, iv. 323, n. 2; as Lord Grey: in Rye House Plot, iv. 322, n. 1, 323 & nn. 1, 2; ~ at Sedgemoor, &c., iv. 451–2 & n.; ~ pardoned, &c., iv. 490 & n. 7; ~ lands of, granted to Rochester, iv. 533 & n. 2; as Tankerville: appointed Lord Privy Seal, v. 432, n. 2; ~ chaplain of: *see* Knaggs, Rev. T.
Grey, Henry, tenth earl of Kent: geneal., i. 3, n. 3.
Grey, Mary, countess of Kent, wife of Anthony Grey, eleventh earl; Baroness Lucas of Crudwell *suo jure*, iii. 372, n. 1; social, iii. 372, 541 & n. 2(?); dies, v. 521 & n. 7.
Grey, Thomas, son of Lord Grey: as member of Council for Foreign Plantations, iii. 578 & n. 7.
Grey, William, first Baron Grey of Warke: son of, iii. 578 & n. 7.
Grey of Warke: Barons: *see* Grey, William, first baron; Grey, Forde, third baron 1675–95, later earl of Tankerville.
Gribelin, S.: engraving by, v. 399, n. 2.
Griffin, Edward; first Baron Griffin 1688, v. 142, n. 3; as Lord Griffith: services in chapel of, v. 142–3 & nn.
Griffin: first Baron, 1688–1710: *see* Griffin, Edward.
Griffith, Captain —: in France, 1652, iii. 55 & n. 2.
Griffith, Dr. —: sermon by, iii. 214 & n. 2.
Griffith, Prince: in Paris, 1650, iii. 7.
Griffith, Rev. —: sermons by, at Wotton, v. 261, 262.
Griffith, George, D.D.; bishop of St. Asaph 1660: sermon by (?), iii. 214 & n. 2.
Griffith, Captain John, iii. 55, n. 2.
Griffith, Sir John: at Gravesend, 1665, iii. 422–3 & n.
Griffith, Matthew, D.D.: sermon by (?), iii. 214 & n. 2.
Griffon: claw of a, ii. 89 & n. 3 (i. 60).
Grillo, Monte, ii. 347, n. 3.
Grimaldi family, of Genoa: rulers of Monaco, ii. 168–9 & n. (i. 106).
Grindal, Edward, archbishop of Canterbury: tomb of, v. 426 & n. 5.
Grinvill, Bernard: *see* Granville.
Grisnez, Cape: sea-fight near, 1653, iii. 81 & n. 9.
Grisons, district: political, ii. 518, n. 1.
Groombridge, Kent: notices, iii. 72 & nn. 1–3; iv. 40 & nn. 1–3; chapel at: sermons in, iii. 72; iv. 40; mentioned, ii. 548, n. 1.
Groot, C. C. de (?), ii. 476 & n. 5.
Groot, Diederik de (?), ii. 476 & n. 5.

Gross, Hans (G. Alto): guide in Rome, ii. 214, n. 2.
Grossi, G. F., called Siface (Cifeccio, &c.), *castrato*, iv. 537, n. 5; character, iv. 547; sings, iv. 537, 547 & n. 1.
Grossolles, François de, marquis de Flamarens: social, iv. 393 & n. 3.
Grosswardein (Great Waradine): taken by Imperialists, 1692, v. 101 & n. 3.
Grosvenor, Mary, Lady Grosvenor, wife of Sir Thomas, iv. 86, n. 3; as Mary Davies: marriage project for, *ib.*; claims against, of Edward Fenwick, v. 528 & n. 8.
Grosvenor, Sir Thomas, third bt.: house of, in Cheshire: architect of, iii. 554, n. 3; geneal., iv. 86, n. 3.
Grotius, Hugo (H. de Groot), ii. 39, n. 2; escape of, from Loevestein, ii. 39 & n. 2 (i. 29); wife of: *see* Reigersberch, M. van; geneal., ii. 476 & n. 5.
Grotta del Cane, Lago di Agnano, ii. 339–40 & nn.
Grottoes: described: Brussels: Cour, ii. 71–2 (i. 47); Cliveden, iv. 177; Enstone: Bushell's Wells, iii. 382 & n. 6; Florence: Pitti palace, ii. 186–7 & n. (i. 117); Pratolino, ii. 418; Rome: Quirinal, ii. 287; ~ Villa Borghese, ii. 251–2 & n.; Rueil, ii. 110 (i. 71); St.-Cloud, ii. 108 (i. 69); St. Germain-en-Laye, ii. 111 & n. 2 (i. 71–2); Tivoli: Villa d'Este, ii. 396.
  not described, ii. 41 (i. 30), 120, 130 (i. 83), 175 (i. 111), 238, 392, 393, 395, 396; iii. 10.
Grove, The, near Watford, Herts.: part of Clarendon collection of portraits at, iii. 520, n. 3.
Grove, Robert, D.D.; bishop of Chichester 1691, iv. 628, n. 1; sermons by, iv. 628(?); v. 14.
Grünheide, Andreas: operation on, &c., ii. 53–4 & n. (i. 37); alluded to, iii. 306.
Gruter (Greuter), Janus, librarian, ii. 302 & n. 4.
Gualdo, Cavaliere Francesco, ii. 314, n. 1; museum of, ii. 314–15 & nn.; gift of, ii. 245.
Guarini, Battista, the poet: portrait of, ii. 365 & n. 1.
Guasconi, Bernardino: *see* Gascoigne, Sir Bernard.
Gudius, M., ii. 462, n. 7.
Guèbres (*gabrs*) (Igniculi), iv. 214 & n. 2.
Guercino, G. F. Barbieri called, painter: St. William assuming the monastic habit, by, ii. 424 & n. 2; mentioned, ii. 420, n. 5.
Guernsey: governor of, 1670–1706: *see* Hatton, Christopher, first Viscount Hatton; deputy-governor of, 1665–70: *see* Atkins, Sir J.
Guernsey (Gernsey): Baron of, 1703–14: *see* Finch, Heneage, later earl of Aylesford.
Guerrino dal Borgo San Sepolcro, architect, ii. 202, n. 8 *ad fin.*
Guglielmo, Maestro, architect at Pisa, ii. 180, n. 3.
Guicciardini, Francesco: supposed portrait of, iv. 102 & n. 2.
Guido: *see* Reni, Guido.
Guildenlow, Lord: *see* Gyldenløve, U. F.
Guildford (Gilford, &c.), Surrey: E visits, &c., ii. 25 (i. 18), 79 (i. 52), 557; iii. 88; iv. 474; distance of Wotton from, ii. 4 & n. 2 (i. 5–6).
  Free School at, v. 358, n. 2, 536, n. 3; George Evelyn educated at, v. 358; master (Rev. S. Piggott) and usher of, v. 536, n. 3; master of: sermons by, v. 545, 546–7, 548; usher(s) of: sermons by, v. 536, 580, 582.
  Friery, The, iv. 35, n. 7; Holy Trinity church: Archbishop Abbot's tomb in, iii. 88 & n. 5; Red Lion inn, iii. 88 & n. 3; river of (Wey), iv. 255 & n. 6; Trinity Hospital, iii. 88 & n. 4.
Guildford: Countess of, 1660–7: *see* Boyle, Elizabeth, formerly Viscountess Boyle of Kinalmeaky.
Guildford: Earl of, 1674–82: *see* Maitland, John, duke of Lauderdale.
Guilford: Barons, &c., of: *see* North, Sir Francis, first baron, 1683–5; North, Francis, second baron, 1685–1729; North, Elizabeth, his baroness.
Guillelmus, architect at Pisa, ii. 180 n. 3.
Guillotine (frame): used for executions, ii. 401 & n. 2, 459.
Guinea (Ginny, Guiny): converts to Christianity in: in sermon, v. 328; Gambo in, v. 174 & n. 5.

Guinea Company (Africa Company): shares in: fall in price of, 1694, v. 174 & n. 6.
Guise, Duke of, the murderer of Coligny: in painting, ii. 297.
Guise, Charles de Lorraine, duke of: houses of, at Aix and Marseilles, ii. 163 & n. 4 (i. 103), 166 (i. 105).
Guise, Louis-Joseph de Lorraine, duke of: visits England, iii. 575 & n. 2.
Guldeford, Edward: geneal., iii. 373, n. 1.
Guldeford, Mary: *see* Tuke, Mary, Lady Tuke.
Gulson, Joseph, D.D.; dean of Chichester 1663, iii. 400, n. 2; sermons by, iii. 400, 432.
Gundamar (Gundimor): *see* Gondomar.
Gunfleet, the, off Essex coast: Dutch ships at, 1665, iii. 425, n. 1.
Gunman, Captain Christopher, R.N., iv. 80, n. 1, 432 & n. 1; yacht commanded by, iv. 80 & n. 1; buried, &c., iv. 432.
Gunning, Peter; D.D. 1660; bishop of Chichester 1670; of Ely 1675, iii. 190, n. 3, 446, n. 4; excellence of, as preacher, &c., iv. 3–4.
life to 1660: officiates at Exeter House chapel, 1657–60, iii. 95, n. 5; dependant of Lady Hatton, &c., iii. 204, n. 1; taken in custody, Christmas 1657, iii. 203–4 & n.; sermons, fast-sermons, and celebrations of Communion, by, iii. 190 *bis*, 193, 194, 202, 203, 211, 225, 226, 230, 233–48 *passim*; social, iii. 235, 237.
later life: as bishop of Chichester: prepares John Evelyn, jnr., for Communion, iv. 6; translation of, to Ely, iv. 61 & n. 3; *Lex Talionis* attributed to, iv. 83, n. 5; on Parliamentary Test Act, iv. 159 & n. 4; sermons by: on conversion of Britain, iii. 333 & n. 4; ~ against *The Naked Truth*, iv. 83 & n. 5; ~ other, iii. 307, 446; iv. 3, 33, 165; dies, iv. 394 & n. 2; chaplain of: sermon by, iv. 359.
Gunpowder and Salt-petre: history of, by T. Henshaw, iii. 294 & n. 3.
gunpowder: experiments with, iii. 473, 474; iv. 83; magazine of, at Tower of London, iii. 458 & n. 4; manufacture of: Evelyn family's concern in, i. *1*, *3* & n. 1, 2–3 & n., 52 & n. 2; iii. 219; ~ at Tivoli, ii. 397 & n. 3; used to fight Great Fire of London, iii. 455 & n. 2, 456; in comparison, iii. 293.
salt-petre: supply of: commission for, 1666, i. *19*; iii. 443–6 & nn. *passim*; at Venice, ii. 458.
Gunpowder Plot [for commemorations *see* Church of England: worship: feasts and fasts]: Roman Catholics deny existence of, iv. 156–7 & n.; mentioned, iv. 204.
Gunson: *see* Gonson.
Gustavus Adolphus, king of Sweden: at Geneva (?), ii. 521 & n. 4; spoils of, from Germany, iv. 221; victories of: in interpretation of prophecy, iv. 636.
Gutenberg (Gottenberg), Johann: invention of printing attributed to, ii. 54 & n. 2 (i. 37).
Guy of Warwick: relics of, iii. 120 & n. 3, 121 & n. 7; chapel, &c., of, at Guy's Cliff, iii. 120–1 & nn.
Guy's Cliff, near Warwick: notice, iii. 120–1 & nn.
Gwinne, Matthew: on use of gold in medicine, iii. 86, n. 6.
Gwyn, Nell *or* Eleanor (Mrs. Nellie), iii. 573, n. 4; mother of, iv. 392 & n. 2; as mistress of Charles Sackville, Lord Buckhurst, later earl of Dorset: alluded to (?), iii. 466 & n. 4; and Charles II: introduction of, to, iii. 230, n. 3; ~ alluded to (?), iii. 466 & n. 5; ~ visited by, iii. 573 & n. 4; ~ death-bed concern for, of, iv. 409 & n. 2; mother of Charles Beauclerk, duke of St. Albans, iv. 374, 392; at supper-party, iv. 268; reported conversion of, to Roman Catholicism, iv. 497 & n. 1.
Gyldenløve (Guildenlow), Ulrik Frederik, iii. 270 & n. 2, 537 & n. 5; as Danish ambassador in England, iii. 270 (error), 537.

Haak (Hake), Theodore: experiment by, with magnet, iv. 315 & n. 3.
Haarlem (Harlaem, &c.): in E's journeys, 1641, ii. 42 (i. 31), 49 (i. 35); notice, ii. 50–1 & nn. (i.

Haarlem (*cont.*)
35–6), 54 & n. 2 (i. 37); church of St. Bavon at, ii. 50–1 & nn. (i. 35–6); ~ peepshow representing, iii. 165 & n. 6; printing invented at, &c., ii. 51 (i. 36), 54 & n. 2 (i. 37).
Hacker, Col. Francis, regicide: executed, iii. 259 & n. 2.
Hacket (Haccket), John, D.D.; bishop of Lichfield 1661: sermon by, iii. 221 & n. 1.
Haddock, Sir Richard: wins prize in lottery, v. 158 & n. 3.
Hadrian, Roman emperor: Pantheon rebuilt by, ii. 371, n. 2; temple of, at Rome, ii. 370 & n. 5; tomb of: objects from, ii. 305 & n. 3; villa of, near Tivoli, ii. 397 & n. 4; statue of, ii. 223 & n. 12; modern head of, ii. 223, n. 9.
Hadrian IV, pope: tomb of, ii. 289 & n. 7.
Hagar (in text as Sarah, in error): in sermon, iii. 525 & n. 4.
Hague, The: E visits, 1641, ii. 33–4 (i. 25–7), 41 & nn. 4, 5 (i. 30–1), 41 (i. 31), 55–6 (i. 38–9).
descriptive, &c.: 'the chief village in Europe', ii. 34 & n. 5 (i. 26–7); Binnenhof, ii. 41 & nn. 4, 5 (i. 30–1); ~ in comparison, ii. 70 & n. 3 (i. 46); Mauritshuis: painting in (1950), iii. 262, n. 6.
historical, &c.: Queen Elizabeth of Bohemia and her court at, ii. 33–4 & nn. (i. 25–6 & nn.); book by C. Wase published at, iii. 55, n. 1; I. Dorislaus killed at, ii. 556 & n. 5; William II of Orange dies at, iii. 23, n. 2; foreign ambassadors at: declaration circulated among, 1688, iv. 604 & n. 2; William III intends to visit, 1690–1, v. 39, n. 6; Archduke Charles at, 1703, v. 548, n. 2, 551, n. 2; Marlborough at, 1704, v. 555 & n. 2.
Haines *or* Heynes, Thomasine: *see* Evelyn, Thomasine, Lady Evelyn.
Haines *or* Heynes, William: geneal., iii. 174, n. 1.
Haiti: *see* Hispaniola.
Hake, —: *see* Haak, T.
Hale (Hales), Sir Matthew, judge: case before, iii. 565 & n. 4, 580 & n. 4.
Hales, —, iii. 370, n. 7.
Hales, Edward, of Chilston, iii. 174, n. 2; visits E at Deptford, iii. 174, 510; at Chilston, iii. 436, 468; geneal., iii. 370, n. 7; v. 218, n. 6; mentioned, iii. 155, n. 7.
Hales, Sir Edward, second bt., iii. 153, n. 6; and Elizabeth Carey (later Lady Mordaunt), iii. 155 & n. 7; social, iii. 153, 159; geneal., iii. 155, n. 7, 174, n. 2.
Hales, Sir Edward; third bt. *c.* 1683; earl of Tenterden (Jacobite creation) 1692, iv. 171, n. 6; as Mr. Hales: commissioner of the Admiralty, iv. 171 & n. 2; becomes a Roman Catholic, iv. 506, n. 4; appointed governor of Dover Castle, iv. 506 & n. 4; as Lieutenant of the Tower: treatment by, of the Seven Bishops, iv. 588 & n. 4; flies with James II, &c., iv. 611 & n. 6; geneal., iv. 510 & n. 3.
Hales, Edward, son of Sir Edward, third bt.: conversion of, to Roman Catholicism, iv. 510 & n. 3.
Hales, Mrs. Elizabeth, born Evelyn, wife of Edward Hales of Chilston, iii. 174, n. 2; social, iii. 174; iv. 552; geneal., iv. 552, n. 1; v. 218, n. 6, 340.
Hales, Frances: *see* Glanville, Mrs. F.
Halford, Sir William: geneal., iv. 461, n. 1.
Halifax, Yorks.: executions at, ii. 401, n. 2; Stansfield township in: property of Lewes Priory, ii. 3, n. 1.
Halifax: Earls and Marquises of, &c.: *see* Savile, Sir George, Viscount Halifax 1668–79, earl 1679–82, and first marquis 1682–95; Savile, William, second marquis, 1695–1700; Savile, Mary, his marchioness; *new creation*: *see* Montagu, Charles, Baron Halifax 1700–14, and first earl 1714–15.
Halkett, Lady Anne, the autobiographer: geneal., iii. 87, n. 1.
Hall, —, cousin of E or Mrs. Evelyn: funeral of, iii. 370 & n. 7.
Hall, —, 1686: *see* Hills, H.
Hall, Dr. —: *see* Hall, John.
Hall, Rev. —, son of Dr. Joseph Hall: sermon by, iii. 222 & n. 2; *see also* iv. 135, critical note.
Hall, Rev. —, 1687: *see* Hayley, W.
Hall, Anne: *see* Gardiner, Mrs. A.

Hall, George, D.D.; bishop of Chester 1662, iii. 222, n. 2.
Hall, John, D.D.; bishop of Bristol 1691, iii. 534, n. 2; sermons by, iii. 534(?); iv. 242(?); v. 228; mentioned, v. 256, n. 7.
Hall, Joseph, D.D.; bishop of Exeter 1627; of Norwich 1641, iii. 222, n. 2; grave of: desire of, regarding, iv. 304 & n. 5; geneal., iii. 222 & n. 2; iv. 135, critical note.
Hallaton, Leics.: rector of: *see* Cradocke, M.
Halley, Edmond, the astronomer, iv. 314, n. 2; magnetic demonstration by (as Mr. Baker, in error), iv. 314; paper by, on variations of the compass, v. 97 & n. 1.
Halstow, Kent: Darell property in, iii. 620, n. 5.
Halton, Timothy, D.D.; provost of Queen's College, Oxford 1677–1704, iv. 67, n. 1; sermon by (?; as Dr. Hamilton), iv. 67.
Haman: in sermon, v. 362.
Hamburg (Hambrow, &c.): besieged by Danes, 1686, iv. 524 & n. 3, 525 & n. 1; storm at, 1699, v. 311 & n. 2; sea-journey from, to England, iv. 398; *see also* Diplomatists.
Hamerton, Hunts.: Sir Richard Fanshawe at, iii. 123, n. 3.
Hamet Lucas, interpreter, &c., iv. 265 & n. 6.
Ham House, Petersham, Surrey: notice, 1678, iv. 143–4 & n.; James II required to reside at, 1688, iv. 611, n. 1.
Hamilton, Rev. —: sermons by, Paris, 1650–1: *see* Hamilton, James, bishop of Galloway.
Hamilton, Dr. — (T. Halton ?): sermon by, iv. 67 & n. 1.
Hamilton, Anne, duchess of Hamilton *suo jure*, wife of William Douglas, earl of Selkirk, created duke of Hamilton 1660, iii. 254, n. 2.
Hamilton, Anthony, author of *Mémoires de Grammont*: geneal., iv. 79, n. 3; v. 28, n. 5.
Hamilton, Elizabeth, countess of Orkney: *see* Villiers, Elizabeth.
Hamilton, Frances, Lady Hamilton, wife of Sir George: *see* Talbot, Frances, duchess of Tyrconnel, &c.
Hamilton, Lord George, earl of Orkney, v. 555, n. 4; chaplain(s) of: sermons by, v. 555, 557, 584, 620.
Hamilton, Sir George, d. 1676: death of, &c., iv. 79 & n. 3.
Hamilton, James, bishop of Galloway 1661, iii. 23, n. 5; sermons by (?), iii. 23, 24, 29.
Hamilton, James, third marquis and first duke of Hamilton, ii. 548, n. 2; accused of betraying Charles I, iii. 50 & n. 3; tried and executed, ii. 548 & n. 2, 552 & n. 1.
Hamilton, Sir John, bt.: social, iii. 94 & n. 2.
Hamilton, Richard, general: captured at Battle of the Boyne, &c., v. 28 & n. 5.
Hamilton: Dukes, &c., of: *see* Hamilton, James, third marquis, 1625–43, and first duke, 1643–9; Douglas, Anne, duchess *suo jure* 1651–1716; Douglas, William, (third) duke 1660–94; Douglas, James, fourth duke 1698–1712.
Hamilton: Countess of, 1677 (error): *see* Talbot, Frances, duchess of Tyrconnel, &c. (iv. 108 & n. 3).
Hammond, Henry, D.D.: Presbyterian attacks in speech, iii. 105 & n. 6.
Hampden, John, the opponent of Ship Money: geneal., iv. 227, n. 8, 322, n. 6.
Hampden (Hambden), John, jnr., iv. 322, n. 6; imprisoned in Tower for Rye-House Plot, &c., iv. 322 & nn. 6, 7; released, iv. 354 & n. 2; tried and fined, iv. 366 & n. 5; views of, on Monmouth's conduct, iv. 353, n. 5 *ad fin.*; character, v. 147.
Hampden (Hamden), Richard, iv. 227, n. 8; activities of, in parliament, iv. 227, 619 & n. 3; alluded to (?), iv. 635 & n. 3.
Hampshire: control of Sick and Wounded in, 1664, iii. 395, n. 1; woods in, iv. 474; receiver of, 1662–7: *see* Scawen, R.
Hampton, Middlesex: W. Blathwayt's house near, iv. 554.
Hampton Court:
— E at: 1647, ii. 537; 1662, iii. 320–5, 329–30; 1665, iii. 415 *bis*; 1666, iii. 428–9; 1679, iv. 177–8; 1681, iv. 248; 1687, iv. 553–5; 1689, iv. 644–5; unspecified visit, v. 182.

Hampton Court (*cont.*)
— general account of, 1662, iii. 322–5 & nn.; in comparison, ii. 116, 117 & n. 1 (i. 75, 76 & n. 1); William and Mary's alterations to, iv. 645 & n. 2.
— places, &c., in: canal, iii. 322, n. 5, 324; chapel, iii. 324; ~ services in, iii. 321, 415; iv. 641, n. 1; Clock Court: colonnade in, iii. 322, n. 5; council chamber, iv. 553; Fountain Court, iii. 322, n. 5; Gallery of Horns, iii. 323 & n. 4; gardens, iii. 322, n. 5, 324–5 & nn.; ~ William and Mary extend, iv. 645; Gatehouse, iii. 322, n. 5; Great Hall, iii. 324; Haunted Gallery, iii. 323, n. 4; King's Long Gallery, iii. 322, n. 5, 325, n. 1; Long Gallery, iii. 323, n. 2; Paradise, iii. 325 & n. 1; park: planted, &c., iii. 324 & n. 4; Prince's Gallery, iii. 323, n. 4; Privy Garden, iii. 324, n. 6; queen's bed-chamber, iii. 322; Tents: office of the, iii. 324 & n. 3; wardrobe, *ib.*; Water Gallery, iii. 322, n. 5.
— furniture, &c.: general, iii. 324 & n. 3; china, v. 147, n. 2; corner fireplace, iii. 554, n. 4; gondolas, iii. 322 & n. 2.
— historical: royal visits, &c.: Charles I, 1647, ii. 537; ~ portrait of, painted at, iii. 216, n. 5; Cromwell acquires, iii. 179, n. 3; Queen Catherine, 1662, iii. 320–2 & nn., 333; Charles II: 1662, iii. 322, 333; ~ 1665, iii. 415 & n. 1; ~ 1666, iii. 428–9 & nn.; ~ 1679, iv. 177–8; ~ 1681, iv. 248; James II, 1687, iv. 553–4; William and Mary, 1689, iv. 641, n. 1, 645, n. 1; William III, 1700, v. 419, n. 2, 430, n. 2; ~ 1701, v. 468, n. 2, 480, n. 2; ~ fatal accident to, near, v. 491, n. 2.
— — other persons at: Sir G. Carteret: apartment of, iii. 320; Mrs. Evelyn, *ib.*; Sir R. Fanshawe, iii. 329 & n. 6; Monmouth, iii. 559.
— works of art at, 1898, &c.: paintings, ii. 549, n. 5; iii. 75, n. 1, 96, n. 5, 166, n. 1, 262, nn. 6, 7, 263, n. 2, 323 n. 2, 375, n. 3; iv. 216, n. 5; tapestries, iii. 323, nn. 1, 3.
Hanmer, Sir Thomas, second bt., iii. 191, n. 2; social, iii. 191, 193; on Col. T. Blount's vineyard, iii. 161, n. 1; portrait of, iv. 402 & n. 6.
Hanmer, Sir Thomas, fourth bt.: geneal., iii. 622, n. 4.
Hannibal: deceives Fabius Maximus, ii. 324 & n. 1; helmet of, ii. 192 & n. 6 (i. 119); statues of, ii. 225 & n. 14 (error), 310 & n. 1.
Hanover: House of: in succession to English throne, iv. 645 & n. 8; v. 464–5 & n.
Hanover: Dukes and Electors, &c., of: *see* Sophia; George I, king of England.
Hans: *see* Bruggen, L. van der.
Hanseatic League: house of, at Antwerp, ii. 66 & n. 3 (i. 44).
Hansley, Rev. John: sermons by, iii. 326 *bis* & nn. 3, 5.
Hanson, Sir Robert, sheriff of London 1665–6: knighted, iii. 429 & n. 3.
Hanson Grange, Thorpe, Derbyshire: part of dowry of Mrs. Martha Evelyn (?), iv. 415 & n. 2.
Hapsburg family: portraits of, ii. 411; owners of Villa d'Este, Tivoli, ii. 394, n. 4.
Harbord, Sir Charles, sen., iii. 175, n. 6; negotiates marriage, iii. 175–6 & n., 184, 193; as surveyor-general of Crown Lands: examines ground claimed by E, iii. 290; ~ grants building to E, iii. 352 & n. 2; *add.*; ~ participates in Treasury business, iv. 24, n. 2; geneal., iii. 616.
Harbord, Sir Charles, jnr.: killed, iii. 616–17 & n.
Harbord, William: dies, v. 117 & n. 4; alluded to (?), iv. 635 & n. 3.
Harbours: *see* Ships and Shipping.
Harcourt, Elizabeth, Viscountess Harcourt, 1657–1724, wife of (1) Richard Anderson; (2) Simon Harcourt, first Viscount Harcourt, iv. 224, n. 3; as Mrs. Anderson: godmother of (Sir) John Evelyn, iv. 272; ~ social, iv. 224; geneal., v. 448, n. 4, 608.
Harcourt, Mrs. Elizabeth, 1684–1760, born Evelyn, wife of Simon Harcourt, iv. 396, n. 1; as Elizabeth Evelyn: birth, &c., iv. 395–6; ~ journey to Ireland, v. 113; *see also* v. 116.

Harcourt, Henri de Lorraine, comte d', called 'Cadet-la-Perle', ii. 168, n. 1; takes Îles de Lérins, ii. 168 (i. 106); in procession, iii. 42.
Harcourt, Sir Simon; Baron, 1711–21, and first Viscount, 1721–7, Harcourt, v. 448, n. 4, 602, n. 2; as Mr. Harcourt: political activities of, v. 466–7; ~ social, v. 448, 466–7; as Sir Simon: concerned in (Sir) John Evelyn's marriage settlement, v. 602, 605, 606; Lady Stonhouse dies at house of, v. 618; social, v. 608; geneal., iv. 224, n. 3, 396, n. 1.
Harcourt, Simon, 1684–1720, son of Sir Simon Harcourt, first Viscount Harcourt: geneal., iv. 396, n. 1.
Harcourt, Simon, second Viscount and first Earl Harcourt: geneal., iv. 396, n. 1.
Harcourt, Lord (*c.* 1800): sees MS. of Diary, i. *54*.
Harcourt: Viscounts, &c.: see Harcourt, Sir Simon, baron 1711–21 and first viscount 1721–7; Harcourt, Elizabeth, his viscountess; Harcourt, Simon, second viscount and first earl.
Hardwick Hall, Derbyshire: floors at, ii. 174, n. 1.
Hardy, Rev. —: sermon by, iii. 195.
Hardy (Harding), Nathaniel, D.D.; dean of Rochester 1660, iii. 314, n. 3; sermons by: printed, iii. 314 & n. 3; ~ unprinted, iii. 435, 444.
Hare, Francis; bishop of St. Asaph 1727; of Chichester 1731: sermon by (?), v. 620 & n. 4.
Hare, Henry, second Baron Coleraine, v. 123, n. 2; chaplain of: sermon by, v. 123.
Harington, James, author of *Oceana*: geneal., iii. 554, n. 3.
Harington, John, first Baron Harington: owns barony of Oakham, iii. 123 & n. 5.
Harington (Harrington): the Barons: *see* Harington, John, first baron.
Harkány, near Mohács, Hungary: Turks defeated at, 1687, iv. 560 & n. 3.
Harlackenden (Harlakinton), —: social, iii. 159 & n. 4.
Harlakenden, Thomas: social (?; as Mr. Harlakingdon), iii. 422 & n. 2.
Harlaxton, Lincs.: rector of: *see* Nash *or* Naish, H.
Harlech, Merionethshire: fiery exhalation near, 1693–4, v. 174 & n. 3.
Harley, Sir Edward: loses timber by storm, v. 550, n. 2 *ad fin.*
Harley (Harlow), Robert; earl of Oxford 1711, v. 446, n. 6; pupil at Foubert's academy, iv. 257, n. 5; elected Speaker, v. 446 & n. 7, 484 & n. 2; buys MSS., v. 323, n. 3.
Harlington (Arlington), Middlesex: Lord Arlington and, iv. 119 & n. 3.
Harman, (Sir) John, admiral: ship of, in Four Days' Battle, iii. 438 & n. 3.
Harnham Hill, near Salisbury, iii. 114, n. 6.
Harold (Herold), king of England: defeat of, by William I: anniversary of, iv. 601.
Harris, —: tenant of E at Preston, ii. 552.
Harris, Rev. —: sermon by, iii. 150.
Harris, Sir J.: *see* Harrison, Sir J.
Harris (Haris), John; D.D. 1706: appointed Boyle Lecturer for 1698, v. 273 & n. 4.
Harris, Richard: at Padua, 1645, ii. 464, n. 2.
Harrison, Ann: *see* Fanshawe, Ann, Lady Fanshawe.
Harrison (Harris), Sir John: house of, ii. 81 & n. 1 (i. 54); geneal., iii. 19, n. 5.
Harrison, General Thomas: executed, iii. 259, n. 2.
Harrogate, Yorks.: the English spa, iii. 129, n. 6.
Harscot, Dr. —: *see* Hascard, G.
Hart, Sir Eustace: geneal., i. 3, n. 3.
Hart, Joan *or* Jane, Lady Hart, born Evelyn, wife of (1) Sir A. Benn; (2) Sir E. Hart: geneal., i. 3, n. 3; iii. 372, n. 1.
Hart, John: buys Great Warley manor, iii. 158 & n. 6.
Hartingford-berry: *see* Hertingfordbury.
Hartington: Marquis of, 1694–1707 (courtesy title): *see* Cavendish, William, second duke of Devonshire.
Hartlib, Samuel: notice, 1655, iii. 162–3 & n.
Hartlip, Kent: Dane-house at, iii. 611 & n. 5.
Hartman, George, steward of Sir K. Digby, iii. 48, n. 2.

Hartop, Mrs. Anne, born Evelyn, wife of John Hartop: geneal., iii. 198, n. 3.
Hartop, Elizabeth: *see* Needham, Elizabeth, Lady Needham.
Hartop, John: geneal., iii. 198, n. 3.
Harvard College, Cambridge, Mass.: Sir G. Downing as teacher at, iii. 445, n. 1.
Harvey, — (John Hervey?): social, iv. 25 & n. 2.
Harvey, Sir Daniel: brings news of Four Days' Battle, iii. 439 & n. 2.
Harvey (Hervy), Edward: in parliamentary election, 1705, v. 595 & n. 4.
Harvey, Frances: *see* Evelyn, Mrs. F.
Harvey (Hervey), Stephen, v. 478, n. 2; acts as steward for E, v. 478; social (?), v. 547 & n. 4, 548, critical note.
Harvey, William, M.D., iii. 338 & n. 2; statue of, *ib.*; questions equivocal generation, iii. 341, n. 4; Harveian orations at Royal College of Physicians, iii. 379 & n. 1; iv. 291 & n. 1.
Harwich, Essex: geographical, iv. 115 & n. 7; English fleet off, 1665, iii. 405, n. 3; William III at: as Prince of Orange, 1677, iv. 122, n. 3; ~ as king, 1691, &c., v. 51, n. 4, 91, n. 2, 136, n. 1; Shaftesbury at, iv. 329, n. 1; master-shipwright at: *see* Deane, Sir A.
Hascard (Harscot, Hitchcock), Gregory, D.D.; dean of Windsor 1684, iv. 537, n. 6; sermons by, iv. 537, 570; v. 44, 243.
Hastings: battle of: alluded to, iv. 601.
Hastings, Ferdinando, sixth earl of Huntingdon: geneal., iii. 543, n. 3.
Hastings, George, eighth earl of Huntingdon: wounded 1702, v. 504 & n. 3.
Hastings, Lucy, countess of Huntingdon, wife of Ferdinando Hastings, sixth earl, iii. 543, n. 3; and Sir Samuel Tuke, iii. 543; godmother of Sir Charles Tuke, iii. 585; social, iii. 550.
Hastings, Theophilus, seventh earl of Huntingdon: social, iii. 550 & n. 6.
Hatfield, Herts.: E at, ii. 81; Hatfield House, ii. 80 & nn. 4, 5 (i. 54 & n. 3); rector of: *see* Lee, Richard.
Hatten *or* Hatton, John: house of, in London, iii. 233, n. 4.
Hatton, Anne: *see* Lechford, Mrs. A.
Hatton, Sir Christopher, lord chancellor: acquires Ely Place, iii. 231, n. 6; builds Holmby House, iv. 70, n. 3.
Hatton, Christopher, first Baron Hatton of Kirby 1643, ii. 562, n. 9; in Paris, &c., 1649–52: lends E money, iii. 13; ~ ill, iii. 22; ~ quarrel of, with Sir R. Browne, iii. 38 & n. 4; ~ social, &c., ii. 558, 562; iii. 6, 21, 24, 26, 54; in London, 1657, &c.: social, iii. 191 & n. 5, 270, 292; owner of Kirby Hall, iii. 133–4 & n.; lets Hatton Garden for building, iii. 231, n. 6.
Hatton, Christopher; second Baron Hatton of Kirby 1670; first Viscount Hatton of Gretton 1683: social, iv. 457 & n. 8.
Hatton, Elizabeth, Baroness Hatton, wife of Christopher Hatton, first baron, ii. 558, n. 1; in London, 1649–50: social, &c., ii. 558; iii. 13; taken in Christmas raid on Exeter House chapel, iii. 203–4; patron of Rev. Peter Gunning, iii. 204, n. 1.
Hatton *or* Hatten, John: *see* Hatten.
Hatton, Mrs. Mary, born Evelyn, wife of Richard Hatton: geneal., i. 2, n. 4; ii. 78, n. 1; iii. 561, n. 4.
Hatton, Richard: geneal., i. 2, n. 4; ii. 78, n. 1; iii. 561, n. 4.
Hatton, Robert, serjeant-at-law, ii. 78, n. 1; advises E to go abroad, ii. 82, n. 2; social, ii. 78 (i. 51), 537; geneal., ii. 562, n. 9.
Hatton: Barons, &c.: *see* Hatton, Christopher, first Baron Hatton of Kirby 1643–70; Hatton, Elizabeth, his baroness; Hatton, Christopher, second Baron Hatton of Kirby 1670–83; first Viscount Hatton of Gretton 1683–1706.
Haughton: *see* Houghton.
Haully, Lord: *see* Hawley.
Haunce, Monsieur: *see* Bruggen, L. van der.
Hausse, M. de: *see* du Houssay.
Haut-Brion (Obrien): vineyard, iv. 329 & n. 3.
Havana, Cuba: Spanish plate fleet from, 1656, iii. 188, n. 3; governor of: *see* Villalba y Toledo, Don Diego de.

Havre de Grace (Le Havre): notice, 1644, ii. 125 & nn. 1–4 (i. 79–80); bombarded, 1694, v. 186 & n. 2.
Hawarde (Haywood, &c.), Sir William, iii. 598 & n. 3; social, iii. 598; iv. 489.
Hawley, Francis, Baron Hawley, iii. 343, n. 6; social, iii. 343–4, 597.
Hawley: Baron, 1645–84: *see* Hawley, Francis.
Hay, John, second earl and first marquis of Tweeddale, iii. 370, n. 2; as Lord Tivedale, &c.: social, &c., iii. 370; iv. 184.
Hayes, Middlesex: Dr. T. Triplet at, iii. 168, n. 5.
Hayes, Sir James, iii. 623, n. 4; gift from, to Royal Society, iii. 566, n. 1; social, iii. 623.
Hayley, William; D.D. 1695, iv. 545, n. 3; sermons by, iv. 545 (as by Mr. Hall in error); v. 504 & n. 8.
Hayward, Captain —, iii. 439, n. 3.
Hayward, Roger, D.D.: sermon by, iv. 135 & n. 1.
Hayward *or* Haywood, Sir William: *see* Hawarde.
Haywood (Hayward, Heywood), William, D.D., iii. 103 & n. 7; sermons by, iii. 103, 265, 275, 307.
Heardman, Rev. —: sermon by, iii. 249.
Hearne (Herne), John, D.D.: sermon by, iv. 652–3 & n.
Heath, —, at Calais, 1652, iii. 55 & n. 6.
Heath, —, schoolfellow of E (Robert Heath ?): wife of, buried, iii. 502 & n. 5; mentioned, iii. 55, n. 6.
Heath, Mrs. — (Mrs. Frances Heath ?): buried, iii. 502 & n. 5.
Heath, Sir Edward, K.B.: owns Cottesmore, iii. 124 & n. 3; mentioned, iii. 55, n. 6.
Heath, Mrs. Frances, wife of Robert Heath, iii. 502, n. 5.
Heath, John, son of Sir Robert, iii. 55, n. 6.
Heath, Robert, iii. 502, n. 5.
Heath, Sir Robert, judge: geneal., iii. 55, n. 6, 124 & n. 3.
Heath, Thomas, E's servant: apprenticed to carpenter, iii. 95.
Heath, Thomas: legend of, v. 13, n. 1.
Heaven, the Third, ii. 198 & n. 12; St. Paul in: painting of, ii. 240; in sermons, v. 490, 500–1, 536.
Hebert, —, valet: robs E, ii. 535.
Hebrew language: MS., ii. 301–2 & n.; study of: Archbishop Ussher's views on, iii. 156; ~ scholars, iii. 359; iv. 172; v. 82; ~ examination, iii. 287; vocabulary: in sermons, iii. 525 & n. 4; iv. 646; *see also* iv. 648; writing, v. 453.
Hedges, Sir Charles: appointed secretary of state, v. 432 & n. 3.
Hedley, Surrey: rector of: *see* Nason, J. (v. 430, n. 1).
Heenvliet: Lord of: *see* Kerckhoven, J. P. à.
Heidelberg: taken by French, &c., 1693, v. 141 & n. 1; Great Tun at, ii. 147 (i. 95); Palatine library from, in Vatican, ii. 302 & nn. 3, 4; C. Cisner at, iii. 171, n. 2; the Spanheims at, iv. 78 & n. 1; William Howard, Viscount Stafford, in prison at, iv. 234, n. 4.
Heinsius, Daniel: at Leyden, ii. 52 & n. 5 (i. 36).
Heinsius (Hiensius), Nicolaas, sen.: library of: sale of, &c., iv. 330 & n. 3.
Heissler (Heustler), Count Donat, Imperial general: killed, v. 258 & n. 6; *add.*
Helena, St., mother of Constantine the Great: finding of the Cross by, ii. 262, 380; gift of, ii. 272–3 & n.; tomb, &c., of, ii. 274 & n. 5; legendary connexion of, with Colchester, iii. 176–7 & n.; statue of, &c., ii. 262 & n. 4.
Heleon: error: *see* Acteon.
Hell: meaning Hades: gates of, ii. 346; Christian: mouth of, ii. 336 & n. 4; ~ in sermons, iii. 12; iv. 549; ~ alluded to, in sermon, iii. 35.
Helmsley, Yorks., N.R.: ownership of, v. 246, n. 2.
Helvetia: *see* Switzerland.
Helvoetsluis: William of Orange sails from, 1688, iv. 604, n. 4.
Henchman (Hinchman, Hienchman), Rev. — (Dr. H. Henchman ?): sermons by, iii. 218 & n. 3, 231 & n. 3, 251.
Henchman (Hensman, Hinchman), Humphrey, D.D.; bishop of Salisbury 1660; of London 1663, iii. 240, n. 2; as bishop of Salisbury: consecrates Dr. Earles, iii. 346; as bishop of London: commissioner for repair of St. Paul's, iii. 448–9

Henchman, Humphrey, D.D. (*cont.*) & nn.; ~ social, iii. 400; sermons by, iii. 218 & n. 3(?), 231 & n. 3(?), 240, 251(?); appointed to preach, iv. 7, n. 2, 61, n. 6.
Heneage, Anne, Lady Heneage, wife of Sir Thomas: antipathy of, to roses (?), iii. 550, n. 5.
Heneage, Sir Thomas: geneal., iii. 550, n. 5.
Hengist: at Leyden, ii. 51 & n. 5 (i. 36).
Henley-on-Thames, Oxon.: E at, iv. 67; Bolney Court (Boyne) near, ii. 540 & n. 5.
Henley, Sir Robert: house of: architect of, iii. 554, n. 3.
Hennage, Lady: *see* Heneage, Anne, Lady Heneage.
Henneberg, Margaret, countess of: legendary parturition of, ii. 55 & n. 3 (i. 38).
Hennequin, Nicolas, sieur de Fresne: *see* Fresne.
Henri II, king of France: tomb of, ii. 86 (i. 58); gift to, ii. 119, n. 2.
Henri III, king of France: at Venice, ii. 445 & n. 8, 457 & n. 7; murder of, ii. 108, n. 1; buildings of, &c.: Fontainebleau: decoration, ii. 117 (i. 76); ~ Louvre, &c.: parts built by, ii. 103, n. 1, 104, n. 2; ~ Pont-Neuf: begun by, ii. 92 (i. 61); statue of, ii. 108 (i. 70).
Henri IV, king of France (Henri le Grand): marriage of, to Queen Marguerite, ii. 297 & n. 3; at Corbeil, ii. 121 & n. 1 (i. 78); consecration of, ii. 147 & n. 1; assassination of, i. 85 & n. 2; v. 196 & n. 1.
buildings of: Blois: gallery in Château garden, ii. 141 & n. 6 (i. 92); Fontainebleau: general, ii. 117 (i. 76); ~ rooms, &c., ii. 117–19, nn. *passim*; Paris: Louvre, &c.: parts built by, ii. 103 & n. 1 (i. 67), 104, n. 2; ~ Place Royale, ii. 101 (i. 66); ~ Pont-Neuf: completed by, ii. 92 (i. 61); St. Germain-en-Laye: New Château, ii. 111 (i. 71).
miscellaneous: crowns, &c., of, ii. 88 (i. 60); drawings made for, iii. 10–11; victories of: paintings of, ii. 117 & n. 2 (i. 76).
statues, &c., of: at: Fontainebleau, ii. 118 & n. 1 (i. 76);

Henri IV (*cont.*)
Paris, Pont-Neuf, ii. 92–3 & n. (i. 61–2), 101 (i. 66); Rome, Lateran, ii. 275 & n. 2; St.-Cloud, ii. 108 (i. 70).
geneal., ii. 57 (i. 39), 152, n. 4, 368, n. 8, 534, n. 3; iv. 318, n. 5.
Henrietta Anne, duchess of Orleans (Madame), i. 97, n. 1; ii. 565, n. 1.
as princess: birth of, i. 96–7; attendant of, at Exeter, iii. 270, n. 3; governess of: *see* Douglas, Anne, countess of Morton; to go to a convent, 1651, iii. 44, n. 5; visit to England, 1660–1: arrives, iii. 261; at Whitehall, *ib.*; at St. James's Palace, iii. 264; Mrs. Evelyn presented to, iii. 261–2; Mrs. Evelyn's character of, &c., iii. 264 & n. 7; returns to France, iii. 265–6 & n., 267, n. 2.
as duchess: Charles II receives letter from, iii. 299; meets Charles II at Dover, &c., 1670, iii. 548 & n. 1, 548–9 & n.; maid of honour to: *see* Kéroualle, Louise de, duchess of Portsmouth; physician of: *see* Yvelin, Dr. P.
geneal., v. 421 & n. 3.
Henrietta Maria, queen of England, consort of Charles I:
— chronological series: 1629: visits Tunbridge Wells, iii. 68, n. 4; 1638–41: visited by Marie de Médicis, ii. 57 (i. 39); 1641: attends Strafford's trial, ii. 27 (i. 20); 1643–4: escapes of, in Civil War: describes, iii. 341 & n. 2; 1644: gives birth to Henrietta Anne at Exeter, i. 97 & n. 1; ~ at Tours, ii. 149 & n. 1 (i. 96–7); ~ at Bourbon-l'Archambault, ii. 155 & n. 6 (i. 100); 1647: in or near Paris, ii. 536; 1649: at St.-Germain-en-Laye, ii. 562; 1649–52: at Louvre: court of, i. *10*; iii. 36 & n. 5; ~ apartments occupied by, &c., in Louvre, ii. 103, n. 1, 105, n. 4; iii. 36, n. 5, 52, 634, 636; 1651: discharges ladies of her household, iii. 44 & n. 5, 634–5; ~ learns of Charles II's escape after Worcester, iii. 47 & n. 4; 1660: marriage of James, duke of York, announced to, iii. 258 & n. 4;

Henrietta Maria (*cont.*)
1660–1: visits England, iii. 259 & n. 3, 261 & n. 3, 265–6 & n., 267, n. 2; 1662: gift of, to Queen Catherine, iii. 323–4; ~ returns to England, iii. 328 & n. 1; ~ court of, iii. 334 & n. 3; ~ absent from Lord Mayor's show, iii. 341; 1665: retires to France, iii. 519, n. 5.
— amusements, &c.: dogs of: sagacity of, iii. 331; wins prize in lottery, iii. 376; visits Bushell's Wells, iii. 382, n. 6.
— household: attorney: Sir P. Ball, iii. 310 & n. 2; confessor: *see* Goffe, S.; groom of privy chamber: P. Church, iii. 6, n. 5; ladies: French: devotions of, &c., iii. 45, 635; lady of bedchamber: Elizabeth Boyle, countess of Guildford, iii. 263, n. 8; laundress: Lady Sanderson, iv. 94, n. 4; maids of honour: *see* Cavendish, Margaret, duchess of Newcastle; Wood, Mary, Lady Wood; treasurer: *see* Wood, Sir H.; vice-chamberlain: Sir T. Stafford, iii. 71; servant: Sir R. Walsh, iii. 6, n. 4.
— letters: to and from Charles I, ii. 538, n. 1; to Charles II, 1660, iii. 247.
— portrait: by J. Hoskins (?), iii. 263 & n. 3.
— property: Nonsuch Palace, iii. 426, n. 4; Oatlands Palace, Byfleet, &c., iv. 141, n. 3, 565, n. 2; Pontefract: house at (?), iii. 127 & n. 8; Somerset House: tenancy of, iii. 334, n. 3, 519, n. 5; iv. 90, n. 4; Wimbledon: sells, &c., iii. 315 & n. 5.
— — Louvre: apartment in: *see* chronological series *above*; debts of: to be settled, 1660, iii. 258.
— relations with E: E pays court to, &c., ii. 149 (i. 97), 536, 562; iii. 261, 328, 331, 334, 341, 345, 369, 396; and conversion of J. Cosin, jnr., iii. 52 & n. 2, 62, 636; E carries letters for, iii. 247; visits Sayes Court, iii. 330, 331; E gives Fréart's *Parallel* to, iii. 380, 389; Mrs. Evelyn presented to, iii. 261–2; John Evelyn, jnr., presented to, iii. 263.

Henrietta Maria (*cont.*)
— religion: attacks Church of England, iii. 45, 635; Anglicans fear offending, iii. 36 & n. 5, 634; establishes convent at Chaillot, &c., ii. 91, n. 1; chapels of: in Louvre, iii. 634; St. James's Palace, iii. 373, n. 2; Capuchins attached to, iii. 602, n. 3.
— geneal., ii. 57; iii. 412.
Henrietta Maria, Princess, daughter of Frederick V of the Palatinate, wife of S. Rákóczi, ii. 34, n. 1.
Henry II, king of England: as ruler of Touraine, ii. 145, n. 3.
Henry V, king of England: founds priory at Sheen, iv. 143, n. 1.
Henry VII, king of England: erects monument to Richard III, iii. 122, n. 6; builds New Hall, Essex (error), iii. 179–80 & n.; founds Savoy Hospital, iii. 410, n. 1; legend relating to court of, *add.* (v. 192); MS. given by, to Queen Margaret of Scotland, iv. 215 & n. 2; portrait of, iii. 166 & n. 1; geneal., iii. 137, n. 3.
Henry VIII, king of England: *Assertio septem sacramentorum* by: copy of, in Vatican Library, ii. 302 & n. 2; divorce proceedings of: alluded to, iii. 546; ~ 'unhappy wife' of, iii. 135; besieges Boulogne, ii. 84 & n. 3 (i. 57); founds: professorship, iii. 533, n. 8; ~ Trinity House of Deptford Strond, iii. 313, n. 6 *ad fin.*; iv. 248 & n. 1; MS. lectionary of, iii. 109 & n. 2; vestments given by, to pope, ii. 298 & n. 3; portraits of, ii. 550 & n. 3; iii. 166 & n. 1; iv. 141 & n. 1 (error).
buildings, &c., of: Blechingley, house at: chimney-piece from, iii. 156 & n. 2; Hampton Court, ii. 117, n. 1; iii. 322, n. 5, 323, n. 3; New Hall, Essex, iii. 179–80 & n.; Nonsuch Palace, iii. 426, n. 4, 427; Windsor Castle: terrace at, iv. 317, n. 4.
Henry VII, Emperor: death of, ii. 206 & n. 6; tomb of, ii. 408 & n. 4.
Henry Frederick, prince of Wales, son of James I: Charlton House built for, iii. 66 & n. 3; Sir Walter Raleigh's cordial given to, iii. 336, n. 4.

Henry, duke of Gloucester, brother of Charles II, iii. 251, n. 3; dines with Charles II, iii. 251; dies, iii. 257 & n. 1; man of war renamed after, iii. 438, n. 3; William III's resemblance to, iii. 563, n. 5 *ad fin.*, 564.

Henry, earl of Lancaster 1327–45: founds hospital at Leicester, iii. 122, n. 8 *ad fin.*

Henry, duke of Lancaster 1351–60: enlarges hospital at Leicester, iii. 122, n. 8 *ad fin.*

Henry Frederick, prince of Orange: error for Maurice, iv. 118; *add.*

Henshaw, Mrs. Anne, wife of Thomas Henshaw and previously of James Darell: social, iii. 201 & nn. 1, 2.

Henshaw (Hienshaw), Joseph, D.D.; bishop of Peterborough 1663: social, iii. 237 & n. 8.

Henshaw, Thomas, ii. 179, n. 6.
- travels in Italy with E: meets E at Pisa, ii. 179 (i. 113); buys Baglione's *Nove chiese*, ii. 575; sees phosphorescent material in Rome, ii. 397–8; iv. 253; E sends drawing to A. Kircher by, ii. 469 & n. 4; iii. 171–2; at Padua: arrives, ii. 470 & n. 3; ~ matriculates, &c., ii. 464, n. 2; ~ shares lodgings with E, iii. 473; mentioned by name, ii. 316, 358, 379, 389 [in many passages in which E uses the first person plural Henshaw is probably implied; but as far as ii. 470 they may refer equally to James Thicknesse; and it is clear that E and Henshaw separated for a time before the latter's arrival at Padua].
- later life: in London, 1649, ii. 546; paintings owned by, *ib.*; succeeds to the Evelyns' chamber in Middle Temple, i. 12; ii. 24, n. 4; iii. 194, n. 1; marriage of, &c., iii. 201, nn. 1, 2; proposed by E as ambassador to Turkey, 1660, iii. 248–9; history of salt-petre, &c., by, iii. 294 & n. 3; appointed French secretary to Charles II, *ib.*; as envoy to Denmark, &c., 1671–4, iv. 76 & n. 1; house of, in Kensington, iii. 255 & n. 4; iv. 76.
- later relations with E: E dedicates *The French Gardiner* to, iii. 225, n. 3; E gives copy of *Numismata* to, v. 283, n. 3; letter from, to E: cited, iii. 186, n. 1; social: parties, ii. 558; iii. 85, 170, 186, 201, 217 *bis*, 450; iv. 96, 205, 310, 454, n. 3(?); ~ alone, &c., iii. 75, 90, 255; iv. 76.
- brother-in-law of, iii. 85 & n. 9.

Heraldry and Heralds:
- — arms [select: those of popes and Italian princes are indexed only under their bearers' names]: the Commonwealth, iii. 57 & n. 3; Evelyn family, i. 9; ii. 89, n. 3; Geneva, ii. 525 & n. 4; grant of, to Royal Society, iii. 332 & n. 2, 336.
- — banners, &c.: ensigns, i. 20; iii. 57; guidons, iii. 57, 224; pendants, iii. 224 & n. 2; sheriff's banners, i. 9.
- — books, &c., on: in Norfolcian library, later in College of Arms, iii. 472, n. 3; iv. 144 & n. 3.
- — Heralds' Office: *see* London: topography: College of Arms.
- — talbots, iii. 336 & n. 1.
- — heralds:
- — — in ceremonies: at funerals, iii. 307; v. 55; state: Ireton's funeral, iii. 57 & n. 3; Cromwell's funeral, iii. 224; creation of peers, iii. 277; Charles II's coronation procession, iii. 279–80 (not indexed in detail); Garter feast, iii. 479.
- — — proclamations by: peace, 1667, iii. 492; James II's accession, iv. 412–13.
- — — individual heralds: *see* Bysshe, Sir E.; Dugdale, Sir W.; Walker, Sir E.

Hérauld, Didier (Desiderius Heraldus): geneal., iii. 339 & n. 7.

Hérault (Herauld), Louis, D.D.: social, iii. 339 & n. 7.

Herbert, earls of Pembroke: as owners of Wilton House, iii. 113, n. 6.

Herbert, Lord, 1654: social, iii. 94 & n. 5.

Herbert, —: executor of Lady Mordaunt's will, iv. 259.

Herbert, — (John Herbert ?): social, iv. 273 & n. 3.

Herbert, Anne, countess of Pembroke, wife of Philip Herbert, fourth earl; *suo jure* Baroness Clifford; formerly countess of Dorset, iii. 203, n. 5.
Herbert, Arthur; earl of Torrington 1689, iv. 609, n. 9; reported defeat of French fleet by, 1688, iv. 609 & n. 9; in battle of Bantry Bay, iv. 639 & n. 1; imprisoned for conduct in battle of Beachy Head, v. 29 & n. 3; *see also* v. 27, n. 2; *add.*; Oatlands estate granted to, iv. 565, n. 2; geneal., iii. 1, n. 2.
Herbert, Sir Edward; Lord Keeper 1653–4: geneal., iii. 1 & n. 1.
Herbert, Sir Edward; earl of Portland (Jacobite creation) 1689; judge, iv. 517, n. 1; as Lord Chief Justice: E takes Test before, iv. 500; ~ judgement of, in *Godden* v. *Hales*, iv. 517 & n. 1; appointed a Commissioner for Ecclesiastical Affairs, iv. 519–20; house of, at Walton-on-Thames (Oatlands), iv. 565–6 & n.; social, iv. 591; geneal., iii. 1, n. 2; iv. 609, n. 9.
Herbert, Edward, first Baron Herbert of Cherbury: geneal., iii. 58; v. 56 & n. 2; *see also* Books mentioned in text.
Herbert, Elizabeth, Lady Herbert, born Offley, wife of Sir Henry: geneal., ii. 537, n. 2; iii. 58, n. 2, 176, n. 2; v. 56, n. 2; as godmother, iii. 63.
Herbert, George, the poet: on celebration of Communion, v. 180, n. 1.
Herbert, Sir Henry, Master of the Revels, iii. 58, n. 2; gives book to E, iii. 58 & n. 3; social, iii. 176, 398; geneal., ii. 537, n. 2; v. 56, n. 2.
Herbert, Henry, created Baron Herbert of Chirbury 1694: at funeral of John Evelyn of Wotton, v. 56 & n. 2.
Herbert, Henry, second earl of Pembroke: institutes Salisbury races, iii. 114, n. 6.
Herbert, John, F.R.S., iv. 273, n. 3; at Royal Society meeting, iv. 325, n. 4; social (?), iv. 273.
Herbert, Margaret, Lady Herbert, wife of Sir Edward Herbert, Lord Keeper, and previously of T. Carey, iii. 1, n. 2; in Paris, 1650–2, iii. 1, 17, 54; geneal., iii. 155, n. 7.
Herbert, Mary, countess of Pembroke, sister of Sir P. Sidney, iii. 72, n. 5.
Herbert, Philip; fourth earl of Pembroke, 1630; &c., ii. 25, n. 2; sent to Tower, 1640, ii. 25 & n. 2; as high steward of Greenwich Park, iii. 64, n. 2; geneal., iii. 203, n. 5.
Herbert, Philip; fifth earl of Pembroke 1650, iii. 100, n. 5; house of, at Ramsbury, iii. 100 & n. 5; as owner of Wilton, iii. 113; employs E. Phillips, iii. 401 & n. 4.
Herbert, Philip; seventh earl of Pembroke 1674: educated by E. Phillips, iii. 401, n. 4.
Herbert, Richard, second Baron Herbert of Cherbury, iii. 94, n. 5.
Herbert, Thomas; eighth earl of Pembroke 1683, iv. 440, n. 3; as Lord Privy Seal, v. 210, n. 2; as commissioner for Greenwich Hospital: at meeting, v. 209–10; as Lord President: appointed, v. 325 & n. 2; ~ second term, v. 532, n. 3; appointed a Lord Justice, 1701, v. 469 & n. 2; as Lord High Admiral: Greenwich Hospital accounts submitted to, v. 496 & n. 1; admitted F.R.S., iv. 440; elected president of Royal Society, iv. 652 & n. 3; art-collection of, v. 245 & nn. 2, 3; as owner of Wilton, v. 586; social: parties, iv. 548; v. 469; ~ alone, &c., v. 292, 325, 363, 469, 532, 609.
Herbert, William; third earl of Pembroke 1601, iii. 107, n. 7; MSS. given by, to Bodleian Library, iii. 107 & n. 7; grandstand built by, iii. 115 & n. 1.
Herbert, William; styled Lord Herbert 1650; sixth earl of Pembroke 1669, iii. 94, n. 5; tutor for (?), iii. 401 & n. 4.
Herbert, William, earl of Powis: as prisoner in Tower, 1678–84: *see* London: Tower: prisoners: the Roman Catholic peers.
Herbert: Lords (courtesy title): *see* Herbert, William, later sixth earl of Pembroke (1650–69); Somerset, Henry, later first marquis of Worcester (*c.* 1604–28); Somerset, Henry, later first duke of Beaufort, &c. (1629–67).

Herbert of Cherbury (Chirbury): Barons: *see* Herbert, Edward, first baron; Herbert, Richard, second baron, 1648–55; *new creation*: *see* Herbert, Henry, first baron, 1694–1709.
Herculaneum, ii. 325, n. 4.
Hercules: places associated with, ii. 228 & n. 1, 341 & n. 2, 345 & nn. 2, 3; labours of, &c.: in paintings, iv. 344; *see also* Sculpture.
Herculis, Portus, Provence, ii. 168 & n. 5 (i. 106).
Hereford: Viscounts: *see* Devereux, Leicester, sixth viscount, 1649–76; Devereux, Leicester, seventh viscount, 1676–83.
Hereford: cathedral clergy:
  bishop-elect, 1633: *see* Juxon, W.
  bishops: *see* Wren, Matthew, D.D. (1634–5); Field, T. (1635–6); Monck, N. (1661); Croft, Herbert (1662–91); Ironside, Gilbert, D.D., jnr. (1691–1701); Humphreys, H. (1701–12).
  dean: *see* Benson, George, D.D. (1672–92).
  archdeacon: *see* Benson, Rev. Samuel (1684–90).
  canon: *see* Sherburne, W., D.D.
Herefordshire: in view, iii. 119.
Herford: abbess of, 1667–80: *see* Elizabeth, Princess Palatine.
Hermann II, count of Henneberg: geneal., ii. 55, n. 3.
Herne, Dr. —: *see* Hearne, J., D.D.
Herod Antipas: palace of: relics of (error), ii. 268–9 & nn.; in sermons, v. 121, 132, 149, 508.
Herod the Great: as slayer of the Innocents, i. 58; ii. 243; in sermons, iii. 238; v. 84.
Herodians: in sermon, v. 288 & n. 4.
Herodias, ii. 267.
Herold: *see* Harold.
Herrick, Robert: friend of Sir C. Crewe, ii. 540, n. 1.
Herring, Thomas, archbishop of Canterbury 1747–57: tomb of, v. 426, n. 5.
Hertford: Christ's Hospital girls' school moved to, iii. 192, n. 2; Balls Park (Sir J. Harrison) near, ii. 81 & n. 1 (i. 54).
Hertford: first Earl of: *see* Seymour, Edward.
Hertford: first Marquis of: *see* Seymour, William, later duke of Somerset.
Hertfordshire: ruled by Coel, iii. 176, n. 5.
Hertingfordbury, Herts.: E visits Mrs. Keightley at, ii. 80 & n. 3 (i. 54), 81.
Hertochs, A.: engraves plates for E's *French Gardiner*, iii. 225, n. 3.
Hervart, Bartholomew: geneal., iv. 517, n. 6.
Hervart, Esther: *see* Gouvernet, Marquise de.
Hervey, —: *see* Harvey, Stephen.
Hervey, John, courtier, iii. 165, n. 2; godfather of Francis Godolphin, second earl of Godolphin, iv. 147; social, iii. 164–5(?); iv. 10, 25 & n. 2(?).
Hervy, —, of Come: *see* Harvey, Edward.
Hesdin: frontier near, ii. 84, nn. 1, 5.
Hesse: Prince of: *see* George, Landgraf of Hesse-Darmstadt (v. 610 & n. 2).
Hesselin (Essling), Louis: house of, at Essones, ii. 120–1 & n. (i. 77–8).
Heusden (Hysdune): notice, 1641, ii. 59 (i. 40).
Heustler, General: *see* Heissler, Count D.
Hevelius, Johannes, astronomer, iii. 583, n. 9; observations, &c., by, of the moon, i. 44 (*and see* ii. 64, n. 2 *ad fin.*); iii. 158 & n. 2, 286, n. 3; letter from, to Royal Society, iii. 583 & n. 9.
Hewer (Ewers, Hewers), William, v. 111 & n. 2; house of, at Clapham, iv. 176, n. 1; v. 111; ~ Pepys resides in, v. 427–8 & n., 538; bequest to, v. 538, n. 2.
Hewett, Elizabeth: *see* Anderson, Elizabeth, Lady Anderson.
Hewett, Sir William: geneal., iv. 224, n. 3.
Hewit *or* Hewett, John, D.D., iii. 88, n. 7; as rector of St. Gregory by St. Paul's, iii. 61, n. 4, 150, n. 2; tried and executed, iii. 214 & n. 4, 216 & n. 9; sermons by, iii. 88, 165, 167, 169, 170, 183, 189, 193.
Heworth Hall, Yorks.: Mary Ward dies at, ii. 400, n. 3.
Hewson, Col. John, regicide: death of, iii. 259 & n. 2.
Heylyn (Hylin), Peter, D.D.: sermon by, iii. 275 & n. 2. *see also* Books: sources.
Heynes: *see* Haines.
Heyward, Sir William: *see* Hawarde.

Heywood, Dr. —: *see* Haywood, W.
Hezekiah: destroys Brazen Serpent, ii. 500, n. 4; in sermons, iv. 348, 447; v. 347, 499.
Hickes, George, D.D., the nonjuror: sermon by, iv. 459 & n. 6.
Hickman, Charles, D.D.; bishop of Derry 1703, v. 137, n. 3; sermons by, v. 136 & n. 3(?), 137, 138, 140 *bis*, 141–2, 159 & n. 3, 166–7 & n.(?), 210.
Hickman, Thomas Windsor; seventh Baron Windsor 1660; earl of Plymouth 1682: social, iii. 564 & n. 5.
Hicks, Dr. —: error for Dr. C. Hickman, v. 159.
Hicks, Baptist, first Viscount Campden: geneal., iii. 124, n. 1.
Hicks, Juliana: *see* Noel, Juliana, Viscountess Campden.
Hicks, Sir William, bt.: house of, &c., iii. 230 & n. 6.
Hide: *see* Hyde.
Hienchman, Rev. —: *see* Henchman.
Hienshaw, Dr. —: *see* Henshaw, Joseph, D.D.
Hiensius: *see* Heinsius.
Hierom, St.: *see* Jerome, St.
Higgons, Bridget, Lady Higgons, wife of Sir Thomas: geneal., iv. 528, n. 3.
Higgons, Grace: *see* Wheler, Grace, Lady Wheler.
Higgons (Higgins), Sir Thomas: geneal., &c., iv. 528 & n. 3.
Higham, Elizabeth: *see* Comber, Mrs. E.
Higham, Rev. George, rector of Wotton 1612–58, ii. 5, n. 7; iv. 377 & n. 2; character, iii. 143; baptizes E, ii. 5–6 (i. 6); as preacher: style of, iii. 88, 143; sermons by, iii. 14, 88, 143, 154, 155, 219 (4), 220 (4).
Higham, Rev. John, rector of Wotton *c.* 1659–84, iii. 244, n. 1; celebrates Communion at Wotton House, iii. 244; sermons by, iii. 244 *ter*, 360, 377, 416, 421, 423, 561 *bis*, 562; catechizes, iv. 111; dies, &c., iv. 377 & n. 2; *see also* ii. 5, n. 7.
Higham, Rev. Robert, rector of Wotton 1583–1612, ii. 5, n. 7; iv. 377 & n. 2.
High Wycombe (Wicckam), Bucks.: E at, iii. 381 & n. 4; *see also* iii. 530, n. 2.
Hilary, pope: chapel built by, ii. 267, n. 2.
Hilary, St., of Poitiers: relics of, ii. 87 (i. 58), 88 (i. 59).
Hildesheim: bishop of, 1714–23: *see* Joseph Clemens, archbishop-elector of Cologne.
Hildyard, Lady Anne, wife of Henry Hildyard, sen., ii. 550, n. 7; social, ii. 551.
Hildyard (Hyldiard, &c.), Charles, ii. 550, n. 7; tutor for, ii. 550; iv. 510; travels of, iii. 50–1, 54, 61, 193 & n. 3.
Hildyard, Sir Christopher: geneal., ii. 550, n. 7.
Hildyard (Hyldiard, &c.), Henry, sen., 1610–74, ii. 550, n. 7; E lends money to (?), ii. 545 & n. 1; E recommends O. Walker to, ii. 550; iv. 510; house of, ii. 551, n. 9; iii. 87 & n. 6; social, ii. 551; iii. 61, 87, 142, 157, 423; geneal., v. 56, n. 1.
Hildyard (Hyldiard, &c.), Henry, jnr., 1636–1705, ii. 550, n. 7; tutor for, ii. 550; iv. 510; travels of, iii. 50–1, 54, 61, 193 & n. 3; converted to Roman Catholicism, &c., iv. 510 & n. 2.
Hildyard (Hyldiard), Philip, v. 56, n. 1; at funeral of John Evelyn of Wotton (?), v. 56; house of, ii. 551, n. 9.
Hill, — (Abraham Hill?), iv. 310 & n. 4.
Hill, Dr. — (Thomas Hill?): sermon by, iii. 287 & n. 4.
Hill, Rev. —: sermon by, iii. 101.
Hill, Abraham, F.R.S., iv. 273, n. 4; reports on sale of stock to Royal Society, iv. 273; social, iv. 299–300, 310(?).
Hill, Captain Richard: murder committed by, v. 129, n. 2.
Hill, Rev. T. P., rector of Abinger, i. 63, n. 1.
Hill, Thomas, B.D.: sermon by (?), iii. 287 & n. 4.
Hills (Hall), Henry, sen., iv. 504, n. 1; seeks right of printing Roman Catholic prayer-books, &c., iv. 503–4; mentioned, iv. 489, n. 4.
Hinchman, Rev. —: *see* Henchman.
Hinde (Hynd), Samuel, D.D.: sermon by, iii. 395 & n. 4.
Hippolytus, St.: statue of, ii. 301 & n. 1.

Hispaniola (Haiti): treasure from sunken ship near, iv. 552 & n. 3; ~ Lord Falkland's share in, v. 182.
Hitchcock, Dr. —: *see* Hascard, G.
Hoare, Richard, calligrapher, E's amanuensis, ii. 559 & n. 2; ill, iii. 84; letter of, cited, iii. 5, n. 1, 9, n. 3; mentioned, iii. 421, n. 2.
Hobart *or* Hubbert, Sir Richard, groom-porter: gaming at table of, iii. 308 & n. 4.
Hobbes, Thomas, the philosopher, iii. 41, n. 1; in Paris, 1651, iii. 41; in London, 1655, iii. 163 & n. 2; *Leviathan*: book against, by A. Rosse, iii. 81 & n. 2; ~ attacked in sermon, iv. 164 & n. 3; influence of, i. *110*.
Hobbs, William, D.D.: as college tutor, ii. 17 & n. 1 (i. 13).
Hobson (Hobbson), John, English consul at Venice, ii. 476, n. 3; social, ii. 469 & n. 6(?), 476.
Hobson, Thomas, the Cambridge carrier: conduit built by, iii. 140 & n. 5.
Höchstädt, on the Danube: battle at, 1703, v. 546 & n. 3.
Hohenems (Altemps), Marcus Sittich von, cardinal: builds villa at Frascati, ii. 393, n. 5.
Holbein, Hans, the younger: paintings by:
identifiable: Henry VII, Henry VIII, &c. (wall-painting in Whitehall), iii. 166 & n. 1; 'Noli me tangere', iv. 216–17 & n.; portrait of Erasmus, iii. 155 & n. 1; copies: portraits of Erasmus and Frobenius (?), iii. 263 & n. 2.
unidentifiable and/or doubtful: Madonna, iv. 115 & n. 6; portraits: Edward VI, ii. 549; ~ Henry VIII, ii. 550 & n. 3; ~ Sir Thomas More, ii. 549; ~ Sir Brian Tuke, iv. 143 & n. 4; unspecified: historical picture, iii. 96 & n. 5; ~ at Kensington Palace, v. 237; ~ at Montague House, iv. 344.
wrongly attributed: Dancers (called Henry VIII, &c.), iv. 141 & n. 1; portrait of Edward VI, iv. 543 & n. 1; *see also* iii. 96, n. 5.
Holbein's Gate, Whitehall: *see* Whitehall.
Holden, Dr. Henry, Roman Catholic divine: discussion with, ii. 567 & n. 3.
Holden, Rebecca: dies, iv. 446 & n. 2.
Holden, Rev. Richard, vicar of Deptford 1673–1702 (our vicar, &c.), iv. 4, n. 5; *add.*; character of, and style of preaching, iv. 4–5; called 'our curate', v. 116; as rector of Great Casterton, &c.: visits parish, iv. 179 & n. 4; ~ resigns, iv. 522 & n. 2; as rector of St. Dunstan in the East: presented, *ib.*; ~ goes to, for winter, iv. 563 *bis*; children of, die, iv. 446 & n. 2; visits Tonbridge (Tunbridge Wells?), iv. 287; ill, iv. 237, 254, 280, 589, 591, 597; E entertains, iv. 495; attends Elizabeth Evelyn on her death-bed, iv. 463, 464; baptizes Thomas Draper, v. 193–4; marries John Evelyn, jnr., iv. 194.
sermons: at St. Nicholas, Deptford, iv. 4–v. 179; v. 191–200, 211–14, all *passim*; v. 239–40; before Lord Mayor: mentioned, iv. 284 & n. 1; to Trinity House, iv. 513; *see also* iv. 4, n. 5; at Whitehall (?), iv. 4 & n. 5; funeral: Sir R. Browne, iv. 302–3; — Cook, iv. 507; Mary Evelyn, iv. 430; Captain C. Gunman, iv. 432; Captain A. Young, v. 158–9.
Holden, Rev. William: geneal., iv. 4, n. 5.
Holdenby House: *see* Holmby.
Holder, William, D.D., iv. 84, n. 7; officiates at Whitehall, iv. 374; social, iv. 84, 124.
Holidays, secular: James II's birthday kept as holiday, iv. 526.
Holland [notices in which Holland is used for the Dutch Republic are indexed under United Provinces]: Gecommitteerde Raden: member of, iii. 470, n. 6 *ad fin.*; States of: levies of troops by, 1684, iv. 367, n. 3, 369 & n. 2; ~ slip for States General, iii. 323 & n. 5.
Holland: first Earl of, 1624–49: *see* Rich, Henry.
Holland (Netherlands): Earl, &c., of: *see* William I, count of Holland (ii. 50 & n. 3; i. 35); Henneberg, Margaret, countess of (i. 38; for identification *see* ii. 55, n. 3).

Holland, Rev. —, curate at Deptford: sermons by, iv. 5 & n. 2, 11, 23 & n. 3(?), 25, 26.
Holland, John, of Deptford: partner of Sir William Petty, iv. 57, n. 2.
Holland, Sir John, bt.: social, iii. 463 & n. 9.
Hollar, Wenceslaus, and his etchings, i. 21–2 & nn.; etches frontispiece of E's *Lucretius*, iii. 173, n. 2.
Holles, Denzil, first Baron Holles: created baron, iii. 277; geneal., iii. 16, n. 3.
Holles, Eleanor: *see* Fitzwilliam, Mrs. Eleanor, later countess of Tyrconnel.
Holles, John, first earl of Clare: geneal., iii. 16, n. 3.
Holles, John, second earl of Clare: house of, at Nottingham, iii. 125 & n. 7.
Holles, John, fourth earl of Clare; first duke of Newcastle 1694: created duke, v. 180 & n. 2.
Holles: first Baron, 1661–80: *see* Holles, Denzil.
Holloway (Hollowell), Sir Richard, judge: in Algernon Sidney's trial, iv. 352, n. 7; in trial of Seven Bishops, iv. 587 & n. 2; ~ dismissed for conduct in, iv. 589 & n. 1, 590 & n. 2; to be heard on Titus Oates's writ of error, iv. 636 & n. 1.
Holman, Mrs. Anastasia: at Stafford's impeachment (?), iv. 226–7 & n.
Holman, George: geneal., iv. 227, n. 1.
Holmby (Holdenby) House, Northants.: ruins of, iv. 70 & n. 3; granted to Lord Duras, later earl of Feversham, iv. 77.
Holme Lacy (Homlacy), Herefordshire: seat of the Viscounts Scudamore of Sligo, iii. 66 & n. 1.
Holme Pierrepont (Home), Notts.: notice, iii. 125 & n. 3.
Holmes, Sir Robert, admiral, iii. 529, n. 3; attacks Dutch Smyrna fleet, 1672, iii. 605–6 & n.; entertains Charles II, &c., at Cranbourn Lodge, iv. 38 & n. 2; entertains E at Portsmouth, iv. 473; social, iii. 529, 626.
Holstein: Duke of, 1689: *see* Christian Albrecht, duke of Gottorp (iv. 642, n. 6 & *add.*).
Holt, Sir T.: error for Sir R. Holte (?), iii. 290 & n. 6.
Holte, Sir Robert, bt.: social (?), iii. 290 & n. 6.
Holten, Carl von, ii. 466 & n. 2.
Holyhead, Anglesey: earthquake at, 1690, v. 36.
Holy Land: *see* Palestine.
Holy Roman Empire: *see* Empire.
Home: *see* Holme Pierrepont.
Homfleur: *see* Honfleur.
Homlacy: *see* Holme Lacy.
Hondius (Hundius), Hendrik (II): maps and printing-press of, ii. 49 & n. 3 (i. 34–5 & n.).
Hondsholredijk, Huis te (Hoff van Hounslers dyck), ii. 56 & nn. 1–3 (i. 38–9).
Honfleur (Homfleur): notice, ii. 125 (i. 80).
Honick, Dr. —: *see* Horneck, A.
Honiton, Devon: William of Orange at, iv. 607 & n. 3.
Honorato II, prince of Monaco, ii. 168–9 & n. (i. 106).
Honorius II, pope: error for Honorius III, ii. 381 & n. 3.
Honorius III, pope: crowns Peter of Auxerre, ii. 381 & n. 3; tomb of, ii. 244.
Honson Grange, Staffs. (Hanson Grange, Thorpe, Derbyshire ?): acquired and sold by E, iv. 415 & n. 2.
Honthorst, Gerard (G. Fiammingo): painting by, ii. 240 & n. 2.
Honywood, Benedict, captain, &c., in Dutch service: courtesy of, ii. 36 & n. 5 (i. 27).
Honywood, Mrs. Mary: geneal., ii. 36, n. 5.
Honywood, Sir Robert: geneal., ii. 36, n. 5.
Hoogstraten, S. van: peepshow painted by, iii. 165, n. 6.
Hooke, Robert; M.D. 1691: the scientist and architect, iii. 356, n. 9.
— as scientist:
— — curator of Royal Society, iii. 370, &c.; secretary of the Society, iv. 263, n. 3.
— — experiments and observations by (mainly for Royal Society): acoustics, iii. 563, n. 3; astronomy, iii. 385, n. 1, 392; geology, v. 30; microscopic observations, iii. 356–7 & n.; physics, iii. 396, 598 & n. 4; iv. 321 & n. 3.

Hooke, Robert (*cont.*)
— — miscellaneous papers by: on memory, iv. 284 & n. 2; on art of music, iii. 599 & n. 4.
— — instruments invented by, &c.: new balance, iv. 361; pendulum clocks, iii. 441 & n. 2, 450 & n. 2, 539; weather-clock, iv. 170 & n. 7; weights, falling: device for checking, iv. 325–6; windmill, iv. 325; miscellaneous, iii. 416.
— as architect: buildings designed by, &c.: new Bethlehem Hospital, iv. 134, n. 1; laboratory for Robert Boyle, iv. 124, n. 6; Montagu House, Bloomsbury, iv. 90 & n. 7, 184, 345; Royal College of Physicians, iv. 133, n. 8, 307, n. 3; Royal Society: plan of building for, iii. 505, n. 1.
— miscellaneous: at Durdans, 1665, iii. 416 & n. 3; social, iii. 370; lodgings of, iii. 433, n. 3.
Hooker, Dr. — (error for Dr. George Hooper?): sermon by, v. 44 & n. 4.
Hooker, Susanna, Lady Hooker, wife of Sir William: social, iv. 349 & n. 1.
Hooker, Sir William, lord mayor 1673–4, iii. 429, n. 3; knighted, iii. 429; social, iv. 349 & n. 1.
Hooper, George, D.D.; bishop of St. Asaph 1703; of Bath and Wells 1704, iv. 260, n. 2; ability of, as preacher, iv. 260; sermons by: printed, iv. 260 & n. 2; ~ unprinted, iv. 370, 537; v. 15, 44 & n. 4(?), 380–1 & n.; appointed to preach, iv. 371, n. 2.
Hope, the, reach of the Thames: Dutch fleet comes to, 1667, iii. 484, n. 1; naval engagement in, iii. 489 & n. 1.
Hopkins, Rev. —: sermons by, iii. 101 *bis*.
Hopton, Sir Arthur, ii. 555, n. 7; in England, 1649, ii. 555–6; account by, of Saludadores, iv. 469.
Hopton, Ralph, Baron Hopton: geneal., ii. 555 & n. 7.
Hopton: Baron, 1643–52: *see* Hopton, Ralph.
Horatii, the, ii. 361; tomb of, ii. 356 & n. 3.
Horatius Cocles: bridge defended by, ii. 357 & n. 3; triumphal arch of, ii. 360 & n. 2; in paintings, ii. 224 & n. 7.
Hore, —, calligrapher (R. Hoare?), ii. 559, n. 2.
Horeb, Mount: stone from: sculpture in, ii. 440 & n. 2.
Horne, Rev. Thomas, iv. 414, n. 1; sermon by, iv. 414 & n. 1; ~ quoted, iv. 407, n. 5; *add.*
Horneck (Honick), Anthony, D.D., iv. 306–7 & nn.; v. 329 & n. 1; attends Col. Vratz at his hanging, iv. 274, n. 1; sermon by, iv. 306; geneal., v. 317 & n. 4.
Horneck, Philip, v. 317, n. 4; sermons by: commemorative, for Lady Guilford, v. 365–6 & n.; ~ unprinted, v. 309 & n. 1(?), 317–18, 327–9, 529 & n. 5(?), 531 & n. 4(?).
Horninghold, Leics.: Sir John Prettyman's house at, iii. 73, n. 3, 121 & n. 8; E and Mrs. Evelyn visit, 1654, iii. 121–3, 133–4.
Horse-baiting, iii. 491–2; *add.*
Horseheath, Cambs.: Lord Alington's house at, iii. 553 & n. 3.
Horse-racing: London: on frozen Thames, 1684, iv. 362; Newmarket: heath, &c., at, iii. 555, 556; ~ races at, iii. 588–9; v. 320; *see also* Newmarket; Rome: carnival races, ii. 370, n. 1, 382; Salisbury: courses near, iii. 114–15 & nn.; Winchester: meeting established at, iv. 341, n. 2.
Horses and Horsemanship [select. Notices of horses used for transport are indexed under Coaches *and* Transport; *see also* Horse-baiting *and* Horse-racing]:
breeds and kinds of horses: various, ii. 195; Barbary, ii. 166 (i. 105); iii. 42; Neapolitan, i. 88 & n. 1; ii. 279–80, 327, 330; iii. 50; Persian, iii. 349; Turkish, iv. 398–9 & nn.; charging horse, iii. 57; great horse, ii. 134 (i. 87), 232; stone-horse, ii. 557; iii. 116, 169.
harness: Turkish, ii. 504; iv. 399; saddle with springs, iii. 435, 444.
horsemanship: 'bel homme de cheval', &c., iv. 400 & n. 5; Arab, iii. 25; French, i. 88; ii. 327, n. 4; Moroccan: displays, iv. 268–9 & n.; Neapolitan, ii. 327 & n. 4; jousting or tournaments, ii. 389 & n. 3, 483 & n. 1; riding-schools (the

Horses and Horsemanship (*cont.*)
buildings; called cavallerizzas or manages, &c.), ii. 71 (i. 47), 112 (i. 72); i. 87; ii. 195 & n. 5 (i. 120), 330 & n. 4, 504; riding-grounds, ii. 204, 232 & n. 6, 484, 527.
riding-academies: general, ii. 134 & n. 2 (i. 87–8 & n.); iv. 290; London (Foubert's), iv. 257–8 & n., 290 & n. 2, 399, 400 & n. 1; Naples, i. 88; Paris, ii. 134 & n. 2 (i. 87–8 & nn.); iii. 2 & nn. 3, 4, 7, 8 & n. 2; iv. 210; Richelieu, ii. 150 & n. 3 (i. 97).
women riders: astride (on mules), ii. 316; pillion: servant rides, iv. 71; riding-habit: Queen Catherine's, iii. 463 & n. 3.
miscellaneous: horse protected against theft by marking, iii. 70; horses: as tribute, ii. 279–80; ~ gentlemen's, requisitioned for army, 1650, iii. 14 & n. 6; ~ killed by highwaymen to stop pursuit, v. 122; riding on French and English roads, ii. 135 (i. 89); hippomanes or mare poison, iii. 337 & n. 2; horse's sperm examined by Royal Society, iv. 171; Captain Wray's nag, ii. 489, 513.
Horsham, Sussex: Christ's Hospital boys' school moved to, iii. 192, nn. 2, 3.
Horsley, Surrey: *see* East Horsley; West Horsley.
Hortensius: villa of, near Baia, ii. 349 & n. 8.
Horton, Surrey: manor of, ii. 542, n. 3.
Hoskins, John, miniaturist: portrait by, of Henrietta Maria, iii. 263 & n. 3.
Hoskins, Sir John, bt., iv. 212, n. 4, 588, n. 5; as F.R.S.: deputed to welcome (Sir) John Chardin, iv. 212 & n. 3; ~ elected president, iv. 296 & n. 6; introduced to Sunderland, iv. 588.
Hospitals and Charitable Institutions [the word hospital comprises institutions of several kinds; its significance in the Diary is difficult to determine because in the seventeenth century some of the older institutions for the care of the aged and infirm poor (asylums) were turning more and more to the treatment of the sick. Here the various institutions are grouped so far as possible according to their functions]:

Hospitals, &c. (*cont.*)
— general: use of words 'hospital' and 'asylum', iii. 77; hospitals and workhouses in United Provinces, i. 25; *see also* ii. 45–6 (i. 32–3); visit to almshouse, iv. 28; Sick and Wounded and: use English hospitals, 1664–7, 1672–4, iii. 388, 405; iv. 24 & n. 5; ~ inspector of, iii. 445; ~ business relating to, iii. 516 & n. 1; ~ projected infirmary for, iii. 430 & n. 2, 431, 432.
— particular institutions:
— — asylum (pensioners, almsfolk): Amsterdam: Gasthuis, &c., ii. 43, n. 2, 45, n. 6; ~ disabled English soldiers at, ii. 45 & n. 6 (i. 32); Charlton: Sir J. Morden's Hospital, v. 212 & n. 5; Deptford: Trinity Hospital (Trinity House almshouses), iii. 577 & n. 6; iv. 303; Guildford: Trinity Hospital, iii. 88 & n. 4; Leicester: Trinity Hospital, iii. 122–3 & nn.; Rome: S. Lorenzo in Miranda, ii. 219 & n. 3; ~ Taberna meritoria, ii. 288–9 & n.; *see also* Greenwich Hospital; London: environs: Chelsea Hospital.
— — asylum and school: Dulwich College, iv. 74 & n. 1; Lee, Kent: Boone's almshouses, &c., iv. 288–9; London: Charterhouse, ii. 45 & n. 3 (i. 32); iii. 192 & n. 1; Lyons: La Charité, ii. 157–8 & n. (i. 101).
— — blind: Paris: Quinze-Vingts, ii. 101 & n. 4 (i. 66).
— — lunatics: Amsterdam: Dolhuys, ii. 45 & n. 5 (i. 32); London: Bethlehem Hospital, ii. 45 (i. 32); iii. 191–2 & n.; iv. 134 & n. 1.
— — pilgrims and travellers: Amsterdam: Gasthuis, ii. 43 & n. 2 (i. 31); Rome: SS. Trinità de' Pellegrini, ii. 366 & n. 3; Siena, ii. 205 & nn. 3, 4; *see also* London: topography: Savoy Hospital.
— — schools and orphanages: Am-

Hospitals, &c. (*cont.*)
sterdam: Wees-huys, ii. 45 & n. 3 (i. 32); Florence: Spedale degli Innocenti, ii. 195 & n. 4 (i. 120); London: Christ's Hospital, ii. 311; iii. 192 & n. 2; iv. 542–3 & nn.
— — sick: Greenwich: King's House, 1692, v. 203, n. 1; London: St. Bartholomew's, iii. 455 & n. 4; ~ St. Thomas's, iii. 391 & n. 4; iv. 560; Milan, ii. 495–6 & n.; Padua, ii. 476 & n. 1; Paris: Hôtel-Dieu, ii. 101 & n. 5 (i. 66); iii. 3, n. 5; ~ La Charité, ii. 101 & n. 6 (i. 66 & n. 1); iii. 3–4, 22; Rome: Incurabili, ii. 373 & n. 7; ~ S. Giovanni Colavita, ii. 358 & n. 10; ~ SS. Rocca e Martino, ii. 375 & n. 4.
— — sick and orphanage: Rome: S. Spirito, ii. 311–12 & nn.; *see also* ii. 292, n. 2.
— — unspecified, &c.: Rome: Spedale di Campo Santo, ii. 290 & n. 2; S. Giovanni in Laterano, ii. 275 & n. 4, 385 & n. 6.
Hostun, Camille d', duc d' Hostun, comte de Tallard: *see* Tallard.
Hotham, Sir John: refusal of, to surrender Hull to Charles I, iii. 130–1 & n.
Hot Springs: *see* Medicinal and Hot Springs.
Houblon, Sir James; knighted 1691, iv. 162, n. 6; houses of: in London, iv. 162–3 & n.; ~ in Epping Forest, iv. 306; Pepys informs, about Charles II's death-bed conversion, iv. 475 ff. & n.; social (?; as Obloor), iv. 128 & n. 6.
Houblon, Sir John, iv. 162, n. 6; as lord mayor: attends Greenwich Hospital committee meeting, v. 236 & n. 2.
Hough (Huff), John, D.D.; bishop of Oxford 1690; of Lichfield 1699; of Worcester 1717: sermon by, v. 40 & n. 2.
Houghton (Haughton), Sussex: E visits J. Michell at, ii. 21 & n. 6 (i. 16).
Hounslers dyck, Hoff van: *see* Hondsholredijk, Huis te.
Hounslow (Hownslow) *and* Hounslow Heath, Middlesex: as post-station, iv. 152, 528; the Priory at, iii. 447, n. 3; encampments
Hounslow (*cont.*)
at: 1678, iv. 136–7; ~ 1686, iv. 513 & n. 5, 514; *see also* iv. 516, 517, 519; ~ 1687, iv. 553 & n. 1; ~ 1688, v. 590 & n. 1; ~ the years 1686–8, iv. 629; ~ movable chapel for Roman Catholic services in, v. 61–2 & n.; review, 1685, iv. 458, n. 1, 463 & n. 2.
Housing: Leicestershire, iii. 122; London: before 1666, ii. 124 (i. 79); Paris, iii. 637, 638; Rhone valley, ii. 156 (i. 100); Rouen, ii. 124 (i. 79); Valais, ii. 517 & n. 2; cave-dwellings, &c.: in England, iii. 120–1 & n., 125 & n. 5; ~ in France, ii. 144 & n. 2 (i. 93); iii. 125.
Howard, — (Henry Howard of Norfolk?): social, iii. 351 & n. 12, 366.
Howard, —, duke of Norfolk (*temp.* Henry VIII): in painting (error), iv. 141 & n. 1.
Howard, —, Lord Howard (Charles Howard, later earl of Carlisle?): social, iii. 252 & n. 7.
Howard, —, Lord Howard of the North (Charles Howard, later earl of Carlisle?): social, iii. 239 & n. 3.
Howard, Alathea, countess of Arundel, born Talbot, wife of Thomas Howard, second earl, ii. 479, n. 4; relations of, with Arundel, ii. 479 & n. 4; resident in Netherlands, *ib.*; ii. 543, n. 4; inherits Worksop Abbey, iii. 127, n. 2; lawsuit following death of, iv. 234, n. 3.
Howard, Anastasia: *see* Holman, Mrs. A.
Howard, Ann, daughter of Mrs. Elizabeth Howard: *see* Sylvius, Ann, Lady Sylvius.
Howard, Mrs. Anne, born Ogle, wife of Craven Howard, iv. 70, 71, n. 1.
Howard, Anne, countess of Carlisle, born Howard, wife of Charles Howard, first earl: godmother of Sir John Chardin, bt. (?), iv. 561 & n. 2.
Howard, Anne, countess of Carlisle, born Capel, wife of Charles Howard, third earl: childhood of, iv. 201 & n. 3.
Howard, Lady Anne, born Somerset, first wife of Henry Howard, later sixth duke of Norfolk: influence of, on Howard, &c., iii. 593 & n. 2; geneal., iv. 142 & n. 5.

Howard, Barbara, countess of Suffolk, born Villiers, wife of James Howard, third earl, iv. 17, n. 4; lends jewel for *Calisto*, iv. 51; social, iv. 17.
Howard, Bernard, brother of Henry Howard, sixth duke of Norfolk, iii. 329, n. 1; social, iii. 329; iv. 403.
Howard, Catherine: *see* Livingston, Catherine, countess of Newburgh.
Howard, Catherine, countess of Nottingham, born Carey, wife of Charles Howard, first earl: geneal., iii. 156, n. 1.
Howard, Charles, of Greystoke, iii. 154, n. 5; garden of, at Dorking (Deepdene), iii. 154 & n. 5; assists Royal Society, iii. 472, n. 2; in lawsuits, iv. 234, n. 3, 450 & n. 2; social, iii. 329, 375, 377, 561.
Howard, Lord Charles: designation applied to Charles Howard, later first earl of Carlisle, iii. 252, n. 7.
Howard, Charles, second earl of Berkshire: heir apparent of, iv. 70–1 & n.
Howard, Charles; first earl of Carlisle 1661, iii. 239, n. 3; created Viscount Howard of Morpeth by Cromwell, *ib.*; designated as Lord Charles Howard, Lord Howard (?), and Lord Howard of the North (?), iii. 239 & n. 3, 252 & n. 7; created earl, iii. 277; speech of, to Tsar Alexis: cited, iii. 344, n. 5 *ad fin.*; vote of, on Stafford's impeachment, iv. 234 & n. 1; proposes marriage between his son and Ann Evelyn (later Mrs. Montague), iii. 475 & nn. 1, 2; social iii. 239 & n. 3(?), 252 & n. 7(?); geneal., iv. 561, nn. 2, 4.
Howard, Charles; third earl of Carlisle 1692, iv. 201, n. 3; as acting Earl Marshal: proclamation by, v. 493, n. 1.
Howard, Charles, Viscount Howard of Morpeth: *see* Howard, Charles, first earl of Carlisle.
Howard, Charles, tenth duke of Norfolk: geneal., iii. 154, n. 5.
Howard, Charles, first earl of Nottingham: geneal., iii. 156, n. 1.
Howard, Craven: brings action against his mother, &c., iv. 70–1 & n.
Howard, Dorothy, daughter of Mrs. Elizabeth Howard: *see* Graham, Mrs. Dorothy.
Howard, Edward, brother of Henry Howard, sixth duke of Norfolk: social, iii. 329 & n. 1.
Howard, Edward; second earl of Carlisle 1685, iii. 475, n. 1; marriage project for, iii. 475; geneal., iv. 561, n. 2.
Howard, Edward, first Baron Howard of Escrick: geneal., iv. 561, n. 2.
Howard, Elizabeth: *see* Mordaunt, Elizabeth, countess of Peterborough.
Howard, Elizabeth: *see* Percy, Elizabeth, countess of Northumberland.
Howard, Mrs. Elizabeth, widow of William Howard, son of the first earl of Berkshire, iii. 345, n. 4; on pleasure journey, iii. 529–30; attends assize at Northampton, iv. 67–71 & nn.; concern in her daughters' marriages, iv. 69, 123; social, iii. 345; iv. 34–5, 36, 47, 50, 64 *bis*, 123; geneal., iii. 529, n. 1; iv. 71, n. 1; daughters of: *see* Graham, Mrs. Dorothy; Sylvius, Anne, Lady Sylvius.
Howard, Elizabeth, countess of Arundel, born Stuart, wife of H. F. Howard, third earl, ii. 543, n. 4; social, ii. 543, 545, 556.
Howard, Elizabeth, countess of Carlisle, born Uvedale, wife of Edward Howard, second earl, and previously of Sir W. Berkeley, iii. 475, n. 1; iv. 561, n. 2; godmother of Sir John Chardin, bt. (?), iv. 561.
Howard, George; fourth earl of Suffolk 1689, v. 3, n. 3; chaplain of: sermon by, v. 3–4.
Howard, Henry, 1628–84; created Baron Howard of Castle Rising 1669; earl of Norwich 1672; sixth duke of Norfolk 1677, ii. 473, n. 1.
— character, iii. 592–3, 593–4, 596; influence on, of his first wife, &c., iii. 593.
— chronological series: 1645–6: at Padua, ii. 473, 479; 1661: obtains restoration of dukedom of Norfolk, iii. 326; *see also* iii. 306 & n. 3; 1663: returns from France, iii. 352; 1668: created D.C.L., Oxford, iii. 500, n. 6; 1669: created baron, iii. 524, n. 8; *see also* iii. 500 & n. 4, 592 & n. 1; 1669–70: goes ambassador

Howard, Henry, 1628–84 (*cont.*)
to Morocco, iii. 528 & n. 4; *see also* iii. 500 & n. 4; 1671: entertains Charles II and Queen Catherine at Norwich, iii. 592, n. 1, 593 & n. 3; 1672: created earl of Norwich and Earl Marshal, iii. 596, n. 1, 625 & n. 4; 1677(?): second marriage of, iii. 592 & n. 5; iv. 128 & n. 2; 1677: succeeds as duke, iv. 127–8 & n.; 1678: visits Windsor, iv. 142; 1680: goes abroad, iv. 235–6.
— art-collection: notices, iii. 155 & nn. 1–4; iv. 141 & n. 1; drawings in: negotiation for purchase of, iv. 312 & nn. 3, 4.
— gifts made by, &c.: general, i. *21* & n. 1; to College of Arms: heraldic MSS., iii. 472, n. 3; iv. 144 & n. 3; Oxford University: Arundel inscriptions, iii. 495–500 & nn., *passim*, 534, n. 4; *see also* iv. 89 & nn. 2–4; Royal Society: invited to meet at Arundel House, 1666, iii. 472 & n. 2; ~ Norfolcian library given to, iii. 472–3 & n., 524; iv. 144–5 & nn.; ~ promised gift (building-site or money), iii. 505, n. 1; ~ venison, iii. 565.
— property: estates, &c.: Albury: in possession of, ii. 77, n. 2; ~ alters house and gardens, iii. 154–5; *see also* ii. 551 & n. 5; ~ E designs garden for, at, iii. 496 & n. 2; iv. 111, 558; ~ sells, iv. 558, n. 1; Arundel House, London: design for rebuilding, 1659, iii. 234 & n. 4; ~ Royal Society at, &c., iii. 472 & n. 2, 505 & n. 1; ~ E advises rebuilding, 1671, iii. 595 & n. 5; Ashtead: sells to Sir R. Howard, iv. 376, n. 3; Norwich: Castle (error), iii. 594 & n. 4, 595; ~ Ducal Palace: alterations to, &c., iii. 593 & n. 3, 595 & nn. 3, 4; Weybridge: house at, iv. 140–1 & n., 142.
— — miscellaneous: settles his grandfather's debts, iii. 326 & n. 2; lawsuit of, with Lord Stafford, iv. 234, n. 3; *see also* art-collection *and* gifts *above*.
— relations with E: gift to, iii. 234; John Evelyn, jnr., brought up with children of, *c.* 1662–3, iii. 326 & n. 6, 329, 355; makes gifts on E's advice, iii. 472, 495–6, 498–500; iv. 144–5; E dedicates book to, iii. 496, n. 1, 514 & n. 2; asks E to receive Venetian ambassador, 1668, iii. 515, n. 1; interest of, in E's *History of the Three Impostors*, iii. 522, n. 2; E negotiates for purchase of his drawings, iv. 312; E visits: at Albury, iii. 88, 154–5, 325–6, 496; *see also* property *above*; ~ at Norwich, 1671, iii. 592–6; ~ at Weybridge, iv. 140–2; further social intercourse, iii. 233, 234, 329, 351 & n. 12(?), 352, 354–5, 366, 504; iv. 88, 235–6; *see also* London: topography: Arundel House.
— religion: intends to become Anglican, iii. 595–6 & n.; views on, iv. 142.
— social, &c.: at dinner-party, iii. 564; at Euston, iii. 592; visits to: Sir R. Clayton, iii. 625; ~ Sir William Ducie, Viscount Downe, iii. 525; relations of, with Sir S. Tuke, iii. 373, 593.
— geneal., iii. 329 & nn. 1, 2, 592; iv. 141, n. 2, 142 & n. 5, 225–6; wives of: *see* Howard, Lady Anne; Howard, Jane, duchess of Norfolk.
Howard, Henry, 1655–1701; styled earl of Arundel 1677–84; seventh duke of Norfolk 1684, iii. 329, n. 2.
character, v. 394.
boyhood: John Evelyn, jnr., brought up with, iii. 326 & n. 6, 329, 355; social, iii. 344; goes to France, iii. 373, 375; returns from France, iii. 482; at Oxford, iii. 535 & n. 3; to become Anglican, iii. 596 & n. 2.
public life: called to house of lords as Lord Mowbray, 1678, iii. 596, n. 2; vote of, on Stafford's impeachment, iv. 234 & n. 1; as Earl Marshal: proclaims James II's accession, iv. 412 & n. 7; ~ issues instructions for mourning for Charles II and for Mary II, iv. 414, n. 3; v. 202, n. 1; as lord lieutenant of Surrey: conduct of, at parliamentary election, 1685, iv. 434; ~ request to, v. 169–70

Howard, Henry, 1655–1701 (*cont.*) & n.; ~ conduct of, at presentation of address, 1697, v. 279.
private life, &c.: projected marriage of, iii. 592 & n. 4; marries, iv. 112 & n. 5; seeks divorce, v. 90 & n. 7, 127 & n. 1, 380 & n. 3; obtains divorce, v. 393–4 & n.; converts Arundel House, London, into tenements, iii. 234, n. 4; sells Arundel sculptures (?), v. 44–5 & n.; in lawsuit, 1685, iv. 450 & n. 2; admitted F.R.S., &c., iv. 396 & n. 3; horsemanship of, iv. 400; at Weybridge, 1678 (?), iv. 141; social: parties, iv. 537; v. 280; ~ alone, &c., iv. 466, 475; dies, v. 453 & n. 3.
duchess of: *see* Mordaunt, Lady Mary.

Howard, Henry; earl of Northampton 1604, iii. 141, n. 2; builds Northumberland House, London, *ib.*; founds Trinity Hospital, Greenwich, ii. 76, n. 4; *see also* i. 50.

Howard, Henry; fifth earl of Suffolk 1691: buys Audley End, iii. 140, n. 7 *ad fin.*

Howard, Henry Frederick; styled Lord Mowbray 1640–6; third earl of Arundel 1646, ii. 470, n. 4; in quarrel, 1640, ii. 25, n. 2; at Venice, ii. 470; dispute of, with Dowager Lady Arundel, ii. 479, n. 4; carving owned by, iii. 155; social, ii. 556; geneal., ii. 473, n. 1, 543, n. 4; iii. 154, n. 5.

Howard, Isabella: *see* Paulet (Powlett), Isabella, marchioness of Winchester.

Howard, James; third earl of Suffolk 1640, iii. 277, n. 3; as Earl Marshal, *ib.*; vote of, on Stafford's impeachment, iv. 234 & n. 1; geneal., iv. 17, n. 4; v. 587.

Howard, Jane, duchess of Norfolk, born Bickerton, second wife of Henry Howard, sixth duke, iii. 592, n. 5; marriage of, character, &c., iii. 592–3 & n.; iv. 128 & n. 2; children of, iii. 592; iv. 141 & n. 2; Norfolk's regard for, iv. 312; and Weybridge: owns house at, iv. 140, n. 8; ~ resident at, iv. 142; ~ art-collection of, at: sale of, iv. 566 & n. 2; sells Arundel sculptures (?), v. 44–5 & n.

Howard, Mary: *see* Winter, Mary, Lady Winter.

Howard, Lady Mary, duchess of Norfolk, born Mordaunt, wife of Henry Howard, seventh duke, and secondly of Sir John Germaine: *see* Mordaunt, Lady Mary.

Howard, Mrs. Mary, wife of Charles Howard of Greystoke, iii. 154, n. 5; social, iii. 375.

Howard, Mary, Lady Howard, born Uphill, wife of Sir Robert: association of, with Howard, &c., iii. 466, n. 2.

Howard, Philip Thomas, cardinal, ii. 479 & n. 3; becomes Dominican, *ib.*; as chaplain, &c., to Queen Catherine, iii. 329 & n. 1, 547 & n. 2; writes to E about Dr. Yvelin, iii. 547–8; social, iii. 329, 577.

Howard, Sir Robert, the dramatist, &c., iii. 466, n. 2; character, iv. 316 & n. 3, 416 & n. 3; mistress or wife of, iii. 465–6 & n.; commissioner for London streets, iii. 319, n. 1; and impeachment of Sir W. Penn, iii. 508 & n. 3; theatrical concern of, iii. 345, n. 3; plays by, acted: *The Committee*, iii. 345 & n. 3; ~ *Indian Queen* (with Dryden), iii. 368–9 & n.; house of, at Ashtead, iv. 376–7 & n.; social, iii. 529; iv. 316, 416; portrait of, iv. 377; geneal., iii. 529, n. 1; v. 55–6.

Howard, Theophilus; second earl of Suffolk 1626: geneal., iii. 141, n. 2 *ad fin.*, 264, n. 5; iv. 400, n. 3.

Howard, Thomas, 1651–1701, son of Sir Robert, v. 55–6 & n.; attends funeral of John Evelyn of Wotton, v. 55; dies, v. 453 & n. 4.

Howard, Thomas, d. 1689; styled Lord Thomas Howard 1677–89, iii. 329, n. 2; iv. 142, n. 4; boyhood: John Evelyn, jnr., brought up with, iii. 326, 329, 355; ~ social, iii. 344; ~ goes to France, iii. 373, 375; ~ returns, &c., iii. 482; ~ at Oxford, iii. 535 & n. 3; at Weybridge, 1678, iv. 142; geneal., v. 394 & n. 1.

Howard, Thomas, 1585–1646, second earl of Arundel [in other reckonings twenty-first or fourteenth earl], the art-collector, ii. 27, n. 4.
— chronological series: 1621: created Earl Marshal, iii. 596, n.

Howard, Thomas, 1585–1646 (*cont.*) 1; 1636: goes on embassy to Vienna, i. 21 & n. 1; 1641: Lord High Steward at Strafford's trial, ii. 27 (i. 20); iv. 226; ~ accompanies Marie de Médicis to Cologne, ii. 57 (i. 39); ~ return journey, Ghent–London, ii. 72, 74–6 (i. 47, 49–51); ~ at Albury, ii. 77 (i. 51); 1645–6: at Padua, ii. 466–7, 473, 479 & nn. 2, 5; ~ family troubles, ii. 479 & nn. 3, 4.

— as art-lover, &c.: 'that great virtuoso', iii. 326; patron of H. van der Borcht and Hollar, i. 21; *see also* ii. 29, n. 1; portrait of, by Rubens, v. 145 & n. 3; gives letter of recommendation to an artist, i. 74; praises Lake of Garda, ii. 488 & n. 6.

— art-collections: formation of: helped by Sir A. Hopton, ii. 555, n. 7; drawing made for, ii. 298, n. 3; attempted purchases: drawings by Leonardo, ii. 498 & nn. 6, 8; ~ obelisk, ii. 362 & n. 5; ~ statues, ii. 217 & n. 1, 415, n. 6.

— — contents: pictures: etchings after, by Hollar, i. 21; statues, *add.* (v. 44, n. 6).

— — dispersal of: inscriptions: given to Oxford University by Henry Howard, sixth duke of Norfolk, iii. 495–500 & nn., *passim*; *see also* i. *21*; iii. 534, n. 4; iv. 89 & nn. 2–4; by embezzlement, iii. 472, n. 3; by sale: drawings, iv. 312 & n. 3; ~ paintings, &c., iv. 566 & n. 2; ~ statues, v. 44–5 & n.

— library: purchase for, iv. 145 & n. 4; dispersed by gifts of Henry Howard, sixth duke of Norfolk, iii. 472–3 & nn., 524; iv. 144–5 & nn.

— property: Albury, ii. 77, n. 2; Worksop Abbey, iii. 127 & n. 2; debts of: settled by Henry Howard, sixth duke of Norfolk, iii. 326 & n. 2.

— relations with E: influence of, on E, i. 5; regard of, for E, i. 74; iii. 326, 593; iv. 226; takes E sight-seeing at Padua, ii. 466–7 & n.; instructions of, for E's journey from Padua to Milan: writes, &c., ii. 479 & n. 5; ~ as source for Diary, i. *87*; ii. 482–99, nn. *passim*; ~ mentioned, iii. 98, n. 5.

— geneal. ii. 470, 473, 479 & nn. 3, 4, 7; iv. 225–6 & n.; countess of: *see* Howard, Alathea, countess of Arundel.

Howard, Thomas; first earl of Berkshire, 1626, iii. 529, n. 1; *add.*; builds Berkshire House, London, iii. 470, n. 5; social, iii. 529; geneal., iii. 345, n. 4; iv. 416.

Howard, Thomas, third earl of Berkshire: vote of, on Stafford's impeachment, iv. 234 & n. 1.

Howard, Thomas, 1536–72, fourth duke of Norfolk: attainder of, iii. 306, n. 3; *add.*

Howard, Thomas, 1627–77; fourth earl of Arundel 1652; fifth duke of Norfolk 1660 or 1661, iii. 306, n. 3; restored to dukedom, iii. 306 & n. 3; insane, &c., iii. 329; brothers of, *ib.*; heirs of, iii. 344; dies, iv. 128 & n. 1.

Howard, Thomas; eighth duke of Norfolk 1701: demolishes Duke's Palace, Norwich, iii. 593, n. 3.

Howard, Thomas; first earl of Suffolk 1603, iii. 140, n. 7; builds: Audley End, iii. 140 & n. 7; ~ Northumberland House, London (error), iii. 141 & n. 2.

Howard, William, son of Thomas Howard, first earl of Berkshire: deceased husband of Mrs. Elizabeth Howard, iii. 345, n. 4; trust created by, iv. 71, n. 1, 105–6, 106.

Howard, Lord William, of Naworth Castle: geneal., ii. 546, n. 8.

Howard, William, d. 1615; styled Lord Howard of Effingham from 1596: geneal., iii. 156, n. 1.

Howard, William, d. 1694; third Baron Howard of Escrick 1678, iv. 322, n. 7; vote of, on Stafford's impeachment, iv. 234 & n. 1; arrested for Rye-House plot, iv. 322 & n. 7; turns informer, iv. 323 & n. 8; at Lord Russell's trial, iv. 327, n. 2; witness against Algernon Sidney, iv. 353 & n. 1.

Howard, William, 1614–80; created Viscount Stafford 1640, iii. 35, n. 5 (his surname given wrongly); *add.*; character of, iv. 234 & nn. 3, 4; disliked by his Howard kin, iv. 234, 236; in Paris, 1651(?),

Howard, William, 1614–80 (*cont.*) iii. 35 & n. 5; at dinner-party, iii. 550; antipathy of, to roses, *ib.*; imprisoned in Tower for Popish Plot, iv. 158 & n. 7; as prisoner, iv. 169, 174 (name not given).
trial of, for treason, iv. 225–34 & nn.; *add.*; counsel of, at, iv. 234 & n. 2; daughters of, at, iv. 226–7 & n.; witnesses of, at, iv. 228 & n. 8, 229, nn. 1, 4; voted guilty by: the Howard peers, iv. 234 & n. 1; ~ Sunderland, iv. 245, n. 5; executed, iv. 236 & n. 2.
Howard *or* Howard of the North: Lord, 1660: *see* Howard, Charles, first earl of Carlisle.
Howard of Castle Rising: Baron, 1669–72: *see* Howard, Henry, later sixth duke of Norfolk.
Howard of Charleton: Baron, 1622–6: *see* Howard, Thomas, later earl of Berkshire.
Howard of Effingham: Lord, 1596–1615 (courtesy title): *see* Howard, William.
Howard of Escrick: Barons: *see* Howard, Edward, first baron; Howard, William, third baron, 1678–94.
Howard of Morpeth: Viscount, 1657–60 (Cromwellian creation): *see* Howard, Charles, later first earl of Carlisle.
Howe (How), John Grubham: attacks Burnet's *Pastoral Letter* in parliament, v. 131 & n. 2.
Howe, Scrope, Viscount Howe, v. 453, critical note & n. 5.
Howe: first Viscount, 1701–13: *see* Howe, Scrope.
Howell, James: as historiographer royal, iii. 523, n. 1.
Hoy (Foy), Thomas, M.D.: recommended for Regius professorship, v. 298 & n. 2.
Hubbard, —: *see* Hubert, Robert.
Hubbert, Sir Richard: *see* Hobart *or* Hubbert.
Hubert, Robert, *alias* Forges: natural history collection of, iii. 433, n. 3.
Hubin, Louis: experiments by, at Royal Society meeting, iv. 293 & n. 2.
Huddlestone (Hurlston), Father John, O.S.B.: attends Charles II on death-bed, iv. 408 & n. 1.
Huff, Dr. —: *see* Hough, John.
Hugenius: *see* Huygens, Christiaan.
Hugh Capet, King of France, ii. 95.
Hughes, Margaret, mistress of Prince Rupert: alluded to (?), iii. 466 & n. 3.
Huguenots: *see* French protestants.
Huis: *see* Huy.
Hull, Yorkshire, E.R.: notice, iii. 130–1 & nn.; declares for William of Orange, iv. 609; executions at: guillotine used for (error), ii. 401 & n. 1.
Hull, river, iii. 130, n. 6.
Humber: passage over, iii. 131 & n. 2.
Humphrey, duke of Gloucester: Gloucester castle granted to, iii. 118, n. 3.
Humphreys, Humphrey, D.D.; bishop of Bangor 1689; of Hereford 1701, iv. 653, n. 1; sermons by, iv. 653; v. 203.
Humphry, Ozias: geneal., i. *52*.
Hundius: *see* Hondius.
Hungary: Turks invade, 1683, iv. 331; recovered by Emperor, 1688, iv. 598; v. 7; rebellion in, 1703–4, v. 544, 546, 553, 572, 581; king of: *see* Joseph I, Emperor.
Hungerford, Berks.: trout at, iii. 104 & n. 2.
Hungerford family: Cadenham branch, iii. 100, n. 6; acquires farm in Great Durnford, iii. 115, n. 3.
Hungerford, —, cousin of E (or Mrs. Evelyn), iii. 161 & n. 4.
Hungerford, Edward, of Cadenham, uncle by marriage of Mrs. Evelyn, iii. 101 & n. 1; house of, at Cadenham, iii. 100–1 & n.; farm of, at Great Durnford, iii. 115 & n. 3; geneal., ii. 22, n. 1; iii. 89, n. 5, 161, n. 4, 176, n. 1; iv. 136, n. 1.
Hungerford, Elizabeth: *see* Moore, Elizabeth, Lady Moore.
Hungerford, Elizabeth: *see* Richards, Elizabeth, Lady Richards.
Hungerford, Frances, Lady Hungerford, wife of Sir George: social, iv. 136 & n. 1.
Hungerford, Sir George: geneal., iv. 136, n. 1.
Hungerford, John: expelled from house of commons, 1695, v. 207, n. 7 *ad fin.*
Hungerford, Sir John, of Downe: geneal., ii. 22, n. 1.

Hungerford, Mrs. Susan (Susanna), born Prettyman, wife of Edward Hungerford of Cadenham ('Aunt Hungerford'), iii. 89, n. 5; godmother of children of E, iii. 89, 421, 528; visits Sayes Court, iii. 93, 167, 193, 318, 367; iv. 109, 136, 290, 291; visited by Mrs. Evelyn and Susanna Evelyn (Mrs. Draper), v. 61; geneal., iv. 136 & n. 1.
Hungerford, Walter, D.D.: sermon by, iii. 101 & n. 2.
Hüningen, in Alsace: projected French fort at, v. 35, n. 8.
Hunniades, the noble, iii. 446, n. 6.
Huns, the: Paris delivered from, ii. 100, n. 6; invasion of Italy by, ii. 431.
Hunsdon: fourth Lord, 1617–28: *see* Carey, Henry, earl of Dover.
Hunter, Dr. Alexander: editions of *Sylva* by, i. 57 & nn. 2, 3.
Huntercombe, Bucks.: Manor House, iv. 177 & n. 2.
Huntingdon: notice, iii. 135 & n. 5.
Huntingdon: Earls, &c., of: *see* Hastings, Ferdinando, sixth earl, 1643–56; Hastings, Lucy, his countess; Hastings, Theophilus, seventh earl, 1656–1701; Hastings, George, eighth earl, 1701–5.
Huntingdonshire: fertility of, iii. 135.
Huntingtower (Huntingtore): Lord, 1651–98 (courtesy title): *see* Tollemache (Talmash), Sir Lionel, later earl of Dysart.
Hurcott, manor, Kidderminster, Worcs.: bought and sold by E, ii. 541 & n. 5, 545 & n. 3.
Hurlston, Father: *see* Huddlestone, J.
Hurlstone, Captain Nicholas: elected Master of Trinity House, iii. 408 & n. 4.
Hurst Castle, Hants: removal to, of Charles I: debate on, ii. 545, n. 6.
Hus, John: martyrdom of: medal showing, iv. 396 & n. 5.
Hussey, John, of Sutton in Shere, iv. 454, n. 5; suitor for Mary Evelyn, iv. 425 & n. 2(?), 454–5; dies, iv. 454–5.
Hussey, Mrs. Margaret, born Evelyn, wife of Peter Hussey of Gumshall: marriage of, v. 202 & n. 5.
Hussey, Peter, of Gumshall, v. 202, n. 5; marries, v. 202 & n. 5; social, v. 480.
Hussey, Peter, of Sutton in Shere, iii. 561 & n. 7; seat of, iii. 561; iv. 255–6 & n.; geneal., iv. 454, n. 5.
Hussey, Sir William, English ambassador to Turkey: dies, v. 71 & n. 6.
Hutcheson, Rev. —: *see* Hutchinson, Dr. Thomas.
Hutchins, Dr. — or Rev. —: *see* Hutchinson, Dr. Thomas.
Hutchinson (Hutchison), Catherine, Lady Hutchinson, wife of Sir Thomas: social (?), iii. 552 & n. 1.
Hutchinson, Col. John: geneal., iii. 552, n. 1.
Hutchinson, Mrs. Lucy, wife of Col. John Hutchinson: geneal., ii. 36, n. 4.
Hutchinson, Dr. Thomas, iv. 72, n. 1; *add.*; [the following entries all presumably refer to this man]: as Mr. Hutcheson: sermon by, iv. 72; as Dr. or Mr. Hutchin or Hutchins: sermons by, iv. 386 & n. 2, 460, 500, 538, 546, 581 *bis*, 589, 591.
Hutchinson, Sir Thomas: geneal., iii. 552, n. 1.
Huy (Huis): castle of: taken by French, 1693, v. 148 & n. 3; town retaken by Confederates, 1694, v. 191 & n. 2.
Huygens, Christiaan, of Zuylichem (Monsieur Zulecum), astronomer, &c., iii. 276 & n. 1; in England, 1661: scientific activities of, iii. 285, 285–6 & nn.; *add.*; ~ social, iii. 276; in England, 1663: elected F.R.S., iii. 276, n. 1; ~ meets E at Lady Needham's, *add.* (iii. 363 & n. 1); on Sir R. Moray, iii. 272, n. 3; pendulum clocks of, iii. 261, n. 1, 276, 285, n. 4; explains Saturn's rings, iii. 276, 286 & n. 3; geneal., iii. 377, n. 1.
Huygens, Constantijn, sen., heer van Zuylichem, iii. 377 & n. 1, 582 & n. 4; visits E, 1664, 1671, iii. 377, 378, 582.
Huygens, Constantijn, jnr.: befriended by L. Lincler, iii. 10, nn. 1, 3.
Hyde (Hide), —: buried, Paris, 1650, iii. 8.
Hyde, — (Laurence Hyde, later earl of Rochester ?): social, iv. 181 & n. 7.

Hyde, Anne, daughter of Edward Hyde, earl of Clarendon: *see* Anne, duchess of York.
Hyde, Anne, daughter of Lawrence Hyde, earl of Rochester: *see* Butler, Anne, countess of Ossory.
Hyde, Bridget: *see* Osborne, Bridget, duchess of Leeds, wife of Peregrine Osborne, second duke.
Hyde, Edward, d. 1702: dies, v. 521 & n. 8.
Hyde, Sir Edward, 1609–74; created Baron Hyde of Hindon 1660; first earl of Clarendon 1661; the Lord Chancellor, ii. 561, n. 5.
— character, iii. 493 & n. 6; iv. 339; conversation of, iii. 331 & n. 1.
— public career, &c.: in Paris, 1649, ii. 561; as ambassador to Spain, 1651 (error), iii. 32–3 *bis* & n.; agent sent by, to England, 1655, iii. 53, n. 4; as chancellor of Oxford University, iii. 384 & n. 3, 474; relations of, with Henrietta Maria, Oct. 1660, iii. 258 & n. 4; created baron, iii. 258, n. 4; created earl, iii. 277 & nn. 2, 3; thanked by Royal Society for services, 1662, iii. 334; at Lord Mayor's banquet, 1664, iii. 389; ill, &c., 1665, iii. 402; as commissioner for repair of St. Paul's, iii. 448 & n. 3; dismissed, &c., 1667, iii. 493–4 & nn.; iv. 338–9 & n.; charges against, iii. 493 & n. 4; iv. 338; condition of, after his fall, iii. 494, 502; fears impeachment, iii. 498 & n. 1; attacked in parliament, iii. 500–1 & n.; flies, iii. 502 & nn. 1, 4.
— property, residences, &c.: Cornbury: grant of, &c., iii. 381, n. 6; London: occupies Worcester House, 1660–7, iii. 264 & n. 3, 379–80; resides at Berkshire House, 1666, iii. 470 & n. 5; Clarendon House: site for, building costs, garden, &c., iii. 379–80 & n., 436, n. 6; first resides in, &c., iii. 481 & n. 2; superintends work at, iii. 502; as builder of, iv. 321, 338–9 & n., 382; *see further* London: topography: Clarendon House.
— — collection of portraits, i. *21*; iii. 520 & n. 3; debts of, iv. 339 & n. 1.
— literary: *History*: copy of, given to E, v. 583 & n. 4; ~ character-drawing in, i. *109* & n. 1; ~ error in, iii. 99, n. 1.
— personal relations: Robert Boyle: invites, to take holy orders, v. 83, n. 1; Sir Richard Browne: friendship with, i. *8*; ~ correspondence with: publication of, i. *56*; Elizabeth Mordaunt, Viscountess Mordaunt: befriended by, iv. 188, n. 5.
— relations with E: (i) as Lord Chancellor: interviews, &c., relating to Sayes Court, 1661–2, iii. 271, 272, 285, 302, 318, 343; E takes qualifying oath before, iii. 319; and nomination of E as J.P., iii. 434 *bis*; E requests use of Star Chamber from, for Commissioners for Sick and Wounded, iii. 444; E asks him to reform Savoy Hospital, iii. 447–8 & n.; receives E's proposal for Thames wharf, iii. 476; other business interviews, iii. 397, 482 *bis*.
— — (ii) private: general, i. *21*; iii. 493; iv. 338; intimacy of, with E, iii. 397; condoles with E on Lady Browne's death, iii. 77; books dedicated to, by E: Naudé's *Instructions*, iii. 303–4 & n., 306 & n. 1 (dedication quoted, i. *42–3*); ~ *New Heresie*, iii. 431, n. 7; E gives books to, iii. 284, 369, 380; consults E about: Clarendon House garden, iii. 379–80; ~ collection of portraits, iii. 520 & n. 3; visits Sayes Court, iii. 330–1; John Evelyn, jnr., presented to, iii. 474.
— social: parties: iii. 327, 355–6, 360, 379, 386, 393, 406; alone, &c., iii. 266, 314, 336, 364, 369, 396, 397, 400, 405, 442, 447, 477.
— miscellaneous: matriculation of, at Oxford, iii. 383, n. 7 *ad fin.*; suffers from gout, iii. 502 & n. 2.
— chaplain of: *see* South, R.; secretary of: *see* Bulteel, J.
Hyde, Edward, 1661–1723; styled Lord Cornbury 1674–1709; third earl of Clarendon 1709, iv. 483, n. 2; gives account of Denmark, iv. 558, n. 7, 559 & n. 1; joins William of Orange, 1688, iv. 607 & n. 3; social, iv. 483.

Hyde, Flower, countess of Clarendon, born Backhouse, wife of Henry Hyde, second earl, and previously of W. Bishop and of Sir W. Backhouse, iv. 2, n. 1; character, iv. 482; wedding-day of, iv. 644 & n. 2; house of, at Swallowfield: E visits, iv. 480–3 & nn.; godmother to converted Jewess, iv. 222; friendship of, with Ashmole, iv. 454 & n. 2; affection, &c., of, for Mary Evelyn, iv. 428 *bis*; social: as Lady Cornbury, iv. 2, 12, 34; ~ as Lady Clarendon, iv. 205, 552; v. 53, 383; dies, v. 383, n. 3.

Hyde, Lady Francis: *see* Keightley, Lady Francis.

Hyde, Frances, countess of Clarendon, born Aylesbury, wife of Sir Edward, first earl, the Lord Chancellor, iii. 263, n. 7; E visits, iii. 263; visits Sayes Court, iii. 330–1; takes E to see her grandchildren, &c., iii. 379–80 & nn.; dies, iii. 493, n. 1. attendant on, 1650, iii. 383, n. 5.

Hyde, Lady Henrietta (Harriette), countess of Rochester, born Boyle, wife of Laurence Hyde, created earl 1682, iii. 446, n. 2; as Lady Henrietta Hyde: at Tunbridge Wells, 1673, iv. 17 *bis*; ~ social: parties, iii. 446; iv. 103, 192; as countess: affection of, &c., for Mary Evelyn, iv. 428 *bis*; ~ social: parties, iv. 483 (here called Lady Treasurer), 517.

Hyde (Hide), Sir Henry: execution of, iii. 384 & n. 2.

Hyde, Henry, 1638–1709; styled Lord Cornbury 1661–74; second earl of Clarendon 1674, iii. 331, n. 2.

— public career, &c.:

— — in Queen Catherine's service: private secretary, iii. 381, n. 2; lord chamberlain: appointed, iii. 436–7 & n.; treasurer, iv. 259, n. 5.

— — Lord Privy Seal, 1685: appointed, iv. 417 & n. 3; attends parliament, iv. 442; at interview between Monmouth and his duchess, iv. 455, n. 4.

— — as Lord Lieutenant of Ireland, 1685–7: appointed, iv. 464 & n. 1; commission sealed, iv. 475; preparations for, and journey to Ireland, iv. 482, 483, 491 *bis*; Tyrconnel's intrigues against, iv. 527, n. 2; superseded by Tyrconnel, iv. 535–6 & n.; returns to London, iv. 539 & n. 4; conduct of: James II approves of, iv. 540; secretary of: *see* Rycaut, Sir P.

— — disappointed of renewed office as Lord Privy Seal, 1687, iv. 540; refuses to sit in Privy Council with Roman Catholics, 1688, iv. 602–3 & n.; at Windsor, Dec. 1688, iv. 610, n. 4; advises James II not to leave England, iv. 612, n. 3; at meeting to discuss settlement of the crown, 1689, iv. 613–15; opposes Revolution settlement, iv. 625–6 & n.; imprisoned in Tower for conspiracy and released on bail: 1690, v. 27 & n. 1, 29 & n. 2, 32 & n. 2; ~ 1691, v. 41–60 & nn., *passim*; implicated in Preston's confessions, v. 52–3 & n.

— private affairs, &c.: visits Cornbury, Oxford, &c., 1664, iii. 381–6; and Cranbourn Lodge, iv. 38, n. 2; sells Clarendon House, &c., iii. 379, n. 8 *ad fin.*; iv. 321, 339 & nn. 1, 2; sells Cornbury, iv. 339, n. 2; lodgings of, in Whitehall, iv. 446; rebuilds Swallowfield, iv. 481, n. 1.

— — elected F.R.S., &c., iv. 393 & n. 4, 396; interest of, in Clarendon collection of portraits, iii. 520 & n. 3; visits Essex in Tower, 1683, iv. 327–8 & n.; as executor of Lady Mordaunt, iv. 188 & n. 5, 202, 259, 275; discusses Bishop Seth Ward, iv. 318.

— relations with E: interest of, in E's *Mystery of Jesuitism*, iii. 393, n. 6 *ad fin.*; attends funeral of Mary Evelyn, iv. 430; gives E lodgings in Whitehall, iv. 446; and E's appointment as commissioner for Privy Seal: presents E to James II, &c., iv. 464–7; i. *31*, *32*; E visits, at Swallowfield, iv. 558; gives E political information (?), iv. 588, n. 1, 603, n. 1; gives E his father's *History of the Rebellion*, v. 583 & n. 4.

Hyde, Henry, 1638–1709 (*cont.*)
— social: gives ball, iv. 30; table of, iii. 436–7; ~ cook for, iv. 483; parties: as Lord Cornbury, iii. 331, 371, 481, 529; iv. 2, 12, 25 & n. 2, 34; ~ as earl, iv. 103, 191, 293, 358, 417, 441, 446, 488, 552, 570 & n. 3, 588 & n. 6, 591, 612 & n. 3, 644 & n. 2 (?); v. 383; alone, &c.: as Lord Cornbury, iii. 436, 440, 466, 470; ~ as earl, iv. 259, 394, 475, 544, 568, 610 & n. 4.
— geneal., iv. 2, n. 1, 328, n. 1, 465, n. 1.
— tutor of: *see* Nash, H. (iii. 383 & n. 5).
Hyde, Henry; second earl of Rochester 1711; fourth earl of Clarendon 1723: geneal., v. 521, n. 8.
Hyde (Hide), James, M.D., iii. 383–4 & n.; entertains E, iii. 383; speech by, iii. 533.
Hyde, Laurence; created Viscount Hyde of Kenilworth, 1681; first earl of Rochester 1682, iv. 188 & n. 6.
public career, &c.: created viscount, iv. 275, n. 1; knows of Charles II's money-treaties with Louis XIV, 1681, iv. 331, n. 5; 'the great favourite', 1682, iv. 293–4 & n., 297; created earl, iv. 297 & n. 5; on Charles II's attitude towards Lord Russell, iv. 328, n. 3; appointed Lord President, 1684, iv. 387 & n. 5; as Lord High Treasurer, 1685–7: appointed, &c., iv. 417 *bis* & nn. 3, 5; ~ attends to E's affairs, iv. 516, 518, 523, 529; ~ dismissal of, and pension for, iv. 533 & n. 2, 535; advises E about licensing Roman Catholic books, iv. 512; appointed a commissioner for Ecclesiastical Affairs, iv. 519; opposes Revolution settlement of crown, iv. 626 & nn. 1, 2; stands bail for his brother, 1691, v. 51; appointed Lord Lieutenant of Ireland, 1700, v. 438 & n. 4; joins in lords' protest, v. 466, n. 2; goes to Ireland, v. 468, n. 3.
private affairs: buys Cornbury House, iv. 339, n. 2; congratulates E on appointment, iv. 465; executor of Lady Mordaunt, iv. 188 & n. 5, 202, 275; friend of A. Newport, iv. 25, n. 3.
social: gives music-party, iv. 404; parties: as Mr. Hyde, iv. 181 & n. 7 (?), 192; ~ as earl, iv. 297–8, 417, 493, 505; alone, &c.: as earl, iv. 475, 503.
geneal., iii. 446, n. 2; iv. 297 & n. 6; v. 521 & n. 8, 588, n. 2.
Hyde, Sir Robert, judge, iii. 384, n. 1; request of, to E (?), iii. 394 & n. 3; geneal., iii. 383–4.
Hyde, Theodosia, Lady Cornbury, born Capel, first wife of Henry Hyde, Lord Cornbury, later second earl of Clarendon, iv. 328, n. 1, 465, n. 1.
Hyde, Sir Thomas: geneal., iv. 354, n. 6.
Hyde of Hindon: Baron, 1660–1: *see* Hyde, Sir Edward, later earl of Clarendon.
Hyde of Kenilworth: Viscount, 1681–2: *see* Hyde, Laurence, later earl of Rochester.
Hyldiard: *see* Hildyard.
Hylin, Dr. —: *see* Heylyn, P.
Hymns: in sermons: compared with Psalms, iii. 367; use of, by Early Christians, iv. 527.
Hynd, Dr. —: *see* Hinde, S.
Hysdune: *see* Heusden.

Ibach (Jbach), Josias, bronze-founder, iv. 207, n. 4; *add.*
Ibbot, Edmund, D.D.: sermon by (?), iii. 410–11 & n.
Ibelinus *or* Evelinus, lord of Baruth, iii. 548, n. 3.
Ibrackan: Lord and Lady: *see* O'Brien, Henry, d. 1678, styled Lord O'Brien and Lord Ibrackan; O'Brien, Katherine, his lady.
Iceland (Iseland): Island dog, iii. 198 & n. 2; minerals from, iii. 563, 601 & n. 2; effect of cold in, iv. 146.
Icklingham, Suffolk: estate of Sir J. Holland at, iii. 463, n. 9.
If, Château d', ii. 164 & n. 4.
Ignatius, St., bishop of Antioch: in sermon, v. 419.
Ignatius Loyola, St.: tomb of, ii. 230.
Île-Bouchard, l', Touraine, ii. 150 (i. 97).
Ilicinus, Mons, ii. 207 & n. 1.

Illnesses [some minor ailments affecting E alone are indexed under Evelyn: health, with no cross-reference under the present heading; epidemics, apart from plague (for which see Plague) and smallpox (indexed below), are indexed under Epidemics]:
general: the Hundreds of Essex, iii. 178 & n. 5.
ague: cause of hot fits in: demonstrated, iv. 324–5, 333; cases, i. 14; ii. 519; iii. 86, 183; v. 196, 491; prevalent, v. 585; tertian, iii. 151; quartan, iii. 206; treatment of, with quinine (Jesuits' bark), iv. 325 & n. 5, 333, 462; v. 197 & n. 3; *see also* Evelyn: health.
angina: *see* Evelyn: health.
apoplexy: cases, iii. 84, 433; apoplectic fit (?), iv. 405 & n. 3; deaths from, v. 85 & n. 3, 453, 521 & nn. 7–9; treatment of, iv. 77.
cancer in the fauces, v. 445.
cold, v. 84; epidemic, iv. 76; frequent, 1705, v. 586; cough, v. 456, 491, 591; rheum, iv. 565; *see also* Evelyn: health.
colic: *see* Evelyn: health.
constipation: *see* Evelyn: health.
consumption, iii. 566 & n. 2.
convulsion fits, iii. 91 *bis*, 92, 557; v. 215.
delirium, iv. 148; v. 102.
diabetes insipidus, iii. 316 & n. 5.
dizziness: *see* Evelyn: health.
dropsy, ii. 26 (i. 19); iii. 211; iv. 302.
epilepsy: symptoms, iv. 406; in sermons, iv. 572; v. 95.
eyes, sore: curative springs for, ii. 345; iii. 119 & n. 1; *see also* Evelyn: health.
fainting fits, iv. 592; *see also* Evelyn: health.
fever [*see also* ague *above*]: theory of, ii. 522, n. 4; cause of hot fits demonstrated, iv. 324–5, 333; cases, iii. 20, 183; iv. 381 *bis*, 383, 386, 446, 463; v. 193, 352, 456, 491; epidemic &c., iv. 148, 386; malignant, ii. 13 (i. 11); iv. 210; v. 618; *see also* Evelyn: health.
fistula *in ano*: operation for, iv. 533 & n. 6.

Illnesses (*cont.*)
flux, v. 282, 283; curative baths for, ii. 348.
gangrene: operation for, iii. 610; death from, iv. 432.
giddiness, &c., v. 93.
goitre, ii. 510 & nn. 3, 4; alluded to, ii. 522, 530.
gout, iii. 482, 502; iv. 302; in stomach, v. 319; curative baths for, ii. 340.
gravel, iv. 607; *see also* Evelyn: health (under kidneys).
gripes, iv. 256; *see also* Evelyn: health.
haemorrhoids: *see* Evelyn: health.
hysteric, iii. 557.
King's Evil (scrofula), ii. 510, n. 3; curative spring for, iii. 119 & n. 1; miraculous cures of, iv. 469, n. 3; touching for, iii. 250–1 & n.; iv. 374 & n. 2, 606 & n. 3; *add.*
leprosy: curative spring for, iii. 119 & n. 1; in United Provinces, ii. 33 & n. 7 (i. 25); in sermon, iv. 572.
liver-grown, iii. 210 & nn. 1, 2.
lunacy: in sermon, iv. 572.
measles, iii. 290.
melancholy, iv. 21; *see also* Evelyn: health.
nerves: cold distempers of: curative baths for, ii. 340.
palsy: dumb, iv. 74; paralytical, v. 195.
perspiration, excessive, iii. 316.
plague (or pestilence): *see* Plague.
plethoric habit of body, iii. 604.
pleurisy, iii. 631; v. 208, 456, 586; bastard, v. 585; *see also* Evelyn: health.
puerperal sepsis: death from, iv. 148, n. 1.
rheumatism, v. 155.
scarlet fever, iii. 76; iv. 653; v. 420, n. 2.
scorbut: *see* Evelyn: health.
scrofula: *see* King's Evil *above*.
smallpox: medical (accounts of cases, treatment, &c.), ii. 519 & n. 4, 520, 521–2 (E); iv. 424–5 & n., 468; v. 431–2; epidemics: 1652, iii. 68; 1684, iv. 359; 1685, iv. 463; 1694–5, v. 196 & n. 2, 199–201 & nn., *passim*; 1698, v. 286 & n. 5; 1705, v. 585, 587; cases: fatal,

Illnesses (*cont.*)
iii. 23, 257, 264 & n. 6; iv. 357 *bis*, 420–5, 455, 463–4, 507; v. 182, 200, 295, n. 2, 340, 420–1 & n. (?), 432, 520, 530, 560, 618; recoveries, iv. 72, 359, 366–74, 432–3; loss of eye due to, ii. 559, n. 2.
spotted fever, ii. 522 & n. 4.
stone: cause of: demonstrated, iv. 355; cases, v. 159, 187; operating for, v. 453; ~ in Paris, ii. 101 & n. 6 (i. 66); iii. 3–4; operations proposed, iii. 529; iv. 52; preventive medicinal spring, ii. 153 & n. 4 (i. 99); autopsy for, iii. 544–5; specimens of, iii. 529; iv. 290; *see also* Evelyn: health (under kidneys).
strangury: *see* Evelyn: health.
struma, ii. 510 & n. 3.
suppression of urine: treatment for, iv. 290.
tooth-ache: in Bantam, iv. 285; *see also* Evelyn: health.
tympane, iv. 646.
vapours: *see* Evelyn: health.
venereal disease: treatment of, ii. 348, 476; alluded to, ii. 332.
Illuminations: *see* Fireworks and Illuminations.
Imperato, Ferrante: museum of, ii. 330–1 & nn.
Inchiquin: Earls, &c., of: *see* O'Brien, Murrough, sixth baron, 1624–54, and first earl, 1654–74; O'Brien, William, second earl, 1674–92.
Independents: occupy parish churches, 1652, iii. 60; Rev. T. Malory as an Independent, iii. 80–1 & n.; *see also* iii. 142, 184, 185; preaching of, iii. 142, 184; in Colchester, 1656, iii. 177, n. 3; in Gauden's project for re-union, iii. 187, n. 6; political activities of ministers, 1659, iii. 231, n. 4; participate in address to James II, iv. 553; appointed to Privy Council, iv. 590; individuals, iii. 104–5 & n., 223 & n. 1; sermon against, iii. 30; *see also* i. 18, n. 1.
India: Dutch East India Company's stock, &c., in, iii. 187; use of lac in, iii. 324, n. 2; chaplain in: *see* Evans, John, D.D.; *see also* Bombay; East India Company.
Indies, Indians [E uses the words loosely to cover the East and West Indies and the Far East, and, more vaguely, any other regions inhabited by savages, &c. Here notices are indexed so far as possible under the more specific headings: Dutch East India Company; East India Company; East Indies; India; Spanish Indies; West Indies; the notices indexed under the present heading are general or indeterminate]: Indian curiosities, iv. 99; ~ collections of, ii. 236 *bis* & n. 2, 310; iv. 142; v. 427; ~ on sale, ii. 49 (i. 35), 100; fruits, ii. 331; ink, ii. 331, n. 6; spices and drugs, i. 35 & n. 2; weapons, &c., ii. 53 (i. 37), 356; iii. 107, 199.
Indian language (Malay, &c.): translations of Bible into, v. 82 & n. 2; pirates, v. 261 & n. 5.
Indians: Leonardo's drawings of (?), ii. 498 & n. 5.
Infidels: sermons against: endowment for, v. 88, n. 3; infidelity, &c.: in sermons, iii. 599; iv. 86, 89, 165, 191–2, 373; v. 164, 258–9; *see also* Libertines.
Ingatestone (Ingulstone), Essex: E at, iii. 176, 180, 226.
Ingle: *see* Engelen.
Inglis *or* Langlois, Esther: *see* Kello, Mrs. E.
Ingoldsby, Sir: house of, at York, iii. 129 & n. 7.
Ingram, Sir Arthur, d. 1642: house of, at York, iii. 129, n. 7.
Ingram, Sir Arthur, d. 1655: house of, at York, iii. 129, n. 7.
Ingram, Sir Arthur, 1617–81: social, iii. 448 & n. 1.
Ingram, Sir Thomas: commissioner for London streets, iii. 319, n. 1.
Ingulstone: *see* Ingatestone.
Innocent VIII, pope: acquires Holy Lance, ii. 262; letter to, from Bajazet II, ii. 499 & n. 2; MS. presented to, ii. 301 & n. 6.
Innocent X, pope (Giambattista Pamfili): election of, ii. 206, n. 2, 207 & n. 4; Possesso of, ii. 279–82 & nn.; ~ preparations for, ii. 227, n. 1, 228 & n. 6; ~ mentioned, ii. 206; creates cardinal, ii. 254.

Innocent X (*cont.*)
religious ceremonies: Lady Day, at S. Maria sopra Minerva, ii. 377–8 & n., 384; benediction of: the Holy Rose, ii. 384 & n. 6; ~ standard of the Roman people, ii. 387 & n. 1; other ceremonies, ii. 291 & n. 1, 300 & n. 2, 385 & n. 5, 386 & n. 5.
secular ceremonies: receives oaths of Roman magistrates, ii. 291; receives ambassadors from Lucca, ii. 391 & n. 2.
buildings, &c., of: obelisk and fountain in Piazza Navona, ii. 270, n. 2; *add.*; ii. 362 & n. 6; pavement, &c., in St. Peter's, ii. 265, n. 4, 266, n. 1; restores inscription in Vatican, ii. 297, n. 5.
relations of, with Bernini, ii. 229 & n. 1.
Innocent XI, pope: attitude of, towards persecution of French protestants, iv. 486, n. 2; decides disputed election to archbishopric-electorate of Cologne, iv. 596, n. 3; reported to have excommunicated Louis XIV, iv. 641; *add.*; as error for Innocent X, ii. 270, n. 2; *add.*
Innocent XII, pope, v. 368, n. 1; endeavours of, for peace, 1693–4, v. 163, n. 4; ill, v. 368; dies, v. 429 & n. 2, 430.
Innocents, Holy: relics of, ii. 87 (i. 58), 243, 456.
Inns and Travellers' Lodgings [for restaurants, &c., see London: topography: taverns; Pleasure Gardens, &c.]:
general: host's album, ii. 354; living in pension, ii. 44 & n. 4 (i. 32); *see also* ii. 149 (i. 97); ~ inclusive terms, ii. 325, n. 5, 429, n. 5; costs of lodgings, ii. 212–13, 534.
England: Guildford: Red Lion, iii. 88 & n. 3.
France: Paris: Ville de Venise, ii. 90 & n. 2 (i. 61); ~ E's other lodgings in (apart from Sir R. Browne's houses), ii. 97 & n. 4 (i. 64), 534 *bis*; iii. 17; Orleans: White Cross, ii. 136 & n. 1; Roanne: Loup, ii. 533 & n. 3; other towns, ii. 116 & n. 3, 122, 126, 152 (i. 98), 156 & n. 8 (i. 100); wayside accommodation, ii. 83–4 (i. 56–7); iii. 54 & n. 3.
Italy: Ferrara: Angel, ii. 428 & n. 4; Florence; Baritiere, ii. 184 (i. 116–17); Genoa: Zachary, ii. 171 (i. 108); Milan: Three Kings, ii. 491 & n. 3; Naples: Three Kings, and its host, ii. 325 & n. 5, 354; Rome: Petit and his house, ii. 212–13 & nn., 232; ~ Spada, Monte Giordano, ii. 214, n. 2; Venice: Aquila Nera (P. Rodomonte), ii. 429 & n. 5; Verona: Cavalletto, ii. 485 & n. 1; post-houses, village inns, &c., ii. 179 (i. 113), 207 *bis* & nn. 2, 6, 208, 209, 318, 427 & n. 2, 452, 488 & n. 4, 489, 507, 509.
Switzerland: Geneva: White Cross, and E's expenses there, ii. 520 & n. 6, 530; Simplon pass: hospice, ii. 511–12 & nn.; places in Valais, ii. 515–17 & n., 518, 519.
United Provinces: Amsterdam: Brownist's house, ii. 44 & n. 3 (i. 32); wayside accommodation, ii. 35.
Innsbruck: John (John Oenipont) and William of, ii. 180 & n. 3 (i. 113).
Inscriptions [on walls and monuments, and ancient inscriptions; modern inscriptions on plate, &c., and inscriptions cited in notes, are not indexed under this heading]:
— collections: Arundel: *see* Oxford: University: institutions; Blois, château (Duke Gaston), ii. 141 (i. 92); Louvre: room in, for, i. 68; Padua, S. Giustina, ii. 456 & n. 7; Sion, Valais, ii. 516 & n. 3.
— individual inscriptions: copied by E or reproduced in notes:
— — Acquapendente: Post-house, ii. 209.
— — Antwerp: Gymnasium, ii. 66 & n. 1 (i. 44).
— — Blois: château: Louis XII, ii. 141 & n. 2.
— — Caen: William the Conqueror: epitaph, &c., ii. 126–7 & n. (i. 80–1).
— — Calais: former Prince's Inn, ii. 83 & n. 3 (i. 56).

Inscriptions (*cont.*)
— — Geneva: Maison de Ville, ii. 525–6 & nn.
— — Lucca: St. Richard, English king: epitaph, ii. 409 & n. 1.
— — Milan: colonnade by S. Lorenzo, ii. 496 & n. 3; S. Ambrogio: chapel near, ii. 500 & n. 3: S. Angelo: epitaph of Col. A. Burnet, ii. 505, n. 1; S. Eustorgio: tomb of Magi, ii. 496.
— — Montefiascone: bishop's epitaph, ii. 210.
— — Naples: Pontano Chapel: arm of Livy, ii. 328–9 & n.; Virgil's tomb, ii. 337 & n. 1.
— — Orleans: monument to Joan of Arc, ii. 137 & n. 3 (i. 90).
— — Padua: monument of Livy, ii. 462–3 & n.; Porta del Portello, ii. 453 & n. 3; tomb of Antenor, ii. 454 & n. 3; University: entrance, ii. 464.
— — Portici: eruption of Vesuvius, 1631, ii. 333 & n. 2.
— — Pozzuoli: temple of Augustus, ii. 343 & n. 7.
— — Rome: Acqua Paola, ii. 313 & n. 1; arches: Constantine, ii. 250; ~ Titus, ii. 248; obelisks: Lateran, ii. 270–1; ~ Piazza del Popolo, ii. 375; ~ S. Maria Maggiore, ii. 245; ~ Vatican, ii. 256–7; pyramid of C. Cestius, ii. 361; S. Giovanni in Laterano: façade, ii. 271 & n. 3; ~ Sancta Sanctorum at, ii. 269; S. Maria Maggiore: Gualdi's gift to, ii. 245 & n. 3; S. Maria del Popolo: epitaph of Tovarvallis, ii. 374 & n. 8; S. Paolo Fuori: F. Eugenius Asellus, ii. 306 & n. 9; St. Peter's: altars of four major relics, ii. 262–3; Semo Sancus, ii. 358–9 & n.; Vatican: armoury, ii. 302; ~ fountain of Urban VIII, ii. 305; ~ Sala Regia, ii. 297 *ter* & nn. 2, 5; ~ Scala Vecchia, ii. 297 & n. 1.
— — Rotterdam: birth-place of Erasmus, ii. 33 (i. 25).
— — Terracina: various, ii. 320–1 & nn.
— — Torre del Epitaffio, ii. 322.
— — Tours, environs: tomb of St. Francis of Paola, ii. 147 & n. 6 (i. 95).
— — Verona: amphitheatre (spurious), ii. 486 & n. 2.

Inscriptions (*cont.*)
— — Vicenza: Teatro Olimpico, ii. 482.
— — Viterbo: Osiris (forgery), ii. 210–11 & n.
— — Wotton: epitaphs: George Evelyn, sen., i. 4; E, v. 623 (note).
— individual inscriptions: mentioned by E or in notes [select]:
— — Blois: bridge, ii. 140 & n. 3 (i. 92).
— — Gaeta: temple of Saturn near, ii. 278, n. 2.
— — Godstone: epitaph of Sir J. Evelyn, &c., iv. 122.
— — Leyden: epitaph of J. J. Scaliger, ii. 52 & n. 2 (i. 36).
— — Loosduinen, ii. 55 & n. 3 (i. 38).
— — Lucca: spurious, ii. 486, n. 2.
— — Lyons: grant of privileges by Claudius, ii. 158 & n. 6 (i. 101).
— — Milan: Ambrosiana: G. Arconati, ii. 497–8 & nn.
— — Naples: museum: Roman laws, ii. 309 & n. 5; Pontano burial-chapel, ii. 328; temple of Castor and Pollux, ii. 327.
— — Padua: house of Livy, ii. 463 & n. 7.
— — Persepolis, iv. 213.
— — Rome: Acqua Felice, ii. 238 & nn. 6, 7; Aerarium (error), ii. 278 & n. 2; Arch of Severus, ii. 220; house of L. de' Manili, ii. 292 & n. 5; Palazzo de' Conservatori: various, ii. 223 & n. 7, 224 & n. 2, 225 & n. 5; Pantheon, ii. 371 *bis* & nn. 3, 5; Possesso of Innocent X, ii. 228, 281; S. Paolo fuori: doors, ii. 306 & n. 7; temple of Antoninus and Faustina, ii. 219; triclinium of Leo III, ii. 275 & n. 5; urn of M. Minucius Felix, ii. 383, n. 1; tomb of the Plautii, near Rome, ii. 394.
— — Rouen: cathedral, ii. 123 & n. 1 (i. 79).
— — Venice: S. Marco: relief in, ii. 440, n. 2.
— — Verona: Vitruvius Cerdo, ii. 486, n. 6 *ad fin.*
— — Windsor Castle: stone from, iii. 566 & n. 1.
Insects [select notices]:
collection of, ii. 133 (i. 86); iii. 33 & n. 3; drawings of, iv. 289;

Insects (*cont.*)
microscopic observations of, iii. 356–7 & n.; iv. 126, 128; paper on, iv. 570.
bees, iv. 122; ~ E's, iii. 321–2; ~ Charles II discusses, iii. 304; ~ transparent apiaries for, iii. 110 & n. 1; bugs (*cimici*), ii. 471 & n. 3; butterflies, ii. 133 (i. 86); iii. 33; caterpillars: damage done by, iv. 446; death-watches, iii. 325; fire-flies (*lucciole*), ii. 427 & n. 3; flesh-flies: in comparison, iii. 325; locusts, iv. 54; millipedes: in medicine, iv. 290; moth, iii. 325 & n. 5; scorpions, iv. 275 & n. 3, 632; v. 81; ~ habits of, iv. 54 & n. 6; spiders: in Ireland, iii. 303; ~ skeleton of, ii. 53 (i. 37); tarantulas, ii. 331.
Inventions and Mechanical Curiosities [*see also* Scientific Instruments]:
miscellaneous, iii. 416; Sir S. Morland's, iii. 488; iv. 257.
bridge, screw, iv. 117; digester (D. Papin), iv. 171–2; ~ meal cooked in, iv. 278–9 & n.; diving-bell, iii. 292; grab for marine specimens, iii. 473; ink, copying, iii. 162–3; ovens, portable iron, iii. 446–7 & n.; sea-water: machine for purifying, iv. 388–9 & n.; springs, iii. 473; stocking-frame, iii. 285 & n. 3; weights: device to check fall of, iv. 325–6; wind-mill, iv. 325.
chair that grips sitter, ii. 254 & n. 3, 285, critical note; jack-in-the-box (satyr), ii. 254 & n. 2; ladder, folding, ii. 277; statue, speaking, iii. 110.
Io: metamorphosis of, ii. 428 & n. 5.
Ipswich, Suffolk: notices: 1656, iii. 178–9 & nn.; ~ 1677, iv. 114–16 & nn.; population of, iii. 178, n. 6; trade of, iv. 115 & n. 8; Quakers at, 1656, iii. 179 & n. 2; recorder, &c., of, iv. 114 & n. 6; Cardinal Wolsey's college, iii. 179 & n. 1; iv. 116; Christ Church, iii. 178 & n. 7; iv. 115 & nn. 4–6; harbour, iv. 115 & n. 7.
Ireland and the Irish:
— chronological series:
— — 1641: Strafford accused of misgoverning, iv. 226; rebellion: begins, ii. 77 & n. 1 (i. 51); ~ project for suppressing, ii. 78 & n. 6 (i. 52).
— — 1649: Cromwell in, ii. 565.
— — 1651: Ireton dies in, &c., iii. 52 & n. 1, 57 & n. 4.
— — 1660: act for restoring Ormond's estates in, iii. 252.
— — 1686: Roman Catholics appointed to office, iv. 514 & n. 5; Tyrconnel: appointed lieutenant-general, iv. 514 & n. 4; ~ influence of, &c., v. 527 & n. 2.
— — 1687: Tyrconnel supersedes Clarendon, iv. 535–6 & n.; Clarendon's conduct in (1685–7), iv. 540.
— — 1689: general condition, iv. 620, 625; ~ William of Orange refuses to hear Clarendon on, iv. 626, n. 1; William and Mary declared king and queen, iv. 621; danger from Tyrconnel, iv. 622, 630–1.
— — 1689–91: war in Ireland, iv. 622, 629–51; v. 6–8, 19, 22, 27–37, 59, 66–70, & nn., *passim & singulatim*.
— — — England and: forces for, iv. 622 & n. 4; v. 6 & n. 4; neglected by William III and parliament, iv. 625, 629, 630, 631–2 & n., 637, 651; troops in: neglected, iv. 651; v. 7; funds for: mismanaged, v. 22; fast for: *see* Church of England: worship: special services, &c.
— — — French activities in: military, iv. 622 & n. 4, 629, 639; v. 6, 19 & n. 2, 28, 31 & n. 1, 33 & n. 3, 35 & n. 3; naval, iv. 639 & n. 1; v. 34 & n. 5; political, iv. 634–5 & n.; general in, 1691, v. 66.
— — — James II in (1689–90): sets out, &c., iv. 629, 631 & n. 1, 634–5 & n.; success and strength of, iv. 637 & n. 2, 651; defeated and leaves, v. 28 & n. 6; attendants on, iii. 329, n. 2; v. 72, n. 2.
— — — Schomberg in (1689–90), iv. 645 & n. 3, 647 & n. 1, 648 & n. 5, 651; v. 6 & n. 4; killed, v. 28.
— — — William III in (1690): prepares for, v. 4, 6, 23; arrives, v. 24 & nn. 1, 4; at the Boyne,

Ireland and the Irish (*cont.*)
&c., v. 27–9 & nn.; advances to Limerick, v. 31 & n. 1; reported to be killed, v. 32 & n. 1; returns to England, v. 34 & n. 1.
— — — principal incidents; &c.: 1689: danger from, to Scotland, iv. 637; battle of Bantry Bay, iv. 639 & n. 1; Londonderry relieved, iv. 643 & n. 4 (false report), 648 & n. 2.
— — — — 1690: fight at Cavan, v. 8 & n. 4; battle of the Boyne, &c., v. 27–9 & nn.; ~ participants in, v. 30 & n. 2, 32–3 & n.; siege of Limerick, v. 31 & n. 1, 32 & n. 5, 33 *bis* & nn. 2, 3; ~ raised, v. 34 & n. 1; Cork taken, v. 35 & n. 1, 37, n. 3; Tyrconnel leaves, v. 35 & n. 3; Jacobites devastate, v. 37.
— — — — 1691: Athlone taken, v. 59 & n. 4; battle of Aughrim, v. 66 & n. 2; Limerick: besieged, v. 68 & n. 3, 69; ~ surrenders, v. 70 *bis* & nn. 2, 3.
— — 1691: West India fleet in, v. 77.
— — 1692: drought in, v. 112; parliament meets, v. 118 & n. 2.
— — 1696: projected French attacks (?), v. 234 & n. 2, 262.
— — 1698: scarcity of corn, v. 301, n. 1.
— — 1699–1700: forfeited estates: parliamentary inquiry into disposal of, begins, v. 324 & n. 4; ~ report on, published, v. 404 & n. 2; ~ act for resumption and sale of, v. 369 & n. 1, 377 & n. 2, 401, n. 1, 402; ~ commissioners for sale of, appointed, v. 394 & n. 2.
— — 1705: floods, v. 620 & n. 1.
— geography, &c.: animals in, &c., iii. 303 & n. 6; Down Survey of, iv. 57 & n. 3; Petty's map of, iv. 58 & n. 2; trade of: Bristol and, iii. 102; wool: patent for export of, 1663, iii. 488, n. 4.
— military [Irish soldiers]: Irish and English-Irish at the Boyne, v. 28; prisoners of war killed in explosion, v. 37 & n. 1; Foot-guards: captain in, iii. 488, n. 4; soldiers: in England, 1688, iv. 596–7 & n., 599 & n. 6, 612, n. 2; ~ in French service, iii. 6, n. 4; iv. 79, n. 3; ~ in Germany (J. Wall), ii. 96–7 (i. 63–4); ~ in Spanish service (Viscount Tara), ii. 35, n. 5.
— miscellaneous: arms of, iii. 57; Irishman on figurehead of *Naseby*, iii. 149–50.
— personal: Thomas Blood in, iii. 576; Donough Maccarty, earl of Clancarty: estate in, of, &c., iv. 595 & n. 4; Sir L. Dyve in, iii. 40, n. 1; John Evelyn, jnr., &c., in: *see* Evelyn, John, jnr.; Evelyn, Mrs. Martha; Harcourt, Mrs. E.; Murrough O'Brien, earl of Inchiquin, leaves, 1651, iii. 26; Ormond leaves, 1651, *ib.* [for Ormond's movements as Lord Lieutenant *see* Butler, James, first duke of Ormond]; Sir W. Petty in, iv. 57–60; Dr. B. Worsley in, iii. 603, n. 1; soldier (J. Thompson) in, iii. 74.
— religion: (i) protestants: primate: *see* Ussher, J.; divines suitable for episcopate presented to Charles II, 1660, iii. 253 & n. 1; in James II's reign: impending ruin of, iv. 535–6 & n., 630–1; ~ privy councillors removed, iv. 635 & n. 1; fugitive clergy, 1689–91: relief of, iv. 647, n. 5; v. 82; ~ sermons by, iv. 641; v. 22, 43; ~ bishop: social, iv. 647.
— — (ii) Roman Catholics: appointments, 1686, iv. 514 & nn. 4, 5; danger from, 1689, iv. 630–1; in Assassination Plot, v. 231; J. Wall, ii. 96, 97 (i. 63, 64); unnamed traveller, ii. 45 (i. 32); clergy: Father P. Walsh, iv. 496 & n. 4; unnamed: in Italy, ii. 170 (i. 107), 504–5.
— officers: Lords Lieutenants, &c.: *see* Wentworth, Thomas, first earl of Strafford (lord deputy 1633–40; lord lieutenant 1640–1); Ireton, Henry (in charge 1650–1); Butler, James, first duke of Ormond (1662–9, 1677–85); Berkeley, Sir John, Baron Berkeley (1670–2); Capel, Arthur, earl of Essex (1672–7); Hyde, Henry, second earl of Clarendon (1685–7); Talbot,

Ireland and the Irish (*cont.*)
Richard, duke of Tyrconnel (lord deputy 1687–9?); (lords justices 1690: appointed, v. 34 & n. 2); Sidney, Henry, earl of Romney (1692–3); (lords justices 1693–5: appointed, v. 150 & n. 5; ~ 1697–1701: mentioned, v. 468, n. 3); Hyde, Laurence, earl of Rochester (1701–3); ~ secretary to, 1692: *see* Wyche, Sir C.
— — secretary to William III for Ireland, 1690–1702: *see* Southwell, Sir R.; lord chancellor, 1686–7, 1690–6: *see* Porter, Sir C.; privy council: appointments, 1686, iv. 514 & n. 5; ~ d'Avaux as member of (error), iv. 634–5 & n.; chief justice of, 1681–7: *see* Davis, Sir W.; surveyor-general, 1660: *see* Broderick, Sir A.; vice-treasurer, 1670–3: *see* Aungier, Francis, earl of Longford; treasury, excise, &c.: commissioner for, 1692–6: see Evelyn, John, jnr.; Act of Settlement, 1662: commissioner for: *see* Cooke, Edward.
Irenæus: in sermon, v. 419; *see also* v. 448, n. 1.
Irene, the Empress: in sermon, iv. 521 & n. 1.
Ireton, Henry, the regicide, iii. 52, n. 1; conduct of, at Colchester, iii. 58 & n. 1, 177; dies, iii. 52 & n. 1, 57 & n. 4; funeral of, iii. 57–8 & nn.; corpse of: exhumed, &c., iii. 269 & n. 2; geneal., iii. 14, n. 9.
Irish (Erse) language: translation of Bible into, v. 82 & n. 2.
Ironside, Gilbert, sen.; D.D.; bishop of Bristol 1660: consecrated, iii. 266 & n. 3.
Ironside, Gilbert, jnr.; D.D. 1666; bishop of Bristol 1689; of Hereford 1691, iv. 87, n. 1; consecrated, iv. 649, n. 1; on the Family of Love, iv. 554, n. 2; sermons by: printed, iv. 395 & n. 3; ~ unprinted, iv. 87.
Isaac: in sermons, iii. 30, 503; v. 271, 397, 414; ~ error for Esau, v. 306 & n. 1.
Isaac, Monsieur, dancing-master, iv. 271, n. 5; *add.*; teaches Mary Evelyn, iv. 271, 423.
Isabella (Isola Bella), island in Lago Maggiore: notice, ii. 506–7 & nn.
Isabella Clara Eugenia, Archduchess, ii. 70, n. 4; hearse of, ii. 70 (i. 46); pictures relating to, ii. 71 & n. 3 (i. 46); and name of colour, iii. 42, n. 4.
Isaiah, the prophet: relics of, ii. 88 (i. 59); in sermons, v. 397, 496.
Ischia: in views, ii. 329, 334.
Iseland: *see* Iceland.
Iselle, Lago Maggiore, ii. 507, n. 1.
Isidore, St., the Martyr (Isidore of Chios): relics of, ii. 438–9 & n.
Isleworth (Thistleworth), Middlesex: houses, &c., at, 1648, ii. 539–40 & nn.; *see also* Syon House.
Isola Bella (Isabella), Lago Maggiore: notice, ii. 506–7 & nn.
Isola Madre *or* Renata, Lago Maggiore, ii. 506, n. 8.
Isola Superiore (dei Pescatori), Lago Maggiore, ii. 507 & nn. 1, 3.
Isolino San Giovanni (Isola di Sant'Angelo), Lago Maggiore, ii. 507 & n. 2.
Ispahan, Persia: plane-trees at, iv. 337 & n. 4.
Israelites: *see* Jews.
Istria: in view, ii. 446 & n. 6.
Italian language: at Geneva, ii. 524; at Lucca, ii. 410; at Siena, ii. 201 & n. 4; in Upper Valais, ii. 511 & n. 2; protestant sermons in: at Geneva, ii. 523 & n. 4; ~ in London, ii. 545 & n. 9; purity of: its improvement, ii. 364; scholar of, iv. 421; speech in, ii. 233; words coined by E: cedrario, ii. 484 & n. 1; citronario, iii. 18 & n. 5; posario, ii. 221 & n. 3.
Italy and the Italians [general statements; Italians outside Italy; strangers in Italy; &c.]:
— E's travels in: account of, ii. 168–509 & nn. (i. 106–21 & nn.); ~ bibliographical note on, ii. 573–4; *see also* i. 7–8.
— buildings, &c.: beds, ornamented: delight in, ii. 236; ceilings of cedar, ii. 308–9; coaches, &c.: splendour of, ii. 257–8 & n.; gardens: provision for maintaining, ii. 362; guns outside princely houses, ii. 253; paintings on house-fronts, ii. 485; palaces: slow building of, ii. 483 & n. 7; towns: in compari-

Italy and the Italians (*cont.*)
son, iv. 596; villas: in comparison, iii. 18; iv. 143–4.
— characteristics of Italians: eloquence, ii. 233, 384; frugality, ii. 187 (i. 118); jealousy, ii. 192 (i. 119); licentiousness, ii. 476; neatness, ii. 311; sober manners, ii. 534; treachery, ii. 254.
— culture: academies, ii. 364 & n. 5; Greek studies: present state of, iii. 156; painters allowed by owners of masterpieces to copy them, ii. 299; virtuosos' collections: in comparison, iii. 35.
— geography, &c.: boy's knowledge of, iv. 618; Geneva in relation to Italy, ii. 524; trade-routes from Switzerland, ii. 506; 'the peculiar joys of Italy', ii. 171 & n. 2; climate: cold, 1669–70, &c., iii. 542; ~ heat, v. 336, 472; earthquakes: *see* Earthquakes; floods, 1705, v. 618 & n. 2, 620 & n. 1.
— history, &c.: Constantine the Great's march through, iv. 618; Huns overrun, ii. 431; kings of: crowned in Milan, ii. 500–1 & n.; Italians in garrison at Genoa, ii. 176, n. 2; Swiss mercenaries in, ii. 517; Venetian conquests in, ii. 431.
— Italians outside Italy [diplomatists are indexed under Diplomatists; Italians in France, &c., apart from performers, are not indexed collectively]:
— — (i) in England [excluding performers]: at Royal Society meeting, iv. 250 & n. 1; Milanese count, iv. 358; sculptor employed at Nonsuch, iii. 427; traveller from Africa, iv. 630; *see also* Cosimo III; Diodati, J.; Donghi, G.; Gascoigne, Sir B.; Monte Feltre, C. Ubaldino, count of.
— — (ii) performers [for musicians *see* Music: personal]: acrobats, &c., iii. 256; comedians, iv. 12 & n. 3; puppet-players, iii. 492 & n. 2; Scaramuccio (T. Fiorilli), iv. 75; water-spouter, iii. 27, n. 5.
— music: *see* Music: general, &c.
— social life [*see also* Rome; Venice]: carnival: at Naples, ii. 331–2 & n.; ~ at Rome, ii.

Italy and the Italians (*cont.*)
381–2 & nn.; *see also* ii. 360, n. 5, 389, n. 3; ~ at Venice, ii. 473–4 & nn.; celebrations: illuminations used in, ii. 282, 391; v. 72; dancing: in disrepute, ii. 534; jousting: at Rome, ii. 389 & n. 3; ~ at Vicenza, ii. 483 & n. 1; ladies: freedom of, at Lucca, ii. 410; maypole: in Rome, ii. 387 & n. 5; pasquinades: in Rome, ii. 369 & n. 3; ~ in Venice, ii. 474; poor: provision for (Monti di Pietà), ii. 366 & n. 8, 463; promenade: at Milan, ii. 503; ~ at Naples, ii. 327 & n. 3; ~ at Venice, ii. 433 & n. 3; ~ at Vicenza, ii. 484; prostitutes or courtesans, ii. 316, 331–2 & n., 375, 382, 476; ~ tax on, ii. 417 & n. 9; snuff-taking, ii. 201 & n. 1.
— travel in Italy: bills of health, ii. 167–8 & n. (i. 106), 426; fire-arms: prohibited in towns, ii. 160, n. 6; road-services, ii. 315, n. 1; shipping for: danger to, ii. 169–70 (i. 107); sightseeing, ii. 214 & nn. 1, 2, 431.
— travellers and strangers in Italy [for diplomatists *see* Diplomatists; persons mentioned by E in his account of his travels in Italy, or in the notes to it, are not indexed collectively. The page-references are to statements relating to the various persons' visits to Italy]: *see* Abell, J. (iv. 270); Bargrave, J. (iii. 614 & n. 6); Compton, Henry, bishop of London (iv. 97 & n. 3); Craford, J. (ii. 22–3 & n.; i. 17); Croyden, G. (iii. 34 & n. 3); Duncon, E. (iii. 30 & n. 3); Elwes, Sir G. (iii. 31, nn. 3, 4); Godfrey, J. (*ib.*); Gustavus Adolphus, king of Sweden (?) (ii. 521 & n. 4); Hildyard, C. and Henry, jnr. (iii. 193, n. 3); Howard, Thomas, fifth duke of Norfolk (iii. 329); Keightley, T. (iii. 35 & n. 6, 36, 633); Knight, Mrs. Mary (iv. 49); Lucretia, Signora (ii. 556); Pate, —, the singer (v. 289); Pope, Walter (iii. 354, n. 2); Pratt, Sir R. (iii. 153 & n. 2); Stanhope, Philip, second earl of Chester-

Italy and the Italians (*cont.*)
field (iii. 22); Thicknesse, J. (i. 14); Villiers, George, first duke of Buckingham (ii. 522 & n. 1); Villiers, George, second duke of Buckingham (ii. 522, n. 1); Wright, J. M. (iii. 338 & n. 5); unnamed Poles, ii. 60 (i. 41).
Ivelin (Yvelin) family, iii. 548 & n. 3.
Ivory: carvings in, ii. 87 (i. 59), 190 & n. 2 (i. 119), 253; iii. 300; ~ on sale, ii. 100 (i. 65–6), 124 (i. 79); turner's work in, ii. 192 & n. 9 (i. 119); iii. 64–5.

Jacatra, Java, ii. 57, n. 7; iii. 108, n. 5.
Jackson, Mrs. Ann: sells portrait of E to (Sir) John Evelyn, *add.* (iv. 479, n. 2).
Jackson, John, nephew of Samuel Pepys: Pepys's heir, &c., v. 538 & nn. 5–7; *add.* (iv. 479, n. 2).
Jackson, Rev. John, rector of Lees, iv. 206, n. 6; sermons by, iv. 166 & n. 1(?), 192, 206–7, 211 & n. 4(?), 335 & n. 3(?); v. 346–8, 348–50.
Jacob: in sermons, iii. 48, 188; iv. 447; v. 63, 219, 271, 308, 564.
Jacob: Well of: in sermon, v. 167.
Jacobites: the name, v. 231, 261; plots, &c. [for further plots against William III, not necessarily Jacobite, *see* England: plots]: supposed, 1690: suspects imprisoned, v. 27 & n. 1, 29, 32; 1691 (Preston, Ashton, &c.), v. 41 & nn. 2–4, 42 & nn. 1–5, 51, 52–3; 1692: suspects arrested during invasion alarm, v. 99, 100 & n. 1; 1696: *see* Assassination Plot (v. 231, &c.); reported, 1696, 1697, v. 261 & n. 2, 273 & nn. 2, 3.
Englishmen active or suspected as Jacobites (apart from participants in plots): Godolphin: accused, 1705, v. 619 & n. 1; Col. James Graham (v. 42 & n. 5, &c.); Edward Griffin, Baron Griffin (v. 142, n. 3); Marlborough (v. 86, n. 1); Col. John Parker (v. 188 & n. 5); — Pate (v. 289, n. 1); Henry Mordaunt, earl of Peterborough (v. 92 & n. 2).
Jacombe, Thomas, D.D.: payment to, iv. 37 & n. 6.
Jacombe, William: payment for, iv. 37 & n. 6.
Jacomo Siciliano: error for T. Laureti, ii. 239 & n. 9.
Jacquet, Mathieu: sculpture by, ii. 118 & n. 1 (i. 76).
Jakatra, Java, ii. 57, n. 7; iii. 108, n. 5.
Jamaica: Charles II decides to retain, 1660, iii. 257 & n. 2; condition of, 1671: report on, iii. 580–1 & n.; ~ discussed by Council for Foreign Plantations, iii. 602; affairs of: discussed by Council of Trade and Plantations, iii. 629 & n. 5; share of, in Sir Henry Morgan's raid on Panama, iii. 583, 585; projected Dutch attack on, 1672, iii. 628; earthquake in (Port Royal), 1692, v. 113 & n. 1, 115, 133; ~ represented at Southwark Fair, v. 115–16 & n.; French attack on, 1694, v. 188 & n. 4; cultivation of nutmegs, &c., in: proposed, iii. 602–3; logwood trade, iii. 613 & n. 2; travels, &c., of Sir Hans Sloane in, v. 48 & n. 1; merchant-ships for: *see* England: merchant shipping; governors, &c.: *see* Massey, Sir Edward (governor-designate, 1660; iii. 257 & n. 3); Modyford, Sir T. (governor 1664–71; iii. 580, n. 1); Lynch, Sir T. (lieutenant-governor 1671–4; governor 1682–4: iii. 574, n. 1).
See also Port Royal.
James I, king of England:
chronological series: ceremonial on his being proclaimed king, 1603, iv. 412 & n. 5; reception of, at Godmanchester, 1603, iii. 135, n. 5; as founder of order of baronets, 1611, iv. 514, n. 1; surrenders cautionary towns to United Provinces, 1616, i. 23, n. 4.
grants, &c.: founds Chelsea College, iii. 397, n. 2; grant for manufacture of gunpowder, i. 52, n. 2; gives his *Opera* to Cambridge University Library, iii. 140 & n. 4; grants Syon House to earl of Northumberland, iii. 414, n. 10.

James I (*cont.*)
household: clerk of the Green Cloth: *see* Browne, Sir Richard, sen. (iv. 303, & n. 3).
miscellaneous: tries to introduce silk-worms into England, iii. 96, n. 7; brings remains of Mary, Queen of Scots, to Westminster Abbey, iii. 135, n. 2; tries to buy drawings by Leonardo (?), ii. 498, n. 8 *ad fin.*; statue of, at St. Paul's: removed, ii. 555, n. 6; plots against: discovery of (in sermon), iv. 336.
palaces: Eltham: occupied by, iii. 170, n. 3; Holmby House: acquired by, iv. 70, n. 3; Newmarket: built by, &c., iii. 138, n. 5, 554, n. 2; Nonsuch, iii. 426, n. 4; Royston: built by, iii. 138, n. 5; Windsor Castle: neglected by, iii. 98, n. 6.
geneal., iii. 316, n. 2; iv. 215 & n. 2.

James II, king of England [b. 1633; duke of York 1633–85; king 1685–8; in exile 1689–1701]:
— character, Sept.–Oct. 1685, iv. 474–5, 479; dislikes profanity, iv. 415.
— chronological series:
— — (1) as duke of York:
— — — 1633: born, ii. 12 & n. 2 (i. 10); 1649–50: in Paris, ii. 563 & n. 7; iii. 19, n. 1, 20, n. 4; 1651–2: in Paris, iii. 36 & n. 4, 37, 38, 51, 53; 1660: marriage of, to Anne Hyde: officiating divine, ii. 564, n. 5; ~ opposed by Henrietta Maria, iii. 258 & n. 4; ~ made public, iii. 264 & n. 1; ~ Clarendon as father-in-law of, iv. 338 & n. 4; 1661: in Charles II's coronation procession, iii. 280.
— — — 1664–7: Second Dutch War: in command of fleet, &c., iii. 389 & n. 2, 404; in battle of Lowestoft, iii. 410 & n. 3, 411 & n. 5; *see also* iii. 412; ~ flagship of, in, iii. 414 & n. 1; ~ protected by Sir J. Smith during, iv. 12 & n. 1; visits fleet, iii. 413; superseded as commander, iii. 414 & n. 2; later visits to fleet, iii. 436, n. 2, 441 & n. 5; informs Charles II about Four Days' Battle, iii. 439, n. 3; orders of, iii. 444; concern of, in defence of the Medway, iii. 484–5 & n.
— — — 1665: at Oxford (Sept.), iii. 423, n. 7; 1666: fights Fire of London, iii. 455, n. 2, 457 & n. 5; 1667: sent to ask Clarendon to retire, iii. 493, n. 1; supports Clarendon, &c., iii. 494, n. 3, 502, n. 1; 1670: in Garter celebration, iii. 559; 1671–2: as member of Council for Foreign Plantations, iii. 571, n. 1, 574, 577, 604–5; 1672 (Third Dutch War): in command of fleet, iii. 614 *bis*; in battle of Solebay: flagship of, iii. 616, n. 5; iv. 432, n. 1; visits fleet, iii. 620, 623.
— — — *c.* 1672: converted to Roman Catholicism: *see* religion *below*; 1673: resigns his offices, iv. 14, n. 1; marriage of, to Mary of Modena: unpopularity of, iv. 26 & n. 2; 1679: retires to Brussels, iv. 167 & n. 6; pamphlets, &c., against, iv. 172; returns from Brussels, iv. 181 & n. 1; sent to Scotland, iv. 189 & n. 6; 1679–81: the Exclusion Bills, i. *28*; ~ second bill, iv. 223, n. 1, 225, n. 3, 236 & n. 1; ~ third bill, iv. 239 & n. 3; ~ supporters of the bills, iv. 245 & nn. 5, 6, 261 & n. 3, 453–4 & n.; 1682: returns from Scotland, iv. 281–2 & n.; in shipwreck: escape of, *ib.*; *see also* iv. 432 & n. 1.
— — — 1682–5: principal adviser of Charles II, iv. 294, n. 1, 323 & n. 6; 1683: plot to assassinate (Rye-House plot), iv. 321–2 & n.; i. *29*; succession of, to the throne: fear of, iv. 323; in Tower at time of Essex's suicide, iv. 326; concern of, in Russell's execution, iv. 328, n. 3; knows of Charles II's money-treaties (1681) with Louis XIV (?), iv. 331, n. 5; 1684: powers of, as Lord High Admiral restored, iv. 377 & n. 3; proceeds against Titus Oates, iv. 636, n. 1; 1685: at Charles II's death-bed, iv. 408 & nn. 2, 3, 409 & n. 2; grief of, for Charles, iv. 411, 412.

James II (*cont.*)
— — — escapes from dangers until 1685: in sermon, iv. 446.
— chronological series (2) as king:
— — the reign: general account, i. *30–3*; popular discontent during, v. 4; errors of, v. 475.
— — — 1685: accession, iv. 411–13 & nn.; ~ Venetian embassy to congratulate him on, iv. 492–3 & nn.; ~ commemorative service for, iv. 499 & nn. 7, 8; declaration of, to Privy Council, iv. 411–12 & n.; ~ reaffirmed to parliament, iv. 442; ~ acts contrary to it, iv. 509–10, 582; proclaimed king, iv. 412–13 & nn.; ~ at Bromley, iv. 414–15 & nn.; reforms the court, iv. 415; appointments (royal household, officers of state), iv. 416–17 & nn.; orders collection of Customs to continue, iv. 417, n. 6 *ad fin.*; coronation of, iv. 436, 437–8 & nn.; ~ scaffolds in Westminster Abbey for, iv. 470; prospects of a good reign, iv. 437, 474–5; speech of, at opening of parliament (May), iv. 442–3 & n.; intervenes in quarrel between Devonshire and Col. Colepeper, iv. 454; interview with Monmouth, iv. 455 & n. 2; Monmouth's last paper for, iv. 456 & n. 3; English, &c., regiments in Dutch service sent to, iv. 458 & n. 1; reviews troops on Blackheath, iv. 458 & n. 1; appoints Jeffreys Lord Chancellor, iv. 466 & n. 5; orders all negroes in Plantations to be baptized, iv. 471 & n. 3; visits Winchester and Portsmouth, iv. 467 & n. 1, 468–73; speech of, to parliament (Nov.), iv. 488, 489.
— — — 1686: grants peerage to Catherine Sedley, iv. 496–7 & n.; hoped that he will control duelling, iv. 501; attends reviews, iv. 504, 526; alienates baronets, iv. 514; proceeds against Dr. J. Sharp, &c., iv. 516 & nn. 1, 2, 524 & n. 1; at Windsor, &c., iv. 526, n. 2; mentioned, iv. 519.
— — — 1687: dismisses Commissioners of Privy Seal and passes over Clarendon, iv. 540; closets members of parliament, iv. 540–1 & n.; prorogues parliament, iv. 544 & n. 2; first Declaration of Indulgence of: effects of, iv. 546–7 & nn.; ~ addresses of thanks for, iv. 553–4 & nn.; *see also* iv. 560 & n. 1; dealings of, with Magdalen College, v. 40 & n. 2; at Windsor, iv. 558, n. 5; at Hampton Court, iv. 553–4; progress of, to Bath, &c., iv. 560 & n. 1; at Lord Mayor's feast, iv. 562–3.
— — — 1688: May and June: alarmed by Dutch naval preparations, iv. 582 & n. 1; goes to Chatham, *ib.*; displays projects for advancement of Roman Catholicism, iv. 582; second Declaration of Indulgence of: the Seven Bishops petition against his order for reading, iv. 583–4 & n.; displeased by celebrations for acquittal of the Seven Bishops, iv. 588 & n. 2.
— — — 1688: July and Aug.: appoints Nonconformists as Privy Councillors, iv. 590 & n. 4; summons parliament, iv. 597 & n. 4.
— — — 1688: Sept.–Oct.: expedition of William of Orange against: alarm at court at news of, iv. 597 & n. 3, 598 & n. 5, 599 & n. 2; conduct of, towards Church of England: declaration promising to maintain it, iv. 597 & n. 4; ~ conciliatory measures, iv. 599 & nn. 3, 4; ~ appeals to bishops, &c., iv. 600 & n. 4, 601 & n. 1; ~ questions bishops about invitation to William, iv. 604 & n. 3, 605; ~ asks bishops to publish declaration against the invasion, iv. 604, n. 3, 605–6 & n.; political conduct: cancels summons of parliament, iv. 599 & n. 2; ~ retains dispensing power, iv. 599 & n. 3; ~ refuses to dismiss Father Edward Petre, iv. 600, n. 1; ~ dismisses Sunderland, iv. 602 & n. 2; ~ vindicates authenticity of James Edward, iv. 602–3 & nn.; ~ E prays that he will adopt a conciliatory policy, iv.

James II (*cont.*)
603, 606; military preparations, iv. 599 & nn. 5, 6.
— — — 1688: Nov. and Dec.: forms army to repel William, iv. 605; goes to Salisbury, iv. 607 & nn. 2, 5; returns to London, iv. 608 & n. 1; petitioned by peers to summon parliament, iv. 608 & n. 4; sends commissioners to William, iv. 608 & n. 8; *add.*; address to, from fleet at Portsmouth, iv. 609 & n. 8; first flight of, iv. 610 & n. 5; ~ carries off Great Seal (?), iv. 616 & n. 1; ~ relic taken from him during, iv. 470, n. 3 *ad fin.*; ~ companion on, iv. 611, n. 6; returns to Whitehall, iv. 610–11 & n.; communications of, with William, *ib.*; goes to Rochester, iv. 611 & n. 1; flight of, to France, iv. 612 & n. 4; ~ Clarendon opposes, iv. 612, n. 3; ministers, &c., of: excepted from pardon, 1690, v. 23, n. 4.
— chronological series: (3) dethronement and exile [for plots for James's restoration *see* Jacobites]:
— — general: peers created by, after abdication, ii. 558, n. 3; iii. 482, n. 1; iv. 171, n. 6, 517, n. 1; v. 41, n. 4, 144, n. 3, 149, n. 6.
— — — 1689: proposals for recall, iv. 614, 619, 625 & n. 3; ~ the bishops' opposition to, iv. 626–7; proposals for a regency, iv. 614, 619 & n. 4; abdication: commons vote that he has abdicated, &c., iv. 616 & n. 1; ~ vote carried to and debated by lords, iv. 619 & nn. 3, 4, 622 & n. 2; ~ spontaneous abdication not proved, &c. iv. 628; ~ Sancroft's dissatisfaction with, iv. 634; Queen Mary II's assumption of crown of, iv. 624 & n. 3; dethronement: mentioned, v. 166; prayers, &c., for: curtailed, iv. 620 & n. 5; ~ before house of commons, 30 Jan., *ib.*; accession-day to be disregarded, iv. 621 & n. 2.
— — — 1689–90: expedition to Ireland: supplied by Louis XIV, iv. 629; v. 6 & n. 4; &c.; Louis's conditions for support (?), iv. 635 & n. 1; arrives in Ireland, iv. 631 & n. 1, 634–5 & n., 637; promotes Tyrconnel to duke, iv. 23, n. 2; said to have taken Londonderry, &c., iv. 637 & n. 2; army of: at the Boyne, v. 28; returns to France, v. 28 & n. 6, 32 & n. 1; attendants on, in Ireland, iii. 329, n. 2; v. 72, n. 2.

James II (*cont.*)
— — — 1689: offer of pardon by, iv. 642 & n. 5; 1692: announces expected birth of a child, v. 96 & n. 1; preparing to invade England, v. 97, n. 2; declaration, v. 141, n. 2; 1693: declaration of, with offer of pardon, &c., v. 140 & n. 2, 141; 1696: at Calais, preparing to invade England, v. 232 & n. 1; concern of, in Assassination Plot: animosity aroused by, v. 233; ~ declared innocent by conspirators, v. 234; abjuration of: required of office-holders, &c., v. 242–3 & n.; attacked by Titus Oates v. 238 & n. 3; 1697: considered dead in law, v. 271; 1699: reported ill, v. 371 & n. 3; 1701: dies, v. 475 & n. 1; ~ heart deposited at Chaillot, ii. 91, n. 1.
— as James VII, king of Scotland: 1686: asks parliament to repeal laws against Roman Catholics, iv. 514 & n. 7; 1688: letter to, from Scottish bishops, iv. 615, n. 1; 1689: letter from, to Convention of Estates: rejected, iv. 631 & n. 2; declared to have forfeited the crown, iv. 635 & n. 2.
— naval: as Lord High Admiral: appointed, iii. 389, n. 2; ~ chaplain of: *see* Woodroffe, B.; yacht belonging to, iii. 297 & n. 1; ship built for, iii. 509; to consider project for naval infirmary, iii. 430 & n. 2; project of, for hospital at Greenwich, v. 203, n. 1; assists Captain G. Collins, the hydrographer, iv. 301 & n. 3 *see & also* chronological series *above*, 1664–7, 1672, 1684.
— religion: (1) as duke of York:

James II (*cont.*)
attends Anglican services, &c.: 1650–2, iii. 19, n. 1, 20, n. 4, 37, 38, 51, 53; ~ 1671, iii. 590; ~ after his conversion to Roman Catholicism, iv. 7, 34 & n. 3; ~ ceases to attend, iv. 87 & n. 4; ~ influence of his absenting himself, iv. 154 & n. 3; hears A. Morus preach, iii. 311; conversion of, to Roman Catholicism, iv. 7 & n. 3; i. *26*; ~ retains his Anglican chaplains after, iii. 624, n. 4; ~ supported by Clifford (?), iv. 14 & n. 1, 16; ~ unpopularity of, iv. 26; ~ attacked by commons on account of, iv. 167; ~ prospective influence of, on politics, iv. 409; excepted from Parliamentary Test Act, 1678, iv. 159, n. 1.
— — (2) as king (for his more political activities *see* chronological series *above*): Chapel Royal services: absence of, from, iv. 416; ~ obeisance in absence of, iv. 433, 491; maintains Anglican worship in Private Oratory, iv. 418; attends Mass, &c., iv. 416 & n. 1, 465; throne of, in Roman Catholic chapel, Whitehall, iv. 534; Roman Catholic chapel of, for camp on Hounslow Heath, v. 61–2 & n.; religion of: influence of, on Monmouth's rebellion, iv. 456; desirability, &c., of his becoming an Anglican, iv. 474–5, 479; gives account of Charles II's conversion to Roman Catholicism, iv. 475–9 & nn.; Louis XIV's ability to protect, iv. 486, n. 3; influence of on commemoration of Gunpowder Plot, iv. 487 & n. 3; and persecution of French protestants: disapproves of, iv. 485, n. 3; ~ permits arrest of refugees on English ships (?), iv. 490, n. 8; ~ issues brief for collection for refugees, iv. 508, n. 3; ~ protects and relieves refugees, iv. 515 & n. 2.
— — (3) general: views of, on miracles, &c., iv. 468–71; touches for king's evil, iv. 606 & n. 3; *add.*; last English king to perform Maundy Thursday

James II (*cont.*)
ceremony in person, ii. 385, n. 5.
— mistresses and illegitimate children: *see* Godfrey, Mrs. A. (Arabella Churchill); Sedley, Catherine, countess of Dorchester; Waldegrave, Henrietta, Baroness Waldegrave; FitzJames, James, duke of Berwick.
— personal relations: with Arlington, iv. 119 & n. 1; *see also* iv. 476; with Clifford, iv. 14 & n. 1, 16, 20 & n. 1; with George Legge, Baron Dartmouth, iv. 311, n. 2, 314; disliked by Essex, iv. 201 & n. 7; betrayed by Marlborough (as Lord Churchill), v. 86, 90; *see also* v. 525; gift of, to Queen Mary of Modena, v. 147, n. 4; displeased by duke of Northumberland's marriage, iv. 505, n. 4; with Henry Mordaunt earl of Peterborough, iv. 417, n. 2.
— relations with E:
— — (1) general intercourse: visits Sayes Court, &c., iii. 312–13 & nn.; greets E after Plague, iii. 429; E informs, about illegal quartering of soldiers, iv. 458; appoints E a commissioner of the Privy Seal, iv. 464–5, 466–7, 493; E consults, about Mary Evelyn's marriage, iv. 502 & n. 5; grant of, in settlement of E's claims on the crown, iv. 551 & n. 1, 553; E pays court, ii. 563; iii. 247, 404, 411, 412; iv. 301, 526; conversations, &c., iii. 306, 343, 463; iv. 2, 480.
— — (2) business: interviews, &c.: unspecified, iii. 402; Sick and Wounded, &c., iii. 406; iv. 93; Lord Berkeley's affairs, iv. 90; E's claim to Sayes Court, iv. 129 & n. 3.
— residences and property: house at Greenwich (?), iii. 515, n. 1; St. James's Palace: as duke, iii. 380, n. 1, 624, n. 4; &c. ~ as king, 1685, iv. 493 & n. 6; Whitehall: as duke, 1664, iii. 389, n. 2; ~ as king: rebuilds part, iv. 480 & n. 2; palace at Winchester: stops work on, iv. 472 & n. 1; collection of books, &c., made for, iii. 44; due from

James II (*cont.*)
Hispaniola treasure, iv. 552 & n. 3; debt of, to Queen Catherine, iv. 585; art-collection of: catalogue cited, iii. 96, n. 5, 263, nn. 1, 3.
— social: (1) general: dines with Charles II, iii. 251; at balls, iii. 350; iv. 30; takes part in military display, iv. 42; pays for jewel lost during performance of *Calisto*, iv. 51; birthdays (as king), iv. 480; *add.*; iv. 526, 601; entertained at: Cranbourn (Sir R. Holmes), iv. 38; Durdans, iii. 334; Euston and Newmarket, iii. 589, 590; New Hall, iv. 287, n. 4.
— — (2) amusements, &c.: attends Christmas revels at Lincoln's Inn, iii. 307–8; musical performances before, iii. 307; iv. 404; views captured Turkish horses, iv. 399; at examination of Saturn's rings, iii. 286, n. 2; company of, of actors: *see* London: topography: theatres; ~ gives his coronation suit to, iii. 303, n. 4.
— household as duke of York: general, iv. 333; ~ Roman Catholic servants to be dismissed, 1678, iv. 159 & n. 2; officers: superintendent, 1651: *see* Byron, John, Baron Byron; chaplains: general, iii. 624, n. 4; iv. 198, n. 3; ~ unnamed: sermons by, iii. 624; iv. 198; ~ *see* Crowther, J.; Doughty, T.; Lake, E.; Turner, Francis; grooms of the bedchamber: *see* Ashton, J.; Slingsby, Col. Henry; housekeeper at Deptford: *see* Howard, Mrs. Elizabeth; keeper of privy purse: *see* Graham, James; physicians: *see* Waldegrave, Sir William; Wedderburn, Sir John; secretaries: *see* Coleman, Edward; Coventry, Sir William; Wren, Matthew.
— miscellaneous: horseguards of, iii. 278–9; life guard of, iii. 298 & n. 2; portrait of, with Charles I, by Lely, iii. 216 & n. 5; statue of, by G. Gibbons, iv. 317, n. 2; ~ (error), v. 53 & n. 2; dog of, iii. 412; eulogy on: in sermon, iv. 440.

James II, king of Scotland: geneal., iv. 39, n. 4.
James IV, king of Scotland: geneal., iv. 215, n. 2.
James, St.: relics of, ii. 267; in sermon, v. 132.
James, St., the Less: relic of, ii. 289.
James, —: at funeral of John Evelyn of Wotton, v. 56.
James, Dr. — (Henry James or John James?): sermon by, v. 321 & n. 3.
James Edward (James Francis Edward Stuart), 1688–1766; Prince of Wales 1688; the Old Pretender: thanksgiving for his mother's pregnancy, iv. 567 & n. 4; birth of, iv. 586 & n. 5; ~ premature, iv. 587 & n. 1; ~ rejoicings for, iv. 587; ~ meeting to authenticate, iv. 602–3 & n.; ~ not proved an imposture, iv. 628; nurse for, iv. 597; movements of, Nov.-Dec. 1688, iv. 607, n. 5, 609 & n. 7; taken to Calais, iv. 612 & n. 4; prayers for: stop, iv. 613 & n. 1; portrait of: shown to E, 1692, v. 92 & n. 2; excluded from succession to English crown, v. 421; proclaimed king of Great Britain, and recognized by Louis XIV, 1701, v. 476 & nn. 3–4; ~ effect of recognition in England, v. 480–1 & n.; marriage of, ii. 210, n. 3; peers created by, iv. 387, n. 5 *ad fin.*; v. 611, n. 3.
James, Henry, D.D., iv. 86, n. 4; sermons by, iv. 86, 506, 544; v. 321 & n. 3(?).
James, John, D.D.: sermon by (?), v. 321 & n. 3.
James, Thomas: on editions of Early Christian Fathers, iv. 145, n. 1.
Jane (Seymour), queen of England: portrait of, iii. 166, n. 1.
Jane (Jeane), William, D.D.; dean of Gloucester 1685, iv. 260, n. 3; sermons by, iv. 260, 262, 263, 395, 484, 538, 571–2, 630; appointed to preach, iv. 503, n. 2.
Janicius, Dr. —: at Padua, 1645, ii. 470.
Janissaries: caps worn by, iv. 137.
Jansen, Cornelius: portrait by, iv. 404, n. 2.
Janssen, Sir Theodore: owner of Wimbledon Park, iii. 315, n. 5.

Januarius (Genuarius), St.: relics of, ii. 328 & n. 3; convent of, near Pozzuoli, ii. 342 & n. 5.
Janus: supposed temple of, at Leicester: ruins of, iii. 123 & n. 2.
Japan: account of: mentioned, iv. 214 & n. 6; works of art, &c., from, iii. 373–4 & nn.; cabinets, iv. 190, 343; lacquer or varnish (japanning), iii. 324, n. 2; iv. 288 & n. 7; Japanese writing, ii. 331.
Japanese language: a grammar of (?), iii. 374.
Jardine, —: *see* Chardin, Sir John.
Jarmine, Henry: *see* Jermyn, Henry, Baron Jermyn, &c.
Java (Java Major), iv. 285–6 & n.; Bantam in: ambassadors from, iv. 284–6 & nn.; Jacatra in, ii. 57, n. 7; iii. 108, n. 5.
Jeakel, Mrs. —: *see* Middleton, Mrs. Elizabeth.
Jean de France, duke of Berry: chapel of, at Bourges, ii. 153 & nn. 10–13 (i. 99).
Jean d'Orléans, count of Angoulême: *see* Angoulême.
Jeane, Dr. —: *see* Jane, W.
Jeffreys (Geoffries, &c.), Sir George; first Baron Jeffreys 1685; the judge, iv. 342, n. 3; character, &c., iv. 342, 484, 500; at Lord Russell's trial, iv. 327, n. 2; as lord chief justice of King's Bench: appointed, iv. 342 & n. 3; ~ conduct of, iv. 445; ~ presides at trials of Algernon Sidney, &c., iv. 352 & n. 7, 466 & n. 5, 484; appointed a Privy Councillor, iv. 342, n. 3; created baron, iv. 445 & n. 5; expected to supersede Lord Keeper Guilford, *ib.*; as Lord Chancellor: appointed, iv. 466 & n. 5, 484 & n. 1; ~ swears in, &c., commissioners for Privy Seal, iv. 493, 494 *bis*; ~ case before, iv. 500; as Commissioner for Ecclesiastical Affairs: appointed, iv. 519–20; ~ in proceedings against Compton, iv. 524; views of, on: reports of Popish Plot trials, iv. 175, n. 3; ~ James II's relations with the bishops, Sept. 1688, iv. 600, n. 4 *ad fin.*; social: connexion of, with Deptford, iv. 484 & n. 2; ~ conversation of, on lawyers' chicanery, iv. 530; ~ at wedding, iv.
Jeffreys, Sir George (*cont.*)
352; ~ at parties, &c., iv. 385 & n. 1(?), 490, 587; flight and capture of, iv. 611 & n. 4; excepted from pardon, 1690, v. 23, n. 4; alluded to (?), v. 408 & n. 2; geneal., iv. 590, n. 4 *ad fin.*
Jeffreys: first Baron, 1685–9: *see* Jeffreys, Sir George.
Jehoram, v. 165, n. 3.
Jehoshaphat: in sermons, v. 165 & n. 3, 505.
Jehovah: use of the name by the Jews: in sermon, v. 424.
Jehu: in sermons, iv. 100, 348, 364.
Jekyl (Jeakel), Mrs. Elizabeth: *see* Middleton, Mrs. E.
Jeliabouisky, Ivan, Russian ambassador to England with Prince P. Prozorovsky, 1662–3: *see* Prozorovsky, Prince P.
Jenkins, Sir Leoline; knighted 1670, iii. 499, n. 3; iv. 222, n. 7; brings thanks of Oxford University to E and Henry Howard, iii. 498–500; diplomatic appointments, iv. 8, n. 2, 76, n. 3; godfather to a Jewess, iv. 222.
Jenner (Genner), Sir Thomas: appointed Recorder of London, iv. 342 & n. 5.
Jennings, Mrs. —, wife of Richard Jennings and mother of the duchess of Marlborough: reputation of, v. 525, n. 4.
Jennings, Frances: *see* Talbot, Frances, duchess of Tyrconnel.
Jennings, Richard, of Sandridge, Herts.: geneal., v. 90, n. 2.
Jennings, Sarah: *see* Churchill, Sarah, duchess of Marlborough.
Jeoly (Jolo, Giolo), Prince, v. 295 & n. 2.
Jeremiah: in sermon, v. 397; death of: in sermon, iv. 45 & n. 4.
Jermyn, Henry; created Baron Dover 1685; earl of Dover 1689 (Jacobite peerage); third Baron Jermyn 1703, iii. 482, n. 1; appointed a commissioner of the Treasury, 1687, iv. 533; appointed governor of Portsmouth, 1688, iv. 609 & n. 7; submits to William III, v. 72 & n. 2; describes French military strength, v. 72; at Newmarket, iii. 588; social, iii. 482; iv. 589; Dover Street named after, v. 37, n. 4.

Jermyn, Henry; first Baron Jermyn 1643; earl of St. Albans 1660, ii. 562, n. 3; in Paris, &c., 1649 (as Lord German), ii. 562 & n. 3; as governor of Jersey: man recommended to, iii. 251 & nn. 4, 6; as ambassador in France: despatch to, iii. 299 & n. 5; commissioner for London streets, iii. 319, n. 1; as Lord Chamberlain of the Household: appointed, iii. 588, n. 7; ~ superseded, iv. 47, n. 2; in old age, iv. 337–8 & n.; property of, at Byfleet and Oatlands, iv. 141 & n. 3, 565, n. 2; visits Sayes Court, iii. 330, 354; greets E after Plague, iii. 429; at Newmarket, iii. 588; gives ball, iv. 30; social, iii. 356, 547; geneal., iii. 588.

Jermyn, Judith, Baroness Dover, later Baroness Jermyn, wife of Henry Jermyn, third Baron Jermyn, &c.: as Lady Dover: social (?), iv. 498 & n. 3.

Jermyn: Barons, &c.: *see* Jermyn, Henry, first baron 1643–60, later earl of St. Albans; Jermyn, Henry, third baron 1703–8, formerly Baron Dover, &c.; Jermyn, Judith, his baroness.

Jerome (Hierom), St.: version by, of Bible: Ussher on, iii. 156; Biblical commentaries by: passage in, ii. 247 & n. 3; views of, on Millenarianism: in sermon, v. 448 & n. 1; relics of, ii. 244.

Jeronimo: *see* Carpi, Girolamo da.

Jersey: natives of: *see* Brevint, D.; Durel, J.; Edward Stowell in, iii. 37, n. 3; governor of, 1644– : *see* Jermyn, Henry, earl of St. Albans; lieutenant-governor, 1643–51: *see* Carteret, Sir George; judge-advocate (?): E recommends — Messervy (Messeroy) for, iii. 251 & n. 4.

Jersey: first Earl of, 1697–1711: *see* Villiers, Edward.

Jerusalem [sometimes called simply 'the City']:

— general: conquest of, by Titus: arch commemorating, in Rome, ii. 247–8; ~ spoils from, ii. 275, n. 3; earth from, ii. 181 (i. 114), 272–3 & n., 290, 380; *see also* i. 85; pilgrim to, ii. 65 (i. 44); E plans to visit, ii. 451; Dr. R. Frampton at, iii. 629 & n. 1; return of the Jews to (Messianic prophecy), ii. 54–5 (i. 37–8); Millenarians expect to return to, v. 177–8.

— — in sermons: annual devotions of the Jews at, v. 576; Christ's entry into, iv. 132; v. 382; Christ's tears over, iv. 33, 168, 250, 281; v. 521; Christ suffers outside, iv. 198; early Church in, v. 74, 80, 341, 342; destruction of, &c., v. 128–9 & n., 146, 306; peace of, iv. 236, 610; v. 194; figurative, iii. 551.

— places in: Bethesda, Pool of: in sermons, v. 249–50 & n., 493; Herod's palace (error), ii. 268–9 & nn.; Moriah, Mount: in sermon, v. 113; Pilate's palace: relics from, ii. 268–9 *bis* & nn., 273, n. 7; Siloam, Tower in: in sermon, v. 113; Solomon's palace: columns from, ii. 438 & n. 5; Temple (or Temple of Solomon): columns from, ii. 264 & nn. 2, 3, 438 & n. 5; ~ sacred objects from: representation of, ii. 247 & n. 3; ~ veil of: relics of, ii. 273 & n. 7; ~ in sermons: geographical, v. 250; ~ general history of, v. 63–4; ~ sacrifices brought to, v. 15; ~ Christ's cleansing of, v. 74, 429; ~ destruction of: omens preceding, iv. 495–6 & n.; ~ general significance, iv. 108; v. 113, 274, 290; ~ courts of, iv. 372; v. 429; ~ Holy of Holies: high priest's entry into, iv. 571, 579; v. 241, 424; ~ veil: rending of, v. 126; Second Temple: in sermon, iv. 652–3; Zion (Sion), Mount: in sermons, iii. 19; v. 99; ~ named in error, iii. 34 & n. 1; ~ figurative, iii. 164.

Jessop, Constantine, D.D.: sermon by, iv. 593 & n. 2.

Jesuits and the Society of Jesus:

— general: in Japan and China, iii. 373 & n. 5; educational system of, ii. 65–6 & n. (i. 44); rule of: adopted for Institute of Blessed Virgin Mary, ii. 400, n. 3; generals of: *see* Oliva, G. P.; Vitelleschi, M.

— attacks on: allegations against: falsification by, of Patristic

Jesuits and the Society of Jesus (*cont.*)
texts, iv. 145 & n. 1; ~ originated Presbyterianism in England, v. 13 & n. 1; ~ permit regicide, iv. 230; v. 165–6 & n.; general: in sermons, iv. 181; v. 381; E hostile to, i. *26*; anti-Jesuit books: translated by E, iii. 393 & n. 6, 431 & n. 7; ~ translated by E. Tonge, iv. 153–4 & n.
— churches: at: Antwerp, ii. 63–4 & n. (i. 43); Genoa, i. 109; ii. 177 (i. 111); Milan, ii. 494–5 & n.; Naples, ii. 329–30 & n.; Paris, ii. 96 & n. 3 (i. 63–4); iii. 34–5, 637; ~ sermon at, iii. 23; Rome, ii. 230 & nn. 1–3; *see also* ii. 281, n. 1.
— colleges, &c.: at: Aix-en-Provence, ii. 163 & n. 5 (i. 103); Antwerp, ii. 65–6 & nn. (i. 44); Bourges, ii. 154 & n. 2 (i. 99); Nevers, ii. 533 & n. 6; Paris, ii. 96 & n. 3 (i. 63–4); ~ Far Eastern collection for, iii. 373–4; Rome: Casa Professa, ii. 230 & n. 5; Collegio Germanico, ii. 290, n. 7; Collegio Romano, ii. 282–3 & n.; *see also* ii. 230, n. 5; Venerable English College, ii. 365–6 & nn.; ~ plays, &c., at, ii. 291 & n. 4, 388; ~ rector of (T. Courtney), ii. 213 & n. 7.
— — St. Omer (English): T. Oates at, iv. 153, n. 4; Tournon, ii. 159 & n. 7 (i. 102); Tours, ii. 148 & n. 5 (i. 96); Valladolid (English): T. Oates at, iv. 153, n. 4.
— conversions effected by: *see* Cosin, John, jnr. (iii. 636, &c.); Hollar, W. (i. 21 & n. 2).
— in English politics, 1678–88: accusations against, by T. Oates, i. *27*; relations of, with T. Oates, iv. 153, n. 4, 174–5, 232; 'the Jesuited party of the Papists': hostility of, to Church of England, iv. 174; suspected of murdering Sir E. B. Godfrey, iv. 175; the five Jesuits executed for the Popish Plot, iv. 170 & n. 10; influence of, on James II, 1687–8, iv. 536 & n. 4, 582, 616; v. 475; James II retains at court, Oct. 1688, iv. 599–600 & n.; intrigue against protestants, iv. 600; Sunderland unwilling to serve, iv. 602; fly, Dec. 1688, iv. 609.
— influence of, &c.: on Spanish policy, 1636, i. 21; on Leopold I, 1690, v. 35, 37; accused of murdering Kyrillos Lukaris, i. 14; ii. 18, n. 3; approve of persecution of French protestants, iv. 486.
— members of the Society: (i) English: confessors of Sir Henry Gage's regiment, ii. 65 & n. 4 (i. 44); officiants in Roman Catholic chapel, Whitehall, &c., iv. 534–5 & n., 606 & n. 3, 610; former occupants of the later Trinity Chapel, v. 63; *see also* Courtney, T.; Petre, C.; Petre, E.; Tomson, —; Warner, J.; Whitbread, T.
— — (ii) unnamed foreign Jesuits: 'the Jesuit of Brussels' (D. Seghers), iii. 216 & n. 6; at Castellanza, ii. 505–6; preacher at Paris, iii. 23.
Jesuits' bark *or* powder: *see* Medicine and Surgery: drugs (quinine).
Jesus Christ: *see* Christ.
Jethro: in sermon, iv. 495.
Jews or Israelites, &c. [*see also* Pharisees; Sadducees; Scribes]:
— (1) in biblical times, &c.:
— — general: straw for making bricks, iv. 214; murmuring for water on Mount Horeb: relic relating to, ii. 440 & n. 2; Brazen Serpent: relic of, ii. 500 & n. 4; Coliseum built by Jewish captives, ii. 249 & n. 7; rabbinical studies, &c., iv. 329.
— — in sermons:
— — — conduct towards Christ: accusations against, v. 1; cruelty or malice towards, iii. 101; iv. 137, 630, 648; v. 21, 47, 563, 596; ~ J. Allington as preacher on, iii. 134 & n. 1; incredulity, v. 293, 512; rejection of, iii. 537; iv. 168, 495–6, 571; v. 81, 152, 276–7, 569–70; ~ punishment for, v. 113, 227, 228; separation from, iv. 287.
— — — conduct, &c., in relation to Christianity: Gospel: revealed to, v. 484; ~ rejected by, v. 570; offer of salvation no

Jews or Israelites, &c. (*cont.*)
longer restricted to, v. 255; St. John the Baptist's place in Jewish church, iv. 356; religion of: St. Paul's knowledge of, v. 395; St. Paul's teaching and, iii. 23; malice of, towards St. Paul, v. 72–3; converts to Christianity: relapsed, iv. 81; ~ St. Peter's exhortations to, v. 93.
— — — customs, worship, &c.: anathema, iii. 337 & n. 1; iv. 164; *see also* iv. 436; circumcision, iii. 350; v. 125, 373–4, 554; corban (vow), v. 303 & n. 3; first fruits: offering of, iii. 435 & n. 9; high priest's entry into Holy of Holies, iv. 571, 579; v. 241, 424; Jehovah: use of name, v. 424; Passover, iii. 292; v. 167, 505; places of public worship, v. 62–4; sabbath: observance of, iii. 574–5 *bis*; v. 14; *see also* iv. 280; sacrifices: described, iv. 198; v. 15–16, 45; Sanhedrin, iii. 30; Scriptures: study of, v. 106; shoes, iii. 542–3; washing before worship, v. 123; worship, daily, v. 573.
— — — history: general: God revealed Himself to, v. 334–5, 344, 385; trust of, in God's promises to Abraham, v. 296; Chosen People, iii. 163–4, 168; deliverances and disobedience of, &c., iii. 222; v. 51, 74–5, 227, 271, 306, 309, 362; kings of: sins of, iv. 168; punishment and destruction of, iii. 305; iv. 250; v. 89, 128–9, 146, 333, 463; dispersal of, iii. 377.
— — — history: particular: gathering of manna, v. 180; Law delivered to, &c., iii. 34 & n. 1, 170; worship of Golden Calf, v. 347; Brazen Serpent, iii. 506, 526; breach of the Covenant, iv. 592; sins in David's time, v. 319; David's census, iv. 165–6; v. 151; sins before Babylonish captivity, iv. 334; stone Jeremiah, iv. 45 & n. 4.
— — — law: Mosaic or ritual law or sacrifice (frequently in contrast with Christian revelation), iii. 366; iv. 29, 37, 81, 137, 198, 264, 271, 297, 392, 544, 571, 579, 650; v. 73, 165, 195, 211,

Jews or Israelites, &c. (*cont.*)
226, 253, 273–4, 295, 348, 356, 373, 379, 386, 397, 421, 442, 449, 454, 469–70, 471 *bis*, 474, 480, 488, 504, 529, 560, 576, 618; ~ contrasted with moral law, v. 162, 248, 470.
— — — morals: charity: limits of, v. 375; ~ obligation to, v. 428; commandments: unknown to, v. 422; ~ to love one's neighbours neglected by, v. 231; commemoration of deliverances, iv. 348; good works: views on, v. 160; hypocrisy and idolatry, iv. 47, 198; v. 474, 492; ingratitude, &c., iv. 373; malice and vindictiveness, v. 425, 471, 506; persistence in sin, iv. 556; piety, iv. 585; sins of: in comparison, iii. 222.
— — — views, &c.: on the Messiah, v. 123, 208, 276, 454–5, 515, 524, 563; on paradise, v. 114; on possession by the devil, v. 95; on gift of prophecy, v. 184; on Sacrament, v. 240–2; on freedom of thought, v. 430; ignorant of immortality of the soul, &c., v. 114, 239–40, 357, 470, 488, 496.
— — — miscellaneous: possess symbols of spiritual food, iii. 23; Holy Spirit and, iv. 205.
— (2) in E's time:
— — communities, &c.: Amsterdam, ii. 42–3 & nn. (i. 31); Avignon, ii. 162 & n. 4 (i. 103); England: resettlement, iii. 163 & n. 3; *see also* ii. 42, n. 2; sermons against: endowment for, v. 82, 88 & n. 3; ~ a sermon, v. 126; France: exclusion from, iv. 162, n. 4; Persia: account of persecution in, iii. 522, n. 2 *ad fin.*; Portugal: Jewesses from, at Venice, ii. 477 & n. 4; Rome: Ghetto, ii. 292 & n. 3; conversions: a Jew baptized annually, ii. 386, n. 4; ~ a convert baptized, ii. 376–7 & n.; dress, ii. 294, 400 & n. 2; *Possesso* of Innocent X: decorations for, provided by, ii. 228 & n. 6, 281; poverty of, ii. 294; sermons to, ii. 291–2 & n., 376; Venice: Ghetto, ii. 477 & nn. 2, 4; in streets, ii. 449.
— — ceremonies: burial customs,

Jews or Israelites, &c. (*cont.*) ii. 42–3 (i. 31); circumcision, ii. 293–4 & n.; marriage, ii. 477 & n. 3; worship in synagogue, ii. 42 (i. 31); dress: hats: red, later yellow, ii. 162 & n. 5 (i. 103), 294, 400 & n. 2; ritual, ii. 42 (i. 31); individuals: Burgundian Jew at Leyden: on metempsychosis, &c., ii. 54–5 & n. (i. 37–8); Jewess from Holland baptized, iv. 222; Duarte family at Antwerp, ii. 67 & n. 6 (i. 45); Shabbethai Zebi, iii. 522, n. 2; Messianic prophecies concerning: calling or conversion of the Jews: imminent, iii. 158; v. 20–1, 26; return to Jerusalem, ii. 54–5 (i. 38); v. 177–8; error in, iv. 652–3.

Jezebel: alluded to, in sermon, iv. 364.

Joachim of Flora: portraits of St. Dominic, &c., made by, ii. 439 & n. 2.

Joan, Pope, ii. 268, n. 2.

Joan of Arc (Jane d'Arc), ii. 137 (i. 90); sword of, ii. 89–90 & n.; portrait of, ii. 89 (i. 60); statue of, at Orleans, ii. 137 & nn. 1–3 (i. 90); alluded to, ii. 100 & n. 6 (i. 66).

Joanna I (Jeane), queen of Naples: gives Avignon to Clement VI, ii. 160 & n. 5 (i. 102).

Joanna Maria, singer (Joanna Maria Lindehleim?), v. 531, n. 2; notice (?), v. 531.

Jo: Battist, harpsichord-player (G. B. Draghi?): performs, iv. 384–5 & n., 404, 422.

Job (Jobe): messengers to (proverbial), v. 550; in sermons, iii. 20; iv. 46, 221, 495; v. 127, 129, 166, 172, 179, 306, 316, 387, 414, 470, 496, 499, 534, 565.

Johann Friedrich, duke of Brunswick-Lüneburg: geneal., v. 317, n. 3.

Johann Wilhelm, Elector Palatine 1690–1716, iv. 65, n. 4; as prince of Neuburg: visits England, iv. 65 & n. 4; as elector: in religious issue, v. 270, n. 7; giant guardsman of, v. 592 & n. 1.

John III (Sobieski), king of Poland: relieves Vienna, iv. 340 & n. 3, 398, n. 2; later conduct and death of, v. 247 & n. 3.

John IV, king of Portugal: geneal., iii. 286, n. 6.

John IV, duke of Brabant: besieges Dordrecht, ii. 32, n. 3.

John IV, pope: oratory built by, ii. 267–8 & n.

John of Gaunt, duke of Lancaster: birth-place of, ii. 73 & n. 7 (i. 48); hospital founded by (error), iii. 122 & n. 8.

John, Roman patrician: tomb of, &c. (in text as Patricius), ii. 242, n. 5, 243 & n. 1.

John, Father: *see* Wilfrid.

John, St., the Baptist: execution of: rule commemorating, ii. 267 & n. 2; relics of, ii. 88 (i. 59), 205 & n. 2; in sermons, iii. 133, 307, 543; iv. 356, 401; v. 123, 149, 162–3, 183, 226, 228, 258, 372, 508, 621.

John, St., Chrysostom: MS. written by, ii. 205 & n. 6; tomb of, ii. 289; works of: edited by Sir Henry Savile, iii. 336–7 & n.; ~ *Education of Children*: translation of, by E, &c., iii. 220 & n. 4; in sermons, v. 106, 155, 168.

John, St., the Evangelist: Gospel of: copy of, written by him, ii. 188 & n. 8 (i. 118); relics of, ii. 88 (i. 59), 275; explanation of Daniel by, v. 26; writes against the Gnostics: in sermon, iv. 363 & n. 7; in sermons, iii. 238, 240; v. 79, 491.

Johnson, Captain —: funeral of, iv. 111.

Johnson, Dr. — (William Johnson?): sermon by, iii. 271 & n. 5.

Johnson, Rev. —: sermon by, iii. 83.

Johnson, Elizabeth: *see* Mordaunt, Elizabeth, Lady Mordaunt.

Johnson, Martin, seal-engraver, iii. 390, n. 3.

Johnson, Nicholas: geneal., iv. 206, n. 1.

Johnson, Rev. Samuel: convicted for seditious libel, iv. 367 & n. 2.

Johnson, William, D.D.: sermon by (?), iii. 271 & n. 5.

Johnston (Johnson), Sir John, bt.: executed, v. 41 & n. 1.

Jolo (Jeoly, Giolo), Prince, v. 295 & n. 2.

Jonah: chronology of, iv. 244, n. 3; in sermons, v. 401, 457, 487; *see also* iii. 613.

Jones, —, of Gray's Inn (William Jones?): E consults, iii. 580 & n. 3.

Jones, Arthur, second Viscount Ranelagh: geneal., v. 26, n. 2.
Jones, Edward; bishop of Cloyne 1683; of St. Asaph 1692: sermon by, v. 212 & n. 1.
Jones, Elizabeth, countess of Ranelagh, wife of Richard Jones, third viscount and first earl: as Elizabeth Willoughby: social, iii. 218 & n. 7.
Jones, Sir Henry: remarks of, on France, iii. 587 & nn. 3–5.
Jones, Inigo, the architect: uses Portland stone, i. 81, n. 1; study of Stonehenge by, iii. 115, n. 6; master of John Webb, iii. 301 & n. 1; buildings, &c.: general, i. *17*, n. 1 *ad fin.*; Greenwich: Queen's House, ii. 543 & n. 2; London: Covent Garden: origin of design of, ii. 184 & n. 5 (i. 116); ~ Marlborough Chapel, iii. 373, n. 2; ~ St. Paul's: repairs and portico, iii. 448, n. 3, 459, n. 1; i. *19–20*; Wilton House: designs for, by (?), iii. 113, n. 6; doubtful and false attributions, iii. 133, n. 8, 140, n. 1.
Jones, Col. John, regicide: executed, iii. 259 & n. 1.
Jones, Katherine, Viscountess Ranelagh, wife of Arthur Jones, second viscount, v. 26, n. 2; house of, iv. 124, n. 6; social, v. 26; dies, v. 83 & n. 2.
Jones, Richard, third Viscount and first earl of Ranelagh: geneal., iii. 218, n. 7.
Jones, Sir Thomas, judge: decision by, iv. 417, n. 6 *ad fin.*
Jones, Sir William, K.C., iii. 580, n. 3; in Stafford's impeachment, iv. 227 & n. 5, 229–30 & nn., 231, nn. 1, 2; counsel for Lady Mordaunt's executors, iv. 259; E consults (?), iii. 580.
Jonson, Ben: at the Devil tavern, v. 5, n. 1; *Catiline* by: performed, iii. 520 & n. 2; *Volpone* by: and mountebanks, ii. 474, n. 5; ~ performed, iii. 341 & n. 1; supposed part-author of *The Widdow*, iii. 313, n. 4.
Jordan, river: in sermon, v. 362.
Jordan, Sir Joseph: conduct of, at Solebay: alluded to, iii. 618 & n. 5.
Joseph I, Emperor, v. 7, n. 2; crowned king of Hungary, v. 7 & n. 2; as king of the Romans:
Joseph I (*cont.*)
elected, &c., *ib.*; marriage of, v. 317, n. 3; at siege of Landau, 1702, v. 510 & n. 2, 512 & n. 3.
Joseph II, patriarch of Constantinople: tomb of, ii. 200 & n. 2.
Joseph (the son of Jacob): particoloured coat of (in Bodleian Library), iii. 107 & n. 9; in sermons, iii. 188; iv. 169; v. 271, 433, 499, 589.
Joseph, St., of Arimathea: in Britain (in sermon), iii. 333 & n. 4; relic of, ii. 290.
Joseph Clemens, archbishop-elector of Cologne, &c., iv. 596, n. 3; disputed election of, 1688, iv. 596 & n.3, 598 & n. 2; delivers Liège to France, 1701, v. 482 & n. 2.
Joseph Ferdinand, Bavarian prince: in first Partition treaty, v. 434, n. 4.
Joshua: in sermon, iv. 132.
Josiah: in sermons, iii. 521; v. 418, 499.
Jouar y Velasco, Don Pedro de, marqués de Fresno: *see* Fresno.
Jousting: tournament at Rome, ii. 389 & n. 3; place suitable for, ii. 483 & n. 1; *see also* ii. 395 & n. 4.
Jovius, Paulus: *see* Giovio, P.
Joyliffe, George, M.D., ii. 551 & n. 2; rattlesnakes of, iii. 200; social, ii. 551; iii. 89, 186.
Judah: kingdom of: in sermon, iv. 358; reformed church of: in sermon, iv. 577–8.
Judas Iscariot: lantern of, ii. 89 (i. 60); one of the thirty pieces of silver, ii. 380 & n. 10; in sermons, iii. 203, 503, 524, 569; v. 84, 128, 172, 195, 281, 345, 393.
Judea: country east of: in sermon, v. 83.
Judgement, Day of [sermons on the Last Judgement are not indexed as such; for its approach *see* Prophecies]: duration of: in sermons, v. 279, 613 & n. 1.
Julamerk, Turkey: orpiment mined at, ii. 430, n. 1.
Julian the Apostate: imitated by Cromwell, iii. 163 & n. 1; in sermon, v. 143.
Jülich and Berg: Duke of: *see* Johann Wilhelm, Elector Palatine.
Juliers: Dukes of: *see* Arnold of Egmont; William V.

Julio: *see* Giulio Romano.
Julius, Portus, near Pozzuoli, ii. 345 & n. 2.
Julius II, pope: starts to rebuild St. Peter's, ii. 258; tomb of, ii. 278 & n. 7.
Julius Caesar [sometimes called Caesar; all references to Julius are collected here; for Caesar used generically *see* Caesar]: conquests of, iv. 486; assassination of, ii. 283; murderers of: in sermon, iv. 336; ashes of, ii. 256 & n. 2; villa of, at Baia, ii. 349 & n. 3; reputed builder of: tower at Geneva, ii. 529 & n. 2; ~ the Châtelets at Paris, ii. 102 (i. 66); portraits of: statue (called Augustus in text), ii. 222 & n. 4; ~ gems, ii. 89 (i. 60), 314; William III compared to, v. 28–9.
Julius Paulus: bust of, ii. 463 & n. 4.
Juno: wood sacred to, ii. 210.
Jupiter: place of sacrifice to, ii. 228, n. 1; *see also* Sculpture.
Jupiter, the planet: observed, iii. 286.
Justel, Henri, D.C.L., iv. 287, n. 2; at Royal Society meeting, iv. 287 & n. 1; sees R. Sheldon's collection of medals, iv. 396–7; arranges MSS. in library at St. James's Palace, v. 44; social, iv. 365–6; v. 150.
Justice: Administration of [outside England. Select: notices of seats of justice and law-courts are generally omitted]:
— miscellaneous notices: Delft: punishment at, for bigamy, ii. 41 (i. 30); France: civil trial in, ii. 149 (i. 96); ~ trial for theft in, ii. 535; ~ use of torture in, iii. 28–9 & n.; Geneva: punishment at, for adultery, ii. 527 & n. 4; Genoa: punishment at, for carrying knives, ii. 173 (i. 109); Simplon: independent jurisdiction on, ii. 512 & n. 1; *see also* ii. 518; Sion: bishops' jurisdiction at, ii. 515 & n. 6.
— punishment: instruments and means of, &c.: methods of execution: in Egypt (?), iv. 206 & n. 5; at Naples, ii. 401 & n. 2; Rome, ii. 400–1 & n.; Venice, ii. 459.
— — *eculeus*, ii. 307 & n. 6; galleys,

Justice (*cont.*)
ii. 173 (i. 109); iii. 29; ~ French protestants sent to, iv. 447, n. 3, 485 *bis*; v. 319; *see also* Ships and Shipping; guillotine (frame), ii. 401 & n. 2, 459; house of correction, ii. 45 & n. 4 (i. 32).
— — places of execution: at Geneva, ii. 527 & n. 3; Rome, ii. 367 & n. 1; Venice, ii. 445, 459.
Justin, St.: in sermon, iv. 361.
Justina, St.: relics of, ii. 455 & n. 7.
Justinian family: *see* Giustiniani.
Justinian, Emperor: *Digesta* (*Pandecta*) of: MS. copy of, at Florence, ii. 188 & n. 9 (i. 118); establishes Candlemas: in sermon, iii. 240–1 & n.; statue of, ii. 383 & n. 3.
Justiniani: *see* Giustinian, A.
Jutland, Denmark: in Charles X's winter march, iii. 211, n. 2.
Juvenal: translator of: *see* Stapleton, Sir R. (iii. 98 & n. 2).
Juxon, William, D.C.L.; bishop of London 1633; archbishop of Canterbury 1660, iii. 274 & n. 1; reads service to Charles I before his execution, iv. 193, n. 2; decision of, in election of warden of Merton College, Oxford, iii. 273 & n. 3; ill, 1661, iii. 281, 282; at coronation of Charles II, iii. 282–4 & n.; repairs, &c., by, at Lambeth Palace, iii. 361, n. 5, 362, n. 9; chaplain of: *see* Frank, M.

Kaiserswerth (Keyserwert, &c.): besieged by Allies, 1702, v. 498 & n. 2, 504 & n. 3; capitulates, v. 515 & n. 2.
Karric firgus: *see* Carrickfergus.
Kauffmann, Nicholas, called Mercator: astronomical clock made by, iii. 450 & n. 1.
Kazaneck: battle near, 1690, v. 6 & n. 5.
Keck, Sir Anthony; knighted 1689: counsel for Lady Mordaunt's executors (?), iv. 259 & n. 4.
Keele: *see* Dordsche-Kil.
Keeling, Josiah: Rye-House Plot informer, iv. 322, n. 1, 323, n. 8.
Keffler, Dr.: *see* Kuffeler, J. S.
Keightley, Lady Frances, wife of Thomas Keightley the youngest: as Lady Frances Hyde: social, iv. 12 & n. 5.

Keightley, Mary: *see* Langley, Mary, Lady Langley.
Keightley, Mrs. Rose, born Evelyn, wife of Thomas Keightley, sen., ii. 5, n. 5; godmother of E, ii. 5 (i. 6); E visits, ii. 80 & n. 3 (i. 54); *see also* ii. 81; laments her sons' conversion to Roman Catholicism, iii. 634; in old age, iv. 238–9 & n.; geneal., ii. 149, n. 2; iii. 394, n. 1.
Keightley, Thomas, sen., 1580–1662, ii. 5, n. 5; acquires Hertingfordbury Park, ii. 80, n. 3; laments his sons' conversion to Roman Catholicism, iii. 634; geneal., ii. 80, n. 3; iii. 394, n. 1.
Keightley, Thomas, jnr., b. 1622, ii. 149, n. 2; student at Peterhouse, Cambridge, iii. 46, n. 4 *ad fin.*, 634; at Tours, ii. 149 & n. 2, 150 (i. 97 *bis*); i. 98; conversion of, to Roman Catholicism, iii. 35 & n. 6, 634; ~ conferences relating to, iii. 36–7 *bis*, 634; social, iii. 85, 175, 633–4.
Keightley, Thomas, the youngest, 1650–1719: geneal., iv. 12, n. 5.
Keightley, William, ii. 149, n. 2; student at Peterhouse, Cambridge, iii. 46, n. 4 *ad fin.*; pass for, to travel abroad, ii. 80, n. 3; at Tours, ii. 149 & n. 2, 150 (i. 97 *bis*); i. 98; converted to Roman Catholicism, iii. 634; geneal., iv. 12, n. 5.
Keller(s), sculptors: statue by, ii. 118, n. 9.
Kello, Bartholomew: geneal., iii. 107, n. 3.
Kello, Mrs. Esther, born Inglis, wife of B. Kello: MS. written by, iii. 107 & n. 3.
Kemp, —: buys impropriation of South Malling, ii. 541.
Kempten: Barbara Ursler born near, iii. 198, n. 1.
Ken (Can, Cann), Thomas, D.D.; bishop of Bath and Wells 1684–90, iv. 302, n. 3; visits Tangier, &c., iv. 379, n. 2; attends Charles II on death-bed, iv. 407; attends Monmouth in Tower, &c., iv. 456 & n. 1; conversation of, with James II at Winchester, iv. 468–71; suspected inclination of, to Roman Catholicism, iv. 504; as one of the Seven Bishops, iv. 583–8 & nn., *passim*; visit to, in Tower, iv. 587; at meeting to discuss settlement of the crown, Jan. 1689, iv. 613–14; superseded as bishop, v. 48–9 & n.; conduct of, after deprivation, v. 52 & n. 2, 289, n. 3; as preacher: style and popularity of, iv. 543, 577, 578; sermons by: printed, iv. 577–8 & n.; ~ unprinted, iv. 302, 379–80 & n., 504 & n. 3, 541–2, 543; appointed to preach, iv. 370, n. 1; social, iv. 543.
Kendal: Duke of: *see* Charles.
Kendal, George, D.D.: speech by, iii. 105 & n. 5.
Kendrick, John, lord mayor of London: social, iii. 63 & n. 2.
Kendrick, Mrs. Katherine, born Evelyn, wife of John Kendrick: geneal., iii. 63, n. 2.
Kendrick, Thomas: geneal., iii. 63, n. 2.
Kennedy, John, earl of Cassillis: social (?; as earl of Castleton), v. 150 & n. 6.
Kensington: Lord: *see* Rich, Henry.
Kent: County of:
chronological series: rising in, 1648, ii. 541 & n. 4; iii. 153, n. 6; control of Sick and Wounded in, 1664–7, &c., iii. 388, 394, 609; i. *18–19*; collections in, for relief of plague, 1666, iii. 445, n. 6; soldiers in, 1666, iii. 422, n. 4; Kentish Petition, 1701, v. 457 & n. 2, 461.
Commission of Sewers: *see* Surrey and Kent Commission of Sewers.
militia: called out: at time of Monmouth's rebellion, iv. 450, 458–9; ~ against French, 1696, v. 233 & n. 1; command in, offered to E, iii. 254 & n. 4; commanders, iii. 484, n. 4; iv. 414.
officers: sheriffs: *see* Leech, Sir W. (1666–7); Rooke, Sir W. (1684–5); deputy-lieutenants: request of, to E, iii. 422 & n. 3.
miscellaneous: beauty of, iii. 422; gigantic ox from, ii. 554; unnamed persons belonging to, ii. 54 (i. 37); iii. 74.
Kent: Earls and Countesses of: *see* Grey, Henry, tenth earl, 1643–51; Grey, Amabella, his countess; Grey, Anthony, eleventh earl; Grey, Mary, Baroness Lucas, his countess.

Kepler, J., astronomer, ii. 64, n. 2 *ad fin*.
Keppel, Arnold Joost van, earl of Albemarle, v. 321, n. 1; commission in Guards granted to, v. 320–1 & n., 323 & n. 2.
Kercherus, Father: *see* Kircher, A.
Kerckhoven (Kirkhoven), John Polyander à, lord of Heenvliet: geneal., iv. 92, n. 2.
Kéroualle: château of, iv. 66 & n. 1.
Kéroualle (Quierwill): Comte (Guillaume de Penancoët) and Comtesse de: visit Sir R. Browne, &c., iv. 66 & nn. 1, 2.
Kéroualle (Quirreval, &c.), Louise-Renée de Penancoët de; created duchess of Portsmouth 1673, iii. 564 & n. 1; comes to court, *ib.*; at Euston: mock-marriage of, to Charles II, iii. 589–90 & n.; in height of favour, iv. 66; entertains Moroccan ambassador, iv. 267–8 & nn.; visited by Charles II, iv. 343; as mother of duke of Richmond, iv. 374, 392; at court, 25 Jan. 1685, iv. 403, 413; Charles II's death-bed concern for, iv. 409 & n. 2; Charles II's expenditure on, iv. 410, n. 2; apartment of, in Whitehall: furniture of, iv. 74 & n. 3, 343 & nn. 1–3; ~ burnt down, v. 47 & n. 2; parents of, iv. 66 & n. 1.
Kerr, William, earl of Lothian, iii. 175, n. 3; social, iii. 175 & n. 3, 254 & n. 3.
Ketch, Jack, executioner: beheads Monmouth, iv. 456 & n. 2.
Kettlewell, Rev. John: burial of, v. 289, n. 3.
Kew (Cew, Cue), Surrey: house and garden of Sir Henry Capel, Baron Capell, at: notices, iv. 144 & n. 1, 347, 576; ~ visit to, iv. 465; Kew Palace, iv. 144, n. 1.
Keyes, Thomas: trial, &c., of, v. 234 *bis* & nn. 4, 8.
Keynes, Geoffrey L.: concern of, in present edition of Diary, i. *64*; bibliography of E's writings by, i. *130*, n. 2, 122–3 & nn.
Keyser, Hendrik de: buildings designed by, ii. 41 & n. 1 (i. 30), 48–9 & n. (i. 34); statue of Erasmus by, ii. 33 & n. 4 (i. 25); tomb of William the Silent by, ii. 40 & n. 5 (i. 30).
Keyserwert: *see* Kaiserswerth.
Kidder, Richard, D.D.; bishop of Bath and Wells 1691, v. 18, n. 4; as dean of Peterborough: sermon by, v. 18; as Boyle Lecturer for 1693: appointed, v. 123 & n. 3, 161 & n. 1; ~ lecture by, v. 126.
Kidderminster, Worcs.: Hurcott in: *see* Hurcott.
Kiel: duchess of Gottorp dies at, v. 582, n. 1.
Kievit (Kiviet), Sir Jan, bt., iii. 470–1 & nn.; project of, for making clinker brick, &c., iii. 471, 476 & n. 3, 477–8, 495; drains Soham Mere, iii. 555–6 & nn.; social, iii. 478, 492, 504.
Kil, the (the Dordsche-Kil; the Keele), ii. 60 *ter* & n. 1 (i. 41 *bis*).
Kildare: Earls, &c., of: *see* Fitzgerald, George, sixteenth earl, 1620–60; Fitzgerald, Joan, his countess; Fitzgerald, John, eighteenth earl, 1664–1707.
Killegrew, William: colonelcy of, in Dutch army, ii. 36, n. 1.
Killiecrankie: battle of: Dundee killed in, iv. 647 & n. 3.
Killigrew, Henry, admiral: commission to, 1693, v. 131 & n. 1, 161 & n. 2.
Killigrew, Henry, D.D., iii. 301, n. 2; as master of the Savoy Hospital, iii. 410, n. 1; sermons by, iii. 301, 310; iv. 35, 82.
Killigrew, Thomas: theatrical company of (King's Company): *see* London: topography: theatres.
Kilmacduagh: bishop of Clonfert and, 1665–84: *see* Wolley, E.
Kilmore and Ardagh: bishops of: *see* Marsh, Francis (1673–82); Wetenhall, E. (1699–1713).
Kilmorey: Viscounts, &c.: *see* Needham, Robert, first viscount; Needham, Charles, fourth viscount, 1657–60; Needham, Bridget, his viscountess.
Kilpeck: Baron (Jacobite peerage): *see* Pye, Walter.
Kinalmeaky, Lady: *see* Boyle, Elizabeth, countess of Guildford.
King, Sir Edmund, M.D.; knighted 1686, iv. 290, n. 1; bleeds Charles II at time of seizure, iv. 406 & n. 1; at Royal Society meeting (?), iv. 290.
King, Edward: trial, &c., of, v. 234 *bis* & nn. 4, 8.

King, Elizabeth: *see* Prettyman, Mrs. E.
King, Henry, D.D., bishop of Chichester, iii. 346, n. 1; consecrates Dr. J. Earles, iii. 346; sermon by, iii. 524 & n. 5.
King, John: geneal., ii. 538, n. 1.
King, John, bishop of London: geneal., ii. 538, n. 1.
King, Philip, D.D.: sermon by, iii. 287 & n. 3.
King, Rev. William, rector of Ashtead: sermon by, iii. 220 & n. 7.
King, William, D.D.; bishop of Derry 1691; archbishop of Dublin 1703: character, v. 597 & n. 2.
King Road (Kings-rode), channel in the Severn: in view, iii. 119 & n. 3.
King's Company: *see* London: topography: theatres.
King's Ferry, across the Swale, Kent: needs fortifying, iii. 487 & n. 2.
King's Lynn, Norfolk, iv. 120 & n. 1.
Kingston (Kingston upon Thames), Surrey: distance of Wotton from, ii. 4 & n. 2 (i. 5–6); the Evelyn family at, i. *1–2*, 2, n. 4; Lord Francis Villiers killed near, ii. 541–2 & n.; E dines at, iv. 178; Coombe House (Come) in, v. 595; *add.*; high steward of, 1707–36: *see* Harvey, E. (v. 595, n. 4).
Kingston: Earls and Dukes, &c., of: *see* Pierrepont, Robert, first earl 1628–43; Pierrepont, Henry, second earl 1643–5, later marquis of Dorchester; Pierrepont, Robert, third earl 1680–2; Pierrepont, William, fourth earl 1682–90; Pierrepont, Evelyn, fifth earl 1690–1706, later marquis of Dorchester and first duke, 1715–26, of Kingston; Pierrepont, Mary, his countess.
Kingstone, —, soldier of fortune, iii. 13.
Kinsale (Kingsale), Cork: James II at, iv. 631, n. 1, 635, n. 1; v. 28, n. 6; taken by English forces, 1690, v. 35 & n. 4, 37; Smyrna fleet at, 1691, v. 67 & n. 1; Sir George Rooke and merchantships at, 1693, v. 150 & n. 2.
Kinzig: valley of the: action in, 1703, v. 535 & n. 1.
Kipping, Anne: *see* Henshaw, Mrs. A.
Kipping, Dorothy: *see* Darell, Mrs. D.
Kipping, Robert: geneal., iii. 201, nn. 1, 2.
Kippis, Dr. A.: on E (1793), i. *39*, n. 3.
Kirby Hall, Gretton, Northants.: notice, iii. 133–4 & n.
Kircher (Kercherus, Kirker), Father Athanasius, S.J., ii. 230 & n. 4; collection of, of scientific instruments, ii. 230 & nn. 5–7; sundial invented by (?), ii. 373 & n. 5; lecture by, ii. 283; Ussher's opinion of, iii. 156 & n. 5; *see also* Books: sources; Books mentioned in text.
Kirke, Captain George: in duel, 1699, v. 331 & n. 1.
Kirke, Percy, general: reported to have relieved Londonderry, iv. 643 & n. 4.
Kirkhoven, Charles Henry; Baron Wotton 1650; earl of Bellomont 1680, iii. 555, n. 3; as Lord Wotton: drains Soham Mere, iii. 555–6 & nn.; ~ house of, in Hampstead, iv. 92 & n. 2.
Kirkhoven: *see also* Kerckhoven.
Kiviet, Monsieur: *see* Kievit, Sir Jan.
Klencke, I.: presents book of maps to Charles II, iii. 260, n. 5.
Knaggs (Nag, &c.), Rev. Thomas, v. 381, n. 2; sermons by, v. 371 & n. 1(?), 440, 489 & n. 1(?), 491, 496, 533; ~ for fast, v. 590; Wednesday lectures at Trinity Chapel, Bond Street, by, v. 381–414, 464, 486–93, 502–8, 523–9, 553, 555, 564, 585 *passim & singulatim*.
Knaresborough, Yorks.: springs at, iii. 129 & n. 6.
Knatchbull, Sir John, bt.: appointed a commissioner of the Privy Seal, v. 7 & n. 5.
Knatchbull, Sir Norton, bt., iii. 359 & n. 2; seat of, *ib.*; chaplain of: sermon by, iii. 359.
Kneller, Sir Godfrey, bt., iv. 479, n. 2; portraits by: E, iv. 479 & n. 2; *add.*; ~ for Pepys, iv. 644 & n. 1, 646; Bishop Gilbert Burnet, iv. 642 & n. 3; William III, iv. 465, n. 7; social, iv. 646.
Knight, —, of Northants., and Mrs. Knight: social, iii. 86.
Knight, Rev. —: sermon by, v. 278–9.

Knight, Francis Maria, actress, iii. 230, n. 3.
Knight, John, M.D.: attends Sick and Wounded, 1672, iii. 611 & n. 2.
Knight, John, M.P.: sister of: killed in fire, 1695, v. 222–3 & n.
Knight, Mrs. Mary, singer, iii. 230, n. 3; sings, &c., iv. 49; social, iii. 230.
Knight, Moll, mistress of Charles II, iii. 230, n. 3.
Knights and Orders of Knighthood:
knighthood: Richard Evelyn, sen., fined for evading, ii. 2, n. 2.
knights of various classes, &c.: Knight Banneret (Sir J. Smith), i. 54 & n. 1; knight-errant (Guy of Warwick), iii. 120; ~ journey of knight-errantry, iv. 71; knight of honour, in Cromwell's funeral procession, iii. 224; Knight Marshal: *see* Royal Household; knights of the Sun, in Christmas revels, iii. 308.
orders: Bath: knights of: creation of, at Charles II's coronation, iii. 276 & nn. 5, 7; ~ in Charles II's coronation procession, iii. 279; ~ later order, iii. 276, n. 5 [individual knights are not indexed collectively]; Elephant: knight of, v. 258, n. 1; Garter: *see* Garter, Order of the; Holy Ghost: crosses of, iii. 42; Malta: *see* Malta, Knights of; St. Jago: knight of, iii. 189; St. Stephen (Pisa): church of, &c., ii. 179–80 & n. (i. 113); ~ knight of, ii. 314, n. 1; Knights Templars: monuments of, iii. 67–8 & n., 113 & n. 3; ~ property of, in Paris, ii. 100 & n. 3 (i. 66).
Knodsenburg (Naseburg), near Nijmegen: fort at, ii. 35 & n. 2 (i. 27).
Knole (Knowle) House, Sevenoaks, Kent, iv. 17 & n. 3.
Knollys, Edward, styled second earl of Banbury: attacked by banditti, ii. 317–18 & n.
Knollys, Sir Francis: builds Wallingford House, London, iii. 490, n. 2.
Knollys, Thomas: commissioner for Sick and Wounded in third Dutch War, iii. 602, n. 1.
Knollys, Sir William; Baron Knollys 1603; Viscount Wallingford 1616; earl of Banbury 1626: as owner of Caversham Park, iii. 99, n. 3; Wallingford House, London, named after, iii. 490, n. 2.
Knollys: Baron: *see* Knollys, sir William, later earl of Banbury, &c.
Knowsley, Lancs.: Lady Ossory at (error), iv. 211 & n. 3.
Knox, Thomas: trial of, for defaming Titus Oates, iv. 188, n. 1.
Königsmarck (Koningsmarke, Coningsmark), Count Karl Johann von: trial of, as accessory to murder of Thomas Thynne, iv. 273, 274, n. 1, 276.
Königsmarck, Count Philipp Christoph von: at Foubert's academy, iv. 257, n. 5, 274, n. 1.
Koran: copy of, on calico, iii. 107–8 & n.
Kracovia: *see* Cracow.
Kruisschans (La Croix, Santa Cruce), fort on the Scheldt, ii. 62 & n. 7 (i. 43).
Krummbach, river, ii. 508, n. 5.
Kuffeler, Mrs. Catherina, wife of Dr. J. S. Kuffeler: geneal., iii. 446 & n. 5.
Kuffeler (Keffler), J. S., M.D.: portable stoves of, &c., iii. 446–7 & nn.
Kukeland: *see* Cuyk: Land van.
Kulmbach: Margrave of: *see* Christian Ernest.
Kyeserswert: *see* Kaiserswerth.

L., Dr. —: sermon by, iv. 366.
Labarum (standard) of Constantine, ii. 236 & n. 8, 383, n. 4, 441–2 & n.
la Caillemotte, Pierre de Massue, sieur de: death of, v. 30 & n. 2.
La Charité: E loses spaniel at, ii. 533 & nn. 7, 8.
La Châtre, Claude de: chapel of, at Bourges, ii. 153 & n. 9 (i. 99).
La Chaussée, near Boulogne: accident at (?), ii. 83 & n. 5 (i. 56).
Lachford, Sir Richard: *see* Lechford.
La Croix (Kruisschans, Santa Cruce), fort on the Scheldt, ii. 62 & n. 7 (i. 43).
Lactantius: views of, on duration of the world: in sermons, v. 448 & n. 1, 613, n. 1.

Lacy, John, actor, iii. 338, n. 7; acts in *The Committee*, iii. 345 & n. 3; portrait of, in three parts, iii. 338–9 & n.; *Sauny the Scott* by, iii. 338, n. 7.
La Doree, —, silk manufacturer (Peter La Dore ?), iii. 65 & n. 8.
La Faiola, near Nemi, ii. 316, n. 3 *ad fin*.
La Ferté-Milon: Spanish forces at, 1650, iii. 17, n. 3.
la Ferté-Nabert, Henri de St.-Nectaire, marquis de: altar built by, &c. (as M. Seneterre), iii. 28 & n. 3; *add.*; ~ mentioned, iii. 27.
la Force, Jacques-Nompar de Caumont, duc de, and his duchess: geneal., iv. 649 & n. 6.
Lago Maggiore: *see* Maggiore, Lago.
la Grange, Jean de, bishop of Amiens and cardinal: tomb of (as Cardinal d'Amboise, in error), ii. 161 & n. 10.
La Hogue: battle of, v. 101 & n. 2; effect of, v. 97, n. 2; thanksgiving for, v. 102 & n. 3, 119 & n. 2; conduct of Admiral Edward Russell (later earl of Orford) in, v. 127, n. 2, 130–1; sick and wounded from, v. 203, n. 1.
Lake (Leake), Edward; D.D. 1676, iv. 36, n. 3; officiates: baptism, iv. 49; ~ administers communion to a sick person, iv. 52; ~ marries Sidney Godolphin to Margaret Blagge, iv. 63; daughter of: baptized, iv. 95; sermons by, iv. 36, 71, 75, 191, 194, 532.
Lake, John, D.D.; bishop of Chichester 1685, iv. 502, n. 4; *add.*; as one of the Seven Bishops, iv. 583–8 & nn., *passim*; at meeting to discuss settlement of the crown, Jan. 1689, iv. 613–14; sermon by, iv. 502; death of (as Dr. Lang, in error), iv. 649 & n. 1.
Lamardati: error for B. Ammanati, ii. 193 & n. 7.
Lamb, Dr. — (John Lambe ?): sermon by, iv. 263 & n. 2.
Lamb, James, D.D.: sermon by, iii. 308 & n. 2.
Lambarde, Jane, Lady Lambarde: *see* Garrard, Jane, Lady Garrard, wife of Sir John, first bt.
Lambarde, Jane: *see* Garrard, Jane, Lady Garrard, wife of Sir John, second bt.
Lambarde, Sir Moulton: geneal., ii. 542, n. 2; iii. 90, n. 4.
Lambarde, Thomas: estate of, at Westerham, iii. 90 & n. 4.
Lambe, John, D.D.; dean of Ely 1693: sermon by (?), iv. 263 & n. 2.
Lamberg, J. H. von, baron in Ortenegg, &c.: issues matriculation certificate at Padua, ii. 465–6 & nn.
Lambert, John, general: occupies Wimbledon Park, iii. 315, n. 5.
Lambesc (Loumas), Provence, ii. 162 & nn. 8, 9 (i. 103).
Lame, Biagio delle: paintings by, ii. 423, n. 7 *ad fin*.
la Meilleraye, Armand de la Porte, marquis de, Duc Mazarin: *see* Mazarin.
la Mothe, C.-G. de, French protestant minister: sermon by (?; as La Mot), iv. 552 & n. 2.
Lamplugh, Thomas, D.D.; bishop of Exeter 1676; archbishop of York 1688, iv. 10, n. 4, 85, n. 2, 633, n. 6; as vicar of St. Martin in the Fields: certifies that E has received Sacrament, iv. 10; as archbishop: takes oath of allegiance to William and Mary, iv. 628, n. 4; ~ takes part in coronation of William and Mary, iv. 633 & n. 3; as preacher: style, &c., iv. 28, 130; sermons by, iv. 10, 28, 34, 44, 61, 85, 104, 130, 168, 195.
Lancashire: part of, in view from York Minster, iii. 129 & n. 6; connexion of Lord Gerard with, iii. 476, n. 1.
Lancashire Plot, 1694: arrests for, v. 188 *bis* & n. 3; trial and release of prisoners, v. 196 & n. 4.
Lancaster, Thomas of, duke of Clarence: *see* Thomas.
Lancaster: Duchy of: chancellors of: *see* Carr, Sir Robert, third bt.; Phelips, Col. R.
Lancaster: Earl of, 1327–45: *see* Henry.
Lancaster: first Duke of, 1351–61: *see* Henry.
Lancaster, William, D.D.; vicar of St. Martin in the Fields 1692–4, 1694–1717; provost of Queen's College, Oxford 1704, v. 121, n. 1; and St. Martin's: as reader (?), *add.* (v. 128); ~ disputed presentation to, v. 112, n. 4, 121,

Lancaster, William, D.D. (*cont.*) n. 1, 169, n. 1; ~ new presentation to, v. 204, n. 5; appointments by, at Trinity Chapel: minister, v. 375–6 & n.; ~ lecturer, v. 591, n. 1; as preacher: uses notes, v. 554–5; ~ doubtful views of, v. 137 & n. 2, 303; ~ plagiarizes, v. 405 & n. 1; sermons by, v. 111–12 & n.(?), 112 & n. 4(?), 121–47, 204, 226, 238–9, 246, 301–413, 435–504, 530, 553–69, 595–619 *passim & singulatim*; see also *add.* (v. 128).

Lance, Holy: *see* Christ: relics.

Landau (Landaw, &c.): besieged and taken by Allies, 1702, v. 510 & nn. 2, 3, 512 & n. 3, 514 & nn. 3, 6, 10; taken by French, 1703, v. 551 & n. 1; besieged and taken by Allies, 1704, v. 577 & n. 3, 579 & n. 6, 580 & n. 3, 582 & n. 2.

Land Drainage: Commissioners of Sewers, iii. 151, n. 6; for E as a commissioner and for Sayes Court business *see* Surrey and Kent Commission of Sewers.
  drainage areas: the Fens (Great Level), iii. 135 & n. 3; Leghorn, ii. 183 (i. 115); 's Hertogenbosch, ii. 58 (i. 39); Soham Mere, iii. 555 & nn. 2, 6; Terracina, ii. 321.

Landen (Landun): battle of, v. 148 & n. 4, 149–50 & nn.; ~ alluded to, v. 150, 151, 175(?).

Landini, T.: statues by, ii. 185 & n. 3 (i. 117).

Land's End, Cornwall: journey of (Sir) John Evelyn to, v. 515 & n. 4.

Landskrona: battle of: Prince George of Denmark, &c., in, iv. 332–3 & n.

Lane, Sir George, bt.; Viscount Lanesborough 1676, iii. 285 & n. 2, 585 & n. 1; social, iii. 285, 585.

Lane, Jane, later Lady Fisher, iii. 51, n. 2; in Paris 1651–2, iii. 51, 54.

Lane, John: trial of, for defaming Titus Oates, iv. 188, n. 1.

Lane, Sir Richard, Lord Keeper of the Great Seal: in Paris, 1649, ii. 562 & n. 8.

Lane, Susan, Lady Lane, wife of Sir George, later Viscount Lanesborough: geneal., iii. 285, n. 2.

Lane, Sir Thomas, lord mayor of London 1694–5, v. 212, n. 3; as commissioner for Greenwich Hospital, v. 212, 219.

Lanesborough: first Viscount, 1676–83: *see* Lane, Sir George.

La Neve, painter (C. de Neve?): art-collection of, ii. 548 & nn. 4, 5.

Laney, Benjamin, D.D.; bishop of Ely 1667; &c.: consecrates Dr. John Wilkins, iii. 517 & n. 8.

Lanfranco, Giovanni, ii. 237, n. 6; paintings by, ii. 237, 307 & n. 5, 369 & n. 8, 376 & n. 6.

Lang, Dr.: error for Dr. John Lake, iv. 649.

Langdale, Sir Marmaduke, first Baron Langdale: in Paris, 1649, ii. 565 & n. 7.

Langdale: first Baron, 1658–61: *see* Langdale, Sir Marmaduke.

Langford, Oxon., iii. 117.

Langham, Lady: error for Lady Langley (?), iii. 143 & n. 5.

l'Angle, J.-M. de: geneal., iv. 318, n. 10.

l'Angle, Samuel Baux, sieur de, D.D.: at Windsor, iv. 318–19 & n.

Langley, Mary, Lady Langley, born Keightley, wife of Sir Roger, iii. 394, n. 1; social (?; as Lady Langham), iii. 143–4 & n.

Langley, Sir Roger, bt.: as candidate for parliament, iii. 394 & n. 1.

Langley, Captain Thomas: letter from, 1666, iii. 438, n. 4.

Langlois *or* Inglis, Esther: *see* Kello, Mrs. E.

Lanham, Captain Humphrey: imprisoned for carrying manifestoes of William of Orange, Oct. 1688, iv. 603–4 & n.

Laniere, family, iii. 74, n. 5.

Laniere (Lennier), Jerome, musician, iii. 74 & n. 5, 79–80; art-collection of, iii. 79–80 & n.; social, iii. 74.

Laniere, Nicholas, d. 1612: geneal., iii. 74, n. 5.

Laniere, Nicholas, 1588–1666, iii. 74, n. 5; wife of: pillaged, ii. 74, n. 4.

Lansdown: Lord, 1661–1701 (courtesy title): *see* Granville, Charles, second earl of Bath.

Lansdowne: Baron, 1711–34: *see* Granville, George.

Laodiceans: in sermon, iv. 254.

La Palisse (Palisse), ii. 156 & n. 1 (i. 100).
La Perle: fort on the Scheldt, ii. 62, n. 7 *ad fin.*
La Poderina: inn at, ii. 207 & n. 2.
la Porte, Armand de, marquis de la Meilleraye, Duc Mazarin: *see* Mazarin.
La Porte du Sex, Valais, ii. 519 & n. 1.
Lares: in sermon, v. 124.
Largillière, N.: portrait by, of Prince James Edward, v. 92, n. 2.
La Roch, —, valet of E, 1650–1, iii. 5; discharged, iii. 44.
la Roche-Guyon, Duc de: *see* Liancourt.
La Rochelle: expedition to relieve, 1627, ii. 9 & n. 1; expedition to, 1628: commander of, ii. 12, n. 1; attack on islands near, 1696, v. 252 & n. 3.
Lassels, Richard: crosses the Simplon pass, ii. 505, n. 2; *see also* Books: sources.
la Strade, Count de: *see* Estrades.
Laterani, family, ii. 271.
Latimer of Danby: Viscount, 1673–4: *see* Osborne, Sir Thomas, later first duke of Leeds, &c.
Latin language [only passages in the text in which Latin is explicitly mentioned are indexed here]:
education in: schools: Eton: boy's speech, iv. 208; French school at Greenwich (?): speeches, &c., v. 79; Westminster: examination in, iii. 287–8; boys' studies, &c.: — Clench, iv. 618; E: begins study of, ii. 8 (i. 8); John Evelyn, jnr., iii. 474; little Richard Evelyn, iii. 206–7 & nn., 208; William Wotton, iv. 172.
scholars, &c.: Arlington, iv. 118; Sir R. Browne, iv. 302; Sir J. Chardin, iv. 213; Richard Evelyn, sen., i. 1; Richard Waller, v. 176; a Spaniard, iii. 188; poets: Sir W. Petty, iv. 58 & n. 3, 61 & n. 2; Constantijn Huygens, sen., iii. 377 & n. 1.
use of: conversations in, iii. 171; iv. 518; disputation in, ii. 97 (i. 64); English pronunciation of, iii. 288 & n. 1; letters in, v. 322 & n. 4; orations, &c., iv. 275–6 & n., 291; sermon, iii. 106; ~ sentences used in, iv. 247, 330.
Latins: chronological reckoning of the, v. 26.
Latium: boundaries of, ii. 208, n. 4, 323.
la Tour: Charles de: *see* Gouvernet, marquis de; Esther de: *see* Gouvernet, marquise de; Esther de, daughter of preceding: *see* Savile, Esther, Lady Eland.
la Tour-d'Auvergne: Elizabeth de: *see under* Duras, G.-A., marquis de (iv. 77, n. 2); Frédéric-Maurice de: *see* Bouillon, duke of; Godefroy-Maurice de: *see* Bouillon, duke of; Henri de: *see* Turenne, vicomte de; Isabella de: *see* Bouillon, duchess of.
la Trémoille, Louis de, comte d' Olonne: *see* Olonne.
Laud (Lawd), William, D.D., archbishop of Canterbury, &c., ii. 19, n. 2; as chancellor of Oxford University: reforms of, ii. 19 & n. 2 (i. 14); ~ pensions N. Conopios, i. 14; palace of, attacked by mob, &c., 1640, ii. 25 & n. 1 (i. 18); trial of: etching of, i. 22 & n. 1.
benefactions, &c.: Lambeth Palace: embellishes chapel, iii. 361, n. 5; Oxford: Bodleian Library: builds part of (?), iii. 107 & n. 5; ~ gifts to, iii. 107, n. 5, 385, n. 3; St. John's College: building at, and gifts to, iii. 108 & n. 6.
letter to (spurious ?), iv. 508, n. 1; geneal., iii. 172, n. 2; chaplain of: *see* Haywood, W.
Lauderdale: Earl and Duke, &c., of: *see* Maitland, John, second earl 1645–72 and duke 1672–82; Maitland, Elizabeth, his duchess.
Laura, mistress of Petrarch: tomb of, ii. 161, n. 11, 162 & n. 1 (i. 103).
Laura (Martinozzi), duchess of Modena, iv. 27, n. 6; in London, 1673, iv. 27, 28, 30(?).
Laurence, St.: martyrdom of, ii. 246; relics of, ii. 246 & n. 7, 381 & n. 4 (as St. Sebastian, in error).
Laurence, Henry: *see* Lawrence.
Laurence (Lawrence), Thomas, D.D., master of Balliol College, Oxford, ii. 17 & n. 3, 18 (i. 13); sermon by, ii. 22.
Laureti, Tommaso: paintings by, ii. 224 & n. 7, 239 & n. 9.
Lauretto: *see* Loreto.

Lauretto, Cavalier: *see* Vittori, L.
Lauzun, Antoine-Nompar de Caumont, count and later duke of: returns from Ireland to France, v. 34, n. 5, 35 & n. 3.
la Varenne (Lavaran), Mlle, singer, iii. 35 & n. 1, 91.
Law: moral and Christian compared: in sermon, iv. 44.
Law (Laws), John, the financier: kills E. Wilson in duel, v. 175, 176, n. 1.
Lawes, Henry, musician: teacher of Mrs. Mary Knight, iii. 230, n. 3.
Lawley, Sir Francis, bt., iv. 566, n. 4; in coronation procession, 1661, iii. 280, n. 1; social, iv. 566, 592 & n. 1(?).
Lawrence (Laurence), Henry, the statesman: visits Sayes Court, iii. 193 & n. 5.
Lawrence, Sir John, lord mayor of London 1664–5: show and banquet of, iii. 388–9 & n.
Lawrence, Thomas, D.D.: *see* Laurence.
Lawson, Sir John, admiral: E takes leave of, iii. 403 & n. 4.
Lazarus, brother of Martha and Mary: in sermons, v. 60, 489, 512.
Lazarus, in the parable: in sermons, iv. 299, 577.
Lea, Mrs. Prudence, murderess, iii. 64, n. 3.
Leach, Mrs. Bridget, wife of Symon Leach: *see* Higgons, Bridget, Lady Higgons.
Leach, Richard, D.D., v. 501, n. 2; sermons by (?), v. 501–2, 506–7.
Leach, Symon: geneal., iv. 528, n. 3.
Leake, Rev. —, chaplain of James, duke of York: *see* Lake, Edward.
Leake, Rev. —: sermon by, 1654, iii. 133 & n. 5.
Leamington Hastings, Warwickshire: vicar of: *see* Allington, J.
Leardini, Alessandro, musician, ii. 450, n. 3.
Learning: hostility of Cromwell's army to, iii. 165 & n. 8; vanity of: in sermon, iv. 502.
Leasam: *see* Lewisham.
Leather: reported imposition on, 1640, i. 39 & n. 1; morocco: books bound in, ii. 128 (i. 82); iii. 11; morocco or Turkey: cabinet of, iii. 34.
Leatherhead, Surrey: election of knights of the shire for Surrey at, 1685, iv. 433–4; river Mole at, ii. 523, n. 3; iii. 157; road through, v. 168, n. 1, 467.
Léau: *see* Leuwe.
le Barbier, Louis, speculative builder in Paris, ii. 93, n. 5 *ad fin.*
le Bouthillier, Victor, archbishop of Tours, ii. 145, n. 7; courtesy of, to E, ii. 145 (i. 94); receives Henrietta Maria, ii. 149 (i. 97).
Le Bouveret (Beveretta), Valais, ii. 519 & nn. 1, 3.
Le Brun, Charles: paintings by (error), i. 84 & n. 2.
Lechford, Mrs. Anne: geneal., iii. 561, n. 4.
Lechford (Lachford), Sir Richard: social, iii. 561 & n. 4.
L'Écluse, defile, near Geneva, ii. 523, n. 3.
le Coq (le Coque, Mr. Cock), François, sieur de Germain, iv. 649 & n. 6; social, *ib.*; wins lottery prize, v. 196 & n. 6.
Le Duchat (Le Chat), Étienne, physician at Geneva, ii. 521–2 & nn.; attends E, *ib.*; fee of, ii. 530; regimen of, for E, ii. 530–2; ~ cited, ii. 511, n. 6 *ad fin.*; iii. 212, n. 4.
Lee, near Blackheath, Kent: Boone's Chapel and hospital at, iv. 180, n. 3, 288–9 & n.; Lee Place in, iv. 180 & n. 3; ~ E visits Christopher Boone at, *ib.*; iv. 180, 288, 337 & n. 4, 386.
  church: divine service or sermons at, iv. 180, 288, 337; v. 346–8, 348–50; (Dr.) Ralph Bohun preaches at, iv. 179; rector of, 1672–1701: *see* Jackson, John; unnamed clergy from: sermons by, at Deptford, iv. 166, 324, 507; *see also* Hutchinson, Rev. Thomas.
Lee family (later earls of Lichfield): as owners of Ditchley Park, iii. 382 & n. 8.
Lee, Dr. — (Richard Lee?): sermon by, iv. 281 & n. 1.
Lee, Lady, 1648, ii. 542.
Lee, Anne, Lady Lee, wife of Sir F. H. Lee, second bt.: *see* Wilmot, Anne, countess of Rochester.
Lee, Anne, Lady Lee, wife of Sir Robert: geneal., ii. 553, n. 3.

Lee, Catherine: *see* Seymour, Catherine, Lady Seymour.
Lee, Sir Charles: social, &c., ii. 553 & n. 3; iii. 213 & nn. 1, 2.
Lee, Charlotte, countess of Lichfield, wife of Edward Henry Lee, first earl: at banquet, iv. 268 & n. 2.
Lee, Sir Edward Henry, first earl of Lichfield: geneal., iv. 268, n. 2.
Lee, Elizabeth, Lady Lee, wife of Sir F. H. Lee, fourth bt.: *see* Bertie, Elizabeth, countess of Lindsey.
Lee, Frances: *see* Elwes, Frances, Lady Elwes.
Lee, Sir Francis Henry, second bt.: geneal., iii. 383, n. 2.
Lee, Sir Francis Henry, fourth bt.: as owner of Ditchley Park, iii. 382–3 & nn.
Lee, Sir Henry, bt.: inherits Ditchley Park, &c., iii. 382, n. 8, 383, n. 4.
Lee, Sir Henry, K.G.: acquires Ditchley Park, iii. 382, n. 8; portraits of, iii. 383 & n. 4.
Lee, Nathaniel, the dramatist: geneal., iv. 281, n. 1.
Lee, Richard, D.D.: sermon by (?), iv. 281 & n. 1.
Lee, Sir Robert, lord mayor of London 1602–3: geneal., iii. 58, n. 4.
Lee, Sir Robert, of Billesley: geneal., ii. 553, n. 3.
Lee, Sir Thomas, bt.: takes part in Stafford's trial, iv. 227 & n. 12.
Lee, Rev. William, inventor of the stocking-frame, iii. 285 & n. 3.
Leech, Dr. — (Richard Leach ?): sermons by, v. 501–2 & n., 506–7 & n.
Leech, Jane, Lady Leech, born Evelyn, wife of Sir William: social, iii. 219 & n. 3; *see also* iii. 90 & n. 3.
Leech, Sir William, iii. 219, n. 3; acquires Squerryes, iii. 90.
Leedes, Father Thomas Courtney *veré* Leedes: *see* Courtney.
Leeds: Dukes and Duchesses of: *see* Osborne, Sir Thomas, earl of Danby, &c., first duke 1694–1712; Osborne, Bridget, his duchess; Osborne, Peregrine, second duke 1712–29; Osborne, Bridget, his duchess.
Leeds Castle, Kent, iii. 422, n. 1; leased for accommodation of prisoners of war, iii. 422 & n. 1; repaired, &c., iii. 436; guards for, *ib.*; prisoners at: mustered, &c., iii. 467–8; ~ ordered to be released, iii. 492 & n. 4.
Leeke, Lady Anne: *see* Hildyard, Lady Anne.
Leeke, Lady Catherine: *see* Morley, Lady Catherine.
Leeke, Sir Francis, first earl of Scarsdale: geneal., ii. 550, n. 7; iv. 11, n. 3.
Leemput, Remigius van (Remeè), iv. 3, n. 3; copy by, of painting by Holbein, iii. 166, n. 1; paintings in house of, iv. 3.
Leeuwenhoek (Lewenhook), Antony van: paper by, iv. 570 & n. 2.
Leeward Islands, iii. 605, n. 1; misgoverned by Sir C. Wheeler, iii. 597; Wheeler recalled, iii. 599 & n. 2; new governor of: instructions for, *ib.*; iii. 613 & n. 2; government of: re-organized, iii. 605 & n. 1; French attack on: danger of, *ib.*
  governors of: *see* Willoughby, William, sixth Baron Willoughby of Parham (1667–71); Wheeler, Sir C. (1671–2); Stapleton, Sir W. (1672–86); Parke, Col. Daniel (1706–10).
  See also St. Christopher.
le Fèvre (Le Febure, &c.), Nicasius, ii. 534, n. 5; English appointments, &c., of, iii. 336, n. 3; an iatrochemist, iii. 48, n. 2; gives courses of chemistry, ii. 534–5; iii. 49; prepares Sir Walter Raleigh's cordial in presence of Charles II, iii. 336 & n. 4; on use of gold in medicine, iii. 86, n. 6; social, iii. 54.
Le Franc, Rev. Jacques, French Protestant divine, iii. 160 & n. 4; sermon by, iii. 160; discusses theology with Jeremy Taylor, iii. 171 & nn. 3, 4; receives Anglican orders, iii. 172 & n. 1.
Legends [folk-tales, &c. Legends relating to the saints, individuals' narratives, miracles performed by saints, &c., ordinary historical errors and false identifications, &c., are not indexed collectively]:
  miscellaneous: anemone-seed

Legends (*cont.*)
stolen, i. 86–7; *add.*; birds deceived by painting, ii. 109 & n. 1 (i. 70); courtesan as foundress of church, ii. 468 & n. 4; painting miraculously completed while artist sleeps, ii. 194 & n. 9 (i. 120); philosopher at the triumph, v. 192; *add.*; pictures of SS. Peter and Paul, v. 328; Roman Catholic emissaries in England (priests disguised as sectaries; *Rosa inter spinas*), iii. 157, n. 2; iv. 507–8 & n.; v. 13 & n. 1; sailor and tulip-bulb, i. 86; *add.*; scent of flowers on coast perceptible at sea, ii. 171 & n. 2 (i. 108).
local and personal: Amyclae, ii. 322 & n. 5; Cimmerians, ii. 338 & n. 3, 349 & n. 7; Colchester: no grass where Sir C. Lucas, &c., were shot, iii. 177 & n. 2; ~ St. Helena, &c., at, iii. 176–7 & n.; Frederick Barbarossa: humiliated by Alexander III, ii. 439 & n. 3; *see also* ii. 297 & n. 5; Gaeta: split rock at, ii. 323 & n. 3; Geneva, Lake of: tritons, &c., in, ii. 520; Guy of Warwick: at Warwick, Coventry, &c., iii. 120–1 & nn.; Hercules: in Rome, at Solfatara, &c., ii. 228 & n. 1, 341 & n. 2, 345 & nn. 2, 3; Leyden: besiegers tricked, ii. 51–2 & n. (i. 36); Loosduinen: woman gives birth to 365 children at, ii. 55 & n. 3 (i. 38); Montefiascone: bishop and wine of, ii. 210 & n. 4; Nemi: Acteon at, ii. 317 & n. 4; Nesis, ii. 351 & n. 5; Padua: Antenor founds, ii. 454 & n. 3; Paris: origin of Château de Madrid at, ii. 112 & n. 2 (i. 72); iii. 2; Pilate, Pontius: at Vienne and Ponsas, ii. 159 & n. 2 (i. 101–2); Po (Eridanus): Phaethon, &c., and, ii. 428 & n. 5; Rome: persons lost in Catacombs, ii. 388 & n. 4; ~ *Sedes Stercoraria*, ii. 268 & n. 2; ~ *Taberna meritoria*, &c., ii. 288–9 & n.; Solfatara: souls from Hell at, ii. 342 & n. 6; Venice: Campanile ascended by king on horse-back, ii. 445 & n. 8; ~ clock-tower: automaton on, kills man, ii. 435 & n. 2; ~ St. Mark's: portraits in, of St. Francis, &c., by Joachim of Flora, ii. 439 & n. 2.

Legg(e), George: error for William Legge, iv. 314.

Legge, George, first Baron Dartmouth, iv. 311, n. 2; character, &c., iv. 314; as Master-general of the Ordnance, iv. 459, n. 5; expedition of, to Tangier, iv. 379 & nn. 2, 3; and Trinity House: elected master, iv. 314; ~ re-elected master, iv. 379, 380; ~ at annual meeting, iv. 459; granted right of holding fair in Lewisham, iv. 311 & n. 2; geneal., v. 182 & n. 3; *add.*

Legge, Robert: geneal., iv. 474, n. 5.

Legge, Col. William, 1609–70, Lieutenant of the Ordnance, &c., iii. 494, n. 5; appointments of, iii. 443, n. 1; *add.*; iv. 314 & n. 3 (called George Legge, in error); assists Col. R. Norton, iv. 474 & n. 5; dines with Clarendon, 1667, iii. 494; geneal. (as George Legge, in error), iv. 314.

Legge (Leg), Col. William, jnr.: reported suicide of, 1694, v. 182 & n. 3.

Leghorn (Ligorne, Livorno): notice, 1644, ii. 183–4 & nn. (i. 115–16 & nn.); galley-slaves at, ii. 183–4 & nn. (i. 116); canal from, to Pisa, ii. 183 & n. 4 (i. 115); ~ alluded to, ii. 182 (i. 114); Grand Duke's park near, ii. 182–3 & nn. (i. 115); view of (mosaic), ii. 191 & n. 11 (i. 119).
E's journeys to, ii. 178 (i. 112), 182 (i. 115), 401–2; E obtains money, &c., at, ii. 182 (i. 115), 408.
English consulage at, iii. 629 & n. 5; consul at: *see* Clutterbuck, Sir T. (iv. 156, n. 2).

Legnano: campaign near, 1701, v. 465, n. 2, 467, n. 1.

Le Grand, Monsieur (Louis de Lorraine, count of Armagnac?), iii. 575 & n. 6.

Leicester: notice, 1654, iii. 122–3 & nn.; ~ source for (?), iii. 98, n. 5, 122, n. 6.
archdeacon of, 1703–15: *see* Rogers, Rev. J.

Leicester: Earls of: *see* Dudley, Robert, earl 1564–88; *new creation*: *see* Sidney, Robert, second earl 1626–77; Sidney, Philip, third earl 1677–98; Sidney, Robert, fourth earl 1698–1702.
Leicestershire: E sets out for, iii. 117; countryside, iii. 121; condition of, 1654, iii. 122 & n. 3; Caldwell family of (error), ii. 24 & n. 2 (i. 18); v. 358 & n. 3; sheriff of, 1653–4: *see* Prettyman, Sir John, bt.
Leighlin: dean of, 1637– : *see* Cressy, H. P.
Leighton, Sir Elisha (Ellis), iii. 516, n. 3; cart designed by, iii. 516; social, iv. 11.
Leijonberg, John Barckmann, Baron, Swedish resident in England, iii. 497, n. 4; anatomical demonstration at house of, iii. 497–8; entertainment given by, for birthday of Charles XI, iv. 295–6 & n.; social, iv. 365.
Leinster: Duke of, 1691–3: *see* Schomberg, Meinhard, later third duke of Schomberg.
Leith (Lyth, Lith) Hill, Surrey, i. 2; view from, &c., ii. 4 & n. 1 (i. 5).
Lely (Lilly), Sir Peter, iii. 216, n. 5; double portrait by, of Charles I and James duke of York, iii. 216 & n. 5; art-collection of: drawings in, from Norfolk (Arundel) collection, iv. 312 & n. 3; ~ painting from (?), iv. 404 & n. 3; pupil of: *see* Gawdy, Sir J.
Lemanus, Lacus: *see* Geneva: Lake of (ii. 519).
Lemercier, Jacques; designs chateau of Richelieu, ii. 151, n. 1.
Leningrad: Hermitage: paintings in, ii. 71, n. 3.
Lennard, Anne, countess of Sussex, wife of Thomas Lennard, earl of Sussex, iii. 592, n. 4; as Anne Palmer or Fitzroy: marriage project for (?), iii. 592; parentage of, iv. 97 & n. 6; social, iv. 97, 268.
Lennard, Elizabeth, Lady Dacre (created countess of Shepey 1680), wife of (1) Francis Lennard, Lord Dacre; (2) David Walter, iii. 56, n. 5.
Lennard, Francis, Lord Dacre: geneal., iii. 56, n. 5.
Lennard, Thomas; fifteenth Lord Dacre 1662; earl of Sussex 1674, iii. 592, n. 4; social, iv. 383 & n. 4.
Lennier, Jerome: *see* Laniere.
Lennox, Charles, first duke of Richmond and of Lennox, iv. 268 & n. 6; the Moroccan ambassador's good wishes for, iv. 268; receives Sacrament at Whitehall, iv. 374; character, &c., iv. 392; recommended by Charles II to James, duke of York, iv. 408 & n. 3.
Lennox: Dukes, &c., of: *see* Stuart, Ludovick, duke of Richmond, second duke 1583–1624; Stuart, Esme, third duke 1624; Stuart, James, duke of Richmond, fourth duke 1624–55; Stuart, Mary, his duchess; Stuart, Charles, duke of Richmond, sixth duke 1660–72; *new creation*: *see* Lennox, Charles, duke of Richmond, first duke 1675–1723.
Lenoncourt: Cardinals de, ii. 113, n. 7.
Le Nôtre, André: garden, &c., laid out by, ii. 106, n. 1, 110, n. 2.
Leo IV, Byzantine emperor: church at Venice built for (?), ii. 460 & n. 3.
Leo V, Byzantine emperor: church at Venice built for (?), ii. 460, n. 3.
Leo III, pope: triclinium of, ii. 275, n. 5.
Leo X, pope: marble ship set up by, ii. 361–2 & n.; copy of Henry VIII's *Assertio septem sacramentorum* presented to, ii. 302 & n. 2; portrait of, by Raphael, ii. 190 & n. 12; statues of: Florence, Palazzo Vecchio, ii. 188 & n. 6 (i. 118); ~ Rome, Capitol, ii. 224 & n. 5.
Leo XIII, pope: reconstructs choir of S. Giovanni in Laterano, ii. 266, n. 4.
Leominster: first Baron, 1692–1711: *see* Fermor, Sir William.
Leonardo da Vinci, ii. 114, n. 4; death of, ii. 497 & n. 1.
drawings by (Ambrosiana and Arundel collections, &c.), ii. 498 & nn. 1–8.
paintings by: Last Supper, ii. 497 & n. 1; Monna Lisa (?), ii. 120 & n. 4; St. John the Baptist (now Bacchus; in Louvre), ii. 120 & n. 3 (i. 77); St. John the

Leonardo da Vinci (*cont.*)
Baptist, half-length (in Louvre), ii. 120, n. 3; Virgin with St. Anne (in Louvre): copy of, at Milan, ii. 495 & n. 5; in Uffizi, ii. 191 (i. 119).
unidentifiable paintings, &c.: Magdalen, in Liancourt collection, ii. 114 (i. 73); Rape of Proserpine, at Fontainebleau, ii. 120 & n. 9 (i. 77); St. Catherine, in Northumberland collection, iii. 216; woman's head, in Arlington collection, iv. 102.
false entry, ii. 423 & n. 7.
Leonius (Leoncenas), Dr. Joannes, called Estensis: makes anatomical tables, &c., ii. 475 & nn. 4, 5.
Leopardi, Alessandro: designs S. Giustina at Padua, ii. 455, n. 6; completes statue of Colleoni at Venice, ii. 459, n. 6.
Leopold I, Emperor [notices relating to Leopold personally; for notices relating to the political activities of the Empire (the Hapsburg state) *see* Empire]: breaks off peace-negotiations with Turkey, v. 6–7, 35–6, 37; influence of Jesuits, &c., on, v. 35, 37; claim of, to Spanish succession: in negotiations, v. 434 & n. 4; ~ England supports, v. 515; ~ resigns to his younger son, v. 545, n. 3; compliments Queen Anne on victory, v. 573 & n. 2; dies, v. 594 & n. 2; geneal., v. 126, n. 1.
Leopold I, grand duke of Tuscany: rebuilds Poggio Imperiale, ii. 410, n. 5.
Leopold William, Archduke, governor of the Spanish Netherlands: invades France, 1650, iii. 17 & n. 3; art-collection of, ii. 70, n. 5.
Lepanto: battle of: paintings of, ii. 297 & n. 6, 444 & n. 5.
Lepanto, Gulf of: Venetians defeat Turks in, 1687, iv. 560 & n. 3.
Lepidus: the four fountains of, ii. 241 & n. 6.
Le Premier, Monsieur (Henri de Beringhen ?), iii. 575 & n. 7.
Le Prévost, Charles, seigneur de Saint-Germain: *see* Saint-Germain.
Lerici: procession at, ii. 179 & nn. 2, 3 (i. 113); site of, ii. 178, n. 10.
Lérins: Îles de: notice, ii. 168 & n. 1 (i. 106); Vincent of: *see* Books mentioned in text.
Lesbia (in Catullus): sparrow of, iv. 336.
Lesdiguières, Charles de Créqui, duke of, prince de Poix, marshal of France: as owner of Poix, iii. 17 & n. 2; *add.*; geneal., *add.* (iii. 575, n. 5).
Lesdiguières, François de Bonne de Créqui, duke of: geneal., iii. 575, n. 5; *add.*
Leslie, Alexander, earl of Leven: besieges York, 1644, iii. 129, n. 1.
Leslie, Henry, bishop of Down and Connor, 1635; of Meath, 1661: ordains J. le Franc (?), iii. 172 & n. 1.
L'Estrange, Sir Roger, the journalist, knighted 1685, iii. 167, n. 2; in Kentish rising, 1648, iii. 153, n. 6; invites E to hear T. Baltzar (Lubicer) perform, iii. 167; conduct of, as author of *The Observator*, 1685, iv. 439 & n. 3; social, iv. 35.
Lether-head: *see* Leatherhead.
Leucogean hills, near Pozzuoli, ii. 341 & n. 2.
Leueson, Lady Jane: *see* Leveson-Gower.
Leusham: *see* Lewisham.
Leuwe (Léau): taken by Allies, 1705, v. 607 & n. 3.
Levant, the: camel from, iii. 292; collection of inscriptions made in, for Arundel, iii. 496, n. 1; Dr. I. Basire as missionary in, iii. 303 & n. 3; Sir Henry Blount's travels in, iii. 233, n. 3; E's projected visit to, ii. 451–2, 468.
Levant Company: appointments: J. Hobson as agent at Venice, ii. 476, n. 3; ~ Lord Winchilsea as ambassador in Turkey, iii. 249, n. 1; deputy-governor of, 1690–1715: *see* Roberts, Sir G.
Levellers: sermon against, iii. 542–3 & n.
Leven: first Earl of, 1641–61: *see* Leslie, Alexander.
Leveson-Gower, Catharine: *see* Wyndham, Catharine, Lady Wyndham.
Leveson-Gower, Jane, Lady Leveson-Gower, wife of Sir William: visits Eton (as Lady Jane Leveson), v. 236–7 & n.
Leveson-Gower, Sir William, fourth bt., 1689, iv. 11, n. 6; social (?; as Mr. Lucie Gore), iv. 11; geneal., v. 237, n. 1.

Levett, Sir Richard, lord mayor of London 1699–1700, v. 392, n. 1; attends special sermons, v. 391, 398–9 & n.
Levinz (Leven), Baptist, D.D., bishop of Sodor and Man: sermon by, iv. 578 & n. 3.
Levinz, Sir Creswell, judge: decision by, iv. 417, n. 6 *ad fin.*; counsel for the Seven Bishops, iv. 587, n. 2.
Lewen, Samuel, sheriff of Surrey 1684–5: conduct of, at parliamentary election, iv. 433–4 & n.
Lewenhook, —: *see* Leeuwenhoek, A. van.
Lewes, Sussex:
E's connexion with: resident at, as boy, 1625–37, ii. 7–16 (i. 7–12); ~ absences from, ii. 11 (i. 8–9), 12–13 (i. 10–11), 13–15 (i. 11–12); later visits to, ii. 20 (i. 16), 21 (i. 16), 23 (i. 17), 27 (i. 20), 77 (i. 51), 78, 79 (i. 52), 80, 543–4; tenants and property of, at or near, ii. 27 & n. 2 (i. 20); *see also* Cliffe *below*, Beddingham, *and* Ripe; the Stansfield-Evelyn connexion with, i. *3–5*; *add.*; Richard Evelyn educated at, ii. 13 (i. 11), 15 (i. 12), 23 (i. 17); *see also* ii. 9, n. 7 *ad fin.*
All Saints (All Souls): J. Stansfield buried in, ii. 7–8 & n. (i. 7).
Cliffe, The, near Lewes: property of J. Stansfield at, ii. 27, n. 2; Mrs. Eleanor Evelyn born at, ii. 3; E resident and at school at, ii. 9 *bis* & n. 4; E's house at, ii. 27, n. 2, 544; ~ sold, iii. 65.
Lewes Priory: owned Halifax church, Yorks., ii. 3, n. 1.
South Malling near Lewes: *see* South Malling.
Southover near Lewes: free school at, ii. 9 & n. 5; ~ E attends, ii. 9 (i. 8), 15–16 (i. 12); *see also* i. *5*; *add.*; ~ Richard Evelyn leaves, ii. 23 (i. 17); Southover Grange, ii. 9 & n. 7; *add.*
Lewes, —: *see* Lewis, William.
Lewis of Baden, Prince (Ludwig Wilhelm I): visits London, v. 163 & n. 1.
Lewis, Mrs. Margaret, wife of William Lewis, ii. 557, n. 2.
Lewis, William, of Levan, ii. 557, n. 2; marriage of, &c. (?; as Mr. Lewes), ii. 557 *bis*.
Lewisham (Leasam, Leusham, &c.), Kent:
fair at: established, &c., iv. 311 & n. 2; manor of: lord of the, iv. 311, n. 2.
church: continues orthodox, 1652, iii. 60 & n. 1, 79; services in, iii. 60, 78, 79, 80; v. 211; vicars of: *see* Colfe, A. (1610–57); Stanhope, G. (1689–1728).
Colfe's School: masters: *see* Day, M.; Turner, John, D.D.
other places in: Blackheath: part of, in, iv. 311 & n. 2; the Bowling Green, Dartmouth Row, &c., iv. 311 & n. 3; Sydenham Wells, iv. 74 & n. 2, 112 & n. 3; Wells Road, iv. 74, n. 2.
Lewkner, —, E's guide at Antwerp, ii. 63 & n. 2 (i. 43).
Lewknor, Mrs. —, 1658: *see* Morley, Anne, Lady Morley.
Lewknor, Anne, Lady Lewknor, wife of Sir John: *see* Morley, Anne, Lady Morley.
Lewknor, John: brings action against William Montague, 1690, v. 3 & n. 2.
Lewknor, Sir John, K.B.: geneal., iii. 218, n. 2.
Ley, river, at Ghent, ii. 74 & n. 2 (i. 48).
Leyburn, John, D.D.; bishop of Adrumetum; vicar-apostolic: officiates in Roman Catholic chapel, Whitehall (?), iv. 534–5 & n.
Leyden: E visits, 1641, ii. 34 (i. 27), 42 (i. 31), 51–5 & nn. (i. 36–8); matriculates at university of, ii. 52 & n. 4 (i. 36).
descriptive, &c.: general, ii. 51–4 & nn. (i. 36–7); the Burcht and its legends, ii. 51–2 & nn. (i. 36); churches, ii. 52 & n. 2 (i. 36); Elzevier press, ii. 52 & n. 6 (i. 36); mall (?), ii. 54 & n. 2 (i. 37); university: its standing, ii. 51 & n. 4 (i. 36); ~ Anatomy School, ii. 53–4 & nn. (i. 37); *add.*; ~ Botanic Garden, ii. 52–3 & n. (i. 36–7); ~ professor at: *see* Sylvius, F. de la Boe.
Jew with Messianic views at, ii. 54–5 & n. (i. 37–8).
Leyden, Lucas van, ii. 114, n. 1; painting by, ii. 114 (i. 73); prints by, ii. 133 (i. 86).

Leyton, Essex: Forest House in, iii. 538 & n. 1; ~ rebuilding of, by (Sir) James Houblon, iv. 306; Rookwood or Ruckholt in, iii. 230 & n. 6.
Liancourt, Oise: Château of, i. 74 & n. 1.
Liancourt, François Rochefoucauld d'Auvergne, Cardinal: portrait of (?), ii. 113 & n. 7 (i. 73).
Liancourt, Roger du Plessis de, duc de la Roche-Guyon: house of, in Paris, ii. 112–14 & nn. (i. 72–4); E's introduction to, i. 74; seat of, at Liancourt, i. 74 & n. 1.
Liane (l'ans), river, at Boulogne, ii. 84 (i. 57).
Libels and Lampoons: attacks on English government, &c.: 1640, ii. 25 & n. 3 (i. 18); ~ 1679, iv. 172 & n. 3; ~ *c.* 1682, iv. 319; against Lady Castlemaine, 1668, iii. 507 & n. 6; pasquinades: at Rome, ii. 369; ~ in Venice, ii. 474.
Liberius, pope: S. Maria Maggiore at Rome founded in time of, ii. 242, n. 5; *add.*
Liberti, Henri, musician: portrait of, by Van Dyck, iv. 102 & n. 6.
Libertines (freethinkers): sermons against: endowment for, v. 82, 88 & n. 3; in catechizing, v. 511.
Libraries:
  Bologna: S. Salvatore, ii. 422 & n. 7.
  Brussels: Cour, ii. 70–1 (i. 46).
  Cambridge: Emmanuel College, iii. 139 & n. 8; King's College, iii. 138 & n. 2; St. John's College, iii. 136 & nn. 2–6; Trinity College, iii. 137 & nn. 1–4; University: *see* Cambridge: University Library.
  Cassiobury Park: Lord Essex, iv. 200, 201.
  Chaillot: Bonshommes, ii. 112 (i. 72).
  Coventry: Free School, iii. 121 & n. 5.
  Dublin: Marsh's Library, v. 323, n. 3.
  Eton: Dr. H. Godolphin: proposed purchase of books by, iv. 589.
  Euston: Arlington, iv. 121.
  Florence: Laurenziana, ii. 198 & nn. 10, 11, 417 & nn. 1–3; S. Marco, ii. 200.

Libraries (*cont.*)
  Geneva: University, ii. 529–30 & n.
  Gloucester: Cathedral (1648), iii. 117 & n. 6.
  Heidelberg: Palatine: in Vatican, ii. 301, n. 2, 302 & n. 3.
  Ipswich: Wolsey's, iv. 116 & n. 2.
  Leyden: J. J. Scaliger (University), ii. 52 (i. 36).
  London (and environs): lack of public libraries in, iv. 367–8 & n.; Arundel: dispersal of, i. *21* & n. 1; iii. 472 & n. 3, 524; iv. 140, n. 7, 144–5 & nn.; E. Ashmole (at Lambeth), iv. 138 & n. 4; British Museum: *see* British Museum; Chelsea Hospital: proposed, iv. 270; Clarendon, iii. 379, n. 8 *ad fin.*, 481; College of Arms: Arundel MSS. in, iii. 472, n. 3; iv. 144 & n. 3; Cottonian, iii. 507 & n. 1; ~ MS. in, iv. 216, n. 3; Kensington Palace, v. 237; Lambeth Palace, iii. 527 & n. 1; iv. 560; *add.* (iii. 140, n. 3); Dom F. de Mello, iv. 2; Dr. J. Moore, bishop of Norwich, &c., v. 325 & n. 8; Sir W. Morice, iii. 363 & n. 4, 477; Pepys, iv. 644; ~ at Clapham, v. 538; Don P. Ronquillo: destroyed, iv. 610; Royal College of Physicians, iii. 338; iv. 307 & n. 3; ~ catalogue of, iii. 337, n. 4 *ad fin.*; Royal Society: *see* Royal Society; St. James's Palace: *see* London: topography: St. James's Palace; St. Martin in the Fields: parochial library (Tenison's), iv. 367–8 & n., 369, 455; v. 66; Sir C. Scarburgh, v. 206 & n. 1; Sunderland (Charles Spencer, Lord Spencer, later third earl), v. 206 & n. 1, 322 & nn. 1, 2; Westminster Abbey, iv. 368, n. 1; Whitehall, iv. 214–16 & nn., 257; v. 147(?).
  Milan: Ambrosiana, ii. 497–500 & nn.
  Norwich: Sir T. Browne, iii. 594.
  Oatlands: Sir E. Herbert, iv. 566.
  Orleans: University, ii. 138 & n. 6 (i. 91).
  Oxford: Balliol College: E's gifts to, &c., ii. 19 & n. 3 (i. 15 & n. 2); Dr. R. Bathurst, v. 571; Bodleian: *see* Oxford: University: institutions: Bodleian

Libraries (*cont.*)
Library; Christ Church, iii. 109 & nn. 1, 2; Magdalen College, iii. 109; St. John's College, iii. 108 & n. 6.
Paris: Collège de Navarre, ii. 97 (i. 64); Dr. J. Cosin, iii. 36, 634; du Houssay, ii. 114–15 & n. (i. 74); Gaston, duke of Orleans, ii. 128 & n. 3 (i. 82); Jesuits, ii. 96 (i. 64).
Rome: Barberini, ii. 229; Collegio Romano, ii. 283; C. dal Pozzo, ii. 277 & n. 3; Oratorians, ii. 284; Vatican, ii. 300–2 & nn.; ~ librarian of, ii. 283 & n. 4.
St. Albans: Rev. E. Carter, iv. 589 & n. 4.
Siena: Cathedral, ii. 205 & n. 1.
Sion (Valais): unnamed, ii. 516.
Swallowfield: second earl of Clarendon, iv. 482.
Tournon: Jesuits, ii. 159 (i. 102).
Urbino: ducal: in Vatican, ii. 301 & n. 2.
Venice: St. Mark, ii. 445 & n. 6; W. or I. Vandervort, ii. 477.
Wimbledon: Lord Bristol, iv. 126 & n. 3.
Wotton: George Evelyn, v. 359.
uncertain places: A. Beverland, v. 322, n. 1; Conde de Castelmelhor: takes collection to Portugal, iv. 454; Dr. J. Cosin, iii. 62 & n. 8, 636; Sir K. Digby, iv. 126, n. 3; N. Heinsius, sen., iv. 330 & n. 3; James, duke of York, iii. 44; Dr. E. Stillingfleet, bishop of Worcester, v. 323 & n. 3, 324.
French protestants' libraries: burnt, iv. 485.
Lichfield: Earls, &c., of: *see* Stuart, Charles, later duke of Richmond, &c., earl 1645–60; *new creation*: *see* Lee, Sir Edward Henry, first earl 1674–1716; Lee, Charlotte, his countess.
Lichfield: cathedral clergy:
bishops: *see* Baylie, R. (proposed, 1661); Hacket, J. (1661–70); Wood, T. (1671–92); Lloyd, William, D.D., the apocalyptic (1692–9); Hough, J. (1699–1717).
dean: *see* Smalwood, M. (1671–83).
prebendary: *see* Offley, G.
Licola, Lago di, near Cuma, ii. 347 & n. 1.
Liefkenshoek (Lifkinshoek), fort on the Scheldt, ii. 62 (i. 42).
Liège: attacked by French, 1691, v. 57 & n. 3; occupied by French, 1701, v. 482 & n. 2; taken by Allies, 1702, v. 517 & n. 2.
Liège: Bishop of, 1694–1723: *see* Joseph Clemens, archbishop-elector of Cologne.
Lighthouses: Eddystone: builder of first, v. 247, n. 1; Genoa, ii. 171 & n. 3 (i. 108), 177 & n. 5 (i. 112); North Foreland, iii. 615 & n. 3; harbour lights at Leghorn, ii. 183 & n. 5 (i. 115).
Lighting [for candlesticks, chandeliers, and sconces, *see* Furniture]: for display of waxworks, iii. 612; lamps: specially designed, iii. 318, 475 *bis* & n. 6; ~ ever-burning, ii. 320 & n. 1; ~ experiment with, iv. 162; wax-lights: manufacture of, iii. 127.
harbour-lights, ii. 183 & n. 5 (i. 115); illuminations: in London, v. 72, 277, 578; ~ at Rome, ii. 282, 391; lamplit road, v. 363 & n. 3.
Ligne (Lignis), Claude-Lamoral, prince de, Spanish ambassador in England, 1660: audience of, iii. 256 & n. 1.
Ligorio, Pirro, archaeologist, &c.: designs Villa d'Este, Tivoli, ii. 396, n. 4; explores Hadrian's Villa, ii. 397, n. 4.
Ligorne: *see* Leghorn.
Lilburne, John: draft Agreement of the People by, discussed, ii. 546, n. 1.
Lille: refugee from, 1567, iv. 475, n. 2.
Lillo, fort on the Scheldt: E's difficulties at, ii. 61–2 & nn. (i. 42).
Lilly, —, painter: *see* Lely, Sir P.
Lilly, William: predictions of, relating to solar eclipse, 1652, v. 354 & n. 2.
Lima, Peru: earthquake(s) at, 1687 (and 1688 ?), iv. 585–6 & n., 598 & n. 4.
Limançon: spring of, near Tours, ii. 148 & n. 2 (i. 96).
Limburg, near Verviers: taken by Allies, 1703, v. 546 & n. 4.
Limburg-Styrum und Bronchorst, Hermann Otto, Graf zu: defeated at Höchstädt, v. 546 & n. 3.

Limerick (Limrick): General Henry Ireton dies at, iii. 52, n. 1; besieged by William III, 1690, v. 31 & n. 1, 32 & n. 5, 33 *bis*; siege raised, v. 34 & n. 1; besieged by English, 1691, v. 68 & n. 3, 69; surrenders, v. 70 *bis* & nn. 2, 3.
governor of, *c.* 1710: *see* Fairfax, General Thomas.
Limerick: Bishops of: *see* Fuller, William, D.C.L. (1664–7); Marsh, Francis (1667–73); Vesey, John (1673–9).
Linch, Sir Thomas: *see* Lynch.
Lincler, Claude, iii. 10, n. 1.
Lincler, Louis, artist, iii. 10, n. 3; drawings by, ii. 578 (note); iii. 10 & n. 3; art-collection, &c., of, beneath Samaritaine, Paris, iii. 10–11 & nn., 20 & n. 6.
Lincoln: notice, 1654, iii. 131–2 & nn.; road from, to Grantham, iii. 132 & n. 5, 133, n. 2.
Lincoln: cathedral clergy, &c.:
bishops: *see* Montaigne *or* Mountain, G. (1617–21); Williams, John, D.D., later archbishop of York (1621–41); Sanderson, Robert (1660–3); Laney, B. (1663–7); Fuller, William, D.C.L. (1667–75); Barlow, Thomas (1675–91); Tenison, T. (1691–4); Gardiner, James (1695–1705); Wake, W. (1705–16); Gibson, E. (1716–23).
deans: *see* Brevint, D. (1681–95); Fuller *or* Fulwar, S. (1695–1700).
chancellor: *see* Fuller *or* Fulwar, S. (1670–95).
archdeacon of Lincoln: *see* Throckmorton, R.
prebendaries: *see* Allington, J.; Gostling, J.
Lincoln Heath, iii. 132 & n. 5.
Lincolnshire: countryside, iii. 131; fens of: drainage of, iii. 135 & n. 3.
Lindehleim, Joanna Maria, singer: notice (?), v. 531 & n. 2.
Lindsey: Earls, &c., of: *see* Bertie, Robert, first earl 1626–42; Bertie, Montague, second earl 1642–66; Bertie, Robert, third earl 1666–1701; Bertie, Elizabeth, his countess.
Linford, Rev. — (Dr. Thomas Lynford?): sermon by, v. 103 & n. 1.
Linge, Abraham van: stained glass by, iii. 109, n. 3.
Lintlaër, Jean, builder of the Samaritaine, Paris, ii. 93, n. 3; iii. 10, n. 1.
Lionberg, Monsieur: *see* Leijonberg, John Barckman, Baron.
Lion-Court: *see* Liancourt.
Lionne, Hugues de, secretary of state to Louis XIV: geneal., iii. 411 & n. 3.
Lionne, Louis-Hugues de, marquis de Berny: social (?; as M. Brizasiere), iii. 411 & n. 3.
Lions: *see* Lyons.
Lippi, Annibale (Nanni): architect of Villa Medici, Rome, ii. 230, n. 8.
Lira y Castillo, Don Manuel Francisco de: visits Royal Society's museum, &c. (?), iv. 133 & n. 6.
Liris, river (Garigliano), ii. 323 & n. 6.
Lisbon: Allied fleet at, 1702, v. 514, n. 2; Archduke Charles (pretender to Spanish throne, later Emperor as Charles VI): expected at, 1704, v. 555 & n. 5; ~ arrives at, v. 560 & n. 1, 561; English merchant-ships home from, 1705, v. 601.
Lady Tuke goes to, iii. 511, n. 2; chaplain to English factory at: *see* Lloyd, William, D.D., the nonjuror.
Lisbon, Rock of: French fleet off, 1693, v. 142, n. 1.
Lisle, Sir George: execution of, iii. 58 & n. 1, 177 & n. 2.
Lisle, John: at trial of John Mordaunt (later Viscount Mordaunt), iii. 214, n. 3.
Lisle: Lords (courtesy title): *see* Sidney, Philip, third earl of Leicester, styled Lord Lisle 1626–77; Sidney, Robert, fourth earl of Leicester, styled Lord Lisle 1677–98.
Lister, Martin, M.D.: at Royal Society meeting, iv. 355 & n. 2.
Litcott (Lytcott), Sir John: appointed secretary to Lord Castlemaine, iv. 498 & n. 1.
Lithuania: natives of: *see* Hartlib, S. (iii. 162 & n. 2); Horneck, Anthony (error; v. 317 & n. 4, 329).
Littlecote, Wilts.: house of Col. A. Popham at, iii. 100 & n. 1; *see also* iii. 99, n. 4; William of Orange at, iv. 609, n. 6.

Littler, Robert, B.D., vicar of Deptford 1659–61 ('our vicar'), iii. 228, n. 6; sermons by, iii. 228–300 *passim*; dies, iii. 300 & n. 2.
Little Saxham, Suffolk: house of Lord Crofts at, iv. 113, n. 4.
Littleton, Adam, D.D., iv. 5, n. 3; sermons by: printed, iv. 5 & n. 3, 33 & n. 1; ~ unprinted, iv. 5, 47, 55, 85, 106 *bis*, 131–2, 166, 198, 505.
Littleton, Sir Charles: *see* Lyttelton.
Littleton, Sir Henry: *see* Lyttelton.
Littleton, John, D.D.: sermon by (?), ii. 78 & n. 3.
Littleton, Sir Thomas, 1422–81, the judge: descendants of, iv. 576 & n. 2.
Littleton, Sir Thomas, bt., 1647–1710, v. 304, n. 2; as speaker of house of commons: elected, v. 304, 306–7; ~ superseded, v. 446 & n. 5; ~ fails to be re-elected, v. 484 & n. 2.
Little Wicckam: error for High Wycombe or West Wycombe (?), iii. 530 & n. 2.
Liverpool: embarkation at, 1689, iv. 643, n. 4.
Livia Quarta: freedman of: inscription commemorating, ii. 462 & n. 7; ~ relic of, ii. 328, n. 10 *ad fin.*
Livingston, Catherine, countess of Newburgh, wife of James Livingston, first earl: geneal., iv. 400, n. 3.
Livingston, Charles, second earl of Newburgh: displays his horsemanship, iv. 400 & n. 3.
Livingstone, Dorothy: *see* Stanhope, Dorothy, Baroness Stanhope.
Livingstone, Sir John: geneal., iv. 13, n. 5.
Livorno: *see* Leghorn.
Livy (Titus Livius), the historian: supposed birth-place of, ii. 463 & n. 7; supposed arm of, ii. 328–9 & n., 462, n. 7; monument to, at Padua, ii. 462–3 & n.; bust (modern) of, ii. 463, n. 4.
Llandaff: Bishops of: *see* Field, Theophilus (1619–27); Lloyd, William, D.D., the nonjuror (1675–9); Beaw, W. (1679–1707).
Lloyd, —: clerk of Council of Trade and Plantations (?), iii. 628.
Lloyd, Dr. —: sermon by, 1652, iii. 53 & n. 4.
Lloyd, Dr. —: bears thanks of Oxford University to E, &c., 1667, iii. 498–500.
Lloyd, Sir Richard: at Calais, 1649–52, ii. 560 & n. 3; iii. 16, 55.
Lloyd, William; D.D. 1667; bishop of St. Asaph 1680; of Lichfield 1692; of Worcester 1699 [distinguished in notes and index as 'the apocalyptic'], iii. 630, n. 3.
chronological series: as dean of Bangor, iv. 55, n. 3; as vicar of St. Martin in the Fields: instituted, iv. 107, n. 6; ~ superseded iv. 224; as bishop of St. Asaph: consecrated, iv. 205, n. 2; ~ house of, in London, iv. 240–1 & n.; ~ goes to his diocese, *ib.*; ~ as one of the Seven Bishops, iv. 583–8 & nn., *passim*; ~ visit to, in Tower, iv. 587; ~ at meeting to discuss settlement of the crown, Jan. 1689, iv. 613–14; ~ appointed Lord Almoner, iv. 630 & n. 2; ~ attends coronation of William and Mary, iv. 633, n. 3; ~ discusses ecclesiastical affairs, &c., iv. 633–4; as bishop of Lichfield: account of Queen Mary's last illness, &c., by, v. 205 & nn. 4, 5; *add.*; as bishop of Worcester: translation, v. 321–2 & n.
views, &c.: zeal against Roman Catholicism, iv. 188 & n. 2; as interpreter of prophecies: identifies the Two Witnesses with the Waldenses, &c., iv. 636–7 & n.; v. 25–6; ~ on Antichrist, the Second Coming, &c., v. 20–1 (sermon), 321–2; ~ general, v. 32 & n. 3; describes origin of Presbyterianism, v. 12–13 & n.
ministrations: attends Ossory on his death-bed, iv. 210; baptizes converted Jewess, iv. 222; consulted on case of conscience, v. 338–9; sermons by: printed, iv. 158 & n. 2, 650–1 & n.; v. 14 & n. 1; ~ unprinted, iii. 630 (?; *see add.*); iv. 55, 80, 107, 109 *bis* & n. 3, 123(?), 134, 137, 157(?), 167, 169, 187–8, 223, 242, 630, 641, n. 1; v. 20–1, 38, 227.
personal relations, &c.: gift to, from J. L. Cappel (?), iv. 641 &

Lloyd, William (*cont.*)
n. 4; controversy with Sir George Mackenzie, v. 12 & n. 2; describes William Wotton's precocity, iv. 172–3.
social: parties, iv. 205, 454, 488 *bis*, 588 & n. 6, 612 & n. 3; v. 7, 8, 105, 224, 238, 383; alone, &c., v. 326, 383, 529.
Lloyd, William; D.D. 1670; bishop of Llandaff 1675; of Peterborough 1679; of Norwich 1685; deprived 1690 [distinguished in notes and index as 'the nonjuror'], iii. 335, n. 3; *add.*; as curate of Deptford, 1662– : sermons by, iii. 334, 335–6, 361 [some other sermons by the curate at Deptford may be by Lloyd, but none can be assigned to him with certainty; the date of his leaving Deptford is unknown]; ~ mentioned as former curate, iii. 552; iv. 3, 86–7, 369; as preacher at Gray's Inn: sermons by, at Deptford, iii. 552 & n. 5, 565; as chaplain to Clifford: sermon by, iv. 3 & n. 8; other sermons by, iii. 630 & n. 3; *add.* (?); iv. 86–7, 157(?), 369; as bishop of Norwich: social, iv. 588 & n. 6; ~ deprived, v. 49, n. 1, 59; as nonjuror: conduct of, at funeral of Dr. T. White, v. 289 & n. 3.
Lo, —: *see* Lowman, J.
Lobes, river (error): *see* Robec.
Locatelli, Luigi: inventor of Lucotellus balsam, iii. 146, n. 1.
Locke, John, the philosopher, iii. 628, n. 3; as secretary of Council of Trade and Plantations: sworn in, iii. 628 & n. 3(?); iv. 25; weather diary of (at Oxford): cited, iii. 451, n. 6, 453, n. 3.
Lockhart, Sir William, of Lee: social, iv. 28 & n. 2.
Loddington, Leics.: Sir J. Prettyman buys estate at, iii. 73, n. 3, 133, n. 5; minister of: *see* Leake, Rev. — (iii. 133).
Loddon, river, Berks., iv. 481 & n. 3.
Lodi: notice, ii. 490 & n. 9.
Loevestein (Lovestine), castle: as state prison, ii. 39 & n. 1 (i. 29).
Loftus, —: negotiates to buy Parsons Green estate, iv. 202.
Loiano, ii. 419, n. 3, 420.
Loire (Loyer, &c.), river: E decides to spend summer in town on, 1644, ii. 135 (i. 89); journeys
Loire, river (*cont.*)
on: from Orleans to Tours, ii. 139, 143, 144 (i. 91, 93); from Roanne to Orleans, ii. 533–4.
cliffs and cave-dwellings in valley of, ii. 144 & n. 2 (i. 93); slate-roofs in towns on, ii. 143 (i. 93).
at Blois, ii. 140 (i. 92); at Orleans, ii. 136–7 (i. 89–90); at Roanne, ii. 156 (i. 100); at Tours, ii. 144 (i. 93).
Lombard (Lombart), Pierre, engraver: sees E's collections, iii. 86 & n. 3.
Lombardelli, G. B., called della Marca, painter, iii. 339, n. 3.
Lombardi, Tullio: sculptures by, at Padua, ii. 454 & n. 7.
Lombardy: Iron Crown of, ii. 500–1 & n.; 'the Paradise of all Lombardy', ii. 491; plains of, ii. 507.
Lomellini family: builds SS. Annunziata, Genoa, ii. 177 & n. 3 (i. 111).
LONDON [London in the Diary means both the general built-up area and the particular local government area formed by the City and its Liberties, and governed by the Lord Mayor and Corporation. Here, except in the sections relating to the political activities and organization of the City and its authorities, the whole built-up area is treated as a unit.
— general: the Diary as a source for its history, i. *112–13*; 'the most august city in the world', iv. 343; fort at Tilbury as a bridle to, iii. 609 & n. 4; danger to, from Gunpowder Plot (in sermon), iv. 348; buildings, streets, &c., *c.* 1660, i. *17*; view of, from Greenwich, iii. 76 & n. 3; growth of: act relating to new buildings in and near, iii. 223, n. 2; ~ general statement, 1684, iv. 382 & n. 2; ~ building of Golden Square district, iv. 400, n. 1; v. 132, n. 2; ~ parish of St. Martin in the Fields, v. 62; ~ building of Seven Dials, v. 193 & n. 1; comparisons: with Bristol, iii. 102; ~ with Norwich, iii. 594 & n. 2; ~ with Paris, ii. 131 (i. 84–5 & n.); iii. 637–8 (extract from *State of France*); public

LONDON (*cont.*)
security in, iii. 638 (extract from *State of France*); distance of Wotton from, ii. 4 & n. 2 (i. 5).
— chronological series: the built-up area:
— — 1640: disorders, &c., and attack on Lambeth Palace, ii. 24–5 & nn. (i. 18).
— — 1642: Prince Charles (later Charles II) leaves, iii. 246, n. 1; alarm in, on royalist advance to Brentford, ii. 79 (i. 52–3).
— — 1643: Cross in Cheapside demolished, ii. 81 & n. 3 (i. 55).
— — 1648: fear of attack by Army, ii. 540 & n. 6.
— — 1649: disturbance in Fleet Street, ii. 556 & n. 1.
— — 1657: the Christmas raid on the Anglican congregations, iii. 203–4 & nn.
— — 1660: arrival and activities of General Monck (later duke of Albemarle), iii. 240, n. 5, 241–2 & nn.; republican troops removed from, iii. 241 & n. 4; the burning of the rumps, iii. 242 & n. 2; Charles II proclaimed in, iii. 244 & n. 3; Charles II returns to, iii. 246 & n. 2.
— — 1661: Venner's rising, iii. 266 & n. 5, 267 & n. 1; Solemn League and Covenant burnt in, iii. 288–9 & n.
— — 1662: guards in streets, to prevent disturbances due to Act of Uniformity, iii. 331 & n. 4; Queen Catherine's entry, iii. 322, n. 2, 333 & n. 2; projected rising (Oct.), iii. 341, 342, n. 1.
— — 1665: celebrations for battle of Lowestoft, iii. 410; plague in: *see* epidemics *below*.
— — 1666: Great Fire of: *see* Great Fire *below*.
— — 1667: fear of attack by Dutch fleet, iii. 484 & n. 2.
— — 1668: apprentices riot, iii. 507, n. 6.
— — 1673: supposed danger to, from army encamped on Blackheath, iv. 13 & n. 1.
— — 1678: Roman Catholics ordered to leave (Oct.), iv. 159, n. 2.
— — 1679: demonstration in, on Monmouth's return, iv. 189 & n. 6.

LONDON (*cont.*)
— — 1683: for proceedings relating to City Charter *see* City *below*; return of Roman Catholics to, iv. 320; disaffected to Charles II, iv. 322.
— — 1688: danger of anti-Roman Catholic riot, iv. 599; mob demolishes Roman Catholic chapels, &c., iv. 602 & n. 1, 607 & n. 4, 610 & n. 2; William of Orange's guards to be quartered in, iv. 610; English, Scottish, and Irish forces, sent away from, iv. 612 & n. 2.
— — 1693: James II's declaration distributed in, v. 140, n. 2.
— — 1696: Roman Catholics required to leave, v. 232 & n. 3.
— — 1704: rejoicings and thanksgiving for Blenheim in, v. 575, 578 & n. 1.
— the City: chronological series [events in which the corporation in general is concerned; *see further* lord mayor *below*]:
— — 1660: city-gates, &c., removed by Monck, iii. 241 & n. 4, 242; Monck joins with the City, iii. 242 & n. 2; letter from Charles II to Common Council, iii. 244, n. 2; City appoints commissioners to invite Charles to return to England, iii. 245, n. 1; lord mayor, &c., in Charles's entry into London, iii. 246.
— — 1662: address and gift from, to Queen Catherine, iii. 321 & n. 7; management by, of finances of Gresham College: inquiry into, iii. 328 & n. 2, 330 & n. 4, 334–5.
— — 1666: welcomes Charles II on his return to Whitehall after the Plague, iii. 429 & n. 3; builds the *Loyal London*, &c., iii. 440.
— — 1667: occupies Gresham College after Great Fire, iii. 472, n. 2.
— — 1673: invites Royal Society to return to Gresham College, iv. 27–8 & n.
— — 1679: congratulates Charles II on recovery from illness, iv. 181.
— — 1682: riots during election of sheriffs in Common Hall, iv. 319 & n. 1.

LONDON (*cont.*)
— — 1683: *Quo Warranto* proceedings against City charter (begin 1681), forfeiture, &c., iv. 319–20 & nn.; judgement entered against the City, &c., iv. 341–3 & nn.; effect on Lord Mayor's powers, iv. 528; *see also* i. *28*, *29*.
— — 1685: lord mayor, &c., at proclamation of James II, iv. 413.
— — 1688: lord mayor, &c., attend meeting to authenticate birth of Prince James Edward, iv. 602 & n. 3; aldermen and common councillors join with members of Charles II's houses of commons in assembly (Dec.), iv. 612, n. 5.
— — 1690: City charter restored, v. 23 & n. 3.
— — 1695: lord mayor, &c., at funeral of Queen Mary, v. 204.
— — 1696: congratulates William III on discovery of Assassination Plot, v. 232 & n. 2.
— — 1701: loyal address to William III, v. 481, n. 1.
— — 1702: congratulates Queen Anne on her accession, v. 493 & n. 3.
— — 1704: lord mayor, &c., in thanksgiving for Blenheim, v. 578 & n. 1.
— the City: officers:
— — general: two to attend opening of prize-ship (?), v. 522 & n. 1.
— — lord mayor:
— — — powers, &c.: to be appointed henceforward by royal commission, 1683, iv. 342 & n. 6; diminution of powers since forfeiture of City charter, iv. 528.
— — — chronological series:
— — — — 1648: proclaims orders for keeping watch, 25, 29 Apr., ii. 540 & n. 6.
— — — — 1649: proclaims abolition of kingship, 30 May, ii. 555 & n. 6.
— — — — 1661: in Charles II's coronation procession, iii. 280, 281 & n. 1.
— — — — 1662: at Queen Catherine's entry into London, iii. 333.

LONDON (*cont.*)
— — — — 1663: at Archbishop Sheldon's translation to Canterbury, iii. 363.
— — — — 1666: activities of, during Great Fire, iii. 452, n. 3, 455, n. 3.
— — — — 1667: and fuel for London, iii. 487.
— — — — 1679: at trial of Sir G. Wakeman, iv. 174.
— — — — 1689: letter to, from William III, for charitable collection, v. 3, n. 1.
— — — — 1692: closes Southwark Fair, v. 116, n. 1.
— — — feasts: Speaker, &c., at, 1649, ii. 556, n. 1; Cromwell at, 1654, iii. 93; Charles II at, 1660, iii. 250; following show, 1664, iii. 388–9; private dinner (?), iii. 443; general statements (Sir R. Clayton's mayoralty), iv. 185 & n. 6, 187.
— — — annual ceremonies: swearing in, iii. 259, n. 4; show: general note, iii. 259, n. 4; ~ accommodation for king and queen to watch, iii. 342 & n. 2; ~ particular shows, iii. 259 & n. 4, 301 & n. 4, 341–2 & nn., 388 & n. 6; iv. 393 & n. 4, 528 & n. 5; attendance at divine service (lord mayor, aldermen, &c.): in course of show, iii. 301, n. 4 *ad fin.*; ~ at opening of law terms, iv. 284 & n. 1; ~ at Spital sermons, v. 398–9 & n.; *see also* v. 391; entertainments: for City Companies (First State Dinner?), iii. 396 & n. 3.
— — — barge of, iii. 333.
— — — individual lord mayors (year begins 29 Oct.): *see* Buckle, Sir C. (1593–4); Lee, Sir Robert (1602–3); Lowe, Sir Thomas (1604–5); Foote, Sir T. (1649–50); Kendrick, J. (1651–2); Dethick, Sir J. (1655–6); Frederick, Sir J. (1661–2); Robinson, Sir John (1662–3); Lawrence, Sir J. (1664–5); Bludworth, Sir T. (1665–6); Bolton, Sir W. (1666–7); Turner, Sir William (1668–9); Hanson, Sir R. (1672–3); Hooker, Sir W. (1673–4); Edwards, Sir J. (1678–9); Clayton, Sir Robert (1679–80);

LONDON (*cont.*)
Moore, Sir John (1681–2); Prichard, Sir William (1682–3); Tulse, Sir H. (1683–4); Smyth, Sir James (1684–5); Peake, Sir J. (1686–7); Shorter, Sir J. (1687–8); Lane, Sir Thomas (1694–5); Houblon, Sir John (1695–6); Edwin, Sir H. (1697–8); Levett, Sir R. (1699–1700); Gore, Sir William (1701–2); Parsons, Sir J. (1703–4).
— — aldermen [notices concerning the aldermen with other members of the City corporation are entered under City: chronological series *and* lord mayor *above*; notices relating to individual aldermen are entered only under their several names]:
— — — conduct of, in Great Fire, iii. 455 & n. 3; removal of, 1683, iv. 342 & n. 6.
— — recorders: *see* Wilde, Sir W. (1659–68); Jeffreys, Sir George, Baron Jeffreys (1678–80); Treby, Sir George (1680–3, 1688–92); Jenner, Sir T. (1683–6); Shower, Sir B. (1688).
— — sheriffs [for notices concerning the sheriffs with the lord mayors and aldermen *see* City: chronological series *and* lord mayor *above*]:
— — — at Archbishop Sheldon's translation to Canterbury, iii. 363; knighted, 1666, iii. 429 & n. 3; riot at election of, 1682, iv. 319 & n. 1; to be appointed henceforward by royal commission, 1683, iv. 342; at executions of: Lord Russell, iv. 332; ~ Algernon Sidney, iv. 353.
— — — feasts, iii. 150, 266 (private?), 425; iv. 179 & n. 1, 210 & n. 1.
— — — individual sheriffs: *see* Bolton, Sir W. (1660–1); Hanson, Sir R. (1665–6); Hooker, Sir W. (1665–6); Gauden, Sir Dennis (1667–8); Clayton, Sir Robert (1671–2); Shorter, Sir J. (1675–6); North, Sir Dudley (1682–3).
— climate and atmosphere:
— — atmosphere in general: effects on some persons, ii. 339, n. 4; 'our accidentally suffocated city', iii. 639 (extract from *State of France*); corrosive effects of: general, iv. 380; ~ on Arundelian inscriptions, iii. 495; smoke in: proposed act of parliament for reducing, iii. 297 & n. 3, 310; ~ *see also* iii. 295 & n. 9.
— — particular occurrences: fogs: the black Sunday, 1679, iv. 161 & n. 1; ~ during great frost, 1684, iv. 363 & n. 2; ~ 1699, v. 363 & n. 2; storms: effects of: 1652, iii. 71; ~ 1703, v. 550; *see also* topography: Thames *below*.
— commercial, &c. [trading companies, &c., of national rather than local character are indexed under their own names; notices relating to particular industries are indexed under Trade and Industry]: 'the City': E sent to, to borrow money for Sick and Wounded, iv. 9; ~ effect on, of loss of Smyrna fleet, 1693, v. 145, 148; ~ concern in Bank of England, v. 185; merchants address Charles II concerning Jamaica, iii. 257 & n. 2.
— environs: *see after* topography *below*.
— epidemics:
— — plague: 1625, ii. 7 & n. 3 (i. 7); 1636, ii. 15 *bis* & n. 6 (i. 12); 1637, ii. 15, n. 6; 1641, ii. 76 & n. 5.
— — — 1665: notices, &c., iii. 412–23 & nn., *passim*; i. *19*; the stricken town, iii. 417–18, 421; deaths from: total number, iii. 435, n. 1; ~ weekly numbers, iii. 412, n. 6 *ad fin.*, 415, nn. 3, 4, 417, nn. 1, 3, 6, 421, n. 6, 423, n. 5; evacuation of officials, &c.: general, iii. 429 & n. 1; ~ king and court, iii. 414–15 & nn., 423 & n. 7, 428 & n. 6; ~ offices, iii. 418 & n. 2, 426–7 & n.; fast for, iii. 415 & n. 5, 421, 423 & n. 4, 424, 430, 432 & n. 3, 443, 446; Nonconformist congregations during, iii. 513, n. 3; Royal Society reassembles after, iii. 432–3 & n.; mentioned, iii. 441, 464, 497 & n. 2; iv. 429; for more general mention *see* Plague.

LONDON (*cont.*)
— — — 1666, iii. 430, n. 1, 435 & n. 1.
— — smallpox: 1652, iii. 68; 1694–5, v. 196 & n. 2, 199 & n. 2, 200 & n. 5, 201 *bis* & n. 2; 1698, v. 286 & n. 5.
— Great Fire, 1666 [notices relating to particular buildings and streets in the general account of the Fire (iii. 450–62) are not indexed in this section; they are all included in the topographical section below]:
— — general: the conflagration and its effects, iii. 450–62 & nn.; i. 20.
— — causes: attributed to: Dutch and French incendiaries, iii. 457, n. 4, 462; ~ Roman Catholics, iv. 243, n. 6.
— — course: carts: orders relating to, iii. 452, n. 3; ~ use of, during, iii. 453; deaths due to, iii. 460 & n. 7; demolition of buildings to check, iii. 452, n. 3, 454 & nn. 6, 8, 455 & nn. 2, 3; ~ use of gunpowder for, iii. 455 & n. 2, 456; ~ houses near Tower demolished, iii. 458 & n. 4; duration of, in cellars, &c., iii. 460 & n. 6; inhabitants: apathy of, iii. 452 & n. 3, 455, 456; ~ begin to fight, iii. 456; ~ flight of, iii. 453 & n. 2; refugees from: in the fields, &c., *ib.*; iii. 457, 461–2 & nn.; ~ number of, iii. 461 & n. 4; ~ alarm among, iii. 462 & n. 1; *add.*; smoke clouds, iii. 453–4 & n.; visibility of, iii. 451 & n. 4, 453 & n. 3; wind during, and its effects, iii. 451 & n. 6, 454 & n. 7, 455, n. 2, 456.
— — effects: general, &c.: area burnt down, iii. 453, n. 5; destruction along Thames, iii. 476; number of houses destroyed by, iii. 453, n. 4, 461, n. 4; statue destroyed by, iii. 338, n. 2; the inhabitants in the ruins, iii. 460; collection for sufferers from, iii. 464; Royal Exchange occupies Gresham College, in place of Royal Society, iii. 472 & n. 2, 487; iv. 27–8 & n.
— — rebuilding: general: acts for: provisions for wharfs in, iii. 476, n. 3; ~ Fire Court established by, iv. 17, n. 5; ~ provision for rebuilding churches, iv. 243, n. 7; replanning: E's suggestions for, iii. 463 & n. 2; ~ failure to replan, iv. 307 & n. 6; progress of: 1669, iii. 537 & n. 4; ~ 1681, iv. 243 & nn. 5–7; London as rebuilt, i. 84–5.
— — — particular buildings: Christ's Hospital, iv. 542, n. 1; churches: Christchurch, Newgate Street, iii. 192, n. 2; ~ St. Alban, Wood Street, iv. 180 & n. 6; ~ St. Clement, Eastcheap, iii. 64, n. 5; ~ St. Martin, Ludgate, iii. 296, n. 1; ~ St. Mary Magdalen, Old Fish Street, iii. 82, n. 4; ~ St. Paul's cathedral, v. 278, 290 & n. 1; College of Arms, iii. 327, n. 4; Customs House, iii. 588 & n. 2; Guildhall, iii. 507, n. 4; Old Bailey Sessions House, iv. 175, n. 2; Painters' Hall, iii. 390, n. 4; Royal College of Physicians, iii. 337, n. 3; iv. 307 & n. 3; Royal Exchange, iv. 28, n. 1; St. Paul's School, v. 127, n. 4; Trinity House, iii. 313, n. 6 *ad fin.*; iv. 64, n. 6.
— — — churches destroyed and not rebuilt: All Hallows, Honey Lane, iv. 72, n. 1; St. Gabriel Fenchurch, ii. 78, n. 2; St. Gregory by St. Paul's, iii. 61, n. 4; St. Mary Woolchurch Haw, iii. 197, n. 3; St. Mary Magdalen, Milk Street, iii. 95, n. 4; St. Peter, Paul's Wharf, ii. 552, n. 5 *ad fin.*
— — commemoration, &c.: fast for, iii. 464 & n. 3; anniversaries, iii. 586; v. 352; the Monument, iv. 243 & n. 6, 449 & n. 4; in sermons, iii. 463, 464, 569; v. 87(?), 227, 293.
— — mentioned or alluded to, i. 79; iii. 130, n. 3, 470, 477, 486 & n. 3(?); iv. 411; v. 148; mentioned incorrectly, iv. 134 & n. 1.
— improvements [for abortive projects *see* Great Fire: rebuilding *and* climate and atmosphere *above*]: streets: Commissioners for Repairing the Highways,

LONDON (*cont.*)
&c. 1662: appointed, &c., iii. 318–19 & n.; ~ meetings and orders of, iii. 319 & n. 3, 327, 328 & nn. 3–5, 333, 335, 358, 364, 379; *see also* i. *17*; lamp-lit road, v. 363 & n. 3.
— Livery Companies [for the Companies' buildings *see* topography *below*]:
— — annual (?) reception by lord mayor, iii. 396 & n. 3.
— — attendance at processions: Charles II's entry into London, iii. 246; coronation procession, 22 Apr. 1661, iii. 280–1; Queen Catherine's entry into London, iii. 333; Russian ambassadors' entry, 1662, iii. 344; thanksgiving for Blenheim, 1704, v. 578.
— — barges of, iii. 333.
— — individual companies: Clothworkers: charter, 1685, iv. 518, n. 3; ~ feast, iv. 518; ~ lecturer: *see* Strengfellow, W.; Drapers: entertainment for, iv. 179 & n. 1; Fishmongers: connexion of, with St. Thomas's Hospital (?), iii. 391, n. 5; ~ feasts, iii. 391; iv. 208, n. 3, 210; Goldsmiths: and recovery of stolen jewellery, iii. 70–1; Ironmongers: feast, iii. 587 & n. 2; Mercers: questioned concerning finances of Gresham College, iii. 330 & n. 4; Painter-Stainers, iii. 390, n. 4; Skinners: governors of Free Grammar School, Tonbridge, iii. 408, n. 1; Stationers: loss of books belonging to, in Great Fire, iii. 459 & n. 3.
— military:
— — defences: line of communication, 1642, ii. 80 & n. 1; ~ fort in, iii. 398, n. 3; chains in streets, iii. 461 & n. 2; *see also* iii. 241, n. 4; against the Dutch, 1667, iii. 485 & n. 5.
— — lieutenancy of: party changes, 1702, v. 511 & n. 2.
— — militia (train-bands): called out: 1648, ii. 540 & n. 6; ~ 1667, iii. 484, n. 2; attendance of, at processions: Charles II's coronation, 1661, iii. 280; ~ Russian ambassadors' entry, 1662, iii. 344; ~ thanksgiving for Blenheim, 1704, v. 578; appointment of colonels of, 1702, v. 511 & n. 2.
— religious:
— — chronological series: the churches occupied by the sectaries, &c., 1650, iii. 15; Anglican services in London during the Protectorate (1654), iii. 144; ordinance against observance of festivals enforced, 1657, iii. 204, n. 5; ministers ejected as result of Act of Uniformity: number of, 1662, iii. 331, n. 4; Declaration of Indulgence read in few churches, 1688, iv. 584 & n. 4.
— — Church of England [for Anglican congregations and services during the Protectorate, &c., *see* Church of England: chronological series *and* topography *below*; for national thanksgivings and fasts observed in London *see* Church of England: worship: special services and fasts; for individual churches *see* topography *below*]: celebration of Communion in London churches, 1692, v. 180, n. 1; *see also* v. 422, n. 2; lenten sermons arranged by bishop of London, iv. 305, n. 1, 436, n. 1; clergy: treatises written by, against Nonconformists, 1683–5, iv. 418 & n. 2; ~ letter to, from bishop of London, for charitable collection, 1690, v. 3 & n. 1; Spital sermons, v. 399, n. 1.
— — Dutch Church: address to Charles II, 1660, iii. 248 & n. 3.
— — French protestants: address from French church to Charles II, 1660, iii. 248 & n. 3; churches established in London, 1685–8, iv. 447, n. 3 *ad fin.*; refugees in London, 1685, iv. 485–6; for individual churches *see* topography: St. Martin Orgar; Savoy; Somerset House; Threadneedle Street *below*.
— — Italian Church: address to Charles II, 1660, iii. 248 & n. 3; *see also* topography: Mercers' Chapel *below*.
— — Jews: Jews resident in London before 1655, iii. 163, n. 3.

LONDON (*cont.*)
— — Nonconformists: meetings held openly during Plague, iii. 513, n. 3; large number of, 1694, v. 178; sermons for, at Salters' Hall, v. 391, n. 1.
— — Roman Catholics: places of worship destroyed, &c., 1688, iv. 599 & n. 1, 602 & n. 1, 607 & n. 4, 610 & n. 2; prevented from attending ambassadors' chapels, 1700, v. 403, n. 2; for individual places of worship *see also* topography: St. James's Palace; Somerset House; Wild House; York House, *below*; Whitehall.
— — Socinians: increase of, 1696, v. 230–1 & n.
— social and miscellaneous: *Bills of Mortality*: *see* Newspapers; charitable collections: for persecuted Anglican divines, 1658, iii. 213–14; ~ for Plague, 1666, iii. 445, n. 6; ~ for poor in great frost, 1684, iv. 361, n. 3, 363; ~ for persecuted Waldenses, 1690, v. 3 & n. 1; clipping: case of, 1696, v. 256 & n. 6; coal: from Newcastle, supplied by Ipswich, iv. 115 & n. 8; coffee-houses: use of, by private chaplains, iv. 367; culture: academy projected by Sir B. Gerbier, ii. 134, n. 2; ~ meetings for scientific discussion prior to formation of Philosophical Society (later Royal Society), iii. 266 & n. 6; ~ lack of a public library (1684), iv. 367–8 & n.; ~ collection of Far Eastern works of art, &c., brought to, iii. 373–4 & n.; disorderly houses: attacked by apprentices, 1668, iii. 507, n. 6; Epsom salts: on sale in, iii. 544, n. 1; feasting, &c., iv. 179; *see also* City: lord mayor; &c., *above*; festivals, &c., in: May Day: the day for visiting Hyde Park, iii. 82, n. 6; ~ Gunpowder Plot: celebrations: 1652, iii. 77 & n. 4; 1673, iv. 26 & n. 2; ~ bonfires forbidden, 1680, &c., iv. 487 & n. 3, 526; fires (conflagrations) in, iii. 150 & n. 4; iv. 649; v. 222–3 & n., 376 & n. 5, 563 & n. 3; fuel for: search to be made for, 1667,

LONDON (*cont.*)
iii. 486 & n. 1, 487 *bis*, 488; gaming ordinaries: raid on, Christmas Eve, 1657, iii. 204, n. 6 *ad fin.*; hackney-coaches: commissioners for regulating, iii. 319 & n. 1, 358 & n. 2, 379; poor: relief for, in great frost, 1684, iv. 361 & n. 3, 363; shops, iii. 638 (extract from *State of France*); ~ closed for king's birthday, 1686, iv. 526; taverns, iii. 638 (extract from *State of France*); ~ use of, by private chaplains, iv. 367; tennis-courts in: Groom Porter's right of licensing, iii. 308, n. 4; theatres: profanity and immorality of, iii. 465; iv. 422; ~ performances, &c.: *see* topography: theatres *below*; watch in, iii. 638 (extract from *State of France*); wintering in, iii. 92 [the practice can be traced in E's movements, &c.]; 'the youths of the city', iv. 26.
— — noise of guns in battle off Lowestoft heard in, iii. 84, n. 5 *ad fin.*; concourse from, to see stranded whale at Greenwich, iii. 214–15.
— topography:
— — general:
— — — chains, &c., in streets: removed by Monck, 1660, iii. 241, n. 4; ~ in Great Fire, iii. 461 & n. 2; churches: number of, destroyed in Great Fire, iii. 459–60 & n.; ~ rebuilding of (1681), iv. 243 & n. 7; fountains: destroyed in Great Fire, iii. 460; gates: removed by Monck, 1660, iii. 241 & n. 4; Livery Companies' halls: destruction of, in Great Fire, iii. 460; pleasure gardens, 1654, iii. 96–7 & nn.; prisons: in Great Fire, iii. 461; public buildings: sites of, iv. 307; squares (piazzas): in comparison, ii. 131 (i. 84); streets: Commissioners for Repair of, 1662: *see* improvements *above*; ~ paving: in comparison, ii. 94 (i. 62); water-supply: New River, iv. 515 & n. 4; ~ ~ Thames water, iv. 313 & n. 1; ~ interrupted by severe winter, 1683–4, iv. 363; wooden part of London, ii. 124 (i. 79).

LONDON (*cont.*)
— — particular buildings, streets, &c.:
— — — Abchurch Lane: Pontack's in, v. 160, n. 4.
— — — Admiralty: visits to, iv. 96, 616.
— — — Admiralty buildings (modern): site, ii. 556, n. 4; iii. 490, n. 2.
— — — Albemarle House: *see* Clarendon House *below.*
— — — Albemarle Street: site, iii. 379, n. 8 *ad fin.*
— — — Aldersgate: after Great Fire, iii. 458.
— — — Aldgate: as terminal for whipping criminals, iv. 440, n. 4, 445, 451, n. 3; Sir J. Friend's head on, v. 235, n. 3.
— — — Amen Corner: Royal College of Physicians in, iii. 337, n. 3; Stationers' Hall in, iii. 459, n. 3.
— — — Apollo tavern: *see* Devil tavern *below.*
— — — Archer Street: G. Geldorp's house in, ii. 554, n. 3.
— — — Arlington House: *see* Goring House *below.*
— — — Artillery Ground ii. 360 & n. 6.
— — — Arundel Buildings: house of John Evelyn, jnr., in, iv. 530; *see also* Evelyn, John, jnr.
— — — Arundel House: notice, iii. 234 & n. 4; projects for rebuilding, *ib.*; iii. 595 & n. 5; iv. 395, n. 5; the Arundelian inscriptions at, iii. 495–6 & n.; the Norfolcian library at, iii. 472, n. 3; ~ removal from, iv. 144 & n. 2; Royal Society at (1667–73): invited to meet at, iii. 472 & n. 2; ~ proposed building for, at, iii. 505 & n. 1, 507; iv. 139 & n. 1; ~ meetings of, stated to be held at, iii. 472–8 *passim,* 489(?), 498–506 *passim* [all meetings in noted period were held here]; ~ leaves, iv. 27–8 & n.; Spanish prisoners dine at, 1657, iii. 189; musical performance at, iii. 310; delegates of Oxford University visit H. Howard at, iii. 500; H. van der Borcht at, i. 21; John Evelyn, jnr., brought up

LONDON (*cont.*)
at, iii. 326 & n. 6, 355; iv. 142; E visits (visits to H. Howard, later sixth duke of Norfolk, &c.), iii. 301–6 *passim,* 352, 357, 375, 482, 489(?), 501, 503; iv. 89.
— — — Arundel Stairs, ii. 76 & n. 6 (i. 51).
— — — Arundel Street: site, ii. 76, n. 6; iii. 234, n. 4; house of John Evelyn, jnr., in, iv. 395 & n. 5; *see also* Evelyn, John, jnr.
— — — Austin Friars: Dutch church in, iii. 248, n. 3.
— — — Bainard Castle: *see* Baynard's Castle *below.*
— — — Bank of England: site, iv. 125, n. 4.
— — — Bankside: view of Great Fire from, iii. 451 & n. 2.
— — — Bartholomew Close: house of Sir N. Strode in, iii. 379 & n. 4.
— — — Bartholomew Fair: visit to, ii. 543 & n. 1; *see also* iii. 492, n. 2.
— — — Baynard's Castle: in Great Fire, iii. 452 & n. 1.
— — — Beak Street: building of, iv. 400, n. 1.
— — — Bear Garden: bear-baiting, &c., in, iii. 549 & n. 4.
— — — Bear Gardens (modern street): site, iii. 549, n. 4.
— — — Beaufort Buildings: site, iii. 264, n. 3; fire in, 1695, v. 222–3 & n.
— — — Bedford House: *see* Southampton House *below.*
— — — Bedford Place (modern): site, iii. 398, n. 3.
— — — Bedlam: *see* Bethlehem Hospital *below.*
— — — Bell Yard, King Street, Westminster: E's new lodging in, 1674, *add.* (iv. 50 & n. 3).
— — — Berkeley House, later Devonshire House: notices, iii. 436 & n. 6, 624–5 & nn.; part of gardens to be built over, iv. 381–2 & n.; Lord Berkeley at (?), iii. 445–6 & n.; iv. 77; Margaret Blagge, later Mrs. Godolphin, resident at, 1673–5, 1676–8: moves to, iv. 1; ~ returns to, 1676, iv. 94 & n. 1; ~ leaves, 1678, iv. 107; ~ visits

LONDON (*cont.*)
to, at (as Berkeley House or my Lord Berkeley's), iv. 1–13, 25–35, 46–78, all *passim*; iv. 94 *bis*, 100, 107 [when no place is given for visits to her at this time she was probably here]; ~ Elizabeth Evelyn (E's daughter) stays with, at, iv. 35; other visits to, iii. 630; iv. 124; *see also* iv. 152; Princess Anne (later queen) resident at, v. 201.
— — — Berkeley Street: laid out, iv. 381–2 & n.; *see also* iii. 436, n. 6; E resident in, 1698–9, v. 292 & n. 5, 340.
— — — Berkshire House: *see* Cleveland House *below*.
— — — Bethlehem Hospital (Bedlam): in comparison, ii. 45 (i. 32); the old building, iii. 191–2 & n.; the new building (1675–6), iv. 134 & n. 1; ~ site, iii. 457, n. 2.
— — — Birdcage Walk: house of Mrs. M. Knight in, iii. 230, n. 3.
— — — Bishopsgate: after Great Fire, iii. 458.
— — — Bishopsgate Street: Sir T. Gresham's house, later Gresham College, in, iii. 266, n. 6 *ad fin*.
— — — Bishopsgate Street Without: old Bethlehem Hospital near, iii. 191, n. 6.
— — — Bishopsgate ward: foreign silk-weavers in, iii. 65, n. 8.
— — — Blackfriars: hat-maker resident in, iii. 143.
— — — Bloomsbury: manor of, iii. 398, n. 2; Southampton's buildings in, iii. 398 & nn. 2, 3; R. Montagu's house near: *see* Montagu House *below*; French Conformist church moved to (1817), iii. 545, n. 3.
— — — Bloomsbury Square, formerly Southampton Square: building of, iii. 398 & n. 2; Dr. Hans Sloane resident in, v. 48, n. 1.
— — — Blue Coat School: *see* Christ's Hospital *below*.
— — — Bond Street (Old Bond Street): site, iii. 379, n. 8 *ad fin.*; Trinity Chapel in, v. 62, n. 1.
— — — Borough High Street, iii. 255, n. 5, 417, n. 7; Marshalsea

LONDON (*cont.*)
in, iii. 420, n. 5; St. Thomas's Hospital in, iii. 391, n. 4.
— — — Botolph Lane: fire in, 1655, iii. 150, n. 4; in Great Fire, iii. 451, n. 3.
— — — Bow Street, Covent Garden: Grinling Gibbons resident at King's Arms in, iv. 179, n. 2; Sir J. Stonhouse's lodging in, iv. 194.
— — — Brewer Street: Foubert's academy in, iv. 257, n. 5; advance of building beyond, iv. 400, n. 1.
— — — Bridges Street, Covent Garden: King's theatre (Theatre Royal) in: *see* theatres *below*.
— — — Bridgewater House (modern): site, iii. 470, n. 5.
— — — British Museum (modern): site, iv. 90, n. 7; for collections in *see* British Museum.
— — — Broad Street, St. Giles: limit of Southampton's property, iii. 398, n. 2.
— — — Brook Buildings, Greville Street: Dr. G. Burnet lodges in, iv. 301, n. 1.
— — — Buckingham House: successor to Goring House, iii. 404, n. 2.
— — — Buckingham Palace: site, iii. 96, n. 7, 404, n. 2.
— — — Buckingham Street: Pepys resident in, iv. 591, n. 2.
— — — Bucklersbury: Carmelites' chapel in, 1688, iv. 602 & n. 1.
— — — Burleigh Street: site, iii. 203, n. 3.
— — — Burlington Gardens, formerly Glasshouse Street: limit of Clarendon's property, iii. 379, n. 8 *ad fin.*; Trinity Chapel near, v. 62, n. 1.
— — — Burlington House: site, iii. 379, n. 7.
— — — Canon *or* Channel Row, Westminster: Derby House adjoining, iii. 222, n. 4; Rhenish wine-house in, iii. 447, n. 2.
— — — Carlton House (after 1706): site, iii. 573, n. 3.
— — — Castle Street, near St. Martin in the Fields: Tenison's Library, &c., in, iv. 368, n. 1.
— — — Chancery Lane: Rolls Chapel in, iii. 14, n. 1; Ser-

LONDON (*cont.*)
jeants' Inn in, iii. 194, n. 2; residents in: Sir R. Fanshawe, iii. 143, n. 3, 182, n. 1; Sir Francis North, later Baron Guilford, iv. 312, n. 5, 365, n. 8(?).

— — — Channel Row: *see* Canon Row *above*.

— — — Chapel Street, Tothill Fields: New Chapel in, v. 394, n. 3.

— — — Charing Cross: St. Martin's Lane formerly ended at, iii. 319, n. 3; execution of the Regicides at, iii. 259; pillory at, iii. 503; iv. 440, n. 4 *ad fin.*; Suffolk House near: *see* Northumberland House *below*; S. Hartlib resident at, iii. 162, n. 2; Punchinello performs at, iii. 492, n. 2.

— — — Charles Street, Hatton Garden: site, iii. 231, n. 6.

— — — Charterhouse: notice, 1657, iii. 192 & n. 1; in comparison, ii. 45 & n. 3 (i. 32); school: nomination for entry to, iv. 511; master of, 1677–85: *see* Erskine, W.; preacher at, 1661–71: *see* Thurscross, T.; Rutland House near, iii. 95, n. 5.

— — — Cheapside: lord mayor's show in, iii. 259, 342 & n. 2; Solemn League and Covenant burnt in, iii. 289, n. 1; in and after Great Fire, iii. 451 & n. 3, 456, n. 6, 458; mentioned, iv. 17; Cross in: demolition of, ii. 81 (i. 55); ~ in comparison, iii. 121; Mercers' Chapel in: *see* Mercers' Chapel *below*; Nag's Head in, iii. 259, n. 4.

— — — Chip Street: *see* Sackville Street *below*.

— — — Christ's Hospital: notices: 1657, iii. 192 & nn. 2, 3; ~ 1687, iv. 542–3 & nn.; childrens' dress at: in comparison, ii. 311; in procession to Spital sermon, v. 398–9 & n.; Mathematical School at, iv. 542 & n. 2; v. 399 & n. 1.

— — — churches [St. Paul's Cathedral, Westminster Abbey, parish churches, and chapels of ease, &c. Royal and private chapels, &c., are indexed under their several names in this section; Anglican services during the Protectorate, &c., under Church of England: chronological series. Non-Anglican places of worship, &c., are indicated above, in religious section. In what follows, ordinary services are those for Sundays and major festivals and fasts; occasional fasts are noted, and minor festivals when they do not fall on Sundays]:

— — — — All Hallows, Honey Lane, iv. 72 n. 1; minister of: *see* Hutchinson, Thomas.

— — — — Christ Church, Newgate Street: notice, iii. 192 & n. 2; destroyed in Great Fire, iii. 460 & n. 4; the new building, iv. 543 & n. 3.

— — — — Christ Church, Westminster (modern): *see* New Chapel *below*.

— — — — church near Garlick Hill: service at, Christmas 1657, iii. 204, n. 6 *ad fin*.

— — — — New Chapel (New Church), Westminster (now Christ Church), v. 394 & n. 3; minister, 1699–1719: *see* Smalridge, G.

— — — — St. Alban, Wood Street: tabernacle used during rebuilding of: service in, iv. 180 & n. 6; rector, 1694–1711: *see* Adams, John.

— — — — St. Andrew, Holborn: John Evelyn, jnr., married at, iv. 194; rector, 1665–89: *see* Stillingfleet, E.

— — — — St. Andrew Undershaft: service for East India Company at, iii. 202 & n. 2; lecturer, *c.* 1714: *see* Strengfellow, W.

— — — — St. Anne, Blackfriars: Edward Darcy married at, ii. 10, n. 7.

— — — — St. Anne, Soho: building, &c., iv. 543–4 & n.; services at, iv. 543–7, 652–4; v. 2–6, 16–22, all *passim*; rector, 1686–1704: *see* Hearne, J.; reader at: sermons by, iv. 654; v. 4.

— — — — St. Antholin, Watling Street: lecturer, *c.* 1692: *see* Strengfellow, W.

— — — — St. Augustine (Austine),

LONDON (*cont.*)
Watling Street: service at (?), v. 221 & n. 5; rector, 1689–1706: *see* Fleetwood, W.
— — — — St. Benet Fink: rector, 1725–31: *see* Goddard, T.
— — — — St. Botolph, Aldersgate: minister, *c.* 1658: *see* Hall, George.
— — — — St. Bride: Spital sermons at, v. 399 & n. 1; Dr. J. Needham buried at, iv. 183; vicar, 1674–95: *see* Dove, H.
— — — — St. Clement Danes: notice, 1684, iv. 392–3 & n.; services at, iii. 212, 249(?); iv. 392–3, 530 & n. 3, 536, 537, 545, 551; v. 228, 237–55, 275–82, 288, 292 *passim & singulatim*; sermon on Thursday in Holy Week, iv. 309 & n. 2; rectors: *see* Dukeson, R. (1634–47, 1660–78); Hascard, G. (1678–1708); ministers: *see* Masterson, G. (1651, 1660); Alsop, J. (error: iii. 314, n. 4 & *add.*); curate: baptizes Elizabeth Evelyn (later Mrs. Harcourt), iv. 395–6; lecturers: *see* Burnet, G. (*c.* 1683); Adams, John (*c.* 1696–*c.* 1712; falsely identified as W. Fleetwood, v. 228 & n. 2: *see add.*); ∼ unnamed: sermons by, iv. 536, 545, 551; v. 228.
— — — — St. Clement Eastcheap (called Eastcheap, &c.), iii. 64, n. 5; services at, iii. 64, 82, 150 *bis* & n. 5, 160, 249(?); rector, 1660–6: *see* Alsop, J.; lecturer, 1654–6: *see* Pearson, J.
— — — — St. Dunstan in the East: rector, 1686–98: *see* Holden, R.; ∼ presentation of, iv. 522 & n. 2; ∼ goes to, for winter, 1687, iv. 563; rector, 1698–1731: *see* Strengfellow, W. (previously, 1686–98, curate and lecturer); lecturer (W. Strengfellow?): sermons by, at Deptford, 1687–8, iv. 549–50 & n., 592, 608.
— — — — St. Dunstan in the West (in Fleet Street), iv. 73, n. 3; statue of Queen Elizabeth at, iii. 461, n. 1; accident near, iv. 301; services, iv. 73; v. 220, 221 & n. 5(?), 222, 235, 249, 272–3; rector, 1677–1736: *see*

LONDON (*cont.*)
Grant, J.; lecturer, 1693– : *see* Fleetwood, W.
— — — — St. Edmund the King: rectors: *see* Bradford, J. (*c.* 1683); Lynford, T. (1685–1724).
— — — — St. Ethelburga: rector 1677–85: *see* Evans, J.; ∼ presentation, iv. 127, n. 2.
— — — — St. Faith beneath St. Paul's: destruction of books in, in Great Fire, iii. 459 & n. 3; in comparison, ii. 289 & n. 6.
— — — — St. Gabriel Fenchurch: baptism at, ii. 78 & n. 2 (i. 51).
— — — — St. Giles (unspecified): service at, iii. 629.
— — — — St. Giles in the Fields: new buildings near, 1694 (Seven Dials), v. 193 & n. 1; marriage-licence for, iii. 551, n. 3; Sharp's controversial sermons at, iv. 516, n. 1, 524, n. 1; services, iv. 368; v. 501–2, 504, 506–7; rectors: *see* Sharp, J. (1676–91); Scott, John (1691–5); Hayley, W. (1695–1715); curate: sermon by, iv. 368; lecturers: *see* Leech, Dr. —; Knaggs, T.; ∼ unnamed (Leech?): sermon by, v. 506–7.
— — — — St. Gregory by St. Paul's, iii. 61, n. 4; Book of Common Prayer used at, during Protectorate, iii. 150 & n. 2; service forbidden, Christmas, 1657, iii. 204, n. 6 *ad fin.*; Dr. T. White, deprived bishop of Peterborough, buried in vault of, v. 289 & n. 3; services: fast-day, 1658, iii. 213; ∼ ordinary, 1652–8, iii. 61, 95, 148–51, 158–64, 187–8, 193, 214, *passim & singulatim* [some other services recorded with no place named in this period probably took place here: *see* iii. 148–52, 159, 160, 214]; ∼ later, 1660–2, iii. 263, 265, 271, 273, 296; ministers at: *see* Hewit, J. (to 1658); Masterson, G.
— — — — St. Helen: error for St. Ethelburga (?), iv. 127 & n. 2.
— — — — St. James, Garlickhithe: rectors: *see* Buck, J. (1661–86); Alderson, S. (1686–96).
— — — — St. James, Piccadilly:

LONDON (*cont.*)
notice, 1684, iv. 397 & nn. 4, 5; parish constituted, iv. 294, n. 2; date of building, iii. 624, n. 4; font, iv. 317, n. 2; congregation: character of, v. 542; services: general note, *add.* (iv. 397, n. 4); ~ ordinary, iv. 397–8, 414, 436, 531, 538, 539, 568, 590, 644; v. 27, 39–55, 69–70, 79, 136–42, 147, 166–7, 170, 193, 210, 213, 353–4(?), 559, n. 3, 589(?), 592(?), *passim & singulatim*; ~ weekday: Thursdays in Lent, iv. 544 & n. 5, 623 & n. 2; v. 43 & n. 4, 44; ~ fast, v. 51; ~ New Year's day, v. 81; rectory: disputed right of presentation to, 1692, v. 112, n. 4, 136, n. 5, 376, n. 1; individual rectors: *see* Tenison, T. (1686–92); Birch, P. (1692–5); Clarke, Samuel (1709–29); lecturer: *see* Hickman, C.

— — — — — Tabernacle (chapel of ease), King Street, Golden Square (sometimes apparently as St. James's Chapel, and not clearly distinguishable from the chapel at St. James's Palace), v. 132, n. 2; services: list, *add.* (iv. 397, n. 4); ~ ordinary, v. 132–3, 136 & n. 4(?), 141 & n. 3(?), 159(?), 160, 164(?), 166(?), 170 & n. 2(?), 173–4(?), 608 & n. 1(?); ~ fast (?), v. 319–20.

— — — — St. Lawrence Jewry: notice, 1682, iv. 282 & n. 4; parish of St. Mary Magdalen, Milk Street, united with, iii. 95, n. 4; service, iv. 282; sermons preached at, iv. 371, n. 1, 641, n. 5; vicar, 1668–83: *see* Whichcote, B.

— — — — St. Margaret, Westminster: sermons at: by Hugh Peters, ii. 547, n. 1; ~ before house of commons (fast-days, &c.), iii. 311–12, 314 & nn. 3, 4, 356; iv. 26 & n. 1, 156–7 & nn., 641 & n. 2; other services, iii. 290, 307, 314–17 *passim*, 355, 605; iv. 188, 207, 223, 238, 244, 258, 263, 281, 286, 292, 378, 416, 528; v. 212; curates and lecturers: *see* Tucker, W. (1661–4); Owtram, W. (1664?–79); Sprat, T. (1679–); curate: sermon by, iii. 355.

LONDON (*cont.*)
— — — — — — chapel of ease, v. 394 & n. 3.

— — — — St. Mark (error for St. Martin in the Fields?): service, v. 273 & n. 1.

— — — — St. Martin in the Fields, iii. 276, n. 8; congregation: size of, iv. 599; man seeks sanctuary in, during service, 1687, iv. 545; Robert Boyle buried in, v. 81–3 & nn.; Boyle Lectures to be delivered at, v. 89; Sacrament to qualify with Test Act received at, iv. 10; v. 568, n. 2; &c.; services: ordinary, iii. 276; iv. 10, 12, 34–6, 43, 51, 61–4, 87, 91, 107, 109, 133–7, 167–9, 222, 223, 240, 258, 279, 292–6, 309, 350–75, 384, 499–506, 529–51, 564–6, 579–80, 589, 598–630, 650–4; v. 1–27, 38–57, 81, 92–3, 103, 137, 204, 226, 238–9, 246, 248, 273 & n. 1(?), 568 & n. 2(?), *passim & singulatim* [some other sermons recorded with no place mentioned probably took place here: so Dr. Meriton's sermons, iv. 351, 359, &c.]; weekday, with Communion: New Year's day, iv. 359, 532–3; ~ Ascension, iv. 10, 35, 63, 90, 109, 134, 244, 313, 512, 549, 584–5; v. 23, 53–4; weekday, without Communion: Candlemas, iv. 538; ~ Lady Day, iv. 630; ~ Ascension, iv. 168, 204; v. 99; ~ Whit Monday, iv. 378–9; ~ St. Matthew, iv. 598; catechizing: Wednesday (?), iv. 286 & n. 4; ~ Friday, iv. 259 & n. 7, 269; baptism, iv. 222; Boyle Lectures, v. 126, 222, 239; fasts, v. 21, 23, 24, 51.

— — — — — clergy: vicarage: disputed right of presentation to, 1692, v. 112, n. 4, 121, n. 1, 169, n. 1, 376 & n. 1; individual vicars: *see* Hardy, N. (1661–70); Lamplugh, T. (1670–6); Lloyd, William, D.D., the apocalyptic (1676–80); Tenison, T. (1680–92); Lancaster, W. (1692–4, 1694–1717); Gouge, N. (1694); curate: sermon by, v. 591; lecturers: *see* Meriton, J. (1660–1704); Gibson, E. (1703–15); ~ unnamed: sermon by, iv.

London (*cont.*)
499 & n. 4; readers: sermons by, iv. 313; v. 112 & n. 3(?), 114 & n. 1, 127–8, 128 & *add.*, 131; schoolmaster of: *see* St. Martin in the Fields: parish *below*.
— — — — — — chapels of ease: Tabernacle near (Oxenden Street): service at, iv. 242 & n. 4; Trinity Chapel, Bond Street: *see* Trinity Chapel *below*.
— — — — — St. Martin, Ludgate, iii. 296, n. 1; parish of St. Mary Magdalene, Old Fish Street, united with, iii. 82, n. 4; marriage at, iii. 367; services, iii. 296, 367; v. 279; rector, 1662–72: *see* Breton, Robert.
— — — — — St. Mary Aldermary: rector, 1694–1708: *see* Blackall, O.
— — — — — St. Mary le Bow, iv. 72, n. 2; parish of All Hallows, Honey Lane, united with, iv. 72, n. 1; special service to be held at, 1686, iv. 524, n. 2; Boyle Lectures: to be delivered at, v. 89; ~ lecture at, v. 94 & n. 1; sermon for Reformation of Manners at, v. 391–2 & nn.; minister, 1675: *see* Hutchinson, Thomas.
— — — — — St. Mary le Strand: parishioners of: use Savoy Chapel, iii. 343, n. 1.
— — — — — St. Mary Woolchurch Haw (Woolchurch), iii. 197, n. 3; services, iii. 197, 212.
— — — — — St. Mary Woolnooth: parish of St. Mary Woolchurch Haw united with, iii. 197, n. 3.
— — — — — St. Mary Magdalen, Milk Street: service, iii. 95 & n. 4.
— — — — — St. Mary Magdalen, Old Fish Street: Communion service, 1653, iii. 82 & n. 4.
— — — — — St. Michael, Cornhill: lecture at, iv. 305 & n. 1; rector, 1664–1704: *see* Meriton, John.
— — — — — St. Michael, Crooked Lane: lecturer, 1659–61: *see* Malory, T.
— — — — — St. Olave, Hart Street: burials at: Mrs. Pepys, iii. 541, n. 1; ~ Pepys, v. 538, n. 7; rector, 1658–89: *see* Mills, D.

London (*cont.*)
— — — — — St. Paul's Cathedral: general: founder of, iii. 459, n. 6; lord mayor at: visit during his show, iii. 301, n. 4 *ad fin.*; ~ services attended by, iv. 284, n. 1; *see also* iii. 165.
— — — — — — Old St. Paul's: height of (as measurement), ii. 513; position of St. Gregory by St. Paul's in relation to, iii. 61, n. 4; statues of James I and Charles I on portico removed, 1649, ii. 555 & n. 6; ordinary services at, iii. 165, 263, 367; thanksgiving for Four Days' Battle at, 1666, iii. 439 & n. 3; commissioners for repair of, 1663, i. *20*; ~ activities of, iii. 448 & n. 3, 449, nn. 1, 2; ~ scaffolds erected by, iii. 452 & n. 2; proposals for repair of, 1666: examination of, and report on, i. *19–20*; iii. 448–9 & nn.; in Great Fire, iii. 452 & n. 2, 454; condition after Great Fire, iii. 458–9 & nn.; Lady Chapel, iii. 459, n. 5; portico after Great Fire, iii. 458–9 & n.; St. Faith beneath: *see* St. Faith *above*.
— — — — — — New St. Paul's: rebuilding, iv. 243 & n. 5; ~ progress of: 1694, v. 192 & n. 2; ~ 1697, v. 278 & n. 3; ~ 1700, i. 84; ~ stone for: supply interrupted, v. 230 & n. 6; suitable position for public library in, iv. 368; reopened for services, 1697, v. 278; ordinary services, v. 278–9, 290 & n. 1; thanksgiving services at: Peace of Ryswick, 1697, v. 277, n. 2; ~ for successful campaign, 1702, v. 521 & n. 5; ~ for Blenheim, 1704, v. 578; Boyle Lectures delivered at, 1698–1703, v. 273, n. 4, 398, 442–3, 528; sermon for Reformation of Manners at (?), v. 391.
— — — — — — clergy: for bishops *see* London: diocese; dean: house of, iii. 449; ~ *ex officio* commissioner for repair of St. Paul's (1663–), iii. 448, n. 3; ~ individual deans: *see* Steward, Richard (1642–51); Sancroft, W. (1664–78); Stillingfleet, E. (1678–89); Tillotson, J. (1689–91); Sherlock, W.

LONDON (*cont.*)
487; telescope at, iii. 286, n. 4; rain-gauge at: readings of, 1695–6, v. 216, n. 5 (also cited in later notes); professor of music at: *see* Petty, Sir W. (iv. 57, n. 2); Richard Waller at, v. 176.
— — — — relations with Philosophical or Royal Society: usual meeting-place of the society, 1660–7, 1673–1710, iii. 266 & n. 6, 286, n. 1, 472, n. 2; iv. 27–8 & n.; Arundel Library brought to, iii. 472, n. 3; iv. 144, n. 2; meetings of the society at (place specified), iii. 343, 364 & n. 4, 392; iv. 380, 400, 488, 530; v. 224, 303; anniversary dinner at, iv. 160; *see also* iii. 378, n. 5.
— — — Greville Street: Brook Buildings in, iv. 301, n. 1.
— — — Guildhall: rebuilding after Great Fire, iii. 507, n. 4; lord mayor sworn in at, iii. 259, n. 4; legal proceedings in, iii. 507, 565; iv. 65; commissioners, &c., for Greenwich Hospital meet at, v. 209–14 *passim*, 220, 236 & n. 2, 240; feasts at, iii. 250, 388–9; iv. 562–3; portraits of Fire Judges at, iii. 338 & n. 5; iv. 17 & n. 5.
— — — Half Moon Street: limit of Clarendon's property, iii. 379, n. 8.
— — — Hatton Garden: laid out for building, iii. 231 & n. 6; First Fruits office in, iii. 565 & n. 2(?), 567 & n. 1; 'Paradise' (exhibition) in, iv. 24 & n. 6.
— — — Hatton House: P. Gunning resident at (?), iii. 204, n. 1.
— — — Hatton Street (Hatton Garden), iii. 231, n. 6.
— — — Hatton Wall: limit of Hatton property, iii. 231, n. 6.
— — — Haymarket: paving of, ordered, iii. 328 & n. 4.
— — — Heralds' College: *see* College of Arms *above*.
— — — Hicks Hall: trial at (error), iv. 327 & n. 1.
— — — Holborn *and* High Holborn: preservation of, from Great Fire, iii. 455; limit of Southampton's property, iii. 398, n. 2; Hatton House and Garden in, iii. 204, n. 1, 231,

LONDON (*cont.*)
n. 6; Red Lion inn in: corpses of Cromwell, &c., at, iii. 269, n. 2; turnstile in: monstrous birth near, iii. 255 & n. 6; house in: marriage-feast at, iv. 194.
— — — Holborn Bridge: in Great Fire, iii. 456, n. 2.
— — — Holborn Viaduct (modern): site, iii. 456, n. 2.
— — — Honourable Artillery Company: ground of, ii. 360 & n. 6.
— — — Horse Ferry, iv. 360 & n. 4, 365; without name, v. 536.
— — — Horseguards' Parade (modern): site, ii. 556, n. 4.
— — — hospitals: *see* Bethlehem *and* Christ's Hospital *above*; St. Anthony's, St. Bartholomew's, St. Thomas's, the Savoy *and* environs: Chelsea Hospital *below*.
— — — Howard Street: site, iii. 234, n. 4; iv. 395, n. 5 *ad fin*.
— — — Inner Temple: in Great Fire, iii. 454 & n. 4, 456, n. 1; members of: in disturbance, 1649, ii. 556 & n. 1; controller of Christmas revels, 1697: *see* Brereton, E.; Sir E. Thurland's chamber in, iii. 509; *see also* Inns of Court *and* Temple *below*.
— — — Inns of Court: Christmas revels at (general remarks), iii. 307, n. 6; v. 280; Readings in, iii. 400, n. 3; searched for Jacobite conspirators, 1697, v. 273; *see also* Gray's Inn *and* Inner Temple *above*; Lincoln's Inn *and* Middle Temple below.
— — — Ironmongers' Hall: feast in, iii. 587 & n. 2.
— — — Kent Street: plague in, iii. 417–18 & n.; trader in, iv. 352.
— — — Ken Wood House (modern): picture in, iii. 96, n. 3.
— — — King's College of Physicians: *see* Royal College of Physicians *below*.
— — — Kingly Street, Golden Square: *see* King Street *below*.
— — — King Street (position not specified), iv. 49 & n. 3.
— — — King Street, Golden Square, now Kingly Street: Tabernacle in: *see* churches:

LONDON (*cont.*)
St. James, Piccadilly: Tabernacle *above*.
— — — King Street, St. James's: house in, iv. 199, n. 3.
— — — King Street, Westminster (Whitehall): project for rebuilding, v. 204 & n. 4; house in, iii. 603, n. 4; *see also* Bell Yard *above*.
— — — Kingsway (modern): limit of Southampton's property, iii. 398, n. 2.
— — — Kirby Street: site, iii. 231, n. 6.
— — — Knightrider Street: use of name, iii. 82, n. 4.
— — — Leadenhall Street: East India House in, iii. 202, n. 1.
— — — Leicester Fields: *see* Leicester Square *below*.
— — — Leicester House, iii. 626, n. 9; Lady Sunderland at, iii. 626, 631.
— — — Leicester Square, iii. 626, n. 9; iv. 241, n. 1; Dr. W. Lloyd's house in, iv. 240–1.
— — — Lime Street: Elector Palatine's chapel in, 1688, iv. 599, n. 1.
— — — Lincoln's Inn: Christmas revels, 1661, iii. 307–8 & nn.; Reader in: last appointed, iii. 400, n. 3; ~ 1665: *see* Rich, Sir E.; official residing in, iii. 587–8 & n.; chapel: services, ii. 553, 556; iii. 61, 95, 152; iv. 529; preachers at: *see* Ussher, J. (1647–54); Ryves, B. (1654–8). *See also* Inns of Court *above*.
— — — Lincoln's Inn Fields: Lord Russell executed in, iv. 332; Great Turnstile leading to, iii. 255, n. 6; theatres adjoining: *see* theatres *below*; houses in, of: Sir J. Bankes, iv. 96; T. Povey, iii. 375 & nn. 2–4.
— — — Little Trinity Lane: Painter-Stainers' Hall in, iii. 390, n. 4.
— — — Liverpool Street Station: site, iii. 191, n. 6.
— — — London Bridge: in comparison, iii. 128; in Great Fire, iii. 451 & n. 3; unusually low tide at, 1687, iv. 549; shooting the bridge: danger when, ii. 547; highway leading to, iii. 450, n. 3; wharfs near, iii. 476, n. 3; mentioned, iii. 458 *bis*.
— — — London Institution (modern): house occupied by, iii. 625, n. 5; W. Upcott's services to, i. 52.
— — — Lower Thames Street: Custom House in, iii. 588, n. 2.
— — — Ludgate: in Great Fire, iii. 460–1 & n.; debtors imprisoned in: gift for, iv. 29 & n. 2.
— — — Ludgate Hill: in Great Fire, iii. 454, 458; Belle Savage Inn on: rhinoceros exhibited at, iv. 390, n. 1; Ludgate in, iii. 461, n. 1.
— — — the Mall, iii. 346, n. 4; site, ii. 556, n. 4; iii. 614, n. 3.
— — — Mansion House (modern): site, iii. 197, n. 3; house used by lord mayors prior to erection of, iii. 625, n. 5.
— — — Marlborough Chapel: *see* St. James's Palace: Roman Catholic chapel *below*.
— — — Marlborough House (modern): site, iii. 573, n. 3.
— — — Marshalsea prison, iii. 420, n. 5; prisoners in: J. Burckhorst, iii. 420; Col. T. Colepeper, iv. 454 & n. 1; Pepys, iv. 169, n. 1, 171, n. 12; W. Sancroft, jnr., v. 59, n. 2.
— — — Marshland Close: site, v. 193, n. 1.
— — — Mercers' Chapel: in Great Fire, iii. 460 & n. 2; Italian church in: sermon to, ii. 545 & n. 9; ~ address from, to Charles II, 1660, iii. 248 & n. 3; ~ lecturer to: *see* Middleton, W.
— — — Merchant Taylors' Hall: East India Company court of election meets at, iii. 203 & n. 1.
— — — the Mews, iii. 487, n. 8 *ad fin.*; Tenison's Library to be built near, iv. 369; resident in, iii. 487 & n. 8.
— — — Middle Temple: members of, in disturbance, 1649, ii. 556 & n. 1; Christmas revels: 1641, ii. 77 (i. 51); ~ 1668, iii. 504; Readers' feasts at, 1667–9, iii. 490, 512, 536–7; last Reading at, iii. 400, n. 3; meeting for business at, iii. 613.
— — — — separate parts: Brick

LONDON (*cont.*)
Court: fire in, 1704, v. 563 & n. 3; Essex Court, ii. 24 & nn. 1, 4; Hall: Caesars' busts placed in, ii. 77 & n. 4 (i. 51); Hall Court, ii. 24; le Little Court, ii. 24, n. 4; Middle Temple Lane, *ib.*; iv. 362, n. 1; museum of W. Charleton or Courten in: *see* Charleton, William. *See also* Inns of Court *above and* Temple *below*.

— — — — the Evelyns and their connexions at: E and his brothers: admitted, ii. 15 & n. 4 (i. 12); ~ chambers of, ii. 24 & nn. 1, 4 (i. 18); *see also* i. 12; surety for E, iii. 470, n. 2; E elected a comptroller of Christmas revels, ii. 77 (i. 51); repairs his chamber, iii. 78; resides in or visits (specific entries; E apparently used his chamber when he was in London, unless Mrs. Evelyn was with him, until about 1657), ii. 24 *bis* (i. 18), 25 (i. 19), 76–7 (i. 51), 78, 538–9, 548; iii. 91, 95, 172, 194 & n. 1; George Evelyn as student at, v. 358; *see also above*; John Evelyn, jnr.: admitted to, iii. 613–14; Richard Evelyn at: *see above*; relations, &c., at: G. Cole, iii. 470, n. 2; R. Hatton, ii. 78, n. 1; T. Henshaw, ii. 24, n. 4.

— — — Milk Street: church in: *see* churches: St. Mary Magdalen, Milk Street *above*.

— — — Millbank: Horseferry at, iv. 365.

— — — Monmouth House, iv. 652, n. 2.

— — — Montague House, Bloomsbury: notices, iv. 90 & n. 7, 184, 344–5 & n.; burnt down, iv. 497 & n. 2.

— — — the Monument, iv. 243 & n. 6; position of, in relation to outbreak of Great Fire, iii. 450, n. 3; inscription on, attributing Fire to Roman Catholics, obliterated, 1685, iv. 449 & n. 4.

— — — Moorfields, iii. 457, n. 2; after Great Fire, iii. 458; refugees from Fire in, iii. 457; ~ Charles II's speech to, iii. 462, n. 1 (as Moorgate, in error: *see add.*); the new Bethlehem Hospital in, iii. 191, n. 6; iv. 134 & n. 1; silk manufacture in, iii. 65 & n. 8.

— — — Moorgate: error for Moorfields, iii. 462, n. 1; *add.*

— — — Mulberry Garden: entertainment at, iii. 96–7 & n.; acquired by Arlington, iii. 404, n. 2.

— — — National Gallery (modern): site, iii. 487, n. 8 *ad fin.*; iv. 368, n. 1; statue of James II outside, iv. 317, n. 2.

— — — New Fish Street: Great Fire starts near, iii. 450, n. 3.

— — — Newgate: in Great Fire, iii. 454; as terminal for whipping criminals, iv. 440, n. 4, 445, 451, n. 3.

— — — Newgate Market: in Great Fire, iii. 456, n. 6.

— — — Newgate Prison: situation, iv. 307; Captain H. Lanham sent to, 1688, iv. 603–4 & n.; prisoners in, awaiting trial, 1699, v. 366, n. 4.

— — — Newgate Street: Christ's Hospital, &c., near, iii. 192, n. 2.

— — — New Scotland Yard (modern): name of, iii. 319, n. 2; site, iii. 222, n. 4.

— — — Norfolk Buildings, Strand, v. 219, n. 6.

— — — Norfolk House: *see* Arundel House *above*.

— — — Norfolk Street: site, iii. 234, n. 4.

— — — Northampton House: *see* Northumberland House *below*.

— — — Northumberland Avenue (modern): site, iii. 141, n. 2 *ad fin.*

— — — Northumberland House, formerly Northampton House and Suffolk House: notice, iii. 141 & n. 2; pictures in, &c., iii. 216 & nn. 3–8; situation of, iii. 319, n. 3.

— — — Old Bailey: in Great Fire, iii. 454; sessions house in, iv. 175 & n. 2; ~ trials at: Sir J. Johnston, v. 41, n. 1; Sir R. Graham, Viscount Preston, v. 41 & n. 4, 42 & n. 1; Lord Russell, iv. 327, n. 1; H. St. John, &c., iv. 401, n. 1; Sir

LONDON (*cont.*)
G. Wakeman, &c., iv. 173–5 & nn.; man sent to, for trial (?), iii. 73; *see also* iii. 74.
— — — Old Bond Street: site, iii. 379, n. 8 *ad fin.*
— — — Old Change, iii. 82, n. 4.
— — — Old Exchange: *see* Royal Exchange *below.*
— — — Old Fish Street: St. Mary Magdalen in: *see* churches *above.*
— — — Old Jewry: Sir R. Clayton's house in, iii. 625, n. 5.
— — — Old Kent Road, iii. 417, n. 7.
— — — Old King's Barge-House (Old Barge-House Wharf), iv. 362, n. 1.
— — — Oxenden Street: chapel of ease, of St. Martin in the Fields, in, iv. 242, n. 4.
— — — Painters' Hall, iii. 390 & n. 4; meeting-place of Commissioners for Sick and Wounded, 1664–6, iii. 390 *bis*, 391, 392, 403, 405, 435, 443, 444; Commissioners wish to leave, iii. 444.
— — — Pall Mall: T. Thynne murdered in, iv. 274, n. 1; houses in, back on to royal garden, iii. 573, n. 3; residents in: Nell Gwyn, iii. 573, n. 4; Moll Knight, iii. 230, n. 3; Lady Ranelagh and Robert Boyle, iv. 124, n. 6; v. 83, n. 2.
— — — Pall Mall East (modern): Royal College of Physicians in (1825), iii. 337, n. 3.
— — — Paul's Chain: in Great Fire, iii. 454.
— — — Piccadilly: Haymarket near, iii. 328 & n. 4; land on north side of: granted to Clarendon, &c., iii. 379, nn. 7, 8; Sir W. Petty's house in, iv. 56, n. 4; Winstanley's waterworks in, v. 247, n. 1. *See also* Berkeley House *and* Clarendon House *above.*
— — — Pontack's (tavern): dinner at, v. 160 & n. 4.
— — — Portugal Street, Lincoln's Inn Fields (modern), iii. 303, n. 4.
— — — the Post-House: despatch sent to, iii. 299.
— — — Post Office: fellows of Royal Society meet at, iii. 378, n. 5.

LONDON (*cont.*)
— — — the Poultry: in Great Fire, iii. 452, n. 1; pope-burning in, 1673, iv. 26, n. 2.
— — — prisons: *see* Fleet; Ludgate; Marshalsea; Newgate *above*; Tower; Westminster: Gatehouse *below.*
— — — Probate Office: document sent to, iii. 509.
— — — Pudding Lane: Great Fire breaks out in, iii. 450, n. 3.
— — — Queenhithe, iii. 451, n. 2.
— — — Queen Street: *see* Great Queen Street *above.*
— — — Red Lion Square: fire in, 1700, v. 376, n. 5.
— — — Rhenish Wine-house: supper at, iii. 447 & n. 2.
— — — Rolls Chapel, iii. 14, n. 1; situation, iii. 194, n. 2; services in, iii. 14, 15; iv. 282; minister at, 1675–84: *see* Burnet, G.
— — — Royal College of Physicians [E generally calls it the College of Physicians, &c.; it became the Royal College in 1663], iii. 337, n. 3; new building, 1670–8: erection of, iv. 133, n. 8, 307, n. 3; ~ situation of, iv. 307 & n. 5; E lends his anatomical tables to, iii. 77–8 & nn.; anatomy lectures at, iii. 77, n. 6, 78, 338, n. 2 (W. Harvey); iv. 308 & n. 3; Harveian orations at, iii. 379; iv. 291 & n. 1; collections of, iii. 337–8 & nn.; library, iii. 338; ~ new building for, iv. 307 & n. 3; officers of, iv. 307 & nn. 2, 4; visits to, iii. 364; iv. 133.
— — — Royal College of Surgeons: site, iii. 303, n. 4; E's anatomical tables at (1809), ii. 475, n. 5.
— — — Royal Exchange (sometimes called Old Exchange), ii. 46, n. 2; in comparisons, ii. 46 (i. 33), 98 (i. 64), 433–4 & n.; statue of Charles I removed from, ii. 555 & n. 6; in Great Fire, iii. 452, 458, 460 & nn. 3, 8; occupies Gresham College, 1667–9, iii. 266, n. 6 *ad fin.*, 487; iv. 27; new building, iv. 27–8 & n.; ~ statue of Charles II in, iv. 317, n. 2; ~ chimes of: mechanism of, iv. 326 & n. 2; pillory outside, iv. 440, n. 4.

LONDON (*cont.*)
— — — — proclamations at: unkingship, 1649, ii. 555 & n. 6; ~ accession of James II, 1685, iv. 413; Solemn League and Covenant burnt at, iii. 289, n. 1; book burnt at, 1686, iv. 510–11 & n.
— — — — Col. W. Webb at, ii. 549.
— — — Russell Street, Covent Garden: E lodges at Three Feathers in, iii. 233 & n. 4.
— — — Rutland House, near Charterhouse, iii. 95, n. 5.
— — — Sackville Street, formerly Chip Street: limit of Clarendon's property, iii. 379, n. 8; Sir W. Petty resides in, iv. 56, n. 4.
— — — St. Alban's Street, iv. 274, n. 1.
— — — St. Anthony's Hospital: church of: use of, granted to French Protestants, iii. 160, n. 3.
— — — St. Bartholomew's Hospital: Sick and Wounded at, iii. 455–6 & n.; preservation of, in Great Fire, *ib.*; i. *20*.
— — — St. Etheldreda, Ely Place, iii. 270, n. 5.
— — — St. Giles: manor of, iii. 398, n. 2.
— — — St. James's: Berkeley's house or lodgings in, 1666, iii. 446.
— — — St. James's Palace:
— — — — chronological series: Puritan preacher in courtyard of, 1650, iii. 14; Henrietta Anne at, 1660, iii. 264; as residence of James, duke of York (1660–85): James's children at, iii. 380 & nn. 1–3, 444; ~ Mary of Modena at, iv. 27, n. 5, 29; ~ Roman Catholics ordered to leave, 1678, iv. 159, n. 2; ~ James at, 1683, iv. 301; court at, Dec. 1685, &c., iv. 493 & n. 6; William of Orange at, 1688–9: invited to, iv. 610, 611, n. 1; ~ occupies, iv. 611 & n. 2, 623, n. 4 *ad fin.*; ~ council of peers at, iv. 611 & n. 3; ~ concourse of visitors at, iv. 611–12 & n.; ball at, 1699, v. 362 & n. 2; Queen Anne keeps her court at, v. 518 & n. 2.

LONDON (*cont.*)
— — — — building and parts: boundary of royal garden, iii. 573, n. 3; apartments in, of: James Graham, iv. 123 & n. 5; ~ Sir G. and Lady Sylvius, iv. 155; Chapel Royal in: *see below*; Roman Catholic chapel (later German Chapel and Marlborough Chapel), iii. 373, n. 2; ~ marriages in, iii. 373, 511, n. 2; royal library at, iv. 214, n. 8 *ad fin.*; v. 44 & n. 3; ~ E's interest in, i. *35*; ~ proposed purchases of books for, v. 206, 323; ~ additional accommodation desired for, v. 224 & n. 2, 323; ~ proposal to make it a public institution, v. 280 & n. 5; ~ keepers: *see* Justel, H. (1689–93); Bentley, R. (1693–17).
— — — — Chapel Royal (not always distinguishable from the chapel of ease of St. James, Piccadilly), iii. 373, n. 2, 624, n. 4; A. Morus preaches at, iv. 310–11 & n.; services at: baptism, iv. 95; ~ fast (?), v. 319–20; ~ ordinary, iii. 624, 630; iv. 35, 36, 43, 71–83, 94–107, 121–40, 157, 164–8, 185, 194, 198, 207, 280, 294–7, 306, 357, 395(?), 529; v. 141 & n. 3(?), 159(?), 160 & n. 5, 164(?), 166; *add.*(?); v. 173–4 (?), 194–5(?), 203 & n. 2, 205 & n. 2, 213–14(?), 222(?), 226, 589(?), 592(?), 608 & n. 1(?), *passim & singulatim*; ~ lenten sermons at court, 1700, v. 380–1 & n., 383–4 & n.(?), 388–90 & n., 394–8 & n.; chaplains attached to, 1694, *add.* (v. 166).
— — — St. James's Park, iii. 346, n. 4; Charles II in, iii. 347, 437, 476, 573, 614; iv. 398–9; admission to: restricted, 1683, iv. 331; amusements: skating, iii. 346–7 & n.; ~ wrestling-match, iii. 476; birds and animals in: collection, 1665, iii. 398–400 & nn.; ~ ostriches, iv. 266, n. 3; ~ Turkish horses, 1684, iv. 398–9; social, v. 331.
— — — — places, &c., in: Albemarle's lodgings in (Cockpit, part of Whitehall), iii. 416 & n. 4, 417–18; canal, iii. 346 & n. 4; T. Chiffinch: house and

LONDON (*cont.*)
garden of, iii. 293, n. 1, 305 & n. 1; Cockpit in: *see* Whitehall; Cockpit near, 1699, v. 317, n. 1; the Decoy, iii. 399–400 & n.; ~ completed, iii. 404; library building, proposed, v. 280, n. 5, 323; the Pall Mall, iii. 614 & n. 3; royal garden, iii. 573 & n. 3; ~ occupied by A. Verrio, iv. 522 & n. 1; Spring Garden: *see* Spring Garden *below*.
— — — St. James's Square: parochial arrangements, iv. 294, n. 2; displays of fireworks in: 1695, v. 223 & n. 4; ~ 1697, v. 269 & n. 4, 277–8; houses in, of: Essex, iv. 199 & n. 3, 238; Halifax, iv. 294, n. 2; Pembroke, v. 245, n. 2; Romney, v. 223 & n. 4.
— — — St. James's Street: paving of: ordered, iii. 328 & n. 3; Clarendon House at end of, iii. 380.
— — — St. Margaret's Hill, Southwark, iii. 255, n. 5; town-hall on, iv. 276, n. 4.
— — — St. Martin in the Fields: parish: division of, 1685, iv. 294, n. 2; proposed division of, 1691, v. 62 & n. 1; library: Tenison's project, iv. 367–8 & n., 369; ~ visit to, iv. 455; ~ mentioned, v. 66; school (Tenison's), iv. 368, n. 1, 584, n. 5 *ad fin.*; ~ master: sermon by (?), v. 139 & n. 5; ~ master, 1688, &c.: *see* Postlethwayt, J.
— — — St. Martin Orgar (French church): minister, 1686–9: *see* la Mothe, C.-G. de.
— — — St. Martin's Lane: improvement of south end of, iii. 319 & n. 3.
— — — St. Paul's Churchyard: booksellers in, iii. 459, n. 3; iv. 301 & n. 2; St. Paul's School in, v. 127, n. 4.
— — — St. Paul's Pier, (modern), iii. 452, n. 1.
— — — St. Paul's School, v. 127, n. 4; T. Gale at, v. 127, 220; high masters of: *see* Gale, T.; Postlethwayt, J.
— — — St. Thomas's Hospital, iii. 391, n. 4; ordered to reserve accommodation for Sick and Wounded, 1664, &c., iii. 391 &

LONDON (*cont.*)
nn. 4, 5; E invited to be a governor, iv. 560; president: *see* Adams, Sir T. (iii. 391 & nn. 4, 5).
— — — Salters' Hall: Reformation of Manners sermons for dissenters at, v. 391, n. 1.
— — — the Savoy: situation, iii. 264, n. 3; parochial arrangements, iii. 343, n. 1.
— — — — French (Conformist) church in (1661–1817), iii. 181, n. 4, 545 & nn. 3, 4; services, iii. 181 & n. 4(?), 202(?), 545, 556, 570 & n. 3(?); iv. 168(?), 531; recantation sermon in, v. 269; ministers: *see* Bréval, F. Durant de; la Mothe, C.–G. de.
— — — — Savoy Chapel, iii. 343, n. 1; situation of, iii. 410, n. 1; marriage in, iii. 343; services, iv. 306; v. 269, 292; ministers of: *see* Horneck, A.; Pratt, S.
— — — — Savoy Hospital, iii. 410, n. 1; Sick and Wounded at, iii. 409–10 & n., 448, 458; iv. 24, n. 5; needs reforming, iii. 447–8; preservation of, in Great Fire, iii. 456 & n. 1; i. *20*; in comparison, i. 31; master of, 1663–1700: *see* Killigrew, Henry, D.D.
— — — Savoy theatre (modern): site, iii. 264, n. 3.
— — — Seething Lane: Navy Office in, iii. 418, n. 2.
— — — Serjeants' Inn: sermon at, iii. 194 & n. 2.
— — — Seven Dials: building of, begins, v. 193 & n. 1.
— — — Sherwood (Sherard) Street: Foubert's academy in, iv. 257, n. 5.
— — — Shoe Lane: 'Paradise' (exhibition) in, iv. 24, n. 6.
— — — Smithfield: murderess burnt in, iii. 64 & n. 3; in Great Fire, iii. 455, 456.
— — — Society of Apothecaries: garden of, iii. 217, n. 1; iv. 462 & nn. 2–5.
— — — Soho: the Tabernacle by, v. 170 & n. 2.
— — — Soho Square: E lodges in, 1689–90, iv. 652 & n. 2.
— — — Somerset House: situation, iii. 234, n. 4, 410, n. 1; Ireton's funeral starts from, iii. 57;

LONDON (*cont.*)
Cromwell's funeral starts from, iii. 224; Henrietta Maria at, iii. 334, n. 3; after Henrietta Maria's retirement to France, iii. 519, n. 5; granted to Queen Catherine, iv. 90, n. 4; Queen Catherine's council meets at, iv. 90, 93, 101; Roman Catholics ordered to leave, 1678, iv. 159, n. 2; Queen Catherine goes to reside in, 1685, iv. 433 & n. 4; Royal Society moves to, 1779, iii. 433, n. 3; chapel: occupied by French church, 1653–60, iii. 181, n. 4; ~ services in (?; in text as Savoy), iii. 181 & n. 4, 202; ~ Roman Catholic Easter ceremonies in, iii. 612.
— — — — residents in, &c.: countess of Arlington, iv. 498, 531, 565; the younger Clarendon, 1681, iv. 259 & n. 5; countess of Devonshire, iv. 498, n. 2; Sir Charles Tuke baptized in, iii. 585; Sir Samuel Tuke, iii. 519, n. 5 *ad fin.*; E and Mrs. Evelyn at, iii. 519.
— — — — keeper of, 1679– : *see* Hyde, Henry, earl of Clarendon (iv. 259, n. 5).
— — — Southampton House (later Bedford House): notice, iii. 398 & n. 3; descent of, iii. 551, n. 4; visit to, iii. 376 & n. 3; in comparison, iv. 345, n. 1; chapel of: marriage in, iii. 551.
— — — Southampton House, old, in Bloomsbury, iii. 376, n. 3.
— — — Southampton Row: limit of Southampton's property, iii. 398, n. 2.
— — — Southampton Square: *see* Bloomsbury Square *above*.
— — — Southwark [particular places in Southwark are entered separately under their own names]: mob from: attacks Lambeth Palace, 1640, ii. 25 & n. 1 (i. 18); Charles II enters, 29 May 1660, iii. 246, n. 2; fire in, 1689, iv. 649; parliamentary election in, 1701, v. 442, n. 1; Southwark Fair: notice, 1660, iii. 255–6 & nn.; ~ shortened for misconduct, 1692, v. 115–16 & n.; town-hall, iv. 276, n. 4; meeting-place of Surrey and

LONDON (*cont.*)
Kent Commission of Sewers, iii. 151, n. 6; iv. 25; assize in, iv. 276 & n. 4; Lord Hawley's quarters in, iii. 343–4; St. George's Fields near, iii. 457, n. 1.
— — — Southwark Bridge (modern), iii. 451, nn. 2, 3.
— — — Spitalfields: old Artillery Ground in, ii. 360, n. 6.
— — — Spring Garden, Charing Cross, ii. 556, n. 4; closed by authorities: 1650, iii. 83, n. 1; ~ 1654, iii. 97 & n. 1; entertainments in, ii. 556; iii. 83, 213 & n. 4; mentioned, iii. 291, n. 2.
— — — Spring Garden, the new: *see* London, environs: Lambeth *below*.
— — — Stationers' Hall, iii. 459, n. 3.
— — — Stoll Picture Theatre (modern): site, iii. 268, n. 6.
— — — the Strand: Charles II's procession in, 29 May 1660, iii. 246; access to, from St. Martin's Lane: improvement of, iii. 319 & n. 3; White Hart in: Anglican divines, &c., in custody at, 1657, iii. 204, n. 6 *ad fin.*
— — — Stratton Street (formerly Stretton Street): construction of, iii. 436, n. 6; iv. 382, n. 1.
— — — Suffolk House: *see* Northumberland House *above*.
— — — Suffolk Place, Southwark: Southwark Fair moved to, 1743, iii. 255, n. 5.
— — — Suffolk Street, iii. 561 & n. 1; Cock tavern in: dinner at, iii. 599 & n. 7.
— — — Surrey Street: site, iii. 234, n. 4; iv. 395, n. 5 *ad fin.*; William Draper resident in, 1696, v. 219, n. 6.
— — — Swallow Street (modern): Henry Foubert's riding-school in, iv. 257, n. 5.
— — — Tabard Street, formerly Kent Street, iii. 417, n. 7.
— — — tabernacles: *see* churches *above*.
— — — taverns, &c.: Belle Savage, Ludgate, iv. 390, n. 1; Cock, Suffolk Street, iii. 599 & n. 7; Crown, Threadneedle Street, iv. 125, n. 4; *add.* (iv. 324); Devil (Apollo or

LONDON (*cont.*)
Dunstan), Fleet Street, v. 5 & n. 1; Globe, Fleet Street, iv. 401, n. 1; Nag's Head, Cheapside, iii. 259, n. 4; Pontack's, v. 160 & n. 4; Red Lion Inn, Holborn, iii. 269, n. 2; Rhenish Wine-house, Canon Row, iii. 447 & n. 2; White Hart, Strand, iii. 204, n. 6 *ad fin.*

— — — Temple: disturbance outside, 1649, ii. 556 & n. 1; in Great Fire, iii. 456 *bis* & nn. 1, 4; gates closed for plot, 1697, v. 273; as terminal of projected quay, iii. 476 & n. 3; W. Ball's rooms in, iii. 286, n. 1; Temple Church: monuments of Knights Templars in, iii. 68 & n. 1; ~ J. Barton buried in, iii. 85, n. 2; ~ Godolphin married in, iv. 63; ~ services, ii. 78 *bis*; iii. 237, 249, 261; iv. 380–1; v. 220–58, 268–81, 288–92 *passim & singulatim*; Masters of the Temple: *see* Ball, Richard (1661–84); Sherlock, W. (1684–1705); lecturer: *see* Buck, J.

— — — Temple Bar: Lord Mayor meets processions at, &c., iii. 281 & n. 1; iv. 413; v. 578; James II proclaimed at, iv. 413; heads and quarters of traitors set up on, 1696, &c., v. 235 & n. 3; pillory at, iv. 440, n. 4 *ad fin.*

— — — Temple Stairs, iv. 362, n. 1.

— — — Thames [at London]: in comparison with Seine at Paris, i. 68; iii. 637 (extract from *State of France*); proposed quay on left bank, iii. 476 & n. 3, 477; i. *20*; water-supply from, iv. 313, n. 1; Sir L. Dyve escapes by, 1649, iii. 40 & n. 1; lord mayor's procession on, 1661, iii. 301 & n. 4; Queen Catherine comes to Whitehall by, 1662, iii. 333 & n. 2; in Great Fire, iii. 451, 453; fireworks on, 1684, iv. 395 (*see also* iv. 591, fireworks, 1688, where place is not stated, but is the Thames); James II's great seal in, iv. 616, n. 1.

— — — — weather: frozen over: Jan. 1649, ii. 547 & n. 5; ~ Jan. 1658, iii. 206 & n. 1; ~ Dec. 1662, iii. 347 & n. 2; ~ Dec. 1676, iv. 103, n. 3; ~ Dec. 1683–Feb. 1684, with frost-fair, iv. 357 & n. 3, 359–66 & nn., *passim* (especially p. 362, n. 1); ~ Jan. 1685, iv. 402 & n. 1; ~ Jan. 1689, iv. 613 & n. 3; ~ Jan. 1692, v. 85, n. 2; ~ Jan. 1695, v. 201; extraordinary low water in, 1687, iv. 549; effects of storm on, 1689(?), iv. 644 & n. 3; fog on: 1670, iii. 565; ~ 1699, v. 363.

— — — — *see also* Horse Ferry *and* London Bridge *above.*

— — — Thames Street: in Great Fire, iii. 451 & n. 3, 456, n. 7.

— — — theatres [unspecified theatres are not entered here; performances by the Duke's and King's Companies are assumed to have been given at their theatres; performances at Whitehall are indexed under Whitehall; theatres later than E's time are indexed under their own names]:

— — — — Cock-pit or Phoenix, Drury Lane, ii. 539, n. 5; performance at, 1648, ii. 539 & n. 5; Davenant's opera at, 1659, iii. 229, n. 2.

— — — — Duke's (Duke's or Davenant's Company): at Lisle's tennis-court near Lincoln's Inn Fields (1661–71), iii. 303, n. 4; ~ performances at, iii. 303 & n. 4, 304 & n. 6, 309 & n. 1, 350 & n. 3, 371 & n. 5, 405 & n. 2; in Dorset Garden (1671–82), iii. 583, n. 3; ~ stage machinery at (?), iii. 583 & n. 3; ~ performances at, iv. 269, n. 2.

— — — — Gibbon's tennis-court: *see next entry.*

— — — — King's or Theatre Royal (King's or Killigrew's Company): at Gibbon's tennis-court, Vere Street (1660–3), iii. 268 & n. 6; ~ performances at, iii. 268 & n. 5, 345 & n. 3; in Bridges Street (1663–72), iii. 368, n. 6; ~ performances at, iii. 368–9 & n., 477 & n. 4, 510 & n. 8, 520 & n. 2, 524 & n. 2, 569–70 & nn., 599 & n. 1; ~ scenery for, iii. 570, n. 2 (*see also* n. 1); in Drury Lane (1674–82): performance at, iv. 30 & n. 1(?).

LONDON (*cont.*)
— — — — Lisle's tennis-court: *see* Duke's theatre *above*.
— — — — Phoenix: *see* Cock-pit *above*.
— — — — Theatre Royal, Drury Lane: performance at, 1694, v. 164, n. 5; *see also* King's theatre *above*.
— — — Threadneedle Street: Crown tavern in: fellows of Royal Society dine at, iv. 125, n. 4; *add* (iv. 324); French church in, iii. 160, n. 3; ~ service (?), iii. 160; ~ G. Tuke married at, iii. 181, n. 6; ~ ministers: *see* Cisner, C.; Hérault, L.; Stouppe, J. B.
— — — Three Cranes: in Great Fire, iii. 451 & n. 3.
— — — the Tower:
— — — — chronological series: project for delivering it to Charles II, Dec. 1659, iii. 237–8 & n.; *see also* iii. 240; Charles II goes to, for procession, 22 Apr. 1661, iii. 278 & n. 4; *see also* iii. 276–7, &c.; encounter of French and Spanish ambassadors near, 1661, iii. 297–8 & n.; during Great Fire: demolitions near, &c., iii. 455, n. 3, 456 & n. 3, 458 & n. 4; Charles II and James, duke of York, at, 1683, iv. 326.
— — — — Royal Mint in: committee (or commission) for Mint meets at, 1663–4, iii. 361, 370; assay of a metal at, iv. 138 & n. 1; for further notices relating to the Mint *see* Royal Mint.
— — — — Ordnance Office in: commissioners for Saltpetre meet at, 1666, iii. 443–6 *passim*; for the officers of the Ordnance *see* England: Ordnance.
— — — — buildings and contents: compared with Bastille, i. 67; as terminal for projected quay, iii. 476 & n. 3; chapel: service in, iii. 240; crown jewels in: T. Blood attempts to steal, iii. 576 & n. 2; the graft, iii. 458; gunpowder magazine in, in Great Fire, iii. 458 & n. 4; guns in (show-pieces), ii. 84 & n. 3 (i. 57); ~ for the Tower guns *see* Tower Wharf *below*; menagerie in, i. 69; ii. 195 & n. 7 (i. 121); ~ lions sent to, 1682, iv. 266, n. 3; plate in, 1649, iii. 148, n. 4; White Tower, iii. 458; wharfs near, iii. 476, n. 3; P. Yvelin visits, iii. 548.
— — — — prisoners in: (1) groups: some of the Regicides, Jan. 1662, iii. 312 & n. 1; the Roman Catholic peers, 1678–84 (Henry Arundell, Baron Arundell of Wardour; John Belasyse, Baron Belasyse; William Petre, Baron Petre; William Herbert, earl of Powis; and William Howard, Viscount Stafford): sent to the Tower, iv. 158 & n. 7; ~ in danger of trial, iv. 174; ~ committee of house of commons to consider evidence against, iv. 227, n. 3; ~ why Stafford was selected for trial, iv. 225, n. 3; ~ release of survivors, iv. 366 & n. 4; ~ proceedings against, annulled, iv. 445 & n. 2; for Rye-House Plot, 1683, iv. 322–3 & nn.; ~ *see further individual names below*; the Seven Bishops, 1688 (not entered separately here), iv. 586–8 & nn., *passim*; Jacobite plotters, &c.: June, 1689, iv. 643 & n. 3; ~ June, 1690, v. 27 & n. 1, 29; ~ Jan. 1691, v. 41; members of parliament accused of corruption, 1695, v. 207, n. 7 *ad fin*.
— — — — — (2) individuals: James Douglas, earl of Arran (later duke of Hamilton, &c.), 1689, iv. 640 & n. 4; Lord Arundell of Wardour: *see* groups *above*; *also* iv. 404 & n. 5; Lord Belasyse: *see* groups *above*; T. Blood, &c., 1671, iii. 576, n. 2; C. Caesar, 1705, v. 619 & n. 1; Roger Palmer, earl of Castlemaine, 1678–80, iv. 158, n. 7 *ad fin.*; Philip Stanhope, earl of Chesterfield, 1658, iii. 219, n. 4; Donogh Maccarty, earl of Clancarty, 1690–4, v. 38, n. 1; Clarendon: imprisonment in, proposed, 1667, iii. 502; Henry Hyde, second earl of Clarendon: 1690, v. 27 & n. 1, 29 & n. 2, 32 & n. 2; ~ 1691, v. 41 & n. 2, 42 & n. 3, 43–4, 45 & n. 1, 57, 60 & n. 5; Danby (Sir T. Osborne, later

LONDON (*cont.*)
duke of Leeds), 1679–84, iv. 354 & n. 4, 366; Sir A. Deane, 1679, iv. 270, n. 5; Sir Charles Duncombe, 1698, v. 284 & n. 4, 285 & n. 5; Arthur Capel, earl of Essex, 1683, iv. 322 & n. 3; ~ suicide of, in, iv. 326 & n. 4, 367 & n. 1; Sir J. Fagg, 1675, iv. 65, n. 1; Sir J. Glanville (the Speaker), *c.* 1645, iii. 111, n. 7; John Hampden, jnr., 1683, iv. 322 & n. 6, 354 & n. 2; Monmouth, 1685, iv. 455 & n. 2; John Mordaunt (later Viscount Mordaunt), 1658, iii. 214; H. Oldenburg, 1667, iii. 491 & n. 2; Col. John Parker: escapes from, 1694, v. 188 & n. 5; William Penn, 1668–9, iii. 521, n. 1; Pepys, 1679, iv. 169 & n. 1, 270, n. 5; Henry Mordaunt, earl of Peterborough, 1688–90, iv. 640 & n. 4; Lord Petre: *see* groups *above*; earl of Powis: *see* groups *above*; Sir Richard Graham, Viscount Preston, 1689, iv. 640 & n. 4; ~ 1691, v. 41, 57 & n. 2; Lord Russell, 1683, iv. 322 & n. 2; Algernon Sidney, 1683, iv. 322 & n. 4; William Howard, Viscount Stafford: *see* groups *above*; Arthur Herbert, earl of Torrington, 1690, v. 29 & n. 3; Sir John Trenchard, 1683, iv. 322 & n. 5, 354 & n. 1; Matthew Wren, bishop of Ely, 1642–60, iii. 186 & n. 4, 271, n. 1.

— — — — officers: general: at ambassadors' encounter, 1661, iii. 299; constables: *see* Compton, James, earl of Northampton (1675–); Alington, W., Baron Alington (1679–85); Lucas, Robert, third Baron Lucas of Shenfield (1689–1702); Bertie, Montagu, second earl of Abingdon (1702–5); Capel, Algernon, earl of Essex (1705–10); deputy-constable, 1675–9: *see* Robinson, Sir John; governor, Jan. 1660: *see* Morley, Herbert; lieutenant: fees due to, from prisoners, iv. 588; individual lieutenants: *see* Morley, Herbert (1660); Robinson, Sir John (1660–79); Cheke, T. (1679–87); Hales, Sir Edward (1687–8); Churchill, Gen. Charles (1702–6).

— — — Tower Hill: Trinity House on (1795), iii. 313, n. 6 *ad fin.*; executions on: Sir John Fenwick, 1697, v. 264; Monmouth, 1685, iv. 456; Algernon Sidney, 1683, iv. 352–3; William Howard, Viscount Stafford, 1680, iv. 236; Strafford, 1641, ii. 28 (i. 20).

— — — Tower Street: in Great Fire, iii. 451, 452, n. 1.

— — — Tower Wharf: E embarks at, 1643, ii. 82 (i. 56); the Seven Bishops at, iv. 586; guns on, *add.* (iii. 480); salutes fired by, iii. 480, 515; iv. 587; v. 28, n. 2, 273, 518 & n. 1; not fired on James II's birthday, 1688, iv. 601.

— — — Trafalgar Square (modern): site, iii. 487, n. 8 *ad fin.*

— — — Treasury Building, Horse Guards' Parade (modern): site, iii. 315, n. 4.

— — — Trinity Almshouses, Mile End Road, iii. 577, n. 6.

— — — Trinity House, Water Lane [the London building; for general activities of the corporation *see* Trinity House], iii. 313, n. 6; rebuilt after Great Fire, iv. 64, n. 6; feasts at: on Trinity Monday, iii. 408; iv. 64, 91, 248, 380, 459–60; ~ on other days, iii. 313–14 & n., 405; iv. 6, 264, 496.

— — — Tyburn river (at Piccadilly): limit of Clarendon's property, iii. 379, n. 8.

— — — Vere Street, Lincoln's Inn Fields: theatre in: *see* theatres *above*.

— — — Villiers Street: site, iii. 162, n. 1; E takes house in, 1683, iv. 350 & n. 1; concert-room in York Buildings in, 1698, v. 289, n. 1.

— — — Wallace Collection (modern): picture in, ii. 548, n. 5.

— — — Wallingford House, iii. 490, n. 2; Cowley lies in state at, iii. 490 & n. 2; residence of Clifford and Danby as Lord Treasurers, iv. 18 & n. 2; divine service at, iv. 71.

LONDON (*cont.*)
— — — Warwick Lane: in Great Fire, iii. 454; Royal College of Physicians in, iii. 337, n. 3; iv. 307, nn. 3, 5.
— — — Water Lane: Trinity House in, iii. 313, n. 6 *ad fin.*; iv. 64, n. 6.
— — — Waterloo Place (modern): boundary of royal garden, iii. 573, n. 3.
— — — Water Street: site, iii. 234, n. 4.
— — — Watling Street: in Great Fire, iii. 454.
— — — Weld House: *see* Wild House.
— — — Westminster:
— — — — the city of Westminster: high bailiff of, and Charles II's coronation procession, iii. 281 & n. 1; Roman Catholics ordered to leave, iv. 159, n. 2; bonfires in, for James II's birthday, iv. 526; election for parliament, 1701, v. 442, n. 1; deputy high steward of, 1705: *see* Bonython, C.; Treaty of, 1674: *see* Wars: Third Dutch War.
— — — — topographical [the neighbourhood of the Abbey and Palace, including the latter]: as synonym for parliament, iii. 540; manor of Ebury in: heiress of, iv. 86, n. 3; ~ Edward Fenwick claims, v. 528 & n. 8; Sir John Evelyns at, ii. 553; Rev. T. Thurscross at, iii. 204, n. 6 *ad fin.*, 237, n. 7.
— — — — — places: Dean's Yard: W. Samwell resident in, iii. 554, n. 3; Gate House: prisoners in: Pepys, v. 27; ~ Richard Power, earl of Tyrone, *add.* (iv. 366, n. 4); Medical Garden, iii. 217 & n. 1; Westminster Abbey: *see* churches *above*; Westminster Palace: *see below*; Westminster School: election of scholars to universities from, iii. 287–8 & n.; ~ Arlington educated at, iv. 119 & n. 3; ~ statues in garden of, iv. 534, n. 1; ~ master of, 1640–95: *see* Busby, R.
— — — — — Westminster Palace [topographical notices only; notices relating to parliamentary and legal activities, if no locality is given, are entered under Parliament, &c.]: Lord Mayor of London: sworn in at, iii. 259, n. 4; ~ water-procession to, iii. 301 & n. 4; ceremonies in, at coronation of Charles II, iii. 281 & nn. 2, 3.

LONDON (*cont.*)
— — — — — — rooms and places in: Court of Requests, iii. 435, n. 5; iv. 443; Court of Wards, iii. 435, n. 5; ~ Mint Commission, 1666, meets in, iii. 435, 444 & n. 5(?); Exchequer Chamber: commons feast in, 1689, iv. 633; house of lords: the king prorogues parliament in, iii. 402 & n. 3; ~ council of peers meets in, Dec. 1688, iv. 611 & n. 3; ~ lobby behind (Prince's Chamber?), ii. 28 & n. 4; iii. 402 & n. 1; iv. 619; New Palace Yard: disturbance in, 1648, ii. 541 & n. 2; ~ Solemn League and Covenant burnt in, iii. 289, n. 1; ~ buildings, &c., adjoining, iii. 284, n. 3, 444, n. 3, 447, n. 2; iv. 360, n. 1; ~ *see also* Palace Yard *below*; Painted Chamber: Hugh Peters in, 1649, ii. 547 & n. 1; ~ creation of Knights of the Bath in, 1661, iii. 276; ~ conference between the two houses of parliament in, 1675, iv. 65; ~ Charles II lies in state in, 1685, iv. 415, n. 3; Palace Yard: executions in, 1649, ii. 552 & n. 1; ~ pillory in, iv. 440, n. 4 *ad fin.*; ~ *see also* New Palace Yard *above*; Parliament Stairs, iii. 281, n. 3; Prince's Chamber, ii. 28, n. 4; iii. 402, n. 1; Princes Lodging, iii. 281, n. 3; iv. 619; Star Chamber, iii. 444, n. 3; ~ Commissioners for Sick and Wounded meet at, iii. 444–50 *passim*, 462–95 *passim*, 612–13 & n.; Westminster Hall: *see below*; Westminster Stairs, iii. 284 & n. 3; iv. 360, 588, n. 1.
— — — — — Westminster Hall: situation, iii. 435, n. 5; in comparisons, ii. 41 & n. 5 (i. 30), 98 & n. 4; i. 65; pillory outside, iv. 440, n. 4; coronation ceremonies in: Charles II, iii. 281,

LONDON (*cont.*)
n. 3, 284, n. 3; ~ James II, iv. 441, n. 3; ~ William and Mary, iv. 632–3; trials in (impeachments, &c.), &c.: Charles I, i. 22; ~ heads of Cromwell, &c., exposed on, iii. 269, n. 2; ~ Strafford's trial: seating, &c., for, ii. 27 & n. 3 (i. 20); iv. 226; ~ Stafford's trial: seating, &c., iv. 225, n. 3, 226–7 & nn.; ~ at time of trial of Titus Oates, iv. 438–9; *see also* iv. 440, n. 4; as seat of various courts of law: proceedings in, 1652, iii. 73; ~ Court of Chancery: trial in, iv. 546; ~ Court of Common Pleas, iv. 105–6; ~ Court of King's Bench: trials in, iv. 438–9 & n., 484, 587–8 & n.; ~ E takes test in, iv. 500; v. 212.

——— Whitechapel, iv. 306.

——— Whitehall: *see* Whitehall.

——— Wild House *or* Weld House, iv. 242, n. 6; as residence of Spanish ambassador, iv. 242 & n. 6; ~ burnt by the mob, 1688, iv. 610 & n. 2.

——— Winchester Street: *see* Great Winchester Street *above*.

——— Woolchurch: *see* churches: St. Mary Woolchurch Haw *above*.

——— Worcester House, iii. 264, n. 3; occupied by Clarendon, iii. 264, 379–80; site, v. 223, n. 1.

——— York Buildings, Villiers Street, iv. 350 & n. 1; E takes house in, *ib.*; concert-room in, 1698, v. 289, n. 1.

——— York House: notice, iii. 162 & n. 1; Russian ambassador at, 1662, iii. 349 & n. 2; French ambassador at: Easter display by, 1672, iii. 612; site, iv. 350, n. 1.

——— York Stairs: Pepys lives near, iv. 591, n. 2.

— environs [the area is based on the 'Circuit Walk' in Strype's Stow, but includes some places outside his limit (Hampstead, Hyde Park, Tyburn), and excludes some places in Essex within his limit; further, some names are non-parochial and appear in Strype only casually, if at all. In comparison with the County of London, it excludes most of the south-east. Deptford and Greenwich are entered separately on account of length]:

—— general: new buildings near: E and commissioners for, 1658–9, iii. 223 & n. 2, 224–5; ~ alluded to, iii. 227; roads near: number of travellers on (in comparison), ii. 324; refugees from Great Fire find shelter in, iii. 457 & nn. 1, 2, 461–2 & nn.; search to be made in, for fuel for London, 1667, iii. 486 & n. 1; mineral springs in: paper on, iv. 170 & n. 6.

—— Battersea: etched view of, by E, ii. 557, n. 3.

—— Belsize House, Hampstead, iv. 92 & n. 2.

—— Bermondsey: St. Saviour's Dock in: fire near, *add.* (v. 330, n. 1); Shad Thames congregation in, iv. 546, n. 6 *ad fin.*

—— Blackwall: East India ship at, iii. 313; Indian curiosities at, iv. 99; E's accident at, iv. 99, 101; v. 299, n. 1.

—— Brompton: Brompton Park (nursery garden), v. 176 & n. 3, 290, n. 6 *ad fin.*, 532, 606, n. 4; Brompton Road, v. 176, n. 3.

—— Camberwell: sepulchral urns found at, iv. 483; Camberwell Road, iii. 197, n. 2; church: services in, iv. 258, 438 & n. 1, 441, 507; ~ vicars: *see* Parr, R. (1653–91); Tipping, I. (1691–1728); ~ Parr's house at, iv. 507; Dulwich College in, iv. 74; ~ *see also* Dulwich *below*; Grammar School: master: *see* Bradford, J. (iii. 562 & n. 3); manor of, iv. 93, n. 2; residents: A. Bowyer (?), iv. 387 & n. 3; ~ Sir E. Bowyer: house of, at, iii. 197 & n. 2, 490; *see also* Dulwich *and* Peckham *below*.

—— Chelsea: Apothecaries' Garden, iv. 462 & nn. 3, 5; ~ plants for, iii. 217, n. 1.

——— Beaufort House, iv. 161, n. 3; as Lady Bristol's house: notice, 1679, iv. 161–2; ~ visits to, iv. 168, 180, 182; ~ projected sale or lease of, iv.

LONDON (*cont.*)
170, 185 & n. 2, 257–8, 335; Beaufort buys and alters, iv. 335 & n. 4.
— — — Beaufort Street (modern): site, iv. 161, n. 3 *ad fin.*
— — — Chelsea College [also called Chelsea House]: history of, to 1682, iii. 397, n. 2; Dutch prisoners of war at, 1665–7, iii. 397–8, 404, n. 4, 406, 496–7 & n.; given to Royal Society, 1667, iii. 496–7 & n., 527 & n. 2; leased for Dutch prisoners of war, 1672(?), iii. 497, n. 1; iv. 257, n. 3; negotiations for leases, 1679, 1681, iv. 257, n. 5 *ad fin.*, 264 & n. 2; negotiation for sale of, to Charles II for hospital, 1681, iv. 257 & n. 3; sold, iii. 497, n. 1; iv. 269 & n. 5; *see further* Chelsea Hospital *below*.
— — — Chelsea Hospital: for earlier history, &c., *see* Chelsea College *above*; foundation of: proposed, iv. 257; establishment for: planned, iv. 269–70 & n. ; *add.*; i. *34*; buildings: plans, &c., iv. 281 & n. 2; ~ foundations of, laid, iv. 289; ~ completed and occupied, v. 53 & n. 2; proposed library for, iv. 270; statue of Charles II at, iv. 317, n. 2; mentioned, ii. 45, n. 6.
— — — Chelsea House: *see* Chelsea College *above*; Little Chelsea, iii. 255, n. 3; Milman's Street (modern): site, iii. 315, n. 2; Oakley Street (modern): site, iv. 81, n. 5; palace of bishops of Winchester, iv. 81 & n. 5.
— — — residents, &c.: Robert Boyle, iii. 255 & n. 3, 272; Charles Cheyne, Lord Cheyne, v. 247; Dutch ambassadors, *c.* 1665, iii. 408 & n. 5; Sir Arthur Gorges, &c., iii. 315 & n. 2; children of John Mordaunt, Viscount Mordaunt, iv. 289, 335; Ormond, iii. 376 & n. 5.
— — Clapham, iv. 462; marriage licence for, iii. 560, n. 6 *ad fin.*; house of Sir Dennis Gauden, later of W. Hewer, at, iv. 176 & n. 1; ~ as Hewer's house: notice, 1692, v. 111; ~ Pepys and his collections at, v. 427–8 & n., 507, 508 & n. 3, 536, 538 & n. 2; Victoria Road (modern): site, iv. 176, n. 1.
— — Clerkenwell: Berkeley Street (modern): site, iv. 607, n. 4; Hicks Hall in, iv. 327 & n. 1; duke of Newcastle's house in, iii. 478 & n. 4; Newcastle Place (modern): site, iii. 478, n. 4; Roman Catholic nunnery (?) in, 1688, iv. 607 & n. 4; St. James's church (modern): site, iii. 478, n. 4; St. John's: earl of Berkeley's house in, iv. 607 & n. 4; ~ house of Robert Berkeley, later of Bishop Gilbert Burnet, in, iv. 363 & n. 4; St. John Street, iv. 327, n. 1; St. Mary's convent in: site, iii. 478, n. 4.
— — Deptford: *see* Deptford.
— — Dulwich: Dulwich College: notice, iv. 74 & n. 1; Dulwich Gallery (modern): pictures in, v. 145, n. 2; waters: *see* Sydenham Wells *below*.
— — Fulham, iv. 523; church: Lord Mordaunt's monument in, iv. 86 & n. 5; ~ Lady Mordaunt buried in, iv. 173, n. 3; ~ service, iii. 305; ~ rector, 1661–88: *see* Stradling, G.; Fulham Palace: notice, 1681, iv. 258 & n. 3; ~ consecration of bishops at, 1689, iv. 649, n. 1; ~ Bishop Henry Compton at, iv. 182, 289, 379; King's Road, iii. 271, n. 6; manor: ownership of, iv. 258, n. 3; *see also* Parson's Green *below*.
— — Greenwich: *see* Greenwich.
— — Hackney: gardens, &c., at: Lady Brooke, iii. 96 & n. 1, 169; ~ Mr. Tombs, iii. 96 & nn. 2, 3.
— — Hammersmith: gardens at, iv. 523; Sir S. Morland's house at, v. 221–2; Thames at: water from, *ib.*
— — Hampstead: in view from Bedford House, iii. 398, n. 3; Belsize Avenue (modern): site, iv. 92, n. 2; Belsize House, iv. 92 & n. 2.
— — Hide Park: *see* Hyde Park *below*.
— — Highgate: in view from Bedford House, iii. 398, n. 3;

LONDON (*cont.*)
refugees from Great Fire at, iii. 457, 461–2 & nn.
— — Hockley in the Hole: Bear Garden moved to, iii. 549, n. 4.
— — Hoxton: A. Woodhead resident at, iii. 182, n. 2.
— — Hyde Park, iii. 82, n. 6; Kensington Palace adjoining, v. 8; ~ road through, to, v. 8 & n. 2, 363 & n. 3; bucks in, iv. 388; charges for admission to, during Commonwealth, iii. 82–3 & n.; coach-race in, 1658, iii. 213; display of horsemanship in, by Moroccan ambassador, 1682, iv. 268–9 & n.; reviews in, iii. 357 & n. 2; iv. 504, 526; Charles II in, iii. 249, 285; promenade in, iv. 171; visits to, iii. 82–3, 175, 213, 447, 481; in comparisons, ii. 106, n. 4, 107 (i. 69), 433.
— — Isle of Dogs: ferry at, iii. 180, n. 4.
— — Islington: refugees from Great Fire at, iii. 461–2 & n.; legacy to poor of, v. 386; Sir Purbeck and Lady Temple buried at, v. 219, n. 1, 385, 386; Cross Street, iii. 96, n. 6; Islington Spa or Wells, iv. 515, n. 5; New River Head, iv. 515 & n. 4; New Tunbridge Wells, iv. 515, n. 5 *ad fin.*; Sadler's Wells, *ib.*; Spa Green (modern), *ib.*; Spa Wells, iv. 515 & n. 5; residents, &c.: Draper family: connexion with, v. 133, n. 2; Sir S. Duncombe: bear-garden, &c., of, at, ii. 14, n. 4; Sir T. Fowler: aviary of, at (?), iii. 96 & n. 6.
— — Kensington: visibility of Great Fire at, iii. 451, n. 4; Jane Evelyn buried at, *c.* 1692, v. 80, n. 1; Kensington Gardens (modern), v. 8, n. 2; Kensington House (?): notice, 1666, iii. 447 & n. 4; Kensington Palace: *see below*; Victoria and Albert Museum: site, v. 176, n. 3; ~ exhibit in, ii. 59, n. 1; West Kensington: St. Paul's School moved to (1880), v. 127, n. 4; West Town, iii. 255, n. 4; residents, &c.: T. Henshaw, iii. 255 & n. 4; iv. 76; ~ T. Tenison at, 1684, iv. 372; *see also* Brompton *above*.

LONDON (*cont.*)
— — — Kensington Palace, v. 8, n. 2; bought by William III, iii. 447, n. 4; v. 8 & n. 2; notices: 1666, iii. 447 & n. 4(?); ~ 1690, v. 8; ~ 1696, v. 237; ~ 1705, v. 606–7 & n.; fire at, 1691, v. 74 & n. 1; Orangery, v. 606, n. 3; road from, to Clarendon House, v. 8 & n. 2, 363 & n. 3; Queen Mary II at, 1692, v. 90, n. 2; William III at: in connexion with Assassination Plot, v. 231; ~ address presented to, 1697, v. 279 & n. 1; ~ model, &c., of Greenwich Hospital shown to, v. 399 & n. 2; ~ arrivals and departures, v. 34, n. 1, 41, n. 5 *ad fin.*, 91, n. 2, 118, n. 1, 135, n. 2, 136, n. 1, 156, n. 1, 177, n. 5, 238, n. 4, 294, n. 2, 304, n. 1, 327, n. 2, 361, n. 1; ~ dies at, v. 491; Queen Anne at, v. 517, n. 3.
— — Knightsbridge: house of Bishop Seth Ward at, iv. 33 & n. 2.
— — Lambeth: situation, iii. 457, n. 1; the horse-ferry to, iv. 360 & n. 4, 365; v. 536; duke of Buckingham's glass-house (factory) at, iv. 98–9 & n.; marble-warehouse at, iv. 98; yacht building at, 1662, iii. 327 & n. 5, 332–3; church: rector, 1675–1703: *see* Hooper, G.; Goding Street (modern), iii. 291, n. 2; Lambeth Bridge (modern), iv. 360, n. 4; Lambeth Palace: *see below*; Lambeth Stairs, iv. 360 & n. 4; St. Oswald's Place (modern), iii. 291, n. 2; new Spring Garden, iii. 291 & n. 2; Tradescant Road (modern), iii. 198, n. 4; Upper Kennington Lane, iii. 291, n. 2; Vauxhall Gardens (modern), iii. 291, n. 2; residents: E. Ashmole: house and collections of, iv. 138–9 & n., 454; Sir Robert and Lady Needham, iii. 198, 232, 264, 363; J. Tradescant: museum of, iii. 198–9 & nn.; iv. 139.
— — — Lambeth Palace: attacked by Southwark mob, 1640, ii. 25 & nn. 1, 3 (i. 18); ceremony at, of Sheldon's translation to Canterbury, iii. 361–3 & nn.; the Seven Bishops' petition

LONDON (*cont.*)
drawn up at, iv. 584, n. 1; discussion at, concerning settlement of the crown, 1689, iv. 613–15 & nn.; Sancroft confines himself to, Feb. 1689, &c., iv. 626; Sancroft leaves, v. 51–2 & n.; Tillotson given possession of, v. 59 & n. 2; consecration at, v. 508, n. 2; marriages at, v. 258, 609; house and garden, 1695, v. 213; chapel, iii. 361, n. 5, 362; v. 609; great hall, iii. 362 & n. 9; (old) library, iii. 527 & n. 1; iv. 560; ~ designer of, iii. 349, n. 3; present library, iii. 362, n. 9; E visits archbishops at: Juxon, iii. 273–4; Sheldon, iii. 419, 621; Sancroft, iv. 281, 360, 395, 488, 518, 560, 591, 633–4, 636–7; Tillotson, v. 80; Tenison, v. 213, 221, 224, 238, 239, 256–7, 280, 291, 293 *bis*, 294, 323, 353, 440, 507, 508 & n. 1, 536, 568, 597.

— — New Cross: *see* Deptford.

— — Newington: minister of: preaches at Deptford, v. 35 & n. 2; rector, 1689–95: *see* Bordley, S.

— — New River Head, iv. 515 & n. 4.

— — Parson's Green, Fulham: Viscount Mordaunt's house at, iii. 271, n. 6; ~ Mordaunt returns to, 1669, iii. 582, n. 3; ~ proposed sale of, iv. 202; ~ Charles Mordaunt, second Viscount Mordaunt (later earl of Peterborough), tries to buy, iv. 259; ~ visits to Lord or Lady Mordaunt at, iii. 271, 275, 305, 315, 355 & n. 3(?), 367, 375, 585; iv. 1, 9, 34, 55, 75, 80–1, 81, 85, 86, 94, 95, 103, 131, 154; ~ visits to Mordaunt's children, &c., at, iv. 173, 180, 258; ~ visits to, presumably to the Mordaunts, iii. 290, 447; iv. 182 [some other visits to the Mordaunts, if no other place is mentioned, probably took place here]; residents, &c., at: Sir John Clayton, iv. 96, n. 2; Rev. — Rowland, iii. 276; *see also* Fulham *above*.

— — Peckham: hamlet in Camberwell, iv. 438 & n. 1; Sir T. Bond's house at, iv. 93 & n. 2, 258.

— — Putney: girls' schools at, ii. 555 & n. 3; E draws views at, ii. 557 & n. 3; error for Puttenham (?), v. 199, n. 5; perpetual curate of: *see* Sclater, E.; Putney Park: *see* Roehampton House *below*.

— — Ratcliffe: explosion near the Hermitage at, iii. 195 & n. 2.

— — Rederith *or* Roderith: *see* Rotherhithe *below*.

— — Roehampton House, formerly Putney Park, iii. 329 & n. 3; notice, iv. 105 & n. 5.

— — Rotherhithe (Roderith, &c.): plague at, 1665–6, iii. 430, n. 1; St. Saviour's Dock in (error for Bermondsey): fire near, v. 330 & n. 1; *add.*; trader at (James Burton, *c.* 1666), iv. 352, n. 1; rector or minister of: sermons by, at Deptford, iv. 140, 153, 249, 250; rector of, 1675–81: *see* Stoodley, G.; curate(s) of: sermons by, at Deptford, iv. 168, 220; v. 117, 155, 167.

— — St. George's Fields: refugees from Great Fire in, iii. 457 & n. 1; Bethlehem Hospital moved to (1815), iv. 134, n. 1.

— — St. John's: *see* Clerkenwell *above*.

— — Sydenham Wells, iv. 74 & n. 2, 112 & n. 3.

— — Tyburn: gallows at: corpses of Cromwell, &c., exposed on, iii. 269 & n. 2; executions at: Sir T. Armstrong, iv. 382; J. Ashton, v. 42, n. 2; Sir J. Friend, i. 8 & n. 2; v. 236; Sir J. Johnston, v. 41 & n. 1; Sir W. Parkyns, i. 8 & n. 2; v. 236; T. Walcot, &c., iv. 332 & n. 4; unnamed, v. 186 & n. 4; pillory at, iv. 440, n. 4; as terminal for whippings, iv. 440, n. 4, 445, 451, n. 3.

— — Vauxhall: duke of Buckingham's glass-house at, iv. 98–9 & n.; Vauxhall Station (modern): site, iii. 291, n. 2.

— — Wapping: cargo landed at, ii. 469; explosion at, 1657, iii. 195 & n. 2; Lord Chancellor Jeffreys arrested at, iv. 611, n. 4; Execution Dock at: pirates executed at, 1696, v. 261, n. 5.

London diocese [for the deans and prebendaries of St. Paul's *see* London: topography: churches: St. Paul's Cathedral]:
bishop: *ex officio*: commissioner for repair of St. Paul's (1663–), iii. 448, n. 3; ~ palace of, at Fulham, iv. 258, n. 3; ~ chaplain of, as licenser of books, iii. 46; individual bishops: *see* Braybroke, R. de (1381–1404); King, John (1611–21); Montaigne *or* Mountain, G. (1621–8); Laud, W. (1628–33); Juxon, W. (1633–60); Sheldon, G. (1660–3); Henchman, H. (1663–75); Compton, Henry (1675–1713); Gibson, E. (1723–48).
archdeacon of London, 1689–91: *see* Tenison, T.
London, George, gardener: reports on damage done by Peter the Great at Sayes Court, v. 290 & n. 6; *see also* v. 176, n. 3.
Londonderry: reported capture of, by James II, iv. 637 & n. 2; reported relief of, iv. 643 & n. 4; Schomberg sets out to relieve, iv. 645 & n. 3, 647 & n. 1; relieved, iv. 647 & n. 2, 648 & n. 2; Dr. G. Walker as defender of, v. 28 & n. 3.
Londonderry: Bishops of: *see* Derry.
Long Ditton, Surrey: powder-mills at, i. *1*; E visits, ii. 78, 79, 81; the Evelyns and their relations at: Sir Edward Evelyn, iv. 434, n. 1; v. 100 & n. 2, 337 & n. 1; George Evelyn, sen.: estate of, at, i. 3; Thomas Evelyn, i. 2, n. 4, 3; Sir Thomas Evelyn, iv. 434, n. 1; Richard Hatton, i. 2, n. 4; Robert Hatton, ii. 78 & n. 1; David Vincent of Cleygate in, i. *1*.
Longford: Viscount, 1675–7, and Earl of, 1677–1700: *see* Aungier, Francis, Baron Aungier.
Longford Castle, Wilts.: painting at, iii. 155, n. 1.
Longhena, Baldassare: staircase designed by, ii. 461 & n. 7.
Longinus: relic of, ii. 290; statue of, &c., ii. 262.
Longobards: destroy Capua, ii. 324.
Longueil, René de: *see* Maisons, marquis of.
Longueville, Charles-Paris d'Orléans, duke of: visits English court, iii. 575 & nn. 3, 4.
Longueville, Henri II d'Orléans, duke of: imprisoned at Vincennes, iii. 1, n. 3.
Longworth, Berks.: epidemic at, v. 298 & n. 1.
Lonsdale: first Viscount, 1696–1700: *see* Lowther, Sir John, of Lowther.
Loo: William III, &c., at, 1699, v. 352, n. 5.
Loon, Anna van, wife of W. Nieupoort: social, iii. 229 & n. 3.
Loosduinen (Lysdune), near The Hague, ii. 55 & n. 3 (i. 38).
Lopez, Don Francisco de, son of marquis of Baides: captive in England, iii. 188–9 & nn.
Lopez de Zuñiga, Don Francisco, marquis of Baides and count of Pedroso: killed with his family, iii. 188–9 & nn.
Lorenzo de' Medici, the Magnificent: geneal., ii. 416, n. 4.
Loreto (Lauretto): E desires to visit, ii. 401; treasury of church at, ii. 412; ~ gold statue for, ii. 105–6 & n. (i. 68).
Lorne, Lord: *see* Campbell, Archibald, ninth earl of Argyll.
Lorraine, Duchy of: seized by France, 1670, iii. 587 & n. 4; treatment of, in Peace of Ryswick, v. 270 & n. 6.
Lorraine: Dukes of: *see* Charles IV, 1632–75 (iii. 67, n. 1); Charles V Leopold, 1675–90.
Lorraine, Charles de: *see* Guise, duke of.
Lorraine, Henri de: *see* Harcourt, comte d'.
Lorraine, Louis de: *see* Armagnac, count of.
Lorraine, Louis-Joseph de: *see* Guise, duke of.
Lort, Sir John, bt.: directs Christmas revels, Lincoln's Inn, 1661–2, iii. 308 & n. 1.
Los Charcas, district in South America, iii. 188–9 & n.
Lostwithiel, Cornwall: Sir Edward Brett knighted at, iii. 422, n. 4.
Lot: in comparison, iii. 457; in sermons, iv. 349; v. 251.
Lothian: Earl of, 1631–75: *see* Kerr, William.
Loton (Lotten), Rev. John, iii. 432, n. 2; sermons by, iii. 432, 468; iv. 310–11.

Lot's wife: in sermons, iv. 142, 176, 526.
Lotteries: Sir A. Slingsby's, iii. 375 & n. 6, 376 & n. 2; T. Neale as organizer of (Venetian style), v. 193 & n. 1; Neale's, 1693, v. 158 & n. 2; Million-pound lottery loan (Neale), 1694, v. 177 & n. 4; ~ alluded to, v. 169 & n. 4; ~ drawing of, v. 196 & n. 6; projected, 1695(?), v. 202 & n. 6; private: rise of, 1696, v. 246 & n. 3; suppressed, 1699, v. 325 & n. 6; for Greenwich Hospital, *ib.*; Royal Oak, v. 325, n. 6.
Loudun: Ursuline nuns at: alleged case of possession, &c., iii. 557–8 & n.
Lough Foyle: Col. P. Kirke in, iv. 643, n. 4.
Louis IX, St., king of France: builds Sainte-Chapelle, Paris, ii. 99 (i. 65); founds Quinze-Vingts, ii. 101, n. 4; regalia of, ii. 88 (i. 59–60); relics of, ii. 88 *bis* (i. 59 *bis*); ~ translation of, to St. Denis, ii. 90, n. 1.
Louis XI, king of France: cage for prisoners made for, ii. 154, n. 1; builds SS. Trinità de' Monti, Rome (error), ii. 373 & n. 2.
Louis XII, king of France: as duke of Orleans: imprisoned at Bourges, ii. 154 & n. 1 (i. 99); fountain built by, at Blois, ii. 141 & n. 8 (i. 92); picture of hart taken by, ii. 141 & n. 9 (i. 92); statue of, ii. 140–1 & n. (i. 92); tomb of, ii. 86 (i. 58).
Louis XIII, king of France: geneal., ii. 43, n. 5 *ad fin.*, 57 (i. 39), 91, n. 3; birth of: day of (error), v. 195–6 & n.; reconciliation of, with Marie de Médicis, ii. 146, n. 2; health of, i. 68; corpse of, at St. Denis, ii. 86 & n. 5 (i. 58); mourning worn for, ii. 98 (i. 64); crowns of, ii. 88 (i. 60); victories of: paintings of, ii. 151 & n. 2 (i. 98); buildings of: at Fontainebleau, ii. 117 (i. 76), 118 & n. 3 (i. 76); ~ parts of Louvre, ii. 103 & n. 1 (i. 67); Palais-Cardinal given to, ii. 133–4 & n. (i. 87); sends painting to Charles I, ii. 120, n. 3; statues of: in Place Royale, Paris, ii. 101 & n. 1 (i. 66); ~ at St. Cloud, ii. 108 (i. 70); gold statuette of (?), ii. 414 & n. 10.
Louis XIV, king of France [E scarcely distinguishes between Louis XIV and the French state in his notices relating to French foreign policy and to the French protestants; France and the king of France are almost synonymous in them. The notices indexed under the present heading are those in which Louis appears as a man and those relating to politics and religion in which his personality is concerned, and not merely his position as head of the state. All the notices relating to politics and religion are included in the more comprehensive entries under France, French protestants, Ireland, and Wars]:
— early life: birth: date of, ii. 91, n. 3; ~ thank-offering for, ii. 106 (i. 68); resides at Palais Royal (Palais-Cardinal), ii. 91 (i. 61), 134 (i. 87), 562, n. 2, 566.
— — 1643: receives ambassador, ii. 91 (i. 61); visits Notre Dame, ii. 96 (i. 63).
— — 1644: attends review, ii. 135 & n. 1 (i. 88).
— — 1649: gives audience to Sir R. Browne, ii. 566; watches bull-baiting, ii. 567.
— — 1650: returns to Paris from Bordeaux, iii. 23 & n. 1.
— — 1651: dances in court ballet, iii. 31–2 *bis*; instruction of, in fortification: model fort for, iii. 44; boats for, *ib.*; majority of: procession, &c., for, iii. 41–3 & nn.; appearance of, iii. 42–3; gives audience to Sir R. Browne, &c., iii. 43–4 & nn.
— — 1652: re-enters Paris (Oct.), iii. 77, n. 1.
— — 1658: enters Dunkirk, iii. 217, n. 3.
— character: account of, given to E, iv. 518; E's hatred of, i. 67, n. 1, 68, n. 2; ambition, v. 130; ~ alluded to, v. 277; ~ aims at universal monarchy, iv. 331, 380; corruption: uses, to obtain conquests, v. 104; cruelty of: initiates bombardment of towns from sea, v. 216; tyranny of: called the French tyrant, &c., iv. 484, 486, 493, 574; v. 559; untrustworthy, v. 545.

Louis XIV (*cont.*)
— culture and patronage: buildings of, at Louvre, ii. 103 & n. 1 (i. 67), 104, n. 2; palaces of: represented on tapestries, iv. 343 & n. 2; court ballets of, iii. 350, n. 2; ~ *Les festes de Bacchus*, iii. 31–2 *bis* & nn.; paintings: one given to, by Venice, ii. 442, n. 5; ~ orders alteration of one, ii. 120, n. 3; burning-glass of, v. 592; as patron of Sir J. Chardin, iv. 213; knights R. Nanteuil (error), iii. 9–10 & n.
— foreign policy and general activities as head of the state: relations with Charles II, i. *27*, *28*, *30*; establishes precedence of French before Spanish ambassadors, iii. 297, n. 4 *ad fin.*; *add.*; health drunk at Lord Mayor's banquet, 1664, iii. 389; instigates second Dutch War, iii. 405 & n. 1; offers to mediate between Spain and Portugal, 1666, iii. 434 & n. 1; gift to French prisoners of war, iii. 468; and Secret Treaty of Dover, iii. 548, n. 1, 559, n. 4; at Dunkirk, 1671, iii. 575 & n. 1; attempt to establish a universal monarchy, 1683, iv. 331 & n. 4; ~ alluded to, iv. 380; hold over Charles II: alluded to, iv. 331 & n. 5, 340; visits Luxemburg, 1687, iv. 549, n. 1; and James II's expedition to Ireland, iv. 629, 635 & n. 1; celebrates supposed death, &c., of William III, v. 32; 'insolent progress' of, 1690, v. 37; promises safe-conducts for English witnesses of Queen Mary of Modena's delivery, 1692, v. 96; initiates bombardment of towns from sea, v. 216; participation in Assassination Plot: animosity aroused by, v. 233; and duke of Savoy: offers peace to, 1696, v. 247; ~ marriage connexion with, v. 260 & n. 3; sends memorial to Charles II of Spain, 1699, v. 316 & n. 3; conduct of, while negotiating Partition treaties, v. 436 & n. 2, 445; acceptance by, of Charles II's will, v. 445, n. 5; claims guardianship of Philip V of Spain, v. 453; recognizes James Edward as king of Great Britain, v. 476 & nn. 3, 4; ~ effect of, in England, v. 480–1 & n.; prohibits English imports, 1701, v. 477 & n. 1; letter of defiance to duke of Savoy, 1703, v. 548, n. 1.
— geneal., iii. 412, n. 4; iv. 184, n. 5; v. 260, n. 3, 434 & n. 2.
— health: recovers from fistula, 1687, iv. 533 & n. 6; ill and reported dead, 1696, v. 258 & n. 3, 259; supposed ill, 1697, v. 270 & n. 4.
— personal relations: with Dauphin, iv. 518 & n. 1; v. 270 & n. 4; E pays court to, &c., ii. 562 & n. 2, 566; with Mme de Maintenon, v. 270 & n. 4; Philip V: form used by, to address Louis, v. 439 & n. 2; duchess of Portsmouth: gift to (?), iv. 343 & n. 2; Russian ambassador: intervenes to defend son of, iv. 263.
— religion: orders baptism of negroes in French West Indies, iv. 471, n. 3; reported excommunication of, iv. 641; *add.*; instigates duke of Savoy to persecute Waldenses, iv. 511 *bis* & n. 2; *see also* iv. 515, 636; v. 3, 25; and French protestants: supports attack on, iv. 447, n. 3; revokes Edict of Nantes, iv. 484 & n. 4; praised by bishop of Valence, iv. 486 & n. 3; as persecutor, iv. 493, 510; v. 403; ignorant of cruelties of persecution, iv. 518; changes method of persecuting, iv. 574; perfidy towards, v. 545.
— miscellaneous: prophecies applicable to, v. 26, 227.
Louis XVI: arrest of, at Varennes-en-Argonne, ii. 155, n. 1.
Louis XVIII: parts of Louvre built by, ii. 103, n. 1.
Louis, son of Dagobert, king of France: tomb of, ii. 86 & n. 3 (i. 58).
Louis de France, 1661–1711, Dauphin: character, &c., iv. 518 & n. 1; v. 270 & n. 4; award to, in second Partition Treaty (1700), v. 434, n. 4; geneal., v. 434, n. 2.

Louis de France, 1682–1712; duke of Burgundy 1682–1711; Dauphin 1711–12, v. 260, n. 3; as duke: marriage of, v. 260 & n. 3, 270 & n. 3.
Louisa Hollandina, Princess Palatine, abbess of Maubuisson: paintings, &c., by, i. 26 & nn. 2, 3; *see also* ii. 34 & n. 1.
Louisa Maria, 1692–1712, daughter of James II: expected birth of, &c., v. 96 & n. 1; heart of: deposited at Chaillot, ii. 91, n. 1; *add.*
Louise Henriette of Nassau, later electress of Brandenburg: meets Marie de Médicis, ii. 57 & n. 5 (i. 39).
Loumas (Lambesc), Provence, ii. 162 & nn. 8, 9 (i. 103).
Loup, — de, innkeeper at Roanne (?), ii. 533 & n. 3.
Louviers: case of possession at, iii. 547, n. 3.
Lovato: epitaph of Antenor by, ii. 454, n. 3.
Love, Captain —: concerned in duel, 1685, iv. 453.
Love, Anne: *see* Tenison, Mrs. A.
Love, Richard, dean of Ely: geneal., v. 239, n. 2.
Lovelace, John, third Baron Lovelace, v. 89, n. 1; as adherent of William of Orange: arrested, iv. 607, n. 1; chaplain of: sermon by, v. 89.
Lovelace: third Baron, 1670–93: *see* Lovelace, John.
Lovestine: *see* Loevestein.
Lowe, Anne: *see* Lee, Anne, Lady Lee.
Lowe, Jane: *see* Garrard, Jane, Lady Garrard.
Lowe, Mary: *see* Offley, Mary, Lady Offley.
Lowe, Sir Thomas: geneal., ii. 537, n. 2, 542, n. 2, 553, n. 3.
Lower, Richard, M.D.: on treatment of Charles II, 1685, v. 197–8 & n.
Lower Hope Reach (in the Thames): Dutch fleet in, 1667, iii. 484, n. 1.
Lowestoft, Suffolk: battle off, 1665: fleets engaged, iii. 409 & n. 3; notice, iii. 410 & n. 3; audible in London, iii. 84, n. 5 *ad fin.*; account of, in E's 'History of the Dutch War', iii. 411; James, duke of York, in, iii. 412, 414, n. 1; iv. 12 & n. 1; C. Evertsen in, iii. 407, n. 2; other officers, &c., in, iii. 182, n. 3, 413 & n. 4, 414 & nn. 3–5; ships taken in, iii. 414 & n. 9.
Lowitz, Poland: conference at, 1698, v. 285, n. 1.
Lowman, John (Mr. Lo), keeper of the Marshalsea, iii. 420 & n. 5.
Lowndes, William, secretary of the Treasury: at meeting of Commissioners for Greenwich Hospital, v. 210 & n. 5.
Lowther, Sir John, bt., of Lowther; first Viscount Lonsdale 1696, iv. 124, n. 8; social (?), iv. 124, 273 & n. 4.
Lowther, Sir John, bt., of Whitehaven, iv. 124, n. 8; social (?), iv. 124, 273 & n. 4.
Loylie, Sir Francis: *see* Lawley (iv. 592).
Loyola, St. Ignatius: tomb of, ii. 230.
Lübeck: Thomas Baltzar born at, iii. 167, n. 3.
Lubicer: *see* Baltzar, T.
Lucan: Earl of, 1691–3 (Jacobite creation): *see* Sarsfield, Patrick.
Lucar, Cyril: *see* Lukaris, K.
Lucas, Rev. Anthony, iv. 557 & n. 2; sermons by, iv. 557–9 *passim*; v. 207 & n. 6.
Lucas, Sir Charles: execution of, iii. 58 & n. 1, 177 & n. 2; geneal., iii. 478, n. 3.
Lucas, John, first Baron Lucas of Shenfield, iii. 480, n. 7; geneal., iii. 372, n. 1, 480.
Lucas, Margaret: *see* Cavendish, Margaret, duchess of Newcastle.
Lucas, Mary: *see* Grey, Mary, countess of Kent.
Lucas, Robert, third Baron Lucas of Shenfield, v. 7, n. 4; as constable of the Tower, v. 7 & n. 4; ~ letter to, v. 45 & n. 1.
Lucas, Sir Thomas, of St. John's: geneal., iii. 478, n. 3.
Lucas van Leyden, ii. 114, n. 1; painting by, ii. 114 (i. 73); prints by, ii. 133 (i. 86).
Lucas of Crudwell: Baroness: *see* Grey, Mary, countess of Kent.
Lucas of Shenfield: Barons: *see* Lucas, John, first baron, 1645–71; Lucas, Robert, third baron, 1688–1705.
Lucca, city and republic: notice, ii. 408–10 & nn.; ambassadors from, to Pope, 1645, ii. 391 & n. 2; in-

Lucca, city and republic (*cont.*) scription at, ii. 486, n. 2; Reformation at, ii. 410, n. 2; protestants from, at Geneva, ii. 523–4 & n.; the Diodatis from, ii. 521, n. 1, 523.
Lucian: death of: in sermon, v. 146 & n. 2.
Lucius, king of England: in Colchester legend, iii. 176, n. 5; tomb of, &c., iv. 472 & n. 3.
Lucius Verus, Roman emperor: in inscription, ii. 496.
Lucretia, Signora, a Greek, ii. 556.
Lucrino, Lago, ii. 345 & nn. 2, 3, 349, nn. 5, 7.
Lucullus: villa of, at Miseno, ii. 350 & nn. 3, 4.
Lucy, Mrs. Catherine: *see* Fitzroy, Catherine, duchess of Northumberland.
Lucy, Thomas, of Charlecote: geneal., iv. 505, n. 4.
Ludlow, Salop: judge in court of Council of the Marches at, ii. 558, n. 4.
Ludovisi, Ludovico, Cardinal: lays out Villa Ludovisi, Rome, ii. 234, n. 4; gift to, ii. 236, n. 1.
Ludwig Wilhelm I, margrave of Baden: visits London, 1694, v. 163 & n. 1, 165.
Lukaris, Kyrillos (Cyril Lucar), patriarch of Constantinople, ii. 18 & n. 3 (i. 14); sends N. Conopios to England, ii. 18 (i. 14); godfather of Sir Cyril Wyche, iv. 351, n. 5; v. 359, n. 4.
Luke, St.: paintings by, ii. 194 & n. 9 (i. 120), 226 & n. 7, 244 & n. 2, 269 & n. 4; relics of, ii. 289, 442, 456 & n. 4.
Lumley, John, Baron Lumley: as owner, &c., of Nonsuch Palace, iii. 426, n. 4, 427; tomb of, iii. 221 & n. 2.
Lumley, Richard; Viscount Lumley 1663; earl of Scarborough 1690; &c., iv. 451, n. 4; takes part in capture of Monmouth, iv. 451–3 & nn.; social, iv. 548; receives Sacrament as required by Test Act, v. 9 & n. 1; *add.*
Lumley: Baron, 1547–1609: *see* Lumley, John.
Lumley of Lumley Castle: Baron, 1681–9, and Viscount, 1689–90: *see* Lumley, Richard, later earl of Scarborough.
Lumley of Waterford: second Viscount: *see* Lumley, Richard, later earl of Scarborough.
Luna: site of, ii. 178 & n. 10 (i. 113).
Lunensis, Portus, near Spezia: as Lunaris, in error, ii. 178–9 & n. (i. 113).
Lunghi, H.: tabernacle designed by, ii. 307 & n. 4.
Luni, near Sarzana, ii. 178, n. 10 *ad fin.*
Lupo, Arnolfo: *see* Cambio, A. di.
Luther, Martin: book by Henry VIII against: copy of, ii. 302 & n. 2; *see also* Books mentioned in text.
Luttrell, Edward: painting by, v. 187 & n. 2.
Luxemburg: threatened by France, 1683, iv. 331, n. 4; siege and capture of, by France, 1684, iv. 378 & n. 1, 380 & n. 3; ~ English apathy regarding, iv. 549; ~ George Fitzroy, duke of Northumberland, at, iv. 391; Louis XIV visits, 1687, iv. 549, n. 1.
Lybia: sands of: in comparison, iv. 120.
Lygonee (Liguanea), Jamaica, iii. 629, n. 5.
Lyme (Lyn) Regis, Dorset: Monmouth lands at, iv. 449 *bis* & nn. 1, 3.
Lynch (Linch), Sir Thomas, governor of Jamaica, iii. 574, n. 1; sets out for Jamaica, iii. 574; letter to, iii. 628; returns to England, &c., iv. 85 & n. 3.
Lynford, Thomas, D.D.: sermon by (?), v. 103 & n. 1.
Lynn Regis: *see* King's Lynn.
Lyons: notice, 1644, ii. 156–8 & nn. (i. 100–1); E at, 1646, ii. 532; misbirth at, iv. 145; burning-glass made at, v. 592.
Lyons: Cardinal of: *see* du Plessis, A. L.
Lyons: Council of, ii. 508, n. 5.
Lyra, Dom Emanuel de: *see* Lira y Castillo, Don M. F. de.
Lysdune: *see* Loosduinen.
Lytcott, —: *see* Litcott, Sir John.
Lyth-hill: *see* Leith Hill.
Lyttelton, Anne, Lady Lyttelton, wife of Sir Charles, iv. 576 & n. 3.
Lyttelton (Littleton), Sir Charles, bt., iv. 575–6 & nn.; house of, at Sheen, iv. 575.

Lyttelton (Littleton), Sir Henry, bt.: estate of, iv. 575–6 & n.
Lytton, Rebecca: *see* Carey, Rebecca, Viscountess of Falkland.
Lytton, Sir Rowland: geneal., iv. 386, n. 1.

M., Dr. —: sermon by, v. 272–3.
Maas, river, ii. 35, nn. 5, 6, 37, n. 2, 57, n. 7; bridges of boats over, ii. 38, n. 3; *see also* Meuse.
Maastricht: fuel made at, iii. 487; siege of, 1673: Sir H. Jones killed at, iii. 587, n. 3; ~ represented at Windsor, iv. 42 & n. 1.
Macao, iii. 324, n. 2.
Macarino: *see* Beccafumi, D.
Macassar: King of: sends poisons to Royal Society, iii. 403 & n. 3.
Maccabean Brethren, the Seven: relics of, ii. 278 & n. 5.
Maccarty, Callaghan, third earl of Clancarty: geneal., iv. 244, n. 5.
Maccarty, Donogh, fourth earl of Clancarty, iv. 595, n. 4; character, iv. 595; v. 38; captured at Cork, &c., v. 38 & n. 1.
Maccarty, Elizabeth, countess of Clancarty (Clancarne), born Fitz-Gerald, wife of Callaghan Maccarty, third earl, and, secondly, of Sir William Davis, iv. 244 & n. 5; social, iv. 244, 249, 385, 527, 529 *bis*, 531, 586 & n. 3(?); E condoles with, on her son's imprisonment, v. 38; house occupied by, *add.* (v. 159); geneal., iv. 247, n. 3, 385, n. 2, 450, n. 5.
Maccarty, Elizabeth, countess of Clancarty, born Spencer, wife of Donogh Maccarty, fourth earl, iv. 450, n. 5; marriage of, iv. 595; social, iv. 450, 586 & n. 3(?).
Maccenigo, —: *see* Mocenigo, S.
Macclesfield: Earls of: *see* Gerard, Charles, first earl, 1679–94; Gerard, Charles, second earl, 1694–1701.
Macedonia: climate of, &c.: in sermon, v. 156; St. Paul in: in sermon, iv. 321.
Machanes, in Morocco: captives at: collection for, v. 485, n. 1.
Mackenzie (Makenzy), Sir George, iii. 475, n. 8; *Moral Essay* by: E replies to, iii. 475 & n. 8; v. 12; controversy of, with W. Lloyd, v. 12 & n. 2; attends meeting held by Sancroft to discuss settlement of English crown, iv. 613–14 & n.; desires maintenance of Scottish episcopate, iv. 614–15 & n.; account of Scotland by, v. 12.
Maclean, Sir John, Jacobite: examination of, by English parliament, &c., v. 561, n. 1.
Madame: *see* Henrietta Anne, duchess of Orleans.
Maddaloni: the Carafa, dukes of: palace of, at Naples, ii. 330 & n. 1.
Maddox, Sir Benjamin, bt., iii. 222, n. 3; E visits (?; as Mr. Madox), iii. 222 & n. 3.
Maderna, Carlo, architect at Rome: work of, in general, ii. 212, n. 2; buildings by, &c.: Palazzo Barberini: begun by, ii. 229, n. 1; S. Giacomo degli Incurabili: completed by, ii. 373, n. 8; St. Peter's: projected towers for, ii. 259, n. 1; S. Susanna: façade, ii. 239 & n. 5; Vatican: fountain with ship, ii. 303, n. 1, 305 & n. 6.
Maderna, Stefano, sculptor: St. Cecilia by, ii. 358 & n. 1.
Madox, —: *see* Maddox, Sir Benjamin.
Madrid: Francis I as captive at (legendary origin of Château de Madrid), ii. 112 & n. 2 (i. 72); iii. 2; Sandwich's residence at, iii. 519; fountain taken to, from Naples, ii. 327, n. 2; Prado (modern): paintings in, ii. 411, n. 3; iii. 15, n. 4, 166, n. 5, 321, n. 2.
Maence: *see* Mainz.
Maggiore, Lago: voyage along, ii. 506–7 & nn.; river flowing into (error), ii. 505 & n. 3; intercourse between, and Upper Valais, ii. 508, n. 5.
Magi, the: relics of, ii. 496 & n. 2; in sermons, v. 83–4, 526.
Magna Carta: in coronation oath, iii. 282 & n. 4; alleged breach of, iv. 65.
Magnani, Marchese: palace of, at Bologna, ii. 424 & n. 6.
Magnetism: loadstones, ii. 187 (i. 117), 192 & n. 7 (i. 119); magnes, iii. 111; terrella, iii. 152–3 & n.; experiments, ii. 230; iii. 313, 435; iv. 314, 315, 316; ~ with terrella, iii. 268 & n. 4.
Magny, Normandy, ii. 121 & n. 6 (i. 78).

Mahomed Bei (J. M. Cigala), impostor, iii. 522, n. 2.
Mahomet: tomb of: representation of, ii. 302 & n. 6.
Mahometans: *see* Mohammedans.
Maidstone, Kent: Kentish insurgents march to, &c., 1648, ii. 541 & n. 4; Sick and Wounded not to be quartered at, 1665, &c., iii. 422 & n. 3; Kentish Petition drawn up at, 1701, v. 457, n. 2; Mr. Harlakingdon of, iii. 422 & n. 2.
Maignan, E.: sundial made by, ii. 373, n. 5.
Maillard, Mary *or* Mariane: miraculous cure of, v. 163–4 & n.
Mainard: *see* Maynard.
Maine: colony of: ownership of, iii. 582, n. 2.
Maintenon, Françoise d'Aubigné, madame de: influence of, on Louis XIV, v. 270 & n. 4.
Mainwaring, Sir William: geneal., iv. 15, n. 2.
Mainz (Maence, Mantes, Mentz): siege of, 1689, iv. 645 & n. 5, 648 & n. 4; English resident at, 1654–61: *see* Curtius, Sir W.
Maison Rouge, near St.-Fargeau: notice, ii. 120 & n. 10 (i. 77); *add.*
Maisons: chateau of: notices, ii. 563 & nn. 3, 4; iii. 18 & nn. 1–7.
Maisons, René de Longueil, marquis of: builds chateau of Maisons, ii. 563 & n. 3.
Maitland, Elizabeth, duchess of Lauderdale and, *sui juris*, countess of Dysart; born Murray; married (1) Sir L. Tollemache (Talmash); (2) John Maitland, duke of Lauderdale: geneal., iv. 114 & n. 7; connexion of, with Ham House, iv. 143, n. 5.
Maitland, John, second earl, 1645, and duke, 1672, of Lauderdale, iii. 354, n. 4; iv. 2, n. 4; as favourite of Charles II, iii. 370; as secretary to Privy Council of Scotland, iii. 370 & n. 1; iv. 15, n. 6; ~ defeats projected union of English and Scottish parliaments, iii. 570, n. 7; as member of Council for Foreign Plantations, iii. 571, n. 1, 574, 578; concurs in Declaration of Indulgence, 1672, iii. 608, n. 1; pamphlets, &c., against, 1679, iv. 172; marriage of, iv. 114, n. 7; owner of Ham House, iv. 143 & n. 5; ranger of
Maitland, John (*cont.*)
New Park, iv. 220, n. 3; social: visits Sayes Court, iii. 354, 369–70; ~ parties, iii. 526, 600; iv. 67; ~ alone, iv. 2.
Makin, Bathsua, school-mistress, ii. 555, n. 3.
Malaga: battle of, 1704, v. 579 & n. 2, 579–80 & n., 580 & n. 4.
Malagigi: *see* Pasqualini, M.A.
Malalbergo, near Ferrara: inn at, ii. 427 & n. 2.
Malamocco: shipping at, &c., ii. 429 & n. 3.
Malay language: translation of Gospels, &c., into, v. 82, n. 2.
Malchus: relic connected with, ii. 205.
Malden: Viscount, 1670–83 (courtesy title): *see* Capel, Algernon, second earl of Essex.
Maldon, Essex: identified as Camulodunum, iii. 180 & n. 2.
Maler (Mollen), Laux, lute-maker, ii. 426 & n. 5.
Mallier, Claude de, seigneur du Houssay: *see* du Houssay.
Malmesbury (Marlesbury), Wilts.: E visits, ii. 23 (i. 17); 'the famous philosopher of': *see* Hobbes, T. (iii. 41, 163).
Malory, Rev. Thomas, vicar of St. Nicholas, Deptford, 1644–59, iii. 80, n. 5; character, ordination, &c., of, iii. 80–1, 185; disuses Anglican ceremonies, iii. 90; becomes lecturer at St. Michael's, Crooked Lane, iii. 226 & n. 4; as preacher: 'a very pious discourse by', iii. 147; ~ 'very tedious in repeating', iii. 160; sermons by (as our minister, our preacher, &c.), iii. 82–98, 142–227 *passim*; ~ preparatory to Communion, iii. 89, &c., 94, &c.; ~ farewell at Deptford, iii. 226.
Malpighi, Marcello, iii. 524, n. 3; sends papers to Royal Society, iii. 524 & n. 3, 599 & n. 4; recommends Italians to Royal Society, iv. 250 & n. 1.
Malta: earthquake at, 1693, v. 134 & n. 2, 135; fossils from, iii. 511; St. Paul at: in sermon, v. 275; Malta cross (jewel), iii. 42.
Malta, Knights of: property of, in Paris, ii. 100, n. 3; in comparison, i. 113.
individual knights: Grand Prieur de France: *see* Vendôme, P. de

Malta, Knights of (*cont.*) (iv. 318 & n. 5); Wignacourt, A. de; Paul de Saumur and his cross, iii. 42; unnamed, iii. 19.
Malvern Hills, Worcs.: view from, iii. 119 & n. 2.
Mammaea: bridge built by, ii. 393–4 & n.; statue of, ii. 223 & n. 4; *add.*
Man: Bishop of: *see* Sodor and Man.
Manasseh, king of Judah: in sermons, iv. 81, 156; v. 110.
Manasseh, son of Joseph: in sermon, iii. 188.
Manchester: trial at, for Lancashire plot, 1694, v. 196, n. 4; Manchester carrier robbed, 1692, v. 122 & n. 2.
Manchester: Earls and Duke of: *see* Montagu, Edward, second earl, 1642–71; Montagu, Robert, third earl, 1671–83; Montagu, Charles, fourth earl, 1683–1719, and first duke, 1719–22.
Mancini, —: house of, in Rome, ii. 364 & n. 3.
Mancini, Hortense: *see* Mazarin, Duchesse.
Mancini, Laura: geneal., iv. 318, n. 5.
Mancini, Maria: *see* Colonna, Maria.
Mancini, Michele Lorenzo, ii. 364, n. 3.
Mander, Roger, D.D., master of Balliol College, Oxford, 1687–1704, iv. 589, n. 3; visits E, iv. 589; takes charge of (Sir) John Evelyn, v. 314 & n. 4; care of (Sir) John when ill, v. 432 & n. 1.
Mandevile (Mandivel), John; D.D. 1694, iv. 539, n. 1; as chaplain to: duchess of Monmouth, iv. 539; ~ duchess of Buckingham, v. 16, 77; sermons by, iv. 535 & n. 1(?), 539, 544 & n. 5(?); v. 6 & n. 2(?), 16–18, 77, 84, 85, 87–8, 97, 98, 100, 105, 109.
Manes, the: place of sacrifices to, ii. 346.
Mann, —, of Ipswich, iv. 114 & n. 6.
Manna: gathering of: in sermon, v. 180.
Manners, Anne, Lady Ros: *see* Pierrepont, Anne.
Manners, Dorothy: *see* Cooper, Dorothy, countess of Shaftesbury.
Manners, Frances, countess of Rutland, wife of George Manners, seventh earl: house belonging to, iii. 95, n. 5.
Manners, Frances, countess of Rutland, wife of John Manners, eighth earl: relations of, with Jeremy Taylor, iii. 95, n. 5.
Manners, John, eighth earl of Rutland, 1641–79, iii. 95, n. 5; owner of Belvoir Castle, iii. 124, n. 4; London house of: *see* London: Exeter House; taken in raid on Exeter House chapel, Christmas, 1657, iii. 203 & nn. 3, 4; geneal., iii. 519, n. 3.
Manners, John; styled Lord Ros (Roos) 1641–79; ninth earl, 1679, and first duke, 1703, of Rutland, &c.: divorce proceedings of, in house of lords, iii. 545–6 & n.
Manners of Haddon: Lord, 1679 (courtesy title): *see* Manners, John, first duke of Rutland, &c.
Manning, Owen, joint-author of *History of Surrey*, i. 52 *bis*.
Manningham, Dr. —: appointed to preach, v. 203, n. 2.
Mansart, François, architect: designs: Blois, wing of Château, ii. 141, n. 4; Maisons, ii. 563, n. 3.
Mansfield, Notts., iii. 126.
Mansfield: Viscount, 1620–8: *see* Cavendish, William, first duke of Newcastle.
Mantegna, Andrea, ii. 113, n. 12; painting by, ii. 113 (i. 73); Triumph of Julius Caesar by, iii. 323 & n. 2.
Mantes: *see* Mainz.
Mantoa, Benavidii family, called: palace of, at Padua, ii. 466–7 & n.
Manton, Thomas, D.D.: sermon by, iii. 213 & n. 5; *see also* iii. 212, n. 6.
Mantua: in view, ii. 487; E fails to visit, ii. 490; operations near, 1702, v. 510; ducal art-collection at, iii. 323 & n. 2; ~ *see also* ii. 443, n. 3; lake of, ii. 488 & n. 5.
Mantumiato, Monte: *see* Amiata, Monte.
Manuscripts: Arundel library, iv. 144 & nn. 3, 4, 145 & n. 2; Bologna, S. Domenico: Esdras, ii. 421; Cambridge: St. John's College, iii. 136 & n. 5, 137, n. 3; Trinity College, iii. 137 & nn. 2, 3; University Library, iii. 140.
Cassiobury: Essex, iv. 200; Florence: Laurenziana, ii. 417; Palazzo Vecchio: Pandects, &c., ii. 188 & nn. 8, 9 (i. 118).

Manuscripts (*cont.*)
Geneva, university library, ii. 529–30 & n.; N. Heinsius: collection of, iv. 330; Hoare, R.: books, &c., written by, ii. 559, n. 2; Lambeth Palace library, iv. 560; London: Cottonian MSS., iii. 507 & n. 1; iv. 216, n. 3; Dr. T. Gale (?): Book of Deer (?), v. 206 & n. 3; St. James's Palace, v. 44; Whitehall, 1680, iv. 215–16 & nn.
Milan: Ambrosiana, ii. 499 & nn. 1, 2; S. Ambrogio: Josephus, ii. 501 & n. 2.
Oxford: Bodleian, iii. 106–7 & nn.; Christ Church library, iii. 109 & n. 2.
Rome: Barberini, ii. 229; Vatican, ii. 301–2 & nn.
Bishop E. Stillingfleet, v. 323, n. 3; Venice, St. Mark's: St. Mark's Gospel, ii. 441 & n. 4.
Manuzio, Aldo: books printed by, iv. 330 & n. 5.
Manwood, Cornelia, Lady Manwood, second wife of Sir John, ii. 316, n. 1.
Manwood, Sir John: in Italy, ii. 316 & n. 1.
Manwood, Livina, Lady Manwood, first wife of Sir John, ii. 316 & n. 1.
Maps and Engraved Views, &c. [mentioned in text, &c.; maps and views cited in notes merely as authorities are not indexed. For views in nature *see* Views]:
maps: and charts in king's library, Whitehall, iv. 215; book of: given to Charles II, iii. 260 & n. 5; by J. Blaeu, ii. 49 & n. 4 (i. 34–5); ~ 'Hollandia illustrata', ii. 37 & n. 4 (i. 28); G. Collins: charts of Great Britain by, iv. 301 & n. 3; Dampier, W.: map of trade-winds in Pacific by, v. 295 & n. 2; J. Gomboust, plan of Paris: known to E, ii. 91, n. 5; by H. Hondius, ii. 49 & n. 3 (i. 34–5); J. Norden: maps of England by, iv. 301 & n. 4; C. Saxton: maps by, iv. 301, n. 4.
frozen Thames, 1683–4: maps and views of, iv. 365; *see further* iv. 360, n. 4, 362, nn. 1, 2.
views: by L. de Lincler, iii. 10 & n. 3; French royal palaces: painted, at Fontainebleau, ii.

Maps, &c. (*cont.*)
117 & n. 3 (i. 76); ~ on tapestries, iv. 343 & n. 2; Italian towns, &c.: painted, in Vatican, ii. 299 & n. 5; Palmyra, v. 224 & n. 3; *see also* Chardin, Sir J.; Evelyn: drawings, &c., by.
Mar: Earls and Duke of; *see* Erskine, John, second earl, 1572–1634; Erskine, John, sixth earl, 1689–1716, and duke (Jacobite creation), 1715–32.
Maratti, Carlo, ii. 223 & n. 10; influence of, on E's taste, ii. 287, n. 7 *ad fin.*, 299, n. 4; drawings made by, for E, ii. 223, 247 & n. 4; i. *7–8*; copies by, of paintings, ii. 223, n. 10, 229 & n. 5; restores Farnesina frescoes, ii. 287, n. 7; drawing by, ii. 356, n. 5.
Marca, della (de la Marca): painters called: *see* Lombardelli, G. B.; Pagani, L.; Pagani, V.
Marc' Antonio, enameller, and his stories about alchemists, iii. 52–3.
Marc' Antonio, singer: *see* Pasqualini, M. A. (Malagigi).
Marcellinus, St.: relics of, ii. 365.
Marcello, Dr.: *see* Muselli.
Marcellus: Theatre of, at Rome, ii. 228 & n. 5.
Marchand, Floram, water-spouter, iii. 27, n. 5.
Marciano: battle of, 1554: column commemorating, ii. 185–6 & n. (i. 117).
Marcius Rex, Q.: aqueduct built by, ii. 317 & n. 1, 381 & n. 8.
Marcus Aurelius: bridge built by, ii. 384 & n. 2; Column and palace of, at Rome, ii. 370 & nn. 3–5; triumph of: in reliefs, ii. 223 & n. 9; equestrian statue of, on Capitol, ii. 221, 404; ~ in comparison, ii. 101 (i. 66); bust of (modern), ii. 235 & n. 9.
Marden, Godstone, Surrey: *see* Godstone.
Mardyke: taken by French and English, 1657, iii. 199, n. 3, 200 & n. 5.
Mare Morto, near Miseno, ii. 351, n. 2.
Margaret, Empress: as Spanish Infanta: coiffure of, iii. 321, n. 2.
Margaret, queen of Scots, queen of James IV, &c.: MS. given to, iv. 215 & n. 2.

Margaret, countess of Henneberg: legend relating to, ii. 55, n. 3.
Margate (Mergate), Kent: notice, iii. 615 & n. 5; E visits, iii. 611, 615; Dutch fleet off, 1667, iii. 486 & n. 2; William III at, v. 273, n. 5, 294, n. 2, 327, n. 2; official at: *see* Glover, J. (iii. 611 & n. 1); vicar of, 1666–85: *see* Chewney, Rev. N. (iii. 615 & n. 4).
Marguerite, queen of Navarre: marriage of, with Henri IV, ii. 297 & n. 3.
Marguzzo: *see* Mergozzo.
Maria, Empress: as Spanish Infanta: proposed marriage of, to Charles I, ii. 6–7 & n. (i. 6–7).
Maria Anna of Neuburg, queen of Spain, v. 2, n. 2; journey of, to Spain, v. 2 & n. 2, 14, n. 5; reported poisoning and pregnancy of, v. 257 & n. 5, 258 & n. 2, 259.
Maria Antonia, electress of Bavaria: mourning for, v. 126 & n. 1.
Maria Maddalena, grand duchess of Tuscany: enlarges Poggio Imperiale, ii. 410, n. 5, 411.
Maria Sophia, queen of Portugal: dies, v. 351 & n. 1, 352 & n. 1, 354.
Maria Theresa, Empress: painting given to, ii. 495, n. 6.
Marie de Médicis, queen of France, ii. 43, n. 5 *ad fin.*; geneal., ii. 93 & n. 1 (i. 62); character and fortunes of, ii. 57 (i. 39); at Tours, 1619, &c., ii. 146 & n. 2 (i. 94); in England: projects monopoly of leather (?), i. 39 & n. 1; journey of, from England to Cologne, 1641: reception of, at Dort, ii. 57 & nn. 1, 2 (i. 39); ~ Arundel as escort during, *ib.*; ii. 72, n. 4.
apartment of, in Louvre, ii. 103, n. 1, 105, n. 4; named as builder of: aqueduct at Arcueil, ii. 129, n. 3; ~ Cours la Reine, Paris, gate, ii. 106; ~ Palais du Luxembourg, ii. 128 & n. 1 (i. 81); ~ Petit-Luxembourg, ii. 131, n. 1; founds La Charité, Paris, ii. 101 & n. 6 (i. 66); statue (Henri IV) given to, ii. 92–3 & n. (i. 62); in paintings: by Rubens, ii. 128 & n. 2 (i. 82); ~ by Sandrart, ii. 43 & n. 5 (i. 32).
Marie-Adelaide of Savoy, Dauphiness, wife of Louis, duke of Burgundy, later Dauphin: marriage of, v. 260 & n. 3, 270 & n. 3.
Marignano (Melegnano), ii. 490 & n. 10.
Marines, François de Créqui, marquis de: as owner of Poix (error ?), iii. 17 & n. 2; *add.*
Marino, Alban Hills: road through, ii. 316, n. 3.
Marius, Caius: victory of, over the Cimbrians, ii. 485 & n. 3; ~ the battle-field, ii. 488; ~ triumphal arch for, at Verona, ii. 486 & n. 3; ~ trophies of, at Rome (sculpture), ii. 221–2 & n., 379 & n. 7; villas of, at Miseno, &c., ii. 349 & n. 8, 350 & n. 3; statue called, ii. 223 & n. 13.
Mark, St.: Gospel of: autograph copy of, ii. 441 & n. 4; relics of, ii. 365, 441 & n. 5; gold crowns dedicated to, ii. 440–1 & n.
Mark Anthony: portrait of, on gem, ii. 89 (i. 60).
Marlborough (Marlborow), Wilts.: notice, 1654, iii. 99–100 & nn.; Grey Wethers near, iii. 116, n. 1.
Marlborough: Dukes of: inherit library of Charles Spencer, third earl of Sunderland, v. 322, n. 1.
Marlborough: Earl and Duke, &c., of: *see* Churchill, John, earl, 1689–1702, and first duke, 1702–22; Churchill, Sarah, his countess and duchess; Godolphin, Lady Henrietta, duchess *sui juris* 1722–33.
Marmoutier, Touraine: abbey of, ii. 146–7 & nn. (i. 95).
Marne river: bridge over, at Charenton, ii. 115 & n. 6 (i. 75); confluence of, with Seine, iii. 38, n. 7.
Marquise, Pas de Calais: E loses dog at, ii. 560.
Marsaglia: battle near, 1693, v. 155 & nn. 4, 5.
Marseilles: notice, 1644, ii. 164–6 & nn. (i. 103–5); galleys and galley-slaves at, ii. 164–5 & nn. (i. 104–5); environs of (the *bastides*), ii. 163–4 & n. (i. 103).
Marsh, Francis; bishop of Limerick, 1667; of Kilmore, 1673; archbishop of Dublin, 1682: visits Royal Society's repository, iv. 195 & n. 2.

Marsh, Mrs. Mary, wife of Bishop Francis Marsh: character, &c., iv. 195 & n. 2.
Marsh, Dr. Narcissus, archbishop of Armagh: buys Stillingfleet's library, v. 323, n. 3.
Marshall, Alexander: drawings of flowers and insects by, iv. 289 & n. 2.
Marsham (Massham), Sir John, bt., iii. 237 & n. 3; geneal., iii. 237, n. 5.
Marston Moor, Yorks., W.R.: battle-field of, in view, iii. 129; battle of, iii. 129, n. 1.
Martha and Mary: in sermon, v. 251.
Martial: gardens of, at Rome, ii. 313 & n. 6.
Martigny, Valais, ii. 517.
Martin I, pope: holds council in Lateran, ii. 274 & n. 4; tomb of, ii. 274 & n. 7.
Martin V, pope: pavement of, in St. John Lateran, ii. 272 & n. 2; tomb of, ii. 274 & n. 7; in painting, ii. 274 & n. 8.
Martin, St., of Tours: relics of, ii. 144 & n. 7 (i. 94), 147 & n. 1 (i. 95); miracle of, ii. 147 & n. 2 (i. 95).
Martin, —, clerk of Stephen Harvey, v. 478.
Martine, Rev. —: sermon by, iii. 152.
Martinozzi, Laura: *see* Laura, duchess of Modena.
Martyn, John: appointed printer to the Royal Society, iii. 340, n. 1.
Mary, Blessed Virgin: prayers to: recommended by Roman Catholic, iv. 243; in sermons, iii. 34, 123, 239, 275; iv. 33; v. 526; in vision, ii. 242 & n. 5; *add.*; relics of, ii. 87 *bis* (i. 59 *bis*), 274 & n. 1, 275; miraculous paintings of: at Florence ii. 194 & n. 9 (i. 120), 412 & n. 4; ~ at Rome, ii. 226 & n. 7, 240 & n. 1, 374 & n. 3; *see also* ii. 244 & n. 2 (subject not stated).
Mary, the sister of Martha: in sermons, iv. 577; v. 251.
Mary I, queen of England: grants York House to archbishops of York, iii. 162, n. 1; woman born in reign of, iii. 130.
Mary II, queen of England [b. 1662; styled the Lady Mary; married, 1677, William III, prince of Orange; William III and Mary II proclaimed king and queen of England 13 Feb. 1689; d. 28 Dec. 1694]:
— character, &c.: in 1689, iv. 624–5 & nn.; obituary, v. 205 & nn. 4–6.
— chronological series: as child, iii. 380; tutor of: *see* Lake, E.; godmother to Lake's daughter, iv. 95; performs in *Calisto*, iv. 49–50 & n.; at sermon, iv. 76; marries William of Orange, iv. 122 & n. 4, 124, n. 1; i. *27*; at court ball, iv. 123–4; goes to Holland, iv. 124; parting with William before his expedition to England, 1688, iv. 604 & n. 4.
— — accession, 1689: future status of, discussed, iv. 614; crown to be conferred on: commons' vote, iv. 616 & n. 1; ~ terms of settlement, iv. 621–2 & n.; arrives in London, iv. 622 & n. 3; conduct of, on arrival, &c., iv. 624–5 & nn.; views of, on settlement of crown, iv. 624, n. 3, 625; proclaimed queen, iv. 623 & n. 4; makes no apology for her conduct, iv. 623–4 & n.; v. 205 & n. 6; refuses to see Clarendon and Rochester, iv. 626, nn. 1, 2; crowned, &c., iv. 632–3 & nn.; in succession bill, iv. 645 & n. 8; reign of, i. *33*.
— — — Scotland: parliament (Convention) declares for, iv. 635 & n. 2; crown offered to, iv. 639 & n. 2.
— — as queen: (1) as regent: acts as regent during William's absences from England, v. 238, n. 4; 1690: appointed, v. 24 & n. 1, 25; 1691: gives E access to Clarendon, v. 45, n. 1; ~ orders Sancroft to leave Lambeth Palace, &c., v. 51, n. 5, 59 & n. 2; ~ orders Clarendon to be released on bail, &c., v. 60 & n. 5; 1692: closes Southwark Fair, v. 115–16 & n.
— — — (2) miscellaneous: popularity of, 1690, v. 14; orders Princess Anne to dismiss Lady Marlborough, 1692, v. 90 & n. 2; quarrel of, with Anne, v.

Mary II (*cont.*)
98 & n. 1, 201 & n. 4; invited to attend Queen Mary of Modena's lying in, 1692, v. 96; accompanies William III towards Gravesend, 1693, v. 136; claims right of presentation to St. Martin in the Fields and St. James, Piccadilly, v. 112, n. 4, 121, n. 1, 136, n. 5, 169 *bis* & n. 1, 376 & n. 1; interest of, in royal library at St. James's Palace, v. 206; project of, for seamen's hospital at Greenwich, v. 203, n. 1, 205 & n. 4(?); residence of: at Whitehall, v. 147, n. 2; ~ at Hampton Court, June 1689, iv. 641, n. 1.
— — last illness, death, funeral, &c., v. 200–5 & nn. *passim*; *add.*; v. 207 & n. 5.
— religion: piety of, iv. 624 & n. 1; as Anglican, iv. 625; reforms administration of Sacrament at Whitehall, iv. 375, n. 1; attends sermons, iv. 623, n. 3, 628, 630, 641, n. 1, 650–1 & n.; v. 7, 9, 20, 43, n. 1, 52, n. 3, 223, n. 2.
— private and miscellaneous: plays basset, iv. 625; furniture, china collection, and library of, v. 147 & nn. 2, 3; private papers of, v. 205 & n. 5; *add.*; *Memoirs*, i. *82*, n. 3; friendship of, with Frances Apsley (later Lady Bathurst), iv. 264, n. 3; regard of, for James II, v. 238; household of: Princess Anne asked to employ former members of, 1695, v. 201; ~ clerk of the closet, 1689–94: *see* Stanley, William.
Mary of Modena, queen of England, consort of James II [Mary Beatrice d'Este; duchess of York 1673; queen 1685; in exile from 1688], iv. 27, n. 5.
— as duchess of York: marriage of, to James: unpopularity of, iv. 26 & n. 2; reputed to be the pope's eldest daughter, iv. 26, n. 2; arrives in England, iv. 27, n. 5; musical performance in honour of (?), iv. 30 & n. 1; conduct of, as duchess, iv. 413; children of: deaths of, in infancy, iv. 597; goes to Brussels, 1679, iv. 167, n. 6; returns to London from Scotland, 1682,

Mary of Modena (*cont.*)
iv. 281–2 & n.; oratory of, at Whitehall, iv. 416, n. 1; social, iv. 27, 28, 29, 30, 38; gives ball, iv. 103; household of, iv. 333, n. 3; ~ member of: *see* Davia, M. V.; secretary of: *see* Coleman, E.
— as queen: conduct of, at James II's accession, iv. 413 & n. 3; in mourning for Charles II, iv. 419; coronation of, iv. 437 & nn. 2–4; ~ crown worn by, at, iv. 441 & n. 3; attends opening of parliament, iv. 442 *bis*; at review on Blackheath, iv. 458; attends sermon and mass, iv. 465; at court function, iv. 480; plays basset, iv. 519, 625.
— — 1686: displeased by grant of peerage to Catherine Sedley, iv. 497; change of manner of, since accession, iv. 519.
— — 1687: at Bath, iv. 560 & n. 2; and Lord Mayor's feast, iv. 562–3 & n.
— — 1688: (1) as mother of James Edward: thanksgiving for her pregnancy, iv. 567 & n. 4; ~ delivery premature, iv. 587 & n. 1; ~ recovery after delivery: fireworks display for, iv. 591; ~ witnesses of delivery testify to it, iv. 602 & n. 3; ~ resemblance of James Edward to, v. 92.
— — — (2) advises James to dismiss Father Petre, iv. 600, n. 1; asked to intercede for Sunderland, iv. 602; prepares to seek refuge at Portsmouth, iv. 607 & n. 5; leaves Whitehall and arrives at Calais, iv. 612 & n. 4.
— later life: prayers for, in Anglican services, curtailed, iv. 620 & n. 5; pregnant, 1692 (Louisa Maria): invitations to witness delivery, v. 96 & n. 1; marriage settlements, &c., on: provision for payment of, in treaty of Ryswick, v. 271 & n. 2; zeal of, for Roman Catholicism, v. 475; buried at Chaillot, ii. 91, n. 1.
— apartments, &c., of: new apartment in Whitehall, iv. 480 & n. 2, 537; ~ occupied by Queen Mary II, iv. 623, n. 4 *ad fin.*, 625; throne of, in Roman

Mary of Modena (*cont.*)
Catholic chapel, Whitehall, iv. 534; furniture, &c., withheld from, after Revolution, v. 147 & n. 4.
— household, &c., of: chamberlain: *see* Godolphin, Sidney, earl of Godolphin; clerk of the council: *see* Ashton, J.; maid of honour: projected appointment of Mary Evelyn (?), iv. 428; physician: *see* Waldegrave, Sir W.
Mary, queen of Scots: tombs of, iii. 135 & n. 2; documents relating to and letters of, iv. 241, n. 3; account of, mentioned, iv. 603.
Mary, princess of Orange, consort of William II, and Princess Royal of England: born, ii. 10 & n. 6 (i. 8); courted by William, ii. 28 & n. 1 (i. 20); comes to England, 1660, iii. 257 & n. 5; last illness and death of, iii. 264–5 *bis* & nn.; ~ in sermon, iii. 265; William III resembles, iii. 563–4 & n.; bed belonging to, iii. 323 & n. 5; attendants on: *see* Anne, duchess of York (iii. 264 & n. 2); Armorer, Sir N.; secretary of: *see* Oudart, N.
Mary Magdalene, St.: penance of, at Ste-Baume, ii. 167 (i. 105); relics of, ii. 267, 442; in sermons, iii. 403; v. 216, 308.
Masaniello: rebellion of, iii. 50, n. 1.
Mason, Rev. John: millenarian movement of, v. 177–8 & nn.
Mason, Robert, LL.D.: house of, at Deptford, iii. 76 & nn. 2, 3.
Masquerades: at Paris, iii. 1–2 & n.; at Venice, ii. 432 & n. 2; *add.*; ii. 473–4 & n.; at court, iii. 357 & n. 1(?), 476 & n. 2(?).
Masques: *see* Plays, &c.
Massa (Mossa), near Carrara, ii. 179 (i. 113).
Massachusetts: relations of, with Charles II, iii. 579, n. 2 *ad fin.*; occupies Maine, iii. 582, n. 2; territory seized by: to be required to surrender, iii. 584; *see also* New England.
Massachusetts Indian: Bible translated into, v. 82, n. 2.
Massacre of St. Bartholomew: painting of, ii. 297 & n. 3.
Massam, Rev. — (identified as Dr. R. Mossom, but probably G. Masterson): sermon by, iii. 214 & n. 1; *add.*
Massey, Sir Edward: governor-designate of Jamaica, iii. 257 & n. 3.
Massey, John: made dean of Christ Church, Oxford, iv. 519, n. 4.
Massham, —: *see* Marsham, Sir J.
Massica *or* Garo, Monte, ii. 323 & n. 6.
Massingberd, Elizabeth: *see* Berkeley, Elizabeth, countess of Berkeley.
Massingberd, John: geneal., iii. 230, n. 1.
Massue, Henri de, baron and first marquis de Ruvigny: *see* Ruvigny.
Massue, Henri de, second marquis de Ruvigny, earl of Galway, &c.: *see* Ruvigny.
Massue, Pierre de, sieur de la Caillemotte: *see* la Caillemotte.
Massys, Quentin (Quintine the blacksmith): paintings by, ii. 285, n. 3, 550 & n. 2.
Masterson (Marsterson), Rev. George, iii. 212, n. 7; sermons by, iii. 212, 213, 214 & n. 1; *add.* (?; in text as by Massam).
Matfeld, Franz, envoy from Hamburg to England 1671–3, iii. 585, n. 3.
Mathematics [*see also* Scientific Instruments]: parabolas: method of describing, iv. 267; school for, at Christ's Hospital, iv. 542 & n. 2; v. 399 & n. 1; at school display, v. 79; Lord Brouncker as mathematician, iii. 332.
Mathews, —, rebel with Monmouth (Captain Edward Mathews?), iv. 452 & n. 8.
Mathew(s), Rev. Robert, rector of Euston, iv. 118 & n. 2.
Matilda, Empress: builds bridge at Rouen, ii. 122, n. 5.
Matilda, countess of Tuscany: lands bequeathed by, to Church, ii. 208 & n. 4; tomb of, ii. 265 & n. 2.
Matteis, Nicola (Signor Nicholao), violinist, iv. 48, n. 1; performs, iv. 48, 49, 51, 186–7(?).
Matthew, St.: relics of, ii. 244 & n. 3, 267; in sermon, iv. 388.
Matthews, Captain Edward, rebel, iv. 452, n. 8.
Matthias, Emperor: rising of Bohemia against, ii. 7 & n. 1 (i. 7).
Matthias, Prince: *see* Medici, Matteo de'.

Maubuisson, convent, near Pontoise, i. 78 & n. 1; abbess of: *see* Louisa Hollandina.
Maundy, —, servant of Anne Howard (later Lady Sylvius): apparition of, iv. 100–1.
Maurice, Prince of Orange, ii. 35, n. 3; fort built by, ii. 35 & n. 2 (i. 27); burial-place of, ii. 40 & n. 5 (i. 30); illegitimate son of, iii. 622, n. 5; *add.* (iv. 118); geneal., ii. 382, n. 3.
Maurice, Prince, Count Palatine, ii. 34, n. 2; at the Hague, ii. 34 (i. 26 & n. 7); death of, i. 26 & n. 6.
Maxentius, Roman emperor: builds circus near Rome, ii. 362, n. 3; defeat of, by Constantine, ii. 383 & n. 4; ~ buildings commemorating, ii. 250, 380; Constantine's expedition against: in comparison, iv. 618.
Maxfield, —: reconciles Sir R. Browne and Lord Hatton, iii. 38 & n. 3.
Maximian, Roman emperor: persecution of Christians by, ii. 307; ~ in sermon, v. 64; statue of (?), ii. 221, n. 6.
Maximilian II Emanuel, elector (duke) of Bavaria, iv. 394, n. 1; at siege of Buda, 1684, iv. 394; in negotiations for Spanish Succession, v. 434 & n. 4; seizes Ulm, 1702, v. 516 & n. 3; captures Augsburg, v. 553, n. 2; attacked by Allies, 1704, v. 572 & n. 1; defeated at the Schellenberg, v. 572 & n. 3, 573 *bis* & nn. 1, 2; defeated at Blenheim, v. 574 & n. 1, 575 & n. 2; pursued by Allies, &c., v. 576 & n. 1, 577; takes refuge at Brussels, v. 580 & n. 5; defeated at Elixem, 1705, v. 604–5; geneal., iv. 596, n. 3; v. 126, n. 1.
Maximus, St.: relics of, ii. 456 & n. 6.
May, Rev. —: sermon by, 1661, iii. 290.
May, Rev. —: sermon by, 1675, iv. 78.
May, Baptist, iv. 49, n. 1; as godfather, iv. 49; lodgings of, in Whitehall, v. 47, n. 2; geneal., iii. 381, n. 3.
May, Hugh, architect, iii. 381, n. 3; commissioner for London streets, iii. 319, n. 1; visits Cornbury, iii. 381; examines proposals for repair of St. Paul's, 1666, iii. 448–9 & nn.; buildings designed
May, Hugh (*cont.*)
by: Cassiobury Park, iv. 199 & n. 2; Chiswick: Sir Stephen Fox's house, iv. 294; Cornbury House: stables, &c., iii. 381, n. 3, 382; Eltham: Sir John Shaw's house (?), iii. 375, n. 8 *ad fin.*; London: Berkeley House, iii. 625; Whitehall: repairs (?), iii. 381, n. 3; Windsor Castle: state apartments, iii. 573 & n. 1.
Maynard, Banastre, third Baron Maynard, v. 587, n. 3; chaplain of (S. Dunster?): sermons by, v. 587, 603.
Maynard, Sir John, serjeant at law, i. 12, n. 2; iv. 227, n. 4; participates in Strafford's and Stafford's impeachments, iv. 227, 229, n. 4; chambers of, in Middle Temple, i. 12.
Maynard, William, second Baron Maynard, iv. 416, n. 4; as comptroller of the household, iv. 416 & n. 4; ~ superseded, iv. 536, n. 2.
Maynard: Barons: *see* Maynard, William, second baron, 1640–99; Maynard, Banastre, third baron, 1699–1718.
Mazarin, Armand de la Porte, marquis de la Meilleraye, Duc, iv. 97, n. 5; wealth of, v. 330.
Mazarin, Hortense Mancini, Duchesse, iv. 97 & n. 5; at court, &c., iv. 97, 403, 413; dies, v. 330 & n. 1; page of, iv. 413, n. 5; geneal., ii. 364, n. 3; v. 330, 472, n. 3; mentioned, iv. 97, n. 6.
Mazarin, Jules, Cardinal (G. R. Mazzarino), iii. 1, n. 5; relations of, with Anne of Austria, alluded to, ii. 133, n. 4 *ad fin.*; at St. Quentin, 1649, ii. 561, n. 1; at siege of Bordeaux, 1650, iii. 23, n. 1; banished from France, 1651, iii. 26 & n. 4; negotiation of, with Queen Christina, for seizing Naples, *c.* 1657, iv. 221, n. 3; induces Henrietta Maria to recognize James, duke of York's marriage, iii. 258, n. 4; death of: mission of condolence for, iii. 274 & n. 4; palace of, in Rome, ii. 379, n. 4; painting given to, ii. 229, n. 5; agent of, in England, for collecting pictures: *see* Richett (iii. 82 & n. 2); musician of: *see* Alessandro (iii. 1); geneal., iv. 27, n. 6; v. 330.

Mazzarino, Margherita: geneal., iv. 27, n. 6.
Mazzoni, Giulio, called Giulio Piacentino: stucco-work by, ii. 366 & n. 5.
Mazzotti, —, maker of Florentine mosaic, ii. 417.
Mead, Rev. Joseph: interpretation of prophecy by, iv. 636, 637, n. 1; v. 26.
Meadows, Mrs. Dorothy, later Lady Meadows, wife of Sir Philip: marriage of, v. 258 & n. 1.
Meadows, Sir Philip, sen., v. 258 & n. 1.
Meadows, Sir Philip, jnr.: marriage of, v. 258 & n. 1.
Meals [select: notices relating to the circumstances or contents of meals; notices containing simple encomiums, such as 'a great feast', are not indexed collectively. Cookery and the various kinds of food, &c., are indexed under Food and Drink; E's Christmastide parties under England: social]:
— kinds of meals [dinner and supper not indexed]: banquets: as a sequel to dinner, iii. 480 & n. 5; ~ other notices, iii. 308, 349, 440; iv. 267–8, 492; v. 220; breaking fast, iii. 297; collations, iii. 103, 123; iv. 6, 27, 115, 176; v. 220, n. 3; 'present of refreshments' for travellers, iv. 79.
— particular meals: (i) royal: coronation feasts, iii. 284 & n. 3; iv. 633; Garter feast, iii. 479 & n. 1, 480 & nn. 1–6; Charles II dines in public, &c., iii. 251, 490–1 & n., 513; Charles II's meals on his yacht, iii. 297; banquet for Charles II at Deptford dockyard (?), iii. 440; banquet for William III at Oxford, v. 220 & n. 3.
— — (ii) civic, &c.: City of London entertains Royal Society, iv. 27; Lord Mayor's feasts, iii. 388–9, 396; Lord Mayor's dinners (Sir R. Clayton): on solemn day, iv. 185; ~ on private day, iv. 187; sheriffs' feasts, iii. 425; iv. 179; dinner with a sheriff, iii. 266; City Companies' feasts, iii. 391 & n. 5, 587 & n. 2; iv. 518; for nobleman's visit, iv. 115.
— — (iii) special occasions: assize dinner, iv. 276–7; consecrations, &c., of bishops: dinners following, iii. 346, 362, 518; diplomatists: suppers, &c., for ambassadors after first audiences, iii. 349, 515; iv. 492; Readers' feasts at Inns of Court, iii. 400, 512, 536–7.
— — (iv) societies: Lincoln's Inn: Christmas revels, iii. 308; Royal College of Physicians: anniversary dinner, iii. 379; *see also* Royal Society; Trinity House.
— — (v) miscellaneous: on man-of-war, iii. 413; on merchant ship, ii. 469; fish, in Lent, ii. 474; at country-houses, &c. (with notes on food), iii. 552; iv. 255, 473; for judges, at Old Bailey, iv. 175 & n. 2; for trial of master-cook, iv. 483; 'a Dutch feast', iv. 296; German feast, iii. 288; at Milan (Col. A. Burnet), ii. 503–4; at City merchants' houses, iii. 448, 625 (Sir R. Clayton); iv. 163; given by divines, iii. 265; iv. 489; followed by fire-eater's displays, iii. 626–7; iv. 359; followed by music, iii. 601; dessert at dinner-party: fruit with roses, iii. 550.
Meal-tub Plot, iv. 188, n. 1.
Meangis, near Mindanao: native from, v. 295, n. 2.
Meath: Bishop of, 1656, iii. 172 & n. 1; bishops of: *see* Ussher, J. (1621–5); Leslie, H. (1661); Evans, John (1716–24).
Meaux: Bishop of: *see* Bossuet, J. B.
Meaws, Dr. —: *see* Mews, Peter.
Mecarin (Meccharini): *see* Beccafumi, D.
Mecca (Méca): pilgrim to, iv. 285; Mahomet's tomb at: representation of, ii. 302 & n. 6.
Medici family: burial-place of, ii. 198 & n. 5; patron saints of, ii. 198.
Medici, Carlo de', cardinal, ii. 257, n. 2; coach of, ii. 257; arrives at Rome, 1645, ii. 389, n. 4 *ad fin.*
Medici, Cosimo de', Pater Patriae: grave of, ii. 198, n. 5; geneal., ii. 416, n. 4.

Medici, Ferdinando de', cardinal: *see* Ferdinand I, grand duke of Tuscany.
Medici, Don Garzia de': portrait of, ii. 191 & n. 7.
Medici, Giovanni de', son of Cosimo, Pater Patriae: tomb of, ii. 416 & n. 4.
Medici, Giovanni Carlo de', cardinal, ii. 257, n. 2; enters Rome, 1645, ii. 389 & n. 4; occupies Palazzo Madama, ii. 391, n. 1.
Medici, Leopold de', Prince, later cardinal: art-collection of, ii. 415 & nn. 2–4.
Medici, Lorenzo de', the Magnificent: geneal., ii. 416, n. 4.
Medici, Matteo de', Prince: bridge built by, ii. 206 & n. 5.
Medici, Piero de', il Gottoso: tomb of, ii. 416 & n. 4.
Medicinal and Hot Springs, &c.: Bagni: sulphurous river at, ii. 394 & n. 3; Bath: *see* Bath; Bourbon-l'Archambault, ii. 155 & n. 6 (i. 100); Bourges: St. Privé, ii. 153 & n. 4 (i. 99); Bristol Hotwells, iii. 103 & n. 5; Dulwich: *see* Sydenham Well *below*; Epsom: water, iii. 544 & n. 1; iv. 74, n. 2; v. 250 & n. 1, 255; Great Malvern: Holy Well, &c., at, iii. 118–19 & n.; Islington: Spa Wells at, iv. 515 & n. 5; Knaresborough: spas of, iii. 129 & n. 6; London environs, in: paper on, iv. 170; Montecatini: Tettuccio at, ii. 410 & n. 4; Naples, near: Volla, ii. 332 & n. 3; Phlegraean Fields: various springs, baths, &c., ii. 340 & n. 5, 341–2 & nn., 344, n. 4, 345, 348 & nn. 1, 2, 351 & n. 4; Rome: Tre Fontane, near, ii. 308; Shooter's Hill, v. 351 & n. 2; Sydenham Wells, also called Dulwich Wells, iv. 74 & n. 2, 112 & n. 3; Tunbridge Wells: *see* Tunbridge Wells; Viterbo: Bullicame, ii. 211 & n. 1.
Medicine and Surgery [for related activities, &c., *see* Commissioners for Sick and Wounded, 1664–7 *and* 1672–4; London: Royal College of Physicians *and* Royal College of Surgeons; and the various cognate subjects]:
— drugs, medicines, &c.: (i) collective [*see also* Gardens: botanical]: dispensaries ('laboratorie', &c.), iii. 28; iv. 118; display of, by apothecary, iii. 235–6 & nn.; collection of, from Far East, iii. 374; trade in, at Marseilles, ii. 166 (i. 105); MS. work on, iv. 215–16; pharmacists: as chymists, ii. 276 & n. 3; iii. 27–8 & n.; ~ distiller, iv. 121; travelling medicine-chest, ii. 451.
— — (ii) particular substances, &c.: amber: spirit of, iv. 77; antimony: mercury of, iii. 28 & nn. 1, 2; ~ in mercury of life, iii. 220, n. 3; *aurum potabile*, iii. 86–7 & n.; balsams from Portugal, iii. 539; camomile: fumes of, ii. 554; *carduus* posset, iv. 272 & n. 1; *diascordium*, iii. 235 & n. 6; electuaries, iii. 235 & n. 7; frankincense: as fumigatory, ii. 519; *lac tygridis*, iii. 374; Lucotellus balsam, iii. 146 & n. 1; manna: origin of, &c., ii. 352, 353 & n. 2; mercury of life, iii. 220 & n. 3; millipedes, iv. 290; *nux vomica*: effect of, on fish, iv. 197; panacea, iv. 252–3; physick: *see* treatment *below*; quinine (cortex, Jesuits' powder or bark, quinquean, &c.), iv. 325 & n. 5, 333, 406, 462; v. 197–8 & n.; resin: as depilatory for pigs, ii. 430 & n. 2; rusma (resina), ii. 430 & n. 1; saffron, iii. 142, n. 1; Sir Walter Raleigh's cordial: preparation of, iii. 336 & n. 4; steel: course of, iii. 464; treacle, iii. 235 & n. 5; ~ Venice, ii. 478 & n. 2.
— treatment [treatment for particular illnesses is indexed under Illnesses (under the various complaints); notices relating to E are indexed under Evelyn: health (partly under illnesses, partly under treatment); in neither case are there cross-references under the present heading; all notices relating to major surgical operations are indexed below]:
— — (i) medical: physick: taking of, on Lord's Day (in sermon), iv. 108 & n. 2; ~ used, iii. 31; iv. 208; ~ course of, iv. 567; purges, iv. 406; vomit, *ib.*

Medicine and Surgery (*cont.*)
— — (ii) surgical: minor operations: bleeding: recommended for young persons, iv. 425 & n. 1; ~ in Portugal, v. 352 & n. 1; ~ used, iii. 367; iv. 406–7, 569, 592, 653; cupping, iv. 77, 406; issue in neck, iii. 91; major operations: amputation of leg, iii. 610; fistula, iv. 533 & n. 6; stomach opened, ii. 53–4 & n. (i. 37); stone: operating for, in Paris, ii. 101 & n. 6 (i. 66); iii. 3–4; ~ operations for, proposed, &c., iii. 529; iv. 52; v. 453; medicaments, &c.: cere-cloth, iii. 295 & n. 4; duck's bill, iii. 4 & n. 1; stupes (stoopes), iii. 610 & n. 2.
— — (iii) miraculous cures, &c.: king's evil: touching for, &c., iii. 250–1 & n.; iv. 374 & n. 2, 606 & n. 3; *add.*; ~ other cures of, iv. 469 & n. 3; the Saludadors, &c., iv. 468–70 & nn.; M. Maillard, v. 163–4 & n.; case at Rome, iii. 634; ~ alluded to, iii. 36; 'strange cures', iii. 306 & n. 2; stone with curative properties, iii. 288.
— miscellaneous: autopsies, iii. 209–10, 544; child fed by hand, iv. 597; crooked leg: treatment for, iii. 317 & n. 4; curative baths and waters: *see* Medicinal and Hot Springs; doctor's regimen for E, ii. 530–2; drinking: death due to heavy, v. 54; fevers: theory of, ii. 522, n. 4; hanged person: recovery of, iv. 57 & n. 1.
Medina de Riosecco, Don J. A. Enriquez de Cabrera, duke of, viceroy of Naples, and his son, ii. 330 & n. 4.
Mediterranean Sea: coast of, near Marseilles, ii. 163 (i. 103); shipping in: in sermon, iv. 379–80; danger and disaster to Smyrna fleet in, 1693, v. 145 & n. 4, 151–2; English fleet in, 1694, v. 186 & n. 3; French fleet leaves, 1696, v. 242; Allied fleet comes from, 1704, v. 580.
Medlicott, Thomas: counsel for John Evelyn, jnr. (?; as Melldecot), iv. 194 & n. 2.
Medway, river (the river of Chatham): shelter from storm in, i. 56; country about: beauty of, iii. 422; tolls from vessels on, iii. 422, n. 5; geographical: position of Buoy of the Nore, &c., iii. 413, n. 2, 436, n. 1, 441, n. 7; Dutch attack on English fleet in, 1667, iii. 484–7 & nn., *passim*, 489, n. 2; ~ defences of, at time of, iii. 441, n. 7, 484, n. 1, 485 & nn. 3, 4, 486 & n. 6; ~ ships destroyed, &c., in, iii. 149, n. 6, 440, n. 6, 486 & nn. 3–5; ~ representation of, in painting, iii. 559, n. 4; defences of, 1672, iii. 610.
Meecham (Mitcham, Surrey ?): road through, v. 190 & n. 2.
Meeres, Sir Thomas: *see* Meres.
Meerman, Johan, Dutch ambassador in England, 1667–8, iii. 502, n. 6.
Meggot (Megot), Richard, D.D.; dean of Winchester 1679–92, iii. 443, n. 5; James II lodges with, iv. 468; sermons by, iii. 443; iv. 85, 94, 131, 138, 166, 197, 364, 371–2, 517, 518, 539, 576–7; v. 15–16.
Mehun: *see* Meung-sur-Loire.
Mehun-sur-Yèvre (Mung), ii. 152 & n. 7 (i. 98).
Melegnano, formerly Marignano, ii. 490 & n. 10.
Melfort: Viscount, 1685–6, Earl, 1686–95, and Duke (Jacobite), 1692–1715, of: *see* Drummond, John.
Melington, Sir Thomas: *see* Millington.
Mell, Davis, violinist, iii. 74 & n. 6; fame of, iii. 168.
Melldecot, — (T. Medlicott ?), iv. 194 & n. 2.
Mellington, Sir Thomas: *see* Millington.
Mello, Dom Francisco de, marquis of Sande; Portuguese ambassador to England, iii. 290, n. 8; entertained by Charles II, iii. 290–1 & n.; successor of, iii. 305.
Mello (Manuel da Camara), Dom Francisco de (Don Francisco de Melos), iii. 481–2 & n.; character, &c., iv. 2; visits Euston, iv. 112; social, iii. 481–2; iv. 95; mentioned, iv. 133, n. 6.
Melton Constable, Norfolk: architect of, iii. 554, n. 3.
Memory: paper on, iv. 284 & n. 2.

Memphis: mummy-pits near, ii. 469 & n. 3.
Mendip Hills, Somerset: lead-miners from, in Monmouth's rebellion, iv. 452 & n. 2.
Mennes (Minnes), Sir John, iii. 570, n. 8; in charge of Dutch prize-ships, iii. 420, n. 3; funeral of, iii. 570.
Mennetou (Muneton, &c.), ii. 152 & n. 5 (i. 98).
Mensuration: experiment in, iii. 541.
various measures of length [select]: *braccio*: Bolognese, ii. 425 & n. 3; ~ Florentine, ii. 196, n. 9; *canna*: Roman, ii. 425 & n. 3; *decempeda*, ii. 486, n. 1; flight shot, ii. 515; foot: ancient Roman, ii. 223 & n. 7; ~ Bolognese (*piede*), ii. 425 & n. 3; pace, ii. 248 & n. 9; *palmo*: Roman, ii. 248–9 & nn., 425, n. 3; *pertica*, ii. 486, n. 1; pistol shot, ii. 509; *stadium*, ii. 459, n. 1; *ulna*, ii. 196, n. 9.
Mentone, ii. 169 (i. 106 & n. 1).
Mercato di Sabato, near Miseno, ii. 351 & n. 2.
Mercator (N. Kauffmann): astronomical clock made by, iii. 450 & n. 1.
Merchant Adventurers: and Colchester cloth trade, iii. 177, n. 4.
Mercure, —, lutanist, ii. 535 & n. 1.
Mercure, John, musician, ii. 535, n. 1.
Mercurius Aurelianensis, musician, ii. 535, n. 1.
Mercury, the planet: transit of: attempt to observe, iii. 384–5 & n.
Mercy *or* Merey, —, musician, ii. 145 & n. 6 (i. 94).
Meres (Meeres), Sir Thomas, iv. 96, n. 1; visits E, iv. 96, 171.
Mergate: *see* Margate.
Mergozzo (Marguzzo): village and lake, of, ii. 507 & n. 4, 508, n. 2.
Meribah: stone from, ii. 440 & n. 2; in sermon, v. 309.
Merick, Sir William: *see* Meyrick.
Merideth, Dr. — (Dr. J. Meriton?): sermon by, iv. 499 & n. 6.
Merionethshire: phenomenon in, 1693–4, v. 174 & n. 3.
Meriton, Rev. —, iv. 333, n. 4; sermons by, at Deptford, iv. 333, 383–4, 463, 523, 649.
Meriton, John, D.D.; rector of St. Michael, Cornhill, and lecturer at St. Martin in the Fields, iv. 180, n. 5, 333, n. 4; character of, as preacher, iv. 180; sermons by, iv. 180; ~ at St. Martin in the Fields, iv. 351, 356–75 *passim*, 384, 499 & n. 6(?); v. 248, 273 & n. 1; ~ as lecturer of St. Martin's (without name), iv. 366, 499.
Merret (Meret, &c.), Christopher, M.D., iii. 337–8 & n.; shows E College of Physicians, iii. 337–8; E visits, iii. 364; inquiries referred to, by Royal Society, iii. 340, n. 1; demonstrations, &c., by, ii. 398, n. 1; iii. 341, n. 3.
Merrington, Durham: vicar of: *see* Knaggs, T.
Mersham, Kent: Mersham Hatch in, iii. 359 & n. 2.
Mesia de Tobar y Paz, Don A. F.: *see* Molina, conde de.
Mesmes, Jean-Antoine de, comte d'Avaux: *see* Avaux.
Mesniam, Cornelia, later Lady Manwood, ii. 316, n. 1.
Mesopotamia: visited by Dr. I. Basire, iii. 303, n. 3.
Messeroy (Messervy), —: recommended by E for office in Jersey, iii. 251 & n. 4.
Metals [select. For gold and silver *see* Gold and Silver; for metals used for arms, &c., and in building and sculpture *see* Arms and Armour; Building Materials; Sculpture: materials. The present section is probably very incomplete]:
general: experiments in refining, iii. 271.
antimony: in medicine, iii. 28 & n. 1, 220 & n. 3.
brass or bronze, ii. 33, n. 4; chandeliers, ii. 47, 50 (i. 35); sepulchral brasses, iii. 132.
copper: gilt: sconces of, ii. 113 (i. 73).
iron: working: beginning of, in sermon, iv. 315; found in Normandy, ii. 122 (i. 78); damasco metal, iv. 285; effects of atmosphere on, iv. 380; little used in Persia, iv. 358 & n. 4; varnish for, iii. 304; used for: aviary, ii. 175 (i. 111); beds, ii. 471; door-locks, &c., iii. 111–12 & n.; gates, iii. 18 & n. 7;

Metals (*cont.*)
iv. 593–4; grille (grate), ii. 93 (i. 62).
lead: coffins, &c., iii. 378; iv. 151, 276; v. 319, 497; miners of, iv. 452 & n. 2.
mercury: in various experiments, iii. 84, 295 & n. 8, 334; in barometer, &c., iii. 268, n. 1; iv. 126, 301–2 & n.; fixing of, iii. 48, 302 & n. 6, 483 & n. 4; in medicine, iii. 220 & n. 3.
pewter: plates, ii. 528.
steel: in medicine, iii. 464.
Metella, Cecilia: tomb of, ii. 362–3 & n.
Methuselah (Methusalem): in sermon, iv. 170 & n. 8.
Metz: Bishop of, 1612–52: *see* Verneuil, Henri de Bourbon, duke of.
Meung-sur-Loire (Mehun), ii. 139 & n. 5 (i. 91).
Meuse, river: operations near, &c., 1702, v. 519 & n. 1; *see also* Maas.
Meverall, Othowell, M.D.: attends Mrs. Eleanor Evelyn, ii. 14 & n. 1 (i. 11).
Mews (Meaws, &c.), Peter, D.C.L.; bishop of Bath and Wells 1673; of Winchester 1684, iii. 536, n. 1; as president of St. John's College, Oxford: social, iii. 536; attends coronation of William and Mary, iv. 633, n. 3; sermons by, iv. 31 & n. 3, 64, 167 & n. 3; appointed to preach, v. 21, n. 1; social, v. 238.
Mexico: books from, ii. 301; MS. from, iii. 107 & n. 4; clergy of: taxing of, v. 345, n. 2.
Meyrick *or* Mericke, Sir William: at Sheldon's translation to Canterbury, iii. 362 & n. 3.
Miana (Margherita Vitturi): chapel founded by, ii. 468, n. 4.
Miani *or* Emiliani, Giovanni, ii. 468, n. 4.
Michael, —: *see* Michell.
Michael, the Archangel: in sermons, v. 362, 614.
Michael VIII, Palaeologus, Byzantine emperor: monument erected by, ii. 440, n. 2.
Michelangelo Buonarroti, ii. 114, n. 10; as reviver of classical architecture, ii. 214 & n. 4; studies Baths of Diocletian, ii. 238; tomb of, ii. 196 & n. 2.
Michelangelo Buonarroti (*cont.*)
buildings, &c., designed by: Florence: Biblioteca Laurenziana, ii. 417, n. 1; Rome: Palazzo Farnese, ii. 214 & n. 4; Piazza del Campidoglio, ii. 226 & n. 3; S. Maria degli Angeli, ii. 240; S. Maria Maggiore: Cappella Sforza in, ii. 244 & n. 6.
paintings by: Holy Family (Uffizi), ii. 190 & n. 11 (i. 119); Last Judgement, ii. 298 & n. 1; Sistine Chapel ceiling, *ib.*; unspecified, ii. 114 (i. 74); school, &c.: Annunciation, ii. 274 & n. 9; Venus, ii. 309–10 & n.; named falsely for: Caravaggio, ii. 113 & n. 4 (i. 73); Cerquozzi, v. 245 & n. 3.
sculpture by: Bacchus, ii. 413 & n. 5; David, ii. 188 & n. 3 (i. 118), 193 (i. 120; as David and Goliath); Gregory I: begun by, ii. 275 & n. 7; Hercules (Fontainebleau), ii. 119 & n. 2 (i. 77); Julius II: tomb of, ii. 278 & n. 7; Madonna (Florence, S. Lorenzo), ii. 198 & n. 7, 416; Medici tombs, ii. 198, n. 5; Moses, ii. 278 & n. 7; Pietà (St. Peter's), ii. 264 & n. 5; Risen Christ (S. Maria sopra Minerva), ii. 378 & n. 2; school and doubtful: SS. Cosmas and Damian (Florence, S. Lorenzo), ii. 198 & n. 9, 416 & n. 5; Pietà (Norfolk collection; copy ?), iv. 566 & n. 2; false attributions: Descent from the Cross, ivory, ii. 414 & n. 1; Dying Adonis, ii. 403, n. 1; Laundress, ii. 419 & n. 1; Medici, P. and G. de': tomb of (Florence, S. Lorenzo), ii. 416 & n. 4.
Michelangelo delle Battaglie (M. Cerquozzi): painting by, v. 245 & n. 3.
Michelino, Domenico di: painting of Dante by, ii. 197, n. 3.
Michell family of Stamerham, Sussex, i. 7 & n. 1.
Michell, Bridget (Mrs. B. Richards): geneal., ii. 22, n. 1.
Michell, Jane: *see* Newton, Mrs. Jane.
Michell (Michael), John, of Houghton (?), ii. 21 & n. 6 (i. 16).
Michell, Robert, of Petersfield: buys North Stoke, v. 441 & n. 5.
Michell, Thomas, of Rudgwick: geneal., ii. 3, n. 1.

Michell (Michael), William, of Houghton (?), ii. 21 & n. 6 (i. 16).
Michieli, Andrea (A. Vicentino): painting by, ii. 444 & n. 5.
Mickleham, Surrey: Mole river at, ii. 523, n. 3; iii. 157; Sir F. Stydolf's seat (Norbury Park) in, iii. 157 & n. 5.
Micklethwaite, Ann, Lady Micklethwaite, widow of Sir John: law-suit against, iv. 368 & n. 6.
Micklethwaite, Sir John, M.D.: geneal., iv. 368, n. 6.
Middelburg (Midelbrogh), ii. 31 (i. 24).
Middlesex, county: justices of the peace for: appointments, 1687, iv. 536, n. 3; sessions house of: *see* London: topography: Hicks Hall.
Middlesex: Earls of: *see* Cranfield, Lionel, first earl, 1622–45; *new creation*: *see* Sackville, Charles, first earl, 1675–7, later sixth earl of Dorset.
Middleton (Midleton): *see also* Myddelton.
Middleton, Charles; second earl of Middleton 1674; earl of Monmouth (Jacobite) 1701, iv. 387, n. 5; appointed secretary of state, iv. 387 & n. 5, 417 & n. 4; social: parties, iv. 466, 490, 548.
Middleton, Mrs. Elizabeth, wife of Col. Thomas: marries, iii. 560–1 & n.
Middleton, John, first earl of Middleton 1660, iii. 484, n. 4; attacks Donnington Castle, 1644, iii. 100, n. 3; opposes Dutch at Chatham, 1667, iii. 484–5, 486–7 & n.
Middleton, Thomas: *see* Plays.
Middleton (Midleton), Col. Thomas, iii. 560, n. 6; marries, iii. 560–1 n.; provides information about New England, iii. 581 & n. 4, 584; social, iii. 614 & n. 5.
Middleton, William, D.D.: sermon in Italian by, ii. 545 & n. 9.
Middleton: Earls of: *see* Middleton, John, first earl, 1660–74; Middleton, Charles, second earl, 1674–1719.
Mignard, Pierre: paintings by, i. 84, n. 2.
Milan: city, duchy, &c.:
— the city: notice, ii. 491–505 & nn.
— — general remarks: destruction of, by Frederick Barbarossa, ii. 496, n. 2; Inquisition at, ii. 491 & n. 2, 503; manufactures at, ii. 501 & n. 8; opera at, ii. 503 & n. 4; population, &c., of, ii. 491, n. 3 *ad fin.*, 501 & n. 6; situation, &c., ii. 501; Spanish government of: effect of, ii. 491, n. 3 *ad fin.*; governors: *see* Feria, duke of; Frias, duke of; Swiss guard at, ii. 494; P. Tibaldi as architect at, ii. 494.
— — buildings, &c.: Biblioteca Ambrosiana, ii. 497–500 & nn.; ~ MS. in, ii. 501, n. 2; ~ Settala collection in, ii. 502, n. 5; ~ prefect of: *see* Ferrari, F. B.; castle (citadel), ii. 501–2 & nn.; churches, &c.: baptistery, ii. 500 & n. 3; cathedral, ii. 492–4 & nn.; ~ portico before, ii. 503; S. Ambrogio, ii. 500–1 & nn.; ~ canon of: *see* Settala, M.; S. Angelo (in Porta Nuova): tomb of Col. A. Burnet in, ii. 505, n. 1; S. Celso, ii. 495 & n. 1; S. Eustorgio, ii. 496 & n. 2; ~ tomb of St. Peter Martyr in, ii. 199, n. 6; S. Fedele, ii. 494–5 & n.; S. Lorenzo, ii. 496; S. Maria delle Grazie: refectory of friary of, ii. 496–7 & n.; S. Maria presso S. Celso, ii. 495 & nn. 1–7; colleges, ii 496 & n. 1; colonnade by S. Lorenzo, ii. 496 & n. 3; *Herculeum lavacrum*, ii. 496, n. 3; Hospital, ii. 495–6 & n.; palaces: of archbishop, ii. 494 & n. 6; ~ of governor (Palazzo Reale), ii. 494 & n. 7; Piazza del Duomo, ii. 494; Settala collection, ii. 502 & nn. 5–7; Temple of Hercules: ruins of, ii. 496 & n. 3; Three Kings inn, ii. 491 & n. 3; Trivulzio collection (modern): MS. in, ii. 498, n. 1; Via Tre Alberghi, ii. 491, n. 3; walls, ii. 491, n. 3 *ad fin.*, 501.
— — environs: fertility of, ii. 491, 501.
— — persons: E infected with smallpox at, ii. 519, n. 4; Rev. W. Petty at, ii. 498, n. 8 *ad fin.*; Scots colonel serving at: *see* Burnet, A. (ii. 503–5 & nn.).
— diocese: archbishops of: and Iron Crown of Lombardy, ii. 500–1 & n.; individuals: *see*

Milan (*cont.*)
Charles, St., Borromeo; Borromeo, F.
— duchy of: boundaries of, &c., ii. 490 *bis* & n. 7, 506, 508–9; as Spanish possession, ii. 477, n. 6, 518, n. 3; ~ pass for travel through, ii. 477–8; claimed by Emperor, 1700–1, v. 440–1; occupied by French, v. 440, 446, 462 & n. 3; Imperialists advance towards, v. 472 & n. 3.
Milanese traveller (Jo: Baptist), ii. 316; *see also* ii. 325.
Military [miscellaneous notices; *see also* Arms and Armour; Fortifications; Processions; and the armies, &c., of the various states]: displays: imitating battle and siege, ii. 135 (i. 88); iv. 42 & n. 1; encamping: method of, ii. 38 (i. 28); iv. 458; flags [excluding those in accounts of processions]: Charles I's, at Edgehill, i. 53–4 & n.; Spanish: captured, ii. 41 & n. 5 (i. 31); Turkish: captured, ii. 180 (i. 113); ~ royal, iv. 399.
frontiers: marauding on, ii. 38–9 & n. (i. 29), 59 (i. 40), 74 & nn. 4, 5 (i. 48–9), 83–5 & nn. (i. 56–7), 560–1 & n.; iii. 12, 17, 54; hospitals: at Amsterdam, ii. 45 & n. 6 (i. 32); ~ *see also* London: environs: Chelsea; marching: bad season for, iv. 605; operations: bombardment of places from sea, iv. 381 & n. 3; v. 160 & n. 1, 186 & n. 2, 216 & n. 3, 218 & n. 2, 252 & n. 3; siege, ii. 31 & n. 4 (i. 24), 35–8 (i. 27–9); iv. 42 & n. 1.
passport, iv. 610; reviews [excluding those in England], ii. 135 & n. 1 (i. 88); v. 352; salutes, &c. [mainly gunfire]: celebrations in camp, ii. 36 (i. 27); compliments to royalty and diplomatists, ii. 74 (i. 49), 76 (i. 50); iv. 80, 472–3; king's birthday: omitted, iv. 601; royal birth, iv. 587; proclamation of new rulers, iv. 623; other public rejoicings, ii. 282, 291, 386, 432; iii. 480; v. 28, n. 2, 518.
shooting: practice with small arms at Geneva, ii. 526–7 & nn.; tents, ii. 36–7 (i. 28); iv. 553; ~ royal office of, iii. 324 & n. 3; trumpeter: as preliminary to parley, iv. 610.
Millenarians: sect of, at Water Stratford, 1694, v. 177–8 & n.; attacked in sermon, v. 448 & n. 1; *see also* Fifth Monarchy Men.
Miller, Rev. John: sermon by, v. 477 & n. 2.
Milles, Rev. —: *see* Mills, Daniel.
Millington (Mellington, &c.), Sir Thomas, M.D., iv. 307, n. 4; social, iv. 307; attends Mrs. Susanna Draper, v. 190.
Mills, Daniel; D.D. 1679, iii. 622, n. 1; sermons by (?): funeral, iii. 622; iv. 111; ~ ordinary, iv. 25, 47.
Milton, near Gravesend, Kent: rector of: *see* Bréval, F. Durant de.
Milton, near Sittingbourne, Kent: vicar of, 1672–95; *see* Turner, Thomas.
Milton, Sir Christopher, brother of the poet: appointed a judge, iv. 514 & n. 6; office of, at Ipswich, iv. 114, n. 6.
Milton, John, the poet: described as defender of the regicides, iii. 364, n. 6, 365; iv. 514; as uncle of Edward Phillips, iii. 364–5 & n.; as brother of Sir Christopher Milton, iv. 514; Leonora of (L. Baroni), ii. 400, n. 1; his friend Charles Diodati, ii. 521, n. 1.
Mincio, river: Imperialists campaign on, 1701, v. 472 *bis* & nn. 1, 3.
Mindanao: *see* Meangis.
Mindelheim: principality of: granted to Marlborough, v. 573, n. 2.
Minerals [*see also* Building Materials; Crystal; &c.]: various: collections, iii. 445; iv. 68; ~ in inscription (not indexed separately), ii. 333; alum, ii. 353; ~ mines, ii. 342; ~ used in paper-making, iv. 141; amiantus or asbestos, ii. 502 & n. 7; iii. 295; Bologna stone (heavy-spar; called by E *lapis illuminabilis*), ii. 422–3 & n.; ~ mentioned, ii. 398, n. 3; iv. 251; brick-earth, iii. 478; coal: *see* Fuel; flints, ii. 467 & n. 5; *lapis obsianus*, iii. 601 & n. 2; lime, ii. 430 & n. 2; marcasites, iii. 10 & n. 2, 445; iv. 68; mineral salt, Lago di Agnano, ii. 339; nitre, ii.

Minerals (*cont.*)
345; orpiment (arsenic trisulphide), ii. 430 & n. 1; pumice, ii. 334, 345; saltpetre: *see* Gunpowder and Saltpetre; salt-pits, Nantwich: account of, mentioned, iii. 540 & n. 1; sulphate of copper (flower of brass): mine, ii. 342 & n. 3; sulphur (brimstone), ii. 334, 336, 353; iv. 138; ~ mine, ii. 342.
Mineral Waters: *see* Medicinal and Hot Springs.
Minerva, Cape of, near Naples, ii. 329 & n. 3, 350 & n. 2.
Mingrelia: traveller to, iv. 213 & n. 1; women of, iv. 214 & n. 3.
Minn: *see* Mynne.
Minnes, Sir John: *see* Mennes.
Mints: Geneva, ii. 529 & n. 3; Venice, ii. 445 & nn. 4, 5; *see also* Royal Mint.
Minturnae (Minterna): ruins of, ii. 323 & n. 6.
Minturno, ii. 323, n. 6.
Minucius Felix, M.: urn of, ii. 383 & n. 1.
Miomus *or* Nicomus, Antonius, ii. 466 & n. 3.
Miracles: views on, of James II, iv. 468–70; cures: *see* Medicine and Surgery; marks on girl's arm, iii. 556–8; rain-storm: representation of, ii. 370 & n. 4.
Mirandola, Giovanni Pico della: *see* Pico.
Miremont, Armand de Bourbon, marquis de: as horseman (?), iv. 400 & n. 4.
Miseno: cape, &c., of: notice, ii. 350–1 & nn.; in views, ii. 329 & n. 3, 334; villa at, ii. 349, n. 8.
Misenus: tomb of, ii. 350 & n. 1.
Mitcham, Surrey: road through (?; as Meecham), v. 190 & n. 2.
Mittau: taken by Sweden, 1701, v. 472 & n. 4.
Mocenigo (Muccinigo, &c.), Piero, Venetian ambassador to England, 1668–70: entry of, iii. 515 & n. 1; social, iii. 537, 542 & n. 2; departs, iii. 564 & n. 2.
Mocenigo (Maccenigo), Sebastian: accompanies embassy, 1685, iv. 492 & n. 1.
Mochi *or* Mocchi, Francesco, sculptor, ii. 262, n. 1; St. Veronica by, ii. 262 & n. 1; ~ niche of, ii. 308, n. 6; statues by, ii. 306, n. 11.
Modena: James, duke of York (later James II) married at, by proxy, iv. 26, n. 2; home of Montecuccoli family, iv. 93, n. 1; sculpture at, ii. 413, n. 7.
Modena: Dukes and Duchesses of: *see* Alfonso IV (1658–62); Laura (Martinozzi), his duchess; Rinaldo (1694–1737); Charlotte Felicitas, his duchess.
Modyford (Mudiford, &c.), Sir Thomas, bt., governor of Jamaica, iii. 579–80 & n.; letters from, *ib.*; iii. 583 & n. 5, 585 & n. 2; at Berkeley House, iv. 46.
Mohammed: *see* Mahomet.
Mohammedans [*see also* Turkey and the Turks]: annual baptisms of, at Rome, ii. 386, n. 4; converted Turk at Rome, ii. 376–7 & n.; the Bantam ambassadors, &c., as, iv. 285, 286 & n. 1; sermons against: endowed, v. 88, n. 3.
Mohun, Charles, fourth Baron Mohun: tried for murder of W. Mountford, v. 129 & n. 2.
Mohun: fourth Baron, 1677–1712: *see* Mohun, Charles.
Moisset, Jean de: owner of Rueil, ii. 108, n. 4.
Mola di Gaeta (Formia), ii. 323 & n. 4.
Mole, river, Surrey, iii. 143, n. 1; the swallows in, ii. 523 & n. 3; iii. 157 & n. 4.
Molgrave, Lord, *rectè* Mulgrave: *see* Sheffield, John, earl of Mulgrave, later duke of the county of Buckingham, &c.
Molina, Don A. F. Mesia de Tobar y Paz, conde de, Spanish ambassador to England: audience for, iii. 412 & n. 5.
Molines (Moulins), —, surgeon, ii. 553 & n. 4; dissection at house of, ii. 553–4.
Molineux, Mrs., friend of Lady Evelyn (1814), i. *53*.
Molino, Francesco da: elected doge of Venice, ii. 473 & n. 5.
Mollen, —, lute-maker (L. Maler ?), ii. 426 & n. 5.
Monaco (Morgus): notice, ii. 168–9 & nn. (i. 106).
Monaldesco, Marquis G. R.: assassination of, iv. 221 & n. 3.
Monarchies, the four ancient, ii. 431 & n. 3.

Monck, Anne, duchess of Albemarle, born Clarges, wife of (1) T. Radford; (2) George Monck, first duke of Albemarle, iii. 425, n. 2; social, iii. 425; second marriage of: validity of, disputed, v. 410–11 & n.
Monck, Christopher, second duke of Albemarle 1670, iv. 248, n. 5; as a gentleman of the Bed-chamber, iv. 296; introduces Surrey gentlemen to Charles II, iv. 248 & n. 5; buys and sells Clarendon House, iii. 379, n. 8 *ad fin.*; iv. 339 & n. 4; entertains Ahmed Hadu at New Hall, iv. 287 & n. 4; gains of, from Hispaniola treasure, iv. 552 & n. 3; social, iv. 295; geneal., iv. 15, n. 7; estate of: inheritance of, disputed, v. 167 & n. 1, 246 & n. 5, 288 & n. 6, 475; legal paternity of: disputed, v. 410–11 & n.
Monck, Elizabeth, duchess of Albemarle, wife of Christopher Monck, second duke: *see* Montagu, Elizabeth, duchess of Montagu.
Monck (Monk), George; first duke of Albemarle 1660, iii. 240, n. 5.
— chronological series:
— — (1) as Monck:
— — — 1653: serves against Dutch, iii. 425 & n. 1, 440.
— — — 1660: march of, from Scotland to London, &c., iii. 240 & n. 5, 241 & n. 2; removes gates, &c., of City of London, iii. 241 & n. 4; demands summoning of new parliament, iii. 242 & n. 2; expected to recall Charles II, iii. 243; letter to, from Charles II, iii. 244 & n. 2; conduct of: Col. H. Morley's compared with, iii. 245; supported by Edward Mountagu, later earl of Sandwich, iii. 619, n. 2.
— — (2) as duke [he is sometimes called the Lord General]:
— — — 1663: at review, iii. 357 & n. 2.
— — — 1664–7: commissioner for prizes, iii. 419 & n. 3.
— — — 1665: attends the king in parliament, iii. 402; stays at Whitehall during Plague, iii. 416 & n. 4; visits Charles II at Oxford, iii. 423, 424 *bis*; appointed with Prince Rupert to chief command at sea, iii. 424–5 & n.; confidence of, in his ability to defeat the Dutch, iii. 425 & n. 1, 440, 618.
— — — 1666: joins the fleet, iii. 435 & n. 3, 436 & n. 2; in Four Days' Battle, iii. 438–40 & nn., *passim*; at Buoy of the Nore, iii. 441 & n. 4; returns from sea, iii. 463 & n. 4.
— — — 1667: appointed a commissioner of the Treasury, iii. 487, n. 7; sent to Chatham to oppose Dutch, iii. 484–5 & n., 486, n. 7.
— marriage: validity of disputed, v. 411, n. 1.
— property and residence: Cressing Temple: purchase of, proposed to, iii. 435 & n. 2; buys New Hall, Essex, iii. 179, n. 3; iv. 287, n. 4; lodgings of, in Cockpit, Whitehall, iii. 416 & n. 4; fortune of: dissipated by his son, iv. 339.
— relations with E [mainly concerned with E's activities as a commissioner for Sick and Wounded]: letter from, carried by E, iii. 395; authorizes E to lease Leeds Castle, iii. 422, n. 1; presents E to Charles II, Jan. 1666, iii. 428–9; to be asked by E to remove soldiers quartered at Deptford, &c., iii. 475; other business or social intercourse, 1665–6, iii. 409–34 & nn., *passim*; social intercourse, 1666–7, iii. 463, 471, 478.
— relations with Sandwich: supported by Sandwich (as E. Mountagu), 1660, iii. 619, n. 2; censures Sandwich for dispersing prize-goods, iii. 424 & n. 1, 425 & n. 1; questions Sandwich's courage, iii. 425, 440, 617–18.
— social: at funeral of Dr. N. Monck, iii. 307; at Sheldon's translation to Canterbury, iii. 363; at feasts, iii. 389, 408, 425.
Monck, Nicholas; bishop of Hereford 1661, iii. 307, n. 3; consecrated, iii. 266 & n. 3; funeral of, iii. 307.
Monconys, Balthasar de: *see* Books: sources *and* Books mentioned in text.
Money: *see* Coins and Medals; Currency.

Monmouth: Earls and Duke of: *see* Carey, Robert, first earl 1626–39; *new creation*: *see* Scott, James, duke 1663–85; Scott, Anne, his duchess; *new creation*: *see* Mordaunt, Charles, earl 1689–97, later third earl of Peterborough; *Jacobite creation*: *see* Middleton, Charles, second earl of Middleton (Scotland), earl 1701–19.
Monmouthshire: in view, iii. 119.
Mons: surrendered to French, 1691, v. 47 & n. 1.
Monsieur: *see* Philip, duke of Anjou and later of Orleans.
Monson (Munson), Sir John, K.B.: social, iii. 473 & nn. 4, 6.
Monsters [malformed animals; for imaginary monsters *see* Animals, fabulous], ii. 40 (i. 30), 72 (i. 47), 136 (i. 89); iii. 93.
Monstrosities (human): abortions, iii. 256; iv. 145–6; dumb man, iv. 113; giants: man, v. 592 & n. 1; ~ women, iii. 132, 521 & n. 4, 615; the Hairy Maid, iii. 198 & n. 1; hermaphrodite, iii. 492 & n. 3; Siamese twins, iii. 255–6 & nn.; boy with words in his eyes, v. 453 & n. 1.
Montagu, Mrs. Anne, daughter of Richard Evelyn, wife of William Montagu, jnr., iii. 77, n. 5.
as Anne Evelyn: baptised, iii. 77; marriage-proposal for, iii. 475 & nn. 1, 2; as heiress, iii. 544; inherits Baynards, ii. 539, n. 4; married, iii. 551 & nn. 3–5.
as Mrs. Montagu: social, iii. 581; iv. 14, 18; breaks entail of Baynards, iv. 569, 582–3 & n.; v. 86; ill-treated by Montagu, iv. 583; v. 3; dies, iv. 569.
Montagu, Sir Charles, of Boughton: geneal., ii. 558, n. 1.
Montagu, Charles; Baron Halifax, 1700; earl of Halifax 1714, v. 221, n. 2; elected president of Royal Society, v. 226 & n. 1; as member of Junto, v. 324, n. 3; impeachment of, 1701: voted, &c., v. 456 & n. 1, 462 & n. 1; ~ dismissed, v. 467–8 & n.; ~ alluded to, v. 466 & n. 1, 481; quarrels with Leeds, 1702, v. 523 & n. 1; attacked in parliament, 1703, v. 530 & n. 1; social, v. 221, 597.
Montague, Charles; fourth earl of Manchester 1683; first duke of Manchester 1719, iv. 356, n. 1; as English ambassador to France: recalled, 1701, v. 472 & n. 5, 476 & n. 4; social, v. 597; chaplain(s) of: sermons by, iv. 356, 357, 373, 378–9.
Montagu, Edward; second earl of Manchester 1642, iii. 251, n. 1; as parliamentary general: storms Lincoln, iii. 132, n. 3; as Lord Chamberlain of the Household: takes part in ceremonies, iii. 251 & n. 1, 277 & n. 6, 283 & n. 5 (error); visits duchess of York, iii. 264; at feast, iii. 389; invites E to a play at court, iii. 466; E visits (?), iii. 380 & n. 5; chaplain of: sermon by, iii. 265.
Montagu, Edward, earl of Sandwich: *see* Mountagu.
Montagu, Elizabeth: *see* Hatton, Elizabeth, Baroness Hatton.
Montagu, Elizabeth, countess of Montagu, born Wriothesley; married (1) Joceline Percy, earl of Northumberland; (2), as his first wife, Ralph Montagu, earl (later duke) of Montagu, iv. 344 & n. 3; as countess of Northumberland, iv. 261, n. 1.
Montagu, Elizabeth, duchess of Montagu; born Cavendish; married (1) Christopher Monck, duke of Albemarle; (2), as his second wife, Ralph Montagu, earl and, later, duke of Montagu, iv. 15, n. 7; as duchess of Albemarle: social, iv. 15, 18; inherits New Hall, iv. 287, n. 4; marries Montagu, &c., v. 167, n. 1.
Montagu, James; bishop of Bath and Wells 1608; of Winchester 1616: edits James I's works, &c., iii. 140, n. 4; mentioned, iv. 216, n. 3.
Montagu, John, D.D., iv. 503, n. 2; sermon by (?), iv. 503; appointed to preach, iv. 372, n. 5.
Montagu, Ralph; third Baron Montagu of Boughton 1684; earl, 1689, and first duke, 1705, of Montagu, iv. 90, n. 7; marriages of: first, iv. 344 & n. 3; ~ second, iv. 15, n. 7; v. 167, n. 1; claims Albemarle inheritance, v. 167 & n. 1, 246 & n. 5, 288 & n. 6, 475; house of, in Bloomsbury, iv. 90 & n. 7, 184, 344–5 & n.; ~ burnt down, iv. 497 & n. 2.

Montagu, Robert; third earl of Manchester 1671: social, iv. 15 & n. 3; chaplain of: sermon by, iv. 89.
Montagu, Walter: conversion of, to Roman Catholicism, iii. 558, n. 1.
Montagu, William, sen., Chief Baron of the Exchequer, iii. 551, n. 3; case before, iv. 368; decision of, iv. 417, n. 6 *ad fin.*; geneal., iii. 551.
Montagu, William, jnr., iii. 551, n. 3; marries Anne Evelyn, iii. 551; character, &c., of, iv. 583; v. 3, 86; acquires Baynards, iv. 582–3 & n.; v. 86; *see also* iv. 569; action against, v. 3 & n. 2.
Montagu: Earl, 1689–1705, and first Duke, 1705–9, of: *see* Montagu, Ralph.
Montagu: third Viscount, 1629–82, and his viscountess: *see* Browne, Francis; Browne, Elizabeth.
Montagu of Boughton: third Baron, 1684–9: *see* Montagu, Ralph, later duke of Montagu.
Montaigne *or* Mountain, George, archbishop of York, &c.: as bishop of London: licenses Cosin's *Collection of private devotions*, iii. 46 & n. 1, 635.
Montalbani, Ovidio, Dr., and his phosphorus, ii. 422–3 & nn.
Montalcino (Mount Alcini), ii. 207 & n. 1.
Montecatini, ii. 410, n. 4.
Montecuccoli, Raimondo, general: nephew of, iv. 93 & n. 1.
Monte Feltre, Charles Ubaldino, count of: notice, iv. 335–6 & n.
Monte Feltre, Elizabeth Ubaldino, countess of, born Savile, and her sister: notice, iv. 335–6 & nn.
Montefiascone, ii. 210 & nn. 3, 4.
Montelupo, Raffaello da, sculptor: works by, ii. 278 & n. 7.
Monte Oliveto: monastery of, ii. 206 & n. 4.
Monterosi (Montrosso), ii. 211, n. 2, 407 & n. 4.
Monteverde, C., *L'incoronazione di Poppea*: performed, ii. 474, n. 6.
Montford, —: *see* Mountford, W.
Montfort, Anthonie van, called van Blocklandt: paintings by, ii. 32 & n. 6 (i. 25).
Montgomery: Earl of, 1605–30: *see* Herbert, Philip, later fourth earl of Pembroke.
Montgomeryshire: error for Merionethshire, v. 174 & n. 3.
Monthey, Valais, ii. 519 & nn. 1, 2.
Montjuich, Fort, near Barcelona: taken by Allies, 1705, v. 610, n. 2.
Montlouis, Touraine: cave-dwellings at, ii. 144 & n. 2 (i. 93).
Montmorency: Château de, ii. 121, n. 3.
Montpelier: Lord Mordaunt goes to, iii. 468, n. 6 *ad fin.*
Montrah, Lord, *rectè* Mountrath: *see* Coote, Charles, earl of Mountrath.
Montreuil: notice, 1643, ii. 84–5 & n. (i. 57); E at: 1650, iii. 12 & n. 4, 17; ~ 1652, iii. 54; *see also* n. 3.
Montrose: fifth Earl and first Marquis of: *see* Graham, James.
Montserrat: *see* Leeward Islands.
Moody, Lively; D.D. 1671: recommended for vicarship of Eltham (?), iii. 195 & n. 3.
Moore, Elizabeth, Lady Moore, wife of Sir George, iii. 176, n. 1; as Elizabeth Hungerford: visits E (?), iii. 161 & n. 4; marriage-proposal for, iii. 175–6 & n., 193; marries Moore, iii. 367 & n. 4.
Moore, Sir George, bt.: as Mr. Moore: marriage of, iii. 367 & n. 4.
Moore, John, D.D.; bishop of Norwich 1691; of Ely 1707, v. 224, n. 6; library of, v. 325 & n. 8; MS. belonging to, v. 206, n. 3; learning of, v. 353 & n. 3; social: parties, v. 224, 238, 353; alone, v. 469, 529; mentioned, v. 59, n. 1; chaplain of: *see* Clarke, Samuel, D.D.
Moore, Sir John, lord mayor of London 1681–2: sermon before, iv. 284 & n. 1.
Moore (Moor), (Sir) Jonas: commissioner for Saltpetre, iii. 443, n. 1.
Moors: galley-slaves, ii. 183 (i. 116); at Venice, ii. 449; for the Moors of Morocco *see* Morocco.
Moray *or* Murray, Sir Robert, iii. 272, n. 3; in projected rising, 1654, iii. 463, n. 6; account by, of Rupert's drops, iii. 272, n. 2; at observation of Saturn, iii. 285–6 & nn.; and Royal Society's meetings, iii. 340, n. 1, 445; visits Burrough Green, iii. 552; and E's *Mystery of Jesuitism*: supplies materials for, iii. 393, n. 6 *ad fin.*; ~ presents to Charles II, iii. 397; social, &c.: parties, iii. 272, 287, 295, 332, 369–70, 378, 463, 623; iv. 11; funeral of, iv. 15 & n. 6.

Morbrun: *see* Embrun.
Mordaunt, —, Lady Mordaunt, at Ashted, iii. 425 & n. 5(?); iv. 557 & n. 1.
Mordaunt, Carey, countess of Peterborough, wife of Charles Mordaunt second Viscount Mordaunt, &c.: as Lady Mordaunt: social, iv. 499 & n. 5.
Mordaunt, Sir Charles, bt.: geneal., iv. 206, n. 1.
Mordaunt, Charles; second Viscount Mordaunt 1675; earl of Monmouth 1689; third earl of Peterborough 1697, iv. 81, n. 1; ill, iv. 80–1; to visit France, iv. 84; proposals of, for settling Viscountess Mordaunt's estate, iv. 259 & n. 2, 273, 275; comes to London, 1688, iv. 612, n. 1; as commissioner for Greenwich Hospital, v. 209–10 & n.; geneal., iii. 155, n. 7; iv. 499, n. 5; mentioned in error (?), iv. 108–9 & n.
Mordaunt, Elizabeth, Lady Mordaunt, wife of (1) Sir Charles Mordaunt, bt.; (2) Francis Godolphin: social, iv. 206 & n. 1.
Mordaunt, Elizabeth, Viscountess Mordaunt, born Carey, wife of John Mordaunt, first viscount, iii. 155, n. 7; character, iii. 469; iv. 9, 140 & n. 6, 173; geneal., iii. 1, n. 2, 156, n. 1, 189, n. 4; acquainted with E in France, iv. 9 & n. 1; marriage proposal for, iii. 155 & n. 7; at Reigate Priory, iii. 156; marries Mordaunt, iii. 194 & n. 4; inherits house at Parson's Green, iii. 271, n. 6; charities of, iv. 81 *bis*, 140; erects monument to Mordaunt, iv. 86 & n. 5; social: as Mrs. Carey: visits E, iii. 158, 189; as Lady Mordaunt: at parties, iv. 85, 140 & n. 3; ~ visits E or Mrs. Evelyn, iii. 329, 363; iv. 34, 95, 109; ~ visits to, at Parson's Green or elsewhere, iii. 315; iv. 9, 75, 80, 81, 85, 86, 94 *bis*, 95, 103 *bis*, 112, 138, 140, 154; ~ *see also* London: environs: Parson's Green; Mordaunt, John, Viscount Mordaunt; ill, iv. 64, 131; last illness and death of, iv. 173 & n. 3; appoints E a trustee for her children, iv. 173; will of: executors' meetings, iv. 188–9 & nn., 202, 259, 273, 275; portrait of, i. 26 & n. 3; *Private Diarie* of: cited, iii. 194, n. 4; iv. 140, n. 6; *see also* iii. 425, n. 5.
Mordaunt, Elizabeth, countess of Peterborough, born Howard, wife of John Mordaunt, first earl, iii. 156, n. 1; geneal., iii. 189 & n. 4; inherits Blechingley, iii. 156, n. 2; house of, at Reigate, iii. 156 & n. 1, 219; social iii. 194, 214, 305.
Mordaunt, Henry, second earl of Peterborough, iii. 305, n. 4; expedition of, to Tangier, 1661–2: sets out, iii. 305 & n. 4, 311 & n. 5; ~ returns, iii. 327 & n. 7; appointed groom of the stole, 1685, iv. 417 & n. 2; converted to Roman Catholicism, iv. 541, n. 2; flight and capture of, 1688, iv. 611 & n. 4; in Tower, iv. 640 & n. 4; shows E portrait of Prince James Edward, v. 92 & n. 2; and Blechingley: sells, &c., iv. 108–9 & n., 110–11; ~ demolishes manor-house, iv. 111, n. 1; executor of will of Elizabeth Mordaunt, Viscountess Mordaunt, iv. 202; social, iii. 377; iv. 112, 465; geneal., iii. 156, n. 1; iv. 112 & n. 5; v. 393–4.
Mordaunt, John; first Viscount Mordaunt of Avalon 1659, iii. 189 & n. 3, 245, n. 3; geneal., iii. 155, n. 7, 156, n. 1; courtship and marriage of, iii. 189, 194 & n. 4; wedding anniversary, iv. 34 & n. 4; imprisoned and tried, 1658, iii. 214 & nn. 3, 4; at Reigate, iii. 219; prepares rising, 1659, iv. 188, n. 7; procures pardon for Col. H. Morley, iii. 245; E recommends secretary to, iii. 263; in Charles II's coronation procession, iii. 278 & n. 3; charges against, by W. Tayleur, heard in house of commons, iii. 468–9 & nn.; ordered to search Windsor Forest for peat, &c., iii. 486, n. 1; returns to England from abroad, 1669, iii. 582, n. 3; house of, at Parson's Green, iii. 271 & n. 6; social: godfather of Richard Evelyn (b. 1664), iii. 368; visits E, iii. 329, 363, 377, 582; visits to, iii. 193; ~ at Parson's Green or elsewhere, iii. 261, 271, 305, 585;

Mordaunt, John, first Viscount Mordaunt (*cont.*)
~ or to Lady Mordaunt, at Parson's Green, &c., iii. 262, 275, 293, 341, 355, 367, 375; iv. 1, 55; ~ *see also* London: environs: Parson's Green; dies, iv. 64, n. 5; monument to, iv. 86 & n. 5; chaplain of: *see* Rowland, Rev. —.

Mordaunt, John and Elizabeth, Viscount and Viscountess Mordaunt: children of: E as trustee for, iv. 173; business meetings, &c., on behalf of, iv. 188–9, 202, 259, 273, 275; visits to, &c., iv. 173, 180, 258, 289, 334 & n. 1, 335; *see also* Mordaunt, Charles, earl of Peterborough.

Mordaunt, John, first earl of Peterborough: geneal., iii. 156, n. 1.

Mordaunt, Lady Mary; Baroness Mordaunt *sui juris* 1697; married (1) 1677, Henry Howard, Lord Arundel, later seventh duke of Norfolk; (2) 1701, Sir John Germaine, iv. 112, n. 5; first marriage, iv. 112 & n. 5; property of, iv. 108–9 & n.; Norfolk tries to divorce, v. 90 & n. 7, 127 & n. 1, 380 & n. 3; ~ divorce effected, v. 393–4 & n.; sells Arundel marbles (?), v. 44 & n. 6.

Mordaunt of Avalon: Viscounts, &c.: *see* Mordaunt, John, first viscount, 1659–75; Mordaunt, Elizabeth, his viscountess; Mordaunt, Charles, second viscount, 1675–89, later earl of Peterborough, &c.; Mordaunt, Carey, his viscountess.

Mordaunt (of Turvey): Baroness 1697–1705: *see* Mordaunt, Lady Mary.

Morden, Sir John, bt.: hospital founded by, v. 212 & n. 5.

More, Alexander: *see* Morus.

More, Sir Thomas: house of, in Chelsea, iv. 161, n. 3; ~ mentioned, iii. 315, n. 2; portrait of, by Holbein, ii. 549.

Morea, the: Thomas Palaeologus, despot of, ii. 205 & n. 2; Venetian possessions in, ii. 439, n. 5; Count K. J. von Königsmark dies in, iv. 274, n. 1.

Morehouse (Morus), Rev. John: sermon by, v. 209 & n. 3.

Morehouse (Morus), Rev. Stephen; curate at Wotton *c.* 1691–8, v. 68, n. 1; character, &c., v. 68, 181; sermons by (some as by our curate), v. 68 *bis*, 69 *bis*, 115 *bis*, 180–9, 206–9, 228–35, 261–8, 282–7 *passim & singulatim*; relative of, v. 209.

Morella, Spanish painter: *see* Murillo, B.E.

Moretus, Balthasar II, ii. 67, n. 2.

Morgan, Edward, botanist, iii. 217 & n. 2.

Morgan, Sir Henry, iii. 583, n. 5; as Col. Morgan: captures Panama, iii. 583 & n. 5, 585 & n. 2; iv. 46 & nn. 3, 4; at Berkeley House, iv. 46 & n. 2.

Morgus (Monaco), ii. 168 & nn. 4, 6 (i. 106).

Morice, —, Lady Morice, iii. 442 & n. 3.

Morice, Gertrude: *see* Cotton, Gertrude, Lady Cotton.

Morice, Sir William, secretary of state, iii. 299, n. 3; character of, iii. 363; in ceremony, iii. 277 & n. 7; interrupts Charles II, iii. 299; and dismissal of Clarendon, iii. 493, n. 1; library of, iii. 363, 477; judge at wrestling-match, iii. 476 & n. 1; social, iii. 415, 448, 491; geneal., iii. 442 & nn. 2, 3.

Morice, Sir William, jnr., iii. 442, n. 3.

Morin, Pierre: garden, art-collection, &c., of, ii. 132–3 & n. (i. 85–7; *add.*); iii. 33 & nn. 2–4.

Morison, Robert, M.D.: botanical lecture by, iv. 68 & n. 3.

Morland, Sir Samuel, bt., iii. 488, n. 2; inventions of, iii. 488; makes water-wheel, &c., at Euston, iii. 591; iv. 117; makes engine for water-supply of Windsor Castle, iv. 317 & n. 5; social, iii. 492; iv. 257; in old age, v. 221–2.

Morley, —, nephew of Dr. George Morley, v. 351 & n. 3.

Morley, Agnes, foundress of Southover free school, ii. 9 (i. 8).

Morley, Anne: *see* Granville, Mrs. A.

Morley, Anne, daughter of James Morley, iv. 11, n. 2.

Morley, Anne, Lady Morley, wife of (1) Sir John Lewknor; (2) Sir William Morley: as Mrs. Lewknor: godmother of George Evelyn, 1658(?), iii. 218 & n. 2.

Morley, Lady Catherine, wife of Cuthbert Morley, iv. 11, n. 3; social, iv. 11, 34–5.
Morley, Cuthbert: geneal., iv. 11, nn. 2, 3.
Morley, George, D.D.; bishop of Worcester 1660; of Winchester 1662, ii. 566, n. 1; in Paris: officiates, &c., in Sir R. Browne's chapel, ii. 566, 567; iii. 1; ~ leaves for Breda, iii. 2 & n. 2; as bishop of Worcester: preaches at Charles II's coronation, iii. 282 & n. 3; as Dean of the Chapel: at service at Whitehall, iii. 439.
as bishop of Winchester: consecrates J. Earles, iii. 346 & n. 1; concerned in T. Pierce's controversy, iii. 360 & n. 5; at Sheldon's translation to Canterbury, iii. 362 *bis*; prelate of Order of the Garter, participating in Grand Feast, iii. 479 *bis* & n. 4; and conversion of Anne (Hyde), duchess of York, to Roman Catholicism, iv. 282–3 & n.; house of, iv. 81 & n. 5; social: visits duchess of Newcastle, iii. 481; ~ parties, iii. 379, 400; iv. 81; alone, &c., iii. 443.
geneal., v. 351 & n. 3.
Morley, Col. Herbert, iii. 65 & n. 9; provides pass, &c., for Mrs. Evelyn, iii. 65–6 *bis*; buys Preston Beckhelvyn from E, iii. 151; urged by E to restore the monarchy, 1659–60, iii. 235, n. 4, 237–40 & nn., *passim*; i. *13–14*; *see also* i. *24*, n. 2; obtains pardon, &c., iii. 245 & n. 3; geneal., iii. 238 & n. 1.
Morley, James: geneal., iv. 11, n. 2.
Morley, Sir William, K.B.: geneal., iii. 218, n. 2.
Morocco: dress in, iv. 266 & nn. 1, 2; public ceremonies in, iv. 266; the Moors attack Tangier, iv. 208 & n. 6, 299 & n. 2, 379, n. 3; negotiates with England about Tangier, &c., 1681, 1682, iv. 266 & n. 4; captives in: collection for, 1701–2, v. 485 & n. 1; *see also* Ahmed Hadu; Moors.
Morocco leather (maroquin), ii. 128 (i. 82); iii. 11, 34.
Morosini, G. F., patriarch of Venice, ii. 476 & n. 4.
Morosini, Michele, Venetian ambassador to France: audience for, iii. 43 & n. 5.
Morris, John, partner of Sir Robert Clayton, iv. 186 & n. 3.
Mortlake (Mortlack), Surrey: pleasure party at, iii. 372 & n. 2.
Morton, Thomas, bishop of Durham: refuge for, 1649, iii. 95, n. 5.
Morton: Earl, &c., of, *c.* 1650: *see* Douglas, Robert; Douglas, Anne, his countess.
Morus, Rev. —: *see* Morehouse, John; Morehouse, Stephen.
Morus *or* More (Morise, &c.), Alexander, divine, ii. 527 & n. 6; shows E university at Geneva, ii. 529; sermons by: at Geneva, ii. 527; ~ in London, iii. 310–11 & n.
Mosaic [for inlaid floors *see* Architecture: features]: in Greek manner, ii. 197, 278; *opus vermiculatum*, ii. 296 & n. 4; painting copied in, ii. 260 & n. 4; portrait in, ii. 80 (i. 54); walls or ceilings decorated with, ii. 197 *bis*, 219, 240, 242, 259, 265, 267, 278, 287, 289, 306, 307, 346, 380, 437 & n. 5.
Florentine, also called *pietra commessa*, ii. 191 & n. 10; makers of, ii. 191 & n. 12 (i. 119), 417; specimens of, ii. 191 & n. 11 (i. 119), 198, 236, 253, 263, 265, 285, 286–7, 308, 396, 411, 414, 455; iii. 136, 260.
Moschino, Simone: statue by, ii. 215 & n. 4; *see also* ii. 308.
Moscow: fires at, 1699, v. 352 & n. 3.
Moses: relics, &c., of: brazen serpent, ii. 500 & n. 4; ~ rod, ii. 275 & n. 3; ~ stone from Meribah, ii. 440 & n. 2; in sermons, iii. 11, 20; iv. 45, 88, 170, 223, 287, 341, 447; v. 126, 215, 280, 309, 333, 334, 344, 397, 437, 442, 470, 509, 576, 581; rod of: in sermon, iv. 540.
Mosse, Jonathan, gardener: apprenticed to E, iv. 521 & n. 3.
Mossom, Robert, D.D.; bishop of Derry: sermon by (?; as Massam), iii. 214 & n. 1; *add.*
Mottoes: *see* Proverbs and Mottoes.
Moulins: notice, ii. 154–5 & nn. (i. 99–100); road through, ii. 152, n. 1, 156, n. 2.
Moulins, —, chirurgion: *see* Molines.

Mountagu, Edward, first earl of Sandwich, iii. 413, n. 1; character, &c., iii. 617–19 & nn.; appointed commander of the fleet, 1665, iii. 413, n. 1; visits fleet at the Nore, iii. 413–14; conduct of, at Bergen, iii. 617 & nn. 2, 4; captures *Phoenix* and *Slothany*, iii. 418 & n. 5, 508; as commissioner for prizes, iii. 419 & n. 3; allows prize-goods to be taken from *Phoenix*, &c., iii. 423–4 & n.; *see also* iii. 419, 425; superseded as commander of the fleet, iii. 424–5 & n.; suspected of cowardice by Albemarle, iii. 425 & n. 1, 440, 617–18; diplomatic career of, iii. 519, n. 1, 618, n. 6; *add.*; observations of, in Spain, iii. 518–19 & nn.; as president of Council for Foreign Plantations, i. *23*; iii. 578, 581, 584, 586, 587, 599; ~ successor to, iii. 627, n. 5; lodgings of, in Whitehall, iii. 586, n. 2, 617; social: parties, iii. 539, 547, 549–50; killed in battle of Solebay, iii. 616 & n. 5, 617; *see also* iii. 401, n. 6, 620; funeral of, iii. 621 & n. 4; geneal., iii. 401, n. 6; iv. 503, n. 2.

Mountagu, Jemima, countess of Sandwich, wife of Edward Mountagu, first earl, iii. 621 & n. 1.

Mountagu, Lady Jemima: *see* Carteret, Lady Jemima.

Mountain, George: *see* Montaigne *or* Mountain, G.

Mountebanks, &c.: in London (J. Punteus), iii. 293 & n. 4; in Paris, ii. 93, 99 (i. 65); ~ impostor, claiming secret of multiplying gold, iii. 24; ~ water-spouter (F. Marchand?), iii. 27 & n. 5; in Rome, ii. 368 & n. 1; ~ man with phosphorescent ring, ii. 397–8 & nn.; iv. 253; in Venice, ii. 474 & n. 5.

Mount-Edgcumbe, Cornwall: as home of the Edgcumbes, iii. 78, 509.

Mountford (Montford), William: murder of: trial for, v. 129 & n. 2.

Mountrath: third Earl of, &c.: *see* Coote, Charles; Coote, Isabella, his countess.

Mourguez, ii. 168, n. 4.

Mowbray: Lords or Barons (title used by eldest sons of the Norfolk Howards when summoned in their fathers' lifetimes to the house of lords): *see* Howard, Henry Frederick, Lord Mowbray 1640–6, later third earl of Arundel; Howard, Henry, Lord Mowbray 1678–84, later seventh duke of Norfolk.

Muccinigo, —: *see* Mocenigo, P.

Muddiman, Henry, journalist, &c., i. *128*.

Mudyford, Sir Thomas: *see* Modyford.

Mugello, the, ii. 419, n. 4.

Mulgrave: third Earl of, 1658–94: *see* Sheffield, John, later duke of the county of Buckingham, &c.

Mulso, Anne: *see* Dolben, Anne, Lady Dolben.

Mulso, Tanfield: geneal., iv. 282, n. 5.

Mulys, Richard, secretary of Ossory, iv. 208 & n. 8.

Mundanus, Theodorus, alchemist, v. 599 & n. 1.

Munderkingen, on the Danube: engagement at, 1703, v. 543, n. 2.

Muneton: *see* Mennetou.

Mung: *see* Mehun-sur-Yèvre.

Munich: Glyptothek: statue of Horus in, ii. 229 & n. 4.

Munson, Sir John: *see* Monson.

Murano: *see* Venice: environs.

Murillo (Morella), B. E.: paintings by, v. 145 & n. 2.

Murray, Elizabeth: *see* Maitland, Elizabeth, duchess of Lauderdale, &c.

Murray, Elizabeth: *see* Puckering, Elizabeth, Lady Puckering, formerly Newton.

Murray, Henry, brother of Lady Puckering (Newton): visits E (?), iii. 169 & n. 1.

Murray, John; marquis of Athole 1676; &c.: chaplain of: sermon by, v. 297 & n. 2.

Murray, Sir Robert: *see* Moray *or* Murray, Sir R.

Murray, Thomas, provost of Eton: geneal., iii. 87, n. 1.

Murray, William, earl of Dysart: owner of Ham House, &c., iv. 143, n. 5.

Murrey, —: *see* Murray, Henry.

Muschamp, — (of East Horsley?): social, iii. 85, n. 4.

Muscovy: *see* Russia.

Muscovy Company: privileges of, in Russia, to be restored, iii. 344, n. 5 *ad fin.*

Muselli family of Verona: art-collection of, ii. 487 & n. 4.
Museums and Miscellaneous Collections [mixed collections of works of art and natural objects (other than those prized for their beauty, such as shells or agates), miscellaneous collections of scientific instruments, and collections of non-European works of art, &c. Collections predominantly of natural objects are indexed as Natural History Collections; collections predominantly of paintings and sculptures (but also possibly containing natural objects prized for their beauty) are indexed as Art Collections; some specialized collections are indexed under Antiquities; Coins and Medals; &c.
 Private collections established since E's time, when mentioned for the present ownership of objects, are not indexed]:
 Clapham: Pepys, v. 427–8 & n., 538.
 Leyden: Anatomy School, ii. 53–4 & nn. (i. 37); *add.*
 London: British Museum: *see* British Museum; W. Charleton or Courten, iv. 531–2 & nn.; v. 13–14 & n., 81, 224; D. Palmer, iii. 293 & n. 3; Royal Society: *see* Royal Society; J. Tradescant, at Lambeth, later E. Ashmole, later Oxford, Ashmolean Museum, iii. 198–9 & nn., 217 & n. 7; iv. 138–9 & n.
 Norwich: Sir Thomas Browne, iii. 594 & n. 1.
 Oxford: Bodleian Library, iii. 107–8 & nn., 385 & nn. 3, 4; St. John's College, iii. 108 & n. 6; Dr. J. Wilkins, iii. 110–11 & nn.
 Paris: Gaston, duke of Orleans, ii. 128 (i. 82); Jesuits: Far Eastern collection for, iii. 373–4 & nn.; P. Morin, ii. 132–3 & nn. (i. 86); iii. 33 & nn. 2–4.
 Rome: F. Angeloni, ii. 236–7 & nn., 356–7 & n.; F. Gualdo, ii. 314–15 & nn.; A. Kircher, ii. 230 & nn. 5–7; Villa Ludovisi, ii. 234–6 & nn., 391–2 & nn.; F. Orsini (in Farnese palace), ii. 215 & n. 5.

Museums, &c. (*cont.*)
 Sion, Valais: E's host, ii. 516, 517.
 Venice: C. Ruzini, ii. 470–1 & nn.
Musgrave, Sir Philip, bt.: in Paris, ii. 565 & n. 6.
Music [for Opera *see* Opera; for individual operas *see* Plays; composers and performers are included below]:
— general and miscellaneous:
— — general: influence of music: on passions, iii. 168 & n. 3; ~ organs played in hospital to alleviate pain, ii. 311; music-rooms, ii. 467 & n. 1; v. 289, n. 1; Neapolitan peasantry and, ii. 353–4; performance as compliment to travellers, ii. 165 & n. 3 (i. 104); profane: rise of (in sermon), iv. 315; Royal Society and: new instrument shown, iii. 378 & n. 5; ~ paper by R. Hooke on art of, iii. 599; singer: engaged to perform in private houses, v. 531 & n. 2; song-books: destroyed, v. 222; drums beaten to guide boats in fog, v. 363.
— — terms: consort: meaning concert (?), iii. 23, 377, 601; iv. 49; ~ meaning a set of instruments, &c., performing together (?), iii. 167 & n. 5, 347, 378; v. 79; division, i. 34 & n. 1; ground, iii. 167 & n. 4; iv. 48; motetto, ii. 233 & n. 12; music meeting, iv. 82; oratorio, ii. 233, n. 12; recitative, ii. 449, 473; iii. 229, 309 & n. 1; ~ Italian, v. 289; ~ Venetian, iv. 403; tablature, ii. 48 & n. 4 (i. 34), 115; thoroughbass, iv. 421 & n. 2.
— — composition: Italian: Cowley's poems set to, iv. 220 & n. 5; ~ of operas, iii. 229; iv. 30; mechanical system of, iii. 377 & n. 4.
— — execution: French style, &c., iii. 23, 347; Italian style of singing, iii. 144; lyra way: viol d'amore played, iv. 187.
— church and sacred music:
— — general: lawfulness of: discussed, ii. 38 & n. 4 (i. 29); ~ in sermon, iv. 351; in United Provinces, ii. 50–1 & n. (i. 35–6); Puritans' hostility to organs, iii. 109 & n. 5; re-instated: at

Music (*cont.*)
Westminster Abbey, iii. 265 & n. 4; ~ at Whitehall, iii. 262 & n. 2.
— — uses: organ-playing: in hospital at Rome, ii. 311; ~ at supper-time at Christ's Hospital, iv. 542; psalms for service displayed, ii. 44 (i. 32); psalmody of French protestants, ii. 115 (i. 75).
— — performances: London: St. Paul's: thanksgiving for Blenheim, v. 578; Westminster Abbey: during coronation of Charles II, iii. 281–4 *passim*; Chapel Royal, Whitehall: innovation at, ii. 347–8 & n.; Queen Catherine's chapel: rehearsal for, iii. 310; at Roman Catholic chapel, Whitehall, iv. 534 & n. 1, 535, 537.
— — — Paris: at Notre Dame, ii. 96 (i. 63); ~ at St.-Paul-St.-Louis, iii. 23; ~ for St. Cecilia's day, *ib.*; Rome: at Oratory (Chiesa Nuova), ii. 232 & n. 7, 233–4 & nn., 277, 283, 291, 387; Tours: at Jesuits, ii. 148 (i. 96).
— instruments:
— — particular instruments:
— — — bells, church, &c.: mechanism of chimes, ii. 48 & n. 4 (i. 34 & n. 2); iv. 326; rung for public rejoicings, iii. 242, 246, 281, 410, 440; iv. 189, 587, 588, 623; silver, at Haarlem, ii. 50 & n. 3 (i. 35); at Lincoln cathedral, iii. 132 & n. 1; at Rouen cathedral, ii. 123 & n. 3 (i. 79).
— — — cornet (cornett), iii. 347–8 & n.
— — — drums, ii. 96 (i. 63), 280; iii. 57, 389; v. 363; kettle-drums, iii. 480; iv. 413, 492.
— — — fifes, ii. 96.
— — — flutes, i. 63; *flûte douce* (English flute, &c.), iv. 187 & n. 2.
— — — guitar, ii. 354; iii. 91, 307; iv. 220, 360.
— — — harp, iii. 322; in comparison, iii. 294; Irish, iii. 92 & n. 2, 518; Welsh, ii. 556 & n. 3; Sir S. Morland's new, iii. 488.
— — — harpsichord, ii. 233, 433, 475; iii. 198; iv. 49, 186, 270, 385, 404, 421, 422, 547; variant form of, iii. 378 & n. 5.

Music (*cont.*)
— — — lute, ii. 535; iii. 283; iv. 186, 370; v. 44; lutanists, iii. 377; iv. 48; in comparisons, iii. 92, 294, 518; iv. 360; makers of, at Bologna, ii. 426 & nn. 4–7; shape of: in comparison, ii. 446 & n. 7.
— — — organ: cornet, &c., and, iii. 347–8 & n.; keyboard of, in comparison, ii. 48 (i. 34); in Dutch churches, ii. 49 (i. 34); at coronation of Charles II, iii. 283; for Queen Catherine's Chapel, iii. 310; in comparison, iii. 378; particular instruments: Haarlem, ii. 50–1 & n. (i. 35–6); London: Christ's Hospital, iv. 542; ~ in private house, ii. 548; ~ St. Paul's, 1697, v. 278 & n. 3; Milan Cathedral, ii. 494 & n. 4; Oxford: Magdalen College, 1654, iii. 109 & n. 5; ~ Sheldonian Theatre, iii. 532; Paris: St.-Paul-St.-Louis, ii. 96 (i. 63); Rome: S. Giovanni in Laterano, ii. 272; ~ S. Maria sopra Minerva, ii. 378; ~ hospital of S. Spirito, ii. 311; 's Hertogenbosch, ii. 58; Siena Cathedral, ii. 204; Tours: St. Martin, ii. 144 (i. 93); Venice: S. Maria dei Miracoli, ii. 460; Windsor: king's chapel, iv. 316 & n. 5.
— — — pipes, iii. 322.
— — — polyphone, iii. 294 & n. 7.
— — — recorder, iv. 187, n. 2.
— — — theorbo, ii. 233, 287 & n. 6 (defined), 473; iii. 23, 106, 144, 310; v. 222; specimen, ii. 426, n. 6; in comparison, iii. 294; theorbo lute, iv. 403.
— — — trumpets, i. 63; ii. 432; iii. 246, 283, 389, 480; iv. 413, 415, 492; v. 578; meaning trumpeters, ii. 281; iii. 41, 42, 43; iv. 414, 610.
— — — viol, ii. 233; iii. 283, 310; in comparison, iii. 518; consort of viols: in comparison, iii. 378; arched, iii. 378, n. 5 *ad fin.*; bass, iii. 23; Naples, ii. 473 & n. 4; *viol d'amore*, iv. 187.
— — — violin, iii. 167; iv. 48, 49, 51, 187; violins: consort of, iii. 347; ~ meaning violinists, iii. 32; as fiddle, ii. 354; fiddlers, iii. 596.

Music (*cont.*)
— — general terms: loud and soft music, ii. 165 & n. 1 (i. 104); loud music, iii. 281, 532; wind music, iii. 347, 349, 480.
— — mechanical instruments: artificial birds, &c., ii. 47 (i. 33), 111 (i. 72), 392, 396 & n. 5; chime of porcelain dishes, ii. 47 (i. 33); phonotactic cylinder, i. 34 & n. 2; water organs, &c., ii. 41, 72 (i. 47), 111 (i. 72), 238, 287, 392, 396, 419.
— military or processional music: playing, ii. 96 (i. 63), 331, 432; iii. 246, 281, 333; iv. 413, 492; v. 578.
— performances [these almost all take place in private houses or at court. They are here distinguished as concerts, in which several professional musicians perform together or in succession; recitals, in which one or perhaps two noted professionals perform; musical parties, in which amateurs and minor professionals perform; and miscellaneous, in which music is only an incident in a larger activity. For operas *see* Opera; Plays; for oratorios and church-music *see* church and sacred music *above; see also* military and processional *above*]:
— — concerts: London: place not mentioned, iii. 377; at court, iii. 474; iv. 82, 480; ~ Queen Catherine's Portuguese musicians (at Hampton Court), iii. 322 & n. 4; at private houses in: Arundel House (H. Howard): rehearsal of music for Queen Catherine's chapel, iii. 310; Lord Arundell of Wardour: Pordage, &c., iv. 404, 422; Lord Falkland: P. Reggio, &c., iv. 384–5; H. Slingsby: Francesco, &c., iv. 49; ~ four performers, iv. 186–7 & nn.; Sir J. Williamson, iii. 601.
— — — Oxford: All Souls College, 1654, iii. 106; ~ Encaenia and Music Act, &c., 1669, iii. 532, 533; Paris: St. Cecilia rehearsal, iii. 23 & nn. 3, 4.
— — recitals [principal performers' names; all in London, except as noted]: J. Abell, &c., iv. 270; T. Baltzar (Lubicer), iii. 167–8 & nn.; Captain Henry Cooke, iii. 144 & n. 1; C. Gibbon, on organ, Magdalen College, Oxford, 1654, iii. 109 & nn. 5, 6; Mlle la Varenne: in Paris, iii. 35 & n. 1; ~ in London, iii. 91; N. Matteis, &c., iv. 48, 51; Pate, v. 289 & n. 1; Pordage, &c., iv. 403; P. Reggio, iv. 220; Siface, iv. 547; Waldegrave, iv. 370.
— — musical parties [performers' names, &c.; all in London, except as noted]: Alessandro, Paris, iii. 1; Mrs. Bridgeman, &c., iv. 360; Carew: on Welsh harp, ii. 556; Clarke: on Irish harp, iii. 92; Duarte family, Antwerp, ii. 67 & n. 6 (i. 45); Mary Evelyn, &c., iv. 404; Mrs. Packer, &c., *ib.*; Sir E. Sutton: on Irish harp, iii. 518; Sir W. Fermor's lutanist, v. 44; Italian singer, iii. 307.
— — miscellaneous: during feasts, parties, &c., iii. 150, 290–1, 349, 389, 480, 534; iv. 268, 277, 413, 492; galley slaves: during visit to galley, ii. 165 & n. 1 (i. 104); ~ outside travellers' lodgings, ii. 165 & n. 3 (i. 104); open air: in Louvre garden, ii. 106 (i. 69); ~ at Rome, ii. 282; ~ at Venice, ii. 433, 468, 473; ~ for water-party, iii. 372; ~ organs played in hospital, ii. 311; during supper at Christ's Hospital, iv. 542; boys sing at school break-up, v. 79; Sir F. Prujean on polyphone, iii. 294 & n. 7.
— personal [the division into professionals and amateurs is not completely reliable. Many professional performers were also composers and teachers; their names are repeated under the latter headings only when they are mentioned as such in the Diary]:
— — professionals: (i) heard by E: named performers: J. Abell, singer, iv. 270 & n. 2; Alessandro (Paris, 1650), singer, iii. 1; T. Baltzar (Lubicer), violinist, iii. 167–8 & n.; Bartholomeo, harpsichord-player, iv. 186 & n. 6; ~ as teacher, iv. 271, 421; J. Birchensha, iii.

Music (*cont.*)
377; Captain H. Cooke, singer, &c., iii. 144 & n. 1, 183; Dery (?), singer, iv. 413 & n. 5; *see also* iv. 404 & n. 7; G. B. Draghi (Jo: Battist), harpsichord-player, &c., iv. 384–5 & n., 404, 422; Du Prue (Du Pre?), lutanist, iv. 186 & n. 5; Francesco, harpsichord-player, iv. 49 & n. 5, 270 & n. 3; C. Gibbons, organist, iii. 109 & n. 6; Rev. J. Gostling, singer, iv. 404 & n. 9; Mrs. Mary Knight, singer, iv. 49; *see also* iii. 230 & n. 3; N. Matteis (Nicholao), violinist and composer, iv. 48 & n. 1, 49, 51, 186–7; Pate, singer, v. 289 & n. 1; Pordage, singer, iv. 403 & n. 6, 404, 422; P. Reggio (Pietro), singer, iv. 220 & n. 7; ~ as composer, *ib.*; ~ as teacher, iv. 421, 427; ~ alluded to (?), iv. 428; Anna Renzi, singer, ii. 450 & n. 3, 474; Siface (G. F. Grossi), *castrato*, iv. 537 & n. 5, 547 & n. 1.

— — — unnamed performers: *castrati* (as eunuchs), ii. 233, 450, 474; iii. 474; English, 1662, iii. 310; ~ at Bath, 1654: acts droll, iii. 102 & n. 2; French, 1662, iii. 310; ~ boy(s) singer(s) (Dery?), iv. 404 & n. 7, 413 & n. 5; ~ singer, iv. 385; Genoese, singer, ii. 450; German, viola-player, iv. 187; Italian, singers, &c., iii. 307, 474 & n. 4; iv. 534; Neapolitan, opera-singers, ii. 503; Portuguese, singers, &c., iii. 322 & n. 4.

— — professionals: (ii) mentioned by E or in notes, but not heard by him: named performers: chief performers in Rome, 1645 (M. A. Pasqualini, &c.), ii. 400 & n. 1; F. Corbetta, guitarist, iv. 49, n. 5; J. Laniere, iii. 74 & n. 5, 79–80; Mrs. J. M. Lindehleim (as Italian singer): success of, in England, v. 531 & n. 2; D. Mell, iii. 74 & n. 6, 168; J. Mercure, &c., ii. 535, n. 1; Polewheel, &c., iii. 168, n. 1; Paul Wheeler, iii. 168 & n. 1; Buckingham's band of fiddlers, iii. 596.

— — professionals: (iii) general mention: Castilian singers: in comparison, iii. 322, n. 4; *castrati*, v. 531; Italian singers: in comparison, iii. 322, n. 4.

— — amateurs and persons of uncertain status [persons giving occasional musical parties are not indexed collectively]: Mrs. Bridgeman, guitarist, iv. 360; Carew, performer on Welsh harp, ii. 556; Clarke, performer on Irish harp, iii. 92 & n. 2, 518; Duarte family, ii. 67 & n. 6 (i. 45); Mary Evelyn, singer: studies, iv. 271, 421–2, 427, 428; ~ sings, iv. 404 *bis*, 422; Anthony Carey, Viscount Falkland, iv. 427; ~ concert at house of, iv. 384–5; Sir Francis North, baron of Guilford, iv. 299, 365; C. Huygens, heer van Zuylichem, lutanist, iii. 377; Mlle la Varenne, iii. 35 & n. 1, 91; Sir R. L'Estrange, iii. 167; Mercy (or Merey), ii. 145 & n. 6 (i. 94); Mrs. Packer, singer, iv. 404 & n. 8; Pepys, v. 538; ~ studies composition, iii. 377, n. 4; ~ concerts at house of, iv. 547 & n. 1; v. 289 & n. 1(?); Dr. T. Pierce, iii. 183 & n. 5; H. Slingsby: concerts at house of, &c., iv. 49, 51, 186–7 & n.; Sir E. Sutton, performer on Irish harp, iii. 518 & n. 6; Dr. (later Sir) W. Waldegrave, lutanist, iv. 48 & n. 2, 370, 403; R. Waller, v. 176; Sir J. Williamson, iv. 39; ~ concerts at house of, iii. 601; iv. 277.

— — — Sir W. Fermor's servant, lutanist, v. 44; Neapolitan peasants: love music, ii. 353–4.

— — composers: D. Bassano's daughter, ii. 473; G. L. Bernini: opera by, ii. 261 & n. 5; J. Birchensha: method of composition of, iii. 377 & n. 4; R. Cambert, iv. 30, n. 1; F. Cavalli, ii. 474, n. 6; G. B. Draghi, iv. 384, n. 6; Prince Gallicano, ii. 388–9 & n.; A. Leardini, ii. 450, n. 3; N. Matteis, iv. 48 & n. 1; C. Monteverde, ii. 474, n. 6; H. Purcell, v. 289 & n. 1; P. Reggio: sets poems by Cowley, iv. 220 & n. 5; G. Rovetta, ii. 450, nn. 2, 3.

Music (*cont.*)
— — inventors, &c.: R. Hooke, iii. 599; Sir S. Morland, iii. 488; ~ in old age, v. 221–2; Sir F. Prujean, iii. 294 & nn. 5, 7.
— — teachers: Alessandro, Rome, 1644, ii. 287; Bartholomeo, iv. 271, 421; D. Bassano, ii. 473; Mercure, ii. 535 & n. 1; P. Reggio, iv. 421 & n. 3, 427; ~ alluded to, iv. 428.
— study and teaching:
— — lessons, &c.: for E, ii. 22, 287, 473, 535; for Mary Evelyn, iv. 271, 421 & n. 3, 427; ~ alluded to, iv. 428; training, iv. 365; ~ for Irish harp, iii. 518.
— — study in schools, &c.: Antwerp: Jesuits, ii. 66 (i. 44); in riding academies, ii. 134 (i. 87); Winchester: boarding-school, iii. 168, n. 1; children taught psalm-singing, ii. 115 (i. 75); *see also* iv. 542; v. 79.
Mustafa II, sultan: deposed, v. 545–6 & n.
Muziano (Mutiano), Girolamo, ii. 233, n. 2; paintings by, ii. 233 & n. 2, 245 & n. 2.
Myddelton, Charles: geneal., iv. 334, n. 5.
Myddelton (Midleton), Sir Hugh: constructor of the New River, iv. 515 & n. 4.
Myddelton (Midleton), Mrs. Jane, wife of Charles Myddelton, iv. 334, n. 5; beauty of, iv. 334; geneal., iii. 198, n. 3, 363, n. 1.
Mynne family, of Horton and Woodcote, ii. 542, n. 3.
Mynne, Anne, sister of Mrs. Elizabeth Evelyn: *see* Morley, Anne, Lady Morley.
Mynne, Elizabeth: *see* Evelyn, Mrs. E.
Mynne, George, sen.: geneal., &c., ii. 542 & n. 3.
Mynne, George, jnr.: death, &c., of, ii. 542–3 & n.
Mynne, Sir William: sells Durdans, iii. 15, n. 1.

Naaman the Syrian: in sermons, iv. 495, 538; v. 380.
Nab, Rev. —: *see* Knaggs, T.
Nabal: in sermon, v. 48.
Naboth: in sermon, v. 128.
Nag, Rev. —: *see* Knaggs, T.
Naish *or* Nash, Rev. Hugh: sermon by (?), iii. 383 & n. 5.
Namur: town and castle of: besieged and taken by French, 1692, v. 102–7 & nn., *passim*; ~ besieged and taken by Confederates, 1695, v. 215 *bis* & nn. 2, 4, 216 *bis* & n. 4; ~ thanksgiving for capture of, v. 218 & n. 3.
Nancy: in peace of Ryswick, v. 270, n. 6.
Nantes: Sir Richard Browne at, iv. 66, n. 2.
Nanteuil, Robert, portrait-engraver, iii. 9–10 & n.; E sits to, *ib.*; gives E drawing for his portrait, iii. 22 & n. 9; portrait-drawings by, of Sir Richard and Lady Browne and Mrs. Evelyn, iii. 9, n. 3.
Nantwich (Namptwich), Cheshire: salt-pits at: account of, iii. 540 & n. 1.
Napier, Margaret: *see* Brisbane, Mrs. Margaret, later Baroness Napier.
Napier of Merchiston: Baroness: *see* Brisbane, Mrs. Margaret.
Naples: city and kingdom:
— the city and its environs: account of, ii. 325–55 & nn.; bibliographical note on, ii. 578–9; visit to: as excursion from Rome, ii. 315, n. 1; E's visit: chronology of, *ib.*; E sets out for, ii. 316.
— the city: general remarks, ii. 325, n. 4, 352 & n. 3, 353–4 & nn.; in comparison, iii. 637 (extract from *State of France*); Carnival at, ii. 331–2 & n.; churches at: splendour and number of, ii. 328 & n. 2, 353 & n. 4; courtesans at, ii. 331–2 & n.; English merchants at, ii. 330 & n. 3; executions at, ii. 401; French: hatred of, at, ii. 354 & n. 1; horses and horsemanship at, i. 88 & n. 1; ii. 279–80, 327 & n. 4, 353; iii. 50; opera-singers from, ii. 503 & n. 4; population of, ii. 325, n. 4, 352 & n. 3; promenade at, ii. 327 & n. 3; provisions: cheapness of, at, ii. 325; sedan-chairs introduced into England from, i. 11 (*see also* ii. 14, n. 4); ii. 353 & n. 6; Spanish dress at, ii. 353 & n. 5; Spanish garrison at, ii. 326; streets and paving at, ii. 353 & n. 3.

Naples (*cont.*)
— — earthquake at, 1688, iv. 598 & n. 4; danger to, from Vesuvius, 1696(?), v. 234 & n. 6.
— — topographical, &c.: Accademia Pontaniana, ii. 328, n. 9; Arsenal, ii. 326, 352; Castel Nuovo, ii. 326 & nn. 5, 6; ~ fountains near, ii. 327, n. 2; Castel Sant'Elmo, ii. 326 & n. 1, 329, n. 1; Cavalleritia, the viceroy's, ii. 330 & n. 4:
— — — churches and monasteries: cathedral, ii. 328 & nn. 1, 3; Gesù Nuovo, ii. 329–30 & n.; Monte Oliveto, ii. 328 & nn. 6, 7; ~ service at, ii. 331, n. 8; S. Domenico, ii. 328 & n. 5; S. Maria Maggiore, ii. 328–9 & nn.; S. Martino, ii. 329 & nn. 1–5; S. Paolo Maggiore, ii. 327–8 & nn.; S. Pietro ad Aram, ii. 328 & n. 4.
— — — fountain (Parthenope), ii. 327 & n. 2; Livy: arm of, ii. 328–9 & n., 462, n. 7; Molo Angioino, ii. 326, 327 & nn. 1, 2; Molo di S. Vincenzo (modern), ii. 326, n. 7, 327, n. 1; museum (modern): statues, &c., in, from Palazzo Farnese, Rome, ii. 214–16 & nn., *passim*, 308–10 & nn., *passim*; ~ bronze horse's head in, ii. 330, n. 1; museum of F. Imperato, ii. 330–1 & nn.
— — — — palaces: Carafa (Duca di Maddaloni; now Santangelo), ii. 330 & n. 1; Duca di Gravina (Orsini), ii. 330 & n. 2; of Viceroy, ii. 326 & n. 8.
— — — — temple of Castor and Pollux, ii. 327–8 & nn.; Three Kings (inn or *pension*), ii. 325 & n. 5; ~ alluded to, ii. 354; Torre di S. Vincenzo, ii. 326 & n. 7; Via Corsea, ii. 325, n. 5.
— — environs [*see also* Vesuvius *and the* Phlegraean Fields]: fertility of, ii. 324–5 & n., 338–9 & nn., 353; populousness of, ii. 324; Labulla (Bolla or Volla), ii. 332 & n. 3; Ponte della Maddalena, ii. 330, n. 4, 332, n. 3, 333, n. 1; Posilipo, ii. 337, 339 & n. 1; ~ in view, ii. 329; ~ Grotta di, ii. 337–8 & n.; alluded to, iii. 561–2 & n.; ~ Grotta di Sejano at, ii. 338, nn.

Naples (*cont.*)
1, 5; ~ Virgil's tomb, ii. 337 & n. 1; S. Maria di Piedigrotta: canons of, ii. 337, n. 1; Sebeto, river, ii. 332, n. 3, 333 & n. 1; Volla (Labulla), ii. 332 & n. 3.
— kingdom of: frontier (with Papal States), ii. 322 & n. 3; ~ convoy for travellers near, ii. 315, n. 1; land in, bought for searching for statues, ii. 283; peasantry: love of music of, ii. 353–4; produce, ii. 352–3 & nn.
— — government of, ii. 352 & nn. 7, 8; Spanish viceroys of, ii. 316, n. 2; ~ Cavalleritia of, at Naples, ii. 330 & n. 4; ~ palace of, at Naples, ii. 326 & n. 8; ~ procession of, on Candlemas, ii. 331 & n. 8; ~ story told by Sir L. Dyve of a viceroy, &c., iii. 50 & n. 1; ~ viceroy, 1645: *see* Medina de Riosecco, duke of; Grand Constables of, ii. 273, n. 3; v. 330, n. 3; tribute of, to Pope, ii. 280, 352 & n. 4; king of: *see* Charles of Anjou; queen of, *see* Joanna I.
— — late civil war in, 1651, iii. 50 & n. 1; Christina of Sweden's project to seize, iv. 221 & nn. 2, 3.
Napoleon: constructs Simplon road, ii. 508, n. 5; buildings of: at Louvre, ii. 103, n. 1; ~ Milan cathedral, ii. 492, n. 2; collections of sculpture: buys old Borghese collection, ii. 252, n. 5; ~ takes statues from Vatican, ii. 303, n. 3; legend concerning, ii. 445, n. 8.
Narva (Nerva) in Livonia: attacked by Russia, 1700, v. 429, n. 4; battle at and relief of, v. 438–9 & n., 440.
Naseburg: *see* Knodsenburg.
Nash *or* Naish, Rev. Hugh: sermon by (?), iii. 383 & n. 5.
Nason, Rev. John: *see* Nasson, Rev. —.
Nassau family: as rulers of Orange, v. 545, n. 1.
Nassau, Frederik van: *see* Zuylestein.
Nassau, Louis van: *see* Beverweerd.
Nasson, Rev. —, curate of Abinger *c.* 1700–5 (Rev. John Nason ?), v. 430, n. 1; sermons by: at Wotton (some as by curate of Abinger, without name), v. 429–34 *passim*,

Nasson, Rev. — (*cont.*)
445, 473, 540, 540–1, 574, 582–3; ~ at Abinger (?), v. 445.
Nathan: in sermons, iv. 205, 638; v. 557.
Nathanael (as Nicodemus, in error): in sermon, iv. 308 & n. 4.
National Debt: mentioned, 1699–1700, v. 369, 394, 402, 404, 408; in King's Speech, 1701, v. 445.
National Gallery, London: Titian, 'Cornaro' family, in, iii. 216, n. 3; peepshow in, iii. 165, n. 6.
National Portrait Gallery, London: portrait of Queen Catherine in, iii. 321, n. 2.
Natural History Collections [collections predominantly of natural history specimens; for more mixed collections see Museums]:
London: R. Hubert *alias* Forges, iii. 433, n. 3; Royal College of Physicians, iii. 338; ~ catalogue, iii. 337, n. 4 *ad fin.*; Royal Society: *see* Royal Society; Dr. H. Sloane: Jamaican collection of, v. 48 & n. 1.
Milan: M. Settala, ii. 502 & nn. 5–7.
Naples: F. Imperato, ii. 330–1 & nn.
Oxford: Anatomy School, iii. 108 & nn. 4, 5; Dr. R. Plot, iv. 68 & n. 4.
Pisa: collection in botanic garden, ii. 181 & n. 8 (i. 114), 408.
Naturalists: atheists and: in sermon, v. 107 & n. 2.
Navigation: instrument for taking soundings, iii. 317; English coastal charts by G. Collins, iv. 301 & n. 3.
Nazareth: in sermon, v. 524.
Neale, Sir Paul: *see* Neile.
Neale, Thomas, v. 158, n. 2; lotteries managed by, v. 158 & n. 2, 177, n. 4, 193 & n. 1; builds Seven Dials, v. 193 & n. 1.
Neapolitano, Carlo: *see* Maratti.
Nebuchadnezzar, ii. 54 (i. 37).
Needham, — (Mr. or Dr.): *see* Needham, Jasper.
Needham, Bridget, Viscountess Kilmorey, wife of Charles Needham, fourth viscount, and later of Sir John Shaw, &c., iii. 218, n. 4; social, iii. 218; geneal., iii. 375, n. 8.
Needham, Charles, fourth Viscount Kilmorey (Killmurrey): social, iii. 218 & nn. 4, 5.
Needham, Elizabeth, Lady Needham, first wife of Sir Robert: geneal., iii. 198, n. 3.
Needham, Jane: *see* Myddelton, Mrs. Jane.
Needham, Jane, Lady Needham, second wife of Sir Robert: social, iii. 363 & n. 1; *add.*
Needham, Jasper, M.D., iii. 60, n. 3; character, iv. 183; returns from France, iii. 175 & n. 1; commendatory poem by, for Sir S. Tuke, iii. 348, n. 4; E consults, about tutor for John Evelyn, jnr., iii. 364; professional: post-mortem examination by, of little Richard Evelyn, iii. 209–10 & nn.; attends E, 1660, iii. 243; attends John Evelyn, jnr., iv. 180; attends Charles II, 1679, iv. 180 & n. 1; social, iii. 60, 181, 183, 187, 203, 218, 296; iv. 35, 48; funeral of, iv. 183 & n. 5.
Needham, Robert, first Viscount Kilmorey: geneal., iii. 198, n. 3.
Needham, Sir Robert, iii. 198, n. 3; social, iii. 198, 218, 232, 257, 264; geneal., iii. 218, n. 5, 363, n. 1; iv. 334.
Needham, William, B.D.: sermon by, iv. 568 & n. 3.
Negro, del: *see* Dinegro.
Nehemiah: in sermon, iii. 202; Temple of: in sermon, v. 64.
Neile, Elizabeth, Lady Neile, wife of Sir Paul, iii. 172, n. 6 *ad fin.*
Neile (Neale), Sir Paul, iii. 172, n. 6; optic-glasses of, iii. 172; telescope(s) of, iii. 286, nn. 2, 4; at observation of Saturn's rings, iii. 285–6 & nn.
Neile, Richard, archbishop of York: geneal., iii. 172, n. 6.
Neile, William, the mathematician: geneal., iii. 172, n. 6 *ad fin.*
Nellie, Mrs.: *see* Gwyn, Eleanor.
Nemi: Lake of, ii. 317 & n. 4.
Neptune: sacrifices to, at Geneva, ii. 523 & n. 1; *add.*
Neri, Philip: *see* Philip Neri, St.
Nero, Roman emperor: orders execution of St. Paul, ii. 306 & n. 2; murders Agrippina, ii. 349 & n. 5; canal from Avernus to Ostia projected by, ii. 347 & n. 1; Quirinal Horse-tamers sent to, ii.

Nero, Roman emperor (*cont.*) 237; tomb of, ii. 374 & n. 1; colossal statue of, ii. 248, n. 7; portrait of, on gem, ii. 89 (i. 60); buildings of: Baia: villa at, ii. 349 & n. 8; Miseno: reservoirs, ii. 350–1 & nn.; Rome: Golden House, ii. 276 & n. 5, 279, n. 1, 357.
Nesis, nymph, ii. 351 & n. 5.
Nestorius: tenets of, iv. 617.
Netherlands [notices are indexed, as far as possible, under Spanish Netherlands and United Provinces]: invention of gunpowder brought from, to England (as from Flanders), i. 3; town-halls in: magnificence of, ii. 31; earthquake in, 1692, v. 115, n. 4; winter in, 1655–6, iii. 165, n. 4.
Neuburg: Princes of: *see* Johann Wilhelm; Philipp Wilhelm.
Neufville, François de, duc de Villeroi, Marshal Villeroi: *see* Villeroi.
Neuhäusel (Newhausel), Hungary: taken by Imperialists, iv. 463 & n. 1.
Neve, Cornelis de: *see* La Neve.
Nevell, John, admiral: dies, v. 268, n. 1.
Nevers, ii. 533 & n. 6.
Nevill, George, twelfth Lord Bergavenny (Abergavenny): social, iv. 490 & n. 3.
Nevis: *see* Leeward Islands.
Newark, Notts., iii. 125 & n. 1.
New Batavia: *see* Batavia.
Newburgh: Earls, &c., of: *see* Livingston, Catherine, wife of the first earl; Livingston, Charles, second earl, 1670–94.
Newbury, Berks., iii. 100 & n. 2; *see also* iii. 99, n. 4; battles of, iii. 100 & n. 3.
Newcastle-on-Tyne: coal from, iv. 115 & n. 8; coal-mines near, iv. 502; lecturers at: *see* Knaggs, T.; Tully, G.
Newcastle: Dukes, &c., of: *see* Cavendish, William, earl 1628–43, marquis 1643–65, and first duke 1665–76; Cavendish, Margaret, his duchess; Cavendish, Henry, second duke 1676–91; *new creation*: *see* Holles, John, duke 1694–1711.
New East India Company, 1698: *see* East India Company.
New England: state of: commissioners sent to investigate, 1664, iii. 581, n. 5; Council for Foreign Plantations and, 1671–2 [notices apply almost exclusively to Massachusetts]: report on, required, iii. 579 & n. 2; information about, from Col. T. Middleton, iii. 581 & n. 4, 584; report on, by Col. G. Cartwright, iii. 581–2 & n.; projects for controlling, iii. 581; letter to be sent to, iii. 584; commissioners to be sent to: proposals for, iii. 584–5 & n., 603; unspecified business, iii. 601.
natural history specimens from, iii. 563; religion in: R. Boyle promotes, v. 82, n. 2, 88, n. 1; trade of, with West Indies, iii. 584; witchcraft in, 1692, v. 130 & n. 1.
New Forest: effects on, of storm, 1703, v. 550, n. 2 *ad fin.*
Newfoundland: attacked by French, 1696, v. 263 & n. 8.
New Hall, Boreham, Essex: notice, 1656, iii. 179–80 & nn.; Ahmed Hadu at, iv. 287 & n. 4.
New Hall, near Pontefract, Yorks., iii. 128 & n. 1.
Newhaven: Viscounts: *see* Cheyne: Lords, &c.
Newmarket, Suffolk: fire at, 1683: brief for sufferers from, iv. 340–1 & n.; in comparison, iv. 341; palace at, iii. 138 & n. 5, 554–5 & nn.; ~ escapes fire, 1683, iv. 341, n. 1; ~ keeper of: *see* Eliot, T. (iii. 588, n. 8); royal visits, &c.: Charles II and his court: 1670, iii. 562; ~ 1671, iii. 588–9, 590, 596; ~ 1675, iv. 55 & n. 5; ~ 1676, iv. 99, n. 2; ~ 1677, with William of Orange, iv. 122, n. 3; ~ 1679, with Queen Catherine, iv. 183 & n. 1; ~ 1682, with James, duke of York, iv. 282, n. 1; ~ 1683, with James, iv. 321, 340–1 & n.; ~ 1684, iv. 372 & n. 1, 373, n. 2; Queen Anne, 1705, v. 591, n. 3; Ahmed Hadu, iv. 269, n. 1; E passes through, iv. 120.
Newmarket Heath, Suffolk: horse-training on, iii. 556; horse-races on, iii. 588–9; v. 320 & n. 1.
New Park (Richmond Park), Surrey: buck from, iv. 220 & n. 3.

Newport, I.O.W.: Charles I's projected escape from, iv. 360, n. 3; Charles I's removal from: debate on, ii. 545, n. 6; Treaty of: debate on (error), ii. 545 & n. 6; ~ letter relating to, ii. 552, n. 4.

Newport, Andrew, iv. 103, n. 6; as executor of Lady Mordaunt, iv. 188 & n. 7, 202, 259, 275; social, iv. 25 & n. 3(?), 103.

Newport, Diana, countess of Bradford, wife of Francis Newport, first earl: as Lady Newport: godmother of William Wren, iv. 169–70 & n.

Newport, Francis; second Baron Newport 1651; Viscount Newport 1675; first earl of Bradford 1694, iii. 526, n. 3; as Treasurer of the Household, iv. 170 & n. 2; ~ reappointed, 1685, iv. 416 & n. 4; ~ superseded, 1687, iv. 536, n. 2; ~ reappointed, 1689, iv. 627 & n. 2; speech of, in parliament, iv. 444–5 & n.; attends James II at Winchester, iv. 468; art-collection of, iv. 402–3 & nn.; social, iii. 526.

Newport, Richard; styled Lord Newport 1694–1708; second earl of Bradford 1708: chaplain of: sermon by, v. 588 & n. 4.

Newport: peerages: *see* Blount, Montjoy, first earl of Newport (I.O.W.) 1628–65; Newport, Francis, second Baron Newport of High Ercall 1651–75, Viscount Newport of Bradford 1675–94, later first earl of Bradford; Newport, Diana, his baroness, &c.; Newport, Richard, styled Lord Newport 1694–1708.

New Romney, Kent: Sir John Fenwich arrested at, 1696, v. 245, n. 4.

Newry (Eure, Nury), Armagh: occupied by Schomberg, iv. 648 & n. 5.

Newspapers, newsletters, and other periodicals [this includes all contemporary newspapers, English and foreign, used or mentioned by E, or cited as authorities, &c.; all notices, in the introduction and notes, relating to manuscript newsletters; and some miscellaneous periodicals mentioned in the introduction and notes. Periodicals published since E's time, when merely cited as authorities, are not indexed]:

— English newspapers in general: E's use of, i. *84*, *89–90* & nn., *127*, *129*; history of, 1620–1706, i. *101–5* & nn.; publication of: during Popish Plot crisis, i. *28*, *29*; iv. 172, n. 3; ~ during Revolution, iv. 609 & n. 5; files of, used for annotation, *add.* (i. *127–9*).

— particular newspapers, English and foreign:

— — *Account of the proceedings of the meeting of the Estates in Scotland*, 1689; *A Continuation of the proceedings*, &c., 1689–9; cited, iv. 631, n. 2, 635, n. 2, 639, n. 2, 646, n. 2.

— — *Certain passages*; cited, iii. 119, n. 4.

— — *City Mercury*: cited, iv. 24, n. 6.

— — *Daily Courant*, i. *105*; cited, v. 289, n. 1; and occasionally, v. 528–614, nn.

— — *Dawks's News-letter*: cited, v. 310, nn. 2, 3, 316, n. 4, 320, n. 1, 354, n. 1.

— — *Domestick Intelligence*: starts, iv. 172, n. 3; cited, iv. 165, n. 1; occasionally, iv. 178–93, nn.; iv. 266, n. 3, 289, n. 3.

— — *English Currant*: cited, iv. 609–13, nn., *passim*.

— — *English Post*: cited, v. 438, n. 2, 453, n. 1, 518, n. 1, 520, n. 3.

— — *Exact accompt*: cited, iii. 249, n. 2.

— — *Faithful Scout*: cited, iii. 57, n. 3.

— — 'Florence gazette', ii. 576–7 (note); cited, ii. 281, n. 1, 330, n. 3, 331, nn. 8, 9, 366, n. 3, 368, n. 8, 378–91, nn., *passim*.

— — *Flying-Post*: used by E, i. *90* & n. 2; mentioned by E, i. *89–90*; v. 215, n. 3; character, &c., of, i. *104–5*; v. 215, n. 3; ~ interest of, in reformation of manners, v. 366, n. 5 *ad fin.*; cited, as source or authority, v. 213–618, nn., *passim*; supplements to, v. 258, n. 6, 267, n. 1.

— — *Foreign Post*: cited, v. 269, n. 3.

— — *Harlem Currant*: cited, iv. 627, n. 3.

Newspapers, &c. (*cont.*)
— — *Impartial Protestant Mercury*: cited, iv. 269, nn. 1, 2.
— — *Intelligencer*: used by E (?), *add.* (iii. 390, n. 7); cited occasionally, iii. 360–423, nn.
— — *Kingdomes Intelligencer*: as source, iii. 266, n. 1, 277, n. 2, &c., 278, n. 4 *ad fin.*, &c., 281, n. 2, &c., 311, n. 1; cited occasionally, iii. 276–353, nn.
— — *Kingdomes Weekly Intelligencer*: cited, ii. 556, n. 1.
— — London 'Bills of Mortality' (weekly), iii. 412, n. 6; cited: for Plague, iii. 412–30, nn., *passim*; for later epidemics, v. 85, n. 3, 196, n. 2, 199, n. 2, 200, n. 5; for deaths in Great Fire, iii. 460, n. 7; for Lord Mayor's assize of bread, v. 528, n. 3.
— — *London Courant*: cited, iv. 611–12, nn.
— — *London Gazette*: origin and character of, i. *102–3* & n., *104*, *128*; used by E, i. *90*, *105*; notes from, by John Evelyn, jnr. (?), i. *84*, n. 3; mentioned or alluded to by E, iii. 620 (*see* iii. 619, n. 3); iv. 406 & n. 3, 434 & n. 2, 635 & n. 2; v. 36 & n. 3, 101 & n. 2; silence of, about persecution of French protestants, 1685, iv. 487 & n. 2; *see also* iv. 447, n. 3 *ad fin.*; complaint about, in parliament, v. 561 & n. 1; cited, as source or authority, iii. 428–v. 618, nn. (also occasional earlier citations; as source, first, iii. 470, n. 1; citations gradually become frequent); supplements, &c., to: cited, v. 70, n. 2, 216, n. 4, 245, n. 6, 495, n. 1, 519, n. 2, 574–80, nn., *passim*.
— — *London Intelligence*: cited, iv. 620–2, nn.
— — *London Mercury* (1688–9): cited, iv. 611, nn. 3, 6.
— — *London Mercury* (1696): cited, v. 246, n. 5.
— — *London News-letter*: cited, v. 238, n. 1.
— — *London Post*: cited, v. 330, n. 1.
— — *Loyal Protestant Intelligence*: cited, iv. 268, n. 1, 269, nn. 1, 2.

Newspapers, &c. (*cont.*)
— — *Mercurius Anglicus*: cited, iv. 189, n. 6.
— — *Mercurius Britannicus*: cited, iii. 112, n. 2.
— — *Mercurius Civicus*: cited, iii. 111, n. 7.
— — *Mercurius Politicus*: cited, iii. 68, n. 3, 163, n. 1, 169, n. 3; and occasionally, iii. 200–24, nn.
— — *Mercurius Publicus*: as source, iii. 256, n. 1 *ad fin.*, 277, n. 2, &c., 311, n. 1; cited occasionally, iii. 244–353, nn., 399, n. 2.
— — *Mercurius Veridicus*: cited, iii. 112, n. 2.
— — *Newes*: as source, iii. 361, n. 5; E's *Parallel of Architecture* advertised in, iii. 380, n. 4; cited occasionally, iii. 376–425, nn.
— — *Observator* (Sir R. L'Estrange), i. *103–4*; notice, iv. 439 & n. 3.
— — *Orange Gazette*: cited, iv. 622, nn., 628–9, nn.
— — *Oxford Gazette* (later *London Gazette*), i. *102*; cited, iii. 428, n. 6, 429, n. 2, 432, n. 1.
— — Paris *Gazette*: as source, iii. 41, n. 2, &c.; cited (as Renaudot, *Recueil*), iii. 43, n. 4, 47, n. 4, 48, n. 7, 52, n. 1.
— — *Parliamentary Intelligencer*: as source, iii. 256, n. 1 *ad fin.*; cited occasionally, iii. 244–61, nn.
— — *Perfect Account*: cited, iii. 149, n. 6, 150, n. 4.
— — *Perfect Diurnall*: cited, iii. 47, n. 4, 61, n. 3.
— — *Perfect Passages*: cited, iii. 111, n. 7.
— — *Perfect Proceedings*: cited, iii. 149, n. 6, 150, n. 4.
— — *Post Boy*: starts, i. *104*; v. 215, n. 3; notices in, of George Evelyn's death, &c.: quoted, v. 357, n. 3, 360, n. 1; cited, v. 215–531, nn.
— — *Post-Man*: starts, i. *104*; v. 215, n. 3; cited, v. 229–620, nn.; postscript to, v. 504, n. 4.
— — *Proceedings . . . Old Bailey* (sessions paper): cited, v. 41, n. 1.
— — *Protestant Mercury*: cited, v. 238, n. 4, 246, n. 5, 257, n. 4.
— — *Publick Intelligencer*: quoted, iii. 204, n. 6 *ad fin.*; cited occasionally, iii. 169–224, nn.

Newspapers, &c. (*cont.*)
— — *Publick Occurrences*: alluded to, i. *104*; cited, iv. 574, n. 2, 582, n. 1, 585, n. 5, 590, n. 1, 591, n. 2.
— — *Severall Proceedings*: cited, iii. 61, n. 3.
— — *True Domestick Intelligence*: cited, iv. 189, n. 6, 193, n. 1.
— — *True Protestant Mercury*: cited, iv. 262, n. 3, 289, n. 3.
— — *Universal Intelligence*: cited, iv. 608–9, nn., 611–12, nn., 622–3, nn.
— — *Votes of the House of Commons*: origin and revival of, i. *103*, *104*; used by E, i. *105*; cited as source or authority, v. 78–621, nn. (citations during sessions of parliament).
— — *Weekly Intelligencer*: cited, iii. 150, n. 4.
— newsletters, manuscript: in England, i. *127–8* & nn.; not used by E, i. *105*, n. 2; use of, in notes, i. *129*; the 'Gazette à la main', i. *127* & n. 1, *128*, *129*; Dyer's newsletters, v. 595, n. 3; Naples *Giornali* (manuscript?): cited from modern editions, ii. 325, n. 5, 331, nn. 8, 9.
— miscellaneous periodicals:
— — *Abinger Monthly Record*: passages from Diary published in, i. *63*, *69*, *119–20*.
— — *Collection for improvement of Trade and Husbandry* (J. Houghton): cited, iv. 653, n. 2; v. 87, n. 2, 90, n. 1, 104, n. 2, 108, n. 2, 112, n. 2, 114, n. 2, 158, n. 2, 174, n. 6 *ad fin*.
— — *Collection of letters for the improvement of Husbandry and Trade* (J. Houghton); cited, iv. 60, n. 2.
— — *Hollandtse Mercurius*: cited, iii. 323, n. 5, 404, n. 4, 575, n. 2; iv. 27, n. 6.
— — *Philosophical Transactions* and *Philosophical Collections*: *see* Royal Society.
— — *Quarterly Review*: notice of Diary (first edition) in, i. *57*.
— — *Term Catalogues*: not indexed.
Newstead Abbey, Notts.: notice, iii. 126 & n. 7.
Newton family, of Sussex: geneal., ii. 63, n. 2.
Newton, —: owns portrait of, E, i. 7.
Newton, Sir Adam, iii. 66 & n. 3; tomb of, *ib.*
Newton, Elizabeth, Lady Newton, later Puckering: *see* Puckering.
Newton, Sir Henry, later Puckering: *see* Puckering.
Newton, Sir Isaac; knighted 1705, v. 560, n. 4; as president of Royal Society, v. 560; knighted, v. 591, n. 3, 592 & n. 2; reflecting telescope of, iii. 601 & n. 2; burning-glass of, v. 592 & n. 3, 600; views of, on relations of religion and science, i. *110*, n. 1.
Newton, Mrs. Jane, born Apsley, first wife of William Newton: geneal., ii. 9, n. 7, 36, n. 4.
Newton, Mrs. Jane, born Michell, wife (1) of John Stansfield (as second wife); (2) of William Newton (as second wife); called by E his grandmother, ii. 3, n. 1; i. *4–5*; character of, iii. 25; erects monument to Stansfield, ii. 7–8 & n. (i. 7); marries Newton, ii. 9 & n. 7; E's affection for, ii. 11; dies, iii. 25 & n. 3; geneal., ii. 21, n. 6, 22, n. 1; v. 441, n. 5; mentioned, ii. 544, n. 3.
Newton, William, sen., ii. 9, n. 7.
Newton, William: marries Mrs. Jane Stansfield, ii. 9 & n. 7; *add.*
New York: shipping at: order to, 1672, iii. 603, n. 2; project for retaking from Dutch, 1673, iv. 25 & n. 6; divine sent to, by Society for Propagation of the Gospel, v. 507; governor of, 1664–8: *see* Nicolls, R.
Niccolò III, marquis of Ferrara: statue of, ii. 428 & n. 1.
Nice, ii. 168 & n. 3 (i. 106); county of, ii. 168, n. 2.
Nicephorus IV, pope: tomb of (error), ii. 244 & n. 7.
Niceron, J. F.: trick-painting by, ii. 373 & n. 5.
Nicholai, singer (B. Nicolini), ii. 400 & n. 1.
Nicholao, painter: *see* Abbate, N. dell'.
Nicholao *or* Nicolao, violinist: *see* Matteis, N.
Nicholas IV, pope: tomb of, ii. 244 & n. 7.
Nicholas, Friar (N. Blanchot?), iii. 27–8 & nn.
Nicholas, Sir Edward, secretary of state ('Mr. Secretary'), ii. 136, n.

Nicholas, Sir Edward (*cont.*) 2; relations of, with Evelyn family, i. 53 & n. 2; obtains pass for E, *ib.*; *see also* ii. 82, n. 2; in Paris, 1649, ii. 561 & n. 6; takes part in creation of peers, 1661, iii. 277 & n. 7; employs Sir J. Williamson, iii. 471, n. 4; iv. 38 & n. 6; buys West Horsley manor, ii. 545, n. 5; at West Horsley, iii. 418 & n. 4; correspondence of, with Charles I: publication of, i. 56; letters to, ii. 560, n. 2; iii. 6, n. 5 *ad fin.*; geneal., ii. 136 (i. 89); i. 99; iii. 285, n. 2.

Nicholas, Sir John, K.B., ii. 136, n. 2; as Mr. Nicholas: at Orleans, ii. 136 (i. 89); ~ at Bourges, ii. 154 (i. 99); as Sir John: inherits West Horsley manor, ii. 545, n. 5; chaplain of: sermon by, iii. 561.

Nicholas, Matthew, D.C.L., i. 53, n. 2.

Nicholas, Susan: *see* Lane, Susan, Lady Lane.

Nichols, Col.: *see* Nicolls, R.

Nicholson, William; bishop of Gloucester 1661: consecrated, iii. 266 & n. 3; funeral sermon by, iii. 307 & n. 2.

Niclaes, Henrick (Henry Nicholas), founder of the Family of Love, iv. 554, n. 2.

Nicodemus: in legend, ii. 409–10 & n.; in sermons, iv. 650; v. 524; error for Nathanael, iv. 308.

Nicolaitans, iv. 363, n. 7.

Nicolini (Nicholai), Bartolommeo, singer, ii. 400 & n. 1.

Nicolls (Nichols), Col. Richard: commissioner to New England, iii. 581, n. 5, 582 & n. 1.

Nicolson (Nicholson), William, D.D.; bishop of Carlisle 1702; &c.: social, &c., v. 508 & n. 2.

Nicomedia: Constantine baptized at, ii. 267, n. 1.

Nicomus *or* Miomus, Antonius, ii. 466 & n. 3.

Niers, river, at Gennep, ii. 35, n. 5, 37, n. 2.

Nieulay, near Calais: sluices at, ii. 560, n. 6.

Nieupoort, Willem, Dutch ambassador to England 1653–60, iii. 174 & n. 3; provides E with information, iii. 200; views and remarks of, iii. 174–5, 187 & nn. 2–4, 236 & n. 5; goes to United Provinces, iii. 200 & n. 6; returns to England, iii. 222 & n. 4; residence of, *ib.*; social, iii. 175, 200, 228, 229 *bis*; wife of, iii. 229 & n. 3.

Nieuport, Flanders: Dutch fleet near, 1652, iii. 68, n. 3.

Nigrita, A. Emmanuele, called: tomb of, ii. 244 & n. 5.

Nijmegen (Nimegen, &c.): notice, ii. 35 & nn. 1–4 (i. 27); mentioned, ii. 38, n. 3; plenipotentiaries, &c., at, 1676–8, iv. 76 & n. 3, 90 & n. 3, 110 & n. 1, 188 & n. 6; ~ men wrongly described as, iv. 8 & n. 2, 310 & n. 3; peace of, i. 27; alluded to, i. 27.

Nile, river: in inscription, ii. 270; *see also* Sculpture, Ancient.

Nineveh: ruins of, iv. 29 & n. 1, 214 & n. 1; traveller to, iv. 213; in sermons, iv. 244 & n. 3; v. 21, 347, 401, 487.

Nisida (Nesis), island, ii. 351 & n. 5.

Noah (Noach): in sermons, iv. 203, 314–15; v. 29, 63, 187, 271, 334, 503, 509; alluded to, v. 336 & n. 1.

Nob: destruction of: in sermon, v. 298 & n. 3.

Noel, Edward, second Viscount Campden: geneal., iii. 124, n. 1.

Noel, Juliana, Viscountess Campden, wife of the second viscount: house of, at Brooke, iii. 124 & n. 1.

Nogari, Paris, called Romano: painting by, ii. 242, n. 7.

Nola, Capo di (cape of Savona), ii. 170 & n. 1 (i. 107).

Nombre de Dios: Col. Henry Morgan at (error), iii. 585 & n. 2; iv. 46.

Nonconformists, Puritans, and Sectaries [general notices. Notices relating to Fanatics, Schismatics, and Sectaries are also indexed under this heading; notices relating to particular sects by name, unless two or more sects are mentioned in one notice, are indexed under the particular sects, and not here. Roughly some of the Puritans develop into Sectaries during the Civil War; after the passing of the Act of Uniformity in 1662 the latter are best described as Nonconformists. Some further notices relating to these bodies

Nonconformists, &c. (*cont.*)
are indexed under Church of England: chronological series, &c.]:
— chronological series:
— — (i) the Puritans, to 1642:
— — — origin of: forgeries relating to, v. 13, n. 1; at Emmanuel College, Cambridge, iii. 139 & n. 5; at Magdalen Hall, Oxford, iii. 383, n. 7 *ad fin.*; Roman Catholic emissaries among: letters concerning, iii. 157, n. 2; iv. 507, 508, n. 1; incite London mob against Laud, i. 18.
— — (ii) the Sectaries, 1642–62:
— — — rise and growth of heresies, &c.; in sermons, iii. 233, 236; v. 546–7; occupy parish churches, 1649, &c., ii. 552 & n. 3; iii. 60, 181, 185; will bring in Roman Catholicism: in prophecy, iii. 157 & n. 2; *see also* iv. 295; speculative preaching of: effects of, iii. 160 & n. 5, 184 & n. 2; at Colchester, 1656, iii. 177 & n. 3; Gauden's scheme for reuniting, iii. 187, n. 6; in Cromwell's army: force Cromwell to refuse the crown, iii. 190–1 & n.; ~ in Christmas raid on Anglican congregation, 1657, iii. 203–4 & nn.; ~ moved out of London, Feb. 1660, iii. 241 & n. 4; political activity of, May 1659, iii. 231 & n. 4.
— — (iii) the Nonconformists, 1662–1706:
— — — general: ministers ejected following Act of Uniformity: number of, iii. 331 & n. 4; meetings of, in London, during Plague, iii. 513, n. 3; Thomas Blood as spy on, iii. 576 & n. 2; repression of, under Charles II, i. *27*, *29*; ~ from 1681 onwards iv. 323 & n. 7; in Monmouth's rebellion, iv. 452 & n. 5; potential danger from, iv. 460; appointed J.P.'s, iv. 536, n. 3; meeting-house of, at Deptford, 1687, iv. 546 & n. 6; appointed Privy Councillors, iv. 590 & n. 4; ally themselves to Church of England, iv. 590; projected Comprehension of, in Church of England, 1689–90: bill in parliament for, iv. 633–4 & n.; ~ proposed alteration of Anglican liturgy, iv. 652 & n. 1; v. 6; ~ in sermon, v. 22; expect England to become a republic, iv. 646; numerousness of, 1694, 1700, v. 178, 408; 'our new sectaries', 1701, v. 482.
— — — toleration of: period of connivance and toleration, 1667, &c., iii. 513, n. 3; granted by Declaration of Indulgence, 1672, iii. 607–8 & n.; E's views on, iii. 608–9 & n.; bill for, 1673, iii. 608, n. 2; Shaftesbury supports, iv. 328, n. 6; opposed by Sir R. L'Estrange, iv. 439, n. 3; granted by Declaration of Indulgence, 1687, iv. 546–7 & n.; Nonconformists thank James II for Declaration, iv. 553–4 & n., 560 & n. 1; views of Seven Bishops on, iv. 583; not mentioned in vote for maintenance of Church, iv. 631 & n. 4; Toleration Act, 1689, iv. 640 & n. 2; ~ alluded to, in sermon, v. 616.
— controversies and disputes with Church of England: *Book of Common Prayer*, &c.: abused by sectaries, iii. 204; 'Cosin's Cozening Devotions': attacked by Puritans, iii. 45–6 & n., 635–6; mixed Communion: in sermons, iii. 514 & n. 4, 524; iv. 346 & n. 2; favouring Roman Catholicism: mutual recriminations, iv. 563; *see also* iv. 504; visibility of Church of England, iii. 247–8 & n.; treatises against Nonconformists, 1683–5, iv. 418 & n. 2; Nonconformists attacked by: Sir R. L'Estrange, iv. 439 & n. 3; ~ Dr. R. South, iii. 531, n. 4.
— miscellaneous: men 'above ordinances', iii. 204; v. 131 & n. 3; 'our little saints', iii. 320; 'precise people', iv. 265; 'professors', iii. 600; charity: Nonconformists entitled to: in Anglican sermons, v. 599, 615–16; Nonconformist preaching, iv. 402, n. 3; sacraments: Puritan views on, v. 180, n. 1; Nonconformists influenced by Socinus, iii. 227, n. 1; sect denying need to fear God: in

Nonconformists, &c. (*cont.*)
sermon, iii. 259; schisms, iv. 254.
— sermons against: general attacks, iv. 131, 295; v. 332, 546–7; special grounds: Donatist views, iv. 346 & n. 2 (for mixed Communion *see* controversies *above*); election: views on, iv. 282; v. 116, 117–18, 118; free Grace: views on, iii. 101; free will (Christian liberty): views on, iii. 31; impeccability: claim to, v. 131 & n. 3, 587; *see also* iii. 363 & n. 2; indifferent matters: refusal to conform in, iv. 264–5, 522; v. 22; ministry: usurpation of, iii. 330; iv. 54; obedience to civil magistrate, iii. 365; iv. 381; peevishness, spiritual pride, &c., iv. 288, 313–14; v. 22; prayer: disuse of set forms of, iv. 135, 298; schism, iv. 73, 106, 250; v. 116, 118, 127; sectarian spirit, iii. 569, 600 *bis*; separatism in worship, iv. 26, 39, 108, 283, 451, 638–9; v. 64–5, 117; 'the spirit': insistence on, &c., iii. 320, 551; v. 348; unreasonableness of dissent, iv. 347.
Nonjurors: penalties for refusing Oath of Allegiance to William and Mary, iv. 648, n. 6; deprivation and supersession of nonjuring bishops, *ib.*; v. 41, n. 3, 48–9 & n.; ~ Sancroft's views on, &c., v. 51–2 & nn.; conduct of deprived bishops, v. 59.
number of, iv. 620, n. 1; alterations made by, in liturgy, v. 142–3 & n.; views of, on attending conforming services, v. 289, n. 3; in Assassination Plot, v. 231; absolve Sir J. Friend and Sir W. Perkins, v. 236 & n. 1; i. 8 & n. 2; conduct of, at burial of T. White, deprived bishop of Peterborough, v. 289 & n. 3.
Nonsuch: Baroness: subsidiary title granted to Barbara Villiers, duchess of Cleveland, iii. 426, n. 4.
Nonsuch Palace, Cuddington, Surrey: notice, 1666, iii. 426–8 & nn.; materials from: used at Durdans, iii. 15, n. 1; Receipt of the Exchequer at, 1665–6, iii. 426–7 & n.; Exchequer ordered to move to, 1666, iii. 454, n. 8.
Nonsuch Press: edition of Diary projected by, i. *64*.
Norbury Park, Mickleham, Surrey: notice, iii. 157 & n. 5.
Norden, John: maps by, iv. 301 & n. 4.
Nore, The, Kent: ship explodes near, iii. 403, n. 1; *see also* Buoy of the Nore.
Norfolk: collection of birds' eggs from, iii. 594 & n. 1; control of Sick and Wounded in, 1664, iii. 395, n. 1; elections to parliament in, 1685, iv. 444 & n. 2; gentry of: visit Euston, iii. 590.
Norfolk: Henry Howard called of Norfolk for distinction, iii. 233, 495 & n. 5.
Norfolk: Cardinal of: *see* Howard, Philip Thomas.
Norfolk: Dukes, &c., of: dukedom restored, 1660–1, iii. 306 & n. 3, 326; future descent of dukedom, 1700, v. 394 & n. 1; individual dukes: *see* Howard, Thomas, fourth duke, 1554–72; Howard, Thomas, fifth duke, 1660 (1661)–77; Howard, Henry, sixth duke, 1677–84; Howard, Jane, his duchess; Howard, Henry, seventh duke, 1684–1701; Mordaunt, Lady Mary, his duchess; Howard, Thomas, eighth duke, 1701–32; Howard, Charles, tenth duke, 1777–86.
Norfolk: Earl of, 1644–6: *see* Howard, Thomas, earl of Arundel.
Normanby: Marquis of, 1694–1703: *see* Sheffield, John, later duke of the county of Buckingham.
Normandy: general remarks on, ii. 121, 122 (i. 78 *bis*); women's dress in, ii. 125–6 & n. (i. 80); James II in, 1692, v. 97, n. 2; Yvelin family in, iii. 548 & n. 3.
Normandy: Dukes of: representative of, in Charles II's coronation procession, iii. 280 & n. 1; individual duke: *see* Robert Curthose.
North, Sir Dudley: brings Great Seal to Windsor, 1685, iv. 466 & n. 4.
North, Dudley; fourth Baron North 1666, iv. 87, n. 3; geneal., iv. 87, 97, 299.

North, Elizabeth, Baroness Guilford, wife of Francis North, second baron: sermon commemorating, v. 365–6 & n.

North, Sir Francis; first Baron of Guilford 1683, iii. 613, n. 6; iv. 97, n. 4; character, iv. 299; appointed Lord Keeper, 1682, iv. 299 & n. 3; created baron, iv. 312, n. 5; speech of, to City authorities on *Quo Warranto* proceedings, 1683, iv. 319 & n. 1; no speech by, at opening of parliament, 1685, iv. 445 & n. 4; dismissal of, expected, iv. 445 & n. 5; dies, iv. 466 & n. 4; as Lord Keeper: hears cases, iv. 361, 393 & n. 1; admits John Evelyn, jnr., to Middle Temple, iii. 613–14; houses of: in London, iv. 312 & n. 5, 365 & n. 8; ~ at Wroxton, iv. 466 & n. 4; culture and conversation of, iv. 299 & n. 4, 312–13 & nn., 365; receives Sir J. Chardin, iv. 372; visits Sayes Court, i. *38*; social, iv. 383; geneal., iv. 97, 340; chaplain of: sermon by, iv. 361.

North, Francis; second Baron Guilford 1685, v. 309, n. 1; influence on, of his wife: in sermon, v. 366; chaplain(s) of: *see* Horneck, P.; ~ sermons by unnamed, v. 309, 529, 531.

North, Dr. John, iv. 87 & n. 3, 97 & n. 4; sermons by, iv. 87, 107; appointed to preach, iv. 132, n. 3; social, iv. 97.

North, Roger, iv. 340, n. 1; as counsel for E, iv. 340; brings Great Seal to Windsor, 1685, iv. 466; account of Sayes Court, &c., by, i. *38*.

North: fourth Baron, 1666–77: *see* North, Dudley.

Northampton: fire at, 1675, iv. 69–70 & n., 596 & n. 1; notice of, 1688, iv. 596 & n. 1; assize at, iv. 67, 70–1 & n.; fair at, ii. 78 (i. 51).

Northampton: Earls of: *see* Howard, Henry, earl 1604–14; *new creation*: *see* Compton, James, third earl, 1643–81; Compton, George, fourth earl, 1681–1727; Compton, Jane, his countess.

North Cray, Kent: Sir P. Warwick's house in (error), iii. 253 & n. 2; rector of: *see* Owen, R.

North Foreland, Kent: lighthouse on, iii. 615 & n. 3; Dutch fleet off, 1667, iii. 486 & n. 2; Dutch and English fleets off, 1672, iii. 614, n. 4, 615; mentioned, iii. 394.

North Stoke, Sussex: sale of, 1701, v. 441 & n. 5.

Northumberland: lands in, belonging to Lord Grey of Warke (later earl of Tankerville), iv. 533, n. 2; —Clarke of, iii. 92, critical note & n. 2, 518.

Northumberland: Earls and Dukes of: *see* Percy, Henry, eighth earl, 1572–85; Percy, Henry, ninth earl, 1585–1632; Percy, Algernon, tenth earl, 1632–68; Percy, Elizabeth, his countess; Percy, Joceline, eleventh earl, 1668–70; Montague, Elizabeth, countess of Montague, previously Elizabeth Percy, his countess; *new creation*: *see* Fitzroy, George, earl, 1674–83, and duke, 1683–1716; Fitzroy, Catherine, his duchess; *titular duke*, 1620–49; *see* Dudley, Sir Robert.

North-West Passage: expedition to discover, iv. 96 & n. 5.

Norton, —, Lady Norton: insults Charles I, &c., iii. 90 & n. 1.

Norton, Sir Gregory, the regicide: widow of, iii. 90, n. 1.

Norton, Col. Richard, and his estate, iv. 474 & n. 5.

Norway: merchant-ships from, ii. 30 (i. 23); governor of, 1664–99: *see* Gyldenløve, U. F.

Norwich, Norfolk: E visits, 1671, iii. 592–5 & nn.; Charles II and Queen Catherine at, 1671, iii. 592, n. 1, 593 & n. 3; Dutch settlers at, iii. 595, n. 1; population of, iii. 594, n. 2; trade, &c., of, iii. 595 & n. 2; places, &c., in: Bridewell wall, iii. 594, n. 3; Castle, iii. 594 & n. 4, 595; churchyards, iii. 595 & n. 6; Duke's Palace: notice, iii. 593 & n. 3; ~ proposed rebuilding of, iii. 594, 595; Marsfeild (error?), iii. 594 & n. 4; St. Clement's, &c.: rector of: *see* Le Franc, J.; St. Peter Mancroft: minister at: *see* Tenison, T.; Walloon church: minister of: *see* Le Franc, J.; Wensum river, iii. 593 & n. 3.

Norwich: Earls, &c., of: *see* Goring, George, sen., first earl, 1644–

Norwich: Earls of (*cont.*)
63; Goring, Charles, second earl, 1663–71; Goring, Alice, his countess; *new creation*: *see* Howard, Henry, earl 1672–7, later sixth duke of Norfolk; Howard, Henry, styled earl 1677, later seventh duke of Norfolk (iv. 112, n. 5).
Norwich: cathedral clergy:
bishops: *see* White, Francis (1629–31); Wren, Matthew, D.D. (1635–8); Hall, Joseph (1641–56); Reynolds, E. (1661–76); Sparrow, A. (1676–85); Lloyd, William, D.D., the nonjuror (1685–91); Moore, John (1691–1707).
deans: *see* Croft, John (1660–70); Astley, H. (1670–81); Sharp, John (1681–9); Prideaux, H. (1702–24).
Norwood, Col. Henry: social, iv. 5 & n. 6.
Nostradamus (M. de Notredame): prophecy by, v. 273 & n. 2.
Nottingham: notice, iii. 125–6 & nn.; St. Mary's at: vicar of: *see* Masterson, G.
Nottingham: Earls, &c., of: *see* Howard, Charles, first earl, 1597–1624; Howard, Catherine, his countess; *new creation*: *see* Finch, Sir Heneage, first earl, 1681–2; Finch, Daniel, second earl, 1682–1729, later sixth earl of Winchilsea.
Nottinghamshire: geology, &c., iii. 125 & n. 5.
Nova fossa: *see* Fossanova.
Novatian (called Novatus in error): heresy of: in sermon, iv. 259 & n. 8.
Novatianists: views of, iii. 363, n. 2.
Novatus: Baths of, in Rome, ii. 247; as error for Novatian, iv. 259 & n. 8.
Nova Zembla: in sermon, v. 49.
Noviomagus: site of, iii. 221, n. 7.
Nozze Aldobrandini, ii. 285 & n. 4.
Numa: tomb of, ii. 313 & n. 7.
Nuovo, Monte, Phlegraean Fields, ii. 344, n. 4, 345–6 & nn.
Nuremburg (Norimburg): taken by French, 1703 (error), v. 553 & n. 2; paintings by Dürer at, ii. 411, n. 3.
Nutfield, Surrey, v. 56, n. 3; George Evelyn of Nutfield and his family at, v. 187 & n. 1; Evelyn estate at: descent of, v. 520 & n. 5; rector of, 1641–6: *see* Middleton, W.

Oagle, Lord, *recte* Ogle: *see* Cavendish, Henry, styled Lord Ogle; Seymour, Elizabeth, duchess of Somerset, previously Lady Ogle.
Oakham (Ockham), Rutland, iii. 122, n. 2; notice, iii. 123–4 & n.; barony of, iii. 123, n. 5 *ad fin.*
Oakwood Chapel: *see* Wotton.
Oates, Titus, iv. 153, n. 4; character and progress of, iv. 153, n. 4 *ad fin.*, 154, 174–5 & n., 320, 439; claim of, to doctorate, iv. 153, n. 4, 228 & n. 2; 'reveals' the Popish Plot, i. *27–8*; iv. 153–4 & n.; the Popish Plot called Oates's plot, iv. 404; accuses Queen Catherine of high treason, iv. 158 & nn. 5, 6; informs against Roman Catholic peers, iv. 158 & n. 7; evidence of, against: E. Coleman, iv. 231 & n. 3, 232; ~ Stafford, iv. 228 & n. 8, 230; ~ Sir G. Wakeman, &c., iv. 174, 435; value of, as witness, iv. 230–2 & nn.; attempt to defame, iv. 188, n. 1; expelled from lodgings in Whitehall, &c., iv. 320, n. 2; action against, by James duke of York, 1684, iv. 636, n. 1; tried for perjury, 1685, iv. 435, n. 2, 438–9 & n.; sentence on, iv. 440 & n. 4; ~ carried out, iv. 445 & n. 3; ~ mentioned, iv. 451; ~ reversal of: attempt to obtain, iv. 636 & n. 1; *see also* iv. 440, n. 4 *ad fin.*; commons' vote in favour of, iv. 643 & n. 1; allowance granted to, 1689, iv. 440, n. 4 *ad fin.*; dedicates book against James II to William III, v. 238 & n. 3; mentioned, iv. 158, n. 4.
Oaths [*see also* England: oaths]:
lawful use of: in sermons, iv. 229, 385; v. 423–4; rash: in sermon, v. 508.
Scottish National Covenant, ii. 22, n. 3.
Oatlands: palace of, Weybridge, Surrey: lease of, &c., of, iv. 141, n. 3, 565, n. 2.
Obloor, Monsieur (Sir James Houblon?), iv. 128 & n. 6.
Obrien, vineyard (Haut-Brion), iv. 329 & n. 3.

O'Brien, Henry, styled Lord O'Brien and Lord Ibrackan, iv. 39, n. 4; as friend of Sir J. Williamson, iv. 39; social, iv. 125, 128.
O'Brien, Henry, sixth earl of Thomond, iii. 555, n. 1; house of, at Newmarket, iii. 554, n. 2, 555; geneal., iv. 39, n. 4.
O'Brien, Katherine, styled Lady O'Brien, &c., Baroness Clifton *suo jure*, wife of Henry O'Brien, Lord O'Brien, &c.: second marriage of, to Sir J. Williamson, iv. 39 & n. 4.
O'Brien, Murrough, sixth Baron and first earl of Inchiquin: in Paris, &c., 1651, iii. 26 & n. 2.
O'Brien, William, second earl of Inchiquin: conduct of, at Tangier, iv. 208 & n. 6.
O'Brien: Lord and Lady (courtesy titles): *see* O'Brien, Henry, also styled Lord Ibrackan; O'Brien, Katherine, Baroness Clifton *suo jure*.
Ockham, Rutland: *see* Oakham.
Ockham (Occham), Surrey: Henry Weston of, i. 13 & n. 2; rector of, 1606–55: *see* Bradshaw, N.
Ockwood (Oakwood): *see* Wotton.
Odart, —: *see* Oudart, N.
Oenipont, John, architect, ii. 180 & n. 3 (i. 113).
Offley family, v. 359.
Offley, Mrs. —: social, iii. 218.
Offley, Elizabeth, daughter of Dr. Gabriel Offley: *see* Crawley, Mrs. E.
Offley, Elizabeth, daughter of Sir Robert: *see* Herbert, Elizabeth, Lady Herbert.
Offley, Mrs. Frances, wife of Dr. Gabriel Offley: geneal., v. 257, n. 1.
Offley, Gabriel, D.D., rector of Abinger, iii. 154, n. 7; sermons by: at Abinger, iii. 423 *bis*, 561; ~ at Whitehall, iv. 140 & n. 1; ~ at Wotton, iii. 154, 155; geneal., ii. 537, n. 2; iv. 377, n. 1; v. 182, n. 1, 257, n. 1; *add.*
Offley, Mary, daughter of Dr. Gabriel Offley: *see* Graham, Mrs. M.
Offley, Mary, daughter of Sir Robert, second wife of George Evelyn: *see* Cotton, Mary, Lady Cotton.
Offley, Mary, Lady Offley, wife of Sir Robert: geneal., ii. 537, n. 2.
Offley, Robert, d. 1663, ii. 537, n. 2.
Offley, Rev. Robert, rector of Abinger, v. 182 & n. 1; character, &c., v. 182, 216; ~ alluded to, v. 207; sermons by, v. 216, 219; geneal., ii. 537, n. 2.
Offley, Sir Robert: geneal., ii. 537, n. 2; iii. 58, n. 2.
Offley, Thomas, Groom Porter, ii. 544, n. 5; godfather of Mary Evelyn (later Lady Wyche), ii. 544; gaming in lodgings of, iii. 504 & n. 1; social, iii. 81(?), 440, 458, 477, 518, 563; geneal., ii. 537, n. 2.
Ogle, Anne: *see* Howard, Mrs. A.
Ogle, Eutretia (Utricia), ii. 316 & n. 1.
Ogle, Sir John: geneal., ii. 316 & n. 1.
Ogle, Livina: *see* Manwood, Livina, Lady Manwood.
Ogle, Thomas: geneal., iv. 71, n. 1.
Ogle: Lord, 1676–80 (courtesy title), and Lady: *see* Cavendish, Henry; Seymour, Elizabeth, duchess of Somerset, previously Lady Ogle.
Oglethorpe, Lewis: fights duel, v. 527 & n. 2.
Oglethorpe, Sir Theophilus: geneal., v. 527 & n. 2.
Oglio, river, ii. 490 & n. 7.
Ogniati, Count: *see* Oñate.
Oise (Oyse), river: at Paris (error), ii. 92 & n. 1 (i. 61); bridge over, at Pontoise, ii. 121 (i. 78).
Okewood (Oakwood): *see* Wotton.
Oldenbarnevelt, Johan van (Barnevelt): imprisonment of, i. 29 & n. 1.
Oldenburg, Henry, iii. 491, n. 2; lends E Monconys's *Journal*, i. *88*, n. 3; imprisoned as suspect, 1667, iii. 491 & n. 2; as secretary of Royal Society, iii. 630, n. 5; social, iv. 84.
Oliva, G. P., Jesuit: in Oates's revelations, iv. 174 & n. 2.
Oliver, Isaac: miniature by (?), iii. 155 & n. 2.
Oliver, Peter, miniaturist, ii. 540, n. 2; works by, ii. 540 & n. 2; iii. 155 & n. 2(?), 260 & n. 2; ~ copy after, by Mrs. Evelyn, iii. 287.
Olivieri, P. P., sculptor: relief by, ii. 248 & n. 4.
Olona, river, ii. 505 & n. 3.
Olonne, Louis de la Trémoille, comte d': in procession, iii. 41 & n. 5.
Olympic games: in sermons, v. 120–1, 217.

Ombrone, river: bridge over, ii. 206 & n. 5.
Oñate (Ogniati), Don Marcos Alberto de, Spanish envoy, &c., to England, iii. 553–4 & n.
Oneglia (Onela), Liguria, ii. 169 & n. 6 (i. 106).
O'Neill (O'Neale), Daniel, iv. 92 & n. 2; builds Belsize House, *ib.*; commissioner for London streets, iii. 319, n. 1.
Onesimus: in sermon, v. 375.
Onley (Onely), Nicholas, D.D.: sermon by, iv. 168 & n. 3.
Onslow, Mrs. —, wife of Arthur or Denzil Onslow: social, iv. 288 & n. 2.
Onslow, Sir Arthur, bt., iii. 540, n. 5; iv. 558, n. 2; in legal proceedings (?), iii. 540; elected M.P. for Surrey, Feb. and Aug. 1679, iv. 165, n. 1; parliamentary candidate for Surrey, 1685, iv. 433–4 & n.; social, iii. 561 & n. 6; iv. 288 & n. 2(?), 558 & n. 2; geneal., iv. 255, n. 1; v. 55, n. 4; seat of: *see* West Clandon.
Onslow, Denzil, iv. 255, n. 1; seat of, at Pyrford, iv. 255 & nn. 2–6; social (?), iv. 288 & n. 2.
Onslow (Anslowe), Sir Richard, 1601–64: commissioner for London streets, iii. 319, n. 1.
Onslow, Sir Richard, bt.; first Baron Onslow 1716, v. 55, n. 4; entertains Surrey gentry, v. 279; as M.P.: speaks for reducing army, 1699, v. 311 & n. 1; ~ candidate for speakership, 1701, v. 446 & n. 7; ~ elected for Surrey, 1701, 1702, v. 482, 511–12 ~ fights duel, v. 527 & n. 2; ~ elected for Surrey 1705, v. 595, n. 4; acquires Baynards, ii. 539, n. 4; at funeral of John Evelyn of Wotton, v. 55; social, v. 312, 469, 473, 478, 480, 548.
Onslow, Thomas; second Baron Onslow 1717: social, v. 312 & n. 3.
Onslow: Barons: *see* Onslow, Sir Richard, bt., first baron, 1716–17; Onslow, Thomas, second baron, 1717–40.
Opera [for theatres and scenery *see* Theatre; for performers *see* Music; for individual operas *see* Plays, &c.]: at: London: Davenant's opera, 1659, &c., iii. 95, n. 5, 229 & n. 2, 268, n. 6; ~ Italian opera, 1674, iv. 30 & n. 1; Milan, 1646, ii. 503 & n. 4; Rome, ii. 261 & n. 5, 388–9 & n.; Siena, ii. 202 & n. 3; Venice, ii. 449–50 & nn., 474 & n. 6, 475.
Opstal, G. van: sculpture by (?), iii. 18 & n. 3.
Optics [for instruments *see* Astronomy *and* Scientific Instruments]: paper on, iv, 370; catoptrics, ii. 230 & n. 6; perspective (device with mirrors), ii. 254.
Orange: Princes of: stadholders of Zeeland, ii. 31, n. 2; attachment to, of Zeeland, iii. 407, n. 3; own: Breda, i. 41 & n. 1; ~ Willemstad, ii. 60 & n. 2 (i. 41); houses of: in Flushing, ii. 31 & n. 2; ~ at Ryswick, ii. 41 & n. 3 (i. 30); party of, iii. 405, n. 1, 471.
a prince (unspecified): portable stoves for army of, iii. 446–7 & n.; individual princes: *see* William I *and* vol. i, app. iii (p. 145); princesses: *see* Amalia von Solms; Mary, Princess Royal of England; Mary II, queen of England.
Orange: principality of: annexed by France, v. 545, n. 1; *see also* v. 559; French protestant refugees expelled from, 1703, v. 544–5 & n., 559 & n. 3.
Orange: town, &c.: in view, ii. 160 (i. 102).
Orbassan: battle near (Marsaglia), 1693, v. 155 & nn. 4, 5.
Orcagna: tabernacle by, at Or San Michele, ii. 196 & n. 6.
Orford: Earl of, 1697–1727: *see* Russell, Edward.
Origen: in sermons, v. 106, 107.
Orinda, the matchless: *see* Philips, Mrs. Katherine.
Orinoco river: electric eel of, iv. 196–7 & n.
Orkney: bishop of, 1662–3: *see* Sydserff, T.
Orkney: Earl and Countess of: *see* Hamilton, Lord George; Villiers, Elizabeth.
Orleans: notice, 1644, ii. 136–9 & nn. (i. 89–91); E at, 1646, ii. 533, 534; journey from Paris to, ii. 135 & n. 2 (i. 89).
historical: coronations at (?), ii.

Orleans (*cont.*)
138 & n. 4 (i. 91); councils at, ii. 138 & n. 4 (i. 90–1); relief of, by Joan of Arc: monument commemorating, &c., ii. 137 & nn. 1–4 (i. 90); Henrietta Maria at, 1644, ii. 149, n. 1.
miscellaneous: Mercure: musicians named, at, ii. 535, n. 1; provost-marshal at, ii. 136 (i. 89); wine of, ii. 138 & n. 1 (i. 90).
topographical: bridge, ii. 136–7 & nn. (i. 89–90); cemetery, ii. 139 & n. 1 (i. 91); Hôtel de Ville, ii. 139 & n. 2 (i. 91); island in Loire, ii. 136 (i. 89); market-place, ii. 136 (i. 89), 139 (i. 91); Ste.-Croix, ii. 138–9 & n. (i. 91); Three Emperors inn, ii. 136, n. 1; university, ii. 136, n. 3, 138 *bis* & nn. 3, 5, 6 (i. 90, 91); White Cross inn, ii. 136 & n. 1.

Orléans: Charles Paris d': *see* Longueville, duke of; Henri II d': *see* Longueville, duke of; Jean d': *see* Angoulême, count of.

Orleans: Duchy of, ii. 138 (i. 90).

Orleans: dukes, &c., of: *see* Charles; Louis XII, king of France; Gaston-Jean-Baptiste (1608–60); Philip (1660–1701); Henrietta Anne, his duchess.

Orleans: Forest of: danger from brigands in, ii. 135–6 (i. 89).

Orleans: kingdom(s) of, ii. 138 & n. 4 (i. 90).

Orley, Bernard van: tapestries designed by, iii. 323, n. 3.

Orlock, Dr. —: *see* Ullock, H.

Ormond: Dukes, &c., of: *see* Butler, James, sen., twelfth earl, 1633–42, marquis, 1642–61, and first duke, 1661–88; Butler, Elizabeth, his duchess, &c.; Butler, James, jnr., second duke, 1688–1745; Butler, Mary, his duchess.

Orne, river: at Caen, ii. 126 (i. 80).

Orrery: Earls of: *see* Boyle, Roger, first earl, 1660–79; Boyle, Lionel, third earl, 1682–1703.

Orsini (Ursini), dukes of Gravina: palace of, at Naples, ii. 330 & n. 2.

Orsini (Ursino), Fulvio: museum of, ii. 215 & n. 5.

Ortenegg: Baron in: *see* Lamberg, J. H. von.

Orthodox Church: *see* Greek Church.

Orwell, river: at Ipswich, iv. 115 & n. 7.

Orzinuovi (Ursa Nova), ii. 490 & n. 6.

Orzivecchi (Ursa Vecchio), ii. 490 & n. 5.

Osborne, Bridget, duchess of Leeds, &c., wife of Peregrine Osborne, second duke: as Viscountess Dunblane: marriages of, iv. 354 & n. 6.

Osborne, Bridget, duchess of Leeds, &c., wife of Sir Thomas Osborne, first duke: as countess of Danby: on Danby's imprisonment, iv. 354 & n. 5.

Osborne, Dorothy: *see* Temple, Dorothy, Lady Temple.

Osborne, Sir Henry: office held by, iii. 602, n. 1.

Osborne, Sir John, bt.: office held by, iii. 602, n. 1.

Osborne, Peregrine; styled Viscount Dunblane 1674–89, earl of Danby 1689–94, marquis of Carmarthen 1694–1712; second duke of Leeds 1712, iv. 354, n. 6 *ad fin.*; *add.*; as Lord Dunblane: marriage of, iv. 354 & n. 6; as Lord Carmarthen: leases Sayes Court, v. 450; ~ challenges Halifax (C. Montagu), v. 523 & n. 1; ~ chaplain of: sermon by, v. 557.

Osborne, Sir Thomas; earl of Danby 1674; marquis of Carmarthen 1689; first duke of Leeds 1694; &c.; lord high treasurer 1673–9, iii. 21, n. 5.

— early life: in Paris, 1650, iii. 21, 22; iv. 14; ~ leaves for England, iii. 22 & n. 8; elected M.P., 1665, iii. 394 & n. 2; opposes Clarendon, iii. 494, n. 2.

— as lord high treasurer (from 1673) and earl of Danby (from 1674): appointed, iv. 14 & n. 1; character, iv. 20 & n. 2, 267 & n. 5; general policy, &c., i. *27*, *28*; method of conducting business of, iv. 24, n. 2; recovery of the Exchequer during administration of, iii. 607, n. 1; opposed to Council of Trade and Plantations, iv. 14; *see also* iv. 50, n. 4; impeached, iv. 160 & n. 4; advises dissolution of parliament, Jan. 1679, iv. 163 & n. 1; dismissed, iv. 166, n. 2.

Osborne, Sir Thomas (*cont.*)
— — personal relations: hates Arlington, iv. 14 & n. 3, 39, n. 1; obligations of, to Sir Richard Browne, iv. 14, 20; seeks Dolben's support, iv. 267; causes Sir J. Duncombe to be superseded, iv. 267 & n. 3; causes Sir Stephen Fox to be superseded, iv. 267 & n. 4; supported by Sir J. Williamson, iv. 39, n. 1.
— — relations with E: general, i. *23*; iv. 14 & n. 1, 20; E obtains funds for Sick and Wounded from, iv. 24 & n. 2, 31; E obtains supplies for Lord Berkeley from, iv. 78, 107; ~ difficulty of obtaining, iv. 110; other business interviews, iv. 18, 28 *bis* & n. 3, 34(?), 41, 48, 49, 88, 90; consults E on private affairs, iv. 126, 130–1.
— — social: parties, iv. 67, 125, 128; alone, &c., iv. 93, 121, 134.
— later life: as earl of Danby: prisoner in Tower, iv. 354 & n. 4; ~ released on bail, 1684, iv. 366 & n. 4, 368; presides in house of lords, 29 Jan. 1689, iv. 619 & n. 4; appointed Lord President, iv. 627 & n. 2.
— — as marquis of Carmarthen: advises prorogation, 1690(?), v. 5 & n. 2; William III's chief adviser, *ib.*; social: party, v. 7.
— — as duke of Leeds: created duke, v. 180 & n. 2; impeached for corruption, 1695, v. 207, n. 7 *ad fin.*, 209, n. 5; as commissioner for Greenwich Hospital: at meeting, v. 209–10; quarrels with Halifax (Montagu), 1702, v. 523 & n. 1.
— residences and property: occupies Wallingford House, iv. 18, n. 2; buys Wimbledon House, &c., iv. 130–1 & n.; ~ purchase of, mentioned, iii. 315, n. 5; iv. 162 & n. 1; proposes buying Lord Bristol's library, iv. 126 & n. 3; petitions for lease of site of Sayes Court, v. 195 & n. 2.
— miscellaneous: surrenders his Scottish peerage, *add.* (iv. 354, n. 6); daughters of, iv. 130–1 & n.; chaplain of (H. Bagshaw?): sermon by, iv. 71 & n. 2.
Osborne of Kiveton: Baron, 1690–4 (1712): *see* Osborne, Peregrine, later second duke of Leeds, &c.
Oseburne of Dunblane: Viscount, 1673: *see* Osborne, Sir Thomas, later first duke of Leeds, &c.
Osiris: forged inscription of, ii. 210–11 & n.
Ossory: Earls and Countesses of (courtesy title): *see* Butler, Thomas (1642–80); Butler, Amelia (Emilia), his countess; Butler, James, later second duke of Ormond (1680–8); Butler, Anne (d. 1685) *and* Butler, Mary, later duchess of Ormond, his countesses.
Ossory: Bishops of: *see* Parry, John (1672–7); Parry, Benjamin (1678).
Ostend: notice, 1641, ii. 75 & nn. 4–6 (i. 49); as cautionary town, i. 23, n. 4; siege of, 1601–4, ii. 75 & n. 7 (i. 49); ~ Archduchess Isabella at, iii. 42, n. 4.
Osteria Nuova, between Vicenza and Verona, ii. 484 & n. 7.
Ostia: projected canal to, from Avernus, ii. 347 & n. 1.
Otho, Roman emperor: coin of, iv. 397 & n. 1.
Otto, son of Frederick Barbarossa: in inscription, ii. 297.
Ottoboni, Pietro, cardinal: elected pope (Alexander VIII), iv. 650 & n. 1, 651.
Ottone, Carlo, Genoese representative in England: social, iv. 365 & n. 7.
Ottwood, —: visits E, iv. 360.
Oudart (Odart), Nicholas, iii. 377, n. 2; social, iii. 377, 378, 447; ill, &c., iii. 546, n. 4.
Ouderkerk (Over-kirk), near Amsterdam: Jewish cemetery at, ii. 42–3 & n. (i. 31).
Oude Tonge (Oude Towne), ii. 61 & n. 3 (i. 41).
Oughtred, Rev. William, mathematician, iii. 88, n. 1; gift to, iii. 87–8; views of, iii. 157–8 & nn.; pupil of, iii. 178, n. 4.
Ouse: *see* Alost.
Ouse, river: at Huntingdon, iii. 135 & n. 5.
Ouse, river: at York, iii. 128.
Ouseley, Sir Charles: *see* Wolseley.
Outram, Dr. —: *see* Owtram, W.
Overflakkee, ii. 61, nn. 2, 3.
Over-kirk: *see* Ouderkerk.

Ovid: statue of, ii. 411 & n. 2; *see also* Books mentioned in text.
Owen, Sir David, sometime owner of Wotton, i. *2–3*, 4, n. 1.
Owen, Henry: sells Wotton to George Evelyn, sen., i. 4 & n. 1.
Owen, Sir John: tried, 1649, ii. 548, n. 2; social, ii. 556 & n. 2.
Owen, John, D.D., vice-chancellor of Oxford: sermon by, iii. 104–5 & n.
Owen, Richard; D.D. 1660, ii. 552 & n. 2; describes Charles I's execution (?), ii. 547 & n. 6; ministrations of, at Sayes Court, 1649, 1652–7: preaches and celebrates Communion, ii. 552; iii. 79, 89, 94, 144–5, 195; ~ baptises E's children, iii. 75, 89, 147; ~ churches Mrs. Evelyn, iii. 76, 90, 147, 195; other sermons by: at Charlton, iii. 154; ~ at Sayes Court, 1659(?), iii. 226 & n. 5; ~ funeral, for Lady Cotton, at Wotton (?), iii. 378 & n. 2; social, iii. 60, 217.
Owtram (Outram), William, D.D., iv. 56, n. 1; sermons by: printed, iv. 160 & n. 2(?); ~ unprinted, iv. 56, 81; appointed to preach, iii. 524, n. 7; dies, &c., iv. 188 & n. 3.
OXFORD: E at: as student, 1637–40, ii. 16–24 & nn. (i. 13–18) *passim*; later visits: 1654, iii. 104–11 & nn.; ~ 1664, iii. 381, 383–6 & nn.; ~ 1669, iii. 530–6 & nn.; ~ 1675, iv. 67–9 & nn.
— political: Charles I retires to, Nov. 1642, ii. 79, n. 6; court, &c., of Charles I at, ii. 549, n. 9 *ad fin.*; iii. 480, n. 8; Charles II, court, and parliament at, autumn 1665, iii. 423 & n. 7; Albemarle visits Charles II at, iii. 423, 424 *bis*; Charles II returns to London from, iii. 428; parliament at, 1681, iv. 239 & n. 3; William of Orange expected at, 1688, iv. 609 & n. 6; William III visits, v. 220 & n. 3; Queen Anne at: 1702, v. 514 & n. 7, 516 & n. 2; ~ 1705 (error), v. 592 & n. 2.
— miscellaneous: meetings for scientific discussion at, *c.* 1648–60, iii. 266 & n. 6; charitable gift from, for Sick and

OXFORD (*cont.*)
Wounded, 1666, iii. 444; in time of Fire of London: wind at, iii. 451, n. 6; ~ evidence of Fire at, iii. 453, n. 3, 454, n. 1; Thames frozen at, 1667, iii. 477, n. 2.
— persons at [casuals; persons normally residing in Oxford, or visiting it in E's company, are excluded]: Dr. R. Bohun: goes into residence, iii. 566; John Evelyn, jnr.: goes to join William of Orange, 1688, iv. 609 & n. 10; Prince Giolo: dies at, v. 295, n. 2; duchess of Newcastle, as Margaret Lucas, iii. 480, n. 8; Ormond, 1677, iv. 111 & n. 7; Bishop Samuel Parker: dies at, iv. 574, n. 2; Sir Walter Pye, ii. 558, n. 3; Lady Isabella Thynne, ii. 549, n. 9 *ad fin.*; Rev. G. Tully: sermon by, at, iv. 516, n. 2; C. Wase: employed at, iii. 525, n. 1.
— town: places in: cathedral, iii. 109 & n. 3; St. Frideswide's convent: former refectory of, iii. 109, n. 1.
— university: general: in comparisons, iii. 140, 531; originally at Cricklade, iii. 117, n. 3; discipline of, under Laud, ii. 19 & n. 2 (i. 14); undergraduates ordered to be confirmed, ii. 23 (i. 17); parliamentary visitors, 1648: appointments by, ii. 17, n. 2; iii. 104, n. 8, 105, n. 8; ~ expulsion by, i. 13–14 (*see* ii. 17, n. 4); Dr. J. Wilkins as preserver of, during Protectorate, iii. 165 & n. 8.
— — academic ceremonies, lectures, &c.: general: ceremonies and dress retained during Commonwealth, iii. 105 & n. 4; creation of a doctor, iii. 533; dress: in comparison, ii. 448; ~ *see also* ii. 19, n. 1; the Act: general note, iii. 104, n. 4; places of celebrating, iii. 104, n. 5, 385, 531; decline of, iii. 530, n. 4; individual acts: 1654, iii. 104–5 & nn.; ~ 1669, iii. 531, 532–4 & nn. (invitation to, iii. 500); ~ 1675, iv. 67–8 & nn.; Latin sermon in, iii. 104, n. 4, 106; *Terrae filius* in, iii.

OXFORD (*cont.*)
104, nn. 4, 6; ~ speeches, &c., of, iii. 104 (as *praevaricator*) 532–3 & n.; Convocation: gift of Arundel inscriptions announced to, iii. 496, n. 1; decree of, 1667, iii. 498–9; meetings of, 1669, iii. 530, n. 4, 535–6; Encaenia, iii. 104, n. 4, 530, n. 4; first celebration of, iii. 530, 531–2 & nn.; lectures: anatomy, iv. 57; botanical, iv. 68; matriculation, ii. 16 & n. 2.

— — institutions, buildings, &c.: *Anatomy School*: collections in, iii. 108 & nn. 4, 5; *Arundel inscriptions*: given to university, i. *21*; iii. 495–6 & n.; thanks returned for, iii. 497, 498–9, 500 & n. 6; arrangements for removal of, to Oxford, iii. 498; as set up: need for protecting, iii. 534 & n. 4; Prideaux's account of: copies given to E, &c., iv. 89 & nn. 2–4; *Arundel sculptures*: given to university, 1755, v. 44, n. 6; *add.*; *Ashmolean collection*: founded by J. Tradescant, &c., iii. 198–9 & n.; gift of, to university, iii. 199 & n. 2, 217 & n. 7; iv. 139 & n. 1; library, iv. 138, n. 4; gift to, by R. Plot, iv. 68, n. 4; building for (Old Ashmolean), iii. 199, n. 2; iv. 139 & n. 1; *Ashmolean Museum* (modern): objects from Ashmolean collection in, iii. 199, n. 2; Arundel inscriptions and sculptures in, iii. 534, n. 4; v. 44, n. 6; *add.*; *Bodleian Library*: MSS. and miscellaneous collections in, iii. 106–8 & nn., 385 & nn. 2–4; visits to, i. 15; iii. 534; iv. 69; Ashmole's library transferred to, iv. 138, n. 4; books given by E to, iii. 385 & n. 2; ~ *see also* ii. 469, n. 4; iii. 11, n. 1; attempts to obtain Norfolcian MSS., iii. 472, n. 3; building: painted ceilings, &c., ii. 300; ~ closet of the tower, iii. 107 & n. 8; ~ Selden end, iii. 107 & n. 5; ~ *see also* Schools *below*; librarian, 1652–60: *see* Barlow, T.; *Clarendon Building* (18th cent.): university press installed in, iii. 531, n. 1; *Congregation House*, old,

OXFORD (*cont.*)
ii. 16, n. 2; *Convocation House*, iii. 108 & n. 3; ~ degrees conferred in, iii. 535 & n. 7; *Divinity School*, iii. 108; *Physick Garden*: notices, 1654, 1664, iii. 109–10 & n., 386 & nn. 5–7; lecture on plants in, iv. 68; superintendent of, 1632–80: *see* Bobart, J., sen.; *Physick School*: see *Anatomy School* above; *Press*, iii. 531 & n. 1; *St. Mary the Virgin*: E confirmed in, ii. 23 (i. 17); the Act held in, iii. 104 & n. 5, 105; ~ formerly, iii. 385, 531; Act sermons in, iii. 104, n. 4, 104–5, 534; iv. 68 *bis*; vestry of, ii. 16 & n. 2; *Schools building*, i. 15; iii. 108, n. 4; tower of: used as observatory, iii. 384 & n. 7; ~ Archive of the: see *Bodleian Library*: closet of the tower *above*; Arundel inscriptions in, iii. 534, n. 4; academic exercises in, iii. 104, 105, 532; *Selden, J.*: inscriptions given to university by, iii. 534, n. 4; *Sheldonian Theatre*: design and commencement of, iii. 385 & n. 5; ceiling painting in, iii. 375, n. 3; cost of, &c., iii. 530–1 & n.; dedication of (Encaenia, 1669), iii. 500, 530 & n. 4, 531–3 & nn.; the Act held in from 1669, iii. 104, n. 5, 531; the Act of 1669 in, iii. 532–4 & nn.; ceremony in, iii. 535; banquet for William III in, v. 220 & n. 3; the area about, iii. 534 & n. 4; *Tradescant's museum*: see *Ashmolean collection* above; *University Galleries*: see *Ashmolean Museum* above; *University Museum* (modern): contains objects from Tradescant's museum, iii. 199, n. 2.

— — officers and servants: *chancellors* [the page-references are to notices of the holders of the office in this capacity]: *see* Laud, W. (1629–41) (ii. 19 & n. 2; i. 14); Cromwell, O. (1651–8) (iii. 105, 165, n. 8); Hyde, Edward, earl of Clarendon (1660–7) (iii. 384 & n. 3, 474); Sheldon, Gilbert (1667–9) (iii. 535, n. 4); Butler, James, first duke of Ormond (1669–88) (iii.

OXFORD (*cont.*)
535 & n. 4; iv. 111–12 & n.); Butler, James, second duke of Ormond (1688–1715) (v. 321, n. 1); *vice-chancellors*: *see* Baylie, R. (1636–8); Owen, John (1652–7); Say, R. (1664–6); Fell, John (1666–9); Mews, P. (1669–73); Bathurst, Ralph (1673–6); Aldrich, H. (1692–5); Mander, R. (1700–2); *proctors*: speeches of, in the Act, iii. 104, 105, 533; *public orator*: *see* South, R. (1660–77); letter of, to E (?), iii. 498–9 & n.; speeches of, iii. 531–2 & n., 535, 536; *registrar*, iii. 498, 499, 531; *bedels*: E lodges with one, iii. 530 & n. 3; in ceremonies, iii. 535 *bis*.

— — professors: *Astronomy*: Savilian; *see* Ward, Seth (1649–60); *Botany*: *see* Morison, R. (1669–83); *Divinity*: Lady Margaret: *see* Laurence, T. (1638–48); Hall, John (1676–91); ~ Regius: *see* Allestree, R. (1663–80); Jane, W. (1680–1707); *Geometry*: Savilian: *see* Wallis, J. (1649–1703); *Greek*: Regius: *see* Crowther, J. (1660–5); *Law*: *see* Sweet, Sir G. (1661–72); *Mathematics*: Seth Ward called professor, 1654, in error, iii. 105 & n. 2; *Physick* (medicine): *see* Clayton, Sir T. (1647–65); Hyde, James (1665–81); Hoy, T. (1698–1718).

— — other members, &c. [*see* further under the various colleges below]: Philip Stanhope, earl of Chesterfield: created D.C.L., iii. 535; the Evelyns: *see* Balliol College *and* Trinity College *below*; the Howards: degrees conferred on, iii. 535 & n. 3; Johann Wilhelm, prince of Neuburg: created D.C.L., iv. 65, n. 4; William Lee, the inventor (?), iii. 285 & n. 3; Sir W. Petty: studies of, at, iv. 56–7 & nn.; Francis Seymour (Seymour-Conway), later Baron Conway, v. 331 & n. 1; Robert Spencer, later Viscount Teviot: created D.C.L., iii. 535; ~ entertains E at Oxford, iv. 67.

— — colleges and halls: general: in comparison, ii. 94 & n. 1 (i. 62); give their plate to Charles I, i. 15 & n. 1.

— — — All Souls: concert at, iii. 106; chapel: painting in, iii. 385–6 & n.; warden, 1686–1702: *see* Finch, L.; fellow: *see* Creech, T.

— — — Balliol: fellow-commoners (or gentlemen-commoners) at, ii. 16 & n. 1, 17 (i. 13 *bis*); chapel: services in, ii. 19–23 *passim* (i. 15); ~ declamations in, ii. 20; hall: exercises in, ii. 20 *bis*; library, i. 15 & n. 2; ~ books given to, by E, ii. 19 & n. 3 (i. 15); ~ almanacs containing notes by E in, i. *48* & n. 2, *75–7*; masters: *see* Parkhurst, J. (1617–37); Laurence, T. (1637–48); Bradshaw, George (1648–51); Savage, H. (1651–72); Mander, R. (1687–1704); fellows: *see* Cowper, E.; Prowse, E.; Thicknesse, J.; other members: N. Conopios, ii. 18 & nn. 2–4 (i. 14); E: as student at, i. *5*; ii. 16–24 *passim* (i. 12–18); ~ reasons for going to, ii. 16–17 (i. 13); ~ tutor of, at, ii. 17 (i. 13); ~ sups at, 1654, iii. 105; (Sir) John Evelyn: enters, v. 314 & n. 4; *see further* Evelyn, Sir John; Richard Evelyn, ii. 23 (i. 17).

— — — Brasenose: fellows of: sermon by, iv. 68; ~ convert to Roman Catholicism, iv. 510, n. 1.

— — — Christ Church: election to, of scholars from Westminster School, iii. 287, n. 5; library, hall, &c., iii. 108–9 & nn.; Tom Quadrangle: in comparison, iii. 136; ~ dimensions of, iv. 281 & n. 2; E entertained at, iv. 67–8; deans of: as electors of Westminster scholars, iii. 287, n. 5; ~ candidates for deanery, 1686, iv. 519; ~ individual deans: *see* Fell, John (1660–86); Massey, J. (1686–8); Aldrich, H. (1689–1710); canons: *see* French, P.; Smith, Henry; other members: *see* Allestree, R. (iii. 288, n. 5); Bennet, Henry, earl of Arlington (iv. 119, n. 3); Conopios, N. (ii. 18, n. 2); Hill, Thomas (iii. 287 & n. 4); Locke, John (iii. 628).

OXFORD (*cont.*)
— — — Corpus Christi: president, 1688–1714: *see* Turner, Thomas.
— — — Exeter (Excester): play acted at, ii. 20 (i. 16); P. Fiott at, iii. 105 & n. 8.
— — — Hertford, iii. 383, n. 7 *ad fin.*
— — — Magdalen: fellows of: ejected by James II, v. 40; ~ reinstated, iv. 599 & n. 4; connexion of, with Magdalen Hall, iii. 383, n. 7 *ad fin.*; chapel, &c., iii. 109 & n. 5, 386 & nn. 3, 4; Grammar Hall, iii. 383, n. 7 *ad fin.*; presidents of: *see* Pierce, T. (1661–72); Hough, J. (1687, 1688–99); the Howards at, iii. 535 & n. 3.
— — — Magdalen Hall, iii. 383, n. 7; principal, 1662–81: *see* Hyde, James; R. Plot at, iv. 68.
— — — Merton: contest for wardenship of, 1661, iii. 273 & n. 3; visitor of, *ib.*; warden, 1661–93: *see* Clayton, Sir T.; fellow of: *see* Dickinson, E.
— — — New College: E visits, iii. 386; chapel, iii. 108 & n. 7, 386, n. 2; fellows of: sermon by, iv. 68; ~ *see* Bohun, Ralph.
— — — Oriel: provost, 1653–91: *see* Say, R.
— — — Pembroke: master, 1664–1710: *see* Hall, John.
— — — Queen's: provosts: *see* Barlow T. (1658–77); Halton, T. (1677–1704); Lancaster, W. (1704–17); Smith, Joseph (1730–56); Sir Joseph Williamson at, iv. 38 & n. 5.
— — — St. John's: E visits, iii. 536; library, &c., iii. 108 & n. 6; presidents: *see* Baylie, R. (1633–48, 1660–7); Mews, P. (1667–73).
— — — St. Mary Hall: principal, 1664–89: *see* Crowther, J.
— — — Trinity: chapel: rebuilt by R. Bathurst, i. 13 & n. 1; v. 571 & n. 2; president, 1664–1704; *see* Bathurst, Ralph; fellows of: *see* Bathurst, George; Hobbs, W.; other members: George Evelyn at, ii. 15 & n. 1, 17, 20 & n. 1 (i. 12, 13, 15–16); v. 358; John Evelyn, jnr.: enters, iii. 474 & n. 5; ~ tutors of, at, iii. 474; iv. 78; *add.*; ~ *see*

OXFORD (*cont.*)
further Evelyn, John, jnr.; proposal to send E to, ii. 16–17 (i. 13).
— — — University: rebuilding of, iv. 69 & n. 1; masters: *see* Walker, O. (1676–89); Charlett, A. (1692–1722); fellows of: converts to Roman Catholicism, iv. 510, n. 1.
— — — Wadham (Waddum): E entertained at, &c., iii. 104, 105–6, 386; Wilkins's lodgings at, iii. 110–11; wardens: *see* Wilkins, J. (1648–59); Ironside, G., jnr. (1665–89); Seth Ward resident at, iii. 105, n. 2.
Oxford: Earls of: the De Veres, i. 24 & n. 1; individual earls: *see* de Vere, Aubrey, twentieth earl, 1632–1703; *new creation*: *see* Harley, Robert, first earl, 1711–24.
Oxford: Bishops of: candidates for see, 1686, iv. 519; individual bishops: *see* Field, T. (error, ii. 8 & n. 2); Bancroft, J. (1632–40); Paul, W. (1663–5); Blandford, W. (1665–71); Crew, N. (1671–4); Compton, H. (1674–5); Fell, John (1676–86); Parker, S. (1686–8); Hough, J. (1690–9); Talbot, W. (1699–1715).
Oxfordshire: natural history collection from, iv. 68 & n. 4; lord lieutenant of (Montagu Bertie, earl of Abingdon): removed, v. 611, n. 4 *ad fin.*; parliamentary election for, 1685: candidate in, iv. 427 & n. 2.
Oye, river: and frontier of France, ii. 84, n. 1.
Oyse: *see* Oise.

Pacific Sea: Dampier's definition of, &c., v. 295 & n. 3.
Packard, —, iii. 183, n. 1.
Packer, Mrs. —: sings, iv. 404 & n. 8.
Packer, Mrs. Isabel, wife of Philip Packer, ii. 548, n. 1; geneal., iv. 345, n. 4.
Packer, John, ii. 548, n. 1; chapel built by, at Groombridge, &c., iii. 72 & nn. 1, 3; iv. 40.
Packer, Philip, ii. 548, n. 1; house and chapel of, at Groombridge, iii. 72 & nn. 1–3; iv. 40 & nn. 1–3, 6;

Packer, Philip (*cont.*)
reversion held by, iii. 427, n. 2; at Nonsuch, iii. 427; social, ii. 547–8; iii. 393; iv. 279, 281, 298, 302, 345, 416; geneal., iii. 100, n. 3; iv. 345 & n. 4, 404 & n. 8.
Packer, Robert, iii. 427, n. 2.
Packer, William, iii. 427, n. 2.
Packhurst, —, iii. 183 & n. 1.
Paddy, Sir William, M.D.: portrait of, iii. 338 & n. 4.
Padova, Alberto di: *see* Eremitano, A.
Padre Ottomano, impostor, iii. 522, n. 2.
Padua:
— E at, 1645–6, ii. 453–80 & nn., *passim*; E's departure from, ii. 511, n. 6 *ad fin.*; bibliographical note, ii. 453, n. 1; *add.*
— journey from Venice to, ii. 452–3 & nn.
— miscellaneous: bishops of, ii. 456 & n. 6; disorders in, 1645, ii. 471–2; fair of St. Anthony, ii. 452 & n. 2, 453–4 & n.; founder of, ii. 453 & n. 2, 454 & n. 3; homicides in, ii. 472 & n. 2; hospitals at: treatment in, ii. 476; market: cheapness of, ii. 462; procession to S. Antonio, ii. 453–4 & n., 455 & n. 4.
— persons at [persons casually mentioned in notes as visitors to Padua are excluded; for students *see* University *below*]: Arundel, ii. 466–7, 479 & nn. 2, 4; J. Digby, iii. 479 & n. 7; Henry Howard, later sixth duke of Norfolk, ii. 473, 479; Thomas Howard, fifth duke of Norfolk: dies at, iv. 128 & n. 1.
— topography: general: arcaded houses, ii. 453, 490; paving, ii. 453.
— — buildings, &c.: amphitheatre: ruins of, ii. 467; *add.*; Casa degli Specchi, ii. 463 & n. 7.
— — churches: cathedral, ii. 454 & n. 1; Giotto's chapel, ii. 467, n. 2; S. Antonio, ii. 454–5 & nn.; S. Caterina, ii. 472, n. 6; ~ nuns at, ii. 472 & n. 1, 473 *bis* & n. 3; S. Giustina and monastery, ii. 455–6 & nn.; S. Lorenzo, ii. 454 & n. 2.
— — Gattamelata: statue of, ii. 454 & n. 5; Livy: arm of, from, ii. 328–9 & n., 462, n. 7; ~ birth-place of, ii. 463 & n. 7; ~ monument to, ii. 462 & n. 7; Monte di Pietà, ii. 463 & n. 6; Orto Botanico, ii. 466 & nn. 4, 6, 480, n. 5.
— — palaces: del Capitanio, ii. 463 & n. 5; Foscari all' Arena, ii. 467 & n. 2; Giustiniani, ii. 467, n. 1; Mantoa, ii. 466–7 & n.; del Podestà, ii. 463 & n. 5; della Ragione (Salone), ii. 462–3 & nn.; ~ copied at Vicenza, ii. 481–2.
— — Piazza (market-place), ii. 462, 463 & n. 5; Piazza del Santo, ii. 454; Porta del Portello, ii. 453 & n. 3; Pozzo Dipinto, ii. 472 & n. 6; Prato della Valle, ii. 455 & n. 5; S. Francesco: hospital of, ii. 476, n. 1; tomb of Antenor, ii. 454 & nn. 3, 4; Via Cesare Battisti, ii. 472, n. 6.
— university, ii. 453, n. 1; buildings, ii. 463–4 & n.; E as student, i. *8*; ~ matriculation certificate of, ii. 464 & n. 2, 465–6 & nn.; ~ elected *syndicus artistarum* (?), ii. 469–70 & n. 1; *add.*; ~ anatomical tables obtained by: *see* Evelyn: collections; anatomy lecture at, ii. 475–6 & n.; professors, &c.: *see* Leonius, J. (ii. 475 & n. 4); Selvatico, B. (ii. 472 & n. 5, 478); Vesling, J. (ii. 466 & n. 6, 472, 475 & n. 3); students at: misconduct of, ii. 472 & n. 2, 483 & n. 6; ~ English: consuls for: *see* Rogers, G. (ii. 464, n. 1); Abdy, Sir J. (ii. 480, n. 4); individual English students at [men casually mentioned in notes as students at Padua are excluded]: *see* Bramston, Sir F. (ii. 470, n. 3, 473); Croyden, G. (iii. 34 & n. 3); Henshaw, T. (ii. 464, n. 2, 470, 473); Rogers, G., (ii. 464 & n. 1; iv. 291); Thicknesse, J. (i. 14 (ii. 17, n. 4 *ad fin.*); ii. 470); Waller, Edmund (ii. 475, n. 3, 478 & n. 3, 480).
Padus, river: *see* Po.
Pagani, Lattanzio, called della Marca, iii. 339, n. 3.
Pagani, Vincenzo, called della Marca, iii. 339, n. 3.
Page, Alice: *see* Snatt, Mrs. A.

Paget, Nathan, M.D.: delivers Harveian oration, iii. 379, n. 1.
Paget, William; sixth Baron Paget, 1678: appointed ambassador to Turkey, v. 117 & n. 4.
Paget: sixth Baron, 1678–1713: *see* Paget, William.
Paine, Captain —: at Calais, 1652, iii. 55.
Painting and Drawing [collections of paintings are indexed under Art-Collections; dealers, under Art-Dealers. Painters, apart from amateurs and persons not named, are not indexed collectively]:
— amateur artists: Mrs. S. Draper (Susanna Evelyn), v. 138; Sir J. Gawdy, iv. 113 & n. 3; Louisa Hollandina, i. 26 & nn. 2, 3; Mrs. J. Myddelton, iv. 334, n. 5; R. Waller, v. 176; names unknown, iv. 336, 363 & n. 5; *see also* Evelyn, John; Evelyn, Mrs. Mary.
— artists: employed by traveller to take views, iv. 213 & n. 2; *see also* Maratti, C.; unnamed, i. 74; iv. 646.
— connoisseurs of, &c.: Francis North, Baron Guilford, iv. 299, 365; Charles II and E discuss painting, iii. 310.
— genres:
— — chiaroscuro painting, ii. 215, 485; iii. 386.
— — drolleries, ii. 39 (i. 29), 56; iii. 262.
— — landscapes or paysages, ii. 39 (i. 29); i. 76; ii. 132 (i. 85), 299 & n. 1; iii. 294; in inlaid marble, &c., ii. 63 (i. 43), 191 (i. 119); landscape-painter, iv. 51–2.
— — peepshows (called perspectives), ii. 254 & n. 4 (?); iii. 165 & n. 6.
— — perspective [E uses the term loosely; *see also* peepshows *above*; trick-pictures *and trompe-l'œil below*]: E consults A. Bosse concerning, ii. 568; perspective pictures: in Florentine mosaic, iii. 136; in gardens, &c., ii. 108 (i. 69), 112 (i. 72–3); iii. 375; iv. 105, 144; *see also* ii. 109 (i. 70); in stage-scenery, ii. 449; iii. 570; by Steenwyck, ii. 546, 548; painter of, iv. 51–2.

Painting and Drawing (*cont.*)
— — trick-paintings, ii. 373 & n. 5, 399, n. 10.
— — *trompe-l'œil*, ii. 56 (i. 38), 108 (i. 70) (?; tempest), 109 (i. 70), 117 (i. 76), 296 & nn. 5–7.
— materials, techniques, &c.:
— — black-lead pen, ii. 208.
— — crayon, ii. 160 (i. 102), 557; iii. 387 & n. 3; distinguished from pen, iii. 10, 22, n. 9; on copper, v. 187 & n. 2.
— — distemper, iii. 294.
— — fresco: in France, ii. 103 (i. 67), 108, 117 (i. 76); in Italy, ii. 184 (i. 116), 195, 246, 288, 298, 308, 407, 412, 423, 454; in England, iii. 591; iv. 116, 176, 316, 344, 347, 377, 534; liability of, to decay, iv. 317; imitated, iii. 385.
— — miniature or miniatures: mezzotint engraving compared with, iii. 274; collections of, ii. 549 *bis*; iii. 10; copies in: of paintings, ii. 540 & n. 2; iii. 260, 287; ~ of landscape-paintings, ii. 132 (i. 85); paintings in, of flowers, insects, &c., ii. 133; iii. 33; iv. 289, 531–2 & n.; used to indicate drugs, &c., iii. 236; iv. 215–16, 330.
— — oil [select notices], ii. 7 (i. 7), 29 (i. 21), 109, 133, 278; of turpentine, iii. 386.
— — paintings on: blue cloth, iii. 386; copper, v. 187 & n. 2; drug-pots, &c., iii. 28; stone, ii. 113 (i. 73), 132 (i. 85); velvet, ii. 277–8.
— — pencil: in general sense, ii. 204.
— — water-colours, ii. 133 (i. 87), 540.
— schools, &c.: Bolognese, ii. 420, n. 5; Florentine, 1645, ii. 417; Roman, ii. 212, n. 2; ~ in comparisons, iv. 316, 344; ~ painters in Rome, 1645, ii. 399 & nn. 8–10; United Provinces: diffusion of paintings in, ii. 39 & n. 4 (i. 29), 174 (i. 110).
— study of: at Milan (Ambrosiana), ii. 497 & n. 4; in Rome, ii. 288, 295 & n. 4; ~ 'the painters academy', ii. 299 & n. 4.
Palaeologus, Thomas, despot of the Morea: gift from, ii. 205 & n. 2.

Palatinate, The: exiled ministers from: collection for, 1635–6, ii. 15 & n. 5 (i. 12); restored to Charles Louis, ii. 567, n. 2; occupied and devastated by French, 1688–9, iv. 608 & n. 6, 632 & n. 2; protestants in: losses of, by Peace of Ryswick, v. 270 & n. 7; reported French invasion of, 1699, v. 345, n. 1; Sir W. Curtius of, iii. 36 & n. 1.
Electors Palatine: *see* Frederick V; Charles Louis (1648–80); Philipp Wilhelm (1685–90); Johann Wilhelm (1690–1716).

Palavicini, Signor: *see* Paravicini, Sir Peter.

Palestina: *see* Pellestrina.

Palestine *or* the Holy Land: St. Helena finds True Cross in, ii. 262; earth from, i. 85; *see also* Jerusalem; ship bound for, 1645: E prepares to sail in, ii. 451–2; I. Basire visits, iii. 303, n. 3.

Palestrina (Praeneste): and Acqua Felice, ii. 238 & n. 7; in view, ii. 397 & n. 4.

Palfi, —, Imperial general: *see* Pollant.

Paliano: Duke and Prince of, &c.: *see* Colonna, F., &c.

Palisse, La, ii. 156 & n. 1 (i. 100).

Palla, G. della, ii. 119, n. 2.

Palladio, Andrea, the architect, ii. 481 & n. 3; account by, of staircase at Chambord, ii. 139–40 & n.; buildings designed by: Venice: S. Giorgio Maggiore, ii. 461 & n. 7; Vicenza, &c.: Basilica Palladiana, ii. 481–2 & nn.; ~ Loggia del Capitanio, ii. 482–3 & n.; ~ Rotonda, ii. 484 & n. 3; ~ Teatro Olimpico, ii. 482 & nn. 2–5; villa designed by: imitated, iii. 625 & n. 3; false attributions: Chambord: Château, i. 91 & n. 1; Padua: S. Giustina, ii. 455 & n. 6; Vicenza: triumphal arch, ii. 484 & n. 6.

Pall mall: malls: at Palais-Royal, Paris, ii. 134 & n. 1 (i. 87), 567; iii. 44; elsewhere in France, ii. 111 (i. 72), 142 & n. 3 (i. 92), 145 & n. 1 (i. 94), 158 & n. 3 (i. 101); at Geneva, ii. 527; in England, iii. 180.

Palma Giovane (Jacopo Palma): painting by, ii. 444, n. 1.

Palma Vecchio (Jacopo Palma), ii. 115, n. 1; paintings by, ii. 115 (i. 74), 549; iv. 102 & n. 4.

Palmer, Anne, otherwise Fitzroy: *see* Lennard, Anne, countess of Sussex.

Palmer, Sir Anthony, K.B.: geneal., iii. 293, n. 3.

Palmer, Barbara, duchess of Cleveland; born Villiers; wife of Roger Palmer, earl of Castlemaine; created duchess *suo jure* 1670; mistress of Charles II, iii. 505, n. 4; iv. 558, n. 6; concern of, in dismissal of Clarendon, iii. 493–4 & n.; ~ alluded to, iv. 338–9; libel on, iii. 507 & n. 6; Charles II visits, iii. 573 & n. 5; acts in play at court, iii. 505 & nn. 2, 4; at court, 1685, iv. 403, 413; Charles II's death-bed concern for, iv. 409 & n. 2; jewels of, iii. 505 & n. 4; property of: Berkshire, later Cleveland House: given to her, iii. 470 & n. 5; ~ Charles II visits (?), iii. 573, n. 5; ~ notice of, &c., iv. 190; Nonsuch Palace: granted to her, &c., iii. 426, n. 4; as mother of: Henry Fitzroy, duke of Grafton, iii. 622; iv. 184 & n. 5; ~ Charlottee Lee, countess of Lichfield, iv. 268, n. 2; ~ Monmouth (error), iv. 97; ~ George Fitzroy, duke of Northumberland, iv. 374, 391, 505; ~ Anne Lennard, countess of Sussex, iii. 592 & n. 4; iv. 97 & n. 6.

Palmer, Dudley: collection of clocks, &c., of, iii. 293 & n. 3.

Palmer, Sir Geoffrey, attorney-general: attends Gresham College commission, iii. 335 & n. 1.

Palmer, Sir James: paintings taken from, ii. 549 & n. 2.

Palmer, Roger; earl of Castlemaine, 1661, iv. 558, n. 6; imprisoned in Tower, 1678, iv. 158, n. 7 *ad fin.*; as ambassador to Pope: secretary of, iv. 498 & n. 1; social, iv. 558; geneal., ii. 549, n. 2; iii. 505, n. 4.

Palmyra: ruins of: drawing of, v. 224 & n. 3.

Pamfili family: arms of, ii. 207, n. 4; inherit Aldobrandini property, ii. 284, n. 2, 392, n. 2.

Pamfili, Camillo, cardinal, later Prince, ii. 254 & n. 5; receives hat as cardinal, ii. 254; at opera, ii. 389; marriage of, ii. 284, n. 2.

Pamfili, Giambattista: *see* Innocent X.
Panama: alligators of, iv. 391, n. 2.
Panama city: capture of, by Col. H. Morgan, iii. 583 & n. 5, 585 & n. 2; ~ described by Morgan, iv. 46 & nn. 3, 4.
Pandects: *see* Justinian.
Panormita, Antonio Beccadelli, called: brings arm of Livy to Naples, ii. 328–9 & n.
Papacy, Papal States, Popes:
territories, &c.: frontiers of, ii. 208 & n. 4, 322 & n. 3; St. Peter's Patrimony: as gift of Countess Matilda, ii. 208–9 & n.; Bologna, ii. 420 & n. 5; Ferrara, ii. 427, n. 5, 428; Avignon, ii. 160 & nn. 4, 5 (i. 102); ~ vice-legate at, ii. 161 *bis* (i. 103 *bis*); Naples and Sicily: tribute for, ii. 280, 352 & n. 4; general: Jews protected in, ii. 228; ~ prostitutes in: tax on, ii. 417 & n. 9.
elections, &c.: conclaves for: place and conduct of, ii. 302 & n. 7; ~ conclave of 1644, ii. 207 & n. 4; coronations in St. Peter's, ii. 279, n. 3; enthronements in Lateran: chairs used for, ii. 268 & n. 2; procession to Lateran (Possesso), ii. 279, n. 3; ~ Innocent X's Possesso, ii. 279–82 & nn.; tiara, slippers, &c., of popes, ii. 298.
household and court: officials in procession, ii. 279–81; Rota: officials of the, ii. 280 & n. 2; Swiss guard: in procession, ii. 279, 280; ~ guard-room of, in Vatican, ii. 296–7 & n.; ~ member of, ii. 214, n. 2.
miscellaneous: popes: from Acquapendente, ii. 209 & n. 4; ~ buried at Viterbo, ii. 210; ~ persecuting: in sermon, iv. 521.
Paper: Chinese, &c.: specimens of, ii. 331; iii. 374; mill for making, iv. 141–2 & n.
Papillon (Papillion), David: negotiation with (?), iii. 172 & n. 3.
Papillon, Mary: *see* Tuke, Mrs. M.
Papillon, Thomas, iii. 172, n. 3; negotiation with (?), iii. 172; candidate for shrievalty, London, 1682, iv. 319 & n. 1; geneal., iii. 172, n. 5.
Papin, Denis, iv. 172, n. 1; digester invented by, iv. 171–2; ~ supper cooked in, iv. 278–9 & n.; residence of, in Venice, iv. 278, 279, n. 1; siphon of: in experiment, iv. 400.
Papplewick, Notts., iii. 126 & n. 6.
Paracelsus, iii. 28, n. 1.
Paravicini (Pallavicini), Sir Peter; knighted 1687: payment to, iii. 508 & n. 2.
Paravicini, Mrs. Rebecca, wife of Peter (later Sir Peter) Paravicini: heritage of, iii. 508 & n. 2.
Parc: William III's forces at, 1693, v. 142, n. 2.
PARIS:
— E: resident in: 1643–4, ii. 85 (i. 58), 90–121 (i. 61–78), 127–35 (i. 81–9); ~ 1646–7, i. *8*; ii. 534–6; ~ 1649–52, i. *10*; ii. 561–8; iii. 1–12, 17–54, 632–6; descriptions by, of: in Diary: general comment on, ii. 91, n. 5; ~ in *State of France*, iii. 637–9; personal: E's chemistry-teacher at, iii. 336; E's collections from, iii. 548; E writes letter to, iii. 55; lodgings at, ii. 90 & n. 2 (i. 61), 97 & n. 4 (i. 64), 534 *bis* & nn. 3, 4; iii. 17, 21 & nn. 2, 3, 634; marriage at, ii. 536; iii. 346; money affairs at, iii. 13, 47 *bis*, 49, 375.
— bibliographical note, ii. 91, n. 5.
— historical: (i) general: besieged by Condé, 1649, ii. 550 & n. 5, 551; treaty of Rueil, 1649, ii. 553, n. 6; alarm at, Aug. 1650, iii. 17 & n. 3; flood at, Jan. 1651, iii. 25 & n. 1; disturbances in, Feb. 1651, iii. 26; Parlement of, banishes Mazarin from France, iii. 26 & n. 4; Louis XIV's procession to Parlement of, on his majority, iii. 41–3 & nn.; siege threatened by Condé, 1652, iii. 66-7 & n.; Condé admitted to, 1652, iii. 77, n. 1.; mishaps at, by lightning, 1687, iv. 560; rejoicings at, for reported death, &c., of William III, 1690, v. 32; earthquake at, 1692, v. 115 & n. 4.
— — (ii) the English in Paris: Paris full of royalist fugitives, 1650, iii. 17; Lady Browne's house as a refuge for the fugitives, iii. 77; Anglican services in, &c.:

Paris (*cont.*)
see Church of England: chronological series; Charles II at: as Prince of Wales, 1646–8, ii. 536 & n. 1; ~ arrives at, 1651, iii. 47, n. 4; ~ leaves, 1654, iv. 218, n. 3; *see also* Charles II; Henrietta Maria at: arrives, 1644, ii. 155, n. 6; ~ *see also* topography: Louvre *below*, and Henrietta Maria; James II, as duke of York, at: 1649–50, ii. 563, n. 7; iii. 20, n. 4; ~ 1651–2, iii. 36, n. 4; ~ *see also* James II [royalists mentioned in the course of E's notices of his residence in Paris are not indexed collectively; for those mentioned in notices elsewhere *see* personal *below*].

— local government: criminal and civil judiciary, iii. 638; ~ seat of, ii. 102 (i. 66); iii. 28, n. 5; ecclesiastical jurisdiction, iii. 638; Parlement: seat of, ii. 98 (i. 65); ~ activities: *see* historical section *above*, treaty of Rueil, &c.; ~ deputy-general of protestant churches in: *see* Ruvigny, Henri de Massue, first marquis of; ~ presidents of: *see* du Houssay; St.-Germain, C. Le Prévost, seigneur de; Thou, J. A. de, jnr.; ~ president for protestants in: *see* le Coq, F.

— personal: persons at or visiting Paris [persons mentioned in text or notes as being in Paris specifically, but excluding all notices in E's account of his residence in Paris, and diplomatists in general]: (i) English: Lady (Elizabeth) Browne: house of, at, iii. 77; Sir Richard Browne at, iv. 14; ~ first permanently resident at, iii. 67, n. 2; Sir John Chardin: intends to visit, iv. 213; Dr. John Durel: educated at, iv. 164; Sir Gervase Elwes at, iii. 58; Mrs. Evelyn: left by E in, 1652, iii. 59; ~ leaves, iii. 66; Mrs. Margaret Godolphin: returns to London from, iv. 88; Dr. Stephen Goffe at, i. 27; Christopher Hatton, Baron Hatton, at, ii. 558; Dr. W. Hayley: embassy chaplain at, iv. 545, n. 3; Henry Howard, later seventh duke of Norfolk, and (Lord) Thomas Howard: go to, iii. 375; Elizabeth Mordaunt, Viscountess Mordaunt: ill at, iv. 173 & n. 3; William and Margaret Cavendish, duke and duchess of Newcastle: married in, iii. 480–1 & n.; Sir Thomas Osborne, later duke of Leeds, at, iv. 14; Thomas Butler, earl of Ossory, at, iv. 210; Henry Percy, Baron Percy, at, iv. 218, n. 3; James Scudamore: relative of, at, iii. 66; Sir Arthur Slingsby at, iii. 375; Robert Spencer, Lord Spencer: dies at, iv. 595, n. 3; William Howard, Viscount Stafford: meets Edward Turberville at, iv. 228, 232, 234; Lady Tuke: dies at, iii. 373, n. 4; Col., later Sir, Samuel Tuke: leaves, iii. 223, n. 5; ~ visits, 1661, iii. 274, n. 4; Dr. William Wake: embassy chaplain at, iv. 532, n. 3; Lucy Walter at, iv. 457; C. Wase: poverty of, at, iii. 55.

— — (ii) French and foreign: Capuchins going to, iii. 54; S. della Bella: working in, iii. 3 & n. 3; S Foubert: leaves, iv. 257–8 & n.; Monsieur Isac, dancing-teacher, at, iv. 271, n. 5 *ad fin.*; Prince P. Potemkin and his son at, iv. 263.

— social and miscellaneous: ball, iii. 30; burghers, iii. 5; court ballet, iii. 31–2 *bis* & n.; dress: fear of Spanish, ii. 97 (i 64); ~ mourning for Louis XIII, ii. 98 (i. 64); exhibitions: animal, water-spouter, &c., iii. 27 & nn. 3–5; ~ the Hairy Maid, iii. 198, n. 1; ~ puppet-shows, ii. 99 (i. 65); impostors living in, iii. 24, 34, 52–3; masquerade, iii. 1–2 & n.; medical: dispute about use of antimony, iii. 28, n. 1; ~ use of aurum potabile at, iii. 86–7 & n.; music: rehearsal for St. Cecilia's day, iii. 23 & n. 4; promenade: at Cours-la-Reine, ii. 106–7 (i. 69); iii. 1; ~ in Luxembourg garden, ii. 130 (i. 83); public order: attack on man in street, iii. 22; ~

PARIS (*cont.*)
murders, iii. 638; religious: Corpus Christi processions, ii. 536 & n. 3; iii. 35; iv. 560; riding academies, ii. 134 & n. 2 (i. 87–8 & nn.); iii. 7; iv. 257, n. 5; ~ displays at, iii. 2, 8; ~ Ossory as pupil at, iv. 210; scientific academy: account of, mentioned, iii. 274, n. 4; street life: mountebanks, &c., on Pont-Neuf, ii. 93, 99 (i. 65); ~ public letter-writers, ii. 132 (i. 85); traffic, ii. 93 (i. 62); miscellaneous: bed made at, iii. 323 & n. 5; ~ design for coach brought from, iii. 65; ~ leather-work at, iii. 34.
— topography: (i) general: general remarks, ii. 94 & n. 3 (i. 62–3); compared with London: general, ii. 131 (i. 84–5 & n.); iii. 638; ~ details, ii. 94 (i. 62), 98 (i. 64), 107 (i. 69); iii. 637, 639; air of: prevents epidemics, iii. 639; ~ stench, ii. 94 & n. 4 (i. 62–3); building-stone in, ii. 92 & n. 6 (i. 61), 131 (i. 84); iii. 637; cupolas and spires, i. 65; defences, iii. 638; divisions and situation of, ii. 91–2 & n. (i. 61), 94; growth of, iii. 637–8; *hôtels*: list, ii. 133 (i. 87); streets: appearance, iii. 638; ~ paving and mud, ii. 94 (i. 62–3); iii. 639; suburbs: general list, ii. 94 (i. 62); views of: in general, i. 65; ~ from Chaillot, ii. 91 (i. 61); iii. 27; ~ from Pont-Neuf, ii. 93 & n. 2 (i. 62); ~ from Tour St.-Jacques, ii. 131 (i. 84); ~ engraved, by L. Lincler (?), iii. 10, n. 3.
— — (ii) particular buildings, streets, &c.:
— — — Arsenal, ii. 102 & n. 4 (i. 67).
— — — Bastille, *ib.*; prisoners in: — Pate, v. 289, n. 1; Sir R. Walsh, iii. 6, n. 4.
— — — Bibliothèque de l'Institut (modern): Leonardo MSS. in, ii. 498, n. 1.
— — — Bibliothèque nationale (modern): *objets d'art* in, ii. 89, nn. 1, 2, 99, n. 2.
— — — Boulevard St.-Germain (modern): site of, iii. 21, n. 2.

PARIS (*cont.*)
— — — Bourse (Exchange), ii. 98 & n. 1 (i. 64).
— — — Châtelets, Grand and Petit, ii. 102 & n. 1 (i. 66); Grand: application of torture at, iii. 28–9 & nn.
— — — churches and convents:
— — — — Notre Dame, ii. 95–6 & nn. (i. 63); *add.*; in view (?), ii. 93 & n. 2 (i. 62); *Te Deum* at, for battle of Malaga, v. 580, n. 4; clergy of, ii. 96 (i. 63); canon of: *see* St.-Germain, C. Le Prévost, seigneur de.
— — — — Notre-Dame de Bon Secours: prioress of, iii. 34 & n. 5.
— — — — St.-Étienne-du-Mont, ii. 567–8 & nn.
— — — — Ste.-Geneviève, ii. 100–1 & n. (i. 66).
— — — — St.-Germain-des-Prés: abbey, ii. 534; abbot: *see* Verneuil, Henri de Bourbon, duke of; *bailli* of, and his guards, iii. 6 & n. 3, 7.
— — — — Saints-Innocents: cemetery and church, ii. 131–2 & nn. (i. 85).
— — — — St.-Jacques: view from tower of, ii. 131 (i. 84).
— — — — St.-Louis (St.-Paul-St.-Louis), ii. 96 & n. 3 (i. 63–4); *add.*; iii. 34–5 & n., 637; sermon, &c., at, iii. 23.
— — — — Sainte-Chapelle, ii. 98, n. 2, 99 & nn. 1–3 (i. 65); in comparison, ii. 153 (i. 99).
— — — — Val-de-Grâce, i. 84 & nn. 1, 2.
— — — Cité, ii. 91–2 & n. (i. 61).
— — — Collèges: de Clermont, ii. 96, n. 3; de Navarre, ii. 97 & n. 1 (i. 64).
— — — Conciergerie: prisoners in, ii. 98 & n. 6.
— — — Cours-la-Reine, ii. 106–7 & n. (i. 69); iii. 1.
— — — Exchange (Bourse), ii. 98 & n. 1 (i. 64).
— — — Faubourg St.-Germain, ii. 94 (i. 62); bridge to, from Tuileries, ii. 93–4 & n. (i. 62); street leading to, i. 66; in view, ii. 93 (i. 62); persons: S. Foubert: academy of, in, iv. 257, n. 5; P. Morin: garden of, in, ii. 132–3 & n. (i. 85–7); iii. 33 &

PARIS (*cont.*)
nn. 2–4; streets in: Rue: des Beaux-Arts (modern): site, ii. 112, n. 4; de Bussy (Buci), ii. 90, n. 2; du Coulombier (Jacob): E lodges in, ii. 534 & n. 4; de l'Échaudé, ii. 534, n. 3; des Esgousts, ii. 134, n. 2; du Four, iii. 2, n. 3; St.-Pierre (now des Saints-Pères): La Charité in, ii. 101, n. 6; iii. 22, n. 7; ~ Sir R. Browne's house in, iii. 21 & n. 3; ~ protestant cemetery in, iii. 48, n. 10 *ad fin.*; de Seine: E lodges in, ii. 97 & n. 4 (i. 64); ~ Hôtel de Liancourt in, ii. 112 (i. 72); de Tarane: Sir R. Browne's house in, iii. 21 & n. 2; Faubourg mentioned, ii. 128 (i. 81), 528; iii. 633; *see also* Hôtel de Liancourt; Luxembourg; Petit Luxembourg *below.*
— — — Fontaine des Innocents, ii. 132 & n. 1 (i. 85).
— — — hospitals:
— — — — La Charité, ii. 101 & n. 6 (i. 66 & n. 1); operations for stone at, iii. 3–4 & nn.; wounded man taken to, iii. 22 & n. 7.
— — — — Hôtel-Dieu, ii. 101 & n. 5 (i. 66); operations for stone at, iii. 3, n. 5.
— — — — Quinze-Vingts, ii. 101 & n. 4 (i. 66).
— — — Hôtel de Liancourt, ii. 112–14 & nn. (i. 72–4).
— — — Hôtel de Nevers, ii. 133 (i. 87).
— — — Hôtel de Venise (Ville de Venise), inn, ii. 90 & n. 2 (i. 61).
— — — Île du Cité, ii. 91–2 & n. (i. 61).
— — — Isle du Palais: *see* Place Dauphine *below.*
— — — Jardin Royal (Jardin des Plantes), ii. 102 & n. 2 (i. 66–7); lecture at, ii. 565; *intendant* of: *see* Davison, W.
— — — Jesuits: college, ii. 96 & n. 3 (i. 63); museum of: Far Eastern collection for, iii. 373–4 & nn.; school: attended by J. Cosin, jnr., iii. 636 & n. 1; church: *see* churches: St.-Louis *above.*
— — — Jeu de la longe Paume de M. de Metz (Place de M. de Metz), ii. 534 & n. 3.

PARIS (*cont.*)
— — — Louvre and Tuileries, ii. 103–7 & nn. (i. 67–9); in view, ii. 93 (i. 62); situation of, iii. 637; building during E's residence in Paris, ii. 134; Anglicans at, iii. 36 & n. 5; ~ chapel of, at: services in, iii. 9, n. 2; Dr. J. Cosin's library at, iii. 36, 634; Henrietta Maria at: apartments, &c., of, ii. 103, n. 1, 105, n. 4; iii. 36 & n. 5, 634; *see also* i. *10*; iii. 52, 636; countess of Morton at, ii. 564; apartments, &c.: *ateliers*, ii. 105–6 (i. 68); Grande Galerie, ii. 103–4 & nn. (i. 67), 105 (i. 68); ~ in comparison, ii. 300 & n. 1; Imprimerie royale, ii. 104 & n. 5 (i. 68); Petite Galerie, ii. 103, n. 1, 104 & n. 6 (i. 68), 105, n. 4; Salle des Antiques, ii. 104–5 & nn. (i. 68); Tuileries, ii. 104 & nn. 2–4 (i. 67–8); ~ garden and zoo, ii. 106 & nn. 1–3, 107 & n. 1 (i. 69); ~ visits to, iii. 1, 20; ~ bridge near, ii. 93–4 & n. (i. 62).
— — — Louvre: the modern museums: paintings in: old French Royal collection, &c., ii. 120, nn. 1–8; by: J. Breughel, ii. 497, n. 5; Caravaggio, ii. 113, n. 4; Correggio, ii. 229, n. 5, 549, n. 6; Leonardo, ii. 495, n. 5; Rubens (the Marie de Médicis series), ii. 128, n. 2; Vandyck, iii. 96, n. 3; Veronese, ii. 442, n. 5; ancient sculpture in: old Borghese collection, ii. 252, n. 5, 253, nn. 2–5, 286, n. 2; Vatican antiques: temporary removal to, ii. 303, n. 3; individual works: Artemis of Gabii, ii. 284, n. 3; Diana with fawn, ii. 105, n. 3, 118, n. 9; Tiber, ii. 304, n. 3; other works: antique chair, ii. 268, n. 1; modern sculpture, ii. 93, n. 1, 118, n. 9; gates from Maisons, iii. 18, n. 7.
— — — Luxembourg, Palais du, ii. 128–31 & nn. (i. 81–4); iii. 20–1 & nn.; imitation of Pitti Palace, ii. 186, n. 5.
— — — Marais, ii. 100 & n. 3 (i. 66).
— — — Noah's Ark, curiosity shop, ii. 100 (i. 65–6).
— — — Palais (Palais de Justice), ii. 98–9 & nn. (i. 64–5); Louis

Paris (*cont.*)
XIV's procession to, 1651: *see* iii. 41, n. 2.
— — — Palais Archiépiscopal, ii. 96 & n. 1 (i. 63).
— — — Palais-Cardinal (Palais-Royal), ii. 133–4 & n. (i. 87), 566–7 & nn.; garden of, ii. 134, 567; iii. 44 & n. 1; Louis XIV and Anne of Austria residing in, ii. 134, 562, n. 2; audiences at, ii. 91 & n. 2. (i. 61), 566 & nn. 2, 3; iii. 43–4 & nn.; masque at, iii. 31 & n. 1, 31–2 & nn.
— — — Palace of Orleans (iii. 20 & n. 7): *see* Luxembourg *above*.
— — — Palace Royal: error for Place Royale, ii. 101 (i. 66).
— — — Panthéon: *see* churches: Ste.-Geneviève *above*.
— — — Petit Luxembourg, ii. 131 & n. 1 (i. 84).
— — — Place Dauphine (Isle du Palais), ii. 92 & n. 4 (i. 61), 93 & n. 2 (i. 62), 99 & nn. 5, 6; views taken from, ii. 92, n. 3.
— — — Place de Monsieur de Metz: E lodges in, ii. 534 & n. 3.
— — — Place Royale (Place des Vosges), called Palace Royal in error, ii. 101 & n. 1 (i. 66); *see also* ii. 100 & n. 4 (i. 66).
— — — Pont au Change, ii. 93 & n. 4 (i. 62).
— — — Pont-Neuf, ii. 92–3 & nn. (i. 61–2); mountebanks, &c., on, ii. 99 & n. 7 (i. 65); Henri IV's statue on, ii. 92–3 & n. (i. 61–2), 101 (i. 66); the Samaritaine on, ii. 93 & n. 3 (i. 62), 94; ~ Lincler's grotto beneath, iii. 10–11 & nn., 20 & n. 6.
— — — Pont Notre-Dame, ii. 93 & n. 4 (i. 62).
— — — Pont-Rouge, otherwise Pont Ste.-Anne, &c., ii. 93–4 & n. (i. 62); view from, by Lincler (?), iii. 10, n. 3.
— — — Pont-Royal, ii. 93, n. 5 *ad fin*.
— — — Port au Foin, ii. 105, n. 4.
— — — Porte Dauphine, ii. 100 & n. 2 (i. 66).
— — — Porte Ste.-Antoine: Condé defeated at, 1652, iii. 67, n. 1.
— — — prisons: *see* Bastille, Châtelets, Conciergerie *above*; environs: Vincennes *below*.

Paris (*cont.*)
— — — Quai de Nesle: R. Nanteuil's house on, iii. 9, n. 3.
— — — Quai des Orfèvres, ii. 99, n. 6.
— — — Rue: de Charonne, iii. 34, n. 5; Dauphine, ii. 100 & n. 2 (i. 66); ~ E lodges in, iii. 17 & n. 4; de la Ferronnerie: Henri IV assassinated in, i. 85 & n. 2; St.-Antoine: Jesuits' church in, ii. 96; St. Denis: ambassador lodges in, ii. 91 & n. 4 (i. 61); St.-Honoré: Quinze-Vingts in, ii. 101; for other streets *see* Faubourg St.-Germain *above*.
— — — La Samaritaine: *see* Pont-Neuf *above*.
— — — Seine, river: and situation of Paris, ii. 92 & n. 1 (i. 61); compared with Thames, iii. 637; bridges over, ii. 92–4 & nn. (i. 61–2); traffic on, ii. 105 & n. 4 (i. 68 & nn. 1, 2); iii. 637; mentioned, ii. 133 (i. 87).
— — — Sorbonne, ii. 97 & n. 2 (i. 64); iii. 637; disputation at, ii. 97 (i. 64); students: *see* Holden, H. (ii. 567); Le Franc, J. (iii. 171).
— — — statues, public: Henri IV, ii. 92–3 & n. (i. 61–2), 101 (i. 66); Louis XIII, ii. 101 & n. 1 (i. 66).
— — — Temple, ii. 100 & n. 3 (i. 66).
— — — Tuileries: *see* Louvre and Tuileries *above*.
— — — Université (division of Paris), ii. 92 (i. 61).
— — — University (academic), ii. 94 & n. 1 (i. 62), 97 & nn. 1, 2 (i. 64).
— — — Vallée de Misère, ii. 99–100 & n. (i. 65).
— — — Ville de Venise, inn, ii. 90 & n. 2 (i. 61).
— environs:
— — Arcueil: aqueduct at, ii. 129 & n. 3 (i. 82).
— — Bois de Boulogne: in view, iii. 3; review in, ii. 135 & n. 1 (i. 88).
— — Chaillot: F. de Bassompierre's house at (later Visitandines' convent), ii. 90–1 & n. (i. 61); the Bonshommes at, ii. 112 & n. 3 (i. 72); iii. 26–7 & n., 27–8 & n.

PARIS (*cont.*)
— — Charenton: *see* Charenton.
— — Conflans: bathing at, iii. 38 & n. 7.
— — Madrid, Château de, ii. 112 & nn. 1, 2 (i. 72); iii. 2–3 & nn.; mentioned, ii. 121, n. 3.
— — Maisons, Château de, ii. 563 & nn. 3, 4; iii. 18 & nn. 1–7.
— — Montjoyes, the, on road to St.-Denis, ii. 90 & n. 1 (i. 60).
— — Montmartre: freestone from, ii. 92 & n. 6 (i. 61); St. Denis martyred on, ii. 90, n. 1.
— — Mont Valérien (Mont Calvarie): hermit on, ii. 564 & n. 3.
— — Rueil: *see* Rueil.
— — St.-Cloud: *see* St.- Cloud.
— — St.-Denis: *see* St.-Denis.
— — St.-Germain: *see* St. Germain-en-Laye.
— — Seine, river: bathing in, iii. 38 & n. 7; in view, iii. 3; at Maisons, ii. 563 & n. 4; iii. 18.
— — Vanves *or* Vanvres: the 'Bataille de Vambre' at, iii. 4–8 & nn.
— — Vincennes: Bois and Château of, ii. 102 & n. 5 (i. 67); Condé, &c., imprisoned at, 1650, iii. 1 & n. 3.
Paris: Archbishops of: estate of, at St.-Cloud, ii. 107 & n. 3 (i. 69); ~ palace of, in Paris, ii. 96 & n. 1 (i. 63).
Paris Romano: *see* Nogari, P.
Parke, Daniel, sen.: geneal., v. 574, n. 2.
Parke, Col. Daniel: brings the news of Blenheim to Queen Anne, v. 574–5 & n.
Parke, Mrs. Rebecca: geneal., v. 574, n. 2.
Parke, William: geneal., v. 574, n. 2.
Parker, Miss E. G.: transcribes Diary, i. *64*.
Parker, Col. John: escapes from Tower, v. 188 & n. 5.
Parker, Matthew, archbishop of Canterbury: geneal., iii. 502, n. 5.
Parker, Samuel, D.D.; bishop of Oxford 1686–8, iv. 519, n. 2; candidate for see of Oxford, iv. 519; *congé d'élire* for, iv. 525; dies, &c., iv. 574 & n. 2.
Parkhurst family of Pyrford, iii. 183, n. 1.
Parkhurst, Ann: *see* Mynne, Mrs. A.
Parkhurst, John, D.D., master of Balliol College, ii. 18 & n. 1 (i. 13).
Parkhurst, Sir Robert, sen.: geneal., ii. 542, n. 3.
Parkhurst, Sir Robert, jnr., iv. 255, n. 4; as owner of Pyrford, iv. 255; mentioned, iii. 183, n. 1.
Parkyns *or* Perkins, Sir William, v. 235, n. 1; tried and executed, v. 235 *bis* & nn. 1, 3; absolution of, i. 8 & n. 2; v. 235, n. 4, 236 & n. 1.
PARLIAMENT [the section includes notices relating to parliament as an institution as well as those relating to particular parliaments; further it includes notices relating to extra-mural political activities of groups of peers (especially in 1688); and some extra-parliamentary matter relating to the political parties, &c. The chronological series gives a general guide to all notices of proceedings, apart from some notices of the passing of acts in the notes]:
— general: list of parliaments and sessions, 1640–1706, i. 146–8 & nn.; private animosities in former parliaments, 1656, iii. 174–5; failure of parliament to provide adequate revenue for Charles II, 1660–81, iv. 410, n. 2; *see also* iii. 361, n. 1.
— chronological series:
— — Short Parliament, 1640: Charles I's opening procession to, ii. 23–4 & n. (i. 17); dissolved, ii. 24 (i. 18).
— — Long Parliament, 1640–53: opening, ii. 25–6 (i. 19); proceeds against Strafford, 1641, ii. 27 & n. 3, 28 & n. 5 (i. 20 *bis*); attacks Ship Money judges, 1641, i. 23 & n. 1; orders Sir J. Hotham to secure Hull, 1642, iii. 131, n. 1; takes possession of Greenwich Palace, ii. 543 & n. 2; petitions to, 1648, ii. 540–1 & nn.; iii. 196, n. 4; all-night sitting, 1648, ii. 545 & n. 6; attends Lord Mayor's feast, 1649, ii. 556, n. 1; Cromwell's mock-parliament men: at Ireton's funeral, 1652, iii. 57.
— — Cromwell's second parliament, 1656–8: elections to, iii. 182 & n. 5; petitions Cromwell

PARLIAMENT (*cont.*)
to take title of king, iii. 190–1 & n.
— — Richard Cromwell's parliament: dissolved, iii. 228, n. 9.
— — Long Parliament restored, 1659–60: meets, iii. 228, n. 9, 231, n. 4; expelled, 13 Oct. 1659, iii. 234 & n. 1; as the Rump: origin of name, iii. 242, n. 2; meets, 26 Dec., dissolved, &c., iii. 241–2 & nn.
— — interim: hope that parliament will restore Charles II, iii. 243.
— — Convention, 1660: Charles II's letters to, iii. 244 & n. 2; invites Charles to return to England, iii. 244–5 & n.; further proceedings, iii. 249–50 & n., 252 & n. 9; attends City feast, iii. 250; orders exhumation, &c., of corpses of Cromwell, &c., iii. 269, n. 2; fixes king's revenue, iii. 361, n. 1; dissolved, iii. 286 & n. 5.
— — Cavalier Parliament, 1661–79: general account of, i. *26–8*; opens, iii. 286 & n. 5; king's speeches to, &c., iii. 286 & nn. 5, 6, 390 & n. 7, 401–2 & n.; meets at Oxford, 1665, iii. 423 & n. 7; attacks Clarendon, 1667, iii. 493–502 & nn., *passim*; iv. 338; dispute between houses, 1675, iv. 65 & nn. 1, 2; excludes Roman Catholic peers from parliament, iv. 158–9 & n.; other proceedings of, &c., iii. 250, n. 1, 289, n. 1, 306 & n. 3, 312 & nn. 1, 2, 410, n. 3, 467 & n. 2, 468–9 & nn., 503, n. 4, 508 & n. 3, 540 & n. 6, 545–6 & n., 608, n. 2; iv. 5 & n. 5, 83, n. 5, 153, n. 3, 158, n. 5, 160 & n. 4; views of: on dispensing power of the crown, 1663, 1673, iv. 583–4; ~ on newly-raised army, 1678, iv. 136 & n. 4; ~ on Popish Plot, &c., iv. 153 & n. 3, 175; character of, *c.* 1678, iv. 154 & n. 2; dissolved, iv. 163 & n. 1.
— — Charles II's first short parliament, 1679: election to, iv. 164–5 & n.; notices, iv. 167, 169 & n. 1, 172 & n. 3, 174–5.
— — Charles II's second short parliament, 1679–81: election to, iv. 165, n. 1; prorogations, iv. 192–3 & n.; expected conduct of, iv. 209; meets, iv. 223, n. 1; impeaches Stafford, iv. 225–34 & nn.; refuses supply for Tangier, iv. 379, n. 3.
— — Charles II's fifth parliament, 1681: notices, iv. 239 & n. 3, 320, n. 2; mentioned in error, iv. 612 & n. 5.
— — James II's parliament, 1685–7: general notice, i. *31*; summoned, &c., iv. 419 & n. 2; elections to: *see* elections *below*; approach of, iv. 436; sessions:
— — — (1) May–July 1685: notices, iv. 442–51 & nn., *passim*.
— — — (2) Nov. 1685: notices, iv. 488–9 & nn.; further notices, iv. 458, n. 2, 486, n. 3 *ad fin.*, 490, n. 5, 495 & n. 2.
— — — later period: members' views on penal laws examined, iv. 540–1 & n., 544; prorogued and dissolved, iv. 544 & n. 2.
— — interim: Seven Bishops refer themselves to parliament, May 1688, iv. 583–4 & n.; James II issues and recalls writs for new parliament, Aug., Oct., iv. 597 & n. 4, 598 & n. 5, 599 & n. 2; petition to James II to summon parliament, 17 Nov., iv. 608 & n. 4; William of Orange consults peers about summoning parliament, iv. 611 & n. 3; peers and former members of commons, &c., invite William to assume government until a convention meets, v. 612 & n. 5.
— — Convention, 1689–90: circular letters summoning, iv. 612 & n. 5; discussion preceding, iv. 614; sessions:
— — — (1) Jan.–Aug.: settlement of the crown, &c., iv. 616 & n. 1, 619 & nn. 3, 4, 621–2 & n., 625–7 & nn.; ~ Sancroft dissatisfied with, iv. 634; converts itself into a parliament, 23 Feb., iv. 627 & n. 1; members assume offices of state, iv. 629 & n. 2, 631 & n. 6; relations of, with William III, iv. 629; neglects Ireland, iv. 631–2 & n., 637; commons attend coronation of William and Mary, &c., iv. 632–3 & n., 633; other proceed-

PARLIAMENT (*cont.*)
ings, iv. 628–46 & nn., *passim*; *add.* (iv. 643).
— — — — adjourned, 20 Sept., iv. 648 & n. 3.
— — — (2) 1689–90: notices, iv. 651 & nn. 2, 3; v. 4 & n. 1, 5 & n. 2.
— — — — dissolved, v. 5 & nn. 4, 5.
— — William and Mary's second parliament, 1690–5: elections to, v. 5 & n. 5, 6; sessions:
— — — (1) 1690: notices, v. 15, 19, 23 & nn. 2–4; conduct of members, v. 22.
— — — (2) 1690–1: notices, v. 35 & n. 6, 36 & n. 4, 39, n. 6, 40 & n. 4, 41 & n. 5.
— — — (3) 1691–2: notices, v. 71 & n. 3, 72, 78 & n. 2, 90 & nn. 5–7.
— — — (4) 1692–3: notices, v. 126 & n. 3, 127 & nn. 1, 2, 131 & n. 2, 135 & nn. 1, 2.
— — — — prorogations, v. 153 & n. 1, 156 & n. 2.
— — — (5) 1693–4: notices, v. 158 & n. 1, 161 & nn. 2–4, 167 & n. 1, 169 & n. 4, 177 & nn. 3, 4.
— — — (6) 1694–5: members attend Queen Mary's funeral, v. 204; other proceedings, v. 196 & n. 5, 200 & n. 1, 202 & n. 6, 207 & n. 7, 209 & nn. 5–7; queen's death may lead to dissolution, v. 200 & n. 7.
— — — — dissolved, v. 221 & n. 6.
— — William III's third parliament, 1695–8: preparations for, v. 220; summoned, v. 221 & n. 6; sessions:
— — — (1) 1695–6: notices, v. 228–32 & nn., *passim*, 242–3 & n.
— — — — prorogued, v. 257 & n. 6.
— — — (2) 1696–7: notices, v. 260–4 & nn., *passim*.
— — — — interim: expected to consider standing army, v. 275.
— — — (3) 1697–8: notices, v. 278–92 & nn., *passim*.
— — — — dissolved, v. 292 & n. 4, 293.
— — William III's fourth parliament, 1698–1700: summoned, v. 292 & n. 4, 293; elections to, v. 294 & n. 4; sessions:

PARLIAMENT (*cont.*)
— — — (1) 1698–9: Speaker elected, v. 304 & n. 2, 306–7; attempt to influence, v. 323; other proceedings, &c., v. 309 & n. 2, 311 & n. 1, 315–16 & n., 317 & n. 1, 321, n. 1, 324 & nn. 2–5, 337–8 & n.
— — — — prorogued, v. 327 & n. 1.
— — — (2) 1699–1700: notices, v. 366 & n. 3, 369 & nn. 1–3, 371 & n. 2, 376–80 & nn., *passim*, 393–4 & nn., 399–408 & nn., *passim*; prorogation of: mentioned, v. 446, n. 2.
— — — — dissolved, v. 439 & n. 3, 440, 446 & n. 2.
— — William III's fifth parliament, 1701: summoned, v. 439 & n. 3, 440; elections to: *see* elections *below*; notices, v. 445–68 & nn., *passim*; dispute between houses, v. 462, n. 1, 466 & nn. 1, 2, 467–8 & n.; dissolved, &c., v. 480–1 & n.
— — William III's sixth parliament, 1701–2; summoned, v. 480–1 & n.; elections to, v. 481–2 & n., 482; notices, v. 484–6 & nn., *passim*, 491–2 & n., 499 & n. 1, 502 & n. 1; dissolved, v. 511, n. 1.
— — Anne's first parliament, 1702–5: summoned, v. 511, n. 1; elections to, v. 511–12 & nn., 513; sessions:
— — — (1) 1702–3: notices, v. 517–30 & nn., *passim*; relations of, with Queen Anne, v. 518, 519–20 & n., 521; attends thanksgiving service, v. 521; opposes grant to Marlborough, v. 525 & n. 2.
— — — (2) 1703–4: notices, v. 549–53 & nn., 559–61 & nn., *passim*.
— — — (3) 1704–5: notices, v. 581 & n. 3, 583 & n. 7, 587 & n. 5.
— — — — dissolved, v. 595, n. 3.
— — Anne's second parliament, 1705–8: elections to, v. 595 & nn. 3, 4; sessions:
— — — (1) 1705–6: notices, v. 614–21 & nn., *passim*.
— acts and bills [the notices indexed under this heading are those relating to the passing of acts (other than those for taxes), to their effects

PARLIAMENT (*cont.*)
immediately in connexion with their passing, or to their repeal; notices relating to their operation as general laws are indexed under England: laws. For acts, &c., relating to taxation *see* England: taxation. Bills mentioned in the text, if they pass as acts, are entered only under acts]:
— — public and general acts [in chronological order]: abolition of kingship, 1649, ii. 555 & n. 6; oblivion, 1652, iii. 61 & n. 3; annual fast for execution of Charles I, 1660, iii. 269 & n. 1; establishing Commission of Accounts, 1667, iii. 536, n. 2; Test Act, 1673: passing &c., iv. 5, n. 5, 7 & n. 4; ~ repeal of: project for, 1687, iv. 540–1 & n., 544; *see also* England: laws; Parliamentary Test Act, 1678, iv. 158–9 & n.; Declaration of Rights, 1689, iv. 616 & n. 1, 621–2 & n.; ~ clause in (later version, passed Dec. 1689), for succession, iv. 645 & n. 8; coronation oath, 1689, iv. 631 & n. 3; oath of allegiance to William and Mary, 1689, iv. 634 & n. 3, 637 & n. 3; Toleration Act, 1689, iv. 640 & n. 2; restoring charter of London, 1690, v. 23 & n. 3; general pardon, 1690, v. 23 & n. 4; Million-pound lottery loan, 1694, v. 169, n. 4, 177 & n. 4; Triennial Act, 1694, v. 200 & n. 1; *see also* bills *below*; continuing parliament after sovereign's death, 1696, v. 232, n. 2; Association, 1696, v. 232 & n. 2, 242–3 & n.; obliging lawyers to swear allegiance, 1696, v. 242–3 & n.; establishing New East India Company, 1698, v. 288, n. 7 *ad fin.*; Disbanding Act, 1699, v. 316, n. 1; suppressing lotteries, 1699, v. 325 & n. 6; resuming forfeited Irish estates, &c., 1700, v. 369 & n. 1, 377 & n. 2, 401, n. 1, 402 & n. 1, 407, n. 1; ~ commissioners under: appointed, v. 394 & n. 2; penalizing Roman Catholics, 1700, v. 403 & n. 1; Act of Settlement,

PARLIAMENT (*cont.*)
1701, v. 448 & n. 5, 464–5 & n.; ~ alluded to (?), v. 468 & n. 3; ~ clause in: repeal of, v. 621 & n. 3; prohibiting importation of Scottish cattle, March 1705: repealed, Dec. 1705, v. 620 & n. 3; Regency Act, 1706: proceedings relating to, v. 620 & n. 2, 621 & nn. 2, 3.
— — private or personal acts [in alphabetical order]: increase in number of, *c.* 1695, v. 209 & n. 7; *add.*; Arundel House, London: for rebuilding, 1671, iii. 234, n. 4, 595, n. 5; ~ for converting into tenements, iii. 234, n. 4; Bodvile estate, 1667, iii. 473, n. 3; annulling marriage of Captain J. Campbell and Mary Wharton, 1690, v. 41, n. 1; earl of Cleveland's estates, 1660, 1667, iii. 467 & n. 2; East India Company, 1700, v. 378 & n. 3, 404 & n. 3; restoring dukedom of Norfolk, 1660, 1661, iii. 306 & n. 3; duke of Norfolk (Henry Howard, seventh duke), divorcing his duchess: bills, 1692, 1693, v. 90 & n. 7, 127 & n. 1; ~ act, 1700, v. 380 & n. 3, 393–4 & n.; earl of Peterborough: sale of lands of, 1677, iv. 108–9 & n., 110–11; John Manners, Lord Ros: for remarriage, &c., 1667, 1670, iii. 545–6 & n.
— — bills [bills presented to parliament and not converted into acts]: execution of regicides, 1662, iii. 312, n. 1; toleration of protestant Nonconformists, 1673, iii. 608, n. 2; Exclusion Bills, 1679–81, i. *28*; iv. 223, n. 1, 225, n. 3, 236 & n. 1, 239 & n. 3; ~ views on, of Lord Cavendish (William Cavendish, later earl and duke of Devonshire), iv. 453, 454, n. 1; ~ Sunderland supports, iv. 245 & nn. 5, 6; Comprehension Bill, 1689, iv. 633–4 & n.; free and impartial proceedings in parliament, 1692–3, v. 126 & n. 3; Triennial Bill, 1693: rejected by king, v. 135; *see also* acts *above*; resettlement of Wotton estate, 1698–9: proposed bill, v. 314 & n. 1, 337;

PARLIAMENT (*cont.*)
~ bill in lords, v. 337–8 & n.; Occasional Conformity Bills, 1702–3, v. 523, n. 1, 527 & n. 4; ~ 1703, v. 552 & n. 1; for taking public accounts, 1704, v. 561, n. 1.
— — projected bills: Boyle lectures: amending trust for, v. 197; library at St. James's Palace, v. 280, n. 5; smoke of London: reducing, iii. 297 & n. 3, 310; Trinity Chapel, v. 65; Wotton estate: *see* bills *above*.
— commissioners and committees:
— — commissioners: to invite Charles II to return to England, 1660, iii. 245, n. 1; to inquire into Irish forfeitures, 1699: act for, v. 324 & n. 4; ~ report of, v. 404 & n. 2; for forfeited estates in Ireland (trustees), 1700, v. 394 & n. 2; for public accounts, 1703: report of, v. 528 & n. 1, 529 & n. 1, 530, n. 1; *see also* Commissioners of Accounts (1667–9).
— — committees: Derby House: source of name of, iii. 222, n. 4; Grievances: hears charges against Lord Mordaunt, 1666, iii. 468–9 & nn.; for Greenwich Hospital, 1701–2, v. 492 & n. 4; ~ visits Greenwich, v. 498 & n. 4; ~ reports, v. 499 & n. 1; parliamentary, 1656: error for Commissioners for Approbation of Public Preachers, iii. 172, n. 1; *add.*
— constitutional:
— — general: petitions for or appeals to a free parliament: in 1660, iii. 241, n. 2; ~ by Monmouth, 1685, iv. 449; ~ in 1688, iv. 606; in James II's declaration, 1693, v. 140.
— — convention parliaments: 1660: acts of: confirmed by later parliament, iii. 306, n. 3; iv. 417, n. 6; 1689–90: summoning of: value of regency to secure legality of, iv. 614; converted into parliament, &c., iv. 627 & n. 1; doubtful status of, v. 4.
— — duration of: Triennial Bill, 1693, v. 135; Triennial Act, 1694, v. 200 & n. 1; effect of Queen Mary II's death on, v. 200, n. 7; continuation of, after sovereign's death: law altered to secure, v. 232 & n. 2, 491–2 & n.; ~ alluded to (?), v. 493 & n. 2.
— — electorate: effect on, of new borough charters, 1683–5, iv. 419 & n. 2, 444.
— — placemen: exclusion of, from house of commons: bill for 1693, v. 126 & n. 3; ~ clause for, in Act of Settlement: repeal of, v. 621 & n. 3.
— — private acts: increase in number of, *c.* 1695, v. 209 & n. 7; *add.*
— — Roman Catholics: excluded from parliament by Parliamentary Test Act, &c., iv. 158–9 & n.
— — royal assent: refused, 1693, v. 135 & n. 1.
— — tacking, v. 401, n. 1; occurrences of, 1699, 1700, v. 324 & nn. 4, 5, 377, n. 2 *ad fin.*, 401 & n. 1, 402 & n. 1.
— house of commons:
— — elections to: notices mentioning conduct, &c.: Feb. 1679: for Surrey, iv. 164–5 & n.; 1685: court influence on, &c., iv. 419 & n. 2, 434 & n. 3, 440, 444 & nn. 1–4; ~ for Oxfordshire, iv. 427; ~ for Surrey, iv. 433–4 & n.; ~ general character of new members, iv. 434 & n. 2, 440, 444; Sept. 1688: declaration for maintaining order in, iv. 597 & n. 4; Dec. 1688: letters for, for Convention, iv. 612 & n. 5; 1690: canvassing for, v. 5 & n. 5, 6; Jan. 1701: general notices, v. 440 & n. 2, 441, 442 & n. 1; ~ corruption, &c., in, v. 446 & n. 4, 450 & n. 3, 452, n. 2; Nov. 1701: general notice, v. 481–2 & n.; ~ for Surrey, v. 482 & n. 3; 1702: general notices and Surrey, v. 511–12 & nn., 513; 1705: general notices and Surrey, v. 595 & nn. 3, 4.
— — — corruption in: general statement, v. 595; ~ act to prevent, v. 446 & n. 3; ~ members expelled for, v. 3, n. 2, 446 & n. 4, 450 & n. 3; ~ men engaged in, v. 452, n. 2; court influence on: *see preceding*

Parliament (*cont.*)
section; expenses, iv. 165 & n. 1; polling: duration of, v. 442 & n. 1; ~ sheriff's trick in, iv. 433–4 & n.
— — members: attendance of: undue absence of, v. 317 & n. 1, 369 & n. 3; ~ order for better, v. 371 & n. 2; ~ exceptional, v. 614 & n. 2; character of various parliaments: Cavalier, 1678, iv. 154 & n. 2; ~ James II's, iv. 434 & n. 2, 440, 444, 489; ~ 1701, v. 480–1 & nn.; corruption of: in Cavalier parliament, i. 27; iv. 136, n. 4, 163 & n. 1; ~ inquiry into, 1695, v. 207 & n. 7, 209 & n. 5; expulsions of, v. 207, n. 7 *ad fin*, 223, n. 1, 285, n. 2; *see also* elections *above*; former: survivors from Charles II's parliaments meet, Dec. 1688, iv. 612, n. 5; ~ Tories: meet, 29 Jan. 1690, v. 5 & n. 1; individual: Sir R. Browne, sen., 1604, iv. 303–4 & n.; ~ George Evelyn as oldest living member, v. 358 & n. 1; new: unusual number of, following general election, iv. 444 & n. 4; propaganda: use of, to influence, v. 323; Roman Catholic: excluded, &c., iv. 159, n. 1; Solemn League and Covenant: taken by, 1643, iii. 289, n. 1; suspended for misconduct, iii. 73, n. 3.
— — officers: Speaker: attends king in parliament, iii. 402 & n. 3; king refuses candidate elected by house for, v. 476, n. 2; individual Speakers: *see* Glanville, Sir John (1640); Turnor, Sir E. (1661–71); Seymour, Sir Edward (1673–8); Powle, H. (1689–90); Trevor, Sir John (1685, 1690–5); Littleton, Sir Thomas (1698–1700; elected, v. 304, 306–7); Harley, Robert, later earl of Oxford (1701–5; elections, v. 446 & n. 7, 484 & n. 2); Smith, John (1705–8); Onslow, Sir Richard, later Baron Onslow (1708–10).
— — — chairman of committee of whole house: *see* Hampden, R. (iv. 619).
— — — clerk: *see* Goldesborough, W. (iii. 588, n. 1); serjeant-at-arms, v. 371, n. 2.

Parliament (*cont.*)
— house of lords:
— — general and miscellaneous notices: bishops: re-admitted, 1661, iii. 312 & n. 2; ~ exclusion of, &c.: proposed, 1689, iv. 620 & n. 2, 631 & n. 5; Charles II attends debates of, iii. 545, 546, n. 1; clerks attached to, iii. 402 & n. 3, 588, n. 1; Cromwell's 'other house', iii. 191, n. 1; ~ members of, at Cromwell's funeral, iii. 224; protests, iv. 622 & n. 2, 626 & n. 3; v. 324, n. 5, 466 & n. 2; seating in house: arrangement of, iii. 402; iv. 442 & n. 2.
— — judicial activities of [for impeachments *see below*; for trials by the Lord High Steward's court *see* England: officers]: cases before: Charles Howard *v.* seventh duke of Norfolk, iv. 450 & n. 2; Titus Oates, iv. 636 & n. 1, 643, n. 1; duchess of Grafton, v. 161 & n. 4; Albemarle inheritance, v. 167 & n. 1, 288, n. 6.
— — extra-parliamentary activities, &c. [chiefly those of the peers or of groups of peers in the crisis of 1688–9; for the bishops as a group *see* Church of England: organization]: creation of peers prior to coronation of Charles II, iii. 277–8 & nn.; peers in Charles II's coronation, iii. 281 & n. 3, 283, 284; peers in procession to opening of parliament, iii. 286.
— — — secular peers, 1688–9: and trial of Seven Bishops, iv. 585, 588 & n. 3; E advises bishops to consult, about form of prayers for time of danger, iv. 600, n. 4; attend meeting to authenticate birth of Prince James Edward, iv. 602, n. 3; declared by William of Orange to have invited him to England, iv. 604 & n. 3, 606; required to declare against William of Orange's expedition (peers in London), iv. 605–6 & n.; petition for parliament, 17 Nov. (peers in London), iv. 608 & n. 4; join or declare for William of Orange, iv. 607 & n. 1, 609; council of: meets, 21 Dec., &c.,

PARLIAMENT (*cont.*)
iv. 611 & n. 3; ~ invites William of Orange to assume government until Convention meets, iv. 612 & n. 5; ~ Sancroft absents himself from all meetings of, iv. 619, n. 5; some dissatisfied with settlement of crown, iv. 625–7.

— impeachments, attainders, &c.:

— — impeachments: effect on, of dissolution of parliament: orders relating to, 1679, 1685, iv. 445 & n. 2; arrangement of Westminster Hall for, iv. 226 & n. 5; in preparation, 1689, iv. 628 & n. 3; orders for: Sir John Finch, Baron Finch, 1641, ii. 34 & n. 3 (i. 23); ~ John Mordaunt, Viscount Mordaunt, 1666, iii. 468, n. 6 *ad fin.*; proceedings against: Clarendon, 1667, iii. 498 & n. 1; ~ Sir W. Penn, 1668, iii. 508 & n. 3; ~ Danby, 1678, iv. 160 & n. 4; ~ same, as duke of Leeds, 1695, v. 207, n. 7 *ad fin.*, 209, n. 5; ~ Somers, &c., 1701 (includes trial), v. 456 & n. 1, 462 & n. 1, 466 & n. 1, 467–8 & n., 481; trials: Strafford, 1641 (including attainder), ii. 27 & n. 3, 28 & n. 5 (i. 20 *bis*); iv. 226; ~ William Howard, Viscount Stafford, 1680, iv. 225–34 & nn.

— — attainders: Strafford: *see above*; Monmouth, 1685, iv. 449, n. 3; Assassination Plot conspirators, 1697, v. 264, n. 2.

— — other proceedings: against: Ship Money judges, 1641, i. 23 & n. 1; (Sir) Charles Duncombe, 1698, v. 284 & n. 4, 285 *bis* & nn. 2, 5.

— parties [including notices relating to their extra-parliamentary conduct, &c.]: party designations a 'hateful distinction', iv. 439; Church of England party: 1690, v. 5 & n. 5; ~ 1702, v. 511 & n. 1; Country party: members bribed by Louis XIV, &c., 1678, iv. 136, n. 4; ~ state of, 1678, iv. 154, n. 2; ~ in 1699–1700, v. 324, n. 3, 369, 402; Court party: state of, 1678, iv. 154, n. 2; ~ in 1690, v. 5 & n. 5; ~ in 1699–1701,

PARLIAMENT (*cont.*)
v. 311, 324 & n. 3, 369, 402, 408, 484; court interest: services to, of Judge Jeffreys, iv. 484; High Churchmen, 1705, v. 612 & n. 1; Low Churchmen, 1705, v. 612 & n. 1, 614; the peevish party, 1702, v. 511; Republicans: views of, on settlement of government, 1689, iv. 614; ~ in new Privy Council, iv. 635 & n. 3; ~ advocate new Oath of Allegiance to William and Mary, iv. 637; ~ expect England to become republic, iv. 646; the more royal part, 1690, v. 5; Tory party: in Revolution settlement, iv. 614; ~ meeting of, 1690, v. 5 & n. 1; Trimmers: attacked by (Sir) R. L'Estrange, *c.* 1682, iv. 439 & n. 3; Whigs: attacked by L'Estrange, *c.* 1682, *ib.*; ~ 'the crafty Whig party', 1705, v. 612.

— petitions to parliament: county of Essex, 1648, ii. 540–1 & n.; county of Surrey, 1648, ii. 541 & n. 2; iii. 196, n. 4; Lady Capel, 1660: proceedings relating to, iii. 250, n. 1; W. Carr, 1667, iii. 503, n. 4; against East India Company, 1689, *add.* (iv. 643); weavers, 1697, v. 263, n. 5; Kentish Petition, 1701, v. 457 & n. 2, 461.

— privilege: house of lords treats printed petition to commons as libel, iii. 503, n. 4; peers claim exemption from giving bail, iv. 586; house of commons accuses lords of breach of, iv. 65 & nn. 1, 2; member suspended for abuse of, iii. 73, n. 3.

— procedure: opening of parliament: preliminary proceedings, oaths, &c., iv. 442–3 & nn.; king in parliament: passes acts, iii. 252 & n. 9; ~ at prorogation, iii. 402 & n. 3; conferences between the two houses, iv. 65 & nn. 1, 2, 621–2 & n., 626, nn. 1, 2, 645 & n. 8; v. 401, n. 1, 530 & n. 1, 560–1 & n.; house of commons: bringing in of candles, iii. 469 & n. 2.

— publications: *List* of members, 1685, iv. 444 & n. 4; *Report of the Commissioners*) (Irish

PARLIAMENT (*cont.*)
forfeitures), 1700, v. 404, n. 2; reports relating to impeachment of Somers, &c., 1701, v. 456, n. 1; *Votes* of house of commons, i. *103, 104, 105*; names of members elected published in *London Gazette*, 1685, iv. 434 & n. 2.
— records: Rolls and Journals: copies of, iv. 200; Journals (of house of commons?): E borrows, for History of Dutch War, iii. 588.
— religious observances: fasts: Richard Cromwell's parliament appoints day for itself, iii. 226, n. 6; ~ for blessing on parliament, 1680, 1701, iv. 236 & n. 1; v. 452 & n. 4, 453; parliament attends thanksgiving service, 1702, v. 521 & n. 5; house of lords: prayers in, before proceedings, iv. 442 & n. 5; ~ sermons to, iv. 31 & n. 4, 157 & n. 4, 641 & n. 1; house of commons: sermons to: order concerning, 1700, v. 378 & n. 2; ~ individual sermons to, iii. 311–12 & nn., 314 & nn. 3, 4, 356; iv. 26 & n. 1, 156, 620 & n. 5, 641; v. 378.
Parma, ii. 487, 490.
Parma: Dukes of: as owners of: Palazzo Farnese collections, ii. 310 & n. 4; ~ Caprarola, ii. 406; man in service of, iii. 13; individual dukes: Alexander Farnese: captures Corbeil, ii. 121, n. 1; ~ statue of, ii. 215 & n. 4, 308; Odoardo Farnese: in war of Castro, ii. 211, n. 2, 371–2 & n.; ~ erects arch for *Possesso* of Innocent X, ii. 228, n. 6, 281 & n. 1.
Parmigianino (Parmensis), Francesco Mazzola called, ii. 114, n. 12; paintings by, ii. 114 (i. 74); drawings by, ii. 487 & n. 4.
Parnell, James, Quaker: death of, iii. 179 & n. 2; remark about, iii. 207–8 & n.
Parr, Richard; D.D. 1660; vicar of Camberwell, iii. 603, n. 6; as Archbishop Ussher's chaplain, &c., iii. 156, n. 3; *Life* of Ussher by: publication of, delayed, iv. 507–8 & n.; ill, iv. 438, 441; sermons by: funeral (Dr. R. Breton), iii. 603–4 & n.; ~ ordinary, iii. 628; iv. 258, 507; social, iii. 628; iv. 291, 334, 387; successor of, v. 146.
Parry, Benjamin, D.D.; bishop of Ossory 1678: sermon by (?), iv. 15 & n. 5.
Parry, John, D.D.; bishop of Ossory 1672–7, iv. 15, n. 5; sermons by, iv. 15(?), 95(?).
Parsons, Sir John, lord mayor of London: at thanksgiving for Blenheim, v. 578 & n. 1.
Parthenope: fountain of, at Naples, ii. 327 & n. 2.
Parthians: wars of Marcus Aurelius against, represented, ii. 370.
Participatio, G.: church built by, ii. 460, n. 3.
Pasqualini, Marc' Antonio, called Malagigi, singer, ii. 400 & n. 1.
Passes and Passports [E generally uses the word pass; passport occurs on iii. 407 and, as a variant for pass, on i. 42, 43]:
— English: for E: licence to travel (Charles I), ii. 82 & n. 2 (i. 53 & n. 2); passes (parliamentary, &c.), ii. 29 & n. 3, 80, n. 3, 557; iii. 14; ~ forged or out of date, iii. 15–16 & n.
— — for Mrs. Evelyn: admission, &c., iii. 65–6.
— foreign: for Spanish territory: transcribed in Diary, ii. 477–8 & n.; ~ mentioned, ii. 508; attempt to make traveller take pass, ii. 508.
— between belligerent states: United Provinces and Spanish Netherlands, ii. 59 *bis* (i. 40 *bis*), 62–3 (i. 42–3); England and United Provinces, iii. 407.
Passignano (Passegna), Domenico, ii. 114, n. 11; painting by, ii. 114 (i. 74); repairs fresco by Sarto, ii. 412 & n. 2.
Paston, Mrs. Rebecca, later Lady Paston, countess of Yarmouth, &c., wife of Sir Robert Paston, first earl of Yarmouth: geneal., iii. 186, n. 2.
Paston, Sir Robert; knighted 1660; viscount, 1673, and first earl, 1679, of Yarmouth, iii. 170, n. 2; as Mr. or Sir Robert Paston: social, iii. 170, 186, 391, 412; geneal., iii. 186, n. 2; iv. 96, n. 2.
Paston, Sir William, bt., iii. 186, n. 1; geneal., iii. 170, 186.
Paston, William, second earl of Yarmouth: social, iv. 537 & n. 1.

Pate, —, singer: performs, v. 289 & n. 1.
Paterson, John, archbishop of Glasgow: at meeting held by Sancroft to discuss settlement of English crown; seeks maintenance of Scottish episcopate, iv. 613–15 & nn.
Patricius (error), ii. 243 & n. 1.
Patrick, Simon, D.D.; bishop of Chichester 1689; of Ely 1691, iii. 519, n. 4; ordination of, iii. 172, n. 1; letters of, to Lady Gauden, iii. 512, n. 1; appointed a chaplain in ordinary, iii. 631, n. 3; appointed dean of Peterborough, 1679, iv. 229, n. 3; informed by Tenison about William of Orange's intended invasion, iv. 592, n. 3; elected bishop of Chichester, iv. 648–9 & n.; translated to Ely, v. 49 & n. 1; advocates: daily public worship, &c., iv. 136, n. 2; ~ frequent communion, i. *30*, n. 1; on case of conscience, v. 338–9; as preacher: manner, iv. 160; ~ sermons by, iii. 519, 520, 540, 541, 543, 544, 612, 627, 631; iv. 29, 33, 103, 136 & n. 2, 160, 190, 224, 229, 237, 297, 397, 398, 414, 491, 526–7, 530, 578; v. 39, 222.
Paul II, pope: procession of (as Paul III, in error), ii. 374 & n. 3.
Paul III, pope: tomb of, ii. 264–5 & n., 265 & n. 2, 308, n. 6; statues of, ii. 221 & n. 2, 422 & n. 2 (as of Paul IV, in error); named in error, ii. 320 (date), 374 & n. 3.
Paul IV, pope: statue of (error for Paul III), ii. 422 & n. 2.
Paul V, pope (Camillo Borghese), ii. 203, n. 6; arms of, ii. 312 & n. 7; chair invented by, ii. 285, critical note; chapel of, at S. Maria Maggiore, ii. 243–4 & nn.; statue of, ii. 244 & n. 4.
buildings of: Acqua Paola, ii. 312, 313; St. Peter's: high altar, ii. 261; ~ fountain before, ii. 255, n. 3; Vatican: clock-tower in, ii. 255, n. 2.
Paul, Chevalier: *see* Saumur, P. de.
Paul, St.: at Puteoli, ii. 343 & n. 3, 351; at Tres Tabernae, ii. 318; martyrdom of, ii. 308; in legend (spurious: E's invention), ii. 306 & n. 2; relics of: body, ii. 263, 306–7 & n., 363, n. 5; head, ii. 274; ~ exhibited, ii. 292, 385; chain, ii. 307.
Paul, St. (*cont.*)
— on orders of angels, iii. 247, n. 1; mentioned, iv. 329; *see also* Heaven, Third.
— in sermons: incidents in his life: conversion, iii. 240; iv. 128, 348; v. 42, 116, 487; preaching of, to Athenians, iii. 22–3; v. 395, 523; at Malta, v. 275; before Agrippa, iii. 249; iv. 531; v. 75, 266; before Felix, iv. 435; v. 209, 294, 477, 586; before Festus, v. 75, 395; journey to Jerusalem with alms, v. 74, 341, 342; afflictions of, v. 72; in Third Heaven, v. 490; legends, &c.: introduces Christianity into Britain, iii. 333 & n. 4; in paintings, v. 328.
— — equal to St. Peter in power, iii. 240; teaching of, iii. 164; iv. 321, 345, 346, 516, 580, 638–9; v. 18, 72–3, 91, 104, 106, 281, 290, 295, 296–7, 350, 356–7, 375, 384, 406, 443, 447, 486, 565; miscellaneous, iii. 185, 240, 598; iv. 43, 287, 447; v. 242, 387, 424, 588.
Paul, William, D.D.; bishop of Oxford: sermon by, iii. 303 & n. 1.
Paule, Monsieur: *see* Pawel-Rammingen, von.
Paulet (Powlett), Charles; styled Lord St. John 1653–75; sixth marquis of Winchester 1675; first duke of Bolton 1689, iii. 529, n. 2; social: as Lord St. John, iii. 529; ~ as marquis of Winchester, iv. 173.
Paulet (Powlett), Isabella, marchioness of Winchester, third wife of John Paulet, fifth marquis: at Stafford's impeachment, iv. 226–7 & n.
Paulet (Powlett), John; fifth marquis of Winchester 1629, ii. 546, n. 7; social, ii. 546; iii. 356; geneal., iv. 227, n. 1.
Paulwheel *or* Powlwheel, — musician (Paul Wheeler?), iii. 168, n. 1.
Pausilippe: *see* Naples: environs: Posilipo.
Pavia: flints from, used in glass-making, ii. 467.
Paving: roads: France and England, ii. 135 & n. 3 (i. 89); Italy, ii. 317, 319; United Provinces, ii. 31 (i. 24).

Paving (*cont.*)
streets, &c., in towns: brick, ii. 202, 434 & n. 3, 435, n. 3, 453; clinker-brick, i. 24; ii. 47–8 & n. (i. 34); *see also* iii. 471, &c.; pebble, ii. 94 (i. 62), 139 (i. 91); stone or marble, ii. 94 (i. 62–3), 200, 435; casual comments, ii. 176, 353 & n. 3, 428 & n. 2; iii. 102, 119, 121, 130, 140 & n. 6.
Pawel-Rammingen, — von (Monsieur Paule), agent of Elector Palatine in Paris, ii. 567 & n. 2.
Paynter, — *verè* Conyers, a friar, iii. 36.
Peake, Sir John, lord mayor: his show, iv. 528 & n. 5; offers E hospital governorship, iv. 560.
Peale, Rev. —: sermon by, v. 244–5.
Pearce, Edward: *see* Pierce *or* Pearce, E.
Pearson (Pierson), John; D.D. 1660; bishop of Chester 1672, iii. 15, n. 2; character, iv. 5–6; at Durdans, iii. 15 & n. 2; lecturer at St. Clement's, Eastcheap, iii. 64 & n. 5; promotes publication of Walton's *Polyglot*, iii. 78 & n. 4; examines scholars from Westminster School, iii. 288 & n. 4; elected bishop, iv. 2, n. 8; officiates at ordination, iv. 54; sermons by, iii. 82, 150, 403; iv. 2, 5–6, 31, 33, 52–3, 83, 107, 165; appointed to preach, iv. 132, n. 4; social, iv. 33.
Peck, Elizabeth: *see* Saladin, Mrs. E.
Peckham, Sir Henry: Reader's feast of, iii. 536–7 & n.
Pedroso: Count of: *see* Lopez de Zuñiga, Don F.
Pegge, Catherine, mistress of Charles II, iv. 181, n. 6.
Peirse, Thomas, D.D.: *see* Pierce *or* Peirse, T.
Pelagians: in sermons, iii. 11; iv. 334 & n. 6.
Pelham, Sir John, bt.: social, iii. 473 & n. 6.
Pelham, Sir Thomas, bt.; first Baron Pelham 1706: as Mr. Pelham: speaks for reducing army, 1699, v. 309 & n. 2, 311, n. 1.
Pelham: first Baron, 1706–12: *see* Pelham, Sir Thomas.
Pellegrini: *see* Tibaldi, P.
Pellestrina (Palestina), ii. 429 & nn. 2, 3.
Pelling, Edward; D.D. 1690, iv. 192, n. 5; sermons by (?; as Dr. Pellin), iv. 192, 360–1 & n.; sermon by, v. 40.
Pelusium: *see* Damietta.
Peloponnesus: king of: *see* Palaeologus, Thomas.
Pemberton, Rev. —: sermons by: at Charlton, 1653, iii. 85 & n. 1; ~ at Greenwich, 1654, iii. 145 & n. 2.
Pemberton, Sir Francis, judge, iv. 342 & n. 2; removed from King's Bench, iv. 320, n. 1; superseded as chief justice of Common Pleas, iv. 342 & n. 2; counsel for Seven Bishops, iv. 587 & n. 2.
Pemberton, Rev. John, minister at Charlton, 1646, 1650: sermons by (?), iii. 85 & n. 1, 145 & n. 2.
Pemberton, Rev. Matthew: sermons by (?), iii. 85 & n. 1, 145 & n. 2.
Pembroke: Earls of: owners of Ramsbury, iii. 100, n. 5; individual earls, &c.: *see* Herbert, Henry, second earl, 1570–1601; Herbert, Mary, his countess; Herbert, William, third earl, 1601–30; Herbert, Philip, fourth earl, 1630–50; Herbert, Philip, fifth earl, 1650–69; Herbert, William, sixth earl, 1669–74; Herbert, Philip, seventh earl, 1674–83; Herbert, Thomas, eighth earl, 1683–1733.
Penaguião, Count of, Portuguese ambassador in England, iii. 83 & n. 2.
Penancoët, Guillaume de: *see* Kéroualle.
Penn, William, the Quaker: imprisoned for blasphemous publication, iii. 521 & n. 1.
Penn, Sir William, the admiral, iii. 147, n. 2; at the Nore, 1665, iii. 414 & n. 4; disposal of prize goods: concerned in, iii. 424, n. 1; ~ impeached for, iii. 508 & n. 3; as Master of Trinity House, iii. 483; geneal., iii. 521; former chaplain of: sermon by, iii. 147.
Penni, F.: painting executed by, ii. 299 & n. 3.
Penshurst, Kent: Chafford in: church near, iv. 40 & n. 7; Penshurst Place in: notice, iii. 72 & nn. 4, 5.
Pentacle: as symbol of E's compact of friendship with Mrs. Godolphin, iii. 628 & n. 1.

Penton Mewsey, Hants: rector of: *see* Row, J.

Pepin, father of Charlemagne: tomb of, ii. 86 (i. 58).

Pepys, Mrs. Elizabeth, wife of Samuel Pepys, iii. 541, n. 1; at a play, iii. 510, n. 8; funeral of, iii. 541 & n. 1.

Pepys, Paulina (Pal) (Mrs. Jackson): geneal., v. 538, n. 5.

Pepys, Samuel, iii. 529, n. 5 [citations of Pepys's Diary in the notes, or quotations from it, are not indexed, even when they are couched in personal form, except in a few cases where there are clear links between Pepys and E]:

— character, v. 537–8 & nn.

— official and public career: as Clerk of the Acts: term of office, iii. 570, n. 5; reports on project for dock at Sayes Court, iii. 313, n. 2; advises selling prize-goods from captured Dutch ships, 1665, iii. 419, n. 3; visits Albemarle on account of Sick and Wounded, iii. 420, n. 1; interest of, in E's project for infirmary, iii. 430, n. 2.

— — as Secretary to the Admiralty, &c.: terms of service, iv. 270, n. 4, 396, n. 3, 616, n. 2; visits Windsor, 1674, iv. 42–3; imprisoned in Tower and Marshalsea, 1679, iv. 169 & n. 1, 171 & n. 12; accompanies expedition to Tangier, 1683, iv. 379, n. 3; visits Spain, iv. 469 & n. 5; visits Winchester and Portsmouth, 1685, iv. 467–74; dismissed, iv. 644 & n. 1.

— — in retirement: defends himself against charge of maladministration (his *Memoires*, 1690), v. 24 & n. 2; *see also* v. 39, 538; imprisoned, 1690, v. 27, 30 & n. 3.

— private life: marriage, &c., iii. 541, n. 1; cut for the stone, iii. 529 & n. 5; visits Grinling Gibbons, iii. 570; informed by James II about Charles II's conversion to Roman Catholicism, iv. 475–9 & nn.; examines Dr. A. Clench's precocious son, iv. 616–19; ill, 1690, v. 30; last

Pepys, Samuel (*cont.*)
illness, death, &c., v. 536, 537–8 & nn.

— — as diarist: characterization of Sandwich, i. *109*.

— — residence and property: at Admiralty, iv. 96; house, 1688: E watches fireworks from, iv. 591 & n. 2 [visits, &c., to Pepys as secretary to the Admiralty, 1684–9, are probably to this house]; at Clapham, in W. Hewer's house, iv. 176, n. 1; v. 427–8 & n., 538; collections, ship models, and library, v. 427–8 & n., 538 & n. 2; parrot (?), iv. 618.

— — interests: (i) maritime and naval: at launching of *Experiment*, iii. 392, n. 7; elected master of Trinity House, 1676, 1685, iv. 91, 459 & n. 2; composes new charter of Trinity House, iv. 459, n. 2; member of Greenwich Hospital committee, v. 236, n. 2; projected history of the Navy by, v. 538 & n. 4.

— — — (ii) musical: singers perform at his house, iv. 547 & n. 1; v. 289 & n. 1; on J. Birchensha's system of composition, iii. 377, n. 4.

— — — (iii) scientific: elected F.R.S., iii. 401, n. 8 *ad fin.*; as president of Royal Society: elected, iv. 396; ~ re-elected, iv. 490; benefactor to Royal Society, *ib.*; demonstration with phosphorus at his house, iv. 491.

— persons: estimate of Dr. R. Breton, iii. 302, n. 4; W. Hewer as clerk of, v. 111 & n. 2; acquainted with R. Hoare, ii. 559, n. 2; J. Scott, cousin of, iii. 317, n. 4; friends: Sir A. Deane, iv. 270, n. 5; &c.; Sir James Houblon, iv. 162, n. 6, 475, n. 2; Lady Mordaunt, iv. 206, n. 1; — Reeves, iii. 64, n. 6.

— relations with E [*see also* official and public career *above*, &c.]: general, i. *19*, *36*; Pepys's notices of E, i. *37–8*; first meeting, iii. 418, n. 1; beginning of friendship, iii. 529, n. 5; shows E Sir A. Deane's work on shipbuilding, iv. 270–1 & nn.; in-

Pepys, Samuel (*cont.*)
forms E about Charles II's conversion, i. *31–2*; iv. 475–9 & nn.; E's portrait painted for, iv. 644 & n. 1; *add.*; borrows E's history of Second Dutch War (MS.), iii. 523, n. 1; obtains Elizabethan state papers from E, iv. 241, n. 3, 303, n. 3; visits Sayes Court, iii. 110, n. 2, 418, n. 1; shows his calculus to Richard Evelyn, iii. 529; godfather of Jane Evelyn, 1692, v. 84; letter to, from (Sir) John Evelyn, v. 322, n. 4.
— social: parties, iii. 419, n. 1, 570; iv. 206 & n. 1, 273; v. 9–11, 27, 32, 59, 124, 295; alone, &c., iv. 96, 503, 565, 585, 603, 641, 646; v. 67, 507; *see also* v. 508 *bis* & n. 3.

Perce, Thomas: *see* Pierce *or* Peirse, T.

Percy, Algernon; tenth earl of Northumberland 1632, iii. 216, n. 2; attends Clarendon at his creation as earl, iii. 277; as owner of: Suffolk (later Northumberland) House, iii. 141, n. 2, 216 & n. 7; ~ Syon House, iii. 414, n. 10 *ad fin.*, 415; art-collection of, iii. 216 & nn. 3–6; geneal., iii. 264, n. 5; iv. 218; v. 586–7; mentioned, ii. 12, n. 1.

Percy, Lady Elizabeth, daughter of Earl Algernon: *see* Capel, Elizabeth, countess of Essex.

Percy, Lady Elizabeth, daughter of Earl Joceline: *see* Seymour, Elizabeth, duchess of Somerset.

Percy, Elizabeth, countess of Northumberland, born Howard, second wife of Algernon Percy, tenth earl, iii. 264, n. 5; visits Anne, duchess of York, iii. 264; complicity of, in marriage of Lady Ogle to T. Thynne, iv. 261 & n. 1; dies, v. 586–7 *bis* & n.; geneal., iii. 141, n. 2.

Percy, Elizabeth, countess of Northumberland, born Wriothesley, wife of Joceline Percy, eleventh earl, and secondly of Ralph Montagu, duke of Montagu: *see* Montagu, Elizabeth, countess of Montagu.

Percy, Henry, eighth earl of Northumberland 1572 (in text as duke): suicide of, iv. 327 & n. 3.

Percy, Henry, ninth earl of Northumberland 1585: acquires Syon House, iii. 414, n. 10.

Percy, Henry, Baron Percy of Alnwick: employs Sir Stephen Fox, iv. 218 & nn. 2, 3.

Percy, Joceline; styled Lord Percy 1644–68; eleventh earl of Northumberland 1668, iii. 481, n. 3; visits duchess of Newcastle, iii. 481; daughter and heiress of, iv. 260 & n. 4; ~ provision in his will relating to, iv. 261, n. 1; geneal., iv. 201 & n. 2.

Percy: Lord, 1644–68 (courtesy title): *see* Percy, Joceline, eleventh earl of Northumberland.

Percy of Alnwick: Baron, 1643–59: *see* Percy, Henry.

Perekop (Procop, Pericop), Crimea: taken by Russians, 1689, iv. 645 & n. 6.

Perelle, Adam, engraver, iii. 3, n. 4.

Perelle, Gabriel, engraver: visit to, iii. 3 & n. 4.

Perelle, Nicolas, engraver, iii. 3, n. 4.

Peretti, Felice: *see* Sixtus V.

Perfectionists: sermon against, iii. 363 & n. 2.

Périgueux: error for Fréjus, ii. 167 & n. 3 (i. 105).

Perishot, — (correctly Perruchot): art-collection, &c., of, ii. 114 & n. 6 (i. 74).

Perkins *or* Parkyns, Sir William: *see* Parkyns.

Perlan, Henri, modeller, ii. 103, n. 3 *ad fin.*

Perpetual motion: machines for, ii. 230, 310; iii. 325, 513 & n. 1.

Perpoint, William: *see* Pierrepont, W.

Perrier, François: etchings by, of statues, &c., iii. 10–11 & n.

Perrin, P.: *see* Plays.

Perrinchief, Richard, D.D., iii. 602, n. 2; sermons by, iii. 602, 623.

Perrott, William, ii. 24, n. 4.

Perruchot (Perishot), —: art-collection, &c., of, ii. 114 & n. 6 (i. 74).

Persepolis: account of, by Sir J. Chardin, iv. 213, 369 & n. 1.

Persia:
ancient: chronological reckoning, v. 26; empire: duration of, ii. 431, n. 3; ~ succession of rulers: boy's knowledge of, iv. 617; ~ conquest of, by Alex-

Persia (*cont.*)
ander: in sermon, v. 156; Angel of: in sermon, v. 362.
modern: climate of, iv. 358 & n. 4; dress: fashion of, in, iii. 465 *bis* & n. 1; fertility of, iv. 214 & n. 5; fire-worshippers in, iv. 214 & n. 2; Jews in: account of persecution of, iii. 522, n. 2 *ad fin.*; king of: gift from, ii. 89 (i. 60); Persian carpet, iv. 262; Sir J. Chardin's travels in, iv. 212–14 & nn., *passim*, 358 & n. 4, 369 & n. 1, 372.
Persians: at Bologna, ii. 422; iii. 465, n. 3; in London, iii. 161; ~ P. Cisij, iii. 516, 522, n. 2; at Venice, ii. 449.
Persian language: scholar, iv. 213.
Peru: earthquake, &c., in, 1687, iv. 585–6 & n.; sea adjoining, v. 295; clergy of: taxing of, v. 345, n. 2; resident in, iii. 188, n. 5; Peruvian bark: *see* Medicine and Surgery: drugs (quinine).
Perugino, Pietro, ii. 120, n. 8; paintings by, ii. 190 & n. 12, 378 & n. 5; ~ false attributions, ii. 224 & n. 3, 407; ~ school-piece, ii. 120, n. 8.
Peruzzi, Baldassare, ii. 202, n. 8; as Baltazar di Sienna: arch built by (?), ii. 202–3 & n.; paintings by, ii. 288 & n. 2.
Peschiera, ii. 488.
Peter of Auxerre, emperor of Byzantium: coronation of, ii. 381 & n. 3.
Peter II (Dom Pedro), king of Portugal: as regent, iv. 130, n. 1; banishes Castelmelhor, iv. 130 & n. 1; recalls Castelmelhor, iv. 454; policy of, 1703, v. 530 & n. 2; joins Allies, v. 539 & n. 1; geneal., v. 351, n. 1, 560, n. 1.
Peter the Great, tsar of Russia, v. 277, n. 4; visits of, to William III, 1697: alluded to, in sermon, v. 277 & n. 4; visit of, to England, 1698: comes to London, v. 284 & n. 1; occupies Sayes Court, v. 284 & n. 5, 286; ~ damage done by, at, v. 290 & n. 6; visits Portsmouth, v. 285 & n. 4; leaves England, v. 286 & n. 2; arrives in Holland, v. 287 & n. 5.
armament, &c., of, against Turkey, 1699, v. 316, 345, 368 &
Peter the Great (*cont.*)
n. 4; declares war against Sweden, 1700, v. 429 & n. 4; Baltic policy of, v. 439; defeated at Narva, v. 438–9 & n., 440; *see also* Wars: Great Northern War; palace of: burnt down, v. 504.
Peter, St.: at Naples, ii. 328; at Rome: as bishop of, ii. 299; appearance of Christ to, ii. 363; place of residence in, ii. 246 & n. 6; opposes Simon Magus at, ii. 248 & n. 3; prison of, ii. 227 & nn. 5, 6, 8; place of martyrdom of, ii. 313; tomb of, ii. 258, n. 3; relics: body, ii. 263, 307 & n. 1, 363, n. 5; head, ii. 274; ~ exhibited, ii. 292, 385; altar used by, ii. 272; chair of, ii. 264; mantle of, ii. 246; sword of, ii. 205; relating to denial of Christ by, ii. 273 & n. 9; statue of, in St. Peter's, ii. 264 & n. 1.
in sermons: St. Paul equal to, in power, iii. 240; coming of, to Rome, iii. 333; not the earliest disciple, v. 80; in paintings, v. 328; incidents in life of, iii. 524; iv. 33, 43, 205; v. 268, 281; teaching, &c., of, v. 93, 447, 588; mentioned, v. 110, 128, 308, 387.
Peter, St.: Patrimony of: *see* St. Peter's Patrimony.
Peter *or* Peters, Mrs. —, E's wet-nurse, ii. 6 & n. 2 (i. 6).
Peter, Daniel, of Wotton, ii. 6, n. 2.
Peter, John, of Wotton: baptized, ii. 6, n. 2.
Peter Martyr, St.: tomb of (error), ii. 199 & n. 6.
Peterborough, Northants.: notice, iii. 134–5 & nn.; Thorpe Hall, near, iii. 134 & n. 2.
Peterborough: Earls, &c., of: *see* Mordaunt, John, first earl, 1628–43; Mordaunt, Elizabeth, his countess; Mordaunt, Henry, second earl, 1643–97; Mordaunt, Charles, third earl, 1697–1735; Mordaunt, Carey, his countess.
— cathedral clergy:
— — bishops of: ruins of palace of, iii. 134 & n. 2; individual bishops: *see* Laney, B. (1660–3); Henshaw, Joseph (1663–

Peterborough (*cont.*)
79); Lloyd, William, D.D., the nonjuror (1679–85); White, Thomas (1685–91); Cumberland, R. (1691–1718).
— — deans of: *see* Cosin, John (1640–60); Duport, J. (1664–79); Patrick, Simon (1679–89); Kidder, R. (1689–91); Freeman, S. (1691–1707); Mandevile, J. (1722–5).
Peters, Rev. Hugh, ii. 547, n. 1; incites rebels against Charles I, 1649, ii. 547 & n. 1; executed, iii. 259 & n. 2.
Petersham, Surrey: manor of, iv. 143, n. 5.
Petit, —: lets lodgings at Rome, ii. 212 & n. 3.
Petit, — ('old Petit'): at Rome, ii. 549 & n. 4.
Petitot (Petito), Jean: portrait in enamel by, iii. 260 & n. 3.
Peto, Edward: social (?), iii. 87 & n. 2.
Petrarch: at Vaucluse, ii. 162 & n. 6 (i. 103); epigrams (*Canzoniere*) of: MS. of, ii. 301 & n. 7; mistress of (Laura): tomb of, ii. 161, n. 11, 162 & n. 1 (i. 103); statue of, ii. 411 & n. 2.
Petre, Father Charles, S.J.: attacks Authorised Version of the Bible, &c., iv. 599 & n. 1.
Petre (Piters), Father Edward, S.J., iv. 606, n. 3; James II advised to dismiss, iv. 600, n. 1; as privy councillor: appointment challenged, iv. 603, n. 1; officiates at touching for king's evil, iv. 606 & n. 3.
Petre, William; fourth Baron Petre 1638, iv. 169, n. 2; imprisoned in Tower, iv. 158 & n. 7, 169; alluded to, as prisoner, iv. 174, 225, n. 3; dies, iv. 366, n. 4.
Petre: fourth Baron, 1638–84: *see* Petre, William.
Petrifactions [*see also* Crystal (ii. 331 & n. 7, &c.)]: man's body, ii. 235 & n. 10, 391; various, ii. 148 (i. 95–6), 288 & n. 3, 331, 349 & n. 6, 408, 471.
Petronilla, St.: tomb of, ii. 289.
Pett, —, of Chatham: error for Peter Pett of Deptford, v. 10 & n. 1.
Pett, Christopher: builds *Anne* yacht, iii. 297, n. 1.
Pett, Peter, 1593–1652, of Deptford: builds *Constant Warwick*, v. 10 & n. 1; i. 22, n. 6 *ad fin.*
Pett, Peter, 1610–70, commissioner of the Navy, iii. 359, n. 4; house of, at Chatham, iii. 359; builds: *Catherine* yacht, iii. 296, n. 6; ~ *Jemmy* yacht, iii. 327, n. 5.
Pett, Phineas: builds *Sovereign of the Seas*, &c., i. 22 & nn. 5, 6.
Pettus, Dr. —: *see* Pittis, T.
Petty, Anthony: geneal., iv. 56 & n. 6.
Petty, Elizabeth, Lady Petty, wife of Sir William, and previously of Sir M. Fenton; created baroness Shelburne 1688: character, &c., iv. 56, 57 & n. 4, 60.
Petty, Rev. William: at Milan, ii. 498, n. 8 *ad fin.*
Petty, Sir William, iii. 304, n. 3; notice of, iv. 56–61 & nn.; in Ireland: makes the Down Survey, iv. 57 & n. 3; ~ makes map of Ireland, iv. 58 & n. 2; ~ quarrels with B. Worsley, iii. 603, n. 1; commissioner for London streets, iii. 319, n. 1; at Durdans, 1665, iii. 416 & n. 3; house of, in London, iv. 56 & n. 4, 60; double-bottomed ships invented by, iii. 369 & n. 4, 392 & n. 7; iv. 58 & n. 1; as inventor, iii. 416; author of *Observations upon the Bills of Mortality* (?), iv. 60 & n. 3; papers for Royal Society and other works by, iii. 304 & n. 3; iv. 60–1 & nn.; social: parties, iv. 84, 299–300; ~ alone, iv. 531.
Peyton, Sir Thomas, bt., iii. 13, n. 5; procures reprieve of man condemned to death, iii. 74; social, iii. 13.
Phaethon: fall of: place of, ii. 428 & n. 5.
Pharaoh, iv. 214; in sermons, iii. 237, 525; iv. 648; v. 181.
Pharisees: in sermons: general, iii. 162; iv. 93, 249, 264; v. 86, 305, 430, 470, 569, 586, 617; ostentation and pride of, iv. 356; v. 78, 258, 428, 589; Pharisee and Publican (parable), iv. 249, 256; v. 95, 116, 248, 304; ~ alluded to, iv. 238, 254; v. 305, 343; *see also* Scribes and Pharisees.
Pharsalia: battle of: alluded to, in sermon (?), v. 179 & n. 2.

Phelips (Philips), Col. Robert, iv. 513, n. 1; as commissioner of the Privy Seal, iv. 493 & n. 7, 513; social, iv. 585.
Phidias: as sculptor of Horse-tamer on Quirinal, ii. 237, 405, n. 1.
Philemon: in sermon, v. 375.
Philip II Augustus, king of France: as builder of: Notre Dame, ii. 95 (i. 63); ~ part of Louvre, ii. 103, n. 1; statue of, ii. 95 (i. 63).
Philip III, king of France: monuments relating to, ii. 90, n. 1.
Philip IV, the Fair, king of France: the Palais at Paris built in time of, ii. 98 (i. 64).
Philip II, king of Spain: employs P. Tibaldi, ii. 494 & n. 6; geneal., ii. 70, n. 4.
Philip IV, king of Spain: acknowledges precedence of French before Spanish ambassadors, iii. 297, n. 4 *ad fin.*; painting relating to, ii. 71 & n. 3 (i. 46); geneal., ii. 59 & n. 7 (i. 40), 368, n. 8.
Philip V, king of Spain, previously duke of Anjou, v. 434, n. 2; Spanish dominions bequeathed to, v. 434 & n. 2, 436 & n. 2; form used by, to address Louis XIV, v. 439 & n. 2; succession of: acknowledged by United Provinces, v. 446 *bis* & n. 1; guardianship of: claimed by Louis XIV, v. 453.
Philip, duke of Anjou 1640–60; of Orleans 1660–1701; Monsieur, iii. 32, n. 2; dances in court ballet, iii. 32; in procession, iii. 43; acquires St. Cloud, ii. 107, n. 3; envoy from, to congratulate Charles II, 1660, iii. 254 & n. 7; geneal., i. 97 & n. 1; ii. 565, n. 1; iii. 257, critical note.
Philip, St.: in sermons, iii. 227; iv. 202.
Philip Neri, St.: as founder of the Oratorians, &c., ii. 232–4 & nn.; portrait of, ii. 233, n. 6; statue of, ii. 234 & n. 2; mentioned, ii. 369, n. 7.
Philippsburg, Baden: invested by French, 1688, iv. 598 & n. 1.
Philipp Wilhelm von Neuburg, Elector Palatine: geneal., v. 2, n. 2, 351, n. 1.
Philips: *see also* Phelips *and* Phillips.
Philips, Mrs. Katherine: translation of *Horace* by: acted, iii. 505 & n. 2, 524 & n. 2.
Philips Norton, Somerset: skirmish at, iv. 450–1 & n., 452, n. 8 *ad fin.*
Philistines: in sermon, v. 227.
Phillips (Philips), Edward, iii. 364–5 & n.; relations with E, i. *23–4*; becomes tutor to John Evelyn, jnr., iii. 364–5; publishes E's account of the ambassadors' encounter (1661), iii. 297, n. 4 *ad fin.*; enters Pembroke's service, iii. 401 & n. 4; in Arlington's service, iv. 120–1 & n.
Phillips (Philips), Michael, consul-designate at Venice: social, iii. 86 & n. 1.
Philocepos: pseudonym used by E, iii. 225, n. 3.
Philology: study of, recommended, iii. 157.
Philosophic Society *or* Assembly: *see* Royal Society.
Phlegræan Fields: notice, ii. 336–52 & nn.; bibliographical note, ii. 336, n. 6; the name, ii. 341.
Phrases: *see* Words and Phrases.
Physics:
  atmosphere: Torricellian experiment, &c., iii. 268 & n. 1, 273, 327; weight of mercury, iii. 295 & n. 8 (?), 334; barometer, iii. 268, n. 1; ~ experiments with, iv. 126, 301–2 & n.
  cold: corpses preserved by, iv. 146; freezing of water, *ib.*; paper on, iv. 370.
  compressed air: experiments relating to, iii. 274–5, 292 *bis*, 295, 318; water-works worked by, ii. 47 & n. 1 (i. 33).
  dynamics: motion: experiments on, iii. 520, 521, 522; ~ velocity of, iii. 351; demonstration, iv. 250.
  ether, the, iv. 297.
  fire and flame: experiments with, iii. 296, 396; combustion during Fire of London, iii. 452 & n. 4.
  siphon: experiment with, iv. 400.
  statics: experiments, iii. 510.
  water: nature of, iv. 313; compression of: experiments relating to, iii. 274–5, 291, 293, 295 & n. 8(?); descent of bodies in, iii. 378; raising of, &c.: experiments relating to, iv. 293, 321.
  weights: experiment in raising, iii. 547.
Piacentino, Giulio (G. Mazzoni): stucco-work by, ii. 366 & n. 5.

Piacenza, ii. 490.
Pianoro, ii. 419, n. 3, 420.
Piazza, Paolo (Fra Cosimo): painting by, ii. 225, n. 3.
Pica, the, iv. 300 & n. 4.
Picardy: regiment of: *see* France: army.
Piccioli: E's spaniel, ii. 533.
Piccolomini family, ii. 203; palaces of: at Rome, ii. 376 & n. 4; ~ at Siena, ii. 203 & n. 7; *see also* Pius II *and* Pius III.
Pichini *or* Pighini, —: palace and art-collection of, ii. 217 & n. 1.
Pico della Mirandola, Giovanni: precocity of, iv. 173; tomb of, ii. 200 & n. 5; portrait of, iii. 538.
Pie: the rules called the (Pica), iv. 300 & n. 4.
Pie, Sir Walter: *see* Pye.
Piedmont: for campaigns in, 1690–5, *see* Wars: War of the League of Augsburg; for persecutions of the Waldenses in, *see* Waldenses.
Pientio, Monte (error), ii. 207 & n. 5.
Pienza, ii. 207, n. 5.
Pierce *or* Pearce, Edward, sen.: paintings by, at Wilton, iii. 114 & n. 2.
Pierce *or* Peirse (Perce), Thomas; D.D. 1660; dean of Salisbury 1675, iii. 183 & n. 5; as tutor of Sunderland, &c., iii. 234 & n. 2; controversy of, with H. P. (S.) Cressy: the bishops' concern in, iii. 360 & n. 5; connexion of, with Earles, iii. 363 & n. 6; in attendance as chaplain in ordinary, iv. 129 & n. 5; as preacher: commended, iv. 271; censured, iv. 131, 197 & n. 4; sermons by: printed, iv. 164 & n. 3, 193 & n. 4(?), 197 & n. 4(?); ~ others, iii. 234, 263; iv. 3, 32, 52, 54, 83, 105, 129, 131, 164, 165, 271; appointed to preach, iv. 3, n. 6, 83, n. 3.
Pierrepont family, earls of Kingston, &c.: connexion of, with Evelyn family, i. 3 & n. 2.
Pierrepont, —: house of, near Pontefract, iii. 128 & n. 1.
Pierrepont, Anne, wife of John Manners, styled Lord Ros, later duke of Rutland: divorce proceedings against, iii. 545–6 & n.
Pierrepont, Mrs. Elizabeth, born Evelyn, wife of Robert Pierrepont, ii. 557–8 & n.; power of memory of, ii. 557; inherits paternal estate, v. 337, n. 1; arranges her son's marriage, iv. 551 & n. 2; dies, &c., v. 310 & n. 1; geneal., i. 3 & n. 2; ii. 553, n. 7 *ad fin.*
Pierrepont, Evelyn; fifth earl of Kingston 1690; marquis of Dorchester 1706; duke of Kingston 1715, iv. 551, n. 2; first marriage of, iv. 551 & n. 2; social, v. 469; geneal., i. 3 & n. 2; v. 310, 518.
Pierrepont, Francis: house of, in Nottingham, iii. 125 & n. 8.
Pierrepont, Gertrude: *see* Cheyne, Mrs. G., later Viscountess Newhaven.
Pierrepont, Henry; second earl of Kingston 1643; marquis of Dorchester 1645, iii. 125, n. 3; visits duchess of Newcastle, iii. 482 & n. 5; houses of, iii. 125 & nn. 3, 8; geneal., v. 310.
Pierrepont, Mary, countess of Kingston, first wife of Evelyn Pierrepont, fifth earl and first duke of Kingston: marriage of, iv. 551 & n. 2.
Pierrepont, Robert, husband of Elizabeth Evelyn: geneal. (generally as W. or William Pierrepont, in error), i. 3 & n. 2; ii. 557 & n. 6; iv. 551; v. 310.
Pierrepont, Robert, first earl of Kingston: house of, near Pontefract, iii. 128, n. 1; geneal., iii. 125, n. 8.
Pierrepont, Robert; third earl of Kingston 1680, iv. 261, n. 4; projected marriage of, iv. 261; geneal., i. 3, n. 2; mentioned (?), ii. 557–8 & n.
Pierrepont, W. *or* William: error for Robert Pierrepont, i. 3; ii. 557; v. 310.
Pierrepont, William ('Wise William'): geneal., i. 3, n. 2.
Pierrepont, William; fourth earl of Kingston 1682: geneal., i. 3, n. 2; iv. 551 & n. 2; mentioned (?), ii. 557–8 & n.
Piers, William, D.D.; bishop of Bath and Wells 1632: in coronation of Charles II, iii. 282, n. 2.
Pierson, —: *see* Pearson, John.
Pietramala, ii. 419, nn. 3–5; Fuochi di, ii. 420 & n. 1.
Pietro, Signor: *see* Reggio, P.
Pietro d'Abano: bust of, ii. 463 & n. 4.

Piggott, Rev. Samuel, master of Guildford Free School, v. 536, n. 3; sermons by (?), v. 545, 546–7, 548.
Pighini, —: *see* Pichini.
Pignatelli, Antonio: *see* Innocent XII.
Pignerol *or* Pignoll: *see* Pinerolo.
Pilate, Pontius: palace and suicide of, at Vienne or Ponsas, ii. 159 & n. 2 (i. 101–2); house of, in Jerusalem: relics of, ii. 268 & n. 2, 269, nn. 1, 2, 273, n. 7; in sermons, iv. 311; v. 236, 490.
Pilgrims: to Rome: treatment of, ii. 205 & n. 4, 366 & n. 3.
Pilton, Devon: payment relating to, iv. 378 & n. 2.
Pinckney, Leonard, clerk of the kitchen, iii. 330, n. 1; social, iii. 330, 355(?).
Pindar, Sir Paul: lodging of, at Milan, ii. 491, n. 3.
Pinerolo (Pignerol, Pignoll): besieged by Confederates, 1693, v. 155 & n. 5.
Pintoricchio, Bernardino: paintings by, at Siena (as by Raphael, &c.), ii. 205 & n. 1, 407.
Piombo, Sebastiano del, ii. 487, n. 3; paintings by (as by Raphael): Dorothea, ii. 487 & n. 3; ~ portrait of Ferry Carondelet, iv. 102 & n. 2.
Piperno, ii. 318 & nn. 2, 6.
Pirates and Privateers:
  Channel: pursue Dover-Calais packet-boat, &c., ii. 559; iii. 13 & n. 1, 16, 54; reported to have stolen E's property, iii. 39; fear of, ii. 30 (i. 23).
  Dunkirk: depredations by, ii. 75 (i. 49); steal Mrs. Evelyn's portrait, &c., ii. 551; iii. 56 & n. 1; alluded to, iii. 71.
  English: executions of, 1696, v. 261 & n. 5; in West Indies, 1699, v. 369 & n. 2; Captain W. Dampier (buccaneer), v. 295; *see also* Morgan, Sir H.
  French: losses inflicted by, 1689, 1694, iv. 652; v. 174–5.
  Spanish: off Ligurian coast, ii. 169–70 & n. (i. 107).
  Turkish: danger from: along Riviera, ii. 166 (i. 105); near Naples, ii. 349, 355 & n. 3.
Pirckheimer, Bilibald: library of, iv. 145 & n. 4.
Pisa: notices, ii. 179–82 & nn. (i. 113–15), 408 & nn. 3–7.
  topography: arsenal, ii. 182 (i. 114); Baptistery, ii. 181 & nn. 5, 6 (i. 114); botanical garden, ii. 181–2 & n. (i. 114), 408 & nn. 6, 7; bridge, ii. 182 & n. 3 (i. 114); Campo Santo, ii. 180–1 & n. (i. 114); cathedral, ii. 180 & nn. 4–6, 181 (i. 114 *bis*); ~ tomb of Emperor Henry VII in, ii. 408 & n. 4; Collegio Ferdinando, ii. 181, n. 8; ducal palace, ii. 182 (i. 114); exchange, ii. 182 (i. 115); Leaning Tower, ii. 180 & nn. 2, 3 (i. 113–14), 408 & n. 5; ~ in comparison, ii. 188 (i. 118); Lungarno, ii. 182 & n. 1 (i. 114); natural history museum, ii. 181 & n. 8 (i. 114), 408; S. Stefano dei Cavalieri, &c., ii. 179–80 & n. (i. 113); Sapienza, ii. 181, n. 8; statues: Cosimo I, ii. 180 & n. 1 (i. 113); ~ Ferdinand I, ii. 182 & n. 4 (i. 114); tribute-vessel, ii. 181 & n. 3 (i. 114); *add.*; university, ii. 181 *bis* & n. 8 (i. 114 *bis*); ~ professor of anatomy at: Sir J. Finch, iii. 289, n. 2.
  canal from, to Leghorn, ii. 183 & n. 4 (i. 115); alluded to, ii. 182 (i. 114).
  historical: wars of, ii. 179 (i. 113); depopulation, &c., of, ii. 182 & n. 6 (i. 115).
  columns from, ii. 198.
Pisanello, Antonio (Vittore): paintings by (?), ii. 271 & n. 6.
Pisano, Niccolò, ii. 181, n. 3.
Pisano, Pietro (error for A. Pisanello ?): paintings by, ii. 271 & n. 6.
Pistoia, ii. 410 & n. 3.
Piters, Father: *see* Petre, Edward.
Pitt, Moses: publishes Sir J. Chardin's travels, iv. 369, n. 1.
Pitt, Thomas: buys Swallowfield, iv. 481, n. 1; *add.*
Pittis (Pettus), Thomas, D.D., iv. 133, n. 5; sermons by, iv. 133, 167, 168, 242.
Pius II, pope (Aeneas Silvius Piccolomini), ii. 203 & n. 6; buildings of, at Siena, ii. 203 & n. 7; relics acquired by, ii. 205 & n. 2, 263; tomb of (error), ii. 407 & n. 9; life of: in paintings (Siena), ii. 205 & n. 1, 407.

Pius III, pope (F. T. Piccolomini), ii. 203 & n. 6.
Pius IV, pope: protects Vatican statues, ii. 305, n. 2.
Pius V, pope: and Vatican statues, ii. 305, n. 2; tomb and statue of, ii. 243 & nn. 5, 7, 245.
Pius VI, pope, ii. 241, n. 3.
Pius IX, pope: *possesso* of, ii. 279, n. 3.
Plaat, De, ii. 61 & n. 2 (i. 41).
Plague: general statements, iii. 412, n. 6; i. *19*; medical, ii. 522 & n. 4.
— in England: 1625, ii. 7 & n. 3 (i. 7); 1636, ii. 15 *bis* & nn. 3, 6 (i. 12); 1658: fast for, iii. 213 & n. 3.
— — 1665–6: in London: *see* London: epidemics; at Deptford: *see* Deptford: chronological series; at Erith, iii. 435, n. 1; at Greenwich, iii. 417, n. 4, 435, n. 1; at Maidstone, iii. 422, n. 3; at Rotherhithe, iii. 430, n. 1; at Woolwich, iii. 417, n. 4, 435, n. 1; collection for, iii. 445, n. 6; Evelyn family evacuated for, iii. 416–30 *passim*; pest-ship, iii. 418; in sermons: during epidemic, iii. 418(?), 425, 432; ~ later, iii. 440–1, 569; v. 87, 227, 293; alluded to or casually mentioned, iii. 424, 477; iv. 411, 429, 478.
— elsewhere: in Ireland, iii. 303, n. 6; ~ Ireton said to have died of, iii. 57 & n. 4; at Isfahan, iv. 337 & n. 4; in Italy: bills of health as guard against, ii. 167, n. 7; at Milan, 1630, ii. 491, n. 3 *ad fin.*; in Paris, iii. 639 (extract from *State of France*).
Plantations, English: French protestants see refuge in, iv. 448; all negroes in, to be baptized, iv. 471 & n. 3; *see also* Council for Foreign Plantations; Council of Trade and Plantations.
Plantin: press at Antwerp, ii. 67 & n. 2 (i. 45).
Plants [the several kinds, apart from those indexed under Flowers, Fruit-trees, Trees and Timber, and Vineyards; general notices are indexed under Botany and Gardening]:
blessed thistle (*carduus benedictus*): posset made from, iv. 272 & n. 1.
Plants (*cont.*)
brazil: preparation of, for dyers, ii. 45 & n. 4 (i. 32).
calamus aromaticus: room hung with, &c., iv. 482 & n. 1.
cane, iii. 110.
caper, ii. 201.
cinchona: in Apothecaries' Garden, iv. 462 & n. 4.
cinnamon: proposed introduction of, into Jamaica, iii. 602–3.
eryngo (sea-holly): candied, iii. 178 & n. 2.
fern-bracken, iv. 452.
ferns: collection of, from Jamaica, v. 48.
flax: proposed introduction of, into America, iii. 602.
galls: proposed introduction of, into America, iii. 602.
grasses: collection of, from Jamaica, v. 48.
humble plant, iii. 109–10 & n., 293.
hyssop: in sermon, iv. 349.
ivy, i. 47; ii. 232, 285, 287, 484; imitated in silverwork, iii. 21.
lavender, ii. 162 (i. 103).
liquorice: grown in Lincolnshire, iii. 131 & n. 3.
logwood: preparation of, for dyers, ii. 45 & n. 4; Jamaicans unable to obtain, iii. 613.
mandragora, ii. 331 & n. 5.
manna-ash, ii. 353, n. 2.
marjoram, iv. 122.
nutmeg: proposed introduction of, into Jamaica, iii. 602–3.
palm-tree, ii. 181 (i. 114), 279; *see also* Fruit-trees.
pepper, Jamaica, v. 48 & n. 1.
rhubarb, iii. 110.
rice, ii. 325.
rosemary, ii. 162 (i. 103); iv. 365.
saffron: grown at Saffron Walden, iii. 141–2 & n.
sedum arborescens (tree-houseleek): at Fulham Palace, iv. 258 & n. 3.
senna: proposed introduction of, into America, iii. 602.
sensitive plant, iii. 109–10 & n., 293.
simples, ii. 52, 102 (i. 67), 167, 408, 466, 480; iv. 462.
sugar-cane, ii. 325.
tea (thea): root of, v. 13–14 & n.
thyme, wild, iv. 122.
Platina: tomb of, ii. 244 & n. 6.

Platonists: writings of, on the Trinity, v. 220–1 & n.
Plautii: tomb of the, near Rome, ii. 394 & nn. 2, 3.
Plays, operas, masques, and ballets [separate pieces; for theatres, acting, &c., *see* Theatre]:
— performances attended by E:
— — Beaumont and Fletcher, *Scornful Lady*, iii. 268 & n. 5.
— — Bisaccioni, M., *Ercole in Lidia* (opera), ii. 450 & n. 2.
— — Buckingham, *Rehearsal*, iii. 599 & n. 1.
— — Businello, G. F., two operas, ii. 474, n. 6.
— — Corneille, *Horace*, translated by Mrs. K. Philips, iii. 505 & n. 2, 524 & n. 2.
— — Crowne, *Calisto*, iv. 49–50 & nn., 50–1 & n.; performers in, iii. 230, n. 3; iv. 186, n. 6, 271, n. 5, 455, n. 5.
— — Davenant, *Cruelty of the Spaniards in Peru* (opera) (?), iii. 229 & n. 2; *History of Sir Francis Drake* (opera) (?), *ib.*; *Law against Lovers* (adaptation from Shakespeare), iii. 347 & n. 4; *Love and Honour*, iii. 303 & n. 4; *Siege of Rhodes*, pt. ii, iii. 309 & n. 1; *see also* Shakespeare *below*.
— — Dryden, *Conquest of Granada*, iii. 569–70 & n.; *Evening's Love*, ii. 510–11 & n.; *Secret Love*, iii. 477 & n. 4; *Wild Gallant*, iii. 351 & n. 14; *see also* Howard *below*. Further entry below.
— — *Engkuklochoreia* (masque), iii. 307–8 & n.
— — Etherege, *Comical Revenge*, iii. 371 & n. 5; takings from, iii. 350, n. 3.
— — *Festes de Bacchus, Les* (French court ballet), iii. 31 & n. 1, 31–2 & n.; performer in, ii. 133, n. 2.
— — Gallicano, Prince of (P. Colonna), *Proserpina rapita* (opera; libretto by O. Castelli), ii. 388–9 & n.
— — Howard, Sir R., *Committee*, iii. 345 & n. 3; *Indian Queen* (with Dryden), iii. 368–9 & n.
— — Jonson, *Catiline*, iii. 520 & n. 2; *Volpone*, iii. 341 & n. 1. Further entry below.
— — Middleton (?), *Widdow*, iii. 313 & n. 4.
Plays, &c. (*cont.*)
— — Orrery, *Mustapha*, iii. 405 & n. 2, 465 & n. 4, 466.
— — Perrin, P., *Ariane* (opera; music by Cambert) (?), iv. 30 & n. 1.
— — Philips, Mrs. K.: *see* Corneille *above*.
— — Shakespeare, *Hamlet* (Davenant's version?), iii. 304 & n. 6; *see also* Davenant *above*. Further entry below.
— — Shirley, *Young Admiral*, iii. 344 & n. 3.
— — Tuke, Sir S., *Adventures of Five Hours*: rehearsal, performance, and takings, iii. 348 & n. 4, 350 & n. 3.
— — unnamed and unidentified: Bath: droll (?), iii. 102 & n. 2; London: tragi-comedy, 1648, ii. 539 & n. 5; other plays, iii. 599, 622; Whitehall: plays at, iii. 315, 475; ~ French comedy at, iii. 306, & n. 5; Milan: opera, ii. 503 & n. 4; Oxford: Exeter College: comedy, Christmas, 1637, ii. 20 (i. 16); Rome: Venerable English College: Italian and English comedies, ii. 291, 388.
— plays, &c., mentioned in text or notes [pieces cited only for biographies of performers or explanations of words are not indexed]:
— — Bernini: opera by, ii. 261 & n. 5.
— — Calderon: play attributed to, iii. 348 & n. 4; play by: quoted, ii. 125, n. 4.
— — Coello y Ochoa, Don A., *Lo que pasa en una noche*: source of Tuke's *Adventures of Five Hours*, iii. 348, n. 4.
— — Dryden, *Love Triumphant*: prologue, &c., v. 164 & n. 5; *see also* Books mentioned in Notes. Further entry above.
— — Guarini, B., *Il Pastor fido*, ii. 365 & n. 1.
— — Jonson, *Volpone*: and mountebanks, ii. 474, n. 5. Further entry above.
— — Lacy, J., *Sauny the Scott* (adaptation from Shakespeare): portrait of Lacy as character in, iii. 338–9 & n.
— — Middleton and Rowley,

Plays, &c. (*cont.*)
Changeling: droll based on (?), iii. 102, n. 2.
— — Newcastle, *Country Captain*: portrait of J. Lacy as character in, iii. 338–9 & n.
— — Racan, *Les Bergeries*: local setting of, ii. 564, n. 3.
— — Shadwell, *Psyche* (opera): performance of, iv. 269, n. 2; *Sullen Lovers*: Sir R. Howard mimicked in, iv. 416 & n. 3; *Tempest* (opera ?): performance of, iv. 269, n. 2.
— — Shakespeare, *Macbeth*: performance of, iv. 269, n. 2; *see also* Lacy *and* Shadwell *above*. Further entry above.
— — Sophocles, *Electra*: translation of, by C. Wase, iii. 55, n. 1; *Oedipus rex:* performance of, Vicenza, 1585, ii. 482, n. 2.
— — *Statira* (opera): performance of, at Siena, ii. 202, n. 3.
— — Wilson, J., *Cheats*: portrait of J. Lacy as character in, iii. 338–9 & n.
— — *Wits, The* (ed. Kirkman), iii. 102, n. 2.
Pleasure-gardens, &c.: Lambeth: new Spring Garden, &c., iii. 291 & n. 2; London: Mulberry Garden, &c., iii. 96–7 & n.; ~ Spring Garden (Charing Cross), ii. 556 & n. 4; iii. 83 & n. 1, 97 & n. 1, 213 & n. 4; St.-Cloud: Durier, ii. 108 & n. 3, 536(?), 563(?).
Plessis, — de, *or* du Plessis: riding academy of, ii. 134 (i. 87–8); iii. 2, n. 4.
Plessis-lez-Tours (Du Plessis): castle, &c., at, ii. 147 & nn. 3–6 (i. 95).
Pliny the elder: death of, ii. 335 & n. 5; statue (modern) of, ii. 486–7 & n.; in sermon, v. 179 & n. 1.
Plœuc de Timeur, Marie-Anne de, comtesse de Kéroualle: *see* Kéroualle, comte de.
Plot, Robert, D.C.L., iv. 68, n. 4; books by and collections of, iv. 68 & n. 4; elected secretary of Royal Society, iv. 263 & n. 6; paper by, iv. 362, n. 4.
Pluckley, Kent: Sir E. Dering of Surrenden in, iv. 203 & n. 1.
Plume, Thomas; D.D. 1673; vicar of Greenwich, iii. 228, n. 2; catechizes, iii. 361; sermons by, iii. 228, 366, 418–28 *passim*, 463 *bis*, 467, 474, 508, 512, 551, 582, 587, 597, 604, 621; iv. 10–11, 56, 89, 108 & n. 2, 532; curate of: sermon by, iii. 428; for sermons by other curates of, *see* Greenwich: St. Alphege.
Pluto: sacrifices to, ii. 346.
Plumtre, Dean E. H.: on E, i. *39* & n. 5.
Plymouth, Devon: declares for William of Orange, 1688, iv. 608–9 & n.; storms at, 1689, iv. 654, n. 2; English merchant-ships at, 1690, v. 31 & n. 2, 33 & n. 5; French fleet near, 1690, v. 31, n. 2; fleet movement near, 1691, v. 69, n. 2; mentioned, iii. 528, n. 4.
Plymouth: Earls of: *see* FitzCharles, Charles, earl 1675–80; *new creation*: *see* Hickman, Thomas Windsor, first earl 1682–7.
Po (Padus), river: course of, &c., ii. 453 & n. 4, 506; legends concerning, ii. 428 & n. 5; in flood, 1705, v. 618 & n. 2.
Pococke, Dr. Edward: translation into Arabic by, v. 82, n. 2.
Poelenburg, Cornelis van: paintings by, ii. 113 & n. 9 (i. 73).
Poeton (Pogton), Rev. John: sermons by, iv. 40 & n. 6.
Poggibonsi, ii. 200, n. 10, 201 & n. 1.
Pogton, Rev. —: *see* Poeton, J.
Poignant, —: art-collection of, iii. 35.
Pointis (Pontis), J. B. L. Desjean, baron de: takes Cartagena, v. 266 *bis* & nn. 2, 4.
Poisons [for snakes *see* Reptiles]:
experiments with, &c., at Royal Society: grand duke of Tuscany's, iii. 289; king of Macassar's, iii. 403; hippomanes, iii. 337; *nux vomica* (strychnine), iii. 289 & n. 4, 290; poisoned arrows, iii. 290; unspecified, iii. 406.
antidotes: sublimate, iii. 290; Venice treacle, ii. 478 & n. 2.
deaths attributed to: Charles II, v. 197–8 & nn.; Maria Anna, queen of Spain (error), v. 257 & n. 5, 258 & n. 2, 259.
Poix (Pois, Poiz), near Amiens, iii. 12, n. 3; ownership of, iii. 17 & n. 2; *add.*; E at, iii. 12, 17, 54 & n. 3; *see also* ii. 85, n. 5.

Poland: curiosities from, v. 205 & n. 1.
— historical: 1655: devastated by Swedes, iii. 161 & n. 3; 1667: makes peace with Russia, iii. 494 & n. 6; 1696–7: election of king: John III Sobieski dies, v. 247 & n. 3; French interest in election, v. 247, 270 & n. 2; Prince of Conti as candidate, v. 259 & n. 5; ~ journey of, to Poland, v. 267 & n. 2, 269 & n. 5, 270, n. 2; preparations for election, v. 263 & n. 9, 266 *bis*; Augustus II elected and crowned, v. 267 & n. 2.
— — 1698: internal troubles, v. 285 & n. 1, 287, 288 & n. 5; 1701–4: participates in Great Northern War, v. 462 & n. 6, 472 *bis* & nn. 1, 4, 546, 561 & n. 2, 572; 1704: disturbances: throne declared vacant, v. 559 & n. 1; Stanislaus Leczinsky elected king, v. 573 & n. 3; further troubles, v. 577 & n. 6, 580 & n. 2.
— individual Poles: Cardinal Primate: M. S. Radziejowski, v. 288 & n. 5, 577 & n. 6; Dr. A. Horneck described as a Pole (error), v. 329; Dr. Janicius, ii. 470; a bishop, ii. 428; unnamed travellers, ii. 60 (i. 41).
Polewheel, —, musician (Paul Wheeler?), iii. 168, n. 1.
Polewheele, Otho, iii. 168, n. 1.
Poley, Sir Edmund: geneal., iv. 498, n. 3.
Poley, Judith: *see* Jermyn, Judith, Baroness Dover, &c.
Polidoro (Polydor): *see* Caldara.
Polidorus, sculptor, ii. 304.
Politian: tomb of, ii. 200 & n. 5.
Politics: general ideas, &c. [*see also* England: politics]:
kingship: Sancroft's views on, iv. 625, n. 3; monarchical government: Algernon Sidney's aversion to, iv. 353; passive obedience: the Anglican clergy and, iv. 620 & n. 1; v. 59; regicide: Roman Catholic and Calvinist views on, iv. 230, 405; v. 165–6 & n., 364–5; universal monarchy: Louis XIV aims at, iv. 331 & n. 4, 380.
sermons relating to: *see* Church of England: doctrines: political teaching.
Pollaiuolo, Antonio, sculptor: work by, ii. 265, n. 2; work falsely attributed to, ii. 258 & n. 6.
Pollaiuolo, Piero: work falsely attributed to, ii. 258 & n. 6.
Pollant, —, Imperial general: killed (as Palfi, in error), v. 258 & n. 6; *add.*
Pollard, Sir Hugh, bt.; Comptroller of the Household, iii. 344, n. 2; social, iii. 344, 351, 355, 358, 360, 435; dies, iii. 469; mentioned, iv. 19 & n. 3.
Pollexfen, Sir Henry: as counsel: in *Quo Warranto* proceedings, iv. 320, n. 1; ~ for Seven Bishops, iv. 587 & n. 2.
Pollio: in sermon, iv. 358.
Pöllnitz, G. B., Freiherr von, envoy from Brandenburg: audience to, iii. 249 & n. 3.
Pomègues: Fort St.-Jean on, ii. 164 & n. 4.
Pomfret: Countess of: *see* Fermor, Henrietta Louisa.
Pompeii, ii. 325, n. 4.
Pompeius, Sextus, ii. 345, n. 2.
Pompeius Mussianus, Sextus: in inscription, ii. 359.
Pompey: statue worshipped by, ii. 253 & n. 2; house of, in Rome, ii. 276 & n. 8; villa of, near Baia, ii. 349 & n. 8; in sermon, v. 179 & n. 2.
Ponsas, near St.-Vallier: castle at, ii. 159, n. 2.
Pontac: vineyard (error), iv. 329 & n. 3.
Pontac, Arnaud de, iv. 329 & n. 3.
Pontac, F.-A. de: Cabbalistic studies of, iv. 329–30 & nn.
Pontack, —, proprietor of Pontack's tavern, v. 160, n. 4.
Pontano, G. G.: burial chapel of, ii. 328–9 & nn.
Pontcharra, ii. 156 & n. 7 (i. 100).
Pont du Charge (Pont de Chargy), ii. 154 & n. 7 (i. 99).
Ponte, Francesco da *and* Giacomo da: *see* Bassano.
Ponte, Il (S. Piero a Sieve), ii. 419 & nn. 3, 4.
Pontefract, Yorks., W.R.: notice, 1654, iii. 127–8 & nn.; liquorice cultivated at, iii. 131, n. 3.
Ponte Gregoriano, ii. 209 & n. 1.
Ponti: *see* Pointis.
Pontine marshes (Pomptini campi), ii. 317, n. 7, 318 & n. 4.

Pontoise, ii. 121 & nn. 4, 5 (i. 78); abbey of Maubuisson near, i. 26 & n. 2, 78 & n. 1(?).
Pontormo, Jacopo Carucci called, ii. 191, n. 5; paintings by, ii. 191, 416 & n. 2.
Pont-St.-Esprit: the bridge at, ii. 160 & n. 2 (i. 102); engagement with Camisards near, v. 563 & n. 1.
Pope, Elizabeth: *see* Bertie, Elizabeth, countess of Lindsey.
Pope, Thomas, second earl of Downe: geneal., iii. 383, n. 1.
Pope, Walter, M.D.: engaged as travelling tutor for George Evelyn, jnr., of Wotton, iii. 354 & n. 2.
Popes: *see* Papacy.
Popham, Col. Alexander: house of, at Littlecote, iii. 99, n. 4, 100 & n. 1.
Popham, Letitia: *see* Seymour, Letitia, Lady Seymour.
Popish Plot, i. *27–8*; first made public, iv. 153–4 & n.; investigated by parliament, iv. 163; fasts for deliverance from, &c., iv. 157 & n. 3, 166 & n. 8, 236 & n. 1; Roman Catholic peers imprisoned for: *see* London: topography: Tower; trials, &c., for: Coleman, iv. 158 & n. 3; Five Jesuits, iv. 170 & n. 10; Stafford, iv. 225–34 & nn.; Sir G. Wakeman, iv. 173–6 & nn., 435.
effect of, on national feeling, iv. 187–8; crisis of the ferment, iv. 223, n. 1; belief in, declines, iv. 320 & n. 2; succeeded by Protestant Plot (Rye-House), iv. 321, 331; called Oates's plot, iv. 404.
Popular Celebrations [processions organized by governments and civic and religious authorities are generally indexed under Processions and not under the present heading]:
— occasional [all in London, except as noted]:
— — 1660: Burning of the Rump, iii. 242 & n. 2.
— — 1665: for battle of Lowestoft, iii. 410.
— — 1666: for Four Days' battle, iii. 440.
— — 1679: for Monmouth's return to London, iv. 189 & n. 6.
— — 1688: for birth of Prince James Edward, iv. 587, 588 & nn. 2, 7, 589 & n. 2; for release on bail, &c., of Seven Bishops, iv. 588 & n. 2; for Queen Mary of Modena's recovery after childbirth, iv. 591 & n. 2.
— — 1690: for battle of the Boyne, v. 28 & n. 2; in France: for supposed defeat and death of William III, v. 32.
— — 1691: for battle of Aughrim, v. 67.
— — 1702: for Vigo, v. 518 & n. 1, 520, 521 & n. 2.
— — 1704: for Blenheim, v. 575.
— carnival, &c.: at: Naples, ii. 331–2 & n.; Paris, iii. 1–2 & n.; Rome, ii. 360, n. 5, 370, n. 1, 381–2 & nn.; Venice, ii. 473–4 & nn.
— other recurrent celebrations:
— — London: Gunpowder Plot and pope-burnings (5 or 17 Nov.), iii. 77; iv. 26 & n. 2, 188, n. 1; v. 72 & n. 1.
— — Rome: May Day, ii. 387 & n. 5; St. Anthony's day, ii. 387 & n. 4.
— — Lupercalia: superseded by Candlemas, iii. 241, n. 1.
Pordage, —, singer: performs, iv. 403 & n. 6, 404.
Pordenone, G. A.: painting by, ii. 414 & n. 5.
Porta, Giacomo della, architect, ii. 230, n. 1; buildings designed by: Frascati, Villa Aldobrandini, ii. 393 & n. 3; Rome: Palazzo Farnese, loggia, ii. 214, n. 4 *ad fin.*; ~ Gesù, façade, ii. 230 & n. 1.
Porta, G. B. della: sculpture by, ii. 246 & n. 4.
Porta, Giuseppe, called Salviati: painting by, ii. 297 & n. 4; mosaic designed by, ii. 437 & n. 7.
Porta, Guglielmo della, sculptor, ii. 265, n. 2; tomb of Paul III by, ii. 264–5 *bis* & nn.; *see also* ii. 308 & n. 6.
Portalegre: Bishop of, 1671–85: *see* Russell, Richard.
Porter, Sir Charles, iv. 556, n. 1; business of, with W. Prettyman and E, iv. 556 & n. 1; v. 33 & n. 1.
Porter, Endymion: visits art-collection, ii. 554–5 & n.
Portici: road to, from Naples, ii. 332, n. 3, 333, n. 2.

Portland, Isle of, Dorset: stone from, i. 81 & n. 1, 84; v. 230; sinking of ground in, v. 230 & n. 6; sea-fight near, 1653, iii. 81 & n. 9.
Portland: Earls of: *see* Weston, Sir Richard, first earl; Weston, Frances, his countess; Weston, Jeronimo, second earl; *new creation*: Bentinck, Hans Willem, first earl, 1689–1709; *Jacobite creation*: Herbert, Sir Edward.
Portman, Sir William, bt., iv. 206, n. 2; takes part in capture of Monmouth, iv. 451 & n. 4, 453; social, iv. 206.
Portmore: Lord, 1699–1703, and earl of, 1703–30: *see* Colyear, Sir David.
Portocarrero, Cardinal, v. 436, n. 2.
Portofino (Cap fino), ii. 178 & n. 9 (i. 113); *add.*
Porto Maurizio, Liguria, ii. 169 (i. 106).
Porto Venere, near Spezia, ii. 178 (i. 112).
Portraits [isolated portraits of individuals are indexed under their subjects, and under their painters, &c., if known; they are not indexed collectively]:
— general: *camera obscura* for taking, iii. 549 & n. 2; modelling, in relief, iii. 85.
— collections of [see *also* Sculpture: ancient: Caesars; Sculpture: medieval and modern: Caesars *and* decorative series]:
— — Ditchley Park, Oxon.: Lee family, iii. 383 & n. 4.
— — Florence: Poggio Imperiale: the Hapsburgs, ii. 411; Uffizi: collection of P. Giovio, ii. 189 & n. 6 (i. 118–19).
— — London: Clarendon collection, iii. 379, n. 8 *ad fin.*, 520 & n. 3; Guildhall: Fire Judges, iii. 338 & n. 5; iv. 17 & n. 5; Royal College of Physicians, iii. 338.
— — Paris: Palais-Royal: French statesmen, &c., ii. 133, n. 4 *ad fin.*, 134 (i. 87), 566 & n. 5.
— — Rome: C. dal Pozzo: men of letters, ii. 277; SS. Trinità del Monte: French kings, ii. 373; Vatican, Library: Fathers, &c., ii. 300–1 & n.
— — Venice: Doges' Palace: Doges, ii. 444 & n. 3.
Portraits (*cont.*)
— — Winchester: King Arthur's knights, i. 52.
Port Royal, Jamaica: earthquake at, 1692, v. 113 & n. 1; destroyed by fire, 1703 (in text as St. James Town), v. 532 & n. 4.
Portsea Bridge, near Portsmouth, Hants: fort at (?), iv. 472 & n. 6.
Portsmouth, Hants: notices: 1638, ii. 21 & n. 7 (i. 16); 1642, ii. 79 (i. 52); 1685, iv. 467, 472–4 & nn.
— chronological series: 1642: siege of, ii. 79 & n. 1 (i. 52).
— — 1661: Henrietta Maria and Henrietta Anne go to, iii. 265–6, 267, n. 2; Charles II goes to, iii. 267, n. 2; 1662: Charles II and Queen Catherine married at, iii. 320 & n. 2; 1664: James, duke of York, goes to, iii. 389, n. 2; 1679: Charles II visits, iv. 178 & n. 3.
— — 1685: James II visits, iv. 467 & n. 1, 472–3; 1688: James II intends to make it a place of retreat, &c., iv. 599, n. 6 *ad fin.*, 609; William of Orange reported to have landed near, iv. 605 & n. 1; Queen Mary of Modena prepares to seek refuge at, iv. 607 & n. 5; Prince James Edward taken to, &c., iv. 607, n. 5, 609 & n. 7.
— — 1690: forces march to, v. 32 & n. 6; 1698: Peter the Great visits, v. 285 & n. 4.
— — 1703–4: Archduke Charles (pretender to Spanish throne) at, v. 548 & n. 2, 554–7 & nn., *passim*; *see also* v. 558 & n. 1.
— garrison: in comparison, iii. 130, n. 5; receives James II, 1685, iv. 472–3; Roman Catholics admitted to, &c., 1688, iv. 599 & n. 6.
— naval: fleet sails from, 1672, iii. 614; Ossory to embark at, 1680, iv. 208; men of war at, 1685, iv. 474; ships at, 1696, v. 233.
— Sick and Wounded at: in district of B. Reymes, iii. 620, n. 1; *see also* iii. 395, n. 1; mentioned, iii. 394.
— places in, &c.: dockyard, iv. 473 *bis*; fortifications: 1638, ii. 21 & n. 7 (i. 16); ~ 1685, iv. 473

Portsmouth, Hants (*cont.*)
bis, 474; God's House, iv. 473 & n. 3; the platform, iv. 473 & n. 2; town-hall, iv. 473 & n. 5; fort outside: James II received at, iv. 472 & n. 6.
— governors, &c.: *see* Goring, George, later Lord Goring (1639–42; ii. 36, n. 1, 79 & n. 1); Fagg (called Fay in error), Sir John (Dec. 1659; error for Col. N. Whetham; iii. 238 & n. 1); Jermyn, Henry, Baron Dover (Nov. 1688; iv. 609 & n. 7); Slingsby, Col. Henry (lieutenant-governor 1682–8?; iv. 473 & n. 4).
— naval officials at: commissioners: *see* Beach, Sir R.; Middleton, Col. T.; Tippets, Sir John; master-attendant at: *see* Tinker, J.
Portsmouth: Duchess of, 1673–1734: *see* Kéroualle, Louise de.
Portugal: chronological: 1661: treaty with England, iii. 290, n. 8, 305, n. 4; 1661–2: English fleet sailing to, iii. 311 & n. 5; 1666: Louis XIV offers to mediate in war between Spain and, iii. 434 & n. 1; 1667: Affonso VI, king of, deposed, &c., iv. 130 & n. 1; 1688: Queen Catherine abandons intention of returning to, iv. 585 & n. 5; 1692: Queen Catherine returns to, v. 93 & n. 5; 1699: earthquakes in, v. 368 & n. 3; 1701: armed forces of, increased, v. 441; ~: policy of, as regards Spanish Succession, v. 462; 1702: joins Allies (false report), v. 514, n. 2; *add.*; ~ Allied fleet off coast of, v. 515; 1703: uncertain policy of, v. 530 & n. 2; ~ joins Allies, v. 539 & n. 1; 1703–4: journey to, of Archduke Charles (pretender to Spanish throne), v. 548–61 & nn., *passim*; 1705: Archduke Charles and Allied fleet sail from, v. 605 & n. 2.
miscellaneous: balsams from, iii. 539 & n. 3; bays and says: use of, in, iii. 177, n. 4; bleeding (surgical) in, v. 352 & n. 1; dress: women's in, iii. 320 & n. 4; furniture: oriental, brought from, by Queen
Portugal (*cont.*)
Catherine, iii. 324 & n. 2; musicians from, iii. 322 & n. 4.
Portuguese: complexions, &c., iii. 320–1 & nn.; individuals: Duarte, at Antwerp, ii. 67 & n. 6 (i. 45); cardinal of, at Rome, ii. 370 & n. 2; donor to Royal Society, iii. 517; Jewesses at Venice, ii. 477 & n. 4; travellers, &c., iii. 12; iv. 191 *bis*.
queen of: *see* Maria Sophia; prime minister of: *see* Castelmelhor, conde de.
Portus Herculis, Provence, ii. 168 & n. 5 (i. 106).
Portus Julius, near Pozzuoli, ii. 345 & n. 2.
Portus Lunensis (Lunaris), near Spezia, ii. 178–9 & n. (i. 113).
Posilipo: *see* Naples: environs.
Postlethwayt, Rev. John, schoolmaster, iv. 584, n. 5; sermons by (?), iv. 584–5; v. 77 & n. 2, 139 & n. 5.
Potemkin, Prince Peter, Russian ambassador to England 1681–2, iv. 262, n. 3, 263; audience for, iv. 262–3 & nn.; son of, iv. 263; entertained by duchess of Portsmouth (?), iv. 268, n. 1; in comparison, iv. 269; mentioned, iv. 284–5 & n.
Potosi (Potisi), iii. 189.
Potter, John, archbishop of Canterbury: tomb of, v. 426, n. 5.
Pottery and Porcelain:
porcelain or china ware [alternative names, iii. 3; usually called porcelain; as china, v. 147]: general note, ii. 100, n. 1; kind of artificial glass or porcelain, iii. 310; chime of porcelain dishes, ii. 47 (i. 33); in comparison, iii. 3; in collections, &c., ii. 133 (i. 86); iii. 11, 35; iv. 92; ~ of Queen Mary II, v. 147 & n. 2; ~ at Kensington Palace, v. 237; used at table, iii. 60 & n. 6; on sale in Paris, &c., ii. 100 (i. 65), 124 (i. 79).
earth: red, jars of, ii. 235; ~ meaning terracotta, iii. 3; iv. 116 & n. 5; *testae*, ii. 235 & n. 5; vases designed by Raphael, iii. 11 & n. 3.
Potts, —, schoolmaster, ii. 9.
Potts, Sir John, bt.: son of, iii. 231 & n. 2.

Poule, —: *see* Powle, H.
Poultney, Thomas: attacked at Cullen, v. 33 & n. 2.
Poultney, Sir William, iii. 529, n. 4; appointed a commissioner of the Privy Seal, v. 7 & n. 5; social, iii. 529; geneal., v. 33.
Poussin, Nicolas, ii. 113, n. 1; as an artist working in Rome, ii. 399; patron of, ii. 277, n. 3; decorations by, in Louvre, ii. 103, n. 3 *ad fin.*; paintings by, ii. 113 (i. 73); iii. 11; iv. 403 & n. 2.
Povey, Justinian: house of, at Hounslow, iii. 447, n. 3.
Povey, Thomas, iii. 327, n. 6; iv. 84, n. 5; character of, iv. 84; houses of: at Brentford, iii. 447 & n. 3; ~ in London, iii. 375 & nn. 2–4, 504; social, iii. 327, 348, 620; iv. 84, 642; geneal., iv. 554, n. 3.
Powell, —, ship's captain at Venice, 1645: E takes passage with, ii. 451; entertains E, ii. 468–9; gives E inscribed Egyptian stone, ii. 469 & nn. 3, 4; iii. 171, n. 6, 172.
Powell, Sir John: judge in trial of Seven Bishops, iv. 587 & n. 2; dismissed, iv. 589 & n. 1, 590.
Power, Richard, earl of Tyrone: released from Tower, 1684, iv. 366, n. 4.
Powis: Earl of: *see* Herbert, William.
Powle (Poule), Henry, iv. 227, n. 10; takes part in Stafford's impeachment, iv. 227, 229, n. 4, 230 & n. 2; geneal., iii. 203, n. 5.
Powlett: *see* Paulet.
Powlwheel, —: *see* Paulwheel.
Powys, Sir Thomas, judge: as solicitor-general: signs warrants for dispensations, iv. 510 & n. 1.
Pozzo, Cassiano dal, Cavaliere, ii. 277, n. 3; collections of, ii. 277–8 & nn.; notes by, ii. 116, n. 4, &c., 283, n. 4; mentioned, ii. 364, n. 2.
Pozzuoli (Puteoli): notice, ii. 342–5 & nn.; landing of St. Paul at, ii. 343, 351; alarm in, during eruption of Monte Nuovo, ii. 346; in views, ii. 329, 334.
Praeneste: *see* Palestrina.
Prague: battle of the White Hill near: commemorated, ii. 239 & n. 11; W. Hollar born near, i. 21.
Pratolino: grand dukes' villa at, ii. 418–19 & nn.; mentioned, ii. 111, n. 2.
Pratt, Sir Roger, architect; knighted 1668, iii. 153, n. 2; travels of, iii. 153 & n. 2; proposals of, for repair of St. Paul's, 1666, iii. 448, n. 3; on Wren's proposals for St. Paul's, iii. 448–9 & nn.; designs: Clarendon House, London, iii. 379, n. 8 *ad fin.*; ~ Horseheath Hall, iii. 553 & n. 3; social, iii. 153.
Pratt, Samuel, D.D.; dean of Rochester: as master of the Savoy: sermon by (?), v. 292 & n. 3.
Praxiteles: as sculptor of Horse-tamer on Quirinal, ii. 237, 405, n. 1; sculpture at Venice attributed to, ii. 460–1 & n.
Preaching and Sermons [select: ordinary comments on individual sermons, notably commendations or the reverse (admirable, elegant, eloquent, excellent, honest, incomparable, plain, weak, well [preached], are the most frequent; ample, apposite, choice, &c.), and notices of the more usual characteristics (pathetic, practical, profitable, useful, are the most frequent; Christian, converting, devout, &c.) are not indexed. A few notices relating to specifically Anglican preaching are indexed under Church of England: worship: preaching]:
— sermons: general notices: importance attached to, during Protectorate, iii. 160 & n. 5; in sermons: importance of, iii. 507; ~ profit of hearing, iii. 151; ~ danger of neglecting, iv. 355; ~ status of, in divine service, iii. 569; v. 603–4; ~ runners after: censured, iv. 288; v. 252, 612.
— style: general notices, &c.: Bishop Andrewes's, iv. 84, n. 2, 166 & n. 6; ~ compared with modern, iv. 330; modern, iv. 5; Sir W. Petty imitates various styles, iv. 59–60; the preacher's qualities, v. 223.
— delivery: action: in Italy, ii. 384; English preachers lack, ii. 233; v. 555; Burnet's, v. 619; Ken's, iv. 578; of other preachers, &c., iv. 59; v. 93, 223, 259.
— — dull, &c., v. 560; extemporary,

Preaching and Sermons (*cont.*)
iv. 47, n. 5, 164, n. 2; fast, v. 620; inaudible, iii. 149; v. 499, 505 (?), 588; Italian, ii. 384 & n. 3; *memoriter*, iv. 164, n. 2, 188 & n. 4; ~ out of use in England, 1704, v. 555; notes, &c., for: not used at all, iv. 188 & n. 4; v. 298, 500; ~ use of: interrupted by weather, iv. 161, n. 1.
— — reading of (from notes, &c.): as usual practice: *c.* 1659, iii. 160, n. 5; ~ 1702, 1704, v. 500, 555; as valid as other forms of delivery: in sermon, iv. 581 & n. 3; particular cases of, iii. 146; iv. 164 & n. 2; v. 68, 155, 207, 295, 593; ~ interrupted by weather, v. 554–5.
— — voice: loud, v. 117; ~ tested v. 27.
— character and contents of particular sermons [select: see note above]: allegorical, iv. 84; in blank verse, iii. 401 & n. 2; busy, iv. 558; Cabbalistic, iii. 630; catechistical, iv. 361; commonplaces in, iv. 197 & n. 4, 211; critical about words, iv. 130; curiosities, pretty, in, iii. 188; the preacher declaims, iv. 592; eucharistical, v. 579; extravagant, iii. 356; florid, iv. 560 *bis*, 568, 581; v. 207, 261, 277; historical, iv. 279, 357, 364, 374, 405; v. 21, 156.
— — learned, iii. 159, 227; iv. 165, 302, 389, 459, 537; v. 283, 520, 522, 542, 556, 564; learning now out of fashion, iv. 5; ostentation of learning, with much Greek, &c., iii. 186; full of Greek, iv. 375; full of Latin sentences, iv. 247, 330.
— — logical, iv. 126, 330; metaphysical, iv. 291; methodical, iv. 392; v. 303; neat, iv. 438, 539; v. 284; passionate, iii. 39; iv. 6; penitential, iv. 306, 502, 503; v. 14; philosophical, iv. 109, 592; v. 148, 386; philosophico-theological, iv. 389; poetical, v. 261; political: *see below*; quaint, iv. 370 & n. 2, 416, 539; rabbinical, iii. 66; repetition in, iii. 160 & n. 5; iv. 402; v. 259; rhetorical, iv. 132; v. 118, 149; scholastical, iv. 166; full of sentences, &c., iii. 549 & n. 3; sententious, iii. 239; witty, iv. 84.
— individual preachers: characterized [remarks on style, matter, &c.]: L. Andrewes, iv. 166 & n. 6, 330; G. Burnet, iv. 47–8 & n.; v. 619; Z. Cradock, iv. 196; J. Dolben, iv. 6, 193; J. Fell, iii. 401 & n. 2; iv. 106; R. Frampton, iii. 629; G. Higham, iii. 88, 143; R. Holden, iv. 5; Ken, iv. 543, 578; J. Prichett, iv. 84, 166; Sprat, iv. 167, 188; G. Stanhope, v. 223.
— — commended: R. Bathurst, iii. 401; S. Bolton, iii. 312; W. Clarke, iii. 605; R. Creighton, sen., iii. 624; J. Earles, iii. 39, 47, 346; P. Gunning, iv. 3–4; G. Hooper, iv. 260; A. Lucas, iv. 557; J. Sharp, iv. 364; Jeremy Taylor, iii. 148; Tenison, iv. 307, 650; G. Thistlethwaite, iii. 626.
— — censured: J. Crowther, iii. 19, 38; J. Duport, iii. 624; J. Meriton, iv. 180; E. Wolley, iii. 47.
— sectarian preaching: Sir W. Petty's imitations, iv. 59; the coventicle, iii. 167; enthusiastic, iii. 150; Independent, iii. 142; Presbyterian, iv. 402 & n. 3; v. 259; speculative matter in, iii. 184 & n. 2; the sectaries' fondness for the Canticles, iii. 184.
— sermons on political subjects: court sermons, iv. 35, 361, 499; loyal, iv. 446; politic, iv. 333; prerogative, iv. 192; theologo-political, iv. 381 & n. 2.
— miscellaneous: dubious views in sermons, v. 137, 162, 219, 303; duration of sermons: mentioned, iii. 159; iv. 197, 593; French protestant divines wear hats when preaching, ii. 527 & n. 5; *see also* i. 75; probation sermon, iii. 302; provisionary sermon, iii. 604; sermons for feoffees for charities: printed specimen, iii. 318, n. 3; sermons repeated [select; repetitions to the same congregations after a lapse of time (as by W. Strengfellow) are not indexed

Preaching and Sermons (*cont.*)
collectively]: sermons at court repeated elsewhere, v. 7, 43, n. 1(?), 52, n. 3; town sermons repeated in country, v. 283, 542; special comments: 'like a country parson', &c., iii. 111; 'of great and solid matter', &c., iv. 484; 'a vehement but hearty preacher', iii. 378; 'a very mean discourse for a bishop', iv. 85.

Prerogative Office: *see* Canterbury: cathedral clergy.

Presbyterians (English): origin of sect: story concerning, v. 13 & n. 1; formerly called Puritans, i. 18 & n. 1; at Amsterdam: service, &c., ii. 44 & n. 1 (i. 32); occupy parish churches, ii. 552; rejoice at proclamation against Anglican clergy, 1655, iii. 164; in Colchester, 1656, iii. 177, n. 3; in Gauden's project for reunion, iii. 187, n. 6; National Assemblies of: disappear, iii. 254 & n. 1; refuse to conform with Act of Uniformity, 1662, iii. 331 & n. 4; participate in address to James II, iv. 553; Presbyterian as lord mayor of London (Sir J. Shorter), iv. 562, n. 4; appointed to Privy Council, iv. 590 & n. 4; displeased at vote of parliament to maintain Church as established, &c., iv. 631 & n. 4; advocate new Oath of Allegiance to William and Mary, iv. 637.
'Presbyterian animosity' (of G. Kendal), iii. 105; church discipline: in comparison, ii. 527; extemporary prayers, iii. 144; ~ in sermon, iii. 440; preaching: content of, iii. 184; ~ style of, iv. 402 & n. 3; v. 259; *see also* iv. 59; signs required by: in sermon, iv. 84; views on election: sermons against, iv. 282; v. 118; *see also* v. 116, 117.
individuals: Sir H. Ashurst, &c., v. 88, nn. 1, 2; Dr. E. Calamy, iv. 229 & n. 2; Rev. T. Malory: Presbyterian leanings of, iii. 185; *see also* iii. 80–1 & n., 184; Dr. T. Manton, iii. 213.

Presbyterians (Scottish): church discipline of: in comparison, ii. 527; hate the Stuarts, the Church of England, &c., v. 12.

Preston, Lancs.: battle of, iii. 178 & n. 1; ~ Sir L. Dyve captured in, iii. 40, n. 1.

Preston, Elizabeth: *see* Butler, Elizabeth, duchess of Ormond.

Preston, Richard, earl of Desmond: geneal., iii. 76, n. 1.

Preston, Thomas, first Viscount Tara: commander in Spanish service, ii. 35, n. 5.

Preston: Viscount, 1681–95 (Scotland): *see* Graham, Sir Richard.

Preston, in Amoundernesse: Viscount (Jacobite creation): *see* Graham, Sir Richard, Viscount Preston.

Preston Beckhelvyn: manor of: *see* Beddingham.

Prettyman, Dorothy: *see* Farrington, Mrs. D.

Prettyman, Elizabeth, daughter of Sir John, sen.: *see* Browne, Elizabeth, Lady Browne.

Prettyman, Elizabeth, daughter of Sir John, bt.: *see* Burton, Elizabeth, Lady Burton.

Prettyman, Elizabeth, Lady Prettyman, wife of Sir John, bt., iii. 73, n. 3.

Prettyman, Mrs. Elizabeth, wife of William Prettyman, ii. 538, n. 1; married, iii. 77 & n. 3; godmother of Elizabeth Evelyn, iii. 495 & n. 4; geneal., iii. 287, n. 3.

Prettyman, Sir John, sen.: house of, at Driffield, iii. 117 & n. 4; geneal., ii. 535, n. 3.

Prettyman, Sir John; baronet 1660, iii. 73, n. 3; sells Driffield, iii. 117 & n. 4; estate of, at Horninghold, iii. 121, n. 8; ~ visit to, at, iii. 121, 123; *see also* iii. 133, 134; owns Loddington rectory, iii. 133, n. 5; godfather of J. S. Evelyn, iii. 89; social, iii. 73; geneal., iii. 89, n. 5, 184, n. 6, 491, n. 6; iv. 382, n. 3, 461, n. 1; mentioned, ii. 538, n. 1.

Prettyman, Mary: *see* Verney, Mrs. M.

Prettyman, Mary, Lady Prettyman, wife of Sir John, sen., ii. 535, n. 3.

Prettyman, Mary: baptized, iii. 166 & n. 4.

Prettyman, Susan: *see* Hungerford, Mrs. S.

Prettyman, William, ii. 538, n. 1; executor for Christopher Browne, &c., ii. 537, n. 6 *ad fin.*;

Prettyman, William (*cont.*)
in charge of Sayes Court, 1647, &c., *ib.*; ii. 538; in treaty to buy Sayes Court, *c.* 1650, iii. 59, n. 1; visits France, 1648–9, ii. 543 & n. 3, 551; robbed at sea, ii. 551; joins with E in bond, iii. 75; marries, iii. 77 & n. 3; godfather of John Evelyn, jnr., iii. 147; leaves Sayes Court, iii. 149 & n. 4; daughter of: baptized, iii. 166 & n. 4; grand account of, with E, 1656, iii. 170–1 & n.; as executor for George Tuke, iii. 491, n. 7; as deputy for Remembrancer of First Fruits, iii. 567, n. 1.
litigation with E, 1683–7 [the notices indexed below presumably all refer to this case; Prettyman is named only occasionally]: proceeds against E and Mrs. Evelyn for payment of claims against Sir R. Browne, iv. 339–40; Chancery proceedings, &c., on this issue: 1683, iv. 340, 344; 1684, iv. 361, 389, 393, 395, 398; 1685, iv. 402, 438, 480; 1686, iv. 500 & nn. 4, 5; 1687, iv. 546 & nn. 2, 3, 547, 548; in connexion with these proceedings the Evelyns in 1684 petitioned the king for settlement of his debt to Sir R. Browne: the petition, iv. 394 & n. 3; ~ business relating to, iv. 398 *bis*, 440; ~ settlement, 1686, iv. 516; ~ further business, iv. 529, 547; settlement of Chancery proceedings and of petition business, 1687, iv. 551 & n. 1, 555; agreement between Prettyman and E, 1687, iv. 550; ~ and Sir C. Porter, iv. 556 & n. 1; ~ business relating to, 1690, v. 33 & n. 1.
letter from: mentioned, iii. 103.
Price, Henrietta Maria: maid of honour to Queen Catherine, iii. 621, n. 5.
Price, Sir Herbert, bt.: in Charles II's coronation procession, iii. 280 & n. 1.
Prichard *or* Pritchard, Sir William, lord mayor 1682–3: offers submission of the City on *Quo Warranto* proceedings, iv. 319 & n. 1; reappointed lord mayor by commission, iv. 342, n. 6.
Prichett *or* Pritchett (Pritchard), John, D.D.; bishop of Gloucester 1672, iv. 84, n. 2; as preacher: style, iv. 84, 166 & n. 6; sermons by, *ib.*
Pride, Col. Thomas: corpse of, ordered to be exhumed, iii. 269, n. 2.
Pride's Purge, ii. 545 & n. 6.
Prideaux, —: trustee of Clifford (?), iv. 21 & n. 3.
Prideaux, Humphrey, servant: ill and dies, iv. 357 *bis* & nn. 1, 2; alluded to (?), iv. 464.
Prideaux, Humphrey; D.D. 1686; dean of Norwich 1702: presents copy of *Marmora Oxoniensia* to sixth duke of Norfolk, iv. 89 & n. 2.
Prieur, B.: statue by, ii. 118 & n. 9 (i. 77).
Primaticcio, Francesco, ii. 113, n. 6; paintings by, ii. 113 (i. 73); ~ at Fontainebleau, ii. 117 & n. 3 (i. 76).
Prince de la Grange: in Lincoln's Inn revels, iii. 307–8 & nn.
Prince Elector: nick-name given to Lord Bath, 1685, iv. 444.
Printing [for licensing of the press *see* Publishing and Bookselling; for newspaper history *see* Newspapers]:
presses: Aldine: books printed by, iv. 330 & n. 5; Basel: editions of Fathers printed at, iv. 145 & n. 1; Elzevier, ii. 52 & n. 6 (i. 36); Geneva: book-trade and printing at, ii. 524 & n. 5; Haarlem: printing invented at, &c., ii. 51 (i. 36), 54 & n. 2 (i. 37); H. Hondius, Amsterdam (engraving?), i. 35; Imprimerie royale, Paris, ii. 104 & n. 5 (i. 68); King's Printer, London, 1686: licence to, iv. 504 & n. 1; Oxford University Press, iii. 531 & n. 1; Plantin, ii. 67 & n. 2 (i. 45).
miscellaneous: early printed books, iv. 144–5 & n.; v. 322; printed tickets: describing stolen property, iii. 70, 71; ~ for persons to be touched for King's Evil, iv. 374; printing-press on Thames, frost-fair, 1684, iv. 362 & n. 2; correction of the press, iii. 173 & n. 2; varieties of type, iii. 206 & n. 3.

Pristina: battle near, 1690, v. 6 & n. 5.
Privateers: *see* Pirates and Privateers.
Privy Council:
— notices relating to general history of: sworn in on James II's accession, iv. 412 & n. 2; Nonconformists, &c., appointed councillors, iv. 590 & n. 4; protestant councillors refuse to sit in, with Roman Catholics, iv. 602–3 & n.; James II holds, 16 Dec. 1688, iv. 610–11 & n.; new council appointed, 1689, iv. 627 & n. 2; republican spirit of, iv. 635 & n. 3.
— proceedings and orders:
— — royal declarations in, &c.: Charles II announces his intended marriage to, iii. 286 & n. 6; Charles II announces adoption of new fashion to, iii. 465, n. 1; proposed marriage of William of Orange and Lady Mary (later William III and Mary II) announced to, iv. 122, n. 4; attests Charles II's declaration about his marriage, iv. 457 & n. 7; attends submission of London corporation on *Quo Warranto* proceedings, iv. 319; James II's declaration to, on his accession, iv. 411–12 & n.; attends meeting to authenticate birth of James Edward, iv. 602–3 & nn.; members of, invited to attend Queen Mary of Modena's delivery, 1692, v. 96 & n. 1.
— — king present in (apart from notices in preceding section; positive statements only), iii. 387–8 & n., 400, 411–12 & n., 419(?), 442–3 & n., 461 & n. 5, 473 & n. 3, 485–6 & n.; iv. 365, 466, 471, 499 & n. 7, 584, n. 1.
— — examinations by: prisoners taken in Venner's revolt, iii. 266 & n. 5; Titus Oates, iv. 153, n. 3, 158, n. 5, 231, n. 2; William Howard, Baron Howard of Escrick, iv. 322, n. 7; Seven Bishops, iv. 586; *see also* iv. 603–4 & n. (Captain H. Lanham before Cabinet Council).
— — orders, &c., relating to Commissioners for Sick and Wounded, &c.: appointment of, instructions for, &c., 1664, iii. 387–8 & nn., 391 & n. 2; letters on behalf of, iii. 391 & n. 4, 395; order to E, iii. 614; and money for, iii. 409–10 & n., 411–12 & n., 412, 419, 431 & nn. 4, 5, 432, n. 7; for release of prisoners of war, iii. 492 & n. 4; E presents his account to members of Council, iv. 248.
— — orders, &c., relating to E: nominates E a commissioner for saltpetre, iii. 442–3 & n.; orders E to search for fuel for London, &c., iii. 485–6 & n., 487; E has business with, &c., iii. 400; iv. 178, 644–5 & n.
— — miscellaneous orders of: for providing for refugees from Fire of London, iii. 461 & n. 5; for Stop of the Exchequer, iii. 607, n. 1; for proclaiming James II's accession, iv. 412; for baptism of negroes in Plantations (?), iv. 471 & n. 3; for commemorating James II's accession, iv. 499 & n. 7; for reading Declaration of Indulgence in churches, 1688, iv. 584, n. 1; ~ irregularities in, iv. 585 & n. 3; minor orders, iii. 390, n. 2, 435, n. 1, 445, n. 6, 486, n. 1; iv. 487, n. 3; v. 30, n. 3.
— — miscellaneous proceedings, &c.: petitions to: from Canary merchants, iii. 388 & n. 5; ~ for poor of Deptford, iv. 365; report to, iii. 631, n. 4; views of, on origin of Fire of London, iii. 457, n. 4; hears counsel on will of J. Bodvile, iii. 473 & n. 3; James II consults, about disposal of Great Seal, 1685, iv. 466; mentioned, iv. 77; and opening of prize-ship, v. 522 & n. 1.
— meeting-places: on board ship, at the Nore (possibly councils of the fleet rather than Privy Council), iii. 414, 441; Hampton Court, iii. 414, n. 10 *ad fin.*; iv. 177–8, 248, 644–5 & n.; ~ council-chamber at, iv. 553; Syon House, iii. 414–15 & n.; Whitehall: meetings at are not indexed collectively; ~ council-chamber at: *see* Whitehall: structure; Windsor Castle, iv.

Privy Council (*cont.*)
319, 466; ~ council-chamber at, iv. 319.
— committees, &c.: Cabinet Council (misnomer?): examines Captain H. Lanham, iv. 603–4 & n.; ~ Godolphin made a member of, v. 438 & n. 2; committees: for Admiralty, 1673–9, iv. 377, n. 3; of Foreign Affairs: announcement to, by king (?), iii. 465, n. 1; ~ proposal to re-admit James, duke of York, to, iv. 323, n. 6; for inspection of Justices of the Peace, 1686, iv. 536, n. 3; Lords of Trade, 1675– , iv. 50, n. 4; ~ secretary of: *see* Blathwayt, W. (iv. 554–5 & n.).
— members: form of councillor's oath, iii. 578; individual members [for the Lords Presidents of the Council *see* England: officers; other members are not indexed collectively (list mentioned, i. *124*), apart from the following, whose membership is specifically mentioned or alluded to in text or notes]: Sir T. Chicheley, iii. 442 & n. 9; Clifford, iii. 526 & n. 8; iv. 19 & n. 3; Sir J. Duncombe, iii. 442 & n. 8; Arthur Capel, earl of Essex: dismissed, iv. 201, n. 7; Godolphin: appointed, Mar. 1679 (error), iv. 166 & n. 2; ~ 1700, v. 438 & n. 2; William Douglas, third duke of Hamilton, iv. 603, n. 3; James, duke of York: rejoins, iv. 323, n. 6; Sir George Jeffreys, Baron Jeffreys, iv. 342, n. 3; Charles Middleton, earl of Middleton, iv. 387, n. 5 *ad fin.*; Col. S. Titus, Sir J. Trevor, and C. Vane (later Baron Barnard), iv. 590 & n. 4.
— — Clerks of the Council: lodgings of, in Whitehall, iii. 572, n. 1; individual clerks: *see* Blathwayt, W. (1686–1717); Bridgeman, W. (1685–8, 1692–9); Browne, Sir Richard (1660?–72); Lane, Sir George, Viscount Lanesborough (1660–4?); Nicholas, Sir J. (1660–1705); Southwell, Sir R. (1665–79); Williamson, Sir J. (1672–4; succession to office, iii. 601 & n. 1).

Processions [*see also* Ceremonies; Popular Celebrations]:
— diplomatic: London: state-entries of foreign ambassadors, iii. 297, n. 4; ~ regulated, iii. 352 & n. 3; individual state-entries, iii. 256 & n. 1, 344 & n. 5, 515 & n. 1; iv. 169 & n. 3; v. 238 & n. 1, 285 & n. 3; processions to Whitehall for first audiences, iii. 513; iv. 492; *see also* iv. 262.
— — Paris: ambassador's entry, ii. 90–1 (i. 61); Rome: ambassadors' entries, ii. 389 & n. 4, 391 & n. 2.
— political, &c.: (i) occasional [all in London, unless other places are named]:
— — — 1640: Charles I opens Short Parliament, ii. 23–4 & n. (i. 17); Charles I returns from north, ii. 25 (i. 19).
— — — 1641: Dordrecht: reception of Marie de Médicis, ii. 57 (i. 39); Charles I returns from Scotland, ii. 77 (i. 51).
— — — 1644: Rome: *possesso* of Innocent X, ii. 279–82 & nn.; *see also* ii. 206, 227, n. 1, 228 & n. 6; ~ route of, ii. 369 & n. 4.
— — — 1645: Rome: Cardinal G. C. de' Medici rides to Vatican, ii. 389 & n. 4.
— — — 1651: Paris: majority of Louis XIV, iii. 41–3 & nn.
— — — 1652: Ireton's funeral, iii. 57–8 & nn.
— — — 1654: Ash Wednesday: Cromwell to feast with Lord Mayor, iii. 93.
— — — 1658: Cromwell's funeral, iii. 224 & nn. 1–4.
— — — 1660: Charles II returns to Whitehall, ii. 246 & n. 2; Charles II goes to City feast, iii. 250 & n. 2.
— — — 1661: Charles II rides from Tower to Whitehall, iii. 278–81 & nn.; *see also* iii. 276–7; Charles II goes from Westminster Hall to Abbey, &c., iii. 281, n. 3, 284 & nn. 2, 3; Charles II rides to open parliament, iii. 286 & n. 5.
— — — 1662: Queen Catherine comes by water to Whitehall, iii. 333 & n. 2; *see also* iii. 322, n. 2.

Processions (*cont.*)
— — — 1685: proclamation of James II as king, iv. 412–13.
— — — 1689: coronation of William and Mary, iv. 632.
— — — 1695: funeral of Queen Mary, v. 204 & n. 6; *see also* v. 201, 205.
— — — 1697: William III returns to London after Peace of Ryswick, v. 273; *see also* v. 267, 269.
— — — 1699: Vienna: entry of Queen of the Romans, v. 317 & n. 3.
— — — 1702: thanksgiving for Vigo, &c., v. 521 & n. 6.
— — — 1704: thanksgiving for Blenheim, v. 578–9 & nn.
— — (ii) recurrent (annual, &c.; including civic processions):
— — — Florence: St. John's day, ii. 193 & n. 1 (i. 119), 199, n. 4.
— — — Ghent: annual humiliation (?), ii. 73 & n. 8 (i. 48).
— — — London: Lord Mayor's Shows, iii. 259 & n. 4, 341–2 & nn., 388 & n. 6; iv. 528 & n. 5; ~ by water, iii. 301 & n. 4.
— — — Orleans: commemoration of relief, ii. 137 & n. 4 (i. 90).
— — — Rome: civic: New Year's day, ii. 291 & n. 5; ~ St. George's day, ii. 387 & n. 1; Sapienza, ii. 387 & n. 3.
— — — Venice: Marriage with the Sea, ii. 431–2 & nn.; *add.*; *see also* ii. 401 & n. 8, 458; iii. 333.
— religious: Lerici, ii. 179 (i. 113); London: to Spital sermon, v. 398–9 & n.; Naples: Candlemas, ii. 331 & n. 8; Padua: to S. Antonio, ii. 453–4 & n., 455 & n. 4; Paris: Corpus Christi (or octave), ii. 536 & n. 3; iii. 35; Rome: Epiphany, ii. 291 & n. 7; ~ Good Friday (*Battuti*), ii. 386 & n. 3; ~ Lady Day, ii. 377–8 & n., 384 & n. 4; ~ Palm Sunday, ii. 385; Rouen: St. Romain, ii. 123 (i. 79); Tours: Corpus Christi, ii. 146 (i. 94–5).
Procida: in views, ii. 329, 334.
Proclamations [proclamations and similar utterances of the English kings or governments, and of claimants to the crown, &c. (including some pieces not recognized by Steele). Those for fasts or thanksgivings, unless mentioned by E, and those cited only as authorities for statements in the notes, are not indexed. The issuer's name is given if it is not the king, the Privy Council, or the central government]:
1649: act for abolishing kingship: proclaimed by lord mayor of London, ii. 555 & n. 6.
1652: forbidding observation of Christmas, iii. 79, n. 1, 145, n. 1.
1655: forbidding royalists to maintain ejected clergy, &c., iii. 163 & n. 1, 164.
1660: Charles II proclaimed king, 6 May, iii. 244; order by house of lords for return of king's goods, 12 May, iii. 249 & n. 2; for surrender of regicides, 6 June, iii. 312, n. 1; peace with Spain, 10/20 Sept., iii. 257, n. 2.
1664: encouraging seamen, iii. 387, n. 5.
1666: for relief of sufferers in Fire of London, and for London markets, 5 and 6 Sept., iii. 461 & n. 5, 462 & n. 2.
1667: peace with United Provinces, iii. 492 & n. 5.
1671: on Sir C. Wheeler's conduct in Leeward Islands: drafting of, iii. 598 *bis* & n. 2.
1672: Declaration of Indulgence, i. *26*; iii. 607–8 & n.
1678: for discovery of murderers of Sir E. B. Godfrey, 20 and 24 Oct., iv. 155, n. 3; restricting residence of Roman Catholics, &c., 30 Oct., 10 Nov., iv. 159, nn. 2, 3.
1679: forbidding tumultuous petitions, iv. 193, n. 1.
1680: *His Majesties Declaration* (concerning Charles II's marriage), iv. 457, n. 7.
1683: for arrest of Rye-House conspirators, 23 and 28 June, iv. 322, n. 1, 323 & n. 1, 350.
1685: accession of James II, 6 Feb.: proclaimed in London, iv. 412–13 & nn.; ~ proclaimed at Bromley, iv. 414–15; office-holders to retain their offices, 6 Feb., iv. 412; collection of customs to continue, &c.,

Proclamations (*cont.*)
9 Feb., iv. 417, n. 6 *ad fin.*, 419, n. 2; Earl Marshal's instructions for mourning, 9 Feb.: alluded to, iv. 414 & n. 3; on validity of farm of the Excise, 16 (17) Feb.: alluded to, iv. 417 & n. 6; Monmouth: declaration by, 11 June, iv. 449 & nn. 1, 3; declaring Monmouth a traitor, 13 June, iv. 449 & n. 1; for killing or taking Monmouth, 16 June, iv. 449 & n. 3, 453; Monmouth: proclaimed king, at Taunton, 20 June, iv. 449, n. 1.
1686: protecting New River Company, iv. 515, n. 4.
1687: Declaration of Indulgence, iv. 546 & n. 5; ~ addresses of thanks for, iv. 553–4 & nn., 560 & n. 1.
1688: Declaration of Indulgence: reissued, &c., 27 Apr., iv. 584, n. 1, 585 & nn. 2, 3; ~ Seven Bishops protest against order for reading, iv. 583–4 & n.; ~ read at Whitehall, &c., iv. 584 & nn. 2, 4; ~ inquiry into reading of, iv. 590, n. 3; ~ Bishop Sprat on clergy not reading, iv. 596; relating to Seven Bishops: expected, 25 May, iv. 585 & n. 4; reasons for summoning parliament, 21 Sept., iv. 597 & n. 4; recalling writs for summoning parliament, 28 Sept., iv. 598, n. 5; pardon, 2 Oct., iv. 601 & n. 3; William of Orange: declarations by, 10 and 24 Oct., N.S., iv. 604, 606 & n. 2; forbidding reading William of Orange's declarations, 2 Nov., iv. 606 & n. 2; reply to William's declarations, 6 Nov., iv. 606, n. 2; pardon, 22 Nov., iv. 608 & n. 5; William of Orange: spurious declaration, 28 Nov., iv. 609 & n. 3.
1689: order by house of lords for not observing day of James II's accession, 2 Feb., iv. 621 & n. 2; William and Mary proclaimed king and queen, 13 Feb., iv. 623 & n. 4; James II: offer of pardon by, 8 May, iv. 642 & n. 5; appointing commissioners for poll-tax, 13 May, iv. 639, n. 3 *ad fin.*; against men distri-

Proclamations (*cont.*)
buting James II's offer of pardon, 24 June, iv. 642, n. 5.
1690: for capture of Sir J. Johnston, &c., v. 41, n. 1.
1691: for apprehending Jacobite conspirators, v. 42, nn. 4, 5; against Roman Catholics, 9 Apr., v. 47 & n. 4.
1692: James II: declaration by, 20 Apr., N.S.: alluded to, v. 141 & n. 2; for apprehending Jacobites, 9 May, v. 100 & n. 1.
1693: James II: declaration by, v. 140 & n. 2, 141.
1694: for arrest of Col. J. Parker, v. 188 & n. 5.
1695: terminating circulation of clipped crowns, &c., v. 228 & n. 3.
1696: for arrest of Assassination Plot conspirators, 23 Feb.: alluded to, v. 232 & n. 1; requiring Roman Catholics to leave London, 25 Feb., v. 232 & n. 3.
1697: Peace of Ryswick, 19 Oct., v. 269 & n. 2; for apprehending Jacobites, 11 Nov., v. 273 & n. 3.
1698: against immorality and profanity, v. 327–8 & n., 391 & n. 1.
1699: for collection for French protestant refugees, 12 Mar., v. 321, n. 2; against immorality, &c. (1698): reissued, 9 Dec., v. 391, n. 1.
1701: for enlisting seamen, v. 449, n. 1; James Edward: proclaimed king, St.-Germain, v. 476 & n. 3.
1702: accession of Queen Anne, 8 Mar. &c., v. 493 & n. 3; Earl Marshal's instructions for mourning, 9 Mar., v. 493 & n. 1; against immorality, 26 Mar., v. 495 & n. 4; orders for coronation, 29 Mar., v. 495 & n. 6; war declared, 4 May, v. 500 & n. 4, 504; for fast, 15 May, v. 504 & n. 2; for thanksgiving for Vigo, v. 519 & n. 2.
For summoning, proroguing, or dissolving parliament: 1679, iv. 163, n. 1, 193, n. 1; 1687, iv. 544, n. 2; 1688: *see* 1688 *above*; 1690, v. 5 & n. 4; 1693, v. 153, n. 1; 1695, v. 221, n. 6; 1700, v. 439, n. 3; 1701, v. 481, n. 1; 1702, v. 511, n. 1.

Procop: *see* Perekop.
Promenade: London: *see* England: social; Milan, ii. 503; Naples, ii. 327 & n. 3; Paris, ii. 106–7 (i. 69), 130 (i. 83); Rome, ii. 217; Tours, i. 94; Venice, ii. 433 & n. 3, 468; Vicenza, ii. 484.
Prophecies [*see also* Sibyls]:
duration of the world, Second Coming, the last times, &c.: Lactantius on: in sermons, v. 448 & n. 1, 613 & n. 1; Bishop W. Lloyd on, iv. 636–7 & n.; v. 20–1, 25–6, 321–2; ~ mentioned, v. 32; J. Mason on, v. 177–8 & n.; Oughtred on, iii. 158 & nn. 3, 4; in various sermons, iv. 163, 271, 308; ~ minor reports, iii. 37, 47, 238, 541, 580; iv. 157, 260, 357.
messianic: views of a Jew, 1641, ii. 54–5 & n. (i. 37–8); in sermons, iii. 238, 630; iv. 652–3.
various: P. Grebner: on Charles I, &c., iii. 137 & n. 2; Nostradamus: alarm caused by, 1697, v. 273 & n. 2; Ussher: on overthrow of protestantism, iii. 157 & n. 2; iv. 487 & n. 1.
Prosdocimus, St.: tomb of, ii. 456 & n. 6.
Protestant Duke: appellation given to Monmouth, iv. 189 & n. 6.
Protestant Plot: Rye-House Plot called the, iv. 321; *see also* iv. 331.
Protestants and Protestantism [general; for the national churches and the various sects see under their own names]:
iconoclasm of: Amsterdam and Geneva escape, ii. 49 & n. 1 (i. 34), 528; in France, ii. 126, 137, n. 1, 147 & n. 6; in England: *see* Church of England: buildings.
protestant interest in Europe: French desire to weaken, 1664, iii. 405 & n. 1; threatened by France, 1684, 1686, iv. 380, 524–5; Charles II neglects, iv. 478.
protestantism: in Europe: French plans to extirpate, iv. 487, 511; ~ neglected in Peace of Ryswick, v. 270–1 & nn.; ~ security of: recommended to parliament, 1701, v. 445; ~ fast for, v. 452 & n. 4, 453; in England: Sunderland's indifference to preserving, iv. 245; ~ declarations for, 1688, iv. 609; protestants: divisions among: in sermon, v. 513; should be passive under persecution: in sermon, iv. 578; in Hungary: persecution of, 1703, v. 553; at Lucca: refugees from, at Geneva, ii. 523 & n. 5; *see also* ii. 410, n. 2, 521, n. 1; at Milan: hostility to (travellers, &c.), ii. 491, 503, 505.
Provence: vegetation in, ii. 162 & n. 10, 163 (i. 103 *bis*).
Provence: Counts of: palace of, ii. 163 & n. 3 (i. 103).
Proverbs and Mottoes: Amor ardens cogit ad impossibile, iv. 104; Decus & tutamen, iii. 335, n. 2; Fac similiter, iii. 390; Non Marte opus est, cui non deficit Mercurius, ii. 84 & n. 3 (i. 57); Nosce teipsum, v. 49; Ratio ultima regum, ii. 125 & n. 4 (i. 80); Rosa inter spinas, v. 13.
Provoste *or* Provote, Rev. John: sermon by (?), v. 374–5 & n.
Prowse, Rev. Edward: sermon by, ii. 20 & n. 2.
Prowse, Richard, agent for Clifford: questioned about Clifford's death (?), iv. 21 & n. 3.
Prozorovsky, Prince Peter, and Ivan Jeliabouisky, Russian ambassadors to England 1662–3: entry, iii. 344 & n. 5; audience to, iii. 349 & n. 1; London residence of, iii. 349 & n. 2; take leave, iii. 356 & n. 7; pelicans given by, to Charles II, iii. 398–9 & n.; mentioned, iv. 262.
Prujean, Sir Francis, M.D.: collections, &c., of, iii. 294 & nn. 5–7.
Prussia: amber found in, v. 147.
Prynne, William: attacks Cosin's *Collection of private devotions*, iii. 45 & nn. 2, 3, 46, n. 3; *see also* iii. 635.
Psalms: distinguished from hymns: in sermon, iii. 367.
Psammetichus III, king of Egypt, ii. 374, n. 10 *ad fin*.
Publishing and Bookselling [*see also* Newspapers *and* Printing]:
booksellers: at: Amsterdam (map-engravers?), ii. 49 & nn. 3, 4 (i. 34–5); London: losses of, in Great Fire, iii. 459 & n. 3; ~

Publishing and Bookselling (*cont.*)
in St. Paul's Churchyard, *c.* 1683, iv. 301 & n. 2; Paris, ii. 94 (i. 62), 98; Rotterdam: at fair, i. 29.
licensing and suppression of books: Licensing Acts, i. *103–4*; ~ act of 1662; expires, &c., iv. 172 & n. 3; ~ act of 1685, iv. 508, n. 1; bishop of London's *imprimatur*, iii. 46, 635; licences for printing Roman Catholic books, iv. 503–4, 512 & n. 1; control breaks down: 1641, ii. 25 & n. 3 (i. 18); ~ 1688, iv. 609 & n. 5; author imprisoned for book, iii. 521 & n. 1; book called in, &c., iv. 41 & n. 1; impression seized, &c., iv. 507–8 & n.; books burnt, iv. 510–11 & n.; v. 131 & n. 2, 376 & n. 4.
difficulties in getting book published (Chardin), iv. 369 & n. 1.
Puckering, Elizabeth, Lady Puckering, previously (until 1654) Newton, wife of Sir Henry, iii. 87, n. 1; as Lady Newton: goes to live at Warwick, iii. 182 & n. 6; ~ social, iii. 87, 94, 145, 169; as Lady Puckering: social, iii. 227, 253.
Puckering, Sir Henry, bt., previously (until 1654) Newton, iii. 66, n. 4; as Newton: owns Charlton House, iii. 66; ~ sells Charlton, iii. 377; as Puckering: at Warwick Priory, iii. 120 & n. 5; as Newton: goes to live at Warwick, iii. 182 & n. 6; ~ social, iii. 85, 159, 290 *bis*; geneal., iii. 87, n. 2.
Pulton, Father Andrew: controversy of, with Tenison, iv. 540, n. 1.
Pulzone, Scipione, called Gaetano, ii. 233, n. 3; paintings by, ii. 233, 274 & n. 8.
Punishments: *see* Justice: administration of; England: justice.
Punta dell' Epitaffio, near Baia: site of Bauli (?), ii. 349, n. 4.
Punteus, J., mountebank, iii. 293 & n. 4.
Purbeck, Isle of, Dorset: stone from (?), i. 81.
Purcell (Pursal), Henry: compositions by, v. 289 & n. 2.
Purford: *see* Pyrford.
Purgatory: gates of (Solfatara), ii. 342 & n. 4; in sermons, iii. 235; iv. 577; v. 130, 306.
Purim, Feast of: in sermon, v. 362.
Puritans: *see* Nonconformists, Puritans, and Sectaries.
Puttenham, Surrey: Rev. W. Wells proposed for minister of, v. 199 & n. 5.
Puzzles: rebuses and anagrams, iv. 300; letter in rebuses, &c., i. 26.
Puzzolo: *see* Pozzuoli.
Pye, Sir Robert: owns Faringdon House, iii. 111, n. 3.
Pye, Walter, Baron Kilpeck (Jacobite peerage): geneal., ii. 558, n. 3.
Pye, Sir Walter, ii. 558, n. 3; house belonging to (?), iii. 111 & n. 3; social, ii. 558.
Pyrenees mountains: the Pyrenean Christians as one of the Two Witnesses, iv. 636–7 & n.
Pyrford (Purford), Surrey: seat of Denzil Onslow at, iv. 255 & nn. 2–5; Parkhurst family of, ii. 542, n. 3; iii. 183, n. 1.
Pythagoras: in sermons, iv. 242; v. 435.

Quakers: notice, 1656, iii. 179 & n. 2; at Colchester, iii. 177, n. 3; Family of Love as a kind of, iv. 554; sermon, &c., against, iv. 402; v. 511; a Quaker interrupts preacher at Ashtead, iii. 220; Quaker fasting at Colchester: *see* Parnell, J.; *see also* Penn, W.
Quarterman, William, M.D.: social, iii. 442 & n. 7.
Queenborough (Quinborow), Kent: E visits, iii. 436, 620.
Queen Mary's Psalter (MS.), iv. 215 & n. 1.
Queensberry: third Earl, later Marquis and first Duke of: *see* Douglas, William.
Quellin, Arnold: sculpture by, iv. 534, n. 1.
Quercia, Jacopo della, sculptor: Fonte Gaia by, ii. 203 & nn. 2, 3.
Quidenham, Norfolk: Sir J. Holland at, iii. 463, n. 9.
Quierwill *or* Quirreval: *see* Kéroualle.
Quin, James: social, v. 170 & n. 3; *add.*
Quin, Mark: suicide of, v. 170 & n. 3.
Quintine the blacksmith: *see* Massys, Q.

Radcliffe *or* Ratcliffe, —: *see* Radcliffe, T.
Radcliffe, Anne, Lady Radcliffe, wife of Sir George, iii. 92, n. 1; in London, 1654, iii. 92; geneal., ii. 564, n. 6.
Radcliffe (Ratcliffe), Sir George, ii. 564 & n. 6; in Paris, &c., 1649–51, ii. 564, 567; iii. 2 & n. 1, 36 & n. 4, 43; letter of condolence from, iii. 77; geneal., iii. 12, n. 1, 63, 92, n. 1.
Radcliffe (Ratcliffe), Thomas, iii. 12, n. 1; witnesses E's will, Paris, 1650(?), iii. 12; in Paris, 1650–1 (?), iii. 19, 24, 47; in London, 1652–3, iii. 63, 91(?).
Radcliffe, Thomas, third earl of Sussex: as owner of New Hall, Essex, iii. 179–80 & n.
Radford, Thomas: in Albemarle inheritance dispute, v. 411, n. 1.
Radicofani: notice, ii. 207–9 & nn.; E passes through, ii. 407.
Radnor: Earls, &c., of: *see* Robartes, John, first earl 1679–85; Robartes, Isabella, his countess; Robartes, Sarah, styled countess.
Radnorshire: in view, iii. 119.
Radziejowski, Michael Stefan, cardinal, v. 288, n. 5; in Polish disputes, v. 288 & n. 5, 577 & n. 6.
Ragni, Charles-Nicolas de Créquy, marquis de: as Marquis Arignie: envoy from Louis XIV to Charles II, iii. 575 & n. 5; *add.*
Ragotski: *see* Rákóczy.
Rainbowe, Edward, D.D.; bishop of Carlisle 1664, iii. 262, n. 1; sermons by, iii. 262, 304, 609; chaplain of: sermon by, iv. 64.
Rákóczi, Sigismond: geneal., ii. 34, n. 1.
Rákóczy (Ragotski), Count Franz: rebellion of, v. 553; *add.*
Raleigh, Carew, iii. 219, n. 5; as owner of: East Horsley (Bishop's manor), ii. 551, n. 9; iii. 87, n. 6; ~ West Horsley, ii. 545, n. 5; social, iii. 219 *bis*.
Raleigh, Elizabeth, Lady Raleigh, wife of Sir Walter: geneal., i. 9, n. 2.
Raleigh, Sir Walter: as owner of East Horsley (error), iii. 87 & n. 6; cordial of: preparation of, iii. 336 & n. 4; geneal., i. 9, n. 2; iii. 219.
Ramenghi, B. (Bagnacavallo): paintings by, ii. 423, n. 7 *ad fin.*
Rameses, king of Egypt: obelisk dedicated to, ii. 269 & n. 8.
Rameses II, king of Egypt: inscription of, ii. 374, n. 10 *ad fin.*
Rammekins, fort, in Zeeland, i. 23 & n. 4.
Ramsbury, Wilts.: earl of Pembroke's house at, iii. 100 & n. 5; *see also* iii. 99, n. 4.
Ramsgate, Kent: Peterborough in custody at, 1688, iv. 611, n. 4.
Rand, Mrs. Frances, wife of Ralph Rand, M.D.: geneal., ii. 14, n. 3.
Rand, Rev. James: geneal., ii. 14, n. 3.
Rand, Ralph, M.D.: attends Mrs. Eleanor Evelyn (?), ii. 14 & n. 3 (i. 11).
Rand, Dr. Ralph, rector of Gatton: geneal., ii. 14, n. 3.
Rand, Dr. William: dedicates translation of Gassendi's *Life of Peiresc* to E, iii. 189 & nn. 5, 6; geneal., ii. 14, n. 3.
Ranelagh: Viscounts, &c.: *see* Jones, Arthur, second viscount; Jones, Katherine, his viscountess; Jones, Richard, third viscount and earl of; Jones, Elizabeth, his countess.
Raphael, ii. 113, n. 7; tomb of, ii. 372 & n. 10; self-portrait of (?), ii. 313 & n. 5.
paintings by: (i) places and collections containing (in E's time; including school and spurious works): Bologna, ii. 423–4 & nn.; Florence, Uffizi, ii. 190 & n. 12 (i. 119), 413 & n. 14, 415 & n. 8; Fontainebleau, French royal collection, ii. 117 & n. 5, 119–20 & nn. (i. 76, 77); Greenwich or London, Laniere, iii. 75; London: Arlington, iv. 102 & n. 2; royal collection: at Whitehall, iv. 216; ~ at Kensington, v. 237; Milan, ii. 495 & n. 6; Paris, Liancourt, ii. 113 & n. 7 (i. 73); Rome: Farnesina, ii. 288 & n. 1, 357 *bis* & n. 6; S. Maria del Popolo, Chigi chapel (mosaics, &c.), ii. 374 & n. 4; S. Pietro in Montorio, ii. 227 & n. 7, 313 & n. 5; Vatican, ii. 295 & n. 4, 299 & nn. 2–4; Villa Aldobrandini, ii. 284 & nn. 4, 6; Siena, cathedral library,

Raphael (*cont.*)
ii. 205 & n. 1, 407; Verona, Curtoni, ii. 487 & n. 3.
— (ii) specific works: Cupid and Psyche, ii. 288 & n. 1; alluded to, ii. 357; Ezekiel, vision of, ii. 413 & n. 14; Galatea, ii. 288 & n. 1, 357 & n. 6; Giovanna of Aragon, ii. 117 & n. 5, 120 & n. 5 (i. 76, 77); Leo X, ii. 190 & n. 12 (i. 119 ?); Loggie, ii. 295 & n. 4; Madonnas (at Fontainebleau), ii. 119 & n. 11, 120 & n. 6 (i. 77 *bis*); portrait of Beazzano, &c., ii. 284, n. 6; St. Cecilia, ii. 424 & n. 1; St. Margaret, ii. 120 & n. 5 (i. 77); St. Michael, ii. 120 & n. 2 (i. 77); St. Sebastian, ii. 284, n. 4; Stanze, ii. 299 & nn. 2–4; Transfiguration, ii. 227 & n. 7, 313, n. 5.
— (iii) unspecified works, ii. 284, 413; iii. 75; iv. 216; v. 237.
school-pieces: Madonna, ii. 495 & n. 6; St. John: copy of, ii. 415 & n. 8.
false attributions: paintings after, at Bologna, ii. 423–4 & n.; Siena Cathedral library, ii. 205 & n. 1, 407; Dorothea, ii. 487 & n. 3; portraits, ii. 113 & n. 7 (i. 73); iv. 102 & n. 2.
drawings by, in Arundel-Norfolk collection, iv. 312 & n. 3.
miscellaneous: as architect: designs Laurenziana (error), ii. 417 & n. 1; mosaics designed by, ii. 374 & n. 4; tapestries designed by (?), iii. 323 & n. 1; vases designed by (?), iii. 11 & n. 3; miniatures after, iii. 260, 287; painters study works by, ii. 288, 295 & n. 4, 299 & n. 4.
Ratcliffe: *see* Radcliffe.
Ratisbon: Imperial Diet at, iv. 622, n. 5.
Ratisbon: bishop of, 1685–1716: *see* Joseph Clemens, archbishop of Cologne.
Ratonneau, fort, near Marseilles, ii. 164 & n. 4.
Raudine plain: battle of the, ii. 485, n. 3; ~ allusions to: *see* Marius, C.
Ravaillac, François: as assassin of Henri IV, i. 85 & n. 2.
Ravenna: Dante buried at, ii. 197, n. 3; sculpture from, ii. 461, n. 1.
Ravensbourne river, Kent, iii. 508, n. 4.
Ray, Rev. John: book edited by, iv. 503 & n. 5.
Raynolds, —, tenant of E at Ripe, ii. 555.
Raynolds, Dr. —: *see* Reynolds, E.
Ré, Isle of: Buckingham's expedition to, ii. 8–9 & n. (i. 8); *see also* St. Martin.
Reade, Dom R. W. Selby, *alias*: *see* Wilfrid, Father John.
Reading, Berks., iii. 99 & nn. 3, 4.
Reading, Sir Robert, bt., iv. 140, n. 7; concerned in transfer of Arundel Library to Royal Society, *ib.*; iv. 144, n. 2; persuades E to visit duke of Norfolk, iv. 140; social, iv. 360.
Reccii, Andrea: *see* Riccio, A.
Reculver, Kent: in view, iii. 616 & n. 1.
Reddish, Alexander: geneal., ii. 11, n. 3.
Reddish, Grace: *see* Darcy, Grace, Lady Darcy.
Rederith: *see* London: environs: Rotherhithe.
Red Sea: crabs from, iii. 33; in sermon, v. 75.
Reede, Godard van: *see* Ginkel.
Reeve *or* Reeves, Dr.—: *see* Ryves, B.
Reeves, —, maker of optical instruments, &c., iii. 64 & n. 6.
Reggio, Pietro, singer, &c. (Signor Pietro), iv. 220 & n. 5; describes Sweden and Queen Christina, iv. 220–1 & nn.; performs, iv. 384–5; teaches Mary Evelyn (?), iv. 421 & n. 3, 427; alluded to (?), iv. 428.
Regicides: *see* Charles I.
Reie, river: at Bruges, ii. 75, n. 2.
Reigate (Rygate), Surrey: the Priory (Lady Peterborough's house), iii. 156 & nn. 1, 2; ~ Mordaunt at, iii. 219; road through, v. 168, n. 1; Archbishop Ussher at, iii. 156–7 & n.; steward of manor of: *see* Thurland, Sir E.; vicar of: *see* Parr, R.
Reigersberch, Maria van, wife of Hugo Grotius: helps Grotius to escape from prison, ii. 39 & n. 2 (i. 29).
Religious Societies, v. 366, n. 5.
Rembrandt: Night-watch by, ii. 43, n. 4.
Remée: *see* Leemput, R. van.

Remigius, Blessed: tomb of, ii. 199 & n. 8.
Remigius, bishop of Lincoln: tomb of, iii. 131–2 & n.
Remus (Rhemus): place where found, ii. 276 & n. 7.
Reni (Rheno, &c.), Guido, ii. 233, n. 6; paintings by: at Bologna, ii. 423 & nn. 4, 5, 424 *bis* & n. 4; ~ in Rome, ii. 233 & n. 6, 244 & n. 1, 276 & n. 1, 308 & n. 1, 379 & n. 6; ~ in Laniere's collection, iii. 75; ~ mosaic copy after, ii. 260, n. 4; imitator of, ii. 424 & n. 3.
Renzi (Rencia, &c.), Anna, singer, ii. 450, n. 3; in opera, ii. 450; social, ii. 474–5.
Reptiles [select notices]:
 chameleons: method of, of capturing prey, iv. 55 & n. 2; ~ preserved, ii. 331; ~ alive, iii. 147; ~ dissected, iii. 302 & n. 6; crocodiles (or alligators), iv. 390–1 & nn.; ~ skins or skeletons of, ii. 53 (i. 37), 164 (i. 104), 331, 414, 529 & n. 5; lizards: in comparison, iv. 391 *bis*; ~ green: anatomy of, iv. 314; salamanders: preserved, ii. 331; ~ in amber, ii. 471 & n. 2; tortoises, ii. 130 (i. 83); ~ worked tortoise-shell, ii. 124 (i. 79).
 snakes or serpents: at Lake Agnano, ii. 339 & n. 3; in experiment, iii. 284–5; aspic or slow-worm, iii. 291; rattlesnakes, iii. 200 & nn. 2–4; vipers, iii. 337; ~ in experiments, iii. 288, 290, 291; ~ supposed teeth of (fossils), iii. 511.
Reresby, Sir John: accounts by, of Halifax's conversations, i. *109*; attempt to corrupt, iv. 274, n. 1.
Resina: error for rusma, ii. 430–1 & n.
Rettenden (Rittington), Essex, iii. 65 & n. 5.
Revocation of the Edict of Nantes: *see* French protestants.
Reymerswaele, M. van: painting by (?), ii. 285 & n. 3.
Reymes (Rhemys, &c.), Bullen, iii. 388, n. 3; as commissioner for Sick and Wounded, 1664–7, 1672: appointed, iii. 387–8, 602, n. 1; ~ district of, iii. 394–5 & n., 620 & n. 1; ~ attends funeral in Rochester, iii. 619, n. 3, 620.
Reynaldo, Prince: *see* Rinaldo, duke of Modena.
Reynolds, Edward, D.D.; bishop of Norwich 1661, iii. 202, n. 2; sermon by, to East India Company, iii. 202 & n. 2; *add.*; consecrated bishop, iii. 266 & n. 3.
Rheims: Sainte-Ampoule at, ii. 147 (i. 95).
Rhemus: *see* Remus.
Rhemys, Bullein: *see* Reymes.
Rhenen (Rynen): palace of Elizabeth, queen of Bohemia, at, ii. 34–5 & n. (i. 27).
Rheni *or* Rheno, Guido: *see* Reni.
Rhine (Rhyne), river: in United Provinces, ii. 35 (i. 27); sources of, ii. 514 & n. 4; Confederates cross, 1689, iv. 645 & n. 5; Marlborough and Eugene cross, after Blenheim, v. 577 & n. 3.
Rhinegrave, ii. 61, n. 4; member of staff of, ii. 61 (i. 42).
Rhodes: Venetian conquest of, ii. 431; sculptors from (Agesandrus, &c.), ii. 304; coin of, ii. 380, n. 10.
Rhodomant, Paulo: *see* Rodomonte, P.
Rhone (Rhodanus), river: source of, ii. 514 & n. 4; in Valais, ii. 515 & n. 3, 519, n. 1; course of, through Lake of Geneva, ii. 520 & n. 4; at Geneva, ii. 528–9 & nn.; the Perte du Rhone, ii. 523 & n. 3; course of, from Geneva to Lyons, ii. 532 & n. 1; at Lyons, ii. 157 (i. 101); journey down, from Lyons to Pont-St.-Esprit, ii. 158–60 (i. 101–2); at Avignon, ii. 161 (i. 102).
Rhyne: *see* Rhine.
Ribbesford, Worcs.: rector of: *see* Lucas, A.
Riccard, Sir Andrew: geneal., iv. 3, n. 2.
Riccard, Christian: *see* Berkeley, Christian, Lady Berkeley.
Riccardi, Marchese, Tuscan ambassador to pope, ii. 389, n. 4.
Ricci, G. B. (da Novara): painting by, ii. 242, n. 7 *ad fin.*
Ricci, Giovanni, cardinal: first owner of Villa Medici, Rome, ii. 230, n. 8.
Riccio (Reccii), Andrea, called Briosco: reliefs, &c., by, ii. 454–5 & n.
Rich, Mrs. Anne: geneal., iii. 400, n. 3.

Rich, Charles, fourth earl of Warwick: attends Clarendon at his creation as earl, iii. 277.

Rich, Sir Edward; knighted 1670: feast of, as Reader at Lincoln's Inn, iii. 400 & nn. 3–6; *add.*

Rich, Henry, earl of Holland: rising led by, 1648, ii. 541, n. 7; tried and executed, ii. 548 & n. 2, 552 & n. 1; geneal., ii. 549, n. 9.

Rich, Henry, styled Lord Kensington: geneal., iv. 3, n. 2.

Rich, Lady Isabella, daughter of Henry Rich, earl of Holland: *see* Thynne, Lady Isabella.

Rich, Lady Isabella, daughter of Robert Rich, earl of Warwick: *see* Smith, Lady Isabella.

Rich, Col. Nathaniel: occupies Eltham Palace, iii. 170 & n. 3.

Rich, Robert, first earl of Warwick: geneal., iii. 73, n. 1.

Richard II, king of England: murdered in Pontefract Castle, iii. 127 & n. 7.

Richard III, king of England: as duke of Gloucester: Gloucester Castle granted to, iii. 118, n. 3; tomb of, iii. 122 & n. 6.

Richard, St., English king: tomb of, at Lucca, ii. 409 & n. 1.

Richards, Mrs. Bridget: geneal., ii. 22, n. 1.

Richards, Elizabeth, Lady Richards, wife of Sir John: house of, ii. 22 & n. 1.

Richards, Sir John: geneal., ii. 22, n. 1.

Richardson, —, fire-eater: display by, iii. 626–7 & n.

Richardson, Sir Thomas, judge: censures Richard Evelyn, sen., ii. 12 & n. 1 (i. 10).

Richaumont, — de: art-collection of, ii. 132 & n. 2 (i. 85).

Richborough, Kent: road near, iii. 616 & n. 1.

Richelieu, Poitou: town and chateau of, ii. 150–1 & nn. (i. 97–8).

Richelieu, Armand-Jean du Plessis, cardinal: ancestors of: home of, ii. 150 & n. 4; birth-place of, i. 97–8; ii. 150, n. 4 *ad fin.*; hostility of, to Marie de Médicis, ii. 146 & n. 2 (i. 94); academy founded by, at Richelieu, ii. 150 & n. 3 (i. 97); gift to, ii. 131, n. 1; paintings relating to, ii. 151 & n. 2 (i. 98); phrase originated

Richelieu, Armand-Jean du Plessis, cardinal (*cont.*)
by, ii. 125, n. 4; geneal., ii. 125 & n. 3 (i. 80), 400, n. 2.
buildings erected by: Le Havre: citadel, ii. 125 (i. 80); Paris: Palais-Royal, ii. 133–4 & n. (i. 87), 566; ~ Sorbonne, church of the, &c., ii. 97 (i. 64); Richelieu: town and chateau, ii. 150–1 & nn. (i. 97–8); Rueil: villa at, ii. 108–10 & nn. (i. 70–1).

Richelieu, Armand-Jean du Plessis, duc de: at Le Havre, ii. 125 & n. 3 (i. 80).

Richer, Pierre, engraver: agent for Mazarin (?), iii. 82, n. 2.

Richett, —, etcher: collecting pictures for Mazarin, ii. 82 & n. 2.

Richmond, Surrey: *see* Sheen.

Richmond, Virginia: Virginia House at, iii. 120, n. 5.

Richmond: Earls and Dukes of: duke of: daughter of (error), iv. 39; individuals: *see* Tudor, Edmund, earl 1453–6; Beaufort, Margaret, his countess; Stuart, Ludovick, duke 1623–4; *new creation*: Stuart, James, first duke, 1641–55; Stuart, Mary, his duchess; Stuart, Charles, third duke, 1660–72; Stuart, Frances, his duchess; *new creation*: Lennox, Charles, first duke, 1675–1723.

Richmond Park (New Park), Surrey: buck from, iv. 220 & n. 3.

Ridpath, George, editor of *The Flying-Post*, i. 105.

Rie: *see* Rye.

Riga: siege of, 1700, v. 386 & n. 1; mentioned, iii. 344, n. 5 *ad fin.*

Right, Rev. —: sermon by, v. 316–17.

Rilie, Andrew: baptized, ii. 567.

Rilie, Sir Hugh; in Paris, ii. 567 & n. 4.

Rimini: miracle of St. Anthony of Padua at, ii. 319, n. 2.

Rinaldo, duke of Modena: as Prince Reynaldo: visits London, iv. 28 & n. 4.

Ringcurran Fort, near Kinsale: governor of: *see* Armorer, Sir N.

Ringwood, Hants.: Monmouth, &c., captured at, iv. 452, nn. 3, 4.

Ripanda, J.: paintings by, ii. 225, n. 14.

Ripe, Sussex: E's farm in, ii. 555 & n. 5; ~ visit to, iv. 40; ~ mentioned, ii. 27, n. 2.
Ripon, Yorks.: in view, iii. 129; collegiate church at: deans of: *see* Wilkins, J. (1660–72); Cartwright, T. (1676–86).
Rittington: *see* Rettenden.
Rivers family of Chafford, Penshurst, Kent, iv. 40 & n. 7.
Rivers: Earl, &c.: *see* Savage, John, second earl; Savage, Catherine, his countess.
Rizzio, David: relations of, with Mary, queen of Scots, iv. 603 & n. 5.
Rizzo, Antonio: statue by, ii. 443 & n. 3.
Roads [select: notices relating to construction, condition, &c.; *see also* Paving]: Alpine: first carriage-road over a Swiss pass, ii. 508, n. 5; ~ marked by poles, ii. 513; ancient: Via Appia, ii. 319 & nn. 4, 5, 322; cuttings, ii. 321 & n. 4, 347, n. 3; slough on road, v. 547 & n. 4, 548, critical note; straight, ii. 324 & n. 7, 410, 491; tunnel, ii. 337–8 & nn.; unfit for army in November, iv. 605.
Roanne (Roan, Rohan, Rouanne): notices: 1644, ii. 156 & n. 3 (i. 100); ~ 1646, ii. 532–3 & nn.; le Loup inn at, ii. 533 & n. 3; mentioned, ii. 152, n. 1.
Robartes, Isabella, countess of Radnor, wife of John Robartes, first earl, and later of Charles Cheyne, Lord Cheyne: chaplain of (?): sermon by, v. 585–6 & n.
Robartes, John; second Baron Robartes 1634; first earl of Radnor 1679, iii. 402, n. 2; as Lord Privy Seal: prorogues parliament, iii. 402; ~ social, iii. 512; geneal., iii. 473 & n. 3; v. 585, n. 2.
Robartes, Robert, styled Lord Bodmin 1679–82, iii. 473, n. 3; action brought by, relating to his father-in-law's will, iii. 473 & n. 3; geneal., v. 585, n. 1.
Robartes, Mrs. Sarah, later styled Lady Bodmin and, later, dowager countess of Radnor, wife of Robert Robartes, styled Lord Bodmin 1679–82, iii. 473, n. 3; v. 585, n. 2; dispute concerning her father's will, iii. 473 & n. 3; chaplain of (?): sermon by, v. 585–6.
Robartes: second Baron, 1634–79: *see* Robartes, John, later earl of Radnor.
Robbia, Girolamo della: work by, at Château de Madrid, iii. 3 & n. 1.
Robec (Lobes), river, at Rouen, ii. 122 & n. 4 (i. 78).
Robert II, king of France: founds Notre-Dame at Paris, ii. 95.
Robert II, king of Scotland: geneal., iv. 39, n. 4.
Robert Curthose, duke of Normandy: tomb of (as King Stephen's), iii. 118 & n. 2.
Robert, Nicolas, flower-painter, iv. 532, n. 1.
Roberts, Sir Gabriel: godfather of Martha Maria Evelyn, iv. 324 & n. 2.
Roberts, Lewis: geneal., iv. 324, n. 2.
Roberts, William, D.D.; bishop of Bangor 1637: ordination by, iii. 254 & n. 6.
Robin Hood's Well, Yorks., W. R., iii. 128 & n. 2.
Robinson, —, and his brother-in-law, 1652, iii. 74.
Robinson, Sir John, bt., iii. 172, n. 2; as Mr. Alderman Robinson: takes part in G. Tuke's marriage negotiation, iii. 172; as Lord Mayor: show of, iii. 341–2 & nn.; as lieutenant of the Tower, &c.; social, iii. 352 & n. 1, 425, 550.
Robusti, Jacopo: *see* Tintoretto.
Rochecorbon (Roche-Corbé), Touraine, ii. 148 & n. 4 (i. 96).
Rochefoucauld d'Auvergne, François, Cardinal Liancourt: portrait of (?), ii. 113 & n. 7 (i. 73).
Rochester, Kent: Charles II at, 29 May 1660, iii. 246 & n. 2; troops quartered at, 1665 (?), iii. 422; James II at, Dec. 1688, iv. 610, 611 & n. 1, 612, n. 4.
E visits: ii. 30 (i. 23), 76 (i. 50); iii. 56, 358; iv. 79, 80; ~ as commissioner for Sick and Wounded: 1665–6: iii. 395 *bis*, 409 *bis*, 410, 436 *bis*, 437, 467, 468; ~ 1672, iii. 609–24 *passim*.
bridge at, i. 23; cathedral, ii. 30 (i. 23); iii. 432 & n. 6; ~ French officer buried in, iii. 619–20 & nn.; ~ sermons preached in, iii. 468, 611–12, 614.
mayors of: 1665, iii. 395; 1672, iii. 619; 1676, &c. (J. Conny), iv. 79 & n. 2, 80.

Rochester: Earls, &c., of: *see* Wilmot, Henry, first earl 1652–8; Wilmot, Anne, his countess; Wilmot, John, second earl 1658–80; *new creation*: Hyde, Laurence, first earl 1682–1711; Hyde, Henrietta, his countess; Hyde, Henry, second earl 1711–23, later fourth earl of Clarendon.
Rochester: cathedral clergy, &c.
bishops: *see* Dolben, J. (1666–83); Turner, Francis (1683–4); Sprat, T. (1684–1713); Atterbury, F. (1713–23).
deans: *see* Hardy, N. (1660–70); Lamplugh, T. (1673–6); Castillion, J. (1676–88); Ullock, H. (1689–1706); Pratt, S. (1706–23).
prebendaries: *see* Bréval, F. Durant de; Codd, J.; Grant, J.; Harris, John.
chancellor: *see* Trumbull, Sir W.
Rochford: Earls of: *see* Zuylestein.
Rock-crystal: *see* Crystal.
Rocroi: battle of, iii. 639 (in extract from *State of France*).
Roderith, —, serjeant-at-law: *see* Rotherham, Sir John.
Rodomonte (Rhodomant), Paolo: lodgings let by, at Venice, ii. 429 & n. 5.
Roe, Rev. J. (Joseph Row?): sermon by (?), v. 353–4 & n.
Roelofsze, Jan: Dutch prisoner of war, iii. 404 & n. 4, 407 & n. 6.
Roettiers, John, iv. 138, n. 2; statuette by, &c. (?; as Monsieur Rotiere), iv. 138 & n. 2; medal by, iv. 633 & n. 2.
Rogers, George, M.D., ii. 464, n. 1; at Padua, ii. 464 & n. 1; iv. 291; poems addressed to, ii. 478, n. 3, 479, n. 2; Harveian oration by, iv. 291 & n. 1.
Rogers, Rev. John, chaplain to the earl of Berkeley, iv. 248, n. 2; sermons by: printed, iv. 248 & n. 2; ~ ordinary (?), iv. 206 & n. 3.
Rohan: *see* Roanne.
Rohan, Henri de, the memoirist: geneal., ii. 562, n. 10.
Rohan, Henri de Chabot, duke of: visits Charles II, ii. 562 & n. 10.
Rokewood family: owners of manor of Euston, iii. 589, n. 1, 591, n. 2.
Romain, St.: legend and commemoration of, ii. 123 & n. 5 (i. 79).
Roman Catholic Church, Roman Catholicism, Roman Catholics [the notices in the Diary relating to Roman Catholicism are divisible into two main groups, those in which the Church in general is concerned, and those in which it is associated with England. The former group contains little of a general character: Evelyn encountered particular manifestations of Roman Catholic life, but does not record the history of the Church. The latter, and more important, group is largely historical: Evelyn records the 'growth of Popery' under Charles II and James II, and the opposition to it. The arrangement of this section of the index is based on these two groups.
All notices relating specifically to the Jesuits are indexed under Jesuits, and not repeated here; notices relating to the Papacy and the Papal States as a political entity are indexed under Papacy; further notices bearing on the Church are to be found under James II, the Popish Plot, and so on. Some notices relating to the Church prior to the Reformation in the sixteenth century are indexed under Church]:
— the Church and England:
— — chronological series: Roman Catholics [or Church]: in exile in Paris, 1649–52, i. *10*; Henrietta Maria's ladies, iii. 44 & n. 5; rejoice at proclamation against Anglican clergy, 1655, iii. 164; hear A. Morus preach, iii. 311; policy of Clifford and Arlington in regard to, i. *22*; effect on, of Declaration of Indulgence, 1672, iii. 607–8 & n., 612; prominence and activity of, 1676–8, iv. 154 & n. 3; in alleged conspiracy against Charles II, 1678, iv. 153–4 & nn.; *see also* Popish Plot; London: topography: Tower; accused of murdering Sir E. B. Godfrey, iv. 155 & n. 3, 175; alleged commissions from, to Viscount Stafford, &c.,

Roman Catholic Church, &c. (*cont.*) iv. 228, 231, 232; recovery of, 1683, after Popish Plot, iv. 320; rejoice on discovery of Rye-House Plot, 1683, iv. 331 & n. 2; policy of James II in regard to, v. 475; at court, 1685, iv. 418, 419; await conviction of Titus Oates, iv. 438–9; defended by Sir R. L'Estrange, iv. 439 & n. 3; hostility of, to Church of England (general reflection), iv. 478; pamphlets written by, &c.; on public sale, iv. 489 & n. 4; ~ licences for printing (including devotional works), 1686, iv. 503–4 & n., 512 & n. 1; angered by grant of peerage to Catherine Sedley, iv. 497; in favour, iv. 503; strength of interest of, iv. 507; obstruct brief for French protestant refugees, v. 508 & n. 3; growing influence of, 1687, iv. 540; free-schools of, in London, 1688, iv. 584, n. 5 *ad fin.*; attitude of, towards Seven Bishops, iv. 585; preach against and try to extirpate Church of England, iv. 590 *bis*; tyranny of: William of Orange as deliverer from, iv. 600; intrigues of, during interregnum, 1689, iv. 614; pleased at dissatisfaction with Revolution settlement, iv. 627; concerned in Assassination Plot, 1696, v. 231, 232, 234 & n. 8; Papal Nuncio in Paris recognizes James Edward as king of Great Britain, 1701, v. 476.

— — appointments of Roman Catholics: governor of Dover Castle, 1686, iv. 506 & n. 4; judge, iv. 514 & n. 6; commissioners of the Treasury, 1687, iv. 533; justices of the peace, iv. 536 & n. 3; Lord Privy Seal, iv. 540; privy councillor, 1688, iv. 590, n. 4 *ad fin.*; protestant privy councillors refuse to sit with Roman Catholics, iv. 602–3 & n.; Roman Catholic office-holders resign and fly, iv. 609.

— — army: Roman Catholics in, &c.: James II's dispensations from Test Act questioned by parliament, iv. 488 *bis*, 489; the

Roman Catholic Church, &c. (*cont.*) army as a means of advancing the Church, iv. 582; Irish soldiers in, iv. 596–7 & n., 599 & n. 6; Roman Catholics: recruited for, iv. 599 & n. 6; ~ in Portsmouth garrison, *ib.*; ~ desert, iv. 620, n. 4.

— — clergy [general notices]: hiding-places for: in house at Weybridge, iv. 142; hierarchy, 1685, 1688, iv. 534, n. 2; officiate when James II touches for king's evil, iv. 606, n. 3; *add.*; flight of, &c., 1688, iv. 609, 611; Protector of the English: *see* Barberini, F.; vicar-apostolic of all England, &c.: *see* Leyburn, J.; individual priests: *see below*.

— — conversions to Roman Catholicism [general notices]: few among Anglican clergy during Great Rebellion, iv. 394; expected announcement of, Jan. 1687, iv. 535 & n. 3; few of importance, iv. 541 & n. 2; few, 1688, iv. 581, 596.

— — public or congregational worship: chapel for, at St. James's Palace (the queens' chapel), iii. 373, n. 2; permitted by Declaration of Indulgence, 1672, iii. 607–8 & n.; established at Whitehall, 1685, iv. 419; in king's chapel, Windsor, iv. 465, 518 & n. 4; chapel for, at Whitehall, opened, iv. 534–5 & n.; permitted by Declaration of Indulgence, 1687, iv. 546–7 & n.; chapel for, in camp at Hounslow, v. 61–2 & n., 63; attitude of Seven Bishops towards, iv. 583; chapels for, in London, demolished, &c., iv. 599 & n. 1, 602 & n. 1, 607 & n. 4, 610 & n. 2; in North of England, &c., 1700, v. 403 & n. 2.

— — religious orders: (i) contemporary:

— — — Benedictines: three monks tried, 1679, iv. 173–4 & n.; individuals: *see* Wilfrid, J. (president of English province, &c.); Huddlestone, J.

— — — Benedictine nuns: at Brussels, ii. 69–70 & n. (i. 46).

— — — Capuchins: French; attached to Henrietta Maria's

Roman Catholic Church, &c. (*cont.*)
chapel, iii. 602, n. 3; ~ convert to Church of England, iii. 602 & n. 3.
— — — Carmelites: chapel of, 1688, iv. 602 & n. 1; individual, at Amsterdam, ii. 45 (i. 32).
— — — Dominicans: Philip Howard (later cardinal) enters the order, ii. 479 & n. 3.
— — — Franciscans: individual: Father Peter Walsh, iv. 496 & n. 4.
— — — Institute of the Blessed Virgin Mary (Jesuitesses): foundress of (Mary Ward), ii. 400 & n. 3.
— — — Jesuits: *see* Jesuits.
— — — Oratorians: convert to protestantism, v. 204; individual: *see* Goffe, Stephen.
— — religious orders: (ii): former establishments of:
— — — Augustinians: priories, iii. 120, n. 5, 124, n. 1, 156, n. 1.
— — — Bridgettines: convent (Syon), iii. 414–15 & n.
— — — Carthusians: priories: in London, iii. 192; at Sheen, iv. 142–3 & n.
— — — Franciscans: convent: in London, iii. 192, n. 2.
— — individual Roman Catholics [the bracketed page-numbers following cross-references indicate the passages associating the persons concerned with the Church]: (i) laymen, other than converts, specifically described by E as Roman Catholics: *see* Arundell, H., Baron Arundell of Wardour (iv. 540); Belasyse, J., Baron Belasyse (iv. 533); Howard, Lord Thomas (iii. 326, &c.); ~ sons of, 1700 (v. 394); Jermyn, H., Baron Dover, later Baron Jermyn (iv. 533); Howard, H., sixth duke of Norfolk ('no bigoted Papist', iv. 142; *see also* iii. 595–6); ~ sons of (iii. 326, 355); Short, Dr. T. (v. 197 & n. 5).
— — — (ii) clergy (other than Jesuits and converts) mentioned by E as such: *see* Carey, P. (ii. 213 & n. 3); Charnock, R. (v. 234 & n. 8); Conyers, —, *alias* Paynter (iii. 36); Holden, H. (ii. 567 & n. 3); Howard, Cardinal P. T.; Huddlestone, J. (iv. 408 & n. 1); Pordage, — (?; iv. 403 & n. 6); Russell, R., bishop of Vizeu, &c. (iii. 305 & n. 2); Sergeant, J. (?; iii. 634 & n. 3); Stuart, Ludovic, seigneur of Aubigny; White, Thomas, *alias* Blacklow (iii. 33 & n. 3).
— — — (iii) converts to: *see* Anne (Hyde), duchess of York (iv. 282–3 & nn.); Bennet, H., earl of Arlington (iii. 608 & n. 1; iv. 475–6 & n.); Digby, G., earl of Bristol (iii. 311, n. 3); Charles II (iv. 407–8 & n., 476–9 & n.; i. *31–2*); Maccarty, D., earl of Clancarty (iv. 595, n. 4); Clifford, Sir T., Baron Clifford (iii. 577 & n. 5, 608; iv. 14 & n. 1, 16); Cosin, John, jnr. (iii. 26, n. 6, 636); Cottington, F., Baron Cottington (iii. 32, n. 5 *ad fin.*); Craford, J. (ii. 22–3 & n. & i. 17); Crashaw, R. (iii. 46, n. 4); Cressy, H.P. (Serenus) (iii. 360, n. 5); Dryden, J., and his sons (iv. 497 & n. 1); Goffe, S. (ii. 36 & i. 27); Boyle, Elizabeth, countess of Guildford (iii. 263, n. 8); Gwyn, Nell (error; iv. 497 & n. 1); Hales, Edward (iv. 510 & n. 3); Hales, Sir Edward (iv. 506 & n. 4); Hildyard, H., jnr. (iv. 510 & n. 2); Hills, H., sen. (iv. 504 & n. 1); Hollar, W. (i. 21 & n. 2); James II (iv. 7 & n. 3; i. *26*); Keightley, T., jnr., iii. 35, 36–7, 633–4; Keightley, W., iii. 634; Massey, J. (iv. 519, n. 4); Milton, Sir C. (iv. 514 & n. 6); Montagu, Walter (iii. 558, n. 1); Mordaunt, Henry, earl of Peterborough (iv. 541, n. 2); Cecil, James, earl of Salisbury (iv. 541, n. 2); Scrope, Mary, Lady Scrope (iii. 275, n. 6); Talbot, Frances, duchess of Tyrconnel (iv. 79 & n. 3); Walker, Obadiah (iv. 509–10 & n.); Woodhead, A. (iii. 182 & n. 2); Wycherley, W. (iv. 541, n. 2); *further*: former fellows of Peterhouse, Cambridge, iii. 46, n. 4; fellows of Oxford colleges, iv. 509–10 & n.
— — — (iv) presumed converts to:

Roman Catholic Church, &c. (*cont.*) *see* Coleman, E. (iv. 155 & n. 4); Litcott, Sir J. (iv. 498 & n. 1); Tuke, Sir Samuel.
— — — (v) converts *manqués*: *see* Evelyn, John, jnr. (iii. 326, 355); Parker, Samuel, bishop of Oxford (iv. 574).
— — — (vi) converts who revert later: *see* Oates, Titus (iv. 153–4 & n., 230–1 & n.); Sclater, E. (iv. 509 & n. 5); Sibbald, Sir R. (iv. 515 & n. 3); Spencer, Robert, earl of Sunderland (iv. 594–5 & n.; v. 226).
— — — (vii) converts from, to Church of England or protestantism: *see* Bréval, F. Durant de (iii. 602 & n. 3); Carey, P. (ii. 213); Le Franc, J. (iii. 160, 171); Ubaldino, C., count of Monte Feltre (iv. 335–6 & n.); Howard, Henry, sixth duke of Norfolk (intended conversion; iii. 595–6 & n.); Howard, Henry, seventh duke of Norfolk (iii. 596 & n. 2); Lumley, Richard, earl of Scarborough (v. 9 & n. 1; *add.*); *further*: French divines, v. 204, 269.
— — opposition to: (i) chronological series: risk of being suspected to be a Roman Catholic, iii. 185; praying for a Roman Catholic objected to, iii. 204; Fire of London: inscription attributing it to Roman Catholics, iv. 243, n. 6, 449 & n. 4; pope-burning, 1673, iv. 26 & n. 2; causes of harsh treatment of Roman Catholics, 1678–9, iv. 175; fear of Roman Catholic influence on government, i. *26*; ~ as cause of Rye-House plot, iv. 323 *bis*, 329; ~ in Sir E. Seymour's speech, 1685, iv. 444; treatises against Roman Catholicism, 1685–8, iv. 418 & n. 2, 541 & n. 3, 590; preaching against Roman Catholicism, 1686–7, iv. 516 & nn. 1, 2, 524 & n. 1, 541; Nonconformists turn against Roman Catholics, 1688, iv. 590; Roman Catholic property in London destroyed, iv. 610 & n. 2; *see also* public worship *above*; declaration against Roman Catholics, iv. 609 & n. 3; popularity of bishops opposing Roman Catholicism, iv. 631.
— — — (ii) penal laws, &c.: Sir S. Tuke's speeches to house of lords for remission of penal laws, iii. 249–50 & n.; iv. 5 & n. 5; Test Act, 1673, iv. 7 & n. 4; ~ declaration against Transubstantiation required by, iv. 10; ~ for compliance with the act, &c., *see* England: laws; Parliamentary Test Act, 1678, iv. 158–9 & n.; ~ declaration against Roman Catholic tenets required by, iv. 442 & n. 4; *see also* England: laws; proclamations against Roman Catholics, 1678, iv. 159 & nn. 2, 3; projected repeal of penal laws, 1687, iv. 540–1 & n., 544; Roman Catholics: excluded from succession to crown, iv. 616 & n. 1; v. 421, n. 2; ~ proclamation against, 1691, v. 47 & n. 4; ~ required to leave London, 1696, v. 232 & n. 3; ~ vote restricting testamentary powers of, 1700, v. 379 & n. 3; ~ act incapacitating, from inheriting lands, 1700, v. 403 & n. 1.
— — — (iii) controversies between Anglicans and Roman Catholics, &c.: college for maintaining protestant controversialists, iii. 397, n. 2; controversial writings in James II's reign, iv. 541 & n. 3, 590; *see also* iv. 418 & n. 2; Roman Catholic accusations: various, iii. 634; ~ in 1651, iii. 633; visibility of Church of England during Great Rebellion, iii. 36–7, 247–8 & n.; iv. 303; first missionaries to Britain (Gunning), iii. 333 & n. 4; T. Pierce against S. Cressy, on Primitive Church and innovations, iii. 360 & n. 5; existence of Gunpowder Plot denied (Tillotson), iv. 156–7 & n.; the Mass idolatrous (Gunning), iv. 159 & n. 4; Roman Catholicism considered idolatrous, iv. 230; Charles II's reasons for his conversion, iv. 476–8; views of Peter Walsh, iv. 496 & n. 4; W. Wake against Bossuet, on Anglican dogma,

Roman Catholic Church, &c. (*cont.*) iv. 532 & n. 3; Tenison against Pulton, on transubstantiation, iv. 540, n. 1; Bishop S. Parker tries to reconcile transubstantiation with Anglican doctrine, iv. 574 & n. 2.

— — — (iv) anti-Catholic mythology: priests disguised as sectaries foment troubles in England, and variants (Bramhall's story, &c.), iii. 157 & n. 2; iv. 507, 508, n. 1; v. 13 & n. 1.

— the Church and Scotland: penal laws maintained, 1686, iv. 514 & n. 7; liberty of conscience granted, 1687, iv. 539 & n. 3.

— the Church and Ireland: Roman Catholic party in Ireland, 1689, iv. 630–1.

— Anglican sermons against Roman Catholicism [reports in which Roman Catholicism or Roman Catholics are mentioned or clearly alluded to; the division by topics, &c., is rough]: angels: worship of, iv. 88, 153, 649 *bis*; apostasy to Roman Catholicism: warnings against, iv. 157, 557, 564; v. 4; auricular confession, v. 132; Bible denied to laity, iv. 448; v. 106, 119, 364, 403, 541, 607; Britain not converted from Rome, iii. 333 & n. 4; v. 80; confirmation as a sacrament, v. 310; England delivered from Roman Catholicism: by the Reformation, iv. 157, 592; ~ in 1688, iv. 650–1; v. 227, 319, 362; errors of Roman Catholicism: general, iv. 302; v. 520; ~ specified, iv. 555; v. 364–5; general attacks, iv. 621; v. 307, 328; good works, v. 593; Gunpowder Plot commemoration: anti-Romanist sermons, iv. 26, 156, 224, 260, 295, 394, 529, 563; v. 271–2, 362–3; idolatry, iv. 295, 520; ~ *latria* and *dulia*, v. 348 & n. 1; infallibility of the Church, iii. 518; iv. 187, 646–7; infallible interpreter of Scripture not needed, iv. 537 & n. 4; innovations, iii. 23; iv. 158, 187, 541–2, 555, 643; ~ additional articles of belief, iv. 570; v. 276, 327; ~ Candlemas customs, iii. 240–1 & n.; ~ half-Communion, iii. 23, 26, 80; Mary, Virgin: adoration of, v. 526; the Mass, iii. 225; iv. 522, 579–80; mediators in addition to Christ, v. 506–7; monasticism, v. 251–2; moral conduct: fraud, iii. 27; moral teaching, iii. 253; iv. 394; ostentatious charities, iv. 437; penance: false or inadequate, iv. 538, 562, 576–7; v. 364–5, 384; pious frauds, v. 73, 76–7; political: allow civil disobedience, iii. 365; ~ approve of massacres, iv. 648; ~ allow regicide, iv. 405; v. 165–6 & n., 364–5; popes: infallibility of, iv. 27; v. 332; ~ primacy claimed by, iii. 551; v. 80, 271–2; priests parallelled with scribes and Pharisees, iv. 541–2; prophetic: fall of papacy, v. 20–1; purgatory, iii. 235; iv. 577; v. 130, 306; Reformation vindicated, iv. 198, 538–9; Roman Catholic: the term, iv. 158; sacraments: only two, iii. 24; saints: invocation of, &c., iii. 562; iv. 153; ~ merits of, v. 280; signs of true church, v. 254; superstition, iv. 522, 533; tradition as opposed to Scripture, iv. 599; transubstantiation, iii. 33, 80, 525; iv. 489, 513, 522, 539–40 & n.; v. 240–2, 459, 483, 535, 591; unity of the Church in spite of its corruption, v. 513; unknown language used in services, iii. 23; iv. 562; v. 604; vows: unlawful, v. 303, 381.

— the Church in general:

— — converts to: Augustus the Strong, v. 270–1 & n.; Christina, queen of Sweden, iv. 221 & nn. 1, 2; Louisa Hollandina, Princess Palatine, i. 26 & n. 2.

— — history of: in paintings, ii. 299 & n. 5; *see also* ii. 297 & nn. 2–5; Pope Joan and papal enthronements, ii. 268 & n. 2.

— — religious observances: (i) celebrations and ceremonies: cardinal: creation of a, ii. 254 & n. 7; *chapelle ardente*, ii. 368–9 & n.; jubilee: doors opened for, ii. 266, 275; ~ 1600, ii. 366; ~ 1700, v. 429; ~ figurative, iii.

Roman Catholic Church, &c. (*cont.*)
1; ~ word used wrongly (?), v. 163; papal benedictions, ii. 258; popes: enthronement of, at Lateran, ii. 268 & n. 2; Rose, Golden: benediction of the, ii. 384 & n. 6; Te Deum: for battle of White Hill, ii. 239; ~ for Louis XIV's recovery, iv. 533, n. 6.
— — — (ii) festivals (mainly at Rome): Candlemas, ii. 331 & n. 8; ~ origins of, iii. 240–1 & n.; Annunciation, ii. 377–8 & n., 384; Carnival, ii. 331–2 & n., 381–2 & nn.; Ash Wednesday, ii. 382; Palm Sunday, ii. 385, 387 & n. 2; Maundy Thursday, ii. 385 & nn. 4, 5; Good Friday, ii. 386 & nn. 2, 3; Holy Saturday, ii. 377, n. 1, 386 & n. 4; Easter day, ii. 386 & n. 5; Easter sepulchres, ii. 123 (i. 79), 385–6 & n.; iii. 612; Corpus Christi, ii. 146 (i. 94–5), 536 & n. 3; iv. 560; Christmas: cribs, &c., ii. 290, 291 & n. 7; procession at Lerici, ii. 179 & n. 3 (i. 113).
— — — (iii) liturgical: Greek rite, ii. 382 & n. 2, 399.
— — — (iv) services: baptism, ii. 376–7; iii. 585; Quarant'ore, ii. 65 & n. 5 (i. 44), 281, n. 1; stations (at Rome), ii. 243 & n. 3.
— — — (v) special devotions, &c.: devotions at various churches in Rome, ii. 226 & n. 5; *add.*; ii. 245–6 *bis*, 264, 268; hermits and hermitages, ii. 116 & n. 1 (i. 75), 250 & n. 2, 564 & n. 3; privileged altars, ii. 65 & n. 1 (i. 44), 251, 381; Rose, Golden, ii. 384 & n. 6; sermons: Italian style, ii. 384 & n. 3; ~ Spanish, ii. 368; ~ to Jews, ii. 291–2 & n., 376; ~ mentioned, ii. 290, 373; shrines, wayside, ii. 69 (i. 46); votive tablets, ii. 64 (i. 43), 194 (i. 120), 413; women excluded from particular chapels, ii. 267 & n. 2, 380.
— — religious orders [*see also* the Church and England *above*]:
— — — Augustinian canons: at Paris (as Canons regular), ii. 101 (i. 66).
— — — Augustinian canonesses: at Padua, ii. 473 *bis* & n. 3.

Roman Catholic Church, &c. (*cont.*)
— — — Augustinian hermits: at Rome, ii. 374, n. 2; claim St. William as member of order, ii. 424, n. 2.
— — — Benedictines: branch of, ii. 206, n. 4; at Venice, ii. 461.
— — — Bernardine nuns: at Rome, ii. 239.
— — — Camaldolese hermits: near Venice, ii. 468 & n. 3.
— — — Camaldolese nuns: at Rome, ii. 358, n. 4.
— — — Capuchins: friars, iii. 54; convents, ii. 75, n. 6, 145 (i. 94), 209 & n. 7, 342, n. 5, 369.
— — — Carmelites: at Venice, ii. 461; procurator of the, ii. 384 & n. 6.
— — — Carthusians: priories, ii. 240, 329.
— — — Celestines: at Avignon, ii. 161 (i. 103).
— — — Charity, Order of: at Paris, ii. 101, n. 6.
— — — Cordeliers: at Avignon, ii. 162, n. 1.
— — — Crosiers: at Gennep, ii. 37, n. 1.
— — — Dominicans: convents, &c., ii. 199, n. 7, 204, 376, 377 & n. 7, 421; *see also* Jacobins *below*.
— — — Feuillants: at Rome (as Fulgentine monks), ii. 363 & n. 8.
— — — Franciscans: Chinese grammar printed by, iii. 374, n. 7; convents, &c., ii. 75 & n. 6 (i. 49), 147 & n. 5 (i. 95), 176–7 & n. (i. 111), 196, 209 & n. 4; ~ (error), ii. 37 & n. 1 (i. 28); *see also* Capuchins *above*; Minims *below*.
— — — Gesuati: at Rome, ii. 276 & n. 3.
— — — Holy Ghost, Order of the: at Rome, ii. 312 & n. 1.
— — — Illuminate: *see* Augustinian canonesses *above*.
— — — Jacobins: churches of, ii. 157 & n. 8 (i. 101), 200 & n. 3.
— — — Jesuits: *see* Jesuits.
— — — Minims: convents, ii. 112, n. 3, 147, n. 5, 314, n. 1.
— — — Mount Calvary, order of: congregation of, ii. 564, n. 3.
— — — Olivetans: monasteries, ii. 206 & n. 4, 328, 462.

Roman Catholic Church, &c. (*cont.*)
— — — Oratorians: musical services held by, ii. 232–3 & n., 283–4.
— — — Paulist Fathers (modern): church of, at Rome, ii. 239, n. 3.
— — — Poor Clares: convent, ii. 58 & n. 3 (i. 40).
— — — Sacred Heart, Fathers of the: church of, at Rome, ii. 368, n. 6.
— — — St. Stephen, Order of: *see* Knights and Orders of Knighthood.
— — — Servites: convents, ii. 195 & n. 3, 442 & n. 5.
— — — Theatines: churches of, ii. 327–8 & n., 376.
— — — Visitandines: convent of, at Chaillot, ii. 91, n. 1.
— — relics [collections and single relics arranged by places]: Antwerp, Jesuits' church, ii. 64 (i. 43); Bologna, S. Domenico, ii. 421; Bourbon-l'Archambault, ii. 155 (i. 100); Bourges, chapel of Jean, duke of Berry, ii. 153; Brescia, cathedral, ii. 490 & n. 3; Calais (?), i. 56; Fossanova, ii. 319; Genoa, S. Lorenzo, ii. 177 & n. 1 (i. 111); Marmoutier, ii. 147 & n. 1 (i. 95); Marseilles, St. Victoire, ii. 165 (i. 105); Milan: cathedral, ii. 493; ~ S. Ambrogio, ii. 500 & nn. 2, 4; ~ S. Eustorgio, ii. 496 & n. 2; Naples: in procession, ii. 331; ~ cathedral, ii. 328 & n. 3; ~ S. Domenico, ii. 328; Padua, S. Antonio, ii. 454; ~ S. Giustina, ii. 455–6 & nn.; Paris, Ste.-Chapelle, ii. 99 (i. 65); Rheims: Ste.-Ampoule at, ii. 147 & n. 1 (i. 95); Rome, Gesù, ii. 230; S. Bartolomeo, ii. 358; S. Cecilia, ii. 357–8; SS. Cosma e Damiano, ii. 219; S. Croce in Gerusalemme, ii. 380, 384–5 & n.; S. Giovanni in Laterano, ii. 272–5 & nn., *passim*, 292 & n. 1, 385; ~ Baptistery, &c., at, ii. 267, 268, n. 1; ~ Scala Santa at, ii. 268; S. Gregorio Magno, ii. 251; S. Lorenzo fuori, ii. 381 & n. 6; S. Lorenzo in Panisperna, ii. 246 & n. 7; S. Maria in Aracœli, ii. 226; S. Maria della Concezione, ii. 369 & n. 7; S. Maria Maggiore, ii. 243,

Roman Catholic Church, &c. (*cont.*)
244, 291 & n. 2; S. Maria sopra Minerva, ii. 204 & n. 3, 377 & n. 4; S. Nicola in Carcere, ii. 365; S. Paolo fuori, ii. 306–7 & nn.; St. Peter's, ii. 260, 262–3 & nn., 289–90 & nn, 292 & n. 2, 385, 386 *bis*; S. Pietro in Carcere, ii. 227 & n. 6; S. Pietro in Vincoli, ii. 278; S. Prassede, ii. 245, n. 7, 246 & n. 2; S. Pudenziana, ii. 245–6 & nn.; S. Sebastiano (Via Appia), ii. 363; S. Susanna, ii. 239; Vatican: obelisk, ii. 256; ~ Sistine Chapel, sacristy, ii. 298; Venerable English College, ii. 365–6; place not specified, iii. 634.
— — — St. Denis, ii. 86–90 & nn. (i. 58–60); Siena: cathedral, ii. 205 & n. 2; ~ hospital, ii. 205 & nn. 5, 6; ~ S. Domenico, ii. 204 & n. 3 ~ staff of St. Francis, ii. 205 & n. 8; Tours, St. Martin, ii. 144–5 (i. 94); Venice, S. Marco, ii. 438–42 & nn.; ~ S. Zaccaria, ii. 460 & n. 4.
— — — place not mentioned, iv. 470; in James II's possession, iv. 470–1 & nn.
— — miraculous paintings and images [places where preserved]: Florence, SS. Annunziata, ii. 194 & n. 9 (i. 120), 412 & n. 4; Lucca, cathedral, ii. 409–10 & n.; Rome, Lateran, Sancta Sanctorum, ii. 269 & n. 4; S. Maria in Aracoeli, ii. 226 & n. 7; S. Maria Maggiore, ii. 244 & n. 2; S. Maria del Popolo, ii. 374 & n. 3; S. Maria della Vittoria, ii. 240 & n. 1.
— — — Venice, S. Marco, ii. 438 & n. 9.
— — miscellaneous and general notices: tenets discussed, &c., iv. 242–3; papal infallibility: in Charles II's papers, iv. 476–7; ~ denied by P. Walsh, iv. 496; visibility of the Church, iii. 37; Bull *In Coena Domini*, ii. 385 & n. 5; *add.* (iv. 641); Cancelleria, &c.: officials of, in procession, ii. 280; ~ vice-chancellor (Cardinal F. Barberini), ii. 367; dispensations, iv. 476 & n. 2; Inquisition: at Milan, ii. 491 & n. 2, 503, 505; ~ palace of, at Rome, ii. 290 & n. 4; kissing the

Roman Catholic Church, &c. (*cont.*)
pope's foot, ii. 391; miracle at Rome, iii. 36, 634; nuns: freedom of, at Lucca, ii. 410; protestants' child baptised by Roman Catholic midwife, iii. 19; anti-Catholic notices: clergy: examples of bad influence of, in politics, v. 35, 47; miracles: danger of fraudulent, &c., iii. 557, 558; iv. 251–2; Papacy: destruction of: prophecy, v. 271–2; ~ destruction imminent (Lloyd's prophecies), v. 20–1, 322; no reliance on Roman Catholic promises possible, iv. 582.

Romances: recalled by natural scenery, iii. 115 & n. 5; alluded to (knight errantry, &c.), iv. 71.

Romanelli, G. F.; painting by, ii. 233 & n. 10.

Romano, Giulio: *see* Giulio Romano.

Romano, Paris: *see* Nogari, P.

Romans: King of the, 1690–1705: *see* Joseph I, Emperor.

Romans: Queen of the, 1699–1705: *see* Wilhelmina Amalia.

Rome: the Republic and Empire:
rulers of: sequence, ii. 401 & n. 3; ~ triumphs of, in sermon, iii. 9; empire: duration of, ii. 431, n. 3; emperors: hereditary succession of, iv. 300; ~ in sermon, v. 165; people of: erect arches in honour of Titus and Constantine, ii. 247, 250; senate: orders statue to be mutilated, ii. 283; history of: boy's knowledge of, iv. 617; decay of: in sermon, v. 89.
relations with: Capua, ii. 324; the Jews: in sermons, iii. 305; v. 21, 227, 276; Pisa, ii. 179 & n. 8 (i. 113); ~ tribute paid by, ii. 181 (i. 114); Valais, ii. 517.
customs, &c.: burials beside highways, ii. 317; children: naming of, in sermon, v. 124–5; games, &c.: biblical text applied to, in sermon, iv. 533; parricide: punishment of, v. 149, n. 1; religious liberty: in sermon, v. 64; soldiers: provision for aged, ii. 288–9 & n.
inscriptions relating to: *Acta triumphorum* and *Fasti consulares*, ii. 225 & n. 5; laws, ii. 224 & n. 2, 309 & n. 5.

Rome: the Republic, &c. (*cont.*)
Roman Britain: site of city near Banstead, iii. 221 & n. 7; Camelodunum: site of, iii. 180 & n. 2; ruins at Leicester, iii. 123 & n. 2; *see also* Helena, St.

Rome: the City:
— E: at (1644–5), ii. 212–316 & nn., 356–405 & nn.; i. *7–8*; poem by, on, ii. 402–5 & nn.; expenses of, at, ii. 401 & n. 6; guide of, at, ii. 214; lodgings of, at, ii. 212 & nn. 3, 4, 232, 286, 306, 362; music-teacher of, at, ii. 287; painter of, at: *see* Maratti, C.; spaniel brought away by, from, ii. 533; English acquaintances of, at: *see* Pratt, Sir R. (iii. 153); White, Mrs. C., *and* White, Richard (iii. 33, 595); *see also* ii. 213 & nn. 2–8, 311, 365 & n. 8, 367; mentioned, ii. 200, 422.
— bibliographical note, ii. 575–8; guide-books for, i. *100–1* & nn.; *see also* pp. *91–100*; ~ instructions concerning, ii. 214.
— in antiquity: historical, &c.: brethren from, meet St. Paul, ii. 318; St. Peter at: altars used by, ii. 246 & n. 6, 272; ~ contest of, with Simon Magus, ii. 248 & n. 3; ~ meets Christ at Domine Quo Vadis, ii. 363 *bis*; ~ prison of, ii. 227; ~ place of execution of, ii. 313; ~ in sermon, iii. 333; persecutions of Christians, &c., at, ii. 238 & n. 4, 240 & n. 3, 307, 364, 388 & n. 3; Constantine the Great's expedition to: in comparison, iv. 618; Horses of St. Mark's, Venice, removed from, ii. 437 & n. 3; Olympic games at, ii. 360 & n. 5; triumph at: in legend (in sermon), v. 192.
— government of: (i) *conservatori* or consuls, ii. 222 & n. 3; ~ swearing in of, ii. 291 & n. 5; ~ in ceremonies, &c., ii. 224, 280, 291, 385; ~ statues of (error), ii. 224 & n. 6; governor(s) of the city: in procession, ii. 280; ~ at entertainment, ii. 389; people of Rome: *conservatori* as officers of, ii. 291; ~ knight gonfalonier and prior of: in procession, ii. 280; ~ standard of: blessed, ii. 387 & n. 1; ~ erect monu-

Rome: the City (*cont.*)
ment commemorating Gregory XI's return from Avignon, ii. 248; senate: arch erected by, for *possesso* of Innocent X, ii. 228, n. 6, 281, n. 2.
— — (ii) administration of justice: courts, ii. 221; ~ executions: places and method of, ii. 367 & n. 1, 400–1 & n.; archives of, ii. 224; granaries, municipal, ii. 239 & n. 2; office of, for issuing bills of health, ii. 167, n. 7; statues, &c., owned by, ii. 226.
— miscellaneous and general notices: earthquakes at, 1703, v. 531 & n. 1; editions of Early Christian Fathers published at, iv. 145, n. 1; illuminations at, ii. 282, 391; medicinal waters at (Tre Fontane), ii. 308; miracle at, *c.* 1650, iii. 36; music at: performers, ii. 400 & n. 1; performances: at Chiesa Nuova, ii. 232–3 & n., 277, 283, 291, 387; ~ opera, ii. 388–9 & n.; teacher of, ii. 287; painting at: the Roman masters, &c.: in comparison, iv. 316, 344; ~ living masters, &c., at, ii. 399 & nn. 8–10; sculptors, &c., at, ii. 399 & nn. 6–7; Swiss guard at, ii. 296–7 & n.; ~ in procession, ii. 279, 280; ~ member of, ii. 214, n. 2; uncommon illness at, iii. 316 & n. 5; final burning of: in prophecy, v. 322.
— personal: Pietro Cisij educated at, iii. 522, n. 2; T. Keightley converted to Roman Catholicism at, iii. 35, 633–4; A. Kircher at: E sends drawing to, iii. 171–2 & n.; Duchesse Mazarin born at, v. 330; Cardinal M. S. Radziejowski summoned to, 1704, v. 577 & n. 6; travellers to and from, &c.: *see* Bruce, Robert, earl of Ailesbury (ii. 449, n. 7); Donghi, Cardinal G. (ii. 207); Ducie, Sir William, Viscount Downe (iii. 181, n. 2); Howard, Lord Thomas (iv. 142 & n. 4); Pordage, — (iv. 403); Siface (G. F. Grossi) (iv. 537); Ward, Mary, ii. 400 & n. 3; Wright, J. M. (iii. 338 & n. 5); *see also* E at Rome *above*; unnamed travellers to, ii. 45 (i. 32).

Rome: the City (*cont.*)
— religion: (i): festivals: Epiphany, ii. 291 & n. 7; St. Anthony's day, ii. 387 & n. 4; Lady Day, ii. 377–8 & n., 384; Shrove Tuesday, ii. 381–2 & nn.; Ash Wednesday, ii. 382; Palm Sunday and Eastertide, ii. 385–7 & nn.; St. George's day, ii. 387 & n. 1; St. Yves's day, ii. 387 & n. 3; Christmas, ii. 226–7 & n., 290–1 & nn.
— — (ii): miscellaneous: bishopric of Rome: cathedral of, ii. 271, 279, n. 3; charities: Compagnia della Dottrina Christiana, ii. 366 & n. 9; Monte di Pietà, ii. 366 & n. 8; orphanage, ii. 311; *zitelle*, ii. 292 & n. 2, 311, 378 & n. 1, 384 & n. 4; *see also* pilgrims *below*; hospitals, *in* topography *below*; Golden Rose: benediction of, ii. 384 & n. 6; pilgrims to: entertainment for: at Siena, ii. 205 & n. 4; ~ at Rome, ii. 366 & n. 3; sermons: general character of preaching, ii. 384 & n. 3; to Jews, ii. 291–2 & n., 376; mentioned, ii. 290, 373; stations (ecclesiastical) of, ii. 243 & n. 3.
— social life, &c.: Carnival: 1645, ii. 381–2 & nn., 389, n. 3; ~ games at Monte Testaccio (medieval), ii. 360, n. 5; charities: *see* religion *above*; coaches, ii. 257–8 & n.; guides, ii. 214, n. 2; horsemanship, ii. 232 & n. 6; Jews at: *see* Jews; May Day, ii. 387 & nn. 3–5; mountebanks, ii. 368, 397–8; iv. 253; mules: blessing of, ii. 387 & n. 4; processions: ambassadors', ii. 389 & n. 4, 391 & n. 2; *possesso*: route of, ii. 369 & n. 4; ~ of Innocent X, ii. 206, 279–82 & nn.; ~ decorations for, ii. 226–7 & n., 228 & n. 6, 281 & nn. 1, 2; promenade, ii. 217; prostitutes: burial-place of, ii. 375; ~ in Carnival, ii. 382; ~ tax on, ii. 417 & n. 9; tournament, ii. 389 & n. 3; Turkish convert at, ii. 377.
— topography: (i) general: area, ii. 401 & n. 4; inhabited area, ii. 212, n. 2; population, *ib.*; *add.*; general observations, ii. 398–401 & nn.; ~ in poem, ii. 403,

Rome: the City (*cont.*)
405; in comparison, iii. 637 (extract from *State of France*).
— — — ancient Rome: model of, at Villa d'Este, ii. 396 & n. 4; ancient tombs beside roads near, ii. 317; antiquities, &c.: drawings of, iii. 10; art-collections at: *see* Art-collections.
— — — churches in: in comparison, ii. 96; number of, ii. 401 & n. 4; the Seven Roman, ii. 243; first and second, dedicated to Virgin Mary, ii. 289 & n. 3, 359 & n. 4.
— — — guides at, ii. 214 & n. 2; obelisks at, ii. 403; ~ transport of, to, ii. 257 & n. 1, 270 & n. 3; ruins: in comparison, iv. 70; sculptures at: in comparison, iv. 213; soil: rise of, since antiquity, ii. 217, n. 2, 220 & n. 1, 379 & n. 3; as starting-point of Via Appia, ii. 319; streets: beauty, &c., of, ii. 234, 237 & n. 4, 241 *bis*, 381; summer in: unhealthy, ii. 387; view of, by Lincler, iii. 10, n. 3; villas, ii. 401; ~ in comparisons, ii. 563; iii. 359; water-mills, ii. 357 & n. 4.
— — (ii): particular buildings, streets, &c. [the area comprises the whole of the city within the walls, and the extramural churches and adjoining monuments, &c.]:
— — — Accademia degli Umoristi, ii. 364–5 & nn.
— — — Aerarium, ii. 278 & n. 2.
— — — Amphitheatrum Castrense (Amphitheatre of Statilius Taurus), ii. 380 & n. 11.
— — — Amphitheatre of Vespasian *or* Titus: *see* Coliseum *below*.
— — — aqueducts:
— — — — Aqua Alsietina *or* Augusta, ii. 312, n. 6, 313.
— — — — Aqua Claudia, ii. 383 & n. 6; outside the walls, ii. 316, n. 3, 317.
— — — — Acqua Felice: course and fountain of, ii. 238–9 & nn.; outside the walls, ii. 316, n. 3, 317 & n. 3.
— — — — Aqua Marcia, ii. 381 & n. 8; outside the walls, ii. 316, n. 3, 317 & n. 1; *add*.

Rome: the City (*cont.*)
— — — — Acqua Paola: fountain of, ii. 312–13 & nn.
— — — — Aqua Traiana, ii. 312, n. 6.
— — — arches:
— — — — Arcus Argentariorum, ii. 228 & n. 4.
— — — — Arch of Constantine, ii. 250 & nn. 3, 4; painted copy of, ii. 109 & n. 3 (i. 70).
— — — — Arch of Horatius, ii. 360 & n. 2.
— — — — Arco di Portogallo, ii. 370 & n. 2.
— — — — Arch of Septimius Severus, ii. 219–20 & n.; mentioned, ii. 217, n. 2.
— — — — Arch of Titus, ii. 247–8 & nn.; mentioned, ii. 217, n. 2.
— — — Atrium Vestae, ii. 219, n. 7.
— — — Augusteo, ii. 375, n. 5 *ad fin.*
— — — Aventine hill, ii. 227, 359.
— — — barracks of papal horse-guards, ii. 290 & n. 5.
— — — Basilica of Constantine: as Temple of Peace, ii. 218 & n. 1; ~ column from, ii. 245 & n. 4; road through, ii. 217, n. 2.
— — — baths:
— — — — of Antoninus *or* Caracalla, ii. 361 & n. 3; fountain-basins from, ii. 216, n. 7.
— — — — of Constantine, ii. 379; statues from, ii. 226.
— — — — of Diocletian, ii. 238 & nn. 2–5, 240 & n. 3; mentioned, ii. 212, n. 2.
— — — — of Novatus, ii. 247.
— — — — of Septimius Severus: columns from, ii. 358 & n. 6.
— — — — of Titus, ii. 278–9 & n.; fountain-basins from (?), ii. 216 & n. 7, 305 & n. 5; statue from, ii. 304.
— — — — of Trajan, ii. 279, n. 1.
— — — — Lavacrum Agrippinae, ii. 247.
— — — Belvedere di Monte Cavallo (Quirinal palace), ii. 238.
— — — Borgo, ii. 212, nn. 1, 2.
— — — bridges:
— — — — Pons Aurelius: *see* Ponte Sisto *below*.
— — — — Pons Mulvius *or* Milvius (Ponte Molle), ii. 383 & n. 4;

Rome: the City (*cont.*)
Constantine's victory at, ii. 250 & n. 4; ~ in comparison, iv. 618; procession from, ii. 389, n. 4 *ad fin.*
— — — — Pons Probi: remains of, ii. 357, n. 3, 359, n. 6.
— — — — Ponte S. Angelo, ii. 357, n. 3; place of execution at, ii. 367, n. 1.
— — — — Ponte Sisto, formerly Pons Aurelius, ii. 384 & nn. 1, 2; oratory near, ii. 291 & n. 8.
— — — — Pons Sublicius: supposed remains of, ii. 357 & n. 3, 360 & n. 3.
— — — — Pons Triumphalis: remains of, ii. 357 & n. 3.
— — — Caelius, the (Celio), ii. 250, 271, 276, 361.
— — — Campo dei Fiori, ii. 366–7 & n.
— — — Campo Marzo *or* Campus Martius: views of, ii. 231 & n. 1, 373; the antique: in comparison, &c., ii. 484, 526; *see also* iii. 594 & n. 4.
— — — Campo Santo dei Tedeschi, ii. 290 & n. 1.
— — — Campo Scelerato, ii. 241 & n. 4.
— — — Campo Vaccino: *see* Forum Romanum *below*.
— — — Capitol, the, ii. 220–7 & nn., 227 & n. 4; the various buildings, monuments, &c., are indexed under their several names; mentioned, ii. 212, n. 2, 217, n. 2, 219, 247, 291, 405.
— — — Capo di Bove, ii. 362–3 & n.
— — — Castel S. Angelo, ii. 357; angel's foot-print from, ii. 226 & n. 8; paintings from, ii. 549; guns at, fired, for celebrations, ii. 291, 384, 385, 386; illuminated, ii. 282; governor of: in procession, ii. 280.
— — — catacombs:
— — — — of Domitilla, ii. 364, n. 1, 387–8 & nn.
— — — — of S. Agnese, ii. 387, n. 6.
— — — — of St. Calixtus (error), ii. 364, n. 1, 387, n. 6.
— — — — of St. Ciriaca (S. Lorenzo), ii. 381, n. 6, 387, n. 6.
— — — — of S. Sebastiano, ii. 363–4 & n., 387 & n. 6.

Rome: the City (*cont.*)
— — — Celio: *see* Caelius *above*.
— — — cemetery for prostitutes, ii. 375.
— — — centre of the city, ii. 219 & n. 5.
— — — Christ's Hospital: *see* hospitals: S. Spirito *below*.
— — — churches [including adjoining convents, &c.]:
— — — — Chiesa Nuova, the Oratory, &c., ii. 232–4 & nn., 283–4; music at, ii. 233 & n. 12, 277, 283, 291, 387.
— — — — Domine Quo Vadis, ii. 363 *bis* & nn. 2, 7.
— — — — Gesù, ii. 230 & nn. 1–3; Casa Professa adjoining, ii. 230 & n. 5.
— — — — Greek church: *see* S. Atanasio *below*.
— — — — Oratory of the Compagnia della SS. Trinità, ii. 291, n. 8.
— — — — S. Adriano, ii. 219 & nn. 4, 6; mentioned, ii. 217, n. 2, 278, n. 2.
— — — — S. Agnese fuori le Mura, ii. 240–1 & nn.
— — — — S. Agnese in Piazza Navona, ii. 368, n. 1.
— — — — St. Anacletus (S. Anastasia ?), ii. 276 & n. 9.
— — — — S. Anastasia, ii. 276, nn. 8, 9.
— — — — S. Andrea della Valle and monastery, ii. 376 & nn. 3–7; Pius II buried in, ii. 407, n. 9; resident near, ii. 277, n. 3.
— — — — S. Angelo in Pescheria (in Piscina), ii. 384, n. 1; sermons to Jews at, ii. 291, n. 8.
— — — — S. Antonio Abbate: blessing of mules, &c., at, ii. 387 & n. 4.
— — — — S. Apollinare: sermon at, ii. 290 & n. 7.
— — — — S. Atanasio de' Greci: services at, ii. 291 & n. 6, 382 & n. 2; usage at, ii. 399.
— — — — St. Augustine: monastery of (error), ii. 374 & n. 2.
— — — — S. Bartolomeo in Isola, ii. 358 & nn. 9, 10.
— — — — S. Bernardo alle Terme, ii. 238.
— — — — S. Carlo alle Quattro Fontane, ii. 242 & n. 1.
— — — — S. Cecilia in Trastevere

Rome: the City (*cont.*)
and convent, ii. 357–8 & nn.; chapel with the bath in, ii. 275, 276, n. 1.
— — — — SS. Cosma e Damiano, ii. 218–19 & nn.
— — — — S. Costanza, ii. 241 & nn. 2, 3; hippodrome adjoining, ii. 360, n. 5.
— — — — S. Crisogono, ii. 288 & n. 3; columns in: source of, ii. 358, n. 6.
— — — — S. Croce in Gerusalemme, ii. 380 & nn. 1–10; monastery adjoining, ii. 380 & n. 11; relic removed from (in inscription), ii. 262; relics at: exhibited, ii. 384–5 & n.; street leading to, ii. 241, n. 5.
— — — — S. Francesca Romana (S. Maria Nuova), ii. 248 & nn. 2–4; mentioned, ii. 217, n. 2.
— — — — S. Giacomo degli Incurabili: sermon at, &c., ii. 373 & nn. 7, 8.
— — — — S. Giacomo degli Spagnuoli: *chapelle ardente* in, &c., ii. 368–9 & nn.
— — — — S. Giorgio in Velabro: procession to, ii. 387, n. 1.
— — — — S. Giovanni in Fonte: *see* S. Giovanni in Laterano: baptistery *below*.
— — — — S. Giovanni in Laterano: the church and surrounding buildings, ii. 266–75.
— — — — — the church, ii. 266 & nn. 4, 5, 271–5 & nn.; papal procession to (*possesso*): *see* social life *above*; Holy Saturday services at, ii. 386 & n. 4; relics at: exhibited, ii. 292 & n. 1, 385 & n. 7; parts of the church, &c.: altars: high (St. Salvator's), ii. 272, 274 & n. 3; ~ of Sacrament, ii. 272–3 & nn.; apse: papal throne in, ii. 268, n. 2; Cappella del Coro, ii. 273 & nn. 2, 3, 274, n. 8; doors: bronze, ii. 219, n. 6; ~ Porta Santa, ii. 275 & n. 1; papal thrones in, ii. 268 & n. 2; pavement, ii. 272 & n. 2; porticoes: uncertain, ii. 268 & n. 2; ~ eastern, ii. 271 & n. 3, 275 & n. 1; ~ northern, ii. 271, n. 3, 275 & n. 2; Portico Leoniano, ii. 266, n. 4, 273, n. 5, 274, n. 5; relics, ii. 273–4 & nn., 275 & n. 3, 307, n. 1; *see also above*; sacristy, ii. 273 & n. 4, 274, nn. 5, 8; statues: Constantine, ii. 222, n. 8; ~ Henri IV, ii. 275 & n. 2; tombs, ii. 273 & n. 3, 274 & nn. 5–8; ~ of Clement XII, ii. 370, n. 6; transept, ii. 272–3 & nn.
— — — — — surrounding buildings: baptistery (S. Giovanni in Fonte) and its oratories, ii. 266–8 & nn.; ~ portico of, ii. 268, n. 2; ~ monument in, ii. 273, n. 9; ~ Holy Saturday baptisms in, ii. 386, n. 4; cloister: relics, &c., in, ii. 268, n. 2, 273, nn. 5, 7, 274, n. 8; obelisk, ii. 269–71 & nn.; palace, old: doorways from, ii. 268, n. 2; ~ staircase from, ii. 268–9 & n.; palace, new, ii. 271; ~ Christian Museum in: statue in, ii. 301, n. 1; Sancta Sanctorum, ii. 269 & nn. 2–4; ~ mentioned, ii. 268, n. 2, 274, n. 2; Scala santa, ii. 268–9 & n.; Triclinium of Leo III, ii. 275, n. 5.
— — — — S. Giovanni Colavita and convent, &c., ii. 358–9 & nn.
— — — — SS. Giovanni e Paolo and monks there, ii. 276 & nn. 2–4.
— — — — S. Gregorio Magno, ii. 251 & nn. 1, 2; the adjoining oratories, ii. 275–6 & nn.
— — — — S. Ignazio, ii. 283 & n. 2.
— — — — S. Ivo, ii. 376, n. 1.
— — — — S. Lorenzo fuori le Mura, ii. 381 & nn. 2–7; mentioned, ii. 246, n. 10 *ad fin.*
— — — — S. Lorenzo in Miranda, ii. 219 & n. 3.
— — — — S. Lorenzo in Panisperna, ii. 246 & nn. 7–10.
— — — — S. Marco, ii. 378 & nn. 4, 5.
— — — — S. Maria degli Angeli and monastery, ii. 240 & n. 4; mentioned, ii. 239, n. 2.
— — — — S. Maria Annunziata (Collegio Romano), ii. 283 & n. 2, 384, n. 5.
— — — — S. Maria in Aracœli, ii. 226 & nn. 4–8; *add.*; in relation to Campidoglio, ii. 220, n. 3; Christmas in: preparations for (?), ii. 226–7 & n.; procession for Bambino in, ii. 291 & n. 7;

Rome: the City (*cont.*)
statues in (since E's time), ii. 221, n. 2, 224, n. 5; steps leading to, ii. 279.
— — — — S. Maria della Concezione and convent, ii. 369 & nn. 5–8.
— — — — S. Maria in Cosmedin (de Schola Græca), ii. 359 & nn. 3, 4.
— — — — S. Maria in Domnica (della Navicella), ii. 361–2 & n.
— — — — S. Maria Liberatrice, ii. 217, n. 2.
— — — — S. Maria Maggiore, ii. 242–5 & nn.; date of foundation of, ii. 242 & n. 5; *add.*; street leading to, ii. 241, n. 5, 381; mentioned, ii. 212, n. 2; Cappella Paolina in, ii. 243–4 & nn.; Cappella Sforza in, ii. 244 & n. 6; Cappella Sistina in, ii. 243 & nn. 4–7, 244–5 & n.; relic exhibited at, ii. 291 & n. 2.
— — — — S. Maria sopra Minerva, ii. 377–8 & nn.; baptisms of Turk and Jew at, ii. 376–7 & n.; Christmas crib at, ii. 290 & n. 6; papal procession to, on Lady Day, ii. 377–8 & n., 384 & n. 4; mentioned, ii. 372, n. 10.
— — — — S. Maria di Monserrato, ii. 369, nn. 1, 2.
— — — — S. Maria della Navicella, ii. 361–2 & n.
— — — — S. Maria Nova: *see* S. Francesca Romana *above*.
— — — — S. Maria della Pietà nel Coliseo, ii. 250 & n. 2.
— — — — S. Maria del Popolo, ii. 373–4 & nn.; mentioned, ii. 389, n. 4 *ad fin.*
— — — — S. Maria della Rotonda: *see* Pantheon *below*.
— — — — S. Maria Scala del Cielo, ii. 307 & n. 9.
— — — — S. Maria de Schola Græca (in Cosmedin), ii. 359 & nn. 3, 4.
— — — — S. Maria del Sole (S. Stefano alle Carrozze), ii. 359 & n. 2; *add.*
— — — — S. Maria in Trastevere, ii. 288–9 & nn.; mentioned, ii. 359, n. 4.
— — — — S. Maria in Vallicella: *see* Chiesa Nuova *above*.
— — — — S. Maria della Vittoria, ii. 239–40 & nn.

Rome: the City (*cont.*)
— — — — S. Maria Egiziaca, ii. 359, n. 1.
— — — — S. Martino al Monte della Pietà, ii. 366 & n. 9.
— — — — S. Martino ai Monti: St. Martin I buried at, ii. 274, n. 7.
— — — — S. Nicola in Carcere, ii. 365 & nn. 3–5.
— — — — S. Omobono, ii. 278, n. 2.
— — — — S. Onofrio: Cardinal of: *see* Barberini, A.
— — — — S. Orsola, ii. 227, n. 4.
— — — — S. Paolo fuori le Mura, ii. 306–7 & nn.; in comparison, ii. 307.
— — — — S. Paolo alle Tre Fontane, ii. 307–8 & nn.
— — — — S. Pietro in Carcere, ii. 227 & nn. 5–8.
— — — — S. Pietro in Montorio, ii. 313 & nn. 2–5; painting in, ii. 227, n. 7.
— — — — St. Peter's (S. Pietro in Vaticano), ii. 255, 258–66 & nn., 289–90 & nn.; bibliography and general note, ii. 255, n. 1; in E's poem, ii. 405; shaken by earthquake, 1703, v. 531; dimensions, ii. 425 & n. 3; in comparisons, i. 84 *bis*; ii. 243 & n. 2, 266, 328, 493.
— — — — — clergy, ii. 266; Congregatione de' Riti, ii. 263, n. 2; Eastertide ceremonies at, ii. 385–6 & nn.; papal coronations in, ii. 279, n. 3; procession to, &c., ii. 292 & n. 2; relics at: exhibited, *ib.*; ii. 385 & nn. 3, 4, 386 *bis* & n. 2; sermons at, ii. 384.
— — — — — altar, high, ii. 260–1 & nn., 263, 264; ~ bronze for, ii. 371–2 & n.; campanile, ii. 255, n. 1, 258–9 & n.; *add.*; Cathedra Petri, ii. 264 & n. 4; ~ festival of, ii. 300, n. 2; *confessio*, ii. 263 & nn. 4, 5; confessionals, ii. 265; ~ on Good Friday, ii. 386; crypt, ii. 289–90 & nn.; dome, ii. 259–60 & nn.; doors: bronze, ii. 258 & n. 6; ~ Porta Santa, ii. 266; façade, ii. 258–9 & nn.; loggia of the benediction, ii. 258 & n. 7, 385, n. 5, 386, n. 5 *ad fin.*; marble incrustation, ii. 255, n. 1, 265–6 & n., 437; *Navicella*

Rome: the City (*cont.*)
mosaic, ii. 265 & n. 3; *add.*; pavement, ii. 265 & n. 4; portico, ii. 258 & n. 6, 264, 266; ~ in comparison, ii. 492–3 & n.; ~ stairs from, to Vatican, ii. 295–6 & n.; relics: four principal, ii. 261–3 & nn.; ~ others, ii. 263, 264, 307, n. 1; ~ exhibited: *see above*; roof, ii. 260; sacristy, ii. 263 & n. 3; statues: Michelangelo's Pietà, ii. 264 & n. 5; iv. 566, n. 2; ~ St. Peter, ii. 264 & n. 1; ~ St. Veronica, &c., ii. 261–3 & nn.; tombs: Adrian IV, ii. 289 & n. 7; Matilda, Countess, ii. 265 & n. 2; Paul III, ii. 264–5 & nn.; ~ statues from, ii. 308 & n. 6; Sixtus IV, ii. 265 & n. 2; Urban VIII, ii. 264.
— — — — S. Pietro in Vincoli, ii. 278 & nn. 3–7; monastery, ii. 279; mentioned, ii. 227 & n. 7.
— — — — S. Prassede, ii. 245, n. 7, 246 & nn. 2, 3.
— — — — S. Prisca, ii. 359, n. 8.
— — — — S. Pudenziana, ii. 245–6 & n., 246 & nn. 4–6.
— — — — SS. Quirico e Giulitta: Easter Sepulchres at, ii. 386, n. 1.
— — — — SS. Rocco e Martino, ii. 375 & n. 4.
— — — — S. Saba, ii. 361 & n. 3.
— — — — S. Sabina, ii. 359 & nn. 7–10.
— — — — S. Sebastiano and monastery, ii. 363 & nn. 3–8; façade of, ii. 276, n. 6; catacombs at, ii. 363–4 & n.; ~ in comparison, ii. 387.
— — — — S. Sebastiano alla Polveriera, ii. 276 & n. 6.
— — — — S. Sebastianus de via papae, ii. 376, n. 5.
— — — — S. Spirito in Sassia, ii. 312 & n. 2.
— — — — S. Stefano alle Carrozze (as S. Stefano Rotondo), ii. 359 & n. 2; *add.*
— — — — S. Susanna, ii. 239 & nn. 3–9.
— — — — S. Tecla, ii. 311, n. 6.
— — — — S. Teodoro, ii. 276, n. 7.
— — — — S. Tommaso degli Inglesi, ii. 365–6 & nn.
— — — — SS. Trinità de' Monti and convent, ii. 373 & nn. 1–6; *add.*; collection of antiquities at, ii. 314, n. 1; road leading to, ii. 241, n. 5.
— — — — SS. Trinità de' Pellegrini: *see* hospitals *below*.
— — — — SS. Vincenzo ed Anastasio, ii. 307 & n. 8.
— — — circuses:
— — — — Circus Agonalis, ii. 368 & n. 3.
— — — — Circus of Caracalla: *see* Circus of Maxentius *below*.
— — — — Circus Flaminius, ii. 365 & n. 6.
— — — — Circus of Gaius and Nero, ii. 256, n. 1, 290 & n. 3.
— — — — Circus of Maxentius (Caracalla), ii. 362 & nn. 3–6, 363, n. 2.
— — — — Circus Maximus, ii. 227–8 & n., 276–7 & n.; mentioned, ii. 361; obelisks from, ii. 269–71 & nn., 374–5 & nn.; falsely identified, iv. 253.
— — — Coliseum (Amphitheatre of Vespasian), ii. 247, 248–50 & nn.; notices in E's sources quoted, i. *91–6*; damaged by earthquake, 1703, v. 531 & n. 1; drawing of, iii. 10.
— — — colleges:
— — — — Collegio Germanico, ii. 290, n. 7.
— — — — Collegio Greco, ii. 291, n. 6.
— — — — Collegio Romano, ii. 282–3 & nn.; Kircher's instruments at, ii. 230, n. 5; celebration at, ii. 384 & n. 5.
— — — — Irish Franciscan College: occupant of St. Isidore's chair at (?), ii. 96 & n. 2 (i. 63); *add.*
— — — — Venerable English College, ii. 365–6 & nn.; plays, &c., at, ii. 291 & n. 4, 388; John Cosin, jnr., admitted to, &c., iii. 26, n. 6; rector of: *see* Courtney, Father T.
— — — columns:
— — — — Marcus Aurelius, ii. 370 & nn. 3, 4.
— — — — Milliary, ii. 219 & n. 5, 222 & n. 2.
— — — — Columna Rostrata of Duilius, ii. 222 & n. 6.
— — — — before S. Maria Maggiore, ii. 245 & n. 4.

Rome: the City (*cont.*)
— — — — Trajan, ii. 378–9 & nn.
— — — Compagnia della SS. Trinità: oratory of, ii. 291, n. 8.
— — — Corso, ii. 370 & nn. 1, 2, 373; as part of Via Flaminia, ii. 389, n. 4 *ad fin.*; carnival races in, ii. 382; resident in, ii. 283, n. 4.
— — — Curia Julia (S. Adriano), ii. 219 & nn. 4, 6.
— — — Esquiline hill, ii. 242, 278 & nn. 1, 4.
— — — Farnesina, the, ii. 287–8 & nn., 357 & nn. 5, 6.
— — — fora:
— — — — Forum Boarium, ii. 228 & nn. 1–4.
— — — — Forum Romanum (Campo Vaccino), ii. 217–20 & nn.; mentioned, ii. 247, 276; arch for Innocent X's *possesso* in, ii. 281 & n. 1; Farnese gardens near, ii. 383–4; milliary column from (?), ii. 222 & n. 2.
— — — — Forum of Trajan, ii. 378–9 & nn.; resident near, ii. 314, n. 1.
— — — fountains:
— — — — Acqua Felice: Fontanone dell', ii. 238–9 & nn.
— — — — Acqua Paola, ii. 312–13 & nn.
— — — — in Campo dei Fiori, ii. 366–7 & n.
— — — — Capitol, Palazzo dei Conservatori, ii. 222.
— — — — Capitol, Palazzo del Senatore, ii. 220 & n. 4, 226, n. 3.
— — — — in Forum, ii. 217, n. 2.
— — — — of Lepidus (Quattro Fontane), ii. 241–2 & n.
— — — — Marforio, ii. 220, n. 3, 221 & n. 1.
— — — — Meta Sudans: *see* Meta Sudans *below*.
— — — — of Numa (error), ii. 313 & n. 7.
— — — — in palace of duke of Bracciano, ii. 288.
— — — — in Palazzo del Quirinale and gardens, ii. 237, 238, 287.
— — — — in Piazza d'Aracœli, ii. 227 & n. 2.
— — — — in Piazza Farnese, ii. 216 & n. 7.
— — — — in Piazza Navona, ii. 368 & nn. 1, 4.

Rome: the City (*cont.*)
— — — — in Piazza del Quirinale (Horse-tamers), ii. 237 & n. 2.
— — — — in Piazza della Rotonda, ii. 370–1 & n.
— — — — in Piazza di S. Maria in Trastevere, ii. 289 & n. 4.
— — — — in Piazza S. Pietro, ii. 255 & n. 3.
— — — — Quattro Fontane, ii. 241–2 & n.; *see also* ii. 237, n. 4.
— — — — at S. Giovanni in Laterano (by obelisk), ii. 271.
— — — — at S. Maria Maggiore (by column before), ii. 245.
— — — — of Trevi: residence near, ii. 282, n. 2.
— — — — in Vatican and gardens, ii. 303, n. 1, 304, n. 4, 305 & nn. 5–7.
— — — — in Villa Borghese, ii. 251–2, 390 *bis* & n. 3.
— — — — in Villa Giustiniani, ii. 383.
— — — — in Villa Medici, ii. 231, 232 & n. 5; ~ in street outside, ii. 232 & n. 5.
— — — — in Villa Montalto, ii. 240.
— — — Galleria Nazionale in Villa Borghese (modern): origin of, ii. 252, n. 5 *ad fin.*
— — — gates, &c.:
— — — — Porta Angelica, ii. 212, n. 1.
— — — — Porta Asinaria, ii. 316, n. 3.
— — — — Porta Furba, ii. 316, n. 3.
— — — — Porta Latina, ii. 316 & n. 3.
— — — — Porta Maggiore, ii. 381, n. 1, 383, n. 6.
— — — — Porta Ostiensis, ii. 361, n. 2.
— — — — Porta Pia, ii. 240, n. 6, 241.
— — — — Porta del Popolo, ii. 375 & n. 1; statues on, ii. 306, n. 11 *ad fin.*; mentioned, ii. 212, n. 2, 389, n. 4.
— — — — Porta S. Giovanni, ii. 316, n. 3.
— — — — Porta S. Lorenzo, ii. 381 & n. 1.
— — — — Porta S. Pancrazio, ii. 312.
— — — — Porta S. Paolo, ii. 361 & n. 2.

Rome: the City (*cont.*)
— — — — Porta S. Spirito, ii. 212, n. 1.
— — — — Porta Tiburtina, ii. 381, n. 1.
— — — — Porta Trigemina, ii. 361 & n. 2.
— — — — Porta Vaticana, ii. 212 & n. 1.
— — — Ghetto, ii. 292 & n. 3.
— — — Golden House of Nero: ruins of, ii. 276 & n. 5, 279, n. 1; nail from, ii. 357.
— — — granaries, municipal, ii. 239 & n. 2, 241, n. 4.
— — — Hercules: altar of, ii. 359 & n. 5.
— — — Hippodrome (Monte Testaccio), ii. 360 & n. 5.
— — — Horti Aciliorum: nymphaeum of, ii. 232, n. 1; wall of, ii. 375, n. 3.
— — — Horti Sallustiani, ii. 234 & n. 5, 239.
— — — hospitals:
— — — — di Campo Santo, ii. 290 & n. 2.
— — — — Incurabili, ii. 373 & n. 7.
— — — — di S. Giacomo degli Spagnuoli, ii. 368, n. 7.
— — — — di S. Giovanni Colavita, ii. 358 & n. 10.
— — — — di S. Giovanni in Laterano, ii. 275 & n. 4; ceremonies at, ii. 291 & n. 3, 385 & n. 6.
— — — — di S. Lorenzo in Miranda, ii. 219 & n. 3.
— — — — di SS. Rocco e Martino, ii. 375 & n. 4.
— — — — di S. Spirito, ii. 311–12 & nn.; *zitelle* of, ii. 292 & n. 2.
— — — — di SS. Trinità de' Pellegrini, ii. 366 & n. 3.
— — — houses: of
— — — — Cicero: ruins of, ii. 219 & n. 7.
— — — — Laterani, ii. 271.
— — — — M. L. Mancini, ii. 364 & n. 3.
— — — — L. de' Manili, ii. 292 & n.5.
— — — — Martial, ii. 313 & n. 6.
— — — — Pompey: ruins of, ii. 276 & n. 8.
— — — Isola Tiberina, ii. 358–9 & nn.
— — — Janiculum, ii. 313.

Rome: the City (*cont.*)
— — — Janus Quadrifrons, ii. 228 & n. 3.
— — — Lacus Curtius, ii. 218 & n. 2.
— — — Lateran: *see* churches: S. Giovanni in Laterano *above*.
— — — Lavacrum Agrippinae, ii. 247.
— — — Lupercal, ii. 276, n. 7.
— — — markets, ii. 366, 367, n. 10, 368, 371, 397–8; iv. 253.
— — — Marmorata, ii. 360 & n. 1.
— — — mausolea: *see* tombs *below*.
— — — Meta Sudans, ii. 248 & n. 5, 250 & n. 3; *add.*
— — — Milliarium Aureum, ii. 219 & n. 5.
— — — Ministry of Justice (modern): palace of, ii. 391, n. 1; *add.*
— — — Monte Cavallo, ii. 237, 241, 287.
— — — Monte Giordano: Spada inn at, ii. 214, n. 2.
— — — Monte Magnanapoli: Villa Aldobrandini at, ii. 284, n. 2.
— — — Monte Mario: road over, ii. 212, n. 1.
— — — Monte di Pietà (institution), ii. 366 & n. 8.
— — — Monte Testaccio, ii. 360 & nn. 4, 5.
— — — Monte Trinità, ii. 212 & n. 4.
— — — Muro Torto, ii. 375 & n. 3.
— — — Museo Capitolino: foundations of, ii. 220, n. 3; modern: statues, &c., in, ii. 221–6, nn., *passim*, 235, n. 6.
— — — Museo Mussolini: site, ii. 227, n. 4.
— — — Museo Petriano: sculpture in, ii. 265, n. 2.
— — — Museo delle Terme: buildings, ii. 240, n. 4; sculptures in (from Ludovisi collection), ii. 234–6, nn., *passim*.
— — — obelisks (situation in modern times, &c.; classical names, &c., omitted):
— — — — Isola Tiberina, ii. 358.
— — — — Lateran, ii. 269–71 & nn.
— — — — Palazzo Barberini, ii. 229 & n. 6.
— — — — Piazza Navona, ii. 270, n. 2; *add.*; ii. 362 & nn. 4–6.

Rome: the City (*cont.*)
— — — — Piazza del Popolo, ii. 374–5 & nn.
— — — — Piazza del Quirinale, ii. 237, n. 2.
— — — — Piazza della Rotonda, ii. 370, n. 6.
— — — — Pincio, ii. 229, n. 6.
— — — — S. Maria Maggiore, ii. 245 & n. 6.
— — — — Vatican, ii. 256–7 & nn.; re-erection of: painting of, ii. 302 & n. 5.
— — — — Villa Mattei, ii. 362 & n. 2.
— — — — Villa Medici, ii. 232 & n. 4.
— — — palaces:
— — — — Antoninus Pius: ruins of, ii. 370 & n. 5.
— — — — Barberini, and its art-collections, ii. 228–9 & nn.; mentioned, ii. 212, n. 2.
— — — — Bentivoglio, Cardinal (Rospigliosi), ii. 379 & nn. 4–6.
— — — — Borghese, ii. 284 & n. 2; art-collection in, ii. 252, n. 5 *ad fin.*
— — — — of duke of Bracciano, ii. 288 & n. 4.
— — — — Caetani (Ruspoli), ii. 372–3 & n.
— — — — Cancelleria, ii. 367 & nn. 3–9; building materials for, ii. 249, n. 10.
— — — — Capodiferro, Cardinal (Spada alla Regola), ii. 366 & nn. 4–7.
— — — — of duke of Ceri: occupied by French ambassador, ii. 282, n. 2.
— — — — Colonna, ii. 389, n. 1.
— — — — dei Conservatori, and its art-collections, ii. 220, n. 3, 222–6 & nn.; further sculpture, &c., in, ii. 221, n. 1, 256, n. 2.
— — — — della Corgnia, ii. 288, n. 4.
— — — — Doria–Pamphili (modern): works of art in, ii. 284–5, nn.
— — — — Farnese, and its art-collections, ii. 214–16 & nn., 308–11 & nn.; building-materials for, ii. 249 & n. 10; gallery of the Carracci in, ii. 215 & n. 1, 310 & n. 2; statues in, ii. 403, 404.

Rome: the City (*cont.*)
— — — — Farnesina, La, ii. 287–8 & nn., 357 & nn. 5, 6.
— — — — of prince of Gallicano, ii. 389, n. 1.
— — — — de Ghisi *or* Gichi (Chigi): *see* Farnesina *above*.
— — — — of Inquisition, ii. 290 & n. 4.
— — — — Lateran: *see* churches: S. Giovanni in Laterano *above*.
— — — — Madama, ii. 391, n. 1.
— — — — Maggiore: *see* Palatine *below*.
— — — — Medici, Cardinal, ii. 390–1 & n.; *add.*
— — — — Panfili, ii. 368 & nn. 1, 5.
— — — — Piccolomini: site of, ii. 376 & n. 4.
— — — — Pichini, and its art-collection, ii. 217 & n. 1.
— — — — Primoli (in note as Parinoli, in error), ii. 391, n. 4; *add.*
— — — — del Quirinale, ii. 237–8 & nn., 287 & nn. 2–4.
— — — — Rospigliosi, formerly Bentivoglio, ii. 379 & nn. 4–6.
— — — — Ruspoli, formerly Caetani, ii. 372–3 & n.
— — — — Salviati al Corso: site of, ii. 364, n. 3.
— — — — Salviati alla Lungara, ii. 288, n. 4.
— — — — Savelli, ii. 228 & n. 5.
— — — — del Senatore, ii. 220, nn. 2, 3, 221 & nn. 2, 3; design of, ii. 226, n. 3.
— — — — Spada alla Regola, ii. 366 & nn. 4–7; painted astrolabe in, ii. 373, n. 5.
— — — — of Spanish ambassadors, ii. 281–2 & n.
— — — — of grand-dukes of Tuscany, ii. 391, n. 1.
— — — — di Venezia, ii. 378 & n. 6.
— — — Palatine, the, ii. 227, 276 & nn. 5–8, 383–4 & nn.; Cicero's house on: ruins of, ii. 219, n. 7; Palazzo Maggiore on, ii. 276 & n. 5; mentioned, ii. 212, n. 2, 217, n. 2.
— — — Pantheon, ii. 371–2 & nn.; in comparison, ii. 259 & n. 5; bronze from, ii. 261 & n. 1, 371–2 & n.; bronze pine-cone associated with, ii. 305, n. 3;

Rome: the City (*cont.*)
sarcophagus from, ii. 370, n. 6; statue from, ii. 309 & n. 4.
— — — Pasquin: statue of, ii. 369 & n. 3.
— — — piazze:
— — — — d'Aracœli: steps leading from, ii. 221, n. 6, 226, n. 4; *add.*; fountain in, ii. 227, n. 2.
— — — — del Campidoglio, ii. 220 & n. 3; design of, ii. 226 & n. 3; balustrade of, and its monuments, ii. 220, n. 3, 221–2 & nn., 226, n. 6, 379 & n. 7, 405, n. 1; steps leading to, ii. 221, 222; arch in, for *possesso* of Innocent X, ii. 281 & n. 2; celebrations in, ii. 387 & nn. 1, 5.
— — — — Colonna, ii. 370.
— — — — Farnese, ii. 216–17 & nn.
— — — — Giudea, ii. 292 & n. 4.
— — — — in Lucina, ii. 370, n. 2.
— — — — Montanara, ii. 228, n. 5.
— — — — del Monte di Pietà, ii. 366, n. 9.
— — — — Navona, ii. 368 & nn. 1–7; Innocent X's fountain, &c., in, ii. 270, n. 2; *add.*; ii. 362 & n. 6; market in, ii. 367, n. 10, 368; mountebank with phosphorescent ring in, ii. 397–8 & nn.; iv. 253.
— — — — del Pianto: site, &c., ii. 292, nn. 4, 5.
— — — — called Piscina, ii. 384 & n. 1.
— — — — Poli: palace in, ii. 282, n. 2.
— — — — della Rotonda, ii. 370–1 & n.
— — — — di S. Pietro, ii. 255–8 & nn.
— — — — di Spagna: E's lodging near, ii. 212 & n. 4; as Piazza della Trinità: Spanish ambassador's palace in, ii. 281–2 & n.
— — — Pincio (Mons Pincius): ascent to, ii. 212 & n. 4; buildings, &c., on, ii. 231, 251, 373, 374, 375, n. 3; modern: obelisk on, ii. 229, n. 6; ~ statues on, ii. 225, n. 6.
— — — Prato del Popolo Romano, ii. 360, n. 5.
— — — Pyramid of Cestius, ii. 360–1 & n.
— — — Quirinal hill, ii. 237; house of Martial on, ii. 313, n. 6; as Monte Cavallo, ii. 241, 287.
— — — Ripetta, the: Borghese palace near, ii. 284, n. 2.
— — — roads and Streets [squares are indexed under piazze *above*]:
— — — — Corso: *see* Corso *above*.
— — — — Scala di Spagna: site, ii. 212, n. 4.
— — — — Strada Felice (Via Felix), ii. 241 & n. 5, 381 & n. 9.
— — — — Strada (via) Pontificia, ii. 369 & n. 4.
— — — — Via Appia, ii. 250 & n. 3; monuments beside, ii. 362–4 & nn.; mile-stone from, ii. 383 & n. 2.
— — — — Via Cavour, ii. 278, n. 1.
— — — — Via Flaminia, ii. 376, 389 & n. 4.
— — — — Via del Governo Vecchio, ii. 369, n. 4.
— — — — Via Larga, ii. 234 & n. 3.
— — — — Via della Lungara, ii. 212, n. 1, 288, n. 4.
— — — — Via Ostiensis, ii. 307.
— — — — Via Pinciana, ii. 251, nn. 5, 6.
— — — — Via di Porta Pia (Venti Settembre), ii. 241 & nn. 4, 5.
— — — — Via del Portico d'Ottavia, ii. 292, n. 3.
— — — — Via del Progresso, ii. 292, nn. 3, 4.
— — — — Via delle Quattro Fontane, ii. 241, n. 5.
— — — — Via Salaria (Piave), ii. 241 & n. 4.
— — — — Via della Sapienza, ii. 368, n. 6.
— — — — Via Triumphalis, ii. 212, n. 1, 312.
— — — — Via Venti Settembre (formerly di Porta Pia), ii. 239, n. 2, 241, nn. 4, 5.
— — — — Via delle Zoccolette, ii. 291, n. 8.
— — — Roma Subterranea (catacomb of Domitilla ?), ii. 387–8 & nn.
— — — salt-houses, papal, ii. 359 & n. 6.
— — — Sancta Sanctorum: *see* churches: S. Giovanni in Laterano *above*.
— — — Sapienza, La, ii. 376 & nn.

Rome: the City (*cont.*)
1, 2; procession at, ii. 387 & n. 3.
— — — Scala Santa: *see* churches: S. Giovanni in Laterano *above*.
— — — Scala di Spagna: site, ii. 212, n. 4.
— — — Septizonium: site, ii. 361 & n. 5.
— — — Sessorium, ii. 380, n. 2; Sessorian basilica: *see* churches: S. Croce in Gerusalemme *above*.
— — — Sette Sale, ii. 279 & n. 1.
— — — Spada inn, Monte Giordano, ii. 214, n. 2.
— — — Stadium Domitiani (Circus Agonalis), ii. 368, n. 3.
— — — statues, public [in streets, &c.; excluding fountain figures, &c.]:
— — — — Commodus (Colossus Neronis; destroyed), ii. 248 & n. 7.
— — — — Constans, ii. 226 & nn. 4, 6.
— — — — Constantine, ii. 226 & nn. 4, 6; colossal head of, ii. 221 & nn. 1, 5.
— — — — Dioscuri (Capitol), ii. 221 & n. 6, 405 & n. 1; in comparison, ii. 237.
— — — — Horse-tamers (Quirinal), ii. 237 & n. 2, 241, 405 & n. 1.
— — — — Marcus Aurelius, ii. 221 & n. 4, 404; imitation of, ii. 101 & n. 2 (i. 66).
— — — — Marforio, ii. 220, n. 3, 221 & n. 1.
— — — — Pasquin, ii. 369 & n. 3.
— — — — Trophies of Marius, ii. 221–2 & n., 379 & n. 7.
— — — Subura, ii. 278 & nn. 1, 2.
— — — Synagogue, ii. 293.
— — — Taberna meritoria, ii. 288–9 & n.
— — — Tarpeian Rock, ii. 227 & n. 4.
— — — Tempietto of Bramante, ii. 313 & nn. 3, 4.
— — — temples:
— — — — Aesculapius, ii. 358 & n. 8.
— — — — Antoninus and Faustina, ii. 217, n. 2, 219 & n. 3.
— — — — Apollo: statues from, ii. 232, n. 3.
— — — — Bacchus: as error for S. Costanza, ii. 241 & n. 2.

Rome: the City (*cont.*)
— — — — Castor and Pollux, ii. 217, n. 2; as Jupiter Stator, ii. 218 & n. 4.
— — — — Diana (Aventine), ii. 359 & n. 8.
— — — — Fortuna Virilis, ii. 359 & n. 1.
— — — — Hadrian: as palace of Marcus Aurelius, ii. 370 & n. 5.
— — — — Hercules (Hercules Victor), ii. 228 & n. 2.
— — — — Janus Quadrifrons, ii. 228 & n. 3.
— — — — Juno, ii. 384 & n. 1.
— — — — Jupiter Stator: as error for Castor and Pollux, ii. 218 & n. 4.
— — — — Jupiter Tonans: as error for Vespasian, ii. 218 & n. 3.
— — — — Mater Matuta, ii. 359, n. 1.
— — — — Minerva (Chalcidica): site, ii. 377 & n. 3.
— — — — Peace: spoils from Jerusalem placed in, ii. 247, n. 3; as error for Basilica of Constantine, ii. 218 & n. 1; ~ column from, ii. 245 & n. 4.
— — — — Portunus, ii. 359, n. 2.
— — — — Romulus, Divus (Urbis fanum ?), ii. 218 & n. 5.
— — — — Saturn, ii. 217, n. 2; as error for Curia Julia, ii. 219 & n. 4; Aerarium in, ii. 278, n. 2.
— — — — Sun, ii. 359 & n. 2.
— — — — Urbis fanum, ii. 218, n. 5.
— — — — Venus and Cupid (error), ii. 380 & n. 2.
— — — — Vespasian, ii. 217, n. 2; as Jupiter Tonans, ii. 218 & n. 3.
— — — Theatre of Marcellus, ii. 228 & n. 5.
— — — Theatre of Pompey, ii. 376 & n. 4; statues from, ii. 221.
— — — Tiber, river: banks (outside walls), ii. 383 & n. 5; bridges over: *see* bridges *above*; buildings near, &c., ii. 228, 375, 376; ferry over, ii. 287, 357; in view, ii. 227; walk beside, ii. 358–60 & nn.; water-mills on, ii. 357 & n. 4; mentioned, ii. 212, n. 2, 292, n. 3.
— — — tombs:
— — — — Augustus, ii. 375–6 & n; obelisk from, ii. 245 & n. 6.

Rome: the City (*cont.*)
— — — — Cecilia Metella, ii. 362–3 & n.
— — — — Cestius, ii. 360–1 & n.
— — — — Hadrian: sculptures, &c., from, ii. 305 & n. 3.
— — — — Numa, ii. 313, n. 7.
— — — — Scipio, ii. 305.
— — — — Vespasian, ii. 361 & n. 3.
— — — Tor Marancia: catacomb at, ii. 364, n. 1.
— — — Trastevere, ii. 212, n. 2, 288, 357.
— — — Tre Fontane: churches at, ii. 307–8 & nn.
— — — Trophies of Marius (the building), ii. 379 & n. 7.
— — — Tullianum, ii. 227 & nn. 5–8.
— — — Umbilicus Romae, ii. 219 & n. 5.
— — — university: *see* Sapienza *above*.
— — — Vatican palace, ii. 294–305 & nn.; bibliography and general note, ii. 294, n. 3; in E's poem, ii. 405; ceremonies in, ii. 254–5, 291 & n. 1, 385 & n. 5, 391 & n. 2; conclaves (papal elections) in, ii. 302 & n. 7; procession to, ii. 389, n. 4 *ad fin.*; route near, ii. 212 & n. 1.
— — — — armoury, ii. 302–3 & n.; Atrio quadrato, ii. 303, n. 1; Belvedere, ii. 294, n. 3 *ad fin.*; ~ Vatican garden called, iii. 303; ~ for court in *see* Court of the Statues *below*; ~ Quirinal as rival of, ii. 238; Concistorio secreto, ii. 299, n. 6 *ad fin.*; conclaves in: rooms occupied by, ii. 302 & n. 7; Consistory, ii. 299–300 & n., 391 & n. 2; Corridore della Cleopatra, ii. 300, n. 1; Cortile di Belvedere, ii. 294, n. 3 *ad fin.*; ~ fountains in, ii. 305, nn. 5, 7; Court of St. Damasus, ii. 295, n. 2; Court of the Statues (in the Belvedere), ii. 294, n. 3 *ad fin.*; ~ statues in, ii. 303–5 & nn.; entrance, principal, ii. 255, n. 2; fountain with ship, ii. 303, n. 1, 305 & n. 6; Galleria Geografica, ii. 299 & n. 5; gallery, long (Galleria Lapidaria, &c., on east side of Cortile di Belvedere), ii. 300 & n. 1, 302, n. 7, 303, 304, n. 4; gardens, ii. 300, 303, 304, n. 7, 305 & nn. 3–6; library, ii. 300–2 & nn., 303, n. 1; ~ librarian: *see* Vitelleschi, H. (ii. 283 & n. 4); loggie: Raphael's, ii. 295 & nn. 3–5, 296, n. 1; ~ on third floor (with maps), ii. 295 & n. 5, 296, n. 1; Museo Chiaramonti (the rooms), ii. 300, n. 1, 303, n. 1; Museo profano (the rooms), ii. 301, n. 2; Pauline chapel: ceremony in, ii. 385, n. 5; pine-cone, bronze, &c., ii. 305 & n. 3; Raphael's Loggie, ii. 295 & nn. 3–5, 296 & n. 1; Raphael's Stanze, ii. 299 & nn. 2–4; relic preserved in, ii. 274, n. 2; Sala de gl'Appostoli, ii. 299, n. 6; Sala dei Chiaroscuri, ii. 299, n. 6 *ad fin.*; Sala Clementina: as Sala di Gregorio XIII, ii. 296–7 & nn.; ~ paintings in, ii. 298–9 & n.; Sala del Concistoro, ii. 299, n. 6 *ad fin.*; Sala del Concistoro publico, ii. 299, n. 6; Sala del Conclave: *see* Sala Regia *below*; Sala Ducale: in E's time, ii. 299, n. 6; ~ ceremonies in, ii. 385, 391 & n. 2; ~ as altered by Bernini, ii. 294, n. 3 *ad fin.*, 299, n. 6; Sala di Gregorio XIII: *see* Sala Clementina *above*; Sala Regia (Sala del Conclave), ii. 297 & nn. 2–6, 299, n. 6 *ad fin.*; ~ stairs leading to, ii. 296, n. 1; Sala vecchia degli Svizzeri, ii. 296, nn. 1, 8; Sistine chapel, ii. 298 & n. 1; ~ as the Pope's chapel: ceremonies in, ii. 254, 291, n. 1, 385 & n. 5; ~ sacristy of, ii. 298 & nn. 2–4; Sixtus V's wing, ii. 295 & n. 2, 296, n. 2; stairs: Bramante's staircase, ii. 303 & n. 1, 305, n. 6; ~ leading to Sala Regia, ii. 295–6 & n.; ~ Scala Regia, ii. 294, n. 3 *ad fin.*, 296, n. 1; ~ Scala vecchia della Floreria, ii. 296, n. 1, 297 & n. 1; stanze: Raphael's, ii. 299 & nn. 2–4; Stanze dei Paramenti, ii. 299, n. 6; Villa Pia: statue in, ii. 304, n. 7.
— — — — museums (modern): sculptures, &c., in: old Vatican collection, ii. 304–5 & nn., 404–

Rome: the City (*cont.*)
5; further: Ariadne, Sleeping (called Cleopatra): copy, ii. 108 & n. 2 (i. 70); Laocoon: copies (?), ii. 107 (i. 69), 413 & n. 6; later additions: chair, red marble, ii. 268, n. 2; inscription, ii. 358, n. 11; lions, Egyptian, ii. 239, n. 1; Meleager, ii. 217, n. 1; Nozze Aldobrandini, ii. 285, n. 4; sarcophagi: of Constantia, ii. 241, n. 3; ~ of St. Helena, ii. 274, n. 5.
— — — — Pinacoteca: paintings in: Raphael: Transfiguration, ii. 227, n. 7, 313, n. 5; by Caravaggio, ii. 233, n. 5; by Guido Reni, ii. 308, n. 1.
— — — Venerable English College: *see* colleges *above*.
— — — villas:
— — — — Aldobrandini, and its art-collection, ii. 284–5 & nn.; succession to, ii. 392, n. 2.
— — — — Borghese, and its art-collection, ii. 251–4 & nn.; *add.*; ii. 389–90 & nn.; modern extension of, ii. 382, n. 4 *ad fin.*; statues in (in E's time), ii. 286, n. 2, 404 & n. 2, 405; statue by Bernini in (since E's time), ii. 236, n. 1.
— — — — Celimontana *or* Mattei, ii. 362 & nn. 1, 2.
— — — — Farnesiana (on Palatine), ii. 217, n. 2, 383–4 & n.
— — — — Giustiniani, and its art-collection, ii. 375, 382–3 & nn.
— — — — Ludovisi, and its art-collection, ii. 234–6 & nn., 391–2.
— — — — Massimo (formerly Montalto), ii. 240 & n. 5.
— — — — Mattei *or* Celimontana, ii. 362 & nn. 1, 2.
— — — — Medici, and its art-collection, ii. 230–2 & nn., 286–7 & nn.; mentioned, ii. 373, 391, n. 1; statues, &c., in, ii. 236, n. 6, 403, n. 1 *ad fin.*, 404, 415; terrace before, ii. 232 & nn. 5, 6.
— — — — Montalto (later Massimo), ii. 240 & n. 5; chair in, ii. 236, n. 6.
— — — Viminal hill, ii. 240, 278, n. 1.
— — — walls [for the individual gates *see* gates *above*]:
— — — — Servian: gates in, as bases for road-mileage, ii. 219, n. 5.
— — — — Aurelian's and later additions: area surrounded by, ii. 401; building-materials for, ii. 249 & n. 10; structures incorporated in, ii. 360–1, 375 & n. 3; mentioned for buildings outside, ii. 251, 307, 380–1.
— environs [beyond the extramural churches, &c., and short of the surrounding hills]:
— — plains of Rome: journey through, ii. 211–12 & nn.
— — Baccano, ii. 211, n. 4.
— — Bagni: sulphurous river at, ii. 394 & n. 3.
— — Ponte Lucano, ii. 394 & n. 3.
— — Ponte Mammolo, ii. 393–4 & n.
— — Prima Porta: Constantine's victory at, ii. 383, n. 4.
— — Teverone, river, ii. 393.
— — Tomb of the Plautii *or* of Valerius Volusi, ii. 394 & nn. 2, 3.
Romney: Earl of, 1694–1704: *see* Sidney, Henry.
Romney Bay, Kent: French fleet in, 1690, v. 29, n. 1.
Romulus, ii. 276 & n. 7.
Romulus, son of Maxentius: buildings dedicated to, ii. 218 & n. 5, 362, n. 3.
Ronciglione: road through, ii. 211, n. 2.
Ronquillo, Don Pedro, Spanish ambassador in England, iv. 242, n. 5; discusses religion with E, iv. 242–3; attends opening of parliament, iv. 442; house of: destroyed by mob, 1688, iv. 610 & n. 2.
Ronsard, Pierre: grave of, ii. 147 & n. 4 (i. 95).
Rooke, —: error for R. Hooke, iii. 450 & n. 2.
Rooke, Sir George, admiral, v. 150, n. 2; commands convoy of Smyrna fleet, 1693, v. 142, n. 1; account by, of French attack on Smyrna fleet, v. 148, n. 2; returns to Kinsale, v. 150 & n. 2; movements: 1696, v. 233 & n. 2; ~ 1702, v. 510 & n. 7, 515 & n. 3; appointed privy councillor, v. 521 & n. 4; at battle of Malaga, 1704, v. 579 & n. 2, 579–80 & n.; returns home, v. 580 & n. 4; geneal., iv. 414, n. 4.

Rooke, Lawrence, iii. 450, n. 2.
Rooke, Sir William, sheriff of Kent 1684–5: proclaims James II's accession, iv. 414–15 & nn.
Rookwood, Sir T.: former owner of Euston (?), iii. 591 & n. 2.
Roomer, Frische, ii. 49–50 & n. (i. 35).
Roos *or* Ros, Lord: *see* Manners, John, duke of Rutland, &c.
Roper, Edward: patron of the living of Eltham (?), iii. 195, n. 3.
Rosa, Monte, ii. 506, n. 3.
Rosas (Roses), in Catalonia: French take, 1693, v. 155 & n. 3.
Roscius, the actor, iii. 338 & n. 7, 345.
Roscommon: Earl, &c., of: *see* Dillon, James, third earl; Dillon, Elizabeth, his countess.
Rosenvinge, H. V., Danish resident in England: social (?), iii. 255 & n. 2.
Rosewell, Thomas, Nonconformist divine, iv. 453, n. 2.
Ross, Rev. Alexander, ii. 558, n. 5; social, ii. 558; gives E book by himself, &c., iii. 81 & nn. 1, 2; commendatory poem by, on E, ii. 547, n. 3.
Rossano, Olimpia, princess of, ii. 284, n. 2.
Rosse (Roos *or* Ros), Lord: *see* Manners, John, duke of Rutland, &c.
Rossi, Vincenzo de', sculptor: work by, ii. 403 & n. 1.
Rosso Fiorentino: paintings by, at Fontainebleau, ii. 119 & n. 10 (i. 77).
Roswell, Rev. Walter: sermon by (?), iii. 414 & n. 8.
Rota, near Cadiz: Allied landing at, 1702, v. 515 & n. 3.
Rotherham, Sir John, serjeant-at-law, v. 88, n. 2; as trustee for Boyle Lectures, v. 88 (called Serjeant Roderith), 123, 161, 238.
Rotiere, Monsieur (John Roettiers ?): modelling a statuette, iv. 138 & n. 2.
Rottenhammer, Hans: painting by, ii. 550 & n. 1.
Rotterdam: E visits, 1641, ii. 33 & nn. 2–5 (i. 25), 39–40 (i. 29–30), 41 (i. 31), 55 (i. 38), 56 (i. 39), 57 (i. 39), 59 (i. 40).
  notice, ii. 33 & nn. 2–5 (i. 25); fair at, ii. 39–40 & nn. (i. 29–30);
Rotterdam (*cont.*)
  Sunderland at, 1688, iv. 610, n. 1; burgomaster of: *see* Kievit, Sir J. (iii. 470 & n. 6); commissary at: pass granted by, ii. 62 & n. 2 (i. 42).
Rouanne: *see* Roanne.
Rouen: notice, 1644, ii. 122–4 & nn. (i. 78–9); E at, 1647, ii. 536; route through, from Paris to England, iii. 53; Joan of Arc burnt at, ii. 137 (i. 90); I. Basire born at, iii. 303, n. 3; E. Waller residing at, ii. 536, n. 7; environs: Grand-Quevilly: protestant church at, ii. 122 & n. 6 (i. 79); Ste.-Catherine, ii. 122 & n. 1 (i. 78).
Rouen: Archbishops of: chateau of, at Gaillon, ii. 121 & n. 3 (i. 78).
Roussell, Col. — (Col. John Russell ?): social, iv. 562 & n. 1.
Rousselle (Roussel), Claude: *aurum potabile* of, iii. 86–7 & nn.
Rovetta, G., composer: operas by, ii. 450, nn. 2, 3.
Row, Rev. Joseph (J. Roe ?): sermon by (?), v. 353–4 & n.
Rowland, Rev. —, chaplain to Lord Mordaunt: sermon by (?), iii. 253–4; ill, iii. 276.
Roxalana, actress (Elizabeth Davenport), iii. 309 & n. 2; alluded to, iii. 466 & n. 1.
Royal African Company: deputy-governor of, 1681–2: *see* Bathurst, Sir Benjamin.
Royal Household [the household of the kings and queens regnant, and its members from 1660 onwards. Members before 1660 are indexed under Charles I and Charles II: early life; members of the queens consorts' households, under their names. Members taking part *ex officio* in Charles II's coronation procession (iii. 278–81) are not indexed separately; and some general notices relating to both household and political office-holders ('white-staff' officers, &c.) are indexed under England: officers. The grouping here follows roughly that used by Chamberlayne in *Angliae notitia*; the heralds are indexed under Heralds; there is more alphabetization; and the clergy, medical attendants, and some

Royal Household (*cont.*)
other office-holders, are detached from the Lord Chamberlain's department.
E uses the term 'the household' (occasionally 'the family': so iv. 5, 9) to distinguish those members of the court who attended the earlier service on Sunday mornings from the king and, presumably, his attendants]:
— general notices: right of purveyance regulated, iv. 303; uses slaughter-house at Deptford, iii. 352, n. 2; diet: re-established, 1660, iii. 261 & n. 5; ~ to stop, iii. 360–1 & n.; Roman Catholic members to be dismissed, 1678, iv. 159 & n. 2.
— clergy and staff of Chapel Royal [for James II's Roman Catholic clergy *see* Whitehall: structure: Roman Catholic chapel; for lenten sermons at court *see* Whitehall: religion]: establishment, iii. 347, n. 3.
— — Lord Almoner: duties of, ii. 385, n. 5; iv. 133, n. 2; individual almoners: *see* Henchman, H. (→1675); Dolben, J. (1675–84); Turner, Francis (1684–9); Lloyd, William, D.D., the apocalyptic (1689–1703); sub-almoners: *see* Perrinchief, R. (→1673); Blagrave, J. (1689–98).
— — Dean of the Chapel: *see* Sheldon, G. (1660–3); Croft, H. (1668–9); Blandford, W. (1669–75); Compton, H. (1675–85); Crew, N. (1685–9); sub-deans: *see* Colebrande, R. (1672–4); Holder, W. (1674–89).
— — Clerk of the Closet: *see* Earles, J. (1660(1651)–4); Crew, N. (1669–85); Sprat, T. (1685–9); Graham, W. (*c.* 1704–13); North, J. (error?: iv. 97 & n. 4).
— — Confessor: *see* Crespion, S. (1675–).
— — Chaplains in ordinary: duties, iii. 347, n. 3; iv. 129, n. 5; at touching for King's Evil, iii. 250–1; devotions of, during Charles II's last illness, iv. 407 & n. 5; individual chaplains: *see* Adams, J.; Aldrich, H.; Ball, R.; Barne, M.; Barrow,

Royal Household (*cont.*)
I.; Basire, I.; Bathurst, R.; Beaumont, J.; Bell, W.; Benson, G.; Beveridge, W.; Birch, P.; Blackall, O.; Blagrave, J.; Bramston, W.; Breton, R.; Brideoake, R.; Bright, G.; Butler, John; Cartwright, T.; Castillion, J.; Cave, W.; Chetwood, K.; Clarke, S.; Cole, —; Comber, Thomas, D.D. 1678; Cradock, Z.; Creighton, R., sen.; Creighton, R., jnr.; Doughty, T.; Dove, H.; Duport, J.; Durel, J.; Fitzwilliam, J.; Fleetwood, W.; Fox, H.; Freeman, S.; Fuller *or* Fulwar, S.; Goodman, J.; Grove, R.; Gunning, P. (iii. 446, n. 4); Hall, John; Hascard, G.; Hayley, W.; Hayward, R.; Hickman, C.; Hooper, G.; Ironside, G., jnr.; James, H.; Jane, W.; Ken, T.; Lambe, J.; Lamplugh, T.; Littleton, A.; Lloyd, William, D.D., the apocalyptic; Lynford, T.; Mandevile, J.; Meggot, R.; Mews, P.; North, J.; Offley, G.; Onley, N.; Patrick, S.; Paul, W.; Pelling, E.; Perrinchief, R.; Pittis, T.; Rainbowe, E.; Scott, John; Sharp, John; Sherlock, W.; Smalwood, M.; Smith, Henry; Standish, J.; Stanhope, G.; Stillingfleet, E.; Stradling, G.; Sudbury, J.; Tenison, T.; Thistlethwaite, G.; Tillotson, J.; Turner, Thomas, D.D. 1683; Warren, R.; Wolley, E.; Wood, T.; Woodroffe, B.; Young, E.
— — — supernumeraries, &c.: *see* Calamy, B.; Glanvill, J. (iv. 53, n. 4); Gregory, F.; Hickes, G.; Horne, T.; Lloyd, William, D.D., the Nonjuror (iii. 552, n. 2).
— — — unnamed: sermons by, iv. 589–90; v. 166 & n. 3; *add.*
— — Gentlemen, &c., of the Chapel Royal: in Garter celebration, iii. 479; individual Gentleman: *see* Gostling, J.
— Lord Chamberlain of the Household; Bed-chamber, Privy Chamber, &c.:
— — Lord Chamberlain: insignia of, iv. 416; lodgings of, iv.

Royal Household (*cont.*)
184, n. 4; in ceremonies: creation of peers, iii. 277 & n. 6; ~ touching for King's Evil, iii. 251 & n. 1; order issued by, for Chapel Royal, iv. 584, n. 2; error for Lord Chancellor (?), iii. 380 & n. 5; individual Lord Chamberlains: *see* Montagu, Edward, earl of Manchester (1660–71); Jermyn, Henry, earl of St. Albans (1671–4); Bennet, Henry, earl of Arlington (1674–85); Sackville, Charles, earl of Dorset (1689–97); Spencer, Robert, earl of Sunderland (1697); Talbot, Charles, duke of Shrewsbury (1699–1700); Villiers, Edward, earl of Jersey (1700–4).
— — Vice-Chamberlain: at touching for King's Evil, iii. 251, n. 1; called Vice-Chancellor in error (?), iii. 492 & n. 1; individual Vice-Chamberlains: *see* Carteret, Sir George (1660 (1647)–80); Savile, Henry (1680–7).
— — Bedchamber: Gentlemen of the: duties, &c., of, iii. 366, n. 4; iv. 296, n. 5; E dines with (?), iii. 366 & n. 4, 599 & n. 3; iv. 2; individual Gentlemen: Groom of the Stole (first Gentleman): *see* Grenville, John, earl of Bath (1660–85); Mordaunt, Henry, earl of Peterborough (1685–8); Sidney, Henry, earl of Romney (1700–2).
— — — other Gentlemen: *see* Monck, Christopher, duke of Albemarle; Butler, Charles, earl of Arran; Churchill, John, duke of Marlborough; Scott, James, duke of Monmouth (?) (iv. 457 & n. 1); Butler, James, second duke of Ormond; Lennard, Thomas, earl of Sussex.
— — — Lady of the (to Queen Anne): Lady Fretcheville, v. 578, n. 1.
— — — Grooms of the: duties, &c., iii. 366, n. 4; E dines with, iii. 366 & n. 4(?), 567, 577, 599 & n. 3(?), 612 & n. 3; iv. 2(?), 82; individual Grooms: *see* Ashburnham, J.; Godolphin, Sidney, earl of Godolphin; Granville, B.; Legge, Col. William

Royal Household (*cont.*)
(iii. 494 & n. 5; called George, in error, iv. 314); Legge, Col. William, jnr. (v. 182, n. 3); Slingsby, Col. Henry (iv. 473, n. 4); Titus, S.; Walter, D.
— — Privy Chamber: Gentlemen of the: *see* Hawarde, Sir W.; Sutton, Sir E.; Temple, Sir P.
— — — Gentleman-Usher of the: *see* Neile, Sir P.
— — — Deputy-Comptroller (later Comptroller) of the: *see* Vanbrugh, W.
— — Carvers: E dines with, iii. 343 & n. 5, 352, 355, 626 & n. 7.
— — Esquire of the Body in ordinary: *see* Norwood, H.
— — Keeper of the King's Closet: *see* Chiffinch, T. (1660–6); Chiffinch, W. (1666–88 ?).
— — Keeper of the Privy Purse: *see* Bennet, Henry, earl of Arlington (1661–2); May, B. (1665–85); Graham, James (1685–8).
— — Page of the Backstairs: as messenger, iii. 299; individual page: *see* Rustat, T.
— — Black Rod: *see* Ayton, Sir J.
— — Groom-porter: duties of, &c., iii. 308, n. 4; individual Groom-porters: *see* Hobart *or* Hubbert, Sir R. (1660–5); Offley, T. (1665–78 ?); Neale, T. (1678–99).
— — Serjeant-Porter: *see* Brett, Sir E.
— — Robes: Master of the: *see* Godolphin, Sidney, earl of Godolphin; Yeoman of the: *see* Rustat, T.
— — Tents: Office of the, iii. 324, n. 3.
— Lord Steward of the Household; Board of Green Cloth, &c.:
— — Board of Green Cloth: functions of, iii. 261, n. 4; iv. 454 & n. 1.
— — Lord Steward: *see* Butler, James, first duke of Ormond (1660–88); Cavendish, William, first duke of Devonshire (1689–1707).
— — Treasurer of the Household: *see* Berkeley, Sir Charles, Viscount Fitzhardinge (1662–8); Clifford, Sir Thomas, Baron Clifford (1668–72); Newport,

Royal Household (*cont.*)
Francis, earl of Bradford (1672–87, 1689–1708).
— — Comptroller of the Household: *see* Berkeley, Sir Charles, Viscount Fitzhardinge (1660–2); Pollard, Sir Hugh (1662–6); Clifford, Sir Thomas, Baron Clifford (1666–8); Newport, Francis, earl of Bradford (1668–72); Maynard, William, Baron Maynard (1672–87); Waldegrave, Sir Henry, Baron Waldegrave (1687–8).
— — Cofferer: *see* Ashburnham, W. (1660–79); Brouncker, Henry, Viscount Brouncker (1679–85); Bathurst, Sir B. (1702–4); reversion of office, iv. 219.
— — Clerks of the Green Cloth: *see* Crane, J. (1660–1); Wood, Sir H. (1661–71 ?); Fox, Sir Stephen (1661–88); Churchill, Sir W. (1686–8).
— — Clerks Comptrollers of the Green Cloth: E dines with, iii. 261 & n. 4; one of them surveys land at Deptford, iii. 262; individual Clerks Comptrollers: *see* Fox, Sir Stephen (1660–1); Wood, Sir H. (1660–1); Boreman, Sir W. (1661–80); Churchill, Sir W. (1664–86).
— — Kitchen: Clerks of the: *see* Boreman, Sir W.; Pinckney, L.; Fox, Sir Stephen (error ?; iv. 218 & n. 4).
— — King's Wine-cellar: Gentleman of the: *see* Bickerton, R.
— Master of the Horse and his subordinates:
— — Master of the Horse: *see* Scott, James, duke of Monmouth (1674–81).
— — Equerry of the Crown Stable: *see* Armourer, Sir W.
— — Farrier: *see* Snape, A.
— medical attendants, &c.:
— — Physicians in ordinary to the king: *see* Fraizer, Sir A.; Needham, Jasper; Quarterman, W.; Scarburgh, Sir C.
— — Physicians in ordinary to the household: *see* Clarke, Timothy; Dickinson, E.; Waldron, T.
— — Surgeons: *see* Knight, John (Serjeant Surgeon); Whittle, S.
— — Apothecary to the household: *see* le Fèvre, N.

Royal Household (*cont.*)
— military:
— — Gentlemen Pensioners: in processions, &c., iii. 280, 480 & n. 3; v. 578.
— — Yeomen of the Guard: Lieutenant of the: *see* Howard, Thomas.
— miscellaneous offices:
— — Astronomer Royal: *see* Flamsteed, J. (1675–1719).
— — Chief Justice in Eyre of royal forests south of Trent: *see* Stanhope, Philip, earl of Chesterfield (iv. 220 & n. 2).
— — Gardeners: *see* London, G.; Wise, H.
— — Historiographer Royal: *see* Howell, J. (1661–6); C. Wase suggested for, iii. 523, n. 1, 525, n. 1.
— — Jewellers in ordinary: *see* Simpson, F. *or* J.
— — King's Printer: *see* Hills, Henry, sen. (1670–88).
— — Knight Marshal: in ceremony, v. 578; individual Knight Marshal: *see* Throckmorton, Sir W. (1660–7).
— — Library-keeper at St. James's Palace: *see* Thynne, H. F. *and* J. (1677–89); Justel, H. (1689–93, &c.); Bentley, R. (1693–1742).
— — Master of Ceremonies: in ceremony, iii. 349; individual Master: *see* Cotterell, Sir C. (1660–86).
— — Master of the Harriers: *see* Eliot, T.
— — Master of the Jewel-House: *see* Talbot, Sir Gilbert (1660–91).
— — Master of the privy pack of Royal Buckhounds: *see* Graham, James.
— — Master of the Revels: *see* Herbert, Sir Henry.
— — Poet Laureate: *see* Dryden, John (1668–88).
— — Secretary for French tongue: *see* de Vic, Sir H. (1660–1); Henshaw, T. (1661–1700).
— — Secretary for Latin: *see* Fanshawe, Sir R. (1659–66); Oudart, N. (1666–81); reversion of office: promised to E, iii. 546–7 & n.
— — Surveyor-general of the Works: office (lodgings) of,

Royal Household (*cont.*)
iii. 319 & n. 2; v. 244 & n. 2; individual Surveyors: *see* Denham, Sir J. (1660–9); Wren, Sir C. (1669–1718).

Royal Mint: commission for regulation of, 1663–4, 1666, iii. 361 *bis* & n. 2, 370 & n. 6, 435, 444 & n. 5; i. *19*; trial of metal at, iv. 138; not producing enough coin, 1696, v. 242.
officers: Masters of the Mint: *see* Slingsby, Henry (1660–80); Neale, Thomas (1686–99); joint-Master, 1660–7: *see* Freeman, Sir R. (iii. 335, n. 2); Assay-master, 1668–92: *see* Brattle, Sir J. (iv. 138 & n. 1); engraver: *see* Roettiers, J. (iv. 138 & n. 2).

Royal Society [the Royal Society was founded on 28 Nov. 1660 as an association of men interested in natural science, and became the Royal Society by a charter of incorporation granted on 15 July 1662. The break in continuity is slight as regards membership and activities, and is generally disregarded here (and in entries under other headings); the section headed 'Philosophical Society' below deals with notices applying to the unincorporated association alone. In the text the effective break occurs at iii. 330]:
— general: general note and bibliography, iii. 266, n. 6; *add.*; notices in Diary: value of, i. *108*; origin, &c., iii. 266 & n. 6; i. *15*.
— Philosophical Society: called Philosophic Society, &c., iii. 266, 268, 306; *see also* i. *15*, n. 1; presidents of, iii. 272, n. 3; R. Boyle as chairman at meeting, iii. 327; register: *see* Croone, W. (iii. 475, n. 4).
— charters: petition to Charles II for incorporation, iii. 296 & n. 3; first charter: read by society, iii. 330 & n. 3; further notice of, &c., iii. 332 & n. 1; society gives thanks for, iii. 334 & n. 2; second charter: arms granted in, iii. 332 & n. 2, 336 & n. 1; mentioned, iii. 355, n. 2, 366, n. 2; third charter: read by society, iii. 527, n. 2; Chelsea College granted to society by, iii. 497, n. 1, 527.
— statutes: in preparation, &c., 1662–4, iii. 332 & n. 1, 334, 335, 336, 343, 355 & n. 2, 364, 390 & n. 5; new laws, 1682, iv. 267; taken to new president, 1698, v. 305.
— name, arms, &c.: first called Royal Society by E, iii. 306 & n. 1; name granted by charter, iii. 330; arms, iii. 332 & n. 2, 336 & n. 1; ~ alluded to (?), iii. 327 & n. 4; motto, iii. 336; ~ suggestion for, i. *41*, n. 2; ~ significance of, i. *86*; mace: presented, iii. 332 & n. 3; ~ in procession, iii. 483; St. Andrew as patron of, iii. 366; iv. 490; ~ cross of, worn at anniversary meeting, iii. 366.
— officers: (i) general: elections of, 1675, 1676: conduct of, iv. 125, n. 3; presidency: dispute concerning, 1677, iv. 125 & n. 3; *see also* iv. 123 & n. 6, 124 & n. 8; vice-president: first sworn, iii. 527 & n. 2; secretaryship, iii. 630, n. 5; ~ candidates for, discussed, 1681, iv. 263.
— — (ii) office-holders [years run from 30 Nov.; page-references give elections, &c.]: president [for presidency before first charter *see* Philosophical Society *above*]: *see* Brouncker, William, Viscount Brouncker (1662–77; iii. 332); Williamson, Sir J. (1677–80; iv. 125 & n. 3); Boyle, Robert (1680; refused to serve; iv. 225 & n. 1); Wren, Sir C. (12 Jan. 1681–2; iv. 225, n. 1, 263); Hoskins, Sir J. (1682–3; iv. 296); Wyche, Sir C. (1683–4; iv. 351); Pepys, S. (1684–6; iv. 396, 490); Vaughan, John, earl of Carbery (1686–9; iv. 564); Herbert, Thomas, earl of Pembroke (1689–90; iv. 652); Southwell, Sir R. (1690–5; v. 39, 77, 160); Montagu, Charles, earl of Halifax (1695–8; v. 226 & n. 1); Somers, John, Baron Somers (1698–1703; v. 304–5 & n., 436); Newton, Sir Isaac (1703–27); E proposed for, &c. (1682,

Royal Society (*cont.*)
1690, 1693), iv. 296 & n. 6; v. 39, 160; vice-presidents: E as, iv. 450; Sir R. Southwell as, v. 304–5; treasurer: *see* Ball, William (1660–3; iii. 366 & n. 3); Hill, Abraham (1663–5, 1679–1700); Colwall, D. (1665–79); secretaries: *see* Oldenburg, H. (1662–77); Evelyn (1672–3; iii. 630); Hill, Abraham (1673–5); Hooke, R. (1677–82); Grew, N. (1677–9); Gale, T. (1679–81); Aston, Francis (1681–5; iv. 263 & n. 6); Plot, R. (1682–4; iv. 263 & n. 6); Waller, Richard (1687–1709, 1710–14); Sloane, Sir Hans (1693–1713); under-secretary: *see* Papin, D. (1679).

— employees: amanuensis, iii. 292, n. 2; curator, iii. 292 & n. 2; curator for engines, iii. 275; *add.*; curator for anatomy of plants (N. Grew), iv. 124, n. 9; curator of experiments (R. Hooke), iii. 356, n. 9; iv. 184; ~ orders for, iii. 392; English itinerant (T. Willisel), iii. 539 & n. 4; praefectus of museum (N. Grew), iv. 124, n. 9.

— council: first council (1662–3): E nominated for and sworn, iii. 332 & n. 1; ~ meets, iii. 334, 335, 336 *bis*, 343, 350; ~ members of, dine together, iii. 343, 350; second council (1663): meets, iii. 355, n. 2; ~ prepares to receive Charles II, iii. 357, 364; later councils: for elections to, *see* anniversary meetings *below*; ~ meet, iii. 524, 527, 528, 573 & n. 6 (?); iv. 191, 264 & n. 2, 265 & n. 2, 267 & n. 6, 277 & n. 1, 296, 503 & n. 5; ~ special meetings of, iv. 125–6 & n. (?), 205 & n. 5; ~ concern of, with Arundelian library, iii. 524; iv. 145; ~ swears in new president, iv. 125; ~ decides on publication of *Philosophical Transactions*, iv. 277 & n. 1; ~ orders E to compliment Ahmed Hadu, iv. 283 & n. 3; ~ concern of, in book printed at the society's expense, iv. 503 & n. 5; for other publications ordered by council *see* publications *below*; council-book, iii. 332, n. 1; individual members: Sir Kenelm Digby, iii. 294, n. 2; Henry Howard, seventh duke of Norfolk, iv. 396; Henry Hyde, earl of Clarendon, *ib.*; for E as member *see* Evelyn: and Royal Society.

— committees: special: for English language, iii. 396 & n. 4; ~ on fruit for cider, iii. 351 & n. 4; ~ georgical, iii. 374 & n. 8, 400–1 & n.; ~ for museum (repository), iii. 433 & n. 3; delegations, iv. 212 & n. 3; v. 304–5, 324.

— fellows: (i) general: Original Fellows: bibliographical note, *add.* (iii. 266, n. 6); candidates for election: rule regarding, iv. 267; honorary: rule regarding, *ib.*; book presented to all, iii. 294 & n. 2.

— — (ii) groups: at astronomical observation, iii. 285–6; building a yacht, iii. 327 & n. 5, 332–3; supping and discussing business at Sir J. Williamson's, iv. 54, 84, 123 & n. 6 (*see also* p. 125, n. 3), 124 & n. 8, 125 & n. 8, 277, 299–300; discussing secretaryship, iv. 263; at supper cooked in Papin's digester, iv. 278–9.

— — (iii) social [for St. Andrew's day dinners *see* anniversary meetings *below*]: dine together before meetings, iv. 275, 293, 299, 301, 380, 400; club of: dines together, iv. 324; *add.*

— — (iv) individual [notices of admissions, &c.; *see also* foreign correspondents *and* visitors *below*]: admissions: W. Bridgeman, iv. 197 & n. 2; (Sir) Philip Carteret, iii. 401 & n. 6; Sir Nicholas Slanning, *ib.*; elections, &c.: Christiaan Huygens, iii. 276 & n. 1; G. A. Sarotti, iv. 279, n. 1; *see also* iv. 278; Sir S. Tuke, iii. 274, n. 4.

— foreign correspondents, &c.: letters, &c., from abroad or overseas, iii. 392 & n. 1, 539, 563, 601 & n. 2; iv. 162, 196–7, 202, 275, 632; enquiry to, from French scientists, iii. 473;

Royal Society (*cont.*)
named individuals: G. F. Borri: specimen sent by, iii. 293–4 & n.; J. Hevelius, F.R.S.: letter from, iii. 583 & n. 9; A. van Leeuwenhoek, F.R.S.: paper by, read, iv. 570 & n. 2; M. Malpighi, F.R.S.: treatises sent by, iii. 524 & n. 3, 599 & n. 4; ~ persons recommended by, iv. 250; F. de la Boe Sylvius: book sent by, &c., iii. 583 & n. 8.
— premises: at Gresham College, iii. 266 & n. 6; moves to Arundel House, iii. 472 & n. 2; returns to Gresham College, iv. 27–8 & n.; projected building for, iii. 505 & n. 1, 507; imitated, iv. 139 & n. 1.
— property, &c.: (i) general: Chelsea College: *see* London: environs; Gresham College: concerned in inquiry relating to (?), iii. 328 & n. 2; East India stock: purchase of, iv. 273 & n. 5 (?), 297(?), 298; iron chest given to, iii. 366 & n. 3; portrait of E, iv. 479, n. 2 *ad fin.*; accounts: audit of, iv. 296; Pepys as benefactor to, iv. 490.
— — (ii) library: Arundelian library: given to, iii. 472–3 & n.; i. *21*; ~ transferred to, iv. 144–5 & n.; *see also* iv. 140, n. 7; individual books given to, iii. 325 & nn. 2, 3, 369 & n. 2, 380, n. 4, 541 & n. 4, 583 & n. 8.
— — (iii) museum (repository): foundation of, iii. 334, n. 9, 433, n. 3; committee for, iii. 433 & n. 3; keeper of, iv. 124, n. 9; gifts to, iii. 110, n. 4 *ad fin.*, 334 & n. 9, 501 & n. 2 (*see also* ii. 475 & n. 5), 517 & n. 4; iv. 483; objects in, iii. 511 & n. 4; iv. 391 & n. 2; gifts to society presumably for, iii. 293–4 & n., 295 & n. 6, 563, 566 & n. 1, 601 & n. 2; iv. 275 & n. 4; v. 303 & n. 1, 592 & nn. 1, 3; visitors to, iv. 34, 133, 195.
— meetings: ordinary [notices may name the society or the place at which the meeting was held (Gresham College or Arundel House), or merely describe the proceedings, with no indication of who held them], iii. 268–75,

Royal Society (*cont.*)
284–378, 390–412, 432–50, 472–526, 538–49, 563–6, 583, 597–601, 629; iv. 1, 54–65, 83, 126–8, 139–47, 162–206, 243–333, 355–81, 395–400, 439–41, 450, 483–8, 498–502, 520–1, 530, 570, 632; v. 30, 97, 205, 224, 303, 487, 560, 592, 600, & nn., *passim & singulatim*; *see also* ii. 398, n. 1, 568, n. 3; vacations: for Plague, iii. 412 & n. 6, 432–3 & n.; ~ summer, *add.* (iii. 412); iii. 539, 563, 597; iv. 259, 290, 293, 333, 483; papers, &c.: planned series of, iv. 62 & n. 4, 205 & n. 5; journal or register, iii. 503; iv. 61.
— anniversary meetings [these were held on St. Andrew's day (30 Nov.) or, if it fell on a Sunday, on its morrow. They consisted of elections of officers and council, and apparently of a dinner. The Diary contains notices, more or less full, for all years from the first, 1663, to 1700, except 1665, 1666, 1686, 1688, 1692, 1696, 1698, and 1699. In 1665 the elections were postponed to 11 Apr. 1666: notice, iii. 434 & n. 3; in 1688 the elections were postponed to 23 Apr. 1689: iv. 608 & n. 7 (no further notice). Dinners were held at the Crown, Threadneedle Street, and later at Pontacks: iv. 125, n. 4; v. 160 & n. 4. For gifts of venison *see* Charles II *below*.]
— visitors: foreign ambassadors: Ahmed Hadu, F.R.S., iv. 283 & n. 3; Frederick Count Ahlefeldt, iii. 270 & nn. 1, 2, 271 & n. 3; Count P. Capponi, iv. 499 & nn. 1, 2; Count G. L. Durazzo, iii. 314 & n. 2; Count von Zinzendorf, iv. 316 & n. 1; other persons: Conde de Castelmelhor, iv. 191; Cosimo III, iii. 527 & n. 3; Ferdinand Albrecht I, duke of Brunswick-Lüneburg-Bevern, F.R.S., iii. 396 & n. 5; Margaret Cavendish, duchess of Newcastle, iii. 482–3 & n.; Prince Rupert, later F.R.S., iii. 318 & n. 4; unnamed Italian(s), iv. 250.
— publications: printers to society

Royal Society (*cont.*)
appointed, iii. 340, n. 1; rules for publications, *ib.*; books ordered to be printed: E: *Sylva*, iii. 340 & n. 1, 353 & n. 3; ~ *Philosophical discourse of Earth*, iv. 62 & n. 4; M. Malpighi: works by, iii. 524, n. 3, 599 & n. 4; F. Willoughby, *Historia Piscium*, iv. 503 & n. 5; orders discourse to be printed, iv. 289 & n. 5; orders microscopic drawings to be engraved, iii. 356–7 & n.; *Philosophic Transactions* (and *Collections*): publication of, iii. 266, n. 6 *ad fin.*; ~ orders relating to, iv. 205 & n. 5(?), 277 & n. 1; ~ papers, &c., in: citations by E, iv. 120 & n. 2, 376 & n. 1; v. 224 & n. 3, 487 & n. 1; notice relating to *Sylva* in, iii. 541, n. 4.

— other activities: scientific, &c.: inquiries concerning: cider-fruit, iii. 340, n. 1; ~ Tenerife, iii. 274 & n. 3; ~ timber-trees, iii. 340 & n. 1; papers for: prepared by E, iii. 271, n. 4; ~ by Sir W. Petty, iv. 60–1 & n.; tries a diving-bell, iii. 292 & n. 2; general: welcomes (Sir) J. Chardin, iv. 212–14 & n.; to supervise Foubert's academy (proposal), iv. 290 & n. 2; *see also* p. 289, n. 4; attacked by R. South, iii. 531–2.

— Charles II and the society [*see also* charters *and* name, &c., *above*]: discusses it with E, iii. 288; proposed visit of, iii. 357, 364; gives Chelsea College to, iii. 496–7 & n.; *see also* London: environs; gifts from, iii. 268 & n. 4, 272 & n. 2, 372 & n. 6; gives venison to, for anniversary meetings, iii. 366, 501, 519, 565; iv. 189–90, 351.

— E and the society [select references; for full series *see* Evelyn: and Royal Society]: influence of, on formation of, i. *15*; thanked by, for calling it the Royal Society, iii. 306 & n. 1; sketches by, for arms of, iii. 332, n. 2; presides at meetings, iv. 128, 259, 275, 299, n. 1, 395 & n. 4, 450 & n. 1; ~ as vice-president, iv. 450 & n. 1; participates in inquiry of, into timber-trees and cider-fruit, iii. 340 & n. 1; presents *Sylva* to, iii. 369 & n. 2; ~ second edition, iii. 541 & n. 4.

Royalists [general notices]: in Paris and France, 1650, iii. 17; ~ received by Lady Browne, iii. 77; vicious lives of: in sermon, iii. 39; Ireton's cruelty towards, iii. 58; forbidden to employ ejected clergy, 1655, iii. 163 & n. 1; the Decimation, *ib.*; arrests of, 1656, iii. 183, n. 3; Clarendon accused of neglecting, iii. 493 & n. 4; iv. 338; impoverished: Charles II failed to remunerate, iii. 609; iv. 410.

Royston, Herts.: palace at, iii. 138 & n. 5.

Rubens, Sir Peter Paul, ii. 64, n. 1; *Palazzi di Genova* by, ii. 173 & n. 1 (i. 109), 176; paintings by: in Jesuits' church, Antwerp, ii. 63, n. 4, 64 (i. 43); *Introitus Ferdinandi* series, ii. 71 & n. 3 (i. 46); Marie de Médicis series, ii. 128 & n. 2 (i. 82); in Chiesa Nuova, Rome, ii. 232, n. 7; portrait of Arundel, v. 145 & n. 3; unspecified, ii. 70 (i. 46); v. 145.

Rubeus, Joannes: *see* Wilfrid, J.

Rueil: Richelieu's villa at, ii. 108–10 & nn. (i. 70–1), 564.

Rueil: Treaty of, 1649, ii. 553, n. 6.

Rugini, — (C. Ruzini): museum of, ii. 470–1 & nn.

Ruishe, Frances: *see* Wentworth, Frances, Lady Wentworth.

Ruishe, Sir Francis: geneal., iii. 187, n. 5.

Rumsey, Col. John, Rye-House Plot informer, iv. 323, n. 8.

Rupel, river, ii. 68, n. 1.

Rupert, Prince, Count Palatine of the Rhine, duke of Cumberland, iii. 271, n. 4; in Civil War: defeats Essex near Worcester, iii. 119, n. 5; conduct of, at Edgehill, i. 53; at Brentford: E rides in his troop, i. 53; capture of Bristol by, iii. 102, n. 5; storms Leicester, &c., iii. 122, n. 4; fleet commanded by, 1652, i. 26; in Second Dutch War: visits fleet at the Nore, 1665, iii. 413; appointed joint-commander of fleet, iii. 425, n. 1; joins fleet, 1666, iii. 435, n. 3,

Rupert, Prince (*cont.*)
436 & n. 2; in Four Days' Battle, iii. 437–8 & n., 438 & n. 4; at the Nore, iii. 441 & n. 4; sent to defend Woolwich, &c., 1667, iii. 485 *bis* & nn. 1, 5; later career: in Garter celebration, 1670, iii. 559; member of Council for Foreign Plantations, iii. 571, n. 1; ~ attends meeting, iii. 604–5.
apartment of, in Windsor Castle, as Constable, iii. 560 & n. 3; shows E process of mezzotint engraving, iii. 271 &, n. 4, 274; i. *16*; visits Philosophical Society, iii. 318 & n. 4; admitted F.R.S., iii. 318, n. 4; presents inscribed stone to Royal Society, iii. 566.
social: dines at Durdans, iii. 334; at dinner-party, iv. 125.
geneal., i. 26 & nn. 5, 7; relations of, with his mother, iii. 316, n. 2; reputed lover of Lady Catherine Scott, ii. 560, n. 1; a mistress of, iii. 466 & n. 3; supposed son of, iii. 358; secretary of: *see* Hayes, Sir J. (iii. 623 & n. 4).
Ruperta, daughter of Prince Rupert, iii. 466, n. 3.
Rupert's drops: discussed by Royal Society, iii. 272 & n. 2.
Ruremonde: taken by Allies, 1702, v. 516 *bis* & n. 6.
Russel, — (William Russell?), undertaker, v. 360, n. 1.
Russell family, dukes of Bedford: standing of, iv. 332; inherits Southampton property in Bloomsbury, iii. 398, nn. 2, 3.
Russell family (baronets): owners of Swallowfield, iv. 481, n. 1.
Russell, Anne: *see* Digby, Anne, countess of Bristol.
Russell, Lady Catherine: *see* Greville, Catherine, Baroness Brooke.
Russell, Diana: *see* Newport, Diana, countess of Bradford, &c.
Russell, Edward; earl of Orford (Alford) 1697; admiral, v. 127, n. 2; movements of, with fleet, 1691, v. 68, n. 4, 69, n. 2; quarrels with Nottingham and retires, 1693, v. 127 & n. 2, 130–1; appointed Admiral of the Fleet, 1693, v. 157 & n. 2; commands fleet in Mediterranean, 1694, v. 186 & n. 3; resigns commissions, 1699,
Russell, Edward (*cont.*)
v. 325 & n. 4; impeached, 1701, v. 456 & n. 1, 462 & n. 1; *see also* v. 466 & n. 1, 481; acquitted, v. 468 & n. 1; chaplain of (Rev. S. Barker?): sermons by, v. 469 & n. 4, 552–3.
Russell, Francis, fourth earl of Bedford: geneal., iii. 96, n. 1; iv. 95, n. 1, 170, n. 2.
Russell, Col. John, iv. 334 & n. 4, 562, n. 1; social, iv. 334, 562(?).
Russell, Mrs. (Martha), widow of T. Russell: funeral of (?), iii. 185, n. 4.
Russell, Rachel, Lady Russell, wife of William Russell, Lord Russell: inherits Southampton House, iii. 551, n. 4; geneal., iv. 344, n. 3.
Russell, Richard, bishop of Portalegre, &c., called bishop of Cabo Verde: diplomatic activity of, iii. 305 & n. 2, 306.
Russell, Thomas, of Charlton: funeral of (?), iii. 185 & n. 4.
Russell, William, coffin-maker, iv. 276, n. 3; method of embalming of, iv. 276; mentioned (?), v. 360, n. 1.
Russell, William, minister at Rye, iii. 67, n. 5.
Russell, William, fifth earl and first duke of Bedford, iii. 512, n. 4; created duke, v. 180 & n. 2; in ceremony, iii. 277; at feast, iii. 512; portrait of, iv. 162 & n. 3, 403–4; geneal., iv. 322, 333, n. 6, 334.
Russell, William, styled Lord Russell 1678–83, iv. 322, n. 2; sells site of Montagu House, iv. 90, n. 7; *see also* iii. 551, n. 4; complicity of, in Rye-House Plot, trial, and execution, &c., iv. 322–3, 326–9, 332, 333 & nn., *passim*; i. *29*; ~ mentioned, iv. 350, 366, 382, 456; geneal., iii. 551, n. 4; iv. 333, 334; chaplain of: *see* Johnson, Samuel.
Russell: Lord, 1678–83 (courtesy title): *see* Russell, William.
Russia *or* Muscovy [for embassies from, to England, *see* Diplomatists]: English merchants banished from, 1649, iii. 344 & n. 5; makes peace with Poland, 1667, iii. 494, n. 6; takes Perekop, 1689, iv. 645 & n. 6; takes Azov, v. 258 & n. 5; *see also* Peter, the Great; Wars: Great Northern War.

Russia (*cont.*)
ships for: taken by French, 1691, v. 67 & n. 3.
cold in: effects of, iv. 146; curiosities from, iii. 107 & nn. 9, 10.
Rustat, Tobias: erects statue of Charles II in Windsor Castle, iv. 207 & nn. 4, 5.
Rusthall, near Tunbridge Wells, Kent: lodgings at, iii. 68, n. 4.
Rusticus, St.: relics of, ii. 86 (i. 58).
Rutland: places in, &c., iii. 122 & n. 2, 123, 133.
Rutland: Earls and Duke of, &c.: see Manners, Frances, wife of George Manners, seventh earl; Manners, John, eighth earl, 1641–79; Manners, Frances, his countess; Manners, John, ninth earl, 1679–1703, and first duke, 1703–11.
Ruvigny (Rouvigny, Rovigny, &c.), Henri de Massue, baron and first marquis de, iv. 522–3 & n.; as diplomatist: visits to England, iii. 254, n. 7, 504–5 & n.; sufferings of, as a protestant, v. 469; as resident at Greenwich, 1686–9: influence of, on E, i. *32*; iv. 447, n. 3 *ad fin.*; occupies Queen's House, iv. 523, n. 1; obtains use of parish church for French congregation, iv. 548; chapel of, in Queen's House: service in, iv. 565; chapel of: services in, iv. 568, 592, 597, 598, 607; as resident, 1686, iv. 522, 523; goes to winter in London, iv. 526; as resident, 1687–9: social, iv. 552, 557, 561, 563, 565, 568, 573, 592, 607, 615; dies, iv. 649, n. 5.
Ruvigny, Henri de Massue, seigneur and, 1689, second marquis de; Viscount, 1692, and earl, 1697, of Galway, iv. 521, n. 2; character of, v. 468–9; as joint deputy-general of protestant churches in France, iv. 523, n. 1; visits Sayes Court, iv. 521, 587, 649 & n. 5; resident at Greenwich: service in his lodgings, v. 23–4; ~ social, v. 30(?), 36; as lord justice of Ireland: superseded, &c., v. 468–9 & n.; wounded, 1705, v. 614 & n. 5; geneal., v. 30.
Ruvigny, Marie de Massue, marquise de, wife of the first marquis, iv. 523, n. 2; social, iv. 523; v. 30, 36.
Ruzini (Rugini), Carlo: museum of, ii. 470–1 & nn.
Rycaut, Sir Paul, iv. 489, n. 2; social, iv. 489; gives E account of Sabatai Sevi, iii. 522, n. 2.
Rye (Rie), Sussex: officials at, requested to assist Mrs. Evelyn, iii. 66; E meets her at, &c., iii. 67–8 & nn.
Rye-House Plot, i. *29*; general notices, iv. 321–4 & nn., 329; projected assassination of Charles II frustrated, iv. 340–1 & n.; individual conspirators in: Monmouth: surrenders himself, iv. 350 & n. 3; ~ retracts confession, iv. 353–4 & n.; Shaftesbury, iv. 328–9 & n.; R. West: pardoned, iv. 494 & n. 5.
trials for, iv. 366 (*see also* p. 354), 466 & n. 5; ~ alluded to (?), iv. 484; *see also* Gerard, Charles, second earl of Macclesfield; executions for, iv. 332 & nn. 4, 5; *see also* Armstrong, Sir T.; Russell, William, Lord Russell; Sidney, Algernon.
king's *Declaration* concerning: read in church, iv. 335 & n. 2, 336; thanksgiving for king's safety, iv. 336–7; in sermons, iv. 332, 333, 360–1.
Rygate: *see* Reigate.
Rynen: *see* Rhenen.
Ryswick: palace of princes of Orange at, ii. 41 & n. 3 (i. 30).
Ryswick, Peace of: convention for, i. 30; negotiating, v. 266 *ter* & nn. 1, 2; treaties signed, v. 267 & n. 1, 270 & nn. 6, 7; terms of, &c., v. 269–71 & nn.; proclaimed in England, v. 269 & n. 2; thanksgiving, &c.: preparations for, v. 269 & n. 4; ~ celebrated, v. 277–8 & nn.; mentioned in king's speech, v. 278; in sermon, v. 283.
Ryves (Reeves), Bruno, D.D.; dean of Windsor 1660, iii. 95, n. 1; in Garter celebrations, iii. 479 & n. 5, 559 & n. 2; sermons by: before house of commons, iii. 311–12 & nn.; ~ ordinary, iii. 95, 213 & n. 6(?), 225 & n. 2(?), 477.

Saba: *see* Sheba.
Sabatai Sevi (Shabbethai Zebi): E's account of, iii. 522, n. 2.

Sabellians: attacked in sermon, iv. 35.
Sabellius: tenets of: mentioned, iv. 617.
Sacheverell (Sechevarell), William: participates in Stafford's impeachment (?), iv. 227 & n. 9.
Sackville family, earls of Dorset: sometime owners of Groombridge Place, iii. 72, n. 1.
Sackville, Anne, countess of Dorset, wife of Richard Sackville, third earl: *see* Herbert, Anne, countess of Pembroke.
Sackville, Charles; styled Lord Buckhurst 1652?–75; earl of Middlesex 1675; sixth earl of Dorset 1677, iii. 466, n. 4; appointed lord chamberlain of the household, 1689, iv. 627; as commissioner for Greenwich Hospital: attends meeting, v. 209–10; mistress of: alluded to (?), iii. 466 & n. 4; geneal., iii. 203, n. 5.
Sackville, Frances, countess of Dorset, wife of Richard Sackville, fifth earl: taken in Christmas raid on Exeter House chapel, iii. 203 & n. 5.
Sackville, Richard, third earl of Dorset: geneal., iii. 203, n. 5.
Sackville, Richard; fifth earl of Dorset 1652: owner of Knole House, iv. 17 & n. 3; geneal., iii. 203, n. 5; mistress of: alluded to (?), iii. 466 & n. 4.
Sacro Catino, ii. 177 & n. 1 (i. 111).
Sadducees: in sermons, iv. 133; v. 96.
Saffron Walden, Essex: saffron grown at, iii. 141–2 & n., 556; Audley End in: *see* Audley End.
St. Albans, Herts.: notice, 1642, ii. 78 & n. 4 (i. 51); E visits, 1685, iv. 491–2; abbey-church: repaired, iv. 589 & n. 5; library of Rev. E. Carter at, iv. 589 & n. 4; archdeacon of: *see* Carter, E.
St. Albans: Viscount, 1621–6: *see* Bacon, Francis; earl of, 1660–84: *see* Jermyn, Henry; first duke of, 1684–1726: *see* Beauclerk Charles.
St. Anne's Hill (Tan Hill), Wilts., iii. 116 & n. 3.
St. Asaph: cathedral clergy:
  bishops: *see* Griffith, G. (1660–6); Lloyd, William, D.D., the apocalyptic (1680–92); Jones, Edward (1692–1703); Hooper, G. (1703–4); Beveridge, W. (1704–8); Fleetwood, W. (1708–14); Hare, F. (1727–31).
  deans: *see* Stratford, N. (1674–89); Bright, G. (1689–96); Stanley, William (1706–31).
Sainte-Baume, Provence, ii. 167 & nn. 1, 4 (i. 105).
St. Bernard, Great, *massif*: in view, ii. 506 & n. 3.
Saint-Chamond, Marquis de: palace of, in Rome: fireworks before, ii. 282 & n. 2.
St. Christopher, Leeward Islands: divided between English and French, iii. 605, n. 1; Sir C. Wheeler's conduct in, iii. 598 *bis*; French part taken, 1702, v. 516 & n. 5; governors of: *see* Leeward Islands.
Saint-Cloud (St. Cloe, &c.), near Paris: chateau, &c., at, ii. 107–8 & nn. (i. 69–70), 564; Cabinet de la Durier (restaurant) at, ii. 108 & n. 3; Charles II sups at, ii. 563; parties at, ii. 536; iii. 21.
Saint-Côme, near Tours: priory of: Ronsard buried in, ii. 147 & n. 4 (i. 95); Franciscan convent near, ii. 147 & n. 5 (i. 95).
St. Davids: diocese:
  bishops: *see* Laud, W. (1621–6); Field, T. (1627–35); Thomas, W. (1677–83); Watson, Thomas (1687–99).
  chancellor: *see* Needham, William (1690–1727).
Saint-Denis, near Paris: exposed to invasion, iii. 638; alarm at, 1650, iii. 17 & n. 3; abbey, treasury, &c., at, ii. 85–90 & nn. (i. 58–60); ~ visit to, ii. 561.
Saint-Dyé (St. Dieu), on the Loire, ii. 139 & n. 5 (i. 91).
St. Edmondsbury: *see* Bury St. Edmunds.
Saint-Fargeau: Maison Rouge near, ii. 120 & n. 10 (i. 77); *add.*
Saint-Germain, Charles Le Prévost, seigneur de, iii. 6 & n. 2; garden, &c., of, at Vanves, iii. 4–7; comes to Vanves, iii. 7; apologizes for Bataille de Vambre, iii. 7–8; geneal., iii. 7, n. 3.
Saint-Germain-en-Laye: situation of, ii. 107 (i. 69); chateaux at, ii. 110–12 & nn. (i. 71–2); ~

Saint-Germain-en-Laye (*cont.*)
represented on tapestry, iv. 343 & n. 2; forest of, ii. 111, 112 (i. 72 *bis*).
Charles II at: as prince, 1647, ii. 536; ~ with his court, 1649, ii. 561–3 & nn.; Henrietta Maria at, ii. 562; E. Waller at, 1651, iii. 39, 40.
the exiled Stuarts at: report from, iv. 622, n. 4; declaration issued at, 1693, v. 140 & n. 2; William III opposes residence of, at, v. 271, n. 2; James II ill at, 1699, v. 371; James Edward proclaimed king of Great Britain at, v. 476 & n. 3; Godolphin accused of corresponding with, v. 619 & n. 1.
Saint-Germain, Peirouse valley, Piedmont: Waldenses at, iv. 515, n. 1.
Saint-Gervais, near Blois: cream at, ii. 142, n. 5.
Saint-Gingolph, Valais, ii. 519, n. 1.
St. Helena: Edmond Halley's visit to, iv. 314 & n. 2.
St. Helen's Road, I.O.W.: Prince Rupert at, 1666, iii. 437–8 & n.; Archduke Charles at, 1704, v. 556, n. 3; Sir G. Rooke at, v. 580, n. 4.
Saint-Honorat, Îles de Lérins, ii. 168 & n. 1 (i. 106).
St. James Town, Jamaica: destroyed by fire (?), v. 532 & n. 4.
Saint-Jean, fort, Pomègues, ii. 164 & n. 4.
St. John, Anne: *see* Wilmot, Anne, countess of Rochester.
St. John, Sir Henry; fourth bt. 1708; Viscount St. John 1716: murder committed by, iv. 401 & n. 1.
St. John, Sir John: geneal., iii. 383, n. 2.
St. John, Oliver, judge, and his house (Thorpe Hall), iii. 134 & n. 2.
St. John, Sir Walter, third bt., iii. 383, n. 3; social, iii. 383; geneal., iv. 401.
St. John: Lord, 1653–75 (courtesy title): *see* Paulet, Charles, duke of Bolton, &c.
St. John: first Viscount, 1716–42: *see* St. John, Sir Henry.
St. John's, Newfoundland: captured by French, 1696, v. 263 & n. 8.
St. Luckar: *see* San Lucar.
Saint-Malo: mishap by lightning at, iv. 560; bombarded: 1693, v. 160 & n. 1; ~ 1695, v. 218 & n. 2.
St. Margaret's Fair, iii. 255–6 & n.
Sainte-Marguerite, Îles de Lérins, ii. 168 & n. 1. (i. 106).
Sainte-Marie, fort on the Scheldt, ii. 62–3 & n. (i. 43).
Saint-Martin, Isle of Ré: bombarded, 1696, v. 252 & n. 3.
Saint-Maurice, Valais, ii. 518; *see also* ii. 519, n. 1; governor of Lower Valais at: receives E, &c., ii. 516, 518–19 & nn.
Saint-Menoux, ii. 154 & n. 10 (i. 99).
St. Michael, Herts.: Bacon's tomb at, ii. 78 & n. 4 (i. 51).
St. Michel, Elizabeth: *see* Pepys, Mrs. E.
Saint-Nectaire, Henri de, marquis de la Ferté-Nabert: altar built by, &c. (as M. Seneterre), iii. 28 & n. 3; *add.*; ~ mentioned, iii. 27.
Saint-Omer: marauding soldiers from, iii. 12; English Jesuit college at: Titus Oates at, iv. 153, n. 4.
St. Peter's Patrimony, ii. 208 & n. 4.
Saint-Philippe, fort on the Scheldt, ii. 62 & n. 7 (i. 43).
Saint-Quentin: Mazarin at, 1649, ii. 561, n. 1.
St. Remes: *see* San Remo.
Saint-Ruth, —, French general: killed, v. 66.
Saint-Symphorien (St. Saforin), ii. 156 & n. 5 (i. 100).
Saint-Valery-in-Caux, ii. 536, n. 7.
Saint-Valery-sur-Somme, ii. 85 (i. 57); E. Waller at (?), ii. 536–7 & n.
St. Vincent, Cape: French fleet off, 1693, v. 142, n. 1, 145, n. 4; ~ attacks Smyrna fleet off, v. 148 & n. 2, 155, n. 7.
Sakkarah: mummy-pits at, ii. 469 & n. 3.
Saladin(e), —, at Geneva, ii. 521 & n. 2, 522 *bis*, 527; wife of, ii. 522; daughter of, ii. 530.
Saladin, Jean and Mrs. Elizabeth, ii. 521, n. 2.
Salaino, Andrea: painting by, ii. 495 & n. 5.
Salem, Massachusetts: witches at, 1692, v. 130 & n. 1.
Salerno, Blessed Giovanni da: tomb of, ii. 199 & n. 7.

Salisbury, Wilts.: notice, 1654, iii. 113 & nn. 2–5, 115 & n. 2; races at: established, iii. 114, n. 6; Charles II at, 1665, iii. 423, n. 7; James II at, 1688, iv. 607 & n. 2, 608 & n. 1; Dr. Ralph Bohun visits, v. 473; Sir Stephen Fox as choir-boy at, iv. 218; *add.*; J. Punteus surgeon at, iii. 293, n. 4.

Salisbury: Earls, &c., of: *see* Cecil, Sir Robert, first earl, 1605–12; Cecil, William, second earl, 1612–68; Cecil, James, fourth earl, 1683–94; Cecil, Frances, his countess.

Salisbury: cathedral clergy, &c.:
- bishops: *see* Fotherby, M. (1618–19); Duppa, Brian (1641–60); Henchman, H. (1660–3); Earles, John (1663–5); Ward, Seth (1667–89); Burnet, Gilbert (1689–1715); Talbot, William (1715–21).
- deans: *see* Baylie, R. (1635–67); Brideoake, R. (1667–75); Pierce, Thomas (1675–91); Young, Edward (1702–5).
- treasurer, 1690– : *see* Allix, P.
- canons: *see* Bohun, Ralph; Hill, Thomas; Hobbs, W.; Young, Edward.

Salisbury Plain, Wilts., iii. 115; in comparisons, iii. 131, 132, 556.

Sallust: gardens of, ii. 234 & n. 5, 239.

Salm: prince of: *see* Frederick Magnus.

Saltine, river, &c., Simplon Pass, ii. 508, n. 5 *ad fin.*, 513, n. 3.

Salt-petre: *see* Gunpowder and Salt-petre.

Saludadores: miracles performed by, iv. 468–70 & nn.

Salvage, —: *see* Savage, John, Earl Rivers.

Salvatico, —: *see* Selvatico, B.

Salviati, Francesco: paintings by, ii. 215 & n. 3, 367 & n. 9.

Salviati, Giuseppe Porta called: *see* Porta.

Samaria: books from, ii. 301; famine in: in sermon, iv. 55 & n. 6; Samaritans: in sermon, v. 598–9; Woman of: relic of, ii. 307; ~ in sermons, v. 80, 167, 251.

Samaritan, the Good: in sermon, v. 599.

Sameis, Rev. — (P. Samways?): sermon by, iii. 248 & n. 4.

Samians: found Puteoli, ii. 343.

Sampierdarena (St. Pietro d'Arena), near Genoa: villas, &c., at, ii. 170–1 & n. (i. 108), 178 (i. 112).

Sampion, Mount: *see* Simplon.

Samson: in sermon, v. 387.

Samuel: in sermon, iii. 20.

Samuel, —, architect: *see* Samwell, W.

Samways, Peter, D.D.: sermon by (?), iii. 248 & n. 4.

Samwell (Samuel), William, architect: builds house at Newmarket for Charles II, iii. 554 & n. 3.

Samwell, Sir William, bt.: geneal., iii. 554, n. 3.

San Casciano, ii. 200 & n. 10.

Sanchez, Don (Zanches d'Avila?), ii. 560 & n. 7.

Sancroft (Sandcroft), William, D.D.; dean of St. Paul's 1664; archbishop of Canterbury 1678; deprived 1690, iii. 432, n. 1.
- as dean: and proposals for repair of St. Paul's, iii. 448–9 & nn.; sermons by, iii. 431–2; iv. 53, 83, 106.
- as archbishop: consecrated, iv. 152, n. 4; political activities, &c.: opposes bill for Parliamentary Test Act, iv. 159, n. 4; at opening of parliament, 1685, iv. 442; as commissioner for Ecclesiastical Affairs: appointed, iv. 519; ~ refuses to act, iv. 520, n. 1, 524; signs petition against reading Declaration of Indulgence, 1688, iv. 584, n. 1; for further proceedings in this connexion *see* Seven Bishops; as prisoner in Tower, iv. 587; warned by E concerning attempts to create disputes among protestants, &c., iv. 600 & n. 4; i. *33*; *see also* iv. 601 & n. 1; ~ thanks E for warning, iv. 614; attends meeting to authenticate birth of James Edward, &c., iv. 602–3 & n.; questioned by James II about invitation to William of Orange, iv. 604 & n. 3; refuses to publish declaration against William's invasion, iv. 604, n. 3, 605–6 & n.; joins in petition for a parliament, iv. 608 & n. 4; absents himself from council of peers, &c., Dec. 1688, &c., iv. 619, n. 5, 626; holds meeting to

Sancroft, William, D.D. (*cont.*)
discuss settlement of the crown, Jan. 1689, iv. 613–15 & nn.; absent from lords' debate on settlement, iv. 619; views of, on kingship, iv. 625, n. 3; dissatisfied with settlement, iv. 626 & n. 3, 634; refuses to attend parliament, Mar. 1689, iv. 631 & n. 5; excuses himself from officiating at coronation of William and Mary, iv. 633; discusses ecclesiastical and political affairs, iv. 633–4 & nn.
as archbishop: general and private activities, &c.: proposals and plans for Chelsea Hospital submitted to, iv. 270, 281; authorized to make collections for London poor, 1683–4, iv. 361, n. 3; attends Charles II on death-bed, iv. 407; attends Chapel Royal service, 1685, iv. 436; and Brief for French protestant refugees: draft submitted to, iv. 508, n. 3; ~ orders of, to clergy, concerning, iv. 509, n. 1; asked to intercede with William of Orange for Scottish episcopalian clergy, iv. 615 & n. 1; book dedicated to, iv. 641, n. 4; discusses prophecy concerning Antichrist, iv. 636–7; advises E in matter of conscience, iv. 512; presents Rev. R. Holden to St. Dunstan in the East, iv. 522 & n. 2; E recommends Rev. W. Strengfellow to, iv. 641 & n. 5; sermons by: printed, iv. 157 & n. 4; ~ unprinted, iv. 308–9; appointed to preach, iv. 277, n. 3, 373, n. 2, 505, n. 2, 578, n. 3; social: parties, iv. 152, 360, 488, 518, 591; ~ alone, &c., iv. 395, 560; manners, v. 80; barge of, iv. 488; chaplain of: *see* Needham, W.
deprivation, &c.: suspended, iv. 648 & n. 6; superseded, v. 48–9 & n.; date of deprivation, v. 195–6 & n.; conduct and views of, v. 51–2 & nn.; leaves Lambeth, v. 51–2 & n., 59 & n. 2; dies, v. 161 & n. 5.
Sancroft, William, jnr., nephew of the archbishop: holds Lambeth Palace for his uncle, 1691, v. 59 & n. 2.
Sancta Clara, Franciscus a (Christopher Davenport): miraculous cure described by, iv. 469 & n. 1.
Sande, Marquis of: *see* Mello, Dom Francisco de.
Sanders, Rev. — (Saunders?): sermon by, iv. 35 & n. 6.
Sanders, Captain —: *see* Sanderson, Ralph.
Sanderson, Bridget, Lady Sanderson, wife of Sir William: geneal., iv. 94 & n. 4.
Sanderson, Ralph: member of site committee of Greenwich Hospital (?; as Captain Sanders), v. 211 & n. 3.
Sanderson, Robert, D.D.; bishop of Lincoln 1660: sermon by, iii. 238 & n. 2.
Sanderson, Sir William: funeral of, &c., iv. 94 & n. 4; *see also* Books: sources.
Sandown Castle, Kent, iii. 395, n. 5.
Sandrart, J. von: painting by, ii. 43 & n. 5 (i. 32).
Sandwich, Kent: E at, as commissioner for Sick and Wounded, iii. 395, 611; customs officer at: see Glover, J.
Sandwich: Earl, &c., of: *see* Mountagu, Edward, first earl, 1660–72; Mountagu, Jemima, his countess.
Sandys, Rev. Thomas, minister of Trinity Chapel, Bond Street: appointed, v. 375–6; sermons by (as our minister, &c.), v. 376–85, 398–413, 435–65, 482–508, 523–36, 553–69, 584–620 *passim*; repeats a sermon, v. 500–1 & v. 535–6.
Sangallo, Antonio da, jnr., architect: begins Farnese Palace, ii. 214, n. 4.
Sankey, Sir Jerome: challenges Sir William Petty (?), iv. 59, n. 1.
San Lorenzo Nuovo *or* Vecchio, near Bolsena, ii. 407 & n. 5.
San Lucar (St. Luckar): arrival of treasure-ship at, 1702, v. 516 & n. 8.
Sanmicheli, M., architect, ii. 485, n. 1.
San Piero a Sieve (il Ponte), ii. 419 & nn. 3, 4.
Sanquirico, P.: statue of Paul V by, ii. 244 & n. 4.
San Quirico d'Orcia (St. Querico), ii. 207 & n. 2.
San Remo (St. Remes), Liguria, ii. 169 (i. 106), 170 (i. 107).

Sansovino, Andrea Contucci, called: tombs in S. Maria del Popolo by, ii. 374 & n. 5.
Sansovino, Francesco, author: geneal., ii. 429, n. 6.
Sansovino, Jacopo d'Antonio Tatti, called, architect and sculptor, ii. 369, n. 1; tomb of, ii. 436 & n. 2; geneal., ii. 429, n. 6; buildings by (all at Venice): Library of St. Mark, ii. 435, n. 3, 445; Loggetta, ii. 435, n. 3, 446 & n. 9; Piazza di S. Marco, ii. 435–6 & n.; S. Geminiano, ii. 435, n. 3, 436 & n. 2; sculpture by: Mars and Neptune, Doges' Palace, ii. 443; St. James, S. Giacomo degli Spagnuoli, Rome, ii. 369 & n. 1; reliefs, S. Antonio, Padua, ii. 454 & n. 7.
Santa Cruce (Kruisschans), fort on the Scheldt, ii. 62 & n. 7 (i. 43).
Sant' Agata, near Sessa Aurunca, ii. 323 & n. 6.
Santa Maria di Capua Vetere: ruins at, ii. 324 & nn. 3–5.
Santa Vittoria *or* Borgoforte: engagement at, 1702, v. 512 & n. 4.
Santen, Jan van, architect: designs casino, Villa Borghese, ii. 251, n. 4.
Santiago de Cabo Verde: bishop elect of, 1661: *see* Russell, Richard.
Santon Downham, Suffolk (in note as Downham): travelling sands (sand-flood) at, iv. 120 & n. 2.
Saône, river: at Lyons, ii. 157 (i. 101).
Sapphira: *see* Ananias.
Saracens: in Venetian legend, ii. 440–1 & n.
Sarah, wife of Abraham: in sermon, v. 347; ~ as error for Hagar, iii. 525 & n. 4.
Sardinia: wars of, with Pisa, ii. 179 (i. 113).
Sargant, —, Roman Catholic priest: *see* Sergeant, J.
Sarmiento de Acuña, Diego: *see* Gondomar, count of.
Sarotti, G. A., F.R.S., iv. 279, n. 1.
Sarotti, Paolo, Venetian resident in England: academy of, in Venice, iv. 278, 279, n. 1.
Sarrazin, Jacques: studio of, and work by, ii. 105–6 & n. (i. 68).
Sarre in Thanet, Kent: road through, iii. 616, n. 1.
Sarsfield, Patrick, titular earl of Lucan, v. 149, n. 6; raid of, at Cullen, v. 33 & n. 2; killed, v. 149, critical note.
Sarto, Andrea d'Agnolo, called Andrea del, ii. 120, n. 1; tomb of, ii. 412 & n. 3; paintings by: Funeral of St. Philip Benizzi: story relating to, ii. 412 & n. 2; Madonna del Sacco, ii. 411–12 & n.; Madonnas or unspecified subjects, &c.: Gaddi collection, Florence, ii. 415 & n. 7; ~ Uffizi, ii. 190 & n. 12, 191 (i. 119), 413; ~ Fontainebleau (French royal collection), ii. 119–20 *bis* & nn. (i. 77); ~ Northumberland collection, London, iii. 216 & n. 4.
Sarzana, ii. 179 (i. 113).
Satan [select; sometimes as the Devil]: in sermons, iii. 30; iv. 8, 53; v. 171–3, 387–8.
Saturn, the planet, iii. 276 & n. 1, 286 & n. 3, 288.
Saul: cured by David's harp, iii. 168 & n. 3; in sermons, iii. 159, 203; iv. 31, 93, 239; v. 73, 298–9 & n.
Saumeur, Monsieur (Paul de Saumur ?), ii. 563.
Saumur (Saumer): students from, iii. 633.
Saumur, Paul de, admiral, iii. 42, n. 1; in procession, iii. 42; in tennis-match (?), ii. 563 & n. 8.
Saunders, Rev. —, curate at Deptford (?): sermons by, iv. 35 & n. 6 (?; as Sanders), 131 & n. 5, 160, 250, 289, 333.
Saunderson, George, Viscount Castleton: social (?), v. 150 & n. 6.
Saunderson, Sarah, Viscountess Castleton, wife of George Saunderson, Viscount Castleton, v. 150, n. 6 *ad fin.*
Savage (Salvage), —, son of Earl Rivers: social, iii. 77 & n. 2.
Savage, Catherine, Countess Rivers: portrait of, iv. 404 & n. 3.
Savage, Henry, master of Balliol, ii. 17, n. 2.
Savage, John, second Earl Rivers, &c.: geneal., iii. 77 & n. 2.
Savage: Viscount, 1635–40: *see* Savage, John, second Earl Rivers.
Savelli family: palace of, in Rome, ii. 228 & n. 5.

Savile (Savell) family, of Yorkshire, iv. 336.
Savile, Elizabeth: *see* Monte Feltre, countess of.
Savile, Esther, Lady Eland, wife of Henry Savile, styled Lord Eland, iv. 517–18 & n.
Savile, Sir George, bt.; Viscount Halifax 1668; earl, 1679, and marquis, 1682, of Halifax, iii. 336, n. 5; character, iii. 336–7; v. 208; as Sir George: social, iii. 336; as Lord Halifax: at Council of Trade and Plantations, iii. 629; messenger between Queen Catherine and Charles II, 1685, iv. 409, n. 1; appointed Lord President, &c., 1685, iv. 417 & n. 3; refuses to sit in Privy Council with Roman Catholics(?), iv. 602–3 & n.; commissioner from James II to William of Orange, iv. 608 & n. 8; *add.*; appointed Lord Privy Seal, 1689, iv. 627; resigns office, 1690, v. 6 & n. 1.
religious views of: sermon against, iv. 294 & n. 2; called the black Marquis, iv. 393, n. 2; social: parties, iii. 512, 586; iv. 96; geneal., iv. 335, n. 5, 517–18 & n.; v. 208 & n. 2; dies, v. 208 *bis* & n. 2.
Savile, Henry, brother of Lord Halifax, iii. 546, n. 2; reappointed vice-chamberlain of the household, iv. 416 & n. 4; social, iii. 546.
Savile, Henry, of Bowlings: geneal., iv. 335, n. 5.
Savile (Savell), Sir Henry, editor of Chrysostom: Halifax as grandson of (error), iii. 336–7 & n.
Savile, Henry; styled Lord Eland 1679–87: marriage of, iv. 517–18 & n.
Savile, James, second earl of Sussex: in ceremony (error), iii. 277 & n. 3.
Savile, Mary, marchioness of Halifax, wife of William Savile, second marquis: marriage of, v. 208 & n. 2.
Savile, William; styled Lord Eland 1687–95; second marquis of Halifax 1695, v. 208, n. 2; second marriage of, v. 208 & n. 2; dies, v. 425 & n. 1.
Savioni, Mario, singer, ii. 400, n. 1.
Savona, ii. 170 (i. 107); Cape of (Capo di Noli): storm near, ii. 170 & n. 1 (i. 107–8); i. 112.
Savoy: Duchy of [the duchy consisted of Savoy and Piedmont. For its political history *see* Victor Amadeus II; for the persecution of the Waldenses in Piedmont *see* Waldenses; for campaigns in the duchy, 1690–5, *see* Wars: War of the League of Augsburg]:
geographical: as neighbour of Geneva, ii. 520, 525; Nice as part of, ii. 168 & n. 2 (i. 106); boundary of, towards Valais, ii. 519 & n. 1; mentioned, iv. 618.
agent of, in France, 1651: audience to, iii. 43–4.
Duchess of, 1684–1713 (later queen of Sicily, &c.): *see* Anna Maria.
Prince Eugene of: *see* Eugene.
Sawyer, Sir Robert, attorney-general 1681–7, iv. 529, n. 4; in *Quo Warranto* proceedings, iv. 320, n. 1; in Lord Russell's trial, iv. 327, n. 2; appears against E, iv. 529, 546; counsel for Seven Bishops, iv. 587 & n. 2.
Sax-Gottorp: Duke of: error for Christian Albrecht, duke of Gottorp, iv. 525 & n. 1.
Saxony: Saxons besiege Riga, 1700, v. 386, n. 1; elector of, 1694–1733: *see* Augustus the Strong.
Saxton, Christopher: maps by, iv. 301, n. 4.
Say, family, owners of Sayes Court, ii. 537, n. 6.
Say, Robert, D.D., provost of Oriel College: as vice-chancellor of Oxford: visits Lord Cornbury, iii. 384 & n. 4.
Saye and Sele: eighth (second) Baron and first Viscount: *see* Fiennes, William.
Sayes Court, Deptford:
general history, ii. 537, n. 6.
manor of: ownership of, ii. 537, n. 6 *ad fin.*; iii. 59, n. 1; court leet of, iv. 346 & n. 1; land belonging to, iii. 508, n. 4 *ad fin.*; site of: duke of Leeds petitions for lease of, v. 195, n. 2.
estate [ownership and claims]: coming of Browne family, ii.

Sayes Court, Deptford (*cont.*)
537, n. 6; iv. 304; W. Prettyman and: in charge, 1647, iii. 537–8 & nn.; ~ in treaty to buy, *c.* 1649, iii. 59, n. 1; ~ ceases to reside at, 1655, iii. 149; E's concern with, 1647, i. *9*; E buys house and grounds, 1652–3, i. *10* & n. 1; iii. 58–9 & n., 74 & n. 4, 80, 81; cost of purchase, iii. 81; [the property reverted to the crown in 1660]; E's desire for permanent ownership, i. *22*; E's and Sir R. Browne's claims to fee-farm of, i. *15*; iii. 59 & n. 1, 600; iv. 129 & n. 3; E petitions for house and grounds, 1660–3, iii. 262 & n. 4, 271, 272, 276, 285, 290, 302, 318, 326, 329(?), 336 & n. 2(?), 343; ~ lease of house, &c., granted, iii. 356 & n. 6; ~ the Slaughter-house granted, iii. 352 & n. 2; pastures leased to Sir R. Browne, 1663, iii. 59, n. 1; E petitions for lease of part of Brick Close, 1667–8, iii. 482 & n. 4, 504 & n. 3, 511; ~ petition granted, iii. 512 & n. 8, 513; ~ new boundary-wall built, iii. 530; pastures: new lease of, to Sir R. Browne, 1672, iii. 600 & n. 2, 601; lands attached to: purchase of, 1656 (?), iii. 171, n. 1; Ravensbourne mills, &c., bought, 1668, iii. 508–9 & n.; iv. 37 & n. 6; E sells land attached to, 1693, v. 153–4 & nn.

as residence [E as occupant or owner; it is called Sayes Court or Deptford or home, &c.; E's and his family's comings and goings, and ordinary domestic events taking place here, between his settlement in 1652 and his removal to Wotton in 1694, are not indexed collectively]: E resides at, 1647–9, ii. 537–58 & nn., *passim*; ~ has 'a lodging and some books' at, ii. 546 & n. 3; E visits, 1650, iii. 13–15 *passim*; E arrives at, 1652, iii. 56; E prepares to settle at, iii. 58–9; Mrs. Evelyn and Lady Browne come to, iii. 73; E starts as housekeeper, iii. 149; baptisms at: E's children, iii. 75, 89, 147, 194 & n. 6, 368, 495; ~ E's grandchildren, iv. 272, 324(?); Mrs. Evelyn churched at, after childbirth, iii. 76, 90, 147, 195; divine service at: with Communion (1653–4, 1657), iii. 79, 89, 94, 97–8(?), 144–5, 195; ~ other services, iii. 183, 184 *bis*, 185, 226, n. 5(?), 450–1; iv. 63, 517, 586; wedding-parties at, iii. 373, 511; soldiers quartered at: 1657, iii. 192 & n. 6; ~ 1688, iv. 613; ~ *see also* iv. 458; burglaries, &c., at, iii. 226, 265, 352; iv. 72, 259; sound of gunfire from sea-fight heard at, 1653, iii. 84 & n. 5; in danger from Dutch, 1667, iii. 484; Venetian ambassador starts his entry from, 1668, iii. 515 & n. 1; Grinling Gibbons working near, iii. 567; Ossory's visits to, iv. 208; Sir R. Browne dies at, iv. 302; E's grandson, &c., left at, winter 1683–4, iv. 350 *bis*; E moves from, to Wotton, 1694, v. 179; i. *34* & n. 1; occupied by William Draper, v. 179, 190–4, 199; E visits: late 1694, v. 190–200 *passim*; ~ 1695, v. 206, 209–14 *passim*, 228; ~ 1696, v. 239–40, 244; ~ later visits, v. 450, 558, 600; E removes his furniture, &c., from, v. 179, 244, 340, 414; let to Admiral J. Benbow, v. 244 & n. 1, 245; *see also* v. 284, n. 5, 290, n. 6; occupied by Peter the Great, v. 284 & n. 5, 286; ~ damage done to, by Peter, v. 290 & n. 6; let to marquis of Carmarthen, v. 450; let to J. Cresset, v. 600 & n. 7.

fabric: general [house and garden]: called 'my poor villa', &c., iii. 312, 330, 354; iv. 344; description of, by R. North, i. *38*; damage to, by storms, iii. 220, 316–17 *bis*; v. 552, 558; shaken by explosion, iii. 195 & n. 2; building work at, 1654, iii. 142 & n. 4; ~ alluded to (?), iii. 223 & n. 2, 224–5, 227.

house, &c.: named rooms, &c.: best parlour, v. 284, n. 5; E's chamber, iv. 235; E's little cell and cabinet, iv. 37 & n. 3; E's study, iii. 195, 352; iv. 423; v. 284, n. 5; great chamber, iii.

Sayes Court, Deptford (*cont.*)
368; hall, iv. 333; library, iii. 89 *bis*, 94, 144; v. 284, n. 5; little drawing-room, iii. 75; nursery, iii. 145; parlour, iii. 75, 316; iv. 37; v. 284, n. 5; withdrawing-room, iii. 194; backyard, court, or forecourt, iii. 504, 511, 512, 530; south court, iv. 37; coach-house, iv. 72, 259.
gardens, fields, &c. [for land-drainage *see* Surrey and Kent Commissioners of Sewers]: E begins laying out garden, 1653, iii. 80 & n. 1; *add.*; planting at (?), 1665, iii. 393 & n. 3; effects on, of winter, 1683–4, iv. 364–5 & n.; gardener for, iv. 521 & n. 3; garden to be maintained by tenant, v. 244; damage done to, by Peter the Great, v. 290 & n. 6; separate parts and features: apiary, transparent, iii. 110 & nn. 1, 2; aviary, iii. 175; Barne Closes, iii. 80, n. 1; bees: swarm on *Oxford* frigate, iii. 321–2 & n.; Broomfield: Kentish insurgents in, 1648, ii. 541 & n. 4; ~ West: lease of, granted to Sir R. Browne, iii. 600, n. 2; ~ mentioned, iii. 80, n. 1; Earl's Sluice, iii. 151, n. 6; holly hedge, &c., iii. 80; iv. 312 & n. 1; home field: planted, 1664, iii. 370 & n. 4; orange-trees: fruit from, iv. 182; *see also* iv. 162; orchard: planted, 1653, iii. 81; oval garden, iii. 80; *add.*; pond, iii. 393; ~ stocked with fish, iv. 108; riverside land, iii. 214; ~ project for a dock in, 1655, 1662, iii. 161 & n. 2, 162, 313 & n. 2; west field: planted, 1664, iii. 370 & n. 4.
visitors [chiefly persons coming to see the garden; ordinary visitors to E are not indexed collectively]: Archibald Campbell, marquis of Argyll, 1656, 1657, iii. 175 & n. 2, 186; Archibald Campbell, later ninth earl of Argyll, 1662, iii. 318 & n. 2; Queen Catherine, 1676, iv. 89; Charles II: intends to visit, 1661, iii. 302; ~ visits, 1663, iii. 354; *see also* iii. 110; Clarendon, &c., 1662, iii. 330–1; William Douglas, third duke of Hamilton, and other Scottish peers, 1660, iii. 254; Henrietta Maria, 1662, iii. 330, 331; James, duke of York, 1662, iii. 312; Henry Lawrence, &c., 1657, iii. 193; William Kerr, earl of Lothian, 1656, 1660, iii. 175 & n. 3, 254; Pepys, 1665, iii. 418, n. 1; Thomas Wriothesley, earl of Southampton, 1656, iii. 175.

Scaliger (della Scala) family, rulers of Verona, ii. 487, n. 1; tombs of, ii. 485 & n. 2.
Scaliger, Joseph Justus: birth-place of, ii. 487, n. 1; friendship of, with Janus Dousa, iv. 312 & n. 4; tomb and bequest of, ii. 52 & n. 2 (i. 36); *see also* Books mentioned in text.
Scaliger, Julius Caesar: birth-place of, ii. 487 & n. 1; *see also* Books mentioned in text.
Scamozzi, Vincenzo, architect: buildings designed, &c., by, ii. 435, n. 3, 482, n. 2, 483, n. 8.
Scapegoat: in sermon, iv. 495–6.
Scaramouche (T. Fiorilli), iv. 12, n. 3; performs at Whitehall, iv. 12 & n. 3, 75 & nn. 4, 5.
Scarborough: first Earl of, 1690–1721: *see* Lumley, Richard.
Scarburgh, Sir Charles, M.D.; knighted 1669, iii. 77, n. 6; wants to lecture on E's anatomical tables, &c., iii. 77–8; social, iii. 546; library of, v. 206 & n. 1.
Scaricalasino, ii. 419, nn. 3–5, 420 & n. 3.
Scarperia, ii. 419 & nn. 3, 4.
Scarsdale: first Earl of: *see* Leeke, Sir Francis.
Scaven, —: *see* Scawen, R.
Scawen, Robert: social (?; as Mr. Scaven), iii. 463–4 & n.
Scawen, Sir William: in parliamentary election, 1705, v. 595, n. 4.
Scedam: *see* Schiedam.
Scenery, stage: *see* Theatre.
Scevenies: *see* Cevennes.
Scheldt, river: forts along, below Antwerp, ii. 61–3 & nn. (i. 42–3); journey on, above Antwerp, ii. 68 & n. 1 (i. 45); at Ghent, ii. 74 & n. 2 (i. 48).
Schellenberg: captured by Allies, 1704, v. 572 & n. 3, 573 *bis* & nn. 1, 2.

Schiedam (Seedam, Scedam): notice, ii. 56 & n. 7 (i. 39).
Schio (Scio): taken by Turks, 1695, v. 209 & n. 1.
Schmidt, Michael, ii. 466, n. 2.
Schomberg, Charles; second duke of Schomberg 1690: social (?), v. 139 & n. 2.
Schomberg (Schönberg; Scomberge, Shomberg), Frederick Henry; count of Schönberg (Empire); field-marshal (France) 1675; first duke of Schomberg (England), 1689; &c., iv. 598, n. 2; in Brandenburg service: occupies Cologne, 1688, iv. 598 & n. 2; in English service: goes to Ireland, 1689, iv. 645 & n. 3, 647 & n. 1; ~ campaign of, in Ireland, iv. 648 & n. 5, 651; ~ reinforcements for, v. 6 & n. 4; killed, v. 28; geneal., v. 139, n. 2.
Schomberg, Meinhard; duke of Leinster 1691; third duke of Schomberg 1693, v. 139, n. 2; as duke of Leinster: on military expedition, 1692, v. 111 & n. 4, 112 & n. 1; social (?; as Lord Shomberg), v. 139.
Schomberg: Dukes of: *see* Schomberg, Frederick Henry, first duke 1689–90; Schomberg, Charles, second duke 1690–3; Schomberg, Meinhard, third duke, 1693–1719.
Schönberg: *see* Schomberg.
Schools and Colleges [Jesuit schools, &c., are indexed under Jesuits: Colleges, &c.; riding-academies, under Horses and Horsemanship]:
  Amsterdam: Wees-huys, ii. 45 & n. 3 (ii. 32).
  Coventry: free school, iii. 121 & n. 5.
  Dulwich, iv. 74 & n. 1.
  Eton: *see* Eton College.
  Greenwich: French school at, iv. 653 & n. 2; v. 79 & n. 3(?); Green Coat school: founder of, iii. 270, n. 3.
  Guildford: free school, v. 358 & n. 2; usher or master of, v. 536 & n. 3; ~ sermons by, v. 536, 545, 546–7, 548, 580, 582.
  Ipswich: school founded by Wolsey, iii. 179, n. 1; iv. 116 & n. 2.
  Lee, Kent: Boone's charity, iv. 289, n. 1.
Schools and Colleges (*cont.*)
  Lewes (Southover): free school, ii. 9 & n. 5 (i. 8 & n. 2), 15–16 (i. 12); alluded to, ii. 11 (i. 9); master of: payment to, ii. 9, n. 7 *ad fin.*; ~ mentioned, v. 236.
  Lewisham: Colfe's school: masters of: *see* Day, M.; Turner, John, D.D.
  London: charity schools: weekly lecture (sermon) for, v. 385, n. 2; Charterhouse, iii. 192, n. 1; ~ nomination for entry to, iv. 511; ~ in comparison, ii. 45 & n. 3 (i. 32); Christ's Hospital, iii. 192 & n. 2; iv. 542–3 & nn.; v. 398–9 & n.; ~ in comparison, ii. 311; ~ Mathematical School at, iv. 542 & n. 2; v. 399 & n. 1; Gerbier's academy, ii. 134, n. 2; Roman Catholic free schools, 1688, iv. 584, n. 5 *ad fin.*; St. Martin in the Fields: Tenison's school, iv. 368, n. 1, 584, n. 5; ~ schoolmaster of: *see* Postlethwayt, J.; St. Paul's, v. 127, n. 4; ~ masters of: *see* Gale, T.; Postlethwayt, J.
  Putney: girls' schools at, ii. 555 & n. 3.
  Richelieu: academy, ii. 150 & n. 3 (i. 97).
  Rome: Ospedale di S. Spirito (foundlings), ii. 311.
  Tonbridge: free grammar school, iii. 408 & n. 1.
  Westminster: exercises of scholars at, iii. 287–8 & n.; Arlington at, iv. 119 & n. 3; master of: *see* Busby, R.
  Winchester, ii. 79 (i. 52); boarding-school at, iii. 168, n. 1.
  miscellaneous: Tenison's foundations, v. 66; vaulting and dancing school, Oxford, ii. 20–1 & n. (i. 16).
Schott, Gaspar, S.J.: inventions, &c., published by, ii. 230 & n. 7.
Schupp, J. B., *add.* (i. 86).
Schwab, Daniel: operation performed by, &c., ii. 53–4 & n. (i. 37).
Science: general and miscellaneous: notices in Diary: value of, i. *108*; progress of scientific studies during Commonwealth, i. *11–12*; gathering of scientists, 1658, iii. 217; E projects scientific college, iii. 232 & n. 2.

Science (*cont.*)
atomism, Epicurean, iii. 173, n. 4; ~ in sermon, iv. 592; Cartesians: views of, on pineal gland, iv. 530 & n. 2; ~ in sermon, v. 412; philosophy, the new, ii. 64; ~ Lord Guilford's interest in, iv. 299 & n. 4; ~ attacked by R. South, iii. 531, n. 4.
Scientific instruments: collections of: miscellaneous, ii. 230 & n. 6; iii. 110–11 & nn.; ~ mathematical, iii. 108 & n. 6, 293; iv. 215.
aeolipyle, iii. 273 & n. 4; balance, iv. 361; barometer: *see* Physics: atmosphere; burning-glasses, iii. 170; v. 592 & n. 3, 600; calculating machine, iii. 488; mathematical, v. 399 & n. 1; microscope: observations with, iii. 356, 629; iv. 126, 128; telescope: *see* Astronomy; thermometers, iii. 110, 314 & n. 2; way-wisers, iii. 110 & n. 4, 196.
Scilly Isles: Charles II in, 1646, iii. 246, n. 1; fleet near, 1702, v. 510 & n. 8; governor of, 1682–1702: *see* Godolphin, Francis (v. 505–6 & n.).
Scio: *see* Schio.
Scipio: monument of: sculpture supposed to come from, ii. 305; portrait of (gem?), iii. 339 & n. 6; statues of, ii. 152 (i. 98), 189 & n. 2 (i. 118).
Scipionis, Mons (Simplon), ii. 511, n. 4.
Sclater, Rev. Edward, of Putney, convert to Roman Catholicism: dispensation for, iv. 509–10 & nn.
Sclavonia, &c.: *see* Slavonia.
Scomberge, Marshal: *see* Schomberg, F. H.
Sconvelt, Nicholas, lute-maker, ii. 426 & n. 7.
Scot, Major —: brings E message from Charles II, 1660, iii. 245.
Scotland and the Scots:
— chronological series:
— — middle ages: attacks by, on York, iii. 129 & n. 1.
— — 1633: Charles I visits, ii. 12 & n. 2 (i. 10).
— — 1638: opposes introduction of Scottish Prayer Book, ii. 22 & n. 3 (i. 17).
— — 1640: second invasion of England by, iii. 50 & n. 2; Charles I returns from expedition against, ii. 25 (i. 19).
— — 1641: Charles I returns from, ii. 77 (i. 51).
— — 1648: Sir Lewis Dyve in, iii. 40 & n. 1; Scots defeated at Preston, iii. 178, n. 1.
— — 1650: Charles II in, iii. 14, n. 6, 20, n. 4; Scots defeated at Dunbar, iii. 19 & n. 7.
— — 1651: Scots defeated at Worcester, iii. 178 & n. 1.
— — 1660: Monck marches from, to London, iii. 240, n. 5, 241; *see also* iii. 245.
— — 1661: Argyll executed in, iii. 318 & n. 2.
— — 1669–71: proposed parliamentary union with England: commissioner for, iii. 570 & n. 7.
— — 1679: Covenanters' rising in, iv. 170–1 & n.; James, duke of York, sent to, iv. 189 & n. 6.
— — 1682: James, duke of York's journey to, &c., iv. 281–2 & n.
— — 1683: disaffected Scots concerned in Rye-House Plot, iv. 322, n. 1.
— — 1685: parliament grants revenues to kings in perpetuity, iv. 440 & n. 1; Argyll's rising in, iv. 443 & n. 1, 446 & n. 3, 450 & n. 4.
— 1686: parliament maintains penal laws against Roman Catholics, iv. 514 & n. 7.
— — 1687: proclamation in, for liberty of conscience, iv. 539 & n. 3.
— 1688: episcopalian clergy dispossessed, &c., iv. 614–15 & n.
— — 1689: condition of, iv. 620, 629; danger to, from Ireland, iv. 637; Convention of Estates and transfer of the crown: views of, iv. 631; ~ declares for William and Mary, &c., iv. 635 & n. 2; ~ commissioners offer crown to William and Mary, iv. 639 & n. 2; *see also* iv. 621; ~ Instrument of Government (Claim of Right), iv. 635, n. 2, 639, n. 2; episcopacy abolished, iv. 646 & n. 2; uncertain news from, iv. 642; Dundee killed in, iv. 647 & n. 3.

Scotland and the Scots (*cont.*)
— — 1692: projected French attack on, v. 97, n. 2.
— — 1696: projected French attack on, v. 234; Company of Scotland trading to Africa, &c.: subscriptions for, v. 245 & n. 5; scarcity of corn in, v. 257, 259.
— — 1699–1700: expedition to Darien from, v. 345 & n. 2; ~ book concerning: English parliament orders it to be burnt, v. 376 & n. 4; ~ house of lords votes against, v. 379 & n. 1.
— — 1703: discontent and French intrigues in, v. 546, 553 & n. 1.
— — 1704: Jacobite conspiracy in: proceedings relating to, in English parliament, v. 560–1 & n.
— — 1705: cattle from: English parliament permits importation of, v. 620 & n. 3.
— religion [*see also* chronological series *above*]: Cameronians, iv. 440, n. 1.
— — episcopate: character of, &c., 1688, iv. 614–15 & n.; ~ hated by Presbyterians, v. 12.
— — field conventiclers: suppression of, advocated, 1685, iv. 440; ~ excluded from proclamation for freedom of conscience, 1687, iv. 539, n. 3.
— — Presbyterians: church discipline of, ii. 527; ~ views of, 1689, v. 12.
— military [Scots in English and foreign service]:
— — in England: troops added to army, Oct. 1688, iv. 599; ~ sent out of London, Dec. 1688, iv. 612, n. 2; ~ Highland dragoon regiments: disorderly conduct of, 1694, v. 175 & n. 1; in Dutch service: regiments come to England, 1685, iv. 458 & n. 1; in French service: Scots guards, iii. 43; ~ regiments: recruits for, iii. 12 & n. 5; Scots colonel serving at Milan (A. Burnet), &c., ii. 503–5 & nn.
— highlanders:
— — — dress of: in painting, iii. 339; translation of Bible for, v. 82, n. 2; dragoon regiments of, in England, v. 175 & n. 1.
— miscellaneous:
— — second sight in, iv. 470; Jesuit (legendary?) buried in, v. 13; a Scot represented on figure-head of *Naseby*, iii. 149–50 & n.; Scotch covenant burnt in London, 1661, iii. 288–9 & n.
— officers: secretaries: *see* Maitland, John, duke of Lauderdale (1660–80); Erskine, John, sixth earl of Mar (1705–9); deputy-secretary: *see* Moray, Sir Robert; lord of session: 'Lowthiel Dundas', iii. 345, n. 4; Lord Advocate: *see* Mackenzie, Sir G.; commander of (English) army in, 1654–9: *see* Monck, George, duke of Albemarle; commander-in-chief, 1685–8: *see* Douglas, Lord George, earl of Dumbarton; physician to Charles II and James VII: *see* Sibbald, Sir R.
— individuals [persons specified as Scotsmen by E]: (i) named: *see* Castleton: earl of, &c. (v. 150 & n. 6); Creighton, R., sen. (ii. 563 & n. 5; iii. 304); Davison, Dr. W. (i. 67; *see* ii. 565, n. 3); Frazier, — (iv. 330 & n. 1); Hamilton, Rev. — (iii. 23 & n. 5); Law, John, the financier (v. 175, 176, n. 1); Middleton, Charles, earl of Middleton (iv. 387 & n. 5); Hay, John, marquis of Tweeddale (iv. 184); Wright, J. M., the painter (iii. 338); *see also* Officers *above*; David II; Margaret, queen of Scotland; Mary, queen of Scots.
— — (ii) unnamed: noblemen, visiting Sayes Court, iii. 175, 186, 254; gentlemen, in London, iii. 447; ~ visiting R. Boyle, iv. 124; archbishop (John Paterson?): at meeting held by Sancroft, Jan. 1689, iv. 613–15 & nn.; colonel (A. Burnet), &c., at Milan, ii. 503–5 & nn.; students, &c., at Padua, ii. 473; divines: minister of Oakwood Chapel, Wotton: sermon by, v. 259; other divines: sermons by, at: Camberwell, iv. 441; Deptford, iii. 397; iv. 250; v. 199; London: St. Clement's, Eastcheap, iii. 160; ~ St. Mary Magdalen, Old Fish Street, iii. 82; ~ Trinity Chapel, v. 486, 562–3, 584, 586, 590, 622; ~

Scotland and the Scots (*cont.*)
Westminster Abbey, iii. 273, 288.
Scot's-Hall, Smeeth, Kent: visit to, 1663, iii. 358–9 & nn.
Scott family, of Scot's-Hall, iii. 358, n. 7, 359, n. 2; monuments of, iii. 359, n. 3.
Scott, —, practitioner for deformities, iii. 317 & n. 4.
Scott, Dr. — (Dr. John Scott?): sermon by, iv. 584 & n. 3.
Scott, Anne, duchess of Monmouth and Buccleugh, wife of James Scott, duke of Monmouth, &c., and secondly of Charles Cornwallis, Baron Cornwallis, iv. 6, n. 1; character of, iv. 6 & n. 1, 456; acts in *Horace*, iii. 505, n. 2; godmother of Dr. E. Lake's daughter, iv. 95; interviews of, with Monmouth in Tower, 1685, iv. 455 & n. 4; commended by Monmouth to James II, iv. 456; appearance of, 1686, iv. 500; at divine service, iv. 357; social, iv. 6; geneal., iv. 219, n. 4, 262 & n. 1; v. 588 & n. 2; chaplain of: *see* Mandevile, J.
Scott, Caroline, Lady Scott, wife of Sir Thomas, and secondly of D. Abercrombie: first marriage of, iii. 358 & n. 5.
Scott, Lady Catherine, wife of Edward Scott of Scot's-Hall, ii. 560 & n. 1; liaison of, with Prince Rupert: alluded to, iii. 358 & n. 5; travels to Paris, 1649, ii. 560 *bis* & n. 1; in Kent and London, 1650, 1652, iii. 13 *bis*, 57.
Scott, Edward, of Scot's-Hall: geneal., ii. 560, n. 1.
Scott, J., 'cousin' of Pepys, iii. 317, n. 4.
Scott, James, duke of Monmouth and Buccleugh, ii. 562, n. 1; titles of, iv. 6, n. 1; character and career of, iv. 456–7 & nn.; mother of: *see* Barlow, Mrs. L.; paternity of, iv. 457 & n. 6; attempt to remove, from Mrs. Barlow, ii. 560, n. 2; at feast, 1665, iii. 400 & n. 4; at Hampton Court, &c., 1670, iii. 559; at siege of Maastricht, 1673, iv. 42, n. 1; commands regiment 'Royal Anglais' (horse), 1673, iii. 587, n. 3; in display representing siege of Maastricht, 1674, iv. 42 & n. 1; performs in *Calisto*, 1674–5, iv. 49, n. 7 *ad fin.*; social, iii. 558 *bis*; iv. 6, 65, 94, 97; 1679: defeats Covenanters at Bothwell Bridge, iv. 171, n. 1; deprived of military command and sent abroad, iv. 181 & n. 1; returns from Holland, iv. 189 & n. 6; 1680: progress of, through Somerset, &c., iv. 189, n. 6; 1681: assists T. Thynne to marry Lady Ogle, iv. 261 & n. 3; 1683: complicity of, in Rye-House Plot: proclamation for his arrest for, iv. 322, n. 1, 323 & n. 1, 350; ~ hides, iv. 323, n. 3; ~ surrenders himself, iv. 350 & n. 3; ~ confesses and withdraws confession, &c., iv. 353–4 & n.; ~ *see also* iv. 382; 1685: Charles II's displeasure at, iv. 408 & n. 3; in Holland, *ib.*
Monmouth's rebellion, 1685: lands at Lyme Regis, iv. 449 *bis* & nn. 1, 3; attainted, iv. 6, n. 1, 449, n. 3; forces sent against, iv. 450–1 & n.; ~ E required to send horseman, &c., iv. 450, 458–9; ~ English and Scottish regiments in Dutch service, iv. 458 & n. 1; defeated and captured, iv. 451–3 & nn.; brought to London, iv. 455 & n. 2; executed, iv. 456 & nn. 2, 3; execution of: foretold, iv. 470; rebellion: alluded to, &c., iv. 322, n. 6, 458; suppression of: thanksgiving for, iv. 460 & nn. 1, 3; trials for: the Bloody Assize, iv. 466 & n. 5, 484; ~ Lord Delamer (Henry Booth, later earl of Warrington), iv. 608, n. 2.
miscellaneous: called 'the Protestant Duke', iv. 189 & n. 6; on Charles II's treatment of Lord Russell, iv. 328, n. 3; alluded to, iv. 391–2 & n.; house built for, iv. 652, n. 2; mistress of: *see* Wentworth, Henrietta Maria, Baroness Wentworth; agent, &c., of, iv. 452, n. 8 *ad fin.*
Scott, James; styled earl of Doncaster 1674–85; of Dalkeith 1685–1705: dies, v. 588 & n. 2.

Scott, John, D.D., iv. 584, n. 3; v. 137, n. 1; as author, v. 9; sermons by: printed (?), v. 9 & n. 2; ~ unprinted, iv. 584(?); v. 137.
Scott, Thomas, regicide: executed, iii. 259 & n. 1.
Scott, Sir Thomas, of Scot's-Hall, iii. 358, n. 5; paternity of, ii. 560, n. 1; iii. 358; marriage of, iii. 358 & n. 5; visit to, iii. 358–9; chaplain of: sermon by, iii. 359.
Scotus: picture of (?), iii. 339 & n. 3.
Scribes and Pharisees: in sermons, iii. 253, 516; iv. 120, 541; v. 121, 132, 183–4, 236, 276, 389, 405, 489, 537, 596.
Scroggs, Sir William, judge: views of, on reports of Popish Plot trials, iv. 175, n. 3.
Scroope, Mary, Lady Scroope: *see* Scrope.
Scrope, Col. Adrian, the regicide: shows Bristol Castle, iii. 102 & n. 6; executed, iii. 259 & n. 1.
Scrope *or* Scroope, Sir Adrian, iii. 351, n. 9; social, iii. 351; geneal., iii. 275, n. 6.
Scrope, Sir Carr, versifier: geneal., iii. 275, n. 6.
Scrope *or* Scroope, Mary, Lady Scrope, wife of Sir Adrian, iii. 275, n. 6; obtains appointment at court, iii. 275 & n. 6; visits Montague House, iv. 345; social, iv. 13.
Scudamor, —: *see* Scudamore, James.
Scudamore, James (either James Scudamore, 1617–59, or James Scudamore, 1624–68), ii. 558, n. 6; consults E, iii. 66 & n. 1; social, ii. 558; iii. 81.
Scudamore, John, first Viscount Scudamore of Sligo: geneal., ii. 558, n. 6; iii. 66 & n. 1.
Scudamore, John, second Viscount Scudamore of Sligo: geneal., ii. 558, n. 6; iii. 66 & n. 1.
Scudamore, William, of Ballingham: geneal., ii. 558, n. 6.
Scudamore: Viscounts: *see* Scudamore, John, first viscount; Scudamore, John, second viscount.
Sculpture: ancient [classical works, &c., until about the sixth century A.D., and modern copies and imitations. In the list of individual works small capitals indicate extant works; they are used for their modern names and for their present locations; lower case is used for E's names and locations or other old names. Notices providing neither names nor other means of identification are not indexed under this heading (e.g. Gaston's collection at Blois, ii. 141); they are traceable under Art-collections and Museums. Names of museums and collections are abbreviated. For carved gems *see* Gems]:
— general:
— — sculptures at Persepolis, iv. 213; statues, &c.: found near Cuma, ii. 347 & n. 4; H. Vitelleschi's excavations for, ii. 283; drawings of, made for Henri IV, iii. 10–11; engravings of, by F. Perrier, iii. 10–11 & n.; described as antique (stylistic term ?), ii. 225 & n. 2; *see also* ii. 220, &c.; iii. 148 & n. 4.
— individual works:
— — ADMIRAL, CONSERVATORI: as Augustus, ii. 222 & n. 4.
— — Adonis: *see* ENDYMION *and* MELEAGER *below*.
— — AELIUS ARISTIDES, VATICAN, library, ii. 301 & n. 1.
— — AGRIPPINA: cyst of, CONSERVATORI, ii. 223 & n. 6.
— — Alexander taming Bucephalus: *see* HORSE-TAMERS *below*.
— — Alexander Severus (?), ii. 223 & n. 4.
— — AMAZON, WOUNDED, NAPLES, ii. 309 & n. 6.
— — Antinous: *see* HERMES *below*.
— — APOLLINO, UFFIZI, ii. 286 & n. 10.
— — APOLLO: BELVEDERE, VATICAN, ii. 304 & n. 9; WITH LYRE, TERME, ii. 236, n. 5.
— — Apollo, Villa Medici, ii. 286; colossus, Conservatori: *see* CONSTANTINE *below*; idol, Uffizi: *see* IDOLINO *below*.
— — ARIADNE, SLEEPING, VATICAN: as Cleopatra, ii. 303, n. 1, 304 & n. 4, 404; copy of, ii. 108 & n. 2 (i. 70).
— — ARRINGATORE, FLORENCE, ARCHAEOL. MUSEUM: as Scipio, ii. 189 & n. 2 (i. 118).

Sculpture (*cont.*)
— — Artemis: *see* DIANA *below*.
— — Augustus: *see* ADMIRAL *above*; JULIUS CAESAR *below*.
— — BACCHANALIA, relief, NAPLES, ii. 309 & n. 7.
— — Bacchus: Conservatori, ii. 225 & n. 15; another work: *see* MAENAD *below*.
— — — *see also* DIONYSUS *below*.
— — BOAR, UFFIZI, ii. 189 & n. 3 (i. 118); copy of, by P. Tacca, ii. 194 & n. 7 (i. 120).
— — BOYS, VENICE, ARCHAEOL. MUSEUM, ii. 460–1 & n.
— — Brutus, heads of: Sunderland, iv. 404; Vitelleschi, ii. 283 & n. 4.
— — Bucephalus: *see* HORSE-TAMERS *below*.
— — Caesars, Twelve, or Emperors, heads of: Villa Borghese, ii. 253 & n. 1, 390; Farnese, ii. 310 & n. 1; Venice, Ruzini, ii. 471.
— — CAMILLUS, CONSERVATORI: as Faustulus, ii. 225 & n. 1.
— — Canopus, Gualdi, ii. 314.
— — CARACALLA, NAPLES: as Hannibal (?), ii. 310 & n. 1.
— — Cicero, Conservatori, ii. 225 & n. 10.
— — Cleopatra: *see* ARIADNE *above*.
— — COMMODUS: warrior with head of, NAPLES, ii. 216, n. 5.
— — Commodus: *see* HERCULES AND TELEPHOS *below*; colossal statues of: *see* CONSTANS *and* Nero *below*.
— — CONSTANS: CAMPIDOGLIO, balustrade: as Constantine, ii. 226 & n. 6; colossal head, &c., of, CONSERVATORI: as Commodus, ii. 223 & n. 2.
— — CONSTANTINE: S. GIOVANNI IN LATERANO, ii. 222 & n. 8, 223, n. 1; colossal head and feet (as of Apollo) of, CONSERVATORI, ii. 221 & nn. 1, 5, 223 & n. 5; two statues (Constantine and Constans), CAMPIDOGLIO, balustrade, ii. 220, n. 3 (as emperors), 226 & nn. 4, 6.
— — Constantine: *see* DIOSCURI *below* (ii. 221, n. 6).
— — Consuls: Villa Borghese, ii. 253; Conservatori, ii. 225 & n. 10.
— — CUPID, of paragon, UFFIZI, ii. 413 & n. 8.

Sculpture (*cont.*)
— — CURTIUS, Mettus or Marcus, relief, CONSERVATORI, ii. 222, n. 6.
— — Curtius, Mettus or Marcus, relief, Villa Borghese, ii. 252 & n. 3.
— — CYBELE, VATICAN, Villa Pia, ii. 304 & n. 7.
— — DIANA: formerly Borghese, LOUVRE, ii. 253 & n. 2; WITH FAWN, LOUVRE: as Diana of the Ephesians, ii. 105 & nn. 1, 3 (i. 68); ~ copies of, ii. 118 & n. 9 (i. 77); known as ARTEMIS OF GABII, LOUVRE: ancient copy of, DORIA, ii. 284 & n. 3; CAPITOLINO, ii. 223, n. 1.
— — DIONYSUS VISITING MORTAL, relief, NAPLES: as Sacrifice to Priapus, ii. 309 & n. 3.
— — DIOSCURI, CAMPIDOGLIO, balustrade, ii. 221 & n. 6, 405 & n. 1; in comparison, ii. 237.
— — DYING GAUL, CAPITOLINO: as Gladiator, ii. 235 & n. 6.
— — Emperors: *see* Caesars *above*.
— — ENDYMION, CAPITOLINO: as Adonis, ii. 225 & n. 8.
— — Europa, rape of, relief, Villa Borghese, ii. 252 & n. 3.
— — Faustulus: *see* CAMILLUS *above*.
— — FLORA, FARNESE, NAPLES, ii. 216 & n. 2, 403.
— — GANYMEDE, UFFIZI, ii. 286 & n. 8.
— — GLADIATOR: BORGHESE, LOUVRE, ii. 253 & n. 4, 404; NAPLES, ii. 216 & n. 5.
— — Gladiators: Farnese, ii. 216 & n. 5, 308 & n. 5.
— — — *see also* DYING GAUL *above*; KNIFE-GRINDER *below*.
— — GRACES, THREE, SIENA, cathedral library, ii. 407 & n. 10.
— — HADRIAN: CAPITOLINO, ii. 223 & n. 12; restored head in relief, CONSERVATORI, ii. 223, n. 9.
— — Hannibal, errors, ii. 225 & n. 14, 310 & n. 1.
— — HERCULES: FARNESE, NAPLES, ii. 216 & n. 1, 403; ~ copy of, Palazzo Farnese, ii. 216 & n. 4; ~ head of: copy of, on gem, ii. 314; TERME, ii. 235 & n. 7; VATICAN: *see* TORSO *below*; bronze, CONSERVATORI, ii. 225 & n. 11; AND CENTAUR, UFFIZI,

Sculpture (*cont.*)
ii. 413 & n. 10; AND TELEPHOS, VATICAN, ii. 304, n. 8.
— — Hercules as child, Farnese, &c., ii. 309 & n. 2.
— — HERMAPHRODITE: LOUVRE, ii. 253 & n. 5, 404; DORIA, ii. 284 & n. 5.
— — HERMES, VATICAN: as Antinous, ii. 305 & n. 1, 405.
— — Horatii and Curiatii, Farnese, ii. 308, n. 5.
— — HORSE: HEAD, bronze, NAPLES, ii. 330, n. 1; AND LION FIGHTING, CONSERVATORI, ii. 223 & n. 3.
— — Horse, bronze, Naples, near cathedral, ii. 326, n. 3.
— — HORSEMAN, NAPLES, ii. 308, n. 7.
— — HORSES: VENICE, St. Mark's, ii. 437 & n. 3, 439 & n. 6.
— — HORSE-TAMERS, QUIRINAL, ii. 237 & n. 2, 241; as Bucephalus, &c., ii. 405 & n. 1.
— — HORUS, GLYPTOTHEK: as Osiris, Barberini, ii. 229 & n. 4.
— — IDOLINO, FLORENCE, ARCHAEOL. MUSEUM: as Apollo, ii. 189 & n. 4 (i. 118).
— — ISIS, NAPLES (?), ii. 309 & n. 4.
— — Isis, Gualdi, ii. 314.
— — JULIUS CAESAR, CONSERVATORI: as Augustus, ii. 222 & n. 4.
— — Jupiter, Villa Medici, ii. 286.
— — JUPITER CAPITOLINUS, altered to ST. PETER, ST. PETER'S (post-classical ?), ii. 264 & n. 1.
— — Justinian, Villa Giustiniani, ii. 383 & n. 3.
— — KNIFE-GRINDER, UFFIZI: as Gladiator, ii. 286 & n. 4.
— — LAOCOON, VATICAN, ii. 304 & n. 1, 404; copies: by B. Bandinelli, ii. 413, n. 6; ~ at St. Cloud, ii. 107 (i. 69).
— — Leda, relief, Villa Borghese, ii. 252 & n. 3.
— — LIONS: pairs: LOGGIA DEI LANZI, ii. 231 & n. 2; VATICAN, Museo egizio, ii. 239 & n. 1.
— — MAENAD, CONSERVATORI: as BACCHUS, ii. 222 & n. 5.
— — Mammea (?), ii. 223 & n. 4.
— — MARCUS AURELIUS: CAMPIDOGLIO, ii. 221 & n. 4, 404; ~ imitated, ii. 101 & n. 2 (i. 66); TRIUMPHS OF, reliefs, CONSERVATORI, ii. 223 & n. 9; modern bronze bust of, TERME, ii. 235 & n. 9.
— — MARFORIO, CAPITOLINO, ii. 220, n. 3, 221 & n. 1.
— — Marius: *see* WRITER *below*.
— — Mars, Villa Medici, ii. 286, n. 2.
— — MARSYAS, UFFIZI, ii. 286 & n. 7.
— — Marsyas bound to tree, Conservatori, ii. 223–4 & n.
— — Maximian, ii. 221, n. 6.
— — MELEAGER, VATICAN: as Adonis, Pichini, ii. 217 & n. 1.
— — MERCURY, UFFIZI, ii. 304 & n. 6.
— — Mercury, Conservatori, ii. 226 & n. 2.
— — — *see also* HERMES *above*.
— — MINERVA, CAPITOLINO: as bronze head, in error, ii. 222–3 & n.
— — Minerva, Vitelleschi, ii. 283.
— — MUSES, two, CONSERVATORI, ii. 223 & n. 11.
— — Nero, colossus of, later Sun, later Commodus (Colossus Neronis), ii. 248 & n. 7.
— — NILE, VATICAN, ii. 303, n. 3, 304 & n. 2, 405.
— — NIOBE AND CHILDREN, UFFIZI, ii. 232 & nn. 2, 3, 404.
— — Osiris, Barberini: *see* HORUS *above*.
— — Pallas: *see* MINERVA *above*.
— — Pan: *see* POLYPHEMUS *below*.
— — PASQUIN, ii. 369 & n. 3.
— — PEACOCKS, VATICAN, ii. 305 & n. 3.
— — Philosophers, heads, Farnese, ii. 309, n. 8, 310 & n. 1.
— — PINE-CONE, VATICAN, ii. 305 & n. 3.
— — POLYPHEMUS, CAPITOLINO: as Pan, ii. 226 & n. 1.
— — PORPHYRY RELIEFS, VENICE, St. Mark's, ii. 439–40 & n.
— — Poverty, error, ii. 225 & n. 6.
— — Priapus: *see* DIONYSUS *above*.
— — PROVINCES, CONSERVATORI OR PINCIO: as Poverty, ii. 225 & n. 6.
— — Ram, Farnese, ii. 308, n. 7.
— — Ram and horseman, Farnese, ii. 308 & n. 7.
— — ROME, PALAZZO DEL SENATORE, ii. 220 & n. 4.
— — SABINES, LOGGIA DEI LANZI, ii. 231 & n. 5, 404.

Sculpture (*cont.*)
— — Sabines: rape of the: *see* sarcophagi: ACHILLES *below*.
— — ST. AGNES (antique torso), S. AGNESE FUORI, ii. 241 & n. 1.
— — ST. HIPPOLYTUS, LATERAN, Christian Museum, ii. 301 & n. 1.
— — sarcophagi: ACHILLES IN SKYROS, CAPITOLINO: as Rape of Sabines, ii. 223 & n. 4; BATTLE, TERME, ii. 234 & n. 6; FOUR SEASONS, CONSERVATORI, ii. 225 & n. 12; CHRISTIAN, PANTHEON, ii. 371, n. 5; of ST. CONSTANTIA, VATICAN, ii. 241 & n. 3; of ST. HELENA, VATICAN, ii. 274 & n. 5; of ST. SIMPLICIUS, &c., S. MARIA MAGGIORE, ii. 245 & n. 3.
— — Saturn: *see* SILENUS *below*.
— — Scipio: *see* ARRINGATORE *above*.
— — SENECA (false name), LOUVRE, ii. 253 & n. 3, 405.
— — SHE-WOLF WITH TWINS, CONSERVATORI, ii. 224–5 & n.
— — SILENUS WITH INFANT BACCHUS, LOUVRE: copy of: as Saturn, ii. 286 & n. 2.
— — Silenus: *see* BACCHANALIA *above*.
— — Sphinxes, four, Villa Borghese, ii. 252 & n. 1.
— — SPINARIO, CONSERVATORI, ii. 225 & n. 2.
— — STATUES PARTLY ANTIQUE, CONSERVATORI, ii. 224 & n. 6.
— — Sun, colossus: *see* Nero *above*.
— — TIBER: LOUVRE, ii. 303, n. 3, 304 & n. 3; ~ copy of, ii. 119 (i. 77); PALAZZO DEL SENATORE, ii. 220 & n. 4.
— — TIGRIS, PALAZZO DEL SENATORE, ii. 220, n. 4 *ad fin*.
— — TORO FARNESE, NAPLES, ii. 216 & n. 6, 404.
— — TORSO, BELVEDERE, VATICAN, ii. 303, n. 3, 369, n. 3; as Hercules, ii. 304 & n. 8.
— — Torso, Gaddi, ii. 415 & n. 6.
— — TRAGIC MASK, red marble, TERME, ii. 235 & n. 8.
— — TROPHIES OF MARIUS, CAMPIDOGLIO, ii. 221–2 & n., 379.
— — VENUS: formerly Prince Leopold, UFFIZI, ii. 415 & n. 4; DE' MEDICI, UFFIZI, ii. 286 & n. 5, 404; ~ sculptor of: statue by (?), ii. 415; CALLIPIGE, NAPLES, ii. 309 & n. 8; AND CUPID, VATICAN, ii. 304 & n. 5.
— — Venus: Farnese, ii. 309; with Cleopatra's pearl, ii. 372 & n. 5.
— — WOMAN, OLD, CAPITOLINO, ii. 225 & n. 6.
— — WOMEN, SEATED, two statues, UFFIZI, ii. 413 & n. 9.
— — WRESTLERS, UFFIZI, ii. 286 *bis* & n. 3.
— — WRITER, CAPITOLINO: as Marius, ii. 223 & n. 13.
— — Zingara, La: *see* CAMILLUS *above*.
Sculpture: materials [select; *see also* Building materials; Gold and Silver]: alabaster, iv. 117; ~ oriental, ii. 151, 152 (i. 98), 241; brass: sepulchral brasses, iii. 132; bronze: as brass, copper, or Corinthian brass or metal, ii. 33 & n. 4, 92 (i. 62), 137 (i. 90), 221, 309, &c.; ~ bronzing, ii. 417; Lydian marble, ii. 380; Parian marble or stone, ii. 176, n. 8, 193 (i. 120), 198, 243 & n. 7, 261 & n. 7, 413 & n. 8 (error); porphyry: method of working, ii. 185 & n. 5 (i. 117).
Sculpture: medieval and modern [works by unknown artists only; select; tombs and devotional sculptures in churches are not indexed collectively]:
— general: sculptors working in 1645: at Florence, ii. 417; in Rome, ii. 399 & nn. 6, 7.
— individual works:
— — Caesars: sets of heads of, i. 51 (*see also* ii. 77 & n. 4), 151 (i. 98), 190 (i. 119); iii. 114 & n. 5; iv. 117 & n. 3.
— — decorative series: London, Royal Exchange: English kings, iii. 460 & n. 8; Padua, Salone, Eremitano, &c., ii. 463 & n. 4; Paris, Notre Dame: French kings, ii. 95 (i. 63); Poggio Imperiale: rivers and poets (from Florence Cathedral), ii. 411 & nn. 1, 2; St.-Cloud: French kings, ii. 108 (i. 70); Verona, Loggia: Pliny, &c., ii. 486–7 & n.; York, Minster: English kings, iii. 129 & n. 2.
— — garden and fountain figures, &c. [special pieces]: Fontaine-

Sculpture (*cont.*)
bleau: Perseus, ii. 118 & n. 7 (i. 76); Genoa, Palazzo Doria: Jupiter, ii. 175 & n. 4 (i. 111); Paris: Samaritaine, &c., ii. 93, 94 (i. 62 *bis*); Rome, Lateran: St. John, ii. 271; Tivoli, Villa d'Este: Neptune, &c., ii. 395–6 & nn.
— public monuments, &c.: commemorative statues:
— — — popes: Bologna: Paul III, ii. 422 & n. 2; Rome, Conservatori: Leo X and Sixtus V, ii. 224 & n. 5; Velletri: Urban VIII, ii. 317 & n. 6.
— — — other rulers, &c.: Ferrara: Niccolò III, ii. 428 & n. 1; Ghent: Charles V, ii. 73 & n. 8 (i. 48); Orleans: Joan of Arc, &c., ii. 137 & nn. 1–3 (i. 90); London: Ludgate: Queen Elizabeth, iii. 460–1 & n.; Physicians' College: Dr. W. Harvey, iii. 338 & n. 2; Royal Exchange: Sir T. Gresham, iii. 460 & n. 8.
— — statues on columns: Florence, ii. 185–6 & nn. (i. 117), 415 & n. 1; Rome, ii. 245, 370, 379; Siena, ii. 202 & n. 4; Venice, ii. 444–5; Vicenza, ii. 483.
— miscellaneous: Antwerp, crucifix, ii. 66 & n. 2 (i. 44); Guy of Warwick, Guy's Cliff, iii. 120–1 & n.; Scipio Africanus, Chenonceaux, ii. 152 (i. 98).
Scythia, iv. 618.
Seagrave, Leics.: rector of: *see* Rogers, John.
Seals: *see* England: officers, &c.: Lord Chancellor; Lord Privy Seal; Secretaries of State.
Seamor: *see* Seymour.
Sebastian, St.: martyrdom of, ii. 376 & n. 5; tomb, &c., of, ii. 363; relics of, ii. 289, 381 & n. 4 (error).
Sechevarell, —: *see* Sacheverell, W.
Sectaries: *see* Nonconformists, Puritans, and Sectaries.
Sedgemoor, Somerset: battle of, iv. 451–3 & nn.
Sedley, Catherine; countess of Dorchester *suo jure* 1686; &c., iv. 13 & n. 6; as Mrs. Sidly: visits E, iv. 13; ~ created countess, iv. 496–7 & n.; house acquired by, iv. 140, n. 8.
Sedley, Sir Charles, dramatist: geneal., iv. 13 & n. 6.
Seedam: *see* Schiedam.
Seghers *or* Segers, Daniel, 'the Jesuit of Brussels': painting by, iii. 216 & n. 6.
Seghers, Gerard: painting by, ii. 560 & n. 5.
Seignelay: Marquis of: *see* Colbert, J.-B.
Seine, river: mouth of, ii. 125 (i. 80); at Rouen, i. 78; ii. 122 & n. 5 (i. 78–9); at Saint-Cloud, ii. 107 (i. 69), 108; at Saint-Germain, ii. 111 *bis* (i. 71, 72); *see also* Paris: topography *and* environs.
Selby, Dom Richard Wilfrid: *see* Wilfrid, Father J.
Selden, John: executors of: inscriptions given by, to Oxford University, iii. 534, n. 4; ~ *see* Vaughan, Sir John (iii. 492–3 & n.); *see also* Books mentioned in text *and* in notes.
Selenger, Lady (error for Lady Heneage ?): antipathy of, to roses, iii. 550 & n. 5.
'Selenographer', the late: *see* Hevelius, J.
Selkirk: Earl of, 1646–60: *see* Douglas, William, later duke of Hamilton.
Selvatico (Salvatico), Benedetto, physician: treats E, &c., ii. 472 & n. 5, 478.
Semneserteus: *see* Sennesertus.
Semo Sancus Dius Fidius: altar to, ii. 358–9 & n.
Semplon, &c.: *see* Simplon.
Sempronii, Mons (Simplon), ii. 511 & n. 4.
Seneca: statue of, ii. 253 & n. 3; in sermons, iv. 242; v. 433, 435.
Seneterre: *see* St.-Nectaire.
Sennacherib: psalm relating to destruction of host of: in sermon, iv. 348 & n. 1.
Senne, river, Belgium, ii. 68, n. 3.
Sennesertus, king of Egypt: obelisk dedicated by, ii. 374 & n. 10.
Sennock: *see* Sevenoaks.
Senuessa: *see* Sinuessa.
Septimius Severus: Arch of, ii. 217, n. 2, 219–20 & n.; Baths of, ii. 358 & n. 6.
Seres, William, publisher, iii. 46, n. 3.
Sergeant, Father John: associates with T. Keightley (?), iii. 634 & n. 3.

Sergius I, pope: cross of, ii. 274 & n. 2.
Sermonea: *see* Sirmione.
Sermoneta: Osteria di, ii. 317 & n. 7; Portone di, ii. 317 & n. 8.
Sermoneta, Girolamo Sicciolante da: painting by, ii. 274 & n. 10.
Sermon on the Mount: in sermon, iv. 572.
Sermons: *see* Preaching and Sermons.
printed [sermons heard by E and also available in print]: *see* Allestree, R.; Atterbury, L.; Bentley, R.; Blackall, O.; Brady, N.; Burnet, G.; Calamy, B.; Cave, W.; Cosin, J.; Dove, H.; Gibson, E.; Glanvill, J.; Hardy, N.; Hickes, G.; Hooper, G.; Horne, T.; Horneck, P.; Ironside, G., jnr.; Ken, T.; Littleton, A.; Lloyd, W., the Apocalyptic; Morley, G.; Owtram, W.; Parr, R.; Pierce, T.; Reynolds, E.; Rogers, J.; Sancroft, W.; Scott, J.; Sharp, John; South, R.; Standish, J.; Stanhope, G.; Stillingfleet, E.; Tenison, T.; Tillotson, J.; Turner, F.; Wake, W.; Williams, J.
Serto, A. de: *see* Sarto, A. del.
Servetus: execution of, ii. 527, n. 3.
Sessa, now Sessa Aurunca, ii. 323 & n. 6; ruin near, ii. 322, n. 9.
Sessac (Sissac), Marquis de: loan made by: repaid, iv. 96 & n. 6.
Sesto (Sesto Calende), ii. 505, n. 3 *ad fin.*, 506 & nn. 1, 3, 511, n. 6 *ad fin.*
Seti I, king of Egypt: inscription of, ii. 374, n. 10 *ad fin.*
Setia: ruins of, ii. 318, n. 2.
Settala (Septalla), Canon Manfredo: natural history collection of, ii. 502 & nn. 5–7.
Seven Bishops, 1688: petition of, proceedings against, &c., iv. 583–90 & nn., *passim*; trial of: report of, published, iv. 615 & n. 2; James II appeals to, to appease discontent, iv. 600 & n. 4; popularity of, 1689, iv. 631.
Sevenes: *see* Cevennes.
Sevenoaks (Sennock), Kent, iii. 67 & n. 3; Knole near, iv. 17 & n. 3.
Severin, Rev. Jean: sermon by, v. 23–4 & n.
Severn river: Bristol near, iii. 102 & n. 7; at Gloucester, iii. 118; at Worcester, iii. 119; King Road channel in, iii. 119 & n. 3.
Sewers: Commissioners of: *see* Commissions *and* Surrey and Kent Commission of Sewers.
Sexby, Edward: author of *Killing no Murder*, iii. 526, n. 5.
Seymour family: house, &c., of, at Marlborough, iii. 99, n. 5.
Seymour (Seamour, &c.), —: social, iii. 87, 91, 154.
Seymour (Seamor), Catherine, Lady Seymour, wife of Francis Seymour, Baron Seymour of Trowbridge: social, iii. 213 & n. 2.
Seymour, Charles; sixth duke of Somerset, iv. 260, n. 4 *ad fin.*; first marriage of, *ib.*; as owner of Syon House, v. 90, n. 2; legacy to, v. 587 *bis*; geneal., iv. 136, n. 1.
Seymour, Conway (Conyers), *also called* Popham Seymour Conway: killed in duel, v. 331 & n. 1.
Seymour (Seamor), Sir Edward; fourth baronet 1685; the Speaker, iii. 501, n. 1; character and career of, v. 476 & n. 2; attacks Clarendon, iii. 500–1 & n.; speech of, in parliament, 1685, iv. 444 & n. 1; interest of, in art, v. 145; concern of, with St. James's Palace library, v. 280, n. 5; death of: false report of, v. 476; geneal., v 331 & n. 1.
Seymour, Edward, first earl of Hertford: tomb of, iii. 113 & n. 4.
Seymour, Elizabeth, duchess of Somerset; born Percy; wife of (1) Henry Cavendish, Lord Ogle; (2) Thomas Thynne; (3) Charles Seymour, sixth duke of Somerset, iv. 260 & n. 4; marriage-project for, iv. 184, n. 5; marriage of, to Thynne, iv. 260–1 & nn.; v. 587, n. 1; ~ validity of, to be examined, iv. 267 & n. 2; Count K. J. von Königsmarck wants to marry, iv. 273, 274, n. 1; geneal., iv. 344, n. 3; v. 587, n. 1.
Seymour, Frances: *see* Hungerford, Frances, Lady Hungerford.
Seymour, Francis, first Baron Seymour of Trowbridge: house of, at Marlborough, iii. 99–100 & n.; geneal., iii. 213, n. 2.

Seymour, Francis, fifth duke of Somerset: geneal., iv. 136, n. 1.
Seymour, *later* Seymour-Conway, Francis; Baron Conway of Ragley 1703, v. 331 & n. 1.
Seymour, Henry, styled Lord Beauchamp: geneal., iii. 159, n. 7.
Seymour, Letitia, Lady Seymour, second wife of Sir Edward, v. 331, n. 1.
Seymour, Mary, Lady Beauchamp, wife of Henry Seymour, styled Lord Beauchamp: *see* Somerset, Mary, duchess of Beaufort.
Seymour, William, marquis of Hertford, later second duke of Somerset: geneal., iii. 159, n. 7.
Seymour of Trowbridge: Baron, &c.: *see* Seymour, Francis, first baron, 1641–4; Seymour, Catherine, his baroness.
Seyssel: Rhone at, ii. 532, n. 1.
Sezze, ii. 318, nn. 2, 3.
Sfondrato, Paolo, cardinal: builds S. Cecilia, Rome, ii. 357 & n. 8.
Sforza, Ascanio Maria, cardinal: tomb of, ii. 374 & n. 5.
Shabbethai Zebi (Sabatai Sevi): E's account of, iii. 522, n. 2.
Shadwell, Thomas: *see* Plays.
Shaen, Frances, Lady Shaen, wife of Sir James: social, iv. 244 & n. 5; geneal., iv. 247, n. 3.
Shaen, Sir James, bt., iv. 84, n. 8; social, iv. 84, 189, 244, 289.
Shaftesbury: Earls, &c., of: *see* Cooper, Sir Anthony Ashley, first earl, 1672–83; Cooper, Anthony Ashley, second earl, 1683–99; Cooper, Dorothy, his countess.
Shakespeare, William: *see* Plays.
Sharp, James, archbishop of St. Andrews: murder of, iv. 171, n. 1.
Sharp, John, D.D.; archbishop of York 1691, iv. 364 & n. 2; proceedings against, for anti-Roman Catholic sermons, iv. 516 & n. 1, 524 & n. 1; restored to favour, iv. 545, n. 1; appointed dean of Canterbury, v. 19 & n. 4; as archbishop: attends William III, 1695, v. 222, n. 3; sermons by: printed, iv. 502 & n. 2(?); v. 19–20 & n.; ~ at Queen Anne's coronation, v. 498 & n. 5; unprinted, iv. 364, 370–1, 545, 573–4; v. 170, 237; ~ before commons, 30 Jan. 1689, iv. 620 & n. 5; appointed to preach, iv. 623, n. 3.
Shaw, Sir John, bt., iii. 375, n. 8; house of, at Eltham, iii. 375–6 & n.; visit to, iii. 437; geneal., iii. 218, n. 4.
Sheba (Saba), Queen of: portrait of, on gem, ii. 89 (i. 60); in sermon, v. 277.
Sheen (Richmond), Surrey: houses at, on site of priory, iv. 142–3 & nn., 575–6 & nn.
Sheere, John: funeral of (?), iv. 292 & n. 1.
's Heerenberg, Isabella de: *see* Bouillon, Isabella, duchess of.
Sheeres, —, of Deptford (John Sheere?): funeral of, iv. 292 & n. 1.
Sheeres (Sheres), Captain —, of Deptford: geneal., iv. 54 & n. 5.
Sheeres, Sir Henry; knighted 1685: describes African animals, iv. 54–5 & nn.
Sheerness, Kent: dockyard and fortifications at: building, 1666, iii. 441 & n. 7; fort at: taken by Dutch, 1667, iii. 484, n. 1; new fortifications at, July, &c., 1667, iii. 487 & n. 1; ~ fossils found in excavations for, iii. 511 & n. 4; new fortifications, 1672, iii. 609–10 & n.; as equivalent to Buoy of the Nore: English fleet at, 1666, iii. 441–2; ~ Charles II, &c., at, 1672, iii. 620; governor of: *see* Darell, Nathaniel (iii. 620 & n. 5).
Sheffield, John; third earl of Mulgrave 1658; marquis of Normanby 1694; duke of the county of Buckingham 1703, iii. 626, n. 5; as Lord Chamberlain: orders Declaration of Indulgence to be read in Chapel Royal, iv. 584, n. 2 (not identified as Mulgrave).
as Mulgrave: interest of, in art, v. 145; picture bought by, v. 147–8 & n.; social: parties, iii. 626; iv. 181; v. 139, 147; ~ alone, &c., v. 141, 164; as Normanby: account by, of Charles II's death, &c., v. 197–8 & nn.; describes Charles II's project for rebuilding King Street, v. 204 & n. 4; buys Goring House, iii. 404, n. 2.
Shelburne, Baroness: *see* Petty, Elizabeth, Lady Petty.
Sheldon, —: social, iv. 281 & n. 3.

Sheldon, Catherine: *see* Dolben, Mrs. C.
Sheldon, Daniel, iv. 142, n. 1; garden of, at Weybridge, iv. 142 & n. 3; geneal., iv. 257, n. 2.
Sheldon, Edward: social, 1694, v. 164 & n. 4.
Sheldon, Edward, of Stratton: geneal., iii. 511, n. 2.
Sheldon, Frances: inherits collection of coins, iv. 396, n. 4.
Sheldon, Gilbert, D.D.; bishop of London 1660; archbishop of Canterbury 1663, iii. 272, n. 1.
as dean of the Chapel: sermon by, iii. 272 & n. 1; participates in creation of Knights of the Bath, iii. 276 & n. 7.
as bishop of London: at coronation of Charles II, iii. 281–2; marries Charles II and Queen Catherine, iii. 320 & n. 2; attends Gresham College inquiry, iii. 335; marries Sir N. Slanning and Anne Carteret, iii. 343; consecrates Dr. J. Earles, iii. 346.
as archbishop: translation of: ceremony, &c., iii. 361–3 & nn.; concern of, in Dr. T. Pierce's controversy, iii. 360 & n. 5; stays at Lambeth during plague, iii. 419; recovers books belonging to Lambeth Palace library, iii. 527, n. 1; founds and endows Sheldonian Theatre, Oxford, iii. 385 & n. 5, 530–1 & n.; ~ grant of: read and praised, iii. 531–2, 533; as Chancellor of Oxford University, iii. 535, n. 4; consecrates Dr. J. Wilkins, iii. 517; officiates at first marriage of Henry FitzRoy (later duke of Grafton) and Isabella Bennet, iii. 622; at feasts, iii. 400, 536–7; tomb of, v. 426 & n. 5.
relations of, with E: E asks him to intervene in presentation of vicar of Deptford, iii. 613; E visits, &c., iii. 443, 527, 621; E and Mrs. Evelyn visit, at Croydon, iv. 73 & n. 6.
geneal., iv. 142, 257, n. 2; chaplains of: *see* Frank, M.; Stradling, G.; Tomkins, T.; secretary of: *see* Tyndale, S.
Sheldon, Mary: *see* Tuke, Mary, Lady Tuke.
Sheldon, Ralph: collection of medals of, iv. 396–7 & nn.
Shelley, Rev. Peter: sermon by (?), v. 290 & n. 2.
Shells: in art-collections, ii. 516; iii. 10, 372; other important collections: Gaston, duke of Orleans, ii. 128 (i. 82); ~ P. Morin, ii. 132 (i. 86); iii. 33 [collections in other museums, &c., are not indexed collectively].
as decoration of grottoes, ii. 108 (i. 69), 110 (i. 71), 396, 418; drawings of, iv. 531; on sale, ii. 49, 100 (i. 65).
Shelter Island, Long Island, New York: owner of, iii. 581, n. 4.
Sheppey, Kent: ferry to, iii. 487 & n. 2; James II at: gold cross taken from, iv. 470, n. 3 *ad fin.*
Sherard, Bennet, second Baron Sherard: social, iii. 550 & n. 7.
Sherard: second Baron: *see* Sherard, Bennet.
Sherborne Castle, Dorset: declaration dated at, 1688, iv. 609 & n. 3.
Sherburne (Sherborn), Sir Edward; knighted 1682: on commission for saltpetre, iii. 443, n. 1.
Sherburne, William, D.D.: geneal., iii. 302, n. 4.
Shere, Surrey: William Bray and his family at, i. *52*; Dr. T. Duncombe's house at, iv. 111 & n. 5; Sutton in, residence of Peter Hussey: notices, iii. 561 & n. 7; iv. 255–6 & n.; ~ inherited by John Hussey, iv. 454, n. 5; rectors of: *see* Duncombe, Thomas (1659–1714); Duncombe, George (1714–46).
Sherley (Shirley?), Mrs. —: visits E, iii. 230 & n. 2, 252, 268.
Sherlock, Richard, D.D.: sermon by (?), iv. 279 & n. 2.
Sherlock, William, D.D.; Master of the Temple 1684–1705; dean of St. Paul's 1691, iv. 488, n. 8; views of, on settlement of crown, 1689, iv. 625, n. 3; appoints minister to read burial service for non-juring bishop, v. 289 & n. 3; preaches in St. Paul's at thanksgiving for Blenheim, v. 578; sermons by, iv. 279 & n. 2(?), 381 & n. 1(?), 570–1; v. 220, 225–6, 235–6, 248 *bis*, 251–2, 253–4(?), 257, 268–9, 273–5, 279, 288, 292;

Sidney, Henry (*cont.*)
appointed Master of the Ordnance, v. 150 & n. 5.
as earl of Romney: firework display before house of, v. 223 & n. 4; dismissed from mastership of the Ordnance (error), v. 438 & n. 3; appointed Groom of the Stole, *ib.*
Sidney, Isabella: *see* Smythe, Isabella, Viscountess Strangford.
Sidney, Sir Philip: at Penshurst, iii. 72 & n. 5; *see also* Books mentioned in notes.
Sidney, Philip; styled Lord Lisle 1626–77; third earl of Leicester 1677, iii. 164–5 & nn.; visits E, iii. 164; house of, at Sheen, iv. 143 & nn. 1, 3; geneal., iv. 143 & n. 3, 254, n. 1.
Sidney, Col. Robert: supposed father of Monmouth, iv. 457 & n. 6.
Sidney, Robert; second earl of Leicester 1626, iii. 72, n. 4; owner of: Penshurst Place, iii. 72 & n. 4; ~ Leicester House, London, iii. 626, n. 9; friend of, iii. 165, n. 2; geneal., iii. 73, n. 1, 164–5, 231 & n. 7; iv. 254, 322.
Sidney, Robert; styled Lord Lisle 1677–98; fourth earl of Leicester 1698: house of, at Sheen (?), iv. 143 & nn. 1, 3.
Sidon: relic of Christ relating to, ii. 438 & n. 8.
Siegen, Ludwig von: inventor of mezzotint engraving, iii. 271, n. 4.
Siena: notices, ii. 201–5 & nn., 407–8 & nn.; mentioned ii. 200, 206.
conquest of, by Cosimo I: monument commemorating, ii. 185–6 & n. (i. 117), 415; garrison at, ii. 204.
general remarks, ii. 201 & nn. 4–6; arms of, ii. 202; brick: beauty of, at, ii. 202; Italian: purely spoken at, ii. 201 & n. 4; popes and scholars from, ii. 203 & n. 6; provisions at, ii. 201, 206.
buildings, &c., at: academies, ii. 202, n. 3; Biblioteca Comunale: MS. in, ii. 205, n. 6; Capella di Piazza, ii. 201 & n. 8, 202; cathedral, ii. 204–5 & nn., 407–8 & nn.; ~ library, ii. 205 & n. 1., 407 & n. 10; churches: S. Domenico, ii. 204 & n. 3; S. Francesco, ii. 205 & n. 8; S. Francesco all' Alberino (extramural): miraculous tree at, *ib.*; Fonte Branda, ii. 205 & n. 7; Fonte Gaia, ii. 203 & nn. 2, 3; Forte S. Barbera (castle), ii. 203–4 & n.; fountains, ii. 203 & n. 4; hospital (S. Maria della Scala), ii. 205 & nn. 3–6; house of St. Catherine, ii. 408 & n. 2; Lizza, ii. 204 & n. 1; Palazzo Piccolomini, ii. 203 & n. 7; Palazzo Pubblico (Signoria), ii. 201–2 & nn., 203, n. 2; Piazza, ii. 201, 202–3 & nn.; Porta Camollia, ii. 201, n. 5; Porta Romana, *ib.*; ii. 206; Portico del Papa, ii. 203 & n. 7; Sapienza, ii. 203 & n. 5; Strada Romana, ii. 203; Torre del Mangia, ii. 201 & n. 7; walls, ii. 201.
environs: game in, ii. 206.
Siena, Baltazar di: *see* Peruzzi, B.
Sieve, river, ii. 419, n. 4.
Siface, G. F. Grossi called, *castrato*: sings (as Cifeccio, &c.), iv. 537 & n. 5, 547 & n. 1.
Sigismond Rákóczi, Transylvanian prince: geneal., ii. 34, n. 1.
Signs and Portents: 'Annus mirabilis', 1660, 1688, iii. 239 & n. 1; iv. 566; year of prodigies, iii. 477 & n. 3; blood on foundation-stone of building, v. 249; dove at election of Innocent X, ii. 207 & n. 4; fountain of oil at time of Christ's birth, ii. 289 & n. 1.
comets, &c., iv. 235; ~ effects of comet, 1618, ii. 7 & n. 1 (i. 7); earthquakes, iv. 598; v. 133; hailstones shaped like crowns, iii. 71; shining cloud or meteor, 1643, ii. 80 (i. 54); iv. 235; solar eclipses, iii. 63 & n. 3; v. 354 & nn. 1, 2; storms: precede deaths of princes, v. 2 & nn. 3, 4.
Silvester I, St., pope: baptizes Constantine (legend), ii. 267 & n. 1, 271.
Silvestre, Israel: etchings by, after L. Lincler's drawings, iii. 10, n. 3.
Simeon: in sermons, iv. 43; v. 483.
Simmachus, pope: *see* Symmachus.
Simon, St.: relic of, ii. 88 (i. 59).
Simon (Symons), Abraham, medallist: visits E, iii. 85 & n. 5.

Simon, Thomas, medallist: geneal., iii. 85, n. 5.
Simon Magus: place associated with legend of, ii. 248 & n. 3; confused with Semo Sancus Dius Fidius, ii. 358, n. 11; in sermons, iii. 569; v. 57 & n. 1, 596.
Simon Zelotes, St.: brings Christianity to Britain: in sermon, iii. 333 & n. 4.
Simplon, village: ii. 508, n. 5.
Simplon Pass: E's crossing, ii. 508–14 & nn.
general note and bibliography, ii. 508, n. 5; *add.*; accounts of crossing, ii. 505, n. 2; hospices, ii. 508, n. 5; ~ old, ii. 511–12 & nn.; ~ E arrested at, ii. 512–13 & nn., 516, 518 & n. 5; inhabitants of district, ii. 296, n. 8, 510–11 & nn., 512 & n. 1; name of, ii. 511 & n. 4.
Simpson (Simson), Francis *or* John, jewellers to Charles I, &c.: shows E agate cup, iii. 148 & nn. 3, 4.
Simson, —, Independent divine (J. Sympson?): sermon by, iii. 223 & n. 1.
Sinai, Mount: in sermons, iii. 34 & n. 1 (called Sion in error), 525; v. 248.
Sinuessa (Senuessa): site of, ii. 323 & n. 6.
Sion: *see* Syon House.
Sion, Valais: notice, ii. 515–16 & nn.; E's host at, ii. 515–17, 518–19; ~ letter from, ii. 516, 518; linguistic boundary near, ii. 511, n. 2.
Sirani, Elisabetta, painter: notice of, ii. 424 & n. 3.
Sirmione (Sermonea), Lake of Garda, ii. 489 & n. 1.
Siruela, Count of: palace of, in Rome: fireworks before, ii. 281–2 & n.
Sissac, Marquis de: *see* Sessac.
Sittingbourne, Kent: E at, ii. 76 (i. 50), 82 (i. 56); iii. 13, 56, 409 *bis*; Lord Berkeley, &c., at, 1675, iv. 79; Obadiah Walker arrested at (?), iv. 611, n. 6; Bobbing near, iii. 417 & n. 5.
Sixtus III, pope: restoration of S. Maria Maggiore by, ii. 242, n. 5.
Sixtus IV, pope: rebuilds Ponte Sisto, ii. 384 & n. 2; tomb of, ii. 265 & n. 2.
Sixtus V, pope (Felice Peretti): architect of: D. Fontana called, ii. 256, 271; buildings, &c., of (all in Rome): Acqua Felice and fountain, ii. 238–9 & nn.; chapel of, at S. Maria Maggiore, ii. 243 & nn. 4–7, 244–5; Horse-tamers, Quirinal: restored, &c., by, ii. 237 & n. 2; ~ inscription on base of, ii. 405, n. 1; Lateran: medieval palace destroyed by, &c., ii. 268, n. 2, 269, n. 1; ~ new palace built by, ii. 271; obelisks, ii. 245, 256–7, 269–71, 375; ~ general statement, ii. 257 & n. 1; Trajan's Column: statue of St. Peter on, ii. 379; Vatican: library, ii. 300, n. 4, 301; ~ private apartments, ii. 295 & n. 2.
destroys Septizonium, ii. 361 & n. 5; tomb of, ii. 243 & n. 7; life of: in paintings, ii. 300, n. 4; statue of, ii. 224 & n. 5.
Skating, iii. 346–7 & nn.; iv. 362 & n. 3.
Skeffington, Leics.: rector of: *see* Waybred, J.
Slankamen (Szalankemen): battle at, v. 69 & n. 1.
Slanning, Anne, Lady Slanning, wife of Sir Nicholas: wedding of, iii. 343 & n. 1.
Slanning, Sir Nicholas, K.B.; bt., iii. 343, n. 1; wedding of, iii. 343 & n. 1; daughter of: baptized, iii. 363; admitted F.R.S., iii. 401 & nn. 6, 7.
Slare (Slaer), Frederick, M.D., iv. 251, n. 2; phosphorus prepared by: demonstrations of, iv. 251–3 & nn., 263, 491; other demonstrations by, iv. 324–5 & n., 333, 355 & n. 1.
Slaves: baptism of: effect of, on status of, iv. 471 & n. 3; captives in Morocco: collection for, v. 485 & n. 1; galley-slaves, ii. 164–5 & nn., 166 (i. 104–5), 183–4 & nn. (i. 116), 458; ~ chains of, ii. 192; Moroccan ambassador as slave, iv. 268.
Slavonia: saints of: relics of, &c., ii. 267–8 & n. ; Venetian conquests in, ii. 431; Slavonians at Venice, ii. 449.
Slingsby, — (Henry Slingsby?), 1659: social, iii. 228 & n. 5.

Slingsby, Mrs. Ann, wife of Henry Slingsby, iii. 335, n. 2; 553 & n. 1; social, &c., iii. 488, 552.
Slingsby, Sir Arthur; baronet 1657, ii. 560, n. 2; character of, iii. 376; travels to Paris, 1649, ii. 560 *bis* & n. 2; lottery conducted by, 1664, iii. 375 & n. 6, 376 & n. 2.
Slingsby, Henry, Master of the Mint, iii. 335, n. 2; examines proposals for repair of St. Paul's, iii. 448–9 & nn.; as secretary and treasurer of Council for Foreign Plantations, iii. 578–9 & n.; ~ quarrels with Sandwich, the president, iii. 587; ~ attends Council dinner, iii. 599; house of, at Burrough Green: visit to, &c., iii. 552–3 & nn., 556; visits R. Sheldon's collection of medals, iv. 396–7; concerts at house of (in London), iv. 49, 51, 186–7 & nn.; social, iii. 228(?), 335, 345, 488, 547; iv. 65, 94, 96, 138, 171, 182 *bis*, 475; in financial difficulties, iv. 567 & n. 1; children of, iv. 187 & n. 3.
Slingsby, Col. Henry: entertains James II at Portsmouth, iv. 473 & n. 4.
Slingsby, Sir Henry (executed 1658): geneal., iii. 335, n. 2; iv. 473, n. 4.
Slingsby, Sir Robert: geneal., ii. 560, n. 2.
Sloane, Sir Hans, M.D.; baronet 1716, v. 48, n. 1; natural history collections from Jamaica, &c., v. 48 & n. 1; as secretary of Royal Society, v. 304–5 & n.; attends Mrs. Evelyn, v. 456; art-collection of, iii. 339, n. 6; house of, in Chelsea, iv. 161, n. 3 *ad fin.*: E gives copy of *Numismata* to, v. 283, n. 3.
Sloterdijk, ii. 50, n. 1.
Smalley, Mrs. —, servant of Lady Evelyn (1814), i. *54*.
Smalridge, George; D.D. 1701; bishop of Bristol 1714: sermon by (as Mr. Walridge), v. 394–8 & n.
Smalwood, Matthew, D.D., iv. 4, n. 3; sermons by (?), iv. 4, 85.
Smeeth, Kent: Scot's-Hall in: *see* Scot's-Hall.
Smith, —, and his son, 1642, ii. 78 (i. 51).
Smith, —, Lady Smith, at Bobbing, 1665, iii. 417.
Smith, Dr. —: *see* Smith, Henry, D.D.
Smith, Rev. —, curate at Deptford: farewell sermon by, 1682, iv. 243.
Smith, Rev. —: sermons by, at Trinity Chapel, Bond Street, 1692, v. 84, 89–90.
Smith, Henry, D.D., canon of Christ Church, Oxford, iv. 240, n. 2; sermons by, iv. 185(?), 240, 262(?), 263(?), 488(?).
Smith, Dr. H. Maynard: as commentator on the Diary, i. *63*, *69*, *117–19* & nn.
Smith, Isabella: *see* Robartes, Isabella, Countess of Radnor.
Smith, Lady Isabella, wife of Sir John Smith of Bidborough: geneal., iii. 73, n. 1.
Smith, J., servant of E: dies, iii. 566.
Smith, J.: mezzotint by, v. 148, n. 1.
Smith, Sir Jeremiah, admiral, &c.: elected master of Trinity House, iv. 12 & n. 1.
Smith, John, of Queens' College, Cambridge: attacks Epicurus's views, iii. 173, n. 4 *ad fin.*
Smith, John, 1655–1723, politician, v. 452, n. 1; resigns from Treasury, &c., 1701, v. 452 & n. 1; elected Speaker, 1705, v. 614 & n. 1; speech of, mentioned, v. 616; chaplain of (Rev. T. Goddard ?): sermons by, v. 615–16 & n., 617–18.
Smith, Sir John, 1616–44: conduct of, at Edgehill, i. 53–4 & n.
Smith, Sir John, of Bidborough: geneal., iii. 73, n. 1; v. 585, n. 1.
Smith, Joseph; D.D. 1708; provost of Queen's College, Oxford, 1730–56, v. 591, n. 1; as lecturer or reader at Trinity Chapel, Bond Street: sermons by (?), v. 588 & n. 1, 591, 595, 607, 621.
Smith, Margaret: *see* Herbert, Margaret, Lady Herbert.
Smith *or* Smythe, Robert, of Bidborough, &c.: marries Lady Sunderland, iii. 72–3 & n.
Smith, Thomas, D.D.; bishop of Carlisle 1684, v. 257, n. 2; expects Seven Bishops to be convicted, iv. 588, n. 3; proposed successor to, v. 257.
Smith, Sir Thomas, 1558–1625, governor of East India Company: geneal., iii. 73, n. 1.
Smith, Sir Thomas, 1556–1609, master of requests: geneal., iii. 1, n. 2.

Smyrna [for merchant-ships sailing to and from Smyrna *see* England: merchant shipping; United Provinces: merchant shipping]: destroyed by earthquake, 1688, iv. 598 & n. 4; English consul at: *see* Rycant, Sir P.
Smyrna: Bishop of: *see* Conopios, N.
Smyth, Sir James, Lord Mayor of London 1684–5: in ceremony, iv. 413 & n. 1.
Smythe, Lady Dorothy, countess of Sunderland: *see* Spencer, Dorothy.
Smythe, Isabella, Viscountess Strangford, wife of Philip Smythe, second viscount: social, iii. 231 & n. 7.
Smythe, Philip, second Viscount Strangford: geneal., iii. 231, n. 7.
Smythe *or* Smith, Robert, of Bidborough, &c.: marries Lady Sunderland, iii. 72–3 & n.
Snape, Andrew: and Blackheath fair, iv. 311 & n. 3.
Snape, Andrew; D.D. 1705: sermon by (?), v. 307–8 & n.
Snatt, Mrs. Alice, wife of Rev. E. Snatt, ii. 9, n. 6.
Snatt, Rev. Edward, E's schoolmaster at Southover, ii. 9 & n. 6 (i. 8); incompetence of, i. 12; geneal., v. 236.
Snatt, Rev. William: absolves Sir William Parkyns, &c., v. 235, n. 4, 236 & n. 1; i. 8 & n. 2.
Sneiders (Sniders), —: paintings by, ii. 114 & n. 8 (i. 74).
Snuff: making and use of, ii. 201 & n. 1.
Snyders, Frans, painter, ii. 114, n. 8.
Soame (Soames), Sir William, diplomatist: social, iv. 466 & n. 3.
Soap: wash-balls, at Bologna, ii. 426.
Societies for the Reformation of Manners: notice, 1699, v. 366 & n. 5; sermon for, v. 391–2 & n.
Society for the Propagation of the Gospel: meeting, v. 507 & n. 1.
Society of Sons of the Clergy: sermon to, v. 79, n. 2.
Socinianism and Socinians: general note, iii. 227, n. 1; Perfectionists compared with, iii. 363, n. 2; increase of, 1691–1701 (notices chiefly in course of reports of sermons), v. 56, 210, 228, 230–1, 465, 481, 482; Trinity Chapel (Bond Street) so named to testify against, v. 65; sermons against: endowment for, v. 82; Socinian publications, 1695–6, v. 228, 230–1 & n.; 'the new Socinians', 1698, v. 290; Socinians call themselves Unitarians, 1702, v. 494 & n. 1; William Glanville, sen., a Socinian, v. 497 *bis*; sermons against (including those against Socinus), iii. 227; iv. 35, 87–8, 169, 378 & n. 4, 402, 435–6, 495–6, 550 & n. 3; v. 1–2, 56–7, 98, 111, 143, 210, 228, 240–2, 278 & n. 6, 290, 307, 319–20, 340, 342, 343–4, 414, 465, 481, 482, 494, 523–4, 537, 557, 570; *see further* Anti-Trinitarianism.
Socinus, Faustus: influence of, in England, iii. 227, n. 1; iv. 378, n. 4; E on, iv. 435, n. 5; in sermons, iv. 378; v. 414.
Socinus, Lælius, iii. 227, n. 1; iv. 378, n. 4.
Socrates: in sermon, iv. 274.
Sodom: in sermons, iii. 466; v. 109, 333, 347, 444; Fire of London compared to, iii. 454; ~ in sermon, iii. 569.
Sodor and Man: Bishop of, 1685–93: *see* Levinz, B.
Soham Mere (Some meeres), Cambs.: draining of, iii. 555–6 & nn.
Solario, Andrea: painting by (?), ii. 114 & n. 5 (i. 73).
Sole Bay (Sold Bay): *see* Southwold Bay.
Solemn League and Covenant: *see* England: oaths.
Solfatara, the, near Pozzuoli, ii. 340, n. 6, 341–2 & nn.; convent near, ii. 342 & n. 5.
Solms, Heinrich Maastricht, count of Solms-Braunfels: killed, v. 149 & n. 4.
Solomon (Salomon): in sermons, iii. 24; iv. 56, 208, 211; v. 48, 81, 128, 277, 323, 383, 387; cup of, ii. 89 & n. 2 (i. 60); Temple of: in comparison, ii. 255; ~ in sermon, v. 63, 64.
Some meres: *see* Soham Mere.
Somerhill, near Tonbridge, Kent: notice, iii. 71–2 & n.
Somers (Summers), Sir John; knighted, 1689; created Baron Somers, 1697, v. 135, n. 3; character of, v. 408 & n. 2; counsel for Seven Bishops, iv. 587, n. 2; as Lord Keeper: appointed, v. 135 & n. 3; as a

Somers, Sir John (*cont.*)
commissioner for Greenwich Hospital: attends meetings, v. 209–10, 212, 219, 236; ~ orders of, to E, v. 211; as Lord Chancellor: appointed, v. 304, n. 3; ~ politics of, v. 324, n. 3; ~ attacked by commons, v. 407 & n. 1; ~ dismissed, v. 406 & n. 1, 407–8 & nn.; impeachment of, 1701, v. 456 & n. 1, 462 & n. 1, 468 & n. 1; ~ acquitted, v. 466 & nn. 1, 2, 468; ~ alluded to, v. 481.
as president of Royal Society: sworn in, 1698, v. 304–5 n.; ~ re-elected, v. 436; ~ to ask William III to buy Stillingfleet's library, v. 324.
E presents *Acetaria* to, &c., v. 361; social, v. 469.
Somers: Baron, 1697–1716: *see* Somers, Sir John.
Somersbury: manor of, in Ewhurst, Surrey: acquired by Richard Evelyn, ii. 539, n. 4.
Somerset: Monmouth's progress through, 1680, iv. 189, n. 6.
Somerset, Lady Anne: *see* Howard, Lady Anne.
Somerset, Charles; styled marquis of Worcester 1682–98: marriage of, iv. 306 & n. 1.
Somerset, Edward, fourth earl of Worcester: granted Great Park of Nonsuch, &c., iii. 428, n. 1; geneal., ii. 213, n. 8.
Somerset, Edward, second marquis of Worcester: lets Worcester House, London, to Clarendon, iii. 264, n. 3; geneal., iii. 593, n. 2.
Somerset, Elizabeth: *see* Browne, Elizabeth, Viscountess Montagu.
Somerset, Henry, fifth earl and first marquis of Worcester: acquires Worcester House, iii. 264, n. 3; geneal., ii. 213 & n. 8, 367 & n. 2, 551, n. 8.
Somerset, Henry: styled Lord Herbert 1629–67; third marquis of Worcester 1667; created duke of Beaufort 1682, iii. 94, n. 5; as owner of Worcester House, iii. 264, n. 3; house of, in Chelsea, iv. 161, n. 3 *ad fin.*, 185, n. 2; ~ repairs, &c., to, iv. 335 & n. 4; social, iii. 94(?), 549–50; dies, v. 379 & n. 4; geneal., iii. 159, n. 7, 593; iv. 306 & n. 1, 483 & n. 1.
Somerset, Lord John: in Rome, ii. 367 & n. 2.
Somerset, Mary: *see* Butler, Mary, duchess of Ormond.
Somerset, Mary, duchess of Beaufort, &c., wife of Henry Somerset, first duke, and previously of Henry Seymour, Lord Beauchamp: social, &c., iii. 159 & nn. 6, 7.
Somerset, Mary, wife of Lord John Somerset, ii. 367, n. 2.
Somerset, Rebecca, marchioness of Worcester, wife of Charles Somerset, styled marquis of Worcester 1682–98, and secondly of John Granville, Baron Granville: first marriage and dowry of, iv. 306 & n. 1.
Somerset, Thomas; created Viscount Somerset of Cashel 1626: in Rome, ii. 213 & n. 8; geneal., ii. 367, n. 2.
Somerset: Dukes, &c., of: *see* Seymour, William, second duke; Seymour, Francis, fifth duke, 1675–8; Seymour, Charles, sixth duke, 1678–1748; Seymour, Elizabeth, his duchess.
Somerset of Cashel: Viscount, 1626–50: *see* Somerset, Thomas.
Somersfield, William, purchaser of Sayes Court, 1650, iii. 59, n. 1, 74 & n. 4(?).
Somma, Vesuvius, ii. 334, n. 4.
Somme, river: at Abbeville, &c., ii. 85 (i. 57).
Sommelsdijk (Sommers Dyke), ii. 61 & n. 3 (i. 41).
Soncino (Sonano), ii. 490 & n. 7.
Sophia, electress of Hanover: as Princess Sophia: at The Hague, 1641, ii. 34, n. 1; in succession to English crown: position not specified, 1689, iv. 645 & n. 8; v. 421, n. 2; ~ position fixed by Act of Settlement, v. 464–5 & n.
Sophia Dorothea, wife of George I: lover of, iv. 274, n. 1; geneal., v. 352, n. 5.
Sophocles: *see* Plays.
Soranzo, Giovanni, doge of Venice: tomb of, ii. 438 & n. 6.
Soranzo, Lorenzo, Venetian ambassador: entry of, v. 238 & n. 1.
Sorbonne, Robert de: founder of the Sorbonne, ii. 97 (i. 64).
Soria, G. B., architect: façades designed by, ii. 239 & n. 10, 251 & n. 2.

Sorore, Blessed (St. Susorius): relic of, ii. 205 & n. 5.
Sound, the: Edward Mountagu (later earl of Sandwich) returns from, 1660, iii. 619 & n. 2; French warships in, 1683, iv. 331–2 & n.; alluded to, i. 50 & n. 1.
Sourches, Jean du Bouchet, marquis of, Grand-Prévot de France: in procession, iii. 41 & n. 7.
Sousa Tavares, Henrique de: *see* Arronches, marquez d'.
South, Robert, D.D., iii. 365, n. 2; speech of, at Encænia, 1669, iii. 531–2 & n.; candidate for promotion, 1686, iv. 519; sermons by: printed, iii. 365 & n. 2; unprinted, iv. 133 & n. 2.
Southampton, Hants: visit to, ii. 79 (i. 52); projected camp near, v. 99, n. 1.
Southampton: fourth Earl of, 1624–67: *see* Wriothesley, Thomas.
Southampton: first Duke of, 1674–1730: *see* Fitzroy, Charles.
Southborough, near Tunbridge Wells, Kent: lodgings at, iii. 68, n. 4; Margaret Blagge (Mrs. Godolphin) at, iv. 40–1.
Southcote (Southcott), Sir John: in Paris, 1651, iii. 37 & n. 2.
South Malling, near Lewes, Sussex: property at, inherited by E, ii. 27, n. 2; St. Michael's church: built and consecrated, ii. 8 & nn. 1, 2 (i. 7); ~ impropriation of: sold by E, ii. 8 & n. 4 (i. 7–8), 27, n. 2, 541; ~ incumbent of: *see* Coxall, E.
South Mimms, Herts.: highway robbery near, 1692, v. 122 & n. 2.
Southover: *see* Lewes.
South Sea, iii. 585; map of winds in, v. 295 & n. 3.
Southwell, Notts.: prebendary of: *see* Masterson, G.
Southwell, Elizabeth, Lady Southwell, wife of Sir Robert: social, iv. 203 & n. 2.
Southwell, Sir George: error for Sir Robert Southwell, iii. 539 & n. 3.
Southwell, Sir Robert, iii. 539, n. 3; diplomatic career of, iv. 203 & n. 2; as secretary for Ireland, v. 39 & n. 4; letters of news from, to Ormond, i. *128*, n. 1; social, iv. 363.
as F.R.S.: presidency of: elected, v. 39 & n. 4; ~ re-elected, v. 77,

Southwell, Sir Robert (*cont.*)
160; ~ superseded, v. 226; as vice-president: on committee, v. 304–5; reads paper, iv. 62 & n. 4; gifts, &c., from, to Royal Society, iii. 539 (called Sir George Southwell in error); iv. 275, n. 4.
Southwick, Hants: Col. R. Norton's house at, iv. 474 & n. 5.
Southwold Bay (Sole Bay), Suffolk: fleet in, 1665, iii. 411 & n. 2; battle of, 1672, iii. 616–17 & nn.; ~ men killed or wounded in, iii. 186 & n. 4(?), 401, n. 6, 509, n. 3, 619 & n. 3; *see also* pp. 616–17 & n.; ~ conduct at, of Captain C. Gunman, iv. 432 & n. 1.
Sozzini: *see* Socinus.
Spain and the Spaniards:
— foreign relations: (i) chronological series: revolt of United Provinces against, i. 23; the Spanish marriage, ii. 6–7 & n. (i. 6–7); Charles I's return from, 1623: chapel built to commemorate, iii. 72 & n. 3; iv. 40; war of, with United Provinces, 1621–48, ii. 62 & n. 4 (i. 42), 74, n. 4, 316 & n. 2; ~ flags captured by Dutch during, ii. 41 & n. 5 (i. 31); ~ Dutch trading with Spain during, iii. 187, n. 3; influence over Emperor, 1636, i. 21; war of, with France, 1635–59, ii. 7, n. 1, 74, n. 4, 83–4 & n.; ~ danger to France from, 1643, iii. 639 (extract from *State of France*); ~ campaign of 1649, ii. 561, n. 1; ~ alarm in Paris, 1650, iii. 17 & n. 3; ~ Condé in alliance with Spain, 1652, iii. 67, n. 1; war of, with England, 1655–60, iii. 204; ~ treaty of, with Charles II, 1656, iii. 257, n. 2; ~ peace between England and, 1660: proclaimed in London, *ib.*; Portugal to be assisted against, by England, iii. 290, n. 8; accepts Louis XIV's mediation in war with Portugal, 1666, iii. 434 & n. 1; colonial disputes with England, 1672, iii. 613 *bis* & nn. 2, 3; French hostility towards, 1683, iv. 331 & n. 4; relations of, with duke of Savoy, 1696, v. 247; gains of, &c., by Peace of Ryswick, v. 266, n. 1, 267 & n. 1, 269–70 & n.; Eng-

Spain and the Spaniards (*cont.*)
lish trade with: Darien scheme damaging to, v. 379 & n. 1; English and Dutch shipping excluded from ports of, 1701, v. 477, n. 1; Dutch trading with: to be stopped, 1703, v. 526, n. 3; *see also* Wars: War of the Spanish Succession.
— — (ii) general: with Lucca, ii. 410; with Switzerland, ii. 518 & n. 3.
— king(s) of (general or unspecified): statues of, at Brussels, ii. 71 & n. 2 (i. 46); included in prayer for all Christian kings, iii. 204; pensions Doria family to maintain a dog, ii. 175 (i. 111).
— maritime: plate fleets: 1656: capture of ships from, iii. 188–9 & nn.; ~ 1702: attack on at Vigo, &c., v. 516 & n. 8, 517 & n. 1, 519 & n. 2, 522 & n. 1; galleon sunk off Hispaniola: treasure recovered from, iv. 552 & n. 3.
— military: garrisons: at Milan, ii. 501; ~ at Naples, ii. 326 & n. 4, 352; Swiss mercenaries in Spain, ii. 517; armed forces of: at Huys te Gennep, 1641, ii. 35, n. 5; ~ at Mons, 1691, v. 47; ~ at Viloví, 1696, v. 245 & n. 6; ~ in Italy, 1702, v. 514; ~ besiege Gibraltar, 1704, v. 583 & n. 2; Spanish colours, iv. 137, n. 1; a Spaniard represented on figurehead of *Naseby*, iii. 149–50 & n.; *see also* Spanish Netherlands.
— possessions: Albenga (error), i. 107 & n. 1; Finale, ii. 169–70 & n. (i. 107); Îles de Lérins: taken and lost, ii. 168 & n. 1 (i. 106); duchy of Milan, ii. 477, n. 6; ~ limits of, ii. 490 & n. 7, 508–9; kingdom of Naples, ii. 316, n. 2; ~ frontier of, ii. 322 & n. 3; ~ tribute to Pope for, ii. 279–80, 352; ~ Queen Christina of Sweden's project to seize, iv. 221 & nn. 2, 3; *see also* Spanish Indies; Spanish Netherlands.
— social, &c.: dress: at Genoa and Naples, ii. 178 (i. 112), 353 & n. 5; ~ disliked in Paris, ii. 97 (i. 64); ~ women's, iii. 320, n. 4, 321, n. 2; ~ export of bays and says to Spain, iii. 177 & n. 4; gravity, i. 47; ~ in dress, ii. 178 (i. 112), 353; Inquisition, ii. 491 & n. 2; music: Castilian singers, iii. 322, n. 4; Saludadores, iv. 468–70 & nn.
— miscellaneous: heat in: in comparison, v. 472, 473; winter, 1683–4, in, iv. 363 & n. 1; orange-trees from, i. 9 & n. 2; wine of, iii. 103 & n. 1; Sandwich's observations in, iii. 519 & nn. 1, 2; drawings by Leonardo in, ii. 498, n. 8 *ad fin.*; paintings brought from, iii. 538; national church, &c., in Rome, ii. 368–9 & nn.; mentioned, iv. 618.
— persons: (i) Spaniards: Don Zanches d' Avila, ii. 560 & n. 7(?); iii. 17; prisoners from plate fleet, 1657, iii. 188–9 & nn.; unnamed: at Brussels, ii. 70 (i. 46); ~ in Rome: anecdote concerning, ii. 264–5.
— — (ii) travellers, &c., in Spain: Francis I: captivity of, in, ii. 112 & n. 2 (i. 72); J. Wall: friar in, ii. 96 (i. 63); *see also* Baker, Thomas (iii. 538 & n. 1); Boone, C. (as Spanish merchant, iv. 180); Cottington, Francis, Baron Cottington (iii. 32, n. 5 *ad fin.*); Elwes, Sir G. (iii. 31); Forster, Sir Humphrey, second bt. (iv. 313); Godfrey, John (iii. 31); Henshaw, T. (ii. 179 & i. 113); Pepys, S. (iv. 469 & n. 5); Potemkin, Prince P. (iv. 262 & n. 3).
Spallanzani, L., iii. 341, n. 4.
Spalding, Lincs.: Mrs. Godolphin's lease at, iv. 90 & n. 5; ~ alluded to, iv. 93 *bis*; ~ sealed, iv. 101.
Spanheim (Spanhemius), Ezechiel: in England, 1675, iv. 78 & n. 1.
Spanheim, Friedrich, sen., iv. 78 & n. 1.
Spanheim, Friedrich, jnr., iv. 78, n. 1.
Spanish Indies: governors in, &c., returning to Spain from, iii. 188–9 & nn.; Jamaicans not allowed to cut logwood on mainland of, iii. 613 & n. 2; possibility of conquering, iv. 46; earthquake(s) in, 1688, iv. 598 & n. 4; alarmed by Scottish expedition to Darien, v. 345 & n. 2.
Spanish language: Arlington's knowledge of, iv. 118.

Spanish Netherlands [E habitually uses the name Flanders to designate the general area, and not merely the province of Flanders; on one occasion (i. 3) he possibly means the Netherlands in general. All notices relating to Flanders, even when the province alone is intended, are entered under the present heading]:
E's travels in, 1641, ii. 62–76 & nn. (i. 43–50 & nn.); bibliographical and chronological note on, ii. 569–71; mentioned, iii. 61.
chronological [for campaigns in, &c., *see* Wars]: invention of gunpowder brought from, to England, i. 3; winter in, 1657–8, iii. 211, n. 2; condition of, 1667, discussed, iii. 502; attacked by France, 1683, iv. 331 & n. 4, 340; winter in, 1696–7, v. 264 & n. 4.
frontiers, &c.: coast: in sight, ii. 31; Spanish forts on Scheldt, ii. 62–3 & n. (i. 43); lands adjoining: incursions into, by soldiers, ii. 38–9 (i. 29), 74 & n. 4 (i. 48), 83–4 & n. (i. 56), 84–5 & n. (i. 57), 561 & n. 1; iii. 12, 16.
personal: John and Mrs. Earles in, &c., iii. 153; — Houblon as refugee from, iv. 475 & n. 2; James, duke of York: goes to, 1679, iv. 167 & n. 6; ~ returns from, iv. 181 & n. 1; Marie de Médicis flies to, ii. 146, n. 2; Henry Howard, sixth duke of Norfolk, goes to, iv. 236; Sir R. Walsh in, iii. 6, n. 4; C. Wase in, iii. 55.
governors of: *see* Albert, Archduke (ii. 70, n. 4); Isabella Clara Eugenia (*ib.*); Ferdinand of Austria (ii. 59 & n. 7); Leopold William, Archduke (iii. 17, n. 3); general of cavalry in: *see* Ligne, C.-L., prince de (iii. 256 & n. 1).
Spanish Succession: *see* Wars: War of the Spanish Succession.
Sparrow, Anthony, D.D.; bishop of Exeter 1667; of Norwich 1676: sermon by, iv. 7 & n. 2.
Sparta: stone from, ii. 460 & n. 7.
Spartacus: on Vesuvius, ii. 335 & n. 6.
Speke, Hugh: tried and fined, 1684, iv. 367 & n. 1.
Speldhurst, Kent: curate of: sermon by, iii. 295; Groombridge in: *see* Groombridge.
Spelman, —, grandson of Sir Henry: recommended to Lord Mordaunt, iii. 263 & n. 10.
Spelman, Clement: commissioner for London streets, iii. 319, n. 1.
Spelman, Dorothea: *see* Whitfield, Dorothea, Lady Whitfield.
Spelman, Sir Henry: geneal., ii. 82, n. 3; iii. 263 & n. 10.
Spelsbury, Oxon.: Ditchley Park in, iii. 382–3 & nn.
Spencer family: acquires Althorp, iv. 69, n. 3.
Spencer, — (Robert Spencer, later Viscount Teviot, throughout?): leaves Paris for England, 1651, iii. 47; in England: social, 1652–6, iii. 74, 175 & n. 4, 181; *see also* iii. 37 & n. 4.
Spencer, Lord: two sons of: in Paris, 1651, iii. 37 & n. 4.
Spencer, Lady Anne: *see* Douglas, Anne, styled countess of Arran.
Spencer, Anne, countess of Sunderland, born Digby, wife of Robert Spencer, second earl, iii. 589, n. 4.
character: general, *ib.*; iv. 595, n. 1; charitable gift by, iv. 81; domestic economy of, iv. 594.
family affairs, &c.: going to France to join Sunderland, 1672, iii. 626 & n. 8; marriage-project of, for her son, iv. 245–7 & nn., 248; grief of, at Sunderland's conversion to Roman Catholicism, iv. 595; asks Queen Mary (of Modena) to save Sunderland from dismissal, iv. 602; goes to United Provinces, Aug. 1689, iv. 647 & n. 4; ~ returns, v. 9.
friendships: with E: general, iii. 587, n. 6, 589, n. 4; desires his help in marriage-project for her son, iv. 245–7; visits him in illness, iv. 271; affection of, &c., for Mary Evelyn, iv. 428, 430, 432; entertains E and John Evelyn, jnr., at Althorp, iv. 593–5; seeks advice, &c., from E, Oct.-Dec. 1688, iv. 602 & n.

Spencer, Anne (*cont.*)
2, 610; gives E account of storm, iv. 644; *see also* social *below*; other friends, &c.: visits Cranbourn Lodge, iv. 527–8, 642; at Euston, 1671, iii. 589; consulted about monument to Lord Mordaunt, iv. 86; visits Mordaunt children, iv. 180 & n. 2; visits Lord and Lady Northampton, iv. 594.
social, &c.: visits W. Charleton's museum, iv. 531–2; dines with Lord Mayor (Sir R. Clayton), iv. 185 & n. 6; gives dinner-parties with entertainers, iii. 626–7; iv. 87; at other parties, &c. (as hostess or guest), iv. 85, 88 *bis*, 161, 202, 207, 266, 283, 333, 437, 450, 549, 586, 643, 646; v. 49, 171, 239, 294; alone, &c., iii. 631; iv. 72, 82, 88, 156, 184, 191, 275, 352, 501, 504, 529, 569, 591, 644; v. 265, 469; *see also* Spencer, Robert, earl of Sunderland: social.

Spencer, Lady Anne, countess of Sunderland, born Churchill, second wife of Charles Spencer, third earl, v. 525 & n. 7.

Spencer, Arabella, Lady Spencer, d. 1698, born Cavendish, first wife of Charles Spencer, styled Lord Spencer, later third earl of Sunderland: marriage of, v. 202 & n. 4, 206.

Spencer, Charles; styled Lord Spencer 1688–1702; third earl of Sunderland 1702, iv. 595, n. 2; character and promise of, iv. 595 & n. 2; marriages of, v. 202 & n. 4, 206, 525 & n. 7; library of, v. 206 & n. 1, 322 & nn. 1, 2; social: as Lord Spencer, v. 238; ~ as earl, v. 597; letter of, to E, v. 36 & n. 3; governor of, iv. 595 & n. 2; tutor of, v. 322 & n. 3.

Spencer, Dorothy, countess of Sunderland, born Sidney, wife of Henry Spencer, second earl, and, secondly, of Robert Smythe: second marriage of, iii. 72–3 & n.; chaplain of: *see* Pierce, T. (iii. 234 & n. 2).

Spencer, Elizabeth: *see* Harcourt, Elizabeth, Viscountess Harcourt.

Spencer, Elizabeth: *see* Maccarty, Elizabeth, countess of Clancarty, wife of the fourth earl.

Spencer, Henry, first earl of Sunderland: geneal., iii. 73 & n. 1, 175 & n. 4, 254, n. 4, 535.

Spencer, Jane, Lady Spencer, wife of Sir Thomas, bt.: geneal., iii. 252, n. 3.

Spencer, Martha, daughter of Richard Spencer: *see* Evelyn, Mrs. M.

Spencer, Mrs. Martha, wife of Richard Spencer: *see* Stonhouse, Martha, Lady Stonhouse.

Spencer (Specer), Richard, colonel of militia: offers E a captaincy, iii. 254 & n. 4.

Spencer, Richard, first husband of Lady Stonhouse: geneal., iv. 189, nn. 3, 4, 194, 224, n. 3.

Spencer, Robert; styled Lord Spencer 1666–88, iv. 245, n. 1; character, iv. 245, 246, 595; marriage-project for, iv. 245–7 & nn., 248; dies, iv. 595, n. 3.

Spencer, Robert, first Baron Spencer of Wormleighton: geneal., iii. 37, n. 4, 254, n. 4.

Spencer, Robert; second earl of Sunderland 1643, iii. 587, n. 6.
character, &c.: ambition of, iv. 594–5 & n.; as gambler, iv. 245 & n. 4; religious views of, iv. 245.
chronological series: at Euston, 1671, iii. 589, n. 4; appointed ambassador to Spain, iii. 587 & n. 6; as ambassador in France, 1672, iii. 626 & n. 8; ~ chaplain of: *see* Jessop, C.; appointed plenipotentiary at Cologne, 1673, iv. 8, n. 2; as secretary of state, iv. 128 & n. 3; ~ appointed, 1679, iv. 181 & n. 3; ~ secretary of: *see* Bridgeman, W. (iv. 197 & n. 2); ~ conduct of, to Ossory regarding Tangier, 1680, iv. 209 & n. 1; ~ joins Exclusionists, iv. 245 & nn. 5, 6; ~ dismissed, 1681, iv. 245 & n. 5; ~ [he was reappointed in 1683] continued by James II, 1685, iv. 417 & n. 4; appointed President of the Council, iv. 490; as premier minister, iv. 501 & n. 4; delays licence for book, 1686, iv. 508, n. 1; order from, to E, iv. 525; appointed a Commissioner for Ecclesiastical Affairs, iv. 519–20; elected K.G., 1687, iv.

Spencer, Robert (*cont.*)
549 & n. 2; converted to Roman Catholicism, 1688, iv. 594–5 & n.; dismissed from office, iv. 602 & n. 2, 603; flies, iv. 610 & n. 1, 611; in exile in Netherlands, 1689, iv. 642, n. 4; returns and is received by William III, &c., 1691, v. 49 & n. 2; entertains William III at Althorp, 1695, v. 223 & n. 3; as favourite, &c., v. 226 & n. 3; as Lord Chamberlain, 1697, v. 226, n. 3; influence of, with William III: asked to use, v. 298 & n. 2; dies, v. 516 & n. 9.
property, &c.: estate of: impaired, &c., iv. 245, 246, 248; seat of: *see* Althorp; lodgings of, in Whitehall, iv. 191, n. 3, 403, n. 5; paintings belonging to, iv. 128 & n. 4, 403–4 & nn.
social: congratulates E on appointment, iv. 465; gives E nomination for Charterhouse, iv. 511; Mrs. Godolphin visits, iv. 67; borrows money from Mrs. Godolphin, iv. 94, 559; Sir J. Hoskins introduced to, iv. 588; gives music-party, iv. 403; at parties, &c. (as host or guest), iv. 181, 254, 283, 317–18, 383, 490, 558; v. 206; alone, &c., iv. 238, 509; v. 403; Lord or Lady Sunderland (indeterminable): alone, iv. 56, 287, 402, 450, 547; v. 134.
geneal., iii. 175, n. 4, 589, n. 4; iv. 67, 254, n. 1, 450, n. 5, 567; tutor of: *see* Pierce, T. (iii. 234, n. 2).
Spencer, Robert; created Viscount of Teviot 1685, iii. 37, n. 4; in Paris, 1651(?), iii. 37; leaves Paris for England (?), iii. 47; in England: social, 1652–6(?), iii. 74, 175 & n. 4, 181; created D.C.L., Oxford, iii. 535; entertains E at Oxford, iv. 67–8; created viscount, iv. 493, n. 7; as commissioner for Privy Seal: appointed, iv. 493; ~ qualifies, iv. 500; commits suicide, v. 182 & n. 2.
Spencer, Sir Thomas, bt.: social, iii. 252 & n. 3.
Spencer, William, second Baron Spencer of Wormleighton: geneal., iii. 37 & n. 4.
Spencer: Lords (courtesy title): *see* Spencer, Robert (1666–88); Spencer, Charles (1688–1702), later third earl of Sunderland.
Spencer of Wormleighton: Barons: *see* Spencer, Robert, first baron; Spencer, William, second baron.
Spenser, Edmund: tomb of, iii. 490.
Speroni, Sperone: monument to, ii. 463 & n. 1.
Speyer: battle near, 1703, v. 551 & n. 1.
Spezia (Specia): Gulf of, ii. 178–9 & nn. (i. 113).
Spie Park: *see* Spye Park.
Spina, Monte, ii. 340, n. 6.
Spinola, Ambrogio, marquis: constructs Ghent-Bruges canal, ii. 74 & n. 5 (i. 48); house of, in Genoa (?), ii. 176 & n. 6 (i. 111).
Spithead, Portsmouth: Queen Maria Anna of Spain at, v. 2, n. 2; Archduke Charles at, v. 558, n. 1.
Spon, Jacob: travels with Sir G. Wheler, iv. 358, n. 1.
Spragge, Sir Edward: and attack on Dutch Smyrna fleet, 1672, iii. 606 & n. 1.
Sprat, Thomas, D.D.; bishop of Rochester 1684, iii. 533, n. 7; inception of, as D.D., iii. 533; chaplain to Buckingham, iv. 73 & n. 1; trustee for Buckingham's estates, iv. 186, n. 4; as prebendary of Westminster, iv. 73 & n. 1; as curate of St. Margaret's, Westminster, iv. 188 & n. 3; as dean of Westminster: appointed, iv. 359, n. 1; ~ authorized to make collections for London poor, winter, 1683–4, iv. 361, n. 3; ~ and cross of Edward the Confessor, iv. 470; ~ and reading of Declaration of Indulgence in Abbey, iv. 584, n. 4; consecrated bishop of Rochester, iv. 436, n. 3; appointed Clerk of the Closet, iv. 495 & n. 2; as a Commissioner for Ecclesiastical Affairs: appointed, iv. 519–20 & n.; ~ joins in proceedings against Bishop Compton, iv. 524; ~ resigns, iv. 596 & n. 2; author of *Form of Prayer* for birth of Prince James Edward, iv. 588 & n. 7; attends coronation of William and Mary, iv. 633, n. 3; as bishop: preaches and confirms at Greenwich, v. 70–1; as preacher: style, iv. 188; ~ ser-

Sprat, Thomas, D.D. (*cont.*) mons by, iv. 73, 131, 167, 188, 191, 207, 223, 238, 292, 309, 359, 373–4, 436–7, 506, 580; ~ appointed to preach, iv. 197, n. 5; v. 394, n. 3; social, v. 440, 597.
Spye (Spie) Park, near Calne, Wilts.: notice, iii. 112 & n. 3.
Squerryes: *see* Westerham.
Stade, near Hamburg: storm at, 1699, v. 311 & n. 2.
Staffarda: battle of, 1690, v. 33 *bis* & nn. 6, 7.
Stafford, —: arrested for highway-robbery, 1692, v. 122, n. 2.
Stafford, Lord (William Howard, Viscount Stafford?): in Paris, 1651, iii. 35 & n. 5.
Stafford, Father Robert Stanford *alias*, S. J.: in Rome, ii. 365 & n. 8.
Stafford, Sir Thomas: on hailstones in storm, 1652, iii. 71 & n. 2.
Stafford, William, Viscount Stafford: error: *see* Howard, William, Viscount Stafford.
Stafford: Baron, 1640, and Viscount of, 1640–80: *see* Howard, William.
Staffordshire: Dr. R. Plot preparing for his history of, iv. 68 & n. 4; Caldwell family of, v. 358, n. 3; Offley family of, v. 359.
Stained glass: process of colouring, iv. 276 & n. 2; windows: not destroyed at Geneva, ii. 528 & n. 2; at Canterbury before destruction, ii. 76 & n. 3 (i. 50); in Oxford Cathedral: damaged, iii. 109 & n. 3; in various churches, &c., ii. 155 (i. 100), 494, 568 & n. 2; iii. 138; domestic, &c., ii. 526–7; iii. 193 & n. 2.
Staley, William, jnr.: tried, &c., iv. 158 & n. 4.
Standing, Dr. — (error): *see* Stanley, William, D.D.
Standish, John; D.D. 1680, iv. 75, n. 3; sermons by: printed, iv. 75 & n. 3; ~ unprinted, iv. 132, 465.
Stanford, Father Robert: *see* Stafford.
Stanhope family: geneal., iii. 553, n. 3.
Stanhope, Alexander: social, iii. 551–2 & n.; *add.*
Stanhope, Catherine: *see* Hutchinson, Catherine, Lady Hutchinson.
Stanhope, Catherine, Lady Stanhope; countess of Chesterfield *suo jure* 1660: geneal., iv. 92 & n. 2.
Stanhope, Charles, second Baron Stanhope of Harrington: geneal., iv. 13, n. 5.
Stanhope, Dorothy, Baroness Stanhope, wife of Charles Stanhope, second Baron Stanhope of Harrington: social, iv. 13 & n. 5.
Stanhope, Elizabeth: *see* Darcy, Mrs. E.
Stanhope, Elizabeth, countess of Chesterfield, second wife of Philip Stanhope, second earl, iii. 4, n. 2.
Stanhope, George; D.D. 1697; dean of Canterbury 1704, v. 34, n. 4, 223, n. 2; as preacher: ability, &c., of, v. 223; ~ sermons by, v. 34 & n. 4(?), 171–3 & n.(?), 223; as Boyle Lecturer, 1701: sermon (printed), v. 442–3 & n.
Stanhope, Henry, styled Lord Stanhope: geneal., iv. 92, n. 2.
Stanhope, James, first Earl Stanhope: geneal., iii. 551, n. 6 *ad fin.*
Stanhope, Philip, first earl of Chesterfield: geneal., ii. 10, n. 7; iii. 551, n. 6, 552, n. 1.
Stanhope, Philip; styled Lord Stanhope 1634–56; second earl of Chesterfield 1656, iii. 4, n. 2 [E calls him either Lord Stanhope or earl of Chesterfield in 1650 and 1655]; in Paris, 1650: in Bataille de Vambre, iii. 4, 5; ~ at de Veau's academy, iii. 8, n. 2; ~ witnesses E's will, iii. 12; ~ social, iii. 8, 21 *bis*; ~ leaves for Italy, iii. 22 & n. 1; in England, 1655: borrows money from E, iii. 151 & n. 3, 152, 153; ~ in mourning for his first wife, iii. 151, n. 3, 153, n. 5; ~ travels to France, iii. 153 & n. 5; settles permanently in England, 1657, iii. 201, n. 4; E visits on business, iii. 201; as lord chamberlain to Queen Catherine, iii. 352, n. 4; created D.C.L., Oxford, iii. 535 & n. 5; forest justiceship of, iv. 220 & n. 2; at demonstration of phosphorus, iv. 263; sends E venison, iii. 219 & n. 4; iv. 220 & n. 3; social, iii. 352 & n. 4; iv. 190, 191; v. 595; geneal., ii. 10, n. 7; iii. 4, n. 2, 154, n. 1, 535, n. 5, 551–2, 555, n. 3; iv. 92, n. 2; servant of, iii. 5.
Stanhope: first Earl: *see* Stanhope, James.

Stanhope: Lords (courtesy title): *see* Stanhope, Henry (1628–34); Stanhope, Philip (1634–56), later second earl of Chesterfield.
Stanhope of Harrington: second Baron, &c.: *see* Stanhope, Charles; Stanhope, Dorothy, his baroness.
Stanislaus Leczinsky: elected king of Poland, v. 573 & n. 3; Clement XI forbids coronation of, v. 577 & n. 6.
Stanley, —, duellist: error for John Talbot, iv. 501 & n. 2.
Stanley, — (Thomas Stanley?): social, iii. 237 & n. 5.
Stanley, Elizabeth, countess of Derby, wife of W. G. R. Stanley, ninth earl, iv. 97–8 & n.; social, iv. 97, 102, 105; visited by Lady Ossory at Knowsley (?), iv. 211 & n. 3.
Stanley, Henry, M.D.: E consults, iii. 62 & n. 3.
Stanley, James, seventh earl of Derby: execution of: news of reaches Paris, iii. 48 & n. 7.
Stanley, Thomas, the scholar: social (?), iii. 237 & n. 5.
Stanley, William, D.D.; dean of St. Asaph 1706: as Dr. Standing: social, v. 221 & n. 3.
Stanley, William, sixth earl of Derby: builds Derby House, Westminster, iii. 222, n. 4.
Stanley, William George Richard, ninth earl of Derby, iv. 97, n. 7; social, iv. 102, 108; dies, v. 521 & n. 9.
Stansfield, township: *see* Halifax.
Stansfield family, ii. 3 & n. 1; extinct in Sussex, &c., iii. 89, n. 3.
Stansfield, Eleanor: *see* Evelyn, Mrs. E.
Stansfield, Mrs. Eleanor (Hellena), born Comber, first wife of John Stansfield: geneal., ii. 3 & n. 1 (i. 4).
Stansfield, Mrs. Jane: *see* Newton, Mrs. J.
Stansfield, John, ii. 3, n. 1; E's maternal grandfather, ii. 3 (i. 4); i. *3*; godfather of E, ii. 5 (i. 6); E spends his childhood with, ii. 7 (i. 7); i. *4*; builds and endows South Malling church, ii. 8 & n. 1 (i. 7); death and tomb of, ii. 7–8 & nn. (i. 7); legacies of, ii. 27, n. 2; property of, in Ripe, ii. 555, n. 5; E and George Evelyn name sons after, iii. 89 & n. 3.
Stapenhill, Derbyshire: Newhall manor in, ii. 10, n. 7.
Stapleton, Sir Robert, translator of Juvenal: social, iii. 98 & n. 2.
Stapleton, Sir William; baronet 1679, iii. 613, n. 2; as Col. Stapleton: powers of, &c., as governor of Leeward Islands, iii. 605 & n. 1, 613 & n. 2.
Starkey, John, publisher: newsletters written by, i. *128*, n. 2.
State Paper Office: *see* England: state papers.
Staughton: *see* Stoughton.
Stawell, Sir Edward: *see* Stowell, Edward.
Steenbergen, ii. 61 & n. 1 (i. 41).
Steenwyck, Hendrick van, jnr., ii. 70, n. 5, 546, n. 4; paintings by (?), ii. 70 (i. 46), 113 (i. 73), 546, 548, 549; iii. 96 & n. 4.
Steinkerk: battle of, v. 111 & n. 3; mentioned, iv. 548, n. 6.
Stephen, king of England: tomb of (error), iii. 118 & n. 2.
Stephen I, pope: controversy of, with St. Cyprian, iv. 617 & n. 1; relics of, ii. 363 & n. 4.
Stephen III, pope: council held by, ii. 274 & n. 4; stole, &c., of, ii. 88 (i. 59).
Stephen, St.: relics of, ii. 381, 442.
Stephen, Sir Leslie: on E, i. *39*.
Stephens, —, of Henley on Thames, attorney for Mrs. Howard, iv. 67.
Stephens, Mrs. Christian: geneal., ii. 558, n. 7.
Stephens, James, of Clowerwall, ii. 558, n. 7; debt of Sir R. Browne to: settlement of, iii. 75; social, ii. 558(?); iii. 81, 117, 183.
Stephens, Matthias: social (?), ii. 558 & n. 7.
Stephens, William, B.D.: sermon (printed) by, on duties of rulers: censured by house of commons, v. 378 & n. 2.
Sterne, Richard, D.D.; archbishop of York 1664: connexion of, with *Whole Duty of Man* (?), v. 112 & n. 5.
Steward, Mrs. —: godmother of Jane Evelyn, 1692, v. 84.
Steward (Stewart), Richard, D.C.L.; dean of St. Paul's 1642, iii. 20, n. 3; character, iii. 49; in Paris, 1650–1: sermons by, iii. 20, 38, 43; social, iii. 37, 40, 44; E obtains money for, iii. 47; dies, &c., iii. 48–9 & n.; commemorated, iii. 49.

Stewart, Sir James, second earl of Galloway: social, &c., iii. 229 & n. 4.
Stiddolph *or* Stidolph: *see* Stydolf.
Stillingfleet, Edward; D.D. 1668; bishop of Worcester 1689, iii. 407, n. 1; as rector of St. Andrew's, Holborn, iv. 194 & n. 3; installed dean of St. Paul's, iv. 134, n. 2; elected bishop of Worcester, iv. 648, 649, n. 1; on case of conscience, v. 338–9; sermons by: printed, iv. 26 & n. 1, 53 & n. 2, 165 & n. 2, 368 & n. 2, 501 & n. 1, 623 & n. 3; ~ unprinted, iii. 407 & n. 1; iv. 9, 34, 89, 134 *bis*, 166, 195, 238, 240, 277, 419–20, 577; appointed to preach, iv. 4, n. 5; social, iv. 182; v. 25, 302; dies, v. 319 & n. 2; library of: project for purchase of, v. 323 & n. 3, 324; chaplain of: *see* Bentley, R. (v. 88 & n. 4).
Stint, Joan: *see* Evelyn, Mrs. J.
Stoics: views of: in sermons, v. 304, 613.
Stoke next Guildford, Surrey: Stoughton (Staughton) in, i. 2 & n. 3.
Stoke Poges, Bucks.: vicar of: *see* Provoste, J.
Stokes (Stoakes), David, D.D., iii. 86 & n. 2; sermon by, iii. 86; social, iii. 142–3; geneal., iii. 178, n. 4.
Stokes, Richard, M.D., iii. 178, n. 4; at Dedham, iii. 178; communicates perpetual motion from Cologne(?), iii. 513 & n. 1.
Stokes, William, teacher of vaulting, at Oxford, ii. 20–1 & n. (i. 16).
Stone, — (Sir Robert Stone?): in Queen of Bohemia's service, ii. 38, n. 1.
Stone, Nicholas, sculptor, &c.: tomb by, iii. 66 & n. 3.
Stone, Sir Robert, and Lady Stone: at siege of Huys te Gennep, ii. 37–8 & n. (i. 28).
Stonehenge: account of, iii. 115–16 & nn.
Stonhouse, —: geneal., v. 358, n. 7.
Stonhouse, Elizabeth: *see* Byron, Elizabeth, Baroness Byron.
Stonhouse (Stonehouse), Sir John, bt., iv. 189, n. 3; negotiates his step-daughter's marriage with John Evelyn, jnr., iv. 189, 192, 194; London house of, iv. 194, 195; social, iv. 211, 286; *see also* iv. 196; geneal., iv. 137, n. 4.
Stonhouse, Martha, Lady Stonhouse, wife of Sir John, and previously of Richard Spencer, iv. 189, n. 3; mother of Mrs. Martha Evelyn, iv. 189, n. 4, 194; as godmother to Evelyn grandchildren, iv. 236, 324; estate belonging to, iv. 415; social, iv. 211, 286; *see also* iv. 196; visits Eton, v. 103; dies, v. 618 & n. 4.
Stonhouse, Mrs. Mary, born Evelyn (?): *see* Evelyn, Mary (v. 54, n. 2, 358, n. 7, 359, n. 8).
Stoodley, Rev. George, rector of Rotherhithe, iv. 140, n. 5; sermons by (?), iv. 140, 153, 249, 250.
Stoughton (Staughton), Mrs. Catherine, i. 2 & n. 3.
Stoughton *or* Staughton, Sir Laurence, bt., v. 77 & n. 1.
Stoughton (Staughton), Thomas: geneal., i. 2 & n. 3, 13, n. 2.
Stouppe (Stoope), J. B., French protestant divine: address of, to Charles II, 1660, iii. 248 & n. 3.
Stowell, Edward (Sir E. Stawell): in Paris, 1651, iii. 37 & n. 3.
Strada, Famianus: E sees, ii. 283 & n. 3.
Stradbroke, Suffolk: vicar of: *see* Buck, J.
Stradling, —, v. 8.
Stradling, George, D.D.; dean of Chichester 1672, iii. 305, n. 3, 614, n. 2; as chaplain to Archbishop Sheldon, iii. 362 & n. 5; sermons by, iii. 305(?), 614; iv. 4, 24, 97, 106, 181.
Stradling, Sir William: at siege of Huys te Gennep (?), ii. 38 & n. 2 (i. 28).
Strafford: Earls of: *see* Wentworth, Thomas, first earl 1640–1; Wentworth, William, first earl, second creation, 1641–62, and second earl, first creation, 1662–95.
Strangford: Viscount, &c.: *see* Smythe, Philip, second viscount, 1635–1708; Smythe, Isabella, his viscountess.
Strassburg: retained by France in treaty of Ryswick, v. 266, n. 2, 270; cathedral of: clock in, ii. 434 & n. 5.
Strassburg: Bishop of, 1682–1704: *see* Fürstenberg, W. E. von.

Stratford, Nicholas, D.D.; bishop of Chester 1689, iv. 371, n. 2; sermons by, iv. 371; v. 240; on case of conscience, v. 338–9.
Stratford-le-Bow, Middlesex: dye-works at (?), iii. 446, nn. 5, 6.
Straw-work: at Milan, ii. 501 & n. 8.
Streater (Streeter), Robert, iii. 375, n. 3; ill with stone, iv. 51–2; paintings by, iii. 375 & n. 3, 386, n. 1(?), 625–6 & n.; iv. 180, 288; scenery by, iii. 570 & n. 2.
Streatham (Streetham), Surrey: Sir John Bodly's house at, i. 10 & n. 1.
Street-lighting: lamp-lit road, v. 363 & n. 3.
Strengfellow (Stringfellow), Rev. William, iv. 641, n. 5; recommended by E to: Sancroft, iv. 641 & n. 5; ~ Tenison, v. 27, 61–2, 376; as minister of Trinity Chapel, Bond Street: appointed, v. 61–2, 376 & n. 1; ~ reappointed, v. 169 & n. 1; ~ dismissed, v. 375–6 & n.
sermons by: at Deptford, iv. 549–50 & n.(?), 592(?), 608(?), 643, 646–7; v. 28 *bis*, 53, 58; trial, for Trinity Chapel, v. 27; at Trinity Chapel: inaugural, v. 65–6; ~ ordinary, v. 72–136, 169, 194, 195, 204, 206, 210, 293–343, 354–74 *passim & singulatim*; at Golden Square tabernacle (?), v. 136 & n. 4; repetitions of, v. 74–5 & v. 341; v. 90–2, 104–5 & v. 294–5, 296–7; v. 94–5 & v. 136; v. 105, &c., & v. 360, &c.; v. 326–7 & v. 331–2.
Strickland, John, E's servant, &c., v. 98, n. 3; ill, v. 98, 101, 102, 103; E settles accounts with, v. 284; E dines with, v. 600.
Strickland, Sir Thomas, iii. 586, n. 1; appointed a Privy Councillor, iv. 590, n. 4 *ad fin.*; social, iii. 586.
Stringfellow, Rev. William: *see* Strengfellow.
Strode (Stroode), Col. John, iii. 395, n. 3; as governor of Dover Castle: entertains E, &c., iii. 395, 409, 411, 610, 615; buried, iv. 506, n. 4.
Strode (Strood), Sir Nicholas, iii. 379 & nn. 3, 4; social, iii. 379, 391 & n. 1(?), 402; geneal., iii. 395, n. 3.
Strongfellow, Rev. William (iv. 641, n. 5): *see* Strengfellow.
Stroode, Sir Edward: error for Sir N. Strode (?), iii. 391 & n. 1.
Stroud, Glos.: road from, to Gloucester, iii. 118, n. 5.
Stuart: house of: approaching extinction of, iv. 646; Presbyterian hatred of, v. 12; in exile: relic belonging to, iv. 470, n. 2.
Stuart of Aubigny family: geneal., iv. 39, n. 4.
Stuart, —: social, v. 27.
Stuart, Charles, third duke of Richmond and sixth duke of Lennox, iii. 354, n. 3; visits Sayes Court, iii. 354; dies during embassy to Denmark, iv. 76 & n. 1; geneal., iii. 310, n. 1; iv. 39, n. 4.
Stuart, Elizabeth: *see* Howard, Elizabeth, countess of Arundel.
Stuart, Esme, third duke of Lennox: geneal., ii. 543, n. 4.
Stuart, Frances, duchess of Richmond, wife of Charles Stuart, third duke, &c.: geneal., iii. 621, n. 5.
Stuart, James, duke of Cambridge, iii. 380 & n. 3.
Stuart, James, fourth duke of Lennox and first duke of Richmond, ii. 28, n. 3; funeral of (?), ii. 28 & n. 3 (i. 20); portraits of, iii. 96, n. 3; geneal., iii. 260, n. 3, 310 & n. 1.
Stuart, Katherine: *see* O'Brien, Katherine, Lady O'Brien, Baroness Clifton.
Stuart, Ludovic, tenth seigneur d'Aubigny, iii. 48, n. 9; character, &c., iii. 310 & n. 1; house of, in Paris: Lord Norwich at, iii. 48; appointed almoner to Queen Catherine, iii. 310; hears A. Morus preach, iii. 311; marries Sir S. Tuke, iii. 373.
Stuart, Ludovick, second duke of Lennox and duke of Richmond: funeral of (?), ii. 28 & n. 3 (i. 20).
Stuart, Mary, duchess of Lennox and of Richmond, wife of James Stuart, fourth duke of Lennox, &c.: portrait of, iii. 260 & n. 3.
Stuart, Sophia, maid of honour to Queen Catherine, iii. 621, n. 5.
Stufe di San Germano, ii. 340 & n. 5.
Stydolf, Elizabeth, Lady Stydolf: *see* Byron, Elizabeth, Baroness Byron.

Stydolf (Stidolph), Sir Francis: estate of, at Mickleham, iii. 157 & n. 5; geneal., iv. 137, n. 4.
Stydolf (Stiddolph), Sir Richard, bt.: geneal., iii. 157, n. 5; iv. 137, n. 4.
Styrum (Stirumm), General (Hermann Otto, Graf zu Limburg-Styrum, &c.): defeated at Höchstädt, 1703, v. 546 & n. 3.
Styx, river: source of, ii. 346 & n. 6.
Suares, Antonio: inscription set up by, ii. 333.
Suarez de Figueróa y Cordóba, Don Gomez: *see* Feria, duke of.
Succari: *see* Zuccari.
Sudbury, John, D.D., dean of Durham, iv. 109, n. 2; sermons by, iv. 109, 167.
Suffolk: control of Sick and Wounded in, iii. 395, n. 1, 620, n. 1; churches of: condition of, iv. 118; gentry of: visit Euston, iii. 590; case of clipping in, v. 256 & n. 6.
Suffolk: Duke of: *see* Brandon, Charles.
Suffolk: Earls, &c., of: *see* Howard, Thomas, first earl, 1603–26; Howard, Theophilus, second earl, 1626–40; Howard, James, third earl, 1640–89; Howard, Barbara, his countess; Howard, George, fourth earl, 1689–91; Howard, Henry, fifth earl, 1691–1709.
Suidas: account by, of Lucian's death, v. 146, n. 2.
Sulaiman the Magnificent: gift to, from Ferdinand I, iii. 112, n. 1.
Summerhill: *see* Somerhill.
Summers, —: *see* Somers, Sir John, Baron Somers.
Sunderland: Earls and Countesses of: *see* Spencer, Henry, first earl, 1643; Spencer, Dorothy, his countess; Spencer, Robert, second earl, 1643–1702; Spencer, Anne, his countess; Spencer, Charles, third earl, 1702–22; Spencer, Anne, his countess.
Sundials, ii. 373, n. 5, 529 & n. 4; iii. 113 & n. 5.
Sunninghill, Berks.: Sir T. Draper of, v. 194.
Surat: Sir J. Chardin at, iv. 212, n. 2.
Surbiton, Surrey: Lord Francis Villiers killed near, ii. 541–2 & n.
Surgery: *see* Medicine and Surgery.
Surinam (Syrenam): conduct of Dutch in, as a cause of Third Dutch War, iii. 606, n. 1; commissioners to be sent to, for removal of Charles II's subjects from, &c., iv. 36 & n. 1, 44, 47, 48; letter from, at Royal Society, iv. 196–7 & n.
Surrenden (in Pluckley, Kent): Sir E. Dering of, iv. 203 & n. 1.
Surrey: 'my sweet and native country', &c., iii. 143, 210; air of, ii. 4.
  controlled by parliament in Civil War, i. 53; petition from, to house of commons, 1648: bearers of, attacked, &c., ii. 541 & n. 2; ~ a bearer, iii. 196, n. 4; addresses from: to Charles II, 1681, iv. 248 & nn. 4, 5; ~ to William III, 1697, v. 279 & n. 1; gentry of: at funeral of George Evelyn, v. 360 & n. 1; parliamentary elections for: Feb. 1679, iv. 164–5 & n.; Aug. 1679, iv. 165, n. 1, 224, n. 2; 1685, iv. 433–4 & nn.; 1701, v. 482 *bis* & n. 3; 1702, v. 511–12 & n.; 1705, v. 595 & n. 4; assize at Southwark for part of, iv. 276, n. 4.
  officers: lord lieutenant, 1682–1701: *see* Howard, Henry seventh duke of Norfolk; deputy-lieutenants: *see* Evelyn, George (v. 169–70, 358); Evelyn, George, of Nutfield (v. 169–70); sheriffs [*see also* Surrey and Sussex: united sheriffdom]: *see* Burton, James (1672–3; iv. 352 & n. 1); Lewen, S. (1684–5; iv. 433–4 & n.); Wessell, L. (1699–1700; v. 512, n. 1); ~ Sir John Evelyn of Godstone excused from serving as, iii. 365; under-sheriff: takes possession of Lambeth Palace, 1691, v. 59 & n. 2; receiver-general: *see* Weston, John (v. 482, n. 3).
  archdeacon of: *see* Stephens, W.
Surrey: fourth Earl of, 1604–46: *see* Howard, Thomas, earl of Arundel.
Surrey and Kent Commission of Sewers, iii. 151, n. 6; E has business with, iii. 151 & n. 6, 153, 191; E declines serving on, 1658, iii. 223; E joins, 1660, iii. 258; case before, iii. 353; sittings of,

Surrey and Kent Commission of Sewers (*cont.*)
iv. 25 & n. 7, 30–1; new commission for, 1685(?): E qualifies for, iv. 490–1, 496.
Surrey and Sussex: united sheriffdom of, ii. 2, n. 1; Richard Evelyn, sen., as sheriff, 1633–4, ii. 2 (i. 1), 11–12 & nn. (i. 9–10).
Susa, in Persia: in sermon, v. 84.
Susa, in Piedmont: taken by French, 1690, v. 39, n. 5; attacked by Victor Amadeus, 1691, v. 71 & n. 4.
Susorius, St.: *see* Sorore, Blessed.
Sussex: marble from: used in Salisbury cathedral, iii. 113, n. 2.
controlled by parliament in Civil War, i. 53; address from, to Charles II, 1660, iii. 249 & n. 5; control of Sick and Wounded in, iii. 388; i. *18*; militia of: called out, to guard against French, 1696, v. 233 & n. 1.
families: Comber, ii. 3 (i. 4); Eversfield (Aresfield), v. 359; Petty: county of Sir William's father (?), iv. 56 & n. 6; Shirley, iii. 230, n. 2; Stansfield: extinct, iii. 89, n. 3.
sheriff of: *see* Surrey and Sussex: united sheriffdom.
Sussex: Earls, &c., of: *see* Radcliffe, Thomas, third earl; *new creation*: *see* Savile, James, second earl, 1659–71; *new creation*: *see* Lennard, Thomas, earl 1674–1715; Lennard, Anne, his countess.
Sutton, Surrey: Lady Darcy's house at, ii. 11 & n. 3 (i. 9); manor of, ii. 10, n. 7, 11, n. 3; rector of: *see* Stephens, W.
Sutton, Sir Edward, bt.: performs on Irish harp, iii. 518 & n. 6.
Sutton at Hone, lathe of, Kent: foot regiment raised in, iii. 254, n. 4.
Sutton on Derwent, Yorks.: estate at, v. 411 & n. 1.
Swale, river, Kent: fortifications along, 1672, iii. 610.
Swallow, river: *see* Mole.
Swallowfield, Berks.: house at, of Henry Hyde, second earl of Clarendon: notice, iv. 480–2 & nn.; ~ visit to, iv. 558–9; church service at, iv. 482; 'maiden of primitive life' at, iv. 482–3.
Sweden: climate of, iv. 220–1; ~ winter, 1661–2, iii. 311; despotic power in, v. 402; king of: prophecy by P. Grebner applied to a, iii. 137 & n. 2; relics of St. Bridget in, ii. 246, n. 8.
invades Germany in Thirty Years' War, ii. 7 & n. 1 (i. 7); invades Poland, 1655, iii. 161 & n. 3; at war with Denmark, 1677, iv. 332–3 & n.; Denmark helped against, 1683, iv. 332; Russia declares war against, 1700, v. 429 & n. 4; *see further* Wars: Great Northern War: campaigns 1700–4.
Sweerts, Michael: painting by (?), iv. 403 & n. 8.
Sweet (Sweat), Sir Giles, D.C.L.; knighted 1664, iii. 362 & n. 1; at Archbishop Sheldon's translation to Canterbury, iii. 362; as law professor at Oxford: speech by, &c., iii. 533 & n. 4, 535.
Swimming, &c.: discussed, iii. 490; experiment in diving, iii. 351; reviving drowned men: letter concerning, iii. 601.
Switzerland and the Swiss:
political: general remarks on, ii. 518 & nn. 1–3; (as Helvetia) trade-route from, to Italy, ii. 506; the cantons: number and religious division of, ii. 518 & n. 1; ~ as allies of Valais and Geneva, ii. 515, n. 1, 520, n. 6, 525–6.
— defeat of, at Marignano, 1515, ii. 490, n. 10; French pressure on, 1690, v. 35 & n. 8; fear French attack, v. 39 & n. 5; subjected to French control by Peace of Ryswick, v. 270; relations of, with France, 1701, v. 441; French protestants seek refuge in: 1685, iv. 448, 485 & n. 1; ~ 1699, v. 321 & n. 2; ~ from Orange, 1703, v. 544; Waldenses seek refuge in protestant cantons, v. 3.
characteristics, &c.: general (Simplon, Valais), ii. 510–11 & nn., 517; the blunt Swiss, ii. 517; the grim Swiss, ii. 512 & n. 1; *add.*; dress, ii. 510–11 & n., 517 & n. 3; iii. 41; goitre, ii. 510 & nn. 3, 4; ~ alluded to, ii. 522, 530; language (Valais, &c), ii. 511 & n. 2; stature, ii. 296 & n. 8, 511; customs: beech-leaves

Switzerland and the Swiss (*cont.*)
used in mattresses, ii. 507, n. 6; wine sent to distinguished travellers, ii. 518 & n. 6.
military service abroad: general, ii. 517 & n. 5, 518; in France, ii. 136 (i. 89), 516; iii. 41–2, 43; at Milan, ii. 494; in Papal service, ii. 214, n. 2, 279, 280, 296–7 & n.; in Tuscany, ii. 187 (i. 118).
individuals [excluding persons at Geneva]: Hans Gross, ii. 214, n. 2; E's guide for Simplon Pass, ii. 508, 513, 515; E's host at Sion, ii. 515–17; 'president' at St. Maurice, ii. 518; hostess at Le Bouveret, ii. 519; travellers in France, iii. 12.
Sydnie, Algernon: *see* Sidney.
Sydney of Penshurst: Baron, 1689–98: *see* Sidney, Robert, fourth earl of Leicester.
Sydney of Sheppey: Viscount, 1689–94: *see* Sidney, Henry, earl of Romney.
Sydserff, Thomas; bishop of Galloway 1635; of Orkney, 1662, iii. 9, n. 1; ordains Anglican divines, Paris, 1650, iii. 8–9, 633.
Sylvius, Ann, Lady Sylvius, born Howard, wife of Sir Gabriel, iii. 529, n. 6 *ad fin.*; as Ann Howard: trust on behalf of, iv. 67, 70, 71, n. 1, 105–6, 106; attends assize at Northampton, iv. 67–71 & nn.; describes an apparition, iv. 100–1; on pleasure-journey, iii. 529; social, iv. 34–5 & n., 50, 67, 88, 109; marries Sylvius, iv. 123 & n. 4; as Lady Sylvius: goes to Holland, iv. 124; E's *Life of Mrs. Godolphin* written for, iv. 429 & n. 1; resident at St. James's Palace, iv. 155; at Bagshot Park, iv. 558; social, iv. 131, 134–5, 155, 185, 192 *bis*, 202, 204, 257 *bis*, 388, 420, 432, 448, 520; v. 171.
Sylvius, Professor Frans de la Boe: presents book to Royal Society, iii. 583 & n. 8.
Sylvius, Sir Gabriel (de); knighted 1670, iii. 471, n. 3; *add.*; granted patent for export of Irish wool, iii. 488, n. 4; marries Ann Howard, iv. 123 & n. 4; as steward to William III of Orange: goes to Holland, iv. 124 & n. 4; resident at St. James's Palace, iv. 155; as envoy to Denmark, 1685: takes leave of E, iv. 447 & n. 2, 448; ~ chaplain of: describes persecution of French protestants, iv. 447–8 & nn.; social, iii. 471; iv. 102, 155, 266, 312.
Symmachus (Simmachus), pope: and S. Giovanni in Laterano, ii. 274 & n. 4; builds Vatican, ii. 295.
Symonds, Richard: lodgings of, at: Naples, ii. 325, n. 5; ~ Roanne, ii. 533, n. 3; ~ Venice, ii. 429, n. 5.
Symons, Abraham: *see* Simon.
Sympson, John, Independent divine: sermon by (?), iii. 223 & n. 1.
Synod of Dort: meeting-place of, ii. 32 & n. 5 (i. 25); member of, ii. 521, n. 1.
Syon House (Sion), Isleworth: notice, iii. 414–15 & nn.; Privy Council meets at, 1665, *ib.*; Princess Anne retires to, 1692, v. 90 & n. 2, 98, n. 1.
Syrenam: *see* Surinam.
Syria: E desires to visit, ii. 451; I. Basire visits, iii. 303, n. 3; imports from, at Marseilles, ii. 166 (i. 105); sea-weed from, used in glass-making, ii. 467 & n. 5.
Syriac language: scholar in, iv. 172.
Syrophoenician woman: in sermons, iii. 273; v. 471.
Szalankemen: *see* Slankamen.

Taafe, Theobald: second Viscount Taafe 1642; earl of Carlingford 1661, iii. 487, n. 4; project of, for making fuel, iii. 487; social, iii. 577 & n. 1.
Taafe: second Viscount, 1642–61: *see* Taafe, Theobald, later earl of Carlingford.
Tabor *or* Talbor, Sir Robert: use of quinine by, iv. 325 & n. 5; v. 197.
Tacca, Pietro, sculptor, ii. 93, n. 1; works by: Boar (bronze), Florence, ii. 194 & n. 7 (i. 120); Slaves, monument to Ferdinand I, Leghorn, ii. 183 & n. 7 (i. 116); finishes Henri IV, Paris, ii. 93, n. 1; false attribution, ii. 194, & n. 6 (i. 120).
Tadcaster (Todcaster), Yorks., iii. 128.

Tadda, Francesco *or* R. di F. del: statue attributed to, ii. 185, n. 5.
Tailor, Rev. —: funeral sermon by, iii. 185.
Tailor, Dr. — (Thomas Taylor?): sermon by, iv. 195 & n. 4.
Tain, on the Rhone, ii. 159 (i. 102).
Talbor: *see* Tabor *or* Talbor, Sir R.
Talbot family: arms of, iii. 336, n. 1.
Talbot, —, married to Robert Pierrepont, first earl of Kingston, iii. 128, n. 1.
Talbot, Alathea: *see* Howard, Alathea, countess of Arundel.
Talbot, Anna Maria, countess of Shrewsbury, wife of Francis Talbot, eleventh earl: as Buckingham's mistress, iii. 596 & n. 4.
Talbot, Charles; twelfth earl, 1668, and duke, 1694, of Shrewsbury, iv. 181, n. 4; appointed secretary of state, &c., v. 177 & n. 2; as commissioner for Greenwich Hospital, v. 209–10; resigns Lord Chamberlainship (error), v. 406 & n. 2; social, iv. 181; geneal., iv. 501 & n. 2.
Talbot, Elizabeth, countess of Shrewsbury ('Bess of Hardwick'), wife of George Talbot, sixth earl: builds Worksop Abbey, iii. 127, n. 2.
Talbot, Frances, duchess of Tyrconnel; born Jennings; wife of (i) Sir George Hamilton; (ii) Col. Richard Talbot, earl, 1685, and duke, 1689, of Tyrconnel: as Lady Hamilton, iv. 79 & n. 3; as countess of Hamilton (?), iv. 108 & n. 3.
Talbot, Francis, eleventh earl of Shrewsbury: duel of, with Buckingham, &c., iii. 596, n. 4; iv. 453, n. 2.
Talbot, Sir Gilbert, master of the Jewel House, iii. 332, n. 3; brings the Royal Society its mace, iii. 332 & n. 3; proposes Bergen expedition, 1665, iii. 618, n. 3; social, iii. 626; iv. 566.
Talbot, Gilbert, seventh earl of Shrewsbury: geneal., ii. 479, n. 4.
Talbot, John: killed in duel (in text as Mr. Stanley, in error), iv. 501 & n. 2.
Talbot, Sir John, of Lacock Abbey: geneal., iv. 453 & n. 2.
Talbot, Mrs. Katherine, born Boynton, first wife of Col. Richard Talbot, later duke of Tyrconnel, iv. 15, n. 8; social, iv. 15(?), 86.
Talbot, Richard; created earl, 1685, and duke, 1689, of Tyrconnel, iv. 23, n. 2; as Col. Talbot: his two wives, iv. 15, n. 8, 79, n. 3; social, iii. 23, 86; as Tyrconnel: appointed lieutenant-general in Ireland, iv. 514 & n. 4; intrigues against Henry Hyde, second earl of Clarendon, iv. 527 & n. 2; appointed lord deputy of Ireland, iv. 535–6 & n.; appointed J. P. for Middlesex, iv. 536, n. 3; army, &c., of: danger to Ireland from, iv. 622, 630–1; Col. R. Hamilton's negotiation with, v. 28 & n. 5; holds Limerick, v. 31 & n. 1; withdraws to France, v. 35.
Talbot, Sharington: killed in duel, iv. 453 & n. 2.
Talbot, William, D.D.; bishop of Oxford 1699; of Salisbury 1715; of Durham 1721: sermon by, v. 558–9 & n.
Tallard, Camille d'Hostun, duc d'Hostun, comte de, v. 285, n. 3; as French ambassador to England, v. 285 & n. 3; captured at Blenheim, v. 574; brought to England, v. 583 & n. 5.
Tallemant, Marie: *see* Ruvigny, Marie de Massue, marquise de.
Talmash: *see* Tollemache.
Tangier: ceded to Charles II, iii. 305 & n. 4; Peterborough to take possession of, *ib.*; iii. 311 & n. 5; Peterborough returns from, iii. 327 & n. 7; Henry Howard, Baron Howard (later sixth duke of Norfolk), at, iii. 528, n. 4; attacked by Moors, iv. 208 & n. 6, 299 & n. 2; considered untenable (1680), iv. 209–10; peace at: embassy from Morocco to negotiate, iv. 266 & n. 4; evacuated, iv. 379 & n. 3.
  garrison: waiting to sail for, 1662, iii. 311 & n. 5; strength of, 1680, iv. 209 & n. 2; men from, killed, iv. 299 & n. 2; deserter from, iv. 265, n. 6; troops from, iv. 354, n. 3.
  mole :builder of, iv. 54 & n. 5.
  governors: *see* Mordaunt, Henry, earl of Peterborough (1662–3;

Tangier (*cont.*)
iii. 305, n. 4, 311, n. 5); O'Brien, William, earl of Inchiquin (1675–80; iv. 208, n. 6); Butler, Thomas, earl of Ossory (governor-designate, 1680; iv. 208 & n. 5, &c.); lieutenant-governor, &c.: *see* Norwood, Col. H.; treasurer for: *see* Hewer, W.
Tan Hill (St. Anne's Hill), Wilts., iii. 116 & n. 3.
Tankersley, Yorks.: Sir Richard Fanshawe at, iii. 123, n. 3.
Tankerville: Earl of, 1695–1701: *see* Grey, Forde, Baron Grey of Warke.
Tapestry *or* Arras: sets described: Hampton Court, iii. 323 & nn. 1, 3; Paris, St. Etienne-du-Mont, ii. 568 & n. 2; Whitehall, duchess of Portsmouth (the *Maisons Royales*), iv. 343 & n. 2.
diplomatic gift of, iv. 262; hung in streets for processions, ii. 146 (i. 94), 536; iii. 246, 280; imitations of: dyed cloth, iii. 539–40; ~ painted, ii. 117 (i. 76); ~ painter of, ii. 399; hangings, &c., mentioned, ii. 70 (i. 46), 151 (i. 98), 418, 494; iii. 480, 560.
word used figuratively, ii. 133; verb, ii. 70 (i. 46), 224, 434.
Taplow, Bucks.: Cliveden Park in, iv. 176–7 & n.
Tara: first Viscount: *see* Preston, Thomas.
Tarare (Tarrara): situation, &c., ii. 156 (i. 100); E at, ii. 533.
Targoni, Pompeo: tabernacle made by, ii. 272 & n. 5.
Tarquin: in sermon, v. 162.
Tarquiniensis Lacus (lake of Bolsena), ii. 209 & nn. 6, 8.
Tartars: Russians take Perekop from, 1689, iv. 645 & n. 6; error for Turks (?), v. 6 & n. 5, 258 & n. 5.
Tatham, John: devises Lord Mayors' shows, iii. 259, n. 4, 301, n. 4, 388, n. 6; *see also* iii. 342, n. 1.
Tattershall, George: geneal., iii. 154, n. 5.
Tattershall, Mary: *see* Howard, Mrs. M.
Tatti, Jacopo d'Antonio: *see* Sansovino.
Taubman, Matthew: devises Lord Mayor's show, iv. 528, n. 5.
Taunton, Somerset: Monmouth proclaimed king at, iv. 449, n. 1; men of, in Monmouth's rebellion, iv. 452, n. 2.
Tauriscus: sculptor of Toro Farnese, ii. 216.
Tayleur, William (Captain Taylor): charges of, against Lord Mordaunt, iii. 468–9 & nn.
Taylor, Jeremy, D.D.; bishop of Down and Connor 1661, iii. 94 & n. 8.
relations with E: becomes E's spiritual father, iii. 149; i. *11*; dines at Sayes Court, iii. 169–70 & n.; E introduces J. Le Franc to, &c., iii. 171 & nn. 3, 4, 172; receives copy of E's *Lucretius*, iii. 173, n. 2; shows E MS. of *Ductor Dubitantium*, iii. 190 & n. 6; baptizes George Evelyn (E's son), iii. 194; recommends L. Moody (?) to E, iii. 195 & n. 3; condoles with E for little Richard Evelyn, iii. 209, n. 1, 211.
house of, in London: divine service at, iii. 212 & n. 1; on Perfectionists, iii. 363, n. 2; relations of, with: countess of Rutland, iii. 95, n. 5; ~ Sir E. Thurland, iii. 219, n. 2.
sermons by, iii. 95 *ter*, 148, 149, 197, 201, 202, 211, 212.
geneal., iv. 195.
See also Books mentioned in text.
Taylor, Mary: *see* Marsh, Mrs. M.
Taylor, Thomas, D.C.L.: sermon by (?), iv. 195 & n. 4.
Te Deum: origin of, ii. 500 & n. 3.
Teignmouth (Tinmouth), Devon: destroyed by French, v. 30 & n. 5.
Teile: *see* Tiel.
Tekely: *see* Tökölyi, Count E.
Tekoah, Woman of: parable of: in sermon, v. 348–9.
Tell: Duke of: *see* Georg Wilhelm, duke of Celle.
Temesvar: battle near (battle on the Bega), 1696, v. 258 & n. 6, 260 & n. 1; *add.*
Tempesta, Antonio, ii. 267, n. 4; paintings by, ii. 267, 406, n. 7; etching by: source for Diary, ii. 279, n. 3.
Temple, Anne: *see* Lyttelton, Anne, Lady Lyttelton.

Temple, Dorothy, Lady Temple, born Osborne, wife of Sir William: on *Merlin* yacht, 1671, iii. 606, n. 1; helps Lady Ogle to escape, iv. 267, n. 2; geneal., iii. 13, n. 5, 602, n. 1.
Temple, John, son of Sir William: occupies Temple's house at Sheen, iv. 576, n. 4.
Temple, Sir John: dies, v. 587 & n. 4.
Temple, Sir Purbeck, v. 214, n. 2; social, v. 214; dies, &c., v. 219 & n. 1; estate of: law-suit relating to, v. 247–8 & n.; burial-place of, v. 386; house of: *see* Addiscombe.
Temple, Sarah, Lady Temple, born Draper, wife of Sir Purbeck, v. 194, n. 1; godmother of Thomas Draper, v. 194; as aunt of William Draper, v. 214, 219; engaged in law-suit, v. 247–8; funeral and will of, v. 385–6; legacy of, to William Draper, v. 383, 385–6; ~ *see also* v. 425.
Temple, Thomas: geneal., iv. 576, n. 3.
Temple, William: contests Sir Purbeck Temple's will(?), v. 247–8 & n.
Temple, Sir William, bt., the diplomatist, iv. 143, n. 2; offered secretaryship of state, 1674, iv. 39, n. 1; appointed ambassador at Nimeguen, 1675, iv. 76, n. 3; concern of, in marriage of Lady Ogle to T. Thynne, iv. 266–7 & n.; house and garden of, at Sheen, iv. 143 & nn. 1, 2, 576 & n. 4; geneal., v. 214, n. 2, 587, n. 4.
Tenda pass, Piedmont: losses of Victor Amadeus II on, 1697, v. 264 & n. 5.
Tenerife (Tenariffe): Peak of: E forwards account of, to Royal Society, iii. 274 & n. 3.
Tenison, Mrs. Anne, wife of Archbishop Tenison, v. 239, n. 2; apartment of, at Lambeth, v. 239, 294.
Tenison, Thomas; D.D. 1680; bishop of Lincoln 1691; archbishop of Canterbury 1694, iv. 106, n. 4.
— benefices, &c.: minister at St. Peter Mancroft, Norwich, *ib.*; vicar of St. Martin in the Fields; appointed, iv. 224, n. 1; rector of St. James, Piccadilly, iv. 500, n. 1; bishop of Lincoln: nominated, &c., v. 79 & n. 2; *commendam* for livings of St. Martin and St. James, v. 376 & n. 1; archbishop of Canterbury: nominated, v. 198 & n. 5; ~ enthroned, v. 213, n. 5.
— character and preaching of, iv. 307–8 & n.; v. 198; relations of, with E, i. *30, 33–4, 35*; views of, i. *105*.
— general activities: (i) warns his friends about William of Orange's projected invasion, iv. 592 & n. 3; as trustee for Boyle Lectures, v. 88, 161, 196–7, 198–9, 224, 238, 273, 362, 536, 583 & n. 3; on Queen Mary's papers, v. 205 & n. 5; *add.*; as commissioner for Greenwich Hospital, v. 209–10, 219; asked to interest himself in royal library, St. James's, v. 224, 323; presents Wren and E to William III, v. 399; as member of Society for Propagation of the Gospel, v. 507.
— — (ii) benefactions: general, v. 66; library for St. Martin in the Fields, iv. 367–8 & n., 369, 455; school for St. Martin in the Fields, iv. 368, n. 1, 584, n. 5; founds Trinity Chapel, Bond Street, v. 61–2 & n., 66; tabernacle erected by (Golden Square ?), v. 136 & n. 4.
— — (iii) patronage: E recommends to him: Dr. Ralph Bohun, v. 256; ~ Dr. W. Graham, v. 256–7; ~ Dr. T. Hoy, v. 298; ~ Rev. W. Strengfellow, v. 27, 61–2, 376; ~ Rev. W. Wells, v. 199.
— religious activities: (i) controversy of, with Father Andrew Pulton, iv. 540, n. 1; opposes Socinians, v. 231, n. 1; ~ in sermon, v. 56–7; dissatisfied with Canon Law, v. 256; on case of conscience, v. 338–9.
— — (ii) ministration: attends Monmouth in the Tower, &c., iv. 456 & n. 1; baptizes Jane Evelyn, 1692, v. 84; administers Sacrament, v. 85; marries: William Draper and Susanna Evelyn, v. 138; ~ Philip Meadows and Dorothy Boscawen, v. 258; ~ (Sir) John

Tenison, Thomas (*cont.*)
Evelyn and Anne Boscawen, v. 609.
— — (iii) sermons by: excellence of, as preacher, iv. 106, 307, 650; power of, on emotions, iv. 544; printed sermons, iv. 641 & n. 2, 652, n. 4; v. 43, n. 1, 79, n. 2; *see also* iv. 308, n. 2; inaugural sermon at Trinity Chapel, v. 62–5; ordinary sermons, iv. 106, 195, 224, 240, 258, 279, 292–6, 307–9, 350–2, 374, 415–16, 433–6, 500–6, 530–51, 564–89, 599–630, 644–54; v. 1–27, 38–109, 132–3 *passim & singulatim*; catechizes, iv. 259–60 & nn., 269, 286 & n. 4; appointed to preach, iv. 372, n. 3; Dr. R. Bohun preaches for, iv. 590; attends sermon, v. 271.
— personal and social: illnesses, iv. 366, 372, 374; v. 291; buys Tillotson's furniture, &c., at Lambeth, v. 213; lodging of, in Whitehall, v. 273; visits Sir S. Morland, v. 221–2; on author of *Whole Duty of Man*, v. 112 & n. 5; account of Mark Quin by, v. 170 & n. 3; social: parties, iv. 388, 420, 454, 520, 543, 643, 646, 647; v. 8, 25, 105, 127; ~ as archbishop, v. 221, 224, 238, 239, 280, 294, 353, 383, 440, 508 (*see also* p. 507), 568, 597; alone, &c., iv. 475, 585, 603; v. 8, 80, 195; ~ as archbishop, v. 203, 205, 213, 293 *bis*, 529, 560.
— chaplain(s) of: sermons by, v. 329–30, 332–3; *see also* Gibson, E.
Tennet: Earls, &c., of: *see* Thanet.
Tennis: courts, ii. 112 (i. 72), 118 (i. 76); iii. 129, 180; match, ii. 563.
Tenterden: Earl of, 1692–5 (Jacobite creation): *see* Hales, Sir Edward.
Terence: MSS. of, ii. 198 & n. 11, 301 & n. 5; read by Mary Evelyn, iv. 423.
Terracina: notice, ii. 320–1 & nn.; Via Appia near, ii. 316, n. 3 *ad fin.*, 319 & n. 3.
Terra di Lavoro (Campania): fertility of, ii. 324–5 & nn.
Terrasso, Marco, lapidary, ii. 480 & n. 2.
Terryll, Sir Timothy: *see* Tyrrell.
Tertullian: in sermons, &c., v. 106, 419.
Tettuccio, river, ii. 410 & n. 4.
Teverone *or* Aniene, river (the ancient Anio): bridges over, ii. 393–4 & nn.; falls of, ii. 397 & n. 1.
Teves y Guzman, Don Gaspar de: *see* Fuente, Marques de la.
Teviot: Viscount of, 1685–94: *see* Spencer, Robert.
Tewkesbury, Glos.: in view, iii. 119.
Texel, the: battles of, 1653, 1673, iii. 87 & n. 3.; iv. 24, n. 5; storm in, 1697, v. 267 & n. 5.
Textiles [select: simple notices of common materials, or materials frequently mentioned, such as silk, are not indexed. *See also* Dress; Embroidery; Tapestry]:
bays and says: manufacture and export of, iii. 177 & n. 4.
blankets, ii. 293; iii. 209.
brocatell, iii. 531 & n. 3.
calico, i. 31; iii. 108 & n. 1; iv. 266; gummed, iii. 374 & n. 4; painted or stained, v. 378, n. 1.
camlet (chamblett), ii. 145, n. 9; manufacture of, ii. 146 (i. 94); iii. 65 & n. 8.
canvas, ii. 165 (i. 104), 174 (i. 110), 184.
carpets: Persian, iii. 349; iv. 262.
chintz, iii. 426, n. 1.
cloth: manufacture of: treatise on, iii. 304 & n. 3; at Bourges, i. 99 & n. 2; at Colchester, &c., iii. 176, n. 4, 177 & n. 4; at Dedham, iii. 178 & n. 3; at Ipswich, iv. 115 & n. 8; at Norwich, iii. 595 & n. 2; Somerset: clothworkers in, iv. 452 & n. 5.
— blue: spread on processional route, iii. 284 & n. 3; ~ in Valais, ii. 517 & n. 3; stained like tapestry, iii. 539–40.
cloth of gold or silver, ii. 434; iii. 246, 280, 349, 373, 531.
cloth of tissue, ii. 422.
damask, ii. 533, n. 2; beds, ii. 533 & n. 2; chair covered with, iii. 633; coach cushions, iv. 72; hangings, &c., ii. 146 (i. 94), 151 (i. 98), 224; manufacture of, ii. 200; robes, ii. 280, 449; iii. 479, 533; for sale, ii. 434.

Textiles (*cont.*)
drap de Berry, i. 99 & n. 2.
flannel, iv. 141.
galloon, silver, i. 9.
grogram: manufacture of, ii. 146 (i. 94); iii. 65 & n. 8.
Indian hangings, ii. 540.
lace: point de Venise, ii. 448.
lawn, ii. 448.
linen, ii. 42 (i. 31), 293, 426; iv. 141, 285.
lustrèe, ii. 448 & n. 4.
mat, i. 110.
muslin, v. 377.
New Draperies, iii. 177, n. 4, 178, n. 3, 595, n. 2.
Norwich stuff, iii. 595 & n. 2.
pintado: hangings of, iii. 425–6 & n.; import of: to be prohibited, v. 377–8 & n.
rug, ii. 125 (i. 80).
sarsenet, i. 9; iii. 494.
satin, ii. 11 (i. 9), 416; glossing of, iii. 65, n. 8.
silk [general; such materials as damask (*see above*) are silks]: Indian, flowered with gold, iv. 285; Moroccan (?), iv. 266; ornamenting Turkish harness, ii. 504; iv. 399; manufacture of or trade in: East Indian, iii. 424; at Florence, ii. 200; at Geneva, ii. 524, n. 5; in London: manufacture of, in Moorfields, iii. 65 & n. 8; ~ sales of: effects on, of William III's death, v. 493; at Marseilles, ii. 166 (i. 105); in kingdom of Naples, ii. 352; at Tours, ii. 145–6 & n. (i. 94); at Venice, ii. 434.
— sleave-silk: used in embroidery, iii. 374 & n. 5; wrought: Indian, v. 378, n. 1; stockings: machine for weaving, iii. 285 & n. 3; silkwork flowers, ii. 447, 473; silkworms: treatise on, iii. 524 & n. 3; attempt to introduce into England, iii. 96, n. 7; proposal to introduce into American colonies, iii. 602.
stockings: made at Doncaster, iii. 127 & n. 5; *see also* silk *above*.
taffeta, ii. 448; iii. 349.
tiffany, ii. 447 & n. 7.
tissue, ii. 151 (i. 98); cloth of, ii. 422.
velvet: books bound in, iii. 129;

Textiles (*cont.*)
dresses or horse-trappings of: in processions, ii. 280, 281; iii. 41, 42, 57, 224, 246, 280; ~ Turkish, iv. 399; furnishings or hangings of, ii. 34, 114 (i 73), 128 (i. 82), 146 (i. 94), 151 (i. 98), 235; iii. 323, 349(?); ~ ecclesiastical, iv. 397; ~ for coach, iv. 259; manufacture of, ii. 200; paintings on, ii. 277; robes, ii. 449.
unspecified: journeymen weavers: petition of, to parliament, 1697, v. 263, n. 5; weaver's reed, iv. 141.
Thames, river: frozen at Oxford, 1667, iii. 477, n. 2; soil about, iii. 471; water from: quality of, iv. 313 & n. 1; whales in, 1658, 1699, iii. 214–15 & nn.; v. 318–19 & n.
Dutch fleet in, 1667: fear of its attacking London, iii. 484; river defences against, iii. 486 & n. 6; in estuary, iii. 489.
E takes views of (Putney, &c.), ii. 557 & n. 3; Mrs. Evelyn's excursion on, iii. 529.
at Cliveden, iv. 177; at Ham House, iv. 144; at Hammersmith: water from, v. 221–2; at Windsor, iii. 99; ~ water from, supplied to Castle, iv. 317, n. 5.
See also London: topography.
Thames Ditton, Surrey: Robert Hatton at, i. 51; ii. 537.
Thanet, Isle of: cultivation of, &c., iii. 610–11 & n., 615–16; *add.*
Thanet (Tennet): Earls, &c., of: *see* Tufton, Nicholas, third earl 1664–79; Tufton, Elizabeth, his countess; Tufton, Thomas, sixth earl 1684–1729; Tufton, Catherine, his countess.
Thapsus: battle of, v. 179, n. 2.
Thayre (Thyer?), Mr. and Mrs.: E trustee for, iv. 446 & n. 6, 489.
Theatre, the [for individual plays, operas, masques, and ballets *see* Plays; for opera in general *see* Opera]:
actors and actresses: actresses: first appear on London stage, iii. 268, n. 5, 465 & n. 5; ~ *liaisons* of, with nobility, &c., iii. 465–6 & nn.; *see also* iii. 230, n. 3, 309; singer engaged to

Theatre (*cont.*)
sing during plays: payment to, v. 531 & n. 2; unnamed actor at Bath, 1654, iii. 102 & n. 2.
scenery and machines: scenery: for operas, ii. 503; iii. 229 & n. 2; for puppet-theatre, ii. 112 (i. 73); for *Indian Queen*: costliness of, iii. 368–9 & n.; painted by R. Streater, iii. 570 & n. 2; in comparisons, ii. 172 & n. 3 (i. 109); iii. 18 & n. 4, 638; with machines: London, iii. 583 & n. 3; ~ Rome (Bernini), ii. 261 & n. 5; ~ Venice, ii. 449–50 & n.
theatres [buildings, including rooms used for theatrical performances; individual ancient Roman theatres, &c., are not included]: shape of: sites of towns, &c., compared to, ii. 172 & nn. 2, 3 (i. 109), 323, 326; ~ balustrade following, ii. 263; ~ ancient Roman, ii. 482 & n. 2; singing theatre: cupola or, ii. 151 (i. 98); water-theatres (pools with fountains), ii. 392–3 *ter* & nn.; individual theatres: at: Florence, ii. 414; London: *see* London: topography: theatres; Whitehall: theatrical; Paris: Palais-Royal, ii. 134 (i. 87); iii. 31–2 & n.; ~ puppet-theatre, ii. 112–13 (i. 73); Siena, ii. 202; Venice, ii. 449–50 & nn., 474, n. 6; Vicenza: Teatro Olimpico, ii. 482 & nn. 2–5; *see also* ii. 389, n. 1.
miscellaneous: London: performances: in 1648, ii. 539 & n. 5; ~ in 1659 (Davenant's opera), iii. 229 & n. 2; immorality, &c., of, iii. 465, 510–11; iv. 422; ~ in sermon, v. 121; rehearsal, iii. 348; takings from a play, iii. 350 & n. 3; Moroccan ambassador as theatre-goer, iv. 269 & n. 2; episode in a theatre, iv. 470; Venice: seasons for performing, ii. 451 & n. 3, 474.
— nondescript performances: Carnival carts for, at Rome, ii. 382 & n. 1; *commedia dell' arte*, ii. 474, n. 5; drolls, iii. 102 & n. 2; v. 116, n. 1; interludes, iv. 362; puppet-plays, ii. 99 (i. 65); iii. 30, 492 & n. 2

Theatre (*cont.*)
(Punchinello); iv. 362; v. 115–16 & n.; ~ theatre for, ii. 112–13 (i. 73).
— theatrical churches, v. 542 & n. 2.
Thebes, in Egypt: obelisk from, ii. 269 & n. 8.
Theists *or* Deists [the two terms are not differentiated in the seventeenth century]: precursors of (of the Deists), iii. 227, n. 1; Shaftesbury a deist, iv. 328, n. 6; prevalence of, 1700, v. 408; sermons against, v. 143 & n. 2, 340, 414; ~ endowment for, v. 88 & n. 3; alluded to, in sermon (?), v. 390.
Themistocles: saying of, ii. 5 & n. 2 (i. 6).
Theobaldi, —: *see* Tibaldi, P.
Theobalds, Herts.: palace at, ii. 81 & n. 2 (i. 54–5).
Theodore, pope: representation of, ii. 268, n. 1.
Theodore II, tsar of Russia: sends embassy to Charles II, iv. 262–3 & n.
Theodoric: and Coliseum, ii. 249, n. 10; drains marshes at Terracina, &c., ii. 320, n. 6, 321.
Theresa Josepha, Donna, princess of Brazil: dies, v. 560 & n. 1.
Thetford, Norfolk: notice, iv. 113–14 & nn.; titular bishop of: *see* Hickes, G.
Theunisz, Jan: *see* Anthonides, J.
Thicknesse, James, ii. 17, n. 4; E's friendship with, at Oxford, ii. 17–18 (i. 13–14); travels with E, 1643, &c., ii. 82 (i. 56), 151 (i. 98); leaves Padua, ii. 470; death of, i. 14; *see also* ii. 464, n. 2.
Thicknesse (Thickens), Ralph: geneal., ii. 17, n. 4.
Thief, the Penitent: in sermons, iii. 561; iv. 91, 195, 348, 370, 506, 577; v. 114, 116, 146–7, 162, 308, 437, 453–4, 570.
Thiene (Tiene), Count M.: palace designed by, ii. 483 & n. 8.
Thimbleby, Lady Elizabeth: portrait of, iv. 404, n. 3.
Thinn, —: *see* Thynne, Thomas.
Thiss cross, —: *see* Thurscross, T.
Thistlethwaite, Gabriel, D.C.L., iii. 626 & n. 3; sermons by, iii. 626, 627; iv. 76, 194, 238.
Thistleworth: *see* Isleworth.

Thomas, St., the Apostle: relics of, ii. 88 (i. 59), 380; in sermon, v. 460.
Thomas, St., Aquinas: death and relics of, ii. 319 & nn. 1, 2; crucifix which spoke to, ii. 328 & n. 5.
Thomas, St., à Becket: feast of, at English College, Rome, ii. 291 & n. 4; relics of, ii. 289 & n. 8, 365–6 & n.
Thomas of Lancaster, duke of Clarence: and Jean d'Orléans, count of Angoulême, iii. 72, n. 2.
Thomas, Rev. —: sermon by, v. 119.
Thomas, Mary: *see* Beckford, Mary, Lady Beckford.
Thomas, William, D.D.; bishop of St. David's 1677; of Worcester 1683, iv. 5, n. 4; sermon by, iv. 5; appointed to preach, iv. 372, n. 2.
Thomason, George, bookseller: copies of books by E, &c., belonging to, iii. 220, n. 4, 225, n. 3, 235, n. 4, 243, n. 3.
Thomond: sixth Earl of, 1657–91: *see* O'Brien, Henry.
Thompson, Rev. —, curate at Wotton: *see* Tomson.
Thompson, John, criminal, iii. 74, n. 2; identified as robber near Bromley (iii. 69–71, 73, 74).
Thoresby, Ralph: account by, of visit to E, i. *39*; elected F.R.S., v. 277, n. 1.
Thorington, Suffolk: rector of: *see* Pearson, J.
Thornhill, —, iii. 159 & n. 4.
Thornhill, Mrs. Frances, first wife of Col. Richard Thornhill: geneal., iv. 9, n. 4.
Thornhill, Mrs. Joanna, second wife of Col. Richard Thornhill, iv. 9, n. 4; shows E Queen Catherine's toilet-set, iv. 9; social, iv. 32; geneal., iv. 11, n. 2.
Thornhill, Col. Richard: geneal., iv. 9, n. 4.
Thorpe, Derbyshire: Hanson Grange in, iv. 415, n. 2.
Thorpe, James: architect of Audley End (?), iii. 140, n. 7.
Thorpe Hall, near Peterborough, Northants.: notice, iii. 134 & n. 2.
Thorpe-le-Soken, Essex: French minister at, 1683–7: *see* Severin, J.
Thothmes III: erects obelisk, ii. 269, n. 8.
Thou, J. A. de, the historian: geneal., iii. 7 & n. 3.
Thou, J. A. de, jnr.: social, iii. 7 & n. 3.
Three Kings, the: relics of, ii. 496 & n. 2; *see also* Magi.
Thriscoe, Rev. —: *see* Thurscross, T.
Throckmorton, Anne, Lady Throckmorton, wife of Sir Nicholas (1515–71): geneal., i. 9, n. 2.
Throckmorton, Elizabeth: *see* Raleigh, Elizabeth, Lady Raleigh.
Throckmorton, Sir Nicholas, 1515–71: as owner of Beddington, i. 9 & n. 2.
Throckmorton, Sir Nicholas, later Carew, 1644: owner of Beddington, i. 9 & n. 2.
Throckmorton, Raphael; D.D. 1660: sermon by, iii. 149 & n. 5.
Throckmorton, Sir William, knight marshal: social, iii. 458 & n. 1.
Thuanus (J.-A. de Thou), the historian: geneal., iii. 7 & n. 3.
Thulden, T. van: engravings by, ii. 117, n. 3.
Thun, Franz Sigmund, Graf von, Imperial resident in England: social, iv. 365 & n. 5.
Thuren: *see* Turenne.
Thurland, Sir Edward; knighted 1665; judge, iii. 219, n. 2; chamber of: deed sealed in, iii. 509; trial before, iv. 70–1 & n.; social, iii. 219; *see also* Evelyn, John: correspondence.
Thurles, Viscount: *see* Butler, Thomas, earl of Ossory.
Thurloe, John: Sir R. Walsh and, iii. 6, n. 4.
Thurneisser zum Thurn, Leonhard: goldsmith's work by, ii. 192 & n. 1 (i. 119).
Thursby, William: counsel for John Evelyn, jnr. (?), iv. 194 & n. 1.
Thurscross (Thriscoe), Timothy; D.D. 1669, iii. 237, n. 7; taken in custody, Christmas 1657, iii. 204, n. 6 *ad fin.*; social, iii. 237.
Thyer: *see* Thayre.
Thynne, Henry Frederick: social, iv. 178 & n. 4.
Thynne, Lady Isabella, wife of Sir James: portrait of, ii. 549 & n. 9.
Thynne, James, iv. 178, n. 4.
Thynne, Sir James: geneal., ii. 549, n. 9.

Thynne (Thinn), Thomas, iv. 260, n. 4 *ad fin.*; marriage of, to Lady Ogle (later duchess of Somerset), iv. 260–1 & nn.; v. 587, n. 1; ~ prospective examination of, iv. 266–7 & nn.; murder of, iv. 273, 274, n. 1, 276.
Thynne, Thomas, second Viscount Weymouth: geneal., iv. 178, n. 4.
Tibaldi (Theobaldi), Pellegrino, sometimes called Pellegrini, architect, ii. 494, n. 6; buildings designed by, ii. 492, n. 2, 494 & nn. 6, 9.
Tiber, river: as boundary of Latium, ii. 208, n. 4; in inscription, ii. 270; *see also* Rome: topography; Sculpture, ancient.
Tiberius, Roman emperor: at Capri, ii. 326; death of: place of, ii. 350 & n. 3; obelisk dedicated to, ii. 256 & n. 2; intaglio portrait of, ii. 471; in sermon, v. 149.
Ticino, district: relations of, with Swiss cantons, ii. 518, n. 1.
Ticino, river, ii. 506; flints from, for glass-making, ii. 467, n. 5.
Tickhill (Tickel), Yorks., W.R., iii. 127 & n. 4.
Tiel (Teile), on the Waal, ii. 38 (i. 29).
Tiene, Count M.: palace designed by, ii. 483 & n. 8.
Tiepolo, Baiamonte: relics of conspiracy of, ii. 458 & n. 9.
Tiger-baiting, v. 317 & n. 1.
Tilbury, Essex: Queen Elizabeth at, ii. 30 & n. 1 (i. 22); fortifications at, *ib.*; iii. 609 & n. 4.
Tillingbourne stream: at Shere, iv. 111, n. 5; at Wotton, i. *2*.
Tillotson, Mrs. Elizabeth, wife of Dr. John Tillotson: geneal., iii. 104, n. 8, 517, n. 10 *ad fin.*
Tillotson, John, D.D.; archbishop of Canterbury 1691, iii. 517, n. 10.
biographical: inception of, as D.D., Oxford (error), iii. 533 & n. 6; appointed dean of Canterbury, iv. 84, n. 1; appointed dean of St. Paul's, iv. 649 & n. 2; nominated, &c., archbishop of Canterbury, v. 48–9 & n., 80, n. 2; given possession of Lambeth Palace, v. 59 & n. 2, 80, n. 3; last illness of, v. 198 & n. 1; dies, v. 195–6 & n.; furniture, &c., of, at Lambeth: sold,
Tillotson, John (*cont.*)
v. 213; manners of, v. 80; social, v. 25.
as preacher: reads his sermons, iv. 581, n. 3; repeats sermons (?), iv. 371 & n. 1; *see also* iv. 308, n. 4; sermons by: printed, iii. 517–18 & n. (?); iv. 53 & n. 3, 84 & n. 1, 107 & n. 5, 134 & n. 3(?), 156–7 & nn., 166 & n. 4, 198 & n. 1, 240 & n. 6, 277 & n. 3(?), 308 & n. 4(?), 373 & n. 1, 434–5 & n., 529 & n. 6, 628 & n. 2; v. 9 & n. 3; unprinted, iv. 131, 244, 305, 371 & n. 1, 505; mentioned, v. 43, n. 3; appointed to preach, iv. 4, n. 2, 578, n. 2.
geneal., iii. 104, n. 8; v. 80 & n. 3.
Tillotson, Mary: *see* Chadwick, Mrs. M.
Timber: *see* Trees and Timber.
Timotheus, the musician, iii. 168, n. 3.
Timothy: in sermon, v. 106.
Tindal, —: *see* Tyndale, S.
Tinker, Captain John: funeral of, iv. 131 & n. 4.
Tinmouth: *see* Teignmouth.
Tintoretto, Jacopo Robusti, called, ii. 444, n. 1; paintings by: Venice, Doges' Palace, ii. 444 & n. 1; Venice, Scuola di S. Rocco, &c., ii. 461 & n. 4; ~ Crucifixion in: imitated by G. Gibbons in carving, iii. 567, n. 4; at Kensington Palace, v. 237; in Laniere collection, iii. 75.
Tippets, Sir John, iv. 460, n. 4; nephew of: elopes with Elizabeth Evelyn, 1685, iv. 460–2.
Tipping (Tippin), Rev. Ichabod: sermon by, v. 146–7 & n.
Titian, ii. 70, n. 5; master of, iii. 262; tomb of, ii. 461 & n. 2.
paintings: (i) identifiable: so-called Cornaro family, iii. 216 & n. 3; Death of St. Peter Martyr, ii. 459 & n. 7; Ecce Homo, ii. 191 & n. 6; Judith, ii. 285 & n. 2; Leda, ii. 284 & n. 7; Venus (two paintings; Uffizi), ii. 414 & n. 3; Venus and Adonis (school-piece; Earl Spencer, later Widener collection), iv. 162 & n. 2, 403; frescoes, Fondaco dei Tedeschi, ii. 434 & n. 1.

Titian (*cont.*)
— (ii) unidentifiable: by collections: Brussels, Cour, ii. 70 & n. 5 (i. 46); Florence: Gaddi, ii. 415; Uffizi, ii. 413 & n. 13; London: Bristol (later Sunderland), iv. 162; Du Bois, ii. 549; Royal: at Whitehall, iv. 216; ~ at Kensington Palace, v. 237; Paris: Liancourt, ii. 113 (i. 73), 114; Perruchot, ii. 114 (i. 74); Rome: Aldobrandini (later Doria-Pamphili), ii. 284–5; Angeloni, ii. 356.
— (iii) copies after, &c.: Andromeda, by Van Dyck, ii. 548 & n. 5; Venus (Prado), iii. 15, n. 4; ~ etching after, iii. 166, n. 5; owned by R. Walker, iii. 15 & n. 4; miniatures after, by P. Oliver, iii. 260.
Titus, Roman emperor: conquest of Jerusalem by: representation of triumph of, after, ii. 247 & n. 3; ~ spoils from, ii. 275, n. 3; buildings of: baths (error), ii. 278–9 & n.; ~ Coliseum, ii. 248 & n. 8; *see also* iii. 10; ~ Templum Pacis, Rome, ii. 218; Arch of, ii. 247–8 & nn.; columns brought to Rome by, ii. 272–3 & n.; tomb of, ii. 361, n. 3.
Titus, in New Testament: in sermon, iv. 321.
Titus, Col. Silius, iii. 526 & n. 5; as member of Council for Foreign Plantations, iii. 578, 599; participates in Stafford's impeachment (?), iv. 227 & n. 11; made a privy councillor, iv. 590 & n. 4; social, iii. 526.
Tiveat *or* Tiveot, *rectè* Teviot: *see* Spencer, Robert, viscount of Teviot.
Tivedale, *rectè* Tweeddale: Earl of: *see* Hay, John, marquis of Tweeddale, &c.
Tivoli: notice, ii. 393–7 & nn.
cascades, ii. 397 & n. 1; Hadrian's villa, near, ii. 397 & n. 4; powder-mills, ii. 397 & n. 3; Temple of the Sibyl, ii. 397 & n. 2; Villa d'Este, ii. 394–6 & nn.
Tixall, Staffs.: Lord Aston's house at, iv. 228, n. 6.
Toads: in amber, iv. 138; toadstones, ii. 398 & n. 1; iv. 253.
Tobacco: use of, in England, i. 14–15; ii. 201, n. 1; E's pipe, ii. 522; taking tobacco, iii. 224; iv. 352; snuff: making and use of, ii. 201 & n. 1.
Toce *or* Tosa, river, ii. 507, n. 4.
Todcaster: *see* Tadcaster.
Tökölyi (Tekelye), Count Emeric: occupies Alba Julia, v. 35 & n. 7, 37.
Toledo, Don Pedro de, marquis of Villafranca, viceroy of Naples, ii. 340, n. 1; at Grotta del Cane, ii. 340 & n. 1; builds castle at Baia, ii. 349, n. 2; palace, &c., of, at Pozzuoli, ii. 343 & n. 6, 344, n. 1.
Toleto (Toledo), Francesco, cardinal: tomb of, ii. 244 & n. 6.
Tollemache (Talmash), Sir Lionel, third bt.: geneal., iv. 114 & n. 7.
Tollemache (Talmash), Sir Lionel; styled Lord Huntingtower 1651–98; earl of Dysart 1698: social, iv. 114 & n. 7; geneal., iv. 115, n. 2.
Tollemache *or* Talmash, Thomas, lieut.-general: killed, v. 184 *bis* & n. 3.
Tomacelli, Lucrezia, wife of the Constable Colonna: tomb of, ii. 273 & n. 3.
Tombs, —: garden of, at Hackney, iii. 96 & n. 2.
Tomkins, Thomas; D.D. 1673: sermon by, iii. 630 & n. 2.
Tompion, Thomas, clockmaker, iii. 112, n. 1.
Tomson, —, Jesuit: brings Far Eastern collections to England, iii. 373–4.
Tomson, —, merchant at Genoa, ii. 172 (i. 108–9).
Tomson (Thompson), Rev. —, curate at Wotton, 1703–, v. 543, n. 3; as our curate, &c.: sermons by, v. 539(?), 543, 546, 552, 571–82 *passim*; ~ catechizes, v. 571–2, 574.
Tonbridge (Tunbridge), Kent: Free Grammar School: exercise at, &c., iii. 408 & n. 1; C. Wase (headmaster) leaves, iii. 525, n. 1.
Tonge (Tongue), Ezereel, D.D., iv. 154, n. 1; with Oates 'reveals' Popish Plot, iv. 153–4; E's connexion with, i. *26*.
Tonson, Jacob, publisher: newsletters written by, i. *128*, n. 2.

Toorns, — (William Toomes?), of Hackney, iii. 96, n. 2.
Tor Bay, Devon: fleet in, 1656, iii. 169, n. 3; William of Orange lands in, iv. 605 & n. 2; ~ in sermon, iv. 650; Queen Maria Anna of Spain in, 1690, v. 2, n. 2, 14, n. 5; French fleet in, 1690, v. 31, n. 7; English or Allied fleets in: 1691, v. 68, n. 4; ~ 1693, v. 150, n. 2; ~ 1702, v. 510 & n. 7.
Torelli, G.: scenery, &c., designed by, ii. 450, nn. 1, 2.
Torre d'Aquapuzza, near Sermoneta, ii. 317 & n. 8.
Torre dell' Epitaffio, near Terracina, ii. 322 & n. 3.
Torre di Francolise, ii. 324 & n. 1.
Torrenieri (Torniero, Turnera), ii. 206 & n. 7, 407 & n. 6.
Torricelli, Evangelista: demonstration by, of weight of atmosphere, iii. 268 & n. 1; ~ discussed, iii. 327.
Torrington: Earl of, 1689–1716: *see* Herbert, Arthur.
Tosa *or* Toce, river, ii. 507, n. 4.
Tostes (Totes), Normandy, ii. 124 (i. 79).
Touchet, James; third earl of Castle haven 1631, iv. 296, n. 4; social, iv. 296, 318.
Toulouse: relics of St. Thomas Aquinas at, ii. 319, n. 1.
Tournai: bishop of: *see* Choiseul, Gilbert de (in text as of Tournon; iii. 548 & n. 2).
Tournon, on the Rhone: notice, ii. 159–60 & nn. (i. 102); bishop of: *see* Tournai.
Tours: E resident at, 1644, ii. 144–51 & nn. (i. 93–8).
  topography, &c.: general, ii. 144 (i. 93), 145 (i. 94); archbishop's palace, ii. 145 & n. 5 (i. 94), 149 (i. 97); bridges, ii. 144 & n. 5 (i. 93); cave-dwellings near, ii. 144 & n. 2 (i. 93); ~ in comparison, iii. 125; churches, &c.: Capuchins' convent, &c., ii. 145 & n. 8 (i. 94); ~ Jesuits' college, ii. 148 & n. 5 (i. 96); ~ St. Gatien, ii. 145 & n. 3 (i. 94); ~ St. Martin, ii. 144–5 (i. 93–4); Hôtel de la Bourdaisière, ii. 146 & n. 1 (i. 94); the mall, ii. 145 & n. 1 (i. 94), 146; *see also* ii. 142 & n. 3; manufacture of silk, &c., at, ii. 145–6 & n. (i. 94); St. Edme, ii. 144 & n. 5; walls, ii. 145 (i. 94); water-supply, ii. 148 (i. 96).
  Henrietta Maria at, ii. 149 & n. 1 (i. 96–7); Marie de Médicis at, ii. 146 & n. 2 (i. 94).
  archbishop of (V. le Bouthillier), ii. 145 & n. 7 (i. 94), 149 (i. 97); *lieutenant civile* at, ii. 149 (i. 96).
  journey from, to Lyons: E's time on, ii. 156 (i. 100).
Tourville, A.-H. de Cotentin, comte de, admiral: defeated at La Hogue, v. 101 & n. 2.
Tovarvallis, Franciscus: epitaph of, ii. 374 & n. 8.
Town-planning [select; see also Paving; Trees and Timber]:
  places noticed by E on account of their planning, &c.: Amsterdam: Keizers-Gracht, &c., ii. 46 (i. 33), 47–8 (i. 33–4); Genoa: Strada Nuova, ii. 176 & n. 3 (i. 111); Leghorn: Piazza, ii. 184 & n. 5 (i. 116); London: E's plan for rebuilding, 1666, iii. 463; piazzas, ii. 131 (i. 84); Berkeley House gardens, iv. 381–2 & n.; Bloomsbury Square, &c., iii. 398 & n. 2; Clarendon (Albemarle) House site, iv. 339, 382; Covent Garden, ii. 100 (i. 66), 184 & n. 5 (i. 116); Hatton Garden, iii. 231 & n. 6; projected quay, iii. 476 & n. 3, 477; Seven Dials, v. 193 & n. 1; lamp-lit road near, v. 363 & n. 3.
  — Naples: street-drainage, ii. 353; Paris: Place Dauphine, ii. 99 & n. 5; ~ Place Royale, ii. 100 & n. 4, 101 & n. 1 (i. 66); ~ Pont-Neuf foot-ways, ii. 92 & n. 5 (i. 61); Richelieu, ii. 150–1 (i. 97, 98); Rome: Monte Cavallo, the Quattro Fontane, &c., ii. 241–2 & n.
  comments, &c., on streets: arcaded, ii. 421–2, 453, 490; *see also* ii. 524 & n. 4; narrow, ii. 178 (i. 112), 502–3 & n.; iii. 102, 130; water-courses in, iii. 115 & n. 2.
Townshend (Townsend), Sir Horatio; first Baron, 1661, and first Viscount, 1682, Townshend: created baron, iii. 277 & n. 4.

Townshend: first Baron, 1661–82, and first Viscount, 1682–7: *see* Townshend, Sir H.
Trade and Industry:
occupations [for other manufacturers, &c., see the particular commodities]: anchorsmith, &c., v. 348; broom-man, iv. 352; carpenter, iii. 593; ~ apprentice to, iii. 95; cutlers, ii. 155 (i. 100); dyeing: at Amsterdam, ii. 45 (i. 32); ~ Bow dye, iii. 446 & n. 6; ~ sandalwood used in, &c., iv. 3 & n. 4; gardener: apprentice, iv. 521; kitchen-stuff: seller of, iv. 352 & n. 2; laundry, iv. 141; laundress: smoothing-box for, iii. 627; pitch-making, ii. 514; pitch and tar: account of preparation of, iii. 326–7 & n.; rosin-making, ii. 514; scrivener, iv. 122, 186; soap-making, ii. 426; spinning: day's earnings by, iv. 482; tile-maker, iv. 597.
at particular places [select: general production and wholesale trade; retail trade and princely and governmental workshops, &c., are not indexed collectively]: Abbeville, ii. 85 (i. 57–8); Amsterdam, ii. 45 & n. 4 (i. 32), 49 & nn. 3–5 (i. 34–5); Blois, ii. 142 (i. 92–3); Bologna, ii. 426 & nn. 1–7; Bourges, i. 99; Brescia, ii. 489 & n. 6; Bristol, iii. 102–3 & nn.; Byfleet, iv. 141–2 & n.; Colchester, iii. 177 & n. 4, 178 & n. 2; Dedham, iii. 178 & n. 3; Dieppe, ii. 124 (i. 79); Doncaster, iii. 127 & n. 5; Dordrecht, ii. 32 (i. 24); Florence, ii. 200; Geneva, ii. 524 & nn. 5–8, 528–9 & n.; Greenwich, iii. 180–1 & n.; iv. 13 & n. 2; v. 348(?); Ipswich, iv. 115 & n. 8; London, iii. 65 & n. 8, 102, n. 8, 456 & n. 7, 459 & n. 3; iv. 98–9 & n., 363; Lyons, ii. 158 (i. 101); Marseilles, ii. 166 (i. 105); Milan, ii. 501 & n. 8; Moulins, ii. 155 (i. 100); Murano, ii. 467 & n. 5; Naples, kingdom of, ii. 352–3; Norwich, iii. 595 & n. 2; Poggibonsi, ii. 201; Somerset, &c., iv. 452 & n. 5; Tours, ii. 145–6 (i. 94); Valais, ii. 514; Vienne, ii. 159 (i. 102).
Tradescant, John, sen.: founds Tradescant's museum, iii. 198, n. 4 *ad fin.*
Tradescant, John, jnr.: house and museum of, iii. 198–9 & nn.; iv. 138, n. 4, 139.
Traètto, now Minturno, ii. 323, n. 6.
Trajan, Roman emperor: ashes of, ii. 379 & n. 1; baths of (called Titus's in text), ii. 278–9 & n.; column and forum of, at Rome, ii. 378–9 & nn.; inscription of, at Terracina, ii. 321 & n. 2.
Trallop, Mrs. —: *see* Trollop, Elizabeth (Mrs. E. Fox).
Transmigration of Souls: views on, of a Jew, ii. 54 (i. 37).
Transport [select; *see also* Coaches; Horses and Horsemanship; Ships and Shipping; *and* Travel.]
— land:
— — vehicles and animals:
— — — ass, ii. 508 *bis.*
— — — caleche: equated with chariot, iii. 475; improvements in, &c., iii. 405, 475 & n. 5; iv. 483, n. 4.
— — — carriage, i. 25, 61; for goods, iii. 53; as part of vehicle, iii. 475 & n. 5.
— — — cart, iii. 70, 411, 453; iv. 360, 364; v. 470; carnival, at Rome, ii. 382 & n. 1; improvement in, iii. 516; for travellers, ii. 61 (i. 42); whipping at tail of, iv. 445.
— — — chair: at Genoa, i. 112.
— — — chariot: defined, iii. 468, n. 2; mentioned, iii. 83 & n. 2, 193; v. 470; accident to, iii. 468; drawn by dogs, ii. 73 (i. 48); flying, with six horses, iii. 592 & n. 3; improvements in, iii. 416, 475; iv. 483–4 & n.; as hearse, ii. 28 (i. 20).
— — — coach: *see* Coaches.
— — — dog: carts drawn by, ii. 72–3 (i. 48).
— — — hearse, ii. 26 (i. 19); iii. 76; v. 289; with six horses, iii. 490; iv. 151, 152, 430.
— — — horse [*see also* Coaches (for coach-teams) *and* Horses and Horsemanship. E travels on horseback (or on mules) fairly frequently until 1652 (iii. 69–70); then only occasionally (iii. 131, 132, 437)]: riding (or

Transport (*cont.*)
taking) post, ii. 25 (i. 18), 76, 82 (i. 56), 156 (i. 100), 179 (i. 113), 537, 559; iii. 15; ~ forbidden on Sundays, iii. 13 & n. 2; riding or driving post, iii. 358.
— — — — horses: in ambassador's train (riders), iv. 79; hire of, in Valais and England, ii. 517 & n. 4; killed by highwaymen, v. 122 & n. 2; lack of, in Provence, &c., i. 105; mishaps with, ii. 83 (i. 56), 513–14, 543–4; sumpter, ii. 513.
— — — — woman-servant riding pillion, iv. 71; riders attacked by thieves, iii. 69–70, 378(?).
— — — litter: for invalid, ii. 25 (i. 18); at Genoa, ii. 178 (i. 112); horse-litter, ii. 280, 281, 303.
— — — mule, ii. 162 (i. 103), 167 (i. 105), 316, 318, 332, 334, 336, 508–15 *passim*; in procession, ii. 280, 281; women riding astride, ii. 316.
— — — sedan chair: introduced into England, &c., i. 11–12; ii. 14, n. 4; at Genoa, ii. 178 (i. 112); at Naples, ii. 353 & n. 6.
— — — sled or sledge: on ice, iv. 362; criminal on, iv. 445.
— — — tumbrel, i. 42.
— — — wagon: for travellers, ii. 31 (i. 24), 33 (i. 25), 42 (i. 31), 57 (i. 39), 75 (i. 49); for baggage, &c., iv. 79(?); v. 537; drawn by dogs, ii. 72–3 (i. 48); covered, at Rome, ii. 257–8.
— — organization:
— — — coach-service, ii. 182, n. 7; guides (for routes), ii. 151–2 & n., 156 (i. 100), 162 (i. 103), 508, 513, 515 *bis*; *messager* (messenger), ii. 83 & n. 4; i. 56; ii. 135 (i. 89); iii. 12; ~ equated with *procaccio*, ii. 315, n. 1; night-journey, ii. 42 (i. 31); post-service, Simplon Pass, ii. 508, n. 5; for riding post, &c., *see* horse *above*; *procaccio*, ii. 315 & n. 1, 323, 355; *vetturino*, ii. 212 & n. 5, 315, n. 1, 334, n. 1, 336.
— — — cost of journeys: Paris-Calais, iii. 12 & n. 2; Paris-Orleans, ii. 135, n. 2; Rome-Venice, ii. 429 & n. 6; Venice-Padua (by canal), ii. 452, n. 2.

Transport (*cont.*)
— — — speed of journeys: London-Althorp in day, and return in day, iv. 592–3 & n.; London-Newmarket in day, iii. 588 & n. 4; Tours-Lyons, ii. 156; in United Provinces, ii. 33 & n. 1 (i. 25); *see also* ii. 31 (i. 24).
— water [for vessels *see* Ships and Shipping]: (i) canals, rivers, and inland seas:
— — organized services:
— — — United Provinces: services, ii. 33, n. 6; journeys with night on board or *en route*, ii. 31–2 (i. 24), 38–9 (i. 28–9), 59 (i. 40); other journeys, ii. 33 (i. 25), 34 (i. 27), 49–50 (i. 35), 58 (i. 40).
— — — Dordrecht to Antwerp, ii. 59–63 & nn. (i. 41–3).
— — — Spanish Netherlands: overnight journey, ii. 67–9 & n. (i. 45–6); other journeys, ii. 74 (i. 48–9), 75 (i. 49).
— — — North Italy: night journeys, ii. 426–7, 428–9; Venice-Padua, ii. 452–3.
— — individual hire:
— — — abroad: Loire, ii. 139 (i. 91), 143 (i. 93), 533–4; Lake of Geneva, ii. 519–20, 522–3; Lake Maggiore, ii. 506–7; Rhone, ii. 158–60 (i. 101–2), 532; Seine, iii. 38.
— — — London, &c., to Gravesend (or reverse), ii. 76 (i. 50–1), 82 & n. 4 (i. 56), 558–9; iii. 56, 409.
— — — London to Deptford, &c., iii. 147, 163, 347, 522; iv. 148; v. 600.
— — ferries:
— — — Greenwich: Potter's Ferry, iii. 180 & n. 4; Havre to Honfleur, ii. 125 (i. 80); Humber, iii. 131 & n. 2; London: Horseferry, iv. 360 & n. 4, 365; v. 536; Rome, ii. 287, 357.
— water: (ii) sea:
— — Channel: packet-services: Dover-Calais, ii. 82 (i. 56), 537, 559–60; iii. 13, 16, 54–5, 56; ~ protection for, ii. 559; Dunkirk-Dover, ii. 76 & n. 1 (i. 50); other journeys, &c.: Gravesend-Flushing, ii. 29–31 (i. 22–3); Dieppe-Rye, iii. 68; embarkation at Dover, iv. 80.
— — — services interrupted by weather (no foreign news, &c.),

Transport (*cont.*)
iv. 366 & n. 3(?); v. 255–6 & n., 493 & n. 4(?), 500 & n. 3, 505 & n. 3, 510 & n. 6, 550 & n. 1, 552 & n. 5, 579 & n. 3.
— — Mediterranean: Cannes–Genoa, ii. 167–71 & nn. (i. 106–8); Genoa-Lerici, ii. 178–9 (i. 112–13); *see also* ii. 166 (i. 105).
— — — Venice-London 'by long sea', ii. 467; *see also* ii. 401–2, 469.
Transylvania: Dr. I. Basire resident in, iii. 303, n. 3; Count E. Tökölyi's campaign in, v. 35 & n. 7, 37; prince of, &c., ii. 34, n. 1.
Trapani: giant's bone from (?), ii. 314 & n. 5.
Trappes, Anne: *see* Radcliffe, Anne, Lady Radcliffe.
Trappes, Sir Frances: geneal., iii. 92, n. 1.
Trarbach: taken by Allies, 1704, v. 583 *bis* & nn. 1, 6.
Trasquéra, ii. 508, n. 5.
Travel [*see also* Bills of Health; Coaches; Inns; Passes and Passports; *and* Transport]:
— accidents and mishaps: arrest, ii. 512–13 & nn., 516, 518; ~ fear of, ii. 505; *see also* ii. 149 (i. 96); iii. 4–8; boats grounding, &c., ii. 58 (i. 40), 82 (i. 56), 547; iii. 16, 522; coaching accidents: *see* Coaches; floods: accidents, &c., by, ii. 83 (i. 56); v. 618 & n. 1; health: E's sore hand, ii. 318; ~ E's smallpox, ii. 519 & n. 4; riding mishaps, ii. 83 (i. 56), 513–14, 543–4.
— admission to territories and towns: United Provinces–Spanish Netherlands frontier, ii. 62–3 (i. 42–3); customs examinations, ii. 429, 491; iii. 13; ~ on departure, iii. 16; examinations for health, &c., ii. 171 & n. 4 (i. 108), 429 & n. 3; fire-arms taken in charge, &c., ii. 160–1 & n. (i. 103), 427 & n. 5.
— crime and security:
— — brigands and banditti: France, ii. 116 (i. 75), 135–6 (i. 89); Lombardy, ii. 490, 491; kingdom of Naples, ii. 322; iii. 50 & n. 1; Papal States, ii. 317–18, 318.
— — England: foot-pads: attacks by, iii. 69–70, 378(?); highwaymen, v. 366; ~ robbery by, v. 122 & n. 2.
— — frontier areas: danger from marauding troops in: contribution land, ii. 38–9 & n. (i. 29), 74 & n. 4 (i. 48); parties, soldiers, or volunteers, ii. 83–4 & n. (i. 56), 84 & n. 4 (i. 57), 85 & n. 2, 561 & n. 1; iii. 12, 16, 17, 54.
— — pirates, privateers, raiders, &c.: fear of, ii. 30–1 (i. 23), 166 (i. 105), 169–70 (i. 107), 355 & n. 3; iii. 54–5; pursuit by, ii. 559; iii. 16; robbery by, ii. 551; iii. 56 & n. 1, 71; ~ reported, iii. 39; security against, iii. 13 & n. 1.
— — protection: convoys: by land, ii. 315, n. 1, 318; ~ for packet-boat, ii. 559; travellers' weapons, ii. 116 (i. 75), 160 & n. 6 (i. 103), 427, 512; *see also* iii. 5.
— educational value: general., i. *41* & n. 3, *80* & n. 1; travelling tutors, ii. 550; iii. 354 & n. 2, 401, n. 4; iv. 38, 96.
— guide-books: selection of, at Rome, ii. 214 & n. 1; E's use of, i. *86–9*, *90–101*; alluded to, i. 60; *add.*
— guides [for towns; for guides for routes *see* Transport]: professional; Bologna, ii. 421; Rome, ii. 214 & n. 2; Phlegræan Fields, ii. 336, 339; Venice, ii. 434; Vesuvius, ii. 336, n. 3; amateur: Antwerp, ii. 63 (i. 43); Genoa, ii. 172 (i. 108–9); Milan, ii. 492 & n. 1, 497; Paris, iii. 10, n. 3.
— parties, &c., travelling [select]: ambassador's train, iv. 79; coach: party in, Rome-Florence, ii. 405–6, 417–18; funereal journey, iv. 151–2; ladies and gentlemen, with servants, iv. 71; *procaccio's* party Rome-Naples, ii. 315–16, &c.; Waller, Wray, &c., Padua-Paris, ii. 480, &c.; travelling companions [not indexed collectively; the most notable are T. Henshaw; Thomas Howard, earl of Arundel; Lady Catherine Scott; and J. Thicknesse]; arrangements for journey, iv. 592–3 & n.; compliments to

Travel (*cont.*)
travellers, ii. 165 & n. 3 (i. 104), 518 & n. 6; provisions for journey, v. 467; Sacrament in preparation for journey, ii. 556.
— miscellaneous: artist employed by traveller: *see* Maratti, C.; baggage: portmanteaus, ii. 429; ~ trunks, iii. 13, 16; Sunday travelling, iii. 13 & n. 2; toll, ii. 506.
Travers, Samuel, surveyor-general of Crown Lands, v. 211, n. 2; on site committee for Greenwich Hospital, &c., v. 210 & n. 6(?), 211.
Trean, —, ii. 548, n. 3.
Treby, Sir George, judge: knighted 1681, iv. 227, n. 7; participates in Stafford's impeachment, iv. 227; participates in *Quo Warranto* proceedings, iv. 320, n. 1; dismissed from recordership of London, iv. 342 & n. 4; dies, v. 438 & n. 1.
Trees and Timber:
— general: (i) timber: supply, &c., in England: felling during Commonwealth, &c., iii. 99, 170 & n. 3, 343, n. 5, 427–8 & nn.; inquiries concerning, iii. 340 & n. 1; *see also* Evelyn: books: *Sylva*; Charles II's love of planting, iv. 409 & n. 5; woods in Hampshire, iv. 474; plantations, &c.: Althorp, iv. 594; Cassiobury, iv. 200; Euston, iii. 591 & n. 3; iv. 117; Greenwich Park, iii. 370 & n. 5; Marden, iv. 121 & n. 4; v. 425–6; Sayes Court, iii. 80 & n. 1, 193, 370 & n. 4, 393 & n. 3; Swallowfield, iv. 481–2; Wanstead, iv. 305–6; Windsor: new park, iv. 317; Wotton, v. 480; ~ felling at, v. 89, 93, 338 & n. 1.
— — (ii) trees: effects of weather on: 1658, iii. 220; 1683–4, iv. 362 & n. 4, 363, 364–5; 1684, iv. 384, 386; 1689, iv. 644 & n. 3; 1692, v. 104; 1699, v. 315; 1701, v. 444; 1703, v. 550 & n. 2, 552; killed by caterpillars, iv. 446; planted as ornaments of streets and ramparts, ii. 46 (i. 33), 47 (i. 34), 60 (i. 41), 67 (i. 45), 106 (i. 69), 139 (i. 91), 369, 409; tree in centre of France,

Trees and Timber (*cont.*)
ii. 153 & n. 5 (i. 99); miraculous tree, ii. 205 & n. 8.
— — (iii) miscellaneous: planting: age of moon, &c., at time of, iii. 81 & n. 3; incombustible wood, iii. 293–4; pollards, iv. 527; worms breeding in timber, iii. 341.
— several [trees and shrubs, &c., described in *Sylva*; all other trees are indexed under Fruit-trees or Plants]: alaternus, ii. 127 & n. 5 (i. 81); ash, iv. 117; bay, ii. 322, 337; beech: leaves of, in mattresses, ii. 507, n. 6; birch, iii. 295; box, iii. 157 *bis*; dwarf, ii. 129 (i. 82); boxwood, v. 14; cedar: in England, iii. 625, n. 1; timber: used in various parts of buildings, ii. 308; iii. 398, 625 *bis* & n. 1; iv. 141; cherry, black (service), iv. 200 & n. 3; cork, ii. 182 (i. 115), 318; cypress: in France and Italy, ii. 105 (i. 68), 106 (i. 69), 175 (i. 111), 231, 234, 238, 240, 252, 390, 411, 488; ~ cut, ii. 132–3 (i. 86), 487; ~ trees planted by St. Dominic, ii. 421; in England, iii. 359; v. 426; ~ at Theobalds, i. 55 (*see also* ii. 81, n. 2); ~ effects of cold on, iv. 365; timber: in parquet, iv. 141; deal: in parquet, iv. 177; elm, ii. 106 (i. 69), 130 (i. 83), 145 (i. 94), 563; iii. 18, 157, 197, 370, 427, 591; iv. 317, 347, 481, 594; v. 480; *see also* ii. 481, n. 1; fir, ii. 156 (i. 100), 506, 509; iii. 359, 591; iv. 117, 347; v. 426; Spanish, iv. 200; as timber, ii. 517; iv. 252; ~ wainscot of, iv. 116; holly, v. 426; hedges, iii. 534, 625; ~ at Sayes Court, iii. 80; iv. 312 & n. 1; hornbeam: cradle-walk of, iii. 324 & n. 7; hedge, ii. 130 & n. 1 (i. 83); ilex, i. 69, 115; jasmine: flowers of, ii. 171 (i. 108); juniper, ii. 287; v. 426; laurel, ii. 252, 287; in England: effect of cold on, iv. 365; lentisk, ii. 162 (i. 103), 175 (i. 111), 322; lime (linden), ii. 41 (i. 30), 46 (i. 33), 47 (i. 34); i. 37; ii. 56, 60 (i. 41), 67, n. 3; i. 69; ii. 130 (i. 83), 139 (i. 91), 153, n. 5; iii.

Trees and Timber (*cont.*)
114, 141, 180, 324, 556, 591; iv. 317, 481; planting of, in United Provinces, i. 41; unusual tree, ii. 58 (i. 40); locust (error for lotus?), iii. 386 & n. 5; lotus: as locust, in error (?), *ib.*; mulberry, ii. 106 (i. 69), 325, 353, n. 2; myrtle, i. 69; ii. 163 (i. 103), 175 (i. 111), 182 (i. 115), 252, 322, 351, 390; hedges, ii. 287; in England, iv. 347; ~ myrtetum, iv. 576; ~ effects of cold on, iv. 365; oak, iii. 121 & n. 1, 197, 383; iv. 481; avenue of, at Baynards, iii. 193 & n. 1; Procession Oak, Bromley, iii. 69 & n. 1; *add.*; project for planting, in Forest of Dean, iii. 343 & n. 3; trees in great storm, 1703, v. 550, n. 2; Irish: carving in, iii. 118; Spanish: for wainscot, iv. 117 & n. 1; olive: *see* Fruit-trees and Fruits; pine, ii. 102 (i. 67), 156 (i. 100), 167 (i. 105), 252, 506, 509; v. 425; garden of pines at Fontainebleau, ii. 119 (i. 77); extracting pitch from, ii. 514; plane (platanus): in England, iii. 386 & n. 6; at Lee and Ispahan, iv. 337 & n. 4; poplar, black, ii. 428, n. 5; quickset, ii. 60 & n. 3 (i. 41); service (black cherry), iv. 200 & n. 3; taxus: *see* yew *below*; thuya, iv. 142 & n. 3; walnut, iii. 157 & n. 5, 221 & n. 5; iv. 121 & n. 4; plantations of, iv. 305–6; willow, sweet, iv. 482; yew, iii. 157; v. 426; large, iii. 359 & n. 3; hedges, iii. 197; poisonous nature of, ii. 408 & n. 7; as timber: in parquet, iv. 141, 199; zinnar: *see* plane *above*.

Trelawney, John, carver in ordinary, iii. 343, n. 5.

Trelawny, Captain John: death of, &c., iv. 299 & n. 2.

Trelawny, Sir Jonathan, bt.; bishop of Bristol 1685; of Exeter 1689; of Winchester 1707, iv. 299 & n. 2; sermon by, iv. 299; as bishop of Bristol: one of the Seven Bishops, iv. 583–8 & nn., *passim*; ~ attends coronation of William and Mary, iv. 633, n. 3; as bishop of Exeter: preaches thanksgiving sermon, 1702, v. 521 & n. 5.

Trenchard, Sir John; knighted 1689, iv. 322, n. 5; imprisoned in Tower for Rye-House Plot, iv. 322 & n. 5; released from Tower, iv. 354 & n. 1; appointed secretary of state, v. 135 & n. 3.

Trent, Dorset: Charles II at, iii. 51, n. 2.

Trent, river, iii. 125; at Nottingham (as the river), iii. 126.

Trent, Council of: innovations, &c., of: in sermons, iv. 187, 541, 555, 570, 580; v. 132, 607.

Trepone, Sicily: *see* Trapani.

Tres Tabernae: ruins of, ii. 318 & n. 2.

Treviso: Marquisate of: geographical, ii. 481.

Trevor, Sir John, 1626–72, iii. 518, n. 2; as secretary of state: attends Council for Foreign Plantations, iii. 578, 584, 604–5; ~ social, iii. 518, 539.

Trevor, Sir John, 1637–1717, the Speaker, iv. 590, n. 4; appointed Privy Councillor, 1688, *ib.*; expelled from house of commons, v. 207, n. 7 *ad fin.*; alluded to (?), v. 408 & n. 2.

Triers, the, *add.* (iii. 172, n. 1).

Trimnell, Charles: as tutor of Charles Spencer, third earl of Sunderland, iv. 595, n. 2; v. 322, n. 3.

Trinity, Holy [sermons asserting the Trinity against Anti-Trinitarians are indexed under Anti-Trinitarians; Arians; and Socinians. Ordinary sermons asserting the doctrine of the Trinity are not indexed.]

Trinity House of Deptford Strond: general account, iii. 313, n. 6; charters of: Henry VIII's, iii. 314; iv. 248 & n. 1; ~ new, 1685, iv. 459 & n. 2; and Deptford: elections held at, iv. 248 & n. 1; ~ hall at, iii. 441 & n. 1; ~ land at, for alms-houses: given to, iii. 577 & n. 6; iv. 303; London headquarters of, iii. 313 & n. 6; iv. 64, n. 6; younger brothers of, sworn: E and Ossory, iv. 6; ~ John Evelyn, jnr., iv. 12; appoints consul, ii. 476, n. 3; re-assembles after Plague, iii. 440–1; assists Captain G. Collins, iv. 301, n. 3; attends Sir R. Browne's funeral, iv. 302.

Trinity House (*cont.*)
Trinity Monday meetings (all held at Deptford), &c.: with feasts at Deptford, iii. 440–1, 483, 581; iv. 11–12 (?), 36(?); with feasts in London, iii. 408; iv. 64, 91, 247–8, 379–80, 459–60; without feasts, iv. 314–15, 513; feast without meeting, iii. 510; feasts at other times, iii. 313–14, 405; iv. 6, 264, 496.
masters: *see* Hurlstone, N. (1665; iii. 408 & n. 4); Penn, Sir W. (1667; iii. 483); Craven, William, earl of Craven (1670–1; iii. 581); Allin, Sir T. (1671–2; iii. 581); Browne, Sir Richard (1672–3; iv. 6, 11–12, 302); Smith, Sir Jeremiah (1673–4; iv. 12); Ossory (T. Butler) (1675–6; iv. 64, 91); Pepys, S. (1676–7, 1685; iv. 91, 459); Berkeley, George, earl of Berkeley (1681; iv. 248); Legge, George, Baron Dartmouth (1683–5; iv. 314, 379).
Trion, Francis: art-collection of, ii. 548, n. 3.
Triple Alliance, 1668: Clifford's attitude towards, iv. 16, n. 1.
Triplet, Thomas; D.D. 1661, iii. 168, n. 5; corrects proofs of E's *Lucretius*, iii. 173 & n. 2; social, iii. 168.
Tritoli, Phlegraean Fields: baths of, ii. 344, n. 4, 348 & nn. 1, 2, 349, n. 4, 351, n. 4.
Troäs: in sermon, iv. 321.
Trollop (Trallop), Elizabeth: *see* Fox, Mrs. E.
Trollop, Sir William, bt.: geneal., iv. 219, n. 5.
Tromp, Cornelis, admiral, iii. 471, n. 2; engagement of, with Blake, 1652, iii. 67, n. 4; geneal., iii. 471 & n. 2.
Trôo, on the Loir: cave-dwellings at, ii. 144, n. 2.
Trott, Martha: *see* Clayton, Martha, Lady Clayton.
Trott, Perient: geneal., iv. 121, n. 5; *see also* iv. 147, n. 1.
Troy: picture of: in comparison, iii. 454.
Trumbull, Sir William, D.C.L.; knighted 1684, iv. 110 & n. 2; social, iv. 110; as ambassador to Turkey: chaplain of: *see* Hayley, W. (in text as Hall; iv. 545 & n. 3).
Tsarskoje-Selo: helmet preserved at, ii. 192, n. 6.
Tuam: archbishops of, named John, iv. 300 & n. 6; archbishop of, 1679–1716: *see* Vesey, J.
Tuchet, Mervyn, second earl of Castlehaven: tried, ii. 10 & n. 4 (i. 8); geneal., iv. 296.
Tucker, Rev. William: sermon by (?), iii. 315 & n. 1.
Tudor, Edmund, earl of Richmond: geneal., iii. 137, n. 3.
Tudor, Owen: geneal., i. *2–3*, 4, n. 1.
Tuffley, Glos.: view of Gloucester from, iii. 118, n. 5.
Tuffnell, —: buys land in Deptford from E, v. 153 & n. 3.
Tufton, Catherine, countess of Thanet, wife of Thomas Tufton, sixth earl: claims of, to knowledge (?), iv. 505 & n. 3.
Tufton, Elizabeth, countess of Thanet, wife of Nicholas Tufton, third earl, iv. 222, n. 8; godmother to a Jewess, iv. 222; claims of, to knowledge (?), iv. 505 & n. 3.
Tufton, Sir John, second bt.: social, iii. 153–4 & n.
Tufton, Nicholas; third earl of Thanet 1664: geneal., iv. 222, n. 8.
Tufton, Thomas, sixth earl of Thanet 1684: geneal., iv. 505, n. 3; chaplain(s) of: sermons by, v. 376, 560.
Tuke, Sir Brian: portrait of, by Holbein, iv. 143 & n. 4.
Tuke, Sir Charles; second bt. 1674: baptized, iii. 585 & n. 4; godmother of, iii. 543, n. 3; killed, &c., v. 32–3.
Tuke, George, iii. 172, n. 4; marries Mrs. Mary Fountaine, iii. 172 & n. 5, 181 & n. 6; estate of, at Cressing Temple, iii. 182, n. 7; ~ Mrs. Evelyn at (?), iii. 182; ~ E and Mrs. Evelyn at, iii. 225–6; proposes to take Baynards, iii. 192–3; godfather of George Evelyn (born 1657), iii. 194; E as trustee or executor for, iii. 190, 358, 435, 491 & nn. 4, 7; estate of: proceedings relating to, iii. 507; iv. 280, 281; goods of: inventory of, iii. 509; step-daughter of (?), iii. 508, n. 2.
Tuke, Mrs. Mary, wife of George Tuke and previously of Peter Fountaine, iii. 172, n. 5; marries Tuke, iii. 172 & n. 5; *see also* iii.

Tuke, Mrs. Mary (*cont.*)
181; burial-place of, iii. 181, n. 6; geneal., iii. 508 & n. 2.
Tuke, Mary, Lady Tuke, born Guldeford, first wife of Sir Samuel: marries Tuke, goes to France with him, &c., iii. 373 *bis* & nn. 1, 4.
Tuke, Mary, Lady Tuke, born Sheldon, second wife of Sir Samuel, iii. 511, n. 2; marries Tuke, iii. 511 & n. 2; appointed dresser to Queen Catherine, iv. 8 *bis* & n. 3; at Windsor: Mary Evelyn stays with, iv. 38, 428; ~ in 1682, iv. 280 & n. 2; ill, and visits Sayes Court, iv. 522, 526; arranges for Siface to perform for Pepys, iv. 547, n. 1; social: gives music-party, iv. 370; ~ parties, iv. 108, 435; ~ alone, iii. 568; iv. 96, 123, 155, 181; in legal proceedings, iii. 547; iv. 80 & n. 4, 109, 276 & n. 4, 280, 281, 489, 530, 535; geneal., iv. 281, n. 3, 396, n. 4; v. 164, n. 4.
Tuke, Sir Samuel; knighted and created baronet 1664, ii. 564, n. 1; visits St.-Cloud, 1649, ii. 564; in England, 1658, iii. 223 & n. 5; brings E message from Charles II, 1660, iii. 245; on mission to Henrietta Maria, iii. 258; as envoy to France, 1661, iii. 274 & n. 4; *add.*; *Adventures of Five Hours* by: rehearsed, performed, &c., iii. 348 & n. 4, 350 & n. 3; *see also* ii. 535, n. 4; takes sons of Henry Howard (later sixth duke of Norfolk) to France, 1664, iii. 373; comes from France, 1667, iii. 488; speech(es) of, in house of lords, iii. 249–50 & n.; iv. 5 & n. 5; as adviser to Henry Howard (later sixth duke of Norfolk), iii. 593; marriages of, iii. 373 & nn. 1, 2, 511 & n. 2; resident at Somerset House, iii. 519, n. 5 *ad fin.*; affairs of, iii. 491 & n. 4, 504; Cressing Temple sold on behalf of, iii. 542; business of, with countess of Huntingdon, iii. 543 & n. 3; visits Epsom, iii. 371; social, iii. 369; dies, iv. 80, n. 4; geneal., iii. 172, n. 4, 585; iv. 15, n. 2; ~ relationship of, to Mrs. Evelyn, ii. 564, n. 1.
Tullibardine: fifth Earl of, 1670–6: *see* Murray, John, later marquis of Athole.
Tulliola: supposed corpse of, ii. 320 & nn. 1, 2.
Tully, Rev. George: proceedings against, iv. 516 & n. 2.
Tulse, Sir Henry, lord mayor: social, iv. 352 & n. 4.
Tumond, Lord: *see* O'Brien, Henry, earl of Thomond.
Tunbridge: *see* Tonbridge.
Tunbridge: Lord: *see* Zuylestein, W. N. de, earl of Rochford.
Tunbridge Wells, Kent: the waters, &c., iii. 68, n. 4; church of King Charles the Martyr at, iii. 295, n. 2; season at, for taking the waters, iii. 295; persons at: E, Mrs. Evelyn, and Lady Browne, 1652, iii. 68–73; Mrs. Evelyn and E, 1661, iii. 292, 294–5 & nn.; Mrs. Evelyn and Mary Evelyn, 1681, iv. 250, 256; John Evelyn, jnr., &c., 1689, iv. 646; Margaret Blagge (Mrs. Godolphin), &c., 1674, iv. 40–1; Clarendon (Henry Hyde), 1689, iv. 644, n. 2; Clifford, 1673, iv. 16–17; Rev. R. Holden, 1682(?), iv. 287; earl of Kent: dies at, 1702, v. 518, n. 3.
environs: High Rocks, iii. 295, n. 1; Rusthall, iii. 68, n. 4, 295, n. 1; Southborough, iii. 68, n. 4; iv. 40.
Turberville, Edward, iv. 228, n. 4; statements of, to house of commons, iv. 225, n. 3; as witness at Stafford's trial, iv. 228 & n. 8, 230; ~ alluded to, iv. 232, 234.
Turenne, Henri de la Tour-d'Auvergne, vicomte de, the general, iv. 77, n. 2; on campaigns, iii. 17, n. 3, 200, n. 5; geneal., ii. 382, n. 3; iv. 77.
Turin: demanded by French as security, 1690, v. 25; earthquake at, 1699, v. 353, n. 1; threatened by French, 1705, v. 600 & n. 2.
Turk, the, rope-dancer: performs, iii. 197–8 & n.
Turkey and the Turks [the Turks are not only the immediate subjects of the sultans (the Ottoman Turks, &c.), but also the North Africans under the sultans' suzerainty, and, more vaguely, the Mediterranean Mohammedans in general]:
geographical: E desires to visit, ii. 451, 468; Dr. I. Basire in, iii.

Turkey and the Turks (*cont.*)
303, n. 3; rusma from, ii. 430 & n. 1.
political: (i) internal: P. Cisij on affairs of, iii. 516; disturbances, &c.: 1688, iv. 581 & n. 2; ~ 1689, iv. 645 & n. 7; ~ 1693, v. 150 & n. 3; Mustafa II deposed, &c., 1703, v. 544, 545–6 & n.
— (ii) foreign relations: Paul II prays for victory against, 1464, ii. 374; with Empire: *see* Wars: Turkish-Imperial war; with France: encouraged to invade Empire, &c., 1683, 1689–90, iv. 331 & n. 4, 340; v. 36, n. 1, 37; with Russia: surrenders Azov, 1696, v. 258 & n. 5; alarmed by, 1699, v. 345; negotiates peace with, 1699, v. 368, n. 4; with Venice: ensigns, &c., taken from, at Venice, ii. 457 & n. 1, 458 & n. 10; wars, 1645–69 (the Cretan War) and 1684–99: *see* Venice: Republic; frontier-dispute, 1699, v. 345, n. 3.
pirates, &c.: danger from, &c.: on Italian coast, ii. 349, 355 & n. 3; ~ on Riviera, ii. 166 (i. 105); knightly order sworn to fight against, ii. 179–80 & n. (i. 113); victories over: paintings of, at Leghorn, ii. 184 (i. 116).
in relation to Christianity, &c.: Turks' views on Christ, ii. 54 (i. 38); Turks scandalized by divisions among Christians: in sermon, v. 513; tyranny of, over Eastern Christians: in sermon, v. 378; fall of: in prophecy, v. 26.
social, &c.: capital punishment: form of, used in, iv. 206, n. 5; dress: a vestment, iii. 108 & n. 1; other garments, iv. 266, 285; horses, grooms, &c., iv. 398–9 & nn.; bridle, &c., ii. 504, 508; manners: sitting cross-legged, iv. 285; public ceremonies, iv. 266; royal standard, iv. 399; Turkey leather, iii. 34; wives of sultans, &c., obtained from Georgia, &c., iv. 214 & n. 3.
individual Turks: at Venice, ii. 449; convert baptized at Exeter

Turkey and the Turks (*cont.*)
House chapel, iii. 203, n. 5; convert at Rome, ii. 376–7 & n.; *see also* ii. 386, n. 4; galley-slaves: at Leghorn, ii. 183 (i. 116); ~ at Marseilles, ii. 165 (i. 104); slaves at Naples, ii. 340.
Turkey merchants: *see* England: merchant shipping; *see also* Levant Company.
Turkish language: translation of New Testament into, v. 82 & n. 2.
Turner, — (Edward Turner of Therfield?), iii. 552 & n. 4.
Turner, Dr. — (Francis Turner?): sermons by, iv. 30 & n. 7, 204 & n. 1.
Turner, Dr. — (Thomas Turner, 1591–1672?): sermon by, iii. 415 & n. 2.
Turner, Dr. — (Thomas Turner, 1645–1714?): sermons by, iv. 372–3 & n., 532 & n. 2.
Turner, Edward, of Therfield: hospitality of (?), iii. 552 & n. 4.
Turner, Francis, D.D.; bishop of Rochester 1683; of Ely 1684; deprived 1691, iii. 630, n. 4; appointed dean of Windsor, iv. 318 & n. 7; consecrated bishop of Rochester, iv. 357, n. 5; appointed Lord Almoner, iv. 374, n. 3; translated to Ely, iv. 394 & n. 2; attends Charles II on death-bed, iv. 407; preaches at James II's coronation, iv. 437 & n. 3; attends Monmouth in Tower, &c., iv. 456 & n. 1; one of the Seven Bishops, iv. 583–8 & nn., *passim*; visit to, in Tower, iv. 587; at meeting to discuss settlement of crown, Jan. 1689, iv. 613–15; search for, on account of Jacobite plot, v. 41 & n. 3, 42 & n. 4; superseded as bishop, v. 48–9 & n.; at burial of deprived bishop of Peterborough, v. 289 & n. 3; sermons by: printed, iv. 237 & n. 2, 374 & n. 3, 394 & n. 2, 404–5 & n.; ~ on Princess Anne's pregnancy, iv. 357–8 & n.; ~ ordinary, iii. 630; iv. 30 & n. 7(?), 204 & n. 1(?), 499 *bis*; *see also* iv. 372–3 & n. (and iv. 532 & n. 2); at Communion service, iv. 374; social, iv. 370, 488, 612 & n. 3; geneal., iv. 493.
Turner, Captain John: funeral sermon for, iii. 622 & n. 2.

Turner, John; D.D. 1706; master of Colfe's Grammar School, Lewisham, iv. 591, n. 1; sermons by, iv. 591, 653(?); v. 30(?).
Turner, Thomas, Dockyard official at Deptford, &c., iii. 622, n. 2; buried, iv. 256; geneal., iii. 622.
Turner, Thomas, D.D., 1591–1672; dean of Canterbury 1644: sermon by (?), iii. 415 & n. 2.
Turner, Thomas, D.D., 1645–1714; president of Corpus Christi, Oxford, iv. 493 & n. 4; *add.*; sermons by, iv. 372–3 & n.(?), 493, 532(?).
Turner, William; D.D. 1683; sermon by (?), iv. 78 & n. 4; *add.*
Turner, Sir William, lord mayor: geneal., iv. 206, n. 1.
Turnera: *see* Torrenieri.
Turnham Green, Middlesex: Sir J. Chardin's house at, v. 594 & n. 4.
Turning: in ivory: pieces of, ii. 192 & n. 9 (i. 119); iii. 64–5; ~ workmen engaged in, ii. 124; workshop for, iii. 294.
Turnor (Turner), Sir Edward, judge, iii. 400, n. 6; as speaker of house of commons: at feast, iii. 400; ~ in parliament, iii. 402 & n. 3; as Chief Baron: social, iv. 45 & n. 1.
Turpin, Elizabeth: *see* Prettyman, Elizabeth, Lady Prettyman.
Turpin, Sir George: geneal., iii. 73, n. 3.
Turquet de Mayerne, Sir Theodore: geneal., iii. 623, n. 3.
Tuscany: the Grand Duchy.
 territories, &c.: about Lucca, ii. 410; Pisa as part of, ii. 182 & n. 6 (i. 115); frontiers, ii. 208 & n. 4, 419 & n. 5.
 grand dukes of: arms of, ii. 208; burial-place of, ii. 198–9 & n.; chair of, for St. John's day ceremony, ii. 193 & n. 1 (i. 119); craftsmen working for, ii. 188 (i. 118); palaces, villas, &c., of: at Florence, ii. 187 (i. 118), 188–93 (i. 118–19); at Pisa, ii. 182 (i. 114); Poggio a Caiano, ii. 410, n. 5 *ad fin.*; Poggio Imperiale, ii. 410–11 & nn.; *add.*; Pratolino, ii. 418–19 & nn.; in Rome, ii. 391, n. 1; *see also* Rome: topography: Villa Medici.
Tuscany (*cont.*)
 — park of, near Leghorn, ii. 182–3 & n. (i. 115); prostitutes taxed by, ii. 417 & n. 9; Swiss guard of, ii. 187 (i. 118); treasury of, ii. 187 & n. 5 (i. 118); sell wine, ii. 187 & n. 7 (i. 118).
 grand duke of: poison belonging to, iii. 289; gift from, iii. 295.
Tuscany: Countess of: *see* Matilda.
Tusculum: Cicero's villa at, &c., ii. 392 & n. 1.
Tweeddale (Tivedale): second Earl, 1654–94, and first Marquis, 1694–7, of: *see* Hay, John.
Twickenham, Middlesex: Col. Richard Talbot (later duke of Tyrconnel) and Mrs. Talbot at, iv. 15 & n. 8, 86; Twickenham Park at, iv. 23, n. 1; ~ Margaret Blagge (Mrs. Godolphin) at, iv. 23, 72–3, 73–4; ~ Lord Berkeley's bailiff, &c., at, iv. 86, 99.
Twysden (Twisden), Sir Roger, bt.: tries to protect Maidstone from plague, iii. 422 & n. 3.
Tyburtine (Tibur, Tybur): *see* Tivoli.
Tyndale (Tindal), Stafford: social, &c., iii. 349 & n. 3.
Tyrconnel: Earls and Dukes, &c., of: *see* Fitzwilliam, Oliver, first earl 1661–7; Fitzwilliam, Eleanor, his countess; *new creation*: *see* Talbot, Richard, first earl 1685–9 and duke 1689–91; Talbot, Frances, his duchess.
Tyre: relic of Christ from, ii. 438 & n. 8.
Tyrell *or* Tyrrell family: geneal., iii. 55, n. 3; iv. 313, n. 3.
Tyrell, Elizabeth: *see* Forster, Mrs. E.
Tyrell, Elizabeth, Lady Tyrell, wife of Sir John: geneal., iii. 91, n. 5.
Tyrell, Sir John, of Springfield: geneal., iii. 91, n. 5.
Tyrone: Earl of, 1673–90: *see* Power, Richard.
Tyrrell family: *see* Tyrell.
Tyrrell (Tyrell), —, brother of Sir Timothy: in France, 1652, iii. 55 & n. 3.
Tyrrell, Bridget: *see* Sanderson, Bridget, Lady Sanderson.
Tyrrell, Sir Edward, bt.: geneal., iv. 94, n. 4.
Tyrrell, Elizabeth, Lady Tyrrell, wife of Sir Timothy: geneal., i . 383 & n. 6.

Tyrrell (Terryll, Tyrill), Sir Timothy, iii. 383 & n. 6; E visits, at Shotover, *ib.*; iv. 67; geneal., iii. 55 & n. 3.
Tyrrhenian Sea, ii. 334, 351.
Tyson, Edward, M.D., iv. 275, n. 5; demonstration, exhibits, &c., by, at Royal Society meetings, iv. 275, 289–90 & n., 297, 314; social, iv. 337.

Ubaldino, Charles, count of Monte Feltre: notice, iv. 335–6 & n.
Ubaldino, Elizabeth, countess of Monte Feltre, and her sister: social, &c., iv. 335–6 & nn.
Ugbrooke, Devon: Clifford's chapel at: consecration of, iii. 577, n. 5.
Ullock (Orlock), Henry, D.D.; dean of Rochester: sermon by, v. 14 & n. 3.
Ulm: seized by Bavarians, 1702, v. 516 & n. 3; taken by Marlborough, 1704, v. 577 & n. 3, 579 & n. 5.
Ulysses: companion of (Baios), ii. 348 & n. 4.
Unitarianism: founders of, and growth of, in England, iii. 227, n. 1; iv. 378, n. 4; Socinians call themselves Unitarians, 1702, v. 494 & n. 1.
United Provinces [E uses various names for the country and its inhabitants, notably Holland, the Hollanders, and the Dutch, and the States to signify the government. Notices naming Holland, &c., if they relate to the United Provinces in general, are indexed here; those relating to the particular province, under Holland. For Dutch participation in the various wars *see* Wars; for William of Orange's expedition to England in 1688 and for his visits, when king, to the United Provinces *see* William III; references to a few select notices are repeated here]:
— E's travels in, 1641, ii. 30–62 & nn. (i. 23–43 & nn.); bibliographical and chronological note, ii. 569–71.
— politics and history: (i) external relations: assisted by Queen Elizabeth against Spain, i. 23 & n. 4; *see also* ii. 43, n. 2; Robert Dudley, earl of

United Provinces (*cont.*)
Leicester, as governor of, iv. 303; *see also* ii. 45, n. 6; the Veres in the war against Spain, i. 24 & n. 1; French desire to weaken, iii. 405 & n. 1; Fire of London attributed to Dutch and French incendiaries, iii. 457, n. 4, 462; Dutch abuse Charles II in pictures, &c., iii. 559 & n. 4; E ordered to write against, iv. 30; displeased with E's *Navigation and Commerce*, iv. 41 & n. 1; treaty with England, 1678, v. 458, n. 1; French hostility to: 1683, iv. 331; ~ 1686, iv. 525; danger to, by French capture of Luxembourg, iv. 378 & n. 1, 380, 549; French protestants seek refuge in, iv. 448, 485 & n. 2; warlike preparations of, May, Aug. 1688, iv. 582 *bis* & n. 1, 596; States General's declaration in support of William of Orange's expedition to England, iv. 604 & n. 2, 606; William III's concern with, 1689, iv. 625; congratulate William III on his accession to English throne, iv. 640 & n. 3; grief in, for Queen Mary, v. 201 & n. 3; English currency transferred to, 1696, v. 245; recognize Philip V as king of Spain, v. 446 *bis* & n. 1; as potential ally of England, 1701, v. 445–6; ask for English forces, v. 458 & n. 1; threatened by France, v. 462, 465; William III prepares defence of, v. 472 *bis* & n. 5; adhere to Grand Alliance, 1702, v. 494–5 & n.; negotiate with Marlborough, 1704, v. 555 & n. 2; prisoners from Blenheim allotted to, v. 577 & n. 4.
— — — gifts from: to Charles I, iii. 260; ~ to Charles II, iii. 262 & n. 6; *add.*; iii. 323 & n. 5; foreign policy of: selfishness of, iii. 236; Dutchman represented on figurehead of *Naseby*, iii. 149–50 & n.
— — (ii) internal affairs: Loevestein or States party, ii. 39 & n. 1 (i. 29); ~ conspiracy against, iii. 471, n. 1; Orange party, iii. 405, n. 1; ~ repressed, 1666, iii. 471; dispute between William

United Provinces (*cont.*)
of Orange and Amsterdam, &c., 1684, iv. 367 & n. 3, 369 & n. 2, 378 & n. 1.
— military: forces at siege of Huys te Gennep, 1641, ii. 35–8 & nn. (i. 27–8); army goes into winter-quarters, ii. 61 (i. 42); English and Scottish regiments in Dutch service sent to James II, 1685, iv. 458 & n. 1; review of forces near Arnhem, 1699, v. 352 & n. 4; forces increased, 1701, v. 441.
— naval: Albemarle's views on Dutch navy, iii. 425 & n. 1, 440, 618; fleet encounters *Merlin* yacht, 1671, iii. 606 & n. 1.
— colonial: *see* Surinam.
— merchant shipping: convoys provided for, 1689, iv. 651–2; losses: by Dunkirk raiders, i. 49; ~ by French action, 1694, v. 175; excluded from Spanish ports, 1701, v. 477, n. 1; East India fleet, 1665: attack on, at Bergen, iii. 562 & n. 5, 617 & nn. 2, 4, 618 & n. 3; iv. 21; ~ ships from, taken by Sandwich: *see* Ships and Shipping: *Golden Phoenix*; Smyrna or Turkish fleets: attacks on, or losses from, &c.: 1664, iii. 404 & n. 4, 407 & n. 6; ~ 1672, iii. 605–6 & n., 607, 609 & n. 3, 618; iv. 21 & n. 4, 211; ~ 1691, v. 67, n. 1; ~ 1693, v. 150 & n. 2; ~ 1694, v. 169 & n. 3.
— commerce and industry: assiduity in, a cause of Third Dutch War, iii. 620; do not trade with enemies, iii. 187 & n. 3; required to stop intercourse with France, &c., 1703, v. 526 & n. 3; Colchester cloth trade with, iii. 177 & n. 4; German commodities at Dort, ii. 32 & n. 4 (i. 24); (Dutch) East India Company: headquarters of, i. 35 & n. 2; ~ stock in India, &c., and business methods of, iii. 187; ~ yacht built for, iii. 296 & n. 5.
— social and miscellaneous: kitchen: in painting, iii. 262 & n. 6; land-drainage: skill in, i. 39; paintings: general buying of, ii. 39 & n. 4 (i. 29), 174 (i. 110); poor: provision for, i. 25;

United Provinces (*cont.*)
ii. 45–6 (i. 32–3); religion: churches protected from iconoclasm, ii. 49 & n. 1 (i. 34); roads: avenues of limes, i. 41; ii. 47, n. 4; ~ paving of, i. 24–5; ii. 31 (i. 24), 47–8 & n. (i. 34); skating, iii. 346–7; taxation: tax on births, &c., called a Dutch tax, 1695, v. 214; towns: built of brick, i. 24; ~ canals, &c., in, ii. 46 (i. 33); witchcraft: trials for, ii. 56, n. 7 *ad fin.*
— personal [persons mentioned by E in his account of his travels in the United Provinces are not indexed collectively]: (i) Dutchmen, &c. [E sometimes applies the word Dutch to Germans; *see further* Germany and Germans]: boy with remarkable eyes, v. 453 & n. 1; favourites of William III, v. 394; Jewess, iv. 222; marble-seller in Lambeth, iv. 98; men killed by Highlander, 1694, v. 175; settlers: at Colchester, iii. 177, n. 4; ~ at Norwich, iii. 595, n. 1; named persons said to be Dutch: *see* Borgh, — (ii. 316); Germain, Sir J. (v. 393); Kievit, Sir J. (iii. 470 & n. 6, &c.).
— — (ii) Englishmen, &c., in United Provinces: Argyll: sails from, 1685, iv. 443; Sir T. Armstrong: taken in, iv. 323, n. 4; Lady Arundel (?), ii. 479 & n. 4; Charles VI, as Archduke, 1703, v. 545; J. Claude, iv. 485; J. Diodati: sailing for, ii. 521 & n. 1; R. Ferguson: escapes to, 1685, iv. 452, n. 7; — Frazier, iv. 330; James, duke of York: comes from, 1651, iii. 36 & n. 4; ~ and his duchess: embark for, 1679, iv. 167, n. 6; Mary, Princess Royal, princess of Orange: comes from, 1660, iii. 257; Monmouth: returns from, 1679, iv. 189 & n. 6; ~ there, 1685, iv. 408; ~ agent for, iv. 452, n. 8 *ad fin.*; Ossory: goes to, 1677, 1678, iv. 112 & n. 2, 127 *bis* & nn. 1, 3, 137 & n. 5; Peter the Great, v. 277, n. 4, 287 & n. 5; Sir G. Radcliffe: returns from, iii. 36 & n. 4; Shaftesbury: dies in, iv. 328–9 & n.; duchess of

United Provinces (*cont.*)
Somerset (as Lady Ogle): takes refuge in, iv. 260, n. 4 *ad fin.*, 267, n. 2; Sunderland, 1688–9, iv. 610, n. 1, 642, n. 4; ~ returned from, v. 49 & n. 2; Lady Sunderland: goes to, 1689, iv. 647 & n. 4; ~ returned from, v. 9; Sir G. and Lady Sylvius: go to, iv. 124.
Universities: Aix-en-Provence, ii. 163 & n. 5 (i. 103); Bologna, ii. 420 & n. 5; Bourges, ii. 152–3 & n. (i. 98); Caen, ii. 127 (i. 81); Cambridge: *see* Cambridge; Cricklade, iii. 117 & n. 3; Ferrara, ii. 428; Geneva, ii. 527, 529–30 & nn.; Leyden, ii. 51 & n. 4 (i. 36); ~ buildings, &c., ii. 52–4 & nn. (i. 36–7); ~ E matriculates at, ii. 52 & n. 4 (i. 36); Orleans, ii. 136, n. 3, 138 *bis* (i. 90, 91); Oxford: *see* Oxford; Padua: *see* Padua; Paris: Sorbonne, &c., ii. 94 & n. 1 (i. 62), 97 & nn. 1, 2 (i. 64); Pisa, ii. 181 *bis* & n. 8 (i. 114 *bis*); Rome: Sapienza, ii. 376; Siena, ii. 203 & n. 5; Valence, ii. 160 & n. 1 (i. 102).
Upcott, William, i. *52*; catalogues Wotton library, i. *53*, *55*; account by, of Evelyn MSS., i. *53–4*; markings of, on Diary MSS., i. *45*, nn. 1, 2, *46*; persuades Lady Evelyn to allow Diary to be published, i. *54*; share of, in first edition of Diary, i. *54–6*, *115*; share of, in second edition, i. *58*, n. 3; transcripts of V made by, i. *56*, *63*, *69*, n. 1, *117* & n. 3; *see also* iii. 625, n. 5.
Uphill, Mary: *see* Howard, Mary, Lady Howard.
Uphill, Susannah, actress, iii. 466, n. 2.
Upman, —, iv. 96.
Upminster, Essex: weather diaries kept at, 1697–9, v. 263, n. 2; weather at, v. 291, n. 3, 302, n. 1.
Upnor Castle, Kent: fortified against Dutch, 1667, iii. 485 & n. 3; ships run aground at, iii. 486, n. 5; defences of, 1672, iii. 610, 620.
Uppingham, Rutland: notice, iii. 122 & n. 2; rector of: *see* Allington, J.
Upsala (Upsall): fire at, 1702, v. 504.
Urban VIII, pope (Maffeo Barberini), ii. 196, n. 5; family of: original home of, ii. 200 & n. 11; birth-place of, ii. 196 & n. 5; relations of, with Venice, ii. 297 & n. 5; in war of Castro, ii. 211, n. 2, 371–2 & n.; knights L. Vittori, ii. 400, n. 1; arms of, ii. 305; depredations of, at Pantheon, ii. 261, 371–2 & nn.; inscription of, ii. 302; alters inscriptions, ii. 297 & n. 5, 405, n. 1; tomb of, ii. 264 & n. 6, 265, n. 2; statue of, at Velletri, ii. 317 & n. 6; geneal., ii. 369.
buildings, &c., of: decorates SS. Cosma e Damiano, ii. 219; St. Peter's: canopy of high altar, ii. 261 & nn. 1, 3; ~ statues, &c., ii. 262–3 & nn.
Urbino: majolica of, iii. 11, n. 3.
Urbino: duke of: library of, in Vatican library, ii. 301 & n. 2.
Uriah: in sermons, iv. 349; v. 414.
Ursa Nova *and* Ursa Vecchio: *see* Orzinuovi, Orzivecchi.
Ursini: *see* Orsini.
Ursler, Barbara, the Hairy Maid: notice, iii. 198 & n. 1.
Ushant, Cape: fleet movements near: 1691, v. 69, n. 2; ~ 1693, v. 150 & n. 2.
Ussher, Elizabeth: *see* Tyrrell, Elizabeth, Lady Tyrell.
Ussher, James, D.D.; archbishop of Armagh 1625, ii. 552–3 & n.; preacher at Lincoln's Inn, ii. 553, n. 1; at Reigate Priory, iii. 156 & nn. 1, 3; death of: Dr. R. Parr's grief for, iii. 604; prophecies of, concerning: destruction of Church of England, iii. 157 & n. 2; ~ persecution of protestant churches, iv. 487 & n. 1; letter to, from Dr. J. Bramhall, iv. 507, 508, n. 1; Psrr's *Life* of: publication of, delayed, ii. 507–8 & n.; views of, on Biblical studies, &c., iii. 156–7 & nn.; sermons by, ii. 553 *bis*, 554, 556; iii. 61; geneal., iii. 383 & n. 6; chaplain of: *see* Parr, R.; *see also* Books mentioned in text.
Uthwat, John: funeral sermon for (?; as Uttart), iv. 43 & n. 2.
Utrecht: notice, ii. 34 & n. 6 (i. 27); *kermis* at, *ib.*
Utrecht: Treaty of: Queen Mary of Modena's interests at, v. 271, n. 2.

Uvedale, Elizabeth: *see* Howard, Elizabeth, countess of Carlisle.
Uvedale, Robert: garden of, at Enfield, iv. 91, n. 4.
Uvedale, Sir William: geneal., iv. 561, n. 2.
Uxbridge, Middlesex, iii. 381.
Uzza: in sermons, iv. 648; v. 73.
Uzziah: in sermon, v. 257.

Vacca, F.; sculpture by, ii. 231 & n. 2.
Vacuum: experiments with Boyle's air-pump, iii. 255 & n. 3, 271 & n. 3, 284–5, 318; iv. 271, 293, 381, 521; adhesive power of polished surfaces demonstrated, iii. 291–2.
Vaga, Pietro Bonaccorsi, called Perino del, ii. 120, n. 8; tomb of, ii. 372; paintings by, ii. 120 & n. 8 (i. 77) (?); iii. 11.
Valais: E's journey through, ii. 511–19 & nn.; as Valtoline, in error, ii. 515 & n. 1; ally of confederate Swiss cantons, ii. 515, n. 1, 518, n. 1; armed forces of, ii. 515, n. 7, 517; boundary of, towards Savoy, ii. 519 & n. 1; fertility of, ii. 515 & n. 4; inhabitants of: dress of, ii. 510–11 & n., 517; ~ manners of, ii. 511 & n. 3, 517.
Valais, Lower: governor (Landvogt) of, ii. 516, 518 & n. 5.
Valais, Upper: and Landvogt of Lower Valais, ii. 518, n. 5; intercourse of, with Lago Maggiore, ii. 508, n. 5.
Valence, on the Rhone: notice, ii. 160 & n. 1 (i. 102).
Valence: Bishop of, 1655–87: *see* Cosnac, D. de (iv. 486 & n. 3).
Valenciennes: military operations round, 1649, ii. 561, n. 1.
Valentia: second Viscount, 1660–1: *see* Annesley, Arthur, later earl of Anglesey.
Valenza (Valentia), in Piedmont: besieged, 1696, v. 259 & n. 4, 260 & n. 3.
Valerio Vincentino: *see* Belli, V.
Valerius Volusi: tomb of (error), ii. 394 & n. 2.
Valla, Lorenzo: tomb of, ii. 274 & n. 8.
Valladolid: English Jesuit college at: Titus Oates at, iv. 153, n. 4.
Valmarano (Ulmarini), Count —: garden of, at Vicenza, ii. 483–4 & nn.
Valtoline (Val Tellina): error for Valais, ii. 515 & n. 1.
Vanbrugh, Sir John: buildings by: Addiscombe House (attributed), v. 541, n. 1; ~ Robin Hood's Well: pavilion near, iii. 128, n. 2; geneal., v. 211, n. 8 *ad fin.*
Vanbrugh, William: appointed secretary to commissioners for Greenwich Hospital, v. 211–12 & n.
Vandall: *see* Vondel, J. van den.
Vandals: destroy Capua, ii. 324, n. 5.
Vanderborcht: *see* Borcht, H. van der.
van der Gucht, M.: engravings by, v. 487, n. 1.
Vandervort, Walter *or* Isaac: at Venice, ii. 477 & n. 1.
Van Dyck, Sir Anthony: art-collection of, iv. 312, n. 3; painting from, iii. 216, n. 3.
paintings by: collections, &c., containing unspecified works: Bristol (later Sunderland), iv. 162; Melfort: in auction, v. 144–5 & n.; Northumberland, iii. 216; royal, at Kensington Palace, v. 237; Wilton House, iii. 114, n. 1; minor collections, iv. 576 & n. 5; portraits by: Lords Bristol and Bedford (together), iv. 162 & n. 3, 403–4; Charles I: copy of, iv. 576, n. 5; ~ children of, ii. 548, n. 3; Charles II, as child; cited, iii. 468, n. 4; Sir Kenelm Digby (false attribution?), iv. 404 & n. 2; Sir T. Hanmer, iv. 402 & n. 6; James Stuart, duke of Lennox and Richmond (as a man in his shirt), iii. 96 & n. 3; Mary Stuart, duchess of Lennox and Richmond: copy of, in enamel, iii. 260 & n. 3; H. Liberti, iv. 102 & n. 6; Catherine, Countess Rivers, &c. (as two ladies), iv. 404 & n. 3; self-portrait, iv. 102 & n. 5; Lady Isabella Thynne, ii. 549 & n. 9.
copy from Titian by, ii. 548 & n. 5; follower of: *see* Neve, C. de (ii. 548, n. 4).
Vane, Christopher; first Baron Barnard 1698: appointed privy councillor, 1688 (in text as Sir H. Vane), iv. 590 & n. 4.
Vane, Frances, Lady Vane, wife of Sir Henry, jnr.: geneal., ii. 480, n. 3.

Vane, Sir H.: error for Christopher Vane, iv. 590 & n. 4.
Vane, Sir Henry, sen.: imprisoned (error), iii. 183 & n. 2.
Vane, Sir Henry, jnr.: imprisoned, 1656, iii. 183 & n. 2; geneal., ii. 480, n. 3; iv. 590 & n. 4.
Vane, Sir Henry, 1693: error for Sir H. Fane, v. 147 & n. 7.
Vanni, Curzio: relief by, ii. 272 & n. 6.
Vanni, Francesco: painting by, ii. 358 & n. 5.
Varennes-sur-Allier, ii. 155 & n. 1 (i. 100).
Varennes-en-Argonne, ii. 155, n. 1.
Varro, Marcus Terentius, iv. 256 & n. 1.
Vasanzio, Giovanni (J. van Santen): designs casino, Villa Borghese, ii. 251, n. 4.
Vasari, Giorgio, ii. 188, n. 7; building completed by, ii. 417, n. 1; paintings by: in Palazzo Vecchio, Florence, ii. 188 & n. 7 (i. 118), 414; ~ elsewhere, ii. 197, 297 & n. 3, 367 & n. 9; pupil of, ii. 267, n. 3.
Vasconcellos e Sousa, Luis de, conde de Castelmelhor: *see* Castelmelhor.
Vasquez Coronadc, Don Juan: at Milan, ii. 502 & n. 4.
Vatteville, Charles, baron de, Spanish ambassador in England: encounter of, with French ambassador, &c., iii. 297–300 & nn.; *add.*
Vauban, Marshal: as critic of French governmental system, i. 88, n. 2.
Vaucluse, near Avignon: in view, ii. 162 & n. 6 (i. 103).
Vaud, canton, ii. 520, n. 2.
Vaudois: *see* Waldenses.
Vaughan, Sir John, judge; knighted 1668, iii. 492–3 & n.; at Greenwich, iii. 492, 497 & n. 2.
Vaughan, John; styled Lord Vaughan 1667–86; third earl of Carbery 1686, iv. 564, n. 3; as Carbery: elected president of Royal Society, iv. 564; social, v. 139.
Vaughan: Lord, 1667–86 (courtesy title): *see* Vaughan, John, later earl of Carbery.
Vaughan of Emlyn: second Baron, 1686–1713: *see* Vaughan, John, earl of Carbery (v. 139, n. 3).
Vau-le-Duc, near Louvain: armies near, 1694, v. 184, n. 1.
Vaux, George: buys Caversham Park, 1653, iii. 99, n. 3.
Veau, — de: riding-academy of, ii. 134 & n. 2 (i. 87); ~ pupil at, iii. 8, n. 2.
Vedra (Dovedro?), ii. 508 & n. 5.
Veere (Der-Veere), in Zealand, ii. 31 (i. 24); the Veres and, i. 24 & n. 1.
Vegetation [*see also* Agriculture]: Provence, ii. 162 & n. 10, 163–4 (i. 103 *bis*), 167; Liguria, ii. 169, 170, 171 & n. 2 (i. 106, 107, 108); near Fondi, ii. 322–3; Phlegraean Fields, ii. 338–9 & n., 351; near Pistoia, ii. 410; Euganean Hills, ii. 480–1 & nn.; north Italy, ii. 485 & n. 3, 488, 489; Simplon Pass, ii. 509, 514; Salisbury Plain, iii. 115.
Vejer, Spain: *see* Wyers Bay.
Velasquez: portraits by: cited, iii. 320, n. 4, 321, n. 2.
Velletri, ii. 317 & nn. 5, 6; road to, ii. 316, n. 3 *ad fin.*
Venantius, St.: relics of, ii. 268, n. 1.
Vendôme, César, duke of: owner of Chenonceaux, ii. 152 & n. 4 (i. 98).
Vendôme, Louis-Joseph, duke of: geneal., iv. 318 & n. 5.
Vendôme, Philippe de, Grand Prieur de France (Knights of Malta): at Windsor, iv. 318 & n. 5.
Venice [Venice is here divided into the City, comprising the social life, topography, &c., and the Republic, comprising the political organization, its history, and its territories].
Venice: the City:
— E at, 1645–6, ii. 429–78 & nn., *passim*; bibliographical and general note, ii. 429, n. 6; E's journey to, from Rome: begins, ii. 401 & n. 8; ~ chronology of, ii. 405, n. 2; ~ cost of, ii. 429; E's journey from, to the Alps, ii. 507; Egyptian inscription given to E at, ii. 469 & n. 4; iii. 172; E's collections from, ii 478.
— personal:
— — Venetians: Pope Alexander VIII (iv. 650 & n. 1, 651).
— — English and other strangers (individuals) at Venice, &c.: (Sir) Francis Bramston, ii. 470 & n. 3; Robert Bruce, Lord

Venice (*cont.*)
Bruce, later earl of Ailesbury, ii. 449; C. C. *or* D. de Groot, ii. 476 & n. 5; T. Henshaw, ii. 470 & n. 3; John Hobson, ii. 476 & n. 3; *see also* ii. 469 & n. 6, 475; Henry Frederick Howard, Lord Mowbray, later earl of Arundel, ii. 470; — Kingston: in Venetian service, iii. 13; A. Panormita, ii. 328, n. 10; Dr. Denis Papin: scientific activities of, iv. 278, 279, n. 1; Captain — Powell, ii. 451, 468; Anna Renzi: sings, &c., ii. 450 & n. 3, 474–5; J. Thicknesse, ii. 470; — Vandervoort, merchant at: library of, &c., ii. 477 & n. 1; Edmund Waller, ii. 478; prince of Wertenberg, ii. 476; (Sir) George Wheler, iv. 528; unnamed: Candiot, ii. 460; Frenchman, ii. 442; Genoese singer, ii. 450, 475; Polish bishop, ii. 428.
— social and miscellaneous:
— — Ascension-tide: Marriage with the Sea at, ii. 401 & n. 8, 431–2 & nn.; *add.*; ii. 458; ~ in comparison, iii. 333; amusements, ii. 433, n. 3, 451 & n. 3; fair, ii. 446 & n. 10.
— — bath, Turkish, ii. 430–1 & nn.
— — carnival, ii. 473–4 & nn.; amusements permitted during, ii. 451 & n. 3.
— — courtesans: dress of, ii. 448 & n. 4.
— — dress: men's, ii. 442, 448–9 & nn.; iv. 493; women's, ii. 446–8 & nn.
— — executions: place and method of, ii. 401, n. 2, 445 & n. 1, 459.
— — glassware: manufacture of, at Murano, ii. 467 & n. 5; E's purchases, ii. 478; in comparisons, iv. 13, 98–9.
— — gondolas, ii. 432–3 & nn.; mentioned, ii. 445, 448, 459, 461, 468, 475; gift of, with gondoliers, to Charles II, iii. 322 & n. 2.
— — guides, ii. 434, 442.
— — illustrissimo, ii. 444 & n. 7.
— — lapidaries, ii. 480 & n. 2.
— — lotteries in Venetian manner v. 158, 193 & n. 1.
— — Marriage with the Sea: *see* Ascension-tide *above*.

Venice (*cont.*)
— — masks: wearing of, ii. 451 & n. 2, 473 & n. 7.
— — masquerading, ii. 432 & n. 2; *add.*; ii. 473–4; in comparison, iii. 1–2.
— — merchants: meeting-places of, ii. 433–4, 442.
— — money: *ducato di banco*: value of, ii. 401, n. 6.
— — mountebanks, ii. 474 & n. 5.
— — nobles: marriages of, ii. 449 & n. 4; attend procession at Padua, ii. 453–4; *see also* ii. 475.
— — opera, ii. 449–50 & nn., 474 & n. 6, 475.
— — popular sports, ii. 474 & nn. 2, 3.
— — population, ii. 429, n. 6 *ad fin.*
— — promenade, ii. 433 & n. 3, 468.
— — ridotto, ii. 451 & nn. 1, 2, 474.
— — scientific academy (P. and G. A. Sarotti), iv. 278, 279, n. 1.
— — strangers in: concourse of, in Piazza, ii. 449; English: consuls, ii. 469 & n. 6, 475, 476, n. 3; iii. 86 & n. 1; ~ consulage, 1672, iii. 629, n. 5, 630 *bis* & n. 1, 631 & n. 4; ~ merchant-ships trading to, ii. 429 & n. 3; ~ *see also* personal *above*; Greeks (Orthodox): church of, ii. 460.
— — sumptuary laws: observance of, ii. 451 & n. 4.
— — theatres, ii. 450, nn. 1–3; seasons for performances, ii. 451 & n. 3, 474.
— — Venice treacle, ii. 478 & n. 2.
— topography: general: architecture: Greek style of, in frequent use, ii. 440 & n. 4; ~ stateliness of, ii. 459; bridges: number of, ii. 446 & n. 8; built on piles, ii. 459; *see also* ii. 446, n. 4; in comparisons: with Ghent, ii. 74 (i. 48); ~ with Paris, iii. 637 (extract from *State of France*); site, ii. 431; ~ shape of, ii. 446 & n. 7; in view (?), ii. 423 & n. 3; water-supply, ii. 431 & n. 2.
— — particular buildings, streets, &c.:
— — — Aquila Nera: lodgings at, ii. 429 & n. 5.
— — — archaeological museum: sculpture in, ii. 461, n. 1.

Venice (*cont.*)
— — — Arsenal: notice, ii. 456–9 & nn.; guns at: fired, ii. 432.
— — — Campanile di S. Marco, ii. 435, n. 3; notice and ascent of, ii. 445–6 & nn.
— — — Campo S. Giacomo di Rialto, ii. 433, n. 4 *ad fin.*
— — — Chetto di S. Felice: *see* Traghetto.
— — — churches [for churches on the more outlying islands *see* environs *below*]:
— — — — Carmini, I, ii. 461 & n. 6.
— — — — Frari, I, ii. 461, n. 2.
— — — — S. Elena, ii. 462.
— — — — S. Geminiano, ii. 435, n. 3; as S. Jacomo, ii. 436 & n. 2.
— — — — S. Giorgio dei Greci: Orthodox service at, &c., ii. 460 & n. 1; *add.*
— — — — S. Giorgio Maggiore and its monastery, ii. 461 & n. 7; *add.*
— — — — S. Giovanni Evangelista, ii. 461 & n. 3.
— — — — SS. Giovanni e Paolo, ii. 459 & nn. 6, 7.
— — — — S. Luca, ii. 460 & n. 5.
— — — — S. Marco: notice, ii. 436–42 & nn.; Atrio: columns in, ii. 438, n. 5; baptistery and font, ii. 438 & n. 8; Capitello, ii. 438, n. 9; chapels: S. Isidoro, ii. 438–9 & n.; ~ Zeno, ii. 438, n. 6, 440, n. 2; doors, ii. 439 & n. 4; façade, ii. 437 & n. 2; Horses, bronze, ii. 437 & n. 3, 439 & n. 6; Pala d'Oro, ii. 438 & n. 3; porphyry reliefs on exterior, ii. 439–40 & n.; treasury, ii. 440–2 & nn.; ~ door of: mosaic over, ii. 439 & n. 2.
— — — — S. Maria dei Miracoli, ii. 460–1 & nn.
— — — — S. Moisè: *ridotti* held near, ii. 451, n. 1.
— — — — S. Polo, ii. 461 & n. 2.
— — — — S. Rocco, ii. 461 & n. 4.
— — — — S. Sebastiano, ii. 461.
— — — — S. Tomà, ii. 461, n. 2.
— — — — S. Zaccaria, ii. 460 & nn. 3, 4.
— — — — Servi, I, ii. 442 & n. 5.
— — — Courts of Justice: *see* Doges' Palace *below*.
— — — Dogana (del Mare?), ii. 429 & n. 4.
— — — Doges' Palace, ii. 436 & n. 5; notice, ii. 442–4 & nn.

Venice (*cont.*)
— — — Exchange: *see* Rialto *below*.
— — — Fondaco dei Tedeschi, ii. 434 & n. 1.
— — — Ghetto, ii. 477 & n. 2.
— — — Grand Canal, ii. 433; evening promenade on, *ib.* & n. 3.
— — — islands [for the more outlying islands *see* environs *below*]:
— — — — S. Elena, ii. 461, n. 9 *ad fin.*, 462.
— — — — S. Giorgio Maggiore: in view, ii. 445; notice, ii. 461 & n. 7.
— — — Library of St. Mark, ii. 435, n. 3, 436 & nn. 1, 3, 4, 445 & nn. 3, 4, 6.
— — — Loggetta, ii. 435, n. 3, 446 & n. 9.
— — — Merceria, ii. 434 & n. 3.
— — — Mint: *see* Zecca *below*.
— — — Palazzo dei Camerlenghi, ii. 433, n. 4 *ad fin.*
— — — Palazzo Grimani, ii. 459 & n. 4.
— — — Piazza di S. Marco: notice, ii. 434–6 & nn.; Ascension-tide fair held in, ii. 446, n. 10; buildings around, ii. 445 & n. 6, 446; concourse of strangers in, ii. 449; flag-staffs in, ii. 436 & n. 6; in comparison, ii. 422.
— — — Piazzetta, ii. 435, n. 3, 436 & n. 4; as St. Mark's: taking gondola at, ii. 461; bull-baiting in, ii. 474, n. 2; daily meetings in, ii. 442 & n. 9; columns in, ii. 444–5 & n.; ~ execution between, ii. 459; ~ imitated at Vicenza, ii. 483; pillars at north end of, ii. 443 & n. 1.
— — — Ponte di Rialto, ii. 433 & n. 2; dimensions of, iii. 128, n. 7; lodgings near, ii. 429.
— — — Procuratie, ii. 445 & n. 6.
— — — Rialto: as the exchange, ii. 433–4 & n.
— — — Scuola di S. Rocco, ii. 461 & n. 4; Tintoretto's Crucifixion in: copy of, &c., iii. 567 & n. 4.
— — — Senate House: *see* Doges' Palace *above*.
— — — statue of B. Colleoni, ii. 459 & n. 6.
— — — Torre dell' Orologio, ii. 434–5 & nn.

Venice (*cont.*)
— — — Traghetto (chetto) di S. Felice, ii. 450, 451, n. 1.
— — — Zecca, ii. 445 & nn. 4, 5.
— environs:
— — Fusina *or* Lizza Fusina, ii. 452; lock at, ii. 452, n. 5.
— — islands [*see also* Murano, &c., *below*]:
— — — S. Cristoforo, ii. 468 & n. 2.
— — — S. Lazzaro: church on (called St. Laurence in error), ii. 461 & n. 9.
— — — S. Michele: church on, ii. 468 & nn. 2–5.
— — — S. Niccolò, ii. 468 & n. 6.
— — — S. Spirito: church on, ii. 461 & nn. 8, 9.
— — Lido: guns at, fired, ii. 432; Porto di: ceremony at, ii. 432, n. 2; S. Niccolò di, ii. 468 & n. 6; ~ ceremony at, ii. 432, n. 2.
— — Mazzorbo: S. Niccolò della Cavana near, ii. 468, n. 6.
— — Murano, ii. 467–8 & nn.; boat-races at, ii. 433, n. 3; glass made at, iv. 13.
— — Terraferma, ii. 452; water brought from, to Venice, ii. 431 & n. 2.
Venice: the Republic: government: Doge or doges: cap of, ii. 441 & n. 2; ~ in ceremony, ii. 432, 458; ~ dress of, ii. 449 & n. 5; ~ election of (F. da Molino), ii. 473 & n. 5; ~ gallows for, ii. 443 & n. 1; ~ portraits of, ii. 444 & n. 3; Great Council, ii. 443, n. 7; Patriarch of: in ceremony, ii. 432, n. 2; ~ *see* Morosini, G. F.; Procurators: dress of, ii. 449 & n. 5; Senate, ii. 443, n. 7; ~ hall for, at Arsenal, ii. 457 & n. 2; Senators: in ceremony, ii. 432; ~ dress of, ii. 442 & n. 9, 449, n. 5.
— — history, &c.: origin of, ii. 431 & n. 3; durability of, *ib.*; patron-saint of, ii. 441; conquests of, ii. 431; Brides of (legend): votive offerings for, ii. 440–1 & n.; submission at, of Frederick I to Pope Alexander III, ii. 439 & n. 3; ~ in painting, ii. 297 & n. 5; plot against, of B. Tiepolo: relics of, ii. 458 & n. 9; relations of, with Pope Urban VIII, ii. 297 & n. 5; in Cretan War (1645–69), ii. 429, n. 6 *ad fin.*, 456, n. 8; ~ English ship pressed for, ii. 451–2 & n., 468; ~ galleys for Candia, ii. 475; ~ soldiers for, ii. 471 & n. 4; ~ Candia taken by Turks, &c., iii. 515 & n. 4; ~ at war with Turkey (1684–99): seeks English help, iv. 492, n. 1; ~ engagements, &c., iv. 560 & n. 3; v. 209 & n. 1, 215 & n. 6; frontier-dispute with Turkey, 1699, v. 345, n. 3; relations of, with France, 1701, v. 441; neutrality of, 1701, v. 462.
— — — gifts made by: to Charles II, iii. 322 & n. 2; to Louis XIV, ii. 442, n. 5.
— — — territories and possessions: travellers in: require bills of health, ii. 426 & n. 9; *see also* ii. 429; frontier, ii. 490 & n. 7; Venetians foment disputes between Vicenza and Brescia, ii. 483 & n. 4; possessions: in Greece, ii. 439 & n. 5; Crema, ii. 490 & n. 7; Orzinuovi, ii. 490 & n. 6; Peschiera, ii. 488.
Venier, Girolamo: Venetian ambassador to England, 1696, v. 238, n. 1.
Venloo: taken by Confederates, 1702, v. 514 & n. 9, 516 & n. 4.
Venner, Thomas: revolt of, iii. 266 & n. 5, 266–7 & n.
Ventimiglia (Vintimiglia), ii. 169 (i. 106).
Venusti, Marcello, ii. 274, n. 9; paintings by, ii. 274 & n. 9, 377 & n. 5.
Ver, near Bayeux: gives name to Vere family, i. 24, n. 1.
Vercelli: Raudine plain near, ii. 485, n. 3.
Vere, earls of Oxford: *see* De Vere.
Vere, Sir Francis: in Dutch wars, i. 24, n. 1.
Vere, Sir Horace, Baron Vere: in Dutch service, i. 24, n. 1; regiment of, ii. 36, n. 1.
Vere: Baron, 1625–35: *see* Vere, Sir Horace.
Verneuil, Henri de Bourbon, bishop of Metz, count and later duke of, ii. 534, n. 3; in England, iii. 412 & n. 4.
Verney, —: social, iv. 382 & n. 3.

Verney, Sir Edmund (called Sir Richard in text): killed, i. 53, 54, n. 1.
Verney, Mrs. Mary, first wife of Richard Verney, later Lord Willoughby de Broke: geneal., iii. 184, n. 6; iv. 382, n. 3.
Verney, Sir Richard: error for Sir Edmund Verney, i. 53, 54, n. 1.
Verney, Richard; third Baron Willoughby de Broke 1696, iii. 184, n. 6; social, iii. 184; son of (?), iv. 382 & n. 3.
Vernon, Sir Henry: London agent for tax-collectors, *c.* 1664–7, iii. 464, n. 1.
Vernon, James: as secretary of state: reported dismissal of, v. 406 & n. 3.
Verona: notice, ii. 485–8 & nn.; E's journey to, from Vicenza, ii. 484.
  Adige at, ii. 485 & n. 4; amphitheatre (Arena), ii. 486 & nn. 1, 2; aqueducts, ii. 486; Arch of Marius, &c., ii. 486 & n. 3; Cavalletto inn, ii. 485 & n. 1; fortifications, ii. 486 & n. 4; Giardino Giusti, ii. 487 & n. 2; Loggia del Consiglio, ii. 486–7 & n.; Palazzo di Fiorio della Seta, &c., ii. 485 & n. 5; Ponte Nuovo, ii. 485, n. 5; S. Tommaso: ruins near, ii. 486, n. 3; temples: ruins of, ii. 486; Tombs of the Scaligers, ii. 485 & n. 2.
  praised by Scaliger, ii. 487–8 & nn.; men of genius born at, ii. 486–7 & n.; Margherita Emiliani of, ii. 468 & n. 4; marble from, ii. 462, n. 4, 463, n. 3.
Veronese, Paolo Caliari called, ii. 113, n. 2; paintings by: identifiable: Christ in house of Simon (Venice, now Louvre), ii. 442 & n. 5; Martyrdom of St. Justina (Padua, S. Giustina), ii. 455–6 & n.; unidentifiable, ii. 113–14 *bis* (i. 73), 115 (i. 74), 284, 415 & n. 3; drawing by (?), iii. 339 & n. 4.
Veronica, St.: sudarium (Volto santo) of, ii. 262 & n. 3; exhibited, ii. 292 & n. 2, 385 & nn. 3, 4, 386 & n. 2.
Verrio (Virrio), Antonio, iii. 591, n. 5; inscription in honour of, iv. 465 & n. 7; garden of, at Windsor, iv. 176 & n. 4, 207–8; occupies royal garden, St. James's, iv. 522 & n. 1; visits E, iv. 182.
  paintings by: self-portrait, iv. 377; decorative: at Ashtead, iv. 377; Cassiobury, iv. 199 & n. 5; Chelsea Hospital: Charles II, v. 53; Chiswick, Sir S. Fox's house: designs for, iv. 316; Euston, iii. 591–2 & n.; Montague House, London, iv. 344; Whitehall, Roman Catholic chapel, iv. 534; Windsor Castle, St. George's Hall, &c.: notices, iv. 316–17 & nn., 465 & n. 7; ~ praised, iv. 176 & n. 3; ~ mentioned, iii. 592; iv. 136 & n. 3; Woodcote Park, ii. 542, n. 3.
Verrocchio, Andrea, sculptor, ii. 459, n. 6; tomb of P. and G. de' Medici by, ii. 416 & n. 4; statue of Colleoni by, ii. 459 & n. 6.
Verrua (Verrue), Piedmont: demanded by France as security, 1690, v. 25; besieged by French, 1705, v. 587 & n. 2.
Versailles: Palace of: imitated in building, iv. 341, n. 2; tapestry representing, iv. 343 & n. 2; Louis XIV's recovery from illness celebrated at, iv. 533, n. 6; James II at, v. 32, n. 1.
Vertue, George: mentions MS. Diary, i. *52*.
Verulam: ruins of, ii. 78 (i. 51).
Verulam: Baron, 1618–21: *see* Bacon, Francis, later Viscount St. Albans.
Vesey, John, D.D.; archbishop of Tuam 1679, v. 21, n. 4; sermons by, v. 21, 44, 55, 69–70.
Vesling, Johann, professor of anatomy, &c., at Padua, ii. 466, n. 6; as keeper of botanic garden, Padua, ii. 466; attends E, ii. 472; dissection by, ii. 475 & n. 3; Waller's poem on, ii. 475, n. 3, 478, n. 3; *see also* iii. 501.
Vespasian, Roman emperor: brings spoils of Jerusalem to Rome, &c., ii. 247, n. 3, 275, n. 3; as builder of: Coliseum, ii. 247, 248, n. 8; ~ Temple of Peace, Rome, ii. 245; inscription of, ii. 224 & n. 2; tomb of, ii. 361 & n. 3.
Vestal virgins: punishment of, for incontinence, ii. 241.

Vesuna: ancient name of Périgueux, ii. 167, n. 3.
Vesuvius, Mount: ascent of, &c., ii. 332–6 & nn.; crater, ii. 335 & nn. 1–4; ~ as mouth of hell, ii. 336 & n. 4; eruptions: A.D. 79, ii. 335 & n. 5; 1631, ii. 332, n. 2, 336 & nn. 1–3; ~ inscription relating to, ii. 333 & n. 2; 1696 (?), v. 234 & n. 6; summit, ii. 334 & nn. 2–5; in views, ii. 326, 329 & n. 2.
Via Appia: E's journeys on (false statements, &c.), ii. 316, n. 3 *ad fin.*, 317, 318, 356, n. 1; course of, ii. 317, n. 7, 318, nn. 2, 4, 8; described, ii. 319 & nn. 3–5, 322 & n. 4; milestone from, ii. 383 & n. 2; paving of, ii. 321; *see also* Rome: topography: roads.
Via Appia Nuova, ii. 316, n. 3 *bis*.
Via Cassia: old and new, ii. 211, n. 2.
Via Herculanea, Phlegraean Fields, ii. 345, nn. 2, 3.
Via Latina, ii. 316, n. 3.
Via Praenestina, ii. 238 & n. 7.
Viareggio (Viregio), ii. 179 (i. 113).
Viaron: *see* Vierzon.
Via Toscolana, ii. 316, n. 3.
Via Triumphalis: journey along, ii. 212, n. 1; *see also* Rome: topography: roads.
Viccars, Dr. — (Rev. John Viccars ?): sermon by, iii. 152 & n. 2.
Vicentino, Andrea Michieli, called: painting by, ii. 444 & n. 5.
Vicenza: notice, ii. 481–4 & nn.; E arrives at, ii. 480.
  disputes of, with Brescia, ii. 483 & nn. 4, 6.
  arch in Campo Marzo, ii. 484 & n. 6; Arco delle Scalette, ii. 484, n. 6; Basilica Palladiana, ii. 481–2 & nn.; Campo Marzo, ii. 484 & nn. 5, 6; garden of Count Valmarana, ii. 483–4 & nn.; Loggia del Capitanio, ii. 482–3 & n.; Palazzo Thiene, now Bonin (as Oleine), ii. 483 & n. 8; Piazza dei Signori, ii. 481 & n. 5, 482, 483 & nn. 1, 2; Rotonda, Palladio's, ii. 484 & n. 3; Teatro Olimpico, ii. 482 & nn. 2–5.
Vico, Lago di (Lacus Ciminus), ii. 211 & nn. 2, 3.
Victor, St.: relic of, ii. 165 & n. 4 (i. 105).
Victor Amadeus II; duke of Savoy 1675; king of Sicily 1713; of Sardinia 1718 [for his persecution of the Piedmontese Waldenses and for the campaigns in Savoy, &c., in his time, *see* Waldenses *and* Wars: War of the League of Augsburg; under the present heading are indexed all notices in which the duke is specified]:
  persecutes the Waldenses, iv. 511 *bis* & n. 2, 636; v. 3; reinstates the survivors, v. 25.
  joins Confederates against France, 1690, v. 25 & n. 2; on campaign, 1690–5, v. 31, 33 *bis* & n. 6, 59–60 & n., 71 & n. 4, 117 & n. 2, 209 & n. 2; leaves Confederates and joins France, 1696, v. 247 & n. 4, 250–1, 252 & n. 1, 256 & n. 2; daughter of, marries Louis, duke of Burgundy, v. 260 & n. 3; on campaign, 1696–7, v. 260, 264 & n. 5; joins Allies against France, 1703, v. 547 *bis*, 548 & n. 1.
  geneal., v. 421, n. 3.
Vienna: Arundel at, i. 21 & n. 1; threatened by Turks, 1683, iv. 331; siege of, by Turks: relieved by John III Sobieski, iv. 340 & n. 3; v. 247; ~ Charles Granville, Lord Lansdown (later second earl of Bath), at, iv. 400–1 & n.; v. 476; ~ captured horses from, iv. 398–9 & nn.; entry into, of Wilhelmina Amalia, queen of the Romans, v. 317 & n. 3; Archduke Charles leaves, v. 545 & n. 3; Kunsthistorisches Hofmuseum at: paintings in, ii. 70, n. 5, 495, n. 6.
Vienne, Dauphiné: notice, ii. 158–9 & nn. (i. 101–2).
Vierzon (Viaron), ii. 152 & n. 6 (i. 98).
Views [those specified by E as prospects (his usual term) or as vistas, &c.; some others, not specified as views, are included on account of the importance of the descriptions. General notices of districts traversed are indexed under Agriculture; Alps; and Vegetation; representations of views, so far as they are indexed at all, under Maps and Engraved Views;

Views (*cont.*)
those by E under Evelyn: drawings and etchings.
The entries below are of viewpoints when the notices permit, otherwise of the views themselves]:
— notices of, in Diary: general interest of, i. *107*.
— individual views: (i) called prospects by E [sometimes in V and not in K]:
— — Antwerp: cathedral tower, ii. 64 & n. 2 (i. 43–4).
— — Belvoir Castle, near, iii. 125.
— — Bologna: S. Michele in Bosco, ii. 423 & n. 3.
— — Burrough Green, iii. 553.
— — Charlton House, iii. 85 & n. 7.
— — Cliveden Park, iv. 176, 177.
— — Cranbourn Lodge, iv. 527.
— — Elysian Fields, near Miseno, ii. 351.
— — Euganean Hills, ii. 480.
— — Fontainebleau, ii. 119 (i. 77).
— — Frascati: Villa Aldobrandini, ii. 392, 393.
— — Gaeta, near, ii. 323.
— — Genoa: from sea, ii. 172 (i. 109).
— — Gloucester, near, iii. 118 & n. 5.
— — Greenwich: Dr. Mason's house, iii. 76 & n. 3.
— — Holmby House, iv. 70.
— — Horseheath, iii. 553.
— — lakes: of Bolsena, ii. 209; of Garda, near, ii. 488; of Geneva, ii. 520; Maggiore, ii. 506.
— — Lambeth: Ashmole's house, iv. 138–9.
— — Leith Hill, ii. 4 (i. 5).
— — Leyden: Burcht, ii. 51 (i. 36).
— — Lyons: St. Jean, ii. 157 (i. 101); Place Bellecour, ii. 158 (i. 101).
— — Maison Rouge, ii. 120.
— — Maisons, Château de, ii. 563; iii. 18.
— — Malvern Hills, iii. 119 & nn. 2, 3.
— — Marseilles: the Bastides, ii. 163–4 (i. 103).
— — Medway valley, iii. 422.
— — Moulins: castle, ii. 154 (i. 99).
— — Naples: Castel Sant'Elmo, ii. 326; mole, ii. 327; S. Martino, ii. 329 & nn. 1–3.
— — Nijmegen, ii. 35.

Views (*cont.*)
— — Norbury Park, iii. 157.
— — Nottingham, iii. 126.
— — Orleans: hill near, ii. 136–7 (i. 89–90).
— — Paris: Louvre, ii. 105 (i. 68); Pont-Neuf, ii. 93 (i. 62); environs: Chaillot: house of Bassompierre, ii. 91 (i. 61); ~ Bonshommes, iii. 27.
— — Peckham: Sir T. Bond's house, iv. 93.
— — Rhône valley, between Geneva and Lyons, ii. 532.
— — Rochecorbon, ii. 148 (i. 96).
— — Roehampton House, iv. 105.
— — Rome: various places, ii. 227, 231, 235, 252, 255, 305, 313, 360, 373.
— — Rouen: Ste.-Catherine near, ii. 122 & n. 1 (i. 78 & n. 2).
— — St.-Cloud, ii. 108 (i. 70).
— — St.-Germain-en-Laye, ii. 111 (i. 72).
— — Salisbury Plain, iii. 115.
— — Siena, ii. 201 & n. 5.
— — Spye Park, iii. 112.
— — Tarare, ii. 156 (i. 100).
— — Tickhill, iii. 127.
— — Tournon, ii. 159–60 (i. 102).
— — Tours: Capuchins' garden, ii. 145 (i. 94).
— — Venice: Campanile, ii. 446; Piazzetta, ii. 445.
— — Verona: Giardino Giusti, ii. 487.
— — Vesuvius: summit, ii. 334 & n. 3.
— — Via Appia, near Fondi, ii. 322.
— — Warwick Castle, iii. 120.
— — Wimbledon Park, iii. 316.
— — Winchester: Charles II's palace, iv. 472.
— — Windsor Castle, i. 72; iii. 99; iv. 177.
— — Worksop Abbey, iii. 127.
— — York Minster, iii. 129 & n. 6.
— individual views: (ii) called aspects, vistas, &c., and some anomalous entries:
— — Abbeville, ii. 85 (i. 57).
— — Cambridge: King's College Chapel, roof, iii. 138.
— — Genoa: new walls, ii. 177–8 & n. (i. 112).
— — Lincoln: cathedral tower, iii. 132.
— — Nice, ii. 168 (i. 106).

Views (*cont.*)
— — Papplewick, iii. 126.
— — Paris: St.-Jacques, tower, ii. 131 (i. 84); environs: Château de Madrid, iii. 3.
— — Radicofani, ii. 207–8.
— — Thetford, iv. 114.
— — Viterbo, ii. 210.
Vignola, Giacomo Barozzi da, ii. 230, n. 1; buildings designed by: Caprarola: palace, ii. 406; Rome: Gesù, ii. 230 & n. 1; Viterbo: fountain, ii. 210 & n. 7.
Vignola, Girolamo, Venetian representative in England: social, iv. 365 & n. 6.
Vigo: French fleet destroyed at, 1702, v. 519 & n. 2, 520; rejoicings, &c., for, v. 518 & n. 1, 519 & n. 2, 521 & nn. 2, 5, 6; treasure-ship from, v. 522 & n. 1.
Villa Alva: *see* Villalba.
Villac, Jacques d'Aubusson, seigneur de: sent to congratulate Charles II, 1660, iii. 254 & n. 7.
Villafranca: Marquis of: *see* Toledo, P. de.
Villalba y Toledo, Don Diego de, governor of Havana: captured and brought to England, iii. 188–9 & nn.; mentioned, v. 158.
Villa Nova, between Vicenza and Verona, ii. 484, n. 7.
Ville Dieu (Eu ?), ii. 536 & n. 6.
Villefranche (-sur-Cher), ii. 152 (i. 98); *see also* ii. 151, n. 3 *ad fin.*
Villefranche (Villa Franca), near Nice, ii. 168 & n. 5 (i. 106).
Villefrow: *see* Vilvorde.
Villeneuve-lès-Avignon, ii. 161 & nn. 2, 4.
Villeroi, François de Neufville, duc de, Marshal Villeroi: taken prisoner, 1702, v. 488 & n. 2.
Villiers, Anne: *see* Douglas, Anne, countess of Morton.
Villiers, Barbara: *see* Howard, Barbara, countess of Suffolk.
Villiers, Barbara: *see* Palmer, Barbara, duchess of Cleveland.
Villiers, Dame Barbara, *d.* 1672: house of, in Whitehall, iii. 603, n. 4.
Villiers, Sir Edward, 1585–1626: geneal., ii. 564, n. 7; iv. 17, n. 4.
Villiers, Edward; created Viscount Villiers 1691; first earl of Jersey 1697, v. 406, n. 2; appointed lord chamberlain, 1700, v. 406 & n. 2;
Villiers, Edward (*cont.*)
impeached, 1701 (error), v. 456 & n. 1; joins in lords' protest, 1701, v. 466 & n. 2.
Villiers, Elizabeth, countess of Orkney, wife of Lord George Hamilton, earl of Orkney: geneal., v. 406, n. 2, 555, n. 4.
Villiers, Lord Francis: killed, ii. 541–2 & n.
Villiers, George, sen., 1592–1628, first duke of Buckingham, &c., ii. 9, n. 1; in France and Italy, ii. 522 & n. 1; journey of, with Prince Charles, to Spain, ii. 6, n. 5; assassination of, ii. 8–9 & n. (i. 8).
property of: Burley-on-the-Hill, iii. 124, n. 2; ~ building of, at, v. 586, n. 2; Chelsea: house of, at, iv. 161 & n. 3; New Hall, Essex: bought by, iii. 179, n. 3, 180; Wallingford House, iii. 490, n. 2; York House, iii. 162 & n. 1.
geneal., ii. 541, n. 7; iii. 260, n. 3.
Villiers, George, jnr., 1628–87; second duke of Buckingham 1628, ii. 562, n. 4; travels of, ii. 522, n. 1; *add.*; in rising at Kingston, 1648, ii. 541, n. 7; property of: sequestered, 1648, iii. 162, n. 1, 179, n. 3; iv. 161, n. 3 *ad fin.*; in Paris, &c., 1649, ii. 562 & n. 4; policy of, towards Nonconformists, 1668, iii. 513, n. 3; influence of, on ecclesiastical affairs, iii. 518, n. 1; as member of Council for Foreign Plantations, 1671–2, iii. 571, n. 1, 574 & n. 2, 578, 604–5; in favour as minister, 1671, iii. 596 & n. 3; concurs in Declaration of Indulgence, 1672, iii. 608, n. 1.
admitted to Philosophical Society (Royal Society), iii. 290; association of, with countess of Shrewsbury, iii. 596 & n. 4; duel of, with Shrewsbury, iii. 596, n. 4; iv. 453, n. 2; band of fiddlers of, iii. 596; *The Rehearsal* by: performed (as *The Recital*), iii. 599 & n. 1; glass-factories of, iv. 13 & n. 2, 98–9 & n.; social: parties, &c., iii. 389, 518, 600; iv. 128.
property, &c.: barony of Oakham: owned by, iii. 123, n. 5 *ad fin.*;

Villiers, George, jnr. (*cont.*)
Burley-on-the-Hill, iii. 124 & n. 2; Chelsea: house of, in, iv. 161 & n. 3; Cliveden Park, iv. 176–7 & n.; Helmsley, v. 246, n. 2; New Hall, Essex: sells, iii. 179, n. 3; iv. 287, n. 4; Wallingford House: resides at, iii. 490, n. 2; York House, iii. 162, n. 1; estate of (in general): Sir R. Clayton as trustee for, iv. 186 & n. 4; ~ Sir Charles Duncombe buys part of, v. 246 & n. 2.
geneal., iii. 162, n. 1; iv. 517, n. 5; agent for: *see* May, Hugh (iii. 381, n. 3); chaplain of: *see* Sprat, T. (iv. 73 & n. 1).

Villiers, Mary: *see* Stuart, Mary, duchess of Lennox and of Richmond.

Villiers, Mary, duchess of Buckingham, wife of George Villiers, second duke, iv. 517, n. 5; *see also* iii. 162, n. 1; social, iv. 517; chaplain of: Rev. J. Mandevile (error ?), v. 16 & n. 2, 77; *see also* iv. 539, n. 1.

Villiers: Viscount, 1616–17: *see* Villiers, George, first duke of Buckingham.

Villiers of Dartford: Viscount, 1691–7: *see* Villiers, Edward, later earl of Jersey.

Viloví, Catalonia: battle at, 1696, v. 245 & n. 6.

Vilvorde (Villefrow), ii. 68–9 & nn. (i. 45–6).

Vincent, David, of Long Ditton (*c.* 1550), i. *1*.

Vincent, Sir Francis, bt.: at funeral of John Evelyn of Wotton, v. 55 & n. 3.

Vincenza: *see* Vicenza.

Vincentino, Valerio: *see* Belli, V.

Vinci, Leonardo da: *see* Leonardo.

Viner, Sir George: *see* Vyner.

Viner, Sir Robert, bt.: social, iv. 170 & nn. 4, 5; geneal., iv. 354, n. 6.

Vineyards and Viticulture [*see also* Wines]:
Brussels: Cour, ii. 71 (i. 46).
England: Albury, iii. 496, n. 2 *ad fin.*, 562; Charlton: Col. Blount, iii. 161 & n. 1; Hackney: — Tombs, iii. 96; Hatfield House, ii. 80 (i. 54).
France: north-west limits of vineyards in, ii. 85 (i. 58), 121 (i. 78); districts, &c.: Bordeaux, iv. 329 & n. 3; central, ii. 153 (i. 98), 156 (i. 100); Île de France, ii. 109 *bis* (i. 70 *bis*); iii. 18, 27; Lyons, ii. 158 (i. 101); Marseilles, ii. 163 (i. 103); Touraine, ii. 144 (i. 93), 148 (i. 96); ~ notable planting in, ii. 148 (i. 95).
Italy: districts, &c.: Campania, ii. 324–5 & n., 336, 339; Frascati, ii. 393; Montalcino, ii. 207; Northern Italy, ii. 481 & n. 1, 488, 491.
in sermon, iv. 84.

Vinstanley, —: *see* Winstanley, H.

Vintimiglia: *see* Ventimiglia.

Viregio: *see* Viareggio.

Virgil: MSS. of, ii. 301 & n. 4; mirror of, ii. 89 (i. 60); tomb of, ii. 337 & n. 1; friend of, ii. 486, n. 6 *ad fin.*; statue of (medieval), ii. 411 & n. 2; *see also* Books mentioned in text.

Virginia: rattlesnakes from, iii. 200 & nn. 2–4; shipping of: in Third Dutch War, iii. 603, n. 2; ~ fleet from, 1702, v. 516 & n. 5; Robert Evelyn, &c., in, i. 2, n. 4; v. 574, n. 2; Parke family of, v. 574, n. 2.

Virrio, —: *see* Verrio, A.

Visse, —: concert at house of, iii. 23 & n. 3.

Vitelleschi, Hippolito: collection of, of statues, ii. 283 & n. 4, 365.

Vitelleschi, Muzio, S.J.: geneal., ii. 283, n. 4.

Viterbo: notice, ii. 210–11 & nn.; journey through, ii. 407; Bullicame near, ii. 211 & n. 1.

Viterbo: Annius of: forgery by (?), ii. 210–11 & n.

Viterbo, Antonio da: painting by, ii. 224 & n. 3.

Vitruvius Cerdo, L.: inscription relating to, ii. 486, n. 6 *ad fin.*

Vitruvius Pollio, L.: MS. of, iv. 145 & n. 2; statue of (modern), ii. 486–7 & n.

Vittori, Cavaliere Loreto, singer, ii. 400 & n. 1.

Vitturi, Margherita: founds chapel, ii. 468, n. 4.

Vizeu: Bishop of, 1685–93: *see* Russell, Richard.

Vladislau: *see* Stanislaus Leczinsky.

Vokins, Richard: buys land in Deptford from E (?; as Mr. Vokey), v. 153 & n. 2.

Volcanoes, &c.: Batavia: eruption in, 1699, v. 357 & n. 2; Etna: eruption of, 1669, iii. 539 & n. 2; Fuorigrotta: subterranean fire at (?), ii. 338, n. 6 *ad fin.*, 339; Monte Nuovo: formation of, ii. 345–6; Pietramala: burning gas at, ii. 420 & n. 1; Solfatara, ii. 341–2 & nn.; Vesuvius: *see* Vesuvius.
Volsci, ii. 317.
Volsinii (Vulsinium), ii. 210 & n. 1.
Volterra, Daniele da, ii. 101, n. 1; paintings by, ii. 224 & n. 9, 366, 373 & n. 3; sculpture by, ii. 101, n. 1.
Volterra, Francesco Capriano called F. da: building designed by, ii. 373 & n. 8.
Volturno (Vulturnus), river: ii. 323–4 & nn.
Vondel, Joost van den: verses by, on painting (as painting by Vandall, &c.), ii. 43 & n. 5 (i. 32).
Vorsterman(s), Johannes: painting by (?; as Vosterman), iv. 128 & n. 4.
Vorsterman(s), Lucas, engraver: plate by, iii. 263, n. 1; alluded to (?), iv. 128 & n. 4.
Vos, Anna, iii. 306, n. 2.
Vossius, Isaac, D.C.L., iv. 6, n. 2; papers by, at Royal Society, iv. 54 & n. 4; social, iv. 6, 78, 89.
Vostermans: *see* Vorstermans.
Vowel, Rev. —: sermon by, iii. 146.
Vratz, Col. Christopher: executed for murder, iv. 273–4 & n.; corpse of: embalmed, iv. 276.
Vrijberghe, Marinus van: as Dutch ambassador in England, 1702, v. 495 & n. 3.
Vulcan: amphitheatre dedicated to, ii. 342–3 & n.; Court of (Vulcan's Forum): *see* Solfatara.
Vulsinium: *see* Volsinii.
Vulturnus, river: *see* Volturno.
Vyner (Viner), Sir George, bt.: buys carving by G. Gibbons, iii. 572–3 & n.

Waal (Wahal), river: at Nijmegen, ii. 35, n. 2; named in error, ii. 35 & n. 5, 38 & n. 3 (i. 28–9); E's journey on, ii. 38–9 (i. 28–9).
Wainsford, —: *see* Wandesford, J.
Wake, William; D.D. 1689; bishop of Lincoln 1705; archbishop of Canterbury 1716, iv. 532, n. 3; character, iv. 543; writes against Bossuet, iv. 532 & n. 3; in Convocation controversy, 1701, v. 460 & n. 1; sermons by: printed, iv. 641 & n. 3; v. 18 & n. 3, 52 & n. 3; ordinary, iv. 532–3, 543–4, 547, 565; *add.*; iv. 654; v. 3, 4, 6, 18, 21, 43; tomb of, v. 426, n. 5.
Wakeman, Sir George, bt., iv. 173, n. 5; tried for high treason, iv. 173–6 & nn.; *see also* iv. 435; in London, 1685, iv. 435 & n. 2.
Walburga, St.: in inscription, ii. 409.
Walcheren, island, ii. 31 (i. 24).
Walcot, Thomas: convicted and hanged for Rye-House Plot, iv. 327, n. 2, 329, n. 1, 332 & n. 4.
Walcot, Sir Thomas, judge: in trial of Algernon Sidney, iv. 352, n. 7.
Waldegrave, Frances: *see* Weston, Frances, countess of Portland.
Waldegrave, Henrietta, Baroness Waldegrave, wife of Sir Henry Waldegrave, first baron, iv. 497–8 & n.
Waldegrave (Walgrave), Sir Henry, first Baron Waldegrave: created baron, iv. 497–8 & n.
Waldegrave (Wallgrave), Sir William, M.D.; knighted 1688, iv. 48, n. 2; plays the lute, iv. 48, 370, 403.
Waldegrave: Baron, &c.: *see* Waldegrave, Sir Henry, first baron, 1686–90; Waldegrave, Henrietta, his baroness.
Waldenses (Vaudois): supposed origin of, iii. 152 & n. 1; persecutions of: 1655: collection for victims, &c., iii. 152 *bis* & n. 1; 1686–9: notices, iv. 511 *bis* & n. 2, 515 & n. 1, 636; ~ collections for, v. 3 & n. 1; ~ reinstatement of victims, v. 25; ~ in Bishop Lloyd's prophecies, iv. 636–7 & n.; v. 25–6; 1699: reception of exiles in Germany (?), v. 317 & n. 2, 321.
Waldron (Waldrond), Thomas, M.D., iii. 442, n. 5; social (?), iii. 442; visits Sick and Wounded, iii. 611.
Wales: boundary-trench of (error), iii. 119 & n. 2; minerals from (?), iii. 445 & n. 5.
Wales: Princes of: *see* Charles II; James Edward.

Wales: Principality of: revenue from, granted to H. W. Bentinck, earl of Portland, &c., v. 229–30 & n.
Walgrave: *see* Waldegrave.
Walker, —, at Rettenden, iii. 65.
Walker, Davie: *see* Walter, David.
Walker, Sir Edward, Garter King of Arms, iii. 277, n. 5; as Garter: in ceremonies, iii. 277, 479; ~ ordered to record arms granted to Royal Society, iii. 336; describes Clifford's horoscope, iv. 22–3 & nn.; social, iii. 335.
Walker, George, D.D.: killed at Battle of the Boyne, v. 28 & n. 3.
Walker, Obadiah, ii. 550 & n. 6; as tutor to sons of H. Hildyard: recommended by E, ii. 550; ~ in Paris, 1651–2, iii. 50–1, 54; ~ at Basle, iii. 193, n. 3; ~ influence of, on, iv. 510 & n. 2; and gift of Arundelian inscriptions to Oxford, iii. 496, n. 1; ~ bears thanks of University to Howard and E, iii. 498–500; ~ letter from, to E, iii. 499–500; as Master of University College, Oxford: rebuilds college, iv. 69 & n. 1; as convert to Roman Catholicism, iv. 509–10 & n., 541, n. 2; ~ dispensation for, to retain Mastership of college, iv. 509–10 & n.; licensed to print Roman Catholic books, iv. 512 & n. 1; influence of, on Oxford appointments, iv. 519; flies and is taken, iv. 611 & n. 6; dedicates book to W. Charleton, iv. 531, n. 3.
Walker, Robert, ii. 541, n. 6; paints E's portrait, ii. 541 & n. 6; shows E copy after Titian, iii. 15 & n. 4.
Wall, John, ex-friar: as disputant, ii. 96 & n. 2, 97; *add.* (i. 63, 64).
Waller, family: owners of Groombridge, iii. 72, n. 1.
Waller, Edmund, the poet, ii. 478, n. 3; plot of, ii. 478 & n. 3; ~ R. Abbot concerned in, iv. 186, n. 1; leaves Venice with E, ii. 478, 480; on the Loire with E, ii. 534; at Rouen, 1646, ii. 536, n. 7; at St.-Valéry, 1647, ii. 536; in Paris, 1649–52: social, ii. 567 *bis*; daughter(s) of: visits relating to, &c., iii. 19 & n. 2, 20, n. 3, 39, 40; permitted to return to England, iii. 53 & n. 3; in London, 1652: social, iii. 57;
Waller, Edmund (*cont.*)
house of, *c.* 1655, iii. 328, n. 3; recommends C. Wase to earl of Devonshire, iii. 65, n. 3; commissioner for London streets, 1662(?), iii. 319, n. 1; as member of Council for Foreign Plantations, iii. 578; owner of manor of Hurcott, ii. 541, n. 5.
poems by: compared with Milton's, iii. 364, n. 6; on Cromwell's death, iii. 220, n. 2; song for Mrs. Mary Knight, iii. 230, n. 3; to Dr. G. Rogers, ii. 478, n. 3, 479, n. 2; on Lady Isabella Thynne, ii. 549, n. 9; on Vesling, ii. 475, n. 3, 478, n. 3; 'Of a war with Spain', &c., *add.* (iii. 188).
Waller, Edward: slip for Edmund Waller (?), iii. 319, n. 1.
Waller, Elizabeth: *see* Petty, Elizabeth, Lady Petty, Baroness Shelburne.
Waller, Sir Hardress: geneal., iv. 57 & n. 4.
Waller, Richard, of Groombridge: has custody of: Jean d'Orléans, count of Angoulême, iii. 72, n. 2; iv. 40, n. 2; ~ Charles, duke of Orleans, iv. 40 & n. 2.
Waller (Waler), Richard, F.R.S., iv. 325, n. 4; at Royal Society meeting, iv. 325; tables of plants made by, iv. 632 & n. 3; accomplishments of, &c., v. 176.
Waller (Waler), Sir William, sen., general, ii. 79, n. 1; besieges Portsmouth, ii. 79 & n. 1 (i. 52); troops of, in Winchester Cathedral, iv. 472 & n. 2.
Waller, Sir William, jnr.: cross seized by, iv. 470, n. 3.
Wallingford: Viscount, 1616–26: *see* Knollys, Sir William, later earl of Banbury.
Wallis, John, D.D., iii. 287, n. 1; social, iii. 287; observes transit of Mercury, iii. 384–5 & n.; speech of, at Act, 1669, iii. 533; presents his *Treatise of Algebra* to Royal Society, iv. 439 & n. 2.
Walpole, Horace: on E, i. *39*; on portraits of Queen Elizabeth, iii. 79, n. 2.
Walridge, Rev. —: error for G. Smalridge, v. 394 & n. 3.
Walsall (Wollsal), Francis, D.D.: sermon by, iii. 291 & n. 1.

Walsh, Sir James, bt.: geneal., iii. 6, n. 4.
Walsh, Peter, Franciscan: views of, on Church of England, iv. 496 & n. 4.
Walsh *or* Welch, Sir Robert: in Bataille de Vambre, iii. 6 & n. 4.
Walsh, William: buys manor of Hurcott, &c., ii. 541, n. 5.
Walsham, Mrs. Elizabeth: *see* Evelyn, Mrs. E.
Walter, David (Davie Walker), courtier, iii. 56 & n. 5; social, iii. 56–7, 583; geneal., iv. 247, n. 1.
Walter, Sir John, judge: geneal., iii. 56, n. 5.
Walter, Lucy: *see* Barlow, Mrs. L.
Walter, William: geneal., ii. 561, n. 12.
Walter, Sir William, bt.: social, iv. 247 & n. 1.
Walton, Brian, D.D.; bishop of Chester 1660: *Polyglot* by: publication of, iii. 78 & nn. 3, 4.
Walton-on-Thames, Surrey: Apps Court in: Bernard Granville at, iv. 24 & n. 4; Ashley Park in, iii. 425, n. 5; part of Oatlands estate in, iv. 565–6 & n.
Wandesford, Christopher, lord deputy: geneal., iii. 24, n. 6.
Wandesford (Wainsford), John: describes the Arabs, iii. 24–5 & n.
Wanstead, Essex: estate of Sir Josiah Child at, iv. 305–6 & n.; rector of: *see* Mills, D.
Warbeck, Perkin: alluded to, iv. 457.
Warcupp, Edmund: letter relating to, ii. 552, n. 4.
Ward, Mary, founder of Institute of the Blessed Virgin Mary: at Rome (error), ii. 400 & n. 3.
Ward, Seth, D.D.; bishop of Exeter 1662; of Salisbury 1667, iii. 105, n. 2; character of, iv. 318 & n. 6; at Oxford, 1654, iii. 105 & n. 2; influences studies of Dr. J. Wilkins, iii. 110, n. 3; at consecration of Wilkins, iii. 517; house of, at Knightsbridge, iv. 33, n. 2; sermon by, iv. 32 & n. 2; appointed to preach, iv. 130 & n. 3; social, iv. 33, 56 & n. 5.
Wardley cum Belton, Rutland: rector of: *see* Allington, J.
Ware, Herts.: vicar of: *see* Wye, R. (v. 67 & n. 5; &c.).
Ware, Robert: forgeries of, v. 13, n. 1.
Warley *or* Warley Magna: *see* Great Warley.
Warner, Mrs. —, wife of Edward Warner, M.D., landlady of Mrs. Godolphin, iv. 90, n. 2.
Warner, Edward, M.D.: geneal., iv. 90, n. 2.
Warner, Father John, S.J.: officiates at touching for king's evil, iv. 606 & n. 3.
Warren, Richard, D.C.L.: sermon by, iv. 528 & n. 1.
Warriner, Rev. John: sermon by, ii. 21 & n. 3.
Warrington: first Earl of, 1690–4: *see* Booth, Henry, Baron Delamer.
Wars [wars represented in the Diary only by isolated notices or casual statements are not indexed as wars; the particular passages are indexed under their several headings]:
— Civil Wars, English: *see* Civil Wars.
— Dutch War, First, 1652–4: use of frigates in, v. 10; Albemarle in, iii. 425 & n. 1, 440; mentioned, v. 354.
— — first encounters, &c., v. 158 & n. 4; iii. 67 & n. 4, 68 & n. 3; relations broken off, iii. 67, n. 4; sea-fights, 1653, iii. 81 & n. 9, 84 & n. 5, 87 & n. 3.
— Dutch War, Second, 1664–7 [for prisoners of war and sick and wounded seamen *see* Commissioners for Sick and Wounded, 1664–7]:
— — general notice, i. *18–21*; cause of, iii. 404–5 & n.; outbreak of, iii. 387 & n. 5; ~ Charles II on, iii. 390 & n. 7.
— — 1664: James, duke of York, prepares for, iii. 389 & n. 2; Dutch Smyrna convoy attacked, iii. 404 & n. 4, 407 & n. 6.
— — 1665: the *London* disaster, iii. 403 & nn. 1, 4, 408; movements of fleets, &c., Mar., Apr., iii. 404, 405, n. 3, 406 & nn. 2, 3; battle of Lowestoft, 3 June, iii. 409 & n. 3, 410 & n. 3, 412; ~ officers in, iii. 407, n. 2, 413 & n. 4; iv. 12 & n. 1; ~ ships taken in, &c., iii. 414 & n. 9; movements of fleets, June–Oct., iii. 410, 411, 413–14, 418, n. 5, 419, 425, n. 1; Dutch East India fleet attacked

Wars (*cont.*)
at Bergen, iii. 562 & n. 5, 617 & nn. 2, 4, 618 & n. 3; iv. 21; ships captured by Sandwich: *see* Ships and Shipping: *Golden Phoenix*.
— — 1666: France declares war on England, iii. 457, n. 4; movements of fleets, Apr.–May, iii. 435 & n. 3, 436 & n. 2; Four Days' battle, 1–4 June, iii. 437–40 & nn.; ~ losses in, iii. 413, n. 3, 441–2 & n.; ~ mentioned, iii. 444, 509, n. 3; movements of fleets, June–July, iii. 441 & nn. 4, 5, 445 & n. 4; St. James's Fight, 26–7 July, iii. 445 & n. 7, 446 & n. 3; reported enemy landing in England, iii. 462 & n. 1; Albemarle returns from fleet, iii. 463 & n. 4.
— — 1667: English government decides not to set out a fleet, iii. 489 & n. 2; peace negotiations begin, &c., iii. 484, n. 1, 489, n. 2; Dutch in Medway and Thames, iii. 484–9 & nn., *passim*; ~ ships taken or burnt by, iii. 149, n. 6, 440, n. 6; ~ in picture, iii. 559, n. 4; ~ mentioned, &c., iii. 441, n. 7, 610; treaties of Breda, iii. 491, n. 1, 492 & n. 5; ~ medal commemorating, iii. 559, n. 4; ~ provision of, iii. 598, 605, n. 1; ~ mentioned in error, iv. 41 & n. 1.
— — miscellaneous: projected history of: *see* Evelyn: books; intercepted letters, iii. 415; Fire of London attributed to enemy incendiaries, iii. 457, n. 4, 462; taxes for: London agents for collectors of, iii. 464, n. 1; English expenditure on: inquiry into, iii. 536, n. 2, 540 & n. 6; effects of, in Leeward Islands, iii. 605, n. 1; mentioned, &c., iii. 434, 441, 464, 477; iv. 48; ~ in sermon, iii. 569.
— Dutch War, Third, 1672–4 [for prisoners of war and sick and wounded seamen *see* Commissioners for Sick and Wounded, 1672–4]:
— — general notice, i. *22–3*; origins of, iii. 559, n. 4; ~ E's views on, iii. 620; responsibility for, iv. 16 & n. 1, 21 & n. 4; Sandwich on, iii. 618; use of fireships in, v. 11.
— — 1672: order for protection of shipping, iii. 603 & n. 2; outbreak of war, iii. 605–6 & n.; attack on Dutch Smyrna fleet, *ib.*; ~ wounded from, iii. 609 & n. 3, 611; ~ responsibility for, iv. 21 & n. 4; ~ disapproval of, iii. 618; iv. 211; movements of fleets, May, iii. 614–15 & nn.; battle of Solebay, 28 May, iii. 616–17 & nn.; ~ casualties in, iii. 186 & n. 4, 401, n. 6, 509, n. 3, 619 & n. 3.; fleet movements, June–Aug., iii. 620, 623; Dutch threaten Jamaica, iii. 628.
— — 1673: army to invade United Provinces, iv. 13 & n. 1, 15; French and English take Maastricht, iv. 42 & n. 1; battle of the Texel, iv. 24, n. 5; Dutch occupy New York, iv. 25 & n. 6; ship taken by Dutch, iii. 296, n. 6.
— — 1674: treaty of Westminster, iv. 8, n. 2; ~ as treaty of Breda (in error), iv. 41 & n. 1; ~ provision of, iv. 36, n. 1, 44 (allusion).
— Great Northern War:
— — 1700: Russia declares war against Sweden, v. 429 & n. 4; campaign, v. 438–9 & n., 440.
— — 1701: Poland involved in, v. 462 & n. 6; campaign, v. 472 *bis* & nn. 1, 4, 474, 486 & n. 2.
— — 1702: campaigns, v. 504 & n. 5, 510 & n. 5.
— — 1703: no prospect of peace, v. 546.
— — 1704: Polish throne declared vacant, v. 559 & n. 1; campaign, v. 561 & n. 2; general notice, v. 572.
— Thirty Years' War: outbreak of, ii. 7 & n. 1 (i. 7); Gustavus Adolphus in Germany: victories of, iv. 636; ~ spoils of, iv. 221.
— Turkish-Imperial war, 1683–99: Turks invade Empire, 1683, iv. 331 & n. 4; Vienna: relieved by John Sobieski, iv. 340 & n. 3; v. 247; ~ Lord Lansdowne at, iv. 400–1 & n.; v. 476; ~

Wars (*cont.*)
Turkish horses taken at, iv. 398–9 & nn.; sieges, &c., 1684–8, iv. 394 & n. 1, 463 & n. 1, 524 & n. 2, 560 & n. 3, 598 & n. 3; peace negotiations, 1688–9, iv. 613 & n. 2; v. 7, 35–6 & n., 37; battles, &c., 1690, v. 6 & n. 5, 37 & n. 2; peace negotiation, 1691, v. 60, 71 *bis*; battles, &c., 1691–7, v. 69 & n. 1, 101 & n. 3, 155 & n. 6, 258 & n. 6; *add.*; v. 260 & n. 1, 267 & n. 4; negotiation at, and peace of, Carlowitz, v. 307 & n. 2, 316 & n. 2.
— Turkish-Venetian wars, 1645–69 (Cretan War) and 1684–99: *see* Venice: Republic.
— War between England and Spain, 1655–60: general, iii. 204; attack on Spanish Plate fleet, 1656, iii. 188–9 & nn.; v. 158; Dunkirk campaign, 1657–8, iii. 192 & n. 6, 199 & n. 3, 200 & n. 5, 217 & n. 3; peace, iii. 257, n. 2.
— War between France and Spain, 1635–59: mentioned or alluded to, ii. 7, n. 1, 97 (i. 64); episodes in, ii. 168 & n. 1 (i. 106); iii. 17 & n. 3; French forces in: at Gennep, 1641, ii. 37 (i. 28); ~ at Dunkirk and Mardyke, 1657–8, iii. 199 & n. 3, 200, n. 5, 217, n. 3; effects of, in frontier areas, &c.: on Ligurian coast, ii. 169–70 (i. 107); ~ northern France, &c., ii. 74, n. 4, 83–4 & n. (i. 56), 84–5 & n. (i. 57), 561 & n. 1; iii. 12, 16, 17, 54.
— War between France, United Provinces, &c., 1672–8 [the Guerre de Hollande; for the earlier part, in which England was also engaged (1672–4), *see* Third Dutch War *above*]: French naval activities in, 1672, iii. 614, 619 & n. 3; Maastricht taken, 1673, iv. 42 & n. 1; English army raised for war against France, 1678, iv. 136 & n. 4.
— — peace negotiations: at Cologne, iv. 8, n. 2, 310, n. 3; at Nimeguen, iv. 76 & n. 3; ~ English plenipotentiaries at, iv. 8 & n. 2 (error), 76 & n. 3, 90 & n. 3, 110 & n. 1, 188 & n. 6, 310 & n. 3 (error).

Wars (*cont.*)
— — peace of Nimeguen, i. *27*; alluded to, i. 27 & n. 1.
— War between Spain and United provinces, 1621–48, ii. 35, n. 5, 62 & n. 4 (i. 42), 74, n. 4, 316 & n. 2; sieges of: 's Hertogenbosch, 1629, ii. 57, n. 7; Huys te Gennep, 1641, ii. 35–8 & nn. (i. 27–9).
— War(s) between Sweden and Poland, Denmark, &c., 1655–60: Charles X: in Poland, 1655, iii. 161 & n. 3; ~ winter march of, 1658, iii. 211, n. 2; Dutch intervention in, 1658, iii. 236 & n. 5; Sandwich as mediator in, *add.* (iii. 618, n. 6).
— War in Ireland, 1689–91: *see* Ireland: chronological series.
— War of Castro: mentioned, ii. 207, n. 4, 211, n. 2, 371–2 & n.
— War of the League of Augsburg [for the campaigns in Ireland, 1689–91, *see* Ireland; for French threats to Scotland *see* Scotland; for William III's movements *see* William III]:
— — 1688: disputed election of archbishop-elector of Cologne, iv. 596 & n. 3; Schomberg occupies Cologne, iv. 598 & n. 2; France declares war on the Emperor, iv. 596, n. 3; campaign on upper Rhine, iv. 598 & n. 1, 608 & n. 6; reported French naval defeat, iv. 609 & n. 9.
— — 1689: preparations to oppose France, iv. 613; Imperial Diet declares war on France, iv. 622, n. 5; William III and the war, iv. 625; Denmark offers to support Confederates, iv. 642 & n. 6; scope of the conflict, iv. 645; campaigns: Spanish Netherlands, iv. 622; upper and middle Rhine, iv. 632 & n. 2, 645 & n. 5, 648 & n. 4, 649 & n. 7.
— — — naval, iv. 639 & n. 1, 642, 645; shipping, iv. 642, 651–2 & n.
— — 1690: duke of Lorraine dies, v. 22; Savoy joins Confederates, v. 25 & n. 2; French pressure on Switzerland, v. 35 & n. 8, 39 & n. 5; apocalyptic views and the war, v. 20–1; cam-

Wars (*cont.*)
paigns: preparations for, v. 6, 7; Spanish Netherlands, v. 31, 39; ~ English regiments from, v. 29–30 & n.; *see also* v. 31, 32 & n. 6; Germany, v. 31, 33, 35–6; Savoy, v. 31, 33 *bis* & n. 6, 36, 39 & n. 5.
— — — naval, v. 2, 27–37 & nn., *passim*; *add.* (v. 27, n. 2); shipping, v. 2, 31 & n. 2, 33, 37.
— — 1691: strength of France: Lord Dover on, v. 72; campaigns: general, v. 70; Spanish Netherlands and Liège, v. 47 & n. 1, 57 & n. 3, 60 & n. 1, 68; Savoy, v. 59–60 & n., 71 & n. 4.
— — — naval, v. 57 & n. 4, 60, 68 & n. 4, 69 & n. 2, 70; shipping, v. 60 & n. 3, 67 *bis* & nn. 1, 3, 68, 77, 79.
— — 1692: expected English landings in France, v. 92 & n. 3, 100, 111 & n. 4, 112 & n. 1; projected invasion of England, v. 97–101 & nn., *passim*; campaigns: Spanish Netherlands, v. 101–7 & nn., *passim*, 111 & n. 3, 117; ~ numbers engaged in, v. 102; Savoy, v. 117 & n. 2.
— — — naval, v. 97 & n. 3, 99, 101 & n. 2, 111 & n. 4, 112 & n. 1.
— — 1693: France offers peace to Emperor, v. 140 & n. 2; France subsidizes Denmark, v. 150; campaigns: Spanish Netherlands, v. 126 & n. 2, 142 & n. 2, 148 & nn. 3, 4, 149–50 & nn., 155 *bis* & nn. 1, 2; ~ numbers engaged in, v. 142, n. 2, 149 & n. 3; Palatinate, v. 141 & n. 1; Savoy, v. 150, 155 & nn. 4, 5; Catalonia, v. 155 & n. 3.
— — — naval, v. 142 & n. 1, 150 & n. 2; ~ French port bombarded, v. 160 & n. 1; shipping, v. 142–58 & nn., *passim*.
— — 1694: peace proposals (Dec. 1693), v. 163 & nn. 3, 4; Danish supplies for France intercepted, v. 163; English conduct of the war, v. 169; campaigns: Spanish Netherlands, v. 184 *bis* & n. 1, 186, 188, 191 & n. 2; Germany (?): false report, v. 185.
— — — naval, v. 169 & n. 3, 175, 184 *bis*, 186 & n. 3; ~ French

Wars (*cont.*)
ports bombarded, v. 186 & n. 2; ~ French attacks in Guinea and Jamaica, v. 174 & n. 5, 188 & n. 4; shipping, v. 169 & n. 3, 174 & n. 4, 175.
— — 1695: campaigns: Spanish Netherlands, v. 215 & nn. 2, 4, 5, 216 *bis* & n. 4; Savoy, v. 209 & n. 2, 215 & n. 3.
— — — naval: French ports bombarded, v. 216 & n. 3, 218 & n. 2; shipping, v. 218 & n. 1, 220 & n. 4.
— — — 1696: Savoy changes sides, v. 247 & n. 4, 250–1, 252, 256, 260 & n. 3; peace proposals: reports of, v. 250, 256–9 *passim*; Assassination Plot and projected invasion of England, v. 231–4 & nn.; campaigns: Spanish Netherlands and Dunkirk, v. 234 & n. 5, 245–6, 251–6 *passim*, 260; ~ English regiments from, v. 233; Catalonia, v. 245 & n. 6; northern Italy, v. 259 & n. 4, 260.
— — — naval, v. 233–4, 242, 262 *bis*; ~ French port bombarded, v. 252 & n. 3; ~ French attack Newfoundland, v. 263 & n. 8; shipping, v. 251.
— — 1697: peace negotiations, Jan., v. 263; campaigns: Spanish Netherlands, v. 264 & n. 4; northern Italy, v. 264 & n. 5; Catalonia, v. 270 & n. 1.
— — — naval: French take Cartagena, v. 266 & nn. 2, 4, 270 & n. 1.
— — — peace of Ryswick, v. 266–71 & nn., *passim*; mentioned, i. 30.
— — miscellaneous: cost of war to France, v. 270, n. 2; the war in sermons, v. 277, 293, 319.
— War of the Spanish Succession [the English notices for 1701–2 indexed below all relate directly to the European situation; for further notices of events in England *see* Parliament; Church of England; &c.]:
— — before the death of Charles II, 1 Nov. 1700, N.S.: French preparations, 1698, v. 287 & n. 3; negotiations for partition of Spanish dominions, 1698–1700, v. 434 & n. 4, 436 & n. 2; ~

Wars (*cont.*)
English ministers impeached for, v. 462; memorial from Louis XIV to Charles II, Jan. 1699, v. 316 & n. 3; French military preparations, v. 323; ~ consultations for defence of Germany against, v. 345 & n. 1; *see also* v. 445–6; *see further* Charles II, king of Spain.
— — from death of Charles II, 1 Nov. 1700, N.S., to declaration of war by England, 15 May 1702, N.S.:
— — — Charles II dies, v. 431 & n. 1; ~ will of, v. 434 & n. 2, 436 & n. 2, 445 & n. 5; Philip V: as king, v. 439 & n. 2; ~ in Charles II's will, v. 434 & n. 2, 436 & n. 2; ~ acknowledged by United Provinces, v. 446 & n. 1; ~ guardianship of: Louis XIV claims, v. 453.
— — — France, Spain, and Maritime Powers: France: occupies Spanish Netherlands, v. 440, 445–6, 458–65 *passim*, 472; prepares for war, &c., v. 450, 453; recalls ambassador to United Provinces, v. 472 & n. 5; James Edward recognized by, as king of Great Britain, v. 476 & nn. 3, 4, 480–1 & n.; prohibits English imports, v. 477 & n. 1; occupies Liège, v. 482 & n. 2.
— — — — Spain: excludes English and Dutch shipping, v. 477, n. 1.
— — — — England: parliamentary proceedings, Jan.–June 1701, v. 445 & n. 4, 446 & n. 8, 450, 462, 466 & n. 1, 468; increases forces, v. 449 & n. 1; fast for peace, v. 452 & n. 4, 453; Kentish Petition, iv. 457 & n. 2, 461; recalls ambassador to France, v. 472 & n. 5 (error), 476 & n. 4; parliament supports alliance, 1702, v. 485 & n. 2, 486 & n. 3.
— — — — United Provinces: increase forces, v. 441, 465, 472 *bis*; acknowledge Philip V as king of Spain, v. 446 & n. 1; claim English aid, v. 458 & n. 1.
— — — — naval: fleets at sea, v. 462 & n. 2.

Wars (*cont.*)
— — — France and the Empire: Emperor claims Milan, v. 440–1; France occupies Milan, &c., *ib.*; v. 446, 462; campaigns in northern Italy: 1701, v. 462–77 & nn., *passim*; ~ 1702, v. 488 & n. 2, 489.
— — — Grand Alliance: forming, v. 485, 491, 494–5; forces of: estimated number of, v. 485–6 & n.; war begins in Germany, v. 498.
— — from the declaration of war, 15 May 1702, N.S., onwards:
— — — 1702: England declares war, v. 500 & n. 4, 504; Portugal joins Allies (error), v. 514, n. 2; *add.*; English declaration in support of Leopold I's claim to Spanish crown, v. 515 & n. 3; campaigns: Spanish Netherlands and Liège, v. 514–19 & nn., *passim*; upper Rhine, Bavaria, &c., v. 498 & n. 2, 504 & n. 3, 510–16 & nn., *passim*, 520; northern Italy, v. 504 & n. 4, 510–14 & nn., *passim*, 520.
— — — — naval, v. 510–20 & nn., *passim*; ~ West Indies, v. 516 & n. 5, 526–7 & n.; shipping, v. 516 & n. 5, 520 & n. 3.
— — — 1703: United Provinces required to stop intercourse with France and Spain, v. 526 & n. 3; Portugal: wavers, v. 530 & n. 2; ~ joins Allies, v. 539 & n. 1; Savoy: joins Allies, v. 547 *bis*, 548 & n. 1; Archduke Charles claims Spanish crown: *see* Charles VI, Emperor (v. 545 & n. 3, &c.); rising in Cevennes, v. 545 & n. 4; Scotland: France foments discontent in, v. 546, 553 & n. 1; campaigns: general: Allied losses in, v. 551; Spanish Netherlands, v. 542–3, 546 & n. 4; upper Rhine, Bavaria, &c., v. 529 & n. 2, 535 & n. 1, 543, n. 2, 544 & n. 3, 546 & n. 3, 551 & n. 1, 553 & n. 2.
— — — — naval, v. 528 & n. 2.
— — — 1704: for Archduke Charles as king of Spain *see* Charles VI, Emperor; Marlborough: at The Hague, Jan., v. 555 & n. 2; ~ goes to Netherlands as com-

Wars (*cont.*)
mander-in-chief, v. 563; rising in Cevennes, v. 563 & n. 1; campaign on Danube and upper Rhine, v. 572–83 & nn., *passim*; naval: expeditions to Spain, &c., v. 548–58 & nn., *passim* (1703–4), 575 & n. 3, 579–80 & nn., 583 & n. 2.
— — — 1705: Marlborough goes to United Provinces, v. 590 *bis* & nn. 1, 3; campaigns: Spanish Netherlands, v. 602 & n. 3, 604–5 & n., 607 & n. 3; upper Rhine (?), v. 600; northern Italy, v. 587 & n. 2, 600 & n. 2, 607 & n. 4; Spain (partly naval): Gibraltar, v. 587 & n. 2, 591 & n. 2, 594 & n. 3; ~ Catalonia, v. 605 & n. 2, 607, 610 & n. 2, 614 & n. 4, 617; ~ Badajoz, v. 614 & n. 5.
— — — — shipping, v. 601 & n. 1, 614 & n. 6.
Warsaw: taken by Swedes, 1655, iii. 161, n. 3; threatened by Swedes, 1701, v. 486 & n. 2; occupied by Swedes, 1702, v. 504 & n. 5; seized by Augustus the Strong, 1704, v. 580 & n. 2.
Warwick: notice, iii. 119–21 & nn.; ~ material used in, iii. 98, n. 5; Castle, iii. 119–20 & nn.; ~ governor of, 1645: *see* Bridges, Col. J.; Guy's Cliff near, iii. 120–1 & nn.; the Priory (called the Abbey, in error), iii. 120 & n. 5; ~ Sir Henry and Lady Puckering (Newton) go to live at, iii. 182 & n. 6; St. Mary's church, iii. 120 & n. 4.
Warwick: Earls of: *see* Rich, Robert, first earl; Rich, Charles, fourth earl, 1659–73.
Warwick: Guy of: *see* Guy.
Warwick, Joan, Lady Warwick, wife of Sir Philip, iii. 253, n. 2, 368, n. 3; godmother of Richard Evelyn, b. 1664, iii. 368.
Warwick, Sir Philip, iii. 253, n. 2; shows E public revenue accounts, iii. 361; house of, at Chislehurst, iii. 253 & n. 2; social, iii. 253, 327, 344, 352, 364, 365, 368 *bis*, 381, 390, 404, 432, 474; iv. 73.
Warwickshire: in view, iii. 119; congratulatory address from, to Charles II, iii. 249 & n. 4.
Wase, Christopher, scholar, iii. 55 & n. 1; comes from France to England, 1652, iii. 55; recommended to earl of Devonshire, iii. 65 & n. 3; author of epitaph of little Richard Evelyn, iii. 210, n. 3; *add.*; commendatory poem by, iii. 348, n. 4; son of: E godfather to, iii. 369; as headmaster of Tonbridge School, iii. 408, n. 1, 525, n. 1; proposed as writer of history of Second Dutch War, iii. 523, n. 1; i. *22*; employed by Arlington or Williamson, iii. 525 & n. 1, 526 & n. 6; geneal., iii. 233, n. 3; iv. 15, n. 2.
Wase, Christopher, of Upper Islington: geneal., iii. 233, n. 3; iv. 15, n. 2.
Wase, Hester: *see* Blount, Hester, Lady Blount.
Washington D.C.: Library of Congress: MS. in, iii. 571, n. 1.
Washington, George: geneal., v. 574, n. 2 *ad fin.*
Waterford: taken by William III, v. 31 & n. 1.
Water-mills: at: Abinger or Wotton, v. 605–6 & n.; Euston, iv. 117; Geneva, ii. 529; Rome, ii. 357 & n. 4; Vienne (?), ii. 159 (i. 102).
Water Stratford, Bucks.: millenarian movement at, v. 177–8 & n.
Water-supply [notices of supply available at country-houses are not indexed]:
aqueducts, &c.: Arcueil, ii. 129 & n. 3 (i. 82); New River, Islington, iv. 515 & n. 4; Rome: *see* Rome: topography: aqueducts; pumps: Hammersmith, v. 221–2; Paris: La Samaritaine, &c., ii. 93–4 & nn. (i. 62); Hooke's, iv. 325; reservoirs: Genoa: Palazzo Doria a Fassolo, ii. 175 (i. 111); Miseno, ii. 350–1 & nn.; waterhouse: Hull, iii. 130 & n. 7; waterwheels, &c. (Sir S. Morland): Euston, iii. 591; iv. 117; Windsor Castle, iv. 317 & n. 5; miscellaneous: Pontoise, ii. 121 (i. 78); Tours: spring, ii. 148 & n. 2 (i. 96); Venice, ii. 431 & n. 2.
street-fountains, &c. [select]: Brescia, ii. 489; Cambridge: Hobson's conduit, iii. 140 & n. 5; ~ Trinity College, iii. 136,

Water-supply (*cont.*)
137, n. 1; London: dried in Great Fire, iii. 460; ~ Standard in Cornhill, iii. 460 & n. 9; Naples: on Molo, &c., ii. 327 & n. 2; Paris: Fontaine des Innocents, ii. 132 & n. 1 (i. 85); Rome: *see* Rome: topography: fountains.
Water-works [fanciful displays, &c.; *see further* Music: instruments: mechanical]: Amsterdam: Bruiloft, ii. 46–7 & nn. (i. 33); Bushell's Wells, Enstone, iii. 382 & n. 6; London: H. Winstanley, v. 247 & n. 1; St.-Germain-en-Laye, ii. 111 & n. 2 (i. 72) [similar devices occur in some of the great gardens where there were fountains, such as Rueil: *see* Fountains].
Watford, Herts.: Cassiobury Park at: notice, iv. 199–200 & nn., 201; ~ Sir H. Capel at, iv. 347.
Watson, Mrs. —, mother of Baptist Watson, iv. 49.
Watson, Baptist: baptized, iv. 49.
Watson, Richard: letter from, to Sir R. Browne: quoted, iii. 248, n. 1.
Watson, Samuel, blacksmith and clockmaker: alluded to (?), iii. 111–12 & n.
Watson, Thomas, D.D.; bishop of St. Davids 1687–99, v. 256, n. 7; proceedings against, for simony, v. 256 & n. 7; deprived, v. 346 & n. 1.
Watton, Norfolk: W. Samwell at, iii. 554, n. 3.
Watts (Wats), John: in charge of Apothecaries' Garden, iv. 462 & n. 2.
Waxworks: funeral effigies, ii. 90 (i. 60); Last Supper represented in, iii. 612.
Waybred (Waybright), Rev. John: sermon by, iii. 122 & n. 1.
Way bridge: *see* Weybridge.
Waysall, —: *see* Wessell, L.
Weather and Climate [*see also* England: weather]:
climate: influence of, on character: Aristotle on (in sermon), v. 156; storms: change of area of frequency, v. 2; winters: variation in severity of, ii. 511, n. 6 *ad fin.*; weather-clock, iv. 170 & n. 7; cold: in Persia, iv. 358; ~ in Sweden, iv. 220–1; wet: in Persia, iv. 358 & n. 4.
miscellaneous notices of weather [many of the notices for England apply also to northern France, the Netherlands, &c.]: 1645–6: snow and cold at Padua, ii. 473; 1646: rain, Sesto, ii. 506, 511, n. 6 *ad fin.*; 1649: sickly autumn, Paris, ii. 565; 1651: flood, Paris, iii. 25 & n. 1; 1652: winter, Paris, &c., iii. 54 & n. 2; 1683–4: winter, Paris, ii. 93, n. 5 *ad fin.*; 1692: rain, Spanish Netherlands, v. 104, 106–7; 1697: cold, &c., Flanders and Savoy, v. 264 & nn. 4, 5; ~ storm, Dutch coast, v. 267 & n. 5; 1699: storms, Germany, v. 311 & n. 2.
Webb, Col. Edmund: murder committed by, iv. 401, n. 1.
Webb, John, architect, iii. 301, n. 1; publishes Inigo Jones's study of Stonehenge, iii. 115, n. 6; assists Sir J. Denham at Greenwich Palace, iii. 300–1 & nn.; employed for repair of St. Paul's, *c.* 1663, iii. 449, n. 2; houses designed by: Ramsbury, iii. 100, n. 5; Thorpe Hall, iii. 134, n. 2; Wilton (part), iii. 113, n. 6, 114, n. 4.
Webb, Col. William: art-collection of, ii. 549 & nn. 1, 2.
Wedderburn (Wetherborn), Sir John, M.D.; knighted *c.* 1661: attends E (?), iii. 243 & n. 1.
Weede, Everard van, heer van Dijkveld: *see* Dijkveld.
Welbeck Abbey, Notts.: notice, iii. 126–7 & nn.; William III at, v. 222, n. 3.
Welch, Sir Robert: *see* Walsh.
Weld, Humphrey: builds Wild House, &c., iv. 242, n. 6.
Wells: cathedral clergy:
deans: *see* Bathurst, Ralph (1670–1704); Graham, William (1704–13).
prebendaries: *see* Creighton, R., jnr.; Hungerford, W.
Wells (Welles), Benjamin, physician: makes post-mortem examination of little Richard Evelyn, iii. 209–10 & nn.
Wells, Rev. William, curate at Abinger, v. 115, n. 2; character, v. 208; sermons by, v. 115, 167–8,

Wells, Rev. William (*cont.*)
183–4, 187, 188, 189, 190(?); recommended to Archbishop Tenison, v. 199; dies, v. 208 & n. 4.
Wells, Winifred, maid of honour to Queen Catherine, iii. 621, n. 5.
Welsh language: similarity of, to Breton, iv. 66.
Welshmen: Prince Griffith, iii. 7.
Welwyn, Herts.: rectory: value of, v. 417, n. 2; rector of: *see* Creech, T. (*ib.*)
Wentworth, Elizabeth: *see* Dillon, Elizabeth, countess of Roscommon.
Wentworth, Frances, Lady Wentworth, wife of Sir George: social, iii. 187 & n. 5.
Wentworth, Sir George: social, iii. 187 & n. 5.
Wentworth, Henrietta Maria; Baroness Wentworth *suo jure* 1665: liaison of, with Monmouth, iv. 455–6 & nn.
Wentworth, Peter, D.D.; dean of Armagh: sermon by (?), ii. 21 & n. 4.
Wentworth, Thomas; fourth Baron Wentworth of Nettlestead 1593; created earl of Cleveland 1626, iii. 356, n. 2; social, iii. 356; in review, iii. 357; estates bill of, iii. 467 & n. 2; geneal., iv. 455, n. 5.
Wentworth, Sir Thomas; created Baron Wentworth of Wentworth Woodhouse 1628; Viscount Wentworth 1628; first earl of Strafford 1640, ii. 27, n. 3; impeachment of, ii. 27 & n. 3 (i. 20); iv. 226; ~ manager of, iv. 227; ~ portent at time of (error), iv. 235 & n. 1; executed, ii. 28 & n. 5 (i. 20 & n. 2); attainder of: reversed, iii. 16, n. 4; etchings by Hollar relating to, i. 21; ii. 27, n. 3, 28, n. 5; favourite of: Sir G. Radcliffe, ii. 564 & n. 6; iii. 43; follower of (Dr. B. Worsley), iii. 603, n. 1; geneal., ii. 21 & n. 4, 564, n. 6; iii. 91, n. 2, 187 & n. 5.
Wentworth, Sir Thomas, styled Lord Wentworth, ii. 562, n. 5; in Paris, 1649, ii. 562 & n. 5; at Calais, 1652, iii. 55; regiment of: in review, iii. 357 & n. 2; geneal., iv. 455, n. 5.
Wentworth, William; first earl of Strafford, second creation, 1641; second earl, first creation, 1662, iii. 16, n. 4; at Calais, 1650, iii. 16; in Paris, 1651: social, iii. 30, 35, 37, 39; ~ *see also* iii. 35, n. 5; in London, 1653: social, iii. 87, 91 & n. 2.
Wentworth: Lord (courtesy title), 1626–65(?): *see* Wentworth, Sir Thomas.
Wentworth of Nettlestead: Barons, &c.: *see* Wentworth, Thomas, fourth baron 1593–1626, later earl of Cleveland; Wentworth, Henrietta Maria, baroness *suo jure* 1667–86.
Wentworth of Wentworth Woodhouse: Baron, 1628, later Viscount Wentworth, 1628–40: *see* Wentworth, Sir Thomas, later earl of Strafford.
Wertenberg: Prince of: at Venice, 1646, ii. 476.
Wessell (Waysall), Leonard: elected M.P. for Surrey, v. 512 & n. 1.
West, Robert, iv. 494, n. 5; betrays Rye-House Plot, iv. 323, n. 8; pardoned, iv. 494.
West Clandon, Surrey: Sir Arthur Onslow at, iii. 561 & n. 6 (called West Horsley in error); iv. 558 & n. 2; paintings by F. Barlow at (Clandon Park), iv. 255, n. 5; church: stained glass from Baynards in, iii. 193, n. 2.
Westcombe: *see* Greenwich.
Westcote, in Dorking, Surrey: coach-accident near, v. 547 & n. 4; manor of (as Westgate): court held, v. 478 & n. 1.
West Dean, Wilts.: Evelyn property at, i. 2, 3 & n. 2; Mrs. Elizabeth Pierrepont buried at, v. 310, n. 1.
Westerham, Kent: Squerryes (Squirrills) in: proposed purchase of, 1653, iii. 90 & n. 4; Mrs. Jane Leech at, iii. 219 & n. 3.
West Horsley, Surrey [called Horsley by E]: manor of: mortgage on, ii. 545 & n. 5; Viscountess Montagu at, ii. 551; Carew Ralegh at, iii. 219; bought by Sir Edward Nicholas, iii. 418 & n. 4; i. 53, n. 2; West Horsley Place in, ii. 545, n. 5; as error for West Clandon, iii. 561 & n. 6.
West Indies [the area is indeterminate, and apparently in some notices much larger than that to which the name is now applied]:

West Indies (*cont.*)
general: (i) Prince Maurice lost at sea in, i. 26; Admiral W. Penn in, 1655, iii. 147, n. 2; treaty relating to, 1656, iii. 257, n. 2; naval casualties by sickness in, 1697, v. 268 & n. 1; Benbow's action in, 1702, v. 526–7 & n.
— (ii) alligator (crocodile) from, iv. 390–1 & n.; horn of fish from, iii. 372 & n. 6; king-pine grows in, iii. 513; piracy in, 1699, v. 369; products from, at Amsterdam, i. 35 & n. 2; shipwreck (Zacharias) in, ii. 172 (i. 108).
English colonies in, in general: instructions for, 1671, iii. 579; trade of, with New England: possibility of interrupting, 1671, iii. 584; shipping of: in Third Dutch War, iii. 603, n. 2; laws of: committee to examine, 1672, iii. 629; fleet provisioning: threatened by French, 1691, v. 67; merchant-ships from: come to Ireland, 1691, v. 77; come home, 1702, v. 516.
French colonies in: negroes in, ordered to be baptized, iv. 471, n. 3.
See also Caribbee Islands and the particular islands, &c.
West Kington, Wilts.: rector of: *see* Bohun, Ralph (iii. 416, n. 1).
Westminster: *see* London.
Westmorland: Earls of: *see* Fane, Francis, first earl; Fane, Charles, third earl, 1666–91; Fane, Vere, fourth earl, 1691–4.
Weston family, earls of Portland: heir of (?), iv. 425–6 & n.
Weston, Catherine: *see* White, Mrs. C.
Weston, Charles: suitor for Mary Evelyn (?), iv. 425–6 & n.
Weston, Frances, countess of Portland: geneal., iii. 33, n. 6.
Weston, Henry, of Ockham: as patron of G. Bradshaw, i. 13 & n. 2.
Weston, Jeronimo, second earl of Portland: commissioner for London streets, iii. 319, n. 1.
Weston, John, of Ockham, v. 482, n. 3; elected M.P. for Surrey, 1701, v. 482; defeated in Surrey election, 1702, v. 512.
Weston, Sir Richard: geneal., iv. 425, n. 3.
Weston, Sir Richard, earl of Portland: geneal., iii. 33, n. 6, 595.
Weston-sub-Edge, Glos.: rector of: *see* Fiennes, P.
West Wycombe, Bucks., iii. 530, n. 2.
Wetenhall, Edward, D.D.; bishop of Cork, &c., 1679; of Kilmore, &c., 1699, iv. 366, n. 2; sermons by, iv. 366, 373.
Wetherborn, Dr. — (Sir John Wedderburn ?): attends E, iii. 243 & n. 1.
Wey, river: as Guildford river: house near, iv. 255 & n. 6.
Weybridge, Surrey: column from Seven Dials re-erected at, v. 193, n. 1; Ham Court in (house of D. Sheldon), iv. 142 & n. 1; house of Henry Howard, sixth duke of Norfolk, at: notice, iv. 140–1 & nn., 142; ~ duchess of Norfolk, &c., at, iv. 142; duchess of Norfolk's art-collection at, iv. 566 & n. 2; Oatlands palace in, iv. 141, n. 3, 565, n. 2.
Weymouth: second Viscount: *see* Thynne, Thomas.
Whalley, Col. Edward, regicide: takes part in Christmas raid on Exeter House chapel, 1657, iii. 204 & nn. 2, 3.
Whaplode, Lincs.: vicar of: *see* Holden, William.
Wharton, Sir George: secretary of Saltpetre commission, 1666, iii. 443 & n. 3.
Wharton, Mary: abduction of, v. 41 & n. 1.
Wharton, Philip, fourth Baron Wharton: social, iii. 564 & n. 4.
Wharton, Thomas, fifth baron, later earl and marquis of, Wharton: race-horse of, v. 320, n. 1; alluded to (?), iv. 635 & n. 3.
Wharton, Thomas, M.D.: joint compiler of *Musæum Tradescantianum*, iii. 198, n. 4 *ad fin*.
Wharton: Barons, &c.: *see* Wharton, Philip, fourth baron, 1625–96; Wharton, Thomas, fifth baron, later earl and first marquis of Wharton.
Wharton House: *see* Wiverton.
Wheatley, Catherine: *see* Fitzroy, Catherine, duchess of Northumberland.

Wheatley, H. B.: as editor of the Diary, i. *63 bis*, *116*, n. 1; on E, i. *39*.
Wheatley, Robert: geneal., iv. 505, n. 4.
Wheeler, Sir Charles, bt., iii. 586, n. 4; as governor of Leeward Islands: resigns, iii. 586–7 & n.; ~ dismissed, &c., iii. 597, 598 *bis* & n. 2, 599, 605, n. 1; as executor of Baroness Mordaunt's will, iv. 188–9.
Wheeler, Paul (Paulwheel?), violinist, iii. 168 & n. 1.
Wheler (Wheeler), Rev. Sir George, the traveller, iv. 358 & n. 1; character, &c., iv. 528; sermon by, *ib.*; social, iv. 358, 360 *bis*, 363.
Wheler, Grace, Lady Wheler, wife of Sir George, iv. 528 & n. 3.
Whetham, Col. Nathaniel: as governor of Portsmouth, iii. 238, n. 1.
Whichcote, Benjamin, D.D.: sermon by (?), iv. 282 & n. 4.
Whinnell, —: *see* Winnell (iv. 582 & n. 2).
Whistler, Daniel, M.D., iii. 341, n. 3; character, &c., iv. 307 & n. 2; observation by, at Royal Society (?), iii. 341 & n. 3; social, iv. 84, 299–300.
Whitbread, Father T., S.J.: executed, &c., iv. 170 & n. 10.
White, —, son of Richard White of Hutton (George White?): geneal., iii. 33, n. 6; social, iii. 595.
White, Dr. — (Thomas White?): sermon by, iv. 292 & n. 2.
White, Rev. —: sermon by, iii. 238.
White, Mrs. Catherine, born Weston, wife of Richard White, iii. 33, n. 6; geneal., iii. 595.
White, Francis, bishop of Ely, &c., iii. 45, n. 4; and Cosin's *Collection of private devotions*, iii. 45–6, 635.
White, George: *see* White, —, son of R. White of Hutton.
White, Richard, of Hutton, iii. 33, n. 6; acquaintance of E at Rome, iii. 33, 595; geneal., *ib.*
White, Thomas: pseudonym of (Sir) Kenrick Eyton (?), ii. 558, n. 4.
White, Father Thomas, *alias* Blacklow: in Paris, 1651, &c., iii. 33 & n. 5.
White, Thomas, D.D.; bishop of Peterborough 1685–90; nonjuror, iv. 505, n. 2; sermons by, iv. 292 & n. 2(?), 505; one of the Seven Bishops, iv. 583–8 & nn., *passim*; at meeting to discuss settlement of the crown, Jan. 1689, iv. 613–14; superseded as bishop, v. 48–9 & n.; burial of, v. 289 & n. 3.
White, Col. Walter: owner of Bishopthorpe, 1654, iii. 128, n. 4.
White Downs (Whitedowne), near Wotton: precipice of, v. 228 & n. 4.
Whitehall, Palace of [Charles II and James II normally resided and kept their courts at Whitehall; although William and Mary spent less time in it, it continued as a royal residence until it was burnt down in 1698. In many notices of the activities of the kings or the court between 1660 and 1688 (or later) E does not name a place: he regarded the terms 'at court' and 'at Whitehall' as almost synonymous (a clear instance, iii. 260); in notices of religious services there is frequently even less indication of place. Notices relating to the religious and social activities of the court, if they took place at Whitehall, are all indexed under the present heading, whether any place is named or not; notices relating to the history and character of the court are indexed under England: court. E's ordinary visits, &c., unless particular rooms or places are mentioned, are indexed under the names of persons whom he saw there, &c.]:
— structure: (i) general: notice, 1656, iii. 166 & n. 1; Inigo Jones's designs for new palace: share in, of J. Webb, iii. 301, n. 1; Charles II's projected alterations, 1664, iii. 387 & n. 4; Hugh May employed at, iii. 381, n. 3; James II's new building, iv. 480 & n. 2, 492–3, 534, n. 1; ~ court moved to St. James's Palace during construction of, iv. 493 & n. 6; furnishing of, iii. 324, n. 3; paintings by J. M. Wright in, iii. 338 & n. 6; fires at: 1662, iii. 316, n. 4; 1691, v. 47 & n. 2;

Whitehall (*cont.*)
1698, v. 283 & n. 5; ~ mentioned, iii. 166, n. 1; iv. 214, n. 8 *ad fin.*, 480, n. 2, 534, n. 1; v. 321.
— structure: (ii): particular rooms, gardens, yards, &c.:
— — Banqueting House: built of Portland stone, i. 81, n. 1; architecture of, iii. 459, n. 1; ~ projects for extending design of, iii. 301, n. 1; balcony inside, iii. 349; ~ as 'the balusters above', iii. 480; escapes fire, 1698, v. 283, n. 5 *ad fin.*; used as a chapel royal, 1698, &c., v. 321 & n. 4; position of, iii. 569, n. 2; iv. 480; events in: Charles I goes through, to his execution, iii. 474, n. 4; creation of peers in, 1661, iii. 277–8 & nn.; Grand Feast of Order of the Garter celebrated in, 1667, iii. 479 & n. 1, 480 & nn. 1–6; commons kiss William and Mary's hands in, 1689, iv. 633; Scottish commissioners offer crown to William and Mary in, iv. 639, n. 2; ceremonies and other activities in: diplomatic audiences, iii. 256, 349, 412, 506, 513, 537; iv. 262, 265–6 & nn., 640, n. 3; touching for King's Evil, iii. 250–1; iv. 606; used for lottery, iii. 376; furniture stored in, 1685, iv. 492–3; art-collection auctioned in, v. 144–5 & n.
— — Chapel Royal: king's closet in, iv. 433, 491; lobby of, iii. 433; Puritan preacher in, 1650, iii. 14; Banqueting House adapted for use as a chapel royal, 1698, v. 321 & n. 4; for services in, *see* religion *below*; for clergy attached to, *see* Royal Household.
— — Cockpit: the buildings, iii. 315, n. 4, 416, n. 4; as theatre: performances in, iii. 306 & n. 5(?), 315 & n. 4; ~ superseded, iii. 569, n. 2; Albemarle's lodging in, iii. 416 & n. 4, 417 (as 'St. James's', *i.e.* the park), 419, 478.
— — Cofferer's Office, iv. 98, n. 1.
— — Council Chamber, iii. 408 & n. 6, 601; iv. 412 *bis*, 512; ~ new, 1685–7: building, iv. 480, 492–3; ~ meeting in (?), iv. 602–3 & nn.
— — Court: coaches not allowed to enter, iv. 262.
— — Duke's Lodgings: little oratory in, 1685, iv. 416 & n. 1, 419 & n. 1(?).
— — Duchess of York's apartment: Mary of Modena in, as queen, iv. 413 & n. 3.
— — Ewery, iii. 572 & n. 1.
— — Gallery: (the Privy Gallery ?), iii. 389; iv. 77; ~ assembly in, iv. 413; (the Stone or Matted Gallery ?), iv. 343; *see also* Privy Gallery, &c., *below*.
— — gates, iv. 266, n. 5.
— — Great Bakehouse, iv. 98, n. 1.
— — Great Hall: used as theatre, iii. 315, n. 4, 569, n. 2; iv. 75, n. 5; ball in, iv. 395; position of, iii. 166, n. 1.
— — Green Chamber, iii. 474 & n. 4.
— — Holbein's Gate: position of, iii. 284, n. 5, 386, n. 8.
— — King's Bed-chamber [Charles II changed his bed-chamber at least once]: Charles II: interviews with, &c., in, iii. 300, 406, 407, 430, 562; iv. 131; taken ill in, iv. 405; dogs of, in, iv. 410 & n. 1; old bed-chamber of: ceiling painting in, iii. 338 & n. 6; withdrawing-room next to: *see* Withdrawing-room *below*; James II: interviews with, &c., in, iv. 454, 526, 540; lobby outside, iv. 453.
— — King's Cabinet: Charles II (probably identical with his closet), iii. 260, n. 1; art-collection in, iii. 260, 287; business in, iii. 299; situation of, iii. 474.
— — King's Closet: Charles II (probably identical with his cabinet): art-collection in, iii. 260–1 & nn., 262, 262–3 & nn., 300; business with, in, iii. 257, 300; portrait of, taken in, by S. Cooper, iii. 309–10; James II: keeps private papers in, iv. 476; James closets M.P.'s in, iv. 540–1 & n.
— — King's Library: notice, 1680, iv. 214–16 & nn.; visit to, iv. 257.
— — King's Lodgings, iv. 453;

Whitehall (*cont.*)
building in, 1663–8, iii. 387, n. 4; pictures, &c., in, iv. 216–17 & nn.; position of, iii. 573, n. 2; iv. 416, n. 1.
— — King's Privy Chamber: *see* Privy Chamber *below*.
— — King Street Gate: occupied by Sandwich, iii. 586, n. 2; position of, v. 204, n. 4.
— — Lobby next the Queen's Side (Queen's Lobby?): interview with Charles II in, iii. 573 & n. 2.
— — Office of Works, v. 244, n. 2; *see also* iii. 319.
— — Presence Chamber: Charles II dines in (?; as 'the Presence'), iii. 513; situation of, iv. 129, n. 5.
— — Prince's Lodgings, iv. 416, n. 1.
— — Private Oratory, iv. 129, n. 5; discussion in, iv. 129–30 & n.; prayers for Charles II in (?), iv. 407 & n. 5; *add.*; maintained by James II for Anglican worship, &c., iv. 418.
— — Privy Chamber: Holbein's painting in, iii. 166 & n. 1; Charles II in, iii. 284; Twelfth Night gaming in, iii. 308; position of, iv. 129, n. 5, 418.
— — Privy Gallery, iii. 386, n. 8; assemblies in, &c., iii. 386–7; iv. 208, 412; *see also* Gallery *above*; situation of, iii. 166, n. 1, 260, n. 1, 408, n. 6, 568, n. 2; iv. 184, n. 4.
— — Privy Garden, iii. 584, n. 1; proposed building in, iii. 584; Sandwich's lodgings in, iii. 586, n. 2, 617; position of, iii. 386, n. 8, 568, n. 2; iv. 534, n. 1.
— — Privy Stairs: position of, iii. 387, n. 4, 463, n. 1; iv. 214, n. 8 *ad fin.*, 216, n. 4.
— — Queen's Bed-chamber: Queen Catherine: interviews in, iii. 463 & n. 1, 572; Queen Mary of Modena, iv. 537; occupied by Queen Mary II, iv. 625; Mary II lies in state in, v. 204 & n. 1.
— — Queen's Dressing-room, iv. 9.
— — Queen's Lobby (Lobby next Queen's Side?), iii. 573 & n. 2.
— — Queen's Lodgings: Queen Catherine, iii. 573, n. 2; iv. 480, n. 2; Queen Mary of Modena: new lodgings built for, iv. 480 & n. 2, 537; occupied by Queen Mary II, iv. 623, n. 4 *ad fin.*, 625.
— — Queen's Presence Chamber, iii. 494, n. 7; Charles II and Queen Catherine dine in, iii. 491, n. 1; diplomatic audiences in, iii. 494; iv. 492.
— — Queen's Privy Chamber: painting by J. M. Wright in, iii. 338.
— — Queen's Side, iii. 572, 573.
— — Queen's Withdrawing-room: assemblies in, iii. 568, 575; *see also* Withdrawing-room *below*.
— — Roman Catholic chapel of James II: in construction, iv. 480 & n. 2, 492–3; notice, iv. 534 & n. 1; service in, iv. 534–5 & n.; clergy attached to, iv. 534, n. 1; musician belonging to, iv. 403, n. 6; Siface sings in, iv. 537.
— — Roman Catholic oratory: opened for public worship, 1685, iv. 419 & n. 1.
— — Scotland Dock, iv. 179 & n. 3.
— — Scotland Yard, iii. 319, n. 2; office of Surveyor of Works in, iii. 319; v. 244, n. 2; demolitions in, during Fire of London, iii. 454, n. 8; outside area of fire, 1698, v. 283, n. 5; position of, iv. 98 & n. 1, 179, n. 3.
— — Shield Gallery, iii. 463, n. 1.
— — Stone Gallery: in fire of 1691, v. 47 & n. 2; *see also* Gallery *above*.
— — theatre, iii. 476, 569 & n. 2; for plays, &c., at court *see* theatrical *below*.
— — Treasury Chamber, 1686, iv. 529 & n. 3.
— — Vane Room: as king's withdrawing-room (?), iii. 288 & n. 7; position of, iii. 166, n. 1, 386, n. 8.
— — Volary Garden: position of, iv. 214, n. 8 *ad fin.*
— — Whitehall Gate: James II proclaimed king at, iv. 412; escapes fire, 1698, v. 283, n. 5; *see also* gates *above*.
— — Whitehall Stairs, iii. 572, n. 1.
— — Withdrawing-room (Queen's?): Charles II in, iii. 397; Queen Catherine in, iv. 89.

Whitehall (*cont.*)
— — Withdrawing-room adjoining King's Bed-chamber (the Vane Room ?): Charles II sups in, iii. 288 & n. 7; assembly in, iii. 300.
— — Wood-yard: Godolphin's house near, iv. 98 & n. 1.
— structure: (iii) official lodgings:
— — Clerk of the Council, iii. 572, n. 1.
— — Groom-porter, iii. 458; gaming in apartments of, iii. 308 & n. 4, 504 & n. 1.
— — Lord Chamberlain, iv. 77, 184 & n. 4.
— — Lord Privy Seal, iv. 446 & n. 5, 500.
— — Secretary of State, iii. 568 & n. 2; iv. 191, n. 3; *see also* iv. 403, n. 5.
— history: (i) chronological series [political activities, &c., of the sovereigns taking place at the palace; *see also* structure: Banqueting House *above*. The sovereigns' ordinary comings and goings are indexed under their own names, and not under this heading]:
— — sometime London residence of archbishops of York, iii. 162, n. 1.
— — 1641: William II of Orange at, ii. 28, n. 1.
— — 1648: parliamentary army quartered in, ii. 540; council of officers at, ii. 546 & n. 1.
— — 1649–60: Sir Lewis Dyve's escape from, iii. 40 & nn. 1, 2; occupied by the rebels, iii. 14; Cromwell resides in, iii. 166, n. 1; persons from, take part in Christmas raid on Exeter House Chapel, iii. 204; 'that nest of robbers': Monck (Albemarle) attacks (?), iii. 242 & n. 2; king's goods pillaged from: return of, iii. 249 & n. 1.
— — 1660: Charles II arrives at, iii. 246, n. 2; letters from Henrietta Maria to be delivered at, iii. 247; Henrietta Maria returns to, iii. 261, n. 3, 262; Henrietta Anne at, iii. 261 *bis*, 262.
— — 1661: mentioned in connexion with coronation processions, iii. 277, 281, 284; coronation feast at (error), iii. 284 & n. 3.

Whitehall (*cont.*)
— — 1662: Queen Catherine comes to, iii. 333; Royal Society thanks Charles II at, for grant of charter, iii. 334.
— — 1664: James, duke of York, resident at, iii. 389, n. 2.
— — 1666: Charles II returns to, after plague, iii. 428, n. 6, 429 & n. 3; gunfire heard at, iii. 445, n. 7; news of St. James's fight brought to, iii. 446, n. 3; alarm of fire at, during Fire of London, iii. 454 & n. 8.
— — 1671: Grinling Gibbons shows specimen of his work to Charles II at, iii. 568, 571–3; T. Blood before Charles II at, iii. 576, n. 2.
— — 1672, &c.: Council for Foreign Plantations (later of Trade and Plantations): starts holding meetings at, iii. 603 & n. 4; ~ proposed building for, at, iii. 582–3 & n., 584; ~ meeting of, at, iv. 22.
— — 1677: William III of Orange at, iv. 122, n. 3.
— — 1678: Dr. E. Tonge and Titus Oates at, iv. 153–4; Roman Catholics ordered to leave, iv. 159, n. 2.
— — 1683: Oates expelled from, iv. 320, n. 2; strongly guarded, iv. 331; Prince George of Denmark and: received at, iv. 332 & n. 3; ~ marries the Lady Anne at, iv. 333; Monmouth and: surrenders himself at, iv. 350 & n. 3; ~ expelled from, iv. 353 & n. 5.
— — 1685: Charles II dies at, &c., iv. 405–14 & nn.; Roman Catholics frequent, iv. 418, 419; Roman Catholic oratory opened for public worship, iv. 419 & n. 1; Queen Catherine leaves, iv. 433 & n. 4; Monmouth brought to, &c., iv. 455 & n. 2.
— — 1688: panic at, on report of William of Orange's landing, iv. 597 & n. 3; Queen Mary of Modena and Prince James Edward leave, iv. 612, n. 4; James II's first flight from (in note as from London), iv. 610, n. 5; James II returns to, iv. 610–11 & n.; occupied by

Whitehall (*cont.*)
William of Orange's guards, iv. 610, 611 & n. 2, 612, n. 2.
— — 1689: Princess Mary (later Mary II) at: arrives, iv. 622, n. 3, 623 & n. 4; ~ conduct of, on days following arrival, iv. 624–5 & nn.; William of Orange first resides at, iv. 623, n. 4 *ad fin*.
— — 1693: William III leaves, v. 136, n. 2; Mary II as resident at, v. 147, n. 2.
— — 1695: Princess Anne invited to reside at, v. 201; Mary II lies in state at, v. 204 & n. 1.
— history: (ii) ceremonies at [for diplomatic audiences and touching for King's Evil *see* Structure: Banqueting House *and* Queen's Presence Chamber *above*]:
— — Grand Feast of the Garter, iii. 479–80 & nn.; Maundy Thursday ceremony at, ii. 385 & n. 5; christening (Roman Catholic ?), iv. 222.
— religion: Chapel Royal [services, &c., in the Anglican Chapel Royal; for the building *see* structure *above*; for the Private Oratory *see* structure *above*; for Roman Catholic worship *see* structure: Roman Catholic Chapel, &c., *above*]:
— — Notices of ordinary services and sermons at Whitehall occur frequently between 1660 (iii. 262) and 1691 (v. 51) and are not indexed in detail; later services here, v. 174, 210, 222, 223, 224, 271–2, 277. In Lent, 1695, the principal Chapel Royal services were apparently held at St. James's Palace (v. 203 & n. 2, 205 & n. 2); in 1698 the chapel there became the principal Chapel Royal (for services *see* London: topography: St. James's Palace). The Banqueting House was also used as a chapel royal from 1698 (notice of a service there, v. 321). General notes on the services, iii. 262, n. 1, 623, n. 7; on the clergy attached to the Chapel, and their duties, iii. 347, n. 3; for the individual clergy *see* Royal Household.
— — — no sermon during absence of court, iv. 73; Anglican services maintained by James II, iv. 419.
— — — Communion service: order of receiving (Charles II and his sons, &c.), iv. 374–5 & n.; evening prayer, iii. 346.
— — — All Saints' Day service, iii. 501 & n. 3; Good Friday: afternoon sermon before king, iv. 309; New Year's Day service, iv. 1.
— — — Lenten sermons at court: general note, iii. 272, n. 1; character of, iv. 6; *add.*; bibliographical notes on annual lists of preachers, iii. 272, n. 1 (1661), 353, n. 2 (1663), 400, n. 2 (1665), 432, n. 1 (1666), 477, n. 5 (1667), 524, n. 5 (1669), 605, n. 2 (1672); iv. 3, n. 6 (1673), 32, n. 2 (1674), 52, n. 5 (1675), 83, n. 1 (1676), 106, n. 1 (1677), 130, n. 2 (1678), 165, n. 2 (1679), 195, n. 1 (1680), 238, n. 2 (1681), 277, n. 3 (1682), 306, n. 3 (1683). 368, n. 2 (1684), 419. n. 4 (1685), 501, n. 1 (1686), 538, n. 1 (1687), 570, n. 4 (1688), 623, n. 3 (1689); v. 9, n. 3 (1690), 43, n. 3 (1693), 203, n. 2 (1695; at St. James's Palace), 380, n. 4 *ad fin* (1700; at St. James's Palace).
— — — — music in: innovations, 1662, iii. 347–8 & n.; musician of the: *see* Comer, H. (iii. 348, n. 3); gentleman of the: *see* Crespion, S. (iv. 207 & n. 1); obeisance to king in, iv. 433, 491; perfume burnt before service in, iv. 375.
— — — congregation at: full, iv. 7; unsuitable sermon for, iv. 131; bishops in, iv. 436; v. 271; service disturbed by incoming congregation, iv. 577.
— — — special occasions and ceremonies in: creation of Knights of the Bath, iii. 276 & n. 7; thanksgiving for Four Days' Battle, iii. 439; Garter services, 1667, iii. 479–80 & nn.; prayers for Charles II during his last illness, iv. 407 & n. 5; *add.*; James II's absence from, after his accession, iv. 416; special service ordered to be held (?),

Whitehall (*cont.*)
iv. 524 & n. 2; Declaration of Indulgence read, 1688, iv. 584 & n. 2; prayers for James II omitted, Feb. 1689, iv. 620, n. 5.
— social [activities of the court taking place at Whitehall; it is generally not named in text or notes]:
— — general account, i. *24*; balls, iii. 350 *bis* & n. 2, 351–2, 360, 569 & n. 2; bear-baiting (?), iii. 549, n. 4; birthday celebrations (balls, &c.): Queen Catherine, iii. 518 (with fireworks), 630; iv. 48, 101 & n. 3, 123–4, 157, 395 (with fireworks); ~ James II, iv. 480, 526; ~ William III, iv. 651 & n. 1; gaming, iv. 403, 413; ~ Twelfth Night, iii. 308 & n. 4, 504 & n. 1; masque, iii. 397 & n. 1; masquerades (?), iii. 357 & n. 1, 476 & n. 2.
— theatrical: buildings used for performances, iii. 315, n. 4, 569, n. 2; charges made for admission, 1675, iv. 75 & n. 5; performances: Corneille, *Horace*, translated by Mrs. K. Philips, iii. 505 & n. 2; Crowne, *Calisto*, iv. 49–50 & nn., 50–1 & n.; Dryden, *Conquest of Granada* (?), iii. 569–70 & n.; Dryden, *Wild Gallant* (?), iii. 351 & n. 14; Jonson, *Volpone*, iii. 341; T. Middleton, *Widdow* (?), iii. 313, n. 4; Orrery, *Mustapha*, iii. 465 & n. 4; unnamed plays, iii. 315, 475; French comedy, iii. 306 & n. 5; Italian comedy (T. Fiorilli ?), iv. 12 & n. 3; T. Fiorilli, iv. 75 & nn. 4, 5; operas, iv. 30, n. 1.
— — ball or masque (masquerade ?) in theatre, iii. 476 & n. 2; ball in, iii. 569 & n. 2.
— personal [residents, &c., in the palace; for persons having official lodgings *see* structure *above*; for royalty and some persons of political note, &c., *see* history *above*]:
— — Albemarle: *see* structure: Cockpit *above*.
— — Sir Richard Browne: chamber of, iii. 571–2 & n.
— — Henry Hyde, second earl of Clarendon: his two sets of lodgings, 1685, iv. 446.
— — E: lodgings of: 1671, iii. 572; 1674: new, in or near the palace (?), iv. 50 & n. 3; *add.*; iv. 72; 1682, iv. 271; 1685: set lent to, by Clarendon, iv. 446, 480 & n. 1, 500 *bis*, 504; implied, iv. 194, 592.
— — Sir Stephen Fox: house of, iv. 179, n. 3, 270.
— — Sidney and Mrs. Margaret Godolphin, iv. 98 & n. 1; *add.*; Mrs. Godolphin moves in, iv. 107.
— — Baptist May: lodgings of, v. 47, n. 2.
— — Ormond: lodgings of, iii. 284, n. 5; occupied by Ossory (?), iv. 208, n. 7.
— — Ossory: lodgings of, iv. 64, 208 & n. 7, 210.
— — Sir Hugh Pollard: dies in, iii. 469.
— — Duchess of Portsmouth: lodgings of, iv. 74 & n. 3, 343 & nn. 1–3; entertainment in, iv. 267–8; burnt down, 1691, v. 47 & n. 2.
— — John Wilmot, earl of Rochester: lodgings of, v. 47, n. 2.
— — Sandwich: lodgings of, iii. 581, 586 & n. 2, 617.
— — Sunderland: lodgings of: as secretary of state, iv. 191, n. 3, 403, n. 5; ~ after dismissal, iv. 610, n. 1.
— — Archbishop Tenison: lodgings of, 1697, v. 273.
— — Dame Barbara Villiers: house of, iii. 603, n. 4.
— — Dr. John Wilkins: visit to, 1656, iii. 172.
— — Sir Christopher Wren: office of, v. 244 & n. 2.
White Hill: Battle of the: *Te Deum* for, &c., ii. 239 & n. 11.
Whitelocke, Bulstrode: at Greenwich, iii. 64 & n. 2.
Whitesheet, Wilts., iii. 114, n. 6.
Whitfield, Dorothea, Lady Whitfield: geneal., ii. 82, n. 3.
Whitfield, Sir Ralph: social, ii. 82 & n. 3 (i. 55).
Whitgift, John, archbishop of Canterbury: tomb of, v. 426 & n. 5.
Whittell, Rev. William: sermon by (?; as Mr. Whittle), v. 593 & n. 1.

Whittle, Elizabeth: *see* Fox, Elizabeth, Lady Fox.
Whittle, Sackville, iv. 219 & n. 6.
Wiburn, Sir John: *see* Wyborne.
Wicckam: *see* High Wycombe.
Wich, Sir Cyril: *see* Wyche.
Wielingen channel: Dutch fleet near, 1652, iii. 68, n. 3.
Wight, Isle of: E visits, 1638, ii. 21–2 (i. 16); ~ visit mentioned, iv. 474 & n. 4; *add.*; vulnerability of, in case of attack, iv. 473–4 & n.; William of Orange reported to have landed in or near, 1688, iv. 605 & n. 1; governor of, 1669–92: *see* Holmes, Sir R.; treaty of: *see* Newport: Treaty of.
Wignacourt, Alof de: portrait of, ii. 113 & n. 4 (i. 73).
Wilanow, Poland: John III Sobieski dies at, v. 247, n. 3.
Wilbraham, Randle, iv. 315, n. 4; at Sayes Court, iv. 315; suitor for Mary Evelyn, iv. 324, 426; geneal., iv. 324, n. 3.
Wilbraham, Roger: demands of, in Randle Wilbraham's marriage-negotiation, iv. 426 & n. 1.
Wild *or* Wilde, George, D.C.L.; bishop of Derry 1661, iii. 150, n. 1; lodgings of (?): services in, iii. 181 & n. 3, 185 & n. 5; ~ arrest of, after sermon in, iii. 204, n. 6 *ad fin.*; sermons by, 1655–9, iii. 150 *bis*, 151, 160, 164, 169, 170, 181, 185, 222, 237; social, iii. 237.
Wilde (Wild), Sir William, bt., judge: social, iv. 45 & n. 2.
Wildman, John: trustee for duke of Buckingham's estates, iv. 186, n. 4.
Wilfrid *or* Wilford, Father John, O.S.B.: in Rome, ii. 213 & n. 2, 251.
Wilhelmina Amalia, queen of the Romans, later empress: entry of, into Vienna, v. 317 & n. 3.
Wilkins, John, D.D.; bishop of Chester 1668, iii. 106, n. 1; character, iii. 165, 518.
as warden of Wadham College: entertains E, &c., iii. 105–6, 110–11; marries Cromwell's sister, iii. 165 & n. 8; *see also* iii. 104, n. 8, 106, n. 1; services of, to Oxford University, iii. 165 & n. 8; sermon by, iii. 165; visits F. Barlow, iii. 166.
as dean of Ripon, iii. 370, n. 3; at Durdans, 1665, iii. 416 & n. 3; consecrated bishop, iii. 517–18 & nn.
scientific studies of: general, i. *12*; scientific instruments, &c., belonging to, iii. 110–11 & nn.; preparations of, for *Essay towards a real character*, iii. 110 & n. 3; as inventor, iii. 416; and Royal Society: Society refers prospective publication to, iii. 340, n. 1; member of English language committee, iii. 396, n. 4; experiment at: account of, by, iii. 292, n. 5; gift by, to Society, iii. 110, n. 4 *ad fin.*
gift to, from E, iii. 170; recommends Dr. R. Bohun to E, iii. 416; social, iii. 169–70, 172, 363, 526, 562; letter from, to E: cited, iii. 173, n. 2.
geneal., iii. 354 & n. 2, 517, n. 10 *ad fin.*
Wilkins, Mrs. Robina, born Cromwell, wife of (1) Dr. P. French; (2) Dr. J. Wilkins, iii. 104, n. 8; marries Wilkins, iii. 106, n. 1, 165 & n. 8; geneal., iii. 517, n. 10 *ad fin.*
Willemstad (William-Stat): notice, ii. 60 & nn. 2–4 (i. 41).
William I, the Conqueror, king of England: tomb and epitaph of, ii. 126–7 & n. (i. 80–1); victory of, over Harold: anniversary of, iv. 601.
William III, king of England (William Henry of Nassau; prince of Orange as William III from birth; king of England 1689), iii. 563, n. 5.
— chronological series:
— — as prince of Orange: (i) before 1688:
— — — 1670–1: visits London, iii. 563–4 & n., 582 & n. 5.
— — — 1677: Ossory goes to, iv. 112, n. 2; visits England, marries the Lady Mary, &c., iv. 122 & nn. 3, 4, 123–4 & nn.; marriage of, i. *27*; ~ in sermon, iv. 650.
— — — 1684: disagreement of, with Amsterdam, iv. 367 & n. 3, 369 & n. 2, 378 & n. 1; ruined by France, iv. 380.
— — — 1685: sends English and

William III (*cont.*)
Scottish regiments in Dutch service to James II, iv. 458 & n. 1.
— — as prince of Orange: (ii) expedition to England, until 11 Dec. 1688:
— — — general, i. *33*; Tenison informs his friends about the project, iv. 592 & n. 3; preparations for expedition, iv. 596; effects of reports of progress of expedition, iv. 597 & n. 3, 598 & n. 5, 599 & nn. 2–4; general eagerness for landing of, iv. 600 & n. 2; form of prayers for the emergency: James II orders issue of, iv. 601 *bis* & n. 6; ~ William to be named in, as invader, iv. 600, n. 4.
— — — declarations of, iv. 609, n. 3; bearer of: imprisoned, iv. 603–4 & n.; first declaration (10 Oct., N.S.), iv. 604 & n. 3, 606 & n. 2; *add.*; ~ counter-declaration, iv. 606, n. 2; ~ deposition of James II requires reconciling with, iv. 624 & n. 1; spurious declaration attributed to, iv. 609 & n. 3; States General's declaration of their reasons for supporting William, iv. 604, n. 2.
— — — first sailing of expedition (19/29 Oct.), iv. 600 & n. 2; expected, iv. 601 *bis*; supposed landing of, iv. 603 & n. 7; reported losses in, *ib.*
— — — invitation to the Prince: the bishops, &c., questioned concerning and asked to disavow, &c. (2 and 6 Nov.), iv. 604 & n. 3, 605–6 & n.; the bishops' conduct regarding, iv. 626–7.
— — — second sailing of expedition (1/11 Nov.), iv. 604 & n. 4; reported landing of, iv. 605 & n. 1; landing of, at Brixham: news of, reaches London, iv. 605 & n. 2; ~ in sermon, iv. 650; fleet in, iv. 605 & n. 2; advance of, towards London: risings on behalf of, &c. iv. 607 & n. 1, 608 & nn. 2, 3, 608–9 & nn.; ~ commissioners sent to, by James II, iv. 608 & n. 8; *add.*
— — as prince of Orange: (iii) the Interregnum, 11 Dec. 1688–13 Feb. 1689.
— — — advances to Windsor and is invited by James II to come to London, iv. 610, 611, n. 1; detains Feversham, *ib.*; Dutch guards of: to occupy Whitehall, &c., iv. 610; ~ occupy Whitehall, iv. 611 & n. 2, 612, n. 2.
— — — occupies St. James's Palace (18 Dec.), iv. 611 & n. 2; ~ court of, at, iv. 611–12 & n.; assumes control of army, iv. 612, n. 2; consults peers about summoning parliament, iv. 611, n. 3; invited to assume government, iv. 612 & n. 5; the expedition in general: deliverance effected by: thanksgiving service for, iv. 621 & n. 1; ~ in sermons, v. 227, 277, 362; ~ compared with Constantine's, iv. 618.
— — — settlement of the crown: proposals for William's future position, iv. 614; commons' vote concerning, iv. 616 & n. 1; crown settled on William and Mary: terms, &c., iv. 621–2 & n.; William's views on, iv. 624, n. 1, 625 & n. 4.
— — — relations of, with Clarendon and Rochester, iv. 626 & nn. 1, 2; wishes concerning Princess Mary's conduct on arrival in London, iv. 624, n. 3.
— — — William and Mary: proclaimed king and queen (13 Feb.), iv. 623 & n. 4; expected to apologize for assuming the crown, iv. 623–4 & n.; reign of, in general, i. *33*.
— — as king: (i) general series:
— — — 1689: seeks popular approval, iv. 628, 629; proposes abolition of Hearth Tax, iv. 628, n. 5; crowned, &c. (with Mary), iv. 632–3 & nn.; congratulated by United Provinces, iv. 640 & n. 3.
— — — 1690: public discontent with, v. 4; Tories support, &c., v. 5 & nn. 1, 2, 5.
— — — 1692: claims right of presentation to St. Martin in the Fields, &c. (with Mary), v. 112, n. 4, 121, n. 1, 136, n. 5, 169 *bis* & n. 1, 376 & n. 1.

William III (*cont.*)
— — — 1693: excluded from Louis XIV's offers of peace, v. 140 & n. 2.
— — — 1694: creates dukes, &c., v. 177 & n. 2, 180 & n. 2.
— — — 1695: progress of, to the north, v. 220 & n. 3, 222 & n. 3, 223 & nn. 3, 4.
— — — 1696: plot against: *see* Assassination Plot; ~ addresses to, on v. 232 & n. 2; ~ effect of, on stability of his throne, v. 233 & n. 3; ~ obligation to avenge, in case of assassination, v. 242; to be acknowledged as rightful and lawful king, v. 243, n. 1; nominates Lords Justices, v. 238 & n. 4; for later nominations *see* v. 294, 327, 469 & nn. 2, 6.
— — — 1697: conspiracies against, v. 264 & n. 2; *add.*; address to, on peace of Ryswick, v. 279 & n. 1; civil list voted to, v. 282 & n. 1.
— — — 1698: takes Sayes Court for Peter the Great, v. 284 & n. 5.
— — — 1700: deceived by negotiations for Partition Treaties, v. 436 & n. 2.
— — — 1701: addresses to, against Old Pretender, v. 480–1 & n.
— — — 1702: accident to, and death of, v. 491–2 & nn.; ~ in sermon, v. 494; mourning for, v. 493 & n. 1, 494; buried, v. 497 & n. 2; no mourning for, at Imperial court, v. 594.
— — as king: (ii) and parliament [as a rule royal assents to bills are not indexed]:
— — — speeches of, to parliament: Jan. 1690, v. 4, n. 1, 5, n. 2; Oct.–Dec. 1690, v. 39, n. 6, 40 & n. 4, 282, n. 1; 1693, v. 135 & nn. 1, 2; 1696, v. 232, nn. 1, 2, 233, n. 1; 1697, v. 278 & n. 2, 282, n. 1; May 1699, v. 324 & n. 2; Nov. 1699, v. 366, nn. 3, 5 *ad fin.*; Feb. 1701, v. 445 & n. 3; June, 1701, v. 468, & n. 2; Dec. 1701, v. 484, n. 2, 486, n. 3.
— — — messages of, to parliament: 1689, iv. 628, n. 5; 1701, v. 458, n. 1.
— — — 1689: passes act converting Convention into a parliament, iv. 627 & n. 1; seeks parliamentary favour, iv. 629; commons kiss his hand, iv. 633.
— — — 1690: general relations, v. 4.
— — — 1693: refuses to receive lords' address and to pass bill, v. 135 & n. 1.
— — — 1695: goes on progress to influence elections, v. 220 & n. 3.
— — — 1696: parliament opposes proposed grant by, to Portland, v. 229–30 & n.; address to, &c., by parliament, on Assassination Plot, v. 232 & n. 2.
— — — 1697–9: dispute between, concerning standing army, v. 275 & n. 1; *add.*; v. 278 & n. 2.
— — — 1699–1700: dispute between, concerning grants of Irish forfeitures: *see* Ireland: chronological series; ~ William directly implicated, v. 324, 394, 402, 404.
— — — 1700: lords' address to William, v. 379, n. 1.
— — — 1701: dispute concerning negotiation of Partition Treaties, ii 462; *see also* Somers, Sir John, Baron Somers.
— — — 1702: addresses to William, v. 485 & n. 2, 486 & n. 3.
— — as king: (iii) campaigns and journeys to Netherlands:
— — — 1690: expedition to Ireland: dilatoriness of, in preparing, v. 4; journey of: preparing, v. 6, 23; sets out and arrives, v. 24 & nn. 1, 4; wounded, v. 27–8 & nn.; conquers Ireland (the Boyne, &c.), v. 28–9 & nn.; advances to Limerick, v. 31 & n. 1; reported defeat and death of: rejoicings for, in France, v. 32; returns to London, v. 34 & n. 1; success, &c., of: thanksgiving for, v. 36.
— — — 1691: journey to United Provinces, Jan.–Apr.: announces, &c., v. 39 & n. 6, 40 & n. 4; delayed by weather, v. 41 & n. 5; arrives, v. 42 & n. 6; on campaign at Mons, v. 47; returns to London, v. 47 *bis* & n. 3.
— — — — campaign in Nether-

William III (*cont.*)
lands, May–Oct.: sets out, v. 51 & n. 4; raises siege of Liége, v. 57 & n. 3; seeks battle with French, v. 60 & n. 1, 68; returns to London, v. 71 & n. 2.
— — — 1692: campaign in Netherlands: sets out, v. 91 & n. 2; expecting battle, v. 101–2; forces and movements of, about Namur, v. 102 & n. 4, 104 & n. 1, 105 & n. 4, 106–7 & n.; at Steinkerk, v. 111 & n. 3; return of, to London, v. 117, 118 & n. 1; ~ thanksgiving for, v. 119 & n. 2.
— — — 1693: campaign in Netherlands: announces departure, v. 135 & n. 2; delayed and departs, v. 136 *bis* & nn. 1, 2; forces with, v. 142 & n. 2; at Landen, v. 149–50 & nn.; returns to London, v. 156 & n. 1.
— — — 1694: campaign in Netherlands: departure of: delayed, v. 177 & n. 5, 180 & n. 2; success in: thanksgiving for, v. 199 & n. 3.
— — — 1695: campaign in Netherlands: sets out, v. 210.
— — — 1696: campaign in Netherlands: sets out, v. 238 & n. 4; obtains money from England, v. 253 & n. 2, 255 & n. 1, 256 & n. 3; returns to London, v. 260 & n. 2.
— — — 1697: return of, to London, after peace of Ryswick: preparations for, v. 267, 269; ~ supposed plot connected with, v. 273 & n. 3; lands and enters London, v. 273 *bis* & nn. 5, 6.
— — — 1698: visit to United Provinces: sets out, v. 294 & n. 2; returns, v. 304 & n. 1.
— — — 1699: visit to United Provinces: sets out, v. 327 & n. 2; reviews forces at Arnhem, v. 352 & n. 4; duke of Celle visits, v. 352 & n. 5; returns to London, v. 361 & n. 1.
— — — 1700: visit to United Provinces: sets out, v. 419 & n. 2; returns, v. 430 & n. 2.
— — — 1701: visit to United Provinces: preparing, v. 468 & n. 2; to be accompanied by Galway, v. 469; organizes defence of United Provinces, v. 472 *bis*; returns to London, v. 480 & n. 2.
— relations of, with Scotland: Scottish Episcopalian clergy seek protection of, iv. 615 & n. 1; fails to provide against disturbances in, iv. 629; likely to be accepted in, iv. 631; Scottish parliament declares for, and offers crown to, William and Mary, iv. 635 & n. 2, 639 & n. 2.
— relations of, with Ireland: fails to provide against disturbances in, iv. 629, 630, 637; campaign of, in: *see* campaigns *above*; grants made by, of forfeited estates in: *see* Ireland: chronological series.
— analytical series:
— — character and conduct:
— — — gravity, reserve, &c., iv. 612, 620 & n. 3, 625 & n. 2; dilatoriness, iv. 631 & n. 7, 646; conduct of, at Revolution, v. 205, n. 6; courage of, at Landen, v. 149 & n. 7.
— — patronage, &c.:
— — — assists Captain G. Collins, iv. 301, n. 3; assists Dampier, v. 295; ~ assistance to: questioned in parliament, v. 369 & n. 2; Dr. T. Hoy recommended to, v. 298 & n. 2; and Greenwich Hospital: interest of, in, i. *34*; v. 203; contribution of, to, v. 244; model, &c., of hospital shown to, v. 399 & n. 2; attempt to interest him in St. James's Palace library, v. 323, 324.
— — personal relations:
— — — favourites (general): grants forfeited Irish estates to, &c., v. 324, 394, 402, 404; gives military commission to earl of Albemarle (A. J. van Keppel), v. 320–1 & n., 323, n. 2; reconciled with Princess Anne, v. 201 & n. 4; grief of, for Charles V Leopold, duke of Lorraine, v. 22; Constantijn Huygens sen., heer van Zuylichem, as secretary to (?), iii. 582; *see also* iii. 377, n. 1; dismisses Marlborough, 1692, v. 86 & n. 1, 90; grief of, for Queen Mary II, v. 200 & n. 8; refuses to pay marriage-settlements of Queen

William III (*cont.*)
Mary of Modena, v. 271, n. 2; attends trial of Charles Mohun, Baron Mohun, v. 129 & n. 2; grants allowance to Titus Oates, iv. 440, n. 4 *ad fin.*; Oates dedicates attack on James II to, v. 238 & n. 3; Elizabeth Villiers, countess of Orkney, as mistress of, v. 406, n. 2; grants made by, to Portland, opposed by parliament, v. 229–30 & n.; employs Portland as messenger, v. 253 & n. 2; receives Sunderland, 1691, v. 49 & n. 2; visits Althorp and favours and employs Sunderland, v. 223 & n. 3, 226 & n. 3; Sir Gabriel Sylvius as steward of, iv. 124; Frederik van Nassau, heer van Zuylestein, as governor of, iii. 565 & n. 6.
— — private and miscellaneous:
— — — appearance of, 1670, iii. 563, n. 5, 564; birth-days: celebrated, iv. 650–1 & n.; v. 362 & n. 2; ~ in sermon, iv. 650; health of: sickly, Feb.–Mar. 1689, iv. 625, n. 2, 631; ~ has ague, 1694, v. 196 & n. 3; as ruler of Orange, v. 545, n. 1; portrait of, by Kneller, iv. 465, n. 7; in succession to crown: in Declaration of Rights, 1689, iv. 621, 622, n. 1; ~ in bill, 1689, iv. 645 & n. 8; geneal., iii. 257 & n. 5; v. 147, n. 3.
— — religious and moral interests:
— — — reforms administration of Sacrament in Chapel Royal, iv. 375, n. 1; sermons before, iv. 641, n. 1, 650–1; v. 20–1, 203 & n. 2, 223, n. 2, 226, 277, 321, n. 4; favours French protestant refugees: in sermon, v. 36; authorizes collection for Waldenses, v. 3, n. 1; letter of, to Bishop Compton, for moral reform, v. 8 & n. 1, 24, n. 3; concern of, in Reformation of Manners, v. 366, n. 5 *ad fin.*; orders collection for redemption of captives, v. 485, n. 1.
— — residences, &c.:
— — — Hampton Court: resides at, 1689, iv. 641, n. 1, 645, n. 1; *see also* Hampton Court; ~ buildings: alterations to, made by, iii. 322, n. 5; iv. 645 & n. 2; Kensington Palace: buys and alters, iii. 447, n. 4; v. 8 & n. 2; ~ for residence at, &c., *see* London: environs: Kensington; St. James's Palace: resides at, 1688–9, iv. 611 & n. 2, 623, n. 4 *ad fin.*; Whitehall: resides at, Feb. 1689, iv. 623, n. 4 *ad fin.*
William I, the Silent, prince of Orange: builds Willemstad, ii. 60, n. 2; tomb of, ii. 40 & n. 5 (i. 30).
William II, prince of Orange: courts Mary, daughter of Charles I, Princess Royal, ii. 28 & n. 1 (i. 20); bed given by, to Princess Mary, iii. 323 & n. 5; death of: news of, reaches Paris, iii. 23 & n. 2; secretary of, iii. 377, n. 1.
William III, prince of Orange (William Henry): *see* William III, king of England.
William, duke of Gloucester: his mother's pregnancy, iv. 645–6 & n.; dies, v. 420–1 & nn.
William I, count of Holland: legendary stratagem of, ii. 50 & n. 3 (i. 35).
William V, duke of Juliers and Cleves, &c., ii. 58, n. 3.
William, St.: in painting, ii. 424, n. 2.
Williams, John; bishop of Lincoln 1621; archbishop of York 1641: kinsman of E, iii. 136 & n. 6; portrait and benefactions of, *ib.*; iii. 137 & n. 4.
Williams, John, D.D.; bishop of Chichester 1696, v. 199, n. 1; as Boyle Lecturer: elected for 1695, v. 198–9 & n.; ~ re-elected for 1696, v. 224 & n. 4; ~ sermons by, v. 222 & n. 5, 239 & n. 1; as bishop: on case of conscience, v. 338–9.
Williams, Sir John: geneal., iii. 136, n. 6.
Williams, Rose: *see* Evelyn, Mrs. R.
Williams, Thomas: geneal., iii. 136, n. 6.
Williamson, Rev. Joseph, father of Sir Joseph, iv. 38 & n. 4.
Williamson, Sir Joseph; knighted 1672; the politician, iii. 392, n. 4; account of, iv. 38–9 & nn.; as secretary to Arlington, iii. 471 & n. 4, 526 & n. 6; alleged ingratitude of, to Arlington, iv. 38–9 & n.; ~ alluded to, iv. 119 & n. 7; as Keeper of the Paper

Williamson, Sir Joseph (*cont.*)
Office, iii. 526 & n. 6; ~ E borrows state papers from, iii. 563 & n. 1; succeeds Sir Richard Browne as Clerk of the Council, iii. 601 & n. 1; knighted, iii. 601; plenipotentiary at Cologne, 1673, iv. 8, n. 2, 310 & n. 3; as secretary of state: appointed, iv. 38 & n. 3, 44; ~ superseded, iv. 162, n. 5; attaches himself to Danby, iv. 39, n. 1; employs C. Wase, iii. 525, n. 1, 526 & n. 6.
marriage of, to Lady O'Brien, iv. 39 & n. 4.
as Fellow of Royal Society: as president: elected, iv. 125 & n. 3; ~ sworn in, iv. 125 & n. 7; ~ presides at meeting, iv. 162; ~ re-elected, iv. 190; ~ Society's Council meets at house of, iv. 191, 205 & n. 5; entertains fellows at supper, &c., iv. 54, 84, 123 & n. 6 (*see also* p. 125, n. 3), 124 & n. 8 (*see also* p. 125, n. 3), 125 & n. 8, 126, 191, 277, 299–300 & nn.
social: parties, &c., iii. 392, 471, 488, 547; iv. 162, 310; v. 238; alone, &c., iv. 56, 93 *bis*, 106, 307.
Willibald, St.: in inscription at Lucca, ii. 409 & n. 1.
Willingale Spain, Essex: rector of: *see* Bramston, William.
Willis, Sir Richard: informs against royalists, iii. 183, n. 3.
Willisel, Thomas, natural history collector for Royal Society: report of, iii. 539 & n. 4.
Willoughby, Elizabeth: *see* Jones, Elizabeth, countess of Ranelagh.
Willoughby, Frances: *see* Brereton, Frances, Baroness Brereton.
Willoughby, Francis, fifth Baron Willoughby of Parham: describes Barbados, iii. 327 & n. 3; geneal., iii. 218 & n. 7.
Willoughby, William, sixth Baron Willoughby of Parham: commission, &c., for, as governor of Barbados, &c., iii. 612 & n. 2.
Willoughby de Broke: third Baron, 1696–1711: *see* Verney, Richard.
Willoughby de Eresby: twelfth Baron, 1601–26: *see* Bertie, Robert, later earl of Lindsey.
Willoughby of Parham: Barons: *see* Willoughby, Francis, fifth baron, 1618–66; Willoughby, William, sixth baron, 1666–73.
Wilmot, Anne, countess of Rochester, wife of Henry Wilmot, first earl, and previously of Sir F. H. Lee: geneal., &c., iii. 383 & nn. 2, 3.
Wilmot, Henry; Baron Wilmot of Adderbury 1643; Viscount Wilmot of Athlone 1644; first earl of Rochester 1652, ii. 561, n. 11; as Lord Wilmot: coach of, at Paris, 1649, ii. 561; ~ attends Charles II, Paris, 1651, iii. 51; geneal., iii. 383, n. 2.
Wilmot, John, second earl of Rochester, the poet, iii. 565, n. 1; character of, iii. 565; lodgings of, in Whitehall, v. 47, n. 2; geneal., iii. 383, n. 2.
Wilmot of Adderbury: Baron, 1643–52: *see* Wilmot, Henry, later earl of Rochester.
Wilmot of Athlone: Viscount 1644–52: *see* Wilmot, Henry, later earl of Rochester.
Wilson, Edmund, M.D.: treats E, iii. 81–2 & n.; social (?; as 'my physician'), iii. 83.
Wilson, Edward: wealth of, killed in duel, &c., v. 175–6 & n.
Wilson, Thomas, of Keythorpe, Leics.: estate of, &c., v. 175, 176, n. 1.
Wilton: as form of Wiltshire, ii. 557.
Wilton House, Wilts.: notice, 1654, iii. 113–14 & nn.; fire at, 1704, v. 586 & n. 3; Sidney's *Arcadia* and, iii. 72, n. 5; painting at, v. 245, n. 3.
Wiltshire: Mrs. Evelyn's relations, &c., in, iii. 76, 98; receiver of: *see* Scawen, R.
Wimbledon, Surrey: Wimbledon House at, iii. 315, n. 5; gardens of: alterations to, iii. 315–16; Bristol at, iii. 315, 322; iv. 72; ~ library of, at, iv. 126 & n. 3; Lady Bristol at, iv. 95; bought by Danby, &c., iv. 130–1 & nn., 162 & n. 1.
Wimbledon: Viscount, 1626–38: *see* Cecil, Sir Edward.
Winch, Sir Humphrey, bt., iii. 393, n. 1; as member of Council for Foreign Plantations, &c., iii. 578, 629; as commissioner of the Admiralty, iv. 171 & n. 2; social, iii. 392–3.

Winchelsea, Sussex: notice, iii. 67–8 & nn.

Winchester, Hants.: notices: 1642, ii. 79 & n. 2 (i. 52); ~ 1685, iv. 471–2 & nn.; Charles II and: projects palace at, &c., iv. 341 & n. 2, 471–2 & n.; ~ visits, 1684, iv. 383, n. 2, 387; James II at, 1685, iv. 467, n. 1, 468–72, 473; boarding-school at, iii. 168, n. 1; miraculous cure at, iv. 469 & n. 2; race-meeting at: established, iv. 341, n. 2; environs of: in comparison, ii. 488 & n. 3.

Winchester: cathedral clergy:

bishops: *ex officio* prelates of Order of the Garter, iii. 479, n. 4; house of, in Chelsea, iv. 81 & n. 5; individual bishops: *see* Beaufort, Henry (1404–47), Montagu, James (1616–18); Andrewes, L. (1619–26); Duppa, B. (1660–2); Morley, George (1662–84); Mews, P. (1684–1706); Trelawny, Sir Jonathan (1707–21).

deans: *see* Clarke, William (1665–79); Meggot, R. (1679–92).

archdeacon of: *see* Fulham, G. (1700–2).

prebendary: *see* Fulham, G.

Winchester: Marquises of, &c.: *see* Paulet, John, fifth marquis 1629–75; Paulet, Isabella, his marchioness; Paulet, Charles, sixth marquis 1675–89, later duke of Bolton.

Winchilsea: Earls of: *see* Finch, Heneage, second earl 1639–89; Finch, Daniel, sixth earl 1729–30, formerly second earl of Nottingham.

Windham, —, iii. 351.

Windham, Sir William: *see* Wyndham.

Windlesham, Surrey: rector of: *see* Piggott, S.

Windsor: town or castle: distance of, from London, i. 69; William of Orange at, 1688, iv. 610, 611, n. 1; Henry Hyde, earl of Clarendon, at, 1688, iv. 610, n. 4; A. Verrio's garden at, iv. 176 & n. 4, 207–8.

Windsor Castle:

— structure: (i) general: notices: 1654, iii. 98–9 & nn.; 1670, iii. 560 & n. 3; 1678, iv. 136 & n. 3; 1680, iv. 207 & nn. 3–5; 1683, iv. 316–17 & nn.; 1685, iv. 465 & n. 7; 1692, v. 103 & n. 4; rebuilding of: projected, 1670, iii. 560 & n. 2; state apartments rebuilt by Hugh May, iii. 381, n. 3, 573 & n. 1; ~ progress of, iv. 136 & n. 3.

— — in comparison, i. 72; view from, iii. 99; iv. 177.

— structure: (ii) particular parts of the castle, rooms, &c.:

— — Council chamber, iv. 319.

— — Devil's Tower: inscribed stone found in (?), iii. 566, n. 1.

— — Guard Chambers: arms decorating: removed, &c., v. 103 & n. 4.

— — Keep: in 1654, iii. 99 & n. 2; Prince Rupert's apartments in, iii. 560 & n. 3; ~ hall in, decorated with arms, *ib.*; iv. 473; arms in, removed, v. 103 & n. 4; inscribed stone found in (?), iii. 566 & n. 1; in view, iv. 527.

— — King's Chapel: in construction, iv. 207, n. 3; paintings and carvings in, iv. 316–17 & nn.; *see also* iv. 176; services in, iv. 317, 383(?); occupied by Roman Catholics, iv. 465, 518 & n. 4.

— — King's Eating Room: painting in, iii. 338–9 & nn.

— — Presence Chamber, iv. 319.

— — St. George's Chapel, iii. 98–9 & n.; Charles I's grave in, *ib.*; services in, iv. 181(?), 383(?), 465, 517, 518 *bis*; v. 110–11; evening prayer in (?), iv. 318, 466; Garter service in, iii. 558–9; special service to be held in, iv. 524 & n. 2; for clergy attached to, *see* Windsor: St. George's Chapel: clergy.

— — St. George's Hall: in construction, iv. 207, n. 3; paintings and carvings in, iv. 316–17 & nn., 465 & n. 7; *see also* iv. 176.

— — Star building: construction of, iv. 136, n. 3; progress of, iv. 207 & n. 3.

— — statue of Charles II, iv. 207 & n. 4.

— — terrace, iii. 99, 559 & n. 3; balcony over the, iii. 559 & n. 3; long terrace below the Castle, iv. 42; additional terraces, 1683, iv. 317 & n. 4.

Windsor Castle (*cont.*)
— — Upper Ward: remodelling of, iv. 207 & n. 3.
— — royal collections (modern): works of art in, ii. 277, n. 3, 498, n. 8 *ad fin.*; iii. 79, n. 2, 260, nn. 2–4.
— officers:
— — comptroller, 1673–84: *see* May, Hugh.
— — constables: John Mordaunt, Viscount Mordaunt, 1660–8, iii. 468, n. 6, 469; Prince Rupert, 1668–82, iii. 560 & n. 3; clerk to: W. Tayleur, iii. 468, n. 6 *ad fin.*
— court and royalty at, &c.:
— — Charles II or his court at: 1670, iii. 558–60; 1671, iii. 580, n. 6; 1674, iv. 38, 41; 1675, iv. 73 & n. 2; 1678, iv. 142 & n. 6, 147; 1679, iv. 171 & n. 10, 176, 177, 180, 181; 1680, iv. 207, n. 6, 214 & n. 7; 1681, iv. 248, n. 4; 1682, iv. 280 & n. 2; 1683, iv. 317–19 & nn.; 1684, iv. 383 & n. 2.
— — Charles II ill at, 1679, iv. 180, 181 & n. 1; James, duke of York, at, 1679, iv. 181 & n. 1; City of London authorities submit to Charles II at, iv. 319–20 & n.
— — James II or his court at: 1685, iv. 465–7, 467, n. 1; 1686, iv. 517, n. 3, 518–19, 526 & n. 2; 1687, iv. 558, n. 5.
— — Queen Anne or her court at: 1702, v. 514, n. 7, 516, n. 2; 1703, v. 543–4 & n. (implied), 555 & n. 3; 1705, v. 602, n. 2.
— — Archduke Charles visits Queen Anne at, v. 554 & n. 1, 555 & n. 3.
— — Garter celebrations at, iii. 558–9 & n., 580 & n. 6; etching of: cited, iii. 480, n. 1.
— — E visits [sometimes the town alone]: 1654, iii 98–9 & nn.; 1669 (transit), iii. 536; 1670, iii. 558–60; 1674, iv. 38–9, 41–3; 1678, iv. 136, 142; 1679, iv. 176–7, 180–1; 1680, iv. 207–8; 1683, iv. 316–20 & nn.; 1684, iv. 383; 1685, iv. 465–7; 1686, iv. 517 & n. 3, 518–19; 1687, iv. 558; 1692, v. 103, 110–11; Mrs. Evelyn, &c., visit, iv. 38, 207; v. 110; Mary Evelyn spends summer at, iv. 38, 428.

Windsor Forest: lieutenancy of: held by B. Whitelocke, iii. 64, n. 2; to be examined as source of peat, &c., iii. 486, n. 1; Bagshot Park in, iv. 467–8 & n.; ~ visits to, iv. 480–1, 558 *ter*, 559; Cranbourn Lodge in, iv. 527–8 & n.; ~ visits to, &c., iv. 38 & n. 2, 558 *bis*, 642; v. 110; New Lodge in, iv. 38, n. 2.

Windsor Park [E scarcely distinguishes the two parks]: in view, iii. 99; incomparable, iv. 177; Great Park: ash in, from Fire of London, iii. 454, n. 1; ~ planting of, &c., iii. 560 & n. 5; Little Park: military display in (?), iv. 42 & n. 1; ~ walking in (?), iv. 318 *bis*; New Park (1683): avenues to, planted, iv. 317.

Windsor: St. George's Chapel: clergy:
 deans: *see* Ryves, B. (1660–77); Durel, J. (1677–83); Turner, Francis, D.D. (1683–4); Hascard, G. (1684–1708).
 canons: *see* Butler, John, D.D.; Doughty, T.; Fitzwilliam, J.; Goddard, T.

Windsor: seventh Baron 1660–82: *see* Hickman, Thomas Windsor, later earl of Plymouth.

Windward Islands: governor of: appointment of, &c., 1672, iii. 612 & n. 2.

Wines [by name or place; *see also* Vineyards and Viticulture]: Albano, ii. 356 & n. 2; Bologna, ii. 421, 425; Bordeaux, iv. 329 & n. 3; Bristol milk, iii. 103, n. 1; canary carried to the Indies and back, iii. 313; Charlton: wine from Col. Blount's vineyard at, iii. 161; Falernian, ii. 210 & n. 3, 323; Florence: Grand Duke of Tuscany sells his wines at, ii. 187 & n. 7 (i. 118); Greco, ii. 287 & n. 5, 336 & n. 2; Montefiascone, ii. 210; muscatello, ii. 207; Naples, kingdom of: as produce of, ii. 353; Orleans, ii. 138 (i. 90); Rhenish: at Dort, ii. 32 & n. 4 (i. 24); sack, i. 14; v. 467; Spanish, iii. 103 & n. 1; Velletri, ii. 317; wine: made by E at Padua, ii. 472–3 *bis*; fountains running, iii. 281.

Winnell, Rev. — (Philip Wynell?): sermon by, iv. 582 & n. 2.

Winnington, Sir Francis: takes part in Stafford's impeachment, iv. 227 & n. 6.
Winstanley (Vinstanley), Henry: water works of, v. 247 & n. 1.
Winter, Sir John, ii. 546, n. 8; project of, for preparing coke, iii. 180–1 & n.; Forest of Dean granted to, iii. 343, n. 3; social, ii. 546.
Winter, Mary, Lady Winter, wife of Sir John; social, ii. 546 & n. 8.
Winthrop, John, jnr., governor of Connecticut: gives Royal Society account of preparation of pitch, iii. 326–7 & n.; inquiries referred to, iii. 340, n. 1.
Winwick, Lancs.: rector of: *see* Sherlock, R.
Wise, Henry, gardener, v. 606, n. 4; partner in Brompton Park nursery, v. 176, n. 3; lays out Kensington Palace garden, v. 606–7; *see also* v. 290, n. 6 *ad fin.*
Wiseman, Mrs. —, v. 84.
Wisley, Surrey: rector of: *see* Bradshaw, G.
Witches: Joan of Arc burnt as a witch, ii. 137 (i. 90); at Salem, 1692, v. 130 & n. 1; at Schiedam, ii. 56 & n. 7.
Withers, —, shipwright: presented to Charles II, iv. 12.
Withings, Mr. Justice: *see* Wythens, Sir F.
Witnesses, the Two: identification of, discussed, iv. 636–7 & n.; identified with Waldenses, v. 25–6.
Wiverton (Wharton House), Notts., iii. 125 & n. 2.
Woldingham, Surrey: church at: rebuilding of, suggested, iv. 121–2 & n.
Wolley, Edward, D.D.; bishop of Clonfert, &c., 1665, iii. 44, n. 2; as preacher, iii. 47; sermons by, iii. 44, 47, 49, 52.
Wollsal, Dr. —: *see* Walsall, F.
Wolseley (Ouseley), Sir Charles, bt.: social, iii. 164–5 & n.
Wolsey, Thomas, cardinal: and Ipswich: born at, and foundations of, at, iii. 179 & n. 1; iv. 116 & n. 2; burial-place of, iii. 122 & n. 7; buildings of: Hampton Court, iii. 322, n. 5; ~ at Whitehall, iii. 569, n. 2; MS. given by, to Christ Church, Oxford, iii. 109 & n. 2.
Wonersh, Surrey: vicar of: *see* Geree, Stephen.
Wood, Sir Henry, bt., iii. 49, n. 1; marries, iii. 49 & n. 1; office held by, iii. 261, n. 4.
Wood, Mary, Lady Wood, born Gardiner, wife of Sir Henry, iii. 22, n. 5; as Mrs. Gardiner (Garder): in Paris, 1650, iii. 22 & n. 5; ~ dismissal of, from Henrietta Maria's service, expected, iii. 44, n. 5; marries Wood, iii. 49 & n. 1.
Wood, Thomas, D.D.; bishop of Lichfield 1671, iii. 290, n. 4; sermons by, iii. 290, 322(?).
Wood-carving [*see also* Gibbons, G.]: carved or inlaid choir-stalls, ii. 421, 423, 455 & n 8, 528 & n. 3; crucifix (wood of True Cross), ii. 87 (i. 58–9); fruit-stones: chaplet of, ii. 114 (i. 74).
Woodcock, Sir Thomas: social, iii. 473 & n. 5.
Woodcote Park, near Epsom, Surrey, ii. 542, n. 3; Richard Evelyn married at, ii. 542–3; as Richard Evelyn's seat, iii. 190, 544; chapel in Epsom church belonging to, iii. 545; Lady Browne dies at, iii. 76; Mrs. Anne Montague dies at, iv. 569; visits to Richard Evelyn, &c., at: 1648–50, ii. 543 *bis*, 544, 552, 557; iii. 15; ~ 1652–8, iii. 61, 76, 92, 146, 155, 218 *bis*, 219; ~ 1660–6, iii. 244, 254, 326, 334, 371, 416, 418, 425–8, 467; ~ 1667–9, iii. 472, 527, 536, 537, 538; visits to Mrs. Elizabeth Evelyn at, iii. 547, 623.
  Ashley near: Lady Mordaunt at (?), iii. 425–6 & nn.
Woodcote, Beddington, Surrey: supposed site of Noviomagus, iii. 221, n. 7.
Woodford, Essex: rector of: *see* Shelley, P.
Woodhead, Abraham: recommended by E as tutor (?), iii. 182 & n. 2.
Woodroffe, Benjamin, D.D., iv. 12, n. 2; sermons by, iv. 12(?), 317.
Woodstock, Oxon.: park, &c., at: damage to, in Civil War, iii. 381 & n. 5.
Woodward, Rev. —; curate at Deptford (?), iii. 365, n. 5; sermons by, iii. 365–6, 372, 375.

Woolwich, Kent: plague at, 1665–6, iii. 417, n. 4, 435, n. 1; visibility of Great Fire of London at, iii. 453, n. 3; defences at, 1667, iii. 485 & n. 5; Dockyard: Jonas Shish, &c., in, iii. 506, n. 5; curate(s) of: sermons by, at Deptford, iv. 647; v. 58.
Worcester: E sets out for, iii. 118; notice, iii. 119 & n. 5; cathedral: boundary of lands of, iii. 119, n. 2; battle of: news of, reaches Paris, iii. 44 & n. 3; mentioned, iii. 178 & n. 1, 212, n. 7; Charles II's escape after: news of, reaches Paris, iii. 47 & n. 4; ~ mentioned, iii. 51, 259, n. 4; iv. 408, n. 1; Sir R. Fanshawe captured in, iii. 57, n. 2.
Worcester: Earls and Marquises, &c., of: *see* Somerset, Edward, fourth earl 1589–1628; Somerset, Henry, fifth earl, 1628–42, and first marquis, 1642–6; Somerset, Edward, second marquis 1646–67; Somerset, Henry, third marquis 1667–82, later duke of Beaufort; Somerset, Mary, his marchioness, later duchess; Somerset, Charles, marquis 1682–98 (courtesy title); Somerset, Rebecca, his marchioness.
Worcester: cathedral clergy:
bishops: *see* Morley, George (1660–2); Gauden, John (1662); Earles, J. (1662–3); Blandford, W. (1671–5); Fleetwood, J. (1675–83); Thomas, William (1683–9); Stillingfleet, E. (1689–99); Lloyd, William, D.D., the apocalyptic (1699–1717); Hough, J. (1717–43); Frampton, R. (called bishop in error, iii. 604 & n. 3).
deans: *see* Thomas, William (1665–83); Hickes, G. (1683–90); Talbot, William (1691–1715); Burgh, — (called dean in error, iii. 239 & n. 4).
canon: *see* Blagrave, J.
Worcester Park, Surrey: felling of trees in, iii. 428 & n. 1.
Worcestershire: in view, iii. 119.
Worcom: *see* Woudrichem.
Words and Phrases [the principal object of this section is to give references to notes explaining words. In some cases, where words possess a special historical interest, or where they are used freely or loosely, references are given to several occurrences; but I have not tried to index all occurrences of any word, and simple repetitions are excluded (as when V reproduces K faithfully, and in the case of words with precise meanings which are used exactly). Terms relating to architectural style are indexed under Architecture; names of musical instruments under Music; and similarly with other technical terms. I have included a few words to which no notes are attached, as being components of E's vocabulary likely to interest readers and consultants; but the section does not attempt to give a general representation of his vocabulary.
In general words are entered under their standard forms; E's forms are added in brackets if they are likely to be difficult to recognize; in a few cases, on account of their special interest, words are entered under E's forms. I have treated foreign and pseudo-foreign words as English when E appears to have been trying to introduce them into the language]:
abide, iv. 46 & n. 6.
abortive parchment, iii. 374 & n. 1.
abrenuntiate, v. 120 & n. 1.
academist, iii. 42 & n. 2.
accend, iv. 253 & n. 2.
acceptions, iii. 168 & n. 4.
accression, iv. 146 & n. 2.
achate, ii. 88 & n. 1.
acquist, v. 270 & n. 1.
actions, v. 174 & n. 6.
addresses, ii. 69 & n. 3.
advantages, ii. 158 & n. 2.
aeolipyle (eolipile), iii. 272 & n. 4.
allogiaments, ii. 125 & n. 2.
Amazon, ii. 89 & n. 4.
amure, i. 110 & n. 1.
amused, v. 434 & n. 3.
anathema maranatha: explained in sermons, iii. 337 & n. 1; iv. 164, 436.
ancient, ii. 234; *see* ii. 225, n. 2; *see further* Architecture: styles, &c.

Words and Phrases (*cont.*)
angust, v. 222 & n. 2.
antepasts, v. 144 & n. 1.
anti-ports, ii. 258 & n. 6.
antique (adjective), ii. 192, 225 & n. 2; iii. 148 & n. 4; *see further* Architecture: styles, &c.
antique (noun), ii. 300; iii. 505 & n. 3.
architrave, ii. 371 & n. 3.
artificial, *add.* (ii. 41); v. 75 & n. 4.
artists, ii. 374 & n. 7; iv. 203 & n. 4.
arts, ii. 489 & n. 5.
aspectable, iv. 269 & n. 4.
attrition, iii. 200 & n. 3; iv. 562 & n. 2.
back fire, iii. 456 & n. 5.
balusters, iii. 480 & n. 2.
banquet, iii. 480 & n. 5.
baptistery, ii. 59 & n. 1, 163 & n. 2, 266.
barathrum, ii. 335 & n. 4.
beach stone, ii. 319 & n. 5.
beamed, iii. 325 & n. 5.
beau (beaw), v. 280 & n. 2.
behether (behither), ii. 490 & n. 11; iv. 177 & n. 3.
belike, iv. 240 & n. 5.
bettle, ii. 459 & n. 3.
blue (blew), ii. 188 & n. 1.
bodied, iii. 446, n. 6.
bole, ii. 293 & n. 2.
boutefeu (Arch-bouttefew), iv. 452 & n. 6.
bow (of a coach), ii. 257, 258, n. 1.
brass, ii. 33 & n. 4.
brazil (brasill) *or* brazil-wood, ii. 45 & n. 4 (i. 32).
break, iii. 258 & n. 3.
breast, on, ii. 338 & n. 2.
bridle, ii. 326 & n. 3, 330, n. 1.
bronze (verb), ii. 417; *see* ii. 33, n. 4.
bust, ii. 327 & n. 6, 369 & n. 3, 415 & n. 6.
cab of pigeon's dung, iv. 55 & n. 6.
cabal, iii. 494 & n. 1.
cancelled, ii. 71 & n. 1, 246.
cane, ii. 342 & n. 1.
cantore (*kantoor*), ii. 62 & n. 3.
captain-lieutenant, ii. 36 & n. 5.
carking, v. 144 & n. 2.
carpet (of grass), iii. 115, 555; iv. 70.
catadupe, ii. 397 & n. 1.
Catholic: explained in sermon, iv. 158.
catoptrics, ii. 230 & n. 6.

Words and Phrases (*cont.*)
caudatari, ii. 279 & n. 4.
causal, iii. 93 & n. 5.
cavallerizza, cavallerizzo, ii. 330 & n. 4; *add.*; i. 54 & n. 2; ii. 195.
cavous, iii. 210 & n. 1.
cedrario, ii. 484 & n. 1.
ceimeliarcha, ii. 188 & n. 13; *see also* cimelia *below*.
cere-cloth, iii. 295 & n. 4.
chair of arms, ii. 378 & n. 1.
chamblett, ii. 145, n. 9, 146.
champion, ii. 210 & n. 5, 485 & n. 3.
chards, iv. 338 & n. 2.
chimelium: *see* cimelia *below*.
Chi va li, ii. 472 & n. 2.
Christmas, the rest of, iii. 146.
Christo in gremio, iv. 566 & n. 2.
cimelia, cimelium (chimelium), ii. 105 & n. 2, 188, n. 13; iii. 261 & n. 2, 373 & n. 6.
citronario, iii. 18 & n. 5.
citroniere, ii. 109 & n. 1.
city in a wood, ii. 47 & n. 4.
civil list, v. 282 & n. 1.
cloudy, iii. 216 & n. 8.
cochlea, ii. 58 & n. 1.
cognation, v. 254 & n. 1.
coin, ii. 223 & n. 8.
collines, iii. 141 & n. 1; i. 103.
compartiments, ii. 295; iv. 215.
compellation, v. 576 & n. 2.
compound, iii. 59 & n. 1.
conceive, iii. 452 & n. 4.
concredited, v. 342 & n. 3.
concurrent leases, iv. 503 & n. 1.
condited, iv. 190 & n. 5.
condole, iii. 620–1 & n.
confragose, iii. 103 & n. 3, 131.
conscience, v. 596 & n. 1.
conserve, ii. 109 & n. 2, 175.
conspiring, iii. 451 & n. 5.
consulage, iii. 630 & n. 1.
contexture, v. 157 & n. 1.
contignation, ii. 203 & n. 1; iii. 138.
contribution land, ii. 38 & n. 7, 74.
conversation, iii. 72 & n. 5; iv. 308 & n. 1.
cornice, ii. 252 & n. 4.
cornua, ii. 302 & n. 1.
correption, iii. 152 & n. 4.
cortege, iv. 171 & n. 11; corteggio, iii. 256.
crisped, ii. 447 & n. 1.
cupulated, ii. 337 & n. 2.
curiosity, ii. 431 & n. 1; iii. 78 & n. 1, 293, 567 & n. 5, 590 & n. 1.

Words and Phrases (*cont.*)
curious, iii. 492 & n. 3, 560 & n. 4.
daring, iv. 342 & n. 3; *see also* iii. 337.
daughter-in-law, iv. 189.
debite, ii. 368 & n. 2.
decussation, iv. 275 & n. 6.
degenerous, iv. 131 & n. 6.
Deipnosophism, iv. 300 & n. 7.
delicate, ii. 50 & n. 2; iii. 127, 139.
deliciis, in, ii. 425 & n. 2.
deputations, iii. 445 & n. 3.
descend, ii. 239 & n. 8.
design (verb), ii. 160, 176 & n. 4, 494 & n. 6.
devast, ii. 336 & n. 2.
devota, ii. 246 & n. 1.
diet (at court), iii. 261 & n. 5.
diffidence, v. 291 & n. 4.
digladiation, v. 120 & n. 2.
disgust, iii. 304 & n. 6.
division (in music), i. 34 & n. 1.
document, ii. 476 & n. 2; v. 122 & n. 1.
dom. (*domesticis*), *coram*, iv. 97 & n. 2.
domo, ii. 56 & n. 2.
doquett (docket), iv. 503 & n. 6, 509.
dormitory, ii. 12 & n. 5.
dorp, v. 160 & n. 2.
dulcorus, iv. 313 & n. 2.
dured, ii. 208 & n. 1.
earth, ii. 235; iii. 3 & n. 1; iv. 116 & n. 5.
eclat, v. 331 & n. 2.
ectype, iii. 196 & n. 1.
elaboratory, iii. 154 & n. 6.
elapses, iii. 510 & n. 6.
elemental, v. 411 & n. 2.
elogy, ii. 21 & n. 2.
embosse, ii. 255 & n. 4.
enorm (inorm), v. 434 & n. 1.
ensigns, ii. 202 & n. 5.
entertainment, iii. 511 & n. 1; v. 167.
entretices, iii. 427 & n. 4.
eucharistical, iii. 431 & n. 6.
evince, v. 360 & n. 2, 458 & n. 2.
eviternal, v. 107 & n. 3.
exact, iii. 140 & n. 1.
exactness, iii. 567 & n. 6.
exaggerate, ii. 512 & n. 3; iii. 7 & n. 1, 9; iv. 230 & n. 1.
exenterated, iii. 255 & n. 7.
exinanition, iii. 190 & n. 5.
exorbitance, exorbitancy, ii. 10 & n. 5, 28.

Words and Phrases (*cont.*)
extravagant, ii. 73 & n. 4; v. 330 & n. 3.
family, v. 509 & n. 2.
fanal, ii. 183 & n. 5.
feathered rain, ii. 514 & n. 1.
fee-farm, iii. 59 & n. 1.
fellow-commoner, ii. 16 & n. 1; i. 13.
fellow-traveller, ii. 23 & n. 1.
feoffee, iii. 223 & n. 4.
flaccid (flaxid), iii. 292 & n. 4.
floats, on, v. 60 & n. 4.
florist, i. 86 & n. 1.
flower of brass, ii. 342 & n. 3.
flub, ii. 447 & n. 5.
foederal right, v. 18 & n. 1.
fonds, iii. 483 & n. 6.
foot padders, iii. 70 & n. 1.
foreman, ii. 31 & n. 7, 33; i. 24.
foretop, iii. 321 & n. 2.
formal hearers, iii. 252 & n. 6.
formalities, ii. 19 & n. 1.
fret, ii. 366 & n. 6.
garnison, ii. 38 & n. 6.
garnito stone, ii. 216 & n. 7.
gaskins, iv. 398 & n. 3.
gentlemen-commoners, i. 13; *see* ii. 16, n. 1.
girandola, ii. 129 & n. 2, 395 & n. 3.
glass-eye, v. 265 & n. 1.
glorious, ii. 497 & n. 6.
graffs, ii. 67 & n. 1.
graft, ii. 46 & n. 3, 457 & n. 3.
granados, ii. 458 & n. 8; iii. 368 & n. 5.
ground (in music), iii. 167 & n. 4; iv. 48.
guidons, iii. 224 & n. 2.
gulio, ii. 229 & n. 6.
gun, ii. 469 & n. 2.
hablador, iv. 329 & n. 4.
Halcyon time, ii. 21 & n. 7.
hamac, iii. 382 & n. 7.
hands a cross: men standing with their, iii. 455 & n. 1.
harping irons, iii. 215 & n. 1.
Heaven, the Third: *see* Third Heaven *below*.
horrid, ii. 116, 119, 170, 173, 178, 208, 506 & n. 7, 509, 517; iii. 103; iv. 175, 326, 449; i. 104.
horror, ii. 208, 547; i. 47.
hortulan, i. 70 & n. 1; v. 151.
housses, ii. 426 & n. 8.
humanity, iii. 376 & n. 4.
hurocan, hurecan, iv. 644; v. 2, 113, 550; i. 26.

Words and Phrases (*cont.*)
(i) (abbreviation), ii. 248 & n. 9.
igniculi, iv. 214 & n. 2.
ignite, iii. 452 & n. 4.
illiberal arts, the, iv. 199 & n. 5.
illiterate, ii. 2 (i. 1); iv. 201 & n. 1.
illustrissimo, ii. 444 & n. 7.
immarcescible, v. 534 & n. 2.
immunities, iv. 459 & n. 3.
impeach, ii. 26 & n. 5.
impress (noun), ii. 239 & n. 12, 354.
incensories, ii. 358 & n. 2.
incornished, ii. 390 & n. 4.
inculk, v. 388 & n. 2.
indagator, iii. 89 & n. 1.
indicible, v. 491 & n. 1.
individuum vagum, ii. 354 & n. 3.
informe, ii. 379 & n. 7.
inorm, v. 434 & n. 1.
insolvable, v. 346; *see* v. 314, n. 2.
institution, ii. 65 & n. 8.
intaglio (intaglia), iii. 79 & n. 2.
inteneration, v. 416 & n. 1.
intent (verb), v. 422 & n. 1.
interdict, iii. 455 & n. 1.
interesse, v. 306 & n. 3.
internodium, ii. 259 & n. 4.
interpreted names, iii. 24 & n. 4.
interwoven, ii. 307 & n. 2.
intromit, iii. 549 & n. 2.
intuition, v. 342 & n. 2.
invectique, iii. 465 & n. 2.
irrespect, v. 296 & n. 1.
irruption, iii. 539 & n. 2.
isabella, iii. 42 & n. 4.
jacatroo, iii. 108 & n. 5.
jack, iii. 200 & n. 2.
jakes, iii. 40 & n. 2.
jealous, ii. 63; iii. 240 & n. 4.
jejunium, iv. 27 & n. 1.
jeu de goblets, iv. 39 & n. 3.
jointure, v. 271 & n. 2.
kitchen-stuff, iv. 352 & n. 2.
knack of the spirit, iii. 551 & n. 2.
landskip, landscip, ii. 113, 156, 191, 208, 299, 326; iv. 114, 128, 288, 365; i. 21, 106.
large, ii. 95 & n. 3, 269 & n. 6, 493 & n. 4.
leaguer, ii. 31 & n. 4.
lecture, ii. 476 & n. 2; iv. 139 & n. 1.
levati, ii. 296 & n. 6, 310.
limnings, iii. 287 & n. 2.
liver-grown, iii. 210 & n. 2.
lodge, ii. 231 & n. 5, 252 & n. 5.
logiaments, ii. 67 & n. 1.

Words and Phrases (*cont.*)
log-wood, ii. 45 & n. 4.
looby, iii. 292 & n. 8.
luciferous, iv. 325 & n. 3.
luculent, ii. 398 & n. 2.
lustration, v. 484 & n. 3.
luxury, iii. 569 & n. 1.
mabbled, ii. 42 & n. 3.
maille, ii. 134 & n. 1.
make: having been very much made, iii. 556 & n. 1.
malice (verb), v. 451 & n. 1.
manage (manège), ii. 71 & n. 5 (i. 47).
manducation, v. 240 & n. 6.
marquess, iii. 76 & n. 1.
mart-ship, ii. 59 & n. 4.
masque, iii. 357 & n. 1.
mass (verb), iv. 511 & n. 3.
matras, iv. 491 & n. 3.
means, iii. 226 & n. 7; living under the means, iii. 232 & n. 1.
melancholy, ii. 71 & n. 4 (i. 47), 159, 209, 250, 319, 515; iii. 99, 120, 127, 399; i. 47, 55; noun, ii. 3; *see also* Illnesses.
menstrue, menstruum, iii. 396 & n. 2; iv. 162, 253 & n. 1.
mercury (of metals), iii. 28 & n. 2.
metaschematism, v. 91 & n. 1, 295.
meubled, ii. 411 & n. 5.
mezzotinto, iii. 271 & n. 4.
mineries, ii. 342 & n. 2.
miss (noun), ii. 448 & n. 3; iii. 309 & n. 4, 590.
mithinks, ii. 412; mithought, mi thought, ii. 156 & n. 6; v. 309.
mizzling (missling), v. 380 & n. 2.
mobile, i. 55 & n. 1.
mond: *see* mundo *below*.
mouth glue, iv. 251 & n. 3.
mundo, mund, mond, ii. 260 & n. 1; iii. 224 & n. 1, 283 & n. 9.
myrtetum, iv. 576 & n. 6.
naked (noun), ii. 114 & n. 8, 298; iii. 386.
nasute, i. 101 & n. 1.
natural, ii. 326 & n. 4, 352.
naturalists, v. 107 & n. 2.
naumachia, iii. 18.
naupegus, iii. 359 & n. 5; i. 22.
navalia, v. 538 & n. 4.
neeze, iii. 209 & n. 3.
negoce, ii. 166 & n. 4.
new lights, iii. 510 & n. 5.
nices, ii. 127 & n. 6.
nidary, ii. 110 & n. 1.
ninehammer, iv. 300 & n. 5.

Words and Phrases (*cont.*)
non ultra, ii. 354 & n. 2.
notation, v. 157 & n. 4.
novelist, v. 75 & n. 3.
numerical, v. 399 & n. 5, 496.
oblations, v. 207 & n. 3.
obtestation, iii. 53 & n. 1.
office, ii. 27 & n. 1; i. 20; iv. 126 & n. 5.
olitory, iii. 225 & n. 4.
olivaster, iii. 321 & n. 1.
olive-branches, i. 9 & n. 1.
one-and-thirtieth, ii. 23 & n. 4.
operator, ii. 99 & n. 7.
ophite, ii. 181 & n. 4 (i. 114).
ordinances, iii. 184 & n. 1, 204.
ordonance, ord'nance, ii. 266; iv. 317 & n. 3.
oriency, ii. 449 & n. 3.
padders, iii. 70 & n. 1.
pageants, iii. 250 & n. 2.
pagod (pagood), iii. 374 & n. 3.
palaferii, ii. 465 & n. 2.
pargeting, ii. 235 & n. 2.
Parian marble, ii. 176 & n. 8, 243 & n. 7, 261 & n. 7, 413 & n. 8, 438.
parque (error for *parquet*), ii. 115 & n. 3.
parquetted, iii. 21 & n. 1; iv. 141, 177.
participal, iv. 652 & n. 5.
party, ii. 59, 84 & n. 4.
passible, iv. 240 & n. 4.
patine, ii. 99 & n. 2.
pausilippe, iii. 561, 562, n. 1.
peak, iii. 399 & n. 1.
penal bond, iii. 75 & n. 7.
pendants, iii. 224 & n. 2.
pension, in, ii. 44 & n. 4; pension, in their, ii. 149.
pererration (parerration), iii. 142 & n. 3.
perflatile, v. 552 & n. 3.
pergolo, pergola, ii. 373 & n. 5; iii. 115 & n. 1.
periaptas, ii. 236 & n. 9.
peristyle, ii. 367 & n. 8.
pernicity, iii. 347 & n. 1.
perstringe, iii. 34 & n. 2.
pharos, ii. 153 & n. 14, 171 & n. 3; iii. 615.
piazza, ii. 481 & n. 5; *see also* ii. 100, 184; iii. 398; iv. 382; &c.
picaroon (pickaron, &c.), ii. 166 & n. 7; i. 49, 50, n. 1.
pick, iv. 278 & n. 1.
picked, ii. 1 & n. 7; iii. 215, n. 2.
piked, iii. 215 & n. 2.

Words and Phrases (*cont.*)
piscina, ii. 106 & n. 2.
Platonic, iv. 328 & n. 5.
plaustrum, ii. 382 & n. 1.
pleasant, ii. 560; iii. 570 & n. 8.
plica polonica, v. 205 & n. 1.
plot, iii. 595 & n. 3.
podestaria, ii. 467 & n. 6.
poincons, iii. 427 & n. 3.
politicians, iv. 163 & n. 1; v. 342 & n. 1.
pomeridiano, &c., iii. 217 & n. 4.
pontificalibus, in, ii. 254 & n. 6; i. 103.
Pontificians, iii. 365 & n. 3.
popular, iv. 629 & n. 3; popularity, iv. 89.
portals, iv. 504 & n. 2.
ports, ii. 48 & n. 2 (i. 34), 67 & n. 5.
posario, ii. 221 & n. 3.
positive, v. 208 & n. 5.
potagere (pottagere), iii. 538 & n. 2.
pozzo, ii. 104 & n. 3 (i. 68).
pratique-house, ii. 171 & n. 4.
preceps, v. 294 & n. 1.
precinct: error for procinct, iv. 77 & n. 3.
premier minister, iv. 501 & n. 4.
prepassion, v. 46 & n. 3.
prime favourite, iv. 549.
prime minister, iv. 118 & n. 4, 130.
primitiæ, iii. 435 & n. 9.
primitives, iii. 207 & n. 2.
procinct, iv. 77, n. 3.
prompt, iii. 336, n. 5 *ad fin.*, 337.
promulged, iv. 537 & n. 3.
property, iv. 456 & n. 4.
protract, v. 444 & n. 2.
public, the, iii. 228 & n. 8.
published, iii. 492; *add.*
punchions, iii. 427 & n. 3.
putti (puti), ii. 261 & n. 2, 549; iii. 11, 18.
pyramid, ii. 199 & n. 4, 269, 487 & n. 2; iii. 427 & n. 6; *see also* ii. 360, 369.
quaint, iii. 551 & n. 1; iv. 370 & n. 2.
quarantine, i. 106.
quarters, iv. 481 & n. 2.
ract (rack), iii. 145 & n. 4.
rapts, v. 253 & n. 5.
ratoon (ratton), iii. 194, 195, n. 1.
receipt (receite), iii. 382 & n. 2.
recidivation, iii. 303 & n. 2.
redargue, v. 114 & n. 3.

Words and Phrases (*cont.*)
refugee, i. 8 & n. 1.
Reg. (abbreviation), iii. 364 & n. 1.
regiment, v. 123 & n. 1.
reliquary, ii. 187 & n. 8, 262 & n. 2, 264, 438, 440.
renitence, v. 392 & n. 2.
report, iii. 625 & n. 2.
republicarian, republicary, iv. 614 & n. 3, 646.
respect (verb), ii. 71 & n. 1.
retrivance, iv. 435 & n. 1.
rhapsody, iii. 599 & n. 1.
riant, iv. 624 & n. 2.
ridigid, v. 6, 22.
romantic, iii. 103 & n. 6, 121; iv. 177, 221.
rounds, ii. 540 & n. 2.
rudes, ii. 323 & n. 1.
rupellary, ii. 110 & n. 1.
rusticities, ii. 324 & n. 8.
St. Paul's seamen, iv. 379 & n. 4.
salett, ii. 235 & n. 4.
sall, iv. 117 & n. 2.
sasse, iii. 161 & n. 2.
sative, iii. 133 & n. 7.
saunders, iv. 3 & n. 4.
scambling, iii. 221 & n. 4.
scarcy, v. 256.
scenario, ii. 482 & n. 3.
scheets (skates), iii. 346 & n. 5.
schemes, v. 121 & n. 2.
sconces (skonces), ii. 57, n. 7, 62, 183 & n. 6.
scratches, ii. 498 & n. 5.
scrutining, iv. 185 & n. 5.
Septuagesima, the, iii. 26 & n. 5.
Settezonio, ii. 180 & n. 2.
shaft, ii. 86; iii. 133 & n. 1.
sham, v. 78 & n. 1.
shark, iii. 376 & n. 2.
sights-man, ii. 214 & n. 2.
signatures, iii. 188 & n. 2.
slabby, v. 202 & n. 2.
sloop, i. 116 & n. 2.
soffitto (*suffitto*), ii. 482 & n. 5.
solitudinary, v. 426 & n. 1.
spa (spau), iii. 129 & n. 6.
spagyrical, iii. 28 & n. 1.
species, iii. 110 & n. 3, 549 & n. 2.
speculatists, v. 436 & n. 1.
spiracles, ii. 341 & n. 5.
spiring, ii. 171 & n. 1.
spiritato'd, iv. 48 & n. 3.
square, iii. 398 & n. 2.
staffieri, ii. 280 & n. 1.
start-blind, v. 221 & n. 8.
state, ii. 141 & n. 1, 391; iii. 412; iv. 262, 442 & n. 3.

Words and Phrases (*cont.*)
station, ii. 243 & n. 3; iv. 115 & n. 7.
statute: loan on a, ii. 545 & n. 2.
stoops: *see* stupes *below*.
strakes, ii. 447 & n. 2.
strumous, ii. 510 & n. 3.
stupes (stoops), iii. 610 & n. 2.
sub dio, ii. 295 & n. 3.
subduce, v. 475 & n. 2.
subreption, iv. 43 & n. 4.
success, v. 149 & n. 2.
suit, iv. 262 & n. 4.
surbated, iii. 461 & n. 3.
surprising, iii. 120 & n. 1; iv. 144.
sustaint, ii. 462 & n. 6.
symbol, iv. 423 & n. 2; v. 419 & n. 1.
synaxis, i. 16 & n. 1: iv. 32 & n. 4.
synecdoche, iv. 160.
syngraph, iii. 342 & n. 5.
tabernacle, iv. 180 & n. 6.
tablature, ii. 48 & n. 4, 115.
tenents, iv. 405 & n. 2.
tentur'd, ii. 53 & n. 3.
terestial, v. 114 & n. 4.
terrella, iii. 152 & n. 5.
theatre of water, ii. 392 *bis* & n. 3; *see also* ii. 393 & n. 6.
theatrical churches, v. 542 & n. 2.
Third Heaven, ii. 198 & n. 12, 240; explained in sermons, v. 500, 536.
tholus, ii. 218 & n. 6.
Threnæ, iii. 295 & n. 5.
tiffany, ii. 447 & n. 7.
touch, keep, with, iv. 218 & n. 6.
trades men, ii. 502 & n. 2, 517; iii. 91.
trail *or* trail-work, ii. 130 & n. 3; i. 83.
transum-part, ii. 259 & n. 4.
trey-table, ii. 527, n. 2.
tribunal, ii. 218 & n. 6, 443 *bis* & n. 9; *add.*; v. 192.
Trishagion (Trisagion), iii. 236 & n. 6.
tropically, iii. 525 & n. 5.
true-table, ii. 527 & n. 2.
trunks, iii. 324 & n. 2.
type (tipes), v. 448 & n. 2.
union, ii. 372 & n. 5.
unperformance, v. 303 & n. 2.
unsolvable, v. 314 & n. 2; *see also* insolvable *above*.
unvaluable, iii. 275 & n. 4.
ustorius, iv. 54 & n. 4.
vacation, iv. 572 & n. 1.
vecture, i. 24 & n. 2.

Words and Phrases (*cont.*)
vesica (vescica), iv. 324 & n. 6.
vigneron, iv. 84 & n. 3.
vindication, iv. 88 & n. 5.
visie, ii. 551 & n. 1.
volunteers, ii. 85 & n. 2.
vorago, ii. 218, 335 & n. 1, 397 & n. 1; iii. 460.
vows, ii. 413 & n. 1.
wall-eyed, ii. 40 & n. 2.
water (verb), ii. 145, n. 9, 146.
weeping, iii. 316 & n. 1.
weir (waire), iv. 197 & n. 1.
well (of a stair-case), i. 68 (*see* ii. 104, n. 3); ii. 229.
whart, iv. 314 & n. 1.
white (running water), iv. 481 & n. 3.
white staff, iii. 470 & n. 1; iv. 536 & n. 2.
wistly, iv. 101 & n. 1.
workhouse, iii. 294 & n. 6.
works, ii. 204, critical note, & n. 6, 296 & n. 3, 477; iv. 391.
Worksop, Notts., iii. 127 & nn. 1, 2.
Worms: pepper-worms, iv. 126 & n. 4; tape-worm, &c., iv. 289–90 & n.; worms in timber, iii. 341.
Worplesdon, Surrey: rector of: *see* Offley, G.
Worsley, Benjamin, M.D. (?), iii. 603, n. 1; makes statement about Jamaica, iii. 603; as secretary of Council of Trade and Plantations, iii. 628, n. 3; ~ resigns, iv. 25 & n. 1.
Wotton, Surrey:
— E at [residence at or visits to Wotton House; further references for his association with Wotton are given in later parts of this section: and under Wotton estate *and* Wotton House]: birth and early life at, ii. 1–7 (i. 1–7); visits to, &c., 1632–41, ii. 11–29 *passim* (i. 8–21 *passim*); residence at, 1641–3, ii. 77–82 *passim* (i. 51–5 *passim*); visits to: 1647–9, ii. 537–43 *passim*, 551, 557; 1650, iii. 14–15; 1652–8, iii. 60–1, 87–8, 142–3, 154–8, 193, 218–21; 1660–4, iii. 244, 326, 360, 377, 378; 1665–6, iii. 416–25 *passim*, 464; 1667–70, iii. 496, 561–2; 1677–87, iv. 111, 219–20, 254–6, 376–7, 557–9; 1691–4, v. 55–6, 67–9, 115–16, 167–8; resident at, 1694–8, v. 179–90, 200–3, 206–9, 214–19,

Wotton, Surrey (*cont.*)
228–35, 259–64, 265–8, 282–8; visit to, v. 360; visits to, or residence at, as owner of Wotton House, 1701–5, v. 377–9, 414–25, 428–34, 445, 456, 470–82, 508–21, 536–52, 569–83, 591, 605.
— the parish: descriptions, i. *2*; ii. 3–5 & nn. (i. 5–6); iii. 244; also called Blackheath, ii. 3 & n. 2 (i. 5); Glanville charity at, iii. 84, n. 1; hills and woods at, ii. 6 & n. 3 (i. 6); iv. 256; inhabitants of: general condition, v. 542; manor of: E's interest in, as part of Wotton estate, v. 337; ~ court of, held, v. 478 & n. 1, 547; mill at, v. 606, n. 1; Oakwood Chapel in: advowson of, ii. 5 & n. 1; ~ E concerned with, v. 257; ~ repair of, v. 603 & n. 1; ~ minister of: preaches at Wotton church, v. 259; pond, iii. 15; powder-mill at (?), i. *1*; roads to: from Deptford, v. 168 & n. 1; from Dorking, v. 547, n. 4; from London, v. 228 & n. 4, 467(?).
— — fatal accident at, v. 470–1; William Comber of, ii. 5 & nn. 5, 7 (i. 6); Peter (Peters) family of, ii. 6 & n. 2 (i. 6).
— church: (i) fabric: the Evelyn chapel (dormitory or vault), ii. 12–13 (i. 10); iii. 210, 378; iv. 430; v. 56, 319; porch: E at school in, ii. 6.
— — (ii) burials, monuments, &c. (in church or churchyard): Mrs. Evelyn Clarke, v. 582, n. 3; Lady Cotton, iii. 378; Elizabeth Darcy, ii. 12, n. 3; Mrs. Elizabeth Darcy, ii. 12–13 (i. 10), 15 (i. 12); E, v. 622, n. 1; ~ epitaph of, v. 623; Mrs. Eleanor Evelyn, ii. 15 (i. 12), 26 (i. 19); George Evelyn, sen.: epitaph of, i. 4; ~ wives of: epitaphs of, cited i. 2, n. 2; George Evelyn, v. 359–60 & n.; George Evelyn of Wotton, jnr., v. 358, n. 7; John Evelyn, jnr., v. 319 & n. 3; John Evelyn of Wotton, v. 55–6; Richard Evelyn, sen., ii. 26 & n. 3 (i. 19); Stansfield Evelyn, iii. 154, n. 4; Mrs. Jane Glanville, iii. 52, n. 3; William Glanville, jnr., iii. 84, n. 1; Rev.

Wotton, Surrey (*cont.*)
John Higham, iv. 377, n. 2; Robert Offley, ii. 537, n. 2; Lady Wyche, ii. 544, n. 6; Rev. Roger Wye, v. 447, n. 2.
— — (iii) clergy, &c.: advowson of, ii. 5 & n. 1; value of living (general statements), iv. 558; v. 216; rectors: *see* Higham, Robert (1583–1612); Higham, George (1612–58); Higham, John (1660–84); Duncombe, Rev. William (1684–99); Wye, R. (1699–1701); Bohun, R. (1701–16; presented, v. 447; introduced, v. 456; instituted, v. 447, n. 3; qualifies, v. 477 & n. 3); curates: *see* Morehouse (Morus), Rev. S. (*c.* 1691–8); Tomson (Thompson), Rev. — (1703–).
— — (iv) congregation: failure of, to attend services: Communion, v. 180, 181, 262, 422, 546, 580; ~ Good Friday, v. 207; ~ 5 Nov., v. 520; irreverence of, at divine service: censured in sermon, v. 576–7; neglects baptism, &c., v. 67–8; rector's neglect of, v. 180, 181, 188, 207, 266–7; *see also* v. 67; unsuitable sermons for, v. 283, 284, 542.
— — (v) parish register: note inserted by E, ii. 1, n. 1.
— — (vi) services [ordinary services (apart from Communion) and sermons are not indexed under this heading; they are traceable through E's visits to Wotton; *see also* congregation *above*]: Communion: recorded celebrations, ii. 20 (i. 16), 22 (i. 16), 23 (i. 17), 28, 77 (i. 51), 80 (i. 54), 81 *bis* (i. 54, 55); iii. 244, 425 (?); v. 181, 207, 228, 262, 282, 286 *bis*, 422, 456, 477, 515, 536, 546, 570, 580; ~ defective celebrations of, v. 181, 207, 477 & n. 4; ~ monthly celebration of, omitted, v. 180, 189; afternoon services (Sundays): no sermons in, iv. 255; v. 67, 180; ~ catechizing in, iv. 111; v. 415–24, 478, 510–14, 542–8, 571–2, 574 *passim & singulatim*; no morning sermon (Sunday), v. 188; no services for: New Year's day, v. 229; ~ Charles I's Martyrdom, v. 284; *add.*; fast-service, v. 184; thanksgiving for Blenheim, v. 578–9 & n.

Wotton estate [including property in Abinger and Dorking]: (i) ownership: bought by George Evelyn, sen., i. *1*, *3*, 3–4; bequeathed to, and extended by, Richard Evelyn, sen., i. *2–3*, 5; as property of George Evelyn, ii. 5; retention of, in Evelyn family, i. *34–5*; alleged entail of, v. 54 & n. 3; *see also* v. 338; E becomes heir to, v. 54–5; business relating to, v. 56, 67(?); settled on E, 1692, v. 103, 105, 359; *see also* v. 89, 93; new settlement of, 1698–9: proposed, v. 288 & n. 3, 292; ~ application to house of commons for, v. 314 & n. 1; ~ settled, v. 336–9 & nn.; concern of William Glanville, sen., in settlements of, v. 103, 497; E takes possession of, v. 377; present owner of: descent of, ii. 553, n. 7 *ad fin.*
(ii) general: description, ii. 5 & nn. 1–4 (i. 4, 6); value of, ii. 2 & n. 3 (i. 2); E's freeholders: at parliamentary election, v. 595; harvests on, v. 422, 514, 574; hay-making, v. 470–1; manorial courts held, v. 478 & n. 1, 547; mill on: repaired, v. 605–6 & n.; tenant's house: burnt down, v. 614; timber on: felling of, v. 89, 93, 338 & n. 1; ~ effects on, of great storm, 1703, v. 550 & n. 2.

Wotton House: (i) general: descriptions, i. *2–3*; ii. 3–5 & nn. (i. 5–6); repairs to, 1702, v. 499; dining-room, ii. 5 (i. 6); red chamber, ii. 4; ~ alluded to, iii. 421; iv. 429; library, &c., at, 1699: bequeathed by George Evelyn to E, v. 359 & n. 9; earthquake shock at, v. 115; divine service at, v. 180, 181, 188 *bis*, 230, 550; social: during shrievalty of Richard Evelyn, sen., ii. 11–12 & n. (i. 9–10); Christmas 1698, v. 283; George Evelyn's hospitality at, v. 357, n. 3, 358; number of inmates of, 1702, 1703, v. 509, 550; servants at, v. 542.

Wotton House (*cont.*)
(ii) gardens: general, ii. 4–5 (i. 5); improvements of, 1643, 1651–2, ii. 81 (i. 55); iii. 24, 60–1 & n.; gardener for, v. 478; damage to, by gales, v. 444, 550 & n. 2; elm avenue planted, v. 480; fruit-trees for, v. 119, 530; garden mount, i. 55; v. 550; meadow, iii. 61; v. 480; park meadow, v. 550; pond: accident to, v. 474; portico, i. 55 & n. 3; ii. 551 & n. 4.
(iii) the Evelyns at: E: born at, ii. 3 (i. 5); iii. 88, 421; iv. 429; intends visiting, 1652, iii. 76; sends Mrs. Evelyn, &c., to, to avoid Plague, iii. 416, 417, &c., 428, 430; goes into residence at, 1694, i. *34–5*; prepares to move to, v. 173, 176; moves to, v. 179; apartment at, assigned to E, *ib.*; unwilling to live at, 1699, v. 339; furniture of, at, v. 340; as owner: moves furniture to, v. 414; George Evelyn: born at, v. 358; dies at, v. 357; Mary Evelyn: born at, iii. 421; iv. 429, 430.
(iv) contents [modern collections; these have now been moved, the principal contents of the library, with some portraits and furniture, to Christ Church, Oxford; the remaining paintings, drawings, and furniture, to Stonor Park, near Henley]: library: W. Upcott catalogues, &c., i. *53*, *55*; ∼ MSS. preserved in: Charles II's engagement to grant Sayes Court to Sir R. Browne, &c., iii. 59, n. 1, 600, n. 2; E's notes of sermons, i. *83* & n. 1; E's 'Officium Sanctæ . . . Trinitatis', ii. 559, n. 2; E's Padua matriculation certificate, ii. 464, n. 2; E's Spanish passport, ii. 477, n. 6; letters, i. *53–4*, *56*; miscellaneous objects at: E's cabinet, ii. 191, n. 13; etching by E (?), ii. 208, n. 3; etched plate by E, ii. 557, n. 3; E's helmet, ii. 55, n. 2; E's *hortus siccus*, ii. 466, n. 5; *add.*; E's onyx seal-ring, iii. 69, n. 2; drawings by Mrs. Evelyn, ii. 535, n. 4; paintings: Correggio, Marriage of St. Catherine: copy of, ii. 229 & n.

Wotton House (*cont.*)
5; by Couwenberch, ii. 56 & n. 4; by Fioravanti (?), ii. 399, n. 10; by C. Maratti, ii. 223, n. 10; portraits: Sir Richard and Lady Browne, by Nanteuil (drawings), iii. 9, n. 3; Mrs. Elizabeth Darcy, v. 359, n. 9; E: by Kneller, iv. 479, n. 2 *ad fin.*; *add.*; ∼ by Nanteuil (drawing), iii. 9, n. 3, 22, n. 9; ∼ by H. van der Borcht (?), ii. 29, n. 1; ∼ by Walker, ii. 541, n. 6; Mrs. Evelyn, ii. 535, n. 4; ∼ by Nanteuil (drawing), *ib.*; iii. 9, n. 3; Mrs. Eleanor Evelyn, v. 359, n. 9; Richard Evelyn, sen., *ib.*; children of George Evelyn of Nutfield, by Luttrell, v. 187, n. 2; Mrs. Godolphin, by Dixon, iv. 13, n. 7; Henry Owen (?), i. 4, n. 1.

Wotton: Hundred of, Surrey, ii. 3, n. 2.

Wotton, family: geneal., iii. 553, n. 3.

Wotton, Catherine: *see* Stanhope, Catherine, Lady Stanhope, countess of Chesterfield.

Wotton, Rev. Henry: as father of Dr. William Wotton, iv. 172 & n. 4, 173.

Wotton, Sir Henry: friend of Sir C. Crewe, ii. 540, n. 1.

Wotton, Thomas, second Baron Wotton of Marley: geneal., iv. 92, n. 2.

Wotton, William; D.D. 1707, iv. 172, n. 4; v. 184 & n. 2; relations of, with E, i. *35*; as precocious child, iv. 172–3; sermons by, v. 184, 202–3, 207–8; E gives copy of *Numismata* to, v. 283, n. 3.

Wotton of Marley: second Baron: *see* Wotton, Thomas.

Wotton of Wotton: Baron: *see* Kirkhoven, C. H.

Woudrichem (Worcom), ii. 39 & n. 3 (i. 29).

Wray, Sir Christopher: fights against Charles I, &c., ii. 480 & n. 3, 530.

Wray, Frances: *see* Vane, Frances, Lady Vane.

Wray, Sir William, bt.; baronet 1660, ii. 480 & n. 3; as Captain Wray: accompanies E from Padua to Orleans: sets out, ii. 480; conduct of (?), ii. 484 & n. 4; buys a

Wray, Sir William (*cont.*)
horse, ii. 489; gift to, ii. 504; dog belonging to, ii. 511, 512; accident to horse of, on Simplon, ii. 513–14; falls in love, ii. 530; parts from E, ii. 534.

Wren, Sir Christopher; D.C.L. 1661; knighted 1673, iii. 106 & n. 3.
relations of, with E: friend of E, i. *12* & n. 1; first meets E, iii. 106; E godfather to son of, iv. 169; E dedicates book to, i. *35*.
as scientist and scholar: views of, on relations of religion and science, i. *110*, n. 1; at Oxford, 1654, iii. 106, 111; and gift of Arundelian inscriptions to Oxford, iii. 496, n. 1; observes transit of Mercury, iii. 384–5 & n.; scientific instruments made by (?), iii. 110–11; lamp invented by, iii. 475 *bis* & n. 6; thermometer of, iii. 314 & n. 2; paper by, on weather-glasses, iii. 314, n. 2; marble coloured by, iii. 111 & n. 1; as fellow of Royal Society: deputed to welcome Sir John Chardin, iv. 212 & n. 3; president, 1681–2, iv. 225, n. 1, 263; negotiates sale of Chelsea College, iv. 257, n. 3.
as Surveyor-general of the King's Works, iii. 570, n. 4; engages to employ Grinling Gibbons, &c., iii. 570 & n. 6, 573; office of, in Whitehall, v. 244 & n. 2; report of, on damage done at Sayes Court by Peter the Great, v. 290 & n. 6.
as architect: buildings designed by, &c.: Chelsea Hospital: plans of, presented to Archbishop Sancroft, iv. 281 & n. 2; Easton Neston, iv. 170, n. 1; Greenwich Hospital, i. *34*; ~ examines King's House for proposed hospital, v. 203, n. 1; ~ as commissioner, &c., v. 209–10, 244; ~ as member of site committee: visits Greenwich, v. 211; ~ lays foundation-stone (with E), v. 249; ~ shows model, &c., of, to William III (with E), v. 399 & n. 2.
— Hampton Court: new buildings at, ii. 117, n. 1; iii. 322, n. 5; *see also* iv. 645 & n. 2; Lee, Kent: Boone's Chapel, iv. 289,

Wren, Sir Christopher (*cont.*)
n. 1; Lincoln: cathedral cloister, iii. 132, n. 2.
— London: proposed replanning of, i. *20*; churches, iv. 243 & n. 7; Arundel House: plan for rebuilding, iii. 234, n. 4; Christchurch, Newgate Street, iii. 192, n. 2; Customs House, iii. 588 & n. 2; Monument, iv. 243 & n. 6; Royal Society building: plan for, iii. 505, n. 1; St. Clement, Eastcheap, iii. 64, n. 5; St. James, Piccadilly, iv. 397 & n. 4; St. Martin in the Fields: parish library for: Wren consulted, iv. 367, 369; St. Paul's: project for repair of, 1666, i. *20*; iii. 448–9 & nn.; ~ report by, on condition of, after Fire of London: cited, iii. 459, n. 1; ~ rebuilding of, iv. 243 & n. 5; ~ choir-stalls designed by, for, v. 192 & n. 2; Whitehall: not associated with alterations made in 1664, iii. 387, n. 4; ~ designs rooms at, for Council for Foreign Plantations, iii. 584 & n. 1; ~ adapts Banqueting House for use as chapel royal, v. 321, n. 4.
— Oxford: Sheldonian Theatre, iii. 385 & n. 5; ~ on cost of, iii. 530–1 & n.; ~ praised as architect of, iii. 532; Winchester: palace at, for Charles II, iv. 341 & n. 2; *see also* iv. 471–2 & n.
social: son of (William Wren), baptized, iv. 169–70 & n.; at parties, iii. 296 & n. 2 (?), 463, 570; iv. 84, 124.
geneal., iii. 271, n. 1; iv. 84, n. 7.
letter of: cited, iii. 110, n. 1.

Wren, Matthew, D.D.; bishop of Ely, &c., iii. 271, n. 1; imprisonment of, iii. 186 & n. 4; officiates in service, iii. 271; geneal., iii. 106 & n. 3, 186 & n. 4, 392; chaplain of: *see* Boldero, E. (iii. 270 & n. 4).

Wren, Matthew, jnr., iii. 186 & n. 4; social, iii. 186, 392 & n. 3.

Wren, William: baptized, iv. 169–70 & nn.

Wrentham, Suffolk: rector of: *see* Wotton, Rev. Henry.

Wrestling-match, iii. 476 & n. 1.

Wricklemarsh: *see* Charlton, Kent.

Wright (Write), John Michael, iii. 228, n. 4; paintings by, iii. 338–9 & nn.; portraits of Fire Judges by, iii. 338 & n. 5; iv. 17 & n. 5; art-collection of, iii. 339 & nn. 3–6; collection of shells of, iii. 372; social, iii. 228.
Wright, Sir Nathan, v. 413, n. 3; appointed lord keeper, v. 413 & n. 3; superseded, v. 611 & n. 1.
Wright, Sir Robert: judge in trial of Seven Bishops, iv. 587 & n. 2.
Wriothesley, Elizabeth: *see* Montagu, Elizabeth, countess of Montagu.
Wriothesley, Rachel: *see* Russell, Rachel, Lady Russell.
Wriothesley, Thomas, fourth earl of Southampton; Lord High Treasurer 1660–7, iii. 175, n. 5; character, iii. 398; appointed Lord High Treasurer, iii. 253, n. 2; controls funds for Sick and Wounded, iii. 411, 431 & n. 4, 432; houses and buildings of, in Bloomsbury, iii. 376 & n. 3, 398 & nn. 2, 3; *see also* iii. 551 & n. 4; social: at parties, iii. 356, 389; ~ alone, &c., iii. 327, 341, 343, 376, 398; visits Sayes Court, iii. 175; E gives copy of *Sylva* to, iii. 369; dies, &c., iii. 487, n. 7; iv. 19 & n. 5; geneal., iii. 551, n. 4; iv. 90, n. 7, 344, n. 3; secretary of: *see* Warwick, Sir P.
Wroxton, Oxon.: Lord Keeper Guilford dies at, iv. 466 & n. 4.
Wurtemburg: Duke of (1696): informs William III about James II's movements, v. 232, n. 1.
Wyatt, James, architect: alters Cassiobury, iv. 199, n. 2.
Wyborne (Wiburn), Sir John: chaplain of: sermon by, iv. 438 & n. 2.
Wyche (Wich), Sir Cyril, iv. 351, n. 5; godfather of, &c., ii. 18, n. 3; v. 359 & n. 4; elected president of Royal Society, iv. 351 & n. 5; Irish appointments of, v. 101 & n. 1, 150 & n. 5, 359 & n. 5; appointed a commissioner for forfeited estates in Ireland, v. 394, n. 2; marries Mary Evelyn of Wotton, v. 101 & n. 1, 359 & n. 3; visits Wotton, v. 282; geneal., v. 237, n. 1, 359 & n. 4.
Wyche, Jane: *see* Grenville, Jane, countess of Bath.
Wyche, Mary, Lady Wyche; daughter of George Evelyn; wife of Sir Cyril Wyche 1692, ii. 544 & n. 6.
  as Mary Evelyn: baptized, ii. 544 & n. 6; at Chiswick, ii. 558; as godmother, iii. 421; iv. 396; social, iii. 360, 547, 550; marries Wyche, v. 101 & n. 1, 359 & n. 3.
  as Lady Wyche: executrix of George Evelyn's will, v. 359–60, 377.
  geneal., &c., ii. 537, n. 2; v. 54, n. 2.
Wyche, Sir Peter, sen.: geneal., &c., v. 359 & n. 4.
Wyche, Sir Peter, jnr.: and Royal Society's English language committee, iii. 396, n. 4; *add.*
Wycherley, William: converted to Roman Catholicism, iv. 541, n. 2.
Wychwood Forest, Oxon.: rangership of, iii. 381, n. 6; Ranger's Lodge in (?), iii. 382 & n. 5.
Wycliffe, John: translation of Bible by: MS. copy of, iii. 106 & n. 5.
Wye, Rev. Roger; rector of Wotton 1699–1701, iv. 220, n. 1; v. 67, n. 5; instituted rector, v. 377, n. 1; sermons by, at Wotton, iv. 220; v. 67–9, 116, 229, 231, 260–1, 377–9, 414–25, 428–30 *passim & singulatim*; officiates at Wotton House, v. 230; ill, v. 445 *bis*; dies, v. 447 & n. 2.
Wyers Bay (Vejer?), Spain: Captain A. Young at, iii. 188, n. 4.
Wyndham, Catherine, Lady Wyndham, wife of Sir Edward, v. 237, n. 1; visits Eton, v. 236–7; dies, v. 588 & n. 3.
Wyndham, Sir Edward, bt.: geneal., v. 237, n. 1.
Wyndham (Windham), Sir William, bt., the politician: goes to Eton, v. 236–7 & n.
Wynell, Rev. Philip: sermon by (?), iv. 582 & n. 2.
Wynnebald, St.: in inscription at Lucca, ii. 409 & n. 1.
Wynter, Mary: *see* Blathwayt, Mrs. M.
Wythens (Withings). Sir Francis, judge: social, &c., iv. 352 & nn. 6, 7.

Xaverius: *see* Francis, St., Xavier.

Yalding, Kent: brief for (?): read, v. 188 & n. 1.
Yale, manor (Denbighshire): granted to Portland, &c., v. 230, n. 1.
Yarborough (Yearbrow, &c.), Henrietta Maria, Lady Yarborough, born Blagge, wife of Sir Thomas, iv. 64, n. 1; informs E about Mrs. Godolphin's marriage (?), iv. 89 & n. 1; social, iv. 63–4 *bis*, 326, 398.
Yarborough (Yarbrow), Sir Thomas: social, iv. 326 & n. 3; geneal., iv. 64, n. 1.
Yard, R.: letters of news written by, i. *128*, n. 1.
Yarmouth: Viscount and Earls of, &c.: *see* Paston, Sir Robert, viscount 1673–9 and first earl 1679–83; Paston, Rebecca, his viscountess, later countess; Paston, William, second earl 1683–1732.
Yaverland, I.O.W.: visit to, ii. 22 & n. 1.
Yearbrow, Lady: *see* Yarborough, H. M.
Yedic Bassa: rebels, iv. 645 & n. 7.
Yeghen Bassa: geneal., iv. 645 & n. 7.
Yèvre (Eure) river, at Bourges, ii. 153 & n. 2 (i. 98).
York: notice, iii. 128–30 & nn.; besieged by parliamentarians, &c., iii. 129 & n. 1; garrison at, iii. 130, n. 2; parliamentary election at, 1665 (in text as Yorkshire), iii. 394 & n. 2; declares for William of Orange, iv. 609 & n. 2; mayor of: attends William III, 1695, v. 222, n. 3.
York: Duke, 1633–85, and Duchesses of: *see* James II, king of England; Anne [Hyde] *and* Mary [of Modena], queen of England, his duchesses.
York: cathedral clergy:
 archbishops of: residences of: at Bishopthorpe, iii. 128 & n. 4; ~ in London, iii. 162, n. 1; individual archbishops: *see* Montaigne, G. (1628); Neile, Richard (1632–40); Williams, John (1641–50); Sterne, Richard (1664–83); Dolben, John (1683–6); Lamplugh, T. (1688–91); Sharp, John (1691–1714).
 dean: *see* Gale, T. (1697–1702).
York: cathedral clergy (*cont.*)
 sub-deans: *see* Feild, R. (1670–80); Tully, G. (1680–6, 1689–95).
 prebendaries: *see* Parry, Benjamin; Thurscross, T.
Yorkshire: parliamentary election for, 1665 (error for York), iii. 394 & n. 2; movement in, on behalf of William of Orange, iv. 608 & n. 3; address of, to William III, 1701, v. 481, n. 1; North Riding: justices of the peace for, 1687, iv. 536, n. 3; South Yorkshire: fertility of, iii. 128 & n. 5; Stansfield family of, i. 4; ~ *see also* ii. 3, n. 1; iii. 89, n. 3.
Young, Dr. —: *see* Young, Rev. Edward.
Young, Captain Anthony, of Deptford, iii. 188, n. 4; captives taken by, iii. 188–9 & nn.; buried, &c., v. 158–9 & n.
Young, Rev. Edward, B.C.L., iv. 239, n. 1; sermons by (?), iv. 239; v. 19, 21, 48, 51.
Yvelin (Evelin), Pierre, M.D.: visits London, &c., iii. 547–8 & nn.

Zaccheus: in sermon, v. 251.
Zacharias, English inn-keeper at Genoa: adventure of, at sea, ii. 171–2 (i. 108).
Zacharias, St.: relics of (?), ii. 460, n. 4.
Zante: J. Hobson in, ii. 476, n. 3; Sir Henry Hyde in, iii. 384, n. 2.
Zebedee: mother of children of: in sermon, iii. 559.
Zechariah: relics of (?), ii. 460 & n. 4.
Zeeland, in Netherlands: submerged towns of, ii. 31–2 & n. (i. 24); princes of Orange hereditary stadholders of, ii. 31 & n. 2; attachment of, to house of Orange: alluded to (?), iii. 407 & n. 3; vice-admirals, &c., of (C. and J. Evertsen), iii. 407 & n. 2.
Zeeland, island, Denmark: Charles X's winter march to, iii. 211, n. 2.
Zen (Zenno), Girolamo, Venetian ambassador to James II: audience, &c., iv. 492–3 & nn.; at court ceremony, iv. 493.
Zeno, Byzantine emperor: coin of, ii. 496, n. 2.
Zeno, Giambattista, cardinal: tomb of, ii. 438 & n. 6.

Zenta: battle of, v. 267 & n. 4.
Zimri: in sermon, iv. 364.
Zinzano, Alexander: horse trained by, i. 54 & n. 2.
Zinzano *alias* Alexander, Richard, i. 54, n. 2.
Zinzano, Sir Sigismund, i. 54, n. 2.
Zinzendorf, &c., Georg Ludwig, Graf von, diplomatist: at Royal Society, iv. 316 & n. 1.
Zoar: figurative, iii. 457; in sermon, iv. 349.
Zoological Gardens [mixed collections of mammals and birds; sometimes called Vivaries by E; for collections of birds alone *see* Aviaries]: Florence, Grand Duke, ii. 195 & n. 6 (i. 120–1); London: St. James's Park, 1665, iii. 398–400 & nn.; *see also* iv. 266, n. 3; ~ Tower, i. 69; ii. 195 & n. 7 (i. 121); iv. 266, n. 3; Paris, Tuileries, ii. 107 & n. 1 (i. 69); Rome, Villa Borghese, ii. 251, 252, 390; smaller collections, ii. 14, n. 4, 66 (i. 44), 72 (i. 47), 187 (i. 117), 467.
Zoroastrians: in Persia, iv. 214 & n. 2.
Zuccari (Zucchero, Succari), Federico, ii. 197, n. 1; tomb of, ii. 372 & n. 10; paintings by, ii. 197, 373 & n. 3, 406, n. 7.
Zuccari (Zuccharo, Succari, &c.), Taddeo, ii. 215, n. 3; tomb of, ii. 372 & n. 10; paintings by, ii. 215 & n. 3, 373 & n. 3, 406 & n. 7, 407, n. 1.
Zulecum, Zulichem, &c.: *see* Zuylichem.
Zulestein, Monsieur: *see* Zuylestein.
Zurich: canton of (Tigurini): alliance of, with Geneva, ii. 526.
Zuylestein (Zulestein), Frederik van Nassau, heer van: social, iii. 565 & n. 6.
Zuylestein, Willem Hendrik van Nassau, heer van, later first earl of Rochford: messenger for William of Orange, iv. 611, n. 1.
Zuylestein, William Nassau de, second earl of Rochford: as Lord Tunbridge: carries despatch from Blenheim, v. 574, n. 1.
Zuylichem (Zulecum, &c.): lords of: *see* Huygens, Christiaan; Huygens, Constantijn, sen.

ADDENDA

ADDITIONAL CORRECTIONS TO THE TEXT

ii. 309, l. 7. *For* Romans *read* Roman.
iii. 89, l. 4 from foot. *For* libary *read* library.
iv. 506, l. 2. *For* Prostestants *read* Protestants.

ADDITIONS TO THE INDEX

Abinger: church: services, iii. 423.
Academies: Intronati, ii. 202, n. 3; Pontaniana, ii. 328, n. 9.
Animals: monkeys, i. 30; mules: blessing of, at Rome, ii. 387 and n. 4; of St. Thomas Aquinas, &c., ii. 319 & n. 2.
Architecture: general: ship-building as branch of, iii. 333; features: staircases: notable, iv. 190, 594.
Arms and Armour: ordnance: great guns, ii. 432.
Art-collections: Paris: Notre Dame: the *Mays*, ii. 95 & nn. 1, 6.
Arundell, Henry, third Baron Arundell of Wardour: social, iv. 445.
Astronomy: comets: as portents, iv. 411.

Bible: criticism: particular passages: Acts iii. 21: disproves Transubstantiation, iv. 129–30.
Birds: general: collection of eggs, iii. 594.
Books: books mentioned in text: general: Anglican pamphlets, &c., against: Nonconformists, iv. 418 & n. 2; ~ Roman Catholics, iv. 418, 541 & n. 3, 590.
— — Gassendi, life of Peiresc, trans. Rand: *read* iii. 189 & n. 6; Sprat, T., bishop of Rochester, *A Form of Prayer* (for birth of James Edward), 1688, iv. 588 & n. 7; Wilkins, J., *Essay towards a Real Character*, 1668: work preparatory to, iii. 110 & n. 3.
Bowls, ii. 130 (i. 83).
Breisach: taken by French, 1703, v. 544 & n. 3.
Browne, Sir Adam, bt.: stands for parliament, 1679, iv. 164–5 & n.
Butler, Thomas, styled earl of Ossory: social: parties: *read* iv. 191 *bis*.

Caleb: in sermon, v. 268.
Cameronians, iv. 440, n. 1.
Charity, &c.: papal donations, ii. 377.
Cheyne, Isabella, wife of Charles Cheyne, Lord Cheyne: *see* Robartes, Isabella, countess of Radnor.
Christ: miraculous image of, ii. 409–10 & n.; the Bambino, ii. 291 & n. 7.
Church of England: buildings: condition of, in Suffolk, iv. 118; iconoclasm, by Puritans, &c.: organs demolished, iii. 109.

Addenda

Church of England: organization: episcopate: (1) chronological series: 1688: bishops petition James for parliament, iv. 608 & n. 4.
— worship: services: Communion: names: Eucharist, iii. 243; v. 322; feasts and fasts: Ascension Sunday, v. 501; preaching, &c.: catechizing: at Wotton: *see* Wotton: church: services.
Cocke, George, Captain: social: parties, iv. 73.

Downs, The: shipping movements in, iii. 614.
Dress: national, &c.: dress worn by poor in Maundy Thursday ceremony, Rome, ii. 385; garments, &c.: gowns: Venetian senators', ii. 432, 442.
Ducie, Sir William, Viscount Downe: social, iii. 231.

England: navy: miscellaneous notices: and control of New England, iii. 584.
— officers: general: white staffs as insignia of office, iii. 470.
— social: tobacco and snuff: use of, i. 14–15; ii. 201 & n. 1; *see also* Tobacco.
Evelyn, John: and architecture: criticism: Old St. Paul's, portico, iii. 458.
— character: humanity: on treatment of galley-slaves, ii. 165 (i. 104–5).
— Diary: composition: Kalendarium: events entered prematurely, v. 220 & n. 3.
— patronage: this omits Evelyn's recommendations of private tutors (E. Philips, &c.)
— property: claims on Crown, iv. 297 [perhaps relating to Evelyn's services for the Sick and Wounded: *see* Commissioners for Sick and Wounded, 1672–4: finance].
— as trustee, &c.: this omits Evelyn's share in negotiations for marriages: *see* England: social: marriages.
Evelyn, Richard, sen.: visits Lewes, 1636, ii. 15.

Fireworks, &c.: bonfires, iv. 189.
Fish: general: book on, iv. 503 & n. 5.
Folklore: elephant, ii. 39–40 & n. (i. 29); pelican, ii. 40 (i. 30); seaman: skin of, ii. 356.
Food and Drink: hot-waters, ii. 377; pancake: in comparison, iv. 141.
Fortifications: castles: near Papplewick (?), iii. 126 & n. 6.
Frampton, Robert, bishop of Gloucester: sermons by, iv. 503.
France: commerce, &c.: tapestry from, iv. 262.
Fruit-trees, &c.: general: crop destroyed by caterpillars, iv. 446.

Giulio Romano: paintings by, iii. 74–5 & n.
Greece: Modern: Greek manner: goldsmiths' work in, ii. 438; ~ mosaics in, ii. 197, 278.
Grottoes: not described, iii. 114.

Additions to the Index

Hampton Court: historical: Privy Council meets at, &c., iii. 414, n. 10 *ad fin.*; iv. 177–8, 248, 644–5 & n.
Holden, Rev. Richard: lecturer of, at St. Dunstan's (W. Strengfellow?): sermons by, iv. 549–50 & n., 592, 608.
Hooper, George, bishop of St. Asaph: attends Monmouth in Tower, &c., iv. 456, n. 1.

Indies, Indians: hammock, iii. 382 & n. 7.
Inns, &c.: England: Dunstable, iv. 593; Euston, iv. 118.

Julius Caesar: life of: in paintings, ii. 151 (i. 98)

Legends: Haarlem: stratagem at siege of Damietta, ii. 50 & n. 3 (i. 35); Venice: brides stolen, ii. 440–1 & n.
Lighting [this section omits ordinary notices of common illuminants]: candle-light: taking portrait by, iii. 309–10; *chapelle ardente*, ii. 368–9; lights for house of commons, iii. 469 & n. 2.
Luzzara: battle of, v. 514 *ter* & nn. 1, 4, 8.

Medicine, &c.: miscellaneous: quacks, ii. 99 & n. 7 (i. 65), 368, 474, n. 5; curative relic, ii. 205.
Milan: persons: E's journey from Padua to, ii. 479; ~ Arundel's instructions for, ii. 479 & n. 5, &c.
Monck, George, duke of Albemarle: address to Charles II, May 1660, iii. 244.
Montagu, Charles, earl of Halifax: nominated a Lord Justice, 1698, v. 294.
Mynne, Mrs. Anne: geneal., ii. 542, n. 3.

Nonconformists, &c.: chronological series: bills against Occasional Conformity, 1702–3, v. 523, n. 1, 527 & n. 4, 552 & n. 1.

Painting, &c.: miscellaneous: 'the old masters', iv. 344; v. 245; 'the old and best masters', ii. 299.
Papacy: miscellaneous: portraits of the popes, ii. 204.
Paris: environs: Seine: at Saint-Cloud, ii. 107 (i. 69), 108; at Saint-Germain, ii. 111 *bis* (i. 71, 72).
Paul, St.: 'St. Paul's seamen' (phrase), iv. 379 & n. 4.
Persia: modern: horses, iii. 349.
Peter, St.: popes as successors of, iv. 477.
Physics: atmosphere: experiments with aeolipyle, iii. 272 & n. 4.
Plants: couch-grass, ii. 31.
Poggio a Caiano *and* Poggio Imperiale: *see* Florence: environs.
Portraits: collections of: Louvre: French kings, &c., ii. 104 (i. 68).
Publishing, &c.: *see also* Royal Society: publications.

Roman Catholic Church: the Church in general: religious observances: carnival, &c., ii. 451 & n. 3, 473–4; *see also* iii. 1 & n. 7.

Royal Household: Lord Steward, &c.: Clerks of the Green Cloth: *see* Boreman, Sir W. (1680–6).

Ships and Shipping: types of ship: barges: in procession, iii. 284: ~ frigates: naval, iii. 584; miscellaneous notices: convoy, v. 169.
Slaves: at Milan, ii. 494; *see also* ii. 340.
Spanish language: E studies, ii. 534.
Spirit, the Holy: allusions, &c. [probably very incomplete list]: in sectarian sermon, iii. 167; in sermons against Nonconformists, iii. 320; v. 348; 'knack of the Spirit', iii. 551; praying by: origin of, v. 13.
Stammerham: Michell family of, i. 7 & n. 1.
Stillingfleet, Edward, bishop of Worcester: sermons by: unprinted, iv. 107.

DATES OF PRINTING

The printing of this work began with vols. ii–v, which were set up consecutively between September 1947 and December 1949 and were machined between September 1948 and December 1951. Vol. i was set up between January 1950 and February 1951 and was machined in December 1951. The present volume was set up between September 1954 and July 1955.

PRINTED IN
GREAT BRITAIN
AT THE
UNIVERSITY PRESS
OXFORD
BY
CHARLES BATEY
PRINTER
TO THE
UNIVERSITY